The **Rough Guide** t

Egypt

written and researched by

Dan Richardson and Daniel Jacobs

with additional contributions from

Shafik Meghji

www.roughguides.com

Contents

◀◀ View over the Nile and the Cairo Tower ◀ Khan el Khalili Bazaar, Cairo

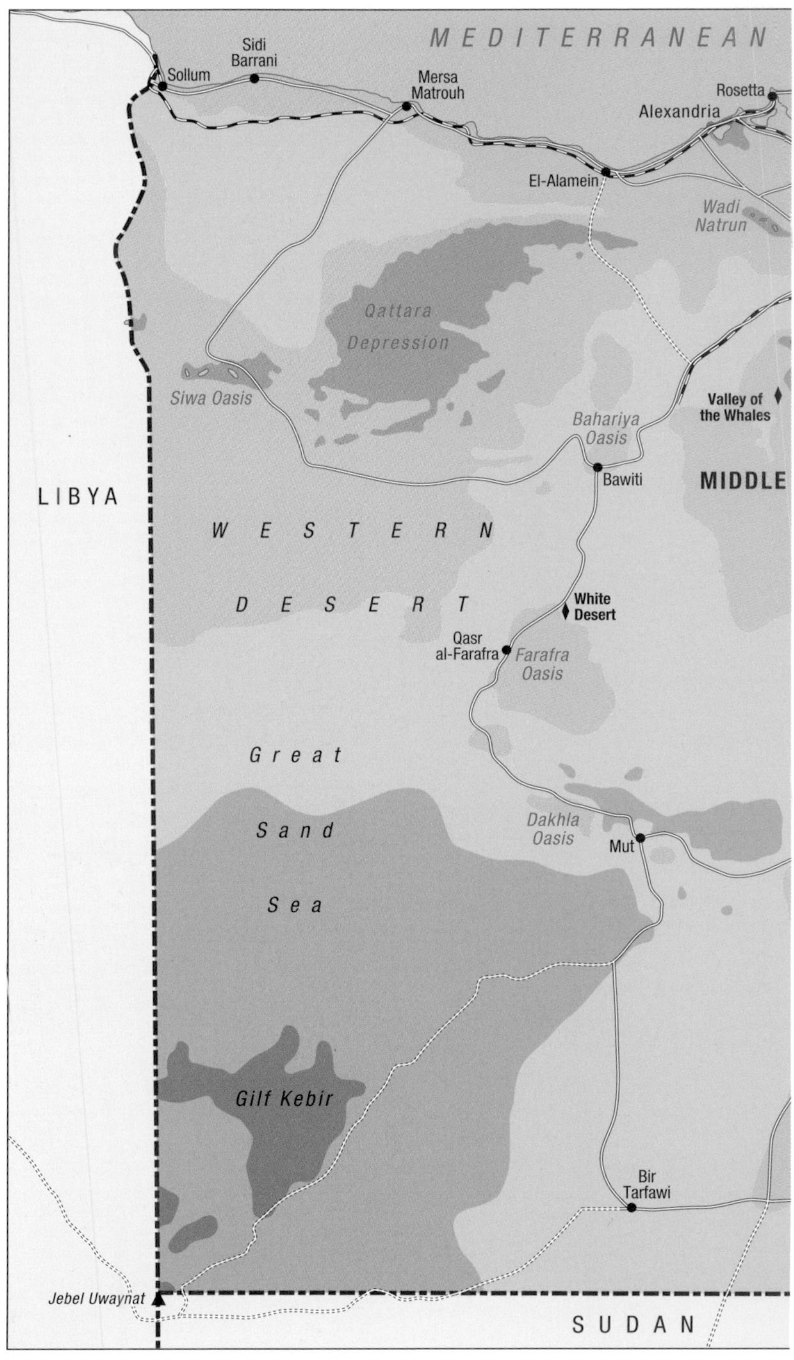
MEDITERRANEAN
Sidi Barrani
Sollum
Mersa Matrouh
Rosetta
Alexandria
El-Alamein
Wadi Natrun
Qattara Depression
Siwa Oasis
Valley of the Whales
Bahariya Oasis
Bawiti
MIDDLE
LIBYA
WESTERN DESERT
White Desert
Qasr al-Farafra
Farafra Oasis
Great Sand Sea
Dakhla Oasis
Mut
Gilf Kebir
Bir Tarfawi
Jebel Uwaynat
SUDAN

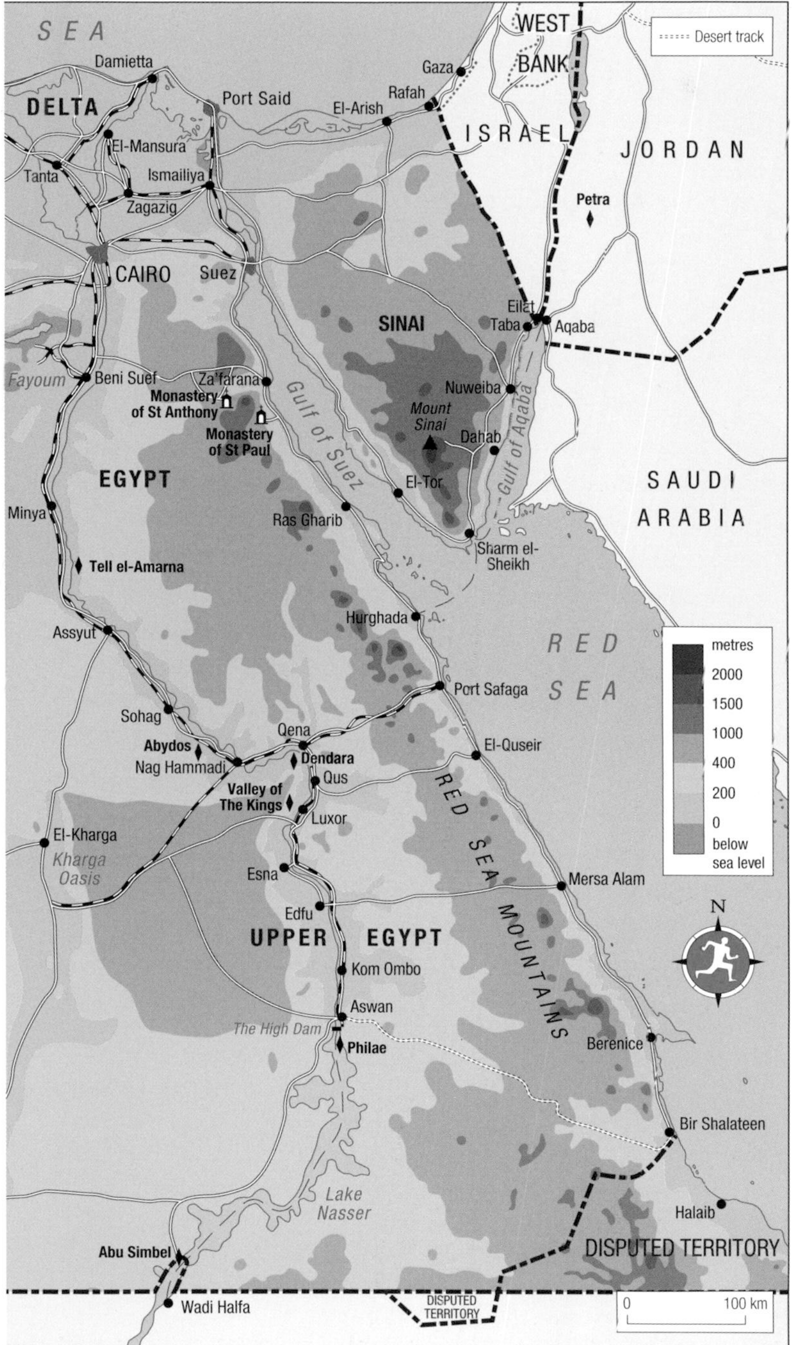
SEA
Desert track
WEST BANK
Gaza
Damietta
Rafah
Port Said
El-Arish
DELTA
ISRAEL
JORDAN
El-Mansura
Tanta
Ismailiya
Zagazig
Petra
CAIRO
Suez
Eilat
Taba
Aqaba
SINAI
Fayoum
Beni Suef
Za'farana
Monastery of St Anthony
Monastery of St Paul
Gulf of Suez
Nuweiba
Mount Sinai
Dahab
Gulf of Aqaba
EGYPT
El-Tor
SAUDI ARABIA
Minya
Ras Gharib
Sharm el-Sheikh
Tell el-Amarna
Hurghada
Assyut
RED SEA
metres
2000
1500
1000
400
200
0
below sea level
Port Safaga
Sohag
Qena
El-Quseir
Abydos
Dendara
Nag Hammadi
Qus
Valley of The Kings
RED SEA MOUNTAINS
Luxor
El-Kharga
Kharga Oasis
Esna
Mersa Alam
N
Edfu
UPPER EGYPT
Kom Ombo
Aswan
The High Dam
Philae
Berenice
Bir Shalateen
Lake Nasser
Halaib
Abu Simbel
DISPUTED TERRITORY
Wadi Halfa
DISPUTED TERRITORY
0
100 km

Introduction to Egypt

Egypt is the oldest tourist destination on earth. Ancient Greeks and Romans started the trend, coming to goggle at the cyclopean scale of the Pyramids and the Colossi of Thebes. During colonial times, Napoleon and the British looted Egypt's treasures to fill their national museums, sparking off a trickle of Grand Tourists that eventually became a flood of travellers, taken on Nile cruises and Egyptological lectures by the enterprising Thomas Cook. Today, the attractions of the country are not only the monuments of the Nile Valley and the souks, mosques and madrassas of Islamic Cairo, but also fantastic coral reefs and tropical fish, dunes, ancient fortresses, monasteries and prehistoric rock art.

The land itself is a freak of nature, its lifeblood the River Nile. From the Sudanese border to the shores of the Mediterranean, the Nile Valley and its Delta are flanked by arid wastes, the latter as empty as the former are teeming with people. This stark duality between fertility and desolation is fundamental to Egypt's character and has shaped its development since prehistoric times, imparting continuity to diverse cultures and peoples over seven millennia. It is a sense of permanence and timelessness that is buttressed by religion, which pervades every aspect of life. Although the pagan cults of ancient Egypt are as moribund as its legacy of mummies and temples, their ancient fertility rites and processions of boats still hold their place in the celebrations of Islam and Christianity.

The result is a multi-layered culture, which seems to accord equal respect to ancient and modern. The peasants of the Nile and Bedouin tribes of the desert live much as their ancestors did a thousand years ago. Other communities include the Nubians of the far south, and the Coptic Christians, who trace their ancestry back to pharaonic times. What unites them is a love of their homeland, extended family ties, dignity, warmth and hospitality towards strangers. Though most visitors are drawn to Egypt by its monuments, the enduring memory is likely to be of its people and their way of life.

▲ Harvesting dates

Fact file

• The Arab Republic of Egypt covers 1,001,450 square kilometres, of which 96.4 percent is **desert**; only the Nile Valley, its Delta and some oases are fertile.

• Egypt's **population** of 83 million is over twice that of the next most populous Arab country (Algeria) and a quarter of the population of the Arab world. Its ethnic profile is Eastern Hamitic and Semitic – Egyptians, Bedouin, Nubians and Berbers account for 99 percent – with tiny minorities of Greeks, Armenians and others. **Arabic** is spoken universally, Nubian around Aswan and Lake Nasser, and Siwi at Siwa Oasis. Islam is the national **religion**, with some 96 percent followers; almost all the rest are Coptic Orthodox Christians. Average **life expectancy** is 70 years.

• A **republic** since 1952, Egypt is divided into 26 governorates or *muhafazat*. President Hosni Mubarak has been head of state since 1981. The National Democratic Party invariably wins tightly regulated elections to the People's Assembly (Maglis al-Shaab) and Advisory Council (Maglis al-Shura). Opposition parties and independent MPs are outspoken, but powerless to change anything.

• **Tourism** is Egypt's largest money-earner, followed by tolls on the Suez Canal, and exports of oil, petroleum products, textiles and natural gas.

Where to go

Egypt's capital, **Cairo**, is a seething megalopolis whose chief sightseeing appeal lies in its **bazaars** and medieval **mosques**, though there is scarcely less fascination in its juxtapositions of medieval and modern life, the city's fortified gates, villas and skyscrapers interwoven by flyovers whose traffic may be halted by donkey carts. The immensity and diversity of this "Mother of Cities" is as staggering as anything you'll encounter in Egypt. Just outside Cairo are the first of the **pyramids** that range across the desert to the edge of the Fayoum, among them the unsurpassable trio at **Giza**, the vast necropolis of **Saqqara** and the recently reopened pyramids at **Dahshur**. Besides all this, there are superb **museums** devoted to Ancient, Coptic and Islamic Egypt, and enough **entertainments** to occupy weeks of your time.

However, the principal tourist lure remains, as ever, the **Nile Valley**, with its **ancient monuments** and timeless river vistas – Nile **cruises** on a luxury vessel or a felucca sailboat being a great way to combine the two. The town of **Luxor** is synonymous with the magnificent temples of **Karnak** and the **Theban Necropolis**, which includes the **Valley of the Kings** where Tutankhamun and other pharaohs were buried. **Aswan**, Egypt's southernmost city, has the loveliest setting on the Nile and a languorous ambience. From here, you can visit the island **Philae temple of Isis** and the rock-hewn colossi at **Abu Simbel**, or embark on a cruise to other temples around **Lake Nasser**. Other sites not to be missed are **Edfu** and **Kom Ombo** between Luxor and Aswan, and **Abydos** and **Dendara** north of Luxor.

▲ Bread vendors, Cairo

▶ Camels cool off in the heat, Nuweiba

Besides monuments, Egypt abounds in natural wonders. Edged by coral reefs teeming with tropical fish, the **Sinai Peninsula** offers superb **diving** and **snorkelling**, and palm-fringed **beaches** where women can swim unmolested. Resorts along the Gulf of Aqaba are varied enough to suit everyone, whether you're into the upmarket hotels of **Sharm el-Sheikh** and nearby **Na'ama Bay**, or **Taba** further north, or cheap, simple living at **Dahab** and **Nuweiba**. From there it's easy to visit **St Catherine's Monastery** and **Mount Sinai** (where Moses received the Ten Commandments) in the mountainous interior. With more time, cash and stamina, you can also embark on **jeep safaris** or **camel treks** to remote oases and spectacular wadis.

Hussein or Houssein?

There's no standard system of transliterating Arabic script into Roman, so you're sure to find that the Arabic words in this book don't always match the versions you'll see elsewhere. Maps and street signs are the biggest sources of confusion, so we've generally gone for the transliteration that's the most common on the spot. However, you'll often need to do a bit of lateral thinking, and it's not unusual to find one spelling posted at one end of a road, with another at the opposite end. See p.639 for an introduction to Egyptian Arabic.

Egypt's **Red Sea Coast** has more reefs further offshore, with snorkelling and diving traditionally centred around **Hurghada**, while barely touched island reefs further south from **Port Safaga** down to **Mersa Alam** beckon serious diving enthusiasts. Inland, the mountainous **Eastern Desert** harbours the **Coptic Monasteries of St Paul and St Anthony**, Roman quarries, and a host of pharaonic and **prehistoric rock art**, seen by few apart from the nomadic Bedouin.

While the Eastern Desert is still barely touched by tourism, the **Western Desert Oases** have been on the tourist trail for forty years and nowadays host safaris into the wilderness. **Siwa**, out towards the Libyan border, has a unique culture and history, limpid pools and bags of charm. Travellers can also follow the "Great Desert Circuit" (starting from Cairo, Luxor or Assyut) through the four "inner" oases. Though **Bahariya** and **Farafra** hold the most appeal, with the lovely **White Desert** between them, the larger oases of

Birdwatching in Egypt

Egypt is a fantastic country for **birdwatching**. Lake Qaroun in the Fayoum is home to 88 of Egypt's 150-odd resident breeding species (including flamingoes) and a wintering ground for grebes, ducks, coots and shorebirds during the great migration of 280 additional species of birds from Siberia, Scandinavia and Eastern Europe. The first wave of **storks** and **raptors** appears in mid-February; **Griffon vultures** and imperial and steppe **eagles** overflying Suez and Ain Sukhna. Spring sees Kittlitz's **sandplover**, Blue-cheeked **bee-eaters**, Rufous **bushchats** and **crested larks** at Wadi Natrun, and nesting osprey and sooty falcons at Ras Mohammed. **Grey heron** live year-round in the marshes and lagoons of the Delta, where Lake Manzala is a wintering ground for **shovellers**, **shelducks** and **coots**. The most striking water-birds on the Nile are the diving pied **kingfisher** (year-round in Aswan), cattle and **little egrets** (common throughout Upper Egypt) and **flamingos** (at Wadi Gimal National Park in spring and autumn).

◀ Flamingos at Wadi Gimal

▶ Wadi Natrun, Western Desert

Dakhla and **Kharga** also have their rewards once you escape their modernized "capitals". And for those into serious desert expeditions, there's the challenge of exploring the **Great Sand Sea** or the remote wadis of the **Gilf Kebir** and **Jebel Uwaynat**, whose prehistoric rock art featured in the film *The English Patient*. In contrast to these deep-desert locations are the quasi-oases of the **Fayoum** and **Wadi Natrun**, featuring the fossil-strewn **Valley of the Whales**, diverse ancient ruins and **Coptic monasteries**.

On the **Mediterranean**, Egypt's second city, **Alexandria**, boasts a string of beaches to which Cairenes flock in summer, and excellent seafood restaurants. Despite being founded by Alexander the Great and lost to the Romans by Cleopatra, the city today betrays little of its ancient glory; however, its magnificent new **library**, featuring statues raised from the sunken remains of **Cleopatra's Palace** and the **Lighthouse of Pharos** (which divers can explore) are restoring an air of majesty. Famous, too, for its decadence during colonial times, Alexandria still allows romantics to indulge in a nostalgic exploration of the city immortalized in Durrell's *Alexandria Quartet*, while further along the Mediterranean coast is the World War II battlefield of **El-Alamein**. For divers, the waters off Alexandria offer an array of sunken cities and wartime wrecks to explore.

The Nile **Delta**, east of Alexandria, musters few archeological monuments given its major role in ancient Egyptian history, and is largely overlooked by tourists. However, for those interested in Egyptian culture, the Delta hosts colourful religious **festivals** at **Tanta**, **Zagazig** and other towns. Further east lies the Canal Zone, dominated by the Suez Canal and its three cities. **Suez** is grim, but a vital transport nexus between Cairo, Sinai and the Red Sea Coast. **Port Said** and **Ismailiya** are pleasant, albeit sleepy places, where you can get a feel of "real Egypt" without tripping over other tourists.

When to go

Egypt's traditional tourist season runs from **late November to late February**, though in recent years Luxor and Aswan have only really been busy with tourists during the peak months of December and January. The Nile Valley is balmy throughout this winter season, although Cairo can be overcast and chilly. The season is also the busiest period for the Sinai resorts, while Hurghada is active year round. Aside from the Easter vacation, when there is a spike in tourism, **March or April** are also good times to visit, with a pleasant climate.

In **May** the heat is still tolerable but, after that, Egyptians rich enough to do so migrate to Alex and the coastal resorts. From **June to September** the south and desert are ferociously hot and the pollution in Cairo is at its worst, with only the coast offering a respite from the heat. During this time, sightseeing is best limited to early morning or evening. **October into early November** is perhaps the best time of all, with easily manageable climate and crowds.

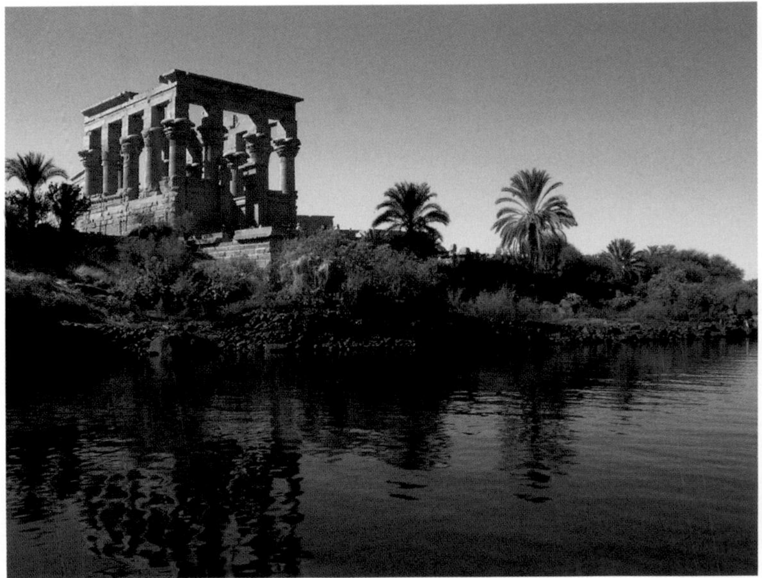

▲ Temple of Philae, Aswan

▲ Sufi followers during a moulid in Tanta

Weather and tourism apart, the **Islamic calendar** and its related festivals can have an effect on your travel. The most important factor is **Ramadan**, the month of daytime fasting, which can be problematic for eating and transport, though the festive evenings do much to compensate. See "Festivals" in the Basics chapter for details of its timing (p.48).

Average daily temperatures

	Jan	March	May	July	Sept	Nov
Alexandria ***Mediterranean***						
Max/Min (°F)	65/51	70/55	79/64	85/73	86/73	77/62
Max/Min (°C)	18/11	21/13	26/18	29/23	30/23	25/17
Aswan ***Southern Nile Valley***						
Max/Min (°F)	74/50	87/58	103/74	106/79	103/75	87/62
Max/Min (°C)	23/10	31/14	39/23	41/26	39/24	31/17
Cairo ***Northern Nile Valley***						
Max/Min (°F)	65/47	75/52	91/63	96/70	90/68	78/58
Max/Min (°C)	18/8	24/11	33/17	36/21	32/20	26/14
Dakhla ***Western Desert***						
Max/Min (°F)	70/41	82/47	99/68	104/74	96/70	82/53
Max/Min (°C)	21/5	28/8	37/20	40/23	36/21	28/12
Hurghada ***Red Sea Coast***						
Max/Min (°F)	70/50	74/61	86/70	90/77	86/74	77/59
Max/Min (°C)	21/10	23/12	30/21	32/25	30/23	25/15

Note that these are *average* daily maximum and minimum temperatures. Summer peaks in Aswan, Hurghada or Sinai, for example, can hit the 120 degrees F (low 50 degrees C) in hot years. The dryness of the air and absence of cloud cover makes for drastic fluctuations, though they do also make the heat tolerably unsticky outside Cairo and the Delta. The Mediterranean Coast can be windy and wet in winter.

28 things not to miss

It's not possible to see everything that Egypt has to offer in one trip – and we don't suggest you try. What follows, in no particular order, is a selective taste of the country's highlights: outstanding temples and tombs, spectacular landscapes and opportunities for Nile cruises. They're all arranged in five colour-coded categories, so that you can browse through to find the very best things to see, do and experience. All highlights have a page reference to take you into the Guide, where you can find out more.

01 Abu Simbel Page **370** • The monumental sun temple of Ramses II is the most spectacular of the Nubian antiquities that were relocated to higher ground on the shores of Lake Nasser.

02 Valley of the Kings Page **302** • The descent into the Underworld, the Judgement of Osiris and the rebirth of the pharaoh are vividly depicted on the walls and ceilings of the royal tombs.

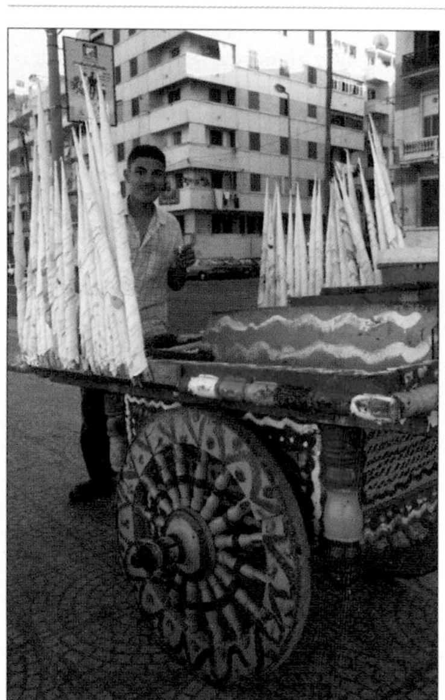

03 Street food Page **39** • Sold from pushcarts or in sit-down diners, *taamiya*, *kushari*, *fuul* and *shawarma* are tasty, cheap and nourishing.

04 Bellydancing Page **193** • The centuries-old tradition of *raqs sharqi* (oriental dance) is best seen at clubs frequented by locals, where the dancers and musicians will set your pulse racing.

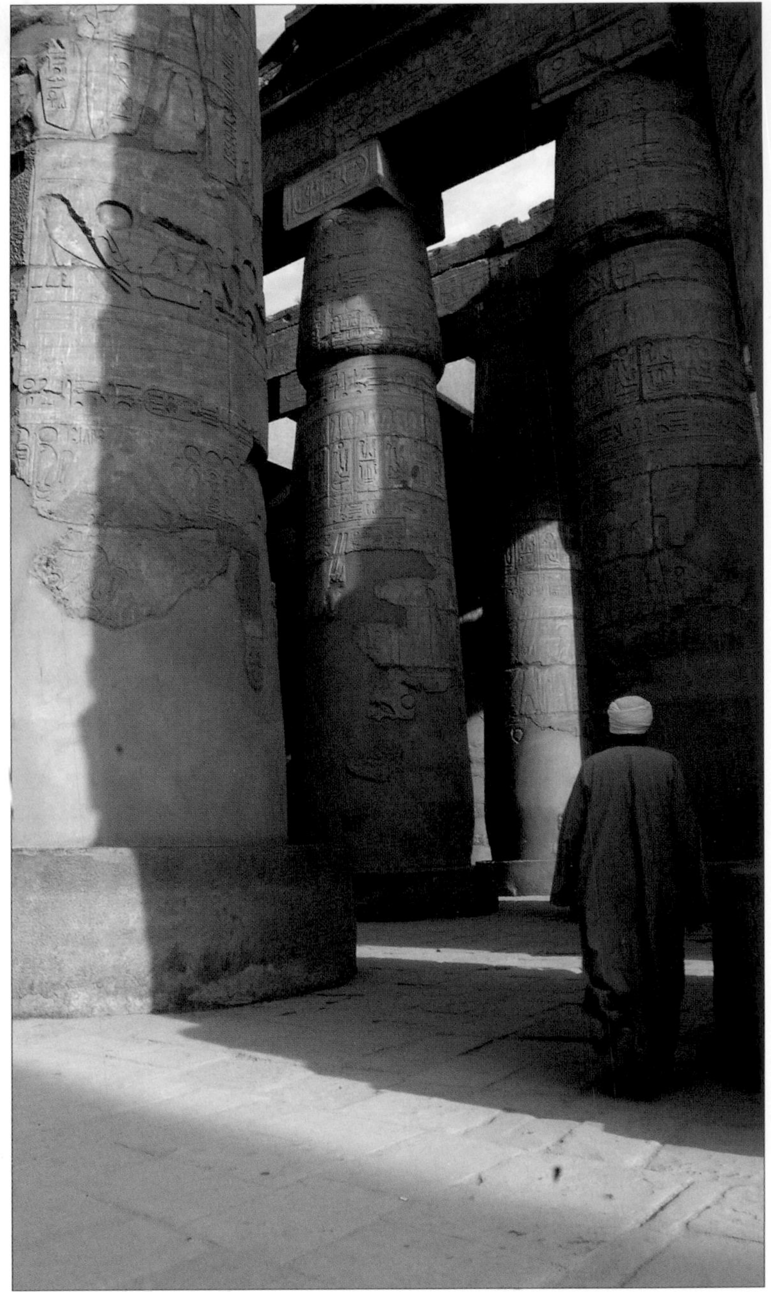

05 **Karnak Temple** Page **283** • Dedicated to the ancient Theban Triad of Amun, Mut and Khonsu, this vast complex reached its zenith during the New Kingdom.

06 Jeep or camel safaris Pages **50** & **379** • Make tracks into the dunes of the Western Desert or the canyons of Sinai – overnight trips or major expeditions are easily arranged.

07 Karkaday Page **42** • This infusion of hibiscus flowers makes a delicious hot or cold drink and tonic.

08 Mezze Page **40** • Dining in a restaurant, try *mezze*, consisting of many delicious, small dishes (particularly good for vegetarians).

09 Islamic Cairo Page **107** • City of a thousand minarets, teeming with life, and chock-full of architectural masterpieces and historic monuments. Head for Khan el-Khalili bazaar, or the Citadel.

10 Feluccas Page **250** • These lateen-sailed boats can be hired for an afternoon lazing on the Nile, or a two- or three-day journey from Aswan, visiting the temples at Kom Ombo and Edfu.

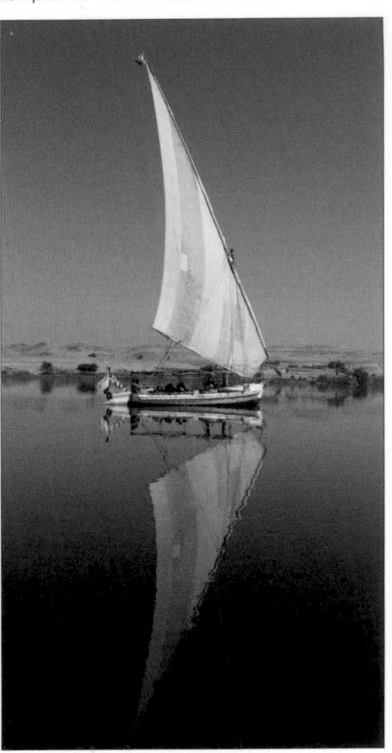

11 Diving and snorkelling See ***Egypt's underwater world* colour section** • Amazing coral reefs, tropical fish and wrecks make the Red Sea a paradise for scuba divers and snorkellers, while Egypt's Mediterranean coast has ancient underwater ruins and warships to explore.

12 Fresh juice Page **42** • Most towns have a sprinkling of juice bars or carts, where you can quench your thirst with whatever's in season, from freshly pressed oranges and mangoes to strawberries and sugar cane.

13 Catacombs of Kom es-Shoqafa Page **473** • Beneath the Karmous quarter of Alexandria are the spookiest tombs in Egypt, with a bizarre fusion of pharaonic, Greek and Roman funerary motifs reflecting the city's ancient diversity.

14 White Desert Page **407** • A tract of weird wind-eroded rock formations in Farafra Oasis, often visited on overnight safaris from the neighbouring oasis of Bahariya.

15 Jewellery Page **55** • There's an endless choice of pharaonic, classical, Islamic and contemporary designs in the bazaars of Cairo, Luxor and Aswan, and oases such as Siwa.

16 Balloon rides Page **280** • Enjoy a magnificent view of the Theban Necropolis on Luxor's west bank.

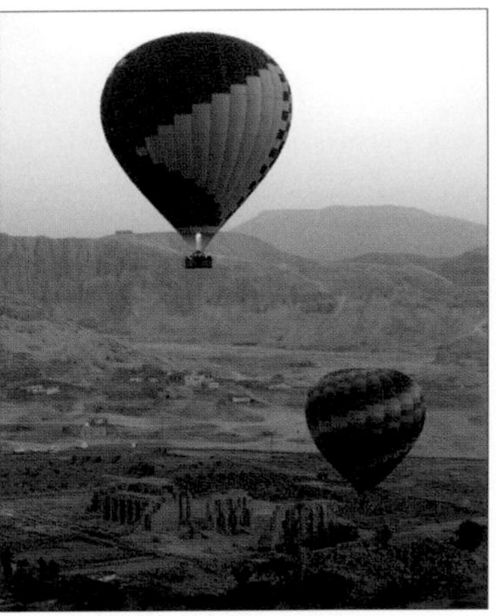

17 Dahabiya cruises Page **249** • These swanky nineteenth-century-style houseboats are perfect for cruising the Nile with a small group of friends.

18 Abydos Page **252** • One of the most ancient cult-centres in Egypt, Abydos' mortuary temple of Seti I contains magnificent bas-reliefs, the finest to have survived from the New Kingdom.

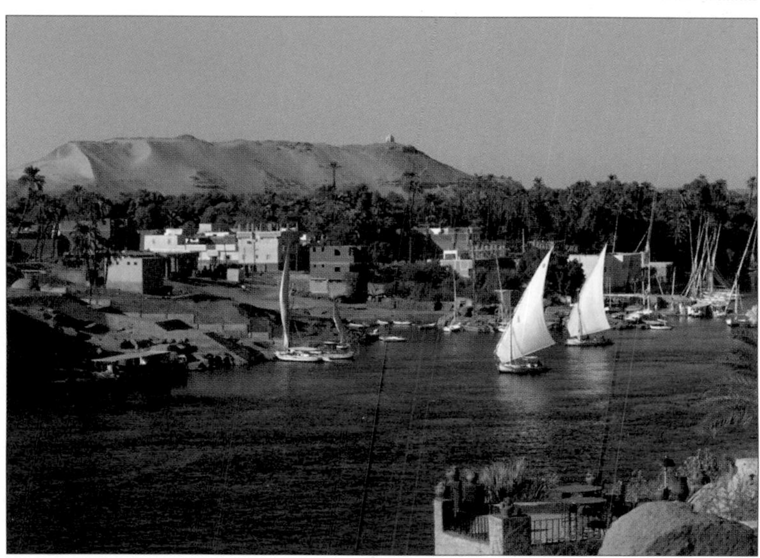

19 Aswan Page **339** • Aswan has been Egypt's gateway to Nubia since ancient times, and its islands, bazaars and riverside restaurants can keep you happy in between excursions to sites such as Abu Simbel.

20 Mount Sinai Page **562** • This awesome peak is revered as the site where Moses received the Ten Commandments from God.

21 The Egyptian Antiquities Museum Page **91** • Home to Tutankhamun's treasures, monumental statues from the Old Kingdom and the Amarna era, a dozen royal mummies and countless other artefacts, some engagingly humble.

22 The pyramids of Dahshur Page **181** • Less famous than the Giza trio but no less fascinating – and far less crowded. The Bent Pyramid, resting place of Snofru, has a distinctive angled top.

23 Ras Mohammed Page **528** • Egypt's oldest marine nature park boasts spectacular shark reefs and the wreck of the Dunraven.

24 Alexandria Page **456** • With its fabulous seafood and vintage coffee houses, its dazzling new library and the chance to dive the ruins of Cleopatra's Palace, there's plenty to discover in this Mediterranean port city.

25 St Catherine's Monastery Page **561** • Secluded beneath Mount Sinai, St Catherine's harbours the burning bush that appeared to Moses, and other holy relics.

26 The Pyramids and Sphinx at Giza Page **163** • The world's most famous monuments have inspired scholarly and crackpot speculations for centuries.

27 Dahab Page **542** • Sinai chill-out zone, renowned for its diving, beach cafés, and camel and jeep safaris into the rugged interior.

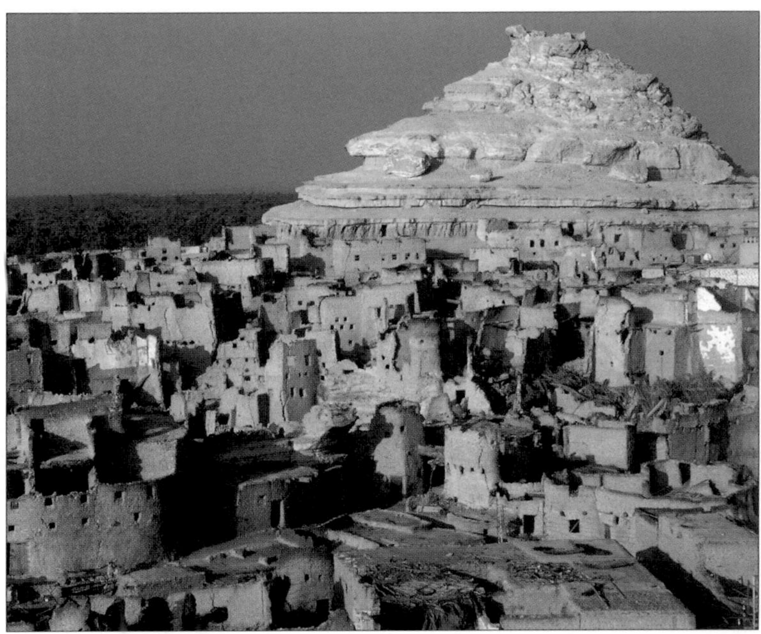

28 Siwa Oasis Page **438** • With its unique culture, hilltop citadel and spring-fed pools, Siwa is rated by many as the best of Egypt's oases.

Basics

Basics

Getting there

It is possible to get to Egypt by land, but most visitors fly in. Cairo has direct scheduled flights from London and New York, with indirect routes from pretty much everywhere, and there are low-cost flights to Luxor and the beach resorts.

The best airfares are available in low season, November through March, excluding Christmas and New Year, which counts as high season along with June, July and August. Flghts at weekends can cost more than on weekdays; prices quoted below are for the cheapest round trip midweek including tax. Many have restrictions such as fixed dates, and may require advance booking.

Note that, should your baggage go astray en route (this is most likely if you have to change flights, especially if the change is tight), you should not leave the airport without filing a report, or you will not be able to reclaim it when it does turn up (and you quite possibly won't even be allowed to re-enter the airport without a departure ticket for that day).

Flights from the UK and Ireland

EgyptAir (ⓦwww.egyptair.com.eg), British Airways (ⓦwww.ba.com) and BMI (ⓦwww.flybmi.com) have scheduled flights to **Cairo** from London Heathrow (5hr). EgyptAir also has weekly direct flights to Luxor and easyJet (ⓦwww.easyjet.com) flies from Luton and Gatwick to Sharm el-Sheikh, and from Gatwick to Hurghada. Flying indirectly, most airlines serve Cairo only, but Olympic (ⓦwww.olympicairlines.com), Royal Jordanian (ⓦwww.rj.com) and Saudi Arabian Airlines (ⓦwww.saudiairlines.com) also fly to Alexandria, while BA, BMI, KLM (ⓦwww.klm.com), Air France (ⓦwww.airfrance.com) and Lufthansa (ⓦwww.lufthansa.com) all offer indirect flights from a number of British and Irish airports. Flights can cost as little as £270 return, though, depending on the airline, you may have to pay more in high season.

From the UK, you may get a better price, or a more convenient flight, with low-cost and charter airlines such as Thomsonfly (ⓦflights.thomson.co.uk), First Choice Airways (ⓦflights.firstchoice.co.uk), or Thomas Cook (ⓦbook.flythomascook.com), who fly from the UK to Luxor and the main resorts – Sharm el-Sheikh, Hurghada and sometimes Mersa Alam and Taba. These may operate only once or twice a week, and prices are generally similar to those on scheduled services, though you may occasionally turn up a bargain out of season. Most flights depart from London Gatwick or Manchester, but a few – particularly to Sharm el-Sheikh – use other UK airports too. Dive companies such as Scubasnacks (ⓦwww.scubasnacks.co.uk), Regal (ⓦwww.regal-diving.co.uk) and Crusader (ⓦwww.crusadertravel.com) occasionally have cheap flight-only deals to the Red Sea resorts, but these are not usually advertised, so you'd need to approach the company direct. You may even find it cheaper to take a package tour than just a flight; there are some amazing bargains to be had among the basic Luxor-plus-Cairo or Luxor-only packages, and many smaller independent operators feature felucca trips on the Nile, diving holidays on the Red Sea or camel trekking in Sinai.

From Ireland, you can either make your own way to London and fly from there, or take an indirect flight, changing planes in Britain or Europe. Fares to Cairo start at around €370, with many (but not all) airlines hiking their prices by around €150 in high season.

Note if using a charter flight that the maximum stay allowed in Egypt for visitors arriving on a charter flight is a month; attempting to circumvent this by buying two one-way tickets, with the return flight happening more than a month after the outbound date, can lead to your being barred from boarding the plane back.

Flights from the US and Canada

From the US, EgyptAir (ⓦwww.egyptair.com.eg) and Delta (ⓦwww.delta.com) fly direct to Cairo from New York (11hr), and several European and Middle Eastern airlines offer indirect flights from a range of departure points, though New York still offers the biggest choice of airlines. West Coast flights are routed via the airlines' hub cities, so check that you won't have to wait overnight for your onward connection. You should be able to pick up a round-trip ticket for as little as $770 out of New York in low season, $820 in high season. Flying from the West Coast, expect to pay at least $160 more.

From Canada there are direct flights to Cairo out of Montreal twice weekly in summer only with EgyptAir, who also offer through tickets from other cities via New York in combination with local airlines. Otherwise, European carriers such as BA (ⓦwww.ba.com) and Air France (ⓦwww.airfrance.com) fly via London or Paris from Toronto, Montreal or Vancouver, while Air Canada (ⓦwww.aircanada.com) offer through tickets from most Canadian airports in combination with Lufthansa (ⓦwww.lufthansa.com). Low-/high-season fares start at around Can$1100/1900 from Montreal or Toronto, Can$1200/2300 from Vancouver.

Flights from Australia, New Zealand and South Africa

A number of European, Middle Eastern and Asian carriers offer indirect flights to Egypt from Australia and New Zealand, changing planes at their hub airports. Cairo fares start at around Aus$1850 in low season, or Aus$2050 in high season from Australia, around NZ$3400 year-round from New Zealand. Emirates (ⓦwww.emirates.com) and Etihad (ⓦwww.etihadairways.com) are usually the cheapest and most convenient airlines, but if flying into Dubai, you might want to investigate low-cost flights on Air Arabia (ⓦwww.airarabia.com) from nearby Sharjah to Alexandria, Assyut and Luxor.

From South Africa, there are direct Cairo flights from Johannesburg with EgyptAir (ⓦwww.egyptair.com.eg), and SAA (ⓦwww.flysaa.com) codeshare this flight, offering through tickets from most South African airports. Otherwise, you can take an indirect flight with an East African airline such as Kenya Airways (ⓦwww.kenya-airways.com) or Ethiopian Airlines (ⓦwww.ethiopianairlines.com), or a Middle Eastern Airline such as Emirates (ⓦwww.emirates.com) or Gulf Air (ⓦwww.gulfair.com). Most serve only Johannesburg, but Emirates flies from Cape Town as well. Fares start at around R5400 year-round.

From Israel and Cyprus by land and sea

At the time of writing, the Rafah border crossing between Gaza and Egypt is closed, and all traffic between Israel and Egypt uses the crossing at Taba near Eilat (open 24/7 except Eid el-Adha and Yom Kippur). Entering Egypt via Taba, you're subject to an Israeli departure tax of US$25 (NIS94.50; NIS4.50 less if you pay at in advance at the main post office in Eilat, Tel Aviv, West Jerusalem, Haifa or Beersheba rather than at the border) and an Egyptian entry tax of £E75 (US$15).

Mazada Tours (141 Rehov Ibn Gvirol, Tel Aviv ⓣ03/544 4544; 15 Jaffa Rd, West Jerusalem ⓣ02/623 5777; ⓦwww.mazada.co.il) runs buses to Cairo twice weekly (Sun and Thurs) from both Tel Aviv and Jerusalem. One-way tickets are US$95 (plus border taxes totalling US$55), return tickets US$110 (plus US$55). It's best to book (and confirm return journeys) at least three days in advance. The company can apply for a visa for you on request, but the Egyptian embassy is just around the corner from its office (see p.60 for the address), and it is cheaper to do it yourself.

Taba makes a fine jumping-off point for the Sinai coast resorts, St Catherine's Monastery or Cairo. From Eilat, a taxi or a #15 bus (which doesn't run on Shabbat) will get you to the Israeli checkpoint at Taba for an exit stamp; you then walk over to the Egyptian side, where Sinai-only visas can be obtained on the spot (for more on visas in general, see p.59). It usually takes a good hour to cross the border, longer at holiday times. A few banks in Sharm el-Sheikh and one or two banks and foreign exchange bureaux in Cairo are the only places in Egypt where you

Six steps to a better kind of travel

At Rough Guides we are passionately committed to travel. We feel strongly that only through travelling do we truly come to understand the world we live in and the people we share it with – plus tourism has brought a great deal of **benefit** to developing economies around the world over the last few decades. But the extraordinary growth in tourism has also damaged some places irreparably, and of course **climate change** is exacerbated by most forms of transport, especially flying. This means that now more than ever it's important to **travel thoughtfully** and **responsibly**, with respect for the cultures you're visiting – not only to derive the most benefit from your trip but also to preserve the best bits of the planet for everyone to enjoy. At Rough Guides we feel there are six main areas in which you can make a difference:

- Consider what you're contributing to the **local economy**, and how much the services you use do the same, whether it's through employing local workers and guides or sourcing locally grown produce and local services.
- Consider the **environment** on holiday as well as at home. Water is scarce in many developing destinations, and the biodiversity of local flora and fauna can be adversely affected by tourism. Try to patronize businesses that take account of this.
- Travel with a purpose, not just to tick off experiences. Consider **spending longer** in a place, and getting to know it and its people.
- Give thought to how often you **fly**. Try to avoid short hops by air and more harmful night flights.
- Consider **alternatives to flying**, travelling instead by bus, train, boat and even by bike or on foot where possible.
- Make your trips "**climate neutral**" via a reputable carbon-offset scheme. All Rough Guide flights are offset, and every year we donate money to a variety of charities devoted to combating the effects of climate change.

can legally exchange Israeli shekels. You are not allowed to drive rented cars or 4WDs across the Israeli–Egyptian border.

The passenger ferry service from Limassol (Cyprus) to Port Said, with some services calling at Haifa (Israel), has often been suspended, but was running at last check, approximately weekly over the summer. For further details contact Varianos Travel, 8C Pantelides Ave, PO Box 22107, 1517 Nicosia, Cyprus ⓣ357/2268 0500, ⓦwww.varianostravel.com/Cruises/ferry_service.htm. The ferry does not carry vehicles. The fare is €200–250 in a shared cabin depending on the season (and regardless of whether you get on in Limassol or Haifa), and takes 16 hour 30 minutes direct, or 38 hour via Haifa (where it stops for 14hr).

From Jordan by land and sea

Direct buses do the 21-hour journey from Amman to Cairo via Aqaba–Nuweiba, but they are neither pleasant nor economical. JETT, on King Hussein Street (ⓣ06/566 4146, ⓦwww.jett.com.jo), 900m north from Abdali station, have two weekly departures (JD75 one-way, plus JD6 border tax). Afana, next door to JETT and at Abdali station (ⓣ06/568 1560), runs weekly buses for the same price. Most buses will leave you in Cairo at Almaza terminal (see p.79), but some arrive at the more convenient Sinai bus terminal (see p.78). Unless time is of the essence, it's better to do the journey in stages, stopping en route at Aqaba or in Sinai.

From Aqaba, the quickest route to Egypt is by land via Eilat in Israel, using local buses. Disincentives are the telltale Taba border stamp (see box, p.59), and the hefty exit and entry taxes (totalling around US$46) payable at Eilat and Taba. Alternatively, there are ferries to Nuweiba in the Sinai operated by the Arab Bridge Maritime Co. (ⓦwww.abmaritime.com.jo): a fast ferry (2 daily; 1hr; $70); and a notoriously unpunctual slow

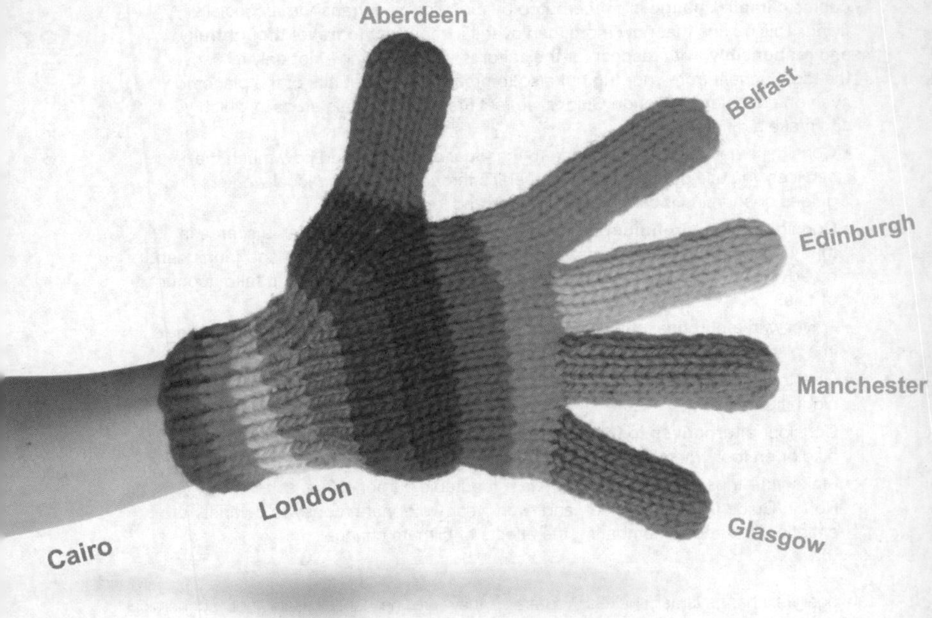

ferry (daily; 3hr 30min; $60); both ferries will take vehicles. You can buy tickets from the company's offices in Amman (beside the Royal Jordanian building just off 7th Circle; ⓣ06/585 9554) or Aqaba (downtown near the *China* restaurant; ⓣ03/209 3237), from agents in Aqaba, or up to an hour before departure at the passenger terminal itself, 5km south of Aqaba (ⓣ03/201 3236). The terminal is served by local buses between Aqaba's fort and the Saudi border at Durra, or costs around JD4 by taxi. You pay a JD6 exit tax when boarding the ferry. Sinai-only visas (see p.60) are available at Nuweiba.

Agents and operators

Ancient World Tours UK ⓣ020/7917 9494, ⓦwww.ancient.co.uk. In-depth archeological and historical tours led by experts to over 120 sites in Egypt, including exclusive access to the tombs of Seti I, Horemheb, Queen Nefertari and the sons of Ramses II (KV5) in the Theban Necropolis, the Golden Mummies of Bahariya Oasis, the interior of the Pyramid of Unas at Saqqara, Hierakonopolis and other sites otherwise off-limits to tourists.

Discover Egypt UK ⓣ0844/880 0462, ⓦwww.discoveregypt.co.uk. Packages and tailor-made itineraries including Nile cruises and multi-centre holidays.

Egypt Tours US ⓣ1-800/TO-EGYPT, ⓦwww.egyptours.com. Packages ranging from a six-night highlights tour to a nineteen-night "In Depth" trip, as well as combined tours with Jordan and Israel.

North South Travel UK ⓣ01245/608 291, ⓦwww.northsouthtravel.co.uk. Friendly, competitive travel agency, offering discounted fares worldwide. Profits are used to support projects in the developing world, especially the promotion of sustainable tourism.

Soliman Travel UK ⓣ020/7244 6855, ⓦwww.solimantravel.co.uk. One of the longest-established UK-based Egypt tour operators, with charter flights and a large range of packages and tailor-made holidays, mainly in five-star accommodation.

STA Travel UK ⓣ0871/230 0040, ⓦwww.statravel.com; US ⓣ1-800/781-4040, Australia ⓣ134 782, New Zealand ⓣ0800/474400, South Africa ⓣ0861/781 781; ⓦwww.statravel.co.za. Specialists in independent travel; also student IDs, travel insurance, and more. Good discounts for students and under-26s.

Trailfinders UK ⓣ0845/058 5858, Republic of Ireland ⓣ01/677 7888, Australia ⓣ1300/780 212; ⓦwww.trailfinders.com. One of the best-informed and most efficient agents for independent travellers.

Travel Cuts Canada ⓣ1-866/246-9762, US ⓣ1-800/592-2887; ⓦwww.travelcuts.com. Canadian youth and student travel firm.

USIT Republic of Ireland ⓣ01/602 1906, Northern Ireland ⓣ028/9032 7111; ⓦwww.usit.ie. Ireland's main student and youth travel specialists.

Ya'lla Tours US ⓣ800/644-1595, ⓦwww.yallatours.com. Egypt and Middle East package specialists offering four-night breaks in Cairo, with optional add-ons to Alexandria, the Fayoum or Mount Sinai.

Getting around

Egyptian public transport is, on the whole, pretty good. There is an efficient rail network linking the Nile Valley, Delta and Canal Zone, and elsewhere you can travel easily enough by bus or collective (service) taxi. On the Nile you can indulge in feluccas or cruise boats, and in the desert there's the chance to test your camel-riding prowess. For those in a hurry, EgyptAir provides a network of flights.

While you can travel without restriction through most areas of Egypt, **travel permits** are required for desert travel between Bahariya and Siwa oases (permits available in Siwa), to Ain Della and the Gilf Kebir/Jebel Uwaynat in the western desert (see p.381), for the desert east of Mersa Alam (see p.594), and to camp around Berenice and the Red Sea coast south of Mersa Alam (see p.594). In principle, permits to visit restricted areas in the eastern and western deserts are obtainable from Military Intelligence (Mukaharabat), whose office is next-door to the Nasser Mosque at Abbassiya in Cairo (you need two photos and photocopies of the identifying pages of your passport and your Egyptian entry visa, plus a detailed intinerary), but in practice, you are very unlikely to get a permit by approaching them directly, and approaches should be made through an authorized travel agency, such as those mentioned in the text, or, failing that, Misr Travel, 1 Sharia Talaat Harb, Cairo ⓣ02/2393 0010, ⓔmisrtrav@link.com.eg. You should not need a permit to travel directly from Mersa Matrouh to the Libyan border, for example if taking a bus or service taxi to Benghazi or Tripoli, but the rules sometimes change, so it is wise to check first.

By rail

Covering a limited network of routes (Cairo to Alexandria, the Delta and the Canal Zone, along the coast to Mersa Matrouh, and up the Nile Valley to Luxor and Aswan), Egypt's trains are best used for long hauls, when air-conditioned services offer a comfier alternative to buses and taxis. For shorter journeys, trains are slower and less reliable.

Timetables can be downloaded from the Egyptian Railways' website (ⓦwww.egyptrail.gov.eg), which also allows you to look up schedules and fares for a/c services between major stations. Schedules for sleeper services are available on the website of the company which operates them, Abela (ⓦwww.sleepingtrains.com).

From Cairo to Alexandria or Aswan, there are fast a/c trains (including sleepers, also called wagons-lits) and snail-like non-a/c local services. However, on the Cairo–Luxor/Aswan route, foreigners are only allowed to use five **"tourist trains"** (three of which are sleepers), whose compartments are guarded by gun-toting plainclothes cops.

Buying tickets can get complicated at the largest stations, where separate queues eixst for different ticket classes.

Air-conditioned trains

Air-conditioned trains nearly always have two classes. The most comfortable option is **first class** (*daraga awla*), with waiter service, reclining armchairs and no standing. They also screen videos until midnight. **Second class superior** (*daraga tania mukayyifa*) is less plush and more crowded – but two-thirds the price of first class. Occasionally a/c trains will be first or second class only. An ordinary first- or a/c second-class carriage should be comfortable enough to allow sleeping on an overnight journey, at a fraction of the cost of a sleeper.

Seats are **reservable** up to seven days in advance. There is occasional double booking but a little baksheesh to the conductor usually sorts out any problem. One common difficulty is that return tickets can't necessarily be booked at the point of origin. The peak seasons for travel are summer for Alexandria and winter for Upper Egypt.

To give an idea of **fares**, a ticket from Cairo to Luxor costs around £E165 in first class (the only class allowed for tourists), while Cairo to Alexandria costs £E41 in first class, £E25 in second. **Students** with ISIC cards (see p.57) get at least a third off on all fares except on sleepers. Most travel agencies sell first-class tickets for a small commission, saving you from having to queue.

Wagons-lits (sleepers)

Many tourists cough up for snazzier wagons-lits, which may comprise an entire train, or be limited to a couple of carriages tacked on to a regular service. Fares are relatively hefty (though still cheaper than flying) at US$60 one-way from Cairo to Luxor or Aswan. Passengers get a comfortable two-bed cabin (a single traveller can book one exclusively for $80, or pay the normal fare and share with someone of the same sex) with a sink, plus breakfast and dinner, and access to a dining car, a bar and sometimes a disco. In summer (mid-June to mid-Sept) there's also a sleeper service from Cairo to Mersa Matrouh.

Bookings for wagons-lits can be done through branches of Thomas Cook or American Express, or with Abela (ⓦwww.sleepingtrains.com), and payment must be made in US dollars or euros.

Non-air-conditioned trains

Non-a/c trains are **ordinary second class** (*daraga tania aadia*), with padded bench seating, or **third class** (*daraga talata*), with wooden benches. Both are invariably crowded, the rolling stock is ancient and often filthy, and schedules fanciful. Few foreigners use them, but on a few routes they are the only services available, and over short distances you might enjoy the disorder.

There is no advance booking for seats on these services and you needn't queue for a ticket at the station. You simply walk on and buy a ticket from the conductor, paying a small penalty fee (£E1–2).

By bus

Egypt's three main bus companies, all based in Cairo, are: Upper Egypt Bus Company (Nile Valley, Fayoum, inner oases, and the Red Sea Coast down to El-Quseir); East Delta Bus Company (Sinai and the Canal Zone); and West and Middle Delta Bus Company (Alexandria, Mersa Matrouh, Siwa and the Nile Delta). Key routes (Cairo to Alexandria, Sharm el-Sheikh and Hurghada) are also covered by Superjet (red, black and gold livery, known as "Golden Arrows" or "Golden Rockets"). Superjet is a subsidiary of the Arab Union Transport Company, which operates international services to Libya, Jordan, Syria and Saudi Arabia. A relatively new operator, El Gouna, runs buses from Cairo to Hurghada and Sharm el-Sheikh.

Major routes are plied by a/c buses, usually new(ish) and fast. Local routes usually have cheaper non-a/c buses, generally old rattletraps. Superjet buses have a/c, toilets, videos and expensive snacks.

Terminals and bookings

Though most towns have a single bus depot for all destinations, cities such as Cairo and Alexandria have several. English- or French-speaking staff are fairly common at the larger ones, but rare in the provinces. **Schedules** – usually posted in Arabic only – change frequently. Bus information can be obtained from hotels in Sinai and the oases, and tourist offices in Luxor, Aswan and the oases.

At city terminals, **tickets** are normally sold from kiosks, up to 24 hours in advance for air-conditioned or long-haul services. In the provinces, tickets may only be available an hour or so before departure, or on the bus itself in the case of through services, which are often standing-room only when they arrive. Passengers on a/c services are usually assigned a seat (the number is written in Arabic on your ticket), but seats on "local" buses are taken on a first-come first-served basis. Fares are very reasonable: Cairo to Alexandria costs £E17 by ordinary bus, or £E35 on the deluxe Superjet service, while Cairo to Luxor is £E100 by Superjet.

By service taxi

Collective **service taxis** (known as *servees*) are one of the best features of Egyptian transport. They operate on a wide variety of routes, are generally quicker than buses and trains, and fares are very reasonable. On the downside, maniacal driving on congested roads calls for strong nerves; accidents are not uncommon.

The taxis are usually big **Peugeot saloons** carrying seven passengers, or **microbuses** (*meecros*) seating a dozen. Most business is along specific routes, with more or less nonstop departures throughout the day on the main ones, while cross-desert traffic is restricted to early morning and late afternoon. Show up at the terminal (locations are detailed in the guide) and ask for a *servees* to your destination, or listen for drivers shouting it out. As soon as the requisite number of people (or less, if you're willing to pay extra) are assembled, the taxi sets off. Fewer people travel after dark in winter or on Friday, when you might have to wait a while for a ride to a distant town; travelling in stages can be quicker.

Service taxis have **fixed fares**, which you can ascertain by asking at your hotel (or the tourist office), or seeing what Egyptians pay. You can also **charter a taxi** – useful for day excursions or on odd routes, but you'll have to bargain hard to get the right price.

By car

Driving in Egypt is not for the faint-hearted or inexperienced motorist. Cities, highways, backroads and *pistes* each pose a challenge to drivers' skills and nerve. Pedestrians and carts seem blithely indifferent to heavy traffic. Though accidents are less frequent than you'd think, the crumpled wrecks alongside highways are a constant reminder of the hazards of motoring.

The **minimum age** for driving in Egypt is 25 years, the **maximum is** 70. Foreigners require an International Driving Licence (obtainable from motoring organizations at home).

The **speed limit** outside towns is 90km per hour (100km on the Cairo–Alexandria Desert Road), but on certain stretches it can be as low as 30km per hour. Road signs are similar to those in Europe, but speed limits are posted in Arabic numerals (see p.642). Although driving on the right is pretty much universal, other **rules of the road** vary. Traffic in cities is relentless and anarchic, with vehicles weaving to and fro between lanes, signalling by horn. Two beeps means "I'm alongside and about to overtake." A single long blast warns "I can't (won't) stop and I'm coming through!" Extending your hand, fingers raised and tips together, is the signal for "Watch out, don't pass now"; spreading your fingers and flipping them forwards indicates "Go ahead." Although the car in front usually has right of way, buses and trams always take precedence. On **country roads** – including the two-lane east- and west-bank "highways" along the Nile Valley – trucks and cars routinely overtake in the face of incoming traffic. The passing car usually flashes its lights as a warning, but not always.

Most roads are bumpy, with potholes and all manner of traffic, including donkey carts and camels. Beware, especially, of children darting into the road. If you injure someone, relatives may take revenge on the spot. Avoid driving **after dark**, when Egyptians drive without lights, only flashing them on to high beam when they see another car approaching. Wandering pedestrians and animals, obstructions and sand drifts present extra hazards. In spring, flash floods can wash away roads in Sinai. On **pistes** (rough, unpaved tracks in the desert or mountains) there are special problems. You need a good deal of driving and mechanical confidence – and shouldn't attempt such routes if you don't feel your car's up to scratch.

Police checkpoints – signposted in English as "Traffic Stations" – occur on the approach roads to towns and oases and along major trunk routes. Foreign motorists are usually waved through, but you might be asked to show your passport or driving licence. In Middle Egypt the checkpoints are militarized.

Car rental

Renting a car pays obvious dividends if you are pushed for time or plan to visit remote sites, but whether you'd want to drive yourself is another matter – it's not much more expensive to hire a car and driver. Any branch of Misr Travel (see p.67), and numerous local tour agencies, can fix you up with one, or you can charter a taxi (see p.37). If you bring your own vehicle, you are required to re-export it when you leave – even if it gets wrecked.

A self-drive car can be rented through one of the international franchise chains, or a local firm (addresses are given in the guide). It's worth shopping around as rates and terms vary considerably. At the cheaper end, you can get a car with unlimited mileage for about £40/US$70 a day. Most companies require a hefty deposit, and not all accept credit cards. You cannot bring a rented car across the border.

Before making a reservation, be sure to find out if you can pick up the car in one city and return it in another. Generally, this is only possible with cars from Hertz, Avis or Budget. Before setting out, make sure the car has a spare tyre, tool kit and full documentation – including insurance cover, which is compulsory with all rentals.

Fuel and breakdowns

Petrol (*benzene*) and diesel stations are plentiful in larger towns but few and far between in rural and desert areas. Replace oil/air filters regularly, lest impurities in the fuel, and Egypt's ubiquitous dust, clog up the engine.

Egyptian **mechanics** are usually excellent at coping with breakdowns, and all medium-sized towns have garages (most with a range of spare parts for French, German and

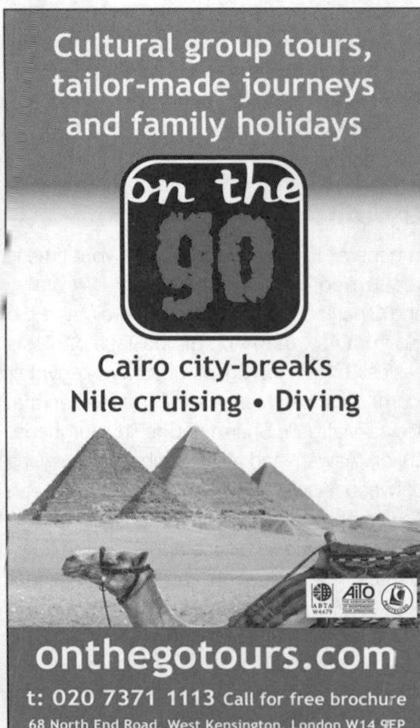
Cultural group tours, tailor-made journeys and family holidays
on the go
Cairo city-breaks
Nile cruising • Diving
onthegotours.com
t: 020 7371 1113 Call for free brochure
68 North End Road, West Kensington, London W14 9EP

egypt uncovered
...specialists in cultural & adventure tours
...small group, private and tailor-made itineraries from economy to luxury level...
email: tours@egypt-uncovered.com
...or visit us at:
www.egypt-uncovered.com
Tel: +44 (0) 845 130 4849
'Egypt Uncovered' is a trading name of Uncover the World Ltd.

adventure of a lifetime
Small group adventures in Egypt & Jordan from 8 to 18 days
Prices start at £325
oasisoverland
+44(0)1963 363400
www.oasisoverland.com

diverseearth
worldwide travel
Travel that doesn't cost the earth
Small group adventures
Tailor-made tours
Exciting family destinations
Call our Egypt experts on
0800 0747 007
ABTA
ABTA No.v3629
climatecare

Japanese cars). But if you break down miles from anywhere, you can pay a lot to get towed back.

Vehicle insurance

All car rentals must by law be sold with third-party insurance. Accident and damage insurance should be included, but make sure. In the case of an **accident**, get a written report from the police and from the doctor who first treats any injuries, without which your insurance may not cover the costs. Reports are written in Arabic.

Driving your own vehicle, you will need to take out **Egyptian insurance**. Policies are sold by Misr Insurance (Ⓣ02/3335-5350 or 19114, Ⓦwww.misrins.com, site in Arabic only); offices are found in most towns and at border crossings. Premiums vary according to the size, horsepower and value of the vehicle.

Motorbikes and bicycles

Motorcycling could be a good way to travel around Egypt, but the red tape involved in bringing your own bike is diabolical (ask your national motoring organization and the Egyptian consulate for details). It's difficult to rent a machine except in Luxor or Hurghada. Bikers should be especially wary of potholes, sand and rocks, and other road-users (see p.34).

Bicycles, useful for getting around small towns and reaching local sights or beaches, can be rented in Luxor, Aswan, Hurghada, Siwa Oasis and other places for a modest sum. Cycling in big cities or over long distances is not advisable. Traffic is murderous, the heat brutal, and foreign cyclists are sometimes stoned by children (particularly in the Delta). If you're determined to cycle the **Nile Valley**, the east bank expressway that runs down as far as Aswan is the safest route.

Most towns have **repair shops**, well used to servicing local bikes and mopeds but unlikely to have the right spare parts (they can usually sort out some kind of temporary solution).

Hitching

Hitching is largely confined to areas with minimal public transport, or trunk routes if passing service taxis or scheduled buses are full. You usually pay anyway, and foreigners who hitch where proper transport is available may inspire contempt rather than sympathy. Women should never hitch without a male companion.

By air

In general, it's only worth flying if your time is very limited, or for the view – the Nile Valley and Sinai look amazing from the air, and the trip from Aswan to Abu Simbel (see p.371) is easiest by plane. EgyptAir (Ⓦwww.egyptair.com) flies between Cairo and Alexandria, Mersa Matrouh, Sharm el-Sheikh, Hurghada, Luxor, Aswan and Abu Simbel, as well as between Aswan and Luxor and between Aswan and Abu Simbel. Details of flights and addresses of local offices appear in the text.

Fares rise as seats on the plane get booked up, so it's best to book early if possible. In winter season, you would be lucky to get any kind of flight between Cairo and Luxor, Aswan, Abu Simbel or Sharm without booking at least a week ahead. Always reconfirm 72 hours prior to the journey, as overbooking is commonplace.

By boat

The colonial tradition of **Nile cruises** has spawned an industry with over two hundred steamers. Most sail from Luxor to Aswan (or the other way), a three- to five-day trip, stopping at Esna, Edfu and Kom Ombo.

The most reliable cruises are sold with package holidays, and week-long cruises plus air fare are available for as little as £500 from the UK or US$2700 from North America. In Egypt you can arrange a four-day trip on the spot for around £220/US$360 (all per person in a twin cabin). Prices escalate dramatically for a luxury cruise.

Looking for a Nile cruise in Egypt, shop around and don't necessarily go for the cheapest deal – some leave a lot to be desired in terms of hygiene and living conditions. If possible, check the vessel first. Deluxe boats with swimming pools can be wonderful, but not all offer value for money. The best deals are available from local agents in Luxor and Aswan (or directly from the boats). Beware in particular of the overpriced trips sold by touts and some hotels in Cairo (see box, p.78).

Feluccas, the lateen-sailed boats used on the Nile since antiquity, still serve as transport along many stretches. Favoured by tourists for sunset cruises, they allow you to experience the changing moods of the Nile while lolling in blissful indolence. Many visitors opt for a felucca cruise between Aswan and Luxor. It's easy to arrange a cruise yourself (see pp.250–252), and several tour operators offer packages.

Local **ferries**, generally battered, crowded and cheap, cross the Nile and Suez Canal at various points. There's also a catamaran service between Hurghada and Sharm el-Sheikh (see p.586 & p.534), and fast and slow ferries from Nuweiba in Sinai to Aqaba in Jordan (see p.553).

City transport

Most Egyptian towns are small enough to cover on foot, especially if your hotel is in the centre. In larger cities, however, local transport is useful. Learn to recognize Arabic numerals (see p.642) to take full advantage of the cheap **buses**, **minibuses** and **trams** that cover most of Alexandria and Cairo (which also has river taxis and an excellent metro).

Four-seater **taxis** often operate on a shared basis, making stops to pick up passengers heading in the same direction. To hail a cab, pick a major thoroughfare with traffic heading in the right direction, stand on the kerb, and wave and holler out your destination as one approaches. If the driver's interested he'll stop, whereupon you can state your destination again, in more detail. If the driver starts talking money, say "*maalesh*" (forget it) and look for another cab.

Don't expect drivers to speak English or know every street; you may need to name a major landmark or thoroughfare in the vicinity instead. If your destination is obscure or hard to pronounce, get it written down in Arabic. Near the end of the journey, direct the driver to stop where you want (bearing in mind one-way systems and other obstacles) with "*h'na/hinak kwayes*" (here/there's okay). You need to know the right fare in advance; hand it over with confidence when you arrive, together with any tip you consider appropriate. If you've underpaid, the driver will let you know. Don't take taxis waiting outside expensive hotels or tourist sites, nor those that hustle you in the street, as these are sure to overcharge you.

Calèches or *hantoor* – horse-drawn buggies – are mainly for tourists, who are often accosted by drivers in Luxor and Aswan, Alexandria, and at other places. Fares are higher than taxis and, regardless of official tariffs, are negotiable. In a few small towns, mostly in Middle Egypt, the *hantoor* remains part of local city transport. Ask locals about fares before climbing on board, or simply pay what you see fit at the end. Some of the horses and buggies are in pristine condition; others painful to behold. Tourists can help by admonishing drivers who abuse their animals or gallop their horses, and by not travelling more than four to a carriage.

Addresses

Words for street (*sharia*), avenue (*tariq*) and square (*midan*) precede the name. Narrower thoroughfares may be termed *darb*, *haret*, *sikket* or *zuqaq*. *Bab* signifies a medieval gate, after which certain quarters are named (for example, Bab el-Khalq in Cairo); *kubri* a bridge; and *souk* a market. Whole blocks often share a single street number, which may be in Arabic numerals (see also p.642), but are commonly not shown at all.

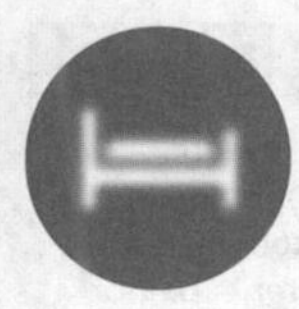

Accommodation

The main tourist centres offer a broad spectrum of accommodation, with everything from luxury palace to homely pensions and flea-ridden dives. Even in high season, in Cairo, Sinai or the Nile Valley, you should be able to find something in your preferred range. Elsewhere, the choice is generally more limited, with only basic lodgings available in most of the desert oases. Cairo is generally more expensive for accommodation of all types.

Hotels

Egyptian hotels are loosely categorized into star ratings, from one-star to five-star deluxe. Below this there are unclassified hotels and pensions, some tailored to foreign backpackers, others mostly used by Egyptians.

Deluxe hotels are almost exclusively modern and chain-owned (Sofitel, Mövenpick, Hilton, etc), with swimming pools, bars, restaurants, air conditioning and all the usual facilities. **Four-star** hotels can be more characterful, including some famous names like the *Old Cataract* in Aswan and the *Winter Palace* in Luxor. There is also the odd gem among **three-star** hotels, though most are slightly shabby 1970s-style towers, where facilities like plumbing and air-conditioning can be less reliable. Upmarket hotels, especially at the top of the range, are invariably much cheaper if booked from home through a travel agent or online than if you simply turn up and pay the rack rate.

At **two- and one-star** level, you rarely get air conditioning, though better places will supply fans, and old-style buildings with balconies, high ceilings and louvred windows are well designed to cope with the heat, but can be chilly in winter, as they rarely have heating.

Some cheaper hotels are classified as **pensions**, which makes little difference in facilities, but may signify family ownership and a friendlier ambience.

Hotel touts

"Fishing" for guests (as Egyptians call it) is common in tourist centres, where new arrivals are approached by touts at train and bus stations, airports and docks. Some work in the hotel they're touting, but most are hustling for commissions and will use trickery to deliver clients to "their" establishment – swearing that other places are full, or closed, or whatever. Usually it's grotty and overpriced places that depend on touts. In any case, their commission will be added to your bill – another reason to avoid using them. In Cairo especially, many touts work for hotels that exist purely to

Accommodation price codes

All the establishments listed in this book have been graded according to the categories listed below, representing the cost, including tax, of the **cheapest double room** in high season (winter in Upper Egypt and Sinai, summer in Alexandria). For places that offer **dorm beds** or charge on a singles basis, rates per person are given in £E. Note that most hotels in categories ❻ to ❾ quote rates in US dollars, but will accept payment in £E.

❶ £E59 (US$10) and under
❷ £E60–119 (US$11–22)
❸ £E120–199 (US$23–37)
❹ £E200–299 (US$38–55)
❺ £E300–410 (US$56–75)
❻ US$76–119 (£E411–655)
❼ US$120–199 (£E656–1090)
❽ US$200–299(£E1091–1635)
❾ US$300 (£E1636) and over.

hand foreigners and sell them overpriced excursions or souvenirs.

Hostels

Egypt's seven official youth hostels are cheap but have daytime lock-outs, night-time curfews and segregation of men from women and (usually) foreigners from Egyptians (which you might appreciate when noisy groups are in residence). The most salubrious hostels are in Cairo, Sharm el-Sheikh and Ismailiya – but all are far from where the action is.

It seems to be up to individual hostels whether you need a Hostelling International (HI) card, and their rules change constantly. Non-HI members, if admitted, are usually charged £E2 extra per night. For more information, contact the Egyptian Youth Hostel Association in Cairo (1 Sharia el-Ibrahimy, Garden City, Cairo ⓣ02/2796 1448, ⓦwww.egyptyha.com; annual membership £E60). There are also a few YMCA hostels, which admit anyone.

Camping

Most campsites are for holidaying Egyptian families on the coast, often shadeless with few facilities, and not recommended. Rather better are the occasional campsites attached to hotels, which may offer ready-pitched tents with camp beds, plus use of hotel shower and toilet facilities. As for camping rough, you should always check with the authorities about any coastal site – some beaches are mined, others patrolled by the military. In the oases it's less of a problem, though any land near water will belong to someone, so again, ask permission.

Food and drink

Egyptian food combines elements of Lebanese, Turkish, Syrian, Greek and French cuisines, modified to suit local conditions and tastes, with more Mediterranean influences, for example, in Alexandria, and spicy Nubian cooking in the south.

Cafés, diners and street stalls offer simpler dishes than more formal restaurants catering to middle-class Egyptians and tourists, with proper menus and a broader range of dishes and, usually, taxes and service charges adding around seventeen percent to the bill.

Restaurant prices do not usually include service and taxes, which may amount to 22 percent. **Tips** are a couple of pounds per person in cheap places, ten to fifteen percent in pricier establishments if service is not included (or even if it is). In the text we've given the price of a sample dish per restaurant, but note that this does not include tax or service.

Cafés and street food

Egypt's staples are bread (*'aish*, which also means "life"), *fuul* and *taamiya*. **Bread**, eaten with all meals and snacks, comes either as pitta-type *'aish shamsi* (sun-raised bread made from white flour) or *'aish baladi* (made from coarse wholewheat flour).

Fuul (pronounced "fool"; fava beans) is extremely cheap and can be prepared in several ways. Boiled and mashed with tomatoes, onions and spices, they are *fuul madammes*, often served with a chopped boiled egg for breakfast. A similar mixture stuffed into *'aish baladi* constitutes the *fuul* sandwiches sold on the street.

Taamiya (falafel) is deep-fried patties of spiced green beans, usually served in pitta bread with salad, pickles and **tahina** (a sauce made from sesame paste), for which you can expect to pay the grand sum of £E1 or so.

Another cheap café perennial is **makarona** – macaroni baked into a cake with minced

Vegetarian eating

Most Egyptians eat vegetables most of the time – meat and fish are luxuries – yet the concept of vegetarianism is incomprehensible. Even if you say that you're vegetarian (in Arabic, *ana nabati* if you're male, *ana nabatiya* if you're female) people may offer you chicken or fish as a substitute. Still, vegetarians and vegans will have no trouble feeding themselves in *kushari* and falafel joints, and *fatatris* offer reasonable pickings too, even for vegans (who can try ordering a veg or mushroom *fiteer* without cheese). Restaurants and hotels that cater particularly to tourists often feature a few vegetarian dishes on the menu, such as omelettes, vegetable tageens, pasta and salads.

lamb and tomato sauce. It's rather bland but very filling. Similarly common is **kushari**, a mixture of noodles, rice, macaroni, lentils and onions, in a spicy tomato sauce (another sauce, made of garlic, is optional). It's served in small, medium and large portions (£E3–5) in tiled stand-up diners, also called *kushari*.

Fiteer, a cross between pizza and pancake, consists of flaky filo pastry stuffed with white cheese, peppers, mince, egg, onion and olives, or with raisins, jams, curds or a dusting of icing sugar, costs £E5–25 (depending on size and ingredients) at café-like establishments known as *fatatri*.

Most **sandwiches** are small rolls with a minute portion of *basturma* (pastrami) or cheese. Other favourite fillings include grilled liver (*kibda*) with spicy green peppers and onions; tiny shrimps; and *mokh* (crumbed sheep's brains).

A common appetizer is *torshi*, a mixture of pickled radishes, turnips, gherkins and carrots; luridly coloured, it is something of an acquired taste, as are pickled lemons, another favourite.

Lastly, there's **shawarma** – slices of marinated lamb, stuffed into pitta bread or a roll and garnished with salad and *tahina* – somewhat superior to the similar-looking doner kebabs sold abroad. A *shawarma* sandwich from a street stall can cost as little as £E2, while a plate of *shawarma* in a cheap diner will set you back around £E5.

On the **hygiene** front, while cafés and tiled eateries with running water are generally safe, street grub is highly suspect unless it's peelable or hot.

Restaurant meals

The classic Egyptian restaurant meal is a lamb **kebab** or **kofta** (spiced mince patties), accompanied or preceded by a couple of mezze (salads and dips) – usually **hummus** (made from chickpeas), *tahina* and **babaghanoug** (*tahina* with aubergine). Many restaurants sell kofta and kebab by weight: a quarter of a kilo is one portion, while a full kilo is usually enough for three to four people. **Chicken** (*firakh*) is a standard, both in cafés and as takeaway food from spit-roast stands. **Pigeon** (*hamam*) is common too, often served with *freek* (spicy wheat) stuffing. There's not much meat on a pigeon, so it's best to order a couple each. In slightly fancier places, you may also encounter pigeon in a **tageen** or *ta'gell*, stewed with onions, tomatoes and rice in an earthenware pot. A meal in an inexpensive restaurant should set you back around £E30–50 per person.

Posher restaurants will offer a larger selection of mezze, often including olives and stuffed vine leaves, as well as soups, and dishes such as **molukhiyya**, (Jew's mallow stewed in stock – a lot tastier than its disconcertingly slimy appearance suggests), **mahshi** (stuffed vegetables), and **torly** (mixed vegetable casserole with lamb or occasionally beef).

Fish (*samak*) – including sea bream, snapper, Nile perch, squid, and prawns – is particularly good in Alexandria, Aswan, the Red Sea Coast and Sinai. You often pick your own from the ice box, priced by weight, then grilled or fried, and served with salad and chips.

Confusingly, pasta, **rice**, **chips** (French fries) and even **crisps** (potato chips) are often considered interchangeable – so you may order rice and get chips instead. Also note that the shaker with one hole is for pepper, the one with several holes for salt.

Snacks, sweets and fruit

There are two main types of cheese: *gibna beyda* (white), which tastes like Greek feta, and *gibna rumi* ("Roman"), which is hard and yellow. For breakfast you will often be given imported processed cheeses such as La Vache Qui Rit ("The Laughing Cow" – a popular nickname for President Mubarak).

Nut shops (*ma'la*) are a street perennial, offering all kinds of peanuts (*fuul sudani*) and edible seeds. *Lib abyad* and *lib asmar* are varieties of pumpkin seeds, *lib battikh* come from watermelon, and chickpeas (hummus) are roasted and sugar-coated or dried and salted; all of these are sold by weight. Most nut shops also stock candies and mineral water.

Cakes are available at patisseries (some attached to quite flash cafés) or street stalls. The classics include baklava (filo pastry soaked in honey and nuts – called *basbousa* in Upper Egypt, though elsewhere the term usually applies to syrup-drenched semolina cake); *katif* (similar but with shredded wheat); and a variety of milk- or cornflour-based puddings, such as *mahalabiyya* (blancmange) and *Um Ali* (made with pastry, milk, sugar, coconut and cinnamon, usually served hot).

Fruits are wonderful in Egypt. In winter there are oranges, bananas and pomegranates, followed by strawberries in March. In summer you get mangoes, melons, peaches, plums and grapes, plus a brief season (Aug & Sept) of prickly pears (cactus fruit). Fresh dates are harvested in late autumn. Only apples are imported, and thus expensive. All are readily available at street stalls, or pressed into juice at juice bars (see p.42).

Drinks

As a predominantly Muslim country, Egypt gives alcohol a low profile. Public drunkenness is unacceptable, and sale of alcohol is prohibited on the Prophet Mohammed's birthday and the first and last days of Ramadan (if not during the whole month).

Tea, coffee and karkaday

Egypt's national beverage is tea (*shai*). Invitations to drink tea (*shurub shai*?) are as much a part of life in Egypt as in Britain, although it is served quite differently, generally prepared by boiling the leaves, and served black and sugared to taste (though an increasing number of cafés use tea-bags and may supply milk). Tea with milk is *shai bi-laban*, tea-bag tea is *shai libton* – to avoid it ask for loose-leaf tea (*shai kushari*). Tea with a sprig of mint (shai *bi-na'ana'*) is refreshing when the weather is hot.

Coffee (*'ahwa*) is traditionally **Turkish** coffee, served in tiny cups pre-sugared to customers' specifications: *saada* (unsugared), *'ariha* (slightly sweetened), *mazboota* (medium sweet) or *ziyaada* (syrupy). In some places you can get it with cardamom (*'ahwa mahawega*). Most middle-class or tourist establishments also serve **instant** coffee, with the option of having it with milk (*'ahwa bi-laban*). Upmarket places increasingly have espresso machines.

Traditional **coffee houses** (*'ahwa*) are usually shabby hole-in-the-wall places with chairs overlooking the street. Until very recently, it was unusual for women to frequent *'ahwas*, and unheard of to see them puffing away on a *sheesha*, but times change, and in more upmarket establishments younger, less inhibited women can now be seen with a waterpipe to their lips. Foreign women won't be turned away from *'ahwas* but may feel uneasy, especially if unaccompanied by a man. For a more

The sheesha

The **sheesha**, or waterpipe, is inseparable from Egyptian café society. It takes *ma'azil*, rough tobacco with molasses, whose distinctive aroma is guaranteed to take you right back to Egypt if you smell it again elsewhere. Posh coffee houses may also stock other flavours of tobacco (apple, strawberry, mint and so forth) and provide disposable plastic mouthpieces. A *sheesha* is normally shared among friends, but you can decline to partake without causing offence. Don't call it a hubbly-bubbly, as the term in Egypt refers to smoking hashish.

relaxed tea or coffee, try one of the middle-class *'ahwas*, found in larger towns and often attached to patisseries.

Karkaday (or *karkadé*) is a deep-red infusion of hibiscus flowers. Most popular in Luxor and Aswan, it is equally refreshing drunk hot or cold. Elsewhere, they may use dehydrated extract instead of real hibiscus, so it doesn't taste as good. Other **infusions** sold in *'ahwas* include *helba* (fenugreek), *yansoon* (aniseed) or *'irfa* (cinnamon).

On cold winter evenings you might enjoy **sahleb**, a thick, creamy drink made from milk thickened with ground orchid root, with cinnamon and nuts sprinkled on top. In hot weather Egyptians imbibe **rayeb** (soured milk), which is something of an acquired taste.

Juice

Every main street has a couple of tiled, stand-up **juice bars**, recognizable by their displays of fruit. Normally, you order and pay at the cash desk, where you're given a plastic token or receipt to exchange at the counter for your drink.

Juices made from seasonal fruit include *burtu'an* (orange), *mohz* (banana; with milk *mohz bi-laban*), *manga* (mango), *farawla* (strawberry), *gazar* (carrot), *rummaan* (pomegranate), *subia* (coconut) and *'asab* (the sickly sweet, creamy, light-green juice of crushed sugar cane). You can also order blends; *nus w nus* (literally "half and half") usually refers to carrot and orange juice, but other combinations can be specified.

Street vendors also ladle out iced *'asiir limoon* (strong, sweet lemonade), bitter-sweet *er'a sous* (liquorice-water), and deliciously refreshing *tamar hindi* (tamarind cordial).

Soft drinks and mineral water

Despite this profusion of cheap fresh juices, the usual **soda** pops – Coca-Cola, Fanta, Sprite and 7-Up (referred to as "Seven") – are widely available in bottles and cans. Local brand Fayrouz offers unusual flavours such as mango or pineapple. Bottled sodas are normally drunk on the spot; you have to pay a deposit on the bottle to take one away.

Bottled **water** (*mayya ma'adaniyya*) is widely available, particularly Baraka; Siwa and Hyat (from Siwa Oasis) are less widely distributed. It's wise to check that the seal is intact, or you may be palmed off with tap water (*mayya baladi*), which is safe to drink in major towns and cities, but highly chlorinated; people with sensitive stomachs should stick to bottled water.

Alcohol

Alcohol can be obtained in most places, but outlets are limited. In the Western Desert oases or Middle Egypt, sale is prohibited or severely restricted. If there are no bars, then hotels or restaurants are the places to try; if you can't see anyone drinking it, there's none to be had. Keep in mind that the hot, dry climate makes for dehydration, and agonizing hangovers can easily result from overindulgence.

Beer, whose consumption goes back to pharaonic times, is the most widely available form of alcohol. Native Stella beer is a light lager (4 percent ABV) which is OK if it hasn't sat in the sun for too long. To check that bottled beer hasn't gone flat, invert the bottle before opening and look for a fizzy head. Stella retails in most places for £E8–12, though discos may charge as much as £E25, and cruise boats even more. Sakkara is a similarly light lager (4 percent) that most foreigners seem to prefer. Premium or "export" versions of Stella and Sakkara have a slightly fuller flavour. Also worth trying is lager, marketed under the name Luxor, which is ten percent alcohol by volume, and there are Egyptian versions of Heineken, Carlsberg, Löwenbrau and Meister, none worth the extra cost, and kamikaze (7–10 percent) versions of Sakkara and Meister, which are worth avoiding. Marzen, a dark bock beer, appears briefly in the spring; Aswali is a dark beer produced in Aswan. There is also Birrel, a non-alcoholic beer.

A half-dozen or so **Egyptian wines**, produced near Alexandria, include Omar Khayyam (a very dry red), Cru des Ptolémées (a decent dry white) and Rubis d'Egypte (an acceptable rosé). Obélisque's Red Cabernet Sauvignon is good; the rosé and white less so. In most restaurants these retail for about £E80 a bottle (but more like £E120 on a cruise boat). Chateau des Rêves, a classy red with complex flavours, goes for £E72 in the shops, and is best left to breathe for a while before drinking.

Spirits are usually mixed with sodas or fruit juice. The favourite is **brandy**, known as *jaz* ("bottle"), and sold under three labels: Ahmar (the cheapest), Maa'tak (the best) and Vin (the most common). **Zibiba** is similar to Greek ouzo. Avoid vile Egyptian-made **gin** and **whisky** whose labels imitate famous Western brands – they may contain wood alcohol and other poisons. A vodka-based alcopop called ID is available in various flavours at liquor stores and some bars and duty-free shops.

Foreigners can buy up to three litres of imported spirits (or two bottles of spirits plus a two-dozen-can carton of beer) at **duty-free** prices within 24 hours of arrival in Egypt, in addition to the two litres allowed in from abroad. There is a black market for duty-free booze (Johnny Walker Black Label is the most sought-after), and Egyptians in the street may ask you to buy them duty-free booze "for my sister's wedding", but never allow them to be involved in the transaction inside the store: the paperwork for any duty-free purchase is in Arabic, and some travellers have discovered on leaving Egypt that a TV or video has been bought duty-free with their passport. Unable to produce the item for customs officials, they've had to pay duty on it, just as if they'd purchased and then sold it.

Health

Change of diet and climate accounts for most visitors' health problems, usually nothing worse than a bout or two of diarrhoea. Some people adapt quickly, others take longer, especially children and older people. If you're only here for a week or two, it makes sense to be cautious, while for longer-staying visitors it is worth trying to acclimatize.

Unless you're coming from an area where yellow fever is endemic (mainly sub-Saharan Africa), there are no compulsory inoculations for Egypt, though you should always be up to date with polio and tetanus, if not typhoid (which occasionally flares up in parts of Egypt). For vaccination clinics see Ⓦwww.masta.org (in Britain), www.cdc.gov/travel (US), www.csih.org (Canada) or www.tmvc.com.au (Australia, New Zealand and South Africa).

Health hazards

Tap water in Egyptian towns and cities is heavily chlorinated and mostly safe to drink, but is unpalatable and rough on tender stomachs. In rural areas, Sinai campsites and desert rest-houses there's a fair risk of contaminated water. Consequently, most tourists stick to bottled mineral water, which is widely available and tastes better. However, excessive fear of tap water is unjustified and hard to sustain in practice if you're here for long. Once your stomach has adjusted, it's usually okay to drink it without going to the hassle of purifying it (which you can do with Halazone tablets or iodine, or by boiling it).

What you should avoid is any contact with stagnant water that might harbour **bilharzia** (schistosomiasis) flukes. These minute worms, which breed in the blood vessels of the abdomen and liver (the main symptom is blood in the urine), infest irrigation canals and the slower stretches of the Nile. Don't drink or swim there, nor walk barefoot in the mud, or even on grass that's wet with Nile water. The saline pools of desert oases are fine to bathe in.

Heat and dust

Many visitors experience problems with Egypt's intense heat, particularly in the south, in summer and in the middle of the day (going out in the early morning and late afternoon is better). Wear a hat and loose-fitting clothes (preferably not synthetic fabrics), and a high-factor sunscreen to protect from sunburn, especially in summer. Wear a T-shirt when snorkelling, for the same reason. Sprinkling water on the ground cools the surrounding area by evaporation, and also levels the dust.

Because sweat evaporates immediately in the dry atmosphere, you can easily become dehydrated without realizing it. Dehydration is exacerbated by both alcohol and caffeine. Drink plenty of other fluids (at least three litres per day; more if you're exerting yourself) and take a bit of extra salt with your food.

Heat exhaustion – signified by headaches, dizziness and nausea – is treated by resting in a cool place and drinking plenty of water or juice with a pinch of salt. An intense headache, heightened body temperature, flushed skin and the cessation of sweating are symptoms of heatstroke, which can be fatal if not treated immediately. The whole body must be cooled by immersion in tepid water, or the application of wet towels, and medical assistance should be sought. If walking long distances in the sun, it is vital to carry drinking water. A sunhat can be drenched with water, wrung to stop it dripping, and worn wet so that the evaporation cools your head – you'll be amazed how quickly it dries out.

Less seriously, visitors may suffer from prickly heat, an itchy rash caused by excessive perspiration trapped beneath the skin. Loose clothing and frequent bathing can reduce it.

Desert dust – or grit and smog in Cairo – can irritate your eyes. Contact-lens users may find switching to glasses helps. If ordinary eye drops don't help, try antihistamine decongestant eye drops such as Vernacel, Vascon-A or Optihist. Persistent irritation may indicate trachoma, a contagious infection which is easily cured by antibiotics at an early stage, but eventually causes blindness if left untreated. Dust can also inflame sinuses. Covering your nose and mouth with a scarf helps prevent this; olbas oil or a nasal decongestant spray can relieve symptoms.

Digestive complaints

Almost every visitor to Egypt gets **diarrhoea** at some stage. Rare meat and raw shellfish top the danger list, which descends via creamy sauces down to salads, juices, raw fruit and vegetables. Visitors who insist on washing everything (and cleaning their teeth) in mineral water are overreacting. Just use common sense, and accustom your stomach gradually to Egyptian cooking. Asking for dishes to be served very hot (*sukhna awi*) will reduce the risk of catching anything.

If you have diarrhoea, the best initial treatment is to simply adapt your diet, eating plain boiled rice and vegetables, while avoiding greasy or spicy food, caffeine, alcohol, and most fruit and dairy products (although some say that bananas and prickly pears can help, while yogurt provides a form of protein that your body can easily absorb). Most importantly, keep your bodily fluids topped up by drinking plenty of bottled water. Especially if children are affected, you may also want to add rehydration salts (brands include Rehydran) to the water, or failing that, half a teaspoon of salt and eight of sugar in a litre of water will help the body to absorb the fluid more efficiently.

Drugs like Imodium or Lomotil can plug you up if you have to travel, but undermine your body's efforts to rid itself of infection. Avoid Enterovioform, which is still available in Egypt despite being suspected of damaging the optic nerve. Antinal (nifuroxazide) is widely prescribed against diarrhoea in Egypt, and available over the counter in pharmacies. Note that having diarrhoea may make orally administered drugs (such as contraceptive pills) less effective, as they can pass straight through you without being absorbed.

If symptoms persist longer than a few days, or if you develop a fever or pass blood in your faeces, get medical help immediately, since acute diarrhoea can also be a symptom of dysentery, cholera or **typhoid.**

Rabies and malaria

Rabies is endemic in Egypt, where many wild animals (including bats, sometimes found in temples, tombs and caves) carry the disease. Avoid touching any strange animal, wild or domestic. Treatment must be given between exposure to the disease and the onset of symptoms; once these appear, rabies is invariably fatal. If you think you've been exposed, seek help immediately.

Malaria, spread by the anopheles mosquito, exists in the Fayoum in summer, but you don't need malaria pills unless you are staying in that area for a while. You should nevertheless take extra steps to avoid mosquito bites in the Fayoum – use repellent and cover bare skin, especially feet and ankles, after dusk (see below).

Mosquitoes and other bugs

Even without malaria, **mosquitoes** are a nuisance, ubiquitous in summer and never entirely absent. Fans, mosquito coils, repellent and plug-in vaporizers (sold at pharmacies) all help. A lot of Egyptians use citronella oil, obtainable from many pharmacies, as a repellent, but tests have shown it to be less effective (and to require more frequent applications) than repellents containing DEET (diethyltoluamide), which are the ones recommended by medical authorities. Xgnat skin gel is an effective natural alternative. Don't forget to put repellent on your feet and ankles if they are uncovered when you go out in the evening. The best guarantee of a bite-less night's sleep is to bring a mosquito net.

Flies transmit various diseases, and only insecticide spray or air conditioning offer protection. Some cheap hotels harbour fleas, scabies, mites, cockroaches and other bugs. Consult a pharmacist if you find yourself with a persistent skin irritation.

Scorpions and snakes

The danger from scorpions and snakes is minimal, as most are nocturnal and avoid people, but don't go barefoot, turn over rocks or stick your hands into dark crevices anywhere off the beaten track. Whereas the sting of larger, darker **scorpions** is no worse than a bad wasp sting, the venom of the pale, slender-clawed fat-tailed scorpion (*Androctonus australis* and a few related species) is highly toxic. If stung, cold-pack the affected area and seek medical help immediately. Photographs of the most danegrous species, plus sound information and advice can be found on the Scorpion Venom website at ⓦweb.singnet.com.sg/~chuaeecc/venom/venom.htm.

Egypt has two main types of poisonous snake: vipers and cobras. Vipers vary in colour from sandy to reddish (or sometimes grey) and leave two-fang punctures. The horned viper, Egypt's deadliest snake, is recognizable by its horns. Cobras have a distinctive hood and bite mark (a single row of teeth plus fang holes). The smaller Egyptian **cobra** (coloured sandy olive) is found throughout the country, the longer black-necked cobra (which can spit its venom up to three metres) only in the south.

All snakebites should be washed immediately. Try not to move the affected body part, get immediate medical help, and stay calm, as panicking sends the venom through your bloodstream more quickly.

HIV and AIDS

Levels of HIV infection are low in Egypt but so is AIDS awareness – even among those involved in sex tourism, an industry catering to Western women or gays (in Luxor, Aswan and Hurghada) and male Gulf Arabs (in Cairo). Pharmacies in these cities plus a few outlets in Sinai are the only places in Egypt sure to sell condoms (*kabout*) – Egyptian brands such as Sportex are cheaper but less reliable than imported Durex. It's best to bring your own supply.

Women's health

Travelling in the heat and taking antibiotics for an upset stomach make women much more susceptible to vaginal infections. The best precautions are to wash regularly with mild soap and wear cotton underwear and loose clothing. **Yeast infections** can be treated with Nystatin pessaries (available at pharmacies), "one-shot" Canesten pessaries (bring some from home if you're prone to thrush), or douches of a weak solution of vinegar or lemon juice. Sea bathing can also help. Trichomonas is usually treated with Flagyl, which should only be taken under medical supervision.

Bring your own **contraceptives**, since the only forms widely available in Egypt are old-fashioned, high-dosage pills, the coil, and not too trusty condoms (see p.45). Cap-users should pack a spare, and enough spermicide and pessaries. Note that persistent diarrhoea can render the pill ineffective. **Sanitary protection** is available from pharmacies in cities and tourist resorts, but seldom anywhere else, so it's wise to bring a supply for your trip.

Medical services in Egypt

Egyptian **pharmacists** are well trained, usually speak English and can dispense a wide range of drugs, including many normally on prescription. If necessary, they can usually recommend a doctor – sometimes on the premises.

Private **doctors** are just as common as pharmacies, and most speak English or French. They charge for consultations: expect to pay about £E100 a session, which doesn't include drugs, but should cover a follow-up visit. There is a call-out charge for private and public ambulances (☎123).

If you get seriously ill, **hospitals** (*mustashfa*) that are privately run are generally preferable to public-sector ones. Those attached to universities are usually well-equipped and competent, but small-town hospitals are often abysmal. Private hospitals usually require a cash deposit of at least £E150 (it can go as high as £E1500) to cover the cost of treatment, and often require payment on the spot; you will then have to claim it back from your insurance provider. Despite several good hospitals in Cairo and Alexandria, Egypt is not a country to fall seriously ill in. In particular, if you need surgery, it's best to get back home for it if you can.

The media

Newspapers

Egyptian papers and magazines are all fairly heavily censored. The **English-language** *Egyptian Gazette* (on Saturday, the *Egyptian Mail*) carries agency reports, articles on Middle Eastern affairs and tourist features, but it's pretty lightweight – you can read it in a few minutes. The same applies to the *Egypt Daily News* (Ⓦwww.thedailynewsegypt.com), though it's more independent and has more foreign news. The English weekly edition of *Al-Ahram* has interesting opinion pieces on politics and international affairs, but tends to reflect government thinking.

Among the **Arabic** papers, *Al-Ahram* ("The Pyramids", founded in 1875 and thus Egypt's oldest newspaper), reflects official thinking, as do *Al-Akhbar* and *Al-Gomhouriya*. Other dailies with a party affiliation include the conservative *Al-Wafd* ("The Delegation"), the socialist *Al-Ahaly* ("The Nation") and *Al-Da'wa* ("The Call"), the journal of the Muslim Brotherhood.

Various British, US, French and German newspapers are available in Cairo, Alexandria, Luxor and Aswan, as are *Newsweek* and *Time* magazines. Elsewhere, however, you'll be lucky to find even the *Egyptian Gazette*.

Radio

With a short-wave radio you can pick up the BBC World Service (Ⓦwww.bbc.co.uk/worldservice), Voice of America (Ⓦwww.voa.gov) and other broadcasters. You can also pick up the BBC on 1323kHz MW on the Mediterranean coast, in Cairo and, when conditions are right, as far south as Luxor or even Aswan.

Cairo has two privately-run **music stations** which are worth a listen: Nogoum Radio (100.6FM) and Radio Misr (88.7FM) play mainly Arabic pop music, while Nile FM (104.2FM) plays Western pop. In addition, the state-owned Music Programme (98.8FM) plays folk and classical music, and Radio Cairo (95.4FM) broadcasts news and talk shows in English daily at 7–9am and 10pm–2am.

TV

Arab music channels with sexy dancing, or news from Al-Jazeera or Al-Arabiya, are staple viewing in coffeehouses. Foreigners may be shocked by their gory reportage, and bored by Egyptian channels, whose programming is heavy on local football matches, Koranic recitations, and chat shows. Nile TV has English subtitles, most notably with classic old Egyptian movies, plus news in English and French. Channels 1 and 2 often screen American films (generally after 10pm, or between midnight and 4.30am during Ramadan). It's not worth paying extra for a TV set in your hotel room unless it gets cable or satellite, and even then, many channels will be Middle Eastern, though you might get the BBC, CNN, Star Plus or sports channels. Daily TV schedules appear in the *Egyptian Gazette*, whose Monday edition lists all the movies for the forthcoming week.

Festivals

Most Islamic holidays and festivals follow the lunar Islamic calendar, with twelve months of 29 or 30 days each. The Islamic year is ten or eleven days shorter than a solar year, so dates move back each year in relation to the Western calendar. You can convert dates at websites such as Ⓦwww.oriold.uzh.ch/static/hegira.html. A day in the Islamic calendar begins at sundown, so Islamic festivals start on the evening before you'd expect.

Ramadan

During the month of **Ramadan**, most Muslims (ninety percent of Egyptians) fast, with no food, drink, smoking or sex from dawn to sunset. This can pose problems for travellers but the celebratory evenings are good times to hear music and share in hospitality.

The ninth month of the Islamic calendar, commemorating the first revelation of the Koran to Mohammed. Ramadan parallels the Christian Lent. Opening times and transport schedules are affected (almost everything pauses at sunset so people can break the fast), and most local cafés and restaurants close during or stop selling food. Ramadan is in many respects a bad time to travel. It is certainly no time to try camel trekking in the Sinai – no guide would undertake the work – and it is probably safer to travel by bus during the mornings only, as drivers will be fasting, too. (Airline pilots are forbidden to observe the fast.)

But there is a compensation in witnessing and becoming absorbed in the pattern of the fast. At sunset, signalled by the sounding of a siren and the lighting of lamps on the minarets, an amazing calm and sense of well-being fall on the streets, as everyone eats *fuul* and *taamiya* and, in the cities at least, gets down to a night of celebration and entertainment. Throughout the evening, urban cafés – and main squares – provide venues for live music and singing, while in small towns and poorer quarters of big cities, you will often come across ritualized *zikrs* – trance-like chanting and swaying.

Ramadan and Islamic holidays

Ramadan and Islamic holidays follow the **lunar calendar**, losing about eleven days a year against the Western (Gregorian) calendar. Exact dates are impossible to predict – they are set by the Islamic authorities on sighting of the new moon – but approximate dates for the next few years are:

	2010	**2011**	**2012**	**2013**	**2014**	**2015**
Eid el-Adha	16 Nov	6 Nov	26 Oct	15 Oct	4 Oct	23 Sept
Ras el-Sana	7 Dec	26 Nov	15 Nov	5 Nov	25 Oct	14 Oct
Moulid el-Nabi	26 Feb	15 Feb	4 Feb	24 Jan	13 Jan	3 Jan
1st Ramadan	11 Aug	1 Aug	20 July	9 July	28 June	18 June
Eid el-Fitr	9 Sept	30 Aug	19 Aug	8 Aug	28 July	17 July

Non-Muslims are not expected to observe Ramadan, but should be sensitive about not breaking the fast (particularly smoking) in public, but the best way to experience Ramadan is to enter into it. You may not be able to last without an occasional glass of water, and you'll probably breakfast later than sunrise, but it is worth an attempt – and you'll win local people's respect.

Islamic holidays

At the end of Ramadan, the feast of **Eid el-Fitr** is a climax to the month's festivities in Cairo, though observed more privately in the villages. Equally important is **Eid el-Adha** (aka Eid el-Kabir or Korban Bairam – the Great Feast), celebrating Abraham's willingness to obey God by sacrificing his son. God didn't make him go through with it, and he ended up sacrificing a sheep instead. In commemoration of this, every household that can afford to, slaughters a sheep, often on the street. For weeks beforehand, you will see sheep tethered everywhere, even on rooftops.

Eid el-Adha is followed, about three weeks later, by **Ras el-Sana el-Hegira**, the Muslim new year, on the first day of the month of Moharrem. The fourth main religious holiday is the **Moulid el-Nabi**, the Prophet Mohammed's birthday. This is widely observed, with processions in many towns and cities. For the approximate dates of these four festivals according to the Western calendar, see the box above.

Moulids

Moulids are the equivalent of medieval European saints' fairs, popular events combining piety, fun and commerce. Their ostensible aim is to obtain blessing (*baraka*) from a local saint, but they are also an opportunity for people to escape the monotony of working life in several days of festivities, and for friends and families from different villages to meet. Farming problems are discussed, as well as family matters – and marriage – as people sing, dance, eat and pray together. Upper-class Egyptians and religious conservatives, however, look down on moulids as vulgar and unorthodox, and in 2009 they used the threat of swine flu as an excuse to ban or severely curtail them. How long these restrictions will last remains to be seen.

Apart from Moulid el-Nabi, most moulids are local affairs, centred around the tomb (*qubba*) of a holy man or woman. Most follow the Islamic calendar, but some start (or finish) on a particular day (eg a Tuesday in a given month), rather than on a specific date, and a few occur at the same time every year, generally following the local harvest. It's wise to verify the (approximate) dates given in this guide by asking local people or the tourist office.

If you are lucky enough to attend a big one, you'll see Egyptian popular culture at its richest. Some draw crowds of over a million, with companies of *mawladiya* (literally, "moulid people") running stalls and rides, and music blaring into the small hours. Smaller, rural moulids tend to be heavier on the practical devotion, with people bringing their children or livestock for blessing, or the sick to be cured.

The largest moulids are in Cairo, Tanta and Luxor. **Cairo** hosts three lengthy festivals in honour of El-Hussein, Saiyida Zeinab and the

Imam el-Shafi'i (held during the months of Rabi el-Tani, Ragab and Sha'ban, respectively), plus numerous smaller festivals (see pp.197–198). Following the cotton harvest in October, the Moulid of El-Bedawi in **Tanta** starts a cycle of lesser **Nile Delta festivals** that runs well into November (see p.494). Equally spectacular is the Moulid of Abu el-Haggag in **Luxor**, held during the month of Sha'ban, and featuring a parade of boats (see p.279). Elsewhere, the procession may be led by camels or floats. Accompanying all this are **traditional entertainments**: mock stick fights, conjurers, acrobats and snake charmers; horses trained to dance to music; and, sometimes, belly dancers. All the longer moulids climax in a *leyla kebira* (literally "big night") on the last evening or the eve of the last day – the most spectacular and crowded phase; some moulids also have a corresponding big day.

Music and singing are a feature of every moulid and people even make cassettes to play back for the rest of the year. At the heart of every moulid is at least one **zikr** – a gathering of worshippers who chant and sway for hours to attain a trance-like state of oneness with God. *Zikr* participants often belong to a **Sufi brotherhood**, identified by coloured banners, sashes or turbans, and named after their founding sheikh. The current incumbent of this office may lead them in a **zaffa** (parade) through town, and in olden times would ride a horse over his followers – a custom known as "the Treading".

Coptic festivals

Egypt's Christian Copts often attend Islamic moulids – and vice versa. Coptic moulids share many of the functions of their Islamic counterparts and usually celebrate a saint's name-day. Major Christian festivals, as in Eastern Orthodox churches, follow the old Julian calendar, so Christmas is on January 6–7, Epiphany (Twelfth Night) on January 19, and the Annunciation on March 21, but Easter and related feast days are reckoned according to the solar Coptic calendar, so differ from Orthodox and Western dates by up to a month (Ⓦwww.copticchurch.net/easter.html has the dates).

Major Coptic **saints' days** include the Feast of the Apostles Peter and Paul (July 12), and various moulids of the Virgin and St George during August. Many of these are celebrated at monasteries in Middle Egypt and the Red Sea Hills.

Lastly, a Coptic festival (of pharaonic origin) celebrated by all Egyptians is the **Sham el-Nessim**, a coming-of-spring festival whose name literally means "Sniffing the Breeze". It provides the excuse for mass picnics in parks and on riverbanks throughout the country.

Sports and outdoor activities

Many tourists visit Egypt simply to dive or snorkel in the Red Sea, whose coral reefs put the Caribbean and the South Pacific in the shade. Besides all kinds of other watersports and some swanky golf courses, Egypt offers horse- and camel-riding, trekking, jeep safaris and hot-air ballooning, but for Egyptians the only sport that counts is football (soccer) – a national obsession.

Watersports

The fantastic coral reefs and tropical fish of the Red Sea (see *Egypt's underwater world* colour section) are the bedrock of tourism from Sinai to Mersa Alam, while the Mediterranean coastline has sunken wrecks and ancient ruins to explore. All this makes Egypt an excellent place to go diving, on a package holiday or through local dive centres (listed under resorts). Many people learn to dive here, gaining a PADI, BSAC or CMAS certificate. The initial step is a five-day open-water (OW) course, starting at around €350/$520 including equipment, plus about €35/$52 for the certificate if it isn't included. You progress from classroom theory to dives in the hotel swimming pool or from the shore, finishing with a few boat dives. Most centres offer a supervised introductory dive (from €40/$60) for those uncertain about shelling out for a full course. Kids aged 8–10 can try the PADI "Bubble Maker" course (€50/$75), which includes a short dive close to the shore. Qualified divers can progress through advanced open-water, dive master and instructor certification, and take specialized courses in night or wreck diving. Note that if you're certified but haven't logged a dive in the past three months, you might have to take a "check dive" before you can go on a sea trip.

Maps and information on dive sites in Sinai and the Red Sea appear on Ⓦwww.goredsea.com, while images of ancient ruins and wrecks in the Med are on Ⓦwww.cealex.org (the practicalities are covered on p.471, p.472, p.477 and p.481. Boat trips to dive sites usually include tanks and weights; lunch on the boat may cost about £E50 extra. Dive packages can be a good deal, costing around €270/$400 for a five-day package (ten dives), with discounts sometimes available for advance or online bookings. **Liveaboards** (safari boats) allow you to spend days or weeks at sea, cruising dive sites and shipwrecks. This can work out cheaper than a hotel and dive package, averaging around €100/$150 per person per day, including full board; where equipment rental isn't covered, expect to pay an extra €25/$38 per day. Most are pre-booked by groups, which may not welcome people joining them at the last moment, so it's better (and cheaper) to buy a package deal at home, though during quiet periods vacant berths might be found by asking around boats in marinas.

If you're aiming to arrange things yourself, be careful when choosing a dive centre. Ones attached to big hotels or with longstanding links with organizations like PADI are safer bets than backstreet outfits, but smart premises are less important than how they treat their equipment. If left lying about, chances are it'll also be poorly maintained. Also note the location of the compressor used to fill the tanks; if it's near a road or other source of pollution, you'll be breathing it in underwater. Misunderstandings can be dangerous underwater, so you need an instructor who speaks your language well.

Anybody who can swim can **snorkel**. Due to its coastal reefs, Sinai (especially Na'ama Bay) offers better snorkelling than further down the Red Sea, where most coral is on islands. Masks and flippers may be rented at any resort, and many also offer windsurfing and kiteboarding (notably Ras Sudr and Dahab), yachting (Hurghada), **water-skiing** and **parasailing** (also at Almaza Bay on the Mediterranean coast).

While a few resorts offer shark-fishing, Egypt is chiefly renowned for angling on Lake Nasser, the vast reservoir behind the Aswan High Dam, which teems with massive Nile perch, carp and tilapia. Fishing trips can be arranged in Aswan or abroad (see p.360 for details).

Riding, trekking and jeep safaris

Around the Pyramids and the major Nile sites, donkeys, horses and camels are all available for hire. Horses are fun if you want to ride across stretches of sand between the Pyramids or in the Sinai desert. Donkeys are best used for visiting the Theban Necropolis, where they traverse mountains that you'd never cross on foot, and enliven the trip no end. Elsewhere they have less appeal, but you might rent a *caretta* (donkey-drawn taxi cart) to explore the pools and ruins in Siwa Oasis.

Camels (the dromedary, or one-humped Arabian camel) make for pretty rigorous but exhilarating riding, and you'll probably want to try them at least once. They are good for short rides around Aswan, but really come into their own in Sinai or the Western Desert oases, where you can go trekking up wadis or across dunes that horses could never cope with. Trips – lasting anything from a half-day to a week – are easily arranged with local operators, or as part of "adventure holiday" packages from home.

If you've never ridden a camel before, try a half-day excursion before committing to a longer trip. Even a few hours in the saddle can leave you with aches in muscles that you never knew existed, so it's advisable to alternate between walking and riding. The mounting is done for you but be sure to hold on to the pommel of the saddle as the camel raises itself in a triple-jerk manoeuvre. Once on, you have a choice of riding it like a horse or cocking a leg around the pommel, as the Bedouin do, in which case you should use a lot of padding around the pommel to avoid soreness. It's easy to get the hang of steering: pull firmly and gradually on the nose rope to change direction; a camel should stop if you turn its head to face sideways.

Trekking on foot requires more stamina, especially in the High Mountain Region of Sinai (see p.563). The ideal number of trekkers is three to five people; larger groups travel more slowly. You'll need comfortable hiking boots, warm clothes, a sleeping bag, sunglasses, sunscreen, lip salve, bug repellent and toilet paper. In the Western Desert, your baggage may be transported by camel or jeep (in which case blankets are provided).

Jeep safaris are the best way to experience the oases, from an overnight stay in the White Desert or the Great Sand Sea to a deep-desert expedition to the Gilf Kebir. See Chapter 3 for details of sites and safari outfits in the Western Desert.

Golf and hot-air ballooning

There are golf courses around Cairo (one in sight of the Pyramids), as well as at Sharm el-Sheikh, Soma Bay, El Gouna and Luxor. For details, visit Ⓦwww.touregypt.net/golfcourses.htm.

From October to May, visitors to Luxor can enjoy the thrill of drifting above the temples and tombs of the Theban Necropolis in a hot-air balloon. Trips can be arranged at short notice for as little as €45/$60 (see p.280).

Football

The only sport screened on Egyptian television, **football** (soccer; *kurat 'adem* in Arabic) transfixes the nation during international and premier matches. The national team won the African Nations' Cup in 1986, 1998, 2006 and 2008, and the two rival Cairo clubs, **Ahly** and **Zamalek**, have long dominated the domestic league, and regularly win African club competitions. Clashes between them can be intense – and have occasionally led to rioting – but games are in general relaxed: Cairo Stadium (see p.205) is the main venue. Should their team win, thousands of supporters drive around Cairo honking horns and waving flags attached to lances – beware of being run over or impaled.

Recently they've been challenged by a new wave of corporate-sponsored teams such as Petrojet and Cement Assyut, which have muscled into the premier league ahead of older local teams like **Ismaily** (from Ismailiya), **Masry** (Port Said) and Al Ittihad (Alexandria). **Santa Katerina** is a team composed entirely of Sinai Bedouin who train by running up Mount Sinai twice a day.

Culture and etiquette

To get the most from a trip to Egypt, it is vital not to assume that anyone who approaches you is on the make. Too many tourists do, and end up making little contact with an extraordinarily friendly people. Even in response to insistent offers or demands, try to avoid being rude or aggressive in refusing.

Intimate behaviour in public (kissing and cuddling) is a no-no, and even holding hands is disapproved of. Be aware, too, of the importance of **dress**: shorts are socially acceptable only at beach resorts (and for women only in private resorts or along the

Gulf of Aqaba coast), while shirts (for both sexes) should cover your shoulders. Many tourists ignore these conventions, unaware of how it demeans them in the eyes of the Egyptians. Women wearing halter-necks, skimpy T-shirts, miniskirts and the like will attract gropers, and the disapproval of both sexes. If you're visiting a mosque, you're expected to be "modestly" dressed (men should be covered from below the shoulder to below the knee, women from wrist to ankle). It's also obligatory to remove shoes (or don overshoes).

When **invited to a home**, it's normal to take your shoes off before entering the reception rooms. It is customary to take a gift: sweet pastries (or tea and sugar in rural areas) are always acceptable.

One important thing to be aware of in Egypt is the different functions of the two hands. Whether you are right- or left-handed, the **left hand** is used for "unclean" functions, such as wiping your bottom or putting on shoes, so it is considered unhygienic to eat with it. You can hold bread in your left hand in order to tear a piece off, but you should never put food into your mouth with your left hand, nor put it into the bowl when eating communally.

Egyptians are likely to feel very strongly about certain subjects – Palestine, Israel and Islam, for instance, and these should be treated diplomatically if they come up in conversation. Some Egyptians are keen to discuss them, others not, but carelessly expressed opinions, and particularly open contempt for religion, can cause serious offence.

Tipping and baksheesh

As a presumed-rich *khawaga* (foreigner), you are expected to be liberal with **baksheesh**, which can be divided into three main varieties. The most common is tipping: a small reward for a small service – anything from waiter service to unlocking a tomb or museum room. Try to strike a balance between defending your own wallet and acquiescing gracefully when appropriate. There's little point getting upset or offending people over what are trifling sums for a Western tourist but an important part of people's livelihood in a country where most people earn less than £50/$82 a month.

Typical tips might be £E1–2 for looking after your shoes while you visit a mosque (though congregants don't usually tip for this), or £E5–10 to a custodian for opening up a door to let you enter a building or climb a minaret. In restaurants, you do not usually leave a percentage of the bill: typical tips (regardless of whether the bill claims to include "service") are as little as £E2 in an ultra-cheap place such as a *kushari* joint, £E2–5 in a typical cheap restaurant, or 10–15 percent in a smarter establishment. Customers also usually give tips of 50pt–£E1.50 in a café, and sometimes 50pt in a juice bar.

A more expensive and common type of *baksheesh* is for rewarding the bending of rules – many of which seem to have been designed for just that purpose. Examples might include letting you into an archeological site after hours (or into a vaguely restricted area), finding you a sleeper on a train when the carriages are "full", and so on. This should not be confused with bribery, which is a more serious business with its own etiquette and risks – best not entered into.

The last kind of *baksheesh* is simply alms-giving. For Egyptians, giving money and goods to the needy is a natural act – and a requirement of Islam. The disabled are traditional recipients of such gifts, and it seems right to join locals in giving out small change. Children, however, are a different case, pressing their demands only on tourists. If someone offers genuine help and asks for an *alum* (pen), it seems fair enough, but to yield to every request encourages a cycle of dependency that Egypt could do without.

Since most Egyptian money is paper, often in the form of well-used banknotes that can be fiddly to separate out, it can make life easier to keep small bills in a separate "baksheesh pocket" specifically for the purpose. If giving baksheesh in foreign currency, give notes rather than coins (which can't be exchanged for Egyptian currency).

Hustlers

Hustling is a necessity for millions of Egyptians – cadging money for errands or knowing a "cousin" who can sort things out. The full-time *khirtiyya* who focus on tourists are versatile, touting for hotels (see p.38),

Female genital mutilation

Most Egyptian women – as many as 97 percent according to one survey – have been subjected to a horrific operation known euphemistically as "female circumcision", and more correctly as female genital mutilation (FGM). In this procedure, typically carried out on girls aged between 7 and 10, the clitoris and sometimes all or part of the inner vaginal lips are cut off to prevent the victim from enjoying sex.

Egypt has the world's highest prevalance of FGM, which is an African rather than an Islamic practice, performed by Copts as much as by Muslims. Nonetheless, spurious religious reasons are sometimes given to justify it, including two disputed hadiths (supposed quotations from Mohammed). In 1951, the Egyptian Fatwa Committee decreed that FGM was desirable because it curbs women's sex drive, and in 1981 the Sheikh of al-Azhar Mosque and University said that it was the duty of parents to have their daughters genitally mutilated.

The good news is that things have changed since then. FGM is now illegal – the government banned it in 1996 and again in 2007. First lady Susanne Mubarak has spoken out against it, and the Islamic religious authorities have issued a fatwa declaring it *haram* (forbidden). The law is hard to enforce, especially in rural communities, but FGM is now in decline, though it remains at high levels: by the time of the 2007 ban, the percentage of teenage girls subjected to it had fallen to just over 50 percent, compared with around 80 percent in 1995.

pushing excursions (often vastly marked up), steering tourists into shops or travel agencies (where their commission will be quietly added to your bill), and even being gigolos (see "Women travellers", below). They'll latch on to you as soon as you arrive (at the airport in Cairo or Luxor), hail you on the street like an old friend ("Hey! Remember me?"), or say anything to grab your attention ("You've dropped your wallet"). If they don't already know, they'll try to discover where you're staying, what your plans are, and pester you regularly.

It's easy to get fed up with being hassled and react with fury to any approach from strangers – even a sincere "Welcome to Egypt". Try to keep your cool and respond politely; intoning *la shukran* (no thanks) with your hand on your heart, while briskly moving on, will dissuade most street peddlers. Or you could try a humorous riposte to classic come-ons like "I know what you need" – *Fil mish mish* ("In your dreams!") works well. If necessary, escalate to a gruff *khalas* ("Enough!") and if that doesn't suffice, bawling *shorta* ("Police!") is sure to send any hustler packing.

Women travellers

Sexual harassment is rife in Egypt: 98 percent of foreign women visitors and 83 percent of Egyptian women have experienced it, according to one survey. The perception that women tourists are "easy" is reinforced by their doing things that no respectable Egyptian woman would: dressing "immodestly", showing shoulders and cleavage, sharing rooms with men to whom they are not married, drinking alcohol in bars or restaurants, smoking in public, even travelling alone on public transport without a relative as an escort. While well-educated Egyptians familiar with Western culture can take these in their stride, less sophisticated ones are liable to assume the worst. Tales of affairs with tourists, and the scandalous Russians of Hurghada, are common currency among Egyptian males. In Sinai, however, unaccompanied women experience few hassles, except from construction workers from "mainland" Egypt.

Without compromising your freedom too greatly, there are a few steps you can take to improve your image. Most important and obvious is **dress**: loose opaque clothes that cover all "immodest" areas (thighs, upper arms, chest) and hide your contours are a big help, and essential if travelling alone or in rural areas (where covering long hair is also advisable). On public transport (buses, trains, service taxis), try to sit with other women – who may invite you to do so. On the Cairo metro and trams in Alexandria there are carriages reserved for women. If travelling with a man, wearing a wedding ring confers respectability, and asserting that you're married is better than admitting to being "just friends".

Looking confident and knowing where you're going always helps, and it's worth avoiding eye contact with Egyptian men (some women wear sunglasses for the purpose), and best to err on the side of standoffishness, as even a friendly smile may be taken as a come-on. Problems – most commonly hissing or groping – tend to come in downtown Cairo and in the public beach resorts (except Sinai's Aqaba coast, or Red Sea holiday villages – probably the only places you'll feel happy sunbathing). In the oases, where attractions include open-air springs and hot pools, it's okay to bathe – but do so in at least a T-shirt and leggings: oasis people are among the most conservative in the country.

Some women find that verbal hassle is best ignored, while others may prefer to use an Egyptian brush-off like *khalas* (finished) or *uskut* (be quiet). If you get groped, the best response is to yell *aram!* (evil!) or *sibnee le wadi* (don't touch me), which will shame any assailant in public, and may attract help, or scare them away by shouting *shorta!* (police!).

Spending time with **Egyptian women** can be a delight. The difficulty is that fewer women than men speak English, and that you won't run into women in traditional cafés. Public transport can be a good meeting ground, as can shops. Asking directions in the street, it's always better to ask a woman than a man.

Gigolos are part of the tourist scene in Luxor, Aswan, Hurghada, Sinai and Cairo. The exchange of sex for cash usually occurs under the guise of true love, with misled women spending money on their boyfriends or "husbands" until their savings run out and the relationship hits the rocks. Enough foreigners blithely rent toyboys and settle into the scene for locals to make the point that neither side is innocent, but be aware that HIV is a big danger on the gigolo scene – always use protection.

Many enter into so-called Orfi (or "Dahab") **marriages**, usually arranged by a lawyer, to circumvent the law that prohibits unmarried couples from sleeping under the same roof. These allow couples to rent a flat without hassle from the Vice Squad and can be annulled without a divorce. However, an Orfi marriage does not confer the same legal rights as a full marriage in a special registry office (Sha'ar el-Aqari) in Cairo, which is the only kind that allows women to bring their spouse to their own country or gives them any rights in child-custody disputes. Women can bolster their position by insisting on a marriage contract (pre-nuptial agreement).

Shopping

Visitors to Egypt are spoilt for choice when it comes to souvenirs: jewellery, textiles, glassware, leatherwork, brass and copperware are traditional crafts which offer good value for money if you're prepared to haggle and be choosy. One thing not to buy is any kind of supposed antiquity. The export of antiquities is strictly prohibited, and you could end up in prison if caught trying to smuggle them out. Another thing to avoid is ivory products: their sale is legal, but almost all Western countries prohibit their importation. Inlaid or carved bone makes an acceptable substitute.

Many Westerners are intimidated by **haggling**, but it needn't be an ordeal. Decide before you start what price you want to pay, offer something much lower, and let the shopkeeper argue you up, but not above your maximum price. If you don't reach an agreement, even after a lengthy session, nothing is lost. But if you state a price and the seller agrees, you are obliged to pay – so it is important not to start bidding for something you don't really want, nor to let a price pass your lips if you are not prepared to pay it. Haggling should be good-natured, not acrimonious, even if you know the seller is trying to overcharge you outrageously.

Don't be put off by theatrics on the part of the seller, which are all part of the game. Buyers' tactics include stressing any flaws that might reduce the object's value; talking of lower quotes received elsewhere; feigning indifference or having a friend urge you to leave. Avoid being tricked into raising your bid twice in a row, or admitting your estimation of the object's worth (just reply that you've made an offer).

Cairo's **bazaars** offer an infinite choice of jewellery, textiles, leatherwork, glassware, brass and copperware and perfumes, plus the world's best selection of bellydancing costumes (see pp.198–201). Alabaster figurines and vases are cheaper on Luxor's west bank (p.300), while Aswan's bazaar (see p.346) is best for spices, incense and basketwork. Siwa Oasis has its own crafts tradition (p.446), as do the thoroughly un-touristy bazaars in Assyut (p.240) and Fayoum City (p.388).

Jewellery, brass and copperware

Jewellery comes in all kinds of styles; gold and silver are sold by the gram, with a percentage added on for workmanship. The current ounce price of gold is printed in the daily *Egyptian Gazette*; one troy ounce equals about 31 grams. Barring antiques, all gold work is stamped with Arabic numerals indicating purity: usually 21 carat for Bedouin, Nubian or *fellaheen* jewellery; 18 carat for Middle Eastern and European-style charms and chains. Sterling silver (80 or 92.5 percent) is likewise stamped, while a gold camel in the shop window indicates that the items are gold-plated brass.

The most popular souvenirs are gold or silver cartouches with names in hieroglyphics. Prices depend on the size, the number of characters and whether they're engraved or glued on, but expect to pay around £E600–900.

Among **brass and copperware** items favoured as souvenirs are candlesticks, waterpipes, gongs, coffee sets, embossed plates and inlaid or repoussé trays (the larger ones are often mounted on stands to serve as tables). Be sure that anything you intend to drink out of is lined with tin or silver, since brass and copper react with certain substances to form toxic compounds. Remember also to test waterpipes for leaky joints.

Perfume and spices

Egypt produces many of the essences used by French perfumiers, sold by the ounce to be diluted 1:9 in alcohol for perfume, 1:20 for eau de toilette and 1:30 for eau de cologne. Local shops will duplicate famous perfumes for you, or you can buy fakes (sometimes unwittingly – always scrutinize labels). Salesmen boasting that their "pure" essence is undiluted by alcohol will omit to mention that oil has been used instead, which is why they rub it into your wrist to remove the sheen.

Spices such as **cinnamon** (*'irfa*) and **sesame** (*simsim*) are piled high in bazaars, but what is sold as **saffron** (*za'faraan*) is actually safflower, which is why it seems ridiculously cheap compared with what you'd pay for the real thing (consisting of fine red strands only, hence the ruse of dying safflower red). You'll also see **dried hibiscus** (*karkaday*); the top grade should consist of whole, healthy-looking flowers.

Textiles, leatherwork and basketwork

Most Egyptian kilims (woven rugs) and knotted carpets have half as many knots (16 per centimetre) as their Turkish counterparts, so should be cheaper – especially ones made from native wool rather than the high-grade imported stuff used in finer kilims. More affordable are tapestries and rugs woven from coarse wool and/or camel hair, which come in two basic styles. Bedouin rugs have geometric patterns in shades of brown and beige and are usually loosely woven, while the other style, deriving from the Wissa Wassef School (see p.170), features images of birds, trees and village life. Beware of stitched-together seams and gaps in the weave (hold pieces up against the light) and unfast colours – if any colour wipes off on a damp cloth, the dyes will run when the rug is washed. Another high-quality brand that's (less widely) imitated is Akhmim silk (see p.246), woven into tapestries or hand-printed scarves and robes, sold by selected shops in major tourist centres. Decorative appliqué work (cushion covers, bedspreads and wall-hangings) and riotously patterned printed tent fabric are best bought in Cairo's Tentmakers Bazaar (p.123).

Although few tourists can wear them outdoors without looking silly, many take home a **kaftan** or *galabiyya* for lounging attire. Women's kaftans are made of cotton, silk or wool, generally A-line, with long, wide sleeves and a round or mandarin collar (often braided). Men's *galabiyyas* come in three basic styles: *Ifrangi* (a floor-length tailored shirt with collar and cuffs), *Saudi* (with a high-buttoned neck and no collar) and *baladi* (very wide sleeves and a low, rounded neckline).

Egyptian **leatherwork** is nice and colourful, if not up to the standards of Turkey. Jackets, sandals, handbags, pouffes (tuffets) and decorative camel saddles are all made in Cairo's workshops, for sale throughout Egypt. Cairo also offers a range of palm-frond basketwork, mostly from the Fayoum and Upper Egypt. Fayoumi baskets (for storage, shopping or laundry) are more practical, but it's hard to resist the woven platters from Luxor and Aswan, as vibrantly colourful as parrots. You may also find baskets from Siwa Oasis, trimmed with tassels.

Glassware

Hand-blown Muski glass, made since medieval times, but nowadays from recycled bottles, is recognizable by its air bubbles and comes in navy blue, turquoise, aquamarine, green and purple, fashioned into glasses, plates, vases, candle holders and ashtrays. Elegant handmade perfume bottles are another popular souvenir. The cheaper ones are made of glass and are as delicate as they look. Pyrex versions cost roughly twice as much and are a little sturdier (they should also be noticeably heavier).

Travelling with children

Children evoke a warm response in Egypt and are welcome more or less everywhere. It's not unusual to see Egyptian children out with their parents in cafés or shops past midnight. The only child-free zones tend to be bars and clubs frequented by foreigners. Most hotels can supply an extra bed and breakfast. Pharmacies sell formula milk, baby food and disposable nappies, and the last two may also be stocked by corner stores in larger towns. Things worth bringing are a mosquito net for a buggy or crib, and a parasol for sun protection.

Potential hazards to guard against include traffic (obviously dangerous), stray animals (possible disease carriers), fenced-off beaches (probably mined – see p.58), elevators with no inner doors (keep small hands away), and poisonous fish and coral in the Red Sea (see *Egypt's underwater world* colour section). Children (especially young ones) are more susceptible than adults to **heatstroke** and **dehydration**, and should always wear a sunhat, and have high-factor sunscreen applied to exposed skin. If swimming, they should do so in a T-shirt, at least for the first few days. Children can also be very susceptible to an **upset tummy**, and antidiarrhoeal drugs should generally not be given to young children; read the literature provided with the medication or consult a doctor for guidance on child dosages.

If children balk at unfamiliar **food**, outlets of all major American fast-food chains are always close at hand. Ice cream is cheap and ubiquitous, as is *ruz bi-laban* (rice pudding) and *mahalabiyya* (a blancmange-like pudding made with powdered rice).

Children should enjoy camel, horse and donkey rides, but choose carefully – AA Stables in Cairo for example (see p.164) has a good reputation. Activities such as felucca rides, snorkelling and visiting a few of the great monuments can also be enjoyable. Activities in Cairo that will especially appeal to younger travellers are listed on pp.195–197. For more travel tips, see *The Rough Guide to Travel with Babies & Young Children*.

Travel essentials

Costs

Egypt is inexpensive and good-value. Providing you avoid luxury hotels and tourist-only services, costs for food, accommodation and transport are very low, though Sinai and Hurghada are pricier than other parts.

Most prices in this book are in Egyptian pounds. The main exceptions – airfares, prices for top-flight accommodation and dive or safari packages – are given in US dollars or euros, depending on what establishments quote. Despite this, you can almost always pay in Egyptian pounds, according to the prevailing exchange rate.

If you're trying to keep expenses down, it is possible to get by on £20/$33 a day by staying in the cheapest hotels and eating street food, but you won't have much left over for sightseeing or activities. On £40/$66 a day, you can eat well and stay in a two- or even three-star hotel. If you want to stay in tip-top accommodation, you could be paying upwards of £100/$165 a night, but even if you travel everywhere by taxi and eat in the very best restaurants, you'll be hard put to add more than £30/$50 a day to that figure.

Although Egypt is cheap, there are hidden costs that can bump up your daily budget. Most restaurant and hotel bills are liable to a **service charge** plus **local taxes** (Cairo, Luxor and Hurghada have the highest), which increase the final cost by 17–25 percent (unless already included in the price). Visiting the Pyramids and the monuments of the Nile Valley entails spending a lot on **site tickets** (typically £E20–60, though holders of student cards get a discount of at least a third). The custodians of tombs and temples and the medieval mosques of Islamic Cairo also expect to be tipped.

Inflation rose to an estimated eighteen percent in 2008, falling back to just over ten percent in 2009. Costs of luxury goods, services and most things in the private sector rise faster than for public transport, petrol and basic foodstuffs, whose prices are held down by subsidies that the government dare not abolish.

Student and other discount cards

ISIC student cards entitle holders to a fifty-percent discount on most museums and sites, a thirty-percent discount on rail fares and around fifteen percent on ferries. It's best to get the card at home (see Ⓦwww.istc.org for outlets) or – with proof that you are a full-time student – for £E80 at Egyptian Student Travel Services (ESTS), 23 Sharia el-Manial, on Roda Island in Cairo (Ⓣ02/2363-7251, Ⓦwww.estsegypt.com; Sat–Thur 8am–6pm, Fri 9am–4pm); you can get there on foot from the El-Malek el-Saleh metro. The International Youth Travel Card (available to anyone under 26), and International Teacher Identity Card (for teachers), at the same price from the same places, give similar discounts. Note however that, due to the number of forged cards now in circulation in Egypt, some archeological sites have stopped accepting them.

Crime and personal safety

While relatively few in number, pickpockets are skilled and concentrate on tourists. Most operate in Cairo, notably in queues. To play safe, keep your valuables in a money belt or a pouch under your shirt (leather or cotton materials are preferable to nylon, which can irritate in the heat). Overall, though, casual theft is more of a problem. Campgrounds and cheap hotels often have poor security, though at most places you can deposit valuables at the reception (always get a receipt for cash). If you are driving, it goes without saying that you shouldn't leave anything you cannot afford to lose visible or accessible in your car.

Minefields (the Arabic for "mines" is *algham*, with the stress on the second syllable) still exist: from World War II along the Mediterranean coast, and from Israeli conflicts in the interior of Sinai and along the Red Sea coast (detailed in chapters 3, 4, 6 and 7). Don't take any risks in venturing into fenced-off territory, unless locals go there often.

Terrorism

Since the 1990s, Egypt's image as a safe country to visit has been shattered by sporadic waves of terrorism. Though the Islamist insurgency in Middle Egypt was crushed in the 1990s, bomb attacks in Cairo and Sinai still occur (two in Cairo in 2009, for example). There are armed police and often metal-detecting arches at tourist sites, stations and upmarket hotels, and plain-clothes agents in bars and bazaars. Along the Nile Valley (see box, pp.216–217 for more), foreigners travelling by rail can only use services designated for tourists, which have plainclothes guards riding shotgun. Tourist buses between Cairo and Israel, and from Aswan to Abu Simbel, must travel in a **convoy** (*kol*) with a police escort. There is no ban on visiting once "risky" areas, but the local police will certainly keep a close eye on you.

Of course the vast majority of tourists spend their stay in Egypt without encountering any kind of terrorist incident, and most parts of the country have never had one. Insofar as any danger can be predicted, visitors should check government travel advisory websites before leaving home (Ⓦwww.fco.gov.uk/travel in Britain; Ⓦwww.foreignaffairs.gov.ie in Ireland; Ⓦwww.travel.state.gov in the US; Ⓦwww.voyage.gc.ca in Canada; Ⓦwww.smartraveller.gov.au in Australia).

To reduce the risk of petty squabbles or misunderstandings developing, always **respect local customs**; see p.51 for more.

The police

Egypt has a plethora of police forces (*shorta*) whose high profile in Cairo (which has more cops per thousand citizens than any other capital in the world) and at checkpoints on trunk roads has been the rule since the 1960s. Whereas ordinary Egyptians fear police brutality, foreign visitors are usually treated with kid gloves and given the benefit of the doubt unless drugs or espionage are suspected.

If you've got a problem or need to report a crime, always go to the **Tourist and Antiquities Police** (Ⓣ126). Found at tourist sites, museums, airports, stations and ports, they are supposedly trained to help tourists in distress, and should speak a foreign language (usually English). Ordinary ranks wear a regular police uniform with a "Tourist Police" armband; officers wear black uniforms in winter and white in summer. The more senior the officer, the better the chance they'll speak English.

The **Municipal Police** (Ⓣ122) handle all crimes and have a monopoly on law and order in smaller towns. Their uniform (khaki in winter, tan or white in summer) resembles that of the **Traffic Police**, who wear striped cuffs. Both get involved in accidents and can render assistance in emergencies, though few speak anything but Arabic.

The largely conscript **Central Security** force (dressed all in black and armed with Kalashnikovs) guard embassies, banks and highways. Though normally genial enough, they shift rapidly from tear gas to live rounds when ordered to crush demonstrations, strikes or civil unrest. To guard vital utilities, there are also Electricity, Airport and **River Police** forces, the last overseeing felucca journeys between Aswan and Luxor.

Egyptian **Military Intelligence** (Mukhabarat) is only relevant to travellers wanting to travel to remote parts of the Western Desert or south beyond Berenice on the Red Sea coast, for which you need travel permits (see p.31). The **State Security Investigations Service** (Amn al-Dawla) may take an interest in foreigners in border areas or Middle Egypt.

All of these forces deploy **plainclothes agents** who hang around near government buildings and crowded places, dressed as vendors or peasants – hence their nickname, the "Galabiyya Police". In hotels or bars, you might be disconcerted to find yourself chatting with a guy who suddenly announces that he's a cop. There are lots of them around.

Drugs

Egypt has its own *bango* (marijuana) industry, based in Sinai, supplemented by hashish from Morocco and Lebanon. Despite a tradition of use stretching back to the thirteenth century, Egypt was one of the first countries in modern times to ban cannabis: possession merits a severe prison sentence and a heavy fine (plus legal costs); trafficking is punishable by up to 25 years' hard labour, or even execution. Nonetheless, many Egyptians still smoke, and though Islam clearly forbids alcohol, the position of hashish is less clear. A few hotels in Luxor and Sinai even facilitate dealing to tourists.

As a foreigner, the least you can expect if caught is immediate deportation and a ban from visiting Egypt. You may be able to buy your way out of trouble, but this should be negotiated discreetly and as soon as possible, while the minimum number of cops are involved: once you're at the police station, it will be a lot more difficult. Needless to say, your embassy will be unsympathetic. The best advice is to steer clear of all illegal drugs while in the country.

Electricity

The current in Egypt is 220V, 50Hz. North American travellers with appliances designed for 110V should bring a converter. Most sockets are for two-pin round-pronged plugs (as in Continental Europe), so you may need an adapter.

Entry requirements

Visitors to Egypt must hold passports valid for at least six months beyond their date of entry. Citizens of most countries also need visas.

Most nationalities, including British, Irish, Americans, Canadians, Australians, New Zealanders and all EU citizens, can obtain visas on arrival at international airports. The process is generally painless and cheaper than getting one through an embassy or consulate (addresses on p.60), but visas issued at the airport are valid for one month only, whereas embassies issue single-visit and multiple-entry visas entitling you to stay in Egypt for three months (the latter allow you to go in and out of the country three times within this period). Visas are not available at overland border

Israeli stamps

At the time of writing, many Arab countries other than Egypt and Jordan – and in particular Syria, Lebanon, Libya and Sudan – will deny entry to anyone whose passport shows evidence of a visit to Israel. Although Israeli immigration officials will usually agree not to stamp your passport if you ask them clearly, an Egyptian entry stamp at Taba or Rafah in the Sinai will give you away – and the Egyptians will insist on stamping your passport. If you are travelling around the Middle East, either visit Israel *after* you have been to Syria, Lebanon, or wherever, or else travel from Jordan to the West Bank and back via Allenby (King Hussein) Bridge, avoid getting any stamps at that border, and visit Israel from the West Bank. This will not of course allow you to travel directly between Israel and Egypt.

crossings or sea ports (apart from Sinai-only visas – see below).

Visa applications can be made in person or by post. If applying in person, turn up early in the day. Postal applications take between seven working days and six weeks to process. Don't be misled by statements on the application form indicating "valid for six months"; this simply means that the visa must be used within six months of the date of issue. When returning the form, you need to include a registered or recorded SAE, your passport, one photo, and a postal or money order (not a personal cheque).

Getting a standard visa on arrival costs US$15, irrespective of your nationality. The cost of getting a visa in advance of your trip varies according to your nationality, and from place to place. Some consulates may demand that you pay in US dollars instead of local currency, or ask you to supply extra photos. It's wise to allow for all these eventualities.

Free **Sinai-only visas**, available at Taba on the Israel–Egypt border, or Sharm el-Sheikh airport, or the seaports at Sharm el-Sheikh and Nuweiba, are valid for fourteen days only, and restrict you to the Gulf of Aqaba coast down to Sharm el-Sheikh, and the vicinity of St Catherine's; they are not valid for Ras Mohammed, the mountains around St Catherine's (except for Mount Sinai), or any other part of Egypt. They can't be extended, and there's no period of grace for overstaying.

In Egypt, carry your passport with you: you'll need it to register at hotels, change money at banks, and possibly to show at police checkpoints. If travelling for any length of time, it may be worth registering with your embassy in Cairo, which will help speed things up if you lose your passport. At the least, it's wise to photocopy the pages recording your particulars and keep them separately (or carry them in the street instead of your passport itself). If travelling to areas of the country that require permits (see p.31), spare sets of photocopies are useful for producing with your application.

Egyptian embassies and consulates

Links to the web pages of Egyptian embassies and consulates worldwide can be found at ⓦwww.mfa.gov.eg (choose English and click on "Sites of Egyptian Missions").

Australia 1 Darwin Ave, Yarralumla, ACT 2600 ⓣ02/6273 4437, ⓔegyembassy@bigpond.com; Level 3, 241 Commonwealth St, Surry Hills, NSW 2010 ⓣ02/9281 4844; Level 9, 124 Exhibition St, Melbourne, Vic 3000 ⓣ03/9654 8634. Visa application forms are available at ⓦwww.egypt.org.au.

Canada 454 Laurier Ave E, Ottawa, ON K1N 6R3 ⓣ613/234 4931, ⓔegyptemb@sympatico.ca; 1000 Rue de la Gauchetière Ouest, Suite 3320, Montreal PQ H3B 4W5 ⓣ514/866 8455, ⓦwww.egyptianconsulatemontreal.org.

Cyprus 14 Ayios Prokopios St, 2406 Nicosia ⓣ2244 9050, ⓦwww.egyptianembassy.org.cy.

Ireland 12 Clyde Rd, Ballsbridge, Dublin 4 ⓣ01/660 6566, ⓦwww.embegyptireland.ie.

Israel 54 Rehov Basel, Tel Aviv 62744 ⓣ03/546 4151 or 2; 68 Rehov Afrouni, Eilat ⓣ08/637 6882.

Jordan 14 Riyad Mefleh St, Amman (between 4th and 5th circles, next to the Dove Hotel) ⓣ06/560 5175 or 6, ⓔembegypt@tedata.net.jo; Al-Wahdat al-'Arabiyya, Sharia al-Istiqlal, Aqaba ⓣ03/201 6171 or 81.

Libya Sharia Omar el-Mokhtar, Tripoli ⓣ021/333 9876, ⓔeg.emb_tripoli@mfa.gov.eg; Sharia Marg Bani Amer, District 19, Western Fuwaihat, Benghazi ⓣ061/223 2522, ⓔegyptian_Consulate_Ben@yahoo.com.

New Zealand c/o the embassy in Australia.

South Africa 270 Bourke St, Muckleneuk, Pretoria ⓣ012/343 1590 or 91, ⓔegyptemb@global.co.za.

Sudan Sharia al-Gomhuria (University Street), Khartoum ⓣ0183/777646, ⓔsphinx-egysud@yahoo.com.

UK 2 Lowndes St, London SW1X 9ET ⓣ020/7235 9777, ⓦwww.egyptianconsulate.co.uk.

USA 3521 International Court NW, Washington DC 20008 ⓣ202/895-5400, ⓦwww.egyptembassy.us; 1110 2nd Ave, Suite 201, New York, NY 10022 ⓣ212/759-7120 to 22, ⓦwww.egyptnyc.net; 3001 Pacific Ave, San Francisco, CA 94115–1013 ⓣ415/346-7352, ⓦwww.egy2000.com; 500 N Michigan Ave, Suite 1900, Chicago, IL 60611 ⓣ312/828-9162 to 4; 1990 Post Oak Blvd, Suite 2180, Houston, TX 77056 ⓣ713/961-4915 or 6.

Visa extensions

Tourists who **overstay** their visa are allowed a fifteen-day period of grace in which to renew it or leave the country. After this, they're fined £E104 unless they can present a letter of apology from their embassy (which may well cost more).

Visa **extensions** cost around £E11, and are obtainable from the Mugamma in Cairo or from passport offices in governorate capitals such as Alexandria, Luxor, Aswan, Suez, El-Tor, Mersa Matrouh and Ismailiya (addresses are detailed in the guide). Depending on how long you wish to extend by, and on the whim of the official, you may have to produce exchange or ATM receipts proving that you've cashed sufficient hard currency during your stay, and you'll need to supply one or two photos. Procedures vary slightly from office to office, but shouldn't take longer than an hour outside Cairo.

Gay and lesbian travellers

As a result of sexual segregation, male homosexuality is relatively common in Egypt, but attitudes towards it are schizophrenic. Few Egyptians will declare themselves gay – which has connotations of femininity and weakness – and the dominant partner in gay sex may well not consider himself to be indulging in a homosexual act. Rather, homosexuality is tacitly accepted as an outlet for urges that can't otherwise be satisfied. Despite this, people are mindful that homosexuality is condemned in the Koran and the Bible, and reject the idea of Egypt as a "gay destination" (although male prostitution is an open secret in Luxor and Aswan). The common term for gay men in Egyptian Arabic, *khawal*, has derogatory connotations.

Homosexuality is not illegal in Egypt, but that doesn't stop the authorities from persecuting gay men (usually on charges of "habitual debauchery"), and places that are well known as gay locales have become dangerous for Egyptians. Foreigners seem to be safe from imprisonment, but if you have a gay relationship with an Egyptian man, be aware that discretion is vital. **Lesbians** do not face this kind of state harassment, but they have never been visible in Egyptian society. As a Western woman, your chances of making contact are virtually zilch.

Online resources

Gay Egypt ⓦwww.gayegypt.com. Practical advice and contacts, but don't log on to it within Egypt, as the Security Police not only monitor the site but may also take an interest in computers which access it.

Globalgayz ⓦwww.globalgayz.com/country/Egypt/EGY. Their Egypt page has articles about the current situation facing gays in Egypt.

International Gay and Lesbian Human Rights Commission ⓦwww.iglhrc.org. Posts information about civil rights for gay people in Egypt.

Hiring guides

Professional guides can be engaged through branches of Misr Travel (see p.67), American Express and Thomas Cook, local tourist offices and large hotels, and on the spot at sights such as the Egyptian Antiquities Museum in Cairo and the Pyramids of Giza. They normally charge a fixed hourly rate, and a tip is also expected.

Guides can be useful at major sites, like the Valley of the Kings, where they will be able to ease your way through queues at the tombs. If you feel intimidated by the culture, too, you might welcome an intermediary for the first couple of days' sightseeing. In general, however, and armed with this book, you shouldn't need a guide.

At ancient sites, there are always plenty of hangers-on posing as "guides", who will offer to show you "secret tombs" or "special reliefs" or just present themselves in tombs or temples, with palms outstretched. They don't have a lot to offer you, and encouraging them makes life more difficult for everyone else.

On the other hand, especially in small towns or villages, you may meet local people, often teenagers, who genuinely want to help out foreigners, and maybe practise their English at the same time. They may offer to lead you from one taxi depot to another, or show you the way to the souks or to a local site. Most people you meet this way don't expect money and you could risk offence by offering – if they want money, they won't be shy about asking.

Insurance

It's frankly reckless to travel without insurance cover. Home insurance policies occasionally cover your possessions when overseas, and some private medical schemes include cover when abroad. Bank and credit cards often have certain levels of medical or other insurance included and you may automatically get travel insurance if you

Rough Guides travel insurance

Rough Guides has teamed up with WorldNomads.com to offer great **travel insurance** deals. Policies are available to residents of over 150 countries, with cover for a wide range of **adventure sports**, 24hr emergency assistance, high levels of medical and evacuation cover and a stream of **travel safety information**. Roughguides.com users can take advantage of their policies online 24/7, from anywhere in the world – even if you're already travelling. And since plans often change when you're on the road, you can extend your policy and even claim online. Roughguides.com users who buy travel insurance with WorldNomads.com can also leave a positive footprint and donate to a community development project. For more information go to Ⓦ**www.roughguides.com/shop**.

use a major credit card to pay for your trip. Otherwise, you should contact a specialist travel insurance company, or consider the travel insurance deal we offer (see above). When choosing a policy, you may want to ask whether you're covered to take part in "dangerous sports" or other activities – in Egypt, this could mean, for example, camel trekking or scuba diving.

If you need to make a claim, you should keep receipts for medicines and medical treatment, and in the event you have anything stolen, you must obtain an official theft report from the police (called a *mahdar*). You may also be required to provide proof that you owned the items that were stolen, in the form of shop receipts or a credit-card statement recording the purchase.

Laundry

Wherever you are staying, there will either be an in-house laundry (*mahwagi*), or one close by to call on, charging piece rates. Some budget hotels in Luxor, Aswan and Hurghada allow guests to use their washing machine for a small charge, or gratis. You can buy washing powder at most pharmacies. Dry cleaners are confined to Cairo, Aswan and Hurghada.

Living in Egypt

Some foreigners make a living in Egypt, teaching English or diving, writing for the English-language media, or even belly-dancing. Getting a work permit involves getting a job offer, then taking evidence of this to Mogamma in Cairo (see p.206) to apply. So long as the offer is for a job where foreigners rather than Egyptians are needed, it is simply then a question of jumping through the necessary bureaucratic hoops.

English **teaching** will be in Cairo or Alexandria, where there are many private language schools. The British Council in Cairo (192 Corniche el-Nil, Aguza Ⓦwww.britishcouncil.org.eg Ⓣ02/19789) may be able to supply a list of schools to approach.

Budding journalists may be able to place work with the local English-language media. *Egypt Today* sometimes accepts articles and photos, and the *Egyptian Gazette* may need sub-editors from time to time.

Most jobs in **tourism** are restricted to Egyptians, and locally based companies usually insist on a work permit, but you can sometimes fix up a season's work with a foreign tour operator as a rep or tour guide. In Sinai, Hurghada and Luxor there may be a demand for people with foreign languages (English, German, French, Italian, Japanese, or – on the Red Sea and Sinai coasts – Russian) to sell dive courses or work on hotel reception desks. Ask around dive centres or upmarket hotels.

Divers with Divemaster or Instructor certificates can often find work with diving centres in Hurghada or Sinai, which may also take on less qualified staff and let them learn on the job, at reduced rates of pay or in return for free tuition. Dive centres commonly turn a blind eye to the lack of a work permit, or might procure one for a valued worker.

Foreign **bellydancers** are much in demand in nightclubs in Cairo, Alexandria, Luxor and Hurghada. The work can be well paid, but you have to be careful: financial or sexual exploitation are real hazards. Aside from work, many foreign dancers come to Egypt to improve their art or buy costumes (see p.194 & p.200).

Studying

The **American University in Cairo** (ⓣ02/2794 2964, ⓦwww.aucegypt.edu) offers year-abroad and non-degree programmes, a summer school and intensive Arabic courses. A full year's tuition (two semesters and summer school) costs roughly US$20,250. US citizens may apply to the Stafford Loan Program, at Office of Admissions, 420 5th Ave, 3rd Floor, New York, NY 10018-2729 (ⓣ212/730-8800).

Foreign students may also attend one- or two-term programmes at **Egyptian universities**, such as Cairo (ⓦwww.cu.edu.eg), Ain Shams (ⓦnet.shams.edu.eg) and Al-Azhar (ⓦwww.azhar.edu.eg). Like the AUC's courses, these are valid for transferable credits at most American and some British universities. In the US, you can get information on exchange programmes from the Egyptian Cultural and Educational Bureau, 1303 New Hampshire Ave NW, Washington DC 20036 (ⓣ202/296-3888, ⓦwww.eecous.net) or AmidEast, 1730 M St NW Suite 1100, Washington DC 20036–4505 (ⓣ202/776-9600, ⓦwww.amideast.org).

A number of schools in Cairo offer courses in **Arabic language**, both in colloquial Egyptian Arabic and Modern Standard Arabic; see p.205 for more.

Mail

Airmail letters from Egypt generally take a week to ten days to reach Western Europe, two to three weeks to North America or Australasia. It speeds up the delivery if you get someone to write the name of the country in Arabic. As a rule, around fifteen percent of correspondence (in either direction) never arrives; letters containing photos or other items are especially prone to go astray.

It's best to send letters from a major city or hotel; blue mailboxes are for overseas airmail, red ones for domestic post. Airmail (*bareed gawwi*) stamps can be purchased at post offices, hotel shops and postcard stands, which may charge a few extra piastres on top of the stamp's official price (£E2.50 for a postcard/letter to anywhere in the world). Registered mail, costing £E10 extra, can be sent from any post office. Selected post offices in the main cities offer an Express Mail Service. Private courier firms such as DHL and UPS are limited to a few cities, and are a lot more expensive. To send a parcel, take it unsealed to a major post office (in Cairo, you'll need to use the one at Ramses Square) for customs inspection, weighing and wrapping.

Post office hours are generally daily except Fridays from 8am to 6pm (Ramadan 9am–3pm), though in big cities post offices may stay open until 8pm.

If receiving mail, note that any package or letter containing goods is likely to be held, and you will have to collect it and pay customs duty; you should be informed that it has arrived and where you need to pick it up. Poste restante (general delivery) services exist, but are unreliable and best avoided if possible (you could have people write to you at a hotel). If you do use the service, have mail addressed clearly, with the surname in capital letters, and bear in mind that even then, it may well be misfiled.

Email can be sent from any internet café, and an increasing number of hotels (even a few cafés) offer wi-fi.

Maps

The best general map of Egypt is published by Rough Guides on a scale of 1:1,125,000, on tear-proof paper, with roads, railways and contours clearly marked; Freytag & Berndt's (1:800,000) is a good second-best, as is Nelles (1:2,500,000, with insets at 1:750,000). Kümmerly & Frey (1:950,000; published in Egypt by Lehnert & Landrock) makes a reasonable alternative.

City maps cover Cairo (see p.79), but few other places. Diving maps of the Red Sea are available in Egypt, but some do not cover sites in the Sinai, the main diving area for most tourists.

Full-blown desert expeditions require detailed maps that can be obtained in Cairo from the Survey Office (*heyat al-misaha*) on Sharia Abdel Salam Arif at the corner of Sharia Giza (daily except Fri 9am–1pm; see map, p.140 for location), who may demand an official letter explaining why you need the maps. Geological maps can be obtained without bureaucratic obstruction (but bring your passport) from the Egyptian Mineral Resources Authority (EMRA) at 3 Sharia Salah Salem, Abbassiya, about 500m south of Midan Abbassiya and Sinai bus terminal (Sun–Thurs 8am–2.30pm; ⓣ02/2628 8013).

Money

Egypt's basic unit of currency is the Egyptian pound (called a *ginay* in Arabic, and written £E or LE), divided into 100 piastres (*'urush*, singular *'irsh*). At the time of writing, exchange rates were around £E8.50 to the pound sterling, £E5.50 to the US dollar, and £E7.50 to the euro.

Egyptian banknotes bear Arabic numerals on one side, Western numerals on the other, and come in denominations of 25pt, 50pt, £E1, £E5, £E10, £E20, £E50, £E100 and £E200. There are coins for 5pt, 10pt, 20pt, 25pt, 50pt and £E1.

Some banknotes are so ragged that merchants refuse them. Trying to palm off (and avoid receiving) decrepit notes can add spice to minor transactions, or be a real nuisance. Conversely, some vendors won't accept high-denomination notes (£E20 upwards) due to a shortage of change. Some offer sweets in lieu of coins, others round prices up. Try to hoard coins and small-value notes for tips, fares and small purchases.

Carrying your money

The easiest way to access your money in Egypt is with plastic, though it's a good idea to also have some back-up in the form of cash or travellers' cheques. Using a Visa, MasterCard, Plus or Cirrus card, you can draw cash using ATMs at branches of the main banks in cities, major towns and tourist resorts. Machines are usually outside banks or inside airports and shopping centres. By using ATMs you get trade exchange rates, which are somewhat better than those charged by banks for changing cash, though your card issuer may well add a foreign transaction fee, sometimes as much as five percent. Note also that there is a daily limit on ATM cash withdrawals, usually £E4000. If you use a credit card rather than a debit card, note also that all cash advances and ATM withdrawals obtained are treated as loans, with interest accruing daily from the date of withdrawal.

It's wise to make sure your card is in good condition and, before you leave home, make sure that the card and PIN will work overseas. Where there is no ATM, cash advances on Visa and MasterCard can be obtained at most branches of the Banque Misr on the same basis.

Credit cards are accepted for payment at major hotels, top-flight restaurants, some shops and airline offices, but virtually nowhere else. American Express, MasterCard and Visa are the likeliest to be accepted.

To have **money wired**, Western Union's main agents are branches of the Arab African International Bank (check on ⓦwww.westernunion.com); Moneygram's (ⓦwww.moneygram.com) are branches of the National Societé Générale Bank, or NSGB.

Banks and exchange

Arriving by land or sea, you should have no trouble changing money at the border, and airport banks are open around the clock. It is illegal to import or export more than £E5000 in local currency.

The best exchange rates for cash can be found at foreign exchange bureaux – private moneychangers found in large towns and tourist resorts – which seldom take travellers' cheques and will offer poor rates if they do, but are open longer hours and perform transactions more quickly than Egyptian banks, where forms are passed among a bevy of clerks. Such extended transactions are less likely at foreign banks in Cairo and Alexandria, branches in hotels, or offices of American Express (in Cairo, Alexandria, Luxor and Aswan) or Thomas Cook (in Cairo, Alexandria, Luxor, Aswan, Port Said, Hurghada and Sharm el-Sheikh; ⓦwww.thomascookegypt.com). **Commission** is not generally charged on currency exchange, but there may be 40pt stamp duty.

Banking hours are generally Sunday to Thursday 8.30am to 2pm, or 9.30am to 1.30pm during Ramadan. Branches in five-star hotels may open longer hours, sometimes even 24/7. For arriving visitors, the banks at Cairo airport and the border crossings from Israel are open 24 hours daily, and those at ports whenever a ship docks.

US dollars, euros and English sterling notes are easy to exchange, but due to forgeries, some banks may not accept worn or pre-1992 US$100 bills. Hard currency (usually US$) may be required for visas, border taxes and suchlike. Don't bring New Zealand dollars, or Scottish or Northern Irish sterling banknotes, which are not accepted; Israeli shekels can only be changed at the Taba border crossing, and at one or two banks (in five-star hotels) and some Cairo foreign exchange bureaux. Sudanese pounds and Libyan dinars are similarly hard to change.

There's sometimes a currency **black market**, but it's best to avoid illegal street money changers, who are usually rip-off artists or *agents provocateurs*.

Opening hours and public holidays

Offices tend to open Sunday to Thursday from 8.30am to 5pm. Shops are usually open from around 10am to around 8pm, sometimes later, with small places often closing briefly for prayers, especially Friday lunchtime between noon and 3pm.

During Ramadan, all these hours go haywire. Since everybody who keeps the fast will want to eat immediately when it ends at sunset, most places close early to allow this, and may open early to compensate. Offices may open 7am–4pm, shops may simply close to break the fast, reopening afterwards, while banks open 9.30am to 1.30pm. Ramadan opening times are given, where available, throughout the text.

Public holidays include Eid el-Adha, Ras el-Sana el-Hegira, the Moulid el-Nabi and Eid el-Fitr, all dated on the Islamic calendar (see p.48). Others, following the Gregorian calendar, are: Coptic Christmas (Jan 7), Sinai Liberation Day (April 25), Labour Day (May 1), Evacuation Day (June 18), Revolution Day (July 23), Flooding of the Nile (Aug 15), Armed Forces Day (Oct 6), Suez Liberation Day (Oct 23), and Victory Day (Dec 23). Sham al-Nassim falls according to the Coptic calendar (see p.49). Banks and offices close on public holidays; most shops and transport operate as usual.

Phones

All towns and cities have at least one 24-hour telephone and telegraph office (*maktab el-telephonat*, or *centraal*) for calling long-distance and abroad, or you can buy a card at grocers or kiosks to use in public phones on the street. Rates are around twenty percent cheaper at night (8pm–8am).

Cards such as Egypt Telecom's Marhaba card, with a scratch-off panel covering a PIN, can be used from private phones by dialling a toll-free number, then the PIN on the card, and finally the number you wish to call. They usually work out cheaper than ordinary phonecards, and are available from the same places, but they generally don't work from public phones.

Mobile phones

If you want to use take your mobile phone with you, you'll need to check with your phone provider whether it will work in Egypt and what the charges are. You may pay extra for international roaming, and to receive calls in Egypt. A US cellphone must be GSM/triband to work in Egypt.

If planning to use your phone a lot in Egypt, especially for local calls, it's worth getting a SIM card from one of the Egyptian providers, Mobinil (prefix ⓣ012) and Vodafone (ⓣ010). You may need to pay a small fee to have the phone unlocked. A typical deal gives you a SIM card for around £E100, including £E70 of free calls. Top-up cards are available in denominations from £E10 to £E200. Mobinil tends to have better coverage than Vodafone, especially in the Western Desert and on the Mediterranean coast, but for optimum coverage in remote areas, you might even consider buying two SIM cards and swapping between them.

Photography

Snap with care. Before taking a picture of someone, ask their permission – especially in rural areas, where you can cause genuine offence, and be wary of photographing anything militarily sensitive (even bridges, train stations, dams, etc). People may also stop you from taking photos that show Egypt in a "poor" or "backward" light.

Usefull telephone numbers

Emergencies and information

Ambulance	ⓣ123
Police	ⓣ122
Tourist police	ⓣ126
Fire brigade	ⓣ180
Directory enquiries	ⓣ140 or 141
International operator	ⓣ120

International calls

Omit the initial zero from the area code when dialling Egypt, the UK, Ireland, Australia, New Zealand or South Africa.

	From Egypt	To Egypt
UK	ⓣ00 44	ⓣ00 20
Ireland	ⓣ00 353	ⓣ00 20
US and Canada	ⓣ001	ⓣ011 20
Australia	ⓣ00 61	ⓣ0011 20
New Zealand	ⓣ00 64	ⓣ00 20
South Africa	ⓣ00 27	ⓣ09 20

Religious buildings

Most of the **mosques** and **madrassas** (Islamic colleges) that you'll want to visit are in Cairo and, apart from El-Hussein and Saiyida Zeinab mosques, are classed as historic monuments, so they're open to non-Muslim sightseers (though you should avoid prayer times, especially at noon on Friday). Elsewhere in Egypt, mosques are not used to seeing tourists and people may object to non-Muslims entering. If you are not Muslim, tread with care and if possible ask someone to take you in.

At all mosques, dress is important. Shorts, short skirts and exposed shoulders are out, and women may be asked to cover their hair (a scarf may even be provided). Above all, remember to remove your shoes upon entering the precinct. They will either be held by a shoe custodian (small baksheesh expected) or you can leave them outside the door, or carry them in by hand (if you do this, place the soles together, as they are considered unclean).

Egyptian **monasteries** (which are Coptic, save for Greek Orthodox St Catherine's in Sinai) admit visitors at all times except during the Lenten or other fasts (local fasts are detailed in the guide where appropriate). Similar rules of dress etiquette to those for mosques apply, though unless you go into the church itself you don't need to remove your shoes.

Smoking

Most Egyptian men smoke, and offering cigarettes around is common practice. The most popular brand is Cleopatra. Matches are *kibreet*; a lighter is a *wallah*. Traditionally, respectable women aren't supposed to smoke in public, but women are increasingly seen nowadays smoking *sheeshas* in Cairo's coffee shops. Don't expect restaurants or public transport to be non-smoking, though Cairo's Metro is.

Time

Egypt is on GMT+2, which means that in principle it is two hours ahead of Britain and Ireland, seven hours ahead of the US East Coast (EST), ten hours ahead of the US West Coast (PST), six hours behind Western Australia, eight hours behind eastern Australia and ten hours behind New Zealand. Daylight Saving Time at home or in Egypt may vary those differences. Egypt's clocks move forward for Daylight Saving on the last Friday in April and back again on the last Friday in September.

Tourist information

The Egyptian Tourist Authority (sometimes abbreviated as EGAPT; ⓦwww.egypt.travel) has offices in several countries. Their website gives a good overview of Egypt's tourist attractions. Better still, ⓦwww .touregypt.net has quite a lot of useful information, including details of main tourist attractions, and listings of hotels, nightclubs and internet cafés.

In Egypt itself, you'll get a variable response from local tourist offices (addresses given throughout the guide), where the level of knowledge and assistance may depend on who exactly you speak to: in some cases (detailed in the text), we recommend contacting a specific member of staff who speaks good English and is well informed.

Egyptian historical and archeological sites are the responsibility of the Supreme Council of Antiquities (SCA; Ⓦwww.sca.gov.eg), whose website carries information about most sites open to the public, and certainly all the important ones. For more detailed archeological information on ancient Egyptian sites, including the more obscure ones, see Ⓦegyptsites.wordpress.com.

Egyptian tourist offices abroad

UK 170 Piccadilly, London W1J 9EJ Ⓣ020/7493 5283, Ⓔinfo.uk@egypt.travel.

USA 630 5th Ave, Suite 2305, New York, NY 10111 Ⓣ1-212/332-2570, Ⓔinfo.us@egypt.travel; 645 N Michigan Ave, Suite 829, Chicago, IL 60611 Ⓣ1-312/280-4666, Ⓔinfo.us@egypt.travel; 8383 Wilshire Blvd, Suite 215, Beverly Hills, Los Angeles, CA 90211 Ⓣ1-213/653-8815, Ⓔinfo.us@egypt.travel.

Canada 2020 University St, Suite 2260, Montreal, PQ H3A 2A5 Ⓣ1-514/861-8071, Ⓔinfo.ca@egypt.travel.

Travel agencies and hotels

Private travel agencies can advise on (and book) transport, accommodation and excursions, though their advice may not be unbiased. The state-run **Misr Travel** (offices in major cities, listed in the guide) operates hotels, buses and limos, and can make bookings for most things. Misr Travel also has offices in London (2 Carshalton Road, Sutton SM1 4RA Ⓣ020/8643 2429, Ⓔmisrtravel@btclick.com) and New York (1270 Ave of The Americas, Suite 604, New York, NY 10020 Ⓣ212/332-2600 or 2601, Ⓦwww.misrtravel.org). American Express and Thomas Cook also offer various travel services. In Luxor, Aswan, Hurghada, Sinai and the Western Desert oases, many hotels and campgrounds double as information exchanges and fixers.

Tourist publications

The monthly magazine *Egypt Today* has features on Egyptian culture and travel, and some useful listings of restaurants, cinemas, theatres, galleries and language schools in Cairo and Alexandria, which are the cities where it's sold. Selected events are listed in the daily *Egyptian Gazette*, and the weekly English-language edition of *Al-Ahram*, which are more widely available (see also p.46).

Toilets

Public toilets are almost always filthy, and there's never any toilet paper (though someone may sell it outside). They're usually known as *toileta*, and marked with WC and Men and Women signs. Expect squat toilets in bus stations, resthouses and fleapit hotels. Sit-down toilets have a nozzle that squirts water into your bottom – make sure you're positioned right before you turn it on. Though it's wise to carry toilet paper (£E2 per double roll in grocers and pharmacies), paper tissues, sold on the streets (50pt), will serve at a pinch.

Travellers with disabilities

Disability is common in Egypt. Many conditions that would be treatable in the West, such as cataracts, cause permanent disabilities here because people can't afford the treatment. People with disabilities are unlikely to get jobs (though there is a tradition of blind singers and preachers), so the choice is usually between staying at home being looked after by your family, and going out on the streets to beg for alms.

For a blind or wheelchair-using tourist, the streets are full of obstacles which, if you walk with difficulty, you will find hard going. Queuing, steep stairs, unreliable elevators, and the heat, will take it out of you if you have a condition that makes you tire quickly. A light, folding camp-stool could be invaluable if you have limited walking or standing power. In that case, it's a good idea to avoid arriving in the summer months.

For wheelchair users, the monuments are a mix of accessible and impossible. Most

Useful things to bring

- **Earplugs** Help muffle the noise of videos on long-distance buses and trains, if you're trying to sleep.
- **Film/memory cards** For a digital camera, it doesn't hurt to bring more memory card capacity than you think you'll need. If using film, Kodak and Fuji film is available in most towns and major resorts, but may be old stock, so bring adequate supplies.
- **Mosquito net** The best guarantee of a mozzie-free night's sleep in the oases and the Nile Valley. Alternatively, buy a plug-in device (such as Ezalo) at any Egyptian pharmacy.
- **Sleeping bag** A decent bag is required if you're planning to sleep out in the desert in spring or autumn, or in any low-budget hotel over winter. In the summer, a sheet sleeping bag or silk sleeping bag liner is handy if you're staying at cheap hotels, where just one (not necessarily clean) sheet is provided.
- **Suitable clothes** Dress should be appropriate given Egypt's conservative sensibilities (see p.51). Northern Egypt can be cold and damp in the winter, while the desert gets freezing at night, even in spring and autumn, so a warm sweater is invaluable.
- **Torch/flashlight** For exploring dark tombs, and for use during power cuts.

major temples are on relatively level sites, with a few steps here and there – manoeuvrable in a wheelchair or with sticks if you have an able-bodied helper. Your frustrations are likely to be with the tombs, which are almost always a struggle to reach – often sited halfway up cliffs, or down steep flights of steps. The Pyramids of Giza (p.163) are fine to view but not enter, though the sound-and-light show is wheelchair accessible; Saqqara (p.170) is difficult, being so sandy. If you opt for a Nile cruise, bear in mind that you'll be among a large throng and will need to be carried on and off the boat if you depend on a wheelchair (often by people who don't understand English), an experience you may well not relish.

Cairo is generally bad news, especially Islamic Cairo, with its narrow, uneven alleys and heavy traffic, but with a car and helper, you could still see the Citadel and other major monuments. There's a lift in the Egyptian Antiquities Museum, and newer metro stations have elevator access from street level to the platforms, though none of the older ones do, which unfortunately includes all those in the city centre. Most five-star hotels in Cairo are wheelchair-accessible and have adapted rooms (see p.85).

Taxis are easily affordable and quite adaptable; if you charter one for the day, the driver is certain to help you in and out, and perhaps even around the sites you visit. If you employ a guide, they may well also be prepared to help you with steps and other obstacles. Some **diving** centres in Sinai and Hurghada accept disabled students on their courses, and the hotels in these resorts tend to be wheelchair-friendly.

There are organized tours and holidays specifically for people with disabilities, and some companies, such as Discover Egypt in the UK (see p.31), offer packages tailor-made to your specific needs. Egypt for All (334 Sharia Sudan, Mohandiseen, Cairo Ⓣ012/396 1991, Ⓦwww.egyptforall.com) run a range of tours, offer tailor-made holidays to your specifications, and may be able to arrange transport or equipment rental.

It's a good idea to carry spares of any clothing or equipment that might be hard to find; if there's an association at home for people with your particular disability, contact them early for more specific advice. And always make sure that travel agencies, package firms and insurance companies, even travelling companions, are aware of, and can cover, your particular needs.

Guide

Guide

Cairo and the Pyramids

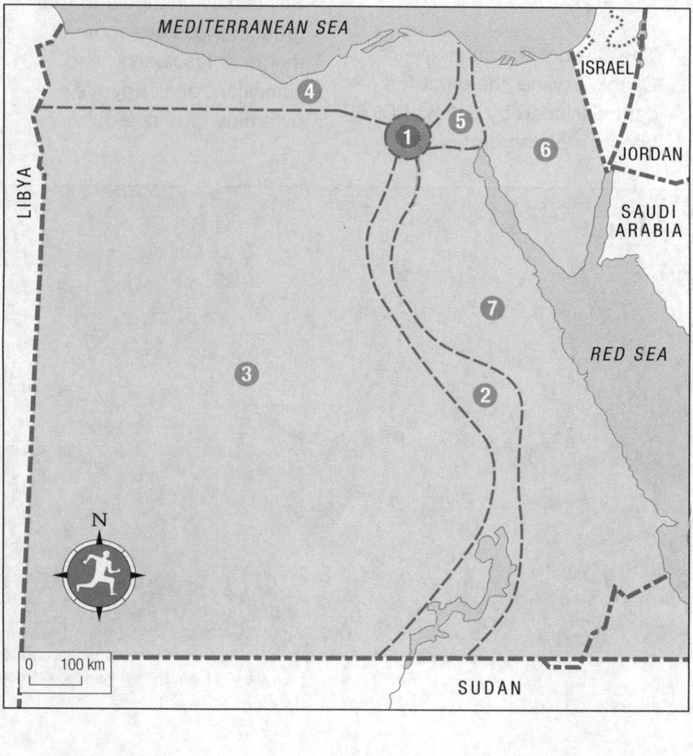

CHAPTER 1

Highlights

* **The Museum of Egyptian Antiquities** One of the world's truly great museums, containing a massive collection of ancient statues, sarcophagi, frescoes, reliefs, and incredible treasures from the tomb of Tutankhamun. See p.91

* **Islamic Cairo** The medieval city of Salah al-Din (Saladin) is Cairo's true heart, teeming with life and chock-a-block with stunning architecture. See p.107

* **The Citadel** Dominating Cairo's skyline, the great fort commissioned by Salah al-Din boasts a plethora of quirky museums, a classic Ottoman mosque, and commanding views of the city. See p.126

* **Old Cairo** This compact quarter contains the city's most ancient Coptic churches and its oldest synagogue. See p.138

* **The Pyramids of Giza** The sole surviving wonder of the ancient world, and still stunning to this day. See p.163

* **The Pyramids of Dahshur** Still largely unknown to tour groups, these are some of the most fascinating and significant of all Egypt's pyramids. See p.181

▲ View of Islamic Cairo from the Citadel

Cairo and the Pyramids

Cairo has been the Islamic world's greatest city since the Mongols sacked Baghdad in 1258. Egyptians have two names for the city: **Masr**, meaning both the capital and the land of Egypt (for Egyptians abroad, "Masr" means Egypt, but within the country it means the capital), is a timeless name rooted in pharaonic civilization; the city's other name, **Al-Qahira** (The Triumphant), is linked specifically to the Fatimid conquest which made it the capital of an Islamic empire embracing modern-day Libya, Tunisia, Palestine and Syria, but the name is rarely used in everyday speech.

In monumental terms the two names are symbolized by two dramatic **landmarks**: the **Pyramids of Giza** at the edge of the Western Desert, and the great **Mosque of Mohammed Ali** – the modernizer of Islamic Egypt – which broods atop the Citadel. Between these two monuments sprawls a vast city, the colour of sand and ashes, of diverse worlds and epochs, and gross inequities. All is subsumed into an organism that somehow thrives in the terminal ward: medieval slums and Art Deco suburbs, garbage-pickers and marbled malls, donkey carts and limos, piousness and "the oaths of men exaggerating in the name of God". Cairo lives by its own contradictions. Its **population** is today estimated at around seventeen million and is swollen by a further million commuters from the Delta and a thousand new migrants every day. An estimated half a million people reside in squatted cemeteries – the famous **Cities of the Dead**. The amount of green space per citizen has been calculated at thirteen square centimetres, not enough to cover a child's palm. Whereas earlier travellers noted that Cairo's air smelt "like hot bricks", visitors now find throat-rasping **air pollution**, chiefly caused by traffic.

Cairo's genius is to humanize these inescapable realities with **social rituals**. The rarity of public violence owes less to the armed police on every corner than to the *dowshah*: when conflicts arise, crowds gather, restraining both parties, encouraging them to rant, sympathizing with their grievances and then finally urging "*Maalesh, maalesh*" ("Never mind"). Everyday life is sweetened by flowery gestures and salutations; misfortunes evoke thanks for Allah's dispensation (after all, things could be worse). Even the poorest can be respected for piety; in the mosque, millionaire and beggar kneel side by side.

Extended-family values and neighbourly intervention prevail throughout the *baladi* quarters where millions of first- and second-generation rural migrants live, while arcane structures underpin life in Islamic Cairo. On a city-wide basis, the

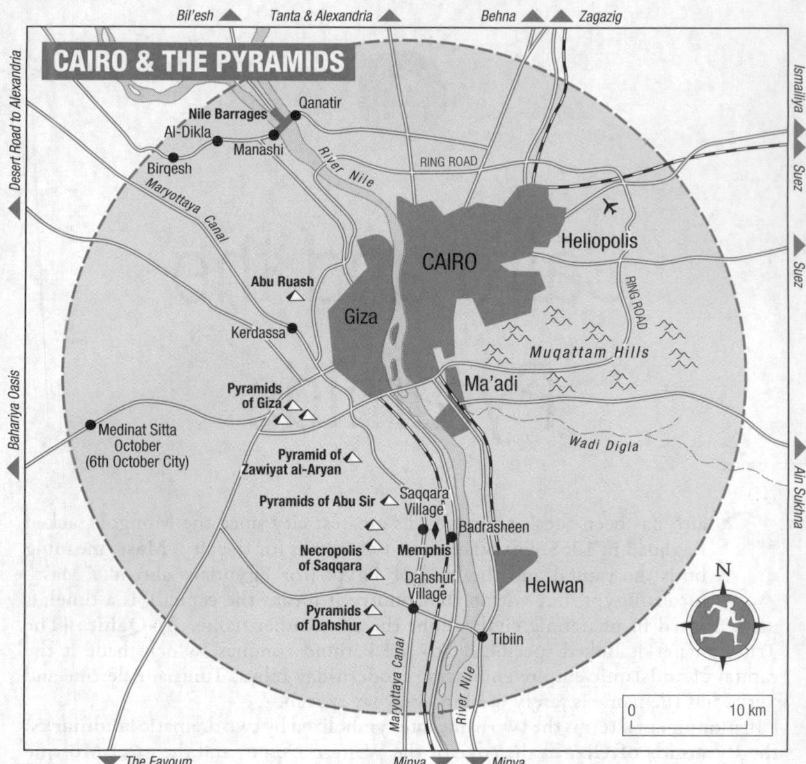

colonial distinction between "native quarters" and *ifrangi* (foreign) districts has given way to a dynamic stasis between rich and poor, westernization and traditionalism, complacency and desperation. Every year its polarities intensify, safety margins narrow and statistics make gloomier reading. The abyss beckons in prognoses of future trends, yet Cairo confounds doomsayers by dancing on the edge.

A brief history

Ancient **Memphis**, the first capital of pharaonic Egypt, was founded around 3100 BC across the river and to the south, but it was 2500 years before a sister city of priests and solar cults, known to posterity as **Ancient Heliopolis** (see p.158), flourished on the east bank. It took centuries of Persian, Greek and Roman rule to efface both cities, by which time a new fortified town had developed on the east side. **Babylon-in-Egypt** was the beginning of the tale of cities that culminates in modern Cairo, the first chapter of which is described under "Old Cairo" (see p.138). Babylon's citizens, oppressed by foreign overlords, almost welcomed the army of Islam that conquered Egypt in 641. For strategic and spiritual reasons, their general, Amr, chose to found a new settlement beyond the walls of Babylon – **Fustat**, the "City of the Tent" (see "Old Cairo", p.148), which evolved into a sophisticated metropolis while Europe was in the Dark Ages.

Under successive dynasties of caliphs who ruled the Islamic Empire from Iraq, three more cities were founded, each to the northeast of the previous one, which itself was either spurned or devastated. When the schismatic Fatimids took control in 969, they created an entirely new walled city – **Al-Qahira** – beyond this teeming, half-derelict conurbation. **Fatimid Cairo** formed the nucleus of the later, vastly expanded and consolidated capital that Salah al-Din (Saladin) left to the Ayyubid dynasty in 1193. But the Ayyubids' reliance on imported slave-warriors – the Mamlukes – brought about their downfall: eventually, the Mamlukes simply seized power for themselves, ushering in a new era.

Mamluke Cairo encompassed all the previous cities, Salah al-Din's Citadel (where the sultans dwelt), the northern port of Bulaq and vast cemeteries and rubbish tips beyond the city walls. Mamluke sultans like Beybars, Qalaoun, Barquq and Qaitbey erected mosques, mausoleums and caravanserais that still ennoble what is now known in English as "Islamic Cairo". The like-named section of this chapter relates their stories, the Turkish takeover, the decline of **Ottoman Cairo** and the rise of Mohammed Ali, who began the modernization of the city. Under Ismail, the most profligate of his successors, a new, increasingly **European Cairo** arose beside the Nile (see "Central Cairo", p.90). By 1920, the city's area was six times greater than that of medieval Cairo, and since then its residential suburbs have expanded relentlessly.

Arrival

Greater Cairo consists of two metropolitan governorates: **Cairo**, on the east bank of the Nile, and **Giza**, on the west. The **River Nile** (*bahr en-nil*, or simply *en-nil*) flows northwards through the city, its waterfront dominated by the **islands** of Gezira and Roda and the **bridges** that connect them to the **Corniche** (embankment) on either side of the Nile. There are four major divisions of the city:

- **Central Cairo** (see map, pp.92–93) spreads inland to the east of the islands. Its **downtown** area – between Ezbekiya Gardens and **Midan Tahrir** – bears the stamp of Western planning, as does **Garden City**, the embassy quarter further south. At the northern end of central Cairo (beyond the downtown area) lies **Ramses Station**, the city's main train terminal. Most of the banks, airlines, cheap hotels and tourist restaurants lie within this part of the city.
- Further east sprawls **Islamic Cairo**, encompassing **Khan el-Khalili** bazaar, the Gamaliya quarter within the **Northern Walls**, and the labyrinthine Darb al-Ahmar district between the **Bab Zwayla** and the **Citadel**. Beyond the latter spread the eerie **Cities of the Dead** – the Northern and Southern cemeteries, and rising up beyond them, the **Muqattam Hills**, a barrier throughout history against Cairo's further eastward spread.
- The Southern Cemetery and the populous **Saiyida Zeinab** quarter merge into the rubbish tips and wasteland bordering the **ruins of Fustat** and the **Coptic quarter** of **Old Cairo**, further to the south. Except for stylish **Heliopolis**, the **northern suburbs** hold little appeal for visitors.
- Across the river on the **west bank**, the residential neighbourhoods of **Aguza** and **Dokki** aren't as smart as nearby **Mohandiseen** or the high-rise northern end of **Gezira** island, known as **Zamalek**. The dusty expanse of **Giza** (which lends its name to the west bank urban zone) is enlivened by **Cairo Zoo** and the nightclub-infested **Pyramids Road** leading to the **Pyramids of Giza**.

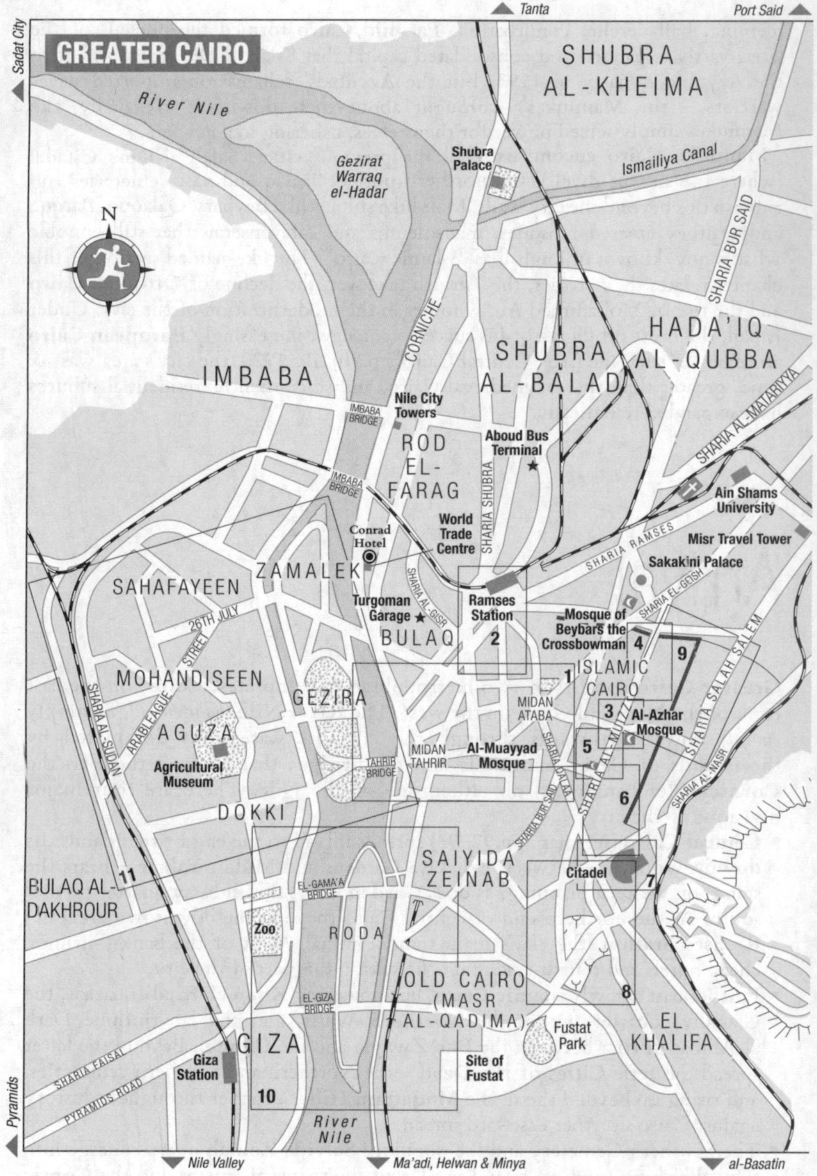

By air

Cairo International Airport, about 15km northeast of the city centre, has three terminals which are roughly 3km apart. **Terminal 1** is known as the old airport, but having been refurbished, is actually more modern than **Terminal 2**; the new **Terminal 3** is used by EgyptAir and other Star Alliance airlines (such as Lufthansa).

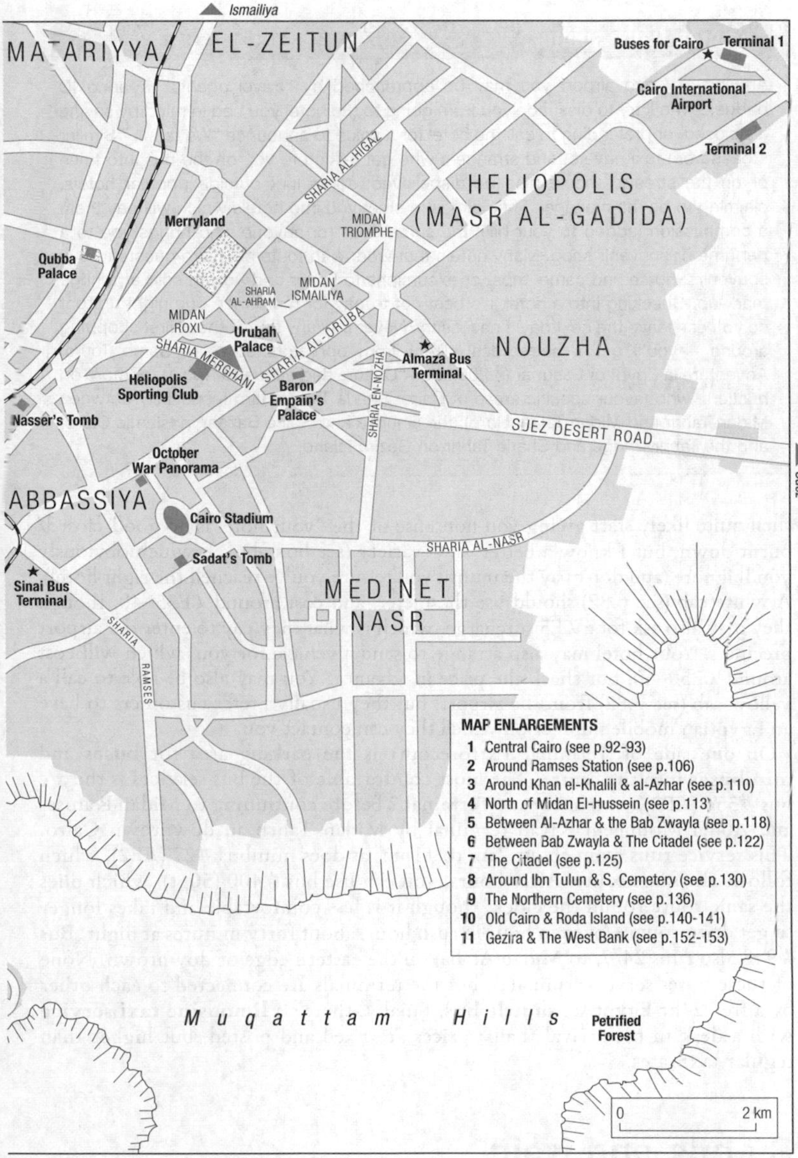
Ismailiya
MATARIYYA
EL-ZEITUN
Buses for Cairo
Terminal 1
Cairo International Airport
Terminal 2
SHARIA AL-HIGAZ
HELIOPOLIS (MASR AL-GADIDA)
Merryland
MIDAN TRIOMPHE
Qubba Palace
MIDAN ISMAILIYA
SHARIA AL-AHRAM
MIDAN ROXI
Urubah Palace
SHARIA AL-ORUBA
SHARIA MERGHANI
Almaza Bus Terminal
NOUZHA
Heliopolis Sporting Club
Baron Empain's Palace
SHARIA EN-NOZHA
Nasser's Tomb
SUEZ DESERT ROAD
Suez
October War Panorama
ABBASSIYA
Cairo Stadium
SHARIA AL-NASR
Sadat's Tomb
Sinai Bus Terminal
MEDINET NASR
SHARIA RAMSES
MAP ENLARGEMENTS
1 Central Cairo (see p.92-93)
2 Around Ramses Station (see p.106)
3 Around Khan el-Khalili & al-Azhar (see p.110)
4 North of Midan El-Hussein (see p.113)
5 Between Al-Azhar & the Bab Zwayla (see p.118)
6 Between Bab Zwayla & The Citadel (see p.122)
7 The Citadel (see p.125)
8 Around Ibn Tulun & S. Cemetery (see p.130)
9 The Northern Cemetery (see p.136)
10 Old Cairo & Roda Island (see p.140-141)
11 Gezira & The West Bank (see p.152-153)
Muqattam Hills
Petrified Forest
0
2 km

For **airport information** call ⓣ 02/265-3333 or 5000 (Terminal 1), or ⓣ 02/265-2222 or 2029 (Terminal 2), or check ⓦ www.cairo-airport.com. You'll find 24-hour currency exchange, ATMs as well as tourist offices at all three terminals.

Emerging from customs, you'll be waylaid by taxi drivers who'll swear that they're the only way of **getting into town**. This isn't so, but you might prefer going by **taxi** anyway. Airport cab drivers will probably demand at least £E60, and

Common Cairo scams

Arriving at Cairo airport you may be approached by "travel agents" wearing ID badges, who'll try to dissuade you from going to the hotel you had in mind by saying it's closed, or pretending to call the hotel for a voice to announce "We're full." Similar stories from taxi drivers, and strangers who get talking to you on the bus into town or on the streets, should also be disbelieved; some lurk outside popular hotels, claiming to be the manager. Their aim is to steer you into hotels which will pay them a commission (added to your bill); the same goes for anyone who brings you to a perfume or souvenir shop. Many hotels that work with touts pressure guests to buy souvenirs, horse and camel trips, or excursions to Luxor and Aswan sold at a huge mark-up. Checking into a hotel, it's best not to pay for more than one night upfront so you can leave the next day if necessary. Never buy any tour without first shopping around – you'll get a better deal direct from operators such as Samo Tours, Adventure in Egypt or Eastmar (p.205). See "Culture and etiquette" (p.51) for more on hustlers, who favour specific areas of Cairo: Sharia Talaat Harb (especially between Midan Tahrir and Midan Talaat Harb); the Ghuriya and Spice Bazaar in Islamic Cairo; and the Tahrir Bridge and Sharia Tahrir on Gezira Island.

then quite likely start giving you nonsense of the "your hotel is no good/closed/burnt down, but I know a better one" variety (see box above), which obviously you'll ignore (and don't pay them until you're sure you've reached the right hotel). A white cab (see p.82) should use the meter, and cost around £E35–40, though they may also ask for a £E5 surcharge, which is what they pay to enter the airport precincts. Your hotel may also arrange to send a vehicle for you, which will cost around £E50–60, but check the price in advance. You may also be able to call a yellow cab (see p.82) from the airport, but they usually prefer customers to have an Egyptian mobile number on which they can contact you.

On one side of Terminal 1's forecourt is the parking area for **buses** and **minibuses** into the centre. The most comfortable of the bus services is the a/c bus #356 (£E2), which stops at Terminal 2 before continuing to Midan Ramses and Abdel Mouneem Riyad terminal by Midan Tahrir in downtown Cairo. This service runs from about 7am to 11pm, as does minibus #27 (£E2), which follows the same route. After hours, you can use bus #400 (50pt), which plies the same route round the clock, though it is less comfortable and takes longer to get downtown – over an hour in rush hour, about forty minutes at night. Bus #948 also runs 24/7, to Midan Ataba, on the eastern edge of downtown. None of these buses serve Terminal 3, but the terminals are connected to each other by a free 24hr EgyptAir **shuttle bus**. Finally, there's a **limousine taxi service** with a desk in the arrivals halls; prices are fixed and posted, but higher than regular taxi rates.

By bus and train

Buses from Sinai, and some from Jordan, arrive at the old **Sinai Bus Terminal** (aka Abbassiya Station), 4km from the centre. The guard at the gate may try to hustle newcomers into one of the taxis waiting outside, which are likely to overcharge (the correct fare into town is £E15–20), and may try to take you to a commission-paying hotel (see box above); it's better to cross the street outside the terminal (Sharia Ramses) and hail a cab that's passing, preferably a white one (see p.82). Alternatively, cross the same street and catch a bus or minibus from the bus stop

100m to the right – buses to Midan Ramses include #14, #69, #178, #710 and #998, and minibus #203 serves Midan Ramses; buses #230, #611 and #998 serve Midan Tahrir (fares 50pt–£E1). Alternatively, if you turn left outside the terminal and walk 300m on past the flyover to the hospital, you have an even wider choice of buses and minibuses to Ramses, Tahrir and Ataba.

Coming from Jordan or Libya on a Superjet bus, you'll arrive at their terminal in **Almaza**, at the back end of Heliopolis. A taxi into town from here costs £E20–25, but the terminal is served by bus #15 to Midan Ataba and Midan Ramses, or minibus #39 to Ramses and Tahrir.

Buses from Tel Aviv and Jerusalem arrive at the **Cairo Sheraton hotel** in Dokki, a fifteen-minute walk or £E3–4 cab ride from downtown.

Certain buses from Alexandria and the Delta, plus Superjet services from Sinai, will drop you at **Cairo Gateway** in Bulaq. To get to downtown Cairo from here the simplest option is to take a taxi (around £E3 to Midan Ramses, £E4–5 to Midan Tahrir), unless you fancy walking, in which case turn right out of the front, then left at the next junction (by a mosque), along Sharia al-Sahafa to the end; cross Sharia al-Galaa (under the flyover), then head right and take the next left (26th July St), and Sharia Talaat Harb is 250m ahead. For Midan Ramses, turn left when you come out of the terminal, to the flyover (Sharia Shanan), then right and right again up Sharia al-Galaa.

Other bus companies coming from Alexandria and the Delta and Upper Egypt arrive at **Aboud Terminal** in Shubra. By far the easiest way into town from here is to climb up the steps to the main road where microbus service taxis await to take you straight to Sharia Orabi by Ramses train station (see below and the map on p.106).

Almost all **trains** into Cairo terminate at **Ramses Station** (see map, p.106), which has a tourist office. There are hotels nearby, but most visitors prefer to head downtown. You can do this by metro (Mubarak Station is beneath Midan Ramses), taxi (£E3–4), or on a bus along Sharia Ramses. Alternatively, it's a ten- to fifteen-minute walk down Sharia Ramses, taking a left at Sharia Emad el-Din or Sharia Orabi, into the main downtown area, where most of the budget hotels are located.

Information

Cairo's downtown **tourist office**, at 5 Sharia Adly (daily 9am–6pm, Ramadan and public holidays 9am–3pm; ⓣ02/2391-3454), is rather useless, but may be able to answer simple queries. There are also 24 hour tourist offices at all the airport terminals and offices at Ramses Station (daily 9am–8pm; ⓣ02/2579-0767), Giza train station (daily 9am–2pm & 5–9pm; ⓣ02/3570-2233), the Giza Pyramids (daily 8.30am–5pm; ⓣ02/3383-8823) and Souk Fustat (supposedly open daily 8.30am–9pm, but in practice often closed for no apparent reason; ⓣ02/2532-5269).

If you can find a copy, the *New Handy Map of Cairo* is generally the best **map** of the city, and Cairo City Key's *Detailed Map of Greater Cairo* comes second, but these were unavailable at last check so your choice is between the Cairo Engineering and

Manufacturing Company's *Cairo Tourist Map*, which extends out to Heliopolis, and Lehnert & Landrock's map of the same name, which is better for downtown. Geodia's *Cairo City* map, on laminated paper, is a lot less detailed. A free map with advertisements can occasionally be found at upmarket hotels, containing reasonable plans of Heliopolis, Ma'adi, Mohandiseen, Zamalek and the downtown area. Of more use for longer stays are the American University in Cairo's (AUC) *Cairo: The Practical Guide Maps* (£E50), which contains a useful set of maps, and the *Cairo City Key* (£E60). The best place to buy maps is at a bookshop such as Lehnert & Landrock (44 Sharia Sherif) or Shorouk (1 Midan Talaat Harb), but Buccellati, at Sharia Qasr el-Nil with Sharia Mohammed Farid, may have maps that other places don't stock.

Don't expect Cairenes themselves to relate to maps; they comprehend their city differently. Also be aware when asking directions that people are unlikely to admit they don't know where something is, and will make up some directions instead; for that reason it's always best to ask more than one person.

City transport

Getting around Cairo is relatively straightforward. The metro is simple to use, and taxis are inexpensive. Familiarize yourself with Arabic numerals (see p.642) and you can also use buses and minibuses, which reach most parts of the city. **Street names** may be posted in English (or French) as well as Arabic, but spellings vary, and often there is no sign at all. The same goes for house **numbers**, rendered in Western and Arabic numerals, or just the latter; note that a single number may denote a whole block with several entrances.

You might as well resign yourself to the fact that everyone here drives like participants in the Paris–Dakar Rally, but accidents are surprisingly rare, all things considered. The streets are busy from 8am to midnight, and, unless you enjoy sweltering in traffic jams, it's best to try and avoid travelling (except by Metro) during **rush hours** (Sun–Thurs 7–10am & 4–7pm). Friday mornings, on the other hand, are a joy, with very little traffic on the roads.

The metro

Cairo's **metro** (for some background, see Ⓦwww.urbanrail.net/af/cairo/cairo.htm) works like nothing else in the city. Trains run every few minutes from 5.30am to midnight; outside of the rush hours they're no more overcrowded than in other cities around the world. The front (and sometimes also the middle) carriage of each train is reserved for women, worth keeping in mind if you're a lone female traveller.

Stations are signposted with a large "M"; signs and route maps appear in Arabic and English. **Tickets** are purchased in the station (£E1 flat fare); twin sets of booths cater for passengers heading in opposite directions, sometimes with separate queues for either sex. Hang on to your ticket to get through the automatic barriers at the other end.

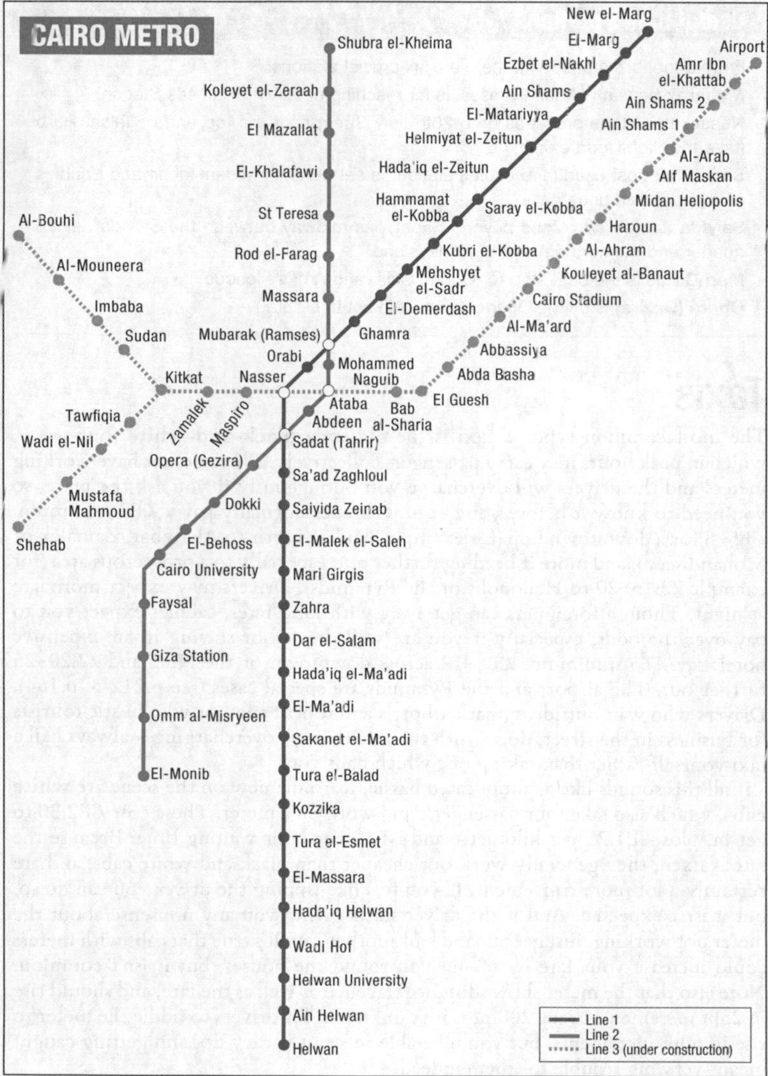

Line One connects the northeastern suburb of **El-Marg** with the southern industrial district of **Helwan** (via Mubarak, Sadat, Saad Zaghoul, Saiyida Zeinab, Mar Girgis and Maadi), with Line Two running from **Shubra** in the north to **El Monib** (via Mubarak, Ataba, Sadat, Opera and Giza). The new stations on Line Two are wheelchair-accessible, but stations on Line One are not. Line Three is now under construction; the first phase will run east from Ataba to Abbassiya, Cairo Stadium and Al-Ahram, but the line should eventually run from the airport via the city centre to Zamalek and Mohandiseen.

Useful metro stations

From a tourist's standpoint, there are six crucial stations:

Mubarak beneath Midan Ramses, is for reaching or leaving Ramses Station.

Nasser two stops on, leads onto 26th July Street near the top end of Talaat Harb (take the High Court exit).

Sadat the most used (and useful) station, is set beneath Midan Tahrir, and doubles as a pedestrian underpass.

Saiyida Zeinab two stops beyond Sadat, lies midway between the Saiyida Zeinab quarter and the northern end of Roda Island.

Mari Girgis is the best stop for Coptic Cairo and Amr's Mosque.

Opera (Gezira) is by the Opera Complex in south Gezira.

Taxis

The most common type of **taxi** is the old-style **black-and-white** four-seater, which in peak hours may carry passengers collectively. These do not have working meters and the drivers will overcharge you outrageously if you ask the price, so you need to know it before you get in. Cairenes normally pay a £E3 minimum, £E5–8 for a downtown hop (for example, Midan Tahrir to Al-Azhar, Zamalek or Mohandiseen), and more if heading further out, especially to a prosperous area (for example £E15–20 to Heliopolis or the Pyramids). Drivers may expect more late at night. Though foreigners can get away with local rates, cabbies expect you to pay over the odds, especially if you are well dressed or staying in an expensive hotel: say £E5 minimum, £E8–12 across downtown or the Nile, and £E20–25 further out. The airport and the Pyramids are special cases (see p.212 & p.164). Drivers who wait outside upmarket hotels and tourist sites, or who hustle tourists for business in the street, do so with the intention of overcharging – always hail a taxi yourself rather than taking one which hails you.

If all this sounds like a complicated hassle, fear not: new on the scene are **white cabs**, which also take four passengers, and work on a meter. These cost £E2.50 to get in, plus £E1.25 per kilometre and £E10 per hour waiting time. Because the rate is fixed, they generally work out cheaper than black and white cabs, and are certainly a lot more convenient. If you feel like tipping the driver you can do so, but it isn't expected. And if the driver starts giving you any nonsense about the meter not working, just get out and hail another cab. It's true that cabs with meters could increase your fare by taking you round the houses, but it isn't common. Note also that the meter shows distance travelled as well as the fare, and should rise in 25pt increments every 200m; it isn't unknown for drivers to fiddle the meter to rise in 60pt increments, but you'll be able to see it if they do, and getting caught means very big trouble for them indeed.

The third kind of taxi are **yellow cabs**, which can be hailed in the street, but are more commonly called by phone. They also use a meter, but are slightly more expensive than white taxis, with a flagfall of £E3.50. Two firms operate yellow cabs: City Cab (Ⓣ16516) and Cairo International Taxi (Ⓣ19155, Ⓦwww.citaxi.com), but they tend to arrive either very early, or late, often phoning several times en route to ask for directions to where you are.

Finally, there are **limousines**, usually Mercedes or Peugeot 406s, operated by firms such as Limousine Misr Travel (Ⓣ02/2269-5675) and Target Limousine (Ⓣ02/3377-2666). They are stationed at five-star hotels and at the airport, with fixed fares (£E66 from the airport to downtown, for example), and are rentable by the day as well as for set routes. A limo for the day (12 hours and 100km) costs around £E500.

Service taxis

Service taxis travel a set route (see box below for some of the most useful) and can be flagged down anywhere along it if there is space aboard. In town they are invariably **microbuses**, known as *arrabeya bin nafar* or just *servees*. **Fares** range from 50pt to £E1 per person, according to the distance travelled. They are especially useful for longer-distance journeys such as from downtown to the Pyramids. Their main terminals are at **Abdel Mouneem Riyad** (behind the Museum of Egyptian Antiquities and in front of the *Ramses Hilton* hotel), and behind and around **Ramses station**. For Saqqara (and occasionally Dahshur), they leave from Maryotteya Canal near its junction with Pyramids Road, easily reached on a pyramids-bound service taxi from Ramses or Abdel Mouneem Riyad.

Buses

Cairo's **buses** mainly operate from 5.30am to 12.30am daily (6.30am–6.30pm & 7.30pm–2am during Ramadan). Fares are cheap enough to be affordable for everyone, so buses are usually full and overflow during rush hour, when passengers hang from doorways. Though many foreigners are deterred from using buses by the crush, not to mention the risk of pickpockets and gropers, the network reaches virtually everywhere. Because buses tend to make slow progress against the traffic, however, service-taxi microbuses are generally a better option, where available, though there are **air-conditioned buses** on some routes to prosperous suburbs such as Heliopolis and Medinet Nasr, and to tourist sights such as the Pyramids.

Buses should have **route numbers** in Arabic numerals on the front, side and back. Those with a slash through the number (represented in this guide as, for example, #13/) may follow different routes from buses with the same number unslashed; some route numbers even have two slashes. **Bus stops** are not always clearly signposted (look for metal shelters, plaques on lampposts or crowds waiting), and buses often just slow down instead of halting, compelling passengers to board and disembark on the run. Some bus stops (at the time of writing, those on the west bank of the river, in and around Mohandiseen) have route information posted, but this is in Arabic only.

Most buses start from (or pass through) at least one of the main city-centre nuclei at Midan Tahrir, Abdel Mouneem Riyad terminal (behind the Museum of Egyptian Antiquities), Midan Ramses or Midan Ataba. At each of these locations, there are several bus stops, and where exactly you pick up your bus will depend on which

Useful service taxi routes

Abdel Mouneem Riyad (behind the Museum of Egyptian Antiquities) to the Pyramids (*Al-Ahram*), Sharia Faisal (near the Pyramids), Midan Giza, Mohandiseen, Bulaq, Bulaq al-Dakrour, Imbaba, Ma'adi and Helwan. Also to Qanatir (Fri & Sat only).

Ramses Ahmed Helmi, behind the station, to Abbassiya, Medinet Nasr, al-Basatin, Ma'adi and Helwan; Sharia al-Gala to Aboud terminal; Sharia Orabi to Midan Giza and the Pyramids; al-Fath Mosque to Midan Ataba.

Midan Giza (at the eastern end of Pyramids Road, and around 1km west of El-Giza bridge) to Ramses, the Pyramids and Badrasheen (for Saqqara).

Maryotteya Canal Pyramids Road to Tahrir, Ramses and sometimes Ataba; west bank of canal to Abu Sir and Saqqara, usually changing at the latter for Dahshur.

Useful bus routes

Abdel Mouneem Riyad and Midan Ramses to Airport #356, #400 (24hr), minibus #27; Abbassiya and Heliopolis (Midan Roxi) #400, #400/, #500, minibus #27.

Abdel Mouneem Riyad to Citadel (Bab Gabal) #951, minibus #105; Midan Salah el-Din #456, #955, minibus #35; Saiyida Zeinab and Ibn Tulun Mosque #72//, #102, #160; Immam al-Shafi'i minibus #154; Manashi #214; Muqattam Hills #951; Pyramids #30, #355, #357, #900; Qanatir #210; Sphinx #997.

direction it is going in and whether it starts there or is simply passing through. If possible, ask the conductor "*Rayih...?*" (Are you going to...?) to make sure.

Except at terminals, you are supposed to enter through the rear door (often removed to facilitate access) and exit from the front. Conductors sell **tickets** (the flat fare on most routes is 50pt–£E1, or £E2 on a/c buses) from behind a crush-bar by the rear door. The front of the bus is usually less crowded, so it's worth squeezing your way forwards; start edging towards the exit well before your destination.

Minibuses

Minibuses run along many of the bus routes, supplemented by privately run green minibuses on new routes. Besides making better headway through traffic and actually halting at stops (usually the same stops as used by ordinary buses), minibuses are far more comfortable than ordinary buses and never crowded, as standing is not permitted. Tickets (£E1–2) are bought from the driver. Minibuses should not be confused with service taxis (usually smaller microbuses, see p.83). There are minibus **terminals** alongside the big bus stations in Midan Tahrir (by the *Nile Hilton* and near Arab League/Omar Makram Mosque) and Midan Ataba.

Trams and river-taxis

As the metro and minibus systems expand, Cairo's original **tram network** (built in colonial times) is being phased out. The Heliopolis tram system remains in use throughout that area (see p.158 for details), but all the other lines into town have been withdrawn. Like buses, the trams are cheap and battered, sometimes with standing room only; their Arabic route numbers are posted above the driver's cab.

River-taxis (aka waterbuses) are the most relaxing way to reach Old Cairo. They leave from the Maspero Dock outside the Television Building, 600m north of the Museum of Egyptian Antiquities. Boats run every hour from 7am to El Gama'a Bridge in Giza (see map, p.140). You can buy tickets (£E1) at the dock. On Fridays and Sundays, they also run up to the Nile barrages at Qanatir (£E5 one-way; see p.207).

Driving

The only thing scarier than **driving in Cairo** is cycling, which is tantamount to suicide. Dashes, crawls and finely judged evasions are the order of the day; jaywalkers trust in motorists' swift reactions. Any collision draws a crowd. Minor dents are often settled by on-the-spot payoffs, but should injury occur, it's wise to involve a cop right away. Multistorey car parks, such as the one on Midan Ataba, are ignored as motorists park bumper-to-bumper along every kerb, leaving their handbrakes off so vehicles can be shifted by the local *minaidy* (street parking attendant), whom they tip £E2 or so. Given all this, it's no surprise that few foreigners drive in Cairo. **Renting a car** with a driver costs around $20 a day more than doing the driving yourself; see p.204 for rental outlets.

Accommodation

Cairo's hotels reflect the city's diversity: deluxe chains overlooking the Nile; functional high-rises; colonial piles and homely *pensions* with the same raddled facades as bug-infested flophouses. Inexpensive hotels tend to be located on the upper floors of downtown office buildings, and one or two are locked at midnight, so if you arrive later you'll have to rouse the doorman (*bowab*), who will probably expect some modest baksheesh for his trouble. Downtown traffic is noisy so you may wish to bring earplugs if staying in the centre. Standards vary within any given price range or star rating – and from room to room in many places, so try to inspect the facilities before checking in, and establish the price and any service tax or extra charges (which should be posted in reception) at the outset. Rates are usually the same all year, though some five-stars have variable rates which change from day to day depending on current demand, and upmarket hotels are of course always cheaper if booked through an agency at home or online.

Nearly all the city's five-star hotels have wheelchair access and adapted rooms. The *El Borg Novotel*, *Four Seasons* (in both Garden City and Giza), *Ramses Hilton*, *Semiramis InterContinental*, *Cairo Marriott*, *Conrad*, *Grand Hyatt*, *Mena House Oberoi* and *Sofitel* all have adapted rooms, as does the *Shepheard*, but without wheel-in showers in the bathroom; the *Nile Ritz-Carlton* should also have adapted rooms when it reopens. Downtown budget hotels tend to have narrow entrances with steps, and small lifts with awkward doors, making access very hard.

Zamalek, the northern half of Gezira Island, is a quieter and fresher place to stay than central Cairo, except along 26th July Street. It's also easier-going for women than the downtown area or Islamic Cairo. There are a couple of good five-stars out by the **Giza Pyramids**, and nearer town in Gezira and on Roda Island, as well as a **youth hostel** (on Roda Island) and a **campsite** (down past the Pyramids on the way to Saqqara).

Central Cairo

Unless otherwise indicated, these hotels are marked on the map on pp.92–93.

Amin 38 Midan Falaki, opposite Bab al-Luq market ⓣ02/2393-3813. Very reasonable rooms with fans on the sixth, seventh and tenth floors. It's worth paying a bit more for a room with private bathroom and constant hot water – the shared facilities aren't so clean. ❶

Berlin Fourth floor, 2 Sharia el-Shawarby ⓣ02/2395-7502, ⓔberlinhotelcairo@hotmail.com. Lofty double and triple rooms, each with its own shower, a/c, and comfortable mattresses; was getting run-down but a facelift is now under way. The owner is full of handy advice, and services include laundry, free wi-fi and use of computer, their own drivers to take you round the pyramid sites or elsewhere at decent rates, and good-value Arabic and bellydancing lessons. BB ❸

Big Ben 33 Sharia Emad el-Din ⓣ02/2590-8881 (see map, p.106). Good-value place with clean fresh rooms, all en suite, not frequented much by foreign tourists, and rather cheaper than its centre-of-downtown equivalents as a result. ❷

Carlton 21 26th July St ⓣ02/2575-5022, ⓦwww.carltonhotelcairo.com. Built in 1935 and still retaining some wood-panelled period charm, albeit rather worn. All rooms are a/c; pricier deluxe rooms have satellite TV and a minibar; rooms at the back are much quieter than those at the front. There's a restaurant on the seventh floor and a very pleasant rooftop garden with a café-bar. You usually have to take half-board, though they may do you a bed-and-breakfast rate. Half-board ❹

Cosmopolitan 1 Sharia Ben Talaab, off Qasr el-Nil ⓣ02/2392-3956, ⓕ2393-3531. This rather grand monumental *belle époque* building is quite stately in a modest way, with sedate, red-carpeted rooms, a European restaurant and English-style bar, but avoid the tours sold at the travel desk. All rooms have a/c and private baths. BB ❺

Dahab Seventh floor, 26 Sharia Bassiouni ⓣ02/2579-9104, ⓦwww.dahabhostel.com. A Dahab tourist camp transported – surprisingly convincingly – to a downtown roof, with poky rooms, friendly staff and lots of backpackers. Plenty of vegetation and an open rooftop area to socialize in make it a pleasant hangout; facilities include a Bedouin-style café, kitchen, laundry service, wi-fi and 24hr hot water. ❶

El Borg Novotel 3 Sharia Saraya el Gezira ⓣ02/3735-6725, ⓦwww.novotel.com (see map, p.153). Just over Tahrir Bridge in Gezira, this refurbished hotel is rather ugly on the outside but cool and stylish inside, with very modern cream and beige rooms, plus the usual deluxe accessories such as a/c and plasma TV. ❾

Fontana Off Midan Ramses ⓣ02/2592-2321 (see map, p.106). A bit scuffed in places, but definitely has a slightly kitsch charm about it, with pink marble in the lobby and a touch of the Louis Farouks in the rooms (that's Louis XIV as interpreted by King Farouk), with a small rooftop swimming pool (summer only), bar, restaurant, café, and nightclub (see p.195). Rooms have TV, fridge and a/c; some have views as far as the Citadel, and the staff are extremely friendly. BB ❹

Four Seasons 1089 Corniche el-Nil, Garden City ⓣ02/2791-7000, ⓦwww.fourseasons.com. Sleek, sophisticated and luxurious to a fault, this branch of the *Four Seasons* chain is better suited to Western tastes than its gaudier sister establishment in Giza. The rooms have little extras like a DVD player and high-speed internet. Two rooms are adapted for wheelchair users. ❾

Garden City House Third floor, 26 Sharia Kamal al-Din Salah ⓣ02/2794-8400, ⓦwww.gardencityhouse.com. 1930s *pension* on the edge of the Garden City, behind the *Semiramis*. Some rooms have Nile views, some have en-suite bathrooms, and some have a/c. For some reason it's quite popular with impecunious egyptologists, but on the downside, the location is rather noisy. BB ❷

Grand 17 26th July St (entrance in the alley off Sharia Talaat Harb) ⓣ02/575-7801 to 5, ⓔgrandhotel@link.net. Characterful Art Deco edifice featuring original lifts and furniture, a fountain, coffee shop and old-fashioned, homely rooms with immaculately varnished wooden floors, attached to large, spotless, bright tiled bathrooms, though the plumbing can be temperamental, and the desk staff a bit surly. They generally insist that you take half-board. Half-board ❹

Happyton 10 Sharia Ali al-Kassar ⓣ02/2592 8600. Two-star hotel with en-suite a/c rooms of variable sizes, all well kept. There's a café and small restaurant, no bar, but you can buy beer in the lobby and drink it on the roof terrace. BB ❷

Isis Marouf Tower, 16th floor, 33B Sharia Ramses ⓣ02/2578-1895, ⓦwww.isiscairo.com. Worth staying at for the spectacular views alone, over the river one side, and over downtown to the Citadel the other. Staff are friendly, rooms are spacious, some en suite, windows large, and there's free internet use. On the downside, some guests don't like the location (two blocks off Talaat Harb among car spares shops – others may see this as a plus), and the lift only reaches the fourteenth floor, so you have to walk the other two. BB ❸

Ismailia House Eighth floor, 1 Midan Tahrir ⓣ02/2796-3122, ⓦwww.ismailiahotel.com. Advance booking is advisable for this cool, cheerful backpackers' haven, with a variety of singles, doubles, triples and dorm beds (£E25), 24hr hot water and plenty of communal areas to hang out in. The Tahrir-facing rooms are noisy at night but have great views. BB ❷

King Tut Hostel Eighth floor, 37 Sharia Talaat Harb ⓣ02/2391-7897, ⓦwww.kingtuthostel.com. Wonderful pharaonic decor in the entrance welcomes you to this well-kept hotel (not really a hostel, despite the name), gleaming bright, and often full, so worth booking ahead (or try *Ramses II Hotel*, four floors up in the same building, run by the same firm). Don't be pressurized into buying their tours, however. BB ❸

Lotus Seventh floor, 12 Sharia Talaat Harb (entrance in the arcade) ⓣ02/2575-0966, ⓦwww.lotushotel.com. Its claim to have "an authentic Art Deco ambiance" is a slight exaggeration, though one or two of the fittings do seem to date from the 1930s. There's a restaurant and a bar, and the staff are friendly; it's worth paying the £E30 extra for a room with a/c and attached bathroom (hot water 6–11am and 6–11pm), but avoid buying tours here. BB ❸

Luna Fifth floor, 27 Sharia Talaat Harb ⓣ02/396-1020, ⓔlunapension@hotmail.com. Well kept and generally cleaner than other hotels in this category, with large a/c rooms, some en suite. It's worth asking for the Egyptian breakfast (*fuul* and falafel) in preference to the Continental. Noisophobes may wish to pay a little extra for a room at the back. BB ❸

New Cecil (or New Cicil) 22 Sharia Emad el-Din ⓣ02/2591-3895 (see map, p.106). A good budget option if you aren't too fussy – the rooms are a bit grimy, but quite OK for the price, with fans and shared bathroom facilities, to the north of the centre, towards Ramses station. ❶

Nile Ritz-Carlton 1113 Corniche el-Nil, backing onto Midan Tahrir ⓣ02/2578-0444 or 0666, ⓦwww.ritzcarlton.com/en/Properties/Cairo. Cairo's most central five-star, closed for refurbishment until 2012, this 1950s building (formerly the *Nile Hilton*) is on the river right by the Egyptian Museum, and boasts the biggest rooms in town. ❾

Odeon Palace 6 Sharia Abdel Hamid Said, just off Sharia Talaat Harb ⓣ02/2577-6637, ⓕ2576-7971. Creaky old place with a certain sombre, old-fashioned charm, but give your room a once-over, and make sure the shower and plug sockets are working. One of the best features is the 24hr room service and 24hr roof bar. ❺

Pension Roma 169 Sharia Mohammed Farid (entrance around the side of Gattegno department store) ⓣ02/2391-1088, ⓦwww.pensionroma.com.eg. The stylish 1940s ambiance, immaculately maintained by Madame Cressaty, is highly recommended and it's wise to book in advance. Some rooms have private bathrooms, but most have shared bathroom facilities. BB ❸

Select Eighth floor, 19 Sharia Adly, beside the synagogue ⓣ02/393-3707, ⓔhostelselect@yahoo.com. A bright little place, homely and very friendly, some rooms en suite, in a 1930s building with one or two period touches. BB ❷

Ramses Hilton Corniche el-Nil ⓣ02/2577-7444, ⓦwww.hilton.com. Cairo's tallest hotel, rooms on the upper storeys giving excellent views over the city and as far as the Pyramids, but it gets rather mixed reports, and is largely used by tour groups, so it isn't quite as posh as you might expect from a *Hilton*, and there always seems to be a queue at the reception desk. ❾

Semiramis Intercontinental Corniche el-Nil ⓣ02/2795-7171, ⓦwww.intercontinental.com. Spacious, elegant rooms, plus a gym, a pool, the *Haroun al-Rashid* nightclub (see p.194), and seven restaurants offering cuisine from around the world. Rooms on the upper floors give excellent views, and in fact the views over Cairo from the slightly cheaper city-side rooms are better than from the Nile side. ❾

Shepheard Corniche el-Nil ⓣ02/2792-1000, ⓦwww.shepheard-hotel.com. Nile-side version of the famous nineteenth-century establishment that stood on Midan Opera, rebuilt on the present site in 1957, and still retaining a certain 1950s feel. Rooms on the quieter side facing the Muqattam Hills are cheaper than those facing the Nile. Facilities include two restaurants, a casino and the *Castle* disco (closed until 2011), but no swimming pool. ❽

Sultan First floor, 4 Sharia Tawfiqia ⓣ02/2577-2258, ⓔhotel.sultan@hotmail.com. Dorm beds only (£E15) in this friendly ultra-cheapy located in a colourful market street near Midan Orabi, very handy for inexpensive eating and groceries, and just the right distance from the centre of downtown. Guests get free use of the kitchen and there's satellite TV.

Talisman in the passage by 39 Sharia Talaat Harb ⓣ02/2393-9431, ⓦwww.talisman-hotel.com. Well-situated boutique hotel claiming to have the facilities of a five-star (a/c, satellite TV, minibar, safe, but no pool or fitness centre), defended against the street noise by double glazing, decorated with antiques and *objets d'art*, with excellent service and attentive staff. BB ❻

Tulip First floor, 3 Midan Talaat Harb ⓣ02/2393-9433, ⓦwww.tulip-hotel.com. Decently refurbished old place facing *Groppi's* across Midan Talaat Harb. The rooms, en suite and some with a/c, are bright and cheerful and the beds have firm mattresses. There's wi-fi but you have to pay £E10 a day for it. BB ❸

Venice Hosokawaya Fourth floor, 4 Sharia Tawfiqia ⓣ02/2773-5307, ⓔinfo@venicehosokawaya.com In the same building as the *Sultan* (see above) but pricier, this is the Japanese backpackers' budget hotel of choice in Cairo, and 90 per cent of its clientele are from Japan. It's very clean and well run, with dorm beds (£E35) and private rooms, free wi-fi, and a laundry service. BB ❷

Victoria 66 Sharia el-Gumhorriya ⓣ02/2589-2290 to 94, ⓦwww.victoria.com.eg (see map, p.106). A three-star 1930s hotel once frequented by George Bernard Shaw. Lots of wood panelling, attractive a/c rooms with shiny wooden floors and a comfortably worn, lived-in feel (some with mahogany furniture), plus a bar, restaurant and spacious lounge area, make this one of the best deals in town. Advance reservation advisable. BB ❻

Windsor 19 Sharia Alfi Bey ⓣ02/2591-5810, ⓦwww.windsorcairo.com. This colonial hotel retains much character and one of the nicest bars in Cairo (the *Barrel Lounge*, see p.190), but has definitely seen better days and is overpriced, not tremendously friendly, and not tremendously clean, and they may insist on your paying for a (not very nice) breakfast. All rooms have a/c and satellite TV; all but the very cheapest have private bathroom. Offers 15 per cent discount for *Rough Guide* readers, but avoid buying tours here. ④

Islamic Cairo

El-Hussein Muski, entered via a passage to *Fishawi's* ⓣ02/2591-8089 (see map, p.110). Rather grimy, and rooms overlooking the square are harangued by Cairo's loudest muezzins, while during festivals the square bops all night, but if you don't mind the noise, a balcony gives you a ringside view. If you want to be in the thick of it, this really is right in the heart of Islamic Cairo. BB ③

El Malky 4 Sharia el-Hussein ⓣ02/2589-0804, ⓦwww.server2002.net/malky (see map, p.110). Behind the Saiyidna Hussein Mosque, with a mainly Muslim clientele, well-kept, good value, and handily located less than 100m from El-Hussein, but out of the noise and bustle. Rooms are carpeted, with a/c and private bathrooms, generally comfortable though the beds are a bit on the hard side. BB ②

Le Riad 114 Sharia al-Muizz ⓣ02/2787-6074, ⓦwww.leriad-hoteldecharme.com (see map, p.113). Immaculate boutique hotel in the heart of Gamaliya, containing seventeen individually themed suites (choose the one you want online), all with sparkling (and generally large) bathrooms, free wi-fi plus loan of a laptop if you need it and plasma TV with DVD player. There's a library of DVDs and books, and a roof terrace with great views. BB ⑨

Elsewhere in the city

Cairo Marriott Sharia Saray al-Gezira, off 26th July St, Zamalek ⓣ02/2728-3000, ⓦwww.cairomarriotthotel.com (see map, p.152). Choose between garden or slightly pricier tower rooms with a better view, all built around a lavish palace constructed to house Napoleon III's wife Empress Eugénie. There are fine restaurants and bars, a casino, nightclub and a pool. Rooms have fast internet connections and the hotel is wi-fi-enabled throughout. ⑨

Conrad 1191 Corniche el-Nil, Bulaq ⓣ02/2580-8000, ⓦwww.conradhotels.com (see map, p.76). Run by the *Hilton* chain, but calmer and more sedate than the *Ramses Hilton*, with some of the most comfortable rooms in Cairo. It has international dining, palm trees in the lobby, a pool and health club. ⑨

Grand Hyatt ⓣ02/2365-1234, ⓦwww.cairo.grand.hyatt.com (see map, p.140). Superior five-star at the northern tip of Roda Island, though best accessed via its own bridge from Garden City, with stylish rooms in a sumptuous new wing (north-facing ones offer killer views of central Cairo and the Nile), with all the facilities you'd expect – sauna, health club, business centre, two pools and nine restaurants, including a revolving one with panoramic views (see p.186). BB ⑨

Longchamps 5th floor, 21 Sharia Ismail Mohammed, Zamalek ⓣ02/2735-2311, ⓦwww.hotellongchamps.com (see map, p.152). Spotless, quiet and well-run three-star hotel with a/c, satellite TV, internet connection and a fridge in all rooms, plus a pleasant terrace and meals available. It's advisable to book at least a couple of weeks ahead, but if it's full, the similarly priced *Horus House* downstairs isn't a bad fallback. BB ⑥

Mena House Oberoi Near the Giza Pyramids ⓣ02/3377-3222, ⓦwww.oberoihotels.com (see map, p.161). Set in lush grounds (of which some rooms have a view), this one-time khedival hunting lodge witnessed Roosevelt and Churchill initiate the D-Day plan, and the formal signing of the peace treaty between Israel and Egypt. Its renovated arabesque halls and nineteenth-century "palace" rooms are delightful; the modern Mena Gardens annexe isn't so grand, though the rooms are plush enough. Facilities include the *Moghul Room* (the best Indian restaurant in Egypt; see p.187), pool, golf course and tennis courts. ⑧

Mayfair 9 Sharia Aziz Osman, 1st floor (see map p.152) ⓣ02/2735-7315, ⓦwww.mayfaircairo.com. Immaculate rooms, some en-suite and a/c, all with balconies, in a quiet location, with a great Art Deco entrance lobby, and a breakfast terrace overlooking the street. 10 percent discount for *Rough Guide* readers, but avoid buying tours here. BB ④

Pension Zamalek 6 Sharia Salah al-Din, Zamalek ⓣ02/2735-9318, ⓔpensionzamalek@msn.com. (see map, p.152) A European-style *pension*, clean, quiet and secluded with a pleasant family atmosphere, and one bathroom to every two rooms, but note that they don't accept unmarried couples. BB ④

Salma Camping Harraniyya, past Giza ⓣ02/3381-5062 or 010 487-1300, ⓔpsalma.camp@yahoo.com (see map, p.161). Cairo's only campsite, a bit run-down, but attracts tourists with camper-vans or bikes, and is handy for the pyramid sites at Giza and Saqqara. Camping or caravanning, it's £E30 per person, including electricity and free hot showers, or there are huts and double rooms, and you can use the kitchen. It's reached by turning off Pyramids Rd towards Saqqara at Maryotteya Canal (1km before the Pyramids), and then after 4km taking a signposted turn-off at

Long stays and flat-hunting

Should you decide to stay a while, it's worth remembering that many hotels reduce their rates after one or two weeks' occupation. Depending on demand for rooms and your rapport with the management, it may be possible to negotiate further discounts for long stays at *pensions*.

In the longer term, however, it's better to rent an **apartment**. The upscale suburb of **Ma'adi** (accessible by metro) is home to most of Egypt's American community and mega-wealthy natives. **Zamalek,** favoured by embassies and European expats, is likewise costly, but always has vacancies. Another focus for the foreign community is **Heliopolis**. Few flats are available downtown except in **Bulaq,** Qasr al-Aini or **Abdin**.

Expect to look at half a dozen places before settling on one. Check the small ads in *Egypt Today*, the *Egyptian Gazette* and *Community Times* and expat community newssheets such as the *Maadi Messenger* or *British Community News*, and look at noticeboards at English-language institutes and cultural centres (see p.204), and the American University. Flats are also advertised online, at Ⓦwww.e-dar.com and Ⓦwww.algomhoria.com. The AUC's regularly updated *Cairo: the Practical Guide* contains much valuable wisdom on apartment rental and Cairo living in general.

Foreigners working or studying in Cairo often seek flatmates or want to sublet during temporary absences. Another way involves using a *simsar* (flat agent), who can be found in any neighbourhood by making enquiries at local shops and cafés (Atef Gamal Ⓣ012 376-6134 has been recommended, but doesn't speak much English). Unless you spend a long, fruitless day together, *simsars* are only paid when you settle on a place; ten percent of your first month's rent is the normal charge. Flat agencies in Ma'adi levy the same commission on both tenant and landlord. You can usually rent a flat in the centre for around £E1500–2500 per person per month, and occasionally even £E1000 or less; prices are a lower in winter than in summer. Additional "key money" (illegal), is rarely demanded for short-term lets.

Harraniyya village; continue for 100m, and the site is about 100m away on your right. ❷

Youth Hostel 135 Sharia Abdel Aziz al-Saoud, by Kobri al-Gamaa, El-Manial Ⓣ02/2364-0729, Ⓔinfo@egyptyha.com (see map, p.140). You can take a place in a six-bed dorm (£E15), or take a three-bed room (£E100), but bookings must be made by e-mail. Rooms are clean and en suite but the location is inconvenient, staff are not very friendly and don't usually speak English, and doors are closed from midnight to 8am, so no carousing unless you aim to make a full night of it. The only advantage, unless you really need the ultra-cheap price, is that you can meet young Egyptians and practise your Arabic. BB ❷

The City

With so much to see, you can spend weeks in **CAIRO** and merely scratch the surface. But as visitors soon realize, there are lots of reasons why people don't stay for long. The city's density, climate and pollution conspire against it, and the culture shock is equally wearing. Tourists unfamiliar with Arab ways can take little for granted, regular visitors expect to be baffled, and not even Cairenes comprehend the whole metropolis. The downside weighs especially on newcomers, since it's the main sights that generate most friction. Generally, however, Cairenes are the warmest, best-natured city dwellers going, and helpful to strangers.

Central Cairo

Most people prefer to get accustomed to **central Cairo** before tackling the older, Islamic quarters, for even in this Westernized downtown area known as *wust al-balad*, the culture shock can be profound. The area is essentially a lopsided triangle, bounded by **Ramses Station**, **Midan Ataba** and **Garden City**, and for the most part it's compact enough to explore on foot. Only the Ramses quarter and the further reaches of Garden City are sufficiently distant to justify using transport. At the heart of central Cairo is the broad, bustling expanse of **Midan Tahrir**, its most famous landmark the domed **Museum of Egyptian Antiquities**, which houses the finest collection of its kind in the world.

Midan Tahrir

At the heart of central Cairo is the broad expanse of **Midan Tahrir** (Liberation Square), created after the 1952 revolution on the site of Britain's Qasr el-Nil Barracks. Dominating its southern side is a concave office block that inspires shuddering memories: the **Mugamma**. A "fraternal gift" from the Soviet Union in the 1960s, this Kafkaesque warren of gloomy corridors, dejected queues and idle bureaucrats houses the public departments of the Interior, Health and Education ministries, and the Cairo Governorate. How many of the fifty thousand people visiting El-Mugamma each day suffer nervous breakdowns from sheer frustration is anyone's guess; an African supposedly flung himself through a window several years ago (for advice on handling the Mugamma, see p.206).

To the left of the Mugamma as you look at it, across Sharia Qasr al-Aini, a handsome pseudo-Islamic facade masks the old campus of the **American University in Cairo** (entered via Sharia Sheikh Rihan). Responsible for publishing some of the best research on Egypt in the English language, the AUC is also a Western-style haven for wealthy Egyptian youths and US students doing a year abroad, its shady gardens and preppy ambiance seeming utterly remote from everyday life in Cairo. Visitors might experience a premonitory shiver that Iran's gilded youth probably looked pretty similar before the Islamic Revolution. Egyptian Marxists and Islamic fundamentalists regard the AUC as a tool of US and Zionist imperialism.

On the other side of the Mugamma (to its right as you look at it) the **Omar Makram Mosque** is where funeral receptions for deceased VIPs are held in brightly coloured marquees. Behind it is Egypt's Ministry of Foreign Affairs. Across Sharia Tahrir from here, the secretariat of the **Arab League**, a tan-coloured edifice built during the 1960s, is a vestige of the time when Egypt was acknowledged leader of the "progressive" Arab cause. After Sadat's treaty with Israel, the Arab League moved its headquarters to Tunis and most of its members severed relations with Egypt. Mubarak's policy of rapprochement was finally rewarded in 1992, when the League returned to Cairo and, with it, posses of limos and gun-toting guards. Sharia Tahrir, the street between Omar Makram Mosque and the Arab League building, leads past two guardian lions and across Tahrir Bridge to Gezira Island (see p.151) and on to Dokki (see p.156). Just south down the Corniche (the road that runs along the bank of the Nile), roughly opposite the **Shepheard Hotel**, was the site of the Thomas Cook landing stage, where generations of tourists embarked on Nile cruises, and where British General Gordon's ill-fated expedition set off for Khartoum in 1883, in a vain attempt to wrest Sudan from the Mahdi's nationalist forces.

North of Sharia Tahrir, in front of the Arab League building and the prestigious **Nile Ritz-Carlton** hotel, what was once a large bus terminus is now a large

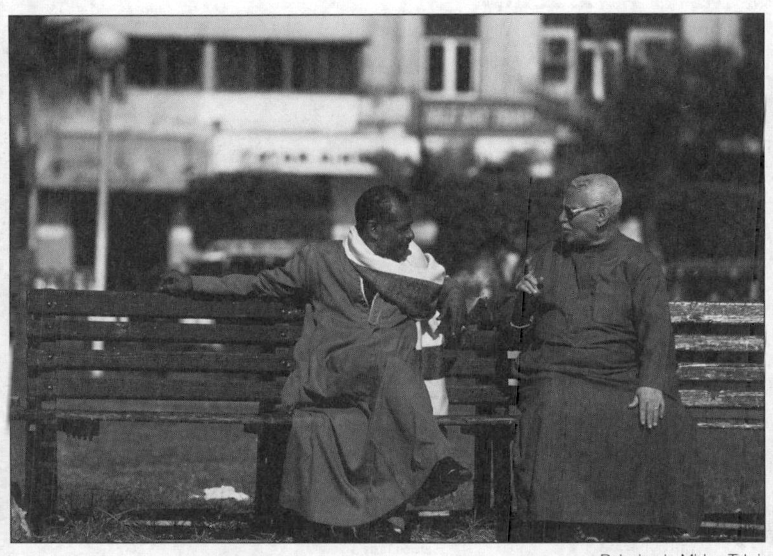

▲ Relaxing in Midan Tahrir

building site, though it should once again serve as a hub for local bus services in the future. To its north is the Egyptian Museum (see below). Across the square, on the east side, Sharia Talaat Harb will take you north through the centre of downtown (see p.103), while Sharia Tahrir continues east to Bab al-Luq and Abdin (see p.105). Heading south, alongside the American University, Sharia Qasr al-Aini leads along the east side of Garden City (see p.105) and on towards Old Cairo (see p.138).

The entrances to **Sadat metro station** serve as pedestrian underpasses linking the various buildings around Tahrir and the main roads that lead off the square. Despite clear labelling in English, it's easy to go astray in the maze of subways and surface at the wrong location. Many Cairenes prefer to take their chances crossing by road – a nerve-wracking experience for newcomers. Though some **landmarks** are obvious, rooftop billboards and neon signs flanking the end of streets like Talaat Harb or Qasr el-Nil also help with orientation. To watch the square over tea, try one of the Arab cafés between Talaat Harb and El-Bustan; the café nearest to Sharia Talaat Harb, the *Wadi el-Nil*, was bombed by Islamic radicals in 1993, apparently because they didn't like the Sudanese cannabis dealers who used to hang out in it.

The Museum of Egyptian Antiquities

Downtown's biggest attraction is the Egyptian Museum, or to give it its full title, the **Museum of Egyptian Antiquities**, at the northern end of Midan Tahrir (daily 9am–6.45pm; Ramadan 9am–4pm; £E60, students £E30, no cameras allowed; Ⓦ www.egyptianmuseum.gov.eg). Founded in 1858 by Auguste Mariette, who excavated the Serapeum at Saqqara and several major temples in Upper Egypt (and who was later buried in the museum grounds), it has long since outgrown its present building, which now scarcely provides warehouse space for the pharaonic artefacts, with 136,000 exhibits, and 40,000 more items crated in the basement. A new Grand Egyptian Museum (see p.169), which will house some

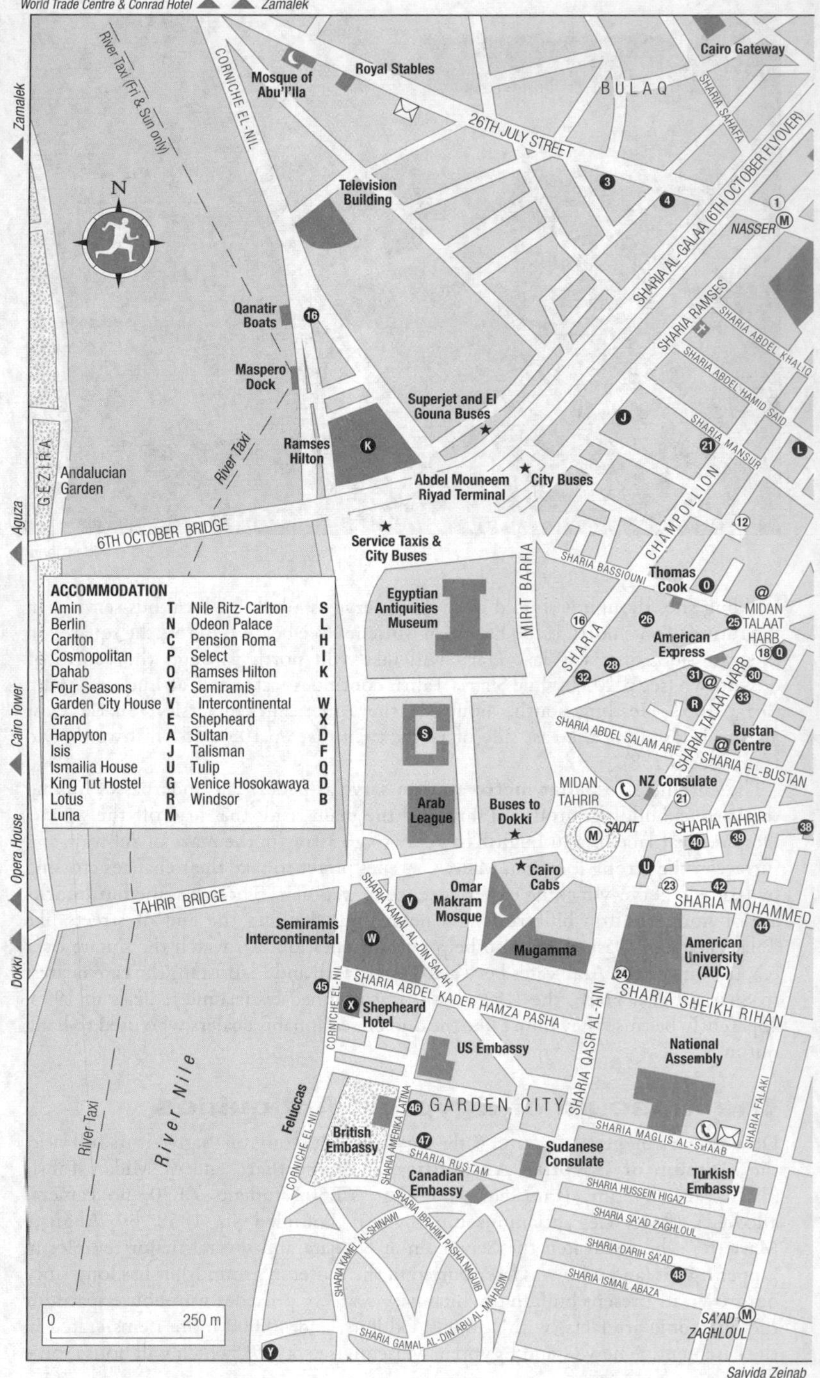
World Trade Centre & Conrad Hotel
Zamalek
Mosque of Abu'l'Ila
Royal Stables
Cairo Gateway
BULAQ
CORNICHE EL-NIL
River Taxi (Fri & Sun only)
26TH JULY STREET
SHARIA SHAHAFA
SHARIA AL-GALAA (6TH OCTOBER FLYOVER)
Television Building
NASSER
Qanatir Boats
Maspero Dock
SHARIA RAMSES
SHARIA ABDEL KHALIQ
SHARIA ABDEL HAMID SAID
SHARIA MANSUR
Superjet and El Gouna Buses
Ramses Hilton
River Taxi
GEZIRA
Andalucian Garden
Abdel Mouneem Riyad Terminal
City Buses
CHAMPOLLION
6TH OCTOBER BRIDGE
Service Taxis & City Buses
MIRIT BARHA
SHARIA BASSIOUNI
Thomas Cook
Egyptian Antiquities Museum
SHARIA
MIDAN TALAAT HARB
American Express
SHARIA TALAAT HARB
SHARIA ABDEL SALAM ARIF
Bustan Centre
SHARIA EL-BUSTAN
NZ Consulate
MIDAN TAHRIR
SADAT
Arab League
Buses to Dokki
SHARIA TAHRIR
Cairo Cabs
SHARIA MOHAMMED
TAHRIR BRIDGE
SHARIA KAMAL AL-DIN SALAH
Omar Makram Mosque
Semiramis Intercontinental
Mugamma
American University (AUC)
SHARIA ABDEL KADER HAMZA PASHA
SHARIA SHEIKH RIHAN
Shepheard Hotel
SHARIA QASR AL-AINI
US Embassy
National Assembly
River Nile
Feluccas
GARDEN CITY
SHARIA FALAKI
British Embassy
SHARIA AMERIKA LATINA
SHARIA MAGLIS AL-SHAAB
Sudanese Consulate
SHARIA RUSTAM
Canadian Embassy
Turkish Embassy
SHARIA HUSSEIN HIGAZI
SHARIA SA'AD ZAGHLOUL
SHARIA KAMEL AL-SHINAWI
SHARIA IBRAHIM PASHA NAGUIB
SHARIA DARIH SA'AD
SHARIA ISMAIL ABAZA
SHARIA ABU AL-MAHASIN
SA'AD ZAGHLOUL
SHARIA GAMAL AL-DIN
0 250 m
Saiyida Zeinab
Aguza
Cairo Tower
Opera House
Dokki
ACCOMMODATION
Amin T
Berlin N
Carlton C
Cosmopolitan P
Dahab O
Four Seasons Y
Garden City House V
Grand E
Happyton A
Isis J
Ismailia House U
King Tut Hostel G
Lotus R
Luna M
Nile Ritz-Carlton S
Odeon Palace L
Pension Roma H
Select I
Ramses Hilton K
Semiramis Intercontinental W
Shepheard X
Sultan D
Talisman F
Tulip Q
Venice Hosokawaya D
Windsor B

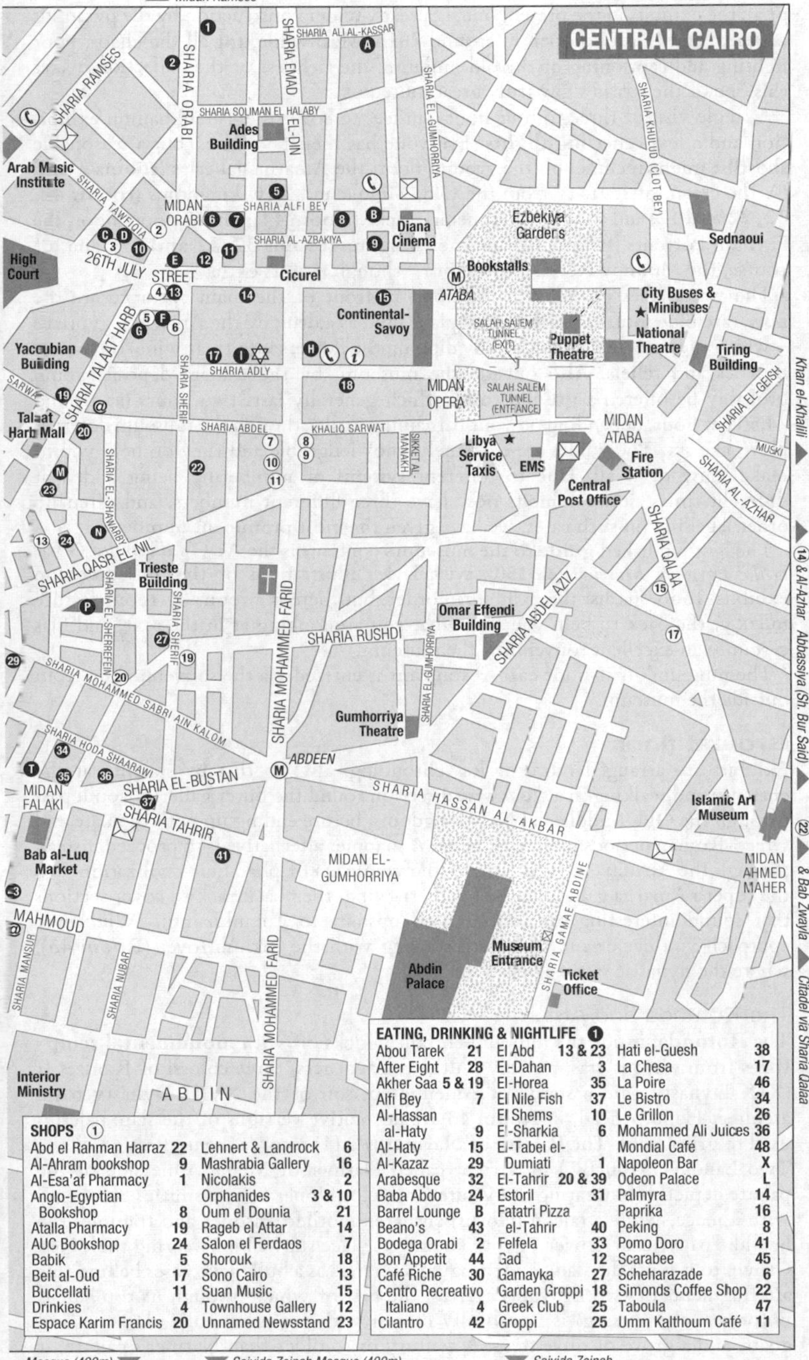
CENTRAL CAIRO
Midan Ramses
Midan Ramses
Sharia Ramses
Sharia Orabi
Sharia Emad el-Din
Sharia Ali al-Kassar
Sharia el-Gumhorriya
Sharia Khulud (Clot Bey)
Sharia Soliman el Halaby
Ades Building
Arab Music Institute
Sharia Tawfiqia
Midan Orabi
Sharia Alfi Bey
Sharia al-Azbakiya
Diana Cinema
Ezbekiya Gardens
Sednaoui
High Court
26th July Street
Cicurel
Bookstalls
Ataba
City Buses & Minibuses
Continental-Savoy
Salah Salem Tunnel (Exit)
Puppet Theatre
National Theatre
Tiring Building
Yacoubian Building
Sharia Talaat Harb
Sharia Sherif
Sharia Adly
Midan Opera
Salah Salem Tunnel (Entrance)
Sarwat
Talaat Harb Mall
Sharia Abdel Khaliq Sarwat
Sikket al-Manakh
Libya Service Taxis
EMS
Midan Ataba
Fire Station
Central Post Office
Sharia el-Geish
Muski
Sharia al-Azhar
Sharia el-Shawarby
Sharia Qalaa
Sharia Qasr el-Nil
Trieste Building
Sharia Mohammed Farid
Sharia Abdel Aziz
Omar Effendi Building
Sharia Rushdi
Sharia el-Sherifein
Sharia Mohammed Sabri Ain Kalom
Gumhorriya Theatre
Sharia Hoda Shaarawi
Abdeen
Sharia el-Bustan
Midan Falaki
Sharia Hassan al-Akbar
Sharia Tahrir
Islamic Art Museum
Midan Ahmed Maher
Bab al-Luq Market
Midan el-Gumhorriya
Mahmoud
Sharia Gamae Abdine
Sharia Mansur
Sharia Nubar
Museum Entrance
Abdin Palace
Ticket Office
Interior Ministry
Abdin
Khan el-Khalili
14 & Al-Azhar
Abbassiya (Sh. Bur Said)
22 & Bab Zwayla
Citadel via Sharia Qalaa
Mosque (400m)
Saiyida Zeinab Mosque (400m)
Saiyida Zeinab
SHOPS 1
Abd el Rahman Harraz 22
Al-Ahram bookshop 9
Al-Esa'af Pharmacy 1
Anglo-Egyptian Bookshop 8
Atalla Pharmacy 19
AUC Bookshop 24
Babik 5
Beit al-Oud 17
Bucellati 11
Drinkies 4
Espace Karim Francis 20
Lehnert & Landrock 6
Mashrabia Gallery 16
Nicolakis 2
Orphanides 3 & 10
Oum el Dounia 21
Rageb el Attar 14
Salon el Ferdaos 7
Shorouk 18
Sono Cairo 13
Suan Music 15
Townhouse Gallery 12
Unnamed Newsstand 23
EATING, DRINKING & NIGHTLIFE 1
Abou Tarek 21
After Eight 28
Akher Saa 5 & 19
Alfi Bey 7
Al-Hassan al-Haty 9
Al-Haty 15
Al-Kazaz 29
Arabesque 32
Baba Abdo 24
Barrel Lounge B
Beano's 43
Bodega Orabi 2
Bon Appetit 44
Café Riche 30
Centro Recreativo Italiano 4
Cilantro 42
El Abd 13 & 23
El-Dahan 3
El-Horea 35
El Nile Fish 37
El Shems 10
El-Sharkia 6
El-Tabei el-Dumiati 1
El-Tahrir 20 & 39
Estoril 31
Fatatri Pizza el-Tahrir 40
Felfela 33
Gad 12
Gamayka 27
Garden Groppi 18
Greek Club 25
Groppi 25
Hati el-Guesh 38
La Chesa 17
La Poire 46
Le Bistro 34
Le Grillon 26
Mohammed Ali Juices 36
Mondial Café 48
Napoleon Bar X
Odeon Palace L
Palmyra 14
Paprika 16
Peking 8
Pomo Doro 41
Scarabee 45
Scheherazade 6
Simonds Coffee Shop 22
Taboula 47
Umm Kalthoum Café 11

or all the exhibits in the present one, is already under construction by the pyramids of Giza, and is due to open in around 2013. Meanwhile, for all the chaos, poor lighting and captioning of the old museum, the richness of the collection makes this one of the world's few truly great museums.

A single visit of three to four hours suffices to cover the Tutankhamun exhibition and a few other **highlights**. Everyone has their favourites, but a reasonable shortlist might include, on the ground floor, the Amarna galleries (**rooms 3 and 8**), the cream of statuary from the Old, Middle and New kingdoms (**rooms 42, 32, 22 and 12**) and the Nubian funerary cache (**Room 44**); on the upper floor, the Fayoum Portraits (**Room 14**) and model figures (**rooms 37, 32 and 27**), and, of course, the Mummy Room (**Room 56**) – though it costs extra.

The water lilies growing in the pond in front of the main entrance are the now-rare blue lotus, a psychoactive plant used as a drug by the Ancient Egyptians – which they are depicted using (by dipping the flowers into their wine) on several frescoes and reliefs. Also outside the museum, by the camera deposit, you'll probably be offered a **guided tour**, which generally lasts two hours (at around £E50 per hour, depending on your bargaining skills), though the museum deserves more like six. The guides are extremely knowledgeable and they do help you to make sense of it all. Due to different systems of numbering being added at different times, some exhibits now have three different numbers, and often no other labelling (in such cases, we have given the most prominent number).

The best published **guide** to the museum's contents is the AUC's *Illustrated Guide to the Egyptian Museum* (£E150), with lavish illustrations of the museum's top exhibits. It doesn't list the exhibits in order, but there is a room-by-room picture index at the back to help you find what you are looking at in the text, and it is certainly an excellent souvenir of the museum.

The museum's first-floor **café-restaurant** is entered via the souvenir shop from outside the museum.

Ground floor

Exhibits are arranged more or less chronologically, so that by starting at the entrance and walking in a clockwise direction round the outer galleries you'll pass through the Old, Middle and New kingdoms, before ending up with the Late and Greco-Roman periods in the east wing. A snappier alternative is to proceed instead through the Atrium – which samples the whole era of pharaonic civilization – to the superb Amarna gallery in the northern wing, then backtrack to cover sections that sound interesting, or instead head upstairs to Tutankhamun. Whichever approach you decide on, it's worth starting with the Atrium foyer (**Room 43**), where the dynastic saga begins.

The Rotunda and Atrium

The **Rotunda**, inside the museum entrance, kicks off with **monumental sculptures** from various eras, notably (in the four corners) three colossi of Ramses II (XIX Dynasty) and a statue of Amenhotep, son of the XVIII Dynasty royal architect Hapu. Ahead, in **Room 43** are decorative versions of the slate palettes used to grind kohl. The **Palette of Narmer** (#111) records the unification of the Two Lands (c.3100 BC) by a ruler called Narmer or Menes. One side of the palette depicts him wearing the White Crown of Upper Egypt, smiting an enemy with a mace, while a falcon (Horus) ensnares another prisoner and tramples the heraldic papyrus of Lower Egypt. The reverse face shows him wearing their Red Crown to inspect the slain, and ravaging a fortress as a bull. Two cases behind this are fragments of two **Libyan Palettes**, the first of which (though its top half is unfortunately missing) is beautifully carved with trains of bulls, donkeys and goats, and a grove of olive trees. A century or so older than Narmer's palette, it

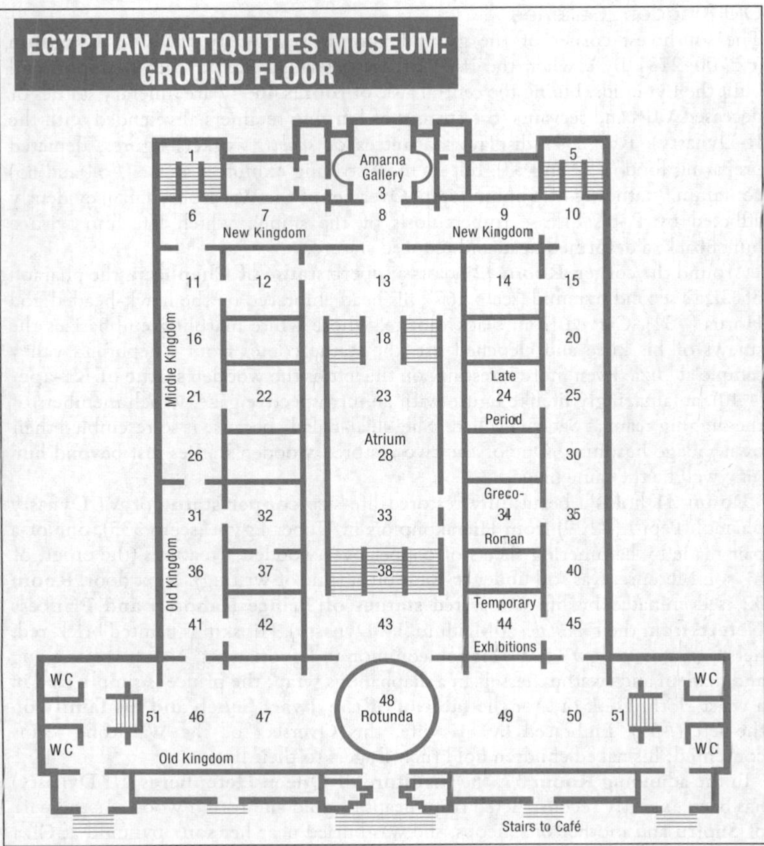

seems to have been made to commemorate the payment of a tribute to the Upper Egyptian ruler by the Tjemehu tribe of Libya.

In **Room 33**, the atrium itself, you'll find **pyramidions** (pyramid capstones) from Dahshur, and more sarcophagi from the New Kingdom, most notably the **sarcophagus of Merneptah** (#213), surmounted by a figure of the XIX Dynasty king as Osiris, protectively embraced from within by a relief of Nut, the sky goddess. At the centre of the Atrium is a **painted floor** from **Akhenaten's** royal palace at **Amarna**. It shows a river brimming with ducks and fish and framed by reeds where waterfowl and cows amble, a fine example of the lyrical naturalism of the Amarna period. For more of this revolutionary epoch in pharaonic history, continue up the stairs at the far end, past the **colossal statues** of Akhenaten's parents, Amenophis III, Queen Tiy and their three daughters, to Rooms 3 and 8 (see p.98).

On the way, **Room 13** contains (on the right) Merneptah's Victory Stele, also called the **Israel Stele** (#134). Its name derives from the boast "Israel is crushed, it has no more seed", from among a list of Merneptah's conquests at the temple of Karnak – the sole known reference to Israel in all the records of Ancient Egypt. Partly on the strength of this, many believe that Merneptah, XIX Dynasty son of Ramses II, was the Pharaoh of the Exodus.

Old Kingdom Galleries

The southwest corner of the ground floor is devoted to the **Old Kingdom** (c.2700–2181 BC), when the III–VI dynasties ruled Egypt from Memphis and built the Pyramids. Lining the central aisle of **rooms 46–47** are funerary statues of deceased VIPs and servants (the custom of burying retainers alive ended with the II Dynasty). Room 47 displays **statuettes** of *shabti* (worker) figures, depicted preparing food (#52 and 53), but its most striking exhibit is a case (#54 and 65) containing statuettes of Khnumhotep, Overseer of the Wardrobe, a man evidently afflicted by Pott's disease (tuberculosis of the spine), which left him with a hunchback, a deformed head and reduced stature.

Around the corner, **Room 42** boasts a superb **statue of Chephren**, the pharaoh of Giza's second pyramid (see p.167), his head embraced by the hawk-headed god Horus (#31). Carved from black diorite, whose white marbling emphasizes the sinews of his knee and clenched fist, the statue comes from Chephren's valley temple at Giza. Even more arresting, on the left, is the wooden **statue of Ka-aper** (#40), an amazingly lifelike figure with an introspective gaze, which members of the digging team at Saqqara called "Sheikh al-Balad" because it so resembled their own village headman. One of the two restored wooden statues just beyond him may well be the same man.

Room 31 holds a beautifully restored life-size **copper statue** of VI Dynasty pharaoh Pepi I (#129) from Hierakonplois in Upper Egypt (see p.335), one of a pair made by hammering sheets of copper over wooden armatures (the other, of his son Merenre, was still under restoration at time of writing). Next door, **Room 32** is dominated by life-size seated **statues of Prince Rahotep and Princess Nefert**, from their *mastaba* at Maidum (IV Dynasty). His skin is painted brick-red, hers a creamy yellow – a distinction common in Egyptian art. Nefert wears a wig and diadem and swathes herself in a diaphanous wrap; the prince is simply clad in a waist cloth. Look out for the **tableau of the dwarf Seneb and his family** on the left (#39). Embraced by his wife, this Overseer of the Wardrobe seems contented; his naked children hold their fingers to their lips.

In the adjoining **Room 37**, the **furniture of Queen Hetepheres** (III Dynasty) has been expertly reconstructed from heaps of gold and rotten wood. As the wife of Snofru and mother of Cheops, she was buried near her son's pyramid at Giza with a sedan chair, gold vessels and a canopied bed. Also in the room, in a cabinet of its own, is a tiny **statuette of Cheops** (#143), the only known likeness of the Great Pyramid pharaoh.

Middle Kingdom Galleries

With **Room 26** you enter the **Middle Kingdom**, when centralized authority was restored and pyramid-building resumed under the XII Dynasty (c.1991–1786 BC), but the **statue of Mentuhotpe Nebhepetre** (on the right) is a relic of the previous era of civil wars, termed the First Intermediate Period (in fact, it was Mentuhotpe Nebhepetre, founder of the XI Dynasty, who finally ended the wars and reunited the country). Glum-faced, and endowed with hulking feet and black skin to symbolize his royal power, plus crossed arms and a curly beard to link him to Osiris, the statue was buried near his funerary shrine at Deir el-Bahri, and was discovered by Howard Carter – whose horse fell through the roof.

The statuettes at the back of **Room 22** (#92) are striking for the uncharacteristic expressiveness of their faces, in contrast to the manic staring eyes of the wooden statue of Nakhti on the right-hand side of the room, but the room's main exhibit is the **burial chamber of Harhotpe** from Deir el-Bahri, covered inside with pictorical objects, charms and texts. Surrounding the chamber are ten limestone **statues of Senusret** from his pyramid complex at Lisht, stiffly formal in contrast to his cedarwood figure in the case to the right as you enter the room (#88). The sides of these statues' thrones bear variations of the *sema-tawy* symbol of unification: Hapy the Nile-god, or Horus and Seth, entwining the heraldic plants of the Two Lands.

New Kingdom Galleries

With **Room 11** you pass into the **New Kingdom**, an era of renewed pharaonic power and imperial expansion under the XVIII and XIX dynasties (c.1567–1200 BC). Egypt's African and Asian empires were forged by Tuthmosis III, who had long been frustrated while his unwarlike stepmother, Hatshepsut, ruled as pharaoh. From one of the Osiride pillars of her great temple at Deir el-Bahri comes a commanding crowned **head of Hatshepsut** (#6184), while on the right of the room stands an unusual wooden *ka* statue of Pharaoh Hor (#75), mounted on a sliding base to signify his posthumous wanderings. In **Room 12** you'll find a grey schist statue of **Tuthmosis III** (#62) and other masterpieces of XVIII Dynasty art. At the back of the room, the **Hathor Shrine** from Tuthmosis III's ruined temple at Deir el-Bahri contains a statue of the goddess in her bovine form, emerging reborn from a papyrus swamp. Tuthmosis stands beneath her cow's head, and is suckled as an infant in the fresco behind Hathor's statue. To the right of the room is a block statue (#418) of Hatshepsut's vizier, **Senenmut**, with the queen's daughter Neferure, with a smaller statue of the same duo in the second recess on the right. The relationship between the queen, her daughter and her vizier has inspired much speculation. From the same period comes a section of the Deir el-Bahri **"Punt relief"** (#130, in the second niche on the left), showing the Queen of Punt, whose oddly shaped body suggests that she may have suffered from elephantiasis, observed by Hatshepsut during her expedition to that fabled land.

To the right of the Punt relief stands a grey granite **statue of the god Khonsu** with a sidelock denoting youth and a face thought to be that of the boy pharaoh Tutankhamun, which was taken from the temple of the moon-god at Karnak. Flanking this statue and the Punt relief, two statues of a man named **Amenhotep** portray him as a young scribe of humble birth (#6014) and as an octogenarian priest (#98), honoured for his direction of massive works like the Colossi of Memnon.

Before turning the corner into the northern wing, you encounter in **Room 6** two **lion-headed statues of Sekhmet**, found at Karnak. Right in the corner is a statue supposedly of the last XVIII Dynasty pharaoh, Horemheb, but the face looks a lot more like that of Tutankhamun, and the suspicion is that Horemheb simply took one of the boy king's statues and had his own cartouche inscribed on it. A **sphinx** with the head of Hatshepsut welcomes you to **Room 7**, where the first set of reliefs on the southern wall come from the Tomb of Maya at Saqqara. The tomb was uncovered in the nineteenth century but subsequently lost until its rediscovery in 1986. **Room 8** is largely an overflow for the Amarna Gallery (see p.98) but also contains a monumental **dyad of Amun and Mut**, smashed to pieces by medieval limestone quarriers and lovingly pieced together from fragments long lost in the vaults of the museum and at Karnak, where it originally stood. Those pieces that could not be fitted into the jigsaw are displayed in a case just behind it.

To the left of the stairs in **Room 10**, note the painted **relief** on a block from Ramses II's temple at Memphis, which shows him subjugating Egypt's foes. In a motif repeated on dozens of temple pylons, the king grabs the hair of a Libyan, Nubian and Syrian, and wields an axe. The room is dominated by a pun (#6245): a **statue of Ramses II** as a child, finger to mouth, holding a plant while protected by the sun-god *Re* or *Ra*, which combines with the word for child (*mes*) and the word for the plant (*sw*) to form his name. From Room 10 you can follow the New Kingdom into the East Wing (covered on p.98), or climb the stairs to the Tutankhamun galleries on the upper floor.

The Amarna Gallery

Room 3 and much of the adjoining **Room 8** focus on the **Amarna period**, a break with centuries of tradition which barely outlasted the reign of Pharaoh Akhenaten (c.1379–1362 BC or 1352–1336 BC) and Queen Nefertiti. Rejecting Amun and the other deities of Thebes, they decreed the supremacy of a single god, the Aten, built a new capital at Amarna in Middle Egypt to escape the old bureaucracy, and left enigmatic works of art that still provoke a reaction.

In the centre of Room 3 is Akhenaten's carnelian-, gold- and glass-inlaid **coffin**, the upper half displayed alongside the gilding from the bottom part of the coffin. This gilding disappeared from the museum at some time between 1915 and 1931, but resurfaced in Switzerland in the 1980s. It has now been restored and mounted on a Plexiglas cast in the presumed shape of the original coffin.

Staring down from the walls of **Room 3** are four **colossi of Akhenaten**, whose attenuated skull and face, flaring lips and nostrils, rounded thighs and belly are suggestive of a hermaphrodite or a primeval earth goddess. Because these characteristics are carried over to the figures of his wife and daughters on certain **stelae** (such as those in the stele case in Room 8), **statuettes** (such as those in case #169 in Room 8) and tomb reliefs, it has been argued that the Amarna style pandered to some physical abnormality in Akhenaten (or the royal family) – the captions hint at perversions. Others retort that the famous head of Nefertiti, in Berlin, proves that it was just a stylistic device. Another feature of Amarna art was its note of intimacy: a **stele of the royal family** (in the stele case in Room 8) portrays Akhenaten dandling their eldest daughter, Meritaten, whilst Nefertiti cradles her sisters. For the first time in Egyptian art, breakfast was depicted. The Amarna focus on this world rather than the afterlife infused traditional subjects with new vitality – witness the freer brush strokes on the fragments of a **marsh scene**, displayed around the walls of Room 3.

A case on the south side of Room 8 contains some of the **Amarna Letters** (others are in London and Berlin), recording pleas for troops to aid the pharaoh's vassals in Palestine. Originally baked into earthen "envelopes" for delivery, these cuneiform tablets were stored in the Foreign Office archives at Amarna.

The East Wing

As an inducement to follow the New Kingdom into the East Wing, **Room 15** starts with, directly facing the statue of Ramses II as a child, a sexy statue of his daughter and consort Merytamun. The centrepiece of **Room 14** is a restored pink granite triple statue of Ramses III being crowned by Horus and Seth, representing order and chaos respectively. Of the diverse statues of deities in **Room 24**, the most striking by far is that of **Taweret** (or Tweri), the pregnant-hippopotamus goddess of childbirth, on the left (#248). Very sleek, in smooth black slate, the statue was found in a sealed shrine at Karnak, which is why it is so well preserved.

Rooms 34 and **35** cover the **Greco-Roman Period** (332 BC onwards), when Classical art engaged with Ancient Egyptian symbolism. Facing you as you enter Room 34 is a coiled serpent, ready to strike, and to the left of it, in case D, an alabaster head of a very young-looking Alexander the Great. At the back of the room, on the right, a Roman fresco depicts the famously Freudian legend of King Oedipus, shown here killing his father, but not doing the other thing that he's famous for. The meld of Egyptian and Greco-Roman styles is typified by the bizarre statues and sarcophagi down the corridor in **Room 49**, especially the **statue of a Ptolemaic king** (possibly Alexander II) at the threshold of the room. Room 44, on your way, is used for temporary exhibitions.

Upper floor

The upper floor is dominated by the Tutankhamun galleries, which occupy the best part of two wings. The other top highlights are the Jewellery Rooms, the Mummy Room and the Fayoum Portraits. Tutankhamun's treasures are best seen together before returning to look at the neighbouring rooms and the rest of the upper floor.

Tutankhamun Galleries

The funerary impedimenta of the boy-king **Tutankhamun** number 1700 items and fills a dozen rooms, laid out roughly as they were packed into his tomb. Given the brevity of his reign (1361–1352 BC or 1336-1327 BC) and the paucity of his tomb in the Valley of the Kings, the mind boggles at the treasure that must have been stashed with great pharaohs like Ramses or Seti. When Howard Carter's team penetrated the sealed corridor of the tomb in 1922 (see p.307), they found an antechamber, stuffed with caskets and detritus, that had been ransacked by robbers, and two life-size **ka statues of Tutankhamun** (flanking the doorway to **Room 45**), whose black skin symbolized his rebirth. Just beyond are golden **statues of Tutankhamun**, mostly depicting him hunting with a harpoon.

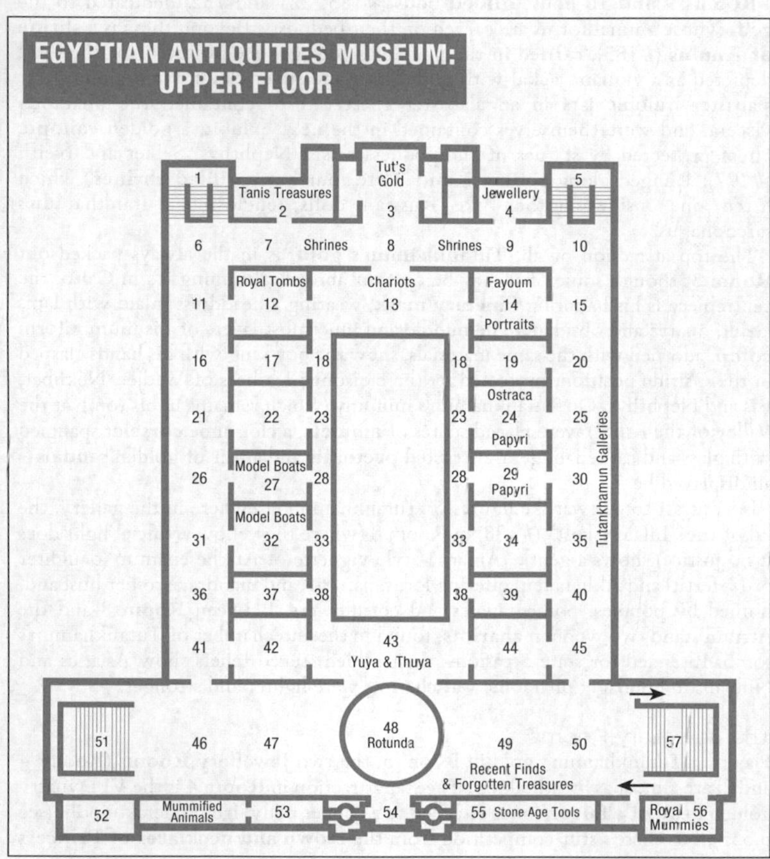

Room 35 is dominated by a **gilded throne** with winged-serpent arms and clawed feet (#179). Its seat back shows the royal couple relaxing in the rays of the Aten, their names given in the Amarna form – dating it to the time when Tutankhamun still observed the Amarna heresy. Among the other worldly goods that the boy pharaoh carried with him into the next world are an ebony and ivory **gaming set** for playing *senet*, a game similar to draughts or checkers (#189), and a host of small **shabti figures** to fulfil any tasks the gods might set him (flanking the door to Room 34). In front of that is the "Painted Chest" (#186), used to store the king's clothes and unguents. On its lid he is depicted hunting ostriches and antelopes and devastating ranks of Syrians in his war chariot, larger than life; the end panels show him trampling other foes in the guise of a sphinx.

Room 30 has a case of **"Prisoners' Canes"** (#187), whose ebony- and ivory-inlaid figures symbolize the unity of north and south. A bust of the boy king emerging from a lotus (#118) shows the continued influence of the Amarna artistic style during Tutankhamun's reign. The **"ecclesiastical throne"** (#181) in **Room 25** is a prototype for episcopal thrones of the Christian Church. Its seat back is exquisitely inlaid with ebony and gold, but looks uncomfortable. More typical of pharaonic design are the wooden Heb-Sed throne and footstools, and an ornate commode.

Rooms 9 and 10 house **gilded beds** (#183, 221 and 732) dedicated to the gods whose animal forms are carved on their bedposts. Beyond these is a **shrine of Anubis** (#185), carried in the pharaoh's cortege: the protector of the dead depicted as a vigilant jackal with gilded ears and silver claws. Next along, four alabaster canopic jars in an alabaster chest (#176) contained the pharaoh's viscera, and were themselves contained in the next exhibit, a golden **canopic chest** protected by statues of the goddesses Isis, Nephthys, Selket and Neith (#177). Ranged along **rooms 7 and 8** are four boxy **gilded shrines**, which fitted one inside another like Russian dolls, enclosing Tutankhamun's sarcophagus.

The top attraction of all, **Tutankhamun's gold**, is in the always packed-out **Room 3**, though some of it may be on tour abroad. Assuming it's in Cairo, the centrepiece is his haunting **funerary mask**, wearing a headdress inlaid with lapis lazuli, quartz and obsidian. The middle and innermost layers of his mummiform **coffin**, adorned with the same materials, show the boy king with his hands clasped in the Osiride position, protected by the cloisonné feathers of Wadjet, Nekhbet, Isis and Nephthys. On Tutankhamun's mummy (which remains in his tomb at the Valley of the Kings) were placed scores of **amulets**, a cloisonné **corselet** spangled with glass and carnelian, gem-encrusted **pectorals** and a pair of golden **sandals** – all displayed here.

In contrast to the warlike figures of Tutankhamun elsewhere in the gallery, the lid of the "Inlaid Chest" (#188) in Room 8 (where the yellow artificial light does it no justice) shows a gentle, Amarna-style vignette of Ankhesenamun (daughter of Nefertiti and Akhenaten) offering lotus, papyrus and mandrake to her husband, framed by poppies, pomegranates and cornflowers. Between **Room 8** and the Atrium stand two wooden **chariots**, found in the antechamber of Tutankhamun's tomb. Intended for state occasions, their gilded stucco reliefs show Asiatics and Nubians in bondage; pharaonic war chariots were lighter and stronger.

The Jewellery Rooms

Flanking Tutankhamun's gold in Room 3, the two **Jewellery Rooms** (Rooms 4 and 2) are almost as breathtaking. The star attraction in **Room 4** is the VI Dynasty golden **head of a falcon** (once attached to a copper body) from Hierakonpolis (see p.335), but there's stiff competition from the **crown and necklaces of Princess**

Khnumyt and the **diadem and pectorals of Princess Set-Hathor**. Buried near the latter at Dahshur were the **amethyst necklace of Mereret**, another XII Dynasty princess. The ceremonial **axe of Ahmosis** (founder of the XVIII Dynasty), commemorating his expulsion of the Hyksos from Egypt, was buried in the tomb of his mother, Queen Ahhotep. From the same cache (discovered by the museum's founder, French Egyptologist Auguste Mariette, in 1859) came some stunning **gold collars** and the bizarre **golden flies** of the Order of Valour – bug-eyed decorations for bravery.

Displayed in **Room 2**, the Treasure of Tanis comes from the XXI–XXII Dynasty, when northern Egypt was ruled from the Delta. Of the three royal caches unearthed by French Egyptologist Pierre Montet in 1939, the richest was that of Psusennes I, whose electrum coffin was found inside the sarcophagus of Merneptah (which is downstairs). His gold necklace is made from rows of discs, in the New Kingdom style.

The Mummy Room

The famous **Mummy Room** (previously Room 52) was closed by President Sadat in 1981 because the exhibition of human remains offended many religious people, but this gave the museum and the Getty Institute an opportunity to restore the badly decomposed royal mummies. The results of their work are now displayed in Room 56, where you have to buy another ticket (£E100, students £E60; closes 6pm) to see them – not really worth the expense unless you have a keen interest in mummies. In deference to the deceased, no guiding is allowed, and the low hum of *sotto voce* chatter is only broken by the attendant periodically calling for "Silence, please!"

Altogether eleven royal mummies are displayed here (clearly labelled and arranged chronologically anticlockwise around the room), including the mortal remains of some of the most famous pharaohs, in particular the great conquerors of the XIX Dynasty, Seti I and his son Ramses II, the latter looking rather slighter in the flesh than the massive statues of him at Memphis and elsewhere. Also here is Ramses's son, Merneptah, whom many believe to be the pharaoh of the biblical Exodus (see box, p.522). All the mummies are kept in sealed cases at controlled humidity, and most of them look remarkably peaceful – Tuthmosis II and Tuthmosis IV could almost be sleeping – and many still have hair. Queen Henut-tawi's curly locks and handsome face suggest Nubian origin.

The mummies were found in the royal cache at Deir el-Bahri (see p.316) and in a spare chamber in the tomb of Amenophis II (see p.311), where they had been reburied during the XXI Dynasty to protect them from grave robbers. For a description of the mummification process, see pp.304–305; and for a graphic demonstration of the hollowness of a mummy, take a look up Ramses V's right nostril – from this angle you'll be able to see straight out through the hole in his skull.

The other galleries

To view the other galleries in approximate chronological order you should start at Room 43 (overlooking the Atrium) and proceed in a clockwise direction, as on the ground floor. However, since most visitors wander in from Tut's galleries, we've described the western and eastern wings from that standpoint.

Room 12's hoard of objects from **XVIII Dynasty royal tombs** includes priestly wigs and wig boxes (in Case L), a libation table flanked by two leopards from the funerary cache of Amenophis II (#3842), and part of the chariot of Tuthmosis IV (#4113). **Room 17** holds the **contents of private tombs**, notably that of Sennedjem, from the Workmen's Village near the Valley of the Kings.

With skills honed on royal tombs, Sennedjem carved himself a stylish vault; its door (#215) depicts him playing *senet* (see p.100). The beautiful gold-painted sarcophagus of his son Khonsu carries a design showing the lions of Today and Yesterday supporting the rising sun, while Anubis embalms his mummy under the protection of Isis and Nephthys.

The museum's **southern wing** is best seen at a trot. By the southeast stairway in Room 50 is the cubic **leather funerary tent** of an XXI Dynasty queen, decorated in red-and-green checkered squares (#3848,). **Room 43** houses objects from the **tomb of Yuya and Thuya**, who, as parents of Queen Tiy (wife of Amenophis III), were buried in the Valley of the Kings; their tomb was found intact in the late nineteenth century. The finest objects from it are the two mummiform coffins, Thuya's gilded funeral mask, and statuettes of the couple. Hidden away by the entrance to Room 42 is a panel of blue faïence tiles from Zoser's burial hall at Saqqara (#17).

Also in Room 48, on the west side, is a display case (#155) containing a stone head of Akhenaten's mum, and Yuya and Thuya's daughter, Queen Tiy, that prefigures the Amarna style. It also contains statues of "dancing dwarves", believed to be modelled on equatorial Forest People ("Pygmies"), who were far more widespread throughout Africa in those days. The same case also holds a beautiful, very lifelike wooden statuette of a Nubian woman, possibly Queen Tiy, with her hair in braids, looking strikingly modern. Next to it, another case (#82) holds a striking bright blue faïence hippopotamus.

Room 53, hidden away off the recess (Room 54) at the southern end of Room 48, contains an odd assortment of **mummified animals and birds** from necropolises across Egypt, evincing the strength of animal cults towards the end of the pagan era, when devotees embalmed everything from bulls to mice and fish, but it is most worth popping into for a look at the **Marsh Scene** from the Sun Temple of Userkaf at Saqqara, the first known example of natural scenes being used as decoration within a royal funerary edifice: a pied kingfisher, purple gallinule and sacred ibis are clearly recognizable.

If approached from the north, the **eastern wing** begins with **Room 14**, containing a couple of mummies and the superbly lifelike but sadly ill-lit "**Fayoum Portraits**" found by British egyptologist Flinders Petrie at Hawara. Painted in encaustic (pigments mixed into molten wax) while their sitters were alive, the portraits were glued onto Greco-Roman mummies (100–250 AD). The staggering diversity of Egypt's pantheon by the late pagan era is suggested by the **statues of deities** in **Room 19**. The tiny statuettes are worth a closer look, especially those of the pregnant hippo goddess Sekhmet (in Case C), Harpocrates (Horus as a child), Ibis-headed Thoth and the dwarf god Ptah-soker (all in Case E), a couple of whose figurines (third shelf down, on the left), look almost Mexican, as do some of the statuettes of Bes in Case P. In the centre of the room, look out for the gold and silver image of Horus in Case V, apparently the case for a mummified hawk.

Room 24 next door, and Room 29 beyond that, are devoted to **ostraca and papyri**. Ostraca were limestone flakes or potsherds, on which were scratched sketches or ephemeral writing; papyrus was used for finished artwork and lasting **manuscripts**. Besides the *Book of the Dead* (**rooms 1 and 24**) and the *Book of Amduat* (depicting the Weighing of the Heart ceremony; on the south side of **Room 29** above Cabinet 51), note the *Satirical Papyrus* (#232 in Cabinet 9 on the north side), showing mice being served by cats. Painted during the Hyksos period (see p.602), the cats represent the Egyptians, the mice their rulers, who came from countries that were part of Egypt's former empire, implying that rule of Egyptians by foreigners is not the natural order.

Downtown Cairo

The layout of **downtown Cairo** goes back to the 1860s, when Khedive Ismail had it rebuilt in the style of Haussmann's new Paris boulevards to impress dignitaries attending the inauguration of the Suez Canal, and had it named the Ismailiya quarter. Cutting an X-shaped swathe through the area are the main thoroughfares of **Talaat Harb** and **Qasr el-Nil** (each about a kilometre long). Almost every visitor gravitates here at least once, while many spend a lot of time checking out the restaurants, shops and bars. Kalashnikov-toting police and Central Security troops are ubiquitous in downtown Cairo, but never threatening.

Talaat Harb and around

By the 1930s, the main boulevard of what was still then the Ismailiya quarter, Suleyman Pasha Street was lined with trees and sidewalk cafés. Since being renamed **Sharia Talaat Harb** (many Cairenes still use its old name), the street has seen its once elegant facades effaced by grime and neglect, tacky billboards and glitzy facings. Yet its vitality and diversity have never been greater, as thousands of Cairenes come here to window-shop, pop into juice bars and surge out of cinemas. Number 17, decorated with old postcards of the city, is the **Café Riche** (see p.190), where the Free Officers supposedly plotted their overthrow of Egypt's monarchy; another version maintains that they communicated over the telephone in **Groppi** (see p.188), a famous coffee house on **Midan Talaat Harb**, at the intersection with Qasr el-Nil. Here stands a statue of Talaat Harb (1876–1941), nationalist lawyer and founder of the National Bank. Further north, Number 34, next door to the Miami Theatre, is the **Yacoubian Building**, immortalized in Alaa Al Aswany's bestselling 2002 novel of the same name (see p.634), though the real building differs somewhat from the fictional version.

A couple of blocks east of Talaat Harb, on the north side of **Sharia Adly**, you'll see a buff, temple-like edifice like something out of a Cecil B. de Mille movie. This is the **Shaar HaShamayim Synagogue** (daily 10am–6pm; donations appreciated; bring your passport to get in), the main house of prayer for Cairo's now much reduced Jewish community. Because of the threat of attack by Islamic fundamentalists, the synagogue is surrounded by armed police, who don't take kindly to tourists pointing cameras at it – which is a pity, because it's actually one of downtown Cairo's most photogenic buildings. Though it looks like a piece of Art Deco, the synagogue was actually built well before that era, in 1905. The palm trees on the facade are a symbol peculiar to Egyptian Jewry; the interior is also impressive, with its high dome, stained-glass windows and opulent marble fittings. Nowadays services are held only at the Jewish New Year (around September), and Yom Kippur (the Day of Atonement, ten days after the New Year).

26th July Street and Midan Opera

The busiest, widest thoroughfare of downtown Cairo is **Sharia Setta w'Ashreen Yulyu** – more easily rendered as **26th July Street** – which runs west across the Nile to Zamalek and Mohandiseen, and east to Midan Opera. It was once called Sharia al-Malik Fouad (a name still quite commonly used), after King Fouad, who reigned 1917–36; the current name commemorates the date on which his son King Farouk abdicated in 1952, following a bloodless coup by the Free Officers three days earlier. The **Cicurel building**, on the corner of Sharia Emad el-Din, and the **Ades building**, with its stylish corner tower, a couple of blocks north, were both originally Jewish-owned department stores, expropriated after the Suez Crisis in 1957.

At the eastern end of 26th July Street is **Midan Opera**, named after an Opera House constructed here in the 1860s, when Cairo's centre was rebuilt; symbolically, the building faced west, overlooking the Ismailiya quarter rather than Islamic Cairo. The square's centrepiece, an equestrian statue of Ibrahim Pasha, by Cordier, honours Ismail's father. The Opera House burned down in 1971; a multistorey car park now occupies the site. It was not the first building hereabouts to have burned down: on "**Black Saturday**" (January 26, 1952), anti-colonial resentments exploded here into arson. The morning after the killing of Egyptian police by British troops in Ismailiya (see p.509), demonstrators were enraged to find an Egyptian police officer drinking on the terrace of *Madame Badia's Opera Casino* (where the Opera Cinema stands today). A scuffle began and the nightclub was wrecked; rioting spread quickly, encouraged by the indifference of Cairo's police force. As ordinary folk took advantage to do a bit of looting, Muslim Brotherhood activists sped around in jeeps torching foreign premises.

Midan Ataba and around

Behind Midan Opera car park, a minibus depot and split-level thoroughfares render **Midan Ataba** just as Yusuf Idris described it in *The Dregs of the City*: "a madhouse of pedestrians and automobiles, screeching wheels, howling klaxons, the whistles of bus conductors and roaring motors". Midan Ataba is a good starting point for several **walking routes into Islamic Cairo** (see p.109), but in the square itself, philatelists might want to pop into the **Post Office Museum** on the second floor of the Central Post Office (Sun–Thurs 8am–3pm; £E2; tickets sold in the post office at the commemorative stamps office, then go upstairs through the guarded entrance on the east side of the building). The museum houses exhibits from Egypt's postal service through the ages, with stamps galore (including the rare Suez Canal commemorative issue).

Ezbekiya Gardens and north to Ramses

The **Ezbekiya Gardens**, to the north of Opera and Ataba squares, were laid out in the 1870s by the former chief gardener of Paris, forming a twenty-acre park. Subsequent extensions to 26th July Street reduced them to trampled islands amid a sea of commerce and traffic, but the western half has now been enclosed to preserve its magnificent banyan tree, while much of the eastern side remains a pitch for hawkers of Islamic arts, gewgaws and incense, as well as a market for secondhand books. Beyond the clothes stalls on the east side stands the **Cairo Puppet Theatre**.

In medieval times a lake fed by the Nasiri Canal and surrounded by orchards existed here, but in 1470 the Mamluke general Ezbek built a palace, inspiring other beys and wealthy merchants to follow suit. During the French occupation Napoleon commandeered the sumptuous palace of Alfi Bey, and his successor Kléber promoted Western innovations such as windmills, printing presses, and a balloon launch which embarrassingly failed. Later in the nineteenth century, two bastions of colonialism overlooked Ezbekiya from a site bounded by Alfi Bey and El-Gumhorriya. Here, *Shepheard's Hotel* (founded in 1841) once flourished alongside the Thomas Cook Agency, which pioneered tourist "expeditions" in the 1870s. Rebuilt more grandly in 1891, *Shepheard's* famous terrace, Moorish Hall and Long Bar were destroyed by Black Saturday rioters in 1952.

Between Ezbekiya and Ramses

When Mohammed Ali created a military high road to link the Citadel with Cairo's new railway station, and named it after the French physician Antoine Clot – whom he ennobled for introducing Western ideas of public health to Egypt – nobody foresaw that **Sharia Clot Bey** (spelt Klot Bek on some street signs, but now officially Sharia Khulud) and the fashionable area north of Ezbekiya would degenerate into a vice-ridden district known to generations of foreign soldiers. During World War II, activities centred on Wagh el-Birket, known as "**the Berka**": a long street with curtained alleys leading off beneath balconies where the (mainly Italian) prostitutes sat fanning themselves.

Nowadays the area is shabbily respectable, with cheap shops and cafés. A stroll up from the gardens along Sharia Khulud towards Ramses will take you past the hulking nineteenth-century **Cathedral of St Mark**, now superseded by the Coptic cathedral in Abbassiya. The run-down porticoed Ottoman pile at no. 117 **Sharia el-Gumhorriya**, at the Ramses end of the street which runs up from the west side of the gardens, was the original premises of *Al-Ahram* ("The Pyramids"), the first newspaper in the Arab world (founded in 1875).

Ramses Station and around

The Ramses Station area is the northern ganglion of Cairo's transport system. Splayed flyovers and arterial roads haemorrhage traffic onto darting pedestrians, keeping **Midan Ramses** busy round the clock. The square took its name from a red granite Colossus of Ramses II, moved here from Memphis in 1955. By 2006 it had become so corroded by pollution that it was relocated out by the Giza Pyramids, at the junction of Pyramids Road and the Alexandria Desert Road.

The square's main focus is **Ramses Station** itself, a quasi-Moorish shoebox to which a major **post office** and the **Egyptian Railways Museum** are appended. At the east end of the station, the museum (daily 8am–2pm; £E10, £E20 on Fri & public holidays) houses model steam engines, stations, engineering works and even the odd airplane, plus a couple of real steam locomotives, most notably Khedive Ismail's private train. For a superb vista over the square, head to the terrace café of the otherwise rather down-at-heel fifteenth-floor *Everest Hotel*, open round the clock.

Garden City and Abdin

Spreading south from the square towards Old Cairo and the Islamic districts are two very different, yet historically interlinked, quarters. Sharia Qasr al-Aini divides the leafy winding streets of **Garden City** from Qasr al-Aini, the grid of blocks where Egypt's ministries and parliament are located. Beyond Qasr al-Aini, the ex-royal, now presidential Abdin Palace lends its name to the **Abdin quarter** that merges on its southern side into Saiyida Zeinab (see p.129).

Since Garden City, Qasr al-Aini and Abdin all meet around Midan Tahrir, each can claim to host Egypt's **National Assembly** (Maglis al-Shaab). In 2008 its Upper House was gutted by fire – fortunately when parliament was taking its summer recess. The road running from here to the Interior Ministry is barricaded at either end against car bombers, floodlit at night and guarded by machine-gunners.

Garden City

When Ibrahim Pasha's al-Dubbarah Palace was demolished in 1906, British planners developed the site for diplomatic and residential use, laying down crescents and cul-de-sacs to create the illusion of lanes meandering through a **Garden City**. Until the Corniche road was ploughed through, embassies and villas boasted gardens running down to the Nile; nowadays, fishermen's shacks and vegetable plots line the river's edge.

Aside from the traffic, it's a pleasant walk along the Corniche towards Roda Island, past a cluster of **feluccas** available for Nile cruises (see p.205). Further inland, Art Deco residences mingle with heavily guarded **embassies** (for addresses, see p.204). Despite being outsized by the US – whose embassy here is the largest

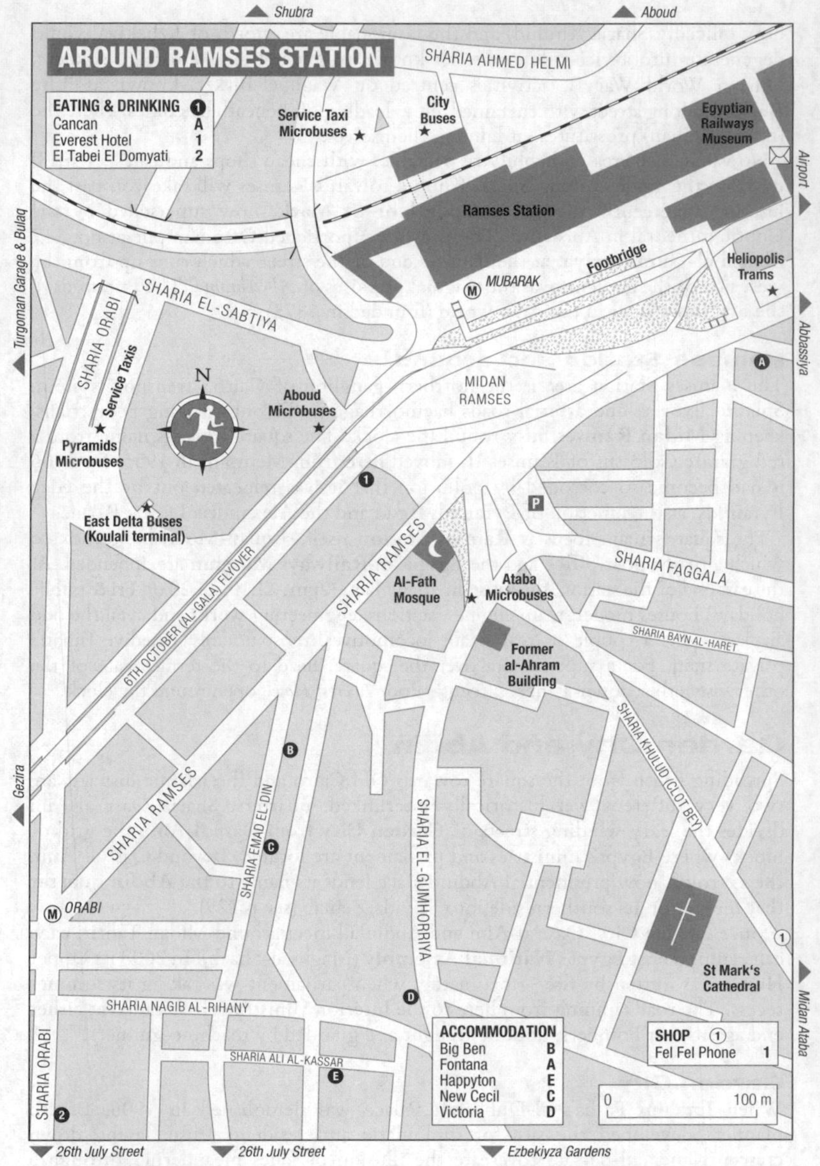

in the world – the British enjoy grander buildings with more spacious grounds, a legacy of their pre-eminence in the days of Lord Cromer and Sir Miles Lampson.

Just south of Garden City, on the east bank of the Nile by Manial Bridge, Cairo's largest public **Qasr al-Aini Hospital**, erected in the 1960s, is Cairo's largest public hospital. It stands on the site of an early nineteenth-century medical school, which itself replaced a palace (*qasr*) erected for a Mamluke emir, Shihabeddin al-Aini, in 1466. The palace gave its name to the hospital, and also to the adjoining

Qasr al-Aini neighbourhood. Antoine Clot (see p.104) was the hospital's first director, and Egypt's most famous short-story writer, Yusuf Idris, practised as a doctor here before dedicating himself to writing.

The Abdin Palace

With hindsight, several rulers must have regretted the move by Khedive Ismail of the seat of state from the Citadel to what is now the **Abdin quarter**. The European-style **Abdin Palace**, flanked to the north by the Cairo Governorate building, is now the state headquarters of Egypt's president. During Ramadan a large tent is pitched outside in the middle of Midan el-Gumhorriya, in which virtuoso performers recite the Koran. The neighbourhood is still chiefly residential and working-class, and divided from the Saiyida Zeinab quarter by **Sharia Bur Said**, which marks the course of the Khalig al-Masri canal that was filled in after the Aswan Dam reduced Cairo's dependency on Nile floodwater. Another effect of the dam's construction was the displacement of much of the Nubian population from the area to its south, many of whom ended up as servants in the palace, and to this day, many of Abdin's residents are of Nubian origin.

The Palace Museum

At the rear of the grounds is the **Abdin Palace Museum** (daily except Fri 9am–3pm; £E15, students £E10, camera £E10), entered from Sharia Gamae Abdine, behind the palace; tickets are sold across the street. A souvenir booklet (£E15) is available at the entrance, though not especially useful.

You begin by walking through the palace grounds to **Mubarak's Hall**, which contains an assortment of weapons presented to President Mubarak by foreign leaders, most notably a set of gold-plated automatic rifles given by Saddam Hussein. From here you cross a courtyard to find the **Arms Museum**. Pavilion 2, on the right, is filled with **daggers**, including Rommel's and some nasty-looking multi-bladed ones used by India's Hindu rajputs against the Mughals in the eighteenth century. Back in the main room, past Mamluke armour, a vast collection of **guns** includes such curios as an 1852 percussion rifle with six revolving barrels, an Apache-Dolene pin-fire revolver which doubles as a knuckleduster and a blade, and a twenty-chamber Belgian revolver.

The next section – devoted to **medals and decorations** – is mainly notable for a set of Napoleonic snuff and tobacco boxes, King Farouk's *sheesha* pipes, and a vial made from a giant crab claw. From here you move on to the **Gifts Museum** containing presents given to Mubarak, including an abalone and mother-of-pearl model of Jerusalem's Dome of the Rock mosque from Yasser Arafat. The **Historical Documents** room displays some letters of condolence sent to King Farouk on the death of his father King Fouad from Hitler, Emperor Hirohito and Britain's ill-fated King Edward VIII.

The last part of the museum is devoted to **silverware, glassware and crockery**, including dinner sets used by the Egyptian royal family, and a tea set belonging to King Fouad, made of solid silver instead of the more customary bone china.

Islamic Cairo

Few foreigners enter Islamic Cairo without equal measures of excitement and trepidation. Streets are narrow and congested, overhung with latticed balconies. Mosques, bazaars and medieval lanes abound; the smell of *sheeshas* and frying offal wafts through alleys where muezzins wail "Allahu akbar!" (God is most great) and beggars entreat "Ya mohannin, ya rabb" (O awakener of pity, O master) – as integral to street life as the artisans and hawkers. The sights, sounds, smells and surprises draw you back time after time, and getting lost or dispensing a little baksheesh is a small price to pay for the experience. You can have a fascinating time exploring this quarter of the city without knowing anything about its history or architecture, but a little knowledge of both will bring it more to life; our potted history section below should help, and architectural expressions used in the text are explained in the glossary on pp.645–648. In 1992 an **earthquake** caused a lot of damage in Islamic Cairo, which ironically led to many mosques and monuments being repaired and restored to their original glory after years of neglect, but one or two are still undergoing restoration and thus closed to the public.

A brief history of Islamic Cairo

New cities in Cairo have invariably been constructed to the north of the old, an east–west spread being prevented by the Muqattam Hills and the Nile, while the prevailing northerly wind blew the smoke and smell of earlier settlements away from newer areas.

Thus when Amr's Muslim troops took Egypt for Islam in 641 AD, they sited their city, **Fustat**, north of Coptic Babylon (see "Old Cairo", p.149). Similarly, when the last Umayyad caliph, Marwan II, burned down Fustat while retreating from the **Abbasids** in 750, they ordered the city rebuilt further north. In 870, the Abbasids' viceroy, Ahmed **Ibn Tulun**, asserting his independence, founded a new city further north again. Inspired by the imperial capital of Samarra, it consisted of a gigantic congregational mosque, palace and hippodrome, surrounded by military quarters. In 905, however, the Abbasids invaded Egypt and razed it, sparing only the great Mosque of Ibn Tulun. After this, people lived wherever they could amid the remains of these earlier cities, together known as **Masr**.

The **Fatimids**, who took Egypt in 969, distanced themselves from Masr by building a new city further north again, which they called **Al-Qahira** (The Triumphant), and key features of their city still remain. It was at the Al-Azhar Mosque that Al-Muizz, Egypt's first Fatimid ruler, delivered a sermon before vanishing into his palaces (which survive only in name); the Mosque of Al-Hakim commemorates the caliph who ordered Masr's destruction after residents objected to proclamations of his divinity. The great Northern Walls and the Bab Zwayla gate date from 1092, when the Armenian-born army commander Al-Gyushi, having reconquered Al-Qahira for the Fatimids following its 1068 fall to the Seljuk Turks, expanded the city's defences northwards.

The disparate areas of Masr and Al-Qahira only assumed a kind of unity after **Salah al-Din** (Saladin) built the **Citadel** on a rocky spur between Al-Qahira and Masr, and walls which linked up with the aqueduct between the Nile and the Citadel, so as to surround the whole. His successors, the **Ayyubids**, erected pepperpot-shaped minarets and the magnificent tombs of the Abbasid caliphs and Imam al-Shafi'i in the Southern Cemetery, but when the sultan died heirless and his widow needed help to stay in power, the Mamlukes who ran the army took control. The Mamluke era is divided into periods named after the garrisons of troops from which the sultans intrigued their way to power: the Qipchak or Tartar **Bahri Mamlukes** (1250–1382), originally stationed by the river (*bahr* in Arabic); and their Circassian successors, the **Burgi Mamlukes** (1382–1517), quartered in a tower (*burg*) of the Citadel.

Despite their brutal politics of assassinations and poisonings, the Mamlukes were also aesthetes, commissioning mosques, mansions and *sabil-kuttabs* (koranic schools featuring fountains) that are still the glory of today's Islamic Cairo. Although urban life was interrupted by their bloody conflicts, the city nevertheless maintained public hospitals, libraries and schools. Caravanserais overflowed with

Approaching and exploring Islamic Cairo: practicalities

The best way **to explore Islamic Cairo** is by walking. Decide on a starting point that's readily accessible, and follow one of our maps on foot from there. The most obvious **starting points** are Khan el-Khalili, Bab Zwayla and the Citadel; see the beginning of each of these sections for details on getting there (and the bus/minibus routes on p.84). The streets of Islamic Cairo are labyrinthine and, while getting lost among them can result in the richest experiences, some visitors prefer to be shown round by a **guide**. The tourist office can put you in touch with authorized guides, and unofficial ones may accost you on the street.

There are four ways to approach Islamic Cairo on foot from **Midan Ataba** in downtown Cairo, using the Ataba post office and fire station for orientation:

SHARIA EL-GEISH Topped by a flyover, "Army Street" runs out towards Abbassiya and Heliopolis. The main reason for venturing beyond the Paper Market is to visit the Mosque of Beybars the Crossbowman on Midan Zahir (see p.157), and the Sakakini Palace beyond (see p.156).

THE MUSKI A narrow bazaar, identifiable by the crowds passing between the *El-Mousky* hotel and a clump of luggage stalls, this is the classic approach to **Khan el-Khalili**, though it takes slightly longer than Sharia al-Azhar. For more details, see p.111.

SHARIA AL-AZHAR Overshadowed by a flyover running to the heart of Islamic Cairo, Sharia al-Azhar buzzes with traffic and cottage industries. It's a ten-to-fifteen-minute walk to **Al-Azhar Mosque** from Midan Ataba.

SHARIA QALAA Across from the fire station, this runs directly to the **Citadel** (2km). The stretch down to Midan Ahmed Maher – where the **Islamic Arts Museum** is located – features musical instrument shops, all-night stalls and cafés.

Most of Islamic Cairo's **monuments** are self-evident and are described in detail in *Islamic Monuments in Cairo: A Practical Guide*, published by the AUC. Although the area **maps** printed in this book should suffice, the AUC book and four fold-out maps published by SPARE (the Society for the Preservation of the Architectural Resources of Egypt) show even more detail. Al-Shorouk, AUC, Buccellati and Lehnert & Landrock (see p.201) are the best places to look for the SPARE maps, which are not always easy to come by.

Historic buildings may charge admission, but mosques generally don't, though unscrupulous custodians and other opportunists may try to charge visitors for entry. If this happens, demand an official ticket – if they have none, the charge is spurious and you should refuse to pay it, though of course custodians may expect baksheesh, especially for looking after shoes (£E1–2) or showing you round and opening things up (£E5–10). **Opening hours** are roughly 9am to 7pm daily (where they're significantly different, specific details are given in the text), though places may well open up later, depending on when the guardian turns up, and they may close an hour or two earlier in winter. During Ramadan, you will not be able to visit after about 4pm. Unless you are Muslim and want to pray, you will also not be welcome during **prayer times**, including the Friday noon assembly, which lasts over an hour but should be finished by 2pm. A couple of mosques (indicated in the text) are closed to non-Muslims completely.

the spices of the East, and with Baghdad laid waste by the Mongols, Cairo had no peer in the Islamic world, its wonders inspiring many of the tales in the *Thousand and One Nights*.

But in 1517 the **Ottoman Turks** reduced Egypt from an independent state to a vassal province in their empire, and the Mamlukes from masters to mere overseers. When the French and British extended the Napoleonic War to Egypt they found a city living on bygone glories, introspective and archaic, its population dwindling as civil disorder increased.

The city's renaissance – and the ultimate shift from Islamic to modern Cairo – is owed to **Mohammed Ali** (1805–48) and his descendants. An Ottoman servant who turned against his masters, Mohammed Ali effortlessly decapitated the vestiges of Mamluke power and raised a huge mosque and palaces upon the Citadel. Foreigners were hired to advise on urban development, and Khedive Ismail's Minister of Public Works ordered Boulevard Mohammed Ali (now Sharia Qalaa) to be ploughed through the old city (asking rhetorically: "Do we need so many monuments? Isn't it enough to preserve a sample?"). As Bulaq, Ezbekiya and other hitherto swampy tracts were developed into a modern, quasi-Western city, Islamic Cairo ceased to be the cockpit of power and the magnet for aspirations. But as visitors soon discover, its contrasts, monuments and vitality remain as compelling as ever.

Around Khan el-Khalili and Al-Azhar

Khan el-Khalili bazaar and the Mosque of Al-Azhar form the commercial and religious heart of Islamic Cairo, and a good starting point for several walking

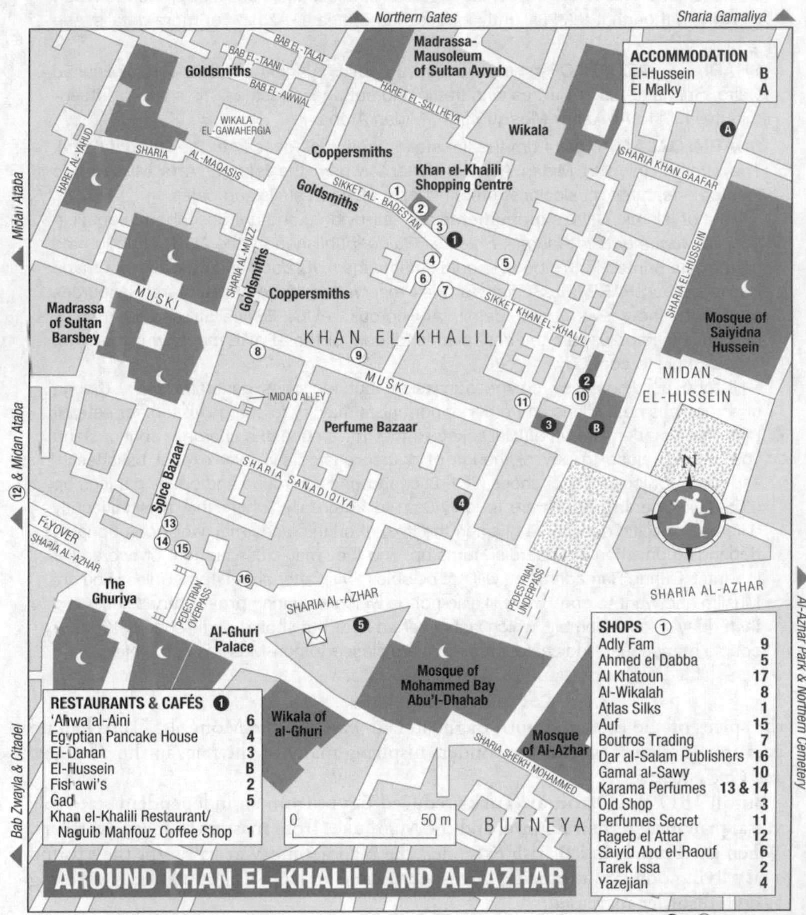

tours. A taxi here from downtown Cairo (usually via the Al-Azhar flyover) shouldn't cost more than £E5, although drivers often try to overcharge tourists bound for Midan el-Hussein – the main square adjoining Khan el-Khalili that's best given as your destination. Bus #66 serves Al-Azhar from Abdel Mouneem Riyad bus station. If you walk from Midan Ataba, it's best to arrive via the Muski and return by Sharia al-Azhar, or vice versa.

The Muski

The Muski is a narrow, incredibly congested street running eastwards from Sharia el-Guesh by Midan Ataba. Worming your way through the crowds, past windows full of wedding gear, and vendors peddling everything from salted fish to socks, beware of mopeds and other traffic thrusting up behind. Barrow-men still yell traditional warnings – "Riglak!" (your foot!), "Dahrik!" (your back!), "Shemalak!" (your left side!). Itinerant drinks-vendors are much in evidence: although water-sellers have been made redundant by modern plumbing, *susi* dispensing liquorice-water and *sherbutli* with their silver-spouted lemonade bottles remain an essential part of street life. Halfway along the Muski you'll cross Sharia Bur Said, which you cannot cross directly (you'll have to take a right and dodge under the flyover, or a left and use the footbridge 100m to the north).

Midan el-Hussein

Midan el-Hussein is a central point of reference. To the north stands the tan-coloured **Mosque of Saiyidna Hussein**, where the Egyptian president and other dignitaries pray on special occasions, and off-limits to non-Muslims. Its cool marble, green and silver interior guards the **head of Hussein**. The grandson of the Prophet Mohammed, Hussein was killed in Iraq in 680 by the Umayyads, who had earlier been recognized as Mohammed's successors against the claims of his son-in-law, Ali, Hussein's father. This generational power struggle over the caliphate caused an enduring schism within Islam. The Muslim world's Sunni ("followers of the way") majority not only recognized the Umayyad caliphate but forbade the office to anyone of Ali's line. Conversely, the Shia ("partisans of Ali") minority refused to accept any leader but a descendant of Ali, and revered Hussein as a martyr. In Egypt, whose Muslim population is almost completely Sunni, Hussein is nevertheless regarded as a popular saint, ranked beside Saiyida Zeinab, the Prophet's granddaughter.

Hussein's annual moulid is one of Cairo's greatest **festivals** – a fortnight of religious devotion and popular revelry climaxing on the *leyla kebira* or "big night", the last Wednesday in the Muslim month of Rabi al-Tani. Here the Sufi brotherhoods parade with their banners and drums, and music blares all night, with vast crowds of Cairenes and *fellaheen* from the Delta (each of whose villages has its own café and dosshouse in the neighbourhood). Midan el-Hussein is also a focal point during the festivals of Moulid al-Nabi, Eid al-Adha, Ramadan and Eid al-Fitr.

The Khan el-Khalili bazaars

Above all, the **Khan el-Khalili** quarter pulses with commerce, as it has since the Middle Ages. Except on Sundays, when most shops are shut, everything from spices to silk is sold in its bazaars. All the bazaars around here are subsumed under the name Khan el-Khalili – after Khalil, a Master of Horse who founded a caravanserai here in 1382, but the *khan* itself is quite compact, bounded by Hussein's Mosque, Sharia al-Muizz and the Muski, with two medieval lanes (Sikket al-Badestan and Sikket Khan el-Khalili) penetrating its maze-like interior.

Most of the shop fronts conceal workshops or warehouses, and the system of selling certain goods in particular areas still applies, if not as rigidly as in the past.

Goldsmiths, jewellers and souvenir-antique shops mostly congregate along the lanes, which retain a few arches and walls from Mamluke times. When you've tired of wandering around, duck into **Fishawi's** (see p.188), Cairo's most famous café, which has been open round the clock every day for over two centuries.

South off the Muski, along Sharia al-Muizz, you'll find the Souk al-Attarin or **Spice Bazaar**, selling dried crushed fruit and flowers besides more familiar spices. On the corner of the same street, screened by T-shirt and *galabiyya* stalls, stands the **Madrassa of Sultan al-Ashraf Barsbey**, who made the spice trade a state monopoly, thus financing his capture of Cyprus in 1426. The *madrassa*, resplendent without in its red-and-white striped stonework, is full of wooden *mashrabiya* -work within, where you can also check out the inlaid wooden *minbar*, and the tombs of Barsbey's wife and son.

Sharia Sanadiqiya (off Sharia al-Muizz) will take you into the **Perfume Bazaar**, a dark, aromatic warren sometimes called the Souk es-Sudan because much of the incense is from there. The first passage on your left off Sharia Sanadiqiya leads up a flight of steps to a tiny cul-de-sac. This is Zuqaq al-Midaq, or **Midaq Alley**, immortalized by Naguib Mahfouz in his novel of the same name, the film adaptation of which was shot here. There is no street sign apparent; it's kept in the tiny (and easy to miss) café, where they'll ask if you want to photograph it – for baksheesh, of course.

Al-Azhar Mosque

To the southwest of Midan el-Hussein, a pedestrian underpass leads towards the **Al-Azhar Mosque**, whose name can be translated as "the radiant", "blooming" or "resplendent". Founded in 970, Al-Azhar claims to be the world's oldest university (a title disputed by the Kairaouine Mosque in Fez, Morocco). As the ultimate theological authority for Egyptian Muslims, the mosque has always been politically significant. Salah al-Din changed it from a Shi'ite hotbed into a bastion of Sunni orthodoxy, while Napoleon's troops savagely desecrated it to demonstrate their power. A nationalist stronghold from the nineteenth century onwards, Al-Azhar was the venue for Nasser's speech of defiance during the Suez invasion of 1956.

The **mosque** (open daily 9am–5pm, except during prayers, including two hours on Friday 11am–1pm) is an accretion of centuries and styles, harmonious if confusing. You come in through the fifteenth-century **Barber's Gate**, where students traditionally had their heads shaved, onto a great **sahn** (courtyard) that's five hundred years older, overlooked by three minarets. The *sahn* facade, with its rosettes and keel-arched panels, is mostly Fatimid, but the latticework-screened *riwaqs* (residential quarters) of the *madrassa*s on your right-hand side date from the Mamluke period. While these are rarely opened for visitors, you can walk into the carpeted, alabaster-pillared prayer hall, where the *mihrab*, or niche facing Mecca, is located. The **roof** and minarets (closed to visitors at time of writing, but it's worth asking if you can go up) offer great views of Islamic Cairo's vista of crumbling, dust-coloured buildings that could have been erected decades or centuries ago, the skyline bristling with dozens of minarets.

North of Midan el-Hussein

You can easily walk from Midan el-Hussein to the Northern Gates and back again in an hour, but checking out the interiors of all the monuments could take half a day or more. If your time is limited, it's best to concentrate on the three big attractions: the Qalaoun–Al-Nasir–Barquq complex, Al-Hakim's Mosque and the Beit al-Sihaymi.

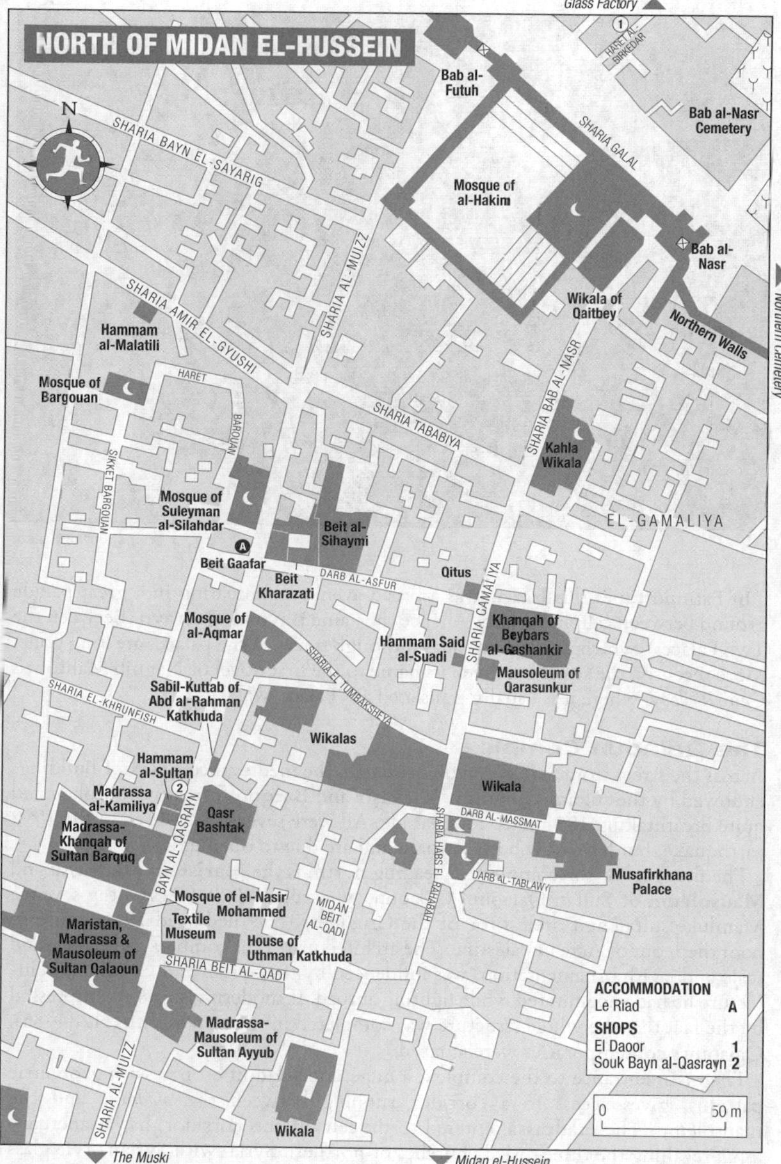

Bayn al-Qasrayn

Sharia al-Muizz crosses the Muski 200m west of Midan el-Hussein, at a crossroads with two mosques (see map, p.110). Heading north from here, jewellers' shops overflowing from the Goldsmiths Bazaar soon give way to vendors of pots, basins and crescent-topped finials, after whom this bit of street is popularly called Al-Nahaseen, the **Coppersmiths Bazaar**.

▲ Coppersmiths Bazaar

In Fatimid times this bazaar was a broad avenue culminating in a great parade ground between caliphal palaces – hence the name **Bayn al-Qasrayn** (Between the Two Palaces), which is still used today although traces of the palaces are long gone. More recently, the street has given its name to the first novel of Naguib Mahfouz's *Cairo Trilogy*, where it is usually translated as "Palace Walk".

The Qalaoun Complex

Across the street from Sultan Ayyub's *madrassa*, the medieval complex of buildings endowed by the sultans **Qalaoun**, **Al-Nasir** and **Barquq** forms an unbroken and quite breathtaking 185-metre-long facade. All were severely damaged in the 1992 earthquake, but have now been restored and are due to open in 2010.

The first part of the complex, if heading north, is the **Maristan**, **Madrassa** and **Mausoleum** of Sultan Qalaoun. Qalaoun, who ruled 1279–90, was the seventh Mamluke sultan and tireless foe of the Crusaders – he died aged 79 en route to boot them out of Acre in Palestine. The architecture of his complex, with its grand scale and lavish ornamentation, was influenced by the Syrian and Crusader architecture he had encountered while fighting abroad. If modern visitors are impressed by the fact that the whole structure was completed in thirteen months (1284–85), Qalaoun's contemporaries were amazed.

The main entrance to the complex, a huge door clad in bronze with geometric patterns, gives access to a corridor running between the *madrassa* and the mausoleum. The **madrassa** (entered to the left off this corridor) has a sanctuary *liwan* recalling the three-aisled churches of northern Syria, with Syrian-style glass mosaics around its prayer niche.

But the real highlight of the ensemble is Qalaoun's **mausoleum**, across the corridor. First comes an atrium court with a *mashrabiya* doorway, surmounted by a beautiful stucco arch worked with interlocking stars and floral and koranic motifs, as intricate as lace. Beyond is the tomb chamber, 30m high, with its soaring dome pierced by stained-glass windows in viridian, ultramarine and golden hues. Elaborately coffered, painted ceilings overhang walls panelled in marble, with mother-of-pearl mosaics spelling out "Mohammed" in abstract calligraphy.

The Al-Nasir Complex

Qalaoun's second son, responsible for the **Mosque of Al-Nasir** next door, had a rough succession. Only nine years old when elected, he was deposed by his regent, then restored but kept in miserable conditions for a decade by Beybars al-Gashankir. He finally had Beybars executed and subsequently enjoyed a lengthy reign (1293–1340, with interregnums), which marked the zenith of Mamluke civilization. Although this **mausoleum** was intended for Al-Nasir, he actually lies next door in Qalaoun's mausoleum, his wife and son being buried in this one. The **minaret** is particularly noteworthy, a superb ensemble of stuccoed Kufic and Naskhi inscriptions, ornate medallions and stalactites, probably made by Moroccan craftsmen.

The Barquq Madrassa and Khanqah

The broad facade of the adjacent **Madrassa and Khanqah of Sultan Barquq**, divided into shallow recesses, echoes Qalaoun's madrassa, although Barquq's complex (1384–86) has the taller dome. It also boasts a minaret, which you may be able to ascend (second door on the right in the entrance passage and over the roof) for excellent views of Islamic Cairo.

Barquq was the first Circassian sultan (1382–98), a Burgi Mamluke who seized power by means of intrigue and assassination. His name, meaning "plum" in Arabic, appears on the raised boss in the centre of the bronze-plated doors, behind which a vaulted passageway leads to an open court. The *madrassa*'s sanctuary *liwan* (on the right as you enter) has a beautiful blue and gold ceiling supported by porphyry columns of pharaonic origin; upstairs are the cells of the Sufi monks who once inhabited the **khanqah** (monastery). To the north of the prayer hall, a splendid domed mausoleum upheld by gilded pendentives contains the tomb of Barquq's daughter.

The Sabil-Kuttab of Abd al-Rahman Katkhuda

At a fork in the road on Bayn al-Qasrayn just north of the Qalaoun, Al-Nasir and Barquq complex, the Sabil-Kuttab of Abd al-Rahman Katkhuda (daily 9am–5pm; £E10, student £E5) rises in tiers of airy wooden fretwork above solid masonry and grilles at street level. The *sabil* (public fountain), and *kuttab* (boys' primary school) are common charitable institutions throughout the Islamic world, but uniquely in Cairo, they were usually combined. At one time there were some three hundred such *sabil-kuttabs* in the city, of which around seventy survive. This one, founded by an eighteenth-century amir who wanted to make amends for his roistering youth, betrays a strong Ottoman influence, notable in the floral carvings between the arches. As usual, the *sabil* is on the ground floor (where the Kaaba at Mecca is depicted in Syrian tilework), with the *kuttab* upstairs giving a bird's-eye view over Bay al-Qasrayn.

The Mosque of al-Aqmar

Taking the left-hand fork at the *sabil-kuttab* and walking 70m north along Sharia Bayn al-Qasrayn, you reach the **Mosque of al-Aqmar**, on the right. Its most salient feature is the facade, whose ribbed shell hood, keel arches and stalactite panels were the first instance of a decorated mosque facade in Cairo. Built between 1121 and 1125 by the Fatimid caliph's grand vizier, the mosque gets its name – "the moonlit" – from the glitter of its masonry under lunar light. The intricate medallion above the door bears the names of both Mohammed and his son-in-law Ali, the Fatimids being Shi'ites who regarded Ali and his descendants as Mohammed's only legitimate successors. The mosque's entrance is at what was the street level when it was built.

Darb al-Asfur and the Mosque of Suleyman al-Silahdar

One block north of the Mosque of Al-Aqmar, the turning on the right is **Darb al-Asfur** ("The Yellow Street"). Thanks to years of loving restoration completed in 1999, it almost seems like a modern reconstruction rather than a genuine Gamaliya street. The first three houses on the left are all open to the public (daily 9am–5pm; £E30, students £E15), entered through the broad wooden door of no.19, **Beit al-Sihaymi**, which is the finest of the three. Its rooms surround a lovely courtyard filled with bird noises and shrubbery, overlooked by a *maq'ad* or loggia, where men enjoyed the cool northerly breezes; the ground-floor reception hall with its marble fountain was used during winter, or for formal occasions. The *haramlik* section, reserved for women, is equally luxurious, adorned with faïence, stained glass, painted ceilings and delicate latticework. From here, you pass through the similarly restored early eighteenth-century **Beit Kharazati**, to emerge via the smaller, nineteenth-century **Beit Gaafar** on the corner at no. 25. The three houses offer a unique chance to see what lies behind the walls of these old-city streets, and view the interior of a traditional wealthy Cairene's home, although the family life that once filled it is missing.

Just 20m north of the junction with Darb al-Asfur on Sharia al-Muizz, the **Mosque of Suleyman al-Silahdar** is recognizable by its "pencil" minaret, a typically Ottoman feature. Built in 1839, the mosque reflects the Baroque and Rococo influences that reached Cairo via Istanbul during Mohammed Ali's reign – notably the fronds and garlands that also characterize *sabil-kuttabs* from the period.

Mosque of al-Hakim

The **Mosque of al-Hakim**, abutting the Northern Walls, commemorates one of Egypt's most notorious rulers. **Al-Hakim bi-Amr Allah** (Ruler by God's Command) was only 11 years old when he became the sixth Fatimid caliph, and 15 when he had his tutor murdered. His reign (996–1021) was characterized by the persecution of Christians, Jews and merchants, and by rabid misogyny: he forbade women to leave their homes and once had a group of noisy females boiled alive in a public bath. Merchants found guilty of cheating during Al-Hakim's inspections were summarily sodomized by his Nubian slave, Masoud, while the caliph stood upon their heads – comparatively restrained behaviour from a man who once dissected a butcher with his own cleaver.

In 1020, followers proclaimed Al-Hakim's divinity in the Mosque of Amr, provoking riots which he answered by ordering Fustat's destruction. Legend ascribes the conflagration to Al-Hakim's revenge on the quarter where his beloved sister, **Sitt al-Mulk** (Lady of Power), took her lovers; only after half of Fustat-Masr was in ruins was she examined by midwives and pronounced a virgin. Allegedly, it was his desire for an incestuous marriage that impelled her to arrange Al-Hakim's "disappearance" during one of his nocturnal jaunts in the Muqattam Hills, though his body was never found.

The **mosque** was thereafter shunned or used for profane purposes until 1980, when it was restored by a group of Bohara Isma'ili Shi'ites from India who have dedicated themselves to looking after Cairo's Fatimid mosques. Their addition of brass lamps, glass chandeliers and a new *mihrab* outraged purists, but the original wooden tie-beams and stucco frieze beneath the ceilings remain. From the roof, you can gaze over Bab al-Nasr Cemetery (see p.117) and admire the mosque's minarets, which resemble bastions and are its only original features. One advantage of modernization is that the courtyard has some degree of wheelchair access (via the side door, to the left of the main one; you'll need to get someone to open it for you).

The Northern Gates

In times past, the annual pilgrim caravan returning from Mecca would enter Cairo via the **Bab al-Futuh** (Open Gate), drawing vast crowds to witness the arrival of the Mahmal, a decorative camel litter symbolizing the sultan's participation in the hajj. Islamic pageantry is still manifest during the **Moulid of Sidi Ali al-Bayoumi**, in early October, when the Rifai brotherhood parades behind its mounted sheikh with scarlet banners flying. The procession starts from El-Hussein, passes through the Bab al-Futuh and north along Sharia Husseiniya, where locals bombard the sheikh and his red-turbanned followers with huge sweets called *arwah*.

The **Northern Walls** are in principle accessible from Al-Hakim's Mosque, but closed at time of writing for restoration. When they reopen, you can gain admission to a **prison** in the dark interior, where the custodian will point out archers' slits and bombardiers' apertures, shafts for pouring boiling oil onto enemies entering through the Bab al-Futuh below, and bits of pharaonic masonry (featuring Ramses II's cartouche and a hippo) filched from Memphis. The ceiling of the two-hundred-metre tunnel is vaulted, which allowed mounted guards passage through. At its end lies a cavernous judgement room where the condemned, if found guilty, were hanged immediately, their corpses dumped through a hole in the floor, into the moat.

Erected in 1087 to replace the original mud-brick ramparts of Fatimid Al-Qahira, the walls were intended to rebuff the Seljuk Turks, but never put to the test, although they later provided a barracks for Napoleonic, and then British, grenadiers. The French attempted to rename the bastions of Bab al-Futuh and the next gate along, **Bab al-Nasr** (Gate of Victory), and titles such as "Tour Julien" and "Tour Pascal" are still inscribed on them. Bab al-Nasr can be reached, like Bab al-Futuh, from the roof of Al-Hakim's Mosque. It was after entering this gate in 1517 that the victorious Ottoman Sultan Selim the Grim had eight hundred Mamlukes decapitated and their heads strung on ropes on Gezira Island. Directly opposite the gate lies **Bab al-Nasr Cemetery**, nowadays so overbuilt with houses that you can hardly see the tombs. At the top end of Haret al-Birkhader, one of the small streets off Sharia Galal opposite Bab al-Futuh, is a traditional **glass factory** (daily except Fri 9am–3pm; free) where they hand-blow Muski glass, and are usually happy for tourists to pop in and have a look: if you can't find it, ask for directions in their shop at no. 10.

From Bab al-Nasr you could catch a taxi or walk 1500m east, following the Walls and then Sharia Galal, to reach Barquq's complex in the Northern Cemetery (see p.137).

South to Bab Zwayla

Heading south from the Muski across Sharia al-Azhar (over the pedestrian bridge), Sharia al-Muizz continues south to the medieval gate known as **Bab Zwayla**. Named after the conquering Fatimid caliph, **al-Muizz** was the chief thoroughfare of Islamic Cairo, running from the Northern Gates down towards the Citadel, and meeting another main road – the Darb al-Ahmar – at Bab Zwayla. Traditionally, each stretch of Al-Muizz had its own name, usually derived from the merchandise sold there. The stretch from Sharia al-Azhar to Bab Zwayla is a short walk of just 300m. Shops along this part sell mostly household goods, making fewer concessions to tourism than Khan el-Khalili.

The Wikala, Mosque-Madrassa and Mausoleum of Al-Ghuri

The lovingly restored **Wikala of Al-Ghuri** (daily 8am–5pm; £E15, students £E8) is the finest example of the merchants' hostels that once characterised the bazaars – built in 1505, just as the new Cape route to the East Indies was diminishing Cairo's role as a spice entrepôt. Its upstairs rooms have been converted into artists' studios, which the custodian will be glad to show you around. With its stables and

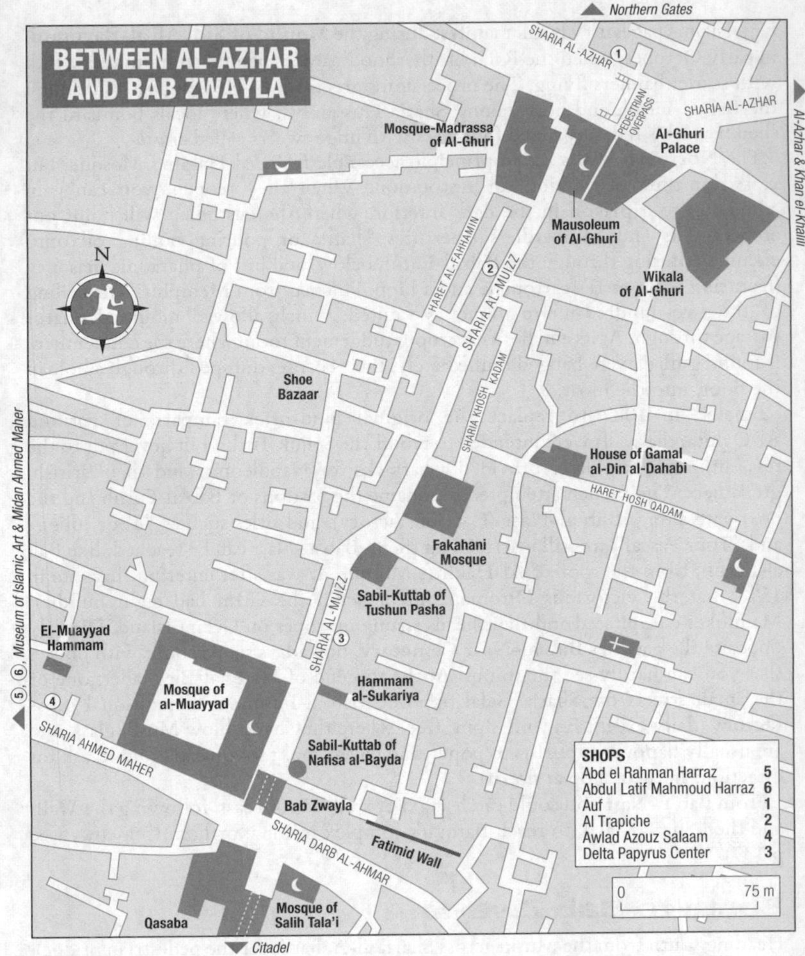

lock-ups beneath tiers of spartan rooms, the *wikala* is uncompromisingly functional, yet the rhythm of *ablaq* (striped) arches muted by the sharp verticals of shutters, and the severe masonry lightened by *mashrabiya*s and a graceful fountain, achieves elegance. On Wednesday and Saturday evenings, it is the venue for a free and spectacular performance of Sufi **dervish dancing** (see p.195), which you shouldn't miss if you are in town.

Located on a side street off Sharia al-Azhar, the *wikala* can be reached by turning left on leaving the Mosque of Al-Azhar, then following the alley round past a market; or you can visit it after seeing the **Ghuriya** – the mausoleum and mosque-*madrassa* of Qansuh Al-Ghuri. Boldly striped in buff and white, this pair of buildings forms a set piece at the junction of Sharia al-Muizz and the Al-Azhar high road, plainly visible from the footbridge. To the right (west) of the bridge stands the **Mosque-Madrassa**, now restored to its full glory. The rooftop offers glimpses of the Spice Bazaar and a grand view of the neighbourhood – the door is diagonally opposite the entrance to the main part of the mosque, but is often closed, so you may have to ask a custodian for access. Across the way is Al-Ghuri's **Mausoleum** (daily 9am–5pm; £E25, students £E15), adjacent to the **Al-Ghuri Palace**, now used to host occasional concerts (details from the Wikala of al-Ghuri). **Qansuh al-Ghuri** became the penultimate Mamluke sultan in 1500, and was killed in 1516 fighting the Ottomans outside Aleppo in Syria; his body was never found and his intended tomb was occupied by his luckless successor, Tumanbey (see p.120).

Towards Bab Zwayla

In olden times the stretch of Sharia al-Muizz between the Ghuriya buildings was roofed over, forming the Silk Bazaar where carpets were sold, the subject of a famous drawing by David Roberts. Some 200m south is the "Fruit Seller" or **Fakahani Mosque**, whose arabesque-panelled doors are all that remain of the twelfth-century original after its reconstruction in 1735. South of the Fakahani Mosque, Sharia al-Muizz curves around the Rococo facade of the 1820 Ottoman-built **Sabil-Kuttab of Tusun Pasha** (daily 10am–8pm; £E20, students £E10, but often closed for no apparent reason), adorned with wrought-iron sunbursts, garlands and fronds. Shortly afterwards, the street passes between two buildings structurally adjacent to Bab Zwayla, whose formidable outline dominates the view ahead.

Al-Muizz continues south to the **Mosque of Al-Muayyad** – also known as the "Red Mosque" for the colour of its exterior – which occupies the site of a prison where its founder was once incarcerated for plotting against Sultan Barquq. Plagued by lice and fleas, he vowed to transform it into a "saintly place for the education of scholars" once he came to power. The building is entered via a nine-tiered stalactite portal with a red-and-turquoise geometric frame around its bronze door. Off the vestibule lies a mausoleum where Al-Muayyad and his son are buried in fittingly sized cenotaphs. The Kufic inscription on Al-Muayyad's reads: "But the god-fearing shall be amidst gardens and fountains: Enter you them, in peace and security" – which seems appropriate for the mosque's spacious courtyard. Beneath the roofed section, a thickly carpeted sanctuary precedes the *qibla* wall, niched and patterned with polychrome marble and blue ceramic tiles. Its minarets are built atop the turrets of Bab Zwayla, the neighbouring city gate.

Bab Zwayla

In Fatimid times, **Bab Zwayla** was the city's main southern gate. It was constructed during the 1090s, when the Fatimid city's defences (including sixty gates) were being reinforced using Anatolian or Mesopotamian Christian architects and Egyptian labour. The minarets of Al-Muayyad's Mosque, added to its turrets some four hundred years after they were built, make it look far mightier than the Northern Gates. In the Mamluke city, which had outgrown the Fatimid walls and pushed up against Salah al-Din's extensions, Bab Zwayla became a central point, but the practice of barring the gates each night continued well into the nineteenth century, maintaining a city within a city. There's a strikingly medieval passage just on the north side of the gate, but the full awesomeness of the Bab itself is best seen from the south side.

The gate was named after Fatimid mercenaries of the Berber al-Zwayla tribe, quartered nearby, whom the Mamlukes displaced. Through the centuries it was the point of departure for caravans to Mecca and the source of the drum rolls that greeted the arrival of senior "Amirs of One Hundred". Dancers and snake charmers performed here, and punishments provided another spectacle. Dishonest merchants might be hung from hooks; garrotting, beheading or impalement were favoured for common criminals; while losers in the Mamluke power struggles were often nailed to the doors. It was here that Tumanbey, the last Mamluke sultan, was hanged in 1517, after a vast crowd had recited the Fatah (the opening sura of the Koran) and the rope had broken twice before his neck did. Bab Zwayla's reputation was subsequently redeemed by its association with Mitwalli al-Qutb, a miracle-working local saint said to manifest himself to the faithful as a gleam of light within the gatehouse.

The **western gatetower**, the **turret** and the **minarets** are now open to the public (daily 8.30am–5pm; £E15, students £E8) and can be visited via a door just next to the al-Muayyad Mosque. Finds from the site are on display, as well as votive offerings left by local residents for Mitwalli al-Qutb. You can also climb to the top of the two minarets for great views over Islamic Cairo and a bird's-eye perspective over the al-Muayyad and Salih Tala'i mosques below. Note the barbells high up on the western gatetower – a relic of medieval keep-fit enthusiasts.

Across the street from the entrance to the gate, the eighteenth-century **Sabil-Kuttub of Nafisa al-Bayda** has been restored and opened to the public (daily 8am–6pm; £E8, students £E4; tickets from the desk at Bab Zwayla), with accounts of the building and some of the artefacts found there, but nothing hugely compelling.

Going through Bab Zwayla, you can now continue south along Sharia al-Muizz (see pp.121–123), or take a left (eastwards) along Sharia Darb al-Ahmar (see pp.123–125), or take a right (westwards) along Sharia Ahmed Maher towards the **Museum of Islamic Art** (see below) and on to Abdin (see p.107). On the way, you'll pass stalls selling waterpipes and braziers, a nineteenth-century *sabil-kuttab* and a fifteenth-century mosque. The neighbourhood between Bab Zwayla and Abdin is known as **Bab el-Khalq** after a long-since-vanished medieval gate.

The Museum of Islamic Art

The **Museum of Islamic Art** stands at the junction of Sharia Ahmed Maher, Sharia Bur Said and Sharia Qalaa, 600m west of Bab Zwayla (see "Central Cairo" map, p.93), and has been closed for some years now for refurbishment, though it is supposed to reopen early in 2010. It was the ruinous state of Cairo's mosques and mansions that impelled Khedive Tewfiq to ask two foreign historians, Hungarian Max Herz and Londoner K.A.C. Creswell, to establish an Islamic collection in 1880. The collection was housed in Al-Hakim's Mosque (see p.116) and grew to over seven thousand pieces before the museum opened to exhibit them in 1903. The exhibits include glassware, jewellery, ceramics and architectural ornaments from Egypt and elsewhere spanning all the major periods of Islamic history, from the early caliphates of the Umayyads, who ruled from Damascus (661–750 AD) and the Abbasids, who presided over the Arab empire from Baghdad (750–1258), as well as Egyptian dynasties such as the Tulunids (868–905 AD), the Fatimids (969–1171), the Ayyubids (1171–1250) and the Mamlukes (1250–1517), to the Ottoman Empire, which supplanted the Caliphates and ruled Egypt from 1517 until its khedives (viceroys) established their de facto independence in 1805.

Noteworthy exhibits in the museum include a bronze ewer with a spout in the form of a crowing cockerel, which probably belonged to the last Umayyad caliph, Marwan II, formerly housed in Room 2 (though this may have changed when the museum reopens). Marwan was slain near Abu Sir, just south of Cairo, his death heralding the end of the Umayyad caliphate and the start of Abbasid rule. From the Fatimid period come **panels from the Western Palace**, one of the two palaces which once stood on Bayn al-Qasrayn (see p.114), which were formerly in Room 4. The same room also exhibited **frescoes** from a Fustat bathhouse depicting people and animals. These are usually absent in Islamic art, as making a graven image was considered to smack of idolatry, but the taboo was not yet established at this early stage. Even under the first Mamlukes, representational art could still be found, as evinced by a **frieze from Qalaoun's Maristan**, formerly in Room 6, which shows hunting, music and dancing. Room 6 also held a pair of original doors from Al-Azhar Mosque.

Room 8 held three wooden **minbars** (pulpits) and a number of wooden panels, mostly from mosques, but one contains a frieze in Hebrew commemorating the building of a synagogue in the twelfth century by one Ibrahim el-Amshati. Among the museum's **metalwork**, previously displayed in Room 9, the most striking pieces are a Persian brass candlestick in the form of two intertwined snakes and, among the **figurines** by the west wall, a little man on a horse in a "Look, no hands" pose. The swords of the Ottoman sultans Mehmet II and Suleyman the Magnificent (the respective conquerors of Constantinople and the Balkans) were formerly displayed in Room 11. Ceramics (formerly in **Room 15**) include tiles found at Fustat that originated in Tunisia, Andalucía and Christian Europe, showing the extent of the city's commercial reach, and including blue Delft tiles from Holland. Room 16 had a blue-tiled nineteenth-century **Turkish fireplace**, and a section of a **kuttab** (koranic school) from Rosetta incorporating a niche for the teacher to sit beneath its *muqarnas* ceiling.

The museum also has a fine collection of books and manuscripts (which were mostly housed in Room 19) illustrating the arts of **calligraphy and bookbinding**, including Persian and Indian illustrated manuscripts, but primacy is accorded to the word of God, with numerous medieval Korans from the personal collection of King Farouk. The first mass-produced Korans were made in Egypt following Napoleon's introduction of the printing press.

Whether these exhibits will remain in the same locations as they were before the museum was renovated is still not certain, but at any rate they should all be there, and the collection is a compelling one for anybody with an interest in art or Islamic history. The museum sits at what was the edge of Islamic Cairo and can easily be reached on foot from Bab Zwayla (see p.120), or from Abdin. Sharia Bur Said, which runs alongside it, was in medieval times a canal marking the western edge of the city (see p.149) although extramural neighbourhoods to the west of it, such as Bab al-Luq, were established as early as the thirteenth century.

Between Bab Zwayla and the Citadel

There are two routes from Bab Zwayla to the Citadel: via the Qasaba, **Sharia al-Muizz** and Sharia Qalaa; or following the old **Darb al-Ahmar** (after which this quarter of Islamic Cairo is named). It's possible to get the best of both worlds by combining the Darb al-Ahmar with a detour into the **Qasaba** and **Saddlemakers Bazaar**, located on the other route, a total distance of about 1500m. If you're starting from Bab Zwayla, it's logical to visit the Qasaba before embarking on the Darb al-Ahmar, but the reverse is true if you're coming from the Citadel, in which case you'll want to start with the "Blue Mosque" of Aqsunqur on Sharia Bab al-Wazir and backtrack through the text from there.

From Bab Zwayla into the Qasaba

Across the street south of Bab Zwayla, where Sharia al-Muizz continues southward, you'll see a cluster of Islamic monuments. On the west side of al-Muizz stands a Sufi establishment, the 1408 Mamluke **Zawiya of Farag ibn Barquq**, whose inlaid marble lintels and *ablaq* panels have now been restored to their original splendour. Opposite the *zawiya*, on the east side of al-Muizz, the **Mosque of Salih Tala'i** withdraws behind an elegant portico with five keel arches – a unique architectural feature. The last of Cairo's Fatimid mosques, the building shows an assured use of the motifs that were first employed on the Mosque of

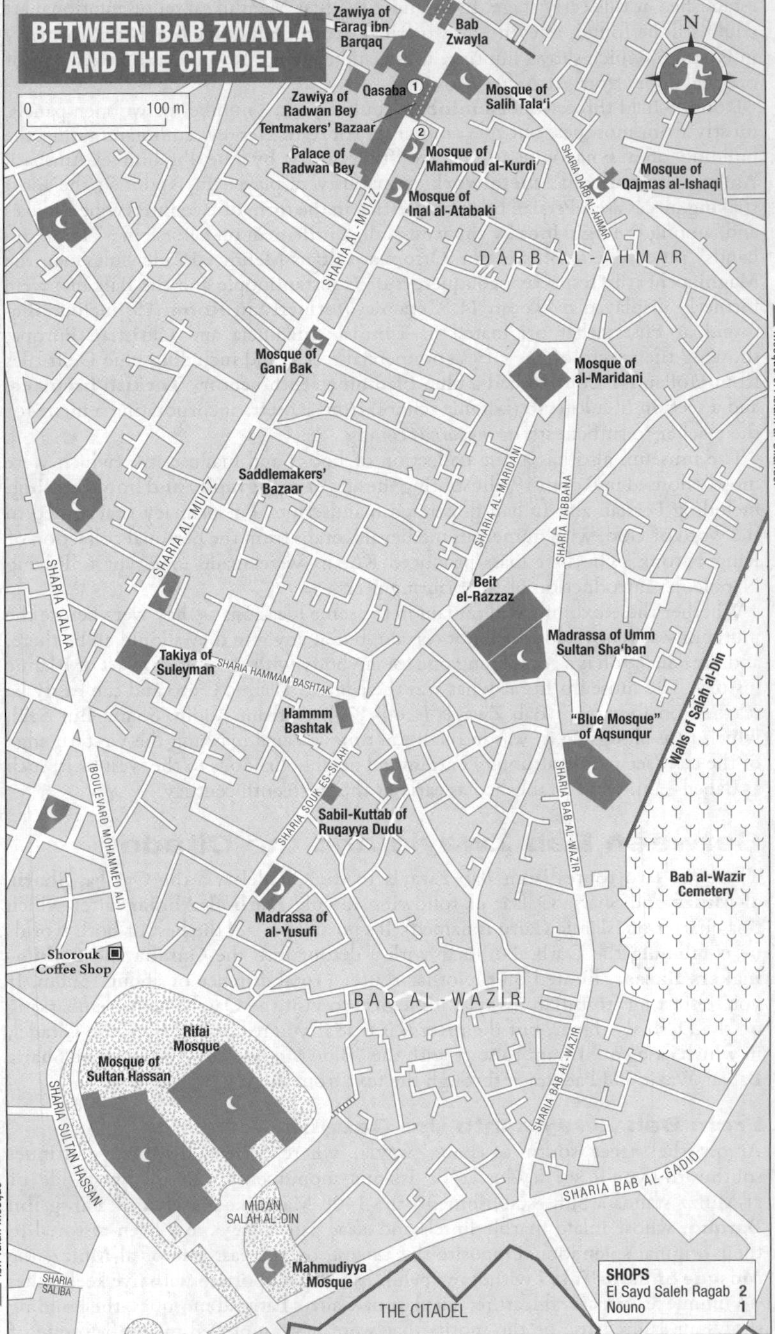
BETWEEN BAB ZWAYLA AND THE CITADEL
0
100 m
Museum of Islamic Art
Al-Ghuri and Al-Azhar
N
Zawiya of Farag ibn Barqaq
Bab Zwayla
Qasaba
Zawiya of Radwan Bey
Tentmakers' Bazaar
Palace of Radwan Bey
Mosque of Salih Tala'i
Mosque of Mahmoud al-Kurdi
Mosque of Inal al-Atabaki
Mosque of Qajmas al-Ishaqi
SHARIA DARB AL-AHMAR
DARB AL-AHMAR
SHARIA AL-MUIZZ
Midan Ataba
Mosque of Aslam al-Silander
Mosque of Gani Bak
Mosque of al-Maridani
SHARIA AL-MARIDANI
SHARIA TABBANA
Saddlemakers' Bazaar
SHARIA AL-MUIZZ
SHARIA QALAA
Beit el-Razzaz
Madrassa of Umm Sultan Sha'ban
Takiya of Suleyman
SHARIA HAMMAM BASHTAK
Hammm Bashtak
"Blue Mosque" of Aqsunqur
Walls of Salah al-Din
(BOULEVARD MOHAMMED ALI)
SHARIA SOUK ES-SILAH
SHARIA BAB AL-WAZIR
Sabil-Kuttab of Ruqayya Dudu
Bab al-Wazir Cemetery
Madrassa of al-Yusufi
Shorouk Coffee Shop
BAB AL-WAZIR
Rifai Mosque
Mosque of Sultan Hassan
SHARIA SULTAN HASSAN
SHARIA BAB AL-WAZIR
SHARIA BAB AL-GADID
MIDAN SALAH AL-DIN
Ibn Tulun Mosque
SHARIA SALIBA
Mahmudiyya Mosque
THE CITADEL
Southern Cemetery
SHOPS
El Sayd Saleh Ragab 2
Nouno 1

Al-Aqmar: ribbed and cusped arches and panels, carved tie beams and rosettes. Rents from the shops around its base (which have been restored, but are as yet unoccupied) contributed to the mosque's upkeep. Originally they were at street level, but this has risen well over a metre since the mosque was built in 1160.

Straight ahead, Sharia al-Muizz passes through the **Qasaba**, erected by Ridwan Bey in 1650, and one of the best-preserved examples of a covered market left in Cairo. Colourful fabrics, appliqué and leatherwork are piled in dens ranked either side of a gloomy, lofty passageway known as the Khiyamiyya, or **Tentmakers Bazaar**, after the printed fabrics used to make tents for moulids and weddings (see p.200)

Beyond the Qasaba

Emerging from the southern end of the Qasaba, **Sharia al-Muizz** extends its path between two mosques and the facade of Ridwan Bey's former palace, beyond which the monuments thin out as vegetable stalls and butchers congest the narrow street. About 150m on you'll pass the **Mosque of Gani Bak**, a protégé of Sultan Barsbey, who was poisoned by rivals at the age of 25. Beyond, a few stalls selling donkey- and camel-wear constitute what remains of the Souk es-Surugiyyah, or **Saddlemakers Bazaar**, formerly the centre of Cairo's leather industry.

Assuming you don't turn back here to pursue the Darb al-Ahmar, it's a fairly mundane 350-metre walk to Al-Muizz's junction with **Sharia Qalaa**. The Sultan Hassan and Rifai mosques below the Citadel are plainly visible at the boulevard's southern end, 300m away. Alternatively, use bus services in the opposite direction to reach the Museum of Islamic Art, 1km up Sharia Qalaa (see p.120). Some of the buses continue on to Midan Ataba, others to Abdin or Al-Azhar.

Along the Darb al-Ahmar

An alternative, more picturesque route between Bab Zwayla and the Citadel follows the "Red Road", or **Darb al-Ahmar**. Originally a cemetery beyond the southern walls of the Fatimid city, this quarter became a fashionable residential area once Al-Nasir developed the Citadel. The thoroughfare acquired its present name in 1805, when Mohammed Ali tricked the Mamlukes into staging a coup before slaughtering them; the street ran red with their blood. Nowadays the neighbourhood is very down-at-heel, with much poverty and unemployment, but has been the object of a regeneration project financed by the Aga Khan Trust along with the building of Al-Azhar Park (see p.137) and the excavation of the Ayyubid city wall which runs along the eastern edge of the quarter, separating it from the park.

Start by walking 150m east from Salih Tila'i's Mosque near Bab Zwayla. On the corner where the Darb turns south, the **Mosque of Qajmas al-Ishaqi** looms over workshops sunk beneath street level. A marble panel with swirling leaf forms in red, black and white surmounts the entrance to a vestibule with a gilded ceiling; left off this is the mosque itself. Notice the *mihrab*'s sinuous decorations (incised grooves filled with red paste or bitumen) and the fine panelling on the floor near the *qibla* wall (ask the custodian to lift a mat). Best of all are the stained-glass windows in the tomb chamber occupied by one Abu Hurayba. A raised passage connects the mosque with a *sabil-kuttab* across the street; both were built in the 1480s.

Al-Silahdar's Mosque

If you're not pushed for time, consider detouring off the Darb to visit the **Mosque of Aslam al-Silahdar**. From Qajmas's Mosque, walk through the tunnel around the side and on past a shrine where the street forks (bear right); Al-Silahdar's Mosque lies 250m ahead. The marble panel outside is typical of exterior decoration during the Bahri Mamluke period; inside, the layout is that of a cruciform

madrassa. Students used to live in rooms above the north and south *liwans*, behind an ornate facade of stucco mouldings and screened windows. The mosque's founder was a Qipchak Mamluke who lost his position as swordbearer after Sultan al-Nasir believed rumours spread by his enemies, and imprisoned him, only to reinstate Aslam as *silahdar* ("swordbearer") six years later. To return to the Darb, either retrace your steps or take the street running southwest off the square, which joins the Darb further south, beyond Al-Maridani's Mosque.

South along the Darb Al-Ahmar

South from the Qajmas Mosque, the Darb al-Ahmar passes the **Mosque of Al-Maridani**, built in 1340 and still a peaceful retreat from the streets. The mosque is usually entered via its northern portal, offset by a stalactite frieze with complex patterns of joggled voussoirs and *ablaq* panels. Inside, a splendid *mashrabiya* screen separates the open courtyard from the prayer hall with its stained-glass windows and variegated columns (Mamluke, pre-Islamic and pharaonic). Architecturally, the minaret marks the replacement of the Ayyubid "pepperpot" finial by a small dome on pillars, which became the hallmark of Mamluke minarets. Below the dome and above the *minbar*, arboreal forms in stucco may allude to the koranic verse, "A good word is as a good tree – its roots firm, its branches in heaven".

Leaving via the southern entrance, you'll need to turn left to rejoin the Darb – or **Sharia Tabbana** as it's called at this point. Roughly 200m on, past a small Turkish mosque, stands the hulking **Madrassa of Um Sultan Sha'ban**. Um Sha'ban was the concubine of a son of Al-Nasir, whose own son erected the *madrassa* (1368–69) as a gesture of gratitude after he became sultan at the age of 10; murdered in 1376, he preceded her to the grave and was buried here since his own *madrassa* was unfinished. A wealth of *muqarnas* and *ablaq* rims the entrance, which is flanked by a *sabil* and a drinking trough for animals. Behind the mosque, and entered through the doorway just to the left of the entrance to the mosque, the **Beit al-Razzaz** (daily except Fri, 9am–5pm) is a rambling palace, now restored. When you go in, the caretaker will probably appear and offer to show you around the upper rooms, with their *mashrabiya* screens, painted ceilings and stained-glass windows, for which he will, of course, expect a tip.

The "Blue Mosque" and the Hammam Bashtak

Further along the street, now called **Sharia Bab al-Wazir** after the Gate of the Vizier that once stood here, lies the **"Blue Mosque"** or **Mosque of Aqsunqur**, which was closed again for restoration on our last check. When originally built in 1347, the mosque was plainer, its *ablaq* arches framing a *sahn*, now battered and dusty, with a palm tree and chirping birds. The Iznik-style tiles (imported from Turkey or Syria) were added in the 1650s by Ibrahim Agha, who usurped and redecorated the fourteenth-century mosque. The indigo and turquoise tiles on the *qibla* wall – with cypresses, tulips and other floral motifs either side of the magnificently inlaid *mihrab* – were added at the same time. Along with similar tiles around the tomb of Ibrahim Agha in the mosque's southwest corner, they were probably made in Damascus, and explain the mosque's name and its popularity with tourists. The marble *minbar*, inlaid with green, grey, salmon and plum stone, is original, as is the circular minaret, which affords a superb **view** of the Citadel (on a clear day you can even make out the Pyramids).

The mosque's founder, Shams al-Din Aqsunqur, intrigued against the successors of Sultan al-Nasir, his father-in-law. Al-Nasir was succeeeded in turn by eight of his sons, one of whom, Al-Ashraf Kuchuk, was enthroned at the age of 6, "reigned" five months, and was strangled by his brother three years later. The reign of another of Al-Nasir's sons, Al-Kamil Sha'ban (not to be confused with

Sha'ban II, who erected the Madrassa of Um Sultan Sha'ban) lasted a year, ending in a palace coup and the crowning of his brother-in-law, Muzaffar Hadji. Muzaffar, recalling how Aqsunqur had manipulated Kuchuk (who's buried just inside the mosque's entrance) and deftly organized the coup against Sha'ban, promptly had him garrotted.

A couple of hundred metres west of the blue mosque, the **Hammam Bashtak** was a bathhouse serving the Darb al-Ahmar quarter, many of whose tenements lack washing facilities, but like most of Islamic Cairo's traditional steam bathhouses, it's now closed. Its elaborate portal is worth a second glance, however, the ribbed keel arch bearing the napkin motif (later used for "diamonds" in a pack of playing cards) of a *jamdar* or "Master of Robes".

The Citadel and around

The **Citadel** is the natural focus of a visit to Islamic Cairo; the area just below it, around Midan Salah al-Din, features two of the city's greatest monuments – the **Sultan Hassan** and **Rifai mosques**. You need a good half a day to do justice to these, and to the Citadel itself. Depending on how much time you have, you may want to visit only the Citadel, but it is well worth stopping in **Midan Salah al-Din** to take in the arresting mix of sounds and the views (see p.128).

To reach the Citadel area, you can either catch a taxi from downtown (£E10–15) or a bus (see p.84 for bus routes) – if you've got the energy, it's also an interesting walk. Note however that, if you ask for the Citadel (Al-Qalaa – usually pronounced "al-'alaa"), most Cairenes will assume you want to go to Midan Salah al-Din, the large square immediately beneath it, but the actual **entrance** to the Citadel is on the other side of it, on Sharia Salah Salem, nearly a kilometre from Midan Salah al-Din.

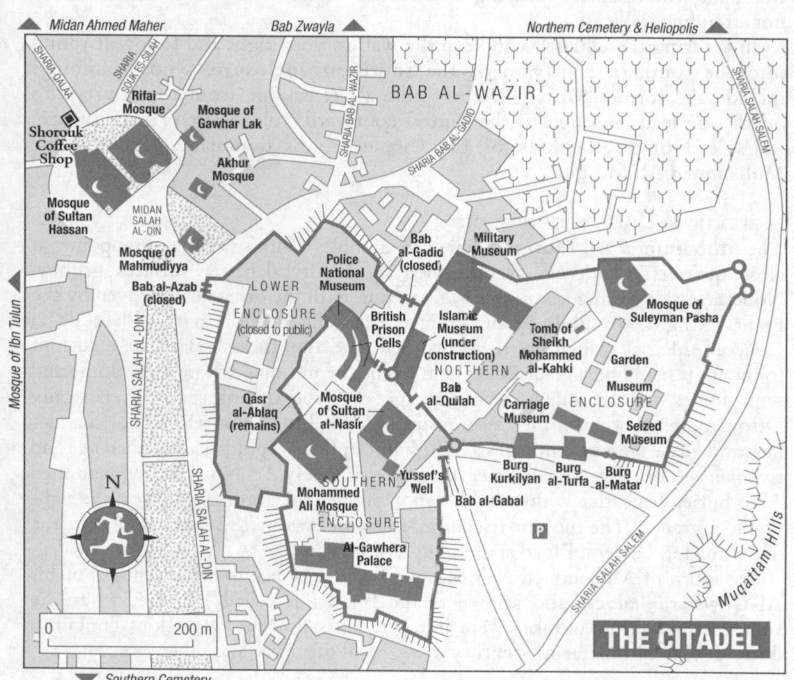

Heading onward from the Citadel, you could continue north from the entrance along Sharia Salah Salem to Al-Azhar Park and the Northern Cemetery (see pp.135–138), or, from Midan Salah al-Din, you could head north up Sharia al-Muizz or Sharia Darb al-Ahmar (covered in the opposite direction on p.123), or west along Sharia Saliba past the Mosque of Ibn Tulun (see p.131).

The Citadel

The Citadel (daily 8am–5pm; mosques closed Fri except for prayer; last entry to museums 30min before closing; £E50, students £E25) presents the most dramatic feature of Cairo's skyline: a centuries-old bastion crowned by the needle-like minarets of the great Mosque of Mohammed Ali. The entrance at Bab al-Gabal, on the opposite side of the Citadel from Midan Salah al-Din, can be reached by bus #951 or minibus #105 from Abdel Mouneem Riyad terminal near Midan Tahrir, or by service-taxi microbuses from Ramses and Ataba along Sharia Salah Salem.

The whole fortified complex was begun by **Salah al-Din**, the founder of the Ayyubid dynasty – known in English as Saladin, the Crusaders' chivalrous foe. Salah al-Din's reign (1171–93) saw much fortification of the city, though it was his nephew, Al-Kamil, who developed the Citadel as a royal residence, later to be replaced by the palaces of Sultan al-Nasir.

The main features of the Citadel as it is today, however, are associated with **Mohammed Ali**, a worthy successor to the Mamlukes and Turks. In 1811 he feasted with 470 leading Mamlukes in the Citadel palace, bade them farewell with honours, then had them ambushed in the sloping lane behind the **Bab al-Azab**, the locked gate (now closed to the public) opposite the Akhur Mosque. An oil painting in the Manial Palace on Roda Island depicts the apocryphal tale of a Mamluke who escaped by leaping the walls on his horse; in reality he survived by not attending the feast.

On entering the Citadel, you keep the wall to your right and follow it round into the southern courtyard of the **southern enclosure**, whose buildings include the former **Mint** (currently closed). A passage from the courtyard's north side leads through to the central courtyard; to the left of this passage, stairs lead up to the back of the Citadel's most dominant structure, the Mohammed Ali Mosque.

Mohammed Ali's monuments

The **Mohammed Ali Mosque**, which so ennobles Cairo's skyline, disappoints at close quarters: its domes are sheathed in tin, its alabaster surfaces grubby. Nonetheless, it exudes *folie de grandeur*, starting with the ornate clock given by the French king Louis Philippe (in exchange for the obelisk in the Place de la Concorde, Paris), which has never worked; and the Turkish Baroque ablutions fountain, resembling a giant Easter egg. Inside the mosque, whose lofty dome and semi-domes are decorated like a Fabergé egg, the use of space is classically Ottoman, reminiscent of the great mosques of Istanbul. A constellation of chandeliers and globe lamps illuminates Thuluth inscriptions, a gold-scalloped *mihrab* and two *minbars*, one faced in alabaster, the other strangely Art Nouveau. Mohammed Ali is buried beneath a white marble cenotaph, behind a bronze grille on the right of the entrance. The mosque itself was erected between 1824 and 1848, but the domes had to be demolished and rebuilt in the 1930s.

Due south of Mohammed Ali's Mosque is the entrance to what remains of his **Al-Gawhara Palace**, also known as the Bijou ("Jewelled") Palace, where he waited while the Mamlukes were butchered. Its French-style salons contain a dusty display of nineteenth-century dress, royal furniture and tableware.

Medieval remains

For an idea of the Citadel's appearance before Mohammed Ali's grandiose reconstruction programme, descend from the Mohammed Ali Mosque's front entrance into the Citadel's central courtyard. On your right, at the end of the passage from the southern courtyard, is the **Mosque of Sultan al-Nasir** (also called the Mosque of Ibn Qalaoun, after Al-Nasir's father).

The Mamlukes and the Mongols of Persia enjoyed good relations when the mosque was constructed (1318–35), and a Tabriz master mason probably designed the corkscrew minarets with their bulbous finials and faïence decorations, if not the dome, which also smacks of Central Asia. Since Selim the Grim carted its marble panelling back to Turkey, the mosque's courtyard has looked ruggedly austere, with rough-hewn pillars supporting *ablaq* arches linked by Fatimid-style tie-beams – although the *mihrab* itself is a feast of gold and marble. Notice the stepped merlons around the parapet, and the blue, white and silver decorations beneath the sanctuary *liwan*.

If as you leave the mosque, you turn right and walk clockwise around it, past one of Mohammed Ali's cannons, you can walk up a ramp to one of the Barbicans and along the adjoining rampart. Just below it (and now filled in) is **Joseph's Well**, dug by prisoners between 1176 and 1182. Dubbed "The Well of the Snail", it spiralled down 97m to the level of the Nile, whence water percolated through fissures in the bedrock. Its steps were strewn with soil to provide a footing for the donkeys that carried up water jars.

The Police National Museum

On the northwestern side of the central enclosure, a gate leads through to another courtyard, at whose northern end is the **Police National Museum**. As you pass through the gateway, the door to your right (with a plaque that reads "Citadel's Prison Museum") leads to **cells** that were used when the Citadel was a prison. Famous detainees included Anwar Sadat, arrested by the British for wartime espionage (see p.156), as well as Osama Bin Laden's mentor, Ayman al-Zawahiri. Although the cells are officially closed to the public, police at the entrance may offer to let you in for a look if you show an interest.

The quirky **exhibition** in the museum covers some of Egypt's most sensational murders and assassinations, although the most infamous of all – Anwar Sadat's – is conspicuously absent. The rooms of the main hall, taken clockwise, begin with one on Pharaonic Egypt, including weapons of the time and an explanation of the conspiracy to assassinate Ramses III. The next room, labelled "Islamic Period", has Ottoman swords, shields and guns and a cartoon of three prisoners from Fatimid times. The next room has a scale model of Ismailiya barracks illustrating the 1952 Battle of Ismailiya (see p.509) that galvanized public opinion against the British occupation. The "Political Assassination" room illustrates three famous political murders, most notably that of British minister Lord Moyne by members of a maverick Zionist paramilitary group, the Stern Gang, in Zamalek in 1944. The next room contains the death mask of murderer Mahmoud Amin Mahmoud Soleiman, and a press for counterfeiting banknotes, which leads into the "Forgery and Counterfeiting" room, whose ancient coins and official seals are all clever fakes.

There is a superb **view** of the entire city from the terrace outside the Police Museum, where you'll also find toilets and a **café**. At the southern end, in a pit, are the excavated remains of the **Qasr al-Ablaq**, or Striped Palace of Sultan al-Nasir. For many of the hapless boy-sultans chosen by the Mamlukes, the palace amounted to a luxury prison, and finally an execution cell. Nevertheless, the Citadel remained the residence of Egypt's rulers for nearly seven hundred years.

Mohammed Ali prophesied that his descendants would rule supreme as long as they resided here, and his grandson Ismail's move to the Abdin Palace did indeed foreshadow an inexorable decline in their power.

The Northern Enclosure

Passing through Bab al-Qullah, you'll enter the Citadel's northern enclosure, open to visitors despite a military presence. Straight ahead, beyond a parade of tanks from four Arab–Israeli Wars, is Mohammed Ali's old Harim Palace, now a **Military Museum** full of ceremonial accoutrements, with spectacular trompe-l'oeil in the main salon. By turning right at the barracks near the enclosure entrance and following the lane around, you'll emerge into the **Garden Museum**, a formal garden decorated with assorted columns, gateways, and the top of a minaret from the mosque of Qaitbey al-Jatkasi.

To its south is a **Carriage Museum**, boasting six royal carriages and two picnic buggies (one an infant prince's); the largest state carriage was a gift to Khedive Ismail by Napoleon and his wife, Empress Eugénie.

The bastions on the other side of these buildings, along the Citadel's ramparts, carry evocative names. Although the derivation of **Burg Kirkilyan** (Tower of the Forty Serpents) is unknown, the **Burg al-Matar** (Tower of the Flight Platform, nowadays used to mean an airport flight tower) probably housed the royal carrier pigeons. Neither can be entered, but it's worth visiting a neglected treasure at the other end of the compound. A cluster of verdigris domes and a pencil-sharp minaret identify the **Mosque of Suleyman Pasha** as an early sixteenth-century Ottoman creation, borne out by the lavish arabesques and rosettes adorning the interior of the cupola and semi-domes. Inside, cross the courtyard to find a **mausoleum** where the tombs of amirs and their families have *tabuts* indicating their rank: turbans or hats for the men, floral-patterned *lingam*-like rods for the women. Adjacent to the courtyard is a **madrassa** where students took examinations beneath a *riwaq* upheld by painted beams.

Midan Salah al-Din

Humdrum traffic islands and monumental grandeur meet beneath the Citadel on **Midan Salah al-Din**, where makeshift swings and colourful tents are pitched for local moulids. The tents have a long pedigree: in 1517, when they took Cairo, the victorious Ottomans set up three large marquees in the square, to supply their troops with, respectively, beer, hashish and young boys. A bevy of small mosques around the square set the scene for a vocal confrontation of its two behemoths, the **Rifai** and **Sultan Hassan mosques**, five times daily when their powerfully-voiced muezzins call the faithful to prayer, their cacophanous duet echoing off the surrounding tenements. This amazing aural experience is best enjoyed from one of the seats on the sidewalk outside the **Shorouk coffee shop**, on the corner of Sharia Sultan Hassan and Sharia Qalaa; check prayer times in the newspapers or by asking around. From this vantage point you can survey both mosques, built so close as to create a knife-sharp, almost perpetually shadowed canyon between them. The dramatic angles and chiaroscuro, coupled with the great stalactite portal on this side of the Rifai, make this facade truly spectacular, although the view from the Citadel itself takes some beating. A few centuries ago, all this area would have been swarming with mounted Mamlukes, escorting the sultan to polo matches or prayers.

The Mosque of Sultan Hassan

Raised at the command of a son of Al-Nasir, the **Mosque of Sultan Hassan** (daily except Fri 8am–4.30pm, Fri 8–10am & 3–4.30pm; tickets from a booth between the Sultan Hassan and Rifai mosques, £E25, students £E15) was unprecedentedly huge in scale when it was begun in 1356, and some design flaws soon became apparent. The plan to have a minaret at each corner was abandoned after the one directly above the entrance collapsed, killing three hundred people. Hassan himself was assassinated in 1391, two years before the mosque's completion. After another minaret toppled in 1659, the weakened dome collapsed; and if this wasn't enough, the roof was also used as an artillery platform during coups against sultans Barquq (1391) and Tumanbey (1517). But the mosque is big enough to withstand a lot of battering: at 150m in length, it covers an area of 7906 square metres, with walls rising to 36m and its tallest minaret to 68m.

The mosque is best seen when the morning sun illuminates its deep courtyard and cavernous mausoleum, revealing subtle colours and textures disguised by shadows later in the day. Entering beneath a towering stalactite hood, you're drawn by instinct through a gloomy domed vestibule with *liwans*, out into the central **sahn** – a stupendous balancing of mass and void. Vaulted **liwans** soar on four sides, their height emphasized by hanging lamp chains, their maws by red-and-black rims, all set off by a bulbous-domed ablutions fountain (probably an Ottoman addition). Each *liwan* was devoted to teaching a rite of Sunni Islam, providing theological justification for the cruciform plan the Mamlukes strove to achieve regardless of the site. At Sultan Hassan, four *madrassa*s have been skilfully fitted into an irregular area behind the *liwans* to maintain the internal cruciform.

Soft-hued marble inlay and a band of monumental Kufic script distinguish the sanctuary *liwan* from its roughly plastered neighbours. To the right of the *mihrab* is a bronze door, exquisitely worked with radiating stars and satellites in gold and silver; on the other side is **Hassan's mausoleum**, cleverly sited to derive *baraka* from prayers to Mecca while overlooking his old stomping grounds. The mausoleum is sombre beneath its restored dome, upheld by stalactite pendentives. Around the chamber runs a carved and painted Thuluth inscription, from the Throne verse of the Koran. Note also the ivory-inlaid *kursi*, or koranic lectern.

The Rifai and Amir Akhur mosques

Adjoining Sultan Hassan, the **Rifai Mosque** (daily except Fri 8am–4.30pm, Fri 8–10am & 3–4.30pm; tickets from the same booth as the Sultan Hassan Mosque, £E25, students £E15) is pseudo-Mamluke, built between 1869 and 1912 for Princess Khushyar, the mother of Khedive Ismail. With the royal entrance now closed, you enter on the side facing Sultan Hassan. Straight ahead in a sandalwood enclosure lies the **tomb of Sheikh Ali al-Rifai**, founder of the Rifai *tariqa* of dervishes, whose moulid occurs during Gumad el-Tani (see p.198). Off to your left are the *mashrabiya*-screened **tombs of King Fouad** (reigned 1917–36), his mother, the last **Shah of Iran** and **King Farouk** of Egypt (who likewise died in exile). The monumental sanctuary (on the left) is impressive, but after Ismail's chief eunuch had overseen its forty-four columns, nineteen types of marble, eighteen window grilles costing £E1000 apiece, and £E25,000 dispersed on gold leaf, dowdiness was scarcely possible: what it lacks is the power of simplicity embodied by the mosques of Ibn Tulun and Sultan Hassan.

Finally, facing the Citadel, you can't miss the **Mosque of Amir Akhur** (on the left), with its bold red-and-white *ablaq*, breast-like dome and double minaret finial, incorporating a *sabil-kuttab* at the lower end of its sloping site.

The Mosque of Ibn Tulun and the Saiyida Zeinab quarter

Two aspects of Islam are strikingly apparent in the great **Mosque of Ibn Tulun** and the quarter of the city named after Egypt's beloved saint, **Saiyida Zeinab**.

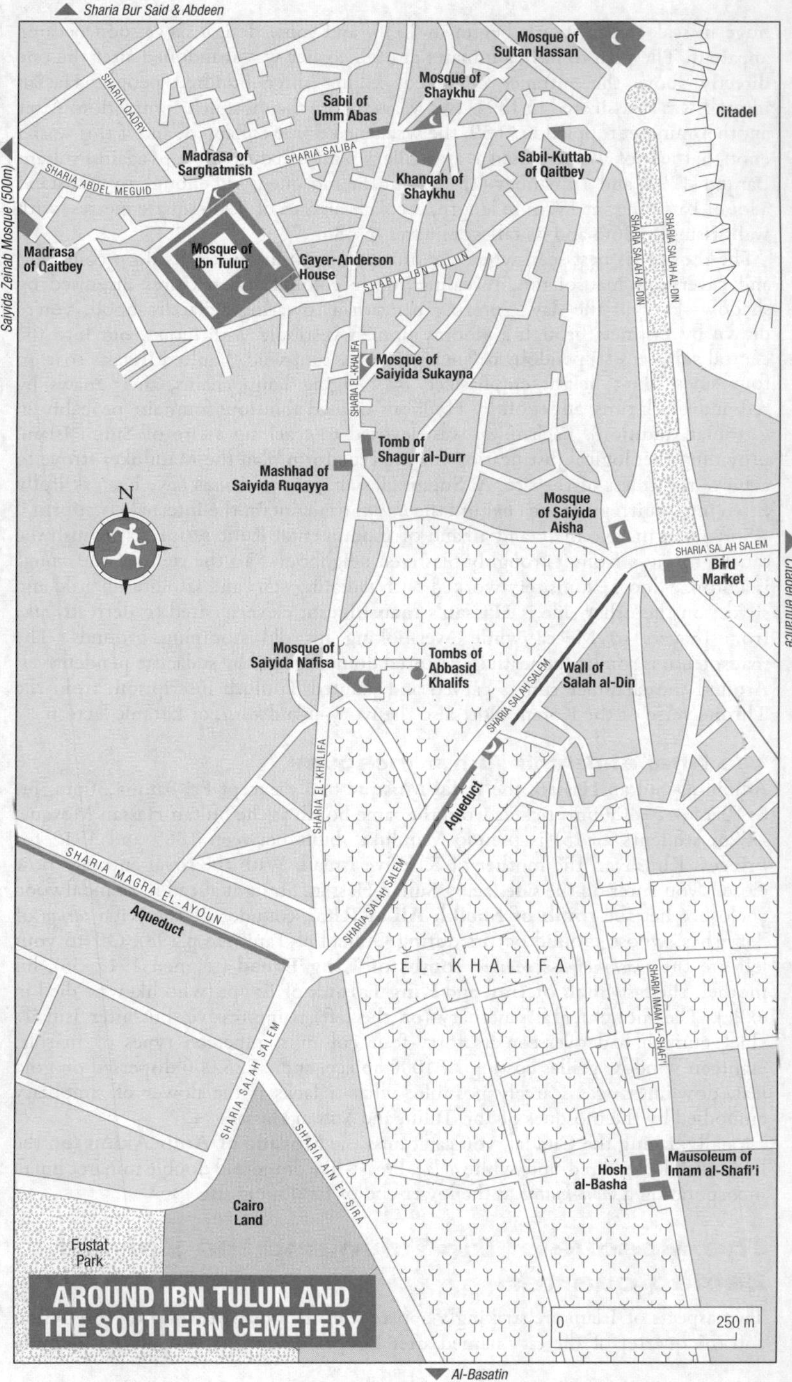
Sharia Bur Said & Abdeen
Mosque of Sultan Hassan
Citadel
Mosque of Shaykhu
Sabil of Umm Abas
SHARIA QADRY
Madrasa of Sarghatmish
SHARIA SALIBA
Sabil-Kuttab of Qaitbey
Khanqah of Shaykhu
SHARIA ABDEL MEGUID
Saiyida Zeinab Mosque (500m)
Madrasa of Qaitbey
Mosque of Ibn Tulun
Gayer-Anderson House
SHARIA IBN TULUN
SHARIA SALAH AL-DIN
Mosque of Saiyida Sukayna
SHARIA EL-KHALIFA
Tomb of Shagur al-Durr
Mashhad of Saiyida Ruqayya
N
Mosque of Saiyida Aisha
SHARIA SALAH SALEM
Bird Market
Citadel entrance
Mosque of Saiyida Nafisa
Tombs of Abbasid Khalifs
Wall of Salah al-Din
SHARIA SALAH SALEM
Aqueduct
SHARIA EL-KHALIFA
SHARIA MAGRA EL-AYOUN
Aqueduct
SHARIA SALAH SALEM
EL-KHALIFA
SHARIA IMAM AL-SHAFI'I
SHARIA SALAH SALEM
SHARIA AIN EL-SIRA
Mausoleum of Imam al-Shafi'i
Hosh al-Basha
Cairo Land
Fustat Park
AROUND IBN TULUN AND THE SOUTHERN CEMETERY
0
250 m
Al-Basatin

The mosque evokes the simplicity of Islam's central tenet, submission to Allah, whereas the surrounding neighbourhoods are urban stews seething with popular cults. **Zeinab's moulid** is the wildest festival in Cairo, its high-octane blend of intense devotion and sheer enjoyment also characteristic of other moulids honouring Saiyida Nafisa, Ruqayya and Aisha, whose shrines lie between Ibn Tulun and El-Khalifa (the Southern Cemetery).

The following section covers only Ibn Tulun, Saiyida Zeinab and sites along Sharia Saliba. You could conceivably visit all of them in a single day. Buses #72// and #160/ provide the easiest access to Saiyida Zeinab **from Midan Tahrir**, running through the quarter past its namesake shrine and within sight of Ibn Tulun's Mosque, towards the Citadel, and on to the Mausoleum of Al-Shafi in the Southern Cemetery. Alternatively, ride the metro to Saiyida Zeinab station, five minutes' walk from Midan Saiyida Zeinab at the heart of the quarter, or take bus #840 **from Midan Ataba**.

Along Sharia Saliba

The fifteen-minute walk from the Mosque of Sultan Hassan to Ibn Tulun takes you along **Sharia Saliba**, past a prison that serves as a barometer of law and order: whenever there's been a crackdown you can see several arms thrust from each cell window. Next comes the lofty **Sabil-Kuttab of Qaitbey**, with its bold red, white and black facade, now beautifully restored and housing an Islamic Civilization Library. Further along, beyond the **Khanqah of Shaykhu**, Sharia el-Khalifa turns off towards the Southern Cemetery (see p.133). By ignoring this and carrying on past the nineteenth-century **sabil of Um Abbas**, with its blue-and-red panels and gilt calligraphy, you'll see the huge walls of Ibn Tulun's Mosque on the left. Its entrance is that way, too.

The portal on the main street belongs not to Ibn Tulun but to the neighbouring **Madrassa of Sarghatmish**. Its courtyard, resplendent in white marble inlaid with red, black and green porphyry, is absolutely stunning, with a cool, light feel that makes a pleasant change from the rather heavy architecture of Cairo's classic mosques. It centres around a fountain surmounted with an *oba* (canopy), and surrounded by the cell-like quarters formerly used by its students. The Sarghatmish who had the *madrassa* built, a Mamluke commander assassinated on the orders of Sultan Hassan in 1358, is interred in a chamber adjoining the courtyard.

The Mosque of Ibn Tulun

Ibn Tulun's Mosque (daily 8am–4.30pm; free) is a rare survivor of the classical Islamic period of the ninth and tenth centuries, when the Abbasid caliphs ruled the Muslim world from Iraq. Their purpose-built capital, Samarra, centred upon a congregational mosque where the entire population assembled for Friday prayer, and this most likely provided the inspiration for the Ibn Tulun. You enter the mosque via a **ziyada**, or enclosure, designed to distance the mosque from its surroundings; to the left stands the Gayer-Anderson House (see p.132). It's only within the inner walls that the vastness of the mosque becomes apparent: the courtyard is 92m square, while the complex measures 140m by 122m.

Besides its sheer size, the **mosque** impresses by its simplicity. Ibn Tulun's architects understood the power of repetition – see how the merlons echo the rhythm of the arcades – and also restraint: small floral capitals and stucco rosettes seem at first glance to be the only decorative motifs. Beneath the arcades you'll find a sycamore-wood frieze over 2km long, relating roughly one-fifth of the Koran in Kufic script. The severely geometric ablutions fountain, an inspired focal point, was added in the thirteenth century, when the *mihrab* was also jazzed up with marble and glass mosaics – the only unsuccessful note in the complex.

▲ Mosque of Ibn Tulun

The **minaret** (entered from the mosque's outer courtyard) is unique for its exterior spiral staircase, which gives the structure a helical shape. Supposedly, Ibn Tulun twisted a scrap of paper into a spiral, and then justified his absent-minded deed by presenting it as the design for a minaret. But the great minaret at Samarra (itself influenced by ancient Babylonian ziggurats) seems a likelier source of inspiration. Expect to pay baksheesh to climb the minaret, and for looking after your shoes or providing shoe covers, but resist excessive demands, especially if you are told (falsely) that they are official charges.

The Gayer-Anderson House

From the *ziyada* of the Ibn Tulun Mosque, a sign directs you to the **Gayer-Anderson House** (daily 9am–7.30pm; £E35, students £E20, video camera £E20), otherwise known as the Beit al-Kritiliya ("House of the Cretan Woman"), which abuts the southeast corner of the mosque.

Gayer-Anderson was a retired British major who, during the 1930s and 1940s, refurbished two mansions dating from the sixteenth and eighteenth centuries, filling them with Oriental bric-a-brac. **Tours** of the house (the buildings are linked by a passage on the third floor) feature Persian, Chinese and Queen Anne rooms, and an amazing guest bedroom named after Damascus, whence its opulent panelling originated. It's possible to sneak through a camouflaged *dulab* (wall cupboard) into the screened gallery overlooking the *salamlik*, as women did in olden days. With its polychrome fountain, decorated ceiling and kilim-covered pillows, this is the finest reception hall left in Islamic Cairo, and served as the set for a tryst and murder in the James Bond film *The Spy Who Loved Me*.

Cities of the Dead

It's thought that at least 500,000 Cairenes live amid the **Cities of the Dead**, two vast cemeteries that stretch away from the Citadel to merge with newer shantytowns below the Muqattam. The Southern Cemetery, sprawling to the southeast of Ibn Tulun's mosque, is only visible from the Muqattam, or at close quarters.

The Northern Cemetery, by contrast, is an unforgettably eerie sight, with dozens of mausoleums rising from a sea of dwellings along the road from Cairo Airport.

Although tourists generally – and understandably – feel uneasy about viewing the cemeteries' splendid **funerary architecture** with squatters living all around or in the tombs, few natives regard the Cities of the Dead as forbidding places. Egyptians have a long tradition of building "houses" near their ancestral graves and picnicking or even staying there overnight; other families have simply occupied them. By Cairene standards these are poor but decent neighbourhoods, with shops, schools and electricity, maybe even piped water and sewers. The saints buried here provide a moral touchstone and *baraka* for their communities, who honour them with **moulids**.

Though these are generally not dangerous quarters, it's best to exercise some caution when **visiting**. Don't flaunt money or costly possessions, and be sure to dress modestly; women should have a male escort, and will seem more respectable if wearing a headscarf. You'll be marginally less conspicuous on Fridays, when many Cairenes visit their family plots; but remember that mosques can't be entered during midday prayers. At all events, leave the cemeteries well before dark, if only to avoid getting lost in their labyrinthine alleys – and don't stray to the east into the inchoate (and far riskier) slums built around the foothills of the Muqattam.

The Southern Cemetery

The older and larger **Southern Cemetery** – known to Egyptians as "the Great Cemetery" (Al-Qarafah al-Kubra) – is broadly synonymous with the residential quarter of **El-Khalifa**, named after the Abbasid caliphs buried amid its mud-brick tenements. The area has become a hotspot for hard drugs and is best avoided after dark. Although the Abbasid tombs aren't half as imposing as those of the Mamlukes in the Northern Cemetery, one of the approach routes passes several shrines famous for their moulids. Another moulid is held at the beautiful **Mausoleum of Imam al-Shafi'i**, which is best reached by bus as a separate excursion.

Sharia Saliba to the Tomb of the Abbasid Khalifs

The route from Sharia Saliba into the southern cemetery passes through one of the oldest poor neighbourhoods in Cairo, where it's thought that people started settling around their saints' graves as early as the tenth century. None of the tombs is remarkable visually, but the stories and moulids attached to them are interesting. The trail begins where **Sharia el-Khalifa** turns south off Sharia Saliba, just after the Khanqah of Shaykhu (see map, p.130). This narrow street passes a succession of tombs. The second on the left, within a yellow-and-white mosque, is that of **Saiyida Sukayna**, a great-granddaughter of Mohammed, whose **moulid** (held during Rabi el-Tani) is attended by several thousand people and features traditional entertainments such as dancing horses and stick-twisters.

Such saintly graves invariably acquired an oratory (*mashhad*) or mosque, unlike the **Tomb of Shagar al-Durr**, 100m further on, a derelict edifice sunk below street level. Shagar al-Durr (Tree of Pearls) was the widow of Sultan Ayyub, who ruled as sultana of Egypt for eighty days (1249–50) until the Abbasid caliph pronounced "Woe unto nations ruled by a woman". This compelled her to marry Aybak, the first Mamluke sultan, and govern "from behind the *mashrabiya*". In 1257 she ordered Aybak's murder after learning that he sought another wife, but then tried to save him; the assassins cried, "If we stop halfway through, he will kill both you and us!" Rejecting her offer to marry Qutuz, their new leader, the Mamlukes handed Shagar al-Durr over to Aybak's former wife, whose servants beat her to death with bath clogs and threw her body to the jackals.

Slightly further down and across the street, the **Mashhad of Saiyida Ruqayya** commemorates the stepsister of Saiyida Zeinab, with whom she came to Egypt; the name of her father, Ali, adorns its rare Fatimid *mihrab*, and the devotion she inspires is particularly evident during Ruqayya's moulid.

Ruqayya's devotion doesn't, however, compare with that accorded to the **Mosque of Saiyida Nafisa**, 100m to the south, by a roundabout planted with grass and flowers. This, Egypt's third-holiest shrine, is closed to non-Muslims, though visitors can still appreciate the good-natured crowd that hangs around after Friday noon prayers, or during Nafisa's **moulid** (see p.198). Honoured during her lifetime as a descendant of the Prophet, and a *hafizat al-Qur'an* (one who knows the Koran by heart), Nafisa was famed for working miracles and conferring *baraka*. Her shrine has been repeatedly enlarged since Fatimid times – the Southern Cemetery possibly began with devotees settling or being buried near her grave – and the present mosque was built in 1897.

If you walk down the alley to its left, and through the passage beyond, a green-painted gate to the right (just before the street turns) leads to a compound enclosing the **Tombs of the Abbasid Caliphs** (in principle open daily 9am–5pm; the caretaker will let you in for a small consideration if he happens to be around). Having been driven from Baghdad by the Mongols, the caliphs gratefully accepted Beybars' offer to re-establish them in Egypt, only to discover that they were mere puppets. Beybars appropriated the domed mausoleum (usually kept locked) for his own sons; the caliphs were buried outdoors in less than grandiose tombs. Notice the beautiful foliate Kufic inscription on the cenotaph of Khadiga, under the wooden shed. In 1517 the last Abbasid caliph was formally divested of his office, which the Ottomans assumed in 1538 and Ataturk abolished in the 1920s.

An alternative route back towards the Citadel passes the **Mosque of Saiyida Aisha**, whose **moulid** occurs during Sha'ban. To get there, retrace your steps to the junction just south of Ruqayya's shrine and take the road leading off to the right. It's roughly 500 metres' walk to Aisha's Mosque. From here, Sharia Salah Salem runs southwest alongside the medieval **Wall of Salah al-Din**, and northeast to the Citadel entrance at Bab al-Gabal, while Sharia Salah al-Din leads north to Midan Salah al-Din. If you happen to be here on Friday, consider making a detour to the **Souk al-Gom'a** (Souk al-Asafeer, also called the bird market because a part of it is dedicated to canaries and budgerigars), an enormous flea market stretching southward from the Salah Salem overpass.

The Mausoleum of Imam al-Shafi'i

The **Mausoleum of Imam al-Shafi'i**, at the southern end of Sharia Imam al-Shafi'i, 2km from the Citadel, is the largest Islamic mortuary complex in Egypt, and is instantly recognizable by its graceful ribbed dome, crowned by a metal boat like a weather vane. It houses the tomb of **Imam al-Shafi'i**, founder of the Shafi'ite school of Islamic law, one of four Sunni schools (*madhab*), and the one whose rulings are followed by most Egyptian Muslims. Born in Gaza in 767 AD, Imam Shafi'i grew up in Mecca and practised law in Baghdad under Caliph Haroun al-Rashid before moving to Cairo, where he eventually died in 820.

The mausoleum was constructed in 1211 on the orders of the Ayyubid sultan Al-Kamil (Salah al-Din's nephew), who was a great propagator of Sunni orthodoxy, like the imam himself. It was the first Sunni monument to be officially commissioned in the city following the demise of the Shi'ite Fatimids fifty years earlier. Within, Al-Shafi'i's teak cenotaph – into which the faithful slip petitions – lies beneath a magnificent dome perched on stalactite squinches and painted red and blue, with gilt designs. The walls are clad in variegated marble, dating from Qaitbey's restoration of the building in the 1480s. Al-Shafi'i's **moulid** (see p.198) attracts many sick and infirm people, seeking his *baraka*. More prosaically, the street leading northwards to the mausoleum from the Al-Basatin quarter is used for scrap, clothing and livestock **markets** every Friday morning.

By walking clockwise around the block in which the Imam's mausoleum is located, you'll find a five-domed complex directly behind it. Inside the courtyard are clumps of cenotaphs decorated with garlands and fronds, topped by a turban, fez or other headdress to indicate the deceased's rank. These constitute the **Hosh al-Basha**, where Mohammed Ali's sons, their wives, children and retainers are buried. The conspicuously plain cenotaph belongs to a princess with radical sympathies, who abhorred ostentation. In a separate room, forty statues commemorate the 470 Mamlukes butchered by Mohammed Ali in the Citadel (see p.126).

You can reach the mausoleum by taxi from Midan Salah al-Din (for about £E7–10), or take bus #81 or #89 from Midan Ataba, or #160 from Midan Ramses, or minibus #154 from Abdel Mouneem Riyad, which turn off Sharia Imam al-Shafi'i 100m short of the mausoleum itself.

The Northern Cemetery

The finest of Cairo's funerary monuments – erected by the Burgi Mamlukes from the fourteenth to sixteenth centuries – are spread around the **Northern Cemetery**. The majority of tourists who venture in from Sharia Salah Salem are content to see three main sites, plus whatever crops up in between, over an hour or so. The opening hours of the monuments in the cemetery seem to change very frequently; some are open until as late as 10pm, while others close at 5pm, but it often seems to depend merely on when the caretaker happens to be around; generally you can access all of them at least between 10am and 5pm but non-Muslims will not be allowed in during prayers.

Aside from catching a taxi (ask for al-*qarafat ash-sharqiyyah* – the Eastern Cemetery – in Arabic), the surest way of **getting there** is to walk from Al-Azhar. This will take around fifteen minutes, following the dual carriageway Bab al-Ghuriyab past university buildings and uphill to its roundabout junction with Salah Salem. Although the tombs of Anuk and Tulbey are among the nearby mausoleums, you might prefer to head 250m north along the highway to the Dirasa bus terminal – also accessible by minibus #102 **from Midan Tahrir** or minibus #10 **from Ramses and Ataba** – and then cut east into the cemetery. That way you start with Qaitbey's Mausoleum, whose ornate dome and minaret are clearly visible. Dirasa can also be reached by service-taxi microbus from Midan Ramses.

Sultan Qaitbey's Mausoleum

Sultan Qaitbey was the last strong Mamluke ruler and a prolific builder of monuments from Mecca to Syria; his funerary complex (depicted on £E1 notes) is among the grandest in the Northern Cemetery. His name means "the restored" or "returned", indicating that he nearly died at birth; as a scrawny lad, he fetched only fifty dinars in the slave market. The rapid turnover in rulers after 1437 accelerated his ascent, and in 1468 he was acclaimed as sultan by the bodyguard of the previous incumbent. His 28-year reign was only exceeded by Al-Nasir's, and Qaitbey remained "tall, handsome and upright as a reed" well into his eighties.

An irregularly shaped complex built in 1474, the **Mausoleum of Sultan Qaitbey** (daily 10am–5pm) is dynamically unified by the bold stripes along its facade, which is best viewed from the north. The trilobed portal carries one's eye to the graceful **minaret**, soaring through fluted niches, stalactite brackets and balconies to a teardrop finial. Inside, the *madrassa liwans*, floors and walls are a feast of marble and geometric patterns, topped by elaborately carved and gilded ceilings,

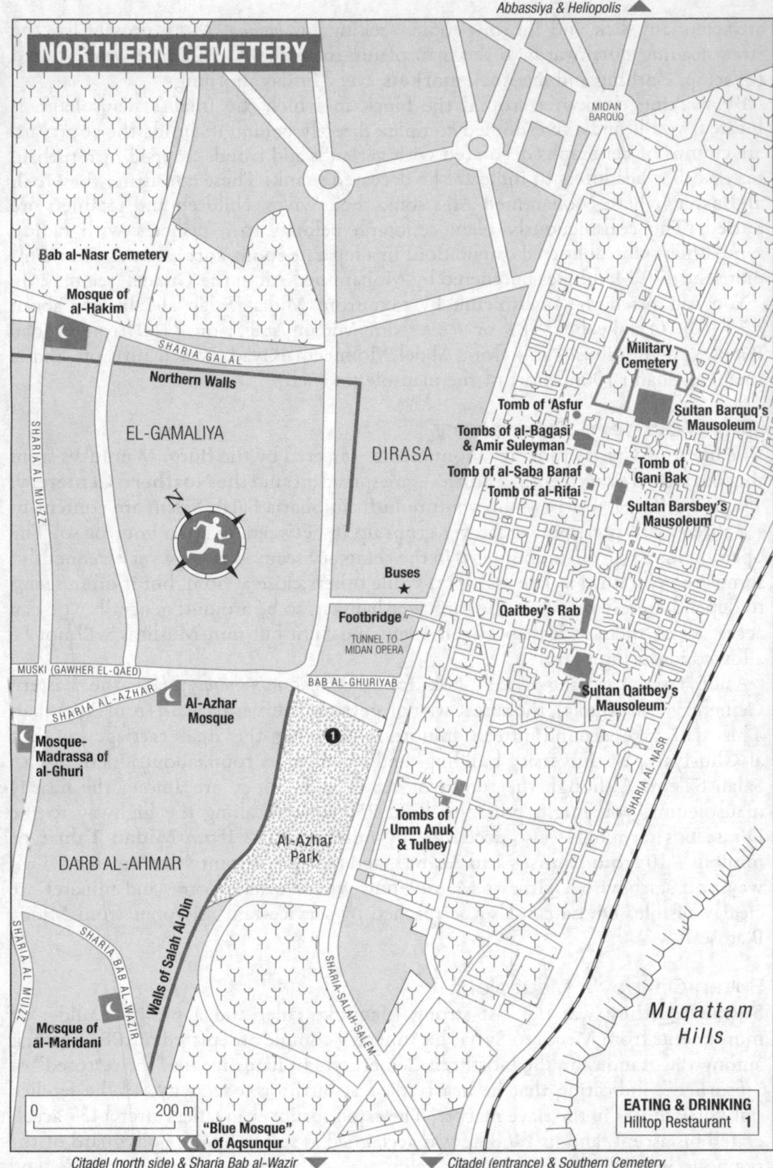

with a lovely octagonal roof lantern. Qaitbey's **tomb chamber** off the prayer hall is similarly decorated, its lofty dome upheld by squinches. One of Mohammed's footprints, brought over from Mecca, is also preserved in the tomb chamber. Ask to climb the minaret for a close view of the marvellous stone carving on the dome's exterior: a raised star-pattern is superimposed over an incised floral one, the two designs shifting as the shadows change. From this minaret vantage point you could also plot a course to Barsbey's complex, further up the narrow, winding street.

The Barsbey and Barquq complexes

As the street jinks northwards from Qaitbey's Mausoleum it passes (on the left) the apartment building that Qaitbey deeded to provide income for the building's upkeep and employment for poor relations. Such bequests could not be confiscated, unlike merchants' and Mamlukes' personal wealth, which partly financed the **Mausoleum of Sultan al-Ashraf Barsbey** (daily 10am–10pm), 200m beyond the building. Barsbey was the sultan who acquired young Qaitbey at a knockdown rate. He himself had been purchased in Damascus for eight hundred dinars, but was "returned to the broker for a filmy defect in one of his blue eyes". Unlike other sultans, who milked the economy, Barsbey troubled to pay his Mamlukes regularly and the reign (1422–38) of this well-spoken teetotaller was characterized by "extreme security and low prices".

Based on a now-ruined *khanqah*, the complex was expanded to include a mausoleum and mosque-*madrassa* (1432) after Barsbey's funerary pile near Khan el-Khalili was found lacking. If there's a curator around, ask him to lift the mat hiding the marble mosaic floor inside the long mosque, which also features a superb *minbar*. At the northern end, a great dome caps Barsbey's tomb, its marble cenotaph and mother-of-pearl-inlaid *mihrab* softly lit by stained-glass windows, added at a later date. The stone carving on the dome's exterior marks a transition between the early chevron patterns and the fluid designs on Qaitbey's Mausoleum. Fifty metres up the street, another finely carved dome surmounts the **Tomb of Gani Bak**, a favourite of Barsbey's, whose mosque stands near the Saddlemakers Bazaar.

The third – and oldest – of the great funerary complexes can be found 50m further north, on the far side of a square with a direct through road onto Sharia Salah Salem. Recognizable by its twin domes and minarets, the **Mausoleum of Sultan Barquq** (daily 9am–10pm) was the first royal tomb in a cemetery that was previously noted for the graves of Sufi sheikhs. Its courtyard is plain, with stunted tamarisks, but the proud chevron-patterned domes above the sanctuary *liwan* uplift the whole ensemble. Barquq and his son Farag are buried in the northern tomb chamber, his daughters Shiriz and Shakra in the southern one, with their faithful nurse in the corner. Both are soaring structures preceded by *mashrabiyas* with designs similar to the window screens in Barquq's *madrassa* on Sharia al-Muizz (see p.115). The sinuously carved *minbar* was donated by Qaitbey to what was then a Sufi *khanqah* (analogous to a monastery); stairs in the northwest corner of the courtyard lead to a warren of dervish cells on the upper floors, long since deserted.

The complex was actually erected by Farag, who transferred his father's body here from the *madrassa*. Farag was crowned at the age of 10 and deposed and killed in Syria after thirteen years of civil strife: it's amazing that the mausoleum was finally completed in 1411.

Depending on your route out, you might pass the minor **tombs of Barsbey al-Bagasi and Amir Suleyman**, or those of **Princess Tulbey and Um Anuk**, nearer Bab al-Ghuriyab and visible from the highway.

Al-Azhar Park

Across Sharia Salah Salem from the northern cemetery, its entrance about 200m south of Dirasa, and 500m north of the Citadel's Bab Gadid, is the new and very welcome **Al-Azhar Park** (daily: summer 9am–midnight; winter 9am–11pm; usually £E5, but £E3 on Tuesdays, £E7 on public holidays). Funded by a US$45m grant from the Aga Khan Trust, the park is part of a regeneration project for the Darb al-Ahmar area, and was built on the site of a filthy and rather dangerous stretch of waste ground, used as a rubbish dump and the haunt of junkies. Now all that has changed: in its place is a scrupulously kept recreational area that has provided local employment and given one of Cairo's most deprived areas a new lease of life. Scattered around the park's lawns and fountains are trees, plants and shrubs from around the world, all labelled, while the western boundary includes a 1300-metre stretch of Ayyubid city wall, most of it newly uncovered during construction of the park, and whose ramparts and bastions will be open to the public when work is complete. The park also contains a lakeside café and a classy **restaurant** (see p.185), and its highest point offers a panoramic view over Islamic Cairo, especially impressive at night when many monuments are illuminated.

Old Cairo and Roda Island

The southern sector of the city is divisible into three main areas, the most interesting of which is **Old Cairo** (Masr al-Qadima). Depending on whether it's broadly or narrowly defined, Old Cairo covers everything south of Garden City and Saiyida Zeinab, or a relatively small area near the Mari Girgis metro station, known to foreigners as "Coptic Cairo". Cairenes themselves distinguish between the general area of Masr al-Qadima and specific localities such as Fumm al-Khalig (where you can see the **Aqueduct** which brought water to the Citadel) or Qasr el-Sham'ah, which was the fortress of **Babylon**, where the Holy Family is thought

Coptic Christianity

While Egypt's **Copts** share a common national culture with their Muslim compatriots, they remain acutely conscious of their separate identity. Intercommunal marriages are extremely rare and bring problems from both sides. **The Coptic church** belongs (along with the Armenian Orthodox and Ethiopian churches) to the Monophysite branch of Christianity, which split from Eastern and Roman Catholic orthodoxy very early on, and the Copts even have their own pope, chosen from the monks of Wadi Natrun. The Coptic Bible (first translated from Greek c.300 AD) predates the Latin version by a century. While Coptic services are conducted in Arabic, portions of the liturgy are sung in the old Coptic language descended from ancient Egyptian, audibly prefiguring the Gregorian chants of Eastern Orthodoxy.

Christianity in Egypt

Tradition holds that **St Mark** made his first Egyptian convert (a Jewish shoemaker from Alexandria) in 45 AD. From Jews and Greeks the religion spread to the Egyptians of the Delta – which teemed with Christian communities by the third century – and thence southwards up the Nile. The Christian faith appealed to Egyptians on many levels. Its message of resurrection offered ordinary folk the eternal life that was previously available only to those who could afford elaborate funerary rituals, and much of the new religion's **symbolism** fitted old myths and images. God created man from clay, as did Khnum on his potter's wheel, and weighed the penitent's heart, like Anubis; Confession echoed the Declaration of Innocence; the conflict of two brothers and the struggle against Satan echoed the myth of Osiris, Seth and Horus. Scholars have traced the **cult of the Virgin** back to that of the Great Mother, Isis, who suckled Horus, and the resemblance between early **Coptic crosses** and pharaonic *ankhs* has also led some to argue that Christianity's principal symbol owes more to Egypt than Golgotha.

Emperor Constantine's 313 AD legalization of Christianity eased matters until 451, when the Copts rejected the decision of the Council of Chalcedon that Christ's human and divine natures were unmixed, insisting that his divinity was paramount. For this **"Monophysite" heresy** (monophysite meaning "single nature") they were expelled from the fold, and persecuted by the Byzantines. Most Egyptians remained to have taken refuge from King Herod. This developed into a powerhouse of native Christianity, and today remains the heart of Cairo's Coptic community. Featuring several medieval churches, the superb **Coptic Museum** and an atmospheric synagogue, it totally eclipses the site of **Fustat** – Egypt's first Islamic settlement, of which little remains but the much-altered **Mosque of Amr**.

Connected by bridge to Old Cairo – and so covered in this section, too – is **Roda Island**, which boasts a venerable Nilometer and the wonderfully kitsch Manial Palace. The Nilometer is best visited in combination with Coptic Cairo, but the palace is more easily accessible from central Cairo.

The Coptic quarter is rapidly accessible by taking the **metro** from downtown Cairo to the **Mari Girgis** station (four stops from Midan Tahrir in the Helwan direction). A **taxi** from downtown Cairo should cost around £E6. **Buses** from Tahrir (#825) and Ramses (#134 and minibus #94) to Amr's Mosque are often packed on the outward journey but fine for getting back. To reach other points, see the directions on p.149 and p.150.

Coptic Cairo

Coptic Cairo recalls the millennial interlude between pharaonic and Islamic civilization and the enduring faith of Egypt's Coptic Christians. Though not a ghetto, the

Christian long after the Arab conquest (640–41) and were treated well by the early Islamic dynasties. Mass **conversions to Islam** followed harsher taxation, abortive revolts, punitive massacres and indignities engendered by the Crusades, until the Muslims attained a nationwide majority (probably during the thirteenth century, earlier in Cairo). Thereafter Copts still participated in Egyptian life at every level, but the community retreated inwards and its monasteries and clergy stagnated until the nineteenth century.

The Copts today

In recent decades the Coptic monasteries have been revitalized by a new generation of well-educated monks, and community work and church attendances are flourishing, but Coptic solidarity reflects alarm at rising Islamic fundamentalism and sectarianism, and the state's policy of trying to placate these by discriminating against non-Muslims. In Egypt religion is recorded on official ID cards (Egyptians may only be Muslim, Christian or Jewish), and it is next to impossible for a Muslim to convert to Christianity – attempting to do brings harassment, death threats and often detention without charge. Meanwhile, there have been several cases of Christian children being abducted and "converted" to Islam, making it extremely difficult for them to return to their original faith. To build or even repair a church requires permission from the local governor, usually denied, and even when given, it often results in sectarian attacks from local Muslims. Egypt's liberal intelligentsia have started to speak out against sectarianism, and it was satirized in a 2008 movie, *Hassan and Morqos*, starring Omar Sharif and Adel Imam, but the liberals are swimming against the tide. All over rural and small-town Egypt, Copts and Muslims are drawing apart; once-mixed communities are becoming polarized, as Copts choose to mix with other Copts, Muslims with other Mulsims. The Coptic diaspora, especially in the US (see ⓦwww.copts.com), rallies international support to counterbalance the Islamist influence at home, but the government is still happy to pander to sectarian sentiment. In 2009, for example, they used the swine flu epidemic as an excuse to slaughter all of the country's pigs and close down all butchers selling pork, despite the fact that swine flu cannot be caught from pigs, and that pigs played a vital role in Egypt's rubbish recycling.

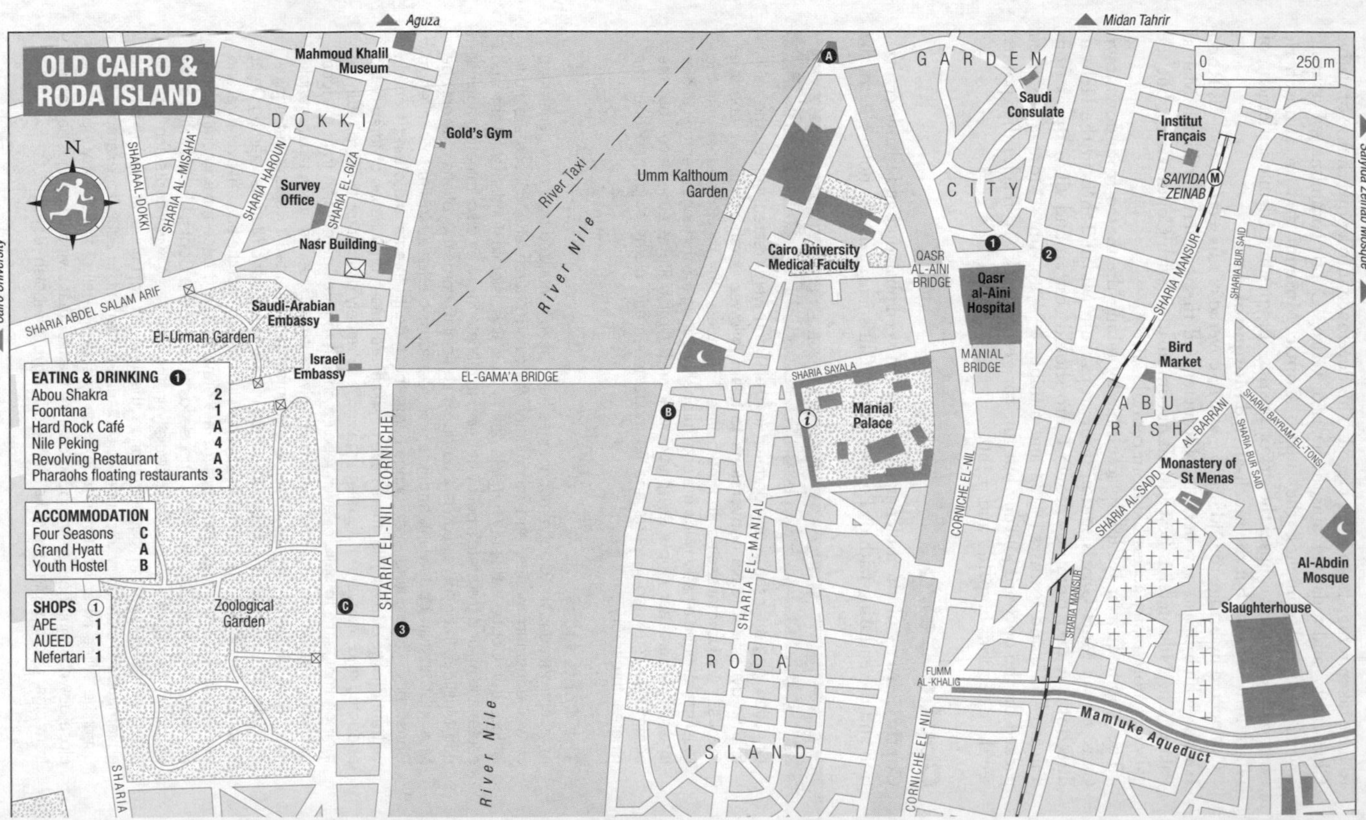
OLD CAIRO & RODA ISLAND
N
0 250 m
Aguza
Midan Tahrir
Saiyida Zeinab Mosque
Cairo University
Mahmoud Khalil Museum
DOKKI
Gold's Gym
River Taxi
River Nile
Umm Kalthoum Garden
GARDEN CITY
Saudi Consulate
Institut Français
SAIYIDA ZEINAB
M
SHARIAAL-DOKKI
SHARIA AL-MISAHA
SHARIA HAROUN
Survey Office
SHARIA EL-GIZA
Nasr Building
Cairo University Medical Faculty
QASR AL-AINI BRIDGE
Qasr al-Aini Hospital
SHARIA MANSUR
SHARIA BUR SAID
SHARIA ABDEL SALAM ARIF
Saudi-Arabian Embassy
El-Urman Garden
Israeli Embassy
EL-GAMA'A BRIDGE
SHARIA SAYALA
Manial Palace
MANIAL BRIDGE
Bird Market
ABU RISH
AL-BARRANI
SHARIA BAYRAM EL-TONSI
Monastery of St Menas
SHARIA AL-SADD
CORNICHE EL-NIL
SHARIA EL-MANIAL
Al-Abdin Mosque
Slaughterhouse
SHARIA EL-NIL (CORNICHE)
Zoological Garden
RODA ISLAND
FUMM AL-KHALIG
Mamluke Aqueduct
SHARIA
River Nile
EATING & DRINKING 1
Abou Shakra 2
Foontana 1
Hard Rock Café A
Nile Peking 4
Revolving Restaurant A
Pharaohs floating restaurants 3
ACCOMMODATION
Four Seasons C
Grand Hyatt A
Youth Hostel B
SHOPS 1
APE 1
AUEED 1
Nefertari 1

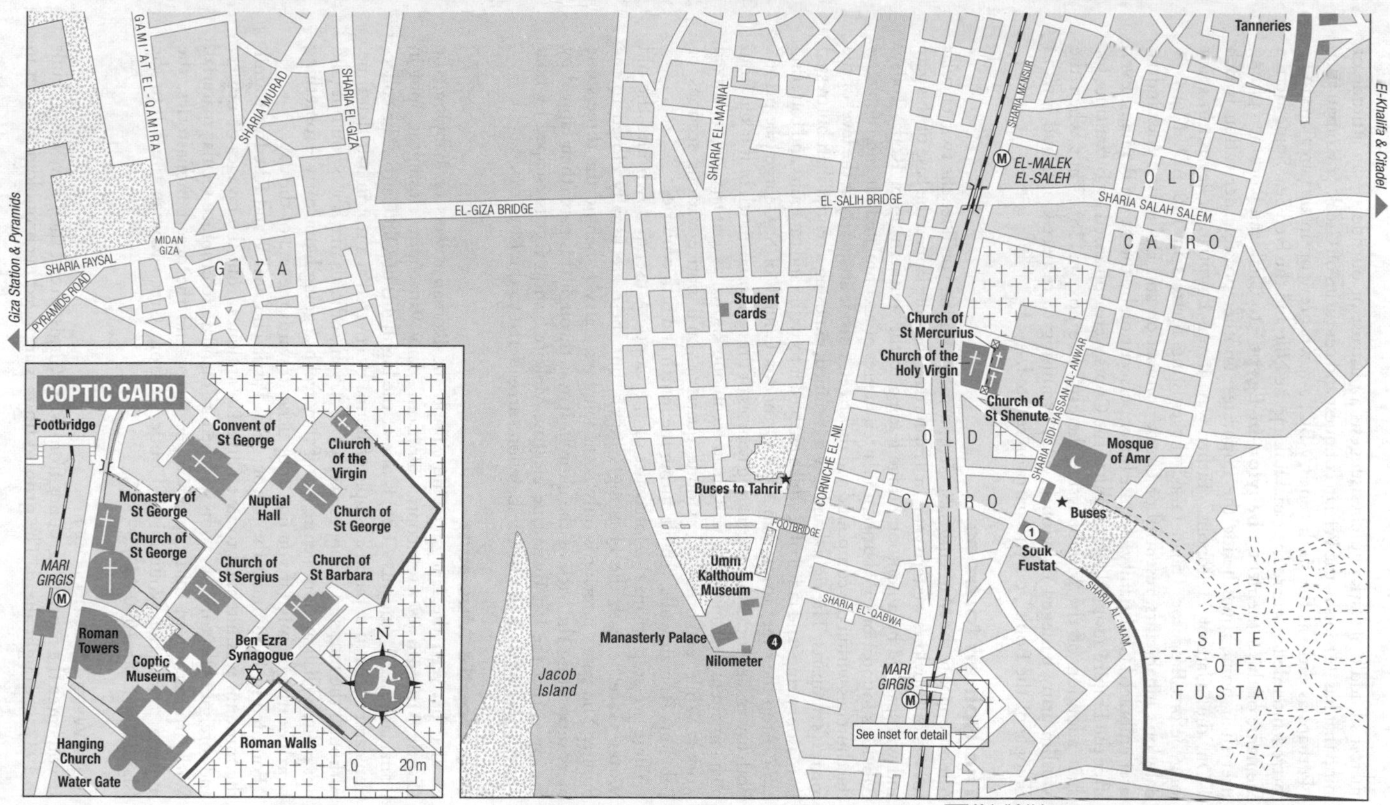
El-Khalifa & Citadel
Giza Station & Pyramids
Ma'adi & Helwan
Tanneries
OLD CAIRO
SHARIA SALAH SALEM
SHARIA MANSUR
EL-MALEK EL-SALEH
EL-SALIH BRIDGE
EL-GIZA BRIDGE
SHARIA EL-MANIAL
GAMI'AT EL-QAMIRA
SHARIA MURAD
SHARIA EL-GIZA
MIDAN GIZA
SHARIA FAYSAL
PYRAMIDS ROAD
GIZA
Student cards
Church of St Mercurius
Church of the Holy Virgin
Church of St Shenute
SHARIA SIDI HASSAN AL-ANWAR
Mosque of Amr
Buses
Souk Fustat
SHARIA AL-IMAM
SITE OF FUSTAT
CORNICHE EL-NIL
Buses to Tahrir
FOOTBRIDGE
Umm Kalthoum Museum
Manasterly Palace
Nilometer
SHARIA EL-QABWA
MARI GIRGIS
See inset for detail
Jacob Island
COPTIC CAIRO
Footbridge
Convent of St George
Church of the Virgin
Monastery of St George
Nuptial Hall
Church of St George
Church of St George
Church of St Sergius
Church of St Barbara
MARI GIRGIS
Roman Towers
Coptic Museum
Ben Ezra Synagogue
N
Roman Walls
Hanging Church
Water Gate
0 20m

quarter's huddle of dark churches suggests a mistrust of outsiders – an attitude of mind that has its roots in the Persian conquest and centuries of Greek or Roman rule.

Perhaps as early as the sixth century BC, a town grew up in this area around a fortress intended to guard the canal linking the Nile and the Red Sea. Some ascribe the name of this settlement – **Babylon-in-Egypt** – to Chaldean workmen pining after their home town beside the Euphrates; another possible derivation is Bab il-On, the "Gate of Heliopolis". Either way, it was Egyptian or Jewish in spirit long before Emperor Trajan raised the existing fortress in 130 AD. Many of Babylon's inhabitants, resentful of Greek domination and Hellenistic Alexandria, later embraced Christianity, despite bitter persecution by the pagan Romans. Even after the Empire adopted Christianity, the Copts were oppressed by Byzantines for their adoption of the Monophysite "heresy" (see box, p.138). Thus when the Muslim army besieged Babylon in 641, promising to respect Copts and Jews as "People of the Book", only its garrison resisted.

The Roman fortress

Almost opposite the Mari Girgis (St George) metro station you'll see the twin circular **towers** of Babylon's western gate. In Trajan's day, the Nile lapped the base of this gate and was spanned by a pontoon bridge leading to the southern tip of Roda. Today, Babylon's foundations are buried under ten metres of accumulated silt and rubble, so the churches within the compound and the streets outside are nearly at the level of the fortress's ramparts. The right-hand tower is ruined, exposing a central shaft buttressed by masonry rings and radial ribs, which enabled it to withstand catapults and battering rams. Atop the other tower stands the Orthodox Church of St George (see p.146). Both towers are encased in alternating courses of dressed stone (much of it taken from pharaonic temples) and brick, a Roman technique known as *opus mixtum* or "mixed work". While exploring the Coptic quarter, you'll notice various sections of Babylon's Roman **walls**, rebuilt during the fourth and fifth centuries.

There are steps from the forecourt of the Coptic Museum down into the old **Water Gate** beneath the Hanging Church, but these are usually closed to the public. The gate's interior is only accessible by a stairway behind the three stone piers supporting the back of the church. It was through this gate (then lapped by the river) that the last Byzantine viceroy, Melkite bishop Cyrus escaped by boat under cover of darkness before Babylon surrendered to the Muslims.

The Coptic Museum

Nestled between the Hanging Church and the Roman towers of Babylon, the **Coptic Museum** (Ⓦwww.coptic-cairo.com; daily 9am–5pm, closing at 3pm in Ramadan; £E50, students £E25) is one of the highlights of Old Cairo. The collection can be seen in detail in a couple of hours, or covered at a trot in half that time. Although the museum is supposed to close at 5pm, officials may shoo you out (and not politely) half an hour before that if they feel like going home early – something worth bearing in mind if you buy your ticket towards the end of the day.

Founded in 1908 under the patronage of Patriarch Cyril V and Khedive Kamil, the museum was intended to save Christian antiques from the ravages of neglect and foreign collectors, but soon widened its mandate to embrace secular material. With artefacts from Old Cairo, Upper Egypt and the desert monasteries, the museum traces the evolution of Coptic art from Greco-Roman times into the Islamic era (300–1000 AD).

New Wing (ground floor)

If you enter the museum grounds from Mari Girgis Street, the **New Wing**, built in 1937, is straight ahead. The **ground floor** is arranged in chronological order in

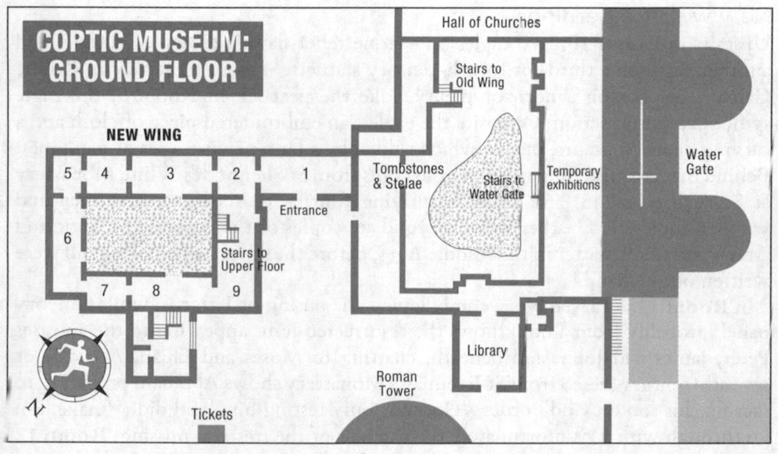

an anticlockwise direction, starting with Room 2 where the exhibits begin (Room 1 is merely the vestibule).

Room 2 kicks off with a fourth- or fifth-century tapestry of (on one side) a piper, possibly African, and (on the other side) people dancing and frolicking. There's also a fresco of saints from the Monastery of St Jeremiah at Saqqara. Amid the shell-shaped cornices in **Room 3**, one relief shows the goddess Aphrodite emerging from a seashell, just as she does in Botticelli's famous painting. Another image of Aphrodite, in the centre of the room, looks almost Indian. Behind her, second-century gravestones still feature the Egyptian gods Anubis and Horus, but in **Room 4** Pharaonic ankhs are transmuted into looped crosses as Christianity begins to take over.

Room 5 displays objects from the **Monastery of St Jeremiah** at Saqqara, as does **Room 6**, which has seven beautiful fresco-painted prayer niches. Some of these depict Jesus holding up a copy of the Bible; others show the Madonna and Child, including two in which Mary is shown breast-feeding the infant Jesus, subtly identifying her with Isis (see box, p.364). In the adjoining **courtyard**, you walk between an avenue of capitals with acanthus leaves and grapevines that mingle with pharaonic palm fronds and lotus motifs, past the earliest known example of a stone pulpit, possibly influenced by the Heb-Sed thrones of Zoser's funerary complex at Saqqara (see p.174).

Three geometric painted panels in **Room 7** (actually a cheap way of imitating a mosaic) kick off the finds from the **Monastery of St. Apollo at Bawit**, near Assyut in Middle Egypt. These continue in **Room 8**, with a series of wonderful fresco-painted prayer niches. The most splendid of these, dating from the sixth or seventh century, depicts Christ enthroned on what appears to be a flaming chariot, surrounded by the creatures of the Apocalypse (eagle, ox, lion and man), and flanked by the archangels Gabriel and Michael. Underneath, the Virgin and Child sit serenely between two phalanxes of saints. In **Room 9**, the finds from Bawit continue with, among other things, a cartoon from the wall of a monk's cell showing three mice – one waving a white flag of peace, and one offering a cup of wine – approaching a cat. It is not clear what the cartoon is meant to represent, but it is reminiscent of the "satirical papyrus" in the Egyptian Museum (see p.102). Directly opposite, a wooden panel shows a haloed monk reaching for a pen from the case hanging on his shoulder (an actual pen case of the same type can be seen in Room 16); in the top-right corner of the panel is a peacock, which was a symbol of resurrection.

New wing (upper floor)

Upstairs in **Room 10**, two eagles on a stone relief flank a crown or rosette, and another eagle on a third- or fourth-century statuette – from right here in Coptic Cairo – perches on a horn of plenty. Like the peacock in Room 9, the eagle symbolizes resurrection. Opposite the eagles, an embroidered piece of cloth and a carving depict centaurs, one of which ridden by a faun playing a set of pan pipes. Behind that is a glistening trove of gold coins from St Shenoudi's White Monastery at Sohag (see p.245) and a case displaying fourth- to sixth-century linen and woollen tunics, and leather shoes. Beyond are copies of the gospels in Coptic and Arabic, no small matter in the Middle Ages, before the advent of printing: all were written out by hand.

In **Room 11**, a carved ivory comb depicts the raising of Lazarus, while an ivory panel (probably from a box) shows the resurrected Jesus appearing to the apostles Peter, James and John, and beneath, chatting to Moses and Elijah. A sixth- or seventh-century fresco from St Jeremiah's Monastery shows Abraham preparing to sacrifice his son on God's orders (God was only testing him, and didn't make him go through with it); unfortunately the top half of the fresco is missing. **Room 12** jumps to the nineteenth century with some liturgical vestments, but we're back in the fourth and fifth centuries in **Room 13**, whose tapestries and embroideries include a very small one of Hercules feeding a lion. A strip of cloth, also from that period, depicts Aphrodite partying, but the goddess is absent from the neighbouring seventh- or eighth-century black-and-white depiction of much the same scenes. In **Room 14**, the textiles get more colourful and elaborate, and include one in red, blue and other colours featuring dancing animals.

Room 15 is dedicated to the **Gospels of Nag Hammadi**, whose 1200 pages shed light on the development of early Christianity and its mystic tradition. These non-canonical Gospels, mostly translated into Coptic from Greek for local members of the heretical Gnostic church, were probably buried during the purges against Gnostics in the fourth and fifth centuries; farmers unearthed the sealed jar in 1945 (see p.257). Unfortunately only two pages are on show, along with the covers in which the gospels were found. The two pages contain the end of a book

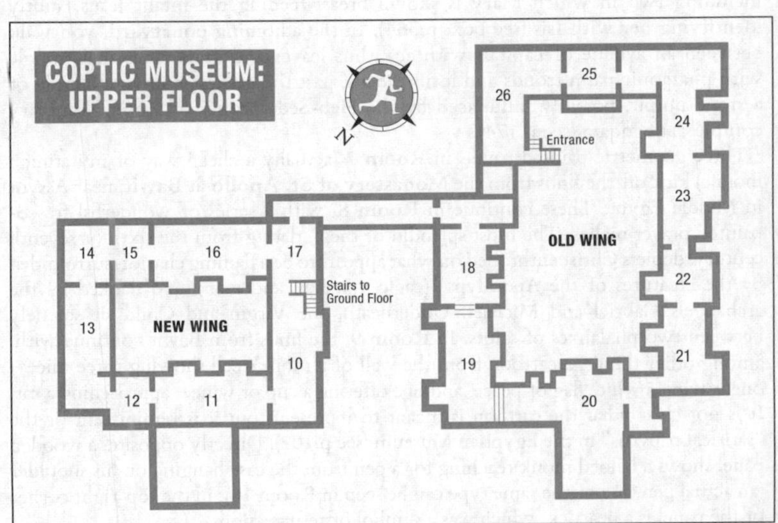

called the Apocryphon of John, and the beginning of the Gospel of Thomas, which may actually be earlier than the official, canonical gospels. Translations of these and other Nag Hammadi gospels can be found on line at ⓦwww.gnosis.org/naghamm/nhl.html.

Into the old wing

The rest of the museum is rather less interesting. **Room 16** has more books, including paper ones from a time before paper was known in Christian Europe, plus inkpots, and a pen sheath similar to the one shown on the wooden panel in Room 9 (see p.143), and ostraca (see p.647) including letters, doodles and orders for grain, mostly on potsherds, but with two on bits of animal bone. **Room 17** has only one exhibit: a fourth- or fifth-century book of Psalms with an ankh-shaped bookmark. You then pass through a corridor to the **old wing**, where **Room 18** has wooden panels carved with Nile scenes including two from the fifth or sixth century that feature crocodiles, still endemic in Egypt at that time. The lovely painted ceiling in **Room 19**, with stained-glass windows, dates from the museum's original construction in 1910, was lovingly restored in 2006, and rather outshines the exhibits, which include some wooden pull-along toys with wheels dating from Byzantine times and a Fayoum-type portrait (see p.102).

Room 20 is dedicated to icons, including a thirteenth-century triptych of Jesus on the cross surrounded by pictures of events (on the left) preceding and (on the right) following his crucifixion. An eighteenth-century image of two saints with the heads of dogs harks back to ancient times, and sits oddly on a Christian icon. Further icons in **Room 21** include one of St Zacharias being throttled to death, and one of John the Baptist holding his own decapitated head on a dish. An eighteenth-century icon on a cloth was a typical souvenir sold to pilgrims in Palestine, which they could roll up and take home. The icons continue in **Room 22**, where one, of St Thomas touching Jesus's stigmata, shows Jesus and the disciples as they probably were – rather swarthier than as usually depicted in European churches. Rooms 23–25 are dedicated to metalware, glassware and ceramics, and Room 26 has an Ottoman litter in which rich female pilgrims were carried to Jerusalem.

You then descend to the courtyard, to pop into the Hall of Churches of Old Cairo, whose prime exhibit is a fifth-century wooden altar from the Church of St Sergius (see p.147) topped by a wooden dome from the Hanging Church (see below), which dates from Fatimid times (tenth to twelfth centuries).

The Hanging Church

Built directly above the water gate, the **Hanging Church** (in Arabic Al-Mu'allaqah, "The Suspended"; daily 9am–4.30pm: Coptic Mass Wed, Fri & Sun 7.30–11am) can be reached via an ornate portal on Mari Girgis street. Ascending a steep stairway, you enter a nineteenth-century vestibule displaying cassettes and videos of Coptic liturgies and papal sermons. Above this are the monks' quarters; beneath it lies a secret repository for valuables, only discovered last century. Through the door and to the right, a glass panel in the floor of the church allows you to see that the church is indeed "suspended" bridge-like, above the water gate.

The main **nave** – whose ceiling is ribbed like an upturned boat or ark – is separated from the side aisles by sixteen pillars, formerly painted with images of saints. Behind the marble pulpit, beautifully carved screens hide three **haikals** (altar areas) from the congregation. Their star patterns, accentuated by inlaid bone and ivory, are similar to those found in mosques. Both pulpit and screens date from the thirteenth century, but the church was founded at least six hundred years earlier and may even have originated in the fourth century as a chapel for the soldiers of the bastion. Among its relics, the church once claimed to own an olive stone chewed by the Virgin Mary, to whom Al-Mu'allaqah is dedicated. The thirteen pillars holding up the pulpit represent Jesus and the twelve disciples: as is customary in Coptic churches, one of the pillars is black, for Judas, and another, perhaps rather unfairly, is grey, for "doubting" Thomas.

The Monastery of St George

Heading north from the Coptic Museum, the first gateway on the right (ignore any demands for cash from "doormen") leads into the precincts of the **Monastery of St George**, now the seat of the Greek Orthodox Patriarchate of Alexandria. The monastery itself rarely admits tourists, but it's worth looking into the neighbouring **Church of St George** (daily 8am–4pm), built in 1904 after a fire destroyed the original tenth-century structure. The only round church in Egypt (it's so shaped because it's built atop one of the old Roman gateway towers), it has a dark interior perfumed with incense and pierced by sunbeams filtered through stained glass. Notwithstanding the church's Greek Orthodox allegiance, its **Moulid of Mari Girgis** (on St George's Day – April 23) is one of the largest Coptic festivals in Cairo.

The Old Quarter

A hundred metres north of the Coptic Museum entrance, steps lead down to a **subterranean gateway** into the oldest part of Old Cairo, whose cobbled lanes flanked by high-walled houses wend between medieval churches and cemeteries. Described as a "constricted slum" by British satirist Evelyn Waugh in 1929, the quarter has been gradually sanitized and tarted up for tourists since the 1970s, and now seems quite spruce compared to Islamic Cairo. The quarter and its churches and synagogue are open daily 8am–4pm.

The Convent of St George

The most interesting of the churches is reached through the first gate on the left after you pass through the subterranean gateway. This is the Coptic **Convent of St George** (Deir Mari Girgis; daily 10am–4pm), whose main building, still a nunnery, is closed to visitors. Underneath however, and usually open to visitors, despite still being under restoration at last check, is a lofty hall that once belonged to a Fatimid mansion. The chapel beyond, with tall, narrow wooden doors, boasts a cedarwood casket containing relics of St George. To the left of this building is the **Chaplet of St George**, a small chapel holding the very chain with which St George was restrained while being tortured by the Romans. Visitors may touch the chain for *baraka*, and the nuns may even offer to wrap it around you for a souvenir photo.

On leaving the convent, turn left and walk on to the end of the lane, where you can turn right for the churches of St Sergius and St Barbara and the Ben Ezra Synagogue, or left to the churches of St George and the Virgin.

The churches of St George and the Virgin

Fifty metres up the alley from the intersection, a doorway on the right leads to yet another **Church of St George**, founded in 681 by Athanasius the Scribe. Of the original foundation, only the Hall of Nuptials survived a conflagration in the mid-nineteenth century, after which the current structure was erected.

Beyond it, at the end of the road, stands the smaller **Church of the Virgin**, also known as Qasriyyat al-Rihan ("Pot of Basil") after the favourite herb of the Orthodox Church. Because Al-Hakim's mother was of that faith, the church was given to the Greek community for the duration of his reign, but later returned to the Copts. Largely rebuilt in the eighteenth century, it's chiefly notable for several icons painted by John the Armenian in 1778.

Church of St Sergius

Heading right from the intersection beyond St George's Convent, you reach, at the next corner, the **Church of St Sergius** (Abu Serga). This is the oldest church in Egypt, its great age attested by its site below modern-day street level. Probably founded in the fifth century, though most of the current building dates from the eleventh, Abu Serga retains the basilical form typical of early Coptic churches. The low ceiling and the antique columns topped with Corinthian capitals support the women's gallery, where you can inspect the thirteenth-century *haikal* screen and bits of frescoes and mosaics in the central apse. Steps to the right of the altar descend into a **crypt** where the Holy Family are believed to have stayed, a sojourn commemorated by a Coptic **festival** (June 1). Unfortunately, the crypt itself is open only for services (Sat 6–7pm). A recently-discovered thirteenth-century painting in the apse of the church's south chapel could not be seen at last check due to restoration work in progress.

From St Sergius, you can wander along to the end of the lane where another thoroughfare leads to the Church of St Barbara (to the left) and Ben Ezra Synagogue (on the right).

Church of St Barbara

The eleventh-century **Church of St Barbara** replaced an earlier Church of Saints Cyrus and John, which was razed during Al-Hakim's assault on Fustat. Unlike others in the quarter, its wooden-vaulted roof is lofty, with skylights and windows illuminating a nave flanked by Arabic arches with Fatimid tie-beams. Its *minbar*-esque pulpit and inlaid *haikal* screen would not look amiss in a mosque. The western sanctuary (remove shoes to enter) contains the relics of Sitt Barbara. Tradition holds that she was the daughter of a pagan merchant who was murdered for preaching Christianity in the third century, but sceptics might note that her belated recognition followed another questionable case (see p.564).

The Ben Ezra Synagogue

Down the road, behind a wrought-iron fence, is the **Ben Ezra Synagogue**, a unique relic of Cairo's ancient Jewish community. Bereft of its former host of worshippers, the synagogue would have crumbled away were it not for the efforts of one "Rabbi" Cohen, who shamelessly overcharged for souvenir postcards to fund repairs for twenty years, until the American Jewish Congress and the Egyptian government stepped in to restore it. Today it is as good as new.

In form, the synagogue resembles a basilical church of the kind that existed here between the fourth and ninth centuries. Sold to the Jews in order that the Copts could pay taxes to finance Ibn Tulun's Mosque, this church was either demolished or incorporated within the synagogue, which Abraham Ben Ezra, the Rabbi of Jerusalem, restored in the twelfth century. The inlaid marble and gilded stalactite niche date from around then, but most of the graceful mouldings and floral swirls are the result of nineteenth-century repairs, which unearthed a huge cache of medieval manuscripts (now dispersed around Western libraries), including a sixth-century Torah written on gazelle hide.

Nevertheless, Jewish and Coptic traditions invest the site with ancient significance. Here, the pharaoh's daughter found Moses in the bulrushes, Jeremiah gathered survivors after Nebuchadnezzar destroyed Jerusalem, and the temple named after him provided a haven for the Holy Family, who lived among the Jews of Babylon for three months. Moreover, the Copts believe that Peter and Mark pursued their apostolic mission in Egypt, whence Peter issued the First Epistle General. The rest of Christendom disagrees, however, arguing that the biblical reference to Babylon (I Peter 5:13) is only a metaphor for Rome.

The Mosque of Amr, Deir Abu'l-Sayfayn, Fustat and the Aqueduct

The Mosque of Amr and Deir Abu'l Sayfayn, plus the western part of Fustat (including its handicrafts souk), can easily be reached on foot from Coptic Cairo. Mari Girgis and El-Malek el-Saleh metro stations are within walking distance, while buses serve the mosque from Midan Tahrir (#825) and Ramses (#134 and minibus #94).

The Mosque of Amr

To get a feel for what happened after Babylon and Egypt surrendered to Islam, return to Mari Girgis Street and follow it northwards, past the turning for Fustat and a small bus depot, to the **Mosque of Amr**, founded by Egypt's Arab conqueror, **Amr Ibn al-As**. Though it was altered several times and doubled in size in 827, this boasts direct descent from Egypt's first-ever mosque, built in 641. A simple mud-brick, thatch-roofed enclosure without a *mihrab*, courtyard or minaret, it was large enough to contain the Muslim army at prayer. The site of the mosque was indicated by Allah, who sent a dove to nest in Amr's tent while he was away at war; on returning he declared it sacrosanct, waited until the dove's brood was raised, then built a mosque.

The existing building follows the classic congregational pattern, arched *liwans* surrounding a pebbled *sahn* centred on an ablutions well. Believers pray or snooze on fine carpets in the sanctuary *liwan*. When Amr introduced a pulpit, he was rebuked by Caliph Omar for raising himself above his Muslim brethren. The *mashrabiya*'d **mausoleum** of his son, Abdullah, marks the site of Amr's house in Fustat. A nearby column bears a gash caused by people licking it until their tongues bled, to obtain miraculous cures. The pair of columns on the left as you come in are said to part to allow the truly righteous to squeeze through, and another was whipped from Mecca by Omar. From the mosque's **well**, it is said, a pilgrim retrieved a goblet dropped into the Well of Zemzem in the Holy City.

Deir Abu'l-Sayfayn

If the Coptic quarter hasn't satisfied your curiosity about medieval churches, pay a visit to **Deir Abu'l-Sayfayn** (daily 9am–5pm), northwest of Amr's Mosque, entered via a door at its southwest corner, on Sharia Ali Salem. Inside, the first church to the right is the early seventh-century **Church of St Shenute** (Anba Shenouda), featuring a beautiful cedarwood and ebony altar screen. Beyond it, the **Church of St Mercurius**, first mentioned in the tenth century (when it served as a sugar-cane warehouse), claims older antecedence, and was totally rebuilt after the burning of Fustat. Beneath its northern aisle you can descend into a tiny crypt where St Barsum the Naked lived with a snake until his death in 317; a special Mass is held here on his name day (September 10).

Across the way, the diminutive, icon-packed **Church of the Holy Virgin** (el-Damshira), originally dating from the seventh century, was destroyed in 785, rebuilt in 809 and restored in the eighteenth century, looking very modern on the outside, and beautifully restored within. It also has a very fine inlaid altar screen, and a cabinet at the back of the anteroom holds some archeological finds, unfortunately unlabelled.

Adjacent to Deir Abu'l-Sayfayn are extensive Protestant and Maronite **cemeteries**, including a military cemetery for Commonwealth servicemen killed in World War II.

Fustat

Behind the Amr Mosque, and stretching all the way to the Citadel, the site of ancient **Fustat** is still partly occupied by rubbish tips and shantytown hovels, but the far side of it (accessible from Sharia Dalah Salem) has been grassed over and landscaped to create **Fustat Park** (see map, pp.140–141; daily 9am–8pm; £E1).

Fustat ("Tent") is the site of Cairo's very first Muslim city, founded by the victorious Arab general Amr Ibn al-As in 640, right by the Roman/Byzantine fortress of Babylon, which had just fallen to his troops. Originally a cluster of tribal encampments around Amr's Mosque, Fustat evolved into a mud-brick beehive of multistorey dwellings with rooftop gardens, fountains, and a piped water and sewage system unequalled in Europe until the eighteenth century. In 750, the last Umayyad Caliph, Marwan II, took his last stand here against the Abbasids, burning the city behind him as he fled to Abu Sir, where he was killed. The Abbasids, Tulunids and Ikhshidids rebuilt Fustat, moving it further to the northeast; a great conurbation known as **Fustat-Masr** was formed, but when the Fatimids moved the administration to their newly-founded city of Al-Qahira, Fustat-Masr's decline began. In 1020, the mad caliph Al-Hakim ordered his troops to sack Fustat-Masr for reasons worthy of Caligula (see p.116). Yet even in 1168, what remained was so vast that Vizier Shawar decided to evacuate and burn it rather than let the Crusaders occupy an unwalled and defenceless old city outside Al-Qahira. Set ablaze with 10,000 torches and 20,000 barrels of naphtha, Fustat smouldered for 55 days.

On the corner of Sharia al-Imam, the road leading down into Fustat, and Sharia Hassan al-Anwar, the relatively new **Souk Fustat** (daily 10am–6pm), showcases handicrafts by local artisans (see p.200).

The Aqueduct

Travelling between Coptic and central Cairo by bus or taxi, you'll catch sight of the great **Aqueduct** that carried water to the Citadel. Originally a mere conduit supported by wooden pillars, it was solidly rebuilt in stone by Sultan al-Nasir in 1311 and subsequently extended in 1505 by Al-Ghuri to accommodate the Nile's westward shift, to a total length of 3405m. River water was lifted by the **Burg al-Saqiyya**, a massive hexagonal water-wheel tower near the Corniche. On its western wall can be seen Al-Ghuri's heraldic emblem and slots for engaging the six oxen-powered water wheels, which remained in use until 1872.

The site of this tower is known as **Fumm al-Khalig** ("Mouth of the Canal"), after the waterway that once ran inland to meet the walls of Fatimid al-Qahira. This Khalig Masri ("Egyptian Canal") supplied most of Cairo's water during Mamluke and Ottoman times, and was also linked to the ancient Nile Delta–Red Sea waterway, re-dug by Amr and Al-Nasir. In an annual ceremony to mark the Nile flood, the dike that separated it from the river was breached, sending fresh water coursing through the city to fill boating lakes near Bab al-Luq and Ezbekiya until the taming of the Nile spelt the end of this practice; in the 1900s the canal was filled in to create Bur Said and Ramses streets.

Roda Island

The narrow channel between **Roda Island** and the mainland is bridged in such a way that the island engages more with Garden City than with Old Cairo – a reversal of historic ties. As the much-rebuilt **Nilometer** suggests, it was the southern end of Roda that was visited by ferries en route between Memphis and Heliopolis, and Roman ships bound for Babylon-in-Egypt. However, Roda reverted to agricultural use as Cairo's focus shifted northeastwards, and nothing remains of the Byzantine fortress that defied the Muslim invasion, nor the vast Ayyubid *qasr* where the Bahri Mamlukes were garrisoned. Its sights are very spread out, and you wouldn't normally visit them together. Manial Palace, at the island's northern end, is most conveniently reached from Garden City, while the Nilometer and Um Kalthoum Museum at its southern end are easiest to get to from Old Cairo.

The closest bridge to downtown leads to the **Grand Hyatt Hotel**, a deluxe five-star job with some of the best views in Cairo. The next crossing, Qasr al-Aini Bridge, leads down to **Cairo University Medical Faculty**. By walking 150m south from here you can reach the palace gates without crossing the Manial Bridge, used by traffic heading for Giza.

The Manial Palace

Built in 1903, the **Manial Palace** (closed for restoration until mid-2010) is a Cairo must. Its fabulously eclectic architecture reflects the taste of King Farouk's uncle, Prince Mohammed Ali, author of *The Breeding of Arabian Horses* and the owner of a flawless emerald that magically alleviated his ill health (so legend has it). Each of the main buildings manifests a different style – Persian, Syrian, Moorish, Ottoman and Rococo – or mixes them together with gay abandon.

Having bought your ticket, make a beeline for the **Reception Palace** just inside the gateway. Its magnificent *salamlik*, adorned with stained glass, polychrome tiles and ornate woodcarving, prepares you for the opulent guest rooms upstairs; the finest is the Syrian Room, which was quite literally transplanted from Damascus. On the stairs you'll notice a scale model of Qaitbey's Mausoleum, made entirely of mother-of-pearl.

Leaving the Reception Palace and turning right, you come upon a pseudo-Moroccan tower harbouring the prince's **mosque**, whose lavish decor is reminiscent of the great mosque of his namesake in the Citadel. Further along, the grotesque **Hunting Museum** features scores of mounted ibex heads, gorgeous butterflies and ineptly stuffed fowl, a hermaphrodite goat, a table made from elephants' ears and a vulture's claw candlestick.

The **Prince's Residence**, deeper into the banyan-shaded garden, is richly decorated in a mixture of Turkish and Occidental styles. The drab-looking building out back contains a long **Throne Hall**, whose red carpet passes life-size royal portraits hung beneath a sunburst ceiling. Around the outside of this hall are the skeletons of the prince's horse and camel, and a stairway to the upper level (often closed). If accessible, visitors can admire the Obsidian Salon and the private apartments of the prince's mother, enriched by a silver four-poster bed from the Abdin Palace. Lastly, signs show the way to the **Private Museum**, a family hoard of manuscripts, carpets, glassware and silver plate, including some huge banqueting trays.

Bus #95 or minibus #58 is the fastest way of getting here from Midan Tahrir (Abdel Mouneem Riyad terminal), and minibus #56 heads here from Ramses; alight on Sharia Sayala, near the palace gates.

The Nilometer and Um Kalthoum Museum

The southern tip of Roda Island features a **museum** dedicated to the life and work of Egypt's most popular singer, **Um Kalthoum** (daily 9am–4pm; £E2). Through audiovisual clips, photos, press cuttings and a filmshow, the museum attempts to recreate the life of this giant of Arabic music (see p.624). Though she died in 1975, her songs, invariably backed by an orchestra of violins, remain massively popular throughout the Arab world. Exhibits include 78rpm wax records, letters from Egyptian and other Arab heads of state including Nasser, Sadat and King Farouk, and, most poignantly, her trademark pink scarf and dark glasses.

In the same compound is the **Nilometer** (daily 9am–4pm; £E15, students £E8). From ancient times into the present century, Egyptian agriculture depended on the annual **flooding of the Nile**. Crop yields were predicted and taxes were set according to the river's level in August, as measured by Nilometers. A reading of 16 *ells* (8.6m) foretold the valley's complete irrigation; significantly more or less meant widespread flooding or drought. Public rejoicing followed the announcement of the Wafa el-Nil ("Abundance of the Nile"), while any other verdict caused gloom and foreboding.

Although the southern tip of Roda has probably featured a Nilometer since pharaonic times, the existing one dates from 861 and its Turkish kiosk is actually a modern replica, built in 1947. Its stone-lined shaft, descending well below the level of the Nile, was connected to the river by three tunnels (now sealed) at different heights – the uppermost is still accessible. Around the shaft's interior are koranic verses in Kufic script, extolling rain as God's blessing; its central column is graduated into 16 *ells* of roughly 54cm each.

The neighbouring **Manasterly Palace** is a Rococo confection dating from 1850. Built as a conference centre, the palace now houses an International Music Center (Ⓦ www.manasterly.com), and is open only for concerts and exhibitions.

Gezira and the west bank

Flowing northwards through Cairo, the Nile divides into channels around the two major islands of Roda and Gezira. **Gezira**, the larger island, is further from the centre than Roda and notably more spacious and verdant than the rest of Cairo. On public holidays, a **fountain** in the middle of the Nile between Gezira and Roda shoots an immense jet of water into the sky. Elevated highways bear cross-town traffic to diverse districts on the **west bank** of the Nile, collectively known as **Giza** and administered as a separate governorate, though transport and utilities are functionally integrated with Cairo's.

Gezira and Zamalek

Gezira (literally "island") dominates the waterfront from Garden City to Bulaq, nearly 4km long, with three sets of bridges spanning the Nile. The southern half is Gezira proper, and includes the **Gezira Sporting Club** (see p.205), laid out by the British Army on land given by Khedive Tewfiq and occupying almost a third of the island. The northern half, **Zamalek**, is full of apartments, villas, offices and embassies, with a Westernized ambiance and nightlife. Both seem so integral to Cairo that it's hard to envisage their absence, yet the island itself only coalesced in the early 1800s and remained unstable until the first Aswan Dam regulated the Nile's flood in the 1900s. For more on the history and architecture of Gezira and Zamalek, check out Samir Raafat's website at Ⓦ www.egy.com/zamalek.

Despite heavy traffic, it's enjoyable to walk across the **Tahrir Bridge** (200m from Midan Tahrir), catching the breeze and watching barges and feluccas on the river. Gaining the island, you can strike 200m northwards past the former *El-Borg Hotel* and turn left down an avenue to reach the Cairo Tower (10min), or follow the traffic heading for Dokki, which brings you to the Cairo Opera House and several museums (5–10min). Alternatively, take a *calèche*, a horse-drawn carriage seating up to five people, on a circuit of Gezira – a short trip, around the Cairo Tower area, will cost around £E40, while a half-hour circuit, all the way round the Gezira Sporting Club, works out at about £E60.

The **6th October Bridge**, high above the Sporting Club, is more of a direct link between Aguza and central Cairo than a viable approach to Gezira (though there are stairs down to both banks of the island).

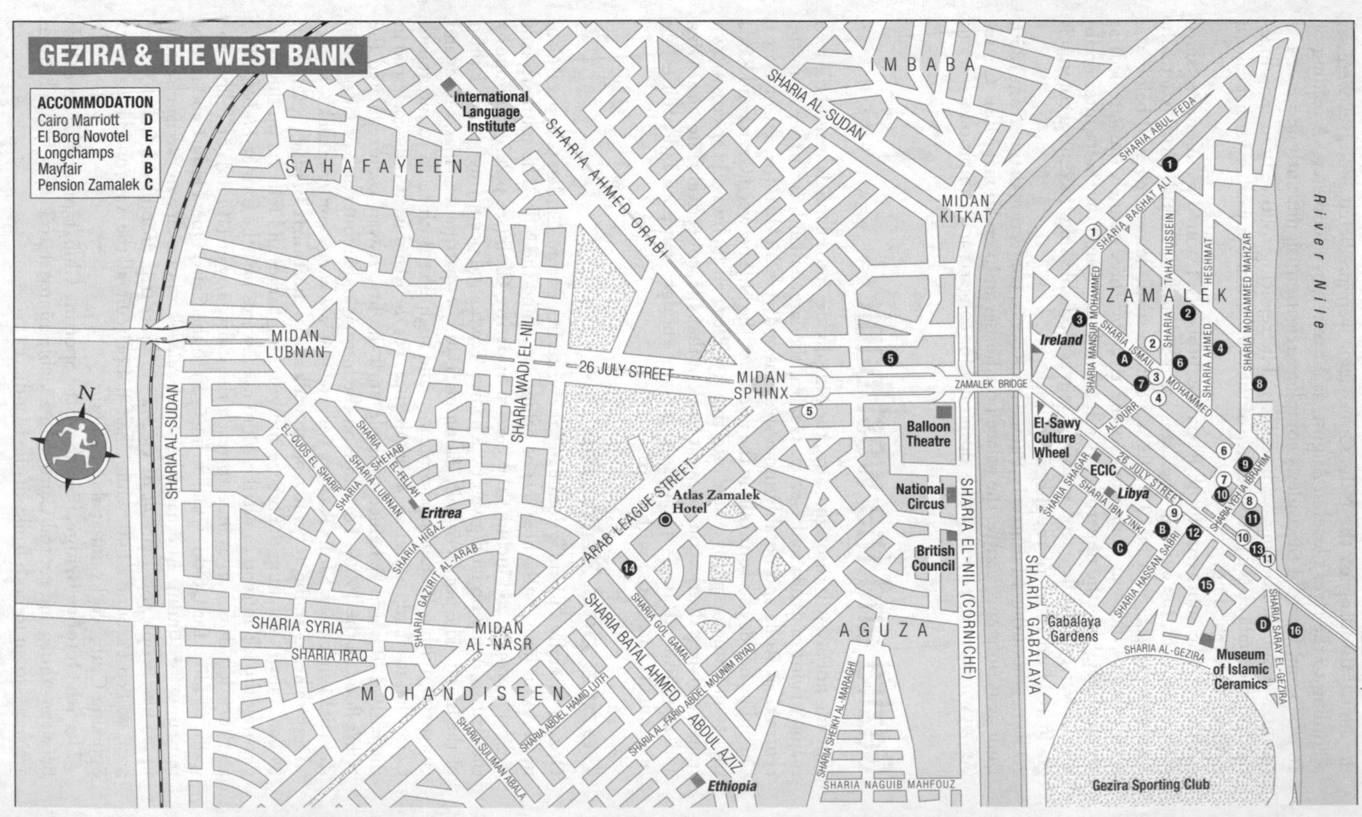
GEZIRA & THE WEST BANK
ACCOMMODATION
Cairo Marriott D
El Borg Novotel E
Longchamps A
Mayfair B
Pension Zamalek C
N
River Nile
Bulaq
IMBABA
ZAMALEK
SAHAFAYEEN
AGUZA
MOHANDISEEN
MIDAN KITKAT
MIDAN LUBNAN
MIDAN SPHINX
MIDAN AL-NASR
SHARIA AL-SUDAN
SHARIA AHMED ORABI
26 JULY STREET
SHARIA WADI EL-NIL
ZAMALEK BRIDGE
SHARIA EL-NIL (CORNICHE)
SHARIA GABALAYA
ARAB LEAGUE STREET
SHARIA BATAL AHMED ABDUL AZIZ
SHARIA SYRIA
SHARIA IRAQ
SHARIA ABUL FEDA
SHARIA BAGHAT ALI
SHARIA TAHA HUSSEIN
HESHMAT
SHARIA MOHAMMED MAHZAR
SHARIA MANSUR MOHAMMED
SHARIA ISMAIL MOHAMMED
SHARIA AHMED
AL-DURR
SHARIA SHAGAR
SHARIA IBN ZINKI
SHARIA HASSAN SABRI
SHARIA YEHIA IBRAHIM
SHARIA AL-GEZIRA
SHARIA SARAY EL-GEZIRA
International Language Institute
Ireland
El-Sawy Culture Wheel
ECIC
Libya
Balloon Theatre
National Circus
British Council
Atlas Zamalek Hotel
Eritrea
Ethiopia
Gabalaya Gardens
Museum of Islamic Ceramics
Gezira Sporting Club
EL-QUDS EL SHARIF
SHARIA SHEHAB
EL-FELLAH
SHARIA LUBNAN
SHARIA HIGAZ
SHARIA GAZIRIT AL-ARAB
SHARIA GOL GAMAL
SHARIA ABDEL MOUNIM RIYAD
SHARIA AL-FARIQ ABDEL
SHARIA ABDEL HAMID LUTFI
SHARIA SULIMAN ABALA
SHARIA SHEIKH AL-MARAGHI
SHARIA NAGUIB MAHFOUZ

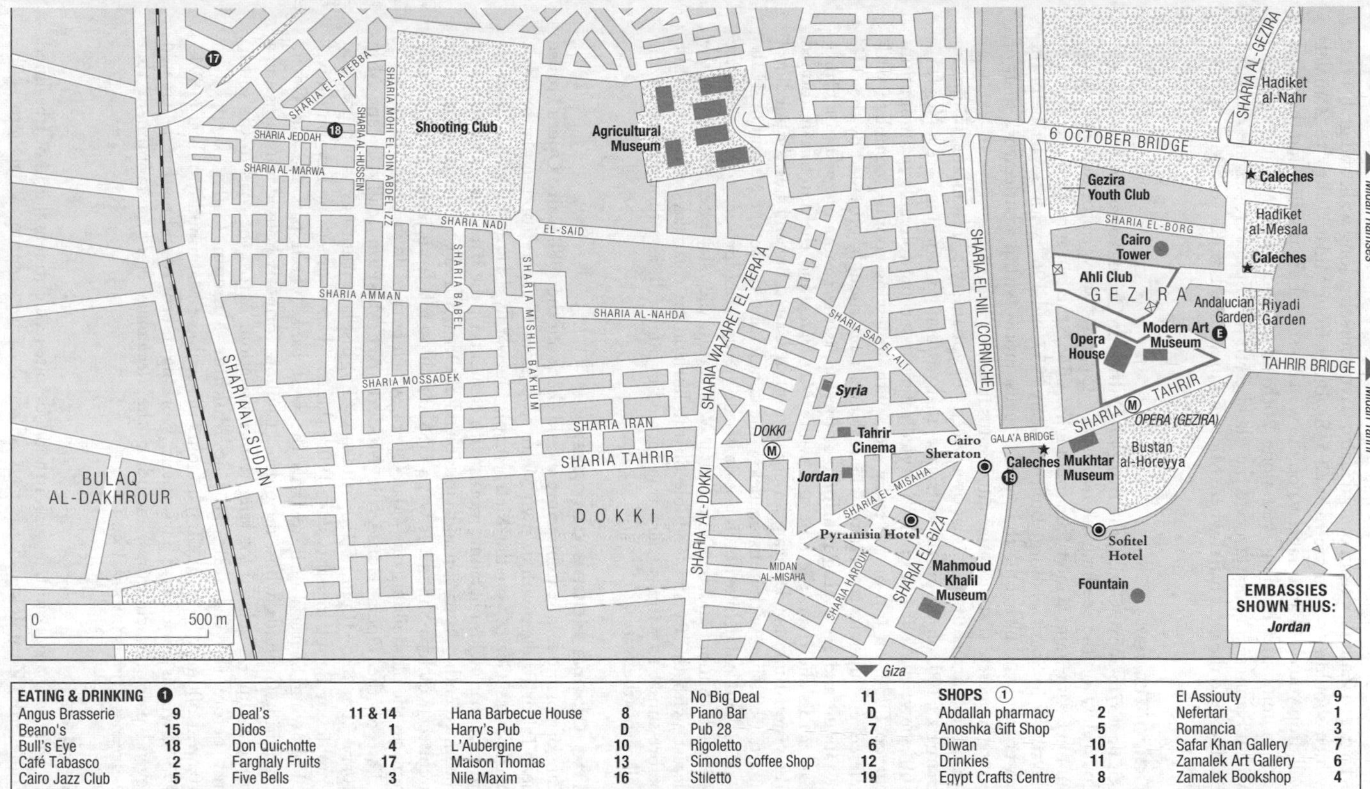

EATING & DRINKING ❶							
Angus Brasserie	9	Deal's	11 & 14	Hana Barbecue House	8	No Big Deal	11
Beano's	15	Didos	1	Harry's Pub	D	Piano Bar	D
Bull's Eye	18	Don Quichotte	4	L'Aubergine	10	Pub 28	7
Café Tabasco	2	Farghaly Fruits	17	Maison Thomas	13	Rigoletto	6
Cairo Jazz Club	5	Five Bells	3	Nile Maxim	16	Simonds Coffee Shop	12
						Stiletto	19

SHOPS ①			
Abdallah pharmacy	2	El Assiouty	9
Anoshka Gift Shop	5	Nefertari	1
Diwan	10	Romancia	3
Drinkies	11	Safar Khan Gallery	7
Egypt Crafts Centre	8	Zamalek Art Gallery	6
		Zamalek Bookshop	4

To get to **Zamalek** from central Cairo, save yourself a long walk and grab a taxi (which shouldn't cost more than £E5–8). Buses from Midan Tahrir to Zamalek will drop you on Sharia Gabalaya on the western side of the district, and there's no lack of minibuses heading west along **26th July Street** from Midan Ataba and Midan Ramses. Having traversed the island, 26th July Street crosses the **Zamalek Bridge** onto the west bank, where Midan Sphinx funnels traffic into Mohandiseen (see p.155).

Cairo Tower

Rising 187m above Gezira, the **Borg al-Qahira** or **Cairo Tower** offers a stupendous view of the seething immensity of Cairo (Ⓦwww.cairotower.net; daily: summer 9am–1am; winter 8am–midnight; £E65); the entrance is to the north of the tower in Sharia el-Borg. Built between 1957 and 1962 with Soviet help, the tower combines pharaonic and socialist realist motifs within a latticework shaft of poured concrete that blossoms into a lotus finial.

On the fourteenth floor is an overpriced "Egyptian-style" restaurant (minimum charge £E100, on top of the entry fee) that – when it's working – revolves for a 360° view; above it is a similarly styled cafeteria serving tolerable tea (minimum charge £E30, on top of the entry fee), with a viewing room – complete with telescopes – upstairs from here. The real attraction, though, provided by the café, restaurant and a **viewing platform** at the top, is the panoramic **vista** of Cairo. East across the river, the blue-and-white *Nile Hilton* and the antenna-festooned Television Building delineate an arc of central Cairo. Beyond lies the medieval quarter, bristling with minarets below the Citadel and the serene Muqattam Hills. Roda Island and deluxe hotels dominate the view south (upriver); to the north are Zamalek, Shubra and the Nile Delta. Westwards, the city extends to meet the desert, with the Pyramids visible on the horizon on clear days. Come a while before sunset to witness Cairo transformed by nightfall, as a thousand muezzins call across the water.

The Opera House complex

Fans of postmodernist architecture should check out the 1988 **Cairo Opera House** near Tahrir Bridge, with its own Metro stop (signed "Opera" on the platform but marked as "Gezira" on the Metro map). Outwardly Islamic in style, it has an interior that melds pharaonic motifs with elements of the Baroque opera houses of the nineteenth century: an audacious blend of Oriental and Occidental by Japanese architect Koichiro Shikida. It was a US$30 million gift from Japan, and belatedly replaces the old building on Midan Opera, which burned down in 1971.

East of the Opera House, the **Modern Art Museum** (daily except Mon 10am–2pm & 5–10pm; £E10, students £E5) displays paintings, sculptures and graphics by Egyptian artists since 1908; there is always something new on show.

Following Sharia Tahrir towards the west bank, you'll pass the old Gezira Exhibition Grounds, whose dilapidated pavilions formerly housed museums and a planetarium – all closed for long-term renovation. Across the road to the south, just before the Galaa Bridge, the **Mukhtar Museum** (daily except Mon 10am–1.30pm & 5–9pm; £E5) honours the sculptor Mahmoud Mukhtar (1891–1934), who is buried in the basement. Working in bronze and marble, he created several patriotic sculptures, including the *Renaissance of Egypt* monument that welcomes drivers into Dokki.

Zamalek

Originally a very British neighbourhood, despite its Continental grid of tree-lined boulevards, **Zamalek** still has bags of social cachet: renting a flat here is the

Cairene equivalent of moving into Manhattan. Unlike most parts of Cairo, the quarter feels very private; residents withdraw into air-conditioned high-rises or 1930s apartment buildings, and with so many foreign companies and **embassies** in the area, most of the streets are lifeless after dark, but paradoxically, Zamalek also features some of the trendiest **nightspots** in Cairo.

Zamalek has less to offer by day, though children may enjoy the **aquarium grotto** in **Gabalaya Gardens** (daily 9.30am–4pm; £E1; see p.196), entered from Sharia Gabalaya. For more cultural pursuits, head for the other end of Sharia al-Gezira as it curves around the northern edge of the Sporting Club, where a graceful nineteenth-century villa houses the Museum of Islamic Ceramics (see below). The modern annexes of the adjacent **Cairo Marriott Hotel** screen what was originally a "madly sumptuous palace" built for Napoleon's wife Empress Eugénie, later sold to wealthy Copts in lieu of Ismail's debts and turned into a hotel. Non-residents can wander in and loll amid khedival splendour for the price of a drink.

Although Zamalek is pretty young by Egyptian standards, it isn't without its history. The portions of Sharia Shagar al-Durr and Sharia Mansur Mohammed south of 26th July Street were once home to nineteen **Edwardian villas** constructed by the British government in 1906–07 to house important official employees. Of the nine still standing, the grandest is at 20 Sharia Ibn Zinki (on the corner of Mansur Mohammed) with its imposing triple-arched portico. Further south, 4 Sharia Hassan Sabry occupies the site of a villa where the UK's senior representative in wartime Egypt, **Lord Moyne**, was shot in 1944, along with his driver, by members of a far-right Zionist paramilitary group known as the Stern Gang. A more recent Zamalek murder, which shocked the Middle East as much, was that of Tunisian singer **Zikra** in November 2003, at her swanky apartment on Sharia Mohammed Mazhar. She was killed by her husband, apparently in a fit of jealousy, after refusing his demand that she give up her career. Having produced two pistols and a machine gun, he pumped Zikra with 25 rounds, then shot two of their friends, and finally himself. Thousands attended the singer's funeral.

Museum of Islamic Ceramics

Housed in a white-domed villa close to the *Cairo Marriott*, the **Museum of Islamic Ceramics** (daily except Fri 10am–1.30pm & 5–9pm; £E25, students £E12) is one of Cairo's most agreeable museums. Built by Prince Amru Ibrahim in the late nineteenth century, the structure itself is worth a look for its elaborate marble inlays and floors. The collection contains pieces from Egypt, Persia, Syria, Turkey, Morocco, Iraq and Andalucía, ranging from the seventh century to the present. Downstairs there's an art gallery (same hours; free) exhibiting original paintings and sculptures as well as prints by modern Egyptian artists such as Asraf and Alzamzami.

The west bank

Crossing over to the west bank of the Nile from Zamalek, you arrive at Mohandiseen, laid out during the 1960s to house Egypt's new technocrats, Medinat Mohandiseen ("Engineers' City"), as the suburb was initially called, responded to an influx of business and media folk during the Sadat era by shortening its name to just **Mohandiseen** and emulating America. Its main axis, **Arab League Street** (Sharia Gameat al-Dowal al-Arabiya) is bisected by palms and shrubbery for its three-kilometre length, and on a clear day (admittedly a rare occurrence in Cairo), you can look down it and see the Giza Pyramids in the distance.

Wedged between Mohandiseen and the Nile, **Aguza** ("Old Woman") was, in the mid-twentieth century, a popular mooring place for houseboats. One of them was occupied by a famous bellydancer, Hekmet Fathy, who used to entice Allied staff officers aboard to inveigle secrets from them on behalf of the Nazis. Also involved was a young Egyptian officer, Anwar Sadat, who attempted to convey messages to Rommel and was subsequently jailed by the British for treason.

Further south, **Dokki** (usually pronounced "Do'i", with a glottal stop in the middle) is notable for the **Mahmoud Khalil Museum** (daily except Mon 10am–5pm; £E25, students £E12; wheelchair access), housed in the refurbished mansion on Sharia el-Giza, where Khalil, a prewar politician and Agriculture Minister, lived with his French-born wife. Together they built up this magnificent collection of art and sculpture, mostly French Impressionist and post-Impressionist works by the likes of Monet, Renoir, Gauguin and Pissarro, but also featuring artists such as Van Gogh, Delacroix and Rodin. There are information sheets on the artists in various languages, but the computer screens that tell you about the Khalils and their home are in Arabic only.

Sharia el-Giza continues to **Giza**, which in pharaonic times lay en route between Heliopolis and Memphis, and probably also housed the skilled corps of pyramid-builders. The extensive grounds which Deschamps laid out for Ismail's palace in Giza, on the west side of the **El-Gama'a Bridge**, are now divided into Cairo's **Zoological Garden** – which is packed on Fridays and public holidays, but fun to visit at other times (see p.196) – and the smaller **El-Urman Garden** (daily 8.30am–4pm); they're shown on the "Old Cairo and Roda Island" map (see pp.140–141). The bridge is named after **Cairo University**, which was founded in 1908 as a counterweight to traditionalist Al-Azhar but has never been any the less political. Access to its scattered faculties is controlled by Central Security, so foreigners may need a letter of introduction (or at least their passports) to pass beyond its gates.

West of the **El-Giza Bridge** and south of the university belt, Cairo's second largest **bus and taxi terminal** agitates **Midan Giza**. Its seething ranks include buses to the Pyramids; minibuses to Tahrir, Ramses and Heliopolis; and service taxis to Fayoum City, Beni Suef and the Red Sea Coast. A few minutes' walk south is **Giza Station**. More flyovers funnel traffic onto the **Pyramids Road** (Sharia al-Ahram), which runs the gauntlet of **nightclubs** and tourist bazaars for 8km. A couple of kilometres before the Pyramids of Giza, Sharia al-Ahram crosses two canals in quick succession, which lead south to Saqqara and Dahshur; service-taxi microbuses for both can be found by the first of these two canals, Maryotteya. See pp.160–183 for details of both these and the Giza pyramid site.

The northern suburbs

During the last century, Cairo's **northern suburbs** swallowed up villages and farmland and expanded far into the desert to form a great arc of residential neighbourhoods stretching from the Nile to the Muqattam. **Heliopolis**, with its handsome boulevards and Art Deco villas, is still favoured above the satellite suburbs that have mushroomed in recent decades, and retains a sizeable foreign community.

Abbassiya

The sprawling **Abbassiya** district gets its name from a palace built by Mohammed Ali's grandson, Pasha Abbas I, who dreaded assassination during his brief reign (1848–54) and kept camels saddled here for rapid flight into the desert. The ornate Rococo **Sakakini Palace**, on Sharia Sakakini near Ghamra metro station, was built in 1898 for an Italian nobleman and supposedly is to be restored and opened to the public, though they have been saying this for years. In the meantime, it is still worth a look if you are in the area for its outrageously kitsch façade, and you may even be able to persuade the caretaker to let you see the marvellous interior with its huge mirrors, murals, painted ceilings and antique elevator.

At the end of Sharia Sakakini, on Midan al-Zahir, the 1268 **Mosque of Beybars the Crossbowman** was the first Cairo mosque to be located outside the city's walls. After it ceased to be a place of worship in the sixteenth century, it was subsequently used as a military storehouse by the Ottomans, a barracks by Napoleon and a slaughterhouse by the British. Restoration started in the early 1990s but soon petered out, and the southeast side is now again in use as a mosque; the rest of it remains a building site.

Medinet Nasr

During the 1960s and 1970s **Medinet Nasr** ("Victory City") was created as a new satellite suburb on the site of the Abbassiya Rifle Ranges, and many government departments were relocated here. Alongside the Sharia al-Nasr boulevard is a landscaped parade ground centred on a pyramid-shaped **Victory Memorial** to the 1973 October (Yom Kippur) War. In 1981, Islamic radicals infiltrated the October 6 anniversary parade and blasted the reviewing stand with machine guns and grenades, fatally wounding President Sadat (Mubarak, who stood beside him, was unharmed). **Sadat's Tomb** is beneath the Victory Memorial.

North of here, on Sharia al-Oruba, the huge **October War Panorama** was built on a suggestion made to Hosni Mubarak by Kim Il Sung of North Korea. Construction was supervised by North Korean technicians, and the building looks like a pavilion in some Communist theme park of the 1950s, decorated with Maoist-style reliefs, but instead of East Asian peasants and workers striding purposefully forward, it's Egyptian soldiers in front of the Pyramids. Shows put on here (daily except Tues 9.30am, 11am and 12.30pm, plus in winter 5pm and 6.30pm, summer 6pm and 7.30pm; £E20, camera £E2) start with two rather silly dioramas illustrating the opening round of the October War, and culminate in an impressive three-dimensional panorama of the war in Sinai, during which the audience is rotated around 360° to take it all in. The commentary (in Arabic, with an English version via headphones) explains the action with such phrases as "the glorious minutes passed rapidly", and the whole thing is so over-the-top in its triumphalism that you might almost think the Egyptians had actually won the October War.

Behind the Panorama is **Cairo Stadium**, where Cairo football clubs Ahly and Zamalek usually play their home matches, and where international ties and cup finals are also held (see p.205).

Heliopolis (Masr al-Gadida)

By the beginning of the twentieth century, the doubling of Cairo's population and the exponential growth of its foreign community had created a huge demand for new accommodation, which fired the imagination of a Belgian entrepreneur, Baron Édouard Empain, itching for new projects after his successful construction of the Paris Metro. Baron Empain proposed creating a garden city in the desert, linked to the downtown area by tram: a venture attractive to investors, since Empain's company would collect both rents and fares from commuting residents of the new suburb, which was named **Heliopolis** after the ancient City of the Sun nearby in Matariyya. The suburb's wide avenues were lined with apartment blocks ennobled by pale yellow Moorish facades and bisected by shrubbery. Wealthy Egyptians settled here from the beginning; merely prosperous ones moved in as foreigners left in droves during the 1950s. Heliopolis is known in Arabic as Masr al-Gadida ("New Cairo").

Transport to Heliopolis

Heliopolis is fifteen to thirty minutes' ride from downtown. You can get here by bus (#400, #400/ and #500) or minibus (#27) from Tahrir and Ramses but, especially during the rush hour, these are slower than the suburb's original tram system, known as the **Heliopolis metro**, which begins at Midan Ramses. From there, its three tram lines follow the same track through Abbassiya, diverging shortly before Midan Roxi. Each has its own colour-coded direction boards:

- The **Abd al-Aziz Fahmi line** (destination written in blue) runs past Midan Roxi and along Sharia al-Ma'had al-Ishtiraki and Sharia al-Higaz, past Merryland and Heliopolis Hospital, to Midan Heliopolis, where it turns off up Abd al-Aziz Fahmi towards Ain Shams.
- More centrally, the **Nouzha line** (destination written in red) veers off Sharia Merghani near the Heliopolis Sporting Club, and follows Al-Ahram and Osman Ibn Affan to Midan Triomphe, then heads up Sharia Nouzha to Midan al-Higaz.
- Initially running alongside the Nouzha line, the **Merghani line** (destination usually written in yellow) follows the street of that name to Midan Triomphe, and out towards the Armed Forces Hospital.

Ancient Heliopolis, the Ennead and the cult of Re

▶ Shu, Nut and Geb

Although Anthony Trollope scoffed "Humbug!" when he saw what little remained of it in 1858, the site of **ancient Heliopolis**, near modern day Matariyya, originally covered some five square kilometres. The City of the Sun (called On by its founders, but better known by its Greek appellation) evolved in tandem with Memphis, the first capital of Dynastic Egypt. As Memphis embodied the political unification of Upper and Lower Egypt, Heliopolis syncretized diverse local cults into a hierarchical cosmogony that surpassed other creation myths of the Old Kingdom. In the **Heliopolitan cosmogony**, the world began as watery chaos (Nun) from which Atum the sun-god emerged onto a primal mound, spitting forth the twin deities Shu (air) and Tefnut (moisture). They engendered Geb (earth) and Nut (sky), whose own union produced Isis, Osiris, Seth and Nephthys. Later texts often regarded this divine **Ennead** (Nine) as a single entity, while the universe was represented by the figures of Shu, Nut and Geb. Meanwhile, the primal deity Atum was subsumed by **Re** (or Ra), a yet mightier aspect of the sun-god, who manifested himself as hawk-headed Re-herakhte (Horus of the Horizon), the beetle Khepri (the rising sun), the disc Aten (the midday sun), or as Atum (the setting sun). From the V Dynasty onwards, pharaohs claimed descent from Re by identifying themselves with Horus and Osiris, and the rituals in Re's sanctuary (exclusively accessible to pharaohs and priests) were adopted by other cults and fused with Osiris-worship (see p.255 & p.285).

▶ Re

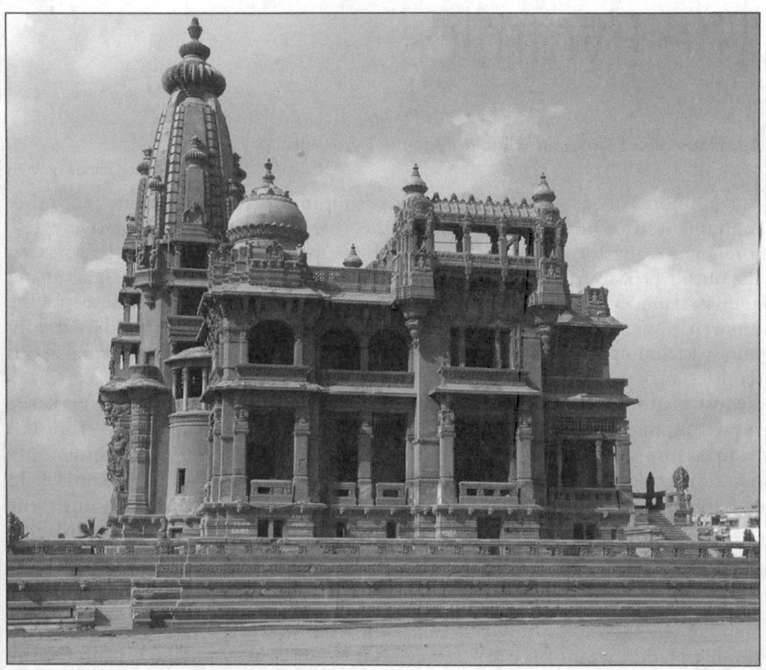

▲ Baron Empain's Palace, Heliopolis

Sights

Nouzha-line trams run through the heart of Heliopolis, up **Sharia al-Ahram**, its handsome villas rich with flowery Art Nouveau and Neoclassical details. Here you'll find classy cafés like *Amphytryon* and a branch of the downtown coffee shop *Groppi* (see p.188), where the bourgeoisie of the district's 1920s heyday would relax with a cake and a coffee, as indeed you can today (unlike its downtown namesake, the Heliopolis branch of *Groppi's* still retains some of its original elegance). At the top of Al-Ahram, the tram sidles to the right to pass around the suburb's centrepiece, the Byzantine-style "jelly-mould" **Basilica**, which is also Baron Empain's last resting place.

Some of Heliopolis's finest neo-Moorish façades can be seen along the streets leading off from Al-Ahram, most notably **Sharia Laqqani**, which leads north to **Midan Roxi**, and **Sharia Ibrahimi**, which crosses Al-Ahram a couple of blocks before the Basilica; both streets are lined by arcades topped with Andalucian-style balconies and pantiles. At the start of Al-Ahram, where it branches off from Sharia Merghani, the wonderful neo-Moorish pile known as the **Urubah Palace** is used as offices by the President, and out of bounds to the public.

The area's most impressive landmark is further southeast, on Sharia al-'Urubah. Modelled on Hindu temples from Cambodia and Orissa, **Baron Empain's Palace** (known to locals as Qasr al-Baron) originally boasted a revolving tower that enabled its owner to follow the sun throughout the day. Although the building, completed in 1910, is generally closed to the public, it has been spruced up, and is illuminated at night. As Sharia al-Oruba is the main road to the airport, you may see it on your way to or from taking a plane.

The Pyramids

All things dread Time, but Time dreads the Pyramids.

Anonymous proverb

For millions of people the **Pyramids** epitomize Ancient Egypt: no other monument is so instantly recognized the world over. Yet comparatively few foreigners realize that at least 118 pyramids are spread across 70km of desert, from the outskirts of Cairo to the edge of the Fayoum. The mass of theories, claims and counterclaims about how and why the Pyramids were built contributes to the sense of mystery that surrounds them. You can read up on some of the wackier ones – including some involving Martians – through links at Ⓦparanormal.about.com/cs/ancientegypt.

Most visitors are content to see the great **Pyramids of Giza** and part of the sprawling necropolis of **Saqqara**, both easily accessible from Cairo (tours to Saqqara often include a visit to the ruins of the ancient city of **Memphis**). Only a minority ride across the sands to Abu Sir, or visit the **Dahshur** pyramid field (see the map opposite for the location of all these sites). Still further south, the dramatic "Collapsed Pyramid" of **Maidum** (see p.392) and the lesser Middle Kingdom pyramids of **Hawara** and **Lahun** (see p.393) are easier to reach from the Fayoum, so for the sake of convenience we've covered them in Chapter 3. There are other pyramid sites, at **Abu Sir** (a group of pyramids between Giza and Saqqara, about £E2 by tuk-tuk from Abu Sir village) and **Abu Ruash** (a single pyramid west of Cairo; service taxis to the nearby village leave from the junction of Sharia Mansureya with Sharia Faisal, north of Pyramids Road), but these are currently closed to the public, though you may be able to make private arrangements with the guards, and Abu Sir may reopen in 2010.

If you're really determined, and very energetic, it's possible to visit the pyramid sites at Giza, Saqqara and Dahshur, plus Memphis, all in one day, starting very early (say 7.30am from town). To do this, you will need to find a taxi driver who will take you, wait at each, and finally bring you back. Make sure the driver understands exactly what you want, and negotiate hard. In principle, you should be able to visit all four sites for around £E200, but £E250–300 would not be an unreasonable rate, especially if there's a group of you. Some hotels (the *Berlin*, for example, see p.85) have their own drivers who are used to taking tourists on such excursions. Alternatively, you could opt for a guided tour (see p.172) that takes in both Giza and Saqqara in one day.

The Pyramids in history

The derivation of the word "pyramid" is obscure. *Per-em-us*, an Ancient Egyptian term meaning "straight up", seems likelier than the Greek *pyramis* – "wheaten cake", a facetious descriptive term for these novel monuments. Then again, "obelisk" comes from *obeliskos*, the ancient Greek for "skewer" or "little spit".

Whatever, the Pyramids' sheer **antiquity** is staggering. When the Greek chronicler Herodotus visited them in 450 BC, as many centuries separated his lifetime from their creation as divide our own time from that of Herodotus, who regarded them as ancient even then. For the Pyramid Age was only an episode in three millennia of pharaonic civilization, reaching its zenith within two hundred years and followed by an inexorable decline, so that later dynasties regarded the works of their ancestors with awe.

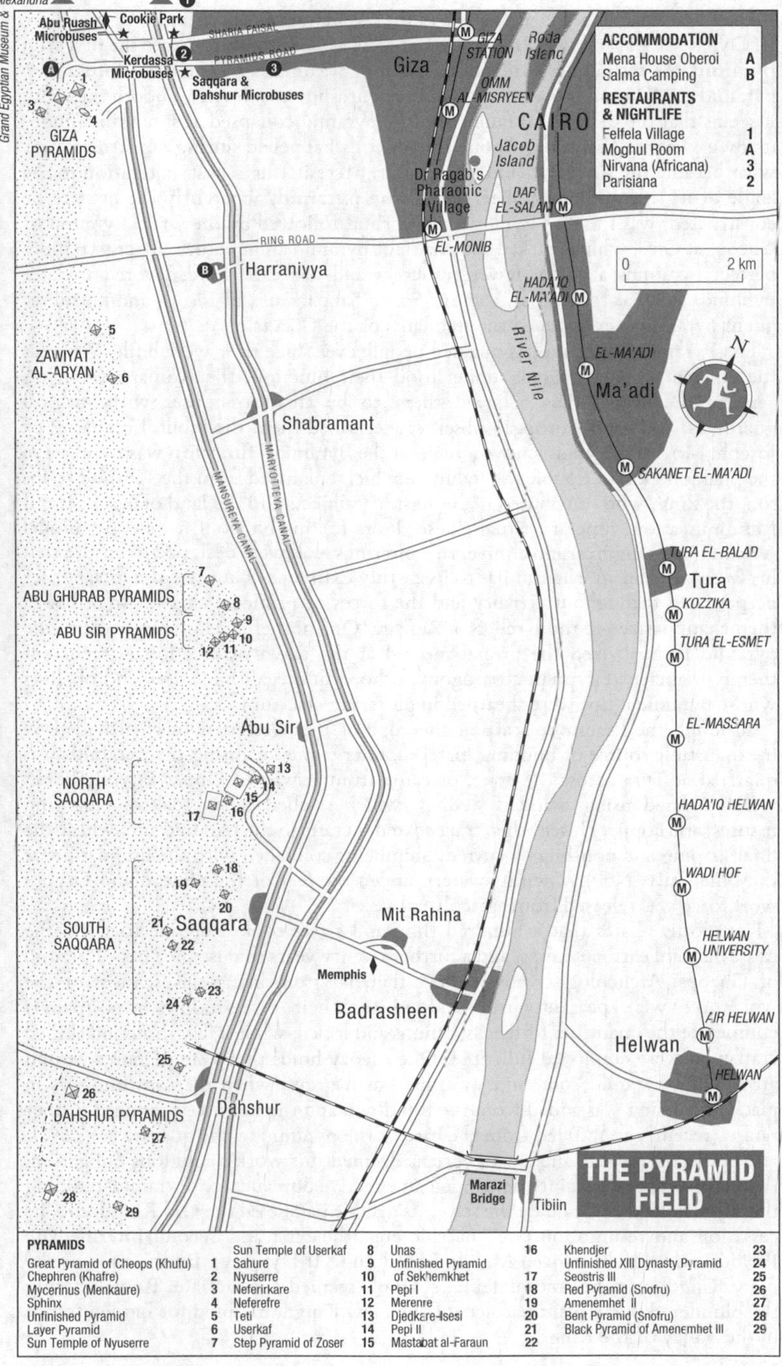

Alexandria
Grand Egyptian Museum &
Abu Ruash Microbuses
Cookie Park
Kerdassa Microbuses
Saqqara & Dahshur Microbuses
SHARIA FAISAL
PYRAMIDS ROAD
GIZA STATION
Roda Island
Giza
OMM AL-MISRYEEN
CAIRO
Jacob Island
Dr Ragab's Pharaonic Village
DAF EL-SALAM
EL-MONIB
RING ROAD
GIZA PYRAMIDS
Harraniyya
ZAWIYAT AL-ARYAN
HADA'IQ EL-MA'ADI
River Nile
EL-MA'ADI
Ma'adi
Shabramant
MANSUREYA CANAL
MARYOTTEYA CANAL
SAKANET EL-MA'ADI
TURA EL-BALAD
Tura
KOZZIKA
TURA EL-ESMET
ABU GHURAB PYRAMIDS
ABU SIR PYRAMIDS
Abu Sir
EL-MASSARA
NORTH SAQQARA
HADA'IQ HELWAN
WADI HOF
SOUTH SAQQARA
Saqqara
Mit Rahina
HELWAN UNIVERSITY
Memphis
Badrasheen
AIR HELWAN
Helwan
HELWAN
Dahshur
DAHSHUR PYRAMIDS
Marazi Bridge
Tibiin
0 2 km
N
ACCOMMODATION
Mena House Oberoi A
Salma Camping B
RESTAURANTS & NIGHTLIFE
Felfela Village 1
Moghul Room A
Nirvana (Africana) 3
Parisiana 2
THE PYRAMID FIELD
PYRAMIDS
Great Pyramid of Cheops (Khufu) 1
Chephren (Khafre) 2
Mycerinus (Menkaure) 3
Sphinx 4
Unfinished Pyramid 5
Layer Pyramid 6
Sun Temple of Nyuserre 7
Sun Temple of Userkaf 8
Sahure 9
Nyuserre 10
Neferirkare 11
Neferefre 12
Teti 13
Userkaf 14
Step Pyramid of Zoser 15
Unas 16
Unfinished Pyramid of Sekhemkhet 17
Pepi I 18
Merenre 19
Djedkare-Isesi 20
Pepi II 21
Mastabat al-Faraun 22
Khendjer 23
Unfinished XIII Dynasty Pyramid 24
Seostris III 25
Red Pyramid (Snofru) 26
Amenemhet II 27
Bent Pyramid (Snofru) 28
Black Pyramid of Amenemhet III 29

The Pyramid Age began at Saqqara in the twenty-seventh century BC, when the III Dynasty royal architect Imhotep enlarged a *mastaba* tomb to create the first **step pyramid**. As techniques evolved, an attempt was made to convert another step pyramid at Maidum into a true pyramid by encasing its sides in a smooth shell, but it seems that the design was faulty and the pyramid collapsed at some time under its own weight. According to one theory, this happened during construction of what became the Bent Pyramid at Dahshur, necessitating a hasty alteration to the angle of its sides. The first sheer-sided **true pyramid**, apparently the next to be constructed, was the Red Pyramid at Dahshur, followed by the Great Pyramid of Cheops at Giza, which marked the zenith of pyramid architecture. After two more perfect pyramids at Giza, fewer resources and less care were devoted to later pyramids (such as those at at Abu Sir, South Saqqara and El-Lisht), and no subsequent pyramid ever matched the standards of the Giza trio.

The Pyramids' **enigma** has puzzled people ever since they were built. Whereas the Ancient Greeks vaguely understood their function, the Romans were less certain; medieval Arabs believed them to be treasure houses with magical guardians; and early European observers reckoned them the biblical granaries of Joseph. Most archeologists now agree that the Pyramids' **function** was to preserve the pharaoh's **ka**, or double: a vital force which emanated from the sun-god to his son, the king, who distributed it amongst his subjects and the land of Egypt itself. Mummification, funerary rituals, false doors for his **ba** (soul) to escape, model servants (*shabti* figures) and anniversary offerings – all were designed to ensure that his *ka* enjoyed an afterlife similar to its earthly existence. Thus was the social order perpetuated throughout eternity and the forces of primeval chaos held at bay, a theme emphasized in tomb reliefs at Saqqara. On another level of **symbolism**, the pyramid form evoked the primal mound at the dawn of creation, a recurrent theme in ancient Egyptian cosmogony, echoed in megalithic *benben* and obelisks whose pyramidal tips were sheathed in glittering electrum.

Although the limestone scarp at the edge of the Western Desert provided an inexhaustible source of building material, finer stone for casing the pyramids was quarried at Tura across the river, or came from Aswan in Upper Egypt. Blocks were quarried using wooden wedges (which swelled when soaked, enlarging fissures) and copper chisels, then transported on rafts to the pyramid site, where the final shaping and polishing occurred. Shipments coincided with the inundation of the Nile (July–Nov), when its waters lapped the feet of the plateau and Egypt's workforce was released from agricultural tasks.

Herodotus relates that a hundred thousand slaves took a decade to build the causeway and earthen ramps, and a further twenty years to raise the Great Pyramid of Cheops. Archeologists now believe that, far from being slaves, most of the workforce were peasants paid in food for their three-month stint (papyri enumerate the quantities of lentils, onions and leeks), while a few thousand skilled craftsmen were employed full-time. One theory holds that a single ramp wound around the pyramid core, and was raised as it grew; when the capstone was in place, the casing was added from the top down and the ramp was reduced. Other ramps (recently found) led from the base of the pyramid to the quarry.

Whether or not the ancient Egyptians deemed this work a religious obligation, the massive levies certainly demanded an effective bureaucracy. Pyramid-building therefore helped consolidate the state. Its decline paralleled the Old Kingdom's, its cessation and resumption two anarchic eras (the First and Second Intermediate Periods) and the short-lived Middle Kingdom (XII Dynasty). By the time of the New Kingdom, other monumental symbols seemed appropriate. Remembering the plundered pyramids, the rulers of the New Kingdom opted for hidden tombs in the Valley of the Kings.

The Pyramids of Giza

Of the Seven Wonders of the ancient world, only the **Pyramids of Giza** have withstood the ravages of time. "From the summit of these monuments, forty centuries look upon you", cried Napoleon. Resembling small triangles from afar and corrugated mountains as you approach, their gigantic mass can seem oddly two-dimensional when viewed from below. Far from being isolated in the desert as carefully angled photos suggest, they rise just beyond the outskirts of Giza City. During daytime, the tourist hordes dispel the mystique (though the site is big enough to escape them), but at sunset, dawn and late at night their brooding majesty returns.

The Pyramids' **orientation** is no accident. Their entrances are aligned with the Pole Star (or rather, its position 4500 years ago); the internal tomb chambers face west, the direction of the Land of the Dead; and the external funerary temples point eastwards towards the rising sun. Less well preserved are the causeways leading to the so-called valley temples, and various subsidiary pyramids and *mastaba* tombs.

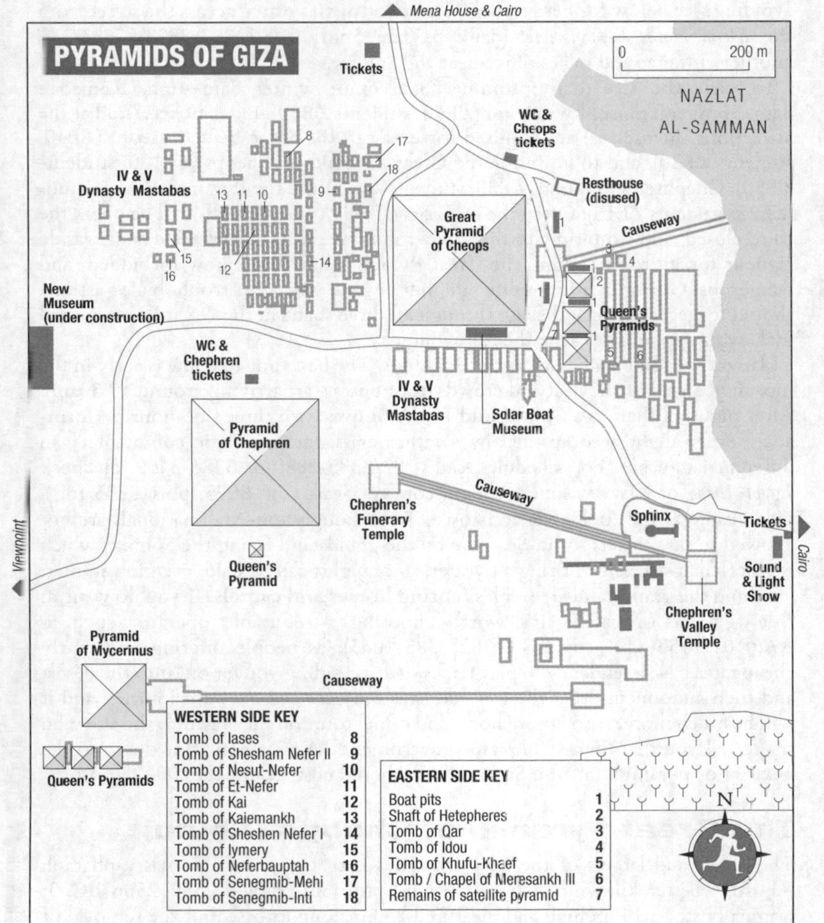

Practicalities

The site is directly accessible from Cairo by the eight-kilometre-long **Sharia al-Ahram** (Pyramids Road) built by Khedive Ismail for Napoleon III's consort, the Empress Eugénie. Though heavy traffic can prolong the journey, getting there is straightforward. Taxi drivers often quote upwards of £E30, but the proper fare is around £E20 for a one-way trip from town. A cheaper option is to take a/c bus #357 (£E2), or ordinary bus #900 (50pt), all from behind Ramses train station or from Al-Esa'af Pharmacy, at the junction of 26th July Street, and Sharia Ramses, or take a microbus service taxi (£E1.25) from Ramses (by Sharia Orabi) or Abdel Mouneem Riyad – drivers heading for the Pyramids shout, "Al-Ahram, al-Ahram", but check they're going all the way. An easier one-day, minimum-effort way to visit the Giza Pyramids, while also taking in Saqqara, is to go on a guided tour (see p.172).

The main entrance to the site is just uphill from the *Mena House Oberoi* hotel. Ignore touts and other dubious characters trying to persuade you that the ticket office is closed, or has moved to the nearby horse stables (which are worth avoiding; see below for better ones). There's a **tourist office** across the street from the *Mena House Oberoi hotel* (daily 8.30am–5pm; ⓣ02/3383-8823). There is another entrance and ticket office near the Sphinx.

To **visit the site** (daily: summer 8am–6pm; winter 8am–4pm, Ramadan 8am–3pm) you must buy a **ticket** (£E60, students £E30). Extra tickets (sold at the attractions themselves) are required for entry to the Solar Boat Museum (£E40, students £E20), and to go inside the Great Pyramid of Cheops (£E100, students £E50), Chephren's Pyramid (£E30, students £E15) and the Pyramid of Mycerinus (£E25, students £E15). Often the interiors of only two pyramids will be open, the third closed, and from time to time they rotate them. In Baedeker's day, it was de rigueur for visitors to climb the Great Pyramid, but this is now forbidden, and dangerous. **Going inside** is quite safe, but anyone with claustrophobia or asthma should forget it, and clambering through all three shafts in the Great Pyramid will make your leg muscles ache the following day.

Plan on spending half a day at the Pyramids. The best time to come is early in the morning, ahead of the heat and crowds (tour buses start arriving around 10.30am). After nightfall there is a **Sound and Light Show**, with three one-hour performances every night accompanied by a rather crass, melodramatic commentary in different languages. For schedules, call ⓣ02/3385-2880 or 3386-3469, or check *Egypt Today* or ⓦwww.soundandlight.com.eg. Seats cost £E75, plus £E35 for a video camera; the Arabic version costs £E11, though non-Arab nationals are not allowed to buy tickets for it. Seats are on the grandstand facing the Sphinx, which is wheelchair-accessible. Bring a sweater, since nights can be cold, even in summer.

Behind the grandstand are stables **renting horses and camels**. If you do want to ride a horse or camel, it's worth choosing a reputable operator such as AA(ⓣ012/153-4142) or KG (ⓣ02/3385-1065), as people offering apparently cheap rates have a tendency to play tricks such as leading you far out into the desert and then announcing that the low rate was only for the outward journey and it will be much more. Also ignore horse and camel touts on the way into the site who try to tell you that their stables are "government". A four-hour ride down to the next set of pyramids (at Abu Sir) and back should cost around £E200–250.

The Great Pyramid of Cheops (Khufu)

The oldest and largest of the Giza Pyramids is that of the IV Dynasty pharaoh **Khufu** – better known as **Cheops** – who probably reigned 2589–2566 BC. It originally stood 140m high and measured 230m along its base, but the removal of its casing stones has reduced these dimensions by three metres. The pyramid is estimated to weigh six million tons and contain over 2,300,000 blocks whose average weight is 2.5 tons (though some weigh almost 15 tons). This gigantic mass actually ensures its stability, since most of the stress is transmitted inwards towards its central core, or downwards into the underlying bedrock. Until recently, the pyramid was thought to contain only three chambers: one in the bedrock and two in the superstructure. Experts believe that its design was changed twice, the subterranean chamber being abandoned in favour of the middle one, which was itself superseded by the uppermost chamber. By the time archeologists got here, their contents had long ago been looted, and the only object left *in situ* was Khufu's sarcophagus. In 1993, a German team using a robot probe accidentally discovered a door with handles supposedly enclosing a fourth chamber, apparently never plundered by thieves, which might contain the mummy and treasures of Cheops himself. Another robot, sent down in 2002, pushed a camera through a hole drilled in the door to reveal another, similar door behind it. A third robot was sent down in 2007, and another in 2009, but so far the results of their explorations have not been announced, though there is said to have been "a major breakthrough".

Inside the Great Pyramid

To keep down humidity inside the pyramid, the number of visitors allowed to enter is limited to 150 in the morning and 150 in the afternoon. If you want to buy **tickets** (£E100, students £E50, no cameras allowed), you will neeed to look sharp. In the morning, tour groups tend to snap up all of them before anyone else can get a look in; it is generally less difficult to get the afternoon tickets, especially if you can be at the ticket office as soon as they go on sale at 1pm, but be prepared to jostle for position (or, if you go in the morning, to sprint to the ticket office as soon as the main gate opens).

You enter the pyramid via an opening created by the treasure-hunting Caliph Ma'mun in 820, some distance below the original entrance on the north face (now

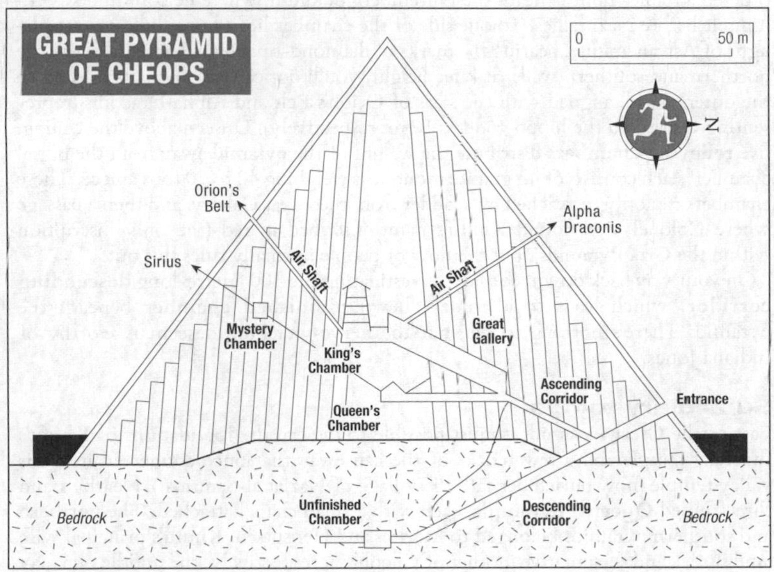

blocked). After following this downwards at a crouch, you'll reach the junction of the ascending and descending corridors. The latter – leading to an unfinished chamber below the pyramid – is best ignored or left until last, and everyone heads up the 1.6-metre-high **ascending corridor**, which runs for 36m until it meets another junction.

To the right of this is a **shaft** that ancient writers believed to be a well connected to the Nile; it's now recognized as leading into the subterranean chamber and thought to have been an escape passage for the workmen. Straight ahead is a horizontal passage 35m long and 1.75m high, leading to a semi-finished limestone chamber with a pointed roof, which Arabs dubbed the "**Queen's Chamber**", though there's no evidence that a queen was ever buried here. In the northern and southern walls are two holes made in 1872 for the purpose of discovering the chamber's ventilation shafts; it was through one of these that the robot probe discovered the "secret chamber", at the end of a 65-metre passageway only twenty centimetres high and the same distance wide, which is aligned with the Dog Star, Sirius (representing the goddess Isis).

However, most people step up into the **Great Gallery**, the finest section of the pyramid. Built of Muqattam limestone, so perfectly cut that a knife blade can't be inserted between its joints, the 47-metre-long shaft narrows to a corbelled roof 8.5m high. The incisions in its walls probably held beams that were used to raise the sarcophagus or granite plug blocks up the steep incline (nowadays overlaid with wooden steps). Though no longer infested by giant bats, as nineteenth-century travellers reported, the Great Gallery is sufficiently hot and airless to be something of an ordeal, and you'll be glad to reach the horizontal antechamber at the top, which is slotted for the insertion of plug blocks designed to thwart entry to the putative burial chamber.

The **King's Chamber** lies 95m beneath the apex of the pyramid and half that distance from its outer walls. Built of red granite blocks, the rectangular chamber is large enough to accommodate a double-decker bus. Its dimensions (5.2m by 10.8m by 5.8m) have inspired many abstruse calculations and wacky prophecies: Hitler ordered a replica built beneath the Nuremberg Stadium, where he communed with himself before Nazi rallies. To one side of the chamber lies a huge, lidless **sarcophagus** of Aswan granite, bearing the marks of diamond-tipped saws and drills. On the northern and southern walls, at knee height, you'll notice two air shafts leading to the outer world, aligned with the stars of Orion's Belt and Alpha Draconis (representing Osiris and the hippo goddess Reret respectively). Unseen above the ceiling, five **relieving chambers** distribute the weight of the pyramid away from the burial chamber; each consists of 43 granite monoliths weighing 40 to 70 tons apiece. These chambers can only be reached by a ladder from the Great Gallery, and then a passage where Colonel Vyse found Khufu's name inscribed in red (the only inscription within the Giza Pyramids), but the flow of people normally rules this out.

On your way back down, consider investigating the 100-metre-long **descending corridor**, which leads to a crudely hewn **unfinished chamber** beneath the pyramid. There's nothing to see, but the nerve-wracking descent is worthy of Indiana Jones.

Subsidiary tombs

East of the Great Pyramid, it's just possible to discern the foundations of Khufu's funerary temple and a few blocks of the causeway that once connected it to his valley temple (now buried beneath the village of Nazlat al-Samman). Nearby stand three ruined **Queens' Pyramids**, each with a small chapel attached. The northern and southern pyramids belonged to Merites and Hensutsen, Khufu's principal wife (and sister), and the putative mother of Chephren, respectively; the middle one may have belonged to the mother of Djedefre, the third ruler of the dynasty. Between that and the Great Pyramid, the remains of a fourth satellite pyramid were discovered in 1993, its capstone the oldest yet found, its purpose so far unknown.

Just northeast of Queen Merites' pyramid is a **shaft** where IV Dynasty pharaoh Snofru's wife Queen Hetepheres' sarcophagus was found, having been stashed here following lootings at its original home in Dahshur. To the east of it are the tombs of Qar and his son Idou, which contain life-size statues of the deceased and various reliefs. To the east of Queen Hensutsen's pyramid are the tombs of Cheops' son Khufu-Khaef, and Chephren's wife (also Hetepheres' daughter) Meres-ankh, the best preserved of all the tombs on the Giza plateau, complete with statues in the niches and reliefs showing scenes of daily life, with much of the paintwork intact. To get into these tombs, ask at the custodian's hut beside Hetepheres' shaft; naturally, he'll expect a tip for opening up.

To the west of the Great Pyramid lie dozens of **IV and V Dynasty mastabas**, where archeologists have uncovered a 4600-year-old mummified princess, whose body had been hollowed out and encased in a thin layer of plaster – a hitherto unknown method of mummification. The **tombs** are less interesting than those on the eastern side, though Neferbauptah's has a dinosaur fossil preserved in the fifth block from the right of the second row up on its north side. Should you want to enter any of these tombs, ask at the Inspectorate office to the north. Beware of deep shafts with no fences around them.

The Solar Boat Museum

Perched to the south of the Great Pyramid, across the road from another cluster of mastabas, is a humidity-controlled pavilion (daily: summer 9am–6pm; winter 9am–4pm; £E40, students £E20) containing a 43-metre-long **boat** from one of the five boat pits sunk around Khufu's Pyramid (another boat has been located by X-rays and video cameras, but remains unexcavated).

When the pit's limestone roofing blocks were removed in 1954, a faint odour of cedarwood arose. Restorer Hagg Ahmed Yussef subsequently spent fourteen years rebuilding a graceful craft from tewlve hundred pieces of wood, originally held together by sycamore pegs and halfa-grass ropes. Archeologists term these vessels "solar boats" (or barques), but their purpose remains uncertain – carrying the pharaoh through the underworld (as shown in XVII–XIX Dynasty tombs at Thebes) or accompanying the sun-god on his daily journey across the heavens are two of the many hypotheses.

The Pyramid of Chephren (Khafre)

Sited on higher ground, with an intact summit and steeper sides, the middle or **Second Pyramid** seems taller than Cheops's. Built for his son **Khafre** (known to posterity as Chephren), its sides once measured 230m but have lost 15m since the removal of its casing stones. Its weight is estimated at 4,883,000 tons. As with Cheops's Pyramid, the original rock-hewn burial chamber was never finished and an upper chamber was subsequently constructed. Roman writer Pliny said that the pyramid had no entrance, but when flamboyant Italian circus strongman turned explorer Giovanni Belzoni located and blasted open the sealed portal on its north face in 1818, he found that Arab tomb robbers had gained access nearly a thousand years earlier, undeterred by legends of an idol "with fierce and sparkling eyes" bent on slaying intruders.

Inside the pyramid (£E30, students £E15, no current limit on numbers, no cameras allowed), you can follow one of the two entry corridors downwards, and then upwards, into a long horizontal passage leading to Chephren's **burial chamber**, where Belzoni celebrated his discovery by writing his name in black letters. Set into the chamber's granite floor is the sarcophagus of Khafre, who reigned c.2558–2533 BC. The square cavity near the southern wall may have marked the position of a canopic chest containing the pharaoh's viscera.

Chephren's Funerary Complex and the Sphinx

The funerary complex of Chephren's Pyramid is the best-preserved example of this typically Old Kingdom arrangement. When a pharaoh died, his body was ferried across the Nile to a riverside valley temple where it was embalmed by priests. Then mourners gathered there to purify themselves before escorting his mummy up the causeway to a funerary (or mortuary) temple, where further rites preceded its interment within the pyramid. Thereafter, the priests ensured his *ka*'s afterlife by making offerings of food and incense in the funerary temple on specific anniversaries.

Chephren's **funerary temple** consists of a pillared hall, central court, niched storerooms and a sanctuary, but most of the outer granite casing has been plundered over centuries and the interior is not usually accessible. Among the remaining blocks is a 13.4-metre-long monster weighing 163,000 kilos. Flanking the temple are what appear to be boat pits, although excavations have yielded nothing but pottery fragments. From here you can trace the foundations of a **causeway** that runs 400m downhill to his valley temple, near the Sphinx.

The **valley temple** lay buried under sand until its discovery by French egyptologist Auguste Mariette in 1852, which accounts for its reasonable state of preservation. Built of limestone and faced with polished Aswan granite, the temple faces east and used to open onto a quay. Beyond a narrow antechamber you'll find a T-shaped hall whose gigantic architraves are supported by square pillars, in front of which stood diorite statues of Chephren.

The Sphinx

This legendary monument, whose enclosure is entered through the Valley Temple, is carved from an outcrop of soft limestone that was supposedly left standing after the harder surrounding stone was quarried for the Great Pyramid; however, since the base stone was too soft to work on directly, it was clad in harder stone before finishing. Conventional archeology credits Chephren with the idea of shaping it into a figure with a lion's body and a human head, which is often identified as his own (complete with royal beard and *uraeus*, see p.648), though it may represent a guardian deity. Some thousand years later, the future Tuthmosis IV is said to have dreamt that if he cleared the sand that engulfed the **Sphinx** it would make him ruler: a prophecy fulfilled, as recorded on a stele that he placed between its paws. All these notions went unchallenged until 1991, when two American geologists argued that the Sphinx was at least 2600 years older than had been imagined, delighting the maverick egyptologist John West, who has long claimed that Egyptian civilization was the inheritor of a more ancient, lost culture – the mythical Atlantis. The name "Sphinx" was actually bestowed by the Ancient Greeks, after the legendary creature that put riddles to passers-by and slew those who answered wrongly; the Arabs call it Abu el-Hol (the awesome or terrible one). During Sound and Light shows, the Sphinx is given the role of narrator.

Used for target practice by Mamluke and Napoleonic troops, the Sphinx lost much of its beard to the British Museum and was sandbagged for protection during World War II. Early modern repairs did more harm than good, since its porous limestone "breathes", unlike the cement that was used to fill its cracks. A more recent **restoration project** (1989–98) involved hand-cutting ten thousand limestone blocks, to refit the paws, legs and haunches of the beast, but it was decided not to replace the missing nose or beard.

Three **tunnels** exist inside the Sphinx, one behind its head, one in its tail and one in its north side. Their function is unknown, but none goes anywhere. Other tunnels have been unearthed in the vicinity of the Sphinx; again, who built them or what they were for is unknown, but one suggestion is that they were created by later Ancient Egyptians looking for buried treasure.

The Pyramid of Mycerinus (Menkaure)

Sited on a gradual slope into undulating desert, the smallest of the Giza Pyramids speaks of waning power and commitment. Though started by Chephren's successor, **Menkaure** (called Mycerinus by the Greeks), it was finished with unseemly haste by his son Shepseskaf, who seemingly enjoyed less power than his predecessors and depended on the priesthood. Herodotus records the legend that an oracle gave Mycerinus only six years to live, so to cheat fate he made merry round the clock, doubling his annual quantum of experience. Another story has it that the pyramid was actually built by Rhodophis, a Thracian courtesan who charged each client the price of a building block (the structure is estimated to contain 200,000 blocks).

Because its lower half was sheathed in Aswan granite, this is sometimes called the Red Pyramid (a name more usually applied to one of Snofru's pyramids at Dahshur). Its relative lack of casing stones is due to a twelfth-century sultan whose courtiers persuaded him to attempt the pyramid's demolition, a project he wisely gave up after eight months. The **interior** (£E25, students £E15) is unusual for having its unfinished chamber in the superstructure and the final burial chamber underground. Here Vyse discovered a basalt sarcophagus later lost at sea en route to Britain, plus human remains that he assumed were Menkaure's, but which are now reckoned to be a XXVI Dynasty replacement and which rest in the British Museum.

The complex also features three subsidiary pyramids, a relatively intact funerary temple, and a causeway to the now-buried valley temple. Northwest of the latter lies the sarcophagus-shaped **Tomb of Queen Khentkawes**, an intriguing figure who appears to have bridged the transition between the IV and V dynasties. Apparently married to Shepseskaf, the last IV Dynasty ruler, she may have wed a priest of the sun-god after his demise and gone on to bear several kings who were buried at Saqqara or Abu Sir (where she also had a pyramid built).

Views of the pyramids

The best **viewpoints** over the pyramids are south of Mycerinus' pyramid. Most tourists gather along the tarmac road some 400m west of the pyramid, which is particularly popular in the late afternoon when the sun is in the right direction. In the morning, however, photos are better taken from the southeast, though it can often be hazy early on. For the best view of the Pyramids close together, the ridge to the south of Mycerinus' pyramid is the place to head for.

The Grand Egyptian Museum

Two kilometres north of the Giza Pyramids site, at the junction of the Alexandria Desert Road with the Cairo Ring Road, a brand new **Grand Egyptian Museum** is under construction, scheduled to open in 2013, insha'Allah. One exhibit, a colossal statue of Ramses II, which formerly graced Midan Ramses in downtown Cairo, has already been shipped down here, and when the museum is opened, will stand at its entrance. The top floor of the museum will have commanding views over the Pyramids. This will all be part of a grandiose development, with an

Kerdassa and Harraniyya

The villages of Kerdassa and Harraniyya have no connection with the Pyramids, but tour groups often pay one or both of them a visit. **Kerdassa** (accessible by microbus from the junction of Pyramids Road with Sharia Mansureya) is where most of the scarves, *galabiyyas* and shirts in Cairo are made, plus carpets, which are sold by the metre. Although no longer a place for bargains, it's still frequented by collectors of ethnic textiles, particularly Bedouin robes and veils (the best-quality ones sell for hundreds of dollars).

Guided tours often take in **Harraniyya**, the site of the famous **Wissa Wassef Art Centre** (daily 10am–5pm; ⓣ02/3381-5746, ⓦwww.wissa-wassef-arts.com and ⓦwww.wissawassef.com). Founded in 1952 by Ramses Wissa Wassef, an architect who wanted to preserve village crafts and alleviate rural unemployment, the centre teaches children to design and weave carpets, and has branched out into batik work and pottery. The pupils, supervised by his widow and the original generation of students, produce beautiful tapestries which now sell for thousands of dollars and are imitated throughout Egypt. You can see them at work (except at lunchtime and on Fridays), and admire a superb collection in the museum designed by Hassan Fathy, a masterpiece of mud-brick architecture. To reach the Art Centre under your own steam, take a taxi or minibus 4km south along the Saqqara road (Maryotteya Canal, west bank) from Pyramids Road; bus #335 from Midan Giza serves Harraniyya, but infrequently.

IMAX cinema, conference and seminar halls, and educational facilities, but according to the project's financial resources development manager, "only one third" of the site's 50 hectares will be occupied by commercial properties. The museum when completed should at any rate take some of the strain off the downtown Egyptian Antiquities Museum (see p.94), and enable items from the warehouse of that venerable institution to be displayed, and also allow the downtown museum to be modernized.

North Saqqara

While Memphis (see p.179) was the capital of the Old Kingdom, Egypt's royalty and nobility were buried at **Saqqara**, the limestone scarp that flanks the Nile Valley to the west – the traditional direction of the Land of the Dead. Although superseded by the Theban necropolis during the New Kingdom, Saqqara remained in use for burying sacred animals and birds, especially in Ptolemaic times, when these cults enjoyed a revival. Over three thousand years it grew to cover 7km of desert – not including the associated necropolises of Abu Sir and Dahshur, or the Giza Pyramids. As such, it is today the largest archeological site in Egypt. Its name – usually pronounced "sa'-*'ah*-rah" by Cairenes, with the q's as glottal stops – probably derives from Sokar, the Memphite god of the dead, though Egyptians may tell you that it comes from *saq*, the Arabic word for a hawk or falcon, the sacred bird of Horus.

The Saqqara necropolis divides into two main sections: **North Saqqara** – the more interesting area (covered here) – and **South Saqqara** (see p.180). North Saqqara boasts a score of sights, so anyone with limited time should be selective. The **highlights** are Zoser's funerary complex, the Mastaba of Ti, and the Double Mastaba of Akhti- and Ptah-Hotep; if time allows, add the museum and some more tombs to your itinerary.

Practicalities

North Saqqara (daily: summer 8am–6pm, winter 8am–4pm, Ramadan 8am–3pm; £E60, student £E30) lies 21km south of the Giza Pyramids as the camel strides, or 32km from Cairo by road. The quickest way here by **public transport** (about an hour) is to take a bus or service taxi to Pyramids Road, and get off at Maryotteya Canal (about 1km before the Pyramids), where you'll find service taxi microbuses to Saqqara village (20min; £E1). An alternative route is to take bus #335 (hourly) from Midan Giza to Saqqara village, or bus #987 from Midan Ramses or Midan Tahrir to Badrasheen, and then a microbus to Saqqara village (15min; 50pt), by

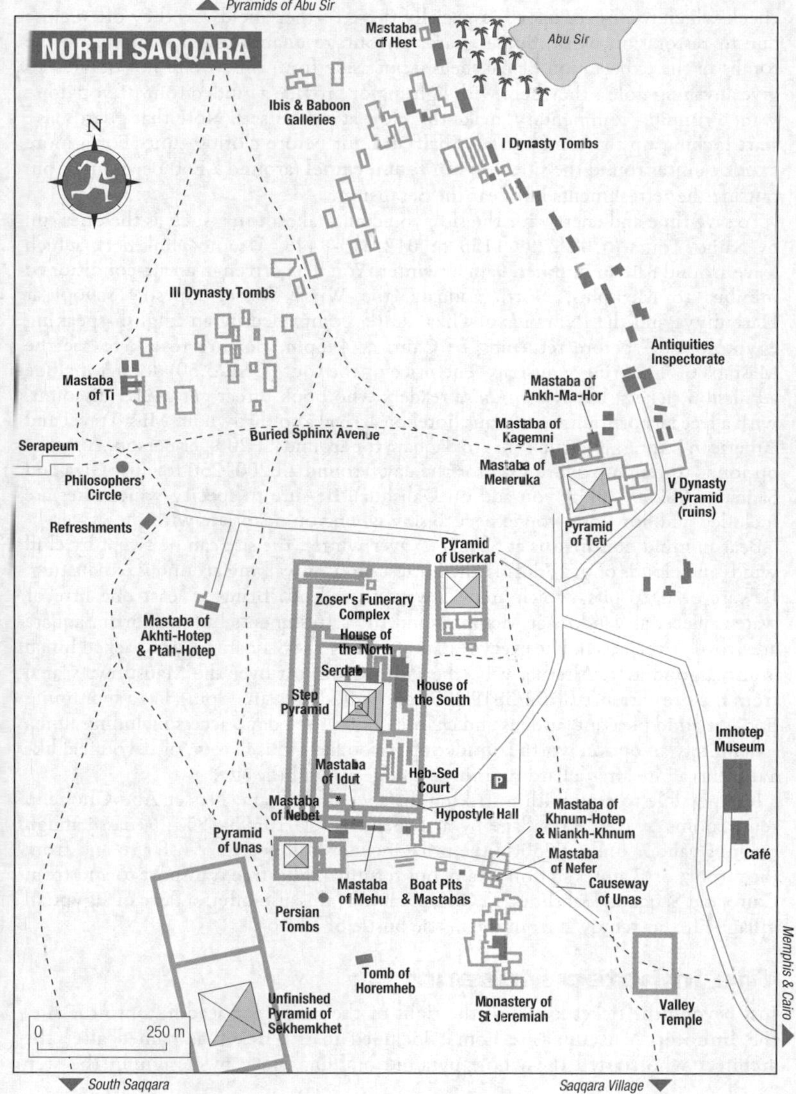

way of Memphis. A final option is to take the metro to Helwan station (30min; £E1), then a minibus to Tibiin, near the Marazi Bridge (15min; £E1); another service taxi (often a Peugeot rather than a microbus) across to Badrasheen on the west bank (15min; £E1); and finally one to Saqqara as above. Unfortunately, all these methods leave you in Saqqara village, still over a kilometre from the site entrance, though the service taxi from Maryotteya will drop you slightly nearer the site entrance if you ask. Getting back to Cairo, don't leave too late or you may not find transport in Saqqara village, and will have either to pay well over the odds for a taxi, or walk another 5km to El-Badrasheen (or at least to the Maryotteya Canal) to pick up a bus or microbus back to Cairo.

Tickets are obtained at the Imhotep Museum (see below). It's a good idea to check which tombs are open – especially those further afield – as they often close due to restoration work. Some guards encourage unauthorized snapping in the tombs in the expectation of baksheesh, but aside from this you're not obliged to give anything unless they help with lighting or provide a guided tour (if you don't want a running commentary, make this clear at the outset). Note that guards also start locking up the tombs at least half an hour before closing time. For a more exotic saunter round the site, you can **rent a camel** (around £E60 per hour) from outside the refreshments hut near the Serapeum.

To save time and energy for the site, you could take a **tour**, such as the ones run by Samo Tours (Ⓣ02/2299-1155 or 012 313-8446, Ⓔsamo@link.net), which leave around 8am in summer, 9am in winter. You'll be driven in an air-conditioned minibus to Memphis, North Saqqara, the Wissa Wassef tapestry school at Harraniyya and the Pyramids of Giza – all accompanied by an English-speaking egyptologist – before returning to Cairo at 4–5pm. Be sure to ask to see the Mastaba of Ti during your trip. The price of the tour (US$23.50) doesn't include admission tickets, but *Rough Guide* readers who book direct get a £E5 discount, with a free airport transfer to your hotel on arrival also thrown in. Misr Travel and American Express also run tours to Saqqara for around £E200 per person. Another option is to rent a **private taxi** for the day (around £E200–250 for just Giza and Saqqara, £E250–300 if you add on Dahshur). Be sure to specify which sites are included and how long you expect to stay when you negotiate with the driver.

Bear in mind **conditions** at Saqqara. Over winter, the site can be swept by chill winds and clouds of grit; during the hottest months walking around is exhausting. Beware of deep pits, which aren't always fenced off. Bring at least one litre of water apiece, as vendors at Memphis and the refreshments hut at North Saqqara are grossly overpriced, like every restaurant along the Saqqara road; a packed lunch is also a good idea. Alternatively, the **Palm Club** just over the Mansureya Canal from the site entrance (Ⓣ02/3819 1555 or 1999; daily 9am–8pm), has a swimming pool set amid pleasant gardens and charges £E95 for a day's access including lunch – definitely an option worth considering if you have kids in tow, or if you feel like a dip and a bite after a hard morning's trudge around the site.

It is possible to **stay** within striking distance of Saqqara: Nasser Abu Ghoneim rents rooms in Abu Sir village by arrangement (Ⓣ010393-1853; Ⓔnasserabughoneim@yahoo.co.uk; £E500); the price includes full board, transfer to and from the airport or Ramses station or any bus terminal, plus free transport to and from Cairo and Saqqara, Dahshur and Giza pyramids; this also offers a taste of Egyptian village life, far removed from the hectic bustle of Cairo.

The Imhotep Museum

Just beyond the ticket kiosk, to the right of the main road leading onto the site, the **Imhotep Museum** (site hours; included in site ticket) is named after the architect who started the whole pyramid building craze by designing the step pyramid for Pharaoh Zoser back in 2650BC or thereabouts. Before you enter the museum, there's a "Viewing Room", where they sometimes show a nine-minute **film** about Imhotep and Saqqara, narrated by Omar Sharif. From here, you can check out the museum itself, which contains a number of interesting items found at the site, and merits a fifteen-minute halt if you aren't pressed for time.

To the right of the entrance hall, the "Expedition Hall" (though the sign on the door says "Saqqara Missions") has a prettily **painted mummy** from the XXX Dynasty, **Imhotep's wooden coffin** (his body has yet to be found), and some copper **surgical instruments** from the tomb of a palace physician called Qar. The main hall, dominated by a reconstruction of the facade from Zoser's tomb, contains the original **green faïence** panels found at the site, a **cobra frieze** similar to the one *in situ*, and a bronze statuette of Imhotep made nearly a millennium after his death. The great architect was revered throughout pharaonic history and worshipped at Saqqara as a god of healing; the Ptolemies associated him with Asclepius, the Greek god of medicine.

To the right of the main hall is a room ("Saqqara Styles") full of stone vessels and **wooden statues**, including two likenesses of a V Dynasty vizier named Ptahotep, modelling two different third-millennium BC hairstyles. The room on the other side of the main hall ("Saqqara Tombs") holds assorted tomb treasures, including the mummy of VI Dynasty pharaoh **Merenra I**, and a canopic jar containing his vital organs. Some of the smaller items are also worth a second glance, among them a dinky XVIII Dynasty goldfish carved in red stone.

Zoser's funerary complex

The funerary complex of King Zoser (or Djoser) is the largest in Saqqara, and its **Step Pyramid** heralded the start of the Pyramid Age. When Imhotep, Zoser's chief architect, raised the pyramid in the 27th century BC, it was the largest structure ever built in stone – the "beginning of architecture", according to one historian. Imhotep's achievement was to break from the tradition of earthbound mastabas, raising level upon level of stones to create a four-step, and then a six-step pyramid, which was clad in dazzling white limestone. None of the blocks was very large, for Zoser's builders still thought in terms of mud-brick rather than megaliths, but the concept, techniques and logistics all pointed towards the true pyramid, finally attained at Giza.

Before it was stripped of its casing stones and rounded off by the elements, Zoser's Pyramid stood 62m high and measured 140m by 118m along its base. The original entrance on the northern side is blocked, but with permission and keys from the site's Antiquities Inspectorate you can enter via a gallery on the opposite side, dug in the XXVI Dynasty. Dark passageways and vertical ladders descend 28m into the bedrock, where a granite plug failed to prevent robbers from plundering the burial chamber of this III Dynasty monarch (c.2667–2648 BC).

Surrounding the pyramid is an extensive **funerary complex**, originally enclosed by a finely cut limestone wall, 544m long and 277m wide, now largely ruined or buried by sand. False doors occur at intervals for the convenience of the pharaoh's *ka*, but visitors can only enter at the southeastern corner, which has largely been rebuilt. Beyond a vestibule with simulated double doors (detailed down to their hinge pins and sockets) lies a narrow colonnaded corridor, whose forty "bundle" columns are ribbed in imitation of palm stems, which culminates in a broader **Hypostyle Hall**.

From here you emerge onto the **Great South Court**, where a rebuilt section of wall (marked ★ on our site plan) is topped by a **frieze of cobras**. Worshipped in the Delta as a fire-spitting goddess of destruction called Wadjet or Edjo, the cobra was adopted as the emblem of royalty and always appeared on pharaonic

▲ Zoser's Step Pyramid

headdresses – a figure known as the *uraeus*. Nearby, a deep shaft plummets into Zoser's **Southern Tomb**, decorated with blue faïence tiles and a relief of the king running the Heb-Sed race. During the Jubilee festival marking the thirtieth year of a pharaoh's reign, he had to sprint between two altars representing Upper and Lower Egypt and re-enact his coronation, seated first on one throne, then upon another, symbolically reuniting the Two Lands.

Although the festival was held at Memphis, a pair of altars, thrones and shrines were incorporated in Zoser's funerary complex to perpetuate its efficacy on a cosmic timescale. The B-shaped structures near the centre of the Great Court are the bases of these altars; the twin thrones probably stood on the platform at the southern end of the adjacent **Heb-Sed Court**. Both shrines were essentially facades, since the actual buildings were filled with rubble. This phoney quality is apparent if you view them from the east: the curvaceous roof line and delicate false columns wouldn't look amiss on a yuppie waterfront development. Notice the four **stone feet** beneath a shelter near the northern end of the court.

Beyond this lies the partially ruined **House of the South**, whose chapel is fronted by proto-Doric columns with lotus capitals, and a spearhead motif above the lintel. Inside you'll find several examples of XVIII–XIX Dynasty tourist graffiti, expressing admiration for Zoser or the equivalent of "Ramses was here". Continuing northwards, you'll pass a relatively intact row of casing stones along the eastern side of Zoser's Pyramid. The **House of the North** has fluted columns with papyrus capitals; the lotus and the papyrus were the heraldic emblems of Upper and Lower Egypt.

On the northern side of the pyramid, a tilted masonry box or **serdab** contains a life-size statue of Zoser gazing blindly towards the North and circumpolar stars, which the ancients associated with immortality; seated thus, his *ka* was assured of eternal life. Zoser's statue is a replica, however, the original having been removed to Cairo's Egyptian Museum, where it's displayed in the Rotunda.

South of the complex

South of Zoser's funerary complex are several tombs and other ruins, dating from various dynasties. During the Old Kingdom, nobles were buried in subterranean tombs covered by large mud-brick superstructures; the name *mastaba* (Arabic for "bench") was bestowed upon them by native workmen during excavations in the nineteenth century. Three such edifices stand outside the southern wall of Zoser's complex; they are often closed for no apparent reason, but it's usually just a question of locating and tipping the caretaker for opening them up. The **Mastaba of Idut** is the most worthwhile, with interesting reliefs in five of its ten rooms. Among the fishing and farming scenes, notice the crocodile eyeing a newborn hippo, and a calf being dragged through the water so that cows will ford a river. The chapel contains a false door painted in imitation of granite, scenes of bulls and buffaloes being sacrificed, and Idut herself. Idut was the daughter of Pharaoh Unas, whose pyramid stands just beyond the **Mastaba of Nebet**, his queen. The reliefs in Nebet's Mastaba are also worth seeing: in one scene, Nebet smells a lotus blossom.

Unas's Pyramid, at the end of the causeway, looks like a mound of rubble from the front, but retains many casing stones around the back, some carved with hieroglyphs. Inside (though it was closed at last check), the walls are covered with Pyramid Texts, on which the Egyptian *Book of the Dead* is based. They speak of the pharaoh becoming a star and travelling to Sirius, and are the earliest-known example of decorative writing within a pharaonic tomb chamber. At time of writing, a kiosk by the car park for the Step Pyramid was selling tickets for further *mastabas* next to the causeway of Unas (£E30, students £E15). The ticket is frankly overpriced: it's supposed to cover three tombs, but once you get there the caretaker says that only two are open (and he's more interested in baksheesh than in seeing a ticket anyway). The one worth seeing is the **Tomb of the Two Brothers**, belonging to Niankh-khnum and Khnum-hotep, two V Dynasty officials depicted kissing each other and performing various activities together. They were probably brothers, and possibly twins, rather than a gay couple, as their families are also pictured in the tomb. The nearby Tomb of Nefer is smaller and less interesting; that of Ruka-Ptah, if the caretaker can be persuaded to open it up, has no lights inside, so you'd need a torch.

Other tombs and ruins

A stone hut to the south of the Unas Pyramid gives access to a spiral staircase that descends 25m underground, to where three low corridors lead into the vaulted **Persian Tombs**. Chief physician Psamtik, Admiral Djenhebu and Psamtik's son Pediese were all officials of the XXVII Dynasty of Persian kings founded in 525 BC, yet the hieroglyphs in their tombs invoke the same spells as those written two thousand years earlier. The dizzying descent and claustrophobic atmosphere make this an exciting tomb to explore. Though often locked, it's not "forbidden" as guards sometimes pretend, hoping to wangle excessive baksheesh.

Further to the southeast lies the **Tomb of Horemheb**. Built when he was a general, it became redundant after Horemheb seized power from Pharaoh Ay in 1348 BC and ordered a new tomb to be dug in the Valley of the Kings, the royal necropolis of the New Kingdom. Many of the finely carved blocks from his original tomb are now in museums around the world. Another set of paving stones and truncated columns marks the nearby **Tomb of Tia**, sister of Ramses II, and the **Tomb of Maya**, Tutankhamun's treasurer, was found nearby in 1986. Unfortunately, all of these were closed to the public at last check.

It's indicative of how much might still be hidden beneath the sands at Saqqara that the **unfinished Pyramid of Sekhemkhet** was only discovered in 1950. Beyond his monuments, nothing is known of Sekhemkhet, whose step pyramid and funerary complex were presumably intended to mimic those of his predecessor, Zoser, and may also have been built by Imhotep. The alabaster sarcophagus inside the pyramid (which is unsafe to enter) was apparently never used, but the body of a child was found inside an auxiliary tomb.

From Sekhemkhet's pyramid it's roughly 700m to the nearest part of South Saqqara.

Around the pyramids of Userkaf and Teti

While neither of these pyramids amounts to much, the mastabas near Teti's edifice contain some fantastic reliefs. If you're starting from Zoser's complex, it's only a short walk to the pulverized **Pyramid of Userkaf**, the founder of the V Dynasty, whose successors were buried at Abu Sir (see p.160). From here, a track runs northwards to the **Pyramid of Teti**, which overlooks the valley from the edge of the plateau. Excavated by Mariette in the 1850s, it has since been engulfed by sand and may be closed; in one of the funeral chambers (accessible by a sloping shaft and low passageway), the star-patterned blocks of its vaulted roof have slipped inwards.

Although most of the VI Dynasty kings who followed Teti chose to be buried at South Saqqara, several of their courtiers were interred in a **"street of tombs"** beside his pyramid, which was linked to the Serapeum by an Avenue of Sphinxes (now sanded over). To do justice to their superbly detailed reliefs takes well over an hour, but it's rare to find all of them open.

The Mastaba of Mereruka

The largest tomb in the street belongs to **Mereruka**, Teti's vizier and son-in-law, whose 32-room complex includes separate funerary suites for his wife Watet-khet-hor, priestess of Hathor, and their son Meri-Teti. In the entry passage, Mereruka is shown playing a board game and painting at an easel; the chamber beyond depicts him hunting in the marshes with Watet-khet-hor (the frogs, birds, hippos and grasshoppers are beautifully rendered), along with the usual farming scenes. Goldsmiths, jewellers and other artisans are inspected by the couple in a room beyond the rear door, which leads into another chamber showing taxation and the punishment of defaulters. A pillared hall to the right portrays them watching sinuous dancers; a room to the left depicts offerings, sacrifices and birds being fed, with a *serdab* at the far end.

Beyond the transverse hall, with its tomb shaft, false door and reliefs of grape-treading and harvesting, lies the main offerings hall, dominated by a statue of Mereruka emerging from a false door. The opposite wall shows his funeral procession; around the corner are boats under full sail, with monkeys playing in their rigging. To the left of the statue, Mereruka is supported by his sons and litter-bearers, accompanied by dwarfs and dogs; on the other side, children frolic while dancers sway above the doorway into Meri-Teti's undecorated funerary suite.

To reach **Watet-khet-hor's suite**, return to the first room in the mastaba and take the other door. After similar scenes to those in her husband's tomb, Watet-khet-hor is carried to her false door in a lion chair.

The Mastabas of Kagemni and Ankh-ma-hor

East of Mereruka's tomb and left around the corner, the smaller **Mastaba of Kagemni** features delicate reliefs in worse shape. The pillared hall beyond the entrance corridor shows dancers and acrobats, the judgement of prisoners, a hippo hunt and agricultural work, all rich in naturalistic detail. Notice the boys feeding a puppy and trussed cows being milked. The door in this wall leads to another chamber where Kagemni inspects his fowl pens while servants trap marsh birds with clap-nets; on the pylon beyond this he relaxes on a palanquin as they tend to his pet dogs and monkeys. As usual in the offerings hall, scenes of butchery appear opposite the false door. On the roof of the mastaba (reached by stairs from the entrance corridor) are two boat pits. As vizier, Kagemni was responsible for overseeing prophets and the estate of Teti's pyramid complex.

The **Mastaba of Ankh-ma-hor** is also known as the "Doctor's Tomb" after its reliefs showing circumcision, toe surgery and suchlike, as practised during the VI Dynasty. If the tomb is open, it's definitely worth a look, unlike the sand-choked **I Dynasty tombs** that straggle along the edge of the scarp beyond the **Antiquities Inspectorate**.

The Double Mastaba of Akhti-Hotep and Ptah-Hotep

This mastaba belonged to **Ptah-Hotep**, a priest of Maat during the reign of Unas's predecessor, Djedkare, and his son **Akhti-Hotep**, who served as vizier, judge and overseer of the granaries and treasury. Though it's smaller than Ti's mastaba, its reliefs are interesting for being at various stages of completion, showing how a finished product was achieved. After the preliminary drawings had been corrected in red by a master artist, the background was chiselled away to leave a silhouette, before details were marked in and cut. The agricultural scenes in the entrance corridor show this process clearly, although with the exception of Ptah-Hotep's chapel, none of these reliefs was ever painted.

Off the pillared hall of Akhti-Hotep is a T-shaped chapel whose inside wall shows workers making papyrus boats and jousting with poles. More impressive is the chapel of his father, covered with exquisitely detailed reliefs. Between the two door-shaped steles representing the entrance to the tomb, Ptah-Hotep enjoys a banquet of offerings, garbed in the panther-skin of a high priest. Similar scenes occur on the facing wall, whose upper registers show animals being slaughtered and women bringing offerings from his estates. The left-hand wall swarms with activity, as boys wrestle and play *khaki la wizza* (a leapfrog game still popular in Nubia); wild animals mate or flee from hunting dogs, while others are caged. A faded mural above the entrance shows the priest being manicured and pedicured.

The Mastaba of Ti

Discovered by Auguste Mariette in 1865, this V Dynasty tomb has been a rich source of information about life in the Old Kingdom. A royal hairdresser who made an advantageous marriage, **Ti** acquired stewardship over several mortuary temples and pyramids, and his children bore the title "royal descendant".

Ti makes his first appearances on either side of the doorway, receiving offerings and asking visitors to respect his tomb **[a]**. The reliefs in the courtyard have been damaged by exposure, but it's possible to discern men butchering an ox **[b]**, Ti on his palanquin accompanied by dogs and dwarfs **[c]**, servants feeding cranes and geese **[d]**, and Ti examining accounts and cargo **[e]**. His unadorned tomb (reached by a shaft from the courtyard) contrasts with the richly decorated interior of the mastaba.

Near his son's false door, variously garbed figures of Ti **[f]** appear above the portal of a corridor where bearers bring food and animals for the sustenance of his *ka* **[g]**. Beyond a doorway **[h]** over which Ti enjoys the marshes with his wife, funerary statues are dragged on sledges above scenes of butchery, and his Delta fleets are arrayed **[i]**. Potters, bakers, brewers and scribes occupy the rear wall of a storage room **[j]**, while dancers shimmy above the doorway to Ti's chapel.

In the harvesting scene, notice the man twisting a donkey's ear to make it behave **[k]**. Further along, Ti inspects shipwrights shaping tree trunks, and sawing and hammering boards **[l]**. Goldsmiths, sculptors, carpenters, tanners and market life are minutely detailed **[m]**, like the musicians who entertain Ti at his offerings table

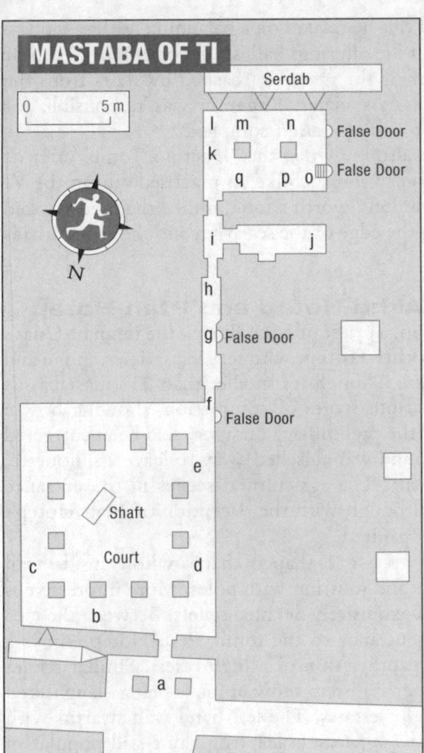

[n]. Peer through one of the apertures and you'll see a cast of his statue inside its *serdab*. The original is in the Egyptian Museum.

Reliefs on the northern wall depict fishing and trapping in the Delta [o]; Ti sailing through the marshes while his servants spear hippopotamuses [p]; harvesting papyrus for boat-building; and ploughing and seeding fields [q]. The scene of hunting in the marshes is also allegorical, pitting Ti against the forces of chaos (represented by fish and birds) and evil (hippos were hated and feared). If you aren't claustrophobic and like cold, dark spaces, it is possible to squeeze down the steps of the shaft into the burial chamber below.

A cluster of **III Dynasty tombs** to the east of Ti's mastaba is now reckoned a likely site for the tomb of Imhotep, as yet undiscovered. Further northeast lie the **Ibis and Baboon Galleries** sacred to Thoth.

The Serapeum

Saqqara's weirdest monument (closed for restoration at the time of writing) lies underground near a derelict building downhill from the refreshments tent. Discovered by Mariette in 1851, the rock-cut galleries of the **Serapeum** held the mummified corpses of the Apis bulls, which the Memphites regarded as manifestations of Ptah's "blessed soul" and identified with Osiris after death. The **cult of the Apis bulls** was assailed by Egypt's Persian conqueror, Cambyses, who stabbed one to disprove its divinity, whilst Artaxerxes I avenged his nickname "the donkey" by having a namesake beast buried here with full honours. But the Ptolemies encouraged native cults and even synthesized their own. "Serapeum" derives from the fusion of the Egyptian Osarapis (Osiris in his Apis form) and the Greeks' Dionysus into the cult of Serapis, whose temple stood in Alexandria.

Although robbers had plundered the galleries centuries before, Auguste Mariette, excavating in 1850, found a single tomb miraculously undisturbed for four thousand years. The oldest of the galleries dates from that era, and is now inaccessible; the second is from the Saite period, and the main one from Ptolemaic times. Enormous granite or basalt **sarcophagi** weighing up to seventy tonnes are ranged either side of the Ptolemaic gallery, at the end of which is a narrow shaft whereby robbers penetrated the Serapeum. The finest sarcophagus squats on the right, while another one lies abandoned near the entrance to the Ramessid gallery. Sadly, none of the mummified bulls remains *in situ*.

En route to the Serapeum you'll notice a concrete slab sheltering broken statues of Plato, Heraclitus, Thales, Protagoras, Homer, Hesiod, Demetrius of Phalerum and Pindar – the **Philosopher's Circle**, now rather rubbish-strewn and neglected. The statues formerly stood near a temple that overlaid the Serapeum, proof that the Ptolemies juxtaposed Hellenistic philosophy and Ancient Egyptian religion with no sense of incongruity.

Memphis

Most tour excursions to Saqqara include a flying visit to the scant **remains of MEMPHIS** in the village of **Mit Rahina**. Sadly, these hardly stir one's imagination to resurrect the ancient city effaced over centuries by Nilotic silt, which now lies metres below rustling palm groves and oxen-ploughed fields. Although something of its glory is evident in the great necropolises ranged across the desert, and the countless objects in Cairo's Egyptian Museum, to appreciate the significance of Memphis you have to recall its history. The city's foundation is attributed to Menes, the quasi-mythical ruler (known also as Narmer – and possibly a conflation of several rulers) who was said to have unified Upper and Lower Egypt and launched the I Dynasty around 3100 BC. At that time, Memphis was sited at the apex of the Delta and thus controlled overland and river communications. Egypt's capital throughout the Old Kingdom, Memphis regained its role after the anarchic Intermediate Period and even after Thebes became capital of the New Kingdom, it remained the nation's second city until well into the Ptolemaic era, only being deserted in early Muslim times after four thousand years of continuous occupation.

Alas for posterity, most of this garden city was built of mud-brick, which returned to the Nile silt whence it came, and everyone from the Romans onwards plundered its stone temples for fine masonry. Nowadays, leftover statues and stelae share a garden (daily 8am–4pm; £E35, students £E20) with souvenir kiosks. The star attraction, found in 1820, is a limestone **Colossus of Ramses II**, similar to the one that used to stand in Midan Ramses, but laid supine within a concrete shelter. A giant **alabaster sphinx** weighing eighty tonnes is also mightily impressive. Both these figures probably stood outside the vast Temple of Ptah, the city's patron deity.

The cults of Ptah and Sokar

In pre-Dynastic times, **Ptah** was the Great Craftsman or Divine Artificer, who invented metallurgy and engineering. However, the people of Memphis esteemed him as the Great Creator who, with a word, brought the universe into being – a concept that never really appealed to other Egyptians. Like most creator gods, he was subsequently linked with death cults and is shown dressed in the shroud of a mummy. The Greeks equated him with Hephaestus, their god of fire and the arts.

Another deity closely associated with Memphis is **Sokar**, originally the god of darkness but subsequently of death, with special responsibility for necropolises. He is often shown, with a falcon's head, seated in the company of Isis and Osiris. Although his major festival occurred at Memphis towards the end of the inundation season, Sokar also rated a shrine at Abydos, where all the Egyptian death gods were represented.

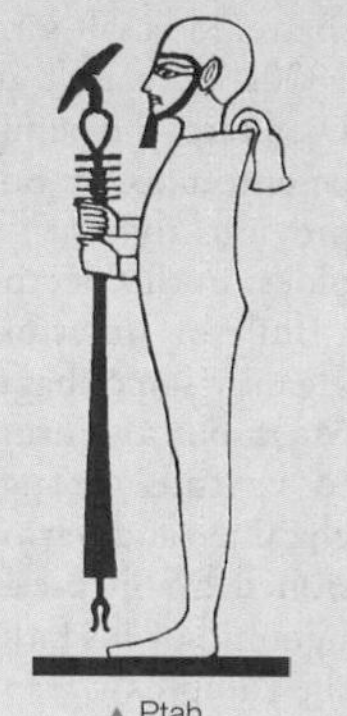

▲ Ptah

By leaving the garden and walking back along the road, you'll notice (on the right) several alabaster **embalming slabs**, where the holy Apis bulls were mummified before burial in the Serapeum at Saqqara. In a pit across the road are excavated chambers from Ptah's temple complex; climb the ridge beyond them and you can gaze across the cultivated valley floor to the Step Pyramid of Saqqara.

South Saqqara

Like their predecessors at Abu Sir, the pharaohs of the VI Dynasty (c.2345–2181 BC) established another necropolis – nowadays called **South Saqqara** – which started 700m beyond Sekhemkhet's unfinished pyramid and extended for over 3km. Alas, the most interesting monuments are those furthest away across the site; renting a donkey, horse or camel (£E30–50 for the round trip) will minimize slogging over soft sand. It's also possible to walk from Saqqara village: just keep heading west until you emerge from the palm trees. If you stop to ask directions, bear in mind that, whatever you say (even if you say it in Arabic), the villagers will almost certainly assume you are looking for the Step Pyramid, and direct you accordingly.

Once you reach the site, two tracks run either side of several pyramids before meeting at the Mastabat al-Faraun. The western one is more direct than the route that goes via Saqqara village, set amid lush palm groves 2km from North Saqqara's ticket office. There is no official entrance fee to the site, and you probably won't see another tourist. Apart from the tranquillity, what you get here – with North Saqqara's pyramids clearly visible to the north, and Dahshur's to the south – is the feeling of being in the midst of a massive pyramid field, somewhere very ancient and vast.

The site

Heading south along either track, you'll pass a low mound of rubble identified as the **Pyramid of Pepi I**. The name "Memphis", which Classical authors bestowed upon Egypt's ancient capital and its environs, was actually derived from one of this pyramid's titles. To the southwest, another insignificant heap indicates the **Pyramid of Merenre**, who succeeded Pepi. French archeologists are excavating the latter's pyramid, but neither site is really worth a detour.

Due west of Saqqara village, sand drifts over the outlying temples of the **Pyramid of Djedkare-Isesi**. Known in Arabic as the "Pyramid of the Sentinel", it stands 25m high and can be entered via a tunnel on the north side. Although a shattered basalt sarcophagus and mummified remains were found here during the 1800s, it wasn't until 1946 that Abdel Hussein identified them as those of Djedkare, the penultimate king of the V Dynasty. Far from being the first ruler to be entombed in South Saqqara, he was merely emulating the last pharaoh of the previous dynasty, whose own mortuary complex is uniquely different, and the oldest in this necropolis.

Built of limestone blocks, the mortuary complex of Shepseskaf resembles a gigantic sarcophagus with a rounded lid; another simile gave rise to its local name, **Mastabat al-Faraun** – the Pharaoh's Bench. If you can find a guard, it's possible to venture through descending and horizontal corridors to reach the burial chamber and various storerooms. The monument was almost certainly commissioned by Shepseskaf, who evidently felt the need to distance himself from the pyramid of his father, Mycerinus. However, the archeologist Jequier doubted that the complex was ever used for any actual burial and Shepseskaf's final resting place remains uncertain.

Northwest of here lies the most complete example of a VI Dynasty mortuary complex, albeit missing casing stones and other masonry that was plundered in medieval times. The usual valley temple and causeway culminate in a mortuary temple whose vestibule and sanctuary retain fragments of their original reliefs. Beyond this rises the **Pyramid of Pepi II**, whose reign supposedly lasted 94 years, after which the VI Dynasty expired. A descending passage leads to his rock-cut **burial chamber**, whose ceiling and walls are inscribed with stars and Pyramid Texts (also found within the subsidiary pyramids of Pepi's queens, Apuit and Neith, which imitate his mortuary complex on a smaller scale).

Dahshur

The **Dahshur pyramid field** (daily 8am–4pm, last ticket sold an hour before closing; £E30, students £E15) contains some of the most impressive of all the pyramids, and some of the most significant in the history of pyramid-building. The easiest way to get to Dahshur is by taxi, but there are service taxi microbuses to Dahshur village from Saqqara village, and occasionally direct ones from Maryotteya Canal by Pyramids Road (otherwise get one from there to Saqqara and change). Infrequent service taxis run the 2km to the site entrance from Dahshur village, but most people will find it easier to walk or take a private taxi. The latter is a good idea since the site is extremely spread out: it's one kilometre from the gate to the Red Pyramid, and another from there to the Bent Pyramid. A tuk-tuk (Indian-style auto-rickshaw) should cost £E3 from the village to the site entrance, but actually it's a pleasant walk. Getting back to Cairo should not be left too late or you may find yourself stranded with the nearest public transport 5km away in Saqqara – transport from Dahshur tends to dry up at around 5pm.

The pyramids are in two groups. To the east are three **Middle Kingdom complexes**, dating from the revival of pyramid-building (c.1991–1790 BC) that culminated near the Fayoum. Though the pyramids proved unrewarding to nineteenth-century excavators, their subsidiary tombs yielded some magnificent jewellery (now in the Egyptian Antiquities Museum). To the north, the pyramids of XII Dynasty pharaohs Seostris III and Amenenmhat II are little more than piles of rubble, but the southernmost of the three, the **Black Pyramid of Amenemhat III** (Joseph's pharoah in the Old Testament, according to some), is at least an interesting shape: though its limestone casing has long gone, a black mud-brick core is still standing (its black basalt capstone is in the Antiquities Museum). More intriguing, however, are the two **Old Kingdom pyramids** further into the desert, which have long tantalized archeologists with a riddle. Both of them are credited to **Snofru** (c.2613–2588 BC), father of Cheops and founder of the IV Dynasty, whose monuments constitute an evolutionary link between the stepped creations of the previous dynasty at North Saqqara and the true pyramids of Giza.

The Red Pyramid

The first pyramid you come to if you follow the road past the ticket office is Snofru's northern **Red Pyramid**, which is named after the colour of the limestone it was built from. Despite its lower angle (43.5°) and height (101m), Snofru's Red Pyramid clearly prefigures Cheops's edifice, which is also the only pyramid that exceeds it in size. It was probably Snofru's third attempt at pyramid building (see p.393), but he was not laid to rest in any of the burial chambers here – all were unused. The **interior** is open to the public; you can climb up and descend into it to check out its three musty chambers. Electric lighting has been installed but it sometimes fails, so bring a torch. The first two chambers are roughly parallel to each other, but the third is on a higher level and perpendicular to the other two. You will probably be alone to absorb the rather eerie, fetid, atmosphere.

The Bent Pyramid

From the Red Pyramid, a track leads south to the **Bent Pyramid**, which is not only the most intriguing of all the pyramids, but, because of its state of preservation, also the most breathtaking. What makes Snofru's final resting place different from all the other pyramids is its change of angle towards the top: it rises more steeply (54.3°) than the Red Pyramid or Giza pyramids for three-quarters of its height, before abruptly tapering at a gentler slope – hence its name. The explanation for its shape, and why Snofru should have built two pyramids only a kilometre apart, is a longstanding conundrum of Egyptology.

Mindful of the truism that a pharaoh required but one sanctuary for his *ka*, many reasoned that the Bent Pyramid resulted from a change of plan prompted by fears for its stability, and when these persisted, a second, safer pyramid was built to guarantee Snofru's afterlife. But for this theory to hold water, it's necessary to dismiss Snofru's claim to have built a *third* pyramid at Maidum as mere usurpation of an earlier structure; and the possibility that its sudden collapse might have caused the modification of the Bent Pyramid must likewise be rejected on the grounds that he needed only one secure monument.

In 1977, a professor of physics at Oxford University reopened the whole debate. Kurt Mendelssohn, arguing that Snofru did, indeed, commission the "Collapsed Pyramid" at Maidum (whose fall resulted in changes to Dahshur's Bent Pyramid), overcame the "one pharaoh–one *ka*–one pyramid" objection by postulating a pyramid production line. As one pyramid neared completion, surplus resources were deployed to start another, despite the satisfaction of the reigning king's requirements. The reason for continuous production was that building a single pyramid required gigantic efforts over ten to thirty years; inevitably, some pharaohs lacked the time and resources. A stockpile of half-constructed, perhaps even finished, pyramids was an insurance policy on the afterlife.

Egyptologists greeted Mendelssohn's theory with delight or derision, but unlike the Great Pyramids, or the lives of Hatshepsut, Nefertiti and Akhenaten, the enigma of Snofru's pyramids has never excited much public interest. Nevertheless, of all the pyramids, the Bent Pyramid is probably the most visually stunning. The reason it seems so impressive lies in the fact that, although its corners have fallen away at the base, the pyramid's limestone casing is still largely intact, giving a clear impression of what it once looked like – smooth and white. All the Old Kingdom pyramids were originally clad in limestone, their surfaces smooth like this one, but most have been stripped, their stone burned for lime. The Bent Pyramid escaped that fate because its narrower angle made it harder to remove the limestone facing, though this has disappeared from much of the base.

The removal of these layers enables you to see not only how closely the blocks were slotted together but also pits and grooves carved into the bedrock at the northwest corner of the pyramid, which were presumably carved before it was begun, marking out a base on the cleared bedrock.

The Bent Pyramid is unusual in one final respect: it has two entrances, one on its west side as well as the more conventional one on its north face. To its south is a subsidiary queen's pyramid, possibly belonging to Snofru's wife Hetepheres. If it did, she didn't stay there too long: after robbers had entered both of Snofru's pyramids at Dahshur, her sarcophagus was moved to Giza for safekeeping, and hidden down a shaft beside the Great Pyramid of her son Cheops. The **interior** of the Bent Pyramid is unlikely to be open to the public in the near future, but you can see inside it on Ⓦwww.guardians.net/egypt.

Eating

Restaurants run the gamut from *nouvelle cuisine* salons to backstreet kebab houses and open-fronted tiled diners. The ones devoted to *kushari* or *fuul* and *taamiya* provide the cheapest nutritious meals going. At the other end of the gastro-cultural spectrum, every hotel rated three stars or above has at least one restaurant and coffee shop that's accessible to non-residents.

Between these extremes there's a huge variation in **standards** of cleanliness and presentation, and whether somewhere seems okay or grotty depends partly on your own values. Running water remains a crucial factor – anywhere without it is risky. A number of places off Ramses, Orabi, Ataba, Falaki, Lazoghli and Giza squares and midway down Sharia Qalaa function **all night**.

Restaurants and street food

The majority of places reviewed here have **menus** in English or French, but others deal only in Arabic; fortunately, many of them display what's on offer, so you only have to point. Increasingly, restaurants in Cairo, from fast-food joints through to posh eateries, offer **home delivery** (or hotel delivery, if your hostelry will allow it). Phone numbers are given for those places, and for establishments where a **reservation** is advisable.

Downtown Cairo

All the restaurants below are marked on the map on pp.92–93 unless otherwise stated.

Al-Haty In the passage by 8 26th July St. Go through the door marked "Salle Orientale" and up the stairs, where a once very grand restaurant, now rather faded and empty, still offers quite posh dishes such as turkey in walnut sauce (£E45) in classic Arabic surrounds. Daily 10am–midnight.

Alfi Bey 3 Sharia Alfi Bey Ⓣ02/577-1888. Another vintage restaurant, founded in 1938. Its panelling, chandeliers and gilt furniture have been here ever since it opened. Best for lamb dishes such as neck of mutton (£E37). No alcohol. Daily 1pm–1am.

Aly Hassan Al-Haty 3 Sharia Halim, off 26th July St, behind the *Windsor Hotel*. Vintage decor, with mirrors and fans, and traditional good-value fare, including mezze, roast lamb, *kofta* and kebab. Try the chargrilled half-chicken (£E18). No alcohol. Daily noon–1am.

Arabesque 6 Sharia Qasr el-Nil Ⓣ02/574-8677. Egyptian, French and Levantine cuisine, strong on soups and meat dishes; if you like Jews' mallow, try the £E55 rabbit *melokheya*. The ambiance is quite chic and there's usually a small exhibition of contemporary art, and you can treat it as a bar and just pop in for a drink. Daily noon–2am.

Bon Appetit Sharia Mohammed Mahmoud, opposite the AUC Library. Downtown branch of the Mohandiseen café-restaurant (see p.152) favoured by students from the AUC. There are sub-style sandwiches (£E18.25–27.25) and dishes such as *shish tawouk* (chicken shish kebab; £E27.50). Daily 9am–1am.

Centro Recreativo Italiano 26th July St, behind the Italian embassy (ring the bell to enter) ⓣ02/2575-9590. This is a club for the city's Italian expats, but they usually let in foreigners on payment of a £E10 guest fee (there's also a £E3 cover charge). As you'd expect, the pizzas (£E25–40) and pasta dishes (£E20–35) are excellent, you eat outside on the terrace in summer, inside in winter, and there's wine, and aperitifs such as Campari and vermouth. Daily 7–11pm. Reservation compulsory on Thurs.

El-Dahan 52 26th July St, Bulaq. Branch of the Muski kebab house (see p.185), but the bill always seems to end up much cheaper here – a quarter kilo of *kofta* and kebab with salad and *tahina* works out around £E25. Daily 1pm–1am.

Estoril 12 Sharia Talaat Harb, in the passage ⓣ02/2574-3102. Mainly French and Lebanese dishes at this cosy bistro-style restaurant, with a vintage bar that merits a Bogart. Dishes include Tripoli-style spicy grouper (£E43), or, for a change from the usual, chicken in ginger and soy sauce (£E38). Daily noon–midnight.

Felfela 15 Sharia Hoda Shaarawi. A tourist favourite, offering Egyptian dishes in a long hall with funky decor, and sells beer. Service can be a little snooty if you're scruffily dressed, and there's nothing you can get here that wouldn't be cheaper elsewhere, but it's reliably good. A portion of *kofta* and kebab goes for £E50, half a grilled chicken for £E27.25. Daily 8am–midnight. *Felfela's* takeaway, around the corner on Talaat Harb (daily 7am–midnight), does *shawarmas* and *taamiya* sandwiches, though again slightly pricier than elsewhere.

Gad 13 26th July St ⓣ02/2576-3353 or 3583. The modern and very popular takeaway downstairs is always crowded, as is the upstairs where you can get a sit-down meal. Excellent standards – *taamiya*, *fuul*, *shawarma* and burgers – plus delicious specialities such as *kibda skanderani* (Alexandrian-style liver with chilli; £E18), wonderful baked-on-the-premises Syrian-style pitta bread (*'aish shaami*), and some of the best *fiteers* in town (£E5–23). They also deliver. Daily 24hr.

Greek Club Above *Groppi* on Midan Talaat Harb; entrance on Sharia Bassiouni. The cuisine isn't particularly Greek, but it's not bad (fried squid and chips for £E26, stuffed vine leaves for £E10), and the summer terrace is pleasant. Serves alcohol, including ouzo. Daily 7pm–midnight.

Hati el-Guesh (aka *Sayed*) 32 Midan Falaki, on the corner of Tahrir and Falaki streets. A bright place serving Egyptian standards such as *kofta* and kebab (£E31) or stuffed pigeon (£E25.50), with the usual mezze and side dishes. Daily noon–midnight.

Le Bistro 8 Sharia Hoda Shaarawi ⓣ02/392-7694. A bright little place with immaculate service and decent French food including sea bass in mustard sauce (£E36), beef tournedos in red wine sauce (£E48), crêpes (£E12) and chocolate mousse (£E12). Serves alcohol. Daily noon–midnight.

La Chesa 21 Sharia Adly ⓣ02/393-9360. Salubrious, Swiss-managed café serving good Western food, including fondues (£E145 for up to four people) and daily specials (£E55), as well as Swiss breakfasts (£E26), scrumptious pastries and great coffee. Daily 7am–midnight.

El Nile Fish 25 Sharia el-Bustan, just off Midan Falaki. Popular fish restaurant with choice of various denizens of the deep freshly caught and fried or grilled to order (£E22–60 per kilo), served with salad, *tahina* and pickles. Daily noon–1am.

Paprika 1129 Corniche el-Nil, just south of the TV Building ⓣ02/2578-9447. Serving a mix of Hungarian and Egyptian food – tasty paprika-based dishes and mezze. The speciality is goulash (£E48). Frequented by media folk (including Omar Sharif) and footballers, it's especially busy at weekends. Daily noon–midnight.

Peking 14 Sharia Saray el-Azbakiya ⓣ02/591-2381, ⓦwww.peking-restaurants.com. Central branch of a citywide chain of Chinese restaurants, not the best or most authentic Chinese food you'll ever taste, but a change at least, and they do takeouts and delivery, with branches in Zamalek, Mohandiseen and Heliopolis, plus a floating restaurant (see p.187). Chicken with ginger and garlic is not bad at £E26.75, prawns with mushrooms and bamboo shoots are pricier at £E43.50. Daily noon–12.30am.

Pomo Doro 197 Sharia Tahrir, Abdin. A hole-in-the-wall place but very clean, with takeaways or seats out on the pavement, serving only spaghetti, with a choice of chicken, bolognaise, vegetarian or (especially recommended) seafood, at £E15 a throw. Everything's cooked fresh, so expect to wait, but it's worth it, and you can watch them cooking it. Daily 3pm–1am.

Very cheap options

Most of the really cheap diners are concentrated around Midan Orabi (especially along the first block of Sharia al-Azbakiya, the small street between the two patisseries) and Midan Falaki (especially on Sharia Mansur, outside Bab al-Luq market). They are not listed individually here, but worth a peruse. At most of the following you can fill up for well under £E20. All are marked on the map on pp.92–93 unless otherwise stated.

Abou Tarek 40 Sharia Champollion, at the corner of Sharia Maarouf www.aboutarek.com. You can't miss this a/c diner on two floors; it's lit up like a Christmas tree. It serves the best *kushari* in Cairo (£E3–7), with rice pudding for afters. Daily 7.30am–11.30pm.

Akher Saa 8 Sharia Alfi Bey, next to the Nile Christian Bookshop. A very popular 24hr *fuul* and falafel takeaway with a sit-down restaurant attached. Not a bad place for breakfast either – *fuul*, omelette, bread and *tahina* for £E10.50. There's a takeaway branch at 14 Sharia Abdel Khaliq Sarwat, just off Talaat Harb (02/2579-8557), which also does home delivery.

Al-Kazaz 38 Sharia Abo Alaam. Clean, inexpensive 24hr diner, just off Midan Talaat Harb. Tasty *shawarma* (£E3 a sandwich), *taamiya* (£E1 a sandwich) and other fried food, served in a tiny a/c dining room upstairs, or downstairs to take away.

Gaba Abdo Sharia Monshaat al-Kataba. Popular downtown kushari joint, hidden away in the backstreets between Talaat Harb and Qasr al-Nil. Also serves spaghetti or macaroni with meat sauce or liver on top (£E5). Daily 7am–midnight.

El Tabei El-Domyati 31 Sharia Orabi, north of Midan Orabi 02/575-4391 (see map, p.106). Pick-and-mix mezze (£E2.50 each) are the best thing in this souped-up *fuul* and *taamiya* diner, though it also does reasonable Egyptian puddings. The takeaway sandwiches, though, are less good. They also deliver, and have a small branch for takeaways in the food court at the bottom of a shopping mall on the corner of Sharia Abdel Hamid Said with Sharia Talaat Harb. Daily 5am–1am.

El-Tahrir Sharia Tahrir between Midan Tahrir and Midan Falaki. A long-established place (*kushari* £E3–8), with a second branch at 19 Sharia Abdel Khaliq Sarwat, just off Sharia Talaat Harb. A rival to *Abou Tarek*, though most *kushari* freaks agree it plays second fiddle nowadays. Daily 8am–2am.

Fatatri Pizza el-Tahrir Sharia Tahrir, one block east of Midan Tahrir (look for the marble facade on the south side). *Fiteers* (with meat and egg) and crustier versions topped with hot sauce, cheese and olives make a delicious meal. Also pancake *fiteers* filled with apple jam and icing sugar. Prices from £E5 to £E25. Daily 24hr.

Islamic Cairo and Saiyida Zeinab

Egyptian Pancake House Between Midan el-Hussein and Al-Azhar (see map, p.110). Made-to-order savoury or sweet *fiteers* filled with meat, egg, cheese, or any combination of coconut, raisins, jam or honey. Soft drinks only. *Fiteers* cost £E15–40, but check for extraneous items on the bill. Daily 24hr.

El-Dahan On the Muski, beneath the *El-Hussein Hotel*. Excellent kebab house, where a quarter kilo of mixed kebab with salad and *tahina* costs £E45. There's also roast lamb and other meat dishes, but no alcohol. Daily 11am–2am.

El-Gahsh Saiyida Zeinab, a block along Sharia Abdel Meguid from Midan Saiyida Zeinab, on the way to Ibn Tulun Mosque (look for the mule-cart cartoon sign). It may not look much, but this insalubrious little takeaway-diner is generally held to do the best *fuul* in Cairo. Best at night, when they lay out tables in the neighbouring streets. A plate of *fuul* with all the trimmings will set you back the princely sum of £E7. Daily 24hr.

El-Hussein On the roof of the *El-Hussein Hotel* (see map, p.110). Fantastic views over Islamic Cairo, but not very good food. They also have juices, teas and *sheeshas* however. Often used for wedding parties. Daily 7am–midnight.

Gad Sharia al-Azhar (see map, p.110). Al-Azhar branch of the popular downtown eatery (see p.184). Daily 24hr.

Hilltop Restaurant Al-Azhar Park, Sharia Salah Salem (see map, p.136). Classy Egyptian eating, subtle background music, grills and kebabs (mixed grill £E58), and on Friday and Saturday evenings, a £E120 eat-all-you-can buffet with soups, salads, half-a-dozen main dishes to sample, and a gluttonous choice of afters. And the toilets are spotless. Expensive. Daily 1–11pm.

Khan el-Khalili Restaurant 5 Sikket al-Badestan. An a/c café-restaurant managed by the *Mena House Oberoi*, near the old gate 40m west of El-Hussein's Mosque. Western and Egyptian snacks (£E16–31) and meals (main dishes from £E55, rabbit *melokheya* £E65) are served in the dining room. Daily 10am–2am.

Rifai 37 Midan Saiyida Zeinab, opposite Saiyida Zeinab Mosque (hidden up an alley by the Sabil Kuttab of Sultan Mustapha, signposted "Mongy Destrict"). A renowned nighttime *kofta* and kebab joint – people are known to drive from Heliopolis for a takeout. A quarter-kilo of *kofta* and kebab with *tahina*, babaghanoug and salad comes to £E35. Daily 5pm–5am.

Zamalek

As befits a high-rent, cosmopolitan neighbourhood, Zamalek boasts several upmarket restaurants devoted to foreign cuisine, plus trendy nightspots like *Deals* and *Pub 28* (see "Drinking" p.191), both of which do good food too. There's also a place that caters especially well for vegetarians, *L'Aubergine*. All these restaurants are on the map on pp.152–153, as is the Zamalek branch of the Chinese *Peking* chain (23b Sharia Ismail Mohammed ⓣ02/2736-3894).

Angus Brasserie 34 Sharia Yehia Ibrahim, inside the *New Star Hotel* ⓣ02/735-1865. Steaks, notably *asado* (Argentinian-style sirloin with chimchurri sauce; £E45.50), or fillet steak with a choice of mustard, blue-cheese or mushroom topping (£E45). Daily 5pm–midnight.

Didos (Al Dente) 26 Sharia Bahgat Ali ⓣ02/2735-9117, ⓦwww.didospasta.com. Besides good pasta (choice of spaghetti, fettuccine, penne or fusilli with a range of sauces, £E13–39), this little place also has excellent salads and specialities such as Portuguese-style fish (£24.50). Delivers anywhere in central Cairo. Daily 24hr.

Don Quichotte 9a Sharia Ahmed Heshmat ⓣ02/2735-6415. Small, elegant, lounge-style restaurant serving great cuisines of the world. Dishes include sole meunière (£E80) and steak in gorgonzola sauce (£E80), with desserts such as chocolate soufflé (£E39). Reservations advisable. Daily 1pm–1am.

Five Bells Corner of Adil Abu Bakr and Ismail Mohammed ⓣ02/2735-8980. It's worth dressing up for this swish Italianate joint, complete with garden and fountain. Specialities include meat fondue, grill-it-yourself charbonnade (£E110 for two), and fish with squid and prawns in red sauce (£E55). Daily 12.30pm–2am.

Hana Barbecue House Sharia Mohammed Mahzar ⓣ02/2738-2972. Small, friendly place offering various Asian dishes. A huge portion of *sukiyaki* (do-it-yourself stir-fry seafood soup) costs £E45. Also does deliveries. Expensive. Daily noon–10.30pm.

L'Aubergine 5 Sharia Sayed el-Bakri. Moderately priced with an adventurous menu, changed weekly and featuring a good variety of vegetarian dishes, such as cheese and spinach crêpes (£E23), or pan-fried halloumi (£E28). The food is usually very good though some of the more ambitious dishes may disappoint. There's also a bar upstairs (see p.191). Daily 10am–1.30am.

Maison Thomas 157 26th July St, opposite the *Marriott Hotel* ⓣ02/735-7057. Deli-diner-takeaway place serving freshly made baguettes and pizzas as well as light meals (from £E40). They make their own mozzarella, as well as doing good breakfasts (7–11am; £E26). They will deliver to anywhere in central Cairo – even beer at £E7.50 a bottle. Daily 24hr.

Garden City and Roda Island

The places reviewed here are keyed on the map on pp.140–141 unless otherwise indicated.

Abou Shakra 69 Sharia Qasr al-Aini, opposite the hospital ⓣ02/531-6111, ⓦwww.aboushakra.com. Decorated in marble and alabaster, this famous establishment specializes in *kofta* and kebab sold by weight (£E94 per kilo), to eat in or take out. Despite the pretensions, the food here isn't as good as in *baladi* establshments such as *el-Dahan* or *Rifai* in Islamic Cairo. Daily 1pm–1am (Ramadan from 7pm).

Revolving Restaurant Fortieth floor, *Grand Hyatt Hotel*, Roda Island ⓣ02/365-1234. "Semi-formal" dress is required (no t-shirts or jeans), and children under 12 are barred at this tip-top French restaurant with the best view in Cairo. Start with the likes of duck liver in ginger and cherry sauce (£E145) or lobster bisque (£E50), follow with salmon in horseradish sauce (£E170) or duck with pink pepper sauce (£E160), and finish with lavender crême brulée (£E60). Daily 7pm–1am.

Taboula 1 Sharia Amerika Latina, Garden City ⓣ02/2792-5261 (see map, p.92). One of Cairo's best Lebanese restaurants, with very grand decor, a massive choice of mezze (£E11–24), various preparations of *kofta*, and Lebanese *fattehs* (dishes made with toasted pitta pieces; £E32–40). Does takeaways and home delivery. Daily noon–2am.

Pyramids area

Felfela Village Maryotteya Canal ⓣ02/3384-1515 or 1616 (see map, p.161). Standard Egyptian fare (falafel £E3.25, *fuul* £E6.50, stuffed pigeon £E35) aimed at tourists in a rambling outdoor complex on a canal that crosses Pyramids Road, 1km north on the east bank. There's a zoo, a playground, and a show with camel rides, acrobats, puppets and bellydancers – even dancing horses. The show (1–7.30pm) is presented daily in summer, Fri in winter. Restaurant daily 8am–1am.

The Moghul Room *Mena House Oberoi* hotel ⓣ02/3377-3222. Cairo's top Indian restaurant. As the name suggests, north Indian Mughal dishes are the mainstay here, notably *rogan josh* (lamb curry with tomato £E98), but they also do veg curries, and Goan fish curry (£E110); they usually go easy on the chilli, so tell them if you want it spicy. Daily sittings at 7pm and 9.30pm, reservation required.

Floating restaurants

Floating restaurants can be an agreeable way to enjoy the Nile, but as cruise schedules change, it is wise to phone and check, and it's worth booking, too.

Nile Maxim ⓣ02/2738-8888. Docked in front of the *Marriott* (see map, p.152), this runs dinner cruises (daily 8pm & 10.30pm), with a choice of set menus (£E260–346) and an impressive floorshow, including some of Cairo's top bellydancers.

Nile Peking ⓣ02/2531-6388, ⓦwww.peking-restaurants.com (see map, p.141). Moored opposite the Nilometer, 200m west of Mari Girgis metro station, this is the floating branch of the *Peking chain* of Chinese restaurants. The boat currently sails Sun 8pm & 10pm, Thurs 10pm & midnight, and Fri 4pm, 6pm, 8pm & 10pm. Each cruise lasts two hours with a £E110 set menu and light music (no floor show). Otherwise, the boat is moored and open daily noon–midnight with an à la carte menu.

The Nile Pharaoh & Golden Pharaoh ⓣ02/3570-1000, ⓦwww.thepharaohs.com.eg (see map, p.140). Pair of mock-pharaonic barges complete with scarab friezes, picture windows, and golden lotus flowers or figures of Horus mounted on the stern and prow. Moored 1km south of the El-Gama'a Bridge and operated by *Oberoi Hotels*, they cruise for lunch (2.30 & 3.30pm in winter, 3pm & 4pm summer; £E170), early dinner (7pm and 7.45pm in winter, 7.45pm & 8.45pm in summer; £E200) or late dinner (10pm & 10.45pm in winter, 10.30pm & 11.30pm in summer; £E250). Cruises last two hours and you should check in half an hour before sailing. The early dinner cruise features music and a bellydancer, the late one features an Arabic stand-up comedian and a shorter bellydance show, while lunch cruises have a Middle Eastern band instead.

Scarabee ⓣ02/2794-3444. Docked on the Corniche near the *Shepheard* Hotel (see map, p.92). Not as posh as the other floating restaurants, the *Scarabee* does two dinner cruises nightly (7.30–9.30pm & 10pm–midnight; £E185) with an "oriental" floor show, bellydancer and a dance band.

Coffee houses, tearooms and buffets

Cairene men have socialized in hole-in-the-wall **coffee houses** (*'ahwas*) ever since the beverage was introduced from Yemen in the early Middle Ages (for a rundown on coffee and tea drinking, see p.41). A few – such as *Fishawi's* in Khan el-Khalili and *El-Horea* in Midan Falaki (see p.190) – are larger and more sophisticated *'ahwas*, with high ceilings and tall mirrors. Some are distinguished by their decor, notably the incredibly kitsch *El Shems*, near Midan Orabi in the passage by 4 Sharia Tawfiqia, and the *Um Kalthoum* café on Sharia al-Azbakiya, filled with memorabilia of the singer and other stars of her day. For football fans, *Mondial Café* at 4 Sharia Darih Sa'd (see map, p.92), is one of the few places that can generally be relied on to show important English and European matches live. **All-night** *'ahwas* can be found around Midan Ramses and Sharia Qalaa and the Saiyida Zeinab end of Sharia Mohammed Farid and Sharia el-Nasireya. There are also modern all-night coffee shops in the *InterContinental*, *Nile Hilton* and other deluxe hotels. Women can increasingly be seen smoking *sheeshas* in *'ahwas*, though generally in more sophisticated, slightly upmarket places rather than old-school hole-in-the-wall ones.

As *'ahwas* are numerous (the downtown ones mentioned above appear on the map on pp.92–93), pretty standard, and don't sell food, the reviews below concentrate on more upmarket Western-style coffee houses and tearooms, whose pastries, rice pudding, crème caramel and suchlike provide an alternative to the monotony of standard hotel breakfasts.

Cairo's best views

The roof of the *Nile Ritz-Carlton* hotel (see p.87) has views of **Midan Tahrir** that only the front rooms at the *Ismailia House* hotel can equal, and which stretch as far east as the Citadel and the Muqattam Hills. The best budget hotel for views is the *Isis* (see p.86). The Citadel (p.125) overlooks **Islamic Cairo**, where certain minarets give you a vista as far as the Pyramids on a clear day if they're open (the Qalaoun complex, the Blue Mosque and the al-Muayyad minarets atop Bab Zwayla), but the finest view is from the high point in al-Azhar Park (p.137). To look down on the mayhem that is **Midan Ramses**, the terrace café of the *Everest Hotel* (see below) is the place. The Cairo Tower on Gezira (p.154) is also great for views, while the revolving restaurant at the *Grand Hyatt* hotel on Roda Island (p.186) offers what must rate as Cairo's best **panoramic view**, encompassing the Pyramids, the Citadel, the Nile and most of downtown.

Downtown

All the places listed are marked on the map on pp.92–93, unless otherwise stated.

Cilantro 31 Sharia Mohammed Mahmoud. All sorts of caffés, frappés, cappuccinos and frappuccinos, plus quiches, toasties, sandwiches (£E10–22) and salads (£E15–22), or cakes and pastries if you want something sweet. Daily 7am–2am. Branches in various upmarket suburbs.

Everest Hotel Midan Ramses (map p.106).The fifteenth-floor terrace café of an otherwise unremarkable cheap hotel, whose coffee isn't the best in town, but you can take a tea or fruit juice and enjoy a view over Midan Ramses and as far as the Citadel and the Muqattam Hills. Daily 24hr.

Garden Groppi 48 Sharia Abdel Khaliq Sarwat/12 Sharia Adly. The more spacious, "garden" branch of the Groppi chain (see below), a favourite with British officers during the war, when non-commissioned ranks were barred. You can sit in the salon with your coffee and pastry, or on the outside terrace and enjoy a *sheesha* with them, though frankly it isn't anything like as elegant as it makes out. Daily 7am–11pm. Minimum charge £E10.

Groppi Midan Talaat Harb. The once-palatial flagship branch of this classic chain was, in its heyday, pretty much synonymous with Cairo's erstwhile European "café society". It's lost much of its charm since renovation, and the coffee itself is pretty terrible, but it has a restful air-conditioned salon, and the pastries are great. Moreover, it's a taste, albeit a very faded one, of what Cairo's elegant downtown Ismailiya quarter was like in the days of King Fouad and King Farouk. Daily 7am–11pm. Minimum charge £E10.

Ibis Café Ground floor, *Nile Hotel*. Cool hotel café-restaurant with an unlimited lunch and dinner buffet bar (£E110 lunchtime, £E120 evening) featuring Lebanese-style mezze, or à la carte dishes such as salmon in lemon butter with two veg (£E95). Daily 11am–6am.

Simonds Coffee Shop 29 Sharia Sherif. A downtown branch of Zamalek's French-style café (see opposite) with espresso coffee and Egyptian or European-style pastries. Daily 7am–10pm.

Islamic Cairo

All the places listed here are marked on the map on p.110.

'Ahwa al-Aini Midan al-Aini, Butneya. You might not even notice, if you come to this little square in the daytime, that there's a café here, but come the evening, especially after around 9pm, the lights are lit, the music plays, and it becomes a lovely open-air hangout, served by the tiny, hole-in-the-wall *'ahwa*. Daily 5pm–2am.

Fishawi's Behind the *El-Hussein Hotel* in Khan el-Khalili. Cairo's oldest tea house has been managed by the same family (and remained perpetually open) since 1773. Imbibe the atmosphere – cracked mirrors, battered furniture, haughty staff and wandering vendors – with a pot of mint tea and a *sheesha*. Prices are posted up in Arabic, but if you don't read it, expect to be overcharged. Daily 24hr.

Naguib Mahfouz Coffee Shop 5 Sikket al-Badestan. Upmarket a/c tourist café in the heart of the bazaar, serving snacks, coffee, mint tea and orange juice. Part of the *Khan el-Khalili Restaurant*. Daily 10am–2am.

Zamalek

All the places listed here are marked on the map on p.152.

Beano's 8 Sharia al-Marsafy. Hot and cold espresso-based coffee concoctions in a lovely a/c space that's cool in both senses, with free wi-fi coverage to boot. Also serves crêpes, pastries, salads and sandwiches, but neither the coffee nor the snacks are cheap. Daily 6am–1am. There's a downtown branch on Sharia Mohammed Mahmoud (map pp.92–93), but it isn't as good.

Café Tabasco 18b Sharia el-Marashly ⓣ02/2735-8465. A sophisticated, Western-style coffee house, wi-fi enabled, where the TV (usually Eurosport) isn't obtrusive, there are magazines to read, and you can get coffee, juices, herb teas and food (salad, mezze, sandwiches, pasta, pizza and ice cream). A good place to hang out, and they even deliver within Zamalek. Daily 7am–3am. Also in Dokki (7 Sharia Mossadek ⓣ02/3762-2060).

No Big Deal Sharia Sayed el-Bakri, next to *Deals* bar ⓦwww.nobigdealcafe.com. Small, San Francisco-style coffee shop, with home-made cakes and such exotic beverages as Earl Grey tea. Pleasant, but somehow not very Egyptian. Daily 7am–1am.

Rigoletto Yamaha Centre, 3 Sharia Taha Hussein. Espresso, cappuccino, cheesecake and by far the best ice cream in town (£E4 a scoop) – try the cinnamon flavour if you fancy something unusual. £E5 minimum charge to eat in (not always enforced). Daily 9am–midnight.

Simonds Coffee Shop 112 26th July St, near the Hassan Sabry intersection. Cairo's original French-style coffee shop, with cappuccino, hot chocolate, lemonade, fresh croissants, pastries and *ramequins* (cheese puffs). Daily 7am–10pm.

Patisseries, juice bars and ice cream

More sophisticated coffeeshops and the upmarket tearooms serve pastries, but they'll be cheaper at **patisseries**, where traditional sticky sweets such as baklava and *burma* (slices of syrup-drenched shredded wheat around a pistachio or hazelnut core) are normally sold by the kilo. Good downtown patisseries (see map, p.93) to try are *El Abd* at 25 Talaat Harb, and on the corner of 26th July and Sherif, and *El-Sharkia* on Sharia Alfi Bey. Even more renowned is the city-wide chain *La Poire*, of which the original and most central branch, at 1 Sharia Amerika Latina (not far from Midan Tahrir; see the map on pp.92–93), offers home-made baklava (£E65 per kilo) and eclairs (£E7 each); other branches can be found in Mohandiseen

▲ *Fishawi's* Café

(see map, p.152), Giza (Sharia el-Nil, 100m south of the Gama'a Bridge), and Heliopolis (92 Sharia al-Higaz, near Midan Heliopolis). Many cafés and not a few *kushari* shops and cheap diners offer puddings such as *mahalabiyya* or rice pudding. One of the best places for the latter, topped if you like with *basbousa* (a confection made with semolina, nuts and syrup), is *Foontana* on Sharia Handusa opposite the north side of Qasr el-Aini Hospital (see map, p.140); it's signed in Arabic only, but look for the honey pots in the window.

As for **juice bars** (usually open 8am–10pm), the ones near the *Café Riche* and *Felfela* charge more than most, but they're never expensive. The best one in Cairo is *Farghaly Fruits*, 71 Arab League St, in Mohandiseen (see map, p.140), but *Mohammed Ali* in Midan Falaki downtown (see map, p.93) is unrivalled for its huge selection, including a wonderful coconut milkshake. **Sobia**, usually sold in juice shops as a kind of rice milk, is available in its original form, as a gloopy dessert, from *Al-Rahmany*, at the corner of Khayrat and Mohedayan streets in Saiyida Zeinab.

Ice cream in Cairo is usually not very good, though you may find interesting flavours like guava and mango. One place that does really good icecream is Rigoletto in Zamalek (see p.189).

Drinking

The cheapest **bars** (always euphemistically named "cafeteria") are rough male-only hard-drinking dens, usually open until around midnight. They're certainly not recommended for women on their own, and even with a male escort you'd be the object of much attention. Other bars are chiefly meeting places for men and prostitutes (the only Egyptian women found there). The more upmarket bars often have a minimum charge, often unadvertised (usually around £E10–20). Inevitably, there's some overlap between bars and nightclubs (covered under "Nightlife and entertainment" on p.192). As throughout Egypt, the sale of alcohol is banned during Ramadan and other major Muslim festivals.

Downtown

Of the bars listed below, women will probably not feel comfortable in the *Gamayka* and *Bodega Orabi*, and may feel happier with a male escort in *Le Grillon*, *Hard Rock Café* and *Odeon Palace*. All the drinking places mentioned above and listed below are marked on the map on pp.92–93.

Barrel Lounge On the first floor of the *Windsor Hotel*, Sharia Alfi Bey. Faded Anglo-Egyptian decor and charming ambiance. Foreigners can buy alcohol during Ramadan. Native rum or brandy (best mixed with Coca-Cola) is the cheapest drink, followed by Stella and *zibiba*. Daily 10am–midnight.

Le Bistro 8 Sharia Hoda Shaarawi ⓣ012 849-1943. Pub run by the neighbouring restaurant (see p.184), with smoochy lighting, soft music and an intimate ambiance; a place for a romantic assignation rather than a booze-up. Daily 7pm–1am.

Bodega Orabi Sharia Orabi (no number apparent, but opposite no.25). Friendly, if rough-and-ready bar with a quieter upstairs section overlooking the street. Daily 11am–4am.

Café Riche 17 Sharia Talaat Harb. This was once a hangout for artists and intellectuals, and practically every Arab revolutionary of the last century has visited at least once – including Saddam Hussein. Although now largely for tourists, it still oozes history, and the outside is decorated with photos of Cairo in days gone by. The owner was a pilot during the wars with Israel. Daily 10am–midnight.

El-Horea Midan Falaki. A mirrored, very 1930s café that's hardly changed since then, and serves beer as well as tea, coffee and *sheesha* pipes. Chess players meet here in the evening and people gather to watch them play – though drinking isn't allowed round the boards. Sun–Thurs 11am–3am, Fri noon–3am.

Gamayka Sharia el-Bank el-Ahly, a small street off Sheria Sharif. Named after the island of Jamaica (the owner's sister went there once), this cosy little dive is really just an ordinary "cafeteria" bar (women won't feel comfortable here), but a cut above most, and you can have a *sheesha* with your beer. Daily 11am–4am.

Le Grillon 8 Sharia Qasr el-Nil, down a small passage between Qasr el-Nil and Sharia Bustan. A cosy, carpeted bar that also serves mediocre food and has a smoking garden in case you want a *sheesha*. Daily noon–2am.

Napoleon Bar *Shepheard* hotel. One of the most comfortable bars in town, with Napoleonic prints on the walls, wood panelling, mezze and light meals, and live music every night. Foreigners can buy alcohol here during Ramadan. Daily 5pm–2am.

Odeon Palace Hotel 6 Sharia Abdel Hamid Said. The 24hr rooftop bar here is a popular and very pleasant location for a bit of after-hours rooftop drinking, with a *sheesha* if you like. Minimum charge £E10 7am–9pm, £E15 9pm–7am.

Zamalek and Mohandiseen

All the places listed here are marked on the map on pp.152–153.

Bull's Eye 32 Sharia Jeddah, Mohandiseen ⓣ02/3761-6888, ⓦwww.bullseyepub.com. English-style pub (well, near as) featuring, as its name suggests, a dartboard, but also food, music (including occasional live bands), cocktails and karaoke nights. See the website for listings. Daily 6pm–2am.

Deals 5 Sharia Sayed el-Bakri, Zamalek. One of Cairo's most congenial drinking spots, and one of the few with any kind of atmosphere, small, homely and popular among expats and Egyptians alike, with no hassling of women. There's cold beer (served with popcorn), and decent food, but the videos never go with the music. Larger branches in Mohandiseen (2 Sharia Gol Gamal) and Heliopolis (40 Sharia Baghdad). Daily 4pm–2am.

Harry's Pub *Marriott Hotel*, Zamalek. British-style bar with live music from 10pm, a favourite with expats despite its obvious phoniness. They do show English football on the telly, however. Minimum charge £E125. Daily 5pm–2am.

Piano Bar *Marriott Hotel*, Zamalek. More refined than *Harry's*, and, as its name suggests, offers live piano music (from 8pm) to enhance the ambiance. Much frequented by expats. Daily 6pm–2am.

Pub 28 28 Shagar al-Durr, Zamalek. A bar that's also popular as a place to eat, with a few different beers, *sangría* by the carafe, plus English coldcuts, mezze, grills and good steaks. Daily noon–2am.

Nightlife and entertainment

Egyptians make a distinction between a **disco**, where you dance to music, and a **nightclub**, where you have dinner and watch a floorshow; should you wish to go clubbing, it's a disco, not a nightclub, that you want. For current information about **what's on** at cinemas, concert halls and nightclubs, get hold of Saturday's *Egyptian Mail*, the weekly English edition of *Al-Ahram* newspaper, the monthly *Egypt Today*, or the free monthly booklets *The Croc* (at various shops and eating places, and on line at ⓦwww.iCroc.com) and *Egypt* (issued by the Egyptian Tourist Authority and available at some hotels).

Nightspots

Cairo has a fair number of **discos** but nowhere to rave about. The music is usually last year's hits back home or current Egyptian stuff; light shows are unsophisticated.

Couples only

Though you might imagine the trend towards a **couples-only policy** is to prevent women from being swamped, locals say that it's to stop discos from becoming gay haunts or pick-up joints for prostitutes. In practice, women can usually get into discos without escorts, but men without women will have more difficulty. Call first to avoid disappointment.

But dance-floor manners are good, boozy boors are at a minimum and casual dress is acceptable at all but the ritziest places.

In addition to the places listed here, one or two **bars** also have dancefloors, notably *Bull's Eye* (see p.191). The *Cancan* at the *Fontana Hotel* (see p.195) is a disco on Monday to Wednesday, Friday and Saturday.

After Eight 6 Sharia Qasr el-Nil, Downtown ⓣ010 339-8000, ⓦwww.after8cairo.com (see map, p.92). Sweaty, smoky and quite atmospheric jazz club, with low lights, and cocktails. Couples over 25 only; reservation compulsory. £E40 "minimum charge" (£E100 Thurs, £E60 Fri), which often seems to mutate into an entry fee. Sat–Wed 8pm–2am, Thurs & Fri 8pm–3am.

Cairo Jazz Club 197 26th July St, Mohandiseen ⓣ02/3345-9939, ⓦwww.cairojazzclub.com (see map, p.152). Food, drink and live musicians most nights, but despite the name, jazz only once a week. The lighting is soft, the seating comfortable and the crowd friendly. Happy hour is 7–9pm, when you get two drinks for the price of one. Saturday is Middle Eastern music, Sunday is jazz, but many reckon the best night is Wednesday, when there's no live band, only a DJ. Couples over 25 only (at least in principle); reservation advisable. Daily 5pm–3am.

Hard Rock Café *Grand Hyatt* hotel, Roda Island (see map, p.140) ⓣ02/2532-1277, ⓦwww.hardrock.com/cairo. The Cairo branch of the international chain, popular with bright young things, and mainly notable for having 1957 Ford (apparently once Gamal Abdel Nasser's) suspended above the tables amid the usual pop paraphernalia. Daily noon–4am, with a DJ from midnight.

Nirvana (Africana) 41 Pyramids Rd (about halfway along; see map, p.161). Officially renamed *Nirvana* but still universally known as *Africana*, plays African and reggae music to a largely sub-Saharan crowd, half of whom seem to be on the game, so it's as much a pick-up joint as a centre for Cairo's African community. It's lively and fun, but don't order spirits here; stick to the beer. £E60 entry. Daily 11pm–3.30am.

Sangria Opposite *Conrad Hotel*, Corniche el-Nil, Bulaq ⓣ02/2579-6511 (see map, p.76). Bar on a boat that doubles as a nightclub after dark. It's quite laid-back, with an outside smoking area, but they sometimes refuse entry to punters they deem too casually dressed. Minimum charge £E100. Daily noon–2.30am.

Stiletto Sharia Corniche el-Nil by Midan Galaa, Dokki (opposite *Cairo Sheraton Hotel*), ⓣ02/3331-1360 (see map, p.153). Upmarket lounge bar with cocktails, music and a dancefloor, popular with Cairo's young and rich. Sunday is Salsa night, Friday jazz night. Minimum charge £E90 Sun–Thurs, £E110 Fri & Sat. Daily 7pm–4am.

Tamarai North Tower, *Nile City Towers*, 2005C Corniche el-Nil, Rod el-Farag ⓣ02/2461-9910, ⓦwww.tamarai-egypt.com (see map, p.76). Very exclusive, über-chic (their own description) bar-restaurant, done out with interior design "concepts", with access strictly by reservation only, and actually pretty slick in a self-consciously upmarket kind of way. The food is good but pricey, the clientele well-heeled, and there's a dancefloor with a mix of chilled music during the week, and uptempo house at weekends. Minimum charge £E250. Daily noon–2am.

Gay venues

In the past, venues such as *Harry's Bar* at the *Marriott* hotel were haunts for **gay men**, but that all changed in 2001, when police raided the *Queen Boat* floating disco, which was popular with both gay and heterosexual couples. Homosexuality as such is not illegal, but fifty-two gay men ("the Cairo 52") were arrested, slung in a cell and charged with offences such as "debauchery" and "contempt of religion", some receiving three-year prison sentences as a result. The religious lobby were delighted, but the gay scene has since gone right underground, and any events that begin to attract a gay crowd (1980s retro nights may be worth checking out) are quickly closed. There are absolutely no venues for **lesbians** in Cairo.

Live music

Aside from at *Cairo Jazz Club* and *After Eight* (see above), tourist restaurants and the Opera House, you're unlikely to hear much live Western music. In 1997, police stormed a heavy metal concert, then raided the homes of over a hundred teenagers on the heavy metal scene, took away anything with skulls and horns on it (including a Chicago Bulls basketball cap), and charged them with "satanic worship" (a criminal offence in Egypt). In the end, after spending some weeks in jail, the teens were released, and Egypt's rock scene is now starting to recover, as the city's occasional **SOS music festivals** (Ⓦ www.sosmusicfestival.com) bear out. For contemporary Arabic music, by far the liveliest time of year is after the school and university exams, from late June to November, but you'll need an Arabic-speaking friend to tell you what's happening, as none of it is advertised in the English press.

Folk, classical Arab and religious music

During the Nasser era, numerous troupes were established to preserve Egyptian folk music and dance in the face of urbanization. Folk doesn't command a wide following today, but traditional rural numbers like *The Gypsy Dance* or *The Mamluke* performed by the **National Troupe** and the **Reda Troupe** can often be seen at the **Balloon Theatre** on the Corniche in Aguza (Ⓣ 02/3347-1718; see map, p.152), which also stages performances of religious and other traditional music.

Another place that often hosts performances of Arabic folk and classical music is the **Abdel Monem el Sawy Culture Wheel** by Zamalek Bridge on Zamalek (Ⓣ 02/2736-8881, Ⓦ www.culturewheel.com; see map, p.152), which holds regular concerts at low prices, advertised on its website. Performances, usually advertised in the weekly English edition of *Al-Ahram*, are also held at the **Gumhorriya Theatre** at 12 Sharia al-Gumhorriya (Ⓣ 02/2390-7707). The Al-Nil Folk Music Troupe performs every Sunday at 8.30pm at Beit al-Sihaymi, on Darb al-Asfar in Gamaliya (Ⓣ 02/2591-3391, Ⓦ www.cdf-eg.org; see map, p.113). Also in Islamic Cairo, Al-Genaina Theatre in al-Azhar Park (Ⓣ 02/2362-5057, Ⓦ www.mawred.org) hosts concerts of Egyptian or foreign classical and folk music on Thursday or Friday evenings.

All the moulids listed on pp.197–198 feature **religious music** in the form of hypnotic Sufi chants. In a similar vein is the **Zar** music of the Sahara, traditionally performed by women to exorcize *jinn* (malevolent spirits) and heal disease; Islamic fundamentalists take a very dim view of it, regarding it as pagan, but you can hear it on Wednesdays at 8pm at **Makan** (Egyptian Centre for Culture and Art), 1 Sharia Saad Zaghloul (Ⓣ 02/2792-0878).

Bellydancing

A Marxist critique of **bellydancing** would point the finger at imperialism, and with good reason. The European appetite for exotica did much to create the art form as it is known today: a sequinned fusion of classical *raqs sharqi* (oriental dance), stylized harem eroticism and the frank sexuality of the *ghawazee* (public dancers). During the nineteenth century, many *ghawazee* moonlighted as prostitutes, and the association has stuck, though most dancers today are dedicated professionals, and the top stars wealthy businesswomen. The resulting social stigma is deterring young Egyptian women from entering the profession, so most up-and-coming bellydancers today are foreigners.

Yet Cairo remains the world's most important bellydancing centre, and every summer, usually in late June or early July, it hosts the world's premier bellydancing event, the **International Oriental Dance Festival**, usually based at the *Mena House Oberoi* hotel. For the latest information on the festival, which features classes and workshops in the daytime and performances in the evenings, plus extra events such as bellydancing costume shows, check Ⓦ www.raqiahassan.net. There is also a smaller and less prestigious rival festival, held three times a year; for further information check Ⓦwww.nilegroup.net. If you're interested in **lessons**, Hisham Youssef at the *Berlin Hotel* (see p.85) can arrange lessons with a number of teachers (including some of Cairo's top dancers) at different levels and prices.

Upmarket venues

To see top acts, the place to go is the nightclub of one of the **five-star hotels**, notably the Haroun al-Rashid at the *Semiramis InterContinental* (Ⓣ02/2795-7171; Tues–Thurs, Sat & Sun 11.30pm–4am; £E400–800); the Empress Show Lounge at the *Cairo Marriott* (Ⓣ02/2728-3000; daily except Mon, 10.30pm–2am, à la carte), and the Abou Nawass at the *Mena House Oberoi* (Ⓣ02/3377-3222; Thurs & Fri 10.30pm–1am). All of these provide a four-course meal to tide you through the warm-up acts until the star comes on sometime after midnight. There's usually a minimum rate or flat charge (£E300–800) for the whole deal. Reservations and smart dress are required. At the *Cairo Sheraton* on Midan Galaa in Dokki (Ⓣ02/3336-9800), bellydancers currently appear on Wednesdays, Thursdays and Saturdays in the Ala al-Din Bar (7pm–midnight; set menus £E130–170), while the hotel's Casablanca nightclub undergoes remodelling work. Floating restaurants are also good, in particular the *Nile Maxim*, and also the *Nile Pharaoh* (see p.187), whose early evening cruise is one of the best bargains at present, for just £E200 (but the late cruise is less worthwhile, as the main act is an Arabic stand-up comedian).

Of the **dancers** at these five-star venues, the big names include **Randa Kamel**, whose sexy moves are very popular with foreigners, though some purists consider them vulgar. Randa currently performs on the *Nile Maxim* (see p.187). Other top stars are **Dina** (who currently performs at the *Semiramis InterContinental Hotel*), Sorraya (at the *Marriott Hotel*) and Nancy (at the *Mena House Oberoi*). Another well-known name, **Lucy**, more or less in retirement, puts in the odd impromptu performance at the *Parisiana* club (Pyramids Rd, north side, just east of Maryotteya Canal Ⓣ02/3383-3911), which she runs with her husband. The *Parisiana* is quite pricey (£E300), but still employs some of the tricks used at cheaper places (see below), involving putting things on your table as if they were complimentary, and then charging stupid prices for them. Lucy is most likely to appear at weekends and if there is a big crowd – don't expect to see her if the place is half-empty.

Cheaper venues

A step down from this are the somewhat sleazy, rip-off nightclubs **along Pyramids Road**, where the entertainments are varied and sometimes good, but the food is usually poor. **Cheaper places**, with no food to speak of, lurk downtown. Most of these are far from pleasant and, if you intend to check them out, you need to be aware of how they operate. Most open their doors at around 10pm, but none really gets going until at least midnight. Most have an entry fee or minimum charge, sometimes both, but be warned that many will also endeavour to rip you off with **hidden charges and sharp practices**. Napkins, for example, may be placed on your table and then charged on your bill; nibbles may be placed on your table unordered, but they are far from free. You need to be on your toes to keep refusing these extras, as the clubs count on customers getting too drunk to notice. Venues may also add spurious taxes, or simply refuse to give change – even for a £E100 note. Women are unlikely to enjoy themselves at most of these places as the atmosphere is generally sleazy, drunken and lecherous. The only **exception** in the list below is the *Cancan*, where women can go, in a group or accompanied by men, and have a good time. All these venues are marked on the map on p.92, except where noted.

Cancan *Fontana Hotel*, off Midan Ramses ⓣ02/592-2321 (see map, p.106). A lower-priced version of the nightclubs in the five-star hotels. It's sufficiently upmarket to be a safe and respectable option. Thurs & Sun 8pm–2am (starts off as a disco; dancer from 11pm). Minimum charge £E38.50.

Palmyra In the passage at 16 26th July St. Dancers, singers and other acts. Used to be free from sharp practices, but has now unfortunately become as bad as the rest. Daily 11pm–4am. Entry £E50 including one beer.

Scheherazade 1 Sharia Alfi Bey. The venue itself is a marvellous old vaudeville-style music hall, with a variety of acts, but the usual tricks are played, and waiters may even try to insist that snacks (lowest price £E20) are compulsory with every beer. Daily midnight–6am. Minimum charge £E45.

Whirling dervishes

The Mowlawiyya are Arab adherents of a Sufi sect known to Westerners as the **whirling dervishes,** founded in Konya, Turkey, during the mid-thirteenth century. Their Turkish name, Mevlevi, refers to their original Master, who extolled music and dancing as a way of shedding earthly ties and abandoning oneself to God's love. The Sufi ideal of attaining union with God has often been regarded by orthodox Muslims as blasphemous, and only during Mamluke and Ottoman times did whirling dervishes flourish without persecution.

In modern Egypt the sect is minuscule compared to other Sufi orders, and rarely appears at moulids, but a tourist version of the famous whirling ceremony is staged at the Wikala al-Ghuri (see map, p.110). Free ninety-minute **performances,** sponsored by the government, are held on Wednesdays and Saturdays starting at 8pm; arrive early to get a good seat, and at least half an hour before the performance in any case. Photos are permitted but not videos.

Each element of the **whirling ceremony** (*samaa*) has symbolic significance. The music symbolizes that of the spheres, and the turning of the dervishes that of the heavenly bodies. The gesture of extending the right arm towards heaven and the left towards the floor denotes that grace is being received from God and distributed to humanity without anything being retained by the dervishes. The camelhair hats represent tombstones; the black cloaks the tomb itself; the white skirts shrouds. During the *samaa* the cloaks are discarded.

Opera and ballet

The **Cairo Opera House** on Gezira (ⓣ02/2739-0132 or 2739-0144) is the chief centre for performing arts. Its main hall hosts performances by prestigious foreign acts (anything from kabuki theatre to Broadway musicals) and the **Cairo Ballet Company** (Sept–June). The smaller hall is used by the **Cairo Symphony Orchestra** (ⓦwww.cairo-symphony.com), which gives concerts here weekly, usually on Saturdays, from September to mid-June. During July and August all events move to the marble-clad open-air theatre where a programme of youth concerts includes everything from Nubian folk-dancing to Egyptian pop to jazz. Programme listings appear in *Egypt Today* and the *Al-Ahram* weekly. Tickets (£E35–75) should be booked several days beforehand (daily 10am–8pm). A jacket and tie are compulsory for men in the main hall. Some chamber-music concerts take place at the **Manasterly Palace** on Roda Island (ⓣ02/2363-1537, ⓦwww.manasterly.com).

Parks and kids' stuff

Cairo has few green spaces. Even in prosperous Mohandiseen, people use the central reservations of the main boulevards for sitting out or picnicking. Most of Cairo's parks are more like gardens, small with well-tended flowerbeds and keep-off-the-grass rules, and they charge small admission fees.

The city's most impressive park by far is **Al-Azhar Park** on Sharia Salah Salem opposite the Northern Cemetery (see p.137). In **Gezira** (see map, p.153), there are a number of small gardens open to the public, mostly open 9am–midnight in summer, 9am–10pm in winter, and charging £E2 entry to foreigners. They include the **Andalucian Garden** just south of Sharia el-Borg (which also has a more exclusive upper section, daily 9am–5pm; £E10), and the **Riyadi Garden** next door, by the river, complete with Cleopatra's Needle-style obelisk. Between them and the 6th October Bridge are two more gardens, the **Hadiket al-Mesala** and, to its north, the **Hadiket al-Nahr**. South of Sharia Tahrir, **Bustan al-Horeyya** is bigger, and decorated with statues.

On Roda Island (see map, p.140), there's the **Um Kalthoum Garden** north of el-Gema'a Bridge (daily: summer 9am–midnight; winter 9am–10pm; £E2), while the **El-Urman Gardens** on Sharia Abdel Salam Aref are a stately remnant of the Khedival Gardens laid out by the French. Other options include Gabalaya Gardens in Zamalek and the zoo in Giza, both covered below.

Besides the following places, most children (and adults) should enjoy felucca (see p.205) and camel rides (see p.164), the Pyramids Sound and Light show (see p.164), and theme restaurants like *Felfela Village* on Maryotteya Canal at Giza.

The aquarium and zoo

The **Aquarium Grotto** in Gabalaya Gardens in Zamalek (daily 9.30am–4pm; £E1) displays assorted live and preserved tropical fish amid a labyrinth of passageways and stairs that children will love to explore. The entrance is on Sharia Galabaya, on the western side of the park.

Cairo Zoo in Giza (daily 9am–5pm; £E1, camera 25pt, also £E1 to walk across the hippo pond) can easily be reached from downtown by bus (#8, #115, #124, #900, #998 and minibus #83 from Abdel Mouneem Riyad terminal behind the Egyptian Museum) is reasonably humane, as zoos go, with quite large enclosures for most animals – the main exception is the lion house. You are greeted on entry by an impressive display of flamingoes, and children will enjoy helping to feed the camels or the elephants. Try to avoid Fridays and public holidays, when it's packed.

Dr Ragab's Pharaonic Village

Dr Ragab's Pharaonic Village at 3 Sharia Bahr al-Azam (daily: summer 9am–9pm; winter 9am–6pm; £E161–204 depending on the length of the tour; ⓣ02/3572-2533, ⓦwww.pharaonicvillage.com) is a kitsch simulation of Ancient Egypt on Jacob Island, upriver from Roda. During the three-hour tour, visitors survey the Canal of Mythology (flanked by statues of gods) and scores of costumed Egyptians performing tasks from their floating "time machines", before being shown around a replica temple and nobleman's villa, and a dozen mini-museums, dedicated to Hellenic, Coptic and Islamic civilization, ancient arts, mummification and (a little incongruously) Nasser, Sadat and Napoleon. There's also a 3-D cinema. If you don't take it too seriously, it's a fun visit, and quite educational, demonstrating such activities as how papyrus is made and how Ancient Egyptians put on their make-up.

You can reach the Pharaonic Village on one of the **boats** that operate half-hourly from the west bank Corniche, 2km south of the Giza Bridge. Alternatively, head there by taxi (£E8–10 from downtown) or metro (the Pharaonic Village is 2km north of El-Monib station) or bus (#987 from Ahmed Helmi behind Ramses station, or #107 from Ataba).

Rides and games

Fun rides and games are on offer at the **Cookie Amusement Park** near the Giza Pyramids, 400m up Mansoreya Canal from Pyramids Road (daily: summer 5pm–1am, winter 3–11pm; entry £E3, rides £E2–3), with dodgems, roundabouts and a big slide, or at **Cairo Land** on Sharia Salah Salem (see map, p.130; daily: winter 8am–11pm, summer 5pm–1am; entry £E3, rides £E3–5). The larger **Sinbad Amusement Park** near Cairo Airport has bumper cars, a small roller coaster and lots of rides for tots (Ⓣ02/2624-4001 or 2; daily 4–11pm; entry £E5, rides £E3–5). Out of town, in 6th October City, 38km southwest of Cairo beyond the Giza pyramids, is a larger amusement park, **Dreampark** (Ⓦwww.dreamparkegypt.com; daily except Fri 10am–7pm, Fri 10am–9pm, Ramadan 9pm–2am), with bigger and better rides and a view of the Pyramids from the top of the two roller coasters.

Religious festivals

Cairo's **religious festivals** (moulids) are quite accessible to outsiders – and lots of fun. Many begin with a *zaffa* (parade) of Sufis carrying banners, drums and tambourines, who later perform marathon *zikrs*, chanting and swaying themselves into the trance-like state known as *gazb*. Meanwhile, the crowd is entertained by acrobats, stick dancers, dancing horses, fortune-tellers and other side shows. The only problem in attending a moulid, aside from the crowds (don't bring valuables, or come alone if you're a woman), is ascertaining the **dates**. Different events are related to the Islamic, Coptic or secular calendars, and sometimes to a particular day or week rather than a certain date, so details below should be double-checked locally.

Muslim festivals

Below is a list of Islamic festivals, broken down by months of the Muslim calendar (see p.47). One Muslim festival is unrelated to the Islamic calendar: the Moulid of Sidi Ali al-Bayoumi, in early October, when a colourful parade of dervishes proceeds from El-Hussein's Mosque to Bab al-Futuh and thence into the Husseiniya quarter.

Moharram The first day of the month is the Islamic New Year, **Ras el-Sana el-Hegira**. The initial ten days of this month are blessed, especially the eve of the tenth day (Leylat Ashura), which commemorates the martyrdom of Hussein. Until well into the last century, it witnessed passionate displays by Cairo's Shia minority – the men would lash themselves with chains. Sunni Muslims observe the next day (Yom Ashura) with prayers and charity; the wealthy often feed poor families, serving them personally to demonstrate humility. But aside from *zikrs* outside Hussein's Mosque, there's little to see.

Safar and Rabi al-Awwal In olden days the return of the pilgrims from Mecca (Nezlet el-Hagg) occasioned great festivities at Bab al-Futuh towards the end of Safar. Nowadays celebrations are localized, as pilgrims are feasted on the evening of their return, their homes festooned with bunting and painted with hajj scenes. However, it's still customary to congregate below the Citadel a week later and render thanksgiving *zikrs* in the evening. Previously, these gatherings blended into celebrations of the Prophet's birthday (Moulid al-Nabi), which run from the third day of Rabi al-Awwal to the night of the twelfth. The eve of the twelfth – known as Leylat Mubarak (Blessed Night) – witnesses spectacular processions and fireworks, with *munshids* (singers of poetry) invoking spiritual aid. Midan el-Hussein, the Rifai Mosque and Ezbekiya Gardens are the best vantage points.

Rabi el-Tani The Moulid of El-Hussein gathers pace over a fortnight, its big day usually a Tuesday, its *leyla kebira* on Wednesday night. Hussein's Mosque in Khan el-Khalili is surrounded by dozens of *zikrs* and amplified *munshids*, plus all the usual sideshows. This month also sees the smaller Moulid of Saiyida Sukayna at her mosque on Sharia el-Khalifa (see map, p.130).

Gumad el-Tani On a Thursday or Friday in the middle of the month, Sufis of the Rifai order attend the Moulid of Al-Rifai at his mosque below the Citadel. Those carrying black flags belong to the mainstream Rifaiyah; subsects include the Awlad Ilwan (once famous for thrusting nails into their eyes and swallowing hot coals) and the Sa'adiya (snake charmers, who used to allow their sheikh to ride over them on horseback). Dervishes are less evident at the Moulid of Saiyida Nafisa (on a Wed or Thurs mid-month, or a Tues towards the end of the month), but the event is equally colourful.

Ragab (Starts around July 4 in 2008). The month is dominated by the great Moulid of Saiyida Zeinab, Cairo's "patron saint", which lasts for fifteen days and attracts up to a million people on its big day and *leyla kebira* (a Tues & Wed in the middle of the month). A much smaller, "local" event is the Moulid of Sheikh al-Dashuti on Rajab 26, at his mosque near the junction of Faggala and Bur Said streets, 1km northwest of Bab al-Futuh. The eve of Rajab 27 is observed by all Muslims as the Leylat el-Mirag or Ascension, with *zikrs* outside the Abdin Palace and principal mosques.

Sha'ban The week-long Moulid of Imam al-Shafi'i enlivens his mausoleum in the Southern Cemetery (see p.134). The starting date varies: normally it's the first Wednesday of the month, but if this falls on the first or second day of the month, the moulid is delayed until the following Wednesday. Either way, it ends on Wednesday evening the following week. The eve of Sha'ban 15 is believed to be the time when Allah determines the fate of every human over the ensuing year, so the faithful hope to gain *baraka* by visiting the mausoleum at this time.

Ramadan A month of fasting from sunrise to sunset, with festivities every night. *Zikrs* and koranic recitations draw crowds to El-Gumhorriya and El-Hussein squares, while secular entertainments are concentrated around Ezbekiya and other areas.

Zoul Qiddah Most pilgrims on the hajj depart during the month, with local send-offs that counterpoint the Nezlet al-Hagg.

Zoul Hagga The twelfth month is notable for Eid al-Adha ("Feast of Sacrifice"), involving the city-wide slaughter of sheep and other livestock on the tenth, commemorating Ibrahim's willingness to sacrifice Isma'il to Allah (the Muslim version of the story of Abraham and Isaac).

Coptic festivals

Coptic festivals are primarily religious, with fewer diversions than Muslim ones; the feasts centred around Easter (see Ⓦ www.copticchurch.net for dates), Christmas (January 7), Epiphany (January 19) and the Feast of Annunciation (March 21) have little to offer, unless you're into church services.

However, there's more to enjoy at two festivals in Old Cairo: the **Moulid of Mari Girgis** at the round Church of St George (April 23, St George's Day) and the **Moulid of the Holy Family** at the Church of St Sergius (June 1). Moreover, all Egyptians observe the ancient pharaonic-Coptic spring festival known as **Sham el-Nessim** (literally "Sniffing the Breeze"), held the day after Coptic Easter Sunday, when families picnic on salted smoked herring, onions and coloured eggs in gardens and cemeteries.

Shopping

Shopping in Cairo is a time-consuming process, which suits most locals fine; Cairenes regard it as a social event involving salutations and dickering, affirmations of status and servility. **Department stores** (generally daily 10am–2pm & 6–10pm) have fixed prices and the tedious system where you select the goods and get a chit, pay the cashier and then claim your purchases from a third counter. **Smaller shops**, usually run by the owner, stay open till 9 or 10pm and tend to specialize in certain wares. Although most of them have fixed prices, tourists who don't understand Arabic price tags are liable to be overcharged in certain places (around the Khan el-Khalili bazaar and Talaat Harb, especially). If you know the correct price, attempts can be thwarted by handing over the exact sum (or as near as possible). In **bazaars** and **markets** bargaining prevails, so it's worth window-shopping around fixed-price stores before haggling (see p.54) for lower rates in bazaar stalls.

During **Ramadan** (see p.47), **shopping hours** go haywire, as some places close all day and operate through the night, while others open later and close earlier. As people splurge after sundown, Cairo's boutiques and bazaars are as busy as Western stores before Christmas.

Crafts, antiques and collectables

Ahmed el Dabba Sikket al-Badestan, Khan el-Khalili (see map, p.111). Lots of belle époque, fin-de-siècle items including cigarette boxes, crockery and chandeliers, plus Egyptian and Middle Eastern inlay and furniture, and Persian rugs. Daily 2–7pm.

Awlad Azouz Salaam 96 Sharia Ahmed Maher, just west of Bab Zwayla, Islamic Cairo (see map, p.118). Riding equipment including decorative saddles, reins, chains and horsewhips. Mon–Sat 10am–9pm.

Delta Papyrus Center 3rd floor, 21 Sharia al-Guriya (part of Sharia al-Muizz), Islamic Cairo (see map, p.111). If you really want a painted papyrus, the next best thing to Dr Ragab (see p.196) is this shop set up by one of his pupils; they quite frankly tell you, "Come by yourself, not with a guide or you'll pay more", which doesn't say much about their ethics, but their papyruses are good, hand painted with pharaonic, Islamic and orientalist motifs, most of which are copied from tombs and paintings. Mon–Sat 11am–9pm, Sun 11am–6pm.

Old Shop Sikket al-Badestan, Khan el-Khalili (see map, p.111). Large, dusty and very browsable mix of old and new knick-knacks, glassware, furniture, 78-record players and lots of stuff hovering between being antiques or just bric-à-brac. Daily noon–10pm.

Oum el Dounia 1st floor, 3 Sharia Talaat Harb, Downtown ⓦ www.oumeldounia.com (see map, p.98). Excellent shop for books, DVDs (classic Egyptian movies with subtitles), muski glass, Bedouin dresses and all kinds of crafts. Daily 10am–9pm.

Salon el Ferdaos 33 Sharia Abdel Khaliq Sarwat (see map, p.93). Barber with a counter at the front selling old stamps, coins and banknotes. Mon–Sat 10am–8pm. There's also usually a man selling stamps, coins and banknotes on the pavement outside the main entrance to the post office in Midan Ataba.

Tarek Issa 58A Khan el-Khalili Shopping Centre, Sikket el-Badestan, Khan el-Khalili (see map, p.111). Superior bric-à-brac shop selling anything from old postcards and banknotes to vintage bakelite telephones. Well worth a browse, though prices are high. Daily 1–9pm.

Jewellery

Adly Fam Muski, Khan el-Khalili (see map, p.111). Jeweller selling silver figurines, chunky bangles, silver rings and gold cartouches, but you'll need good bargaining skills. Mon–Sat noon–8pm.

Boutros Trading Sikket Khan el-Khalili ⓦ www.boutrostrading.com (see map, p.111). Old family firm selling silver jewellery and other silverware, mostly priced by weight, including rings, bracelets, spoons, plates, bowls and some lovely little pillboxes inlaid with mother-of-pearl and abalone. Mon–Sat 11am–8.30pm.

Goldsmiths' bazaar (Souk es-Sagha) Sharia al-Muizz (between the Muski and Sultan Qalaoun's complex). The traditional centre of Cairo's gold jewellery trade. There are also good silversmiths nearby in the Wikala al-Gawarhergia. Daily, approximately 10am–8pm.

Yazejian Opposite the *Khan el-Khalili* Restaurant on Sikket al-Badestan, Khan el-Khalili (see map, p.111). Reliable address for gold jewellery, including gold cartouche pendants. The price of the cartouche will depend on the size, which in turn will depend to a large extent on the number of syllables in the name you want to have put on it, but expect to pay around £E600–800. Daily 1.30–8.30pm.

Clothes

Al Trapiche 36 al-Ghuriya Sharia al-Muizz, Islamic Cairo (see map, p.118). The last fez workshop in Cairo, kept alive by sales to five-star hotels and tourists. Various grades of fez are available, the cheapest going for just £E20. The fez, or *tarboush fassi*, originally of course from Fez in Morocco, was a mark of Ottoman allegiance, which came to represent the secular, Westernized *effendi*, as opposed to the turbaned traditionalist. Under Nasser it fell from fashion, stigmatized as a badge of the old regime. Waiters and entertainers are the main wearers nowadays, and this is where they get them. Mon–Sat 10am–9pm.

Al-Wikalah 73 Sharia Gawhar al-Qayid, just off the Muski, Islamic Cairo (see map, p.111). Well-made and good-value bellydancing costumes: a lavishly beaded and sequinned bra and hipband, with a skirt and veil, costs £E1500–3000; the more you buy, the lower the price. There's a woman to help fit you, and anything they don't have in stock they can make within a few days. Mon–Sat 11am–9pm.

Amira el-Khattan 27 Sharia Basra, Mohandiseen ⓣ02/3749-0322 (see map, p.152). Top-notch but pricey bespoke, tailor-made bellydancing costumes. A full costume will set you back US$300–400. Visits by appointment.

Atlas Silks Sikket al-Badestan, Khan el-Khalili (see map, p.111). Made-to-order garments in handwoven fabrics with intricate braidwork, and can make slippers to order too (allow several weeks; keep all receipts). Their cheapest kaftans and galabiyyas are dearer than most garments in other shops, but much higher quality of course. Mon–Sat 10am–9pm.

Auf 116–118 Sharia al-Azhar, Islamic Cairo (on the north side by the pedestrian bridge; see map, p.111). Large store stocking a wide assortment of ready-made clothes at reasonable prices, including black dresses with Bedouin-style embroidery, plain white cotton galabiyyas, shirts, headscarfs, pyjamas and cloth by the metre, all at fixed prices. Daily 7am–10pm.

Carpets, textiles and furnishings

Al Khatoun 3 Sharia Mohammed Abdo, Midan el-Aini, Butneya ⓦwww.alkhatoun.net (see map, p.111). Chic and arty boutique selling a range of furnishings and home accessories including lampshades, candles, little boxes, side tables, trays and coasters, very Egyptian, with calligraphic and cinematic motifs. Daily 11am–9pm.

APE (Association for the Protection of the Environment) Souk Fustat ⓦwww.ape-egypt.com (see map, p.141). NGO working with the garbage collectors, communities at the bottom of Cairo's pecking order, who recycle rubbish, and recycled rubbish is what their shop sells, in the form of bags, soft toys, patchwork quilts and other products. Profits go towards education, healthcare and improving the lives of Cairo's poorest social group. Daily 10am–6pm.

AUEED (Association of Upper Egypt for Education and Development) 26 Souk Fustat (see map, p.141). Embroidery and wood-carvings by women from Upper Egyptian villages, marketed by an NGO. Daily 10am–6pm.

Egypt Crafts Centre Apartment 8, 27 Sharia Yehia Ibrahim, Zamalek ⓦwww.fairtradeegypt.org (see map, p.152). Non-profit organization selling crafts made by people from poor communities across Egypt, with a particularly good line in clothes, textiles and kilims. Sat–Thurs 9am–8pm, Fri 10am–6pm.

El Assiouty 118 26th July St, Zamalek (entrance in Sharia Aziz Osman; see map, p.152). Upmarket carpet shop founded in 1949, whose customers include embassies and diplomats. All the carpets and kilims are Egyptian (though some incorporate Persian designs), and priced by the square metre. Mon–Sat 10am–9.30pm.

El Sayd Saleh Ragab Tentmakers' bazaar (next to Mahmoud al-Kurdi mosque), Sharia al-Muizz, Islamic Cairo (see map, p.122). Slightly different from the other shops in the tentmakers' bazaar, selling bags, pouches and pocketed wall-hangings made out of moulid tent material. No fixed hours, but usually there at least noon–5pm daily.

Nouno Tentmakers' bazaar (north end, west side), Sharia al-Muizz, Islamic Cairo (see map, p.122). One of a number of shops in the tentmakers' bazaar selling appliqué pillowcases (£E20–35), bedspreads (£E700–1500) and wall hangings (£E200–400), a traditional Cairene craft. Much cheaper is the riotously patterned printed tent fabric used for marquees at moulids (£E8 per metre). It's worth looking around at what the neighbours have as well, and comparing quality and prices. Daily 10am–10pm.

Wissa Wassef Art Centre Harraniyya ⓣ02/3381-5746, ⓦwww.wissa-wassef-arts.com (see box, p.170). The carpet factories around Sakkara – where many a tour will waste your time – are all imitations of this, the original and best. Daily 10am–5pm.

Glass and ceramics

El Daoor 14 Haret al-Birkedar, outside Bab al-Futuh (see map, p.113). Outlet for a factory producing Muski glass, traditional hand-blown glassware full of little bubbles at very low prices. Their factory is just up the street, and they usually allow tourists in (Sat–Thurs 9am–3pm) to watch the glass being blown. To find Haret al-Birkedar, come out of Bab al-Futuh from Sharia al-Muizz, cross the main street (Sharia Galal), and it's about 20m to your right. Daily 9am–10pm.

Perfumes Secret Khan el-Khalili, just off the Muski in the lane opposite the *Radwan Hotel* (see map, p.111). A good and hassle-free place to buy handmade perfume bottles, elegant and very ladylike. The cheaper ones are made of glass and as delicate as they look (£E3–10). Pyrex versions cost about twice as much and are a little sturdier (they should also be noticeably heavier). Daily 10am–1pm.

Saiyid Abd el-Raouf 8 Sikket Khan el-Khalili (see map, p.111). Main outlet for hand-blown Muski glass in the Khan, selling products from a number of small factories, some of them now defunct. Daily 11am–9pm.

Spices, herbs, soaps and perfumes

Abd el Rahman Harraz 1 Midan Bab el-Khalq, Islamic Cairo (100m east of the Islamic Arts Museum towards Bab Zwayla; off the map on p.93 & p.110). Old-established herb and spice shop with an attractive window display of pharaonic and medieval scenes. Sells everything from rice and beans to elderflower and pink peppercorns, as well as medicinal herbs, and even flowers of sulphur and dried lizards. Mon–Sat 9am–9pm.

Abdul Latif Mahmoud Harraz 39 Sharia Ahmed Maher (opposite a *sabil* 200m west of Bab Zwayla; off the map on p.118). The most famous herbalist in Cairo, run by the same family since 1885, a dusty, atmospheric place with drawers and jars full of all sorts of herbs, spices, seeds and resins, from *karkaday* and ginseng to gum arabic and frankincense. Mon–Sat 10am–8pm.

Karama perfumes 114 Sharia al-Azhar (corner of Sharia al-Muizz), and also two doors north on Sharia al-Muizz, Islamic Cairo (see map, p.111). Most of the other perfume shops in Cairo buy their essential oils from here, and then adulterate them with cooking oil and sell them with a massive mark-up to tourists, so avoid the cheats and get your perfume from source. Essential oils such as rose or jasmine should cost around 60pt a gram, though they sometimes try to overcharge tourists. Mon–Sat 10am–10pm.

Nefertari 26A Sharia el-Gezira el-Wosta, Zamalek (see map, p.152) and 27 Souk Fustat (see map, p.141) ⓦwww.nefertaribodycare.com. Handmade soaps, organic cotton towels, loofahs, back brushes and massagers, and other bathtime luxuries, all Egyptian made and cruelty-free. Mon–Sat 10am–6pm.

Rageb el Attar 40 & 62 Sharia al-Azhar (by Midan Ataba and further east by Sharia Bur Said; off the map on p.93 & p.118). Excellent spice shop selling whole and ground spices, joss-sticks and *'amar al-din* (Syrian apricot fruit leather). Mon–Sat 10am–10pm.

Books, maps and newspapers

Al-Ahram 165 Sharia Mohammed Farid, Downtown (see map, p.93). Mostly academic books, and not a great selection, but does have a few maps, and there's a section of classic English literature downstairs. Daily except Fri 9am–5pm.

Anglo-Egyptian Bookshop 169 Sharia Mohammed Farid, Downtown (see map, p.93). Mostly academic books, specializing in Arab politics, history and culture, but has a good all-round selection, plus maps. Mon–Sat 9am–8pm.

AUC Bookshop AUC old campus, corner of Sharia Qasr al-Aini with Sharia Sheikh Rihan, Downtown ⓦwww.aucpress.com (see map, p.92). The obvious place to look for AUC publications, with a huge range of material on all things Egyptian, plus novels, travel guides and dictionaries. Note that you need your passport to get in. Sat–Thurs 9am–6pm. There's another branch at 16 Sharia Mohammed Ibn Thakib, Zamalek (Sat–Thurs 9am–6pm, Fri 1–6pm).

Buccellati At the northwest corner of the junction of Sharia Qasr el-Nil and Sharia Mohammed Farid (see map, p.93). An art shop, but mainly of interest because it sells maps, and books such as *Cairo City Key*, which other bookshops may not have. Mon–Sat 11am–8pm.

Dar al-Salam Publishers 120 Sharia al-Azhar, opposite Al-Ghuri Palace (see map, p.111) ⓦwww.dar-alsalam.com. Islamic publisher, frequented by lots of earnest young men in beards and crocheted skullcaps, with some books and pamphlets in English (just next to the door). Among their publications, *Islam and Sex* by 'Abdullah Nasih 'Ulwan (£E5) is worth a peruse. Daily 9am–8pm.

Diwan 159 26th July St, on the corner of Sharia Ishaq Yaakoub, Zamalek (see map, p.152). Bright, modern store with a wide selection of books, CDs and DVDs (including a small selection of classic and modern Egyptian films on DVD with subtitles, as well as many on video-CD without), and a coffee shop to sit and check out your new buy over a cup of espresso. Daily 9am–midnight.

Ezbekiya book market Ezbekiya Gardens (northeast corner), off Midan Ataba (see map, p.93). The best place to look for secondhand books, whether in Arabic or English. Daily Fri 9am–5pm.

Lehnert & Landrock 44 Sharia Sherif, Downtown (see map, p.93). Lots and lots of postcards and greetings cards, including some vintage ones of their own publication, and one of the best places to look for maps of Cairo and Egypt. At the back, they also have a section selling prints of old photos of Cairo and Egypt. Mon–Sat 10am–7pm.

Romancia Sharia Shagar al-Durr, on the corner of Sharia Ismail Mohammed, Zamalek (see map, p.152). For such a poky little shop this place packs in an awful lot – paperback novels (pulp and literary), coffee-table books on Egypt, maps, British newspapers, and magazines such as *Time*,

Cairo's markets

Although the bazaars deal in more exotic goods, Cairo's **markets** provide an arresting spectacle, free of the touristy slickness that prevails around Khan el-Khalili. Street markets in central Cairo can be found at Bab al-Luq (on the south side of Midan Falaki), Sharia Tawfiqia (off Midan Orabi), at the eastern end of Sheikh Rihan (by Sharia Bur Said), and the northern end of Sharia Qalaa – all of which do business through the night, accompanied by local coffee houses. With the kilo price displayed on stalls, you shouldn't have to bargain unless they try to overcharge. Elsewhere haggling is *de rigueur*.

Secondhand clothing can be found in the **Imam al-Shafi'i Market**, which straggles for 1km along the road leading from Al-Basatin to the Imam's mausoleum in the area of the Southern Cemetery. On Sharia el-Geish near Midan Ataba there's a daily **paper market**, selling all types of paper, dyed leather and art materials, and for **fabrics** (from hand-loomed silk to cheap offcuts), **tools** and much else, you can't beat the daily **Wikalat al-Bulah**, on Sharia Abu'l'Ila in the Bulaq district.

Canary and budgerigar fanciers may want to check out Cairo's **bird markets** (10am–2.30pm), which are named after the days on which they're held: Souk al-Ahad (Sun; Giza Station), Souk al-Gom'a (Fri; by the Salah Salem overpass, south of the Citadel, see map, p.130) and Souk Itnayn w Khamis (Mon & Thurs; in the Abu Rish area of Saiyida Zeinab, see map, p.140). In fact, the Souk al-Gom'a is much more than a bird market: it's a huge flea market full of junk, bric-à-brac and secondhand goods, where you can find all sorts of treasures, and all sorts of rubbish.

Newsweek and *The Economist*, and stationery as well. Sat–Thurs 8am–8pm, Fri 9.30am–8pm.

Shorouk 1 Midan Talaat Harb, Downtown (see map, p.92). Centrally located and very handy for maps, Egyptian novels in translation, books on Egypt, and latest books in English. Daily 9am–11pm.

Unnamed newsstand Sharia Mohammed Mahmoud, opposite the AUC entrance and by *McDonald's* (see map, p.92). Cairo's best newsstand for foreign papers, carries British dailies (usually one day late), the *International Herald Tribune*, *USA Today* and even sometimes the *New York Times*. It also has a big pile of secondhand books. Daily 9am–5pm.

Zamalek Bookshop Sharia Shagar al-Durr, opposite *Pub 28* (see map, p.152). A good place to look for AUC publications, Egyptian novels in English translation, books on Egypt and Cairo in general, plus stationery and British newspapers. Mon–Sat 9am–8pm.

Liquor and smokers' supplies

Anoshka Gift Shop 162 26th July St, by Midan Sphinx, Mohandiseen (see map, p.152). One of the few places in town to sell little metal pipes, but no screens. Daily 10am–7pm.

Babik in the passage by 39 Sharia Talaat Harb (see map, p.93). Wooden tobacco pipes, lighters and numerous brands of cigarette papers and other smokers' requisites. Mon–Sat 9am–9pm.

Drinkies 41 Sharia Talaat Harb, at 26th July St, Downtown ☎19330 (see map, p.93). Retail outlet for Al Ahram, Egypt's biggest booze company, selling all their brands, including Stella, Sakkara and Heineken, as well as their wines and spirits. Other branches include 162A 26th of July St by Maison Thomas in Zamalek (see map, p.152). Also does home delivery, even during Ramadan. Daily 8.30am–4am.

Nicolakis Corner of Sharia Talaat Harb and Sharia Suq al-Tawfiqia (see map, p.93). A decent selection of wines, sometimes at slightly better prices than Drinkies; also beer, zbiba and dodgy lookalike spirits. Daily 7am–10.30pm.

Orphanides 4 Sharia Emad el-Din, and 9 26th July St (opposite the High Court), Downtown (see map, p.93). Booze store selling beer, wine, zbiba and Egyptian brandy, but mostly of interest for the outrageous lookalike brands of spirit it sells (Chefas Rigal, Gorodons, Finelandia Vodka of Egypt and the like), which you definitely wouldn't want to drink. Daily noon–1am.

Souk Bayn al-Qasrayn Bayn al-Qasrayn (on the east side, just south of the Sabil-Kuttab of Abd al-Rahman; see map, p.113). A covered passage full of shops selling *sheesha* pipes. Prices range from £E25 to £E150, depending on the size; the ones with stainless steel rather than brass fittings are better made and more durable. Neighbouring shops also sell *sheeshas*, but are usually slightly pricier. Mon–Sat 11am–11pm.

Musical instruments and recordings

Beit al-Oud 164 Sharia Mohammed Ali aka Sharia Qalaa, off Midan Ataba (see map, p.93). The most renowned and well established of the several *oud* (lute) makers along this stretch of Sharia Qalaa. An *oud* here will set you back anywhere from £E150 to over ten times that much, depending on quality and decoration. Daily 11am–11pm.

Fel Fel Phone 47 Sharia Khulud (Clot Bey), Downtown (see map, p.106). Retail outlet for the Fel Fel Phone record label, though it sells only cassettes, no vinyl or CDs. It isn't really browsable, but there's a representative selection in the window. Mon–Sat 11am–10pm.

Gamal el-Sawy Next to *Fishawi's*, Khan el-Khalili (see map, p.111). Small shop selling bellydancing tapes and videos of the great artistes. Daily 24hr.

Sono Cairo 3 Sharia al-Borsa al-Gadida (an alley between Sharia Talaat Harb and Sharia Qasr el-Nil), Downtown, and in the arcade of the *Continental-Savoy Hotel* on Midan Opera (see map, p.92). Retail outlets for the Sono Cairo label, selling their recordings (including quality recordings of Um Kalthoum, Abdel Wahaab and orchestral music), plus a good selection of CDs, cassettes, and DVDs and video CDs of Egyptian and foreign movies (video CDs are much cheaper than DVDs, but don't offer subtitles). Daily 10am–11pm.

Suan Music 168 Sharia Mohammed Ali aka Sharia Qalaa, off Midan Ataba (see map, p.93). One of the better musical instrument stores at the top end of Sharia Qalaa. This shop (whose name means "Sound of Music") sells drums, ouds (lutes) and other instruments. Daily 10am–midnight.

Contemporary art

Espace Karim Francis 1 Sharia el-Sherifein, Downtown ⓦwww.karimfrancis.com (see map, p.94). Not just painting and sculpture, but installations, video art, and anything new and fresh. Daily except Mon 5–8pm.

Mashrabia Gallery 1st floor, 8 Sharia Champollion, Downtown ⓦwww.mashrabiagallery.org (see map, p.92). Well-established gallery exhibiting works by Egypt's top contemporary artists, especially those working with indigenous styles and materials, and now also showing works by foreign artists. Daily except Fri 11am–8pm.

Safar Khan Gallery 6 Sharia Brazil, Zamalek ⓦwww.safarkhan.com (see map, p.152). Fine modern art by prominent Egyptian artists, with a permanent collection going back to the 1930s as well as regular exhibitions. Mon–Sat 10am–2pm & 5–9pm.

Townhouse Gallery 10 Sharia Nabrawy, off Sharia Champollion, Downtown ⓦwww.thetownhousegallery.com (see map, p.92). Cairo's leading gallery for contemporary art, with regular exhibitions, a stable of good artists, and a library. Sat–Wed 10am–2pm & 6–9pm, Fri 6–9pm.

Zamalek Art Gallery 2nd floor, 11 Sharia Brazil, Zamalek ⓦwww.zamalekartgallery.com (see map, p.152). One of the best places to see (and buy) work by contemporary Egyptian painters and sculptors. Holds monthly exhibitions, promotes up-and-coming young talent and has a permanent collection of work by pioneering Egyptian artists. Daily except Fri 10am–9pm.

Listings

Airlines Air Canada, c/o Imperial Travel Center, 26 Sharia Bassiouni ⓣ02/2578-4658; Air France, 2 Midan Talaat Harb ⓣ02/2394-3938; Austrian Airlines, 5th floor, 4D Sharia Gezira, Zamalek ⓣ02/2735-2777; BMI Sharia el-Bustan (in front of el-Bustan Mall) ⓣ02/2395-4888; British Airways, City Star Complex, Sharia al-Forsan, Heliopolis ⓣ02/2480-0380; CSA Czech Airlines, 9 Sharia Talaat Harb ⓣ02/2393-0395; Cyprus Airways, 4th floor, 17 Sharia Qasr el-Nil ⓣ02/2395-4730; Delta, 17 Sharia Ismail Mohammed, Zamalek ⓣ02/2736-2039; EgyptAir, 9 Sharia Talaat Harb ⓣ02/2392-7664, and 6 Sharia Adly ⓣ02/2390-0999, and at *Cairo Sheraton Hotel*, Midan Galaa, Dokki ⓣ02/3336-2020; El Al, 1st floor, 5 Sharia el-Makrizi, just south of Zamalek Bridge, Zamalek ⓣ02/2736-1795; Emirates, 18 Sharia Batal Ahmed Abdel Aziz, Mohandiseen ⓣ19899; Ethiopian Airlines, 3A Sharia Rafat Saleh Tawfik (off Farid Semeka Hegaz), Heliopolis ⓣ02/2621-4934; Etihad, World Trade Center, 1191 Corniche el-Nil, Bulaq ⓣ02/2578-1303; Iberia, 15 Midan Tahrir ⓣ02/2578-9955; KLM/Kenya Airways, 11 Sharia Qasr el-Nil ⓣ02/2579-8530; Lufthansa, 6 Sharia Sheikh el-Marsafi, Zamalek ⓣ19380; Malaysia Airlines, 21 Sharia Mohammed Bassiouni ⓣ02/2579-9714; Olympic Airways, 23 Sharia Qasr el-Nil ⓣ02/2393-1318; Royal Jordanian, 6 Sharia Qasr el-Nil ⓣ02/2575-0614;

Saudi Arabian Airlines, 8 Sharia Qasr el-Nil ⓣ02/2574-1200; Sudan Airways, 1 Sharia Abdel Salam Arif ⓣ02/2578-7398; Swiss, c/o Lufthansa; TAROM, c/o Red Sea Tours, 8a Sharia Qasr el-Nil ⓣ02/2576-6655; United, c/o Lufthansa.

Banks and exchange There are plenty of ATMs that accept foreign cards, especially around Sharia Talaat Harb, but also in Zamalek, Mohandiseen and Dokki. Changing cash or travellers' cheques is usually quick and easy at the 24hr Bank Misr exchange bureaux in the *Ramses Hilton* and the *Shepheard.* Alternatively there are Forex bureaux dotted around town, including one on Abdel Khalek Sarwat, just east of Sharia Talaat Harb, and another further down at no.38, one on Sharia Abdel Salem Arif between Sharia Talaat Harb and the north end of Midan Tahrir, a handful around the junction of Sharia Qasr el-Nil and Sharia Mohammed Farid, and on the stretch of Qasr el-Nil heading east from there towards Sharia el-Gumhoriyya, and another group on the corner of Sharia el-Gumhoriyya with Midan Opera, which are your best bet for changing currencies such as Israeli shekels or Sudanese pounds. Thomas Cook's main office is at 17 Sharia Bassiouni ⓣ02/2576 6982 (daily 8am–5pm; full branch list at ⓦwww.thomascookegypt.com/our_branches.aspx), American Express at 15 Sharia Qasr el-Nil (daily except Fri 9am–4pm; Ramadan 9am–2.30pm). For international transfers, MoneyGram's agents in Cairo include Sphinx Trading at 2 Sharia Sherif, and Piraeus Bank at 9 Sharia Adly; Western Union's agents are International Business Associates (for example at 1079 Corniche el-Nil in Garden City or downtown at 4 Sharia Hassan Basha al-Memmary off Sharia Bassiouni) and branches of the Arab African International Bank (for example downtown at 44 Sharia Abdel Khaliq Sarwat, or 54d Sharia el-Gumhorriya at Sharia Alfi Bey).

Car rental Avis, 16A Sharia Maamal el-Sukar, Garden City ⓣ02/2794-7400, ⓦwww.avisegypt.com, and Midan Simon Bolivar, Garden City ⓣ02/2793-2400; Budget, 22 Sharia al-Mathaf al-Zira'i, Dokki ⓣ02/3762-0518 and airport Terminal 2 ⓣ02/2265-2395; Hertz, 195 26th July St, Aguza ⓣ02/3347-4172, ⓦwww.hertzegypt.com, and airport Terminal 2 ⓣ02/2265-2430 and at *Ramses Hilton* hotel ⓣ02/2575-8914. A number of local agencies can be found on Sharia el-Misaha in Dokki.

Cinemas Cheap downtown venues (£E10–15) include Cosmos, 12 Emad al-Din (ⓣ02/2577-9537); Diana, 17 Sharia Alfi Bey (ⓣ02/2592-4727); Metro, 35 Sharia Talaat Harb (ⓣ02/2393-7566); Rivoli, 26th July St opposite the law courts (ⓣ02/2575-5053). Plusher venues (£E15–25), with a/c and no-smoking, no-chattering rules, include Al-Tahrir, on Sharia Tahrir, Dokki (ⓣ02/3335-4726), and Ramses Hilton cinema in the mall opposite the *Ramses Hilton* hotel (ⓣ02/2574-7435). For cinema listings, see the weekly English edition of *Al-Ahram*. The Cairo International Film Festival (ⓦwww.cairofilmfest.com) is held in late autumn.

Courier services EMS, opposite the west side of Ataba post office, in Sharia al-Bedak, (daily 24hr) promises worldwide delivery in three to four working days. Private firms (faster but more expensive) include DHL, 38 Abdel Khaliq Sarwat (ⓣ02/3308-6330), with branches citywide, and UPS, c/o Maadi Express Center, 8 Road 78, Ma'adi (ⓣ02/2981-5099 or 5328).

Cultural centres American Research Center in Egypt, 1st floor, 2 Midan Simon Bolivar, Garden City (ⓣ02/2794-8239, ⓦwww.arce.org) has lectures on Egyptology and Islamic art. The Egyptian Centre for International Cultural Cooperation (ECIC), 11 Sharia Shagar al-Durr, Zamalek (ⓣ02/2736-5419, ⓔegycenter2008@yahoo.com; daily except Fri 9am–2.40pm); organizes exhibitions, recitals and occasional tours. Maulana Azad Centre for Indian Culture (MACIC), by 23 Sharia Talaat Harb (ⓣ02/2393-3396; Sun–Thurss 10.30am–5.30pm), has a library (borrowing for members only), and also offers yoga classes. The Netherlands–Flemish Institute, 1 Sharia Mahmoud Azmi, Zamalek (ⓣ02/2738-2522, ⓦwww.institutes.leiden.edu/nvic), has lectures in English about Egypt (Sept–June Thurss 6pm).

Dentists Dr Avedis Djeghalian, 6 Sharia Abdel Hamid Said ⓣ02/2577-7909; Dr Samih Barsoum, 7 26th July St (at Sharia Emad el-Din) ⓣ02/2589-8303.

Doctors Dr Magdi Francis, 20 Sharia Mossadek, Dokki ⓣ02/3749-0818; Dr Moustafa Chakankiry, Jedda Tower, 17 Sharia Ismail Mohammed, Zamalek ⓣ02/2739-4625.

Embassies and consulates Some embassies only isues visas to people with letters of recommendations from their home country's embassy, which may charge for this service. Australia, 11th floor, World Trade Centre, 1191 Corniche el-Nil, Bulaq, 200m north of the 26th July Bridge ⓣ02/2575-0444, ⓦwww.egypt.embassy.gov.au; Canada, 26 Sharia Kamel el-Shenawi, Garden City ⓣ02/2791-8700, ⓦwww.canadainternational.gc.ca/egypt-egypte; Ireland, 22 Sharia Hassan Assem, Zamalek ⓣ02/2735-8264, ⓦwww.embassyofireland.org.eg; Israel, 6 Sharia Ibn Malek, Giza, near El-Gama'a Bridge ⓣ02/3332-1500, ⓔisremcai@internetegypt.com; Jordan, 6 Sharia Gohini (aka Sharia Bassem el-Kateb), Dokki, two blocks west of the *Sheraton* ⓣ02/3749-9912, ⓔjocairo2@ie-eg.com; Libya, 7 Sharia Saleh el-Ayoub, Zamalek

Ⓣ02/2736-7863 (visas not normally issued to non-residents of Egypt); New Zealand, 8th floor, North Tower, Nile City Towers, 2005C Corniche El Nil, Rod el-Farag Ⓣ02/2461-6000, Ⓦwww.nzembassy.com/egypt; South Africa, 6th floor, 55 Rd 18, Ma'adi Ⓣ02/2359-4365, Ⓔcairo.embassy@foreign.gov.za; Sudan, 1 Sharia Mohammed Fahmi el-Sayed, Garden City Ⓣ02/2794-9661 (visas issued in 24hr; apply mornings, with two passport photos and a letter of recommendation from your embassy); Syria, 18 Sharia Abdel Raheem Sabry, Dokki Ⓣ02/3335-8320; UK, 7 Sharia Ahmed Ragheb, Garden City Ⓣ02/2791 6133, Ⓦukinegypt.fco.gov.uk; USA, 5 Sharia Amerika Latina, Garden City Ⓣ02/2797-3300, Ⓦcairo.usembassy.gov.

Ferry companies International Fast Ferries (Hurghada–Sharm el-Sheikh), 2nd floor, 46 Sharia Suriya, Mohandiseen Ⓣ02/3749-8927; Arab Bridge Maritime (Nuweiba–Aqaba), 7 Sharia Abdel Khalaq Sarwat Ⓣ02/2260 4949. Tickets can also be purchased from downtown travel agents such as De Castro Tours, 12 Sharia Talaat Harb Ⓣ02/2574-3144, Ⓦwww.decastrotours.com.

Felucca trips Most of the feluccas moored along the river bank opposite the *Shepheard* and the northern tip of Roda can seat eight people and charge around £E60 per hour. Bring a picnic and lots of mosquito repellent. For rather less cost, you can join one of the boats just south of Maspero Dock, which do round trips to the Nile barrages at Qanatir (£E10 per person). Shorter jaunts are available on boats from the quay just south of Tahrir Bridge on the Corniche (£E2 for 30min). For an even cheaper no-frills ride on the Nile, catch a river-taxi (£E1) from Maspero Dock up to Giza or down to Qanatir (£E5 each way).

Film developing Mitry Colour, 3rd floor, 127 Sharia Ramses, at the corner of Sharia Khan el-Khouly (Mon–Sat 10am–10pm).

Football Cairo's two premier league teams Ahly and Zamalek play in season (Sept–May) at the Cairo Stadium in Medinet Nasr, the most exciting fixture being the Ahly vs Zamalek derby (buy tickets well in advance).

Golf Cairo and the surrounding region have a number of golf courses, of which the most central is the 18-hole course at the Gezira Sporting Club (Ⓣ02/2735-6000; £E50 plus day membership of £E100). The *Mena House Oberoi* by the Pyramids (Ⓣ02/3377-3222) also has an 18-hole course (£E150 for non-residents), and there are a couple more around the ring road out past Heliopolis: the 18-hole course at Katameya Heights (Ⓣ02/2758-0512 to 17, Ⓦwww.katameyaheights.com), and an 18-hole course at the *JW Marriott Hotel* (Ⓣ 02/2411-5588, Ⓦgolf.jwmarriottcairo.com/golf). You'll find further information on Cairo's golf courses at Ⓦwww.touregypt.net/golfcourses.htm.

Hammams The only traditional bathhouse now open in Islamic Cairo is Hammam al-Malatili at 40 Sharia Emir el-Gyushi (women 9am–5pm, men 7pm–5am; see map, p.113), dating from the sixteenth century and none too salubrious. A better option, in Bulaq, is the Hammam el Arbaa at 5 Sharia el-Ansari (aka Sharia al-Hammamat; Ⓣ02/2986-0588; daily women 9am–5pm, men 6pm–6am). The street is by a juice shop on the left (west) side 400m up Sharia Bulaq al-Gadid, which runs north from 26th July St opposite the Abu'l'Ila Mosque.

Hospitals Anglo-American Hospital, 3 Sharia Hadiqet El Zohreya by Cairo Tower, Gezira Ⓣ02/2735-6162 or 3 or 5; Al-Salam International Hospital, on the Corniche in Ma'adi Ⓣ02/2524-0250 or 0077; Cairo Medical Centre, on Sharia al-Ansari, just off Sharia Higaz by Midan Roxi, Heliopolis Ⓣ02/2450-9800. Public ambulances (Ⓣ123) will take you for free to whatever hospital is the nearest, or to one of your choice for £E25.

Internet access Hany, 16 Abdel Khaliq Sarwat (daily 10.30am–8pm; £E2/hr); Concord Net, Sharia Mohammed Mahmoud, between Sharia Falaky and Sharia Mansour (daily 9am–2am; £E4/hr); Five Stars, 3 Sharia Talaat Harb (daily 9am–midnight; £E5/hr); Inter Club, in the passage by 12 Sharia Talaat Harb (by *Estoril* restaurant; Sat–Thurs 9am–midnight, Fri 4.30pm–midnight; £E5/hr); Zamalek Center, 25 Sharia Ismail Mohammed, Zamalek (daily 8am–midnight; £E5/hr); Café Paris, in the Bustan Centre, Sharia Bustan (daily 8am–10pm; £E6/hr).

Language schools Arabic lessons are offered by: International Language Institute (ILI), 4 Sharia Mahmoud Azmi, Sahafayeen (north of Mohandiseen) (Ⓣ02/3346-3087, Ⓦwww.arabicegypt.com); Kalimat Language and Cultural Centre, 22 Sharia al-Koroum, behind Mohammed Mustafa Mosque, Mohandiseen (Ⓣ02/3761-8136, Ⓦwww.kalimategypt.com), which was set up by former British Council teachers; AUC, 113 Sharia Qasr al-Aini (Ⓣ02/2797-6872 or 3, Ⓔsami@aucegypt.edu), which is well-respected, though its teaching methods may not be as up-to-date as at Kalimat or the ILI. ILI charges €215 for 32hr of tuition over four weeks in Egyptian Colloquial Arabic, and also offers Modern Standard Arabic, or a combination of both. The *Berlin Hotel* (see p.85) can also organize low-priced one-to-one tuition.

Nile cruises Luxury cruises offered by five-star hotels are extremely expensive. Budget travellers may consider less ritzy boats run by agencies such as Eastmar Tours, in the passage of 13 Sharia Qasr el-Nil (Ⓣ02/2579-7686, Ⓦwww.eastmar-travel.com), which charges – depending on season –

US$90–120 a night per person for a four-to-seven-night cruise. Be aware that better deals could well be available from local agents in Luxor or Aswan. For more on Nile cruises, see pp.247–250; for details of felucca trips in Cairo, see p.305.

Passport photos Mitry Colour charges £E15 for eight photos while you wait, or £E10 for a dozen photos plus one large print ready the next day. There's an automatic booth in room #99 on the ground floor of the Mugamma (six photos for £E15 while you wait).

Pharmacies All over town, with some 24hr outlets: Al-Esa'af, 27 26th July St, at the junction with Sharia Ramses (ⓣ02/2574-3369); Atalla, 13 Sharia Sherif, at the junction with Sharia Rushdi (ⓣ02/2393-9029); El-Ezaby, in Ramses station (ⓣ02/2575-6272); and Abdallah, 2 Sharia Tahar Hussein, Zamalek (ⓣ02/2738-1988). In cases of emergency, these pharmacies will also deliver medicines.

Police An alleyway to the left of the Sharia Adly tourist office gives access to an office of the tourist police, though their main office is now at Midan al-Fustat (ⓣ126).

Post offices The central post office is on Midan Ataba (daily except Fri 8am–9pm, Ramadan 9am–2pm), with branches (daily except Fri 8am–6pm, Ramadan 9am–3pm) citywide, including on Sharia Tahrir by Midan Falaki, on Sharia Ramses by the junction with 26th July St, and in Ramses station. Poste restante is in Sharia al-Bedak, round the corner from the main entrance to Ataba post office, on the west side of the building – enter the last door, signposted "Private boxes", and ask at counter #10 (Sun–Thurs 8am–9pm, Ramadan 9am–2pm; bring your passport). Mail should be addressed to you, with surname in capitals and underlined, at Poste Restante, Post Office Ataba, 11511 Cairo. Letters are held for a month, often filed under the wrong name. Parcels can only be mailed abroad from the Ramses Square post office, round the back (the north side of the building), in an office marked "Foreign Parcels Office" (daily except Fri 8am–4pm). To receive a parcel, go to the main entrance (east side) of the same building, fourth floor.

Swimming pools Best of the hotel pools is at the *Semiramis InterContinental* (£E200), with an alternative at the *Cairo Marriott* (£E240). The rooftop pool of the *Fontana Hotel*, off Midan Ramses (summer only, £E20), is OK for dipping but barely big enough for a swim. For more serious swimmers, the Ahli Club (ⓣ02/2735-2202; monthly membership $100) behind the Opera House on Sharia Om Kalthoum offers an Olympic-size pool and women-only sessions. In Heliopolis, there's the Heliopolis Sporting Club on Sharia Merghani (ⓣ02/2417-0061–3; £E35 entry, £E35 for a swim). At Saqqara, there's the Palm Club (see p.172).

Telephone and fax offices Phone calls can be made, and faxes sent (at per-minute phone rates) and received (for £E1 per page), at the following telecom offices: 8 Sharia Adly (ⓕ02/2239-7580); Sharia Alfi Bey by the *Windsor Hotel* (ⓕ02/2589-7635); Sharia Ramses, opposite Sharia Tawfiqia (no fax service at last check); 13 Midan Tahrir; Midan Ataba by the National Theatre (ⓕ02/2578-0979). All are open 24hr. EMS and the phone offices will inform you of your fax's arrival if your name and phone number are at the top of the page.

Visa extensions Issued at Mugamma on Midan Tahrir (daily except Fri 8am–2pm). For a tourist visa extension, go to windows #13–14 of the immigration section on the first floor (these numbers may change so check at the information desk on the landing) – accessed via entrance 4 on the same floor, and down the corridor to the end – and pick up a form. You need to provide a passport photo plus a photocopy of the pages in your passport bearing your personal details and your Egyptian visa – there are copying facilities on the ground floor. Take your form to window #43 to get a stamp (£E11.10), then back to window #13 or #14 where your new visa will be issued. This may be done the same day or next day, or could take longer depending on your nationality and the length of stay requested. A re-entry visa will cost £E51.10 (£E61.10 for two re-entries). Display patience and good humour when dealing with the Mugamma; only stage a tantrum or nervous breakdown as a last resort.

Excursions from Cairo

The Nile Valley – most people's target after Cairo – is too distant for a **day excursion** from the city. Elsewhere, however, you can choose between such possibilities as a jaunt to the seaside or remoter pyramids, a river trip or desert monasteries – and still be back in Cairo the same night. See Chapter 3 for details of the "Collapsed Pyramid" of Maidum (p.392) and the Monasteries of Wadi Natrun (p.381); Chapter 4 for Alexandria (p.456); Chapter 6 for the Canal city of Ismailiya (p.509); and Chapter 8 for the Red Sea monasteries (p.569) and beaches of Ain Sukhna (p.573).

Those without the time to organize their own excursions might consider taking a set or **tailor-made tour**. There are plenty of disreputable tour operators about, so beware; those worth trying include: Samo Tours, 28 Sharia Quday, Shubra ⓣ012 313-8446, ⓦwww.first24hours.com; Eastmar Tours, in the passage of 13 Sharia Qasr el-Nil ⓣ02/2574-5024, ⓦwww.eastmar-travel.com; Adventure in Egypt, *Talisman Hotel*, 39 Sharia Talaat Harb ⓣ010 106-7673, ⓦwww.adventureinegypt.com. Eastmar also offers Nile cruises (see p.248).

The Nile barrages at Qanatir

Roughly 20km downriver from Cairo, the Nile divides into two great branches which define the Delta, whose flow is controlled by the **Nile barrages** at **Qanatir**. Decoratively arched and turreted, this splendid piece of Victorian civil engineering is surrounded by shady parks and lush islets – an ideal spot for a picnic. Providing you don't come on Friday, when the area is ridiculously crowded, the barrages make a pleasant excursion.

Originally conceived by Mohammed Ali's French hydro-engineer, Mougel Bey, the barrages were later realized as part of the nationwide hydrological system designed by Scottish military engineer Colin Scott-Moncrieff. At the eastern end of the 438-metre-long Rosetta Barrage lies the Istarahah al-Qanatir or **Presidential Villa**. Egypt's **State Yacht** (originally King Farouk's, on which he sailed into exile) is often moored at the quay.

Qanatir is accessible by bus #210 from the Abdel Mouneem Riyad terminal on Midan Tahrir, or by ferry from the Maspero Dock (hourly 8–10am, returning 2–4pm; £E5) in front of the Television Building, or by pleasure boat (daily round trips departing around 9am; £E10) from just north of the Maspero Dock. Travelling by felucca is slow, since the mast has to be lowered at every bridge.

The Muqattam Hills and Wadi Digla

The **Muqattam Hills** plateau, rising beyond Cairo, are seldom visited by tourists but readily accessible by #951 bus from Abdel Mouneem Riyad, or #401 from Midan Ataba. Zigzagging up the hillside past caves and quarries, ruined shrines and guarded outposts, buses terminate at **Medinet Muqattam**, an upmarket suburb whose avenues are flanked by villas and casinos. The Muqattam Corniche, circling the edge of the plateau, offers spectacular views across the Citadel and most of Cairo – an unforgettable vista at sunset.

People planning self-drive desert expeditions might consider a few training runs below the Muqattam. Victorian travellers used to engage a dragoman to lead them to the **Petrified Forests** – two expanses littered with broken, fossilized trunks, thought to date from the Miocene Period. The larger one (marked on the map of Greater Cairo) is really only accessible with a guide, but would-be explorers can easily find the "Little Forest" on the Jebel el-Khasab plateau, north of the Digla–Ain Sukhna road, which turns east off the Nile Valley expressway near a *zebaleen* village beyond Ma'adi.

The **Digla–Ain Sukhna road** turns east off the Nile Valley expressway near a *zebaleen* village beyond Ma'adi. Roughly 25km from the turn-off, you'll pass the Jebel el-Khasab on the left; if you keep on, you'll notice various tracks leading off to the right, which eventually converge on a main desert track running east–west. By following it west, back towards Digla, you'll pass through several meandering *wadis* before the way is blocked by **Wadi Digla**. This miniature canyon is good for **rock-climbing** and **bird-watching**; bring water, food and shade.

Birqesh Camel Market

Held 35km north of the city at **Birqesh** (pronounced "Bir'esh"), Cairo's **Camel Market** is a twice-weekly feast of drama and cruelty. Beaten into defecating ranks, the hobbled camels are assessed by traders who disregard their emaciation (caused by a month-long trek from northwestern Sudan to Aswan, followed by an overnight truck ride to Cairo), unperturbed by throat-slittings and disembowelments in the vicinity. An adjacent compound hosts a furniture and bric-à-brac market.

The Souk el-Gamal (pronounced "Gah*mell*") lasts from dawn till early afternoon every Friday (and also Monday, when the market is smaller), but is busiest between 6am and 8.30am; tourists pay a £E20 entry fee. To **get there** by taxi will cost around £E100–150 for the round trip. In theory, you can catch the #214 bus from Abdel Mouneem Riyad to Manashi by the Nile barrage at Qanatir (45min) and take a service taxi microbus from there, or get a service taxi microbus from Sharia Sabtiya, off Midan Ramses, changing vehicles at Imbaba (and maybe again at Manashi), but in practice you may well find there are no connecting services once you get to Manashi, so you may then have to take a service taxi to Al-Dikla, and if there's nothing there, take a taxi (£E5, though they'll try to charge you more).

Moving on from Cairo

Cairo is the linchpin of Egypt's transport network and its main link to the outside world. Many parts of the country are accessible from the capital by several forms of transport.

Trains

Most trains depart from **Ramses Station** (Mahatat Ramses). Almost all southbound trains halt at **Giza Station** (Mahatat Giza), 15min after leaving Ramses, and some start at Giza, so you will have to go there to pick them up (Giza Station is around £E15 from downtown by taxi, and can also be reached by Metro). Entering Ramses Station from Midan Ramses, you'll find the **tourist office** (☎02/2579-0767), tourist police and sleeper booking offices on the left; to your right are platforms 1–4, serving Alexandria, the Delta and Canal Zone. Tickets for air-conditioned services to these destinations are sold at the far end of the main hall, directly opposite the main entrance from Midan Ramses, but if you want to use a slow, non-air-conditioned train, you'll find the ticket office outside, through the doorway to the left of the a/c ticket office.

To the right of the a/c ticket office is the doorway through to platforms 8–11, where southbound trains depart for Middle and Upper Egypt. All tickets for trains on this route, bar sleepers, are sold from offices alongside platform 11 (the furthest platform, accessible via an underpass). Note that foreigners travelling to Upper Egypt are only allowed to use certain services (see p.216).

Timetables are not available in leaflet or booklet form, but can be looked up on line at Ⓦwww.egyptrail.gov.eg, though this does not cover slow (3rd and ordinary 2nd class only) trains. A full list of train times is posted up, in Arabic only, at various points around the station, most prominently by the round **information kiosk** (Ⓣ02/2575-3555) opposite platform 4. Staff here should in theory be able to advise on departures, schedules and any problems you may have with ticket buying, but you may need to fall back on the tourist office. There is a **left luggage** office by platform 1, open 24/7 and charging £E2.50 per item per day (you need your passport to use it).

Buying tickets at Ramses is rarely easy. The two non-sleeper ticket offices both have separate windows for 1st class/2nd class superior seating (which is reservable) and ordinary 2nd class/3rd class (which isn't). You have to find the right queue and get your requirements (it helps to have them written down in Arabic) across to clerks who may not give a damn. Tickets can be booked up to a week in advance and should be booked at least a day in advance; 1st and 2nd class superior seats sell out first.

Regular services

Twenty trains a day to **Alexandria** are air-conditioned, with limited stops, and reservations required. Of these, ten are either non-stop or halt only at Tanta, and take around 2 hours 25 minutes. Three more stop at Benha, Tanta and Damanhur, reaching Alexandria in just under three hours. The remainder stop at five to eight stations en route and arrive in Alex in 3 hours to 3 hours 30 minutes. There are some forty non-air-conditioned trains to Alexandria every day, with second and third class carriages only; they cost a fraction of the price of the a/c services, stop everywhere, and can take four hours or more to reach Alex.

Apart from the sleeper service (see below), there are seven daily departures for **Aswan** (14–17hr) and three more for **Luxor** (11–12hr). Tourists are allowed to use two of these trains, currently departing at 8.40pm from Giza, and 10.15pm from Ramses.

Direct services to **Mersa Matrouh** only run in summer: there's a thrice-weekly sleeper, and a daily a/c service leaving early in the morning. Failing this, it is far better to travel by bus from Cairo or Alex than to endure the interminable journey in ordinary 2nd or 3rd class from Alexandria.

Sleeper services

There are three daily **sleeper services** to Upper Egypt. The cost per person for a double cabin including dinner and breakfast is US$60 one-way to Luxor or Aswan. Solo travellers can reserve the entire cabin for US$80, or consent to share it with a stranger of the same sex and pay the normal fare. Note that only one train starts from Ramses (currently at 9.10pm): the other two start from Giza. From mid-June until mid-September, there are also three weekly sleeper trains from Ramses to Mersa Matrouh (Mon, Wed & Sat 11pm, arriving 6am).

You can book at the sleeper office (cash only; daily 9am–8pm; ⓣ02/2576-1319) until around 5pm on the day of departure, but you're best off reserving a sleeper a few days in advance if possible. This can be done at the station or through Abela, who operate the sleeper trains (ⓣ02/2574-9274, ⓦwww.sleepingtrains.com), whose office is just outside the station, in the building by the third-class ticket office for Alexandria. Their staff tend to be somewhat more helpful than those in the station sleeper office, but it is not yet certain whether Abela will continue to have the franchise for these sales after 2010.

Inter-city buses

Inter-city buses are often faster than trains. They depart from three main terminals: Cairo Gateway (aka Turgoman; for most Egyptian destinations, especially the Canal Zone), Aboud (especially to Alexandria, the Delta, Middle and Upper Egypt), and Sinai Terminal (aka Abbassiya Terminal; for services to the Sinai). Some services (particularly Superjet buses to Alexandria and the Canal Zone, as well as international services to Jordan and Libya) leave from, or call at, Almaza Terminal in Heliopolis (see p.211). A few buses also leave from Sharia al-Galaa near the *Ramses Hilton*, and one or two services from Aboud may be picked up off Sharia Orabi near Ramses station. Some destinations may be served by buses from more than one departure point, notably Alexandria (Aboud, Turgoman, Almaza and the *Ramses Hilton*), Hurghada (Cairo Gateway, Aboud and *Ramses Hilton*), Sharm el-Sheikh and Dahab (Sinai and Cairo Gateway), and Tanta and Mahalla (Aboud and Cairo Gateway).

None of the bus companies will take bookings over the phone – tickets must be purchased at the terminal (though, in the case of Mansura and Damietta, you can also buy tickets and board at the old Koulali terminal off Sharia Orabi).

Cairo Gateway (Turgoman)

Cairo Gateway in Bulaq – 600m southwest of Ramses Station on Sharia Waboor al-Turgoman (see map, p.76), and often referred to by its old name, Turgoman – is not really served by local public transport, but it's an easy walk from Ramses station or from downtown (see p.79). A taxi from Midan Tahrir should cost around £E5, and certainly not more than £E8.

The terminal is brand-new and incorporates a cavernous shopping mall, with a barely functioning "food court" at the far end. Tickets are sold to your right and left as you enter, and the buses depart downstairs in the basement. The information desk, right in the middle, in front of you as you enter, is usually unstaffed. Electronic boards announce the next few departures, swapping between Arabic and English every few minutes.

Destinations include: on the **Mediterranean coast**, Alexandria (hourly 5.30am–8.30pm, last departure at 1am; 3hr) and Mersa Matrouh (7 daily; 6hr); in the **Delta**, Mahalla (hourly 7am–10pm; 2hr) via Tanta (1hr 30min); in the **Canal Zone**, Port Said (half-hourly 6am–9.30pm; 3hr), Ismailiya (half-hourly 6am–8.30pm; 2hr) and Suez (half-hourly 6am–8pm; 2hr); in **Sinai**, Sharm el-Sheikh (6 daily; 5hr), Dahab (4 daily; 9hr), St Catherine's Monastery (1 daily; 9hr), and Taba (3 daily; 10hr) via Nuweiba (9hr); on the **Red Sea coast**, Hurghada (8 daily; 6hr); in **Upper Egypt**, Luxor (2 daily; 9hr) and Aswan (1 daily; 12hr); and in the **Western Desert**, Bahariya (6 daily; 5–6 hr); Farafra (2–3 daily; 9hr), Dakhla (4 daily; 14hr), Kharga (3 daily; 9hr), and Siwa oasis (8pm daily; 9hr).

Aboud Terminal

Aboud Terminal, 3km north of Ramses station, up Sharia Ahmed Helmi by the Sharia Shubra intersection, is most easily reached by service taxi microbus from Sharia al-Galaa near Ramses station (see map, p.106; £E1). A taxi will cost around £E5 from Ramses Station, £E10 from downtown.

The West and Middle Delta Bus Co runs buses to **Alexandria** (hourly 7am–7pm; 3hr) via **Damanhur** (2hr), to **Tanta** (half-hourly 7am–8pm; 1hr 30min), and to **Mahalla** (hourly 9am–7pm; 2hr 30min); and the East Delta Bus Co covers **Zagazig** (half-hourly 7.30am–11pm; 1hr 30min), **Faqus** (hourly 9.15am–7pm; 2hr) and **Mansura** (half-hourly 6am–7pm; 2hr).

For destinations southwards up the Nile Valley, the Upper Egypt Bus Co has departures to **Fayoum** (every 45min 6.30am–6.30pm; 2hr), to **Qena** (hourly 6.30am–1.30am; 9–10hrs) via **Minya** (4hr), **Mallawi** (4hr 30min), **Assyut** (6–7hrs) and **Sohag** (8–9hrs), and to **Aswan** (1 daily; 12hr) via **Luxor** (9hr). Almost all these destinations, however, are more comfortable by train.

Sinai (Abbassiya) Terminal

The **Sinai Bus Terminal** (Mahattat Seena), 4km from the centre in Abbassiya, can be reached by bus from Abdel Mounem Riyad (#230, #611 and #998) or Midan Ramses (#14, #69, #178, #710 and #998, and minibus #203), with more buses to Midan Abbassiya, a short walk away. A taxi will cost around £E15 from downtown. Buses from here serve **El-Arish** (2 daily; 5hr), **Taba** (3 daily; 10hr), **Dahab** (4 daily; 9hr) and **Sharm el-Sheikh** (7 daily; 5hr). All stop additionally at Almaza Terminal (see below).

Ramses Hilton departures

Superjet runs deluxe buses to **Alexandria** (hourly 7am–11pm; 3hr) from Sharia al-Galaa near the *Ramses Hilton* hotel (see map, p.92). A few doors down, El Gouna (Ⓣ19567) runs buses to **Hurghada** (17 daily; 6hr) and **Sharm el-Sheikh** (9 daily; 6hr 30min).

International buses

Buses to **Tel Aviv** and **Jerusalem** take fourteen hours, routed via Taba and Eilat. At the time of writing, two buses a week depart from the *Cairo Sheraton* in Dokki (Thurs & Sun 7.30am; $100 one-way, $120 return, plus border taxes of around $20 each way). For tickets and information, contact Misr Travel at the *Pyramisa Hotel*, 60 Sharia el-Giza (see map, p.153) Ⓣ02/3335-5470.

East Delta has a weekly service to **Amman** and **Damascus**, travelling via the Nuweiba–Aqaba ferry, from Sinai Terminal (Sat 10pm; US$60 plus £E300 to Amman, 22hr; US$60 plus £E380 to Damascus, 36hr). Superjet also runs twice-weekly buses to Amman (Tues & Sun; US$105 plus £E20) from their terminal at **Almaza** at the far end of Heliopolis, which can be reached by bus #39 from Abdel Mouneem Riyad, minibus #15 from Midan Ramses, or on the Heliopolis metro (the Merghani line; see p.158), from Ramses to the junction of Sharia Merghani with Sharia Abu Bakr al-Siddiq (under the flyover), following the latter street 300m right (south) to the terminal. Superjet also runs buses from Almaza to **Tripoli** (Tues & Fri; 36hr; US$130 plus £E5).

Inter-city and international service taxis

Aboud Terminal (see p.211) has service taxis to Alex, Damanhur, Faqus, Mahalla, Mansura, Tanta and Zagazig, with very frequent departures and a direct route out of town. Vehicles to several of these destinations, in particular Alex and Tanta, can sometimes be picked up around Ramses rail station too, especially during rush hours, but they may take a roundabout route out of town, and end up taking longer than vehicles from Aboud.

Service taxis for **Suez** and **Ismailiya** leave from Sharia Orabi near Ramses station (see map, p.106). For **Fayoum**, the best place to pick up a *servees* is at Midan Giza (see p.86 for service taxis from Abdel Mouneem Riyad), though you can also get them from Sharia Orabi near Ramses station (see map, p.106). Service taxis to Fayoum, and to **Beni Suef** and **Middle Egypt**, also leave from El Mouneeb, under a flyover 300m north of El-Monib metro station.

Service taxis to **Tripoli** (30hr) leave daily around 8pm from the office of operators Wikala Suessi on Midan Opera (Ⓣ02/2395-4480; see map on p.93). It's wise to book your place a day or two ahead if possible.

Flights

Taxi drivers may demand over £E50 to the airport, but it will only be £E35–40 on the meter, plus £E5 to enter the airport precincts. Airport Terminals 1 and 2 are served by air-conditioned bus #356, minibus #27 and 24-hour bus #400, all from Abdel Mouneem Riyad terminal (in front of the *Ramses Hilton*) and Midan Ramses, and also by 24-hour bus #948 from Midan Ataba. During rush hour, and especially by bus, the journey can take well over an hour, so always allow plenty of time. From Terminal 1 (where the buses terminate), you can take a free shuttle bus to Terminal 3.

Domestic flights

Domestic flights leave from Terminal 3. **EgyptAir** (Ⓣ02/2390-0999 or 0900/70000) has flights to Abu Simbel (2–4 daily, mostly very early morning; 2hr 45min), Alexandria (6 weekly; 50min), Assyut (3 weekly; 1hr), Aswan (11–15 daily; 1hr 20min), Hurghada (6–8 daily; 1hr), Luxor (9–18 daily; 1hr 10min), Mersa Alam (6 weekly; 1hr 25min), and Sharm el-Sheikh (10–12 daily; 1hr).

In addition, the oil company Salit Khadramaat Betrol, based at 45 Akfit al-Mahdi, off Sharia al-Azhar (Ⓣ02/2392-1674) runs weekly flights for their personnel from hall 2 at Cairo airport's Terminal 1 to Kharga (Sun) and Dakhla (Tues), which will take passengers for £E500 if there's room.

International flights

Check which terminal you are flying from (there are three – EgyptAir and other Star Alliance airlines tend to use the new Terminal 3; other airlines generally use Terminals 1 or 2). Some reservations require reconfirmation 72 hours before departure.

Agents such as Spring Tours (3 Sharia Sayed el-Bakry, Zamalek Ⓣ02/2736-5972, Ⓦwww.springtours.com) may offer discounts and can often find seats when the airline itself swears that none exist. Some agents and airlines may accept credit card payments for tickets, but don't bank on it.

2

The Nile Valley

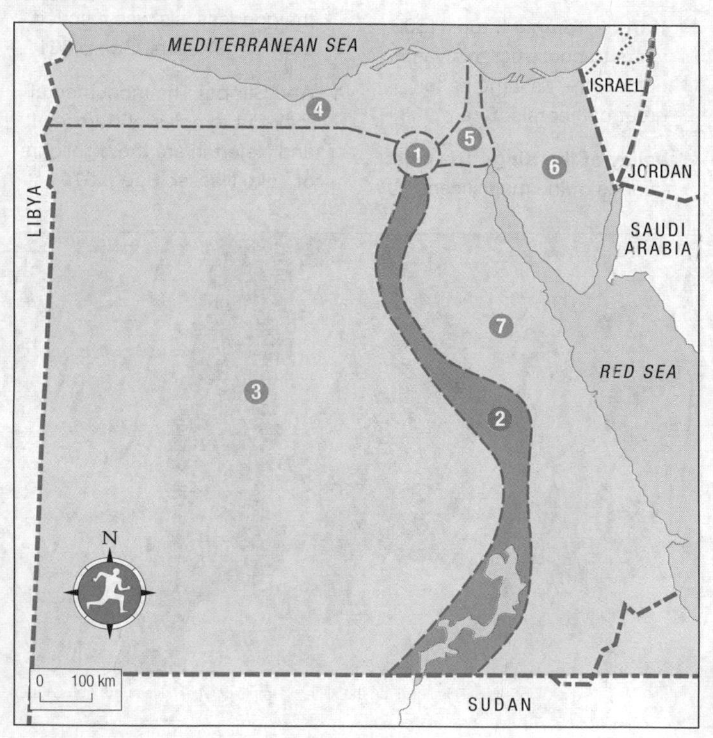

CHAPTER 2

Highlights

* **Dahabiyas** Cruise the Nile in style, aboard a chartered houseboat sailing between Esna and Aswan. See p.249
* **Feluccas** A timeless way to view the Nile's scenery and temples, sailing downriver from Aswan to Edfu. See p.250
* **Abydos** The carvings in Seti I's mortuary temple are among the greatest produced by pharaonic civilization. See p.252
* **Karnak Temple** It took 1300 years to construct this vast cult centre, as large as ten great cathedrals. See p.283
* **Valley of the Kings** The most famous of the magnificent burial complexes and mortuary temples that make up the Theban Necropolis. See p.291
* **Aswan's bazaar** This wonderful marketplace sells all kinds of handicrafts, souvenirs and spices. See p.346
* **Nubian music and dance** Exuberant and haunting by turns, they're best enjoyed on Sehel or Elephantine Island. See p.354
* **Philae** This island sanctuary of the goddess Isis was rescued from Lake Nasser. See p.361
* **Abu Simbel** The monumental rock-cut temples of Ramses II and Nefertari are the highlights of Lake Nasser. See p.370

▲ Colossus of Ramses II, on the Hathor Temple of Queen Nefertari, Abu Simbel

2 The Nile Valley

Egypt has been called the gift of the Nile, for without the river it could not exist as a fertile, populous country, let alone have sustained a great civilization five thousand years ago. Its character and history have been shaped by the stark contrast between the fecund **Nile Valley** and its Delta (covered in Chapter 4), and the arid wastes that surround them. To the ancient Egyptians, this was the homeland or Kemet – the Black Land of dark alluvium, where life and civilization flourished as the benign gods intended – as opposed to the desert that represented death and chaos, ruled by Seth, the bringer of storms and catastrophes.

Kemet's existence depended on an annual miracle of rebirth from aridity, as the Nile rose to spread its life-giving waters and fertilizing silt over the exhausted land during the season of inundation. Once the flood had subsided, the *fellaheen* (peasants) simply planted crops in the mud, waited for an abundant harvest, and then relaxed over summer. While empires rose and fell this way of life persisted essentially unchanged for over 240 generations, until the Aswan High Dam put an end to the inundation in 1967 – a breathtaking period of continuity considering that Jesus lived only eighty generations ago.

Almost every Nile town is built upon layers of previous settlements – pharaonic, Ptolemaic, Roman and Coptic – whose ancient names, modified and Arabized, have often survived. After a century and a half of excavation by a dozen Western nations – and by the Egyptians since independence – the Valley's ancient **monuments** constitute the greatest open-air museum in the world. Revealed along its banks are several thousand **tombs** (over nine hundred in Luxor's Theban Necropolis alone) and scores of **temples**: so many, in fact, that most visitors feel satiated by just a fraction of this legacy.

To enjoy the Valley, it's best to be selective and mix sightseeing with felucca rides on the river, roaming around bazaars and camel markets, or attending the odd moulid. Most visitors succeed in this by heading straight for **Upper Egypt**, travelling by train or air to **Luxor** or **Aswan**, then making day-trips to the sights within easy range of either base – most notably the cult temple at **Edfu** – in addition to exploring the New Kingdom temples and tombs of **Karnak** and the **Theban Necropolis** from Luxor. Inexpensive **Nile cruises** can be found by shopping around before you leave home, through agents in Cairo, Luxor and Aswan (see p.248–249); or on boats moored at Aswan, which is also the point of departure for **felucca** cruises to Kom Ombo and Edfu (see pp.250–252). Further north, **Middle Egypt** is chiefly known for its temples at **Abydos** and **Dendara**, but adventurous travellers also visit the tombs of **Beni Hassan** and the ruins of Akhenaten's capital at **Tell el-Amarna**.

And lastly, a word on the **terms from Egyptology** that fill this chapter: many may be unfamiliar and need a fuller explanation than a glossary allows (see p.645), hence the boxes at intervals in the text: on statehood and symbolism on p.219; funerary beliefs and practices under "The Valley of the Kings" (pp.304–305); and gods and goddesses under their respective cult temples (see the main index for a list). Temple architecture is featured in its own colour section.

The river, its gods and pharaohs

The **Nile** is the world's longest river (6695km), originating in the highland lakes of Uganda and Ethiopia, which give rise to the White and Blue Niles. At Khartoum in Sudan these join into a single river which flows northwards over a series of cataracts through the Nubian desert, before forming Egypt's Nile Valley and Delta, through which it travels 1545km to the Mediterranean Sea. The river's northward flow, coupled with a prevailing wind towards the south, made it a natural highway.

As the source of life, the Nile influenced much of ancient Egyptian **society and mythology**. Creation myths of a primal mound emerging from the waters of chaos reflect how villages huddled on mounds till the flood subsided and they could plant their crops. The need for large-scale irrigation works in the Valley and the consequent mobilization of labour consolidated local, regional and ultimately centralized authority – in effect, the state.

Both the Valley and its Delta were divided into **nomes** or provinces, each with a **nomarch** or governor, and one or more **local deities**. As power ebbed and flowed between regions and dynasties, certain of the deities assumed national significance and absorbed the attributes of lesser gods in a perpetual process of religious

Travel restrictions and routes into the Nile Valley

Setting out from Cairo or the Red Sea Coast, you are faced with a variety of approaches to the Valley, but you need to bear in mind certain **travel restrictions**, imposed in response to the terrorist attacks on tourists in the Valley in the 1990s, and more recently in Sinai. The system relies on police checkpoints to filter traffic and ensure that tourists respect the restrictions listed below. Officially, tourists can visit any place in the Valley providing they get there in a way that stays within the rules, but in reality it can be hard, if not impossible, to reach some places. Whereas tourists are unbothered by controls within the security "bubble" of Luxor and Aswan, in **Middle Egypt** the police insist on **escorting** them on excursions, or around town. While you have little choice but to comply and should certainly never get angry, the system is sufficiently inconsistent and fallible enough that you can sometimes persuade them to cut you some slack. For details of **tickets**, **departure** and **journey times** from Cairo, see the "Moving on" section at the end of the Chapter 1.

The following rules **specifically apply to the Nile Valley**:

• **Trains** Many tourists starting from Cairo catch an overnight train all the way to Aswan, visiting Luxor later. At Cairo's Ramses Station, they only sell foreigners tickets for a single first- and second-class train, or costlier Abela sleepers, a restriction that also applies to travelling to Cairo from Luxor or Aswan. However, for shorter journeys in the Valley you can usually get away with boarding any train and buying a ticket from the conductor – reservations are only mandatory on Abela sleepers. For details of ticket classes and other rail information, see p.208.

• Foreigners can now **drive** a car or motorbike the length of the Valley, instead of having to detour via the Red Sea highway to travel between Cairo and Luxor. Nonetheless, you should expect scrutiny at checkpoints, if not a police escort at some stage – and beware of farm vehicles on the road. The same goes for **cyclists**.

• **Tourist coaches and hired taxis** may now travel freely in Upper Egypt from 6am–6pm, except between Aswan and Abu Simbel, where they must join a convoy mergers and takeovers. Thus, for example, Re, the chief god of the Old Kingdom, ended up being assimilated with Amun, the prime divinity of Thebes during the New Kingdom. Yet for all its complexity, Ancient Egyptian religion was essentially practical: its pre-eminent concerns were to perpetuate the beneficent sun and river, maintain the righteous order personified by the goddess Maat, and achieve resurrection in the afterlife.

Abundant crops could normally be taken for granted, as prayers to Hapy the Nile-god were followed by a green wave of humus-rich water around June. However, if the Nile failed to rise for a succession of years there ensued the "years of the hyena when men went hungry". Archeologists reckon that it was **famine** – caused by overworking of the land, as well as lack of the flood waters – that caused the collapse of the Old and Middle Kingdoms, and subsequent anarchy. But each time some new dynasty arose to reunite the land and re-establish the old order. This remarkable conservatism persisted even under foreign rule: the Nubians, Persians, Ptolemies and Romans all continued building temples dedicated to the old gods, and styled themselves as pharaohs.

The people of the Nile Valley

Although the Nile Valley and its Delta represents a mere four percent of Egypt's surface area, it is home to 95 percent of the country's population. While Cairo and Alexandria account for about a quarter of this, the bulk of the people still live in small towns and villages and, as in pharaonic times, the **fellaheen** or peasant farmers remain the bedrock of Egyptian society.

departing at a set time. In Middle Egypt, a police escort is often mandatory, but rules vary in each governorate and may change at short notice, so it's worth checking with the local tourist office. Coming from Sinai or Hurghada, privately-hired air-conditioned minibuses or cars provide a faster, more comfortable alternative to buses.

• **Buses** from Cairo's Aboud and Cairo Gateway (Turgoman) terminals to Luxor and Aswan are routed via the Red Sea Coast rather than Middle Egypt. Buses to Beni Suef, Minya, Assyut and Sohag in Middle Egypt do exist, but tourists trying to buy tickets for these may be refused. If you do reach Middle Egypt by train, local cops may tolerate you using inter-city buses within the region or heading south to Luxor, from which point on you may use any bus. Superjet buses are invariably more comfortable than regular Upper Egypt Bus Co. services.

• **Service taxis** are generally out of bounds to tourists throughout the Valley, so we have not detailed routes or prices in this chapter.

• **Planes** are the fastest way to travel from one end of the Valley to the other. Depending on demand, there can be from one to a dozen flights a day from Cairo to Luxor, Aswan and Abu Simbel, affording amazing views over the belt of cultivated land surrounded by desert. You can also fly from Aswan to Abu Simbel, and Luxor to Sharm el-Sheikh.

Package tours

Package tours booked abroad are generally good value, but visitors buying tours in Cairo often pay over the odds for substandard hotels and excursions. Many have complained about touts selling or adapting itineraries from Amigo Tours at huge mark-ups; for more on this racket, see p.78. If you *do* want a tour, talk to Samo Tours (p.172) or Eastmar Tours (p.205) in Cairo – Eastmar also does cruises between Luxor and Aswan and on Lake Nasser, and has offices in Luxor and Aswan.

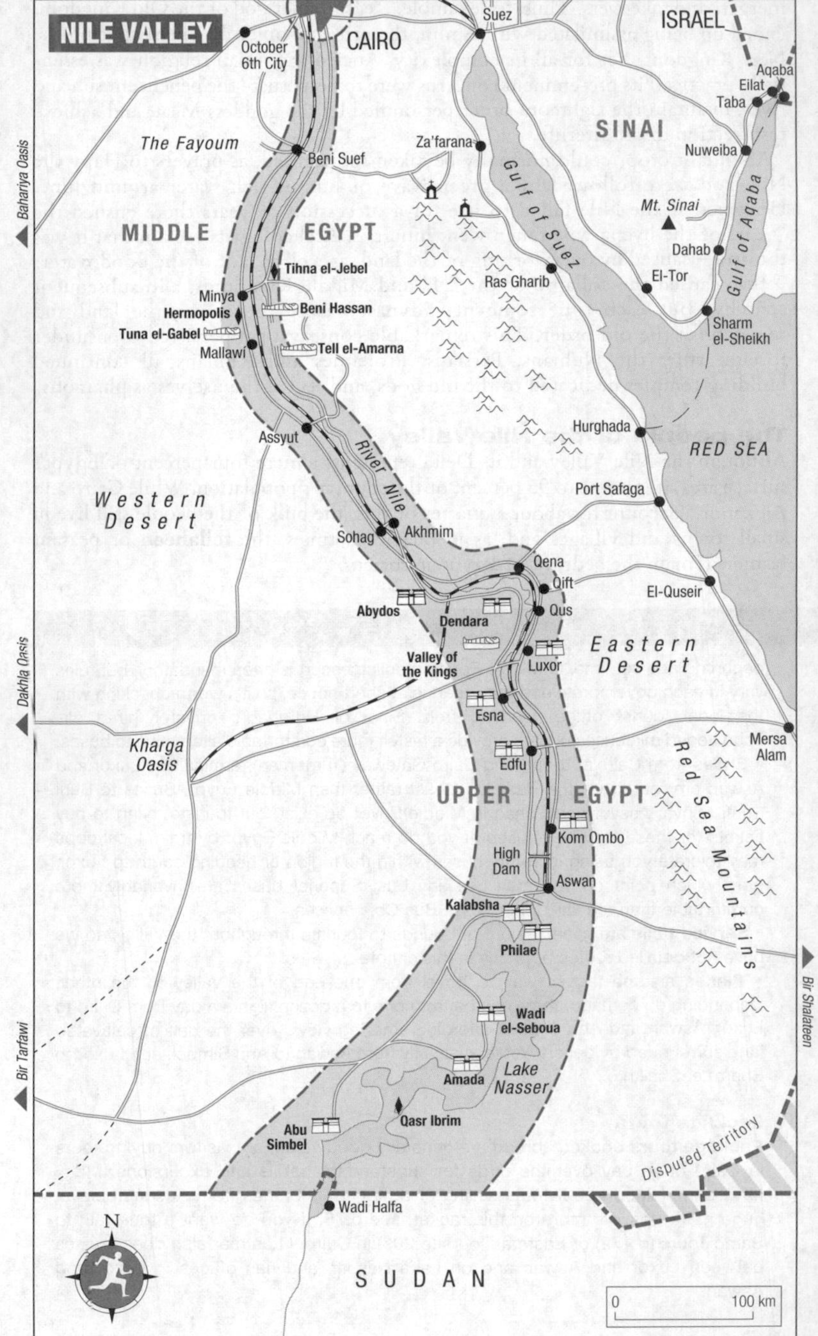
NILE VALLEY
CAIRO
October 6th City
Suez
ISRAEL
Eilat
Aqaba
Taba
SINAI
Nuweiba
Za'farana
The Fayoum
Beni Suef
Bahariya Oasis
Gulf of Suez
Gulf of Aqaba
Mt. Sinai
MIDDLE EGYPT
Dahab
Tihna el-Jebel
El-Tor
Ras Gharib
Minya
Beni Hassan
Hermopolis
Sharm el-Sheikh
Tuna el-Gabel
Tell el-Amarna
Mallawi
Hurghada
Assyut
River Nile
RED SEA
Western Desert
Port Safaga
Sohag
Akhmim
Qena
Qift
El-Quseir
Abydos
Dendara
Qus
Valley of the Kings
Luxor
Eastern Desert
Dakhla Oasis
Esna
Kharga Oasis
Mersa Alam
Edfu
Red Sea Mountains
UPPER EGYPT
Kom Ombo
High Dam
Aswan
Kalabsha
Philae
Bir Shalateen
Wadi el-Seboua
Bir Tarfawi
Lake Nasser
Amada
Qasr Ibrim
Abu Simbel
Disputed Territory
Wadi Halfa
N
SUDAN
0
100 km

The Two Lands: pharaonic symbols and cartouches

Much of the symbolism of Ancient Egypt referred to the union of the **Two Lands**, the **Nile Valley** (Upper Egypt) and its **Delta** (Lower Egypt; in native usage and current administration there's no such area as Middle Egypt). The establishment of this union was what marked the onset of the Old Kingdom (c.3100 BC), and the Middle and New Kingdoms which reunited the Two Lands after eras of political dissolution that Egyptologists call Intermediate Periods.

▲ Winged sun-disc

Each Land had its own deity – the Delta had **Wadjet**, the cobra goddess, while the Valley had **Nekhbet**, the vulture goddess. With union, their images were combined with the sun-disc of the god Re to form the **winged sun-disc**, which often appeared on the lintels of temple doors. Another common image was that of the Nile-god, **Hapy**, binding together the **heraldic plants** of the Two Lands, the papyrus of the Delta and the lotus of the Valley.

▲ Hapy binding the two lands

Much the same process can be observed in the evolution of **pharaonic crowns**. At state rituals, the pharaoh customarily wore first the **White Crown** of Upper Egypt and then the **Red Crown** of Lower Egypt, although by the time of the New Kingdom (c.1570 BC) these were often subsumed into the **Combined Crown**. Pharaonic crowns also featured the **uraeus** or fire-spitting cobra, an incarnation of Wadjet believed to be a guardian of the kings.

Another image that referred to the act of union was the **Djed pillar**, a symbol of steadfastness. Additional symbols of royal authority included the **crook** (or staff) and the **flail** (or scourge), which are often shown crossed over the chest – in the so-called Osiride position – on pharaonic statues. A ubiquitous motif was the **ankh**, symbolizing breath or life, which pharaohs are often depicted receiving from gods in tombs or funerary texts.

However, the archetypal symbol of kingship was the **cartouche**, an oval formed by a loop of rope, enclosing the hieroglyphs of the pharaoh's **nomen** and **prenomen**. The **prenomen** (usually compounded with the name of Re, the sun-god) was one of four names adopted on accession to the throne, while the **nomen** roughly corresponded to a family name, and is the name by which pharaohs are known to posterity (eg Ramses or Seti).

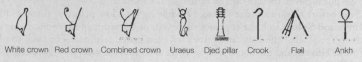

White crown

Red crown

Combined crown

Uraeus

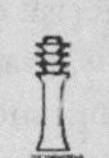

Djed pillar

Crook

Flail

Ankh

Most **villages** consist of flat-roofed mud-brick houses, with chickens, goats, cows and water buffalo roaming the unpaved streets, and elaborate multistorey pigeon coops (the birds are eaten and their droppings used as fertilizer). Children begin work at an early age: girls feed the animals, fetch water and do housework, while by the age of 9 or 10, boys are learning how to farm the land that will one day be theirs.

Rural life might appear the same throughout the Valley, but its character changes as you go further south. The northern reaches of the Valley are unconstrained by the desert hills but fertile land is scarcer; people here have a reputation for being quietly spoken, yet prone to vendettas. By contrast, Egyptians characterize the **Saiyidis** of Upper Egypt as mercurial in character, alternating between hot-blooded passion and a state known as *kismet* – a kind of fatalistic stasis. To non-Saiyidis, they are also the butt of jokes mocking their stubbornness and stupidity. A further ethnic contingent of the southern reaches of the Valley are the black-skinned **Nubians**, whose traditional homeland stretching far into Sudan was submerged by Lake Nasser in the 1960s.

Nile wildlife

The exotic Nile wildlife depicted on ancient tomb reliefs – hippos, crocodiles, elephants and gazelles – is largely a thing of the past, though you might just see a croc on Lake Nasser. However, the Valley has a rich diversity of **birds**. Amid the groves of palms (dates all along the Valley and dom palms south of Assyut), fruit and flame trees, sycamores and eucalyptus, and fields of *besoom* (Egyptian clover) and sugar cane, you can spot hoopoes, turtle- and laughing-doves, bulbuls, bluethroats, redstarts, wheatears and dark-backed stonechats. Purple gallinules, egrets and all kinds of waders are to be seen in the river, while common birds of prey include a range of kestrels, hawks and falcons.

Middle Egypt

It was nineteenth-century archeologists who coined the term **Middle Egypt** for the stretch of river between Cairo and the Qena Bend – a handy label for a region that's subtly distinct from Upper Egypt, further south. (In this guide, we've drawn the "border" just beyond Sohag, assigning the temples of Abydos and Dendara to the Upper Egypt account as access to them is easiest from Luxor.) Owing little to tourism, Middle Egypt's towns are solidly provincial, with social conservatism providing common ground for the Muslim majority and Coptic minority (about twenty percent of the local population, roughly double the national average), though relations were badly strained by Islamic militants in the 1990s. Although adventure-tour groups are returning, the restrictions intended to ensure security for independent travellers can be off-putting even though the risk of danger has receded.

Even before this, most tourists rated Middle Egypt a low priority, as towns like **Minya** and **Sohag** lack the romance of Aswan or the stupendous monuments of Luxor, for all that the local antiquities have fascinated scholars. The rock tombs of **Beni Hassan** and the necropolis of **Tuna al-Gabel** are well-preserved relics of Middle Kingdom artistry and Ptolemaic cult-worship, while the desolate remains

Beni Suef connections

The city of **Beni Suef**, 120km from Cairo, is a **transport hub** from which you can reach the Red Sea, the Fayoum or the Pyramid of Maidum (though it's easier from Cairo). By heading north from the **train station**, crossing the canal bridge, carrying on for 200m and then turning right, you'll find a depot for **minibuses** to El-Wasta, from where a service taxi can get you within range of the Pyramid of Maidum (see p.392). Hourly **buses** to Minya and the Fayoum, and one daily to Za'farana on the Red Sea – running past the turn-off for St Anthony's Monastery (see p.571) – leave from the bus station on Sharia Bur Said, 400m south of (and on the other side of the canal from) the train station.

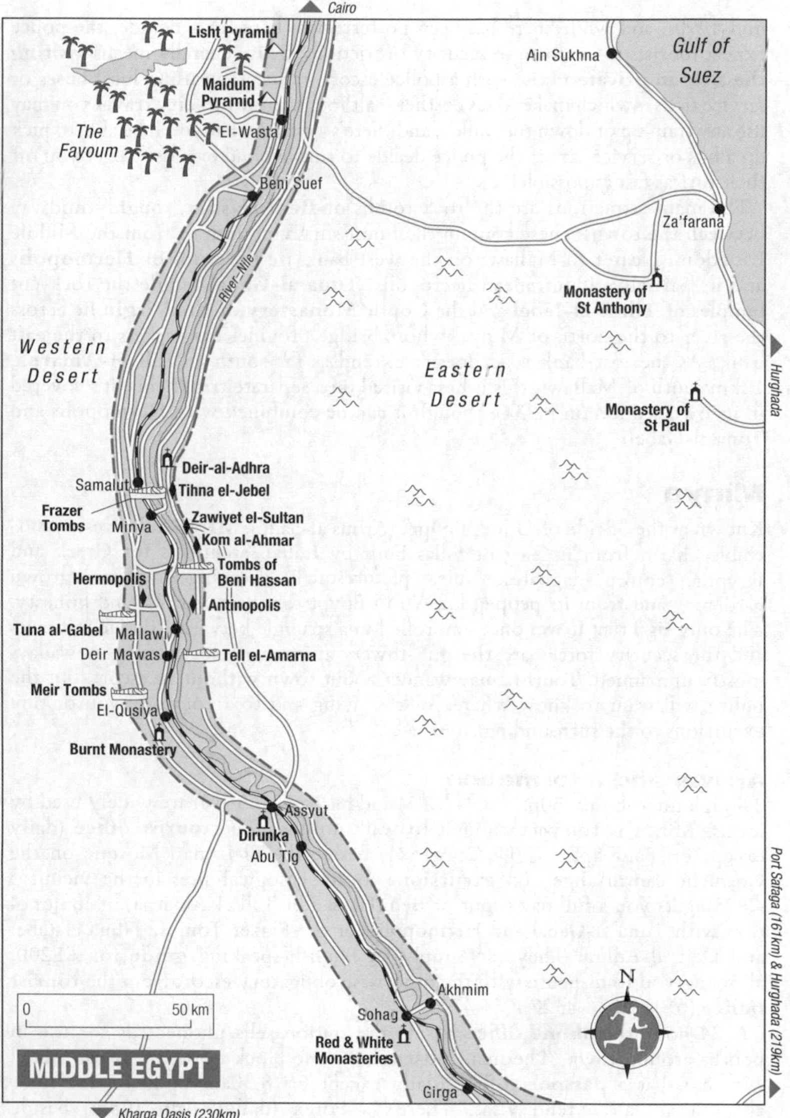

at **Tell el-Amarna** stand as an evocative reminder of the "heretic" Pharaoh Akhenaten. All these sites may be visited with a police escort (see box, p.216).

Minya and around

The best archeological sites in Middle Egypt are around **Minya**, 229km (and 3hr 30min by train) from Cairo, and **Mallawi**, 47km further south. This area was the epicentre of the conflict between Islamic militants and the security forces in the mid-1990s, and while there has been no terrorism here for a decade, the police expect tourists to conform to security restrictions. This generally means **visiting the sites in private taxis**, with a police escort, rather than using local buses or service taxis – which makes trips costlier – although for **inter-city travel** you may use any train up or down the Valley, and there's a chance that you'll be able to pick up a bus or service taxi if the police decide to turn a blind eye just to get you off their turf as fast as possible.

The main attractions are the rock tombs of **Beni Hassan**, roughly midway between the towns; these contain the finest surviving murals from the Middle Kingdom. Nearer to Mallawi on the west bank are the ruins of **Hermopolis** and its partially subterranean necropolis, **Tuna al-Gabel**, while the rock-cut temples of **Tihna el-Jebel** and the Coptic **Monastery of the Virgin** lie across the river to the north of Minya, whose bridge provides easy access to the east bank. As the east bank road doesn't extend as far south as **Tell el-Amarna**, 12km south of Mallawi, this is best visited on a separate trip (hence it's covered in its own section on p.231), though it can be combined with Hermopolis and Tuna al-Gabel.

Minya

Known as the "Bride of Upper Egypt" (Arous al-Sa'id), **MINYA** derives considerable charm from its elegant villas built by Italian architects for Greek and Egyptian cotton magnates – now picturesquely decaying amid overgrown gardens – and from its people, known in Egypt for their warmth and honesty. The only sign that it was once embroiled in a struggle between Islamic militants and the security forces are the gun-towers at strategic locations – nowadays mostly unmanned. Tourists may wander about town without an escort, but the police will want to know where you're staying and to accompany you on any excursions to the surrounding sites.

Arrival and information

Though microbuses (50pt), taxis (£E5) and *calèches* (£E5–10) are widely used by locals, Minya is compact enough to walk around. The **tourist office** (daily except Fri 8am–5pm; Ⓣ086/237-1521) beside the El-Lamati Mosque on the Corniche can arrange taxi **excursions** to archeological sites in the vicinity: £E250 gets you a full day's tour of Beni Hassan or Tell el-Amarna, in conjunction with Tuna al-Gabal and Hermopolis, or the Frazer Tombs, Tihna el-Jebel and Deir al-Adhra. They can supply an English-speaking **guide** for £E200, allowing you to dispense with the otherwise obligatory escort from the **tourist police** (Ⓣ086/236-4527).

A 24-hour **telephone office** beside the station sells phonecards for use in booths around town. The main **post office**, one block north of Sharia Abdel Moniem, has a **passport office** (daily except Fri 8.30am–2pm) on the floor above that can extend visas. There's a Forex (daily 10am–10pm) beside EgyptAir, and most of the banks have ATMs. The University **hospital** (Ⓣ086/236-6743) on Midan Suzanne Mubarak is the best in the region. Dot on Sharia Abdel Moniem and Net in an alley behind Midan al-Mahatta both offer **internet** access (daily 11am–midnight).

Accommodation

None of the old-fashioned hotels near the train station want foreign guests, so visitors are limited to the places listed below. Most have cops outside, who'll ask where you're going whenever you leave and become nervous if you're out late after dark. Breakfast is included in all the places listed.

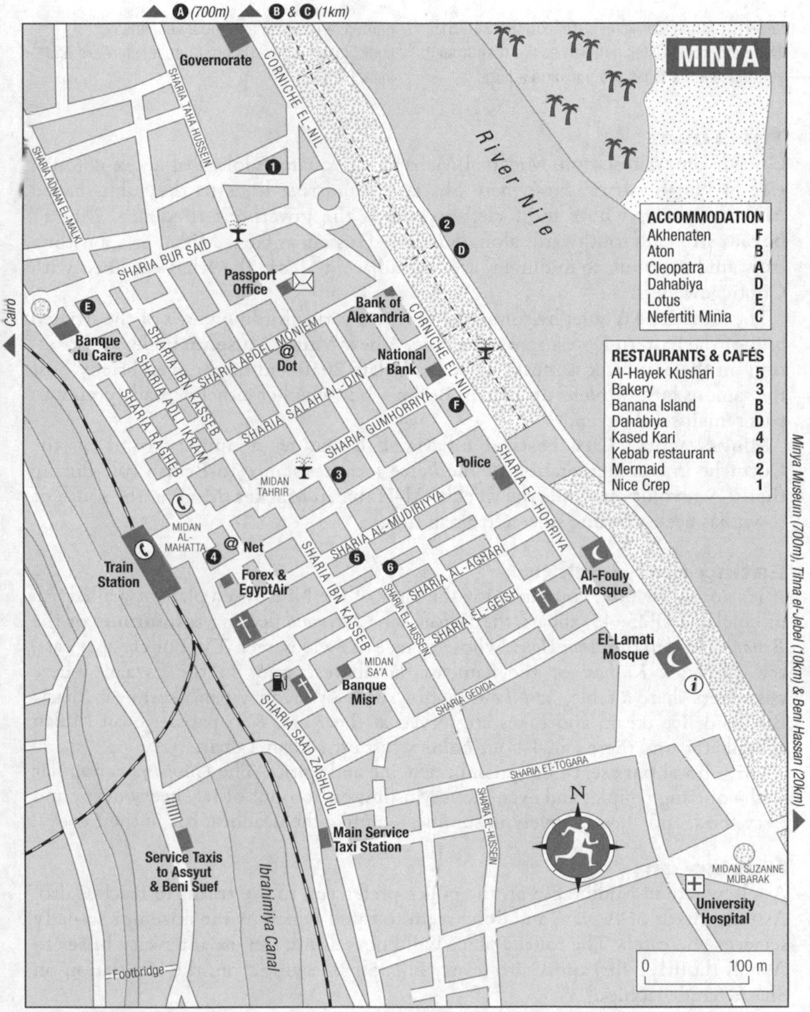

MINYA

ACCOMMODATION

Akhenaten	F
Aton	B
Cleopatra	A
Dahabiya	D
Lotus	E
Nefertiti Minia	C

RESTAURANTS & CAFÉS

Al-Hayek Kushari	5
Bakery	3
Banana Island	B
Dahabiya	D
Kased Kari	4
Kebab restaurant	6
Mermaid	2
Nice Crep	1

Akhenaten Corniche el-Nil ⓣ086/236-5918, ⓔkingakhenaton@hotmail.com. Friendly staff, comfy en-suite a/c rooms with satellite TV, and a fine view of the Nile from its sixth-floor restaurant. Their breakfast is better than most. BB ❸

Aton Corniche el-Nil ⓣ086/234-2293. Beside the Nile about 1km north of the centre, this former *Etap* (still locally known as such) has comfy bungalows (many with river views), a small pool, a bar and restaurant, making it Minya's most agreeable hotel. BB ❻

Cleopatra Sharia Taha Hussein ⓣ086/237-0800. A 20min walk from the centre, this high-rise three-star has a fabulously kitsch lobby, cosy a/c en-suite rooms and a bar on the seventh floor. BB ❹

Dahabiya Moored on the Nile ⓣ086/236-5596 or 010 199-6829. Minya's most unusual lodgings: a restored vintage houseboat, with four small cabins with fans, TV and a shared bathroom – right underneath a noisy restaurant on the top deck, often busy till midnight. BB ❸

Lotus 1 Sharia Bur Said ⓣ086/236-4500. In a quiet-ish part of town, 10min walk from the centre. Decent a/c rooms with showers and TV, and a top-floor restaurant serving alcohol. BB ❷

Nefertiti Minia Corniche el-Nil ⓣ086/234-1515, ⓔmercureminia@link.net. Across the road from the *Aton*, with a fair-sized pool and a large garden, a/c rooms and musty chalets out back. Takes Amex, Diners Club, MasterCard and Visa. BB ❻

The Town

Outside the train station, Midan al-Mahatta is a square redolent of an ex-colonial *ville* in North Africa. From here Sharia Gumhorriya leads to the palm-shaded **Midan Tahrir**, whose most elegant villa is the governor's residence. Minya's **bazaar** stretches southwards along Sharia el-Hussein as far as Midan Sa'a, bustling from mid-morning to midnight, as is the adjacent Sharia Ibn Khasseb, lined with Coptic jewellers.

The **Corniche** is quiet by comparison, with a park affording views of the striated hills of the Eastern Desert across the Nile. A new **Minya Museum** under construction on the east bank is meant to be ready late 2010 and might even briefly host the famous bust of Nefertiti held in Berlin – but whether either actually comes to pass remains to be seen.

Minya's annual **City Festival** on March 8 features a military band on the Corniche in commemoration of the fierce local resistance to British rule during the 1919 revolution, while the weekly **Al-Habashi Market** (Mon) in the south of town has been a fixture since Ottoman times.

Eating and drinking

If it's not too windy, you can enjoy the view of the Nile over a plate of grilled fish or chicken (£E25–45) aboard the *Dahabiya* or *Mermaid* floating **restaurants** or the *Banana Island* in the *Aton Hotel*, whose terrace has widescreen TV. For cheaper eats, try *Al-Hayek Kushari* or the nameless kebab restaurant in the bazaar, where customers share a table, or *Nice Crep* (for sweet or savoury pancakes) near Sharia Bur Said. Ice cream and cakes are served at the *Kased Kari* patisserie on Midan al-Mahatta, and there's a 24-hour **bakery** just off Midan Tahrir.

Three hotel **bars** serve Egyptian beer, wine and spirits. The *Cleopatra* is popular with courting couples and even pious Muslims on account of its cheery decor and tasty food, and *Aton*'s is lively in summer – unlike the deadbeat bar in the *Lotus*.

Moving on

As elsewhere in Middle Egypt, the police prefer you to use **trains** to reach Cairo, Assyut, Luxor or Aswan, and don't seem to mind which of the dozen or so daily services you catch. The tourist office will know if you can use inter-city **buses** to Assyut (hourly; 4hr) and Cairo (every 2hr; 5hr), leaving from the bus station on Sharia Sa'ad Zaghloul.

The Frazer Tombs and Tihna el-Jebel

Six kilometres north of Minya, a turning east onto a side road leads towards some cliffs, where fallen rocks as big as houses mark the start of a path to the **Frazer Tombs** (daily 9am–5pm; free). Named after their excavator, Gary Frazer, these V and VI Dynasty rock-cut tombs are reached by sunken passageways. The two that are open to visitors once belonged to two dignitaries both named Nika-Ankh. The first contains damaged statues of Nika-Ankh, his wife, their children and grandson, interspersed by hieroglyphs. The effigies in the second tomb are better preserved; note the finely carved pleats on the kilt of Nika-Ankh's statue.

Two kilometres further north, another spur road runs to the village of **TIHNA EL-JEBEL**, beside mounds of earth and the mud-brick **ruins** of the pharaonic town of Dehenet (Forehead), known to the Greeks as Acoris. A long stairway once flanked by altars and statues leads to a craggy massif with two unfinished **rock-cut** temples dedicated to Amun and Suchos (the Greek name for the crocodile-god Sobek). In the penultimate chamber of the first temple are two niches that once held mummified crocodiles: if you carefully circumvent a deep shaft right outside, you can see a remaining croc in a chamber beyond the second temple. Further round the cliff-face, a chapel to the goddess Hathor is so high up it seems unbelievable that it was ever used for offerings.

Deir al-Adhra: the Monastery of the Virgin

Beyond Tihna the main road hugs the base of the cliffs, where men cut limestone boulders into kerb-stones, and a flight of 166 steps ascends to the cliff-top village of **Gabel et-Teir**, nowadays also accessible by road. The village is renowned for its **Monastery of the Virgin** (Deir al-Adhra in Arabic), otherwise once known as the Monastery of the Pulley, after a hoist that was the only means of access before steps were cut into the cliff.

A simple nineteenth-century edifice encloses a **rock-hewn church**, reputedly founded in 328 AD by Helena, mother of the Byzantine emperor Constantine. Its sanctity derives from a tiny **cave** where the Holy Family is believed to have hidden for three days, that now contains an icon of the Virgin credited with miraculous powers. Similar tales surround a baptismal font carved into one of the church's Greco-Roman columns. Usually only visited by local villagers, the church receives thousands of pilgrims during the week-long **Feast of the Assumption**, forty days after the Coptic Easter: during the festival, minibuses run here directly from Minya.

The Church of Aba Hur, Zawiyet el-Sultan and Kom al-Ahmar

Four kilometres south of Minya, the road to Beni Hassan runs past the predominantly Coptic village of **AL-SAWADAH**, where a sign in English welcomes visitors to the **Church of Aba Hur**. You can't miss the modern church that stands in front of a tunnel leading to its subterranean rock-hewn namesake. A blacksmith's son who was born in 310 AD, Aba Hur became a hermit at the age of 20 and took up residence in a disused Ptolemaic temple; his faith under torture converted the Roman governor of Pelusium to Christianity.

On July 6, hordes of pilgrims attend the **Moulid of Aba Hur**, camping out in the **cemetery** beyond Al-Sawadah. This vast cemetery, called **Zawiyet el-Sultan** (after the next village) or Zawiyet el-Mayyiteen, consists of thousands of domed mausolea in confessional enclaves, the Coptic ones topped by a forest of crosses, the Muslim section harbouring the tomb of **Hoda Shaarawi**, an early-twentieth-century feminist who was the first Egyptian woman to publicly remove her veil (in Cairo's Ramses station).

Beyond this the road passes **Kom al-Ahmar** (daily 9am–5pm; free), the site of ancient Hebenu, capital of the Oryx nome. The name Hebenu comes from the Ancient Egyptian word *hbn*, meaning to kill with a knife, and refers to the revenge of the god Horus on his father's murderer, Seth. The site's most interesting feature is a ruined III Dynasty **pyramid** whose symbolic tomb was never used as such, unlike another tomb dating from the New Kingdom, containing the defaced funerary statue of a local nomarch, Nefer-Skheru.

Beni Hassan

Some 20km south of Minya, barren cliffs on the east bank harbour the **rock tombs of Beni Hassan** (daily 8am–5pm; £E30), named after an Arab tribe that once settled hereabouts. The vivid murals in this necropolis shed light on the Middle

Kingdom (2050–1650 BC), a period when provincial dignitaries showed their greater independence by having grand burials locally, rather than at Saqqara. Beni Hassan is also memorable for the stark contrast between the fertile banks of the Nile and the desert, close to the river.

At present, the only way of visiting the tombs is by **private taxi** from Minya, escorted by a policeman or a guide from the tourist office (see p.222). A road along the east bank enables cars to get there directly in 25 minutes. Alternatively, you can combine Beni Hassan with Tuna al-Gabal and Hermopolis in a longer excursion, travelling via Abu Qirkus on the west bank and taking a ferry across the Nile. In this case, the taxi will drop you at the ferry stage 3km from Abu Qirkus and wait for your return from Beni Hassan; the **ferry** (daily 8am–5pm) takes fifteen minutes (costing from £E10 for one person down to £E2 per person for more than eight people).

The ticket office at Beni Hassan is 300m from the landing stage, with a resthouse selling soft drinks. A guard will accompany you up the steps to the tombs and unlock them: a tip (about £E10) is expected at the end.

The tombs of Beni Hassan

Most of Beni Hassan's 39 tombs are unfinished. The four shown to visitors evince a **stylistic evolution** during the XI–XII Dynasties, their variously shaped chambers representing a transitional stage between the lateral mastaba tombs of the Old Kingdom and the deep shafts in the Valley of the Kings, gradually acquiring vestibules and sunken corridors to heighten the impact of the funerary effigies at the back. The actual mummies were secreted at the bottom of shafts, accompanied by funerary texts derived from the royal burials of the Old Kingdom. Pharaonic iconography and contemporary reportage are blended in the **murals**, whose innovative wrestling scenes presaged the battle vistas of the New Kingdom. Though battered and faded in parts, their details reward careful study; the following descriptions are keyed to the tomb plans on p.227. To prevent further fading, **photography** is no longer allowed inside the tombs.

▲ The entrance to a tomb at Beni Hassan

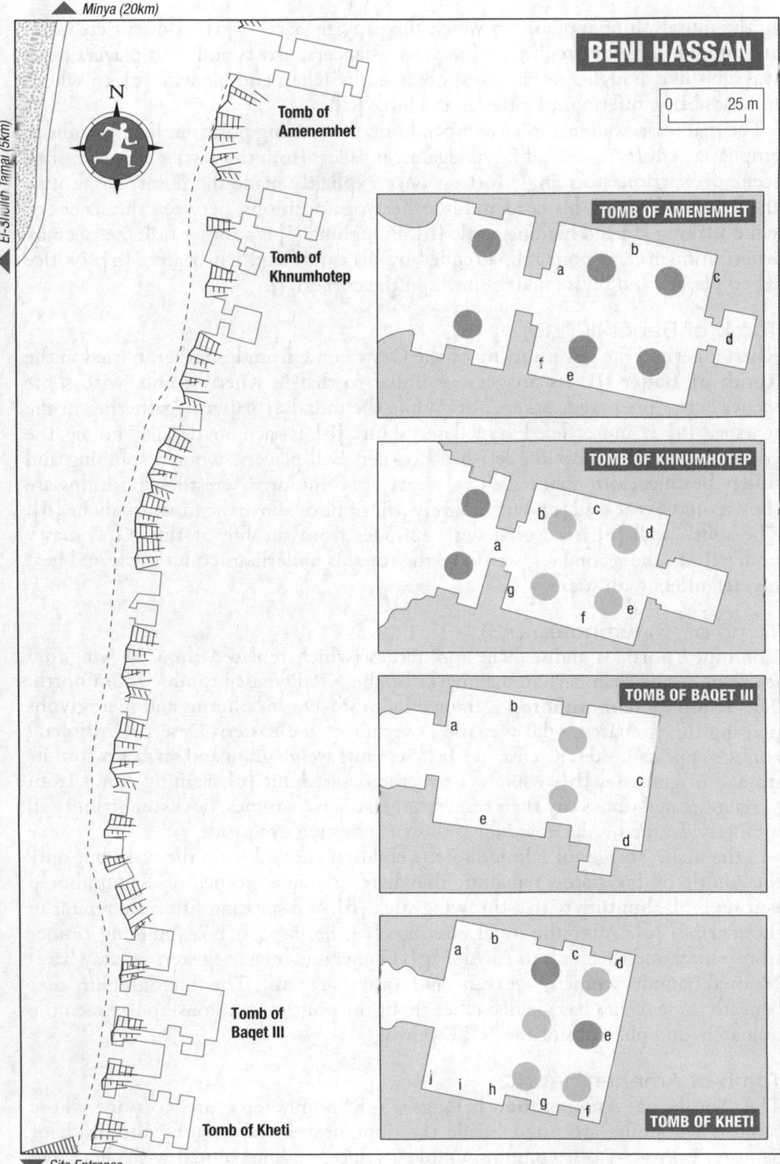

Tomb of Kheti (#17)

Of the many chambers hewn into the cliff-side, the first you'll come to is the **Tomb of Kheti**, which retains two of its papyrus-bud columns, painted in places – the colours are quite fresh. As in most tombs of Ancient Egyptian dignitaries, its images are arranged in "registers" (rows), whose height above floor level reflects their spatial relationship. Thus, Nile scenes go below those involving the Valley, above which come desert vistas, the highest ones most distant.

In the murals, hippopotamuses watch the papyrus harvest **[a]**, as desert creatures are hunted **[b]** above registers of weavers, dancers, artists and *senet* players (*senet* was a bit like draughts or checkers) observed by Kheti and his wife **[c]**, to whom minions bring offerings of gazelles and birds **[d]**.

The rear (east) wall features a compendium of wrestling positions **[e]**, thought to emphasize efforts to defend Egypt against invaders from the east; a now-vanished scene of warriors storming a fortress once explicitly made the point. Don't miss the man standing on his head and in other yoga positions, between the scenes of wine-making **[f]** and herding cattle **[h]**. Ploughing **[i]** is another task overseen by Kheti in his role as nomarch, attended by his dwarf and fan-bearers **[g]**. Notice Kheti's boats, and bulls locking horns, in the corner **[j]**.

Tomb of Baqet III (#15)

Kheti inherited the governorship of the Oryx nome from his father, buried in the **Tomb of Baqet III**. Its imagery is similar to that in Kheti's tomb, with some scenes better preserved, others not. While the mural of papyrus-gathering in the marshes **[a]** is quite faded, the desert hunt **[b]** is rich in details: notice the copulating gazelles near the left-hand corner. Ball players, women spinning and fullers beating cloth appear below. Nearly two hundred wrestling positions are shown on the rear wall **[c]**, with a lovely pair of birds above the funerary niche **[d]**. The south wall **[e]** is covered with episodes from the life of this XI Dynasty nomarch. In the second register from the top, his underlings count cattle and beat tax defaulters with sticks.

Tomb of Khnumhotep (#3)

Columned porticos and a niche for statues (which replaced the Old Kingdom *serdab* or secret chamber) are hallmarks of the XII Dynasty tombs, 150m north. The **Tomb of Khnumhotep** is framed by proto-Doric columns and hieroglyphs praising this nomarch, who was also governor of the Eastern Desert. His funeral cortege appears inside the entrance **[a]**. Servants weigh grain and scribes record its storage in granaries **[b]**, while beneath the desert hunt **[c]**, Semitic Amus from Syria in striped tunics pay their respects, their alien costumes, flocks and tribute all minutely detailed – the governor is shown accepting eye paint.

In the niche, images of Khnumhotep's children are visible on the walls but only the plinth of his statue remains. Elsewhere are vivid scenes of Khnumhotep netting birds, hunting with a throwing stick **[d]**, and spearing fish from a punt in the marshes **[e]**. After the usual offerings **[f]**, he inspects boat-building timber from a litter and then sails to Abydos **[g]**. Higher and lower registers portray bare-breasted laundrywomen, weavers and other artisans. The hieroglyphic text beneath these scenes has yielded clues about the political relationship between the nomarchs and pharaohs of the XII Dynasty.

Tomb of Amenemhet (#2)

The **Tomb of Amenemhet** belongs to Khnumhotep's predecessor, whose campaign honours are listed beside the door near a text relating the death of Senusret I. Proto-Doric columns uphold a vaulted ceiling painted with checkered reed-mat patterns. A mural **[a]** of armourers, leatherworkers (at the top) and weavers (below) precedes the customary hunting scene **[b]**, beneath which Amenemhet collects tribute from his estates. Note the scribes berating defaulters on the second register from the bottom. Below the wrestling and siege tableaux, boats escort him towards Abydos **[c]**. The niche **[d]** contains mutilated effigies of Amenemhet, his mother and his wife Heptet, who sits at her own table to receive offerings **[e]**. Fish are netted and spit-roasted above a painted false door flanked by scenes of music making, cattle fording and baking **[f]**.

Hermopolis and Tuna al-Gabel

Across the river on the west bank are two sites whose remains are less dramatic than their mythical associations. According to one tradition, Creation began on a primordial mound near **Hermopolis**, where two giant stone baboons recall the long-vanished Temple of Thoth. More impressive is the city's necropolis, **Tuna al-Gabel**, where thousands of sacred baboons and ibises were buried in catacombs in the desert.

Due to travel restrictions, both sites are only accessible **by private taxi**, escorted by a policeman or tour guide. Reckon on six or seven hours to see either Beni Hassan or Tell el-Armana, in conjunction with Tuna al-Gabel and Hermopolis – it's not feasible to do them all in a single day excursion.

The ruins of Hermopolis

The pulverized ruins of Hermopolis spread beyond the village of **ASHMUNEIN**, 8km from Mallawi. Turning right off the village's main street you'll come to an outdoor **museum** (free) of antique stone-carvings, fronted by two **giant sandstone baboons** that once sported erect phalluses (hacked off by early Christians) and upheld the ceiling of the Temple of Thoth. Built by Ramses II using masonry from Tell el-Amarna, the temple stood within an enclosure covering 640 square metres, the spiritual heart of the city of the moon-god.

Hermopolis was a cult centre from early Dynastic times, venerated as the site of the primeval mound where the sun-god emerged from a cosmic egg. Like Heliopolis (which made similar claims) its priesthood evolved an elaborate cosmogony, known as the Hermopolitan Ogdoad (see box below). Though Ancient Egyptians called the city Khmunu, history remembers it as **Hermopolis Magna**; its Ptolemaic title reflects the Greek association of Thoth with their own god Hermes. However, there's little to see except 24 slender **columns** further south,

Thoth and the Hermopolitan Ogdoad

In Egyptian mythology, **Thoth** was the divine scribe and reckoner of time, the inventor of writing and the patron god of scribes. His cult probably originated in the Delta, but achieved the greatest following in Middle Egypt; later, by association with Khonsu, he acquired the attributes of the moon-god and mastery over science and knowledge. Though usually depicted with a man's body and the head of an ibis (his sacred bird), Thoth also assumed the form of a great white baboon, invariably endowed with an outsize penis. Baboons habitually shriek just before dawn, and the Egyptians believed that a pair of them uttered the first greetings to the sun from the sand dunes at the edge of the world.

▲ Thoth

Thoth's role is rather more complex in relation to the Hermopolitan cosmogony, which ordained that the chaos preceding the world's creation had four characteristics, each identified with a pair of gods and goddesses: primordial water (Nun/Nanuet), infinite space (Heh/Hehet), darkness (Kek/Keket) and invisibility (Amun/Amunet). From this chaos arose the primeval mound and the cosmic egg from which the sun-god hatched and proceeded to organize the world. While stressing the role of this **Hermopolitan Ogdoad** (company of eight), Thoth's devotees credited him with laying the cosmic egg in the guise of the "Great Cackler", so it's difficult to know who got star billing in this Creation myth. By the New Kingdom it had generally succumbed to the version espoused at Heliopolis (see p.158), but Thoth's cult continued into Ptolemaic times.

which were re-erected by archeologists who mistook the ruins for a Greek *agora*. The columns previously supported a fifth-century Coptic basilica, but originally belonged to a Ptolemaic temple.

Tuna al-Gabel

From Ashmunein, a tarmac road continues to the village of **TUNA AL-GABEL**, which takes its name from the ancient **necropolis** (daily 8am–5pm; £E25) 5km further on into the desert. Along the way, notice the **boundary stele** on a distant cliff, marking the edge of the agricultural land that was claimed by Tell el-Amarna, across the river (see below). The name "Tuna" may derive from the Ancient Egyptian *ta-wnt* (the hare) or *ta-hnt* (a place where many ibis birds gather). For millennia it was a cult-centre where pilgrims gave homage to Thoth by paying the priests to embalm ibises – over two million were sacrificed, mostly bred for the chop. Today this necropolis is awash with sand, wind-rippled drifts casting its angular mausolea into high relief, but obscuring other features. Past the resthouse at the entrance (which sells drinks and has toilets), a path to the right leads to the **catacombs**, which some believe stretch as far as Hermopolis. The accessible portion consists of rough-hewn corridors with blocked-off side passages, where the mummified baboons, which were sacred to Thoth, and ibises were stacked (a few bandages remain). A shrine near the ladder contains a baboon fetish and a pathetic-looking mummy. You can also see the limestone sarcophagus of a high priest of mummification.

Further along the main track are several mausolea excavated by Gustav Lefebvre in 1920. The finest is the **Tomb of Petosiris**, High Priest of Thoth (whose coffin is in the Cairo Antiquities Museum), dating from 350 BC. Its vestibule walls depict traditional activities such as brick-making, sewing and reaping (left), milking, husbandry and wine-making (right) – with all the figures wearing Greek costume. Inside the tomb are colourful scenes from the *Book of Gates* and the *Book of the Dead*. The most vivid scene (on the right-hand wall near the back) shows nine baboons, twelve women and a dozen cobras, each set representing a temporal cycle. Notice the Nubians at the bottom of the opposite wall.

In the desert off to the right you'll spot some columns from the Temple of Thoth that once dominated the site. You can also see the brick superstructure of a **well** that used to supply the necropolis and its sacred aviary with fresh water, drawn up from 70m below the desert by a huge **waterwheel** which still exists, though it no longer works. A spiral staircase gives access to the well-head.

Mallawi

MALLAWI has gone to the dogs ever since Minya supplanted it as the regional capital in the 1960s. Many streets are still unpaved, and hovels are more prevalent than villas. Known to Egyptians as the birthplace of President Sadat's assassin, Khalid al-Islambouli, it bore the brunt of the state's counter-insurgency campaign in the 1990s. The police want foreigners to pass through as quickly as possible, but will tolerate a visit to the small **museum** on Sharia Banque Misr (daily except Wed 9am–2pm, Fri 9am–noon; £E10), exhibiting artefacts from Hermopolis and Tuna al-Gabel, and maybe a quick look at the derelict Hindu-Gothic-style **feudal palace** a few blocks away. Mallawi's terminals are dispersed on either side of the Ibrahimiya Canal that runs through the middle of town, separating the main drag, Sharia Essim, from the **train station** and service taxi depots on the other bank.

Tell el-Amarna

TELL EL-AMARNA is the familiar name for the site where **Pharaoh Akhenaten** and **Queen Nefertiti** founded a city dedicated to a revolutionary idea of God, which later rulers assailed as heretical. During their brief reign, Egyptian art cast off its preoccupation with death and the afterlife to revel in human concerns; bellicose imperialism gave way to pacifistic retrenchment; and the old gods were toppled from their pedestals. The interplay between personalities, beliefs and art anticipates the Renaissance – and their story beats Shakespeare for sheer drama.

The remains of Akhenaten's city lie on the east bank of the Nile, 12km from Mallawi and roughly halfway between Minya and Assyut, and spread across a desert plain girdled by an arc of cliffs. Away from the palm groves beside the Nile, the site is utterly desolate, a tawny expanse of low mounds and narrow trenches littered with potshards. Because the city was created from scratch and deserted after Tut moved the court back to Thebes, its era of glory lasted only twelve years, and many buildings were never completed. Everything of value found during excavations has been removed to museums, leaving only the faintest outlines of the city and the desecrated tombs of Akhenaten and his courtiers to see – yet the site strikes some visitors as a place of mystery whose enchantment grows the more you know about it.

The story of Akhenaten and Nefertiti

Few figures from ancient history have inspired as much conjecture as Akhenaten and Nefertiti, as scholars dispute even fundamental aspects of their story – let alone the interpretation of the events. The tale begins with Pharaoh **Amenophis III**, who flouted convention by making Tiy, his Nubian concubine, Great Wife, despite her lack of royal blood. **Queen Tiy** remained formidable long after Amenophis entered his dotage and their eldest son ascended the throne as **Amenophis IV**. Some believe this event followed his father's death, others that mother and son ruled jointly for twelve years. To square the former theory with the period of his reign (c.1379–1362 BC) and his demise around the age of 30 would mean accepting that Amenophis Jr embarked on his religious reformation between the ages of 9 and 13, though a marriage at 13 is quite likely.

The origins of Amenophis's wife, **Nefertiti**, are obscure. Her name – meaning "A Beautiful Woman Has Come" – suits the romantic legend that she was a Mesopotamian princess originally betrothed to Amenophis III. However, others identify her as Amenophis III's child by a secondary wife, or as the daughter of his vizier **Ay**, whose wife, **Tey**, was almost certainly Nefertiti's wet nurse. The pharaonic custom of sister–brother and father–daughter marriages allows plenty of scope for speculation, but the fair-skinned bust of Nefertiti in the Berlin Museum suggests that she wasn't Tiy's child, at any rate. (Amid all the fuss about Cleopatra being black, nobody seems to have noticed that Queen Tiy – and therefore her son, Amenophis IV – were indubitably so.)

Early in his reign, Amenophis IV began to espouse the **worship of Aten** (see p.232), whose ascendancy threatened the priesthoods of other cults. The bureaucracy was equally alarmed by his decree that the spoken language should be used in official documents, contrary to all tradition. To escape their influence and realize his vision of a city dedicated to Aten, the pharaoh founded a **new capital** upon an empty plain beside the Nile, halfway between Memphis and Thebes, which he named **Akhetaten**, the "Horizon of the Aten". It was here that the royal couple settled in the fifth year of their reign and took Aten's name in honour of their faith. He discarded Amenophis IV for **Akhenaten** (Servant of the Aten) and vowed

Aten-worship and Amarna art.

Many herald **Aten-worship** as a breakthrough in human spirituality and cultural evolution: the world's first monotheistic religion. Aten was originally just an aspect of the sun-god (the "Globe" or "Disc" of the midday sun), ranking low in the Theban pantheon until Amenophis III privately adopted it as a personal deity. Then Akhenaten publicly exalted Aten above other gods, subsuming all their attributes into this newly omnipotent being. Invocations to Maat (representing truth) were retained, but otherwise the whole cast of underworld and celestial deities was jettisoned. Morbid Osirian rites were also replaced by paeans to life in the joyous warmth of Aten's rays (which are usually shown ending in a hand clasping an ankh), as in the famous *Hymn to Aten*.

Similarities between the *Hymn* and *The Song of Solomon* (supposedly written 500 years later) have encouraged speculation about the influence of Atenism on early Jewish monotheism. Sigmund Freud argued that Moses was an Egyptian nobleman and the biblical Exodus a "pious fiction", while Ahmed Osman advances the theory that Akhenaten's deity derived from tales of the Jewish God related to him by his maternal grandfather Yuya, the Joseph of the Old Testament (see "Books", p.632).

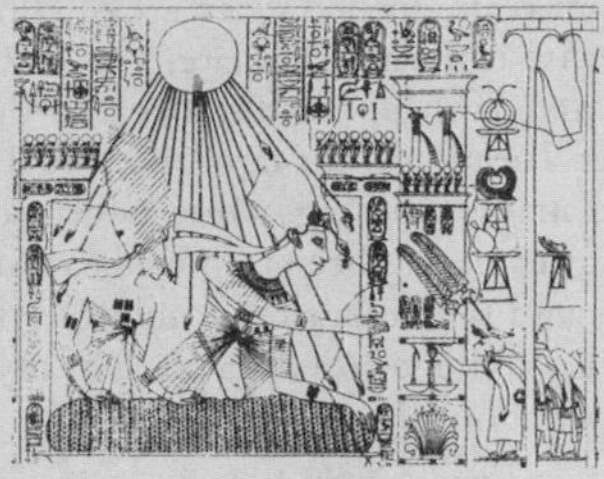

▲ Nefertiti and Akhenaten

Equally intriguing is the artwork of the Amarna period and the questions it raises about Akhenaten. **Amarna art** focused on nature and human life rather than the netherworld and resurrection. Royal portraiture, previously impersonally formalized, was suffused by naturalism (a process which began late in the reign of Amenophis III). While marshes and wildlife remained a popular subject, these scenes no longer implicitly associated birds and fish with the forces of chaos. The roofless Aten temples made new demands on sculptors and painters, who mixed sunk- and bas-relief carving to highlight features with shifting shadows and illumination.

Most striking is the rendering of **human figures**, especially Akhenaten's, whose attenuated cranium, curvaceous spine and belly, and matronly pelvis and buttocks prompted speculation that the pharaoh may have suffered from Marfan's syndrome – a rare genetic disorder that leads to feelings of alienation and a slight oddness in physical appearance – or was possibly a hermaphrodite: theories only disproved by DNA testing of royal mummies in 2009. Some argue that the Amarna style reflected Akhenaten's physiognomy, others that such distortions were simply a device that could be eschewed, as in the exquisite bust of Nefertiti. Advocates of the "Akhenaten was sick" theory point out that this was the only time when vomiting was ever represented in Egyptian art; however, Amarna art also uniquely depicted royalty eating, yet nobody asserts that other pharaohs never ate.

never to leave the city, while she took a forename meaning "Beautiful are the Beauties of the Aten", styling herself **Nefernefruaten-Nefertiti**. Her status surpassed that of any previous Great Wife, approaching that of Akhenaten himself. Bas-reliefs and stelae show her participating in state festivals, and her own cartouche was coupled with Aten's – an unprecedented association.

There's no sign that their happiness was marred by his decision to take a second wife, **Kiya**, nor of the degenerative condition that supposedly afflicted Akhenaten in later life. However, the great ceremony held at Akhetaten in their twelfth regnal year marked a turning point. Whether or not this was Akhenaten's true coronation following his father's death, he subsequently launched a **purge against the old**

cults. From Kom Ombo to Bubastis, temples were closed and statues disfigured, causing public unrest. Although this was quelled by Akhenaten's chief of police, **Mahu**, his foreign minister apparently ignored pleas from foreign vassals menaced by the Hittites and Habiru, and the army was less than zealous in defending Egypt's frontiers. Akhenaten was consequently blamed for squandering the territorial gains of his forefathers.

What happened in the last years of Akhenaten and Nefertiti's reign is subject to various interpretations. The consensus is that Nefertiti and Akhenaten became estranged, and he took as co-regent **Smenkhkare**, a mysterious youth married to their eldest daughter, **Meritaten**. While Nefertiti withdrew to her Northern Palace, Akhenaten and his regent lived together at the other end of the city; the poses struck by them in mural scenes of the period have prompted suggestions of a homosexual relationship. Whatever the truth of this, it's known that Smenkhkare ruled alone for some time after the **death of Akhenaten** (c.1362 BC), before dying himself (see p.313). Nefertiti's fate is less certain, but it's generally believed that she also died around the same time. To date, none of their mummies have been found (or, rather, definitely identified).

The geneaology of Smenkhkare's successor – the boy-king known to posterity as **Tutankhamun** – is obscure. Some hold that his parents were Amenophis III and his half-sister Sitamun; others favour Ay and Tey, or Akhenaten and Kiya, or even (based on DNA analysis) that he was of Hyksos or Jewish descent. About the only certainty is that he was originally raised to worship Aten, and named Tutankh*aten*. By renouncing this name for one honouring Amun, he heralded a return to Thebes and the old gods, fronting a **Theban counter-revolution** executed by Vizier Ay and General Horemheb. Some think this was relatively benign while Tut and his successor Ay ruled Egypt, blaming **Horemheb** and Seti I for a later, ruthless extirpation of Atenism. Seti plundered the abandoned city of Akhetaten for masonry to build new temples, ordered its site cursed by priests to deter reoccupation, and excised the cartouches of every ruler tainted with the "Amarna heresy" from their monuments and the List of Kings. So thorough was this cover-up that Akhenaten and Nefertiti remained unknown to history until the nineteenth century.

The site

While tour groups are now visiting Tell el-Amarna, independent travellers are still rare and presently only allowed access **by private taxi** from Minya or Assyut, accompanied by a police escort or tour guide (see p.222). The site is far too large to explore on foot and there's nobody to drive you around, so you'll need a taxi anyway. Be sure the driver knows which tombs you want to visit or he may balk at going to the remoter ones (though only the Southern Tombs lack a proper access road).

The east bank road from Minya peters out 15km beyond Beni Hassan (see p.226), so access to Tell el-Amarna is via the west bank, using a car ferry 9km from Mallawi. To visit both sites on the same day, you must double back to Minya, or use another car ferry between El-Sheikh Tamai (4–5km south of Beni Hassan) and the west bank, before proceeding to Mallawi to cross back over to the eastern side. Mallawi's landing stage has a choice of craft: a car ferry (£E20 per vehicle with passengers; retain the ticket for the return journey); a green motor-launch (£E10 for up to six people, or £E1 each for more than six); and an occasional blue tourist boat – all landing at **El-Till**, on the east bank. Here the tourist police will assign a cop to ride with you to the ticket office near the Northern Tombs, and a custodian to ride with you to the Royal Tomb if you wish to visit it. The office sells separate **tickets** for the Northern and Southern Tombs (£E30) and the Royal Tomb (£E20).

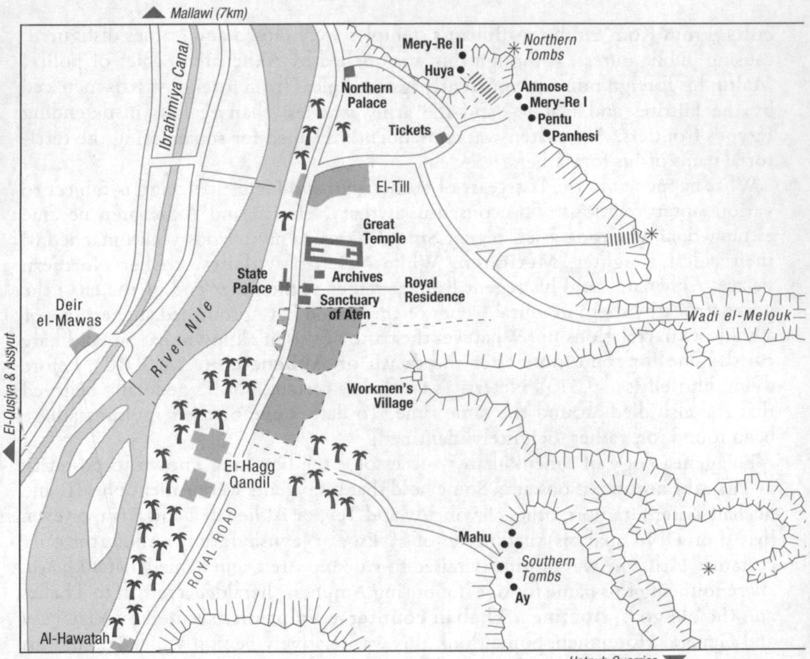

The City

The track running south from El-Till follows the old **Royal Road** that formed ancient Akhetaten's main axis, and is known locally as the Sikket es-Sultan, the Road of the Sultan. Alongside is a Muslim cemetery, overlying part of a rectangle stretching towards the ridge. This was once the **Great Temple of Aten**, whose northern wall incorporated the Hall of Foreign Tribute where emissaries proffered treasure (as depicted in tombs). Unlike traditional temples, which got darker as one approached the sanctuary, Aten's was roofless, admitting the rays of its namesake. After Akhenaten's death Horemheb ordered the temple's destruction, and Ramses II quarried its foundations for his temples at Hermopolis, across the Nile. Today, replicas of a complete and a partial lotus-bundle **column** (erected by Barry Kemp of the Tell el-Amarna Project, who has been working here for decades) tower incongruously above the low walls.

Further south (and hard to distinguish beneath shifting sands) are the remnants of the Foreign Office **Archives**, where the **Amarna Letters** were discovered. Written in the Akkadian script used for diplomatic correspondence with Asiatic states, these clay tablets have revealed much about the period. Over 360 letters have been found, but more were undoubtedly lost, leaving an incomplete puzzle for archeologists to piece together and argue over.

Next come three excavated rectangles that were once the **Royal Residence**. Their private apartments were separated from the stately reception halls that ran through the centre of the huge palace compound. Across the Royal Road stood an even larger **State Palace**, with a dock for the royal barge. Both palaces were connected by a covered "flyover" spanning the road (part of one pylon remains), into which was set the **Window of Appearances**, whence Nefertiti and Akhenaten showered favoured courtiers with gold collars and other rewards.

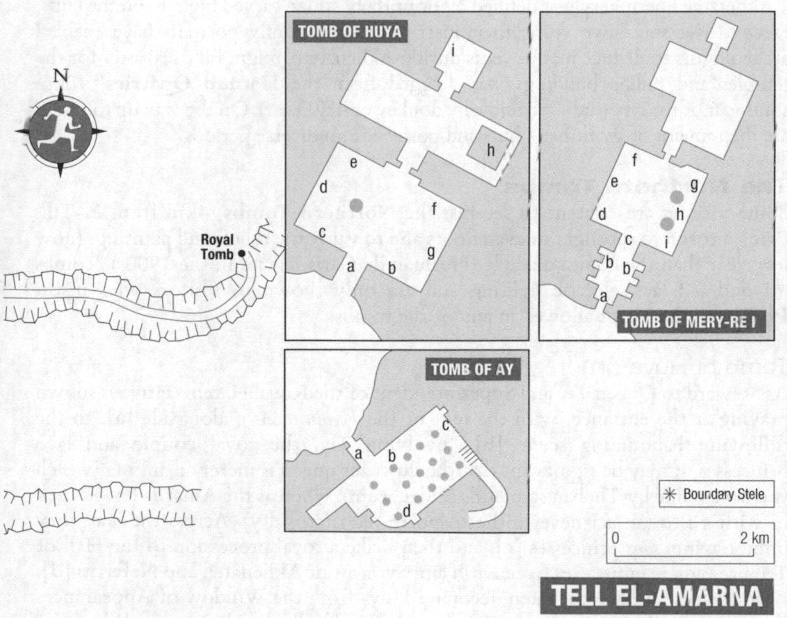

To the south of their residence lay the **Sanctuary of Aten**, probably used for private worship by the royal family, and the home of the High Priest, Panehsi. Beyond spread the city's **residential quarters**: the richest homes beside the road, the poorest hovels backing onto desert. Also in this quarter was the workshop of the sculptor Tuthmosis, where the famous bust of Nefertiti was uncovered in 1912, before being smuggled to Berlin's Ägyptisches Museum – Egypt is now campaigning for its return.

Outlying palaces and stelae

The best-preserved outline of an Amarna building is Nefertiti's **Northern Palace** or summer residence, 1500m from El-Till. Low walls and hollows delineate rooms and courtyards grouped around a garden which once contained a pool that cooled the palace by evaporation. Like all Amarna residences, it was divided into public and private quarters, with north-facing doors to catch the prevailing wind. Rooms were plastered and painted, lit by oil lamps hung from pegs or set in niches, and warmed by braziers over winter. Fitted toilets and bathrooms also featured in the homes of the well-to-do. A magnificent painted floor depicting wildfowl and fish was found here, and is now in the Antiquities Museum in Cairo. Unlike traditional marsh scenes, Amarna tableaux rarely feature hunting, suggesting that Akhenaten abjured the sport of kings.

In summer, Akhenaten and Nefertiti would ride in their electrum-plated chariot to the other end of the Royal Road, where another palace called Maru-Aten stood near the modern-day hamlet of Al-Hawatah. Alongside this **Southern Palace** lay a pleasure lake surrounded by trees and shrubs, which fed smaller pools within the palace. The walls of its columned hall were painted with flowers and inlaid with figures and Aten symbols.

Akhetaten's periphery was defined by **boundary stelae** carved high up on the cliffs, erected over successive years; their inscriptions and family portraits have enabled archeologists to deduce many events during Akhenaten's reign. Fine alabaster for the temples and public buildings was dragged from the **Hatnub Quarries**, 10km southeast of the city (only accessible by donkey or 4WD car). On the way up the wadi are the remains of workmen's huts and pottery from diverse periods.

The Northern Tombs

Some visitors are content to see just the **Northern Tombs**, 4km from El-Till. Bring a **torch** to spotlight uneven floors and to study the reliefs and paintings (now less clear than the copies made by Norman de Garis Davies in the 1900s). Tombs #1 and #2 lack electric lighting and are only shown to visitors who insist. **Photography** is not allowed in any of the tombs.

Tomb of Huya (#1)

As Steward to Queen Tiy and Superintendent of the Royal Harem, **Huya** is shown praying at the entrance, with the text of the *Hymn to Aten* alongside **[a]**. In the following banqueting scene **[b]**, involving Tiy, the royal couple and two princesses, it may be significant that the dowager queen is merely drinking (which was acceptable by Theban standards of decorum), whereas the Amarna brood tuck in with gusto (an act never hitherto portrayed of royalty). Across the way they imbibe wine, *sans* princesses **[c]**, and then make a royal procession to the Hall of Tribute, where emissaries from Kush and Syria await Akhenaten and Nefertiti **[d]**.

On the rear wall, Akhenaten decorates Huya from the Window of Appearances (notice the sculptor's studio, lower down **[e]**), who displays his awards **[f]** on the other side of the portal, the lintel of which portrays three generations of the royal family, including Amenophis III. Along the east wall, Akhenaten leads Tiy to the temple built for his parents **[g]**. Huya's mummy was stashed in a burial shaft **[h]** below the transverse hall, beyond which is a shrine painted with offerings, containing an unfinished statue of Huya **[i]**.

Tomb of Mery-Re II (#2)

The last resting place of **Mery-Re II**, Overseer of the Two Treasuries, is similar in shape to Huya's tomb, but was constructed late in Akhenaten's reign, since his cartouches have been replaced by Smenkhkare's, and Nefertiti's by Meritaten's. Beyond the entrance (whose adoration scene and *Hymn to Aten* are largely destroyed), the inner walls portray Nefertiti straining a drink for the king, who is seated beneath a sunshade (to the left); and Mery-Re receiving a golden crown, followed by a warm welcome from his household (right). The rear wall bears an unfinished scene of Mery-Re being rewarded by Smenkhkare and Meritaten, drawn in black ink.

Tomb of Ahmose (#3)

This battered tomb is one of the four that visitors usually see. The entrance walls show **Ahmose**, Akhenaten's fan-bearer, praying to Aten, with a now-illegible inscription enjoining the deity to ensure "that there is sand on the shore, that fishes in the stream have scales, and cattle have hair. Let him sojourn here until the swan turns black and the raven white". Inside, you can just discern Ahmose carrying an axe and a fan, his official regalia. On the left-hand wall are bas-reliefs of shield-bearers and pikemen, followed by an outsized horse and chariot outlined in red pigment (presumably intended to represent Akhenaten leading his army into battle, which never happened). In the transverse hall are two false doors, a deep vertical shaft, and a defaced, life-size statue of Ahmose in a niche.

Tomb of Mery-Re I (#4)

High Priest **Mery-Re I** (father of Mery-Re II) rated a superior tomb, with a coloured cornice around its entrance **[a]** and false columns of painted flowers at the rear of the vestibule **[b]**. Reliefs of Mery-Re and his wife, Tenro, at prayer flank the portal **[c]** into the main chamber, which retains two of its original papyrus-bud columns. Proceeding clockwise round the room, you see Mery-Re's investiture with a golden collar **[d]**, the royal family leaving the palace **[e]**, and Akhenaten in a chariot (his face and the Aten symbol have been chiselled out, as usual). Scenes of offerings **[f]** and Aten-worship **[g]** flank the left side of a doorway into the unfinished rear chamber, which lacks any decoration. More interesting is the eastern wall **[h]**, depicting Akhenaten and the Great Temple (which has helped archeologists visualize the city's appearance). Notice the sensitive relief of blind beggars awaiting alms, low down in the corner **[i]**.

Tombs of Pentu (#5) and Panehsi (#6)

The third tomb in this cluster belongs to **Pentu**, the royal physician. Its papyrus-bundle columns retain traces of paint with chariots visible on the right-hand wall, but there's little else to see. It's better to head 300m south along the cliff path to the isolated tomb of **Panehsi**, overseer of the royal herds and granaries. Unlike most of the others, its decorative facade has remained intact, but the interior has been modified by Copts who used it as a chapel. To the left of the entrance, the royal family prays above their servants. The painted, apse-like recess in the main chamber is probably a Coptic addition – notice the angel's wings.

The Royal Tomb

It's an easy ten-minute drive to the subterranean **Royal Tomb**, in a desolate ravine 5.5km from the plain. A custodian will ride with you to unlock the tomb. Dug into the bed of the wadi, this tomb was the first from the XVIII Dynasty to run directly from a corridor to a burial chamber. Its burial scene and text were virtually obliterated by Amun's priests, and no mummies were ever found there, but in a chamber off the first descending passage, fragmentary bas-reliefs (now clumsily "restored") depict the funerary rites of one of the royal daughters (either Meketaten or Ankesbaten), and a granite sarcophagus bearing Tiy's cartouche was found, suggesting this might have been a family vault. No one knows whether Akhenaten and Nefertiti were interred in the main burial chamber beyond a deep pit (and perhaps dragged out to rot a few years later) or in the Valley of the Kings. Some believe that the mysterious mummy found in tomb KV55 is Akhenaten's (see p.313), or that Nefertiti's has been discovered in tomb KV35 (see p.311).

The Southern Tombs

From El-Hagg Qandil beyond the ancient Workmen's Village, a poorly surfaced road runs between palm-groves to the **Southern Tombs**, scattered over seven low hills in two clusters: #7–15 and #16–25. Amarna notables buried here include Tutu, the foreign minister, and Ramose, Steward of Amenophis III, but the ones to see are Ay and Mahu.

Tomb of Ay (#25)

Ay's Tomb was never finished, since he built himself a new one at Thebes after the court returned there under Tutankhamun, but such carvings as were executed show the Amarna style at its apogee and the ceiling of its central aisle is painted with a fetching checkerboard pattern.

Both sides of the tomb's vestibule **[a]** are decorated. On the left, the king and queen, three princesses, Nefertiti's sister Mutnedjmet and her dwarfs lead the court in the worship of Aten. Across the way is a superb relief of Ay and his wife Tey rendering homage and the most complete text of the *Hymn to Aten*; every fold of their skirts and braid in their hair are meticulously depicted. The really intriguing scenes, however, are in the main chamber. On the left side of the entrance wall, Ay and Tey are showered with decorations from the Window of Appearances, acclaimed by fan-bearers, scribes and guards **[b]**. Palace life is depicted in ink or sunk-relief: a concubine has her hair done, while girls play the harp, dance, cook and sweep. The depth of bowing by courtiers is the most servile ever found in Egyptian art **[c]**. Along the rear wall are a ruined door-shaped stele **[d]** and a stairway leading to an unfinished burial shaft.

Ay and Tey are mysterious figures, honoured as "Divine Father and Mother", but never directly identified as being royal. Some reckon Ay was a son of Yuya and Thuya, Akhenaten's maternal grandparents; others that Tey was Nefertiti's wet-nurse, or that both conceived Tutankhamun. Certainly, Ay was vizier to Amenophis III, Akhenaten and Tutankhamun, and reigned briefly himself (1352–1348 BC). He was ultimately buried in the Western Valley of the Theban Necropolis (see p.313).

Tomb of Mahu (#9)

Ten minutes' walk away, the **Tomb of Mahu**, Akhenaten's chief of police and frontier security, opens with a rough-cut transverse hall featuring a scene of Mahu standing before the vizier with two intruders, whom he accuses of being "agitated by some foreign power", as minions heat irons in a brazier for their torture (to the left as you enter). Further in are two more chambers at different levels, linked by a winding stairway – mind your head on the low ceiling.

Assyut and around

ASSYUT (pronounced "As-*yoot*") was the first part of Middle Egypt to become a no-go zone for tourists in the 1990s, as local Islamic militants targeted foreigners as well as the security forces in their war against the state. The city endured nearly a decade of curfews and arrests until the conflict fizzled out, leaving Assyut with an overwhelming police presence and the mother of bad reputations. So it's not surprising that citizens – and the Christian population especially – rejoiced at **apparitions** of the Virgin Mary that occurred (so people swear) in 2000 and 2005, in the form of a light above two churches. Another cause for optimism is the success of the city's **football** team Cement Assyut, sponsored by the cement factory across the river. Residents are more ambivalent about the fame of Assyut-born sex bomb **Ruby** – whose pop-videos make Britney Spears look like a nun – and local Mafioso Izzat Hanafi (hanged in 2008). Elsewhere, you'll meet many Egyptian men who recall doing their military service here at the vast Mangabat training depot.

Aside from the atmospheric **bazaar** and a **Governorate Festival** (April 18) commemorating the defeat of French forces by local villagers in 1799 – marked by folklore shows and a flotilla of boats on the Nile – the only reasons to come here are a couple of monasteries and tombs within the governorate. As in Minya, supervision by the **police** can be off-putting – though in Assyut they're weirdly inconsistent, giving you a motorcycle escort one time and totally ignoring you the next.

Arrival and information

While the **train and bus stations** are both central, **service taxis** use the Arba'in terminal beside the El-Mallah Canal on the edge of the old quarter (£E10 by taxi

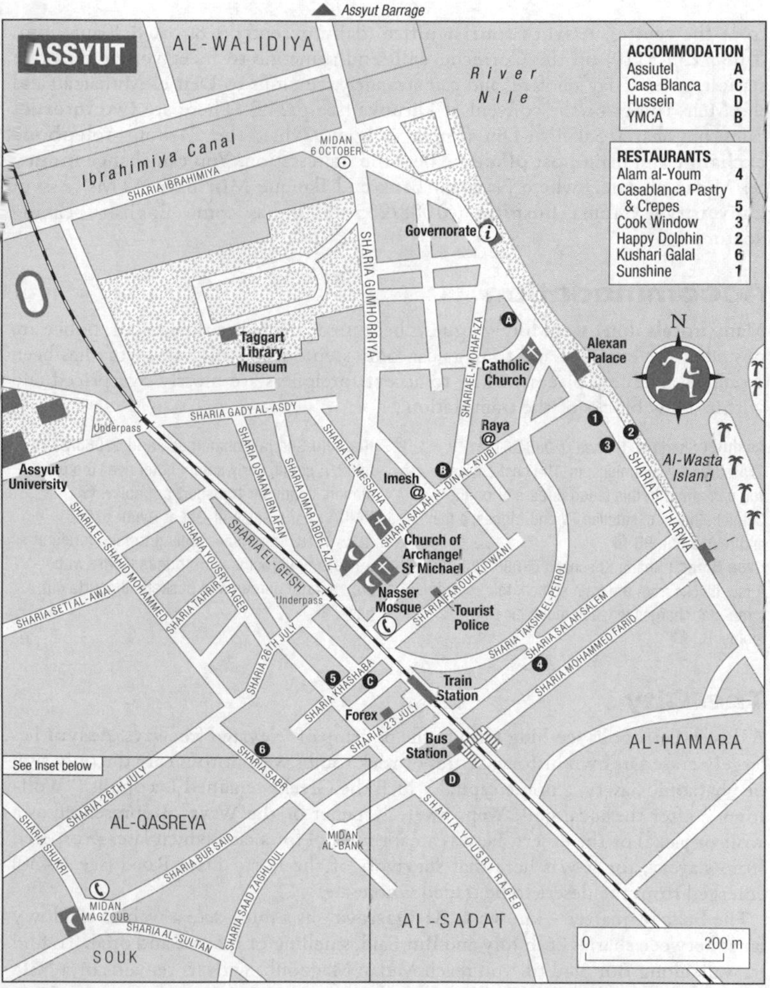

Assyut Barrage
ASSYUT
AL-WALIDIYA
River Nile
ACCOMMODATION
Assiutel A
Casa Blanca C
Hussein D
YMCA B
RESTAURANTS
Alam al-Youm 4
Casablanca Pastry & Crepes 5
Cook Window 3
Happy Dolphin 2
Kushari Galal 6
Sunshine 1
Ibrahimiya Canal
SHARIA IBRAHIMIYA
MIDAN 6 OCTOBER
Governorate
SHARIA GUMHORRIYA
Taggart Library Museum
Catholic Church
Alexan Palace
SHARIA EL-MOHAFAZA
N
SHARIA GADY AL-ASDY
Underpass
Raya
Assyut University
University Hospital
SHARIA OSMAN IBN AFAN
SHARIA OMAR ABDEL AZIZ
SHARIA EL-MESSAHA
Imesh
SHARIA SALAH AL-DIN AL-AYUBI
SHARIA EL-THARWA
Al-Wasta Island
SHARIA EL-SHAHID MOHAMMED
SHARIA YOUSRY RAGEB
SHARIA EL-GEISH
Church of Archangel St Michael
SHARIA FAROUK KIDWANI
SHARIA SETI AL-AWAL
SHARIA TAHRIR
Underpass
Nasser Mosque
Tourist Police
SHARIA TAKSIM EL-PETROL
SHARIA SALAH SALEM
SHARIA MOHAMMED FARID
SHARIA 26TH JULY
SHARIA KHASHABA
Train Station
Forex
SHARIA 23 JULY
Bus Station
AL-HAMARA
See Inset below
SHARIA SABR
SHARIA 26TH JULY
AL-QASREYA
SHARIA YOUSRY RAGEB
MIDAN AL-BANK
SHARIA SHUKRI
SHARIA BUR SAID
Wikalas
MIDAN MAGZOUB
SHARIA SAAD ZAGHLOUL
AL-SADAT
SHARIA AL-SULTAN
SOUK
0 200 m

Al-Awimy Mosque
0 100 m
AL-QASREYA
SHARIA 26TH JULY
SHARIA
SHARIA SHUKRI
N
SHARIA SABR
MIDAN TALAT HARB
Wikala Lotfi
National Bank
Hammam Sabit
MIDAN AL-BANK
SHARIA 26TH JULY
AL-QASREYA
Renaissance Cinema
SHARIA BUR SAID
SHARIA SAAD ZAGHLOUL
Wikala Chalabi
MIDAN MAGZOUB
Wikala Thabat
Nile Barrage
SHARIA AL-SULTAN
Arba'in Taxi Station (600m)

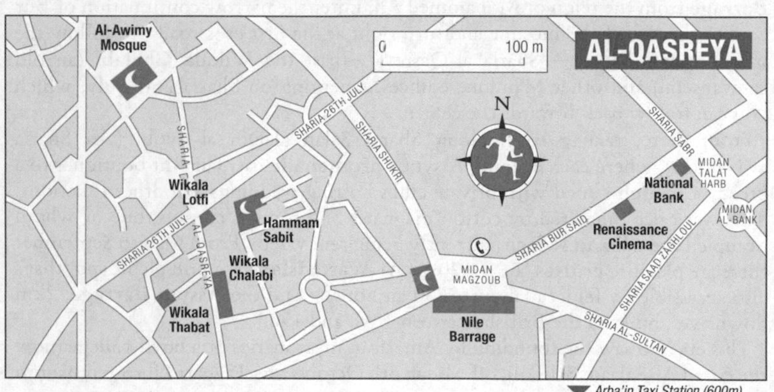

from the centre). Assyut's **tourist office** (daily except Fri & Sat 8.30am–3pm; ⓣ088/230-5110) on the Corniche will send someone to meet you at the train station, given a day's notice, and can arrange excursions to Deir el-Muharraq and the Meir Tombs or the convent at Dirunka (see p.242). There are two **internet** cafes on Sharia Salah al-Din (Imesh is open 24hr); the 24-hour **telephone exchange** and main **post office** are near the train station. You can change **money** on Midan al-Bank, where National Bank and Banque Misr have ATMs. Assyut University's Ga'ama **hospital** (ⓣ088/235-4500) has some English-speaking doctors.

Accommodation

Many **hotels** don't want foreign guests because of the hassle they entail: police are posted at the entrance and tourists can only step outside after an escort has been arranged. The few places willing to accept foreigners are mostly overpriced and within a few blocks of the train station.

Assiutel Sharia el-Tharwa ⓣ088/231-2121, ⓔassiuthotel@hotmail.com. The best choice if you can afford it, this faded three-star on the Corniche has a/c, satellite TV and fridges, a bar and restaurant. BB ❻

Casa Blanca Sharia Khashaba ⓣ088/233-7662. A few blocks from the train station, this overrated three-star charges way too much for dingy rooms. BB ❸

Hussein Sharia Mohammed Farid ⓣ088/234-2532. A small, fairly comfy hotel near the bus station, handy for transport but noisy. ❷

YMCA Sharia Salah al-Din al-Ayubi ⓣ088/232-3218. Sometimes willing to take foreigners, it has simple rooms with fridges (some with a/c), a large garden and basketball courts out back. ❶

The City

A dusty metropolis seething with traffic pouring off elevated freeways, **Assyut** has largely erased its own history. Scores of rock tombs west of town are the only sign of pharaonic Sawty, a nome capital which the Greeks renamed Lycopolis ("Wolf-town") after the local god, Wepwawet, "Opener of the Ways". Represented as a wolf or jackal of the desert, he was an apt symbol for a city which later prospered from slavery, for it was here that survivors of the Forty Days Road (see p.430) emerged from the desert to be traded wholesale.

The **bazaar** quarter – known as **Al-Qasreya** – is a must-see: a web of shadowy lanes between sharias 26th July and Bur Said, smelling of incense and offal. To find it, walk along Bur Said till you reach Midan Magzoub, with its remains of a **Nile Barrage** from the reign of Mohammed Ali. Enter the narrow continuation of Bur Said to the left of the mosque and turn right at the first crossroads, to follow the bazaar's main artery – Sharia al-Qasreya – past the **Wikala Chalabi** (an old caravanserai) and other Mamluke edifices, emerging on Sharia 26th July, which you can follow back towards the centre.

From there, take a stroll along Sharia Salah al-Din al-Ayubi (aka Sharia al-Namees), where each evening Assyutis **promenade** past fairy-lit boutiques to a breezy **Corniche** lined with private clubs hosting weddings and other functions. This was once inhabited by cotton magnates and foreign consuls, one of whom occupied the **Alexan Palace** (currently being renovated). From May to September there are pleasure **cruises** (£E10–20) to **Al-Wasta Island** – a lush picnic spot that's also accessible by felucca (about £E30 an hour) – and the **Assyut Barrage**, 2km downriver, built by the British between 1898 and 1903.

This era also saw the founding by American missionaries of a boys' college (now the co-ed Al-Salaam School), off Midan 6th October: its Taggart Library **museum**

▲ Grain merchants in Assyut's bazaar

(daily except Fri, Sun and school vacations 8am–2pm; free) displays such curios as mummified dogs and fish, and pharaonic soldiers' dog-tags.

Eating, drinking and nightlife

The Corniche offers the best choice for **eating**, with the *Happy Dolphin* floating restaurant serving grilled fish or meat alfresco, the *Cook Window* and *Sunshine Restaurant* burgers, pizzas and *shawarma* indoors – both open till midnight. Downtown, *Casablanca Pastry and Crepes* does takeaway pizzas and pancakes (savoury or sweet), *Alam al-Youm* is the place for kebabs, or you can dig in at *Kushari Galal* (till 1am or later). There are coffeehouses and juice-bars all over the centre, but you can only **drink** alcohol in the lifeless mock-Tudor bar of the *Assuitel* (which doesn't do take-outs). Aside from promenading, **nightlife** is limited to whatever's on at the Renaissance cinema on Sharia Bur Said, or hanging out in coffeehouses.

Moving on from Assyut

The police prefer tourists to leave town by train, so they don't restrict them to any particular service. About nine **trains** a day run to Cairo (5–7hr), stopping at Mallawi (2hr), Minya (3hr) and Beni Suef (5hr) along the way, and a dozen trains call at Sohag (2hr), Qena (4hr) and Luxor (6hr) en route to Aswan (12hr). The tourist office can say whether or not foreigners are allowed to use **buses,** running more or less hourly to Cairo (6–7hr) and Sohag (2hr); every two hours to Minya (2–3hr); and twice daily to Qena (4hr), Alexandria (10hr) and Hurghada (8hr). Additionally, there are four buses daily to Kharga oasis (4hr), two of which run on to Dakhla Oasis (7–8hr). Although **service taxis** run to every town along the Valley from Minya to Qena, foreigners may only take them to Kharga (4hr).

Around Assyut

Two **monasteries** in the vicinity of Assyut testify to the roots Christianity put down in this region in the fourth century. Copts believe that these and other sites were actually visited by the **Holy Family** during the four years that Mary, Joseph and the infant Jesus stayed in Egypt to escape King Herod's massacre of the first-born. Although the Bible says little about this period, details of their wanderings were revealed in a dream to Patriarch Theophilus in AD 500, and Copts have made much of this tradition ever since. Indeed, most tourism in the Assyut region involves Copts from other parts of Egypt, making pilgrimages on holy days – although Assyut's tourist office hopes to lure foreigners with the little-visited **Meir Tombs**.

Dirunka: the Convent of the Virgin

Copts believe that the Holy Family sought refuge in caves at **DIRUNKA**, 12km outside Assyut – as did later Christians. From such troglodyte origins, the present **Convent of the Virgin** (aka Deir el-Adhra, or Santa Maria) on the site has grown into what resembles a fortified campus – cynics might say a refuge for Assyut's Coptic population, should the worst ever occur.

The expansion is justified by the nearly one million pilgrims who attend the **Moulid of the Virgin** (Aug 15–30). This occasions the parading of icons around the spacious cave church where they stand for most of the year. Pilgrims are photographed against a huge portrait of the Virgin, or the verdant plain overlooked by the convent's terrace, below which is a Coptic village where nuns operate a dispensary. About fifty nuns and monks live in the convent.

As the police might wish to escort visitors and may frown on you travelling by minibus (£E1–2) from Assyut, a private taxi (£E40–50 round-trip with 1hr waiting) is the best way of **getting here**, and saves you a fifteen-minute uphill slog from the roadside. If you don't retain your taxi, returning minibuses can be flagged down on the main road.

El-Qusiya: the Burnt Monastery and the Meir Tombs

It's the police who decide whether foreigners can enter the area around El-Qusiya. If you get the go-ahead, the tourist office can arrange an excursion **by private taxi** to both the Burnt Monastery and the Meir Tombs for £E150.

EL-QUSIYA, 42km north of Assyut, has a decade-old history of sectarian strife and police brutality; its Coptic community (nearly half the population) has many grievances which the authorities prefer to hide.

Five kilometres outside town, the **Burnt Monastery** (Deir el-Muharraq) stands near the desert's edge. Its tinderbox surroundings explain the name and protective walls; the crenellated inner rampart is still blackened from a conflagration that occurred during the **Moulid of the Virgin** (June 21–28) twenty years ago. Visitors are shown around the thriving modernized establishment, except on fast days. Many of the hundred students at its Theological College will become monks when they turn 25. Within the compound are grouped the Abbot's residence, a fourth-century keep and two churches. Believers maintain that the **cave sanctuary** of the **Church of the Anointed** (El-Azraq) once hid the Holy Family for six months and ten days, and that the church was the first in the world (consecrated in AD 60), foretold in the Old Testament as "an altar to the Lord in the midst of the land of Egypt" (Isaiah 19:19–21). It's also said that what is now the altar stone was once used to block the cave's entrance. When an abbot ordered its replacement, the mason's hand was paralysed and a vision of Jesus appeared, intoning "Leave it alone." The icon of the Virgin and Child is said to be painted by St Luke; the apostles in the **Church of St George** come from Ethiopia. Remove your shoes before entering the churches.

The **Meir Tombs** are further north, 6km from the village of **Meir** (or Mayr), reached by a secondary road. This rock-hewn necropolis belonged to the rulers of the fourteenth nome, whose capital Qis or Cusae was the ancestor of El-Qusiya. Nine of its seventeen tombs are open to the public (daily except Thurs & Fri 9am–5pm; £E25), several of them still vividly coloured. Tombs #1 and #2 are inscribed with 720 deities, defaced by the Christian hermits that once dwelt there, while in tomb #4 the original grid drawn on the wall to help the artists execute their designs is faintly visible. Best of all are the splendid desert hunting scene in the tomb of **Senbi-Sa-Ukh-hotep**, and the women's fashions of the XII Dynasty depicted in Chancellor **Ukh-hotep**'s tomb. Model boats from these tombs are exhibited in the Luxor Museum (see p.274).

Sohag and around

Set on a rich agricultural plain bounded by the hills of the Eastern and Western deserts, **SOHAG** (pronounced "So*haj*") is a city of 221,000 people with a large Christian community and a small university. Before the troubles of the 1990s, many tourists used Sohag as a base for visiting the nearby **Red and White monasteries** or Abydos Temple, further away (see p.252), having first seen a colossal statue of an ancient Egyptian princess in the satellite town of **Akhmim**, beyond the east bank district of **Medinet Nasr**. Though few visitors come nowadays, the authorities hope tourism will pick up with the opening of the **Sohag Museum**, intended to showcase some five thousand artefacts found within the governorate, from the Middle Kingdom until Greco-Roman times. Its inauguration date keeps slipping but is currently forecast for 2010. Otherwise, the only attractions are Sohag's Monday-morning Souk el-Itnayn – a huge **animal market** held just off the Girga road – and the annual **Moulid of Al-Aref** a few weeks before the nationwide feast of Eid al-Adha.

Arrival and information

Arriving at the train station, you'll be detained by the **tourist police** and assigned an escort for the duration of your stay. The police will insist that you travel everywhere by **taxi** (roughly £E25 an hour), rather than local minibuses or service taxis (£E1–2) from depots on either side of the river – though you may be able to use them on the way back. The inconsistency arises because each municipality has its own police command; taxis may have to wait for a change of escort cars at the "border", marked by a statue of a princess with a harp.

The **tourist office** (Sun–Thurs 8.30am–3pm; Ⓣ093/460-4453) near the museum can arrange excursions by taxi to the monasteries if you call a day ahead. You can change **money** at the Forex (daily 10am–10pm) on Sharia al-Mahatta, or two banks (with ATMs) on the Corniche, where a **post** and **telephone office** is also located. Salam **Internet**, opposite the station, is open 24 hours. The University **hospital** (Ⓣ093/231-9101) and **police** (Ⓣ122) are in Medinet Nasr.

Accommodation

At the time of writing the only **hotel** in Sohag willing to take foreigners was the three-star *Al-Safa* (Ⓣ093/230-7701; BB ④) on Sharia el-Gumhorriya, 200m past the bridge north of the centre. Though its Nile terrace and air-conditioned en-suite rooms are pleasant (with satellite TV, fridges and balconies facing the Nile), you can't help regretting the lack of cheaper alternatives. The *El-Nil* – a yet more upmarket hotel beside the museum – is set to open in 2010.

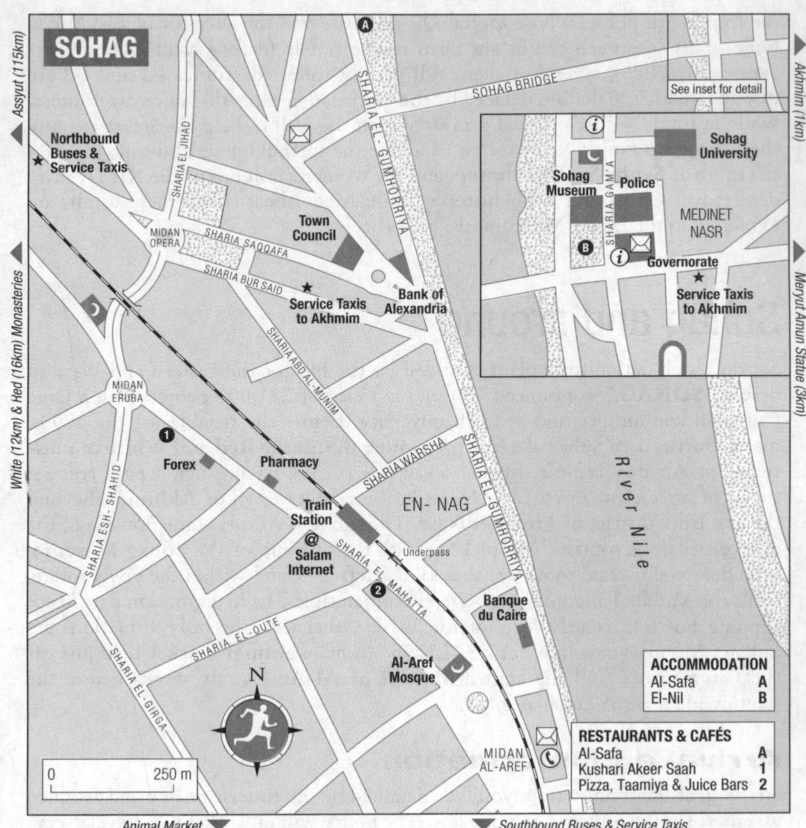

Eating and drinking

The *Al Safa* has the best **restaurant** in town, serving fish, grills and pizzas; a full meal costs about £E70. For cheaper eats try the late-night *Kushari Akeer Saah* or the nameless pizza, *fuul* and *taamiya* joints further down Sharia al-Mahatta, where there's also a juice bar. Or you could buy a spit-roast chicken to take back to your room from a rotisserie near the station. You can buy Egyptian beer and spirits at low-key **alcohol** shops on Midan Opera, to drink in your room.

Moving on

The police prefer you to travel by **train** to Luxor (4hr), Cairo (8–10hr) or anywhere else, and set no restriction on which train you take. If you're allowed to use them, there are six **buses** daily to Minya and Cairo (5am–10pm), and hourly services to Qena.

Monasteries near Sohag

The **Red and White monasteries** to the south of Sohag are both small and dilapidated, yet their near-desolation seems more evocative of the early Christians who sought God in the desert than busier establishments like Dirunka. Only a handful of acolytes tend the chapels, timeworn stones and plastic medallions attesting to the thousands of Copts who visit them during Shenoudi's moulid in the first two weeks of July, when minibuses shuttle in the pilgrims. Although local service taxis run to the White Monastery (12km), the police will make you take a **private taxi** (arranged by the tourist office for £E25 an hour), which enables you also to visit the Red Monastery, 4km further on. There's no admission charge, but baksheesh is expected.

The White Monastery

Across the plain from Sohag, high limestone walls enclose the **White Monastery** (Deir al-Abyad; daily 7am–dusk), named for the colour of its masonry, mostly taken from pharaonic or Roman buildings. Supposedly founded by St Helena on her way back from Jerusalem, the monastery once possessed the greatest Coptic library in Egypt (now dispersed among museums worldwide) and was home to over two thousand monks. Today it has only twenty residents, and its courtyard is flanked by ruined cloisters and cells. Despite its fortress-like walls – which are much thicker at the base and topped with a Cavetto cornice in the ancient Egyptian style – the monastery was often sacked by marauders.

Remove your shoes before entering the **Church of St Shenoudi**, a lofty basilica admitting breezes and birdsong, observed by a stern-faced Christ Pantokrator. Note the monolithic granite pulpit halfway along the northern wall, Roman columns in the apses, and pharaonic hieroglyphics on the outer rear wall. The monastery is also known as Deir Anba Shenouda after its fifth-century founder, who enforced the monastic rule with legendary beatings – on one occasion, fatally. Shenoudi condemned bathing as an upper-class luxury maintained by the sweat of the poor; early monks cleansed themselves by rolling naked in the sand. During **Shenoudi's moulid** (which reaches its climax on July 14), childless women roll down nearby hills in sacks, hoping to obtain divine intervention.

The Red Monastery

Down the road past walled Coptic and Muslim cemeteries, a straggling village conceals the **Red Monastery** (Deir al-Ahmar; 7am–dusk). Built of dark red brick, the monastery is attributed to St Bishoi, a penitent armed robber who became Shenoudi's disciple (retaining his club as a reminder); hence its other sobriquet, Deir Anba Bishoi.

The principal **Church of SS Bishoi and Bigol** is remarkable for its tenth-century **murals** – covering the walls, pillars and niches – which the American Research Center in Egypt has restored to their original colours. Saints glower from the south apse; peacocks and gazelles graze among the flora and fauna in the eastern apse. In the courtyard's far corner squats the smaller **Red Church**, whose inner sanctum is barred to women; notice the intricate peg-locks on the doors.

Akhmim

The sixteenth-century Moorish geographer-historian Leo Africanus reckoned **AKHMIM** "the oldest city in Egypt". Akhmimis have built on the rubble of their ancestors since Pre-Dynastic times. Its name comes from the Coptic "Khmim", recalling a local fertility god, Khente-Min, often represented by a giant **phallus**. Legend has it all the town's men were killed at war, except for one lucky youth who had to re-stock the population and was later deified. The Greeks called the town Panopolis, after their own priapic god, Pan. Egyptologists also associate it with the Akhmim Tablet, a kind of worksheet for scribes, defining mathematical units.

In 1981 excavations to build a school uncovered a colossal **statue of Meryut Amun** (daily 8am–6pm; £E20), now displayed in a pit. Since you can see it from street level, it's only worth buying a ticket to examine the statue's finely carved wig and skirt and the cartouches that identify it as Nefertari's eldest daughter, who had to marry her father, Ramses II, after the death of his second wife, Istnofret (as did her half-sister). When found, the eleven-metre-tall limestone figure had rouged lips, but the colour has since faded.

Across the street behind her head, another pit reveals the plinth and legs of a seated **colossus of Ramses II**. The colossus is reckoned to weigh 700 tonnes and to be nearly as large as the ones at Abu Simbel; it probably stood at the entrance to a vast temple whose ruins awed the Arab explorer Ibn Batuta, which is thought to lie beneath the town's Muslim cemetery.

Having seen the plinth, you can visit a **weaving factory** in the building with green gates, to the right. It's one of four built in the 1900s, using power-looms from England, that nearly wiped out the local hand-weaving industry – a tradition going back to the pharaohs, who were buried in shrouds of Akhmim silk. Hand-weaving was only preserved by a missionary-inspired **Women's Cooperative** (Rahabaat), whose weavers forgo celebrity in order not to irritate their menfolk. The factory, however, may let you see its (male) weavers at work and has a shop downstairs, selling tablecloths, sheets and cuts from bolts of silk or cotton – all in 1950s' patterns.

Upper Egypt

In antiquity, **Upper Egypt** started at Memphis and ran as far south as Aswan on the border with Nubia. Nowadays, with the designation of Middle Egypt, borders are a bit hazy, though the **Qena Bend** is generally taken as the region's beginning and **Aswan** is still effectively the end of the line.

Within this stretch of the Nile is the world's most intensive concentration of ancient monuments – temples, tombs and palaces constructed from the onset of the Middle Kingdom (c.2050 BC) up until Roman and Byzantine times. The greatest of the buildings are the **cult temples** of **Abydos**, **Dendara**, **Karnak**, **Esna**, **Edfu**, **Kom Ombo**, **Philae** and **Abu Simbel**, each conceived as "homes" for their respective deities and an accretion of centuries of building. Scarcely less impressive are the multitude of tombs in the **Theban Necropolis**, most famously in the **Valley of the Kings**, across the river from **Luxor**, where Tutankhamun's resting place is merely a hole in the ground by comparison with those of such great pharaohs as Seti I and Ramses II.

Monuments aside, Upper Egypt marks a subtle shift of character, with the desert closing in on the river, and dom palms growing alongside barrel-roofed houses, designed to reflect the intense heat. One of the greatest pleasures to be had here – indeed one of the highlights of any Egyptian trip – is to absorb the river-scape slowly from the vantage point of a **felucca**. This is easily arranged in Aswan, whence you can sail downriver with no fear of being becalmed; Nile **cruise boats** and **dahabiyas** provide a more luxurious experience. While cruises can be booked at short notice in either city, better deals are usually available in Aswan.

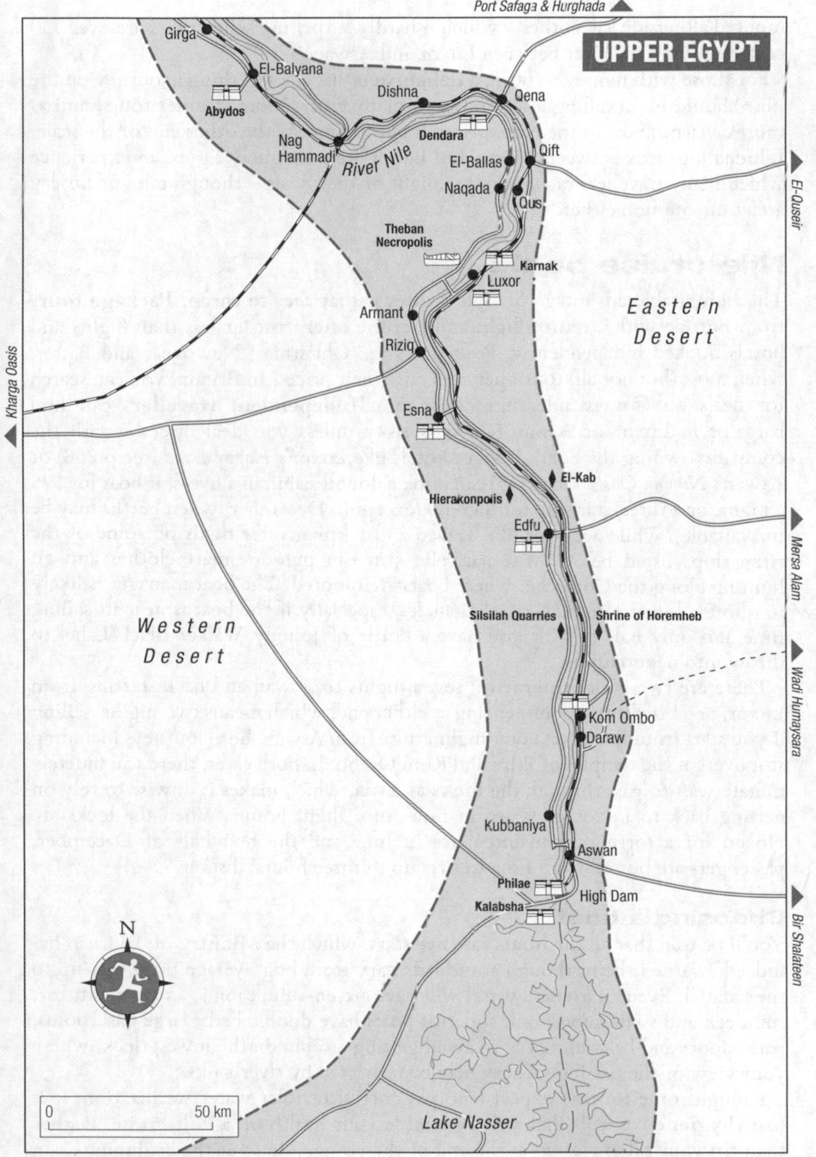

Nile trips

Some people love **Nile cruise boats**, others hate them. On the plus side they offer the chance to travel the river with all the comforts of a four- or five-star hotel. The downside is that you'll visit temples with hundreds of other tourists according to a rigid timetable, amid much noise and air pollution wherever dozens of boats are moored alongside each other – which is hardly surprising when there are over 330 cruisers plying the river between Luxor and Aswan.

For those with money to burn, a **dahabiya** cruise is everything a journey on the Nile should be, recalling a leisurely age of tourism before steamer tours, and as more *dahabiyas* take to the Nile, prices are dropping. At the other end of the scale, **felucca** journeys between Aswan and Luxor are a uniquely Egyptian experience which many travellers rate as the highlight of their visit – though tales of misery aren't uncommon either.

Nile cruise boats

The indubitable advantage of Nile cruises is that they're cheap. **Package tours** from Europe with a return flight and a cruise often cost far less than flights and hotels booked independently. Peak times are Christmas, New Year and Easter, when most (but not all) tour operators raise their prices. In Britain, you can search for deals on Ⓦ www.nilecruisesdirect.com. **Independent travellers** can find bargains in Luxor or Aswan (Cairo is risky unless you deal directly with the company owning the boat). Budget hotels like Luxor's *Happy Land* (see p.268) or Aswan's *Nubian Oasis* (see p.345) can book a double cabin in a five-star boat for $75 a night, or a three-star ship for $55–65 (except in December, when berths may be unavailable), while agencies like Travco and Eastmar offer **deals** on some of the ritzy ships listed below. Alternatively, you can put on smart clothes and go hunting along the Corniche, where boats are moored. The boat manager is likely to quote a lower rate than travel agencies, especially if the boat is near its sailing time and only half full, or you have a bottle of Johnny Walker Black Label to throw into negotiations.

There are two basic **itineraries**: seven nights to Aswan and back starting from Luxor, or a briefer trip commencing at either end, which means two nights' sailing if you start from Luxor or a one-night cruise from Aswan, both journeys including stopovers at the temples of Edfu and Kom Ombo. In both cases, there's an indeterminate wait to pass through the **locks at Esna**, which makes it unwise to rely on getting back to Luxor or Cairo in time for a flight home. When the locks are **closed** for a fortnight's maintenance in June and the first half of December, passengers are bussed from Esna to sites up to three hours' distant.

Choosing a boat

You'll be told that all the **boats** rate five stars, which the Ministry of Tourism has indeed awarded them, though **standards** vary from bog-average three-star up to the palatial. Even an average vessel will have a/c en-suite cabins, a restaurant, bar, sun deck and swimming pool; superior boats have double beds, large bathrooms, patio doors and balconies. Try to avoid getting a cabin on the lowest deck, where your view of the passing scenery may be restricted by riverbanks.

Though some tourists expect (and pay for) ultraviolet water sterilization, it is basic **hygiene** controls that will determine your health on a Nile cruise. Rather than **tip** your cabin cleaner at the end of the voyage, do so at the beginning as an incentive; cleaners are paid less than £E20 a day.

Other things to consider are the quality of **meals** (included in the price, but ranging from mediocre to sumptuous), the inflated cost of **alcohol** (many people smuggle booze aboard despite prohibition), seating arrangements (independent travellers are obliged to eat at the same table) and **moorings**. Boats in Luxor and Aswan are gradually being moved to new berths far outside town, but those belonging to chains like *Sonesta*, *Sofitel* and *Mövenpick* may continue to dock by their respective hotels.

Boats grossly overcharge for **onshore excursions** in Luxor or Aswan. The management won't mind if you find a cheaper way unless you tell other passengers about it.

The following cruise boats are a cut above the rest – and costlier.

Philae ⓦwww.oberoihotels.com. Like a Mississippi paddle-steamer, with teak panelling and antiques galore, this Oberoi-managed boat has all mod cons and is unusual in that each cabin has its own balcony. Rates for one person sharing a cabin start from €275 a night.

St George I ⓦwww.sonesta.com. The flagship of the *Sonesta* fleet, with a full-service spa and fitness centre, nightly entertainment, and over-the-top decor. Cruises start at $400 per person per night. The *Sonesta* also runs the *Star Goddess* – whose cabins are all suites (from $340 per person a night) – *Moon Goddess* (from $284) and *Sun Goddess* (from $130), which are less opulent but still extremely comfortable.

Shehrayar and Shehrazad Also managed by the Oberoi chain but marketed by other travel agencies, these two boats each have forty spacious cabins and all the usual amenities; rates for a three- or four-night cruise range from €225–295/295–325 per person.

Sudan ⓦwww.steam-ship-sudan.com. Commissioned in 1885 for Cook's fleet, this vintage paddle steamer once belonged to King Fouad and was later used as a set in *Death on the Nile*. With only 22 cabins, it has bags of character, which makes up for the lack of a pool. No children under 7. Four- and five-day cruises from €960/1200 per person.

Sun Boat III ⓦwww.akegypt.com. This luxurious boat, managed by Abercrombie & Kent, carries only 36 passengers, with a more intimate ambience than on *Sun Boat IV*, carrying 80, or the *Nile Adventurer*, sleeping 68. Their three, four or seven-day cruises have an Egyptologist on board and enjoy private moorings at Luxor, Aswan and Kom Ombo.

Triton Bookable through ⓦwww.capecairo.com and other upmarket tour agencies. Perhaps the ritziest boat on the Nile, with an indoor and outdoor pool, a spa, a gourmet à la carte restaurant, and a steward for each of its twenty staterooms (from $450–550 per person per night).

Dahabiyas

Egypt's pharaohs loved their pleasure-barges: Cleopatra and Julius Caesar spent *nine months* sailing round Egypt escorted by four hundred ships. Some of this luxury rubbed off on the houseboats that conveyed Ottoman officials up and downriver, dubbed **dahabiya** (from the Arabic for "gold") after their gilded railings. Despite the advent of Cook's tours in the 1860s, some Europeans still preferred to choose one of the two hundred *dahabiyas* for hire at the Cairo port of Bulaq, but by the 1900s steamers and railways had relegated them to Cairo love nests, which later went to the scrap-yard or were left to rot in the 1960s.

Thirty years later, a few entrepreneurs began refurbishing *dahabiyas* to run exclusive cruises, which proved so successful that replicas are now being built at Esna, Rosetta and Cairo. Though sometimes rented to tour groups, they are often **chartered** for a private cruise by newlyweds, families or friends. Passengers are less constrained by schedules and moorings than on cruise boats, making it feasible to visit sites at quiet times or where larger ships can't moor, so besides the temples at Esna, Edfu and Kom Ombo, you get to explore **El-Kab** and **Silsilah**, which are otherwise difficult to reach (see p.335).

A typical *dahabiya* has a spacious salon; wood-panelled cabins ventilated by sliding louvres, with brass fittings and tiled bathrooms; and an upper deck where meals are eaten, whose awning can be rolled back for sunbathing. Besides sightseeing and stopovers there is backgammon, a library of books and CDs, and maybe live music or dancing after supper for entertainment. Meals are lavish, washed down with fruit juices, beer or cocktails. Filtered water and rigorous hygiene mean that sickness is seldom a problem. Unless carefully designed, boats over 38m long can't travel by sails alone and have to use engines (thus technically disqualifying them from being called *dahabiyas*) or be towed by a tug.

Three- to five-day **itineraries** start or end in Esna or Aswan; longer voyages from Luxor to Aswan and back (or vice versa) are also available. If finishing or starting at Esna, transport to or from Luxor is provided. The **price** usually includes transfers, meals and soft drinks, excursions and tickets to the temples en route (but not necessarily in and around Aswan and Luxor) – read the small print carefully.

Among the thirty-odd boats on the Nile are:

Amira (*Princess*) ⓦ www.elamira.com. At 45m long it has to be pulled by a tug, and purists may also be dismayed by the on-deck jacuzzi and TVs in its cabins. Mainly chartered by travel companies, but berths for €100 per person per day might be available if you talk to its owner, Mohammed el-Husseiny (ⓣ010 606-1446).

Assouan, **El-Nil**, **Meröe** and **Melouka** ⓦ www.nourelnil.com. At 53m, *Meröe* is the largest *dahabiya* on the Nile, with ten spacious cabins and a huge suite. *Melouka*'s six cabins are also on the generous size, while *El-Nil* has room for twenty passengers, and the smaller *Assouan* up to sixteen. Rates start at €1100 per person.

El-Bey (*His Lordship*), **El-Hanem** (*Her Ladyship*), **Nesma** (*Breeze*), **Zahra** (*Flower*), **Amber** and **Musk** ⓦ www.dahabiya.com. Run by Belle Époque Travel in Cairo, these 38m-long replica antique vessels each sleep up to twelve passengers in six cabins, panelled in dark wood.

Neferu-Ra ⓦ www.museum-tours.com. Built for Omar Pasha in 1910, this 23m-long vessel sleeps up to seven people in three cabins and a suite. Three, four or five-night cruises cost $2500/3000/3500 for up to three people, $500/700/900 for each extra passenger; there's a $1000 surcharge for private charters.

Orient and **Zekrayaat** (*Memories*) ⓦ www.nile-dahabiya.com. Run by the owner of *Sofra* in Luxor (see p.277), these two replica boats are tastefully furnished with antiques. Each has six cabins and a suite; rates range from €150–190 per person per day.

Vivant Denon ⓦ www.dahabeya.net. Restored by ex-hotel manager Didier Caille, this 30m-long craft built in 1889 (named after the artist on Napoleon's expedition to Egypt) sleeps up to six passengers in four cabins. The ten cruises a year from October to April are mainly booked by French tourists, though Didier and his crew also speak English. Exclusively for chartering.

Princess Donia ⓦ www.princessdonia.com. With its MFI-style décor and TVs in its cabins, this boat bears little resemblance to an antique *dahabiya*, but is nonetheless comfortable. Cabins from €110–150 per person a day; you can charter the boat for €5000–6000.

Royal Cleopatra ⓦ www.nubiannilecruises.com. A converted *sandale* (cargo felucca) rather than a proper *dahabiya*, so the owners call it a "yacht", which is what it looks like, with a bar, salon and two air-conditioned staterooms (sleeping up to six people). Three-, four- or six-night itineraries cost $2495/2595/2725 per person.

Scheherazade and **Malika Merit** (*Queen Merit*) ⓦ www.nileboat.com. Two replica vessels with slightly kitsch pharaonic décor; *Malika Merit* has six cabins and a suite, *Scheherazade* is smaller. Both are exclusively for charter at €5000–6000 a time.

Zarafa (*Giraffe*) and **Dongola** ⓦ www.nubiannilecruises.com. Marketed separately from the same company's replica vessels, these *dahabiyas* were built for Egyptian royalty in the 1830s and owned by 1950s film stars. Cruises start in Cairo, with one night's hotel accommodation included in the price (from $3680/person). *Zarafa* is air conditioned.

Feluccas

Whether your **felucca** trip is blissful or boring, tragicomic or unpleasant depends on a host of factors. Conditions on the river are crucial. Nights are chilly in winter and otherwise cool except in summer, when days are scorching. Nile breezes may be cooling, but winds from the desert can suck you dry and the effect of ultraviolet rays is magnified by water.

As the wind nearly always blows south, travelling downstream (towards Luxor) involves constant tacking, unless you simply drift with the sluggish current, but there's no chance of being becalmed, unlike sailing upriver, where the cliffs between Esna, Edfu and Kom Ombo block the wind – which is why most journeys start **from Aswan**. Since feluccas were forbidden to sail on the Nile after dark, the distance covered on **itineraries** has shrunk and tourists' expectations often exceed reality. Short daylight hours in winter and the low water level between October and May may also cause delay.

Unless the wind is especially strong, a one-day one-night trip usually only gets you to **Kubbaniya** – a few miles beyond the Aswan Bridge – where many boatmen have their family homes, to which you'll be invited for dinner. A two-day two-night trip should take you at least as far as **Darow** if not all the way to **Kom Ombo**, while three days and three nights should include a visit to **Silsilah** and end up somewhere short of **Edfu**. Whatever your final landfall, **onwards travel by minibus** to Luxor–with **stopovers** at Kom Ombo and/or Edfu temples – is often included in the deal (if not, drivers charge £E35 per person; call Ali on ⓣ012 106-5771 to arrange a pick-up at any point from Kubbaniya onwards).

When you're sailing low in the water, the Nile's horizon recedes like an infinity pool, its stillness broken only by passing cruise boats. Evenings often end round a campfire, enlivened by singing and drumming. Most people sleep on mattresses aboard the felucca, but some prefer camping ashore. Each day will be different from the last: stow your watch and take things as they come.

Note that it's also possible to hire a felucca for a half-day outing or day-trip, as detailed in the accounts of Luxor and Aswan.

Arranging a felucca trip

Typically, a vessel has an English-speaking Nubian captain and carries six to eight passengers (the largest boats take twelve). Arranging a trip **through a hotel** is easier than doing it yourself, but some places use unreliable captains, or take such large commissions that the disgruntled crew pester passengers for baksheesh. Ahmed at the *Nubian Oasis* (see p.345) acts as a felucca consolidator, quoting £E100 per person for a one-night trip, £E125 for two nights (meals and a minibus on to Kom Ombo, Edfu and Luxor are included in the price).

Or you can **find a captain yourself** after gathering some would-be fellow passengers together. Beware of people claiming to be from this or that family or felucca, who approach you in waterfront restaurants or are recommended by the tourist office. Two respected outfits can be contacted directly: the Jamaica family under Captain "JJ", and Nour and Ashraf of the *Bob Marley* (see p.344 for details of both). The Jamaica family quotes £E75 per person for one night, £E150 for two nights and £E225 for three (plus £E25 for the minibus on to Luxor). *Bob Marley*'s one-, two- and three-night trips cost £E100/£E150/£E250 per person respectively, with the option of chartering the boat for yourself (£E250/400/600 per person for a minimum of two people) rather than sharing it with strangers – an onwards minibus ride is included in the deal.

The cost should also cover three **meals** a day: simple vegetarian food, usually. It's up to passengers to buy their own bottled **water**, snacks and sweets; crews will purchase **beer** for you if asked. While smoking **dope** is tolerated or encouraged on many boats, the Jamaica family has a "no *bango*" rule on its trips. If you're not sure about a crew, **women** will benefit from teaming up with some men for the duration: an all-female group might have problems.

Establish the number of **passengers** before you go and don't be talked into accepting others later on, or food supplies and space will be more limited than you'd expected. It helps if everyone knows what has been negotiated, to ensure solidarity in the event of a dispute with the crew. Before departing, you might be asked for a photocopy of your passport for **registration** with the River Police, but many captains don't bother, knowing that the rule is rarely enforced.

Blankets are provided but seldom enough to keep you warm at night during winter, when a sleeping bag is advisable. Ensure that the boat has a canvas awning to protect you from the sun and double as a tent at night; adequate mattresses, a kerosene stove and lamp, and a padlocked luggage hold. For those wanting more **comfort**, Ahmed Abd el-Nabi (Ⓣ012 281-3932) has a deluxe felucca sleeping up to twelve people in private canvas "cabins", with a fridge to supply cold drinks and fresh food, costing £E500 per person per day.

Unknown captains can be careless of **hygiene**, resulting in passengers getting sick. Buy plenty of bottled water, or the crew may dip into the Nile for drinking or cooking purposes. Bring sterilizing tablets to purify the jerry can of Nile water used for washing up, and carbolic soap for handwashing. Also essential are a hat, sunscreen and bug repellent (especially during summer).

Abydos

As Muslims endeavour to visit Mecca once in their lifetime and Hindus aspire to die at Benares, the Ancient Egyptians devoutly wished to make a pilgrimage to **ABYDOS** (pronounced "Abi-dos"), cult centre of the god Osiris. Those who failed to make it hoped to do so posthumously; relatives brought bodies for burial, or embellished distant tombs with scenes of the journey to Abydos (represented by a boat under sail, travelling upriver). Egyptians averred that the dead "went west", for the entrance to the underworld was believed to lie amid the desert hills beyond Abydos. By bringing other deities into the Osirian fold, Abydos acquired a near monopoly on death cults, which persisted into Ptolemaic times. Its superbly carved **Temple of Seti I** has been a tourist attraction since the 1830s, and many rate its artwork as the finest in Egypt.

Practicalities

Most travellers visit Abydos in conjunction with Dendara (see p.257) on a 6–7 hour **excursion** from Luxor, costing £E275–300 by taxi, shared between passengers, which can be arranged by *Happy Land*, *Bob Marley House* and other budget hotels with a day or two's notice (you might have to wait longer to assemble a group in summertime). This allows you an hour at each site (which most visitors find sufficient) and avoids the effort and time wasted getting there **independently**. This involves catching a second-class stopping train from Luxor (2hr 40min) or Qena (2hr) to the town of **El-Balyana** and hiring a taxi to drive you 10km to Abydos (£E30–40 return with an hour's waiting time). The temple is in the village of **Al-Araba-El-Madfuna** ("Araba the buried"), where an ugly concrete visitors' centre is set to displace the shady café-bazaar that still greeted visitors at the time of writing.

If you wish **to stay** at Abydos – as New Age pilgrims often do – contact Amir Elkarim's *House of the Companions* (Ⓣ010 331-2188, Ⓔameer558@yahoo.com; ❺), which offers spacious rooms and self-contained flats on a half-board basis (£E150 a day per person); or Kevin Wiles (Ⓣ010 069-0683, Ⓔkevinabydos@hotmail.com; ❸), who rents out two nicely furnished rooms in his flat (£E75 per person; lunch £E35; supper £E65) beneath the "House of Life" sign facing the visitors' centre.

The Temple of Seti I

While the temples of Karnak and Deir el-Bahri at Luxor are breathtaking conceptions executed on a colossal scale, it is the exquisite quality of its bas-reliefs that distinguishes Abydos' **Temple of Seti I** (daily 8am–5pm; £E30). The reliefs are among the finest works of the New Kingdom, harking back to Old Kingdom forms in an artistic revival that mirrored Seti's political efforts to

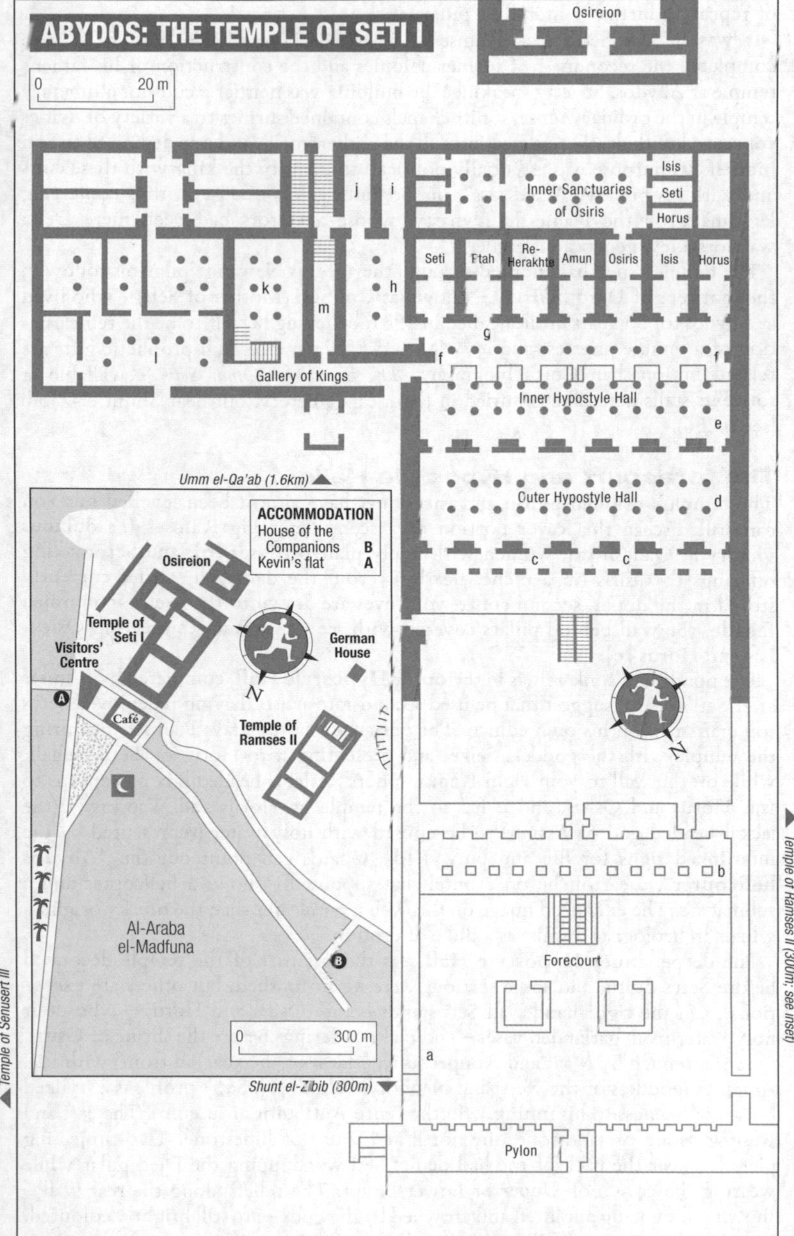
ABYDOS: THE TEMPLE OF SETI I
0 20 m
Osireion
Isis
Seti
Horus
Inner Sanctuaries of Osiris
j
i
Seti
Ptah
Re-Herakhte
Amun
Osiris
Isis
Horus
k
h
m
l
g
f
f
Gallery of Kings
Inner Hypostyle Hall
e
Umm el-Qa'ab (1.6km)
Outer Hypostyle Hall
d
c
c
ACCOMMODATION
House of the Companions B
Kevin's flat A
Osireion
Temple of Seti I
Visitors' Centre
German House
N
Café
Temple of Ramses II
N
Temple of Ramses II (300m; see inset)
b
Al-Araba el-Madfuna
Forecourt
0 300 m
a
Temple of Senusert III
Shunt el-Zibib (300m)
Pylon
Al-Araba el-Madfuna (see inset)

consolidate the XIX Dynasty and recover territories lost under Akhenaten. The official designation of Seti's reign (1318–1304 or 1294–1279 BC) was "the era of repeating births" – literally a renaissance.

It was in fact Seti's son, Ramses II (1304–1237 or 1279–1213 BC), who completed the reconquest of former colonies and the construction of his father's temple at Abydos. Strictly speaking, the building was neither a cult nor a funerary temple in the ordinary sense, for its chapels contained shrines to a variety of deities concerned with death, resurrection and the netherworld, and one dedicated to Seti himself. Its purpose was essentially political: to identify the king with these cults and with his putative "ancestors", the previous rulers of Egypt, thus conferring legitimacy on the Ramessid Dynasty, whose ancestors had been mere Delta warriors a few generations earlier.

The temple's spell has endured through the ages, as New Age pilgrims follow in the footsteps of Dorothy Eady – known as **Um Seti** (Mother of Seti) – who lived at Abydos for 35 years until she died in 1981, believing herself to be the reincarnation of a temple priestess and lover of Seti I. Her trances and prophetic gifts are related in Jonathan Cott's biography, *The Search for Omm Sety* – available at souvenir stalls here. She is buried in the local cemetery, out near Shunt el-Zibib (see p.256).

The forecourt and Hypostyle Halls

The temple's original **pylon** and **forecourt** have almost been levelled but you can still discern the lower portion of a scene depicting Ramses II's dubious victory at Qadesh **[a]**, women with finely plaited tresses **[b]**, and Seti making offerings to Osiris (in a niche, nearby). From the damaged statues currently stored in the upper, second court, your eyes are drawn to the square-columned **facade**, the wall behind pillars covered with scenes of Ramses greeting Osiris, Isis and Horus **[c]**.

The ponderous sunk-reliefs in the **outer Hypostyle Hall**, completed by Ramses after Seti's death, suggest that he used second-rate artists, having redeployed Seti's top craftsmen on his own edifice. The entrance wall portrays Ramses measuring the temple with the goddess Selket and presenting it to Horus on Seti's behalf, while on the wall to your right Ramses offers a falcon-headed box of papyrus to Isis, Horus and Osiris, and is led to the temple by Horus and Wepwawet (the jackal-headed god of Assyut) to be doused with holy water (represented by the interlinked signs for life and purity) **[d]**. Guards can point out the **"Abydos helicopter"**, a cartouche on a lintel that supposedly shows a helicopter and a submarine. The enhanced image on the Web is far clearer than the murky original, which archeologists dismiss as a fluke of erosion.

The deeper **inner Hypostyle Hall** was the last part of the temple decorated before Seti's death, and some sections were never finished, but others are exceptional. On the right-hand wall Seti stands before Osiris and Horus – who pour holy water from garlanded vases – and makes offerings before the shrine of Osiris, who is attended by Maat and Ronpet (the goddess of the year) in front, with Isis, Amentet (goddess of the west) and Nephthys behind **[e]**. Seti's profile is a stylized but close likeness to his mummy (in the Cairo Antiquities Museum). The east and west walls are of sandstone, the north and south of limestone. Two projecting piers **[f]** near the back of the hall depict Seti worshipping the Djed pillar while wearing the crown of Upper or Lower Egypt. The reliefs along the rear wall – showing him being anointed and crowned by the gods – are still brightly coloured. Best of all is a scene of Seti kneeling before Osiris and Horus, with the sacred persea tree in the background, which appears above head height on the wall between the sanctuaries of Ptah and Re-Herakhte **[g]**.

The sanctuaries

The finest **bas-reliefs** at Abydos are inside the sanctuaries dedicated to Seti and six deities. Though retaining much of their original colouring (showing how most temple reliefs once looked), their graceful lines and subtle moulding are best appreciated on the unpainted reliefs. Seti's classical revival eschewed both Amarna expressionism and the bombastic XVIII Dynasty imperial style. The seven sanctuaries are roofed with false vaults carved from rectangular slabs, and culminate in false doors (except for Osiris's chamber, which leads into his inner sanctuaries). To Ancient Egyptians, these chambers constituted the abode of the gods, whom the king (or his priests) propitiated with daily rituals, shown on the walls.

An exception to this rule is the **Sanctuary of Seti**, which emphasizes his recognition by the gods, who lead him into the temple and ceremonially unite the Two Lands along the northern wall. Below the barque near the back of the left-hand wall, Seti receives a list of offerings from Thoth and the High Priest Iunmutef, wearing the leopardskin and braided sidelock of his office. Finally, Seti leaves the temple, his palanquin borne by the souls of jackal-headed deities from the Upper Egyptian town of Nekhen and hawk-headed gods from the Delta capital of Pi-Ramses.

The fine unpainted reliefs of Seti and seated deities in Re-Herakhte's chamber make interesting comparison with similar painted scenes in the sanctuaries of Ptah, Amun, Osiris and Isis. On the side wall just outside the Sanctuary of Horus, the pharaoh presents Maat to Osiris, Isis and Horus, a XIX Dynasty motif symbolizing righteous order and the restoration of royal legitimacy.

The **inner sanctuaries of Osiris** boast three side chapels whose colours were still fresh and shiny in the 1980s, but are now blackened by mould – a rapid rate of deterioration affecting many of the temples and tombs in the Nile Valley.

The cult of Osiris

Originally the corn-god of Busiris in the Delta, **Osiris** attained national significance early in the Old Kingdom, when he was co-opted into the Heliopolitan Ennead. According to legend, Re (or Geb) divided the world between Osiris and his brother Seth, who resented being given all the deserts and murdered Osiris to usurp his domain. Although the god's body was recovered by **Isis**, the sister-wife of Osiris, Seth recaptured and dismembered it, burying the pieces at different locations and feeding the penis to a crocodile. Aided by her sister Nephthys, Isis collected the bits and bandaged them together to create the first mummy, which they briefly resurrected with the help of Thoth and Anubis. By transforming herself into a hawk, Isis managed to conceive a child with Osiris before he returned to the netherworld to rule as lord and judge of the dead. Secretly raised to manhood in the Delta, their child **Horus** later avenged his father and cast Seth back into the wilderness (see p.334).

▲ Osiris

As the "place of the head" of Osiris (the meaning of its ancient name, Abdjw), Abydos was the setting for two annual **festivals**. The "Great Going Forth" celebrated the search for and discovery of his remains, while the Osiris Festival re-enacted his myth in a series of Mystery Plays. In one scene, the god's barque was "attacked" by minions of Seth and "protected" by **Wepwawet**, the jackal-headed god of Assyut. The total identification of Abydos with **death cults** was completed by its association with **Anubis**, the jackal-headed god of embalming, always present in funerary scenes.

The southern wing

From the inner Hypostyle Hall you can enter the southern wing of Seti's temple. The portal nearest his sanctuary leads into the columned **Hall of Sokar and Nefertum**, two deities of the north representing the life-giving forces of the earth and the cycle of death and rebirth. Reliefs on the right-hand wall depict Seti receiving a hawk-headed Sokar **[h]**; Nefertum is shown on the opposite wall in both his human and leonine forms (crowned with a lotus blossom). In the **Chapel of Sokar [i]**, Osiris appears in his bier and returns to life grasping his penis (near the back of the right-hand wall), while Isis hovers over him in the form of a hawk on the opposite wall. The **Chapel of Nefertum** is next door **[j]**.

The other portal leads through into the **Gallery of Kings**, so called after the list of Seti's predecessors carved on the right-hand wall – the earliest (Zoser) on the far left of the top row, with Seti at the far end of the bottom register. For political reasons, the Hyksos pharaohs, Hatshepsut, Akhenaten and his heirs have all been omitted, yet the list has proved immensely useful to archeologists, naming 34 kings (chiefly from the VI, VII, XII, XVIII and XIX dynasties) in roughly chronological order.

Running off from the gallery are the **Sanctuary of the Boats [k]**, where the deities' barques were kept on platforms; the **Hall of Sacrifices [l]** (closed); and a corridor **[m]** with vivid sunk-reliefs of Seti and Ramses harnessing a bull to present to Wepwawet, and hauling birds in a net. This will bring you out through a rear door to the Osireion, behind the temple.

The Osireion and other remains

The **site of Abydos** covers a huge area, with ruins and mounds scattered across the edge of the desert. Egyptologists from the Penn Museum (Ⓦ www.penn.museum) and the German Archeological Institute (Ⓦ www.dainst.org) are excavating several sites, officially off-limits. You can, however, visit two structures near Seti's temple, and Kevin Wiles or Amir Elkarim might be able to arrange trips to others if you're staying at Abydos (see p.252).

When Flinders Petrie excavated here in the 1900s, he uncovered numerous mastabas which he belived to be royal tombs, but which later Egyptologists held to be cenotaphs or Osirian burial places – dummy tombs, built to promote a closer association between the pharaoh's *ka* and Osiris, while his mummy reposed elsewhere. Seti's Cenotaph, known as the **Osireion**, is the only one now visible, albeit half-buried and rendered partly inaccessible by stagnant water. Built of massive blocks, it once enclosed a room containing a mound surrounded by a moat (symbolizing the first land arising from the waters of Chaos at the dawn of Creation), where a pseudo-sarcophagus awaited resurrection. Nearby is a long underground passage that once led to the cenotaph.

Some 300m northwest is a ruined **Temple of Ramses II**, Seti's father, where scenes of the Battle of Qadesh (see p.373) are rendered in exceptional detail on the enclosure walls and pillared courtyard. Ground-penetrating radar has detected a massive structure underneath the sand between Ramses' and Seti's temples, that some suspect is another Osireion. Its existence has yet to be announced.

Elsewhere, the Germans have been excavating the Early Dynastic royal cemetery at **Um el-Qa'ab** and funerary enclosures at **Shunt el-Zebib**. The complex of Khasekhemwy, last king of the II Dynasty, who died about 2686 BC, was surrounded by walls 122m long and 65m wide. It's thought that the pyramids at Saqqara evolved from the enclosure of sunken brick-lined tombs at Abydos, where hieroglyphic writing predating Saqqara's has been found, suggesting the existence of a Predynastic king Hor or Horus, who conquered

The Gnostic Gospels

Driving between Abydos and Dendara you'll pass Nag Hammadi, a town that has given its name to the **Nag Hammadi Codices** found nearby in 1945. Commonly called the **Gnostic Gospels**, they are fourth-century Coptic translations of second-century Greek originals, although the Gospel of Thomas might date from 50–100 AD, and therefore be as early as – or even older than – the gospels of Matthew, Mark, Luke and John. Gnostics (from *gnosis*, Greek for "knowledge") were early mystics who believed that God could only be known through self-understanding and that the world was illusory. Regarding self and the divine as one, they saw Jesus as a spiritual guide rather than the crucified son of God, pointing to his words in the Gospel of Thomas: *"If you bring forth what is within you, what you bring forth will save you. If you do not bring forth what is within you, what is within you will destroy you."* But the official church thought otherwise and condemned Gnosticism as a heresy; hence the burial of these codices (some of which can be seen today in Cairo's Coptic Museum).

the Delta and united the Two Lands a century before Narmer. Six **Solar Boats** found within Khasekhemwy's enclosure in 1991 may date from the reign of the I Dynasty ruler Aha. All this raises the possibility that the Early Dynastic burials attributed to Saqqara may have occurred at Abydos instead, and that an intact royal tomb may exist. Since 2004 the Penn Museum has found evidence that the XII Dynasty **Osirieon of Senusret III** may have really been a royal tomb, looted long ago. 2009 saw the discovery of a 30m-long shaft.

Dendara

The **Temple of Hathor** at **Dendara** lacks the sublime quality of Seti's edifice at Abydos, but its fabulous astronomical ceiling and nearly intact rooftop sanctuaries offer a unique insight into the solar rituals at other cult sites where they have not survived. Dendara also shows how Egypt's Greek and Roman rulers identified themselves with the pharaohs and deities of Ancient Egypt by copying their temples, rituals and iconography down to the last hieroglyph – though they did tinker with a few details of reliefs and murals. Goddesses and queens became bustier, and the feet of royalty were shown with all their toes (instead of only the big toe, as the Ancient Egyptians did).

The temple is also pleasing for the completeness of its mud-brick enclosure walls and its rural setting, with rooftop views of lush countryside and the arid hills of the Western Desert. Approaching it by road from Qena, across the Nile, you'll pass fields of onions and clover, donkey carts and camels – an enjoyable ride by *calèche* if you've got time to spare or decide to stay in Qena (see p.262). Most tourists visit Dendara together with the temple at Abydos (see p.252). **Taxi excursions** from Luxor (£E275–300 shared among passengers; tickets not included) stop here for an hour on the way back from Abydos. Alternatively, the *Lotus Boat* and *Tiba Star* run **day cruises** from Luxor to Dendara on Tuesdays, Fridays and Sundays: tickets are sold through the *Nefertiti* (£E320) and *Iberotel* (£E425) hotels and local travel agencies (the cost per person includes transfers, entrance fee, lunch and tea) up to three days in advance. Coming **by public transport** is only worth the effort if you want to stay longer at Dendara – trying to combine this with a visit to Abydos means starting at the crack of dawn: be sure to check that your train stops in Qena.

The Temple of Hathor

Although there have been shrines to Hathor, the goddess of joy, at Dendara since Predynastic times, the existing **Temple of Hathor** (daily: summer 7am–6pm; winter 7am–5pm; £E35) is a Greco-Roman creation, built between 125 BC and 60 AD. Since the object of the exercise was to confer legitimacy on Egypt's foreign rulers, it emulates the pharaonic pattern of Hypostyle Halls and vestibules preceding a darkened sanctuary, with vast mud-brick enclosure walls surrounding the complex.

The temple **facade** is shaped like a pylon, with six Hathor-headed columns rising from a screen, their head-dresses still blue, red and white. Here and inside, Hathor appears in human form rather than her bovine aspect (see p.260). Because this section was built during the reign of Tiberius, its reliefs depict Roman emperors making offerings to the gods, namely Tiberius and Claudius before Horus, Hathor and their son Ihy **[a]**, and Tiberius as a sphinx before Hathor and Horus **[b]** (hard to see). Nineteenth-century engravings show the temple buried in sand almost to the lintel of its portal, which explains why its upper sections bore the brunt of Coptic iconoclasm.

The Hypostyle Hall

Entering the **Hypostyle Hall** with its eighteen Hathor-headed columns, you'll be transfixed by its **astronomical ceiling**, now largely restored to its vibrant original colours. This is not a sky chart in the modern sense, but a symbolic representation of the heavenly bodies, the hours of the day and night, and the realms of the sun and moon.

Above the central aisle, a row of flying vultures and winged discs separates the left-hand bays representing the southern heavens from those to the right, dedicated to the northern sky. Here, the first row **[c]** begins with the Eye of Re in its barque, above which appear the fourteen days of the waning moon. Beyond the full moon in the centre come the fourteen stages of the waxing moon (each with its own deity), culminating in the full disc worshipped by Thoth, and lastly the moon as Osiris, protected by Isis and Nephthys. Souls in the form of jackals and birds adorn Re's barque as it journeys across the sun's register **[d]**.

Following these are two bands **[e]** showing the planets, the stars of the twelve hours of the night, and the signs of the zodiac (adopted from Babylonia). The end rows **[f]** are dominated by Nut, who gives birth to the sun at dawn and swallows it at dusk. On one side, the rising sun Khepri (the scarab beetle) is born **[g]**; on the other, the sun shines down on Hathor **[h]**.

The Hall of Appearances

The Ptolemaic section of the temple begins with the six-columned **Hall of Appearances**, where Hathor consorted with fellow deities before her voyage to Edfu (see overleaf). With a torch, you can examine reliefs on the entrance wall depicting offerings **[i]**, and the foundation of the temple and its presentation to the gods **[j]**. Notice the "blank" cartouches, which attest to the high turnover of rulers in late Ptolemaic times, when stonemasons were loath to inscribe the names of Ptolemies who might not last for long. Nonetheless, rituals continued at Dendara, where the priests kept holy objects of precious metal in the Treasury **[k]** and drew water for purification ceremonies from a well reached by the so-called Nile Room **[l]**.

Corresponding chambers across the hall include the laboratory **[m]**, where perfumes and unguents were mixed and stored (notice the reliefs showing recipes, and bearers bringing exotic materials from afar); and another room for storing valuables **[n]**. A liturgical calendar listing festivals celebrated at the temple appears on the inner side of its doorway.

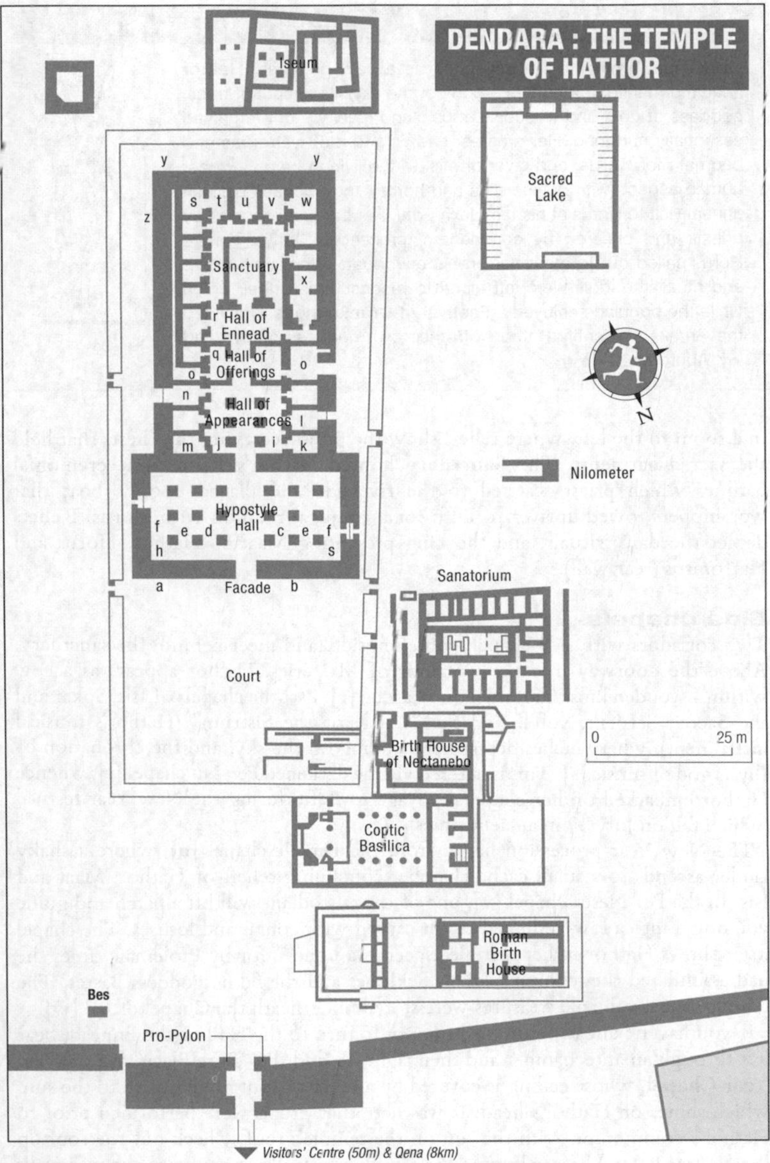

The Hall of Offerings and the Hall of Ennead

Beyond lies the **Hall of Offerings**, the entrance to the temple proper, with twin **stairways** to the roof (see below) up which sacrificial animals were led **[o]**. A list of offerings appears on the rear wall **[p]**, across the way from a relief showing the king offering Hathor her favourite tipple **[q]**.

Next comes the **Hall of the Ennead**, where statues of the gods and kings involved in ceremonies dedicated to Hathor once stood. Her wardrobe was stored

The cult of Hathor

Worshipped from the earliest times as a cow goddess, **Hathor** acquired manifold attributes – body of the sky, living soul of trees, goddess of gold and turquoise, music and revelry – but remained essentially nurturing. Her greatest role was that of wet nurse and bedmate for **Horus**, and giver of milk to the living pharaoh. In her human aspect (with bovine ears and horns), the goddess paid an annual visit to Horus at his temple in Edfu. Her barque, escorted by priests and cheered by commoners, proceeded upriver, where Horus sailed out to meet her on his own boat. After much pomp and ritual, the idols were left alone to reconsummate their union while the populace enjoyed a **Festival of Drunkenness**, which led the Greeks to identify Hathor with their own goddess of love and joy, Aphrodite.

▲ Hathor

in a room to the left, where reliefs show the priests carrying the chests that held the sacred garments. The **Sanctuary** housed Hathor's statue and ceremonial barque, which priests carried to the riverside and placed upon a boat that worshippers towed upriver to Edfu for a conjugal reunion with Horus. Reliefs depict the daily rituals, and the king presenting Maat to Hathor, Horus and Harsomtus (rear wall).

Side chapels

Two corridors with side chapels run alongside (and meet behind) the sanctuary. Above the doorway into the Corridor of Mysteries, Hathor appears as a cow within a wooden kiosk mounted on a barque **[r]**. Past the chapels of Isis, Sokar and the Sacred Serpent, you'll find the "Castle of the Sistrum" (Hathor's musical instrument), where niches depict her standing on the sky, and the coronation of Ihy as god of music **[s]**. This is entered via the darkened Per-Nu chapel **[t]**, whence Hathor embarked on her conjugal voyage to Edfu during the New Year festival (which fell on July 19 in ancient times).

The New Year procession began from the Per-Ur chapel **[u]**, where a shaky ladder ascends to a small cache chamber containing reliefs of Hathor, Maat and Isis. In the Per-Neser chapel **[v]**, one of the custodians will lift a hatch and guide you down into a low-ceilinged **crypt** carved with cobras and lotuses. The chapel itself shows Hathor in her terrible aspect as a lioness, for by Ptolemaic times she had assimilated the leonine goddess Sekhmet and the feline goddess Bastet. The temple's most valuable treasures were stored underneath the Chapel of Re **[w]**.

If you haven't already stumbled upon it, return to the Hall of the Ennead, bear left through an antechamber and then right, to find the "Pure Place" **[x]** or **New Year Chapel**, whose ceiling is covered by a relief of Nut giving birth to the sun, which shines on Hathor's head. It was here that rituals were performed prior to Hathor's communion with the sun on the temple's roof. Check out the rooftop shrines (see below) before leaving the temple and walking round to the rear wall, where two defaced sunk-reliefs **[y]** of Cleopatra and her son Caesarion feature in a procession of deities. The chubby face is so unlike the beautiful queen of legend that most people prefer to regard this as a stylized image rather than a lifelike **portrait of Cleopatra**. The lion-headed **waterspouts** below the cornice were a Roman innovation.

One last bit of iconography worth noting is the array of royal **crowns** – 22 different kinds appear on the third register of the east wall **[z]**.

Rooftop sanctuaries

From either side of the Hall of Offerings, a stairway ascends to the roof of the temple; the scenes on the walls depict the New Year procession, when Hathor's statue was carried up to an open kiosk on the rooftop to await the dawn; touched by the rays of the sun, Hathor's *ba* (soul) was revitalized for the coming year. Besides the sun kiosk there are two suites of rooms dedicated to the death and resurrection of Osiris, behind the facade of the Hypostyle Hall. Although such **rooftop sanctuaries** were a feature of most temples, those at Dendara are uniquely intact.

The one on the left (as you face south) is notable for the reliefs in its inner chamber, which show Osiris being mourned by Isis and Nephthys, passing through the gates of the netherworld, and finally bringing himself to erection to impregnate Isis, who appears as a hovering kite. The other suite contains a plaster cast of the famous **Dendara Zodiac** ceiling filched by Lelorrain in 1820 and now in the Louvre. Upheld by four goddesses, the circular carving features a zodiac which only differs from our own by the substitution of a scarab for the scorpion and the inclusion of the hippo goddess Tweri. The zodiac was introduced to Egypt (and other lands) by the Romans, who copied it from Babylonia. Mind your head on the low doorway.

Best of all is the magnificent **view** of the temple and the countryside from the rooftop. Also notice the **graffiti** left by French troops in 1799, including the names of their commander Desaix and the artist Denon, who sketched frenziedly at Dendara as the Mamlukes drew nearer, melting down bullets for lead when he ran out of pencils.

Outlying buildings

Surrounding the temple are various other structures, now largely ruined. Ptolemaic temples were distinguished by the addition of *mamissi* or Birth Houses, which associated the pharaoh with Horus, the deified king. When the Romans surrounded the temple with an enclosure wall, it split in two the **Birth**

▲ Hathor suckling Horus on the Roman Birth House at Dendara

House of Nectanebo (XXX Dynasty), compelling them to build a replacement. The **Roman Birth House** has some fine carvings of Hathor suckling Horus on its south wall, and tiny figures of Bes and Tweri on the column capitals and architraves. Between the two *mamissi* lies a ruined, fifth-century **Coptic Basilica**, built with masonry from the adjacent structures; notice the incised Coptic crosses.

As a compassionate goddess, Hathor had a reputation for healing and her temple attracted pilgrimages from the sick. In the **Sanatorium** here patients were prescribed cures during dreams, induced by narcotics. Water for ritual ablutions was drawn from a **Sacred Lake** now drained of liquid and full of palm trees and birds.

Nearby stands a ruined **Iseum** used for the worship of Isis and Osiris, built by Cleopatra's mortal enemy, Octavian, after he became Emperor Augustus.

On your way out of the temple, don't miss the scowling **Bes** – god of dancing girls and licentiousness – carved on a chunk of masonry displayed near the Pro-Pylon.

Qena

QENA is a city of 200,000 people, whose tidy streets and civic amenities are the legacy of former governor Adel Labib (now in charge of Alexandria), who wooed back residents embittered by decades of neglect, to prevent any resurgence of sympathy for the militant Islamists who staged Egypt's first terrorist attack on tourists back in 1992. Today, Qena is totally safe to visit and the authorities are even allowing tourists to stay here once again.

Outside its train station you can hire a **taxi** (£E30–40) or a **calèche** (£E25–30) to drive you to Dendara and back (if you want to spent more than an hour at the temple, say so at the outset and expect to pay more). The *New Palace* **hotel** (Ⓣ096/532-2509; ❸) behind the Mobil garage facing the station has air-conditioned rooms with fridges and wrap-around balconies. By following Sharia el-Gumhorriya away from the station you'll find a roundabout, where the *El-Prince* **restaurant** serves meals of salad, rice, chicken or *kofta*, and beer.

Should you be around at the time, Qena's oldest mosque (on the main drag beyond *El-Prince*) hosts the **Moulid of Abdel Rahim el-Qenawi**, featuring *zikrs* and dancing horses. The festival kicks off on Sha'ban 14 (the eighth month in the Islamic lunar calender) and finishes the day before the start of Abu el-Haggag's moulid in Luxor (see p.279).

Buses to Cairo, Port Safaga, Hurghada and Suez leave from the bus terminal near the train station. Middle Egypt and Luxor are better reached by **train**; the journey to (or from) Luxor takes around forty minutes.

Luxor

LUXOR has been a tourist mecca ever since Nile steamers began calling in the nineteenth century to view the remains of **Thebes**, ancient Egypt's New Kingdom capital, and its associated sites – the concentration of relics in this area is overwhelming. The town itself boasts **Luxor Temple**, a graceful ornament to its waterfront and "downtown", while a mile or so north is **Karnak Temple**, a stupendous complex built over 1300 years. Across the river are the amazing tombs and mortuary temples of the **Theban Necropolis**, and as if this wasn't enough, Luxor also serves as a base for trips to Esna, Edfu, Dendara and Abydos temples, up and down the Nile Valley.

In a town where **tourism** accounts for 85 percent of the economy, it's hardly surprising that you can't move without being importuned to step inside a shop or rent a *calèche*, but once you get to know a few characters and begin to understand the score Luxor becomes a funky soap opera with a cast of thousands. See the advice on hotel touts (p.38), hustlers (p.52) and gigolos (p.54) for an idea of how things are.

Most foreigners come between October and February, when the **climate** is cooler than you might imagine, with chilly nights and early mornings. Around the end of March the temperature shoots up 10°C, making April the nicest time of the year to visit, though the weather remains agreeable until May, after which the daytime heat is brutal till late October, when the temperatures start mellowing out to April levels.

Some history

The name Luxor derives from the Arabic El-Uqsur – meaning "the palaces" or "the castles" – a name which may have referred to a Roman *castrum* or the town's appearance in medieval times, when it squatted amid the ruins of **Thebes**. This, in turn, was the Greek name for the city known to the ancient Egyptians as Weset, originally an obscure provincial town during the Old Kingdom, that gained ascendancy in Upper Egypt under Mentuhotep II (c.2100 BC) and later became a power base for local princes who eventually liberated Egypt from the Hyksos invaders and founded the XVIII Dynasty (c.1567 BC).

As the capital of the **New Kingdom**, whose empire stretched from Nubia to Palestine, Thebes enjoyed an ascendancy paralleled by that of **Amun**, whose cult temple at Karnak became the greatest in Egypt. At its zenith under the XVIII and XIX dynasties, Thebes may have had a population of around a million; Homer's *Iliad* describes it as a "city with a hundred gates". Excluding the brief **Amarna Period** (c.1379–1362 BC), when the "heretic" Akhenaten moved the capital northwards and forbade the worship of Amun, the dynasty's – and city's – supremacy lasted some five hundred years. Even after the end of the Ramessid line, when the capital returned to Memphis and thence moved to the Delta, Thebes remained the foremost city of Upper Egypt, enjoying a final fling as a royal seat under the **Nubian** rulers of the XXV Dynasty (c.747–645 BC).

Though Thebes persisted through **Ptolemaic** into **Roman** times, it retained but a shadow of its former glory, and might have been abandoned like Memphis were it not for Christian settlements. During Muslim times its only claim to fame was the tomb of Abu el-Haggag, a twelfth-century sheikh. However, Napoleon's expedition to Egypt awakened foreign interest in its **antiquities**, which were gradually cleared during the nineteenth century and have drawn visitors ever since.

Not every visitor has been impressed: during the filming of *Death on the Nile*, Hollywood icon Bette Davis remarked that "In my day we'd have built all this at the studio – and better." In a sense she had a point: the temple was half hidden by ramshackle bazaars, and downtown was a mess. Now, people wonder if the **transformation** wrought by Governor Samir Farag has enhanced or ruined Luxor. Streets have been widened and houses demolished to create an all-round view of Luxor Temple and reveal more of the Avenue of Sphinxes that once ran out to Karnak; a seven-star hotel-mall by the Corniche and a tourist railway are said to be on the cards. Bizarrely, this Disney-fication of Luxor has been funded by UNESCO, whose remit is to preserve the integrity of historic sites.

Arrival

Arriving in Luxor can be stressful, especially at the **train station**, where you're mobbed by hotel touts thrusting cards under your nose and bad-mouthing rival

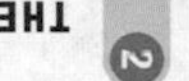

LUXOR

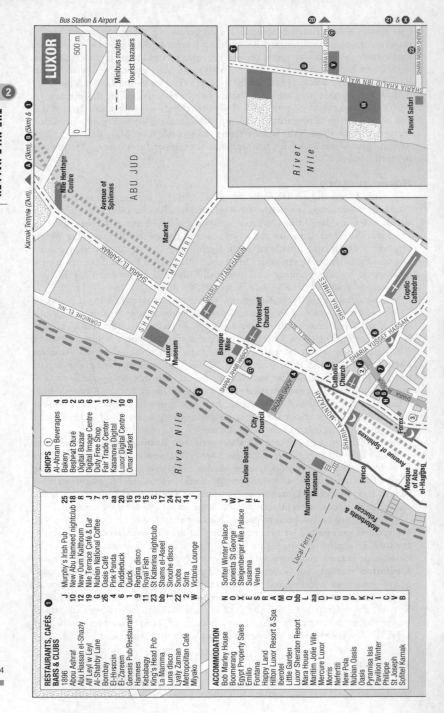

Karnak Temple (2km), A (3km), B (5km) & 1

Bus Station & Airport

0 500 m

Minibus routes

Tourist bazaars

RESTAURANTS, CAFÉS, BARS & CLUBS 1

1896	J	Murphy's Irish Pub	25
Abou Ashraf	10	New Abu Hameed nightclub	18
Abu Hassan el-Shazly	12	New Oum Kalthoum	8
Alf Leyl w Leyl	19	Nile Terrace Café & Bar	J
Al-Shahby Lane	G	Nubian National Coffee	7
Bombay	26	Oasis Café	3
El-Hussein	4	Pink Panda	aa
El-Zareem	6	Puddleduck	20
Genesis Pub/Restaurant	1	Quick	16
Hamees	9	Regina disco	13
Kebabagy	11	Royal Fish	15
King's Head Pub	23	St Katerina nightclub	5
La Mamma	bb	Shams el-Aseel	17
Luna disco	T	Sinouhe disco	24
Lyaly Zaman	22	Snobs	21
Metropolitan Café	2	Sofra	14
Miyako	W	Victoria Lounge	J

SHOPS (1)

Al-Ahram Beverages	4
Bakery	8
Besheat Store	2
Digital Bazaar	5
Digital Image Centre	6
Duty Free Shop	1
Fair Trade Center	3
Kasanova Digital	7
Luxor Digital Centre	10
Omar Market	9

ACCOMMODATION

Bob Marley House	N	Sofitel Winter Palace	J
Boomerang	O	Sonesta St George	W
Egypt Property Sales	X	Steigenberger Nile Palace	Y
Emilio	E	Susanna	H
Fontana	S	Venus	F
Happy Land	R		
Hilton Luxor Resort & Spa	A		
Iberotel	M		
Little Garden	Q		
Luxor Sheraton Resort	bb		
Mara House	L		
Maritim Jolie Ville	aa		
Mercure Luxor	D		
Morris	T		
Nefertiti	G		
New Pola	U		
Nubian Oasis	P		
Oasis	K		
Pyramisa Isis	Z		
Pavilion Winter	I		
Philippe	C		
St Joseph	V		
Sofitel Karnak	B		

River Nile
Nile Heritage Centre
Avenue of Sphinxes
ABU JUD
Corniche el-Nil
Sharia el-Karnak
Sharia Al-Mathari
Market
Luxor Museum
Sharia Tutankhamun
Banque Misr
Sharia Lahaib Habachi
Protestant Church
Cruise Boats
City Council
Bazaar Savoy
Local Ferry
Mummification Museum
Sharia el-Sehi
Sharia Ahmes
Sharia Al-Montazah
Catholic Church
Motorboats & Feluccas
Fence
Sharia Yussef Hassan
Avenue of Sphinxes
Sharia Al-Souk
Forex
Mosque of Abu el-Haggag
Coptic Cathedral
Sharia Khalid Ibn Walid
Sharia St. Joseph
Sharia Radwa Sherifa
Planet Safari
20
21 & X

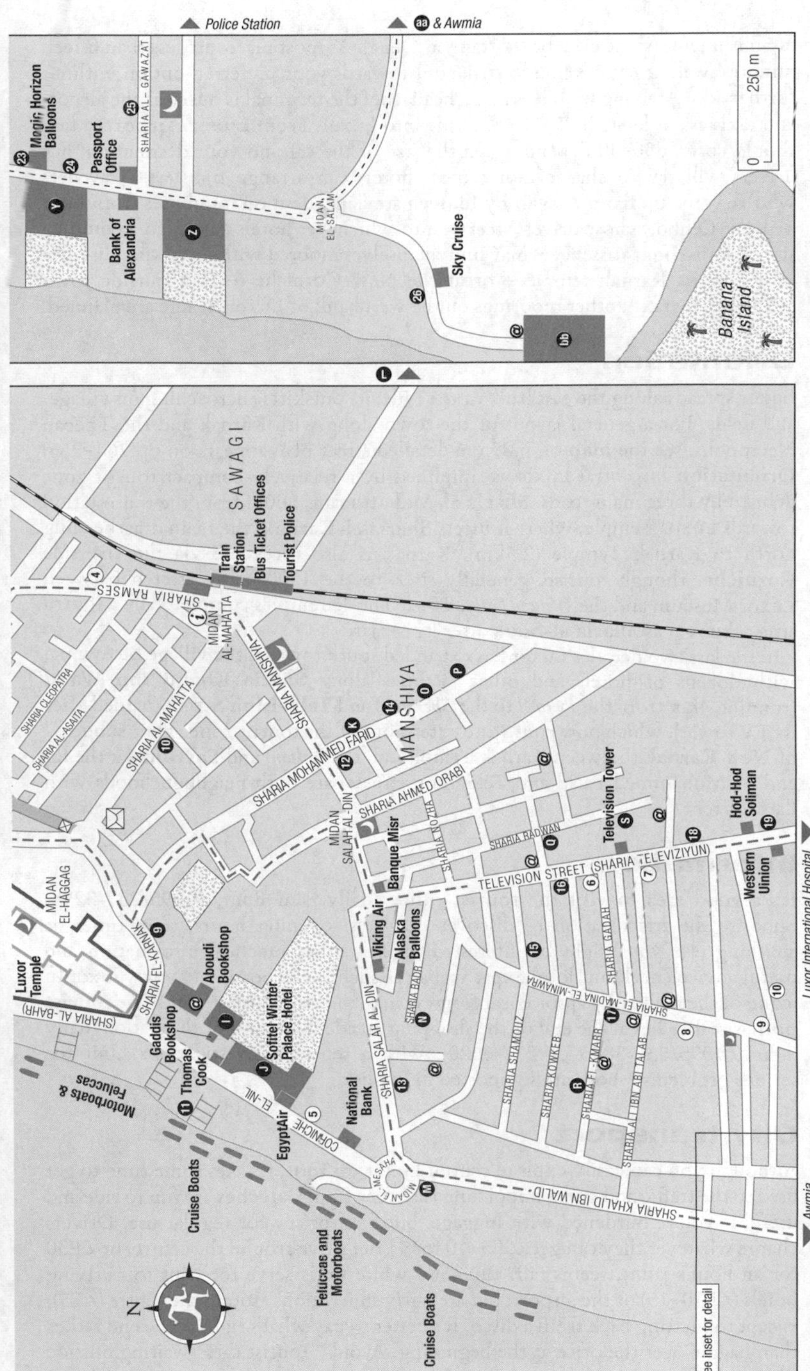
Police Station
aa & Awmia
Magic Horizon Balloons
Passport Office
Bank of Alexandria
SHARIA AL-GAWAZAT
MIDAN EL-SALAM
Sky Cruise
Banana Island
0 250 m
SAWAGI
Train Station
Bus Ticket Offices
Tourist Police
SHARIA RAMSES
MIDAN AL-MAHATTA
SHARIA CLEOPATRA
SHARIA AL-ASAITA
SHARIA AL-MAHATTA
SHARIA MANSHIYA
MANSHIYA
SHARIA MOHAMMED FARID
MIDAN SALAH AL-DIN
SHARIA AHMED ORABI
SHARIA NOZHA
SHARIA RADWAN
Television Tower
Banque Misr
TELEVISION STREET (SHARIA TELEVIZIYUN)
Hod-Hod Soliman
Western Union
Luxor International Hospital
MIDAN EL-HAGGAG
Luxor Temple
Aboudi Bookshop
SHARIA EL-KARNAK
(SHARIA AL-BAHR)
Gaddis Bookshop
Thomas Cook
Sofitel Winter Palace Hotel
Viking Air
Alaska Balloons
SHARIA BADR
SHARIA SALAH AL-DIN
SHARIA SHAMOUZ
SHARIA KOWKEB
SHARIA EL-KMARR
SHARIA GADAH
SHARIA EL-MADINA EL-MINAWRA
SHARIA ALI IBN ABI TALAB
Motorboats & Feluccas
EgyptAir
CORNICHE EL-NIL
National Bank
MIDAN EL-MESAHA
SHARIA KHALID IBN WALID
Awmia
Cruise Boats
Feluccas and Motorboats
Cruise Boats
See inset for detail
N

establishments (some even board trains at Qena). As most places are less than fifteen minutes' walk away, it's fine to strike out towards your preferred option without further ado. Arriving **by bus** is also a headache: the terminal is out near the airport and taxis ask at least £E25–30 for a ride into Luxor. From **Luxor Airport**, a taxi should cost £E30–40 depending on the size of the car and your destination, but drivers will try to charge more; most hotels can arrange transfers. Travellers who've come up **from Aswan by felucca** are dependent on minibuses from Edfu or Kom Ombo, whose drivers steer you to whichever hotels pay them a commission. **Cruise boat** passengers may find themselves moored within walking distance of Luxor or Karnak temple – or at the New Corniche 6–7km outside town (£E30–40 by taxi); other moorings on the west bank of Luxor Bridge are planned.

Orientation

Luxor spreads along the east bank of the Nile, its outskirts encroaching on villages and fields. For a general layout of the town along with Karnak and the Theban Necropolis, see the **map** on p.295; a detailed street plan appears on pp.264–265. **Orientation** in central Luxor is simplified by a relatively compact tourist zone defined by three main roads. **Sharia al-Mahatta** runs 500m from the train station towards Luxor Temple, where it meets **Sharia el-Karnak**, the main drag heading north to Karnak Temple (2.5km). Karnak is also accessible via the riverside **Corniche**, though tourists generally stick to the 1500-metre stretch between Luxor Museum and the *Winter Palace Hotel*. The "circuit" is completed by a fourth street, known as **Sharia al-Souk** after its bazaar.

In the last two decades Luxor has expanded south towards the village of Awmia, with dozens of hotels and other facilities along **Sharia Khalid Ibn Walid** (running 4km from the *Iberotel* to the *Sheraton*) and **Television Street** (named after its TV tower), which now constitute extensions of the tourist zone. The "suburbs" of **New Karnak** (between Karnak Temple and the *Hilton*) and **Fayrouz** (at the far end of Mohammed Farid and Television streets) are both neighbourhoods with flats for rent.

Information

It's a good idea to visit the **tourist office** (daily 8am–8pm; ⓣ095/237-3294) opposite the train station to discover the latest opening hours, train times or anything else you might be interested in. For other practical information and useful advice check out local expat **websites** such as the gossipy ⓦwww.luxor4u.com, or the mainly Egyptological ⓦwww.luxor-news.blogspot.com. The **tourist police**'s office lies at the end of the shopping arcade due south of the station (daily 24hr; ⓣ095/237-3845 or 237-6620), with a separate Investigations Unit for serious problems – both are signposted in English.

City transport

Although you can easily explore central Luxor **on foot**, it takes some time to get used to the traffic and being importuned at every step. **Calèches** are fun to ride and useful if you're burdened with luggage, but a bit pricey for regular use. Drivers charge whatever they can get: £E5–10 for a brief drive around the centre, or £E30 for an hour's jaunt, seems fair. Blue-and-white **taxis** serve for trips to outlying hotels (£E10–15) or the airport, but are fairly superfluous around the centre (£E5), except for getting back from a disco. It's better to pay what's right at the end rather than haggle over the price at the beginning. Avoid "Tourist cars" waiting outside discos; thefts by drivers have occurred.

Surprisingly few visitors take advantage of the fleet of blue-and-white **minibuses** that shuttle between outlying points, constantly passing through the centre along Sharia el-Karnak. Northbound minibuses either turn off towards the taxi depot (*mogaf*) at the end of Sharia al-Mathari, or run straight on to Karnak and the *Nile Hilton*. Heading in the opposite direction, they terminate at the public hospital (*mustashfa*) far down Television Street, or at Awmia, out near the *Sheraton*. The *mustashfa*-bound ones detour inland via the train station, while Awmia buses stick to Sharia Khalid Ibn Walid. The tactic is to wave down any minibus heading in the right direction, holler "*Hilton*" (or whatever), and hop in if they're going there. There's a flat fare of 50pt on all routes.

While cycling in Luxor isn't advisable, many tourists rent **bicycles** to use on the west bank, for getting around the Theban Necropolis (see p.296). They can be carried on local ferries. Shops on Sharia al-Mahatta and Television Street, and many low-budget hotels, rent them for £E10 a day. Most bikes are one-speed only and may be defective in some respect, so it's always wise to check the machine and have a short test ride. You can also rent **motorbikes** from several places, including the *Bob Marley House* (ask for Amr; ⓣ010 646-5503): a 100cc bike costs £E50 per day, 150cc £E75 per day. A passport, student card or other ID is generally required as security.

Accommodation

Officially, there are just "high" (Nov–May) and "low" (June–Oct) **seasons**. In practice, prices rise or fall depending on **demand**, which is affected both by the number of tourists and competition from cruise boats. Many low-budget places employ **hotel touts**, who refer to netting tourists as "fishing" and happily poach them from rivals by telling outrageous lies.

Searching the internet you can get **discounts** of up to fifty percent off the walk-in rack rates at almost any hotel rated three stars or above. Most backpackers' hotels can be booked through ⓦwww.hostelworld.com or www.hostelbookers.com, but you're unlikely to save money and might even pay more than if you simply walk in, ask, and try haggling. Note that a Rasta-themed rooftop signifies a partiality to dope.

The following hotels are all in **Luxor** itself. It's also worth considering staying on the **west bank**, where there are some great hotels (see p.297). We've taken **downtown** to mean anywhere within five minutes' walk of Luxor Temple – an area that includes the main tourist bazaar and the central swath of the Corniche. Inexpensive hotels cluster around **Television Street** and parallel side streets – all no more than fifteen minutes' walk from Luxor Temple or the train station. Despite its littered backstreets, this is an up-and-coming area that's safe to stay in and quieter than the centre of town (to which it's connected by minibus). Running parallel to the Nile out to Awmia, **Sharia Khalid Ibn Walid** is lined with four- and five-star hotels backing on to the Nile, and restaurants, bars and discos further inland. Even if you end up staying several kilometres from the centre there's never a problem finding a taxi or *calèche*, and minibuses run till midnight.

Downtown

Emilio Sharia Yussef Hassan ⓣ095/237-6666, ⓦwww.emiliotravel.com. This large tour-group oriented hotel has comfy a/c rooms with fridge and satellite TV; a rooftop pool, bar and disco, Sunday buffet and dance show. Reservations essential. Accepts major credit cards. BB ❺

Iberotel Midan el-Mesaha, 600m south of Luxor Temple ⓣ095/238-0925, ⓦwww.iberotel-eg.com. This former *Novotel* (still widely known as that) has a large atrium, and a pool and terrace overlooking the Nile; a Nile-view room costs $16 extra. Rooms are small and bland, but the location is good. Breakfast (£E41) not included. ❻

Mercure Luxor Corniche el-Nil, between Luxor Temple and Luxor Museum ⓣ095/238-0944, ⓦwww.mercure.com. Still known to locals as the *Etap*, this 1970s four-star is mainly used by tour operators. Its proximity to the Luxor Museum and a swimming pool are its main advantages. BB 5

Nefertiti Sharia es-Sahbi, between Sharia el-Karnak and the bazaar ⓣ 095/237-2386, ⓦ www.nefertitihotel.com. A friendly semi-boutique hotel in the heart of town, with a/c en-suite rooms with fridge and satellite TV; free wi-fi, a rooftop overlooking Luxor Temple, and a fine restaurant, *Al-Sahaby Lane* (see p.276). Its engaging owner Ala el-Din organizes tours to the oases, Cairo, Sinai and Jordan. BB 3

Pavilion Winter Corniche el-Nil, 75m from Luxor Temple ⓣ 095/238-0422, ⓦ www.sofitel.com. This modern annexe to the *Sofitel Winter Palace* (see below) lacks the original's elegance, but shares its garden and pool. All rooms have balconies and garden views; singles cost the same as doubles. Buffet breakfast (£E95) not included. Amex, MC and Visa. 8

Philippe Sharia Labaib Habachi, near the Corniche ⓣ 095/237-3604, ⓦ www.philippeluxorhotel.com. En-suite a/c rooms with fridge and satellite TV; "superior" ones have fancier decor and balconies with a Nile view. Rooftop pool, billiards (£E25/hr), internet (£E25/hr) and massage (£E130/hr). Mainly used by tour groups. BB 3

Sofitel Winter Palace Corniche el-Nil, 100m from Luxor Temple ⓣ 095/238-0422, ⓦ www.sofitel.com. The doyen of Luxor's hotels, founded in 1887, this Victorian pile has played host to heads of state, Noël Coward and Agatha Christie (parts of *Death on the Nile* were written and filmed here). Rooms overlook the Nile or a vast garden with a heated pool (from €300 for a standard garden view up to €1500 for the royal suite). Buffet breakfast (£E130) not included. Amex, MC and Visa. 9

Susanna Sharia el-Karnak ⓣ 095/236-9915, ⓦ www.susannahotelluxor.com. This new, super-clean mini-hotel has a/c rooms with satellite TV and proper bath-tubs, an a/c restaurant and a rooftop with a tiny pool, affording superb views of Luxor Temple. Accepts Visa cards. BB 3

Venus Sharia Yussef Hassan ⓣ 095/237-2625 or 018 928-0085, ⓦ http://venus-hotel-luxor.webs.com. Under energetic new Colombian-Egyptian management, this legendary hotel is recovering its mojo. Clean a/c rooms, mostly en-suite; also dorm beds and a self-contained flat sleeping up to five people (€30). Free transfer from the station or airport for pre-booked guests; free internet, sports TV and a laidback rooftop Balloon rides, quad-biking and excursions arranged. BB 2

Around Television Street

Bob Marley House Sharia Badr, off Television St ⓣ 010 646-5503, ⓔ bobmarleyhostel2008@hotmail.com. At the end of a quiet cul-de-sac, Ziggy and Amr's welcoming den is Rasta-ed from its lobby to its rooftop, where you can get mellow (or sleep out for £E10), with a free evening meal on Fridays. Clean rooms with fans or a/c and shared or en-suite bathrooms (£E5 extra). Bicycles and motorbikes rented; cheap excursions and balloon rides. BB 1

Boomerang Sharia Mohammed Farid ⓣ 019 136-1544, ⓦ www.boomerangluxor.com. Managed by an Australian woman and her Egyptian husband, *Boomerang* aims to cater for families and backpackers, with en-suite rooms and apartments, a laundry service and wi-fi throughout. BB 1

Fontana Sharia Radwan, off Television St ⓣ 095/238-0663. A longtime backpackers' choice: clean and well furnished, with a notice-board, library and free washing machine; it's worth paying £E10 more for an a/c room with a bathroom. Whatever they say at reception, all prices for rooms and tours are negotiable – bargain hard. BB 1

Happy Land Sharia el-Kamrr, off Sharia el-Madina el-Minarwa ⓣ 095/227-1828 or 010 705-7676, ⓦ www.luxorhappyland.com. Not the cheapest but an established favourite for its cleanliness, honesty and fixed prices. All rooms with fans, some a/c and en-suite with fridges; rooftop jacuzzi and free wi-fi. Bike rental, cheap excursions to the Valley temples and the west bank, balloon trips and cruises; bus, train and ferry tickets. BB 2

Little Garden Sharia Radwan ⓣ 095/227-9090, ⓦ www.littlegardenhotel.com. Aptly named for its garden, this small hotel is a/c, clean and cosy, but some rooms are a bit claustrophobic so it's worth paying €23 for a suite with a private terrace. Transfers from the airport or bus station (€8) for prebooked guests. BB 3

Nubian Oasis Sharia Mohammed Farid ⓣ 095/236-2671 or 012 369-4130, ⓦ www.nubianoasis.com. Cheap clean rooms with a/c or fans and slightly shabby bathrooms. Their Rasta-themed rooftop often serves communal meals (£E10 per person) and they have free wi-fi in the lobby. Cheap excursions to the west bank, Edfu and Kom Ombo. BB 1

Oasis Sharia Mohammed Farid ⓣ 010 380-5882, ⓔ luxoroasis@hotmail.com. Painted blue throughout, its big rooms have fans and shared facilities, or a/c and private bathrooms – some have double beds. Laundry service, free wi-fi, and a sociable rooftop with beer, where free tea and cake is served at sunset. Cheap excursions to the west bank and Valley temples. BB 1

Along Sharia Khalid Ibn Walid

Luxor Sheraton Resort 4.2km from Luxor Temple ⓣ095/237-4544, ⓦwww.sheraton.com/luxor. Tranquilly secluded at the far end of Khalid Ibn Walid, the *Sheraton* has good facilities and service. Go for a room in the main building rather than a garden one; "Nile-view" rooms only live up to their billing on the upper floors. Access by free bus from the Luxor Museum seven times daily, or by minibus as far as Midan el-Salam. BB ❻

Maritim Jolie Ville Crocodile Island, 6km from Luxor Temple ⓣ095/227-4855, ⓦwww.jolieville-hotels.com/luxor. Known to all as the *Mövenpick*, this resort is ideal for families, with 320 bungalows in luxuriant grounds, tennis courts, a pool, playground and mini-zoo. There are hourly buses to the *Sofitel Winter Palace* in town, and a motorboat three times daily. All major cards. BB ❼

Morris Sharia El-Hurriya, 1.7km from Luxor Temple ⓣ095/227-9833, ⓦwww.hotelmorrisluxor.com. This high-rise four-star off the main drag has a rooftop pool with Nile views, a piano bar and a disco; large a/c rooms have fridges, satellite TV and balconies – ask for one with a river view. Breakfast not included. ❼

New Pola 2.2km from Luxor Temple ⓣ095/236-5081, ⓦwww.newpolahotel.com. Probably the best value mid-range hotel on the street, with spotless a/c rooms, a rooftop with a small pool and fabulous Nile views, and agreeably kitsch decor throughout. Ask for a room facing the river. BB ❹

Pyramisa Isis 3.5km from Luxor Temple ⓣ095/237-0100, ⓦwww.pyramisaegypt.com. Significantly cheaper than other five-stars on the street, this anodyne complex (owned by President Mubarak's son, Ala) backs onto lush grounds with a big pool and superb views of the river, but its a/c rooms are on the small side. Visa cards only. BB ❻

St Joseph 2.3km from Luxor Temple ⓣ095/238-1707, ⓔstjosephhotel@yahoo.com. A popular three-star with a heated rooftop pool and a bar facing the Theban Hills. All rooms en suite with a/c and free wi-fi; ask for one with a Nile view. They hold Saturday night Saiyidi parties with snakecharming and a buffet. Friendly staff, and an excellent buffet breakfast. BB ❸

Sonesta St George 2.7km from Luxor Temple ⓣ095/238-2575, ⓦwww.sonesta.com. The fanciest five-star on the street, with oodles of marble, Japanese and Italian restaurants, a heated pool by the Nile, and great service. The top three floors have deluxe rooms with jacuzzis, large screen TVs and power showers. Amex, MC, Visa. BB ❽

Steigenberger Nile Palace 3.7km from Luxor Temple ⓣ095/236-6999, ⓦwww.luxor.steigenberger.com. Awash with fake marble, this five-star behemoth overlooks a heated pool beside a Nile terrace, with disabled access throughout. Street-facing rooms for only €50, €180 for a superior Nile view room, €480 for a deluxe suite. Gym, massage and sauna; Italian and Lebanese restaurants. All major cards. BB ❺

Sawagi

If you fancy staying somewhere untouristy and hassle-free, **Sawagi**, behind the train station, is an artisans' quarter only 15–20 minutes' walk from Luxor Temple. To get there, exit the station by an underpass and follow Sharia Salakhana nearly to the end, before bearing left onto a parallel sidestreet to find *Mara House* (Sharia Salah al-Din al-Ayubi, see map, p.295 ⓣ010 546-2480, ⓦwww.egyptwithmara.com). Run by an Irish family, this child-friendly apart-hotel has large a/c en-suite rooms and a restaurant decorated in the khedival style; a bar with wi-fi, Swingball on a roof-garden overlooking mountains, and a library reflecting Mara's passion for Egyptology and spiritual healing. Takes MasterCard and Visa. ❼

Out beyond Karnak

If you don't mind being far from Luxor there are two deluxe hotels out past Karnak (see map, pp.294–295), both linked to town by free shuttle buses. The *Hilton* is adjacent to a mini tourist-zone of restaurants and bars in New Karnak (also accessible by public minibus from Luxor), while the *Sofitel* exists in splendid isolation.

Hilton Luxor Resort & Spa 4km north of Luxor Temple, 1.5km from Karnak Temple ⓣ095/237-4933, ⓔluxor@hilton.com. Totally refurbished in 2007, this five-star resort features a top-class spa and two infinity pools beside the Nile, with double rooms from $360. Hourly shuttle bus into town. ❽

Sofitel Karnak 5km north of Luxor, 3km from Karnak ⓣ095/237-8020, ⓦwww.sofitel.com. Secluded amid palms and bougainvilleas, this stylish hotel has bungalows, a big heated Nile-side pool, tennis, squash, a sauna and jacuzzi. Advertised abroad as a child-free resort, but not necessarily so. Shuttle bus to the *Sofitel Winter Palace* in Luxor. Takes Visa cards. Dbl from €67 ❼

Apartments

Renting an **apartment** in Luxor is easy; many regular visitors prefer this to staying at a hotel, for more privacy or to save money. Two reputable local **agencies** are Flats in Luxor (ⓣ010 356-4540, ⓦwww.flatsinluxor.co.uk) – which owns several fully-equipped flats near the *Pyramisa Isis* and deluxe flats with a pool and jacuzzi on the west bank (from $40 per night for a one-bedroom flat in low season to $75 for a three-bedroom flat with a pool in high season) – and Egypt Property Sales (ⓣ095/238-1723 or 010 614-2722, ⓦwww.egyptpropertysales.com) on Sharia Radwa Sherifa, off Sharia Khalid Ibn Walid, with dozens of properties on both sides of the river, from two-bedroom apartments (from £E1800 per month) to deluxe villas (£E8000-9000 per month). Both can arrange transfers from the airport. Or you can deal directly with **landlords** like Tito (ⓣ010 549-4647, ⓦwww.luxor-apartment.de), with two- or four-bedroomed flats in New Karnak opposite the *Hilton* for £E1000/1500 a month, or Hosny (ⓣ010 283-4602, ⓔmralis2002@yahoo.com, whose two-bedroom flat in Sawagi has a waterbed, and costs £E600 a week.

Luxor Temple

Luxor Temple (daily: summer 6am–10pm; winter 6am–9pm; £E50) stands aloof in the heart of town, ennobling the view from the waterfront and Midan el-Haggag with its grand colonnades and pylons, which are spotlit at night till 10pm. Though it's best explored by day – when its details can be thoroughly examined in a couple of hours – you could come back after dark to imbibe its atmosphere and drama with fewer people around.

Dedicated to the **Theban Triad** of Amun-Min, Mut and Khonsu (see p.285), Luxor Temple was the "Harem of the South" where Amun's consort Mut and their son Khonsu resided. Every spring a flotilla of barques escorted Amun's effigy from Karnak Temple to this site for a conjugal reunion with Mut in an Optet, or fertility festival, noted for its public debauchery.

Whereas Karnak is the work of many dynasties, most of Luxor Temple was built by two rulers during a period when New Kingdom art reached its apogee. The temple's founder was **Amenophis III** (1417–1379 or 1390–1352 BC) of the XVIII Dynasty, whose other monuments include the Third Pylon at Karnak and the Colossi of Memnon across the river. Work halted under his son Akhenaten (who erased his father's cartouches and built a sanctuary to Aten alongside the temple), but resumed under Tutankhamun and Horemheb, who decorated its court and colonnade with their own reliefs. To this, **Ramses II** (1304–1237 or 1279–1213 BC) of the XIX Dynasty added a double colonnaded court and a great pylon flanked by obelisks and colossi. Despite additions by later pharaohs and the rebuilding of its sanctuary under Alexander the Great, the temple has a coherence that reproaches Karnak's inchoate giganticism. When the French army first sighted it in 1799, the troops spontaneously presented arms.

The clarity of its **reliefs** is due to the temple having been half-buried by sand and silt, and overlaid by Luxor itself. Nineteenth-century visitors found a "labyrinthine maze of mud structures" nesting within its court. When the French wanted to remove an obelisk, and archeologists to excavate the temple, they had to pay compensation for the demolition of scores of homes.

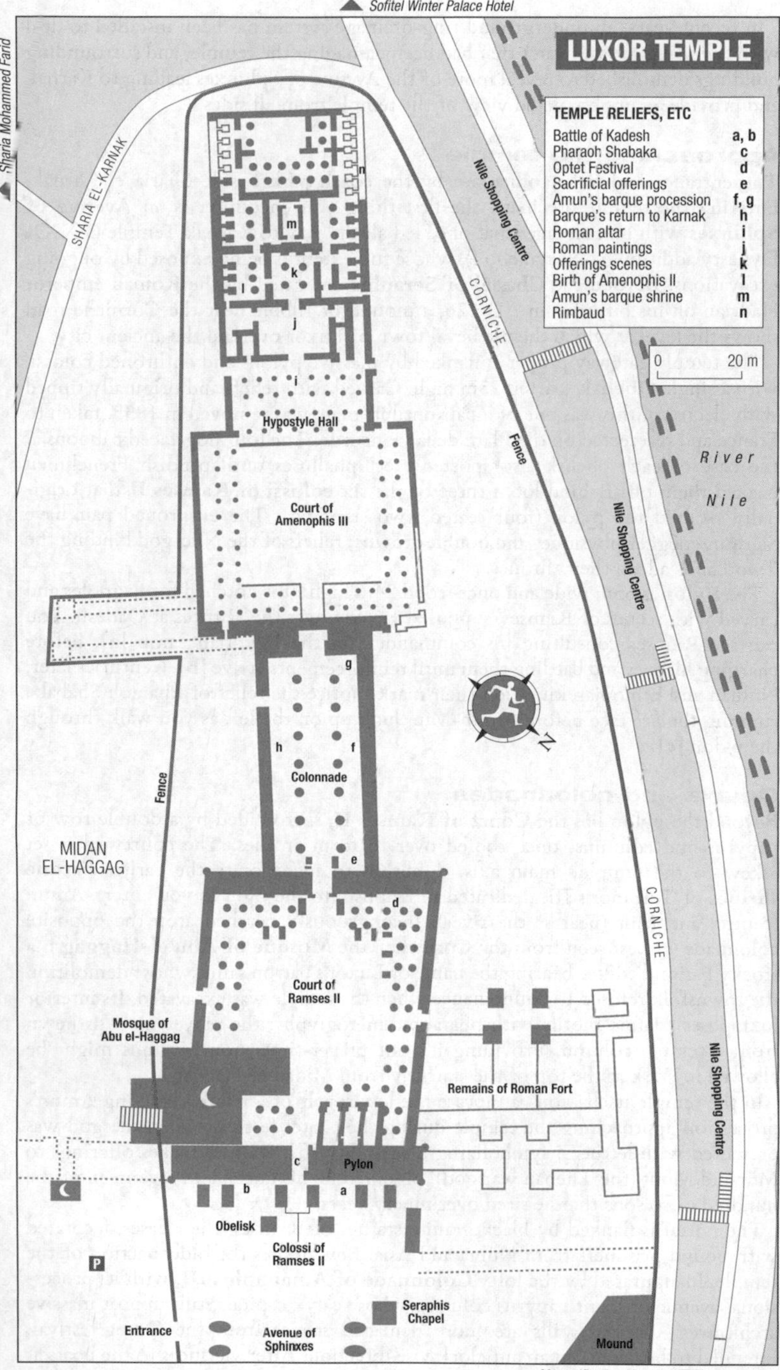
LUXOR TEMPLE
TEMPLE RELIEFS, ETC
Battle of Kadesh a, b
Pharaoh Shabaka c
Optet Festival d
Sacrificial offerings e
Amun's barque procession f, g
Barque's return to Karnak h
Roman altar i
Roman paintings j
Offerings scenes k
Birth of Amenophis II l
Amun's barque shrine m
Rimbaud n
0 20 m
Sofitel Winter Palace Hotel
Sharia Mohammed Farid
SHARIA EL-KARNAK
Nile Shopping Centre
CORNICHE
Fence
River Nile
Hypostyle Hall
Court of Amenophis III
Colonnade
MIDAN EL-HAGGAG
Court of Ramses II
Mosque of Abu el-Haggag
Remains of Roman Fort
Pylon
Obelisk
Colossi of Ramses II
Seraphis Chapel
Entrance
Avenue of Sphinxes
Mound
Mummification Museum
P
N
a b c d e f g h i j k l m n

In recent years, an underground ring-drainage system has been installed to deal with the rising groundwater that had been damaging the temple, and surrounding buildings demolished to reveal more of the Avenue of Sphinxes leading to Karnak and provide an unobstructed view of the temple from all sides.

Approaching the temple

The entrance and ticket office are by the coach park beside Sharia el-Karnak. Entering the temple precincts, the first thing you encounter is an **Avenue of Sphinxes** with human faces that once led all the way to Karnak Temple (a XXX Dynasty addition by Nectanebo I), whose full extent is being exposed by ongoing excavations. Beyond the **Chapel of Seraphis** dedicated by the Roman emperor Hadrian on his birthday in AD 126, a mound of rubble near the Corniche road shows the level at which the medieval town of Luxor overlaid the ancient city.

The temple gateway proper is flanked by massive pylons and enthroned colossi, with a single **Obelisk** soaring 25m high. Carved with reliefs and originally tipped with electrum, this was one of a pair until its mate was removed in 1835, taken to France and re-erected on the Place de la Concorde. The four dog-faced baboons at the base of each obelisk also sported erect phalluses until prudish Frenchmen hacked them off. Behind loom three of the six **colossi of Ramses II** that originally fronted the pylon (four seated, two standing). The enthroned pair have Schwarzenegger physiques and double crowns; reliefs of the Nile-god binding the Two Lands adorn their thrones.

The **Pylon** is 65m wide and once stood 24m high; it is notched for flagpoles and carved with scenes of Ramses' supposed victory over the Hittites at Qadesh. You can see Ramses consulting his commanders in the Egyptian camp **[a]**, before charging his foes and battling them until reinforcements arrive **[b]**. Centuries later, Nubian and Ethiopian kings left their mark: notice the relief of Pharaoh Shabaka running the *heb* race before Amun-Min, high up on the left as you walk through the pylon **[c]**.

Courts and colonnades

Beyond the pylon lies the **Court of Ramses II**, surrounded by a double row of papyrus-bud columns, once roofed over to form arcades. The courtyard is set askew to the temple's main axis, doubtless to incorporate the earlier **barque shrines** of Tuthmosis III, dedicated to Khonsu (to the right as you enter), Amun (centre) and Mut (nearest the river). Incongruously perched atop the opposite colonnade (as best seen from the Corniche), the **Mosque of Abu el-Haggag** is a stocky Fatimid edifice bearing the name of Luxor's patron saint, whose demolition the townsfolk refused to countenance when the temple was excavated. Its interior juxtaposes Islamic motifs with pharaonic hieroglyphs; the prayer niche is hewn from a temple column. Providing it's not prayer-time, non-Muslims might be allowed in – ask at the top of the stairway from Midan el-Haggag.

In the temple itself, you can locate the lower half of a frieze depicting Amun's procession approaching the temple during the Optet festival, when the god was presented with lettuces, symbolizing his fertility **[d]**. Ramses makes offerings to Mut and Mont (the Theban war god), observed by his queen and seventeen of the hundred or so sons that he sired over ninety years.

The portal is flanked by black granite statues of Ramses, their bases decorated with bound prisoners from Nubia and Asia. Beyond lies the older section of the temple, inaugurated by the lofty **Colonnade of Amenophis III**, with its processional avenue of giant papyrus columns whose calyx capitals still support massive architraves. On the walls are more damaged scenes from the Optet festival, intended to be "read" in an anticlockwise direction. After sacrifices to the boats at

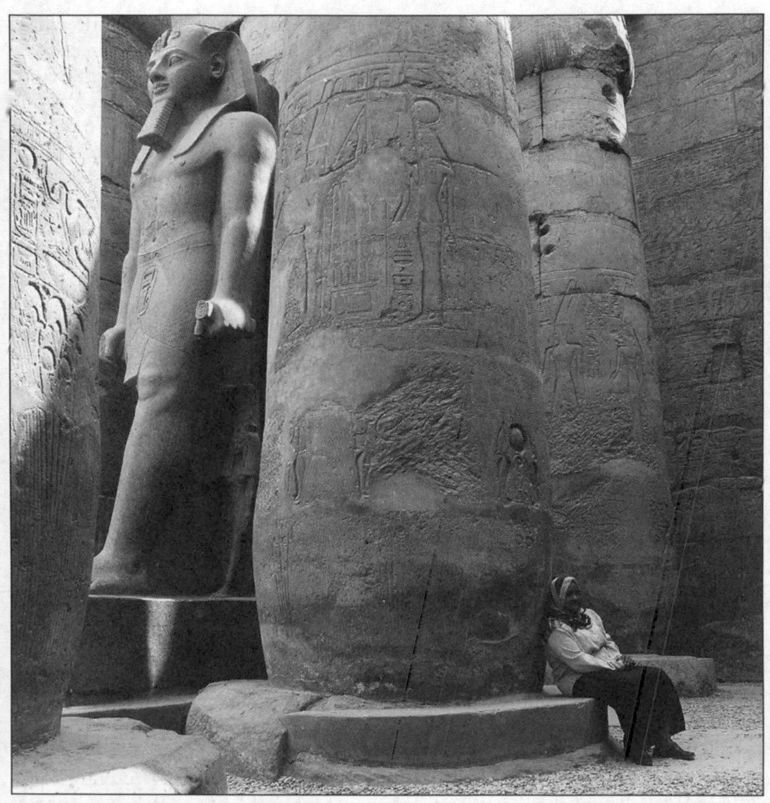

▲ The Court of Ramses II, Luxor Temple

Karnak [e], Amun's procession [f] arrives at Luxor Temple [g], returning to Karnak 24 days later [h]. The pharaoh shown here is Tutankhamun, who had the colonnade decorated, but the cartouches honour his successor, Horemheb.

At the end of the colonnade lies the great **Court of Amenophis III**, surrounded on three sides by colonnades of papyrus-bundle columns with bud capitals. The southern one merges into a **Hypostyle Hall** with 32 papyrus columns, serving as a vestibule to the temple proper. Between the last two columns on the left of its central aisle [i] is a Roman altar dedicated to Emperor Constantine, before his conversion to Christianity.

The inner sanctums

Beyond the hall lies a columned **portico** or antechamber, whose central aisle was flanked by the barque shrines of Mut and Khonsu. Roman legionaries later plastered over the pharaonic reliefs and turned it into a chapel where local Christians were offered a choice between martyrdom or obeisance to the imperial cults. Paintings of Roman emperors are visible near the top of the walls, and around the niche on the south wall [j]; elsewhere the stucco has fallen away to reveal Amenophis offering sacrifices to Amun. In the smaller, four-columned **Hall of Offerings**, beyond, reliefs show the pharaoh leading sacrificial cows and presenting incense and sceptres [k].

More interesting reliefs occur in the **Birth Room** of Amenophis III, whose north wall **[l]** emphasizes his divine paternity, since he was not of direct royal descent. The ravaged lower register shows Thoth leading Amun (disguised as Tuthmosis IV) into the queen's bedchamber, where, the hieroglyphic caption states, "his dew filled her body". Examined from left to right, the middle register depicts Thoth foretelling Amenophis's birth; Mutemuia's pregnancy and confinement; Isis presenting the child to Amun; and the god cradling his son.

If the Birth Room is inaccessible from the Hall of Offerings you can reach it via the next hall, which Alexander the Great converted into the **Sanctuary of Amun's Barque** by removing four columns and installing a granite shrine **[m]**.

The remaining chambers to the south constituted the private apartments of the gods, but are badly damaged and really only notable for the name Rimbaud, carved high up on the wall near the river **[n]**. Rimbaud spent the last sixteen years of his life roaming the Near and Far East; while living in Ethiopia he was feared dead, so Verlaine published his poems (all written by the age of 21), which took Paris by storm and inspired the Decadent movement.

Outside the walls, assorted pharaonic, Roman and Christian **stonework** is stored near the spot where, in 1989, workers uncovered a cache of 26 New Kingdom statues, sixteen of which are on show in the Luxor Museum.

Mummification Museum

At the northern end of the Nile Shopping Centre below the Corniche, Luxor's **Mummification Museum** (daily: summer 9am–1pm & 5–10pm; winter 9am–1pm & 4–9pm; £E50; no photography) devotes more space to the beliefs surrounding death and the afterlife than to the actual practice of mummification (see pp.304–305) and hardly breaks new ground. It does, however, display a spoon and spatula used to remove the deceased's brain (which was discarded by the Egyptians as an unimportant organ), and a finely-preserved mummy of Maserharti, a XXI Dynasty high priest of Amun. In wintertime on Sundays at 7pm there is a free **archeological lecture** by such experts as Kent Weeks (studying tomb KV5 in the Valley of the Kings) and Zbigniew Szafranski (of the Polish Mission at Deir el-Bahri). Visitors can consult the museum's Egyptology reference **library** (daily 9am–6pm; free).

Luxor Museum

Luxor Museum (daily: summer 6am–1pm & 5–10pm; winter 9am–1pm & 4–9pm; £E80), at the northern end of the Corniche, complements the town's monumental assets with a superb collection of statues and funerary goods from the Theban Necropolis and various temples. The museum is wheelchair-accessible, well laid out and labelled in English, though some names are rendered differently from those in this book (for example: Amenhotep for Amenophis). **Photography** is not allowed inside the museum, but illustrated guides are on sale at the bookshop. There is an overpriced café attached.

To the right as you enter is a ramp down to the sunken **Cachette Hall**, displaying sixteen of the statues found beneath Luxor Temple in 1987. It's uncertain whether they were hidden at the start of the Roman occupation or nine hundred years earlier, when Egypt was invaded by the Assyrians. They include an alabaster sphinx of Tutankhamun; Amenophis III and Horus enthroned, in basalt; a headless cobra poised to strike in the name of the Nubian pharaoh Taharqa; Horemheb kneeling before the god Atum; and a processional effigy of Amenophis III, its rose quartzite left unpolished to highlight the texture of his kilt, armbands and Combined Crown.

The **first level** opens with a sensitive-faced statue of the adolescent Tutankhamun and a gilded head of the cow deity Mehit-Weret from his tomb in the Valley of the Kings. A colossal head of Amenophis III, found on the west bank in 1957, leads you on to a raised level showcasing more works in stone. Compare the careworn face of Sesostris II and the watchfulness of bureaucrat Yamo-Nedjeh with the serenity of the boy Tut beside the crocodile god Sobek, or the diorite head of Sekhmet from a colossal statue in the Precinct of Mut at Karnak.

An extension entitled **Thebes Glory** displays artefacts related to the New Kingdom war machine. Tut's war chariot, a relief of Amenophis II target-shooting, and royal bows (some recurved and composite) show how the Egyptians mastered the tactics and technology of the Hyksos invaders. A statue of Horemheb and his wife from their unfinished tomb at Memphis, a granite head of Ramses II and a super-sized alabaster Seti I recall the hard men of the XVIII and XIX dynasties.

Best of all, there are two **royal mummies**. That of **Ahmosis I** has a surprisingly delicate physique for the ruler who expelled the Hyksos. His gold-and-electrum axe (found at Dra' Abul Naga on the west bank) and a gold collar with Flies of Valour, from the tomb of Queen Ahhotep (who may have led the Theban army when Ahmosis was a child), are exhibited nearby. The other mummy was returned to Egypt from a museum at Niagara Falls, and might belong to **Ramses I** (see p.313).

On the **top level** are model boats from the Meir Tombs at Assyut, gilded *shabti* figures from Tut's tomb, and architects' tools from the Workmen's Village at Deir el-Medina. Between two haunting heads of **Akhenaten** from his Aten temple at Karnak is a **wall** from the same temple, made of small blocks called *talatat* ("thirds"), that were later used as filler for the Ninth Pylon, wherein they were discovered in the 1960s. Reassembled, the painted sunk-reliefs depict Akhenaten's *Sed* festival, with the king and Queen Nefertiti in a litter surrounded by fan-bearers. Their figures have the strange physiognomy associated with Akhenaten's reign (see box, p.232). A **multimedia display** shows how papyrus was harvested and pressed into sheets for writing, and how scribes were trained.

Eating and drinking

Luxor's culinary scene is less diverse than Cairo's, but there's no shortage of places to eat. Upmarket **hotel restaurants** offer various world cuisines and elsewhere you'll mainly find pizzas, kebabs, omelettes and other tourist fodder. Be prepared for the additional service charges and tax (up to 24 percent), though many places don't actually levy them.

All the usual **street food** can be found along El-Karnak, Ramses and Yussef Hassan streets. A 24-hour **bakery** near the corner of Sharia al-Mahatta and the souk turns out pretzels and rolls, while *Twinky*, at the station end of Sharia el-Manshiya, sells confectionery. If you're self-catering, there's no shortage of small **grocery shops** and self-service **mini-markets** on Sharia el-Madina el-Minarwa – Omar Market is the best. There's a 24-hour bakery just up the road and another near the junction with Television Street.

Restaurants and cafés

Most of the **restaurants** and **cafés** below are open from mid-morning (or earlier) till 9–10pm (or later), though the range of dishes may diminish as the evening wears on. Unless otherwise stated, they don't sell **alcohol**. Additionally, there are some excellent places to eat on the **west bank**, near the ferry landing stage in Gezira (see p.299 for details).

1896 Restaurant *Sofitel Winter Palace Hotel*, Corniche el-Nil ⓣ095/238-0422. Its grand decor and silver service are matched by its haute cuisine: crab stuffed with mushrooms and herbs (£E90), lobster with saffron sauce (£E250), veal fillet with cloves in coconut milk (£E120), and crêpes with orange cream, vanilla and strawberry sauce (£E45), accompanied by French, Italian or South African wines (£E420–1600). Smart dress (a jacket and tie for men) and reservations for sittings at 7pm & 9pm required. Accepts Amex, Diners Club, MasterCard and Visa.

Abou Ashraf Sharia al-Mahatta. Brightly lit take-away and sit-down diner, serving *kushari* (£E3–5), *shawarma* (£E4), *kofta* and roast chicken (£E10–15). You pay at the cashiers before eating. Open till midnight.

Abu Hassan el-Shazly Sharia el-Manshiya. A kerbside joint in the spice and hardware souk, where a delicious meal of *kofta*, grilled chicken or stuffed pigeon, salad, rice and dips, costs about £E30, with a/c seating indoors if you'd rather escape the street-life.

Al-Shahaby Lane Between Sharia el-Karnak and Sharia al-Souk. With its trellised roof and *mashrabiya* fittings, this airy outdoor restaurant is a pefect retreat from the bazaar. Try the spring rolls (£E10–14), the Al-Sahaby chicken (£E38), beef (£E55) or seafood (£E60) *tageen*, or the Fishermen's Net seafood platter (£E70). All are delicious.

Bombay Sharia Khalid Ibn Walid ⓣ095/236-6117, ⓔbombay_luxor@yahoo.com. Mughal cuisine (with veggie options) in a homely Bollywood setting, conjured up by a charming Indian couple. Try the spicy black lentils (£E20), chicken with cashews and almonds (£E50) or a lamb *biryani* (£E45), with a mango ice cream (£E18) for afters. Daily 11am–11pm.

El-Hussein On the second floor of the Bazaar Savoy, off Sharia el-Karnak. Although its new setting in a tourist mall is far less funky than its old location beside Luxor Temple, this a/c restaurant still serves excellent Egyptian fare (£E40–60 for a full meal).

El-Zareem Sharia Yussef Hassan. A busy sitdown diner and takeaway serving *taamiya*, *kofta* or shrimp sandwiches, *kushari* and other Egyptian staples, all freshly cooked and costing from £E5–10. Daily 24hr.

Kebabagy Nile Shopping Centre, below the Corniche. Despite boasting of having hosted President Sarkozy, their garlic bread (£E15), club sandwiches (£E40) and pizzas (£E30–50) aren't so hot; stick to ice cream, beer (£E15–20) or cocktails (£E40) while you enjoy the view. Takes Visa and MasterCard.

La Mamma *Sheraton Luxor Resort*, Sharia Khalid Ibn Walid. For those with kids, this Italian restaurant is a good choice, with pizzas (£E60–90) and pasta (£E65–100) just like you'd get at home and space to play outside. Their beef carpaccio (£E50) is fabulous.

Metropolitan Café Nile Shopping Centre, near the *Mercure Luxor Hotel*. Like its sister bistro *Kebabagy*, it has a view across the Nile and breezes from the river (which may be spoilt by diesel-belching cruise boats). The menu and prices are much the same too.

Miyako *Sonesta St George Hotel*, Sharia Khalid Ibn Walid ⓣ095/238-2575. Offers a fairly limited Japanese menu of seafood (£E45–180), sushi appetizers (£E146), seafood noodles (£E60) and beef teriyaki (£E75) – the teriyaki chef whirls his knives at your table. Smartish dress expected. Serves alcohol. Most cards accepted. Daily 5–11pm.

Oasis Café Sharia Labaib Habachi. A restful retreat (think *Casablanca*) with recorded jazz and 1940s vocals. Try their Steak Hero (£E40), the Oasis salad (£E30), or specials such as mushroom, chicken and apple crêpes (£E35), home-made pasta and pesto, or gazpacho and other cold soups in the summer. No cards. Daily 10am–10pm.

Pink Panda *Pyramisa Isis Hotel*, Sharia Khalid Ibn Walid ⓣ095/237-2750. One of Luxor's posher restaurants, serving a bland approximation of Szechuan cuisine: Wonton soup (£E25), shrimps with cashew nuts (£E95) and crispy duck with pancakes and Hoisen sauce (£E76) are the tastiest options. Sells alcohol. Most cards accepted. Daily 6–11pm.

Puddleduck Sharia el-Madina el-Minarwa ⓣ016 716-8473. A friendly non-smoking restaurant, run by a British couple experimenting with Jamie Oliver recipes: try their chicken liver pâté (£E25), steak (£E55), roast beef (£E55) or lamb (£E60), followed by fudge cake with fudge sauce (£E25). Serves alcohol; no cards. Daily except Wed noon–4pm & 5.30–10pm.

Quick Television Street. Popular with local families, *Quick* dishes up all kinds of pizzas, pasta, grills and other high-cholesterol favourites (£E20–40) to eat in or take away, and has a balcony for people-watching. Daily 11am–1am.

Royal Fish Sharia el-Haggag, off Television Street. A humble a/c eatery favoured by locals for its seafood platter (£E40), calamari (£E30) and grilled or fried shrimp (£E40–45). Daily noon–10pm.

Shams el-Aseel Sharia el-Kmarr, off Television Street. If you're looking for a tasty snack, this nearly round-the-clock *shawarma*, salad, and *taamiya* takeaway fits the bill, with most dishes costing £E1–5, and a few tables upstairs. Daily 6am–2am.

Snobs Sharia Radwa Sherifa, off Sharia Khalid Ibn Walid ⓣ010 280-2880. Popular with British expats, this a/c restaurant offers stir-fried chicken with ginger and mango (£E44), an all-day Sunday roast (£E48), and a huge mezze selection for two people (£E280). No alcohol served, but you can bring your own. Daily 11am–11pm.

Sofra Sharia Mohammed Farid ⓣ095/235-9752, ⓦwww.sofra.com.eg. A *sofra* is a round brass table, which typifies the decor of this romantic restaurant in the backstreets, serving delicious mezze (£E70), stuffed duck (£E55), flambéed calf's liver (£E20) and other Middle Eastern specialities. They have a lovely rooftop terrace, a covered garden with divans for smoking *sheesha*, and two Khedival-style private dining rooms. Reservations are essential in the winter. Daily 11am–11pm.

Coffee houses

Though traditional **coffee shops** are exclusively masculine territory, women should feel comfortable in the places listed below.

Alf Leyl w Leyl Television St. With its private booths hung with gilded Arabesque tent-fabric, its fresh juices and big choice of *sheesha* flavours, the "Thousand and One Nights" is popular with Egyptian newlyweds and families.

Lyaly Zaman Off Sharia Khalid Ibn Walid. Named "Olden Days" in Arabic, this large, airy tent-covered teahouse has divans for reclining while watching international sports on wide-screen TV. Daily 10am–2am.

New Oum Kalthoum Sharia al-Souk. An outdoor coffee shop in the heart of the tourist bazaar, that's great for people-watching, and cooled by mist-sprayers. They do proper espresso (£E10), fresh juices and flavoured *sheeshas*. Food can be ordered in from the *Al-Shahaby Lane* restaurant (see p.276).

Nubian National Coffee Sharia al-Souk. This funky tearoom decorated with blankets and fake boulders is the place to hear Nubian sounds and meet guys from Aswan. Try the coffee spiced with cardamom or the juices.

Victoria Lounge *Sofitel Winter Palace Hotel*, Corniche el-Nil. For the princely sum of £E70 per person, you can enjoy being served cucumber sandwiches, fruit cake and tea, as if the sun had never set on the British Empire. Daily 4–6pm.

Drinking and duty-free shops

If you don't mind paying £E30–40 plus tax, the classiest places to **drink** a cold Stella beer are the Nile-side terraces of the *Sheraton*, *Pyramisa Isis*, or *Sonesta St George*, which all have fabulous views. In the centre of town, the Nile Shopping Centre below the Corniche has two places serving beer but the view (and fresh air) may be spoilt by cruise boats moored alongside. Otherwise, hotel **bars** are seldom anything special, but there are a few fun **pubs** and a pleasant beer garden to enjoy.

Cheap imported booze can be bought at **duty-free shops** within 24 hours of arrival, in the arrivals lounge at Luxor airport and the duty-free shop on the street behind the *Emilio Hotel* (daily 10am–3pm & 7pm–midnight). You'll need your passport, in which the transaction(s) will be noted. Otherwise, fall back on Egyptian beer, wine or spirits, sold at low-profile **outlets** like Besheat Store on Sharia al-Souk, Al-Ahram Beverages on Sharia Ramses, or two nameless shops near the tourist police office (10am–midnight, closed Sun).

Genesis Pub/Restaurant New Karnak, near the *Hilton Luxor Resort & Spa* (see map, p.294–295). If a swimming pool with a waterfall isn't tempting enough – and you don't mind bubble-blowers, clouds of dry ice and a prowling Great Dane – Gamal and his Ukrainian wife offer karaoke, bingo, BBQ parties, sports TV, pool and wi-fi; cocktails (£E35–55), spicy chicken (£E55), peppered steak (£E55) and a full English breakfast (£E65). Parties on request; children very welcome. Daily 9am–4am.

Hamees Sharia el-Karnak, near Luxor Temple. Billed as a restaurant and coffee house but actually a leafy beer garden where British expats gather to whinge. Stella costs £E8, Heineken £E10, Egyptian wine £E13/£E50 by the glass or bottle, shish kebab with rice or fries £E35 – plus 22 percent tax, waived if they like you. The only drinking spot in Luxor open 24/7.

King's Head Pub Sharia Khalid Ibn Walid. Though the king in question is Akhenaten, this place looks and feels like an English pub, offering club sandwiches (£E28) and a Sunday lunch of roast beef and Yorkshire pud (£E40), cocktails (£E23–38), beer (£E15) and wine (£E24). Happy hour from 7–8pm and 10–11pm; billiards (£E20/hr) and satellite TV. Daily noon–2am (later if there are customers).

Murphy's Irish Pub Sharia al-Gawazat, off Sharia Khalid Ibn Walid. Previously livelier than the *King's Head* – with singalongs, Mexican waves, pool matches and sports TV, cheered on by boisterous Brits – *Murphy's* has been a lot quieter since it imposed a £E50 minimum charge on its Egyptian customers. Daily noon–2am or later.

Nile Terrace Café & Bar *Sofitel Winter Palace, Corniche el-Nil.* The hotel's lofty terrace is an elegant vantage point to watch the sun set over the Theban Hills, while quaffing a G&T or a cold Stella (£E40). Smartish dress expected (no shorts). Daily noon–10pm.

Nightlife

Luxor's nightlife is a paler shadow of Hurghada's, if only because most tourists are too tired from sightseeing to fancy clubbing. Many **discos** are empty, and even at the most popular ones local men outnumber foreigners. There's little difference between the *Regina* disco in the *Tuthotel* on Sharia Salah al-Din, the *Luna* in the *Morris Hotel* off Sharia Khalid Ibn Walid, or *Sinouhe* near the *King's Head Pub*. All three are open till 5am every night, with no entry or minimum charge.

A dozen or so hotels stage weekly "Oriental shows" of **Saiyidi music** and **folk dancing** (stick-fights or whirling dervishes), sometimes also with a bellydancer (if the hotel's licence allows it) or a snakecharmer (at the *Nefertiti* on Sat & Wed and the *St Joseph* on Sat). Non-residents can enjoy them for free (but must buy drinks) unless a buffet meal is included – as at the *Iberotel* (£E150), the *St Joseph* (£E85) or *Nefertiti* (£E75), in which case reservations are advisable – or there's a minimum charge (£E100 at the *Luxor Sheraton* on Thurs).

Bellydancing fans might also enjoy visiting a **real Egyptian nightclub** (any night, though Thursdays are best) where the decor is seedy, the clientele raucous (women are best-off going with male companions), and the dancers tease local bigshots into throwing banknotes around. At *St Katerina*, off Sharia Ahmes in the centre, and *New Abu Hameed* on Television Street, the dancing starts at midnight and runs through till 5am if patrons are still spending. It's best to go with an Egyptian friend to get past the doorman who might claim there's an entry charge, or to argue if they add it to your bill – there isn't one; you should only pay for drinks.

Shopping

Under the governor's masterplan, many tourist shops have been relocated to air-conditioned **malls** (beside the train station and city council), and the traditional tourist **bazaar** on Sharia al-Souk has been totally refurbished, with overhead trellises to provide shade and an ornamental wooden gateway facing Midan el-Haggag.

Fixed-price shops are rare, but provide a benchmark for bargaining at other places. **Crafts** include humble handmade clay cooking pots, Garagos pottery, wooden bowls from Hegaza and textiles from Akhmim. **Alabaster** and **papyrus** are generally cheaper on the west bank, where the Nefertari Papyrus Institute is one of the few fixed-price shops. **Gold and silver** are usually sold by weight and so real prices are roughly fixed. Other buys include *karkaday* (often better here than in Aswan), *duom* (gingerbread shell, to nibble or make tea), fresh cumin and vegetable dyes. Food, spices and clothing stalls cluster on Sharia Ahmes. On Tuesdays and Sundays there's a **fruit and veg market** on Sharia el-Madina el-Minawra, off Television Street, or you could try shopping at the covered market hall on Sharia al-Mathari (open daily).

Most non-tourist shops close for a **siesta** (2–5pm).

Caravanserai Nag Lolah, on the west bank ⓣ012 327-8771, ⓦwww.caravanserailuxor.com. Worth a detour after visiting Medinet Habu Temple, this shop sells handicrafts from the Western Desert oases, Aswan, Sinai and other parts of Egypt. See map, p.294–295.

Fair Trade Center Sharia el-Karnak, near Midan el-Haggag ⓣ010 034-7900, ⓔFTC@EgyptFairtrade.org. The local outlet for a Cairo-based NGO marketing the work of nine handicrafts cooperatives, including Hegaza bowls carved from lemon, orange or tamarisk wood; Garagos pottery; beadwork from Sinai; recycled paper from Cairo; and cottons, silks and linens from Akhmim (see p.246). Accepts cards. Daily 9.30am–10.30pm.

Nashat Aiad Gaied Sharia al-Souk, between Cleopatra and Yussef Hassan streets ⓣ010 397-0457. This tailor can run up a high-quality made-to-measure *galabiyya*, kaftan, shirt or blouse in a few hours, for a reasonable price.

Radwan Bazaar Sharia Khalid Ibn Walid, opposite the *Pyramisa Isis Hotel*. Stocks perhaps the widest choice of styles of jewellery in Luxor. Prices are nominally fixed, but they'll negotiate over sizeable orders.

Winter Akhmeen Gallery Corniche el-Nil, beside the stairway to the *Sofitel Winter Palace Hotel* ⓣ095/238-0422. A small shop stuffed with bolts of hand-woven cotton, silk and linen from the women's weaving cooperative in Akhmim (p.246), from £E150 per metre. Besides selling bedcovers, they also make *galabiyyas* and shirts and can copy any other garment to order with in 48 hours. No cards. Daily 11am–11pm.

Festivals

Luxor has surprisingly few events aimed at tourists, which are always liable to be cancelled. Visitors in February have a chance of seeing the **West Bank marathon** (ⓣ02/260-6930, ⓦwww.egyptianmarathon.com), starting and finishing at Deir el-Bahri – but plans to stage Verdi's **opera** *Aïda* at Luxor Temple went awry in 2005, and the **Nile Heritage Centre** billed as Luxor's answer to the Library at Alexandria has never fulfilled its promise and may even be demolished soon.

Locals have always cared far more about **moulids** (see p.48), generally held during the two months preceding Ramadan (people can rarely tell you the exact date, but know when one is due) – so there was universal dismay when Luxor's biggest moulid was cancelled in 2009 to avoid the spread of swine flu.

Assuming it resumes in the future, the **Moulid of Abu el-Haggag** (pronounced "Hajjaj") pays homage to Luxor's patron sheikh – born in Damascus c.1150 – whose mosque nestles atop the temple. Giant floats move through the packed streets, some dedicated to trades (the *calèche* drivers' bears a carriage), others in the form of **boats** (often compared to the solar barque processions of pharaonic times, though in Islamic symbolism boats represent the quest for spiritual enlightenment). There are *zikrs* outside Abu el-Haggag's Mosque, **stick fights** (*tahtib*) to the music of drums and *mizmars* (a kind of oboe), and **horse races** (*mirmah*). The festival runs during the first two weeks of Sha'ban, the month before Ramadan.

During **Ramadan** itself, townsfolk compensate for its daytime rigours by gathering to hear *zikrs* and musicians on Midan el-Haggag in the evening, where families picnic en masse for three days after the end of Ramadan.

Other moulids are smaller, local events. **Sheikh Ali Musa of Karnak**'s lasts a week, its *leyla kebira* falling on Rajeb 6. During the moulid you can't miss the music, swings and lights around his tomb, near the entrance to Karnak village. Meanwhile, on the other side of town, Awmia village honours its own **Sheikh Ahmed al-Adasi** with a week-long festival, whose curtain raiser is a day of stick fights, horse and **camel races**. Following its *leyla kebira* on Rageb 14, there's a final day of celebrations, when camels and horses are paraded through the streets and villagers throw candies at each other.

There's also a moulid at Gurna Ta'rif (p.301) on the west bank.

Activities

Sailing on the river in a **felucca** is a relaxing way to spend an afternoon, while a sunset cruise is the perfect way to end the day. After haggling, expect to pay around £E20 an hour for a "local" cruise or £E70 for a two-hour trip to Banana Island; somewhat more if there are several passengers.

Banana Island (Gezira el-Moz), 4km upriver, is a title loosely applied to two banana plantations either side of the river, whose owners charge visitors £E5 each to land. It's enjoyable to wander through the cool, shady groves of mature banana trees, with their vaulting fronds and pendant flowers; a handful of bananas are included in the price. The round trip takes between two and three hours depending on the wind, or about half-an-hour each way by **motorboat**. You should be able to rent one for about £E60 an hour by negotiating with boatmen.

A little nearer town, **Crocodile Island** is a great for **birdwatching**, with Nile sunbirds, glossy ibises, purple herons, pied kingfishers, African rock martins, Sardinian warblers, hooded wheatears and black and whiskered terns in its reed-beds and coves. The *Maritim Jolie Ville's* bird-watching guide, Abdou Yussef (☎012 239-5467), can show you the best spots in his boat.

For hands-on thrills you can go **quad-biking** in the desert for £E200. The three-hour trip includes pick-up and drop-off at your hotel, a brief camel ride and tea in a Bedouin tent. For bookings, contact Planet Safari (☎010 081-7400) in the subterranean mall outside the *Lotus Hotel* on Sharia Khalid Ibn Walid. **Horse-riding** on the west bank can be arranged through stables in Gezira (see p.296).

Listings

American Express In the arcade outside the *Sofitel Winter Palace.* Changes money and travellers' cheques, makes cash advances on Amex cards, sells cheques and holds mail for Amex cardholders (daily except Fri 9am–5pm; ☎095/237-8333, ⓦwww.amexfranchise.com).

Banks and exchange Forex bureaux (daily 8am–9pm) on Sharia al-Montazah and Sharia el-Karnak have better rates and faster service than Luxor's banks. There are ATMs outside Banque Misr and the Bank of Alexandria on Sharia Labaib Habachi, and the National Bank of Egypt and Banque du Caire on the Corniche.

Barber Yehiya's salon, in the arcade between the train station and the tourist police, does a sharp haircut and the facial exfoliation (*fatla*) that's favoured by Egyptian men, for £E10–20.

Luxor by air

Don't miss the experience of drifting over the Theban Necropolis in a **hot-air balloon**, which affords an awesome view of the temples, villages and mountains – you'll probably spend 40–60 minutes aloft. Compare quotes from Magic Horizon Balloons (Sharia Khalid Ibn Walid, below *Sinouhe* disco; ☎095/227-4060 or 012 226-1697, ⓦwww.magichorizon.com), Hod Hod Soliman (Television St; ☎095/227-1116, ⓔhodhodoffice@yahoo.co.uk), Sky Cruise (Sharia Khalid Ibn Walid; ☎095/236-0407), Viking Air (Sharia Saleh el-Din; ☎095/238-0988) and Alaska (behind Viking Air; ☎095/227-3777, ⓔbookingalaskaballoons@hotmail.com) with the discounted deals on offer at the *Happy Land* and *Bob Marley* hotels – you might pay as little as $60–70. The deal should include an early-morning transfer from your hotel to the launch site near Hatshepsut's temple. The first flights each day are timed to catch sunrise, but the second series may provide a finer view of the Necropolis in winter time, when mist often lingers over the west bank.

If you'd rather fly over Luxor, there's the Legend of the Nile **floatplane** that takes off and lands on the river – though this only operates sporadically. Phone their office (☎010 005-5713) at the *El-Nile Restaurant* near Karnak Temple for details.

Books Gaddis, outside the *Pavilion Winter Hotel*, is the finest bookshop in Upper Egypt, with heaps of Egyptology, repro prints, guidebooks and novels (Mon–Sat 9am–10pm, Sun 10.30am–10pm ⓣ095/238-7042). Aboudi Bookshop, nearby beside Sharia el-Karnak, also has a decent selection of books, magazines and newspapers (daily 8am–10pm ⓣ095/237-3390).
Dentist Dr Fawzi Henri, opposite the post office on Sharia al-Mahatta, speaks good English and comes well recommended (ⓣ010 678-0298).
Doctors Dr Hosam el-Arab's clinic on Television St (Tues, Thurs & Sun 7am–11pm, Fri 10am–3pm; ⓣ095/237-0032 or ⓣ010 694-4022, ⓔhosam_elazab@yahoo.com) will treat patients with insurance without charging upfront. Other practitioners include paediatrician Dr Bernaba El-Malah, Sharia Ramses ⓣ095 /236-9125; dermatologist Dr Selim Fakhri ⓣ095/237-2028; and urologist Dr Samy Fakhri ⓣ095/237-4964.
EgyptAir In the arcade outside the *Sofitel Winter Palace* (daily 8am–8pm; ⓣ095/238-0580 or 238-0581); at Luxor airport (ⓣ095/238-0588). See "Flights" on p.282.
Golf The ritzy Royal Valley Golf Club (ⓣ012 246-5017, ⓦwww.golfluxor.com), out near the airoprt, has an 18-hole desert course.
Gym Non-residents may use the facilities at the *Steigenberger Nile Palace* for £E200 a day.
Hospitals Luxor International, off Television St (ⓣ095/238-7194) is hardly up to European standards but is the best in Upper Egypt.
Internet Many hotels around Television Street have free internet access or wi-fi for guests; otherwise you can pay £E5–10 per hour in backstreet cyber-cafes, or £E25 per hour in a four- or five-star hotel.
Photography Digital Bazaar (daily 8am–11pm) on the Corniche can burn photos onto a CD (£E25) or print images on a T-shirt (£E45–60) Digital Image Centre and Kasanova Digital on Television St (both daily 9am–midnight) burn CDs for £E15.
Post office At the temple end of Sharia al-Mahatta (Mon–Thurs & Sun 8am–2pm), with a branch in the station (daily 8am–8pm). A reliable courier firm is Aramex (daily except Fri 8am–5pm, ⓣ095/227-3643), next door to Western Union (see below).
Spas The *Sonesta St George* offers mud baths (€50), a Turkish hammam (€45), and various types of massage (€20-50), as do the *Luxor Hilton Resort & Spa* and *Sofitel Karnak*.
Swimming pools Many hotels allow non-residents to use theirs for a fee – from the smallish pools at the *New Pola* (£E25), *Emilio* (£E30), *Philippe* (£E40) and *Mercure Luxor* (£E50) to the full-sized affair at the *Steigenberger Nile Palace* (£E100).
Thomas Cook Outside the *Sofitel Winter Palace*. Changes currency, sells travellers' cheques, does tours and reservations (daily 8am–8pm; ⓣ095/237-2402, ⓔtcluxor@thomascook.com.eg).
Visa extensions The passport office is on Sharia Khalid Ibn Walid (Mon–Thurs & Sat 8am–2pm; ⓣ095/238-0885). Visa extensions require one photo plus a photocopy of your passport.
Western Union Television St (daily 8.30am–10pm, Fri 3–10pm; ⓣ095/227-1187).

Excursions from Luxor - and moving on

With Karnak Temple and the Theban Necropolis in the immediate vicinity, it'll be a while before you start considering **excursions** to other sites in the Nile Valley – the **temples of Esna, Edfu** and **Kom Ombo** along the way to Aswan, or **Abydos** and **Dendara** to the north of Luxor – any of which makes a feasible day-trip. Foreigners travelling by road can now move freely from 6am–6pm rather than having to travel all together at set times, but as most excursions start at 8am people still refer to the ensuing caravans of vehicles as "convoys", and the cost of excursions now includes an obligatory "licence" from the government (costing £E50–100 per vehicle).

Many hotels offer **taxi or minibus excursions**, the cost split between passengers – the more involved, the less each one pays. Edfu and Kom Ombo cost from £E250–300 for one person, down to as little as £E85 each if ten people share a minibus; prices for Dendara and Abydos range from £E250–300 for a solo trip to £E50–85 a head for six to ten people (excluding tickets for the temples). Compare quotes from *Bob Marley House*, *Happy Land,* the *Oasis*, *Nubian Oasis*, *Nefertiti* and *Fontana* hotels. **Day cruises** to Dendara on the *Lotus Boat* or *Tiba Star* (Tues, Fri & Sun) involve five hours on the river (with lunch) and an hour at the temple: tickets are sold by the *Iberotel* (£E425), American Express ($85) and other travel agents, inclusive of admission charges and lunch.

With the road to **Kharga Oasis** open until 4pm daily, a few operators offer **small-group safaris** into the Western Desert (see p.396). The cost per person depends on the size of the group, and includes meals and camping gear. Ala el-Din at the *Nefertiti Hotel* (Ⓣ010 601-6132, Ⓔtours@nefertitihotel.com) in Luxor and Hamada El-Khalifa at the *Nile Valley Hotel* (Ⓣ012 796-4473, Ⓦwww.nile-valley.nl) on the west bank stick to the four oases on the "Great Desert Circuit", while Abu El Naga Gabriel (Ⓣ010 124-0080, Ⓦwww.egypt-westerndesert.net) and Azab Safari (Ⓣ012 385-0227, Ⓦwww.azabdesertsafari.com) also offer more ambitious trips to the Great Sand Sea or the Gilf Kebir. Otherwise, you should be able to hire a **taxi** to drive to Kharga for £E350–500 – ask Tayeb Umran (Ⓣ012 4166-4821) for a quote.

Air-conditioned cars are a faster alternative to buses to **Hurghada**, with costs also shared between passengers – expect to pay £E275–300 for a car through *Happy Land*, *Bob Marley House* and other backpackers' hotels. To reach **Aswan**, you'll find it faster and cheaper (£E45) to travel by minibus with Ali (Ⓣ012 106-5771) on his afternoon return trip from Luxor.

Buses

Luxor's **bus station** (Ⓣ095/232-3218 or 237–2118) is 5km outside town near the airport, but you can buy tickets for some services – and board them – near the train station downtown. The 8pm Superjet to **Hurghada** (£E35) and **Cairo** (£E100) only leaves from outside their office (Ⓣ095/236-7732) there, whereas Upper Egypt Bus Co. services to Cairo (6.30pm; £E100), **Dahab** (4.30pm; £E130), **Sharm el-Sheikh** (4.30pm; £E120) and **Port Said** (6.30pm; £E75) collect passengers outside their own station office 30 minutes before they depart from the bus terminal. For all other buses to **Qena** (5 daily; £E5), **Port Safaga** (3 daily; £E25–30), **Suez** (5 daily; £E60–70), **Edfu** (2 daily; £E5) and **Aswan** (2 daily; £E20), you can only buy tickets and board at the bus station. To avoid the hassle of two trips out there, buy tickets through *Happy Land Hotel*, which doesn't take any commission and can arrange a **transfer** to the bus station for £E30.

Trains

Staff at Luxor station will try to restrict foreigners to the most expensive trains to **Cairo** (12–14hr): #85 (departing at 10.15pm; £E165) and the Abela sleeper-services ($80/€62 for a single cabin, $60/€47 to share; payment in dollars or euros only) – often claiming that no other tickets are available. You can, in fact, board any first- or second-class train and buy a ticket from the conductor (paying £E6 surcharge); all trains to Cairo depart from platform 1. The same applies to trains to **Aswan** (3hr), which routinely arrive 1–3 hours late at Luxor; ask your hotel to phone (Ⓣ095/237-2018) to check when one is due to arrive at platform 2. Seat reservations are only mandatory on the Abela sleepers.

Flights

Luxor Airport (Ⓣ095/237-4655) is 6km southeast of town (£E30–40 by taxi). The latest domestic schedules and fares can be obtained from **EgyptAir** (daily 8am–8pm; Ⓣ095/238-0580) near the *Sofitel Winter Palace*. Destinations include **Cairo** (daily), **Aswan** (daily), **Sharm el-Sheikh** (Tues–Sat), **London** (Mon), **Paris** (Sat) and **Brussels** (Sun). There may also be vacant seats on **charter flights** to Europe. Ask reps at the airport and big hotels, or travel agencies in Luxor. Travellers who overstay the four-week limit on charter return tickets may not get past check-in at the airport.

Karnak

The temple complex of **Karnak** beats every other pharaonic monument bar the Pyramids of Giza. Built on a leviathan scale to house the gods, it comprises three separate temple enclosures, the grandest being the **Precinct of Amun**, dedicated to the supreme god of the New Kingdom – a structure large enough to accommodate ten great cathedrals.

Karnak's magnitude and complexity is due to 1300 years of aggrandizement. From its XII Dynasty core, Amun's temple expanded along two axes – west towards the river and south towards the **Temple of Mut** – while its enclosure wall approached the **Temple of Mont**. Though Pharaoh Akhenaten abjured Amun, defaced his images and erected an Aten Temple at Karnak, the status quo ante was soon restored at the behest of Amun's priesthood.

At the zenith of its supremacy Karnak's wealth was staggering. A list of its assets during the reign of Ramses III includes 65 villages, 433 gardens, 421,662 head of cattle, 2395 square kilometres of fields, 46 building sites, 83 ships, and 81,322 workers and slaves. Yet ordinary folk were barred from its precincts and none but the pharaoh or his representative could enter Amun's sanctuary. The whole area was known to the Ancient Egyptians as Ipet-Isut, meaning the most perfect or esteemed of places.

Practicalities

The **site** of Karnak covers nearly 3 square kilometres, 2.5km north of central Luxor. The only part that's readily accessible is the Precinct of Amun (daily: summer 6am–6pm; winter 6am–5pm; £E65), which hosts nightly Sound and Light shows. This alone requires two hours to look round; with little shade, make sure you wear a hat and bring water. Usually the temple is busy with tour groups from 10am to late afternoon, so come early to beat the crowds. An overpriced café by the Sacred Lake sells tea and soft drinks, and toilets can be found near the grandstand and the open-air museum. A separate ticket (£E25) for the open-air museum is sold at the main ticket office.

There are two **approaches** from town: via the Corniche, which turns inland further north, or along Sharia el-Karnak, roughly following the **Avenue of Sphinxes** that once connected Luxor and Karnak temples, past the towering **Gateway of Euergetes II** and the precinct's **enclosure wall**. You could cycle along the Corniche, but it's best to conserve your energy for the site. The cheapest way there (and back) is by local **minibus** (50pt per person): services returning to Luxor follow the road nearest the river. After haggling, you should be able to pay £E10–15 by **taxi** or £E15–20 by **calèche**; if you want your driver for the **return** trip (£E30 including 2hr waiting time), be sure to remember their licence number.

Expect to pay slightly more for rides to the **Sound and Light Show** (£E100; under sixes free; sold near the Karnak ticket office). Many find the show a letdown – the commentary is bombastic and the lights half-hearted – but in any case, spectators should come armed with mosquito repellent and a torch to light their footsteps. There are three shows each night, at least one of them in English; schedules are posted in the tourist office and less reliably on Ⓦwww.soundandlight.com.eg. Go for the later ones to avoid an aural conflict with local muezzins around sunset.

Approaching Karnak via the Corniche, you'll be steered by police through a coach park to a **visitors' centre** (free), featuring photos showing Karnak's former ruination, an antique train used to haul masonry during its reconstruction, and scale models of the temple and its modern-day surroundings – without mentioning that local residents rioted in protest against the demolition of their homes to create the parking lots, malls and marbled plaza that stretch as far as Sharia Hilton.

The Temple of Amun

The great **Temple of Amun** seemingly recedes towards infinity in an overwhelming succession of pylons, courts and columned halls, obelisks and colossi, spanning some thirteen centuries of ancient history. Half-buried in silt for as long again, the ruins were subsequently squatted by *fellaheen*, before being cleared by archeologists in the mid-nineteenth century. Ever since then, the temple has been undergoing slow but systematic restoration, epigraphic study and (in some places) excavation.

Since map-boards were installed it's become easier to grasp the temple's convoluted layout; the ruins get denser and more jumbled the further in you go. To simplify **orientation**, we've assumed that the temple's alignment towards the Nile corresponds with the cardinal points, so that its main axis runs east–west, and the subsidiary axis north–south.

It's worth following the main axis all the way back to the **Festival Hall**, and at least seeing the **Cachette Court** of the other wing. A break for refreshments by the lake is advisable if your itinerary includes the **open-air museum** or the **Temple of Khonsu**, off the main circuit.

Entering the temple

Walking towards the Precinct of Amun from the ticket office, and crossing over a dry moat, you'll pass the remains of an **ancient dock**, from where Amun sailed for Luxor Temple during the Optet festival. Before being loaded aboard a full-size boat, his sacred barque rested in the small **chapel** to the right, which was erected (and graffitied by mercenaries) during the brief XXIX Dynasty. Beyond lies a short **Processional Way** flanked by ram-headed sphinxes (after Amun's sacred animal) enfolding statues of Ramses II, which once joined the main avenue linking the two temples.

Ahead of this rises the gigantic **First Pylon**, whose yawning gateway exposes a vista of receding portals, dwarfing all who walk between them. The 43-metre-high towers, composed of regular courses of sandstone masonry, are often attributed to the Nubian and Ethiopian kings of the XXV Dynasty, but may have been erected as late as the XXX Dynasty (when Nectanebo I added the enclosure wall). Although the northern tower is unfinished and neither is decorated, their 130-metre width makes this the largest pylon in Egypt.

The **Forecourt** is another late addition, enclosing three earlier structures. In the centre stands a single papyriform pillar from the **Kiosk of Taharqa** (an Ethiopian king of the XXV Dynasty), thought to have been a roofless pavilion where Amun's effigy was placed for its revivifying union with the sun at New Year. Off to the left stands the so-called **Shrine of Seti II**, actually a way station for the sacred barques of Amun, Mut and Khonsu, built of grey sandstone and rose granite.

The Temple of Ramses III to the Second Pylon

The first really impressive structure in the precinct is the columned **Temple of Ramses III**, which also held the Theban Triad barques during processions. Beyond its pylon, flanked by two colossi, is a festival hall with mummiform pillar statues, behind which are carvings of the annual festival of Amun-Min.

Though the pink granite **Colossus of Ramses II** beside the vestibule to the Second Pylon **[a]** is an immediate attention-grabber, it's worth detouring round the side of his temple to pass through the **Bubastite Portal**, named after the XXII Dynasty that hailed from Bubastis in the Delta. En route you'll pass a fish-shaped aperture in the Second Pylon, where in 1820 Henri Crevier uncovered a host of

Amun and the Theban Triad

Originally merely one of the deities in the Hermopolitan Ogdoad (see p.229), **Amun** gained ascendancy at Thebes shortly before the Middle Kingdom, presumably because his cult was adopted by powerful local rulers during the First Intermediate Period. After the expulsion of the Hyksos (c.1567 BC), the rulers of the XVIII Dynasty elevated Amun to a victorious national god, and set about making Karnak his principal cult centre in Egypt.

As the "Unseen One" (whose name in hieroglyphic script was accompanied by a blank space instead of the usual explicatory sign), Amun assimilated other deities into such incarnations as **Amun-Re** (the supreme Creator), **Amun-Min** (the "bull which serves the cows" with a perpetual erection) or ram-headed **Auf-Re** ("Re made Flesh"), who sailed through the underworld revitalizing the souls of the dead, emerging reborn as Khepri. However, Amun most commonly appears as a human wearing ram's horns and the twin-feathered *atef* crown.

His consort, **Mut**, was a local goddess in Predynastic times, who became linked with Nekhbet, the vulture protectress of Upper Egypt. Early in the XVIII Dynasty she was "married" to Amun, assimilated his previous consort Amunet and became Mistress of Heaven. She is customarily depicted wearing a vulture head-dress and *uraeus* and the Combined Crown of the Two Lands.

Amun and Mut's son **Khonsu**, "the Traveller", crossed the night sky as the moon-god, issued prophecies and assisted Thoth, the divine scribe. He was portrayed either with a hawk's head, or as a young boy with the sidelock of youth.

Karnak was the largest of several temples consecrated to this **Theban Triad** of deities.

▲ Amun

▲ Mut

▲ Khonsu

statues and blocks from the demolished Aten Temple (including the colossi of Akhenaten in the Luxor and Cairo museums), which Horemheb used as in-fill for his pylon.

Pass through the Portal and turn left to find the **Shoshenk relief**, commemorating the triumphs of the XXII Dynasty Pharaoh Shoshenk. Traditionally, scholars have identified him as the biblical Shishak (I Kings 14:25–26) who plundered Jerusalem in 925 BC, thus establishing a crucial link between the chronologies of Ancient Egypt and the Old Testament – an orthodoxy challenged by David Rohl's book, *A Test of Time* (see p.600). Although Shoshenk's figure is almost invisible, you can still see Amun, presiding over the slaughter of Rheoboamite prisoners in Palestine **[b]**. The scenes further along the wall are best seen after visiting the Great Hypostyle Hall.

To reach this, return to the forecourt and pass through the **Second Pylon**, one of several jerry-built structures begun by Horemheb, the last king of the XVIII Dynasty. The cartouches of Seti I (who completed the pylon) and Ramses I and II (Seti's father and son) appear just inside the doorway.

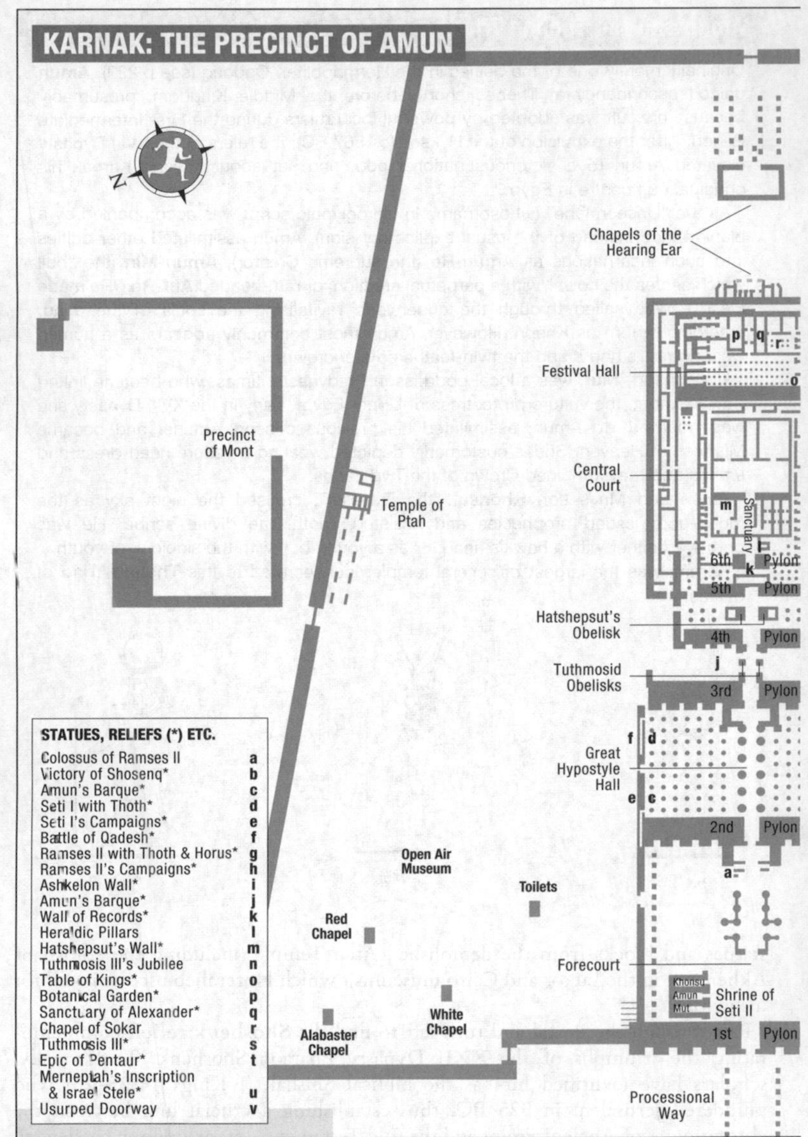

The Great Hypostyle Hall

The **Great Hypostyle Hall** is Karnak's glory, a forest of titanic columns covering an area of 6000 square metres – large enough to contain both St Peter's Cathedral in Rome and St Paul's Cathedral in London. Its grandeur is best appreciated early in the morning or late in the afternoon, when diagonal shadows enhance the effect of the columns. In pharaonic times the hall was roofed with sandstone slabs, its gloom interspersed by sunbeams falling through windows above the central aisle.

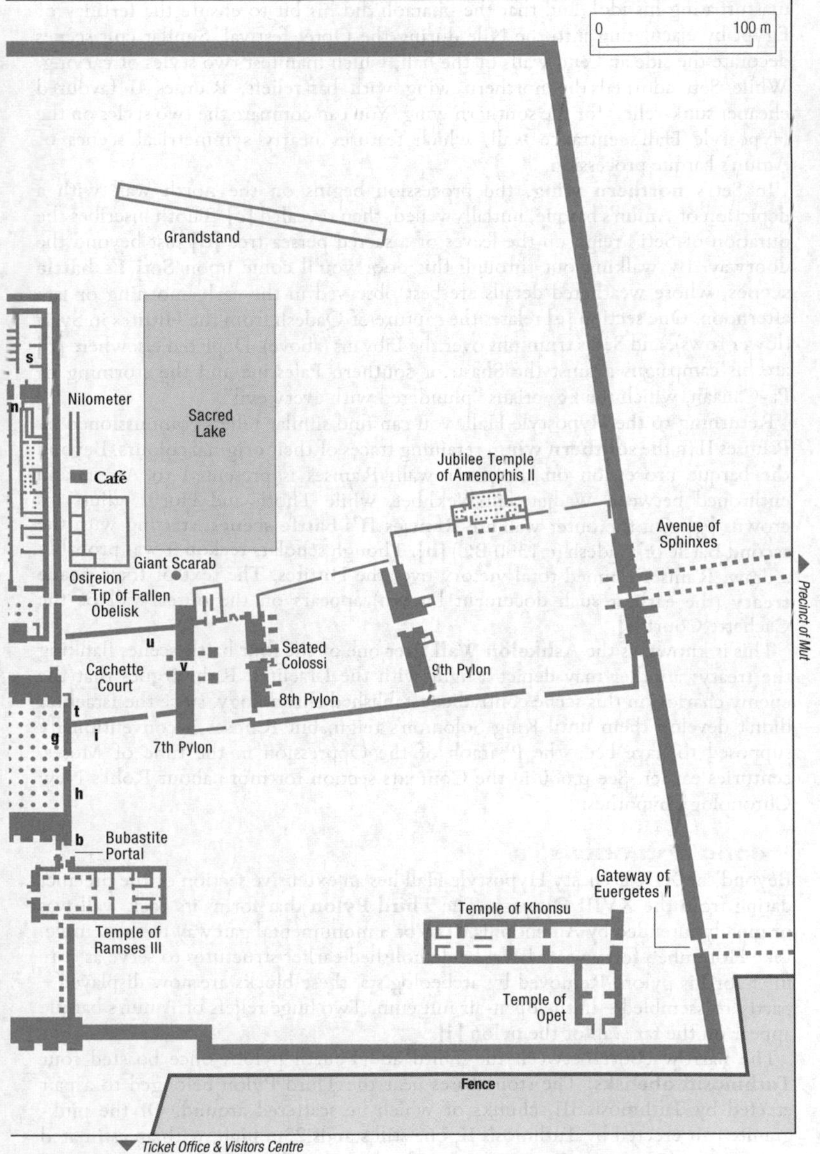

The hall probably began as a processional avenue of twelve or fourteen **columns**, each 23m high and 15m round (requiring six people with outstretched arms to encircle their girth). To this, Seti I and Ramses II added 122 smaller columns in two flanking wings, plus walls and a roof. All the columns consist of semi-drums, fitted together without mortar. Their **carvings** show the king making offerings to Theban deities, most notably Amun, who frequently appears in a sexually aroused state. Some Egyptologists believe that the temple priestesses kept Amun happy by masturbating his idol, and that the pharaoh did his bit to ensure the fertility of Egypt by ejaculating into the Nile during the Optet festival. Similar cult scenes decorate the side and end walls of the hall, which manifest two styles of carving. While Seti adorned the northern wing with bas-reliefs, Ramses II favoured cheaper sunk-reliefs for the southern wing. You can compare the two styles on the Hypostyle Hall's entrance wall, which features nearly symmetrical scenes of Amun's barque procession.

In Seti's **northern wing**, the procession begins on the north wall with a depiction of Amun's barque, initially veiled, then revealed **[c]**. Thoth inscribes the duration of Seti's reign on the leaves of a sacred persea tree **[d]** just beyond the doorway. By walking out through this door you'll come upon **Seti I's battle scenes**, whose weathered details are best observed in the early morning or late afternoon. One section **[e]** relates the capture of Qadesh from the Hittites in Syria (lower rows), and Seti's triumphs over the Libyans (above). Depicted elsewhere **[f]** are his campaigns against the Shasu of southern Palestine and the storming of Pa-Canaan, which the Egyptians "plundered with every evil".

Returning to the Hypostyle Hall, you can find similar reliefs commissioned by Ramses II in the **southern wing**, retaining traces of their original colours. Beyond the barque procession on the inner wall, Ramses is presented to Amun and enthroned between Wadjet and Nekhbet, while Thoth and Horus adjust his crowns **[g]**. On the outer wall are **Ramses II's battle scenes**, starting with the second Battle of Qadesh (c.1300 BC) **[h]**. Though scholars reckon it was probably a draw, Ramses claimed total victory over the Hittites. The text of their **peace treaty** (the earliest such document known) appears on the outer wall of the Cachette Court **[i]**.

This is known as the **Ashkelon Wall** after one of the four battle scenes flanking the treaty; another may depict a fight with the Israelites. Rohl argues that the enemy chariots in this scene contradict established chronology, since the Israelites didn't develop them until King Solomon's reign, but Ramses is conventionally supposed to have been the Pharaoh of the Oppression in the time of Moses, centuries earlier. See p.600 in the Contexts section for more about Rohl's New Chronology hypothesis.

Pylons and obelisks

Beyond the XIX Dynasty Hypostyle Hall lies an extensive section of the precinct dating from the XVIII Dynasty. The **Third Pylon** that forms its back wall was originally intended by Amenophis III to be a monumental gateway to the temple. Like Horemheb forty years later, he demolished earlier structures to serve as core filler for his pylon. Removed by archeologists, these blocks are now displayed – partly reassembled – in the open-air museum. Two huge reliefs of Amun's barque appear on the far wall of the pylon **[j]**.

The narrow court between the Third and Fourth pylons once boasted four **Tuthmosid obelisks**. The stone bases near the Third Pylon belonged to a pair erected by Tuthmosis III, chunks of which lie scattered around. Of the pink-granite pair erected by Tuthmosis II, one still stands 23m high, with an estimated weight of 143 tonnes. Once tipped with glittering electrum, the finely carved obelisk was later appropriated by Ramses IV and VI, who added their own cartouches.

At this stage it's best to carry on through the **Fourth Pylon** rather than get sidetracked into the Cachette Court on the temple's secondary axis. Beyond the pylon are numerous columns which probably formed another hypostyle hall, dominated by the rose-granite **Obelisk of Hatshepsut**, the only woman to rule as pharaoh. To mark her sixteenth regnal year, Hatshepsut had two obelisks quarried in Aswan and erected at Karnak, a task completed in seven months. The standing obelisk is more than 27m high and weighs 320 tons, with a dedicatory inscription running its full height. Its fallen mate has broken into sections, now dispersed around the temple.

The fallen obelisk's carved **tip** can be examined near the Osireion and Sacred Lake. On the way there, you'll pass a granite bas-relief of Amenophis II target-shooting from a moving chariot, protruding from the **Fifth Pylon**. Built of limestone, this pylon is attributed to Hatshepsut's father, Tuthmosis I.

Though the **Sixth Pylon** has largely disappeared, a portion either side of the granite doorway remains. Its outer face is known as the *Wall of Records* **[k]** after its list of peoples conquered by Tuthmosis III: Nubians to the right, Asiatics to the left. Beyond the latter is a text extolling the king's victory at Megiddo (Armageddon) in 1479 BC. By organizing tribute from his vanquished foes rather than simply destroying them, Tuthmosis III was arguably the world's first imperialist.

Around the Sanctuary

The section beyond the Sixth Pylon gets increasingly confusing, but a few features are unmistakable. Ahead stand a pair of square-sectioned **heraldic pillars**, their fronts carved with the lotus and papyrus of the Two Lands, their sides showing Amun embracing Tuthmosis III **[l]**. On the left are two **Colossi of Amun and Amunet**, dedicated by Tutankhamun (whose likeness appears with them) when orthodoxy was re-established after the Amarna Period. There's also a seated **statue of Amenophis II**.

Next comes a granite **Sanctuary** built by Philip Arrhidaeus, the cretinous half-brother of Alexander the Great, on the site of a Tuthmosid-era shrine which similarly held Amun's barque. The interior bas-reliefs show Philip making offerings to Amun in his various aspects, topped by a star-spangled ceiling.

Around to the left of the Sanctuary and further back is a wall inscribed with Tuthmosis III's victories, which he built to hide a wall of reliefs by Queen Hatshepsut, now removed to another room **[m]**. **Hatshepsut's Wall** has reopened after lengthy restoration, as has the facing portion, where Tuthmosis replaced her image by offerings tables or bouquets, and substituted his father's and grandfather's names for her cartouches.

Beyond here lies an open space or **Central Court**, thought to mark the site of the original temple of Amun built in the XII Dynasty, whose weathered alabaster foundations poke from the pebbly ground.

The Jubilee Temple of Tuthmosis III

At the rear of this court rises the **Jubilee Temple of Tuthmosis III**, a personal cult shrine in Amun's back yard. As at Saqqara during the Old Kingdom, the Theban kings periodically renewed their temporal and spiritual authority with jubilee festivals. The original entrance **[n]** is flanked by reliefs and broken statues of Tuthmosis in *hed-seb* regalia. A left turn brings you into the **Festival Hall**, with its unusual tentpole-style columns, their capitals adorned with blue-and-yellow chevrons. During Christian times the hall was used as a church, hence the haloed saints on some of the pillars.

A chamber off the southwest corner **[o]** contains an eroded replica of the **Table of Kings** (the original is in the Louvre), depicting Tuthmosis making offerings to previous rulers – Hatshepsut is naturally omitted from the roll call. The so-called **Botanical Garden** is a roofless enclosure containing painted reliefs of plants and animals which Tuthmosis encountered on his campaigns in Syria **[p]**. Across the way is a roofed chamber decorated by Alexander the Great, who appears before

Amun and other deities **[q]**. The **Chapel of Sokar** constitutes a miniature temple to the Memphite god of darkness **[r]**, juxtaposed against a (now inaccessible) shrine to the sun. A further suite of rooms is dedicated to Tuthmosis **[s]**.

Chapels of the Hearing Ear

Excluded from Amun's Precinct and lacking a direct line to the Theban Triad, the inhabitants of Thebes used intermediary deities to transmit their petitions. These lesser deities rated their own shrines, known as **Chapels of the Hearing Ear** (sometimes actually decorated with carved ears), which straddled the temple's enclosure wall, presenting one face to the outside world. At Karnak, however, they became steadily less approachable and were finally surrounded by the present enclosure wall.

Directly behind the Jubilee Temple is a series of chapels built by Tuthmosis III, centred upon a large alabaster statue of the king and Amun. Further east lie the ruined halls and colonnades of a Temple of the Hearing Ear built by Ramses II. Behind this stands the pedestal of the tallest obelisk known (31m), which Emperor Constantine had shipped to Rome and erected in the Circus Maximus; it was later moved to Lateran Square, hence its name, the **Lateran Obelisk**. As the ancient Egyptians rarely erected single obelisks, it was probably intended to be accompanied by the Unfinished Obelisk that lies in a quarry outside Aswan, abandoned after the discovery of flaws in the rock.

Around the Sacred Lake

A short walk from Hatshepsut's Obelisk or the Cachette Court brings you to Karnak's **Sacred Lake**, which looks about as holy as a municipal boating pond, with the grandstand for the Sound and Light Show at the far end. The main attraction is a shady (and very pricey) **café** where you can take a break from touring the complex and imagine the scene in ancient times. At sunrise, Amun's priests would take a sacred goose from the fowl-yards which now lie beneath the mound to the south of the lake, and set it free on the waters. As at Hermopolis, the goose or Great Cackler was credited with laying a cosmic egg at the dawn of Creation; but at Karnak the Great Cackler was identified with Amun rather than Thoth. During the Late Period, Pharaoh Taharqa added a subterranean **Osireion**, linking the resurrection of Osiris with that of the sun. The **giant scarab beetle** nearby represents Khepri, the reborn sun at dawn.

The north–south axis

The temple's **north–south axis** is sparser and less variegated than the main section, so if time is limited there's little reason to go beyond the Seventh Pylon. The Gate of Ramses IX, at the southern end of the court between the Third and Fourth pylons, gives access to this wing of the temple, which starts with the Cachette Court.

The **Cachette Court** gets its title from the discovery of a buried hoard of statues early in the twentieth century. Nearly 17,000 bronze statues and votive tablets, and 800 figures in stone, seem to have been cached in a "clearance" of sacred knick-knacks during Ptolemaic times. The finest statues (dating from the Old Kingdom to the Late Period) are now in the Luxor and Cairo museums. The court's northwest corner incorporates a mass of hieroglyphics known as the *Epic of Pentaur* **[t]**, which recaps the battles of Ramses II depicted on the outside of the Great Hypostyle Hall. Diagonally across the court are an eighty-line inscription by Merneptah and a copy of the **Israel Stele [u]** that's in Cairo, which contains among a list of conquests the only known pharaonic reference to Israel: "Israel is crushed, it has no more seed". Rohl argues that the stele has been misread and

Sekhmet

Sekhmet – "the Powerful" – was the violent counterpart of the Delta goddess Bastet (see p.497). As the daughter of Re, she personified the sun's destructive force, making her a worthy consort for Ptah, the Memphite creator-god. In one myth, Re feared that humanity was plotting against him and unleashed his avenging Eye in the form of Sekhmet, who would have massacred all life had not Re relented and slaked her thirst with red beer, which the drunken goddess mistook for blood.

With the rise of Thebes and Amun's association with Ptah, a corresponding relationship was made between their consorts, Mut and Sekhmet. The New Kingdom pharaohs adopted Sekhmet as a symbol of their indomitable prowess in battle: the statues of the goddess at Karnak bear inscriptions such as "smiter of the Nubians". As "Lady of the Messengers of Death", Sekhmet could send – or prevent – plagues, so her priestesses also served as healers and veterinarians.

▲ Sekhmet

really relates the achievements of Merneptah's father and grandfather, Ramses II and Seti I.

More proof of the complexities of Egyptology is provided by the **Seventh Pylon**, which was built by Tuthmosis III, but decorated and usurped during the XIX Dynasty, a century or so later, when the cartouches on its door jambs **[v]** were altered to proclaim false ownership. It is fronted by seven statues of Middle Kingdom pharaohs, salvaged from pylon cores. On the far side are the lower portions of two **Colossi of Tuthmosis III**.

The open-air museum

The northern sector of Amun's Precinct contains an **open-air museum**, for which a separate ticket (£E25) must be bought before entering Karnak. Its prime attractions are two early barque shrines, reassembled from blocks found inside the Third Pylon. From the XII Dynasty comes a lovely **White Chapel**, carved all over with bas-reliefs. While most depict Djed columns, ankhs and other symbols, it's the scenes of Senusret I embracing a priapic Amun-Min that you remember. The plainer **Alabaster Chapel** of Amenophis I contains more innocuous scenes of the pharaoh making offerings to Amun and his barque. Along the way you'll pass rows of blocks from Hatshepsut's **Red Chapel**, which archeologists have been unable to reconstruct since each block features a self-contained design rather than a segment of a large relief. This hasn't deterred Egyptologists from trying the same feat with the **Shrine of Tuthmosis III**, with more success. You'll also notice some granite **statues of Sekhmet**, taken from a small **Temple of Ptah** alongside Karnak's enclosure wall, whose ruins aren't much reward for a three-hundred-metre trek across broken ground, though the finest statues of Sekhmet are now in the Luxor Museum.

The Theban Necropolis

Across the Nile from Luxor, the **Theban Necropolis** testifies to the same obsession with death and resurrection that produced the Pyramids. Mindful of how these had failed to protect the mummies of the Old Kingdom pharaohs, later rulers opted for concealment, sinking their tombs in the arid Theban Hills while perpetuating their memory with gigantic mortuary temples on the plain below.

The Necropolis straddled the border between the lands of the living and the dead, verdant flood plain giving way to boundless desert, echoing the path of the dead "going west" to meet Osiris as the sun set over the mountains and descended into the underworld.

Though stripped of its treasures over millennia, the Necropolis retains a peerless array of funerary monuments. The grandest of its tombs are in the **Valley of the Kings** and the **Valley of the Queens**, but there's also a wealth of vivid detail in the smaller **Tombs of the Nobles**. Equally amazing are the mortuary temples which enshrined the deceased pharaoh's cult: among these, **Deir el-Bahri** is timelessly magnificent and **Medinet Habu** rivals Karnak for grandeur, while the shattered **Ramesseum** and **Colossi of Memnon** mock the pretensions of their founders. On a humbler level, but still executed with great artistry, are the funerary monuments of the craftsmen who built the royal tombs, and the ruins of their homes at **Deir el-Medina**.

Visiting the Necropolis

Spread across wadis and hills beyond the edge of the cultivated plain, the Theban Necropolis is too diffuse and complex to take in on a single visit. Even limiting yourself to the Valley of the Kings, Deir el-Bahri and one or other of the major sites, you're likely to feel overwhelmed by the end of the day. Most people favour a series of visits, taking into account the climate and crowds – both major factors in the enjoyment of a trip. In **winter**, mornings are pleasantly hot, afternoons baking but bearable, and most coach tours are scheduled accordingly, making the principal sites crowded between 9am and 2pm. As lots of people come early "to beat the crowds", the royal tombs are actually emptiest in the late afternoon. In **summer**, it's simply too hot throughout the afternoon, and you should get here as early as possible.

The **opening hours** of the sites may change with the season and security restrictions, but are generally from 7am to 5pm daily, except for the Valley of the Kings, which opens at 6am year round, and closes at 4pm in the winter. Making a full tour of the Necropolis is expensive – although a **student card** entitles you to a fifty percent discount. If you wanted to see all the sites in the Necropolis, you'd end up spending around $120/€80 on tickets at the full rate; most people are satisfied to see far less than that.

Guided tours, typically featuring the Colossi of Memnon, the valleys of the Kings and Queens and Deir el-Bahri, are bookable through any hotel or travel agency. Thomas Cook or Karnak Travel charge €30–40 per person (including tickets) for an air-conditioned coach tour, while budget hotels ask £E210–250 per person (students £E140–200) to share a minibus or taxi (including tickets and a guide). Even if you like the idea of a tour, don't sign up for the first one offered – at least, not without an idea of what's available elsewhere and the scope for **independent travel** (see p.293). If you want to hire a personal **guide**, Mahmoud Abd Allah alias "Mr Sunshine" (Ⓣ012 215-7145, Ⓔsunshineluxor@mailcity.com) is a master Egyptologist with forty years' experience, who charges only £E100 for his services (excluding transport and tickets).

Useful **things to bring** include a torch, plenty of water and small change. If you're planning to cycle or donkey it, a hat and double rations of water are vital. A snack, too, is a good idea, as the choice of food and drink is limited, and prices are higher than in Luxor.

Photography is now prohibited in the tombs to protect their fragile murals, which are widely reproduced in print and on the Theban Mapping Project website (Ⓦwww.kv5.com) anyway. Dusk and early morning are the best times to capture the landscape and temples of the west bank.

Crossing the Nile

There are several ways of crossing **from Luxor** to the west bank. Since the opening of **Luxor Bridge**, 7km south of town at Bogdadi, all coaches, minibuses and taxis from Luxor use this circuitous route, which can take an hour if traffic is heavy. Some operators get round this by sending the vehicle on ahead, to meet passengers taken across the Nile by motorboat – and crossing by boat remains by far the most pleasant option.

Local ferries done up like pharaonic barges sail frequently during daytime, hourly after 6pm and sporadically after midnight from the landing stage on the Corniche signposted "National Ferryboat", to dock near **Gezira village** on the west bank. Locals pay 25pt for the ride, tourists £E1. Alternatively, dozens of **motorboats** and **feluccas** inveigle for custom by the water's edge, charging £E5 per boatload (£E10 for more than six passengers) after a brief haggle. Motorboats (called "lunches" in English or *zobak* in Arabic) are the fastest way to cross the river and may land or leave from anywhere along either riverbank, whereas crossing the Nile by **felucca** is more of a leisurely experience than a quick journey.

You should be able to take **bicycles** for free on all these vessels. Keep **safety** in mind: overcrowded boats are a recipe for disaster, as was proved in 2001, when 35 passengers drowned after a ferry hit their motorboat in the dark. Stepping across rickety wharfs after dark is a more mundane hazard – watch out for mooring lines and gaps in the planking.

West bank transport and activities

Once across the Nile, how you choose to get around will depend on the time of year and what you plan to see, your budget and your sense of adventure. If you intend to visit the Necropolis more than once, try using various modes of transport.

It's quite feasible to explore the Necropolis **on foot**, utilizing public transport. From the taxi depot in Gezira, **pick-ups** or minibuses shuttle passengers to Old Gurna (known to drivers as Gurna Foq), bringing you within fifteen minutes' walk of Medinet Habu, the Valley of the Queens or the Ramesseum, for only 50pt per person. Many run on to Dra' Abu Naga, leaving you closer to the Tombs of the Nobles or Deir el-Bahri. Pick-ups can also be engaged **as taxis**, to whisk up to six passengers from one site to another for £E5 without paying for the driver to hang around while you explore.

Hiring a **private taxi** is the easiest way of visiting sites according to your own itinerary, but you may feel constrained about hiking over the hills between the Valley of the Kings and Deir el-Bahri (see p.314), and will pay for waiting time in any case. Taxis are usually hired for four to six hours, at £E20–30 an hour.

Short itineraries around the Necropolis

For those who like to linger over every carving, the tombs and temples on the west bank could easily fill three or four days. If you're forced to cram the highlights into **half a day**, a minimalist schedule might run: Valley of the Kings (1hr 30min), Deir el-Bahri (20min), the Tombs of the Nobles (30min–1hr), Medinet Habu (30min), and/or the Ramesseum (30min). If you have a **full day**, catch a taxi to the Valley of the Kings before 9am, spend a couple of hours there and then walk over the hills to Deir el-Bahri, arranging to be met there for another ride to Medinet Habu or Deir el-Medina and the Valley of the Queens. Alternatively, you could spend time at the Tombs of the Nobles and the Ramesseum before returning to the landing stage.

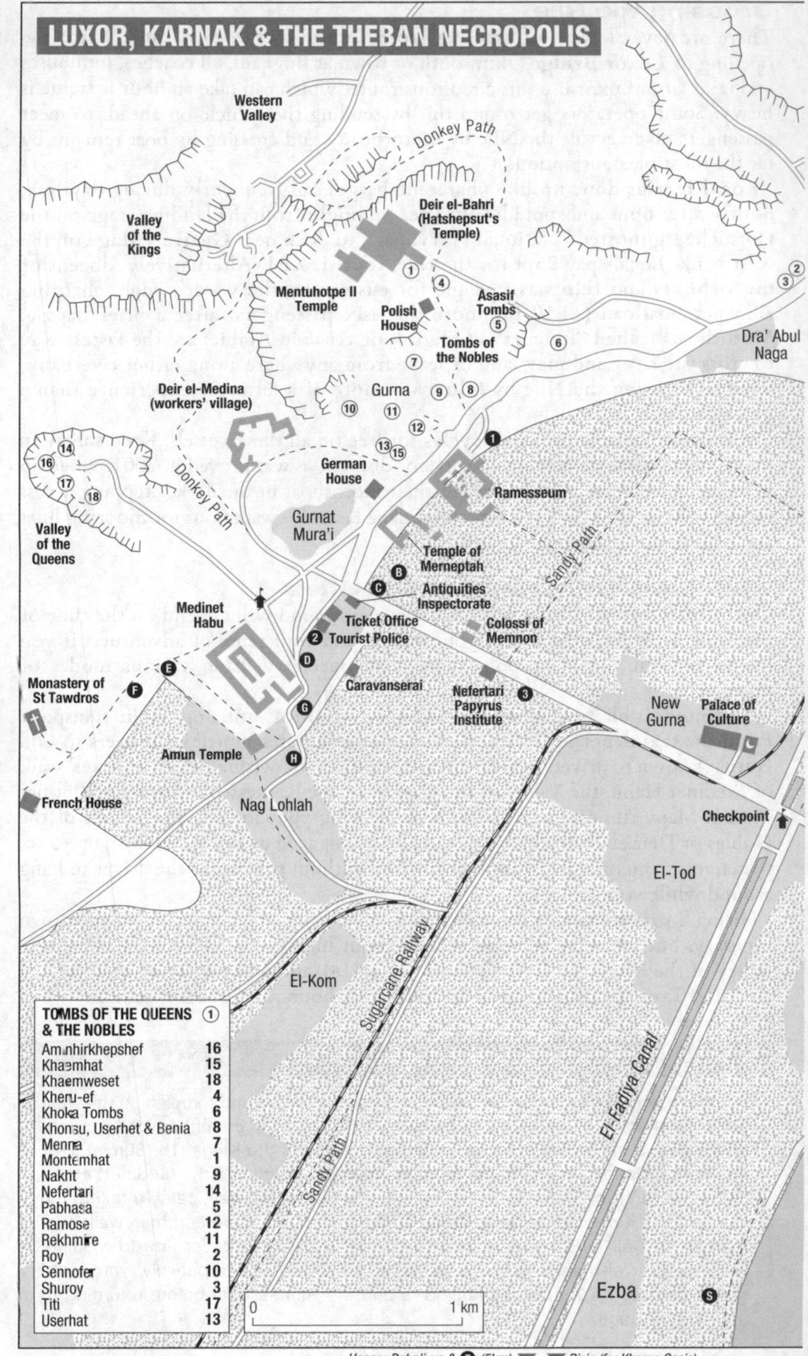
Valley of the Kings
LUXOR, KARNAK & THE THEBAN NECROPOLIS
Western Valley
Donkey Path
Valley of the Kings
Deir el-Bahri (Hatshepsut's Temple)
Mentuhotpe II Temple
Polish House
Asasif Tombs
Tombs of the Nobles
Dra' Abul Naga
Deir el-Medina (workers' village)
Gurna
German House
Ramesseum
Donkey Path
Gurnat Mura'i
Valley of the Queens
Temple of Merneptah
Antiquities Inspectorate
Sandy Path
Medinet Habu
Ticket Office
Tourist Police
Colossi of Memnon
Caravanserai
Nefertari Papyrus Institute
Monastery of St Tawdros
New Gurna
Palace of Culture
Amun Temple
French House
Nag Lohlah
Checkpoint
El-Tod
El-Kom
Sugarcane Railway
El-Fadiya Canal
Sandy Path
Ezba
0
1 km
TOMBS OF THE QUEENS & THE NOBLES
Amunhirkhepshef 16
Khaemhat 15
Khaemweset 18
Kheru-ef 4
Khoka Tombs 6
Khonsu, Userhet & Benia 8
Menna 7
Montemhat 1
Nakht 9
Nefertari 14
Pabhasa 5
Ramose 12
Rekhmire 11
Roy 2
Sennofer 10
Shuroy 3
Titi 17
Userhat 13
Haggar Daba'iyya & T (5km)
Riziq (for Kharga Oasis)

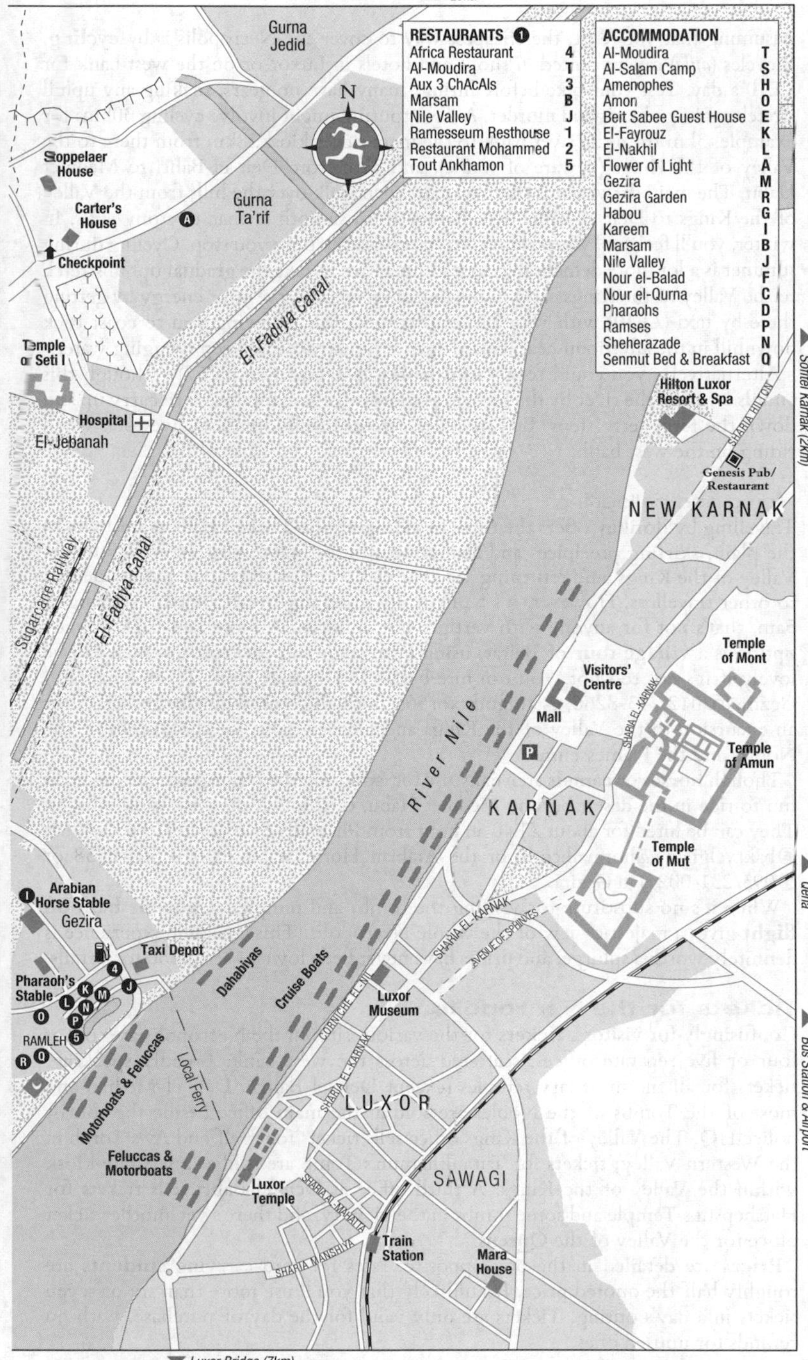

Qena
Gurna Jedid
N
RESTAURANTS 1
Africa Restaurant 4
Al-Moudira T
Aux 3 ChAcAls 3
Marsam B
Nile Valley J
Ramesseum Resthouse 1
Restaurant Mohammed 2
Tout Ankhamon 5
ACCOMMODATION
Al-Moudira T
Al-Salam Camp S
Amenophes H
Amon O
Beit Sabee Guest House E
El-Fayrouz K
El-Nakhil L
Flower of Light A
Gezira M
Gezira Garden R
Habou G
Kareem I
Marsam B
Nile Valley J
Nour el-Balad F
Nour el-Qurna C
Pharaohs D
Ramses P
Sheherazade N
Senmut Bed & Breakfast Q
Stoppelaer House
Carter's House
Gurna Ta'rif
Checkpoint
El-Fadiya Canal
Temple of Seti I
Hospital
El-Jebanah
Hilton Luxor Resort & Spa
Sharia Hilton
Genesis Pub/ Restaurant
NEW KARNAK
Sofitel Karnak (2km)
Sugarcane Railway
El-Fadiya Canal
Temple of Mont
Visitors' Centre
Mall
P
Sharia el-Karnak
Temple of Amun
River Nile
KARNAK
Temple of Mut
Qena
Arabian Horse Stable
Gezira
Sharia el-Karnak
Avenue of Sphinxes
Taxi Depot
Dahabiyas
Cruise Boats
Pharaoh's Stable
Corniche el-Nil
Luxor Museum
RAMLEH
Motorboats & Feluccas
Local Ferry
Sharia el-Karnak
LUXOR
Bus Station & Airport
Feluccas & Motorboats
Luxor Temple
Sharia al-Mahatta
SAWAGI
Train Station
Sharia Manshiya
Mara House
Luxor Bridge (7km)

Cycling and motorbiking

Assuming that you're fit, the cheapest way to cover the Necropolis is by **cycling**. Bicycles (*ajila*) can be rented in shops and hotels in Luxor or on the west bank for £E10 a day. Test your bike before hiring; many have no gears, making any uphill stretch against a headwind murder. A day's touring might involve cycling 30km: for example, 3km from the river bank to the main ticket kiosk, 8km from there to the Valley of the Kings (beware of traffic), and 3km from Deir el-Bahri to Medinet Habu. The main drawback is that you can't then walk over the hills from the Valley of the Kings to Deir el-Bahri. Roads vary from smooth tarmac to stony *pistes*. In winter, you'll feel cool when riding but start sweating once you stop. Cycling during summer is a lot more demanding, so it's imperative to take the gradual uphill stretch to the Valley of the Kings early in the morning, or conserve your energy by getting there by taxi (£E10) with your bike on its roof rack, allowing you to coast back downhill in the afternoon heat. Guard against heatstroke and keep swigging water.

Alternatively, you could rent a **motorbike** in Luxor (see p.267) – though this entails crossing the river by the bridge, as motorbikes are too heavy to carry up and down the ferry jetty steps. Be especially careful of children and livestock when riding on the west bank.

Riding and ballooning

Travelling by **donkey** offers the thrill of riding up the Theban Hills as mist cloaks the plain, skirting precipices and abandoned tombs before you descend into the Valley of the Kings, and returning via Deir el-Bahri – with fantastic views denied to other travellers. However, it's a physically gruelling five-hour trip, starting at 5am, that's not for anyone with vertigo, nor children. A more laid-back donkey option is a **village tour** of Beirat, using farm trails and backroads, which can be lovely if it's not too hot. You can hire beasts and a guide from Tayeb Khalifa in Gezira (Ⓣ012 743-8266, Ⓔkingofluxor66@hotmail.com), who charges £E35 for an excursion to the Valley of the Kings and Deir el-Bahri, or the Tombs of the Nobles and the Ramesseum.

Though **horses** or **camels** aren't any use for exploring the Necropolis, they're great fun to ride in the desert beyond Medinet Habu, or through the west bank villages. They can be hired for about £E40 an hour from Pharaoh's Stables (Ⓣ010 632-4961, Ⓔbakryelgilany@hotmail.com) or the Arabian Horse Stable (Ⓣ010 504-8558 or Ⓣ095/231-0024) in Gezira.

While it's no substitute for visiting the tombs and temples, a **hot-air balloon flight** gives a majestic view of the whole Necropolis. This amazing experience is definitely worth a splurge, and prices have never been lower – see p.280 for details.

Tickets for the Necropolis

Confusingly for visitors, **tickets** for the various sites in the Necropolis are sold at four or five separate offices, scattered across the west bank. Broadly speaking, tickets for all the mortuary temples (except Deir el-Bahri), Deir el-Medina and most of the Tombs of the Nobles are sold at the main office beside the tourist police HQ. The Valley of the Kings office sells tickets for itself and Ay's Tomb in the Western Valley; tickets for Tutankhamun's Tomb are sold at a separate kiosk within the Valley of the Kings. A third office at Deir el-Bahri sells tickets for Hatshepsut's Temple and some tombs in the vicinity, and there's yet another ticket office for the Valley of the Queens.

Prices are detailed in the box opposite; rates for card-carrying **students** are roughly half the quoted price. It's unlikely that you'll use more than six or seven tickets in a day's outing. Tickets are only valid for the day of purchase, with no refunds for unused ones.

Necropolis ticket prices

Main office

#1	Medinet Habu (Temple of Ramses III)	£E30
#2	Ramesseum	£E30
#3	Tombs of Nakht and Menna	£E25
#4	Tombs of Rekhmire and Sennofer	£E25
#5	Tombs of Ramose, Userhat and Khaemhat	£E30
#6	Deir el-Medina (any two tombs)	£E30
#7	Khokha Tombs	£E25
#8	Temple of Seti I	£E30
#9	Tombs of Khonsu, Userhet and Benia	£E15
#10	Tombs of Roy and Shuroy (Dra' Abul Naga)	£E15
#11	Tomb of Peshedu (Deir el-Medina)	£E15
#12	Temple of Merneptah	£E15

Deir el-Bahri office

Deir el-Bahri (Hatshepsut's temple)	£E30
Asasif Tombs (Kheru-ef, Ankh-hor)	£E30
Tomb of Pabhasa	£E25

Valley of the Kings office

Valley of the Kings (any three tombs except Tutankhamun and Ramses VI)	£E80
Tomb of Tutankhamun (sold inside the valley)	£E100
Tomb of Ramses VI	£E50
Tomb of Ay (Western Valley)	£E25

Valley of the Queens office

Valley of the Queens (excluding Nefertari's tomb)	£E35

West bank practicalities

You can find most things on Gezira's main street; **bicycle rental** (£E10 per day), **internet access**, and a **dry cleaners** further up the street. If you need medical treatment, go to Luxor's International Hospital rather than the **hospital** in the west bank village of El-Jebanah. There are no currency exchanges on the west bank, but most hotels will **change money** unofficially.

Generally, the **police** leave tourists alone, but the checkpoint at the El-Fadiya Canal won't allow traffic to pass up the road to the Necropolis before 6am – which spoils things for donkey-groups hoping to catch the sunrise, unless they sneak through the fields – and service taxi drivers at Gezira's depot have been told not to take foreigners beyond the west bank **security zone**, which ends at Haggar Daba'iyya (to the south) and Gurna Ta'rif (to the north).

Accommodation

Staying on the west bank, you experience far less hassle and noise than in Luxor, and some places afford superb views of Luxor Temple or the Theban Hills. Gezira is only five minutes by motorboat from Luxor Temple and on the road to the Theban Necropolis, while other west bank localities are close to a variety of tombs and temples.

Though prices are comparatively higher than in Luxor, the view or ambience more than compensates. Unless stated otherwise, all the following have rooms with private bathrooms and include breakfast in the price. There's also a **campsite** in a rural setting, to the south of Gezira. See the **map** on p.294–295 for locations, and phone ahead before crossing the Nile with your baggage. Only two hotels are okay for guests with limited mobility; *El-Nakhil* has a room for **wheelchair users**, and the *Nile Valley* has a lift to its rooftop restaurant.

Some six hundred foreigners live on the west bank, so renting and selling **apartments** is big business – especially in the Ramleh district of Gezira. Mohammed El-Qadi (ⓣ010 666-9462) owns several blocks of air-conditioned flats with nice bathrooms and simple kitchens, some sharing a rooftop with fine views, or a garden: a two-bedroom flat costs €60 a week. Other landlords include Sayed Mohammed (ⓣ010 615-2234) and Mr Osman (ⓣ012 337-1799); rates start at £E500 per week, £E2000 per month. Many others are available through Egypt Property Sales or Flats in Luxor (see p.270). Or you can find a basic *baladi* flat for about £E300 a month by asking around.

Gezira and around

Al-Salam Camp By the Nile 1600m from the ferry dock ⓣ010 682-4067, ⓦwww.alsalamcamp.com. This laid-back Dahab-style campground of circular huts with mosquito-netted sleeping platforms and tiled floors has clean washrooms, a shady yard, rock music and beer. Almost cut off by water when the Nile rises, it exists in a zonked-out world of its own. The genial owner, Ahmed, can arrange camel rides. BB ❶

Amon Gezira ⓣ010 639-4585, ⓦwww.amon-hotel-luxor.com. This quiet backstreet hotel has two blocks flanking a lush garden with a weird silk-cotton tree; the south-facing one has large cool rooms with balconies, the other block a sun terrace. Most rooms en-suite and a/c. They sell beer and wine, and use filtered water for cooking. Wi-fi (£E10/hr). BB ❸

El-Fayrouz ⓣ095/231-2709 or 012 277-0565, ⓦwww.elfayrouz.com. A salmon-pink tower of spacious rooms with fans (some are a/c) and balconies, with a gorgeous garden and a rooftop overlooking the Theban Hills. Internet access (£E7/hr), meals and alcohol. BB ❸

El-Nakhil On the edge of Gezira ⓣ095/231-3922 or 012 382-1007, ⓔoffice@el-nakhil.com. A Moorish array of a/c chalets, rooms and suites (some equipped for disabled guests), with a pretty garden and a view of fields. Gezira's most restful hotel, it's deservedly popular – beware of the surcharge over Christmas, New Year and Easter. BB ❹

Gezira ⓣ095/231-0034, ⓦwww.el-gezira.com. Down the first turning off the main street, this pleasant hotel has a/c en-suite rooms with fridges and balconies, an attractive rooftop and terrace. Guests get free use of the pool at *Gezira Garden*. Meals, beer and wine served. BB ❸

Gezira Garden ⓣ095/231-2505, ⓦwww.el-gezira.com. A little way in from the Nile, this immaculate three-star mini holiday village has a/c rooms or self-catering apartments sleeping up to four (€50) with mosquito nets and balconies. Swimming pool, bars and restaurants, billiards, darts, table tennis, laundry service, satellite TV and internet (£E15/hr). BB ❺

Kareem ⓣ010 184-2083, ⓦwww.elhakim-lodges.net. At the back of Gezira near the Arabian Horse Stable, with fake waterfalls and naïve murals in its lobby, clean en-suite a/c rooms, free internet access, and a distant view of Hatshepsut's temple from the rooftop. BB ❸

Nile Valley ⓣ095/231-1477 or 012 796-4473, ⓦwww.nilevalley.nl. Located near the ferry dock, their rooftop restaurant boasts the world's finest view of Luxor Temple. Mostly en-suite a/c rooms with balconies; the ones at the back are quieter and overlook the hotel's swimming pool and wet-bar. Well managed and friendly; sells beer, wine and spirits. Free wi-fi for guests. Takes Visa and MasterCard. BB ❹

Ramses ⓣ095/231-2748 or 016 957-2356, ⓦwww.ramseshotel.net. Across the way from the *Gezira*, this rather faded hotel has mostly a/c rooms, and a view of Luxor from its roof, which has internet. BB ❸

Sheherazade ⓣ012 464-4047, ⓦwww.hotel-sheherazade.com. Virtually next door to *El-Nakhil*, its best features are its huge garden and lofty domed atrium painted with scenes from the *1001 Nights*. All rooms with showers and fans; some have double beds. BB ❹

Senmut Bed & Breakfast Ramleh ⓣ095/231-3077 or 012 736-9159, ⓦwww.senmut-luxor.com. This family-friendly B&B in Gezira's villa quarter has soothing rooms with fans or a/c and bathrooms, a communal living room with a library, satellite TV and internet (£E5/hr); a kitchen for guests' use, service wash and a rooftop overlooking the river. BB ❸

Near the temples

Amenophes Nag Lohlah ⓣ095/206-0680 or 012 232-7613, ⓔsayedm25@hotmail.com. Pleasantly faded a/c rooms with TV and balconies, a few minutes' walk from Medinet Habu; the view from its rooftop is marred by houses. Internet (£E3/hr). Takes Visa. BB ❸

Beit Sabee Guest House Nag Lohah ⓣ010 147-2819, ⓔbeitsabee@gmail.com. A chic mud-brick pile on the far side of Medinet Habu temple, featuring colourful en-suite rooms with a/c or fans, cotton sheets and duvets. Its location is very quiet but not too remote. BB ❺

Habou Nag Lolah ⓣ095/231-1611 or 012 358-0242. Immortalized in Critchfield's *Shahhat*, this seedy mud-brick labyrinth of stuffy barrel-vaulted rooms with shared bathrooms is only worth considering for its fabulous view of Medinet Habu temple, directly opposite. BB ❸

Marsam Gurnat Mura'i ⓣ095/237-2403 or 010 342-6471, ⓔmarsam@africamail.com. Built for US archeologists and later owned by Sheikh Ali Abdul Rasoul, who helped discover the tomb of Seti I, this west-bank institution has simple mud-brick rooms with fans (a private shower costs £E50 extra) and an Egyptology library. Fully booked by archeologists in Jan, reservations essential in Dec & Feb. BB ❷

Nour el-Balad On the edge of the desert 500m beyond Medinet Habu ⓣ095/242-6111 or 010 129-5812, ⓦwww.nourelgournahotel.com. Casbah chic rules in this mud-brick palace of "rustic" rooms with cotton duvets, mosquito nets and fancy bathrooms. Upstairs rooms cost £E50–100 more, rooftop suites £E450–500. Its isolation is its main drawback (or selling point). BB ❹

Nour el-Qurna Gurnat Mura'i ⓣ095/231-1430 or 014 428-1119, ⓦwww.nourelgournahotel.com. The *Nour el-Balad*'s little sister hotel lurks in a palm grove across the road from the Antiquities Inspectorate. The mud-brick rooms have beds with cotton duvets, mosquito net, stereo and bathrooms. Rates vary according to the view. BB ❹

Pharaohs Nag Lohlah ⓣ095/231-0702 or 010 613-1436, ⓦwww.hotelpharaohs.com. Mostly en-suite a/c rooms; the roof has a few larger ones costing £E40 more, and a side view of Medinet Habu temple. Free wi-fi. Beer and meals served on a shady patio. BB ❸

Elsewhere on the west bank

Al-Moudira Haggar Daba'iyya, 5km from Medinet Habu and 5km from Luxor Bridge ⓣ012 325-1307, ⓦwww.moudira.com. The classiest hotel in Egypt, it resembles an Ottoman palace, with exquisite courtyards, vast gardens and pool, a Lebanese restaurant, bar, and horseriding. Its 54 individually-styled a/c suites are furnished with antiques, mosquito nets, satellite TV and CD player; some have a fountain and a sunken Turkish hammam. The only drawback is that it is miles from anywhere; a taxi from Luxor or to the Necropolis costs around £E70. There's a twenty percent surcharge at Christmas and New Year. ❽

Flower of Light Gurna Ta'rif ⓣ010 232-4475, ⓦwww.floweroflight.com. Run by an Irish family, it doubles as a spiritual retreat. Variously sized en-suite rooms (some a/c and domed) with mosquito nets, set around a garden with a pool. Accessible by pick-up from Gezira or the road past the Tombs of the Nobles. BB ❸

Eating and drinking

You can get a decent **meal** of *kofta* or chicken with rice and salad at almost any of the hotels on the west bank for £E35–50. The sale of **alcohol** is limited to the *Al-Moudira*, *Amon*, *El-Fayrouz*, *Gezira*, *Gezira Garden*, *Nile Valley*, *Ramses* and *Pharaohs* hotels, the *Resturant Mohammed* and the *Ramesseum Resthouse*.

Africa Restaurant Gezira. Not to be confused with like-named rivals near the taxi depot, it offers grilled duck (£E40), mixed grill (£E50) and a late Egyptian breakfast (£E20), served on a shady rooftop overlooking Gezira. Daily 11am–11.30pm.

Al-Moudira Haggar Daba'iyya, ⓣ012 325-1307. If you want to splurge this is the place, with swanky decor and service to match. Delicious salads and grills at lunchtime, and a fuller dinner menu of Mediterranean-Lebanese cuisine (dishes from £E40–215).

Aux 3 ChAcAls 300m from the Colossi of Memnon ⓣ016 106-1198. This friendly French-managed place serves Gallic and Oriental dishes and has a great view of the Theban Hills from its rooftop. Try their duck curry (£E60). Call ahead to confirm they're open. Daily 9.30am–9pm.

Marsam Gurnat Mura'i. The hotel's courtyard restaurant serves a hearty Egyptian set lunch (£E50) and dinner (£E40), often featuring veggie tempura options.

Nile Valley Gezira. The hotel's rooftop restaurant (accessible by lift) has a fabulous view of Luxor Temple and an extensive menu (most dishes £E20–35). On Sundays at 7.30pm there's a lavish all-you-can-eat buffet (£E65) with Saiyidi music and dervish dancing.

Ramesseum Resthouse This venerable Egyptologists' haunt (see p.321) beside the Ramesseum serves cold beer, soft drinks, spaghetti bolognese and other simple dishes (about £E30).

Restaurant Mohammed Near the main ticket office ⓣ018 204-2226. Home-cooking in a rustic garden with a 600-year-old acacia tree.

Try their home-made goat's cheese, or call two hours ahead to order stuffed pigeon (£E35). Daily 24hr.

Tout Ankhamon Gezira. Impossibly vast helpings of coconut curry or duck with rosemary, spicy lentil and vegetable stews (£E60–70), served on a rooftop beside the Nile.

The west bank villages

The **west bank villages** are incidental to most tourists visiting the Theban Necropolis, but integral to the landscape and atmosphere. Their fields stretch from the river banks to the temples on the desert's edge; their goats root amid the Tombs of the Nobles. Though land remains paramount, almost every family is involved in tourism, renting out donkeys or making souvenirs on the west bank, commuting to hotel jobs in Luxor, or sailing motorboats or feluccas on the Nile. Family and village ties bind them together and help them exploit the stream of rich visitors that flows across their land. Richard Critchfield's *Shahhat* (sold in most Luxor bookshops) gives a fascinating glimpse into their lives two generations ago, before tourism really changed things.

Your first encounter will be with **GEZIRA**, where ferries disgorge villagers returning from Luxor, and tourists arrive in motorboats. The depot for private and service **taxis** to villages on the west bank is behind the white shopping mall, inland. Traditionally Gezira's role in tourism was to ferry tourists about or guide them on donkeys through the Necropolis, but the village now also has half-a-dozen hotels and flats for rent. Luxor Council tried to claim all the land along the waterfront but met fierce resistance from locals who'd built houses and hotels there, as well as from foreigners who'd bought apartments in the chic new district of **Ramleh**. Some only escaped demolition after the matriarch of the Khalifa family lay down in front of the bulldozers – after which Ramleh was nicknamed "Ramallah".

Gezira straggles to the **El-Fadiya Canal**, whose murky depths harbour giant **monitor lizards** (*warran*), which sometimes get sucked into irrigation pumps. Beyond lies **EL-TOD**, with its busy police checkpoint, across the main road from **NEW GURNA**, built in the 1940s with government funds to wean villagers away from Old Gurna in the hills. Designed by Hassan Fathy, an early advocate of creating architecture suited to local conditions, the settlement contains two superbly proportioned public buildings – the **mosque** and **Palace of Culture** – made of Fathy's favourite material, mud-brick. However, the village failed to attract many Gurnawis, and others moved in instead, to find that Fathy's houses were too small for their extended families, obliging them to add breeze-block extensions.

Beyond the Colossi of Memnon, the barren, windswept foothills are pockmarked with the Tombs of the Nobles and traces of Old **GURNA** (often spelt "Qurna" but pronounced with a "G"). For generations this ramshackle village supplied the workforce for archeological digs while quietly **robbing tombs** beneath its own homes. After years of protests, the authorities finally bulldozed the entire village in 2007, compelling its inhabitants to move to the purpose-built settlement of Gurna Jedid.

The road runs on past **DRA' ABUL NAGA**, another largely demolished village whose remaining houses squat in an arid moonscape glittering with light reflected off mica and alabaster dust. Traditionally, it manufactured the statues and ashtrays sold in tourist shops throughout Egypt, in **alabaster workshops** decorated with garish murals.

At this point a spur road turns off towards Hatshepsut's temple, while the main one carries on to a crossroads beside a cemetery, where the road to the Valley of the Kings begins. In a grove of trees you'll see a mud-brick complex that was

Howard Carter's house during his search for Tutankhamun's tomb, now a **museum** (daily 6am–5pm; free) recreating his lodgings, with an exhibition centre in the pipeline. More ambitious is the SCA's plan to construct life-size replicas of the royal tombs here, starting with Tutankhamun's and Seti I's – though a date has yet to be set for work to begin. Nearby is another archeological residence called the **Stoppelaer House**, designed by Hassan Fathy. Japanese, French, German and Polish Egyptologists also have their residences on the west bank.

The wasteland at the crossroads near **GURNA TA'RIF** is the site for the annual **Moulid of Abu Qusman** on Sha'ban 27, commemorating a local holy man known for his miracles and outspokenness, who died in 1984. His moulid used to last all night, but the police now end it at midnight.

The Colossi of Memnon

Looming nearly 18 metres above the fields, the two enthroned **Colossi of Memnon** originally fronted the mortuary temple of Amenophis III, once the largest complex on the west bank – which later pharaohs plundered for masonry until nothing remained but the king's colossi. Both have lost their faces and crowns, and the northern one was cleaved to the waist by an earthquake in 27 BC. Subsequently, this colossus was heard to "sing" at dawn – a sound probably caused by particles breaking off as the stone expanded, or wind reverberating through the cracks. Before the colossus ceased "singing" after repairs to the statue in 199 AD, the sound was attributed to the legendary Memnon (whom Achilles killed outside the walls of Troy) greeting his mother, Eos, the Dawn, with a sigh. The Greeks identified the colossi with Memnon in the belief that his father, Tithonus, had been an Egyptian king. Before this, the colossi had been identified with Amenhotep, Steward of Amenophis III, whom posterity honoured as a demigod long after his master was forgotten.

Standing beside the barrier rope you can appreciate what **details** remain on the thrones and legs of the sandstone colossi. On the sides of the nearer one, the Nile-gods of Upper and Lower Egypt bind the heraldic plants of the Two Lands

▲ The Colossi of Memnon, en route to the Theban Necropolis

together. The legs of each colossus are flanked by smaller statues of Queen Tiy (right) and the king's mother, Mutemuia (left). They are covered in graffiti, including Roman epigrams, as high as you can reach.

Behind them, the long-lost **Mortuary Temple of Amenophis III** is being excavated to form a new archeological park and is currently off-limits to the public.

The Valley of the Kings

Secluded amid the bone-dry Theban Hills, removed from other parts of the Necropolis, the **Valley of the Kings** (daily: summer 6am–5pm; winter 6am–4pm) was intended as the ultimate insurance policy on life eternal. These secretive tombs of New Kingdom pharaohs were planned to preserve their mummies and funerary impedimenta for eternity. While most failed the test, their dramatic shafts and phantasmagorical murals are truly amazing. The descent into the underworld and the fear of robbers who braved the traps is still imaginable in the less crowded, darker tombs.

Royal burials in the "Place of Truth" (as the Ancient Egyptians called it) date from the early XVIII to the late XX dynasties. The first to be buried here was probably Tuthmosis I (1525–1512 or 1504–1492 BC). Until the time of Ramses I, queens and royal children were entombed here. The tombs were hewn and decorated by skilled craftsmen (known as "Servants at the Place of Truth") who dwelt at nearby Deir el-Medina. Work began early in a pharaoh's reign and never exceeded six years' duration; even so, some tombs were hastily pressed into service, or usurped by later kings. Broadly speaking, there are two types: the convoluted, split-level ones of early XVIII Dynasty rulers such as Tuthmosis I and Amenophis II, and the straighter, longer tombs of the XIX and XX dynasties.

The weaker rulers of the XX Dynasty were unable to prevent **tomb-robbing** on a massive scale. Both the vizier and police chief of Thebes were implicated in the disposal of treasure, while many of the robbers were the workmen who had built the tombs, embittered over arrears in pay. In desperation, the priests reburied many sarcophagi and objects in two **secret caches** that were only discovered in the late nineteenth century (see p.316).

The exploration of the Valley began in earnest with a series of **excavations** sponsored by Theodore Davis in 1902–14, when more than thirty tombs and pits were cleared (sometimes all too literally). In 1922, Howard Carter's discovery of Tutankhamun's tomb made headlines around the world. Nothing more was found till 1995, when clues from a papyrus in Turin led Kent Weeks to clear the debris from tomb **KV5** – which Carter had dismissed as looted in antiquity – and uncover the entrance to a mass tomb for the **sons of Ramses II,** reckoned to contain one hundred and fifty chambers, some huge. While inscriptions suggest that fifty of Ramses' one hundred or so sons were meant to be interred here, the remains of only four adults have been found so far and the excavation is set to run for years (see the Theban Mapping Project website, Ⓦwww.kv5.com, for news plus images of other royal tombs).

More recently, in 2006, Otto Schaden uncovered an XVIII Dynasty tomb designated **KV63**, containing empty child-coffins and embalmers' gear (Ⓦwww.kv-63.com). Nicholas Reeves of the Amarna Royal Tombs Project had detected it six years earlier using ground-penetrating radar, but kept it secret. He has since announced that another, as-yet uncovered tomb exists near Tutankhamun's, which he calls **KV64** and which he believes to be a royal tomb from the post-Amarna period (see Ⓦwww.valleyofthekings.org). Meanwhile the Valley of the Kings remains acutely vulnerable. Flash **floods** present a grave danger to the tombs, but clearing the wadis of debris and digging drainage channels risks destroying

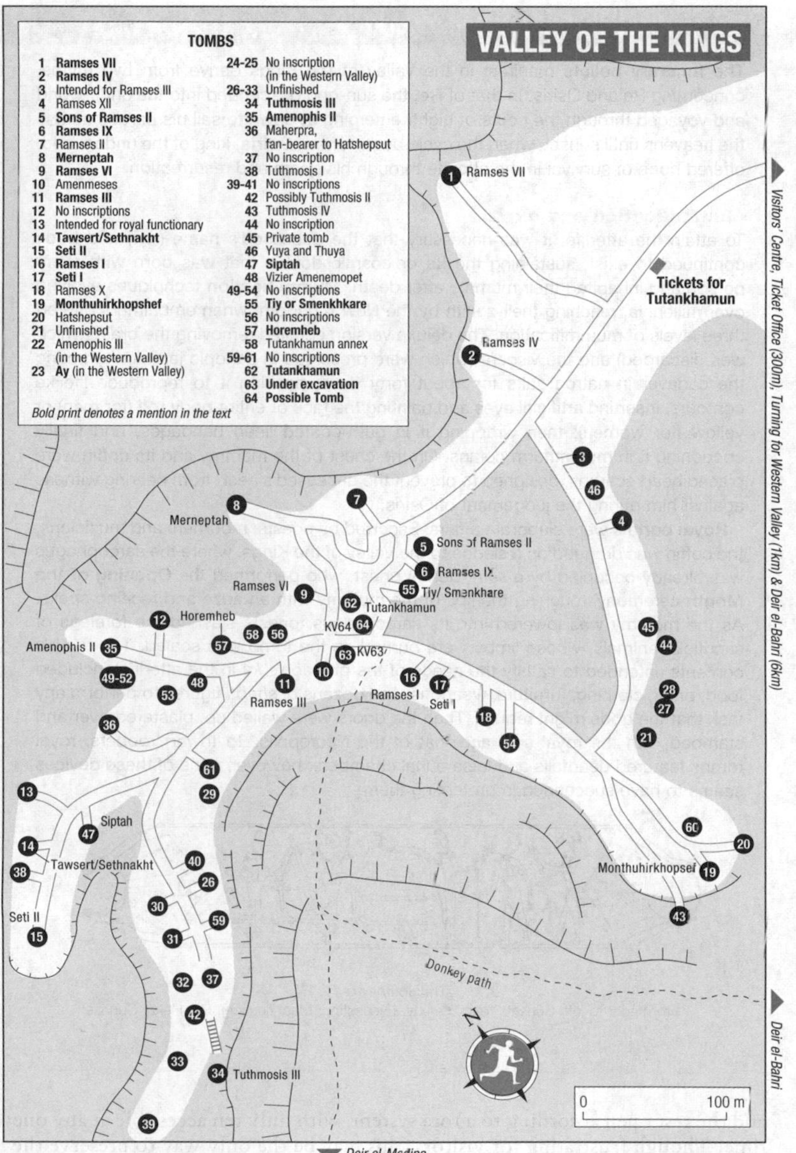

evidence that might point to undiscovered tombs. The SCA and foreign donors have already spent millions tackling an expanding sub-stratum of grey shale which ruptured several tombs in the 1990s, and installing glass screens and dehumidifiers to reduce the harm caused by **tourism** (the average visitor leaves behind 2.8g of sweat to corrode the murals).

The upshot is that some tombs are permanently **closed** except to VIPs and clients of Ancient World Tours (see p.31) – notably Seti I's and Horemheb's –

Mummification and the Underworld

The **funerary beliefs** manifest in the Valley of the Kings derive from two myths, concerning Re and Osiris. In that of **Re**, the sun-god descended into the underworld and voyaged through the hours of night, emerging at dawn to sail his barque across the heavens until sunset, when the cycle began anew. **Osiris**, king of the underworld, offered hope of survival in the afterlife through his death and resurrection.

Mummification and burial

To attain the afterlife, it was necessary that the deceased's name (*ren*) and body continued to exist, sustaining the **ka** or cosmic double that was born with every person and inhabited their mummy after death. **Mummification** techniques evolved over millennia, reaching their zenith by the New Kingdom, when embalmers offered three levels of mummification. The deluxe version entailed removing the brain (which was discarded) and the viscera (which were preserved in canopic jars); dehydrating the cadaver in natron salts for about forty days; packing it to reproduce lifelike contours, inserting artificial eyes and painting the face or entire body red (for men) or yellow (for women); then wrapping it in gum-coated linen bandages, and finally cocooning it in mummiform coffins. On the chest of the mummy and its coffin were placed heart scarabs, designed to prevent the deceased's heart from bearing witness against him during the judgement of Osiris.

Royal burials were elaborate affairs. Escorted by priests, mourners and musicians, the coffin was dragged on a sledge to the Valley of the Kings, where the sarcophagus was already occupied by a *sem* (death) priest, who performed the **Opening of the Mouth** ceremony, touching the lips of the mummy with an adze and reciting spells. As the mummy was lowered into its sarcophagus, priests slashed the forelegs of sacrificial animals, whose limbs were burned as the tomb was sealed. The tomb's contents (intended to satisfy the needs of the pharaoh's *ka* in the afterlife) included food, drink, clothing, furniture, weapons, and dozens of *shabti* figures to perform any task that the gods might require. Then the doors were walled up, plastered over and stamped with the royal seal and that of the Necropolis. To thwart robbers, royal tombs featured deadfalls and false burial chambers; however, none of these devices seems to have succeeded in protecting them.

The Journey of Re
From right to left: Sunset; Year; Eternity; Everlasting; Maat (justice); Re; Heka; Sunrise

and the rest open according to a rota system, with only ten accessible at any one time. Though frustrating for visitors, this may be the only way to preserve the tombs' fragile artwork for future generations, and it's everyone's duty to refrain from touching the walls. **Photography** is no longer allowed inside any of the tombs, nor in the Valley itself; cameras must be handed in at the entrance, and anyone caught breaking the rule may be heavily fined and have their camera confiscated.

As a long-term goal the SCA intends to create life-size replicas of all the royal tombs on a site near the Carter house (see p.301). The originals have already been laser-scanned, to be replicated by digital milling machines. Ultimately,

The journey through the underworld and judgement of Osiris

Funerary artwork dwelt on the journey through the underworld, whose pictorial representation inverted the normal order, so that each register was topped by sand instead of sky. The **descent** into the underworld (*Duat*) echoed that of a sarcophagus into its tomb, involving ramps, ropes and gateways. Each of the twelve **gates** was personified as a goddess and guarded by ferocious deities. In the darkness between them lay twelve **caverns** inhabited by beings such as the jackal-headed gods who fed on rottenness or the wailing goddesses with bloody axes.

It was Maat's Feather of Truth that was weighed against the deceased's heart (believed to be the seat of intelligence) during the **Judgement of Osiris**. With Anubis operating the scales and Thoth waiting to record the verdict, the deceased had to recite the **negative confession** before a tribunal of 42 **assessor gods**, each attuned to a sin. While the hearts of the guilty were devoured by crocodile-headed Ammut, the righteous were pronounced "true of voice" and led into the presence of Osiris to begin their **resurrection**, which paralleled **Re's passage through the underworld**. Voyaging through the twelve *decans* (hours or "divisions") of the night in his solar barque, Re had to overcome the serpent Apopis and other lesser denizens of **primeval chaos**, which threatened the **righteous order** personified by the goddess Maat. Re, helped by Anubis, Isis and Nephthys (often shown as serpents), Aker the earth-god (whose back bore Re's barque) and Khepri the scarab beetle, achieves rebirth in the fifth hour, and is fully restored to life by the tenth. Here the two myths part company, for whereas Re emerges from the body of the sky-goddess Nut to travel the heavens again, the Osirian journey (that of the righteous deceased) concludes by passing through the reedy **Fields of Yaru** (an Ancient Egyptian metaphor for death, also synonymous with fertility).

Since many of the scenes were supplemented by papyri buried with the mummy, funerary **artwork** is categorized in literary terms. The *Book of the Dead* is the name now given to the compendium of Old and Middle Kingdom Pyramid Texts and Spells, known in the New Kingdom as the *Book of Coming Forth*. Other **texts** associated with the New Kingdom include the *Book of Gates*, *Book of Caverns*, *Book of Hours*, *Book of Day and Night* and *Book of Amduat* (That which is in the Underworld).

The Judgement of Osiris
From left to right: Anubis escorts the deceased and weighs his heart before Ammut and Thoth; then Horus leads him to Osiris, Isis and Nephthys

access to the Valley will be restricted to a few premium-paying visitors, and ordinary tourists obliged to settle for the replica tombs – so visit the genuine ones while you can.

Visiting the tombs

The main **approach** to the valley (known as Biban el-Melouk, "Gates of the Kings" in Arabic) is via a serpentine road that follows the route of ancient funeral processions. Just before the ticket office is a **visitors' centre** (daily: summer 6am–5pm; winter 6am–4pm; free) featuring a scale model of the valley, crafted from glass to show each tomb's depth and alignment. You can watch a film of the official opening of Tutankhamun's tomb in 1922, and access the Theban Mapping Project's website. Beyond this are a cloakroom for stashing cameras (free) and an office selling **tickets** for the Valley of the Kings and Ay's tomb in the Western Valley (see p.297 for prices). From here, you can walk or ride an open-sided *tuf-tuf* train (£E4) 500m to the site entrance, just inside which is another kiosk selling tickets for Tutankhamun's tomb.

The valley is surrounded by limestone crags (the loftiest of which was the abode of Meretseger, snake-goddess of the Necropolis) and a natural suntrap, hot even in winter, the heat permeating the deepest tombs, whose air is musty and humid. The signposted **tombs** are **numbered** in order of their discovery, starting with the tomb of Ramses VII (known in antiquity) – #1 – and ending with the most recent discovery, #63. Egyptologists assign them the prefix KV (short for Kings Valley) to distinguish them from other numbered tombs in the Valley of the Queens. When you've had enough of royal tombs you might enjoy **hiking** over the ridge to Deir el-Bahri, for a matchless view of Hatshepsut's temple (see box, p.314).

Tomb of Ramses VII (#1)

Set apart near the entrance to the valley, the short tomb of **Ramses VII** lay wide open for millennia, and is now glassed over. Greek and Roman graffiti mar its sunk-reliefs and vivid colours (red, yellow and blue on white), whose freshness is due to restoration. Amid the standard imagery are odd details like the figures entombed in cartouches on the walls of the final corridor, while the hippo-goddess Tweri is prominent in the nocturnal pantheon on the ceiling of the burial chamber, whose sarcophagus is veined with blue imagery. Other Ramessid tombs are finer, however.

Tomb of Ramses IV (#2)

The next tomb, created for **Ramses IV**, is more of a crowd pleaser. Its cheerful colours make amends for the inferior sunk-reliefs and abundant Greek and Coptic **graffiti** (notice the haloed saints on the right near the entrance). The ceiling of the burial chamber is adorned with twin figures of Nut. On the enormous pink-granite **sarcophagus** are magical texts and carvings of Isis and Nephthys, to protect the mummy from harm. When these seemed insufficient, the priests stashed Ramses in the tomb of Amenophis II, whence the now empty sarcophagus has been returned. His mummy in the Cairo Museum shows him to have been a short, bald man with a long nose. He became pharaoh in his forties after the failure of a conspiracy to usurp the throne from his father, Ramses III (whose "testament" was recorded in the *Great Harris Papyrus*).

Tomb of Ramses IX (#6)

The tomb of **Ramses IX** belonged to one of the last rulers (1140–1123 or 1126–1108 BC) of the XX Dynasty, towards the end of the New Kingdom. It's indicative of waning majesty that the initial scenes in sunk-relief soon give way to flat paintings, akin to drawings. The walls of its stepped corridor (originally bisected by ramps, for moving the sarcophagus) depict Ramses before the gods and symbolic extracts from the *Book of Caverns*. Notice the solar barques bearing crocodiles, heads and other oddities, on the left-hand wall. The burial chamber is memorable for its *Book of Night* in yellow upon a dark blue background. Two sky-goddesses stretch back-to-back across the ceiling, encompassing voids swirling with creatures, stars and heavenly barques. While the king's sarcophagus pit gapes empty, his resurrection is still heralded on the walls by Khepri, the scarab incarnation of the reborn sun at dawn.

Tomb of Tutankhamun (#62)

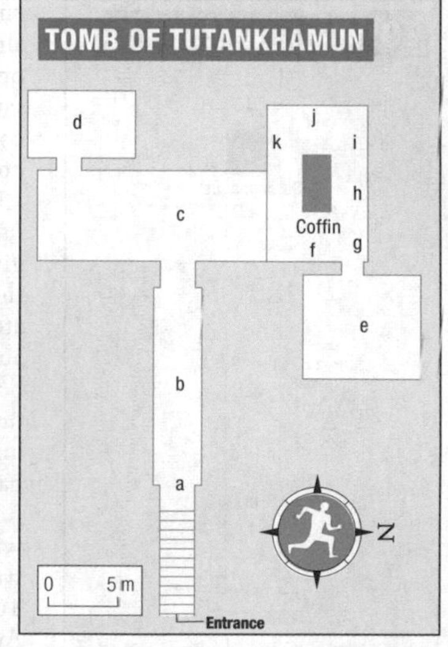

One of the world's most famous tombs, the tomb of **Tutankhamun** is neither large nor imposing by the standards of the Valley of the Kings, reflecting Tut's short reign (c.1361–1352 or 1336–1327 BC; see p.233) as an XVIII Dynasty boy-pharaoh. Its renown stems from its belated discovery and its amazing hoard of treasures (now mostly in the Cairo Museum). After archeologist **Howard Carter** had dug in vain for five seasons, his backer, **Lord Carnarvon**, was on the point of giving up when the tomb was found on November 4, 1922. Fears that it had been plundered were dispelled when they broke through the second sealed door – officially on November 26, though in fact Carter and Carnarvon secretly entered the previous night, stole several items and resealed the door. Unpacking everything took nearly ten years, the whole process being recorded in more than 1800 superb photographs by Harry Burton, who converted an empty tomb into a darkroom. As for the tomb itself, it is now glassed over to protect its paintings, and the number of visitors has been reduced by a steep admission charge (you might well decide that the tomb isn't worth the £E100 fee); **tickets** for Tut's tomb are available at a separate kiosk within the entrance to the Valley of the Kings.

In 1922, Carter found the door at the bottom of the stairway **[a]** walled up and sealed with Tut's cartouche and the seal of the Necropolis, but signs of repairs, the detritus in the corridor **[b]** and another resealed door at the end indicated that robbers had penetrated the antechamber **[c]** during the XX Dynasty. Most of the funerary objects now in the Cairo Museum were crammed into the undecorated chambers **[c, d** (now walled up) and **e]**. Another wall (now replaced by a barrier)

The curse of Tutankhamun

Lord Carnarvon's death in Cairo from an infected mosquito bite in April 1923 focused world attention on a warning by the novelist Marie Corelli, that "dire punishment follows any intruder into the tomb". (At the moment of Carnarvon's death, all the lights in Cairo went out.) The **curse of Tutankhamun** gained popular credence with this and each successive "mysterious" death. The US magnate Jay Gould died of pneumonia resulting from a cold contracted at the tomb; a famous Bey was shot by his wife in London after viewing the discovery; a French Egyptologist suffered a fatal fall; Carter's secretary died in unusual circumstances at the Bath Club in London; and his right-hand man Arthur Mace sickened and died before the tomb had been fully cleared. However, of the 22 who had witnessed the opening of Tut's sarcophagus, only two were dead ten years later. Howard Carter died in 1939 at the age of 64, while others closely involved lived into their 80s – not least Dr Derry, who performed the autopsy which suggested that Tut died from a blow to the head, aged about 19. If the most recent explanation for Tut's death is correct, mosquitoes were instrumental in the demise of both the boy-king and Carnarvon (see p.308).

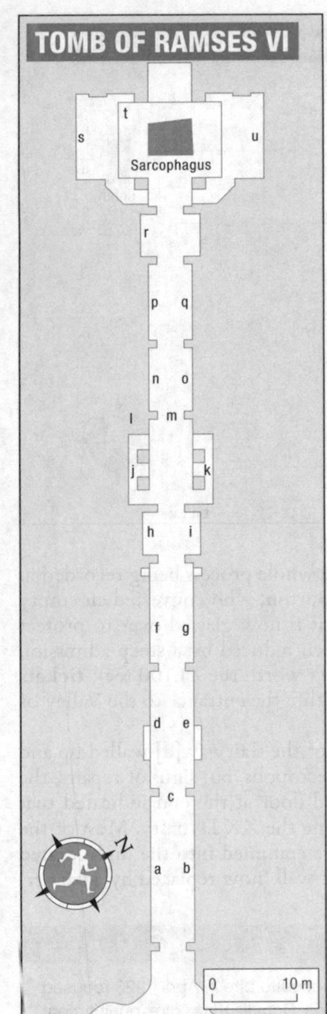

enclosed the burial chamber, which was almost filled by four golden shrines packed one inside another, containing Tut's stone sarcophagus and triple-layer mummiform coffin, of which the innermost, solid **gold coffin** and **Tut's mummy** remain.

In 2005 the mummy was CT-scanned *in situ*, revealing a broken leg that might have given rise to a fatal infection, casting doubt on the theory of a head injury that some had attributed to murder. More recent DNA analysis has revealed that Tut had a hereditary bone disorder and malaria (supported by the discovery of walking sticks and medicines in his tomb), the combination of which may have proved fatal.

The tomb's colourful **murals** run anticlockwise, starting with the funeral procession where nine friends and three officials drag Tut's coffin on a sledge **[f]**. Next, his successor Ay performs the Opening of the Mouth ceremony **[g]** and makes sacrifices to the sky-goddess Nut **[h]**. The deceased king embraces Osiris, followed by his *ka* (in the black wig) **[i]**. His solar boat and sun-worshipping baboons appear on the left wall **[j]**. On the hard-to-see entrance wall, Anubis and Isis escort Tutankhamun to receive life from Hathor **[k]**.

Tomb of Ramses VI (#9)

One reason why Tut's tomb stayed hidden for so long was that it lay beneath mounds of rubble from the tomb of **Ramses VI** (1156–1148 or 1143–1136 BC), which has been a tourist attraction since antiquity, when the Greeks called it the "Tomb of Memnon". The first two corridors have suffered from centuries of graffiti, but far worse occurred in 1992, when the ceiling fell down and had to be glued back on in nearly one thousand pieces. Today, as with Tut's tomb, there's a separate admission charge (£E50); **tickets** are sold at the entrance to the site.

The tomb was begun by Ramses V but usurped and enlarged by his successor, whose offering of a lamp to Horus of the Horizon opens the *Book of Gates* **[a]**, which faces other sunk-reliefs from the *Book of Caverns* **[b]**. Its astronomical ceiling continues through a series of corridors (note the winged sun-disc over the lintel and Ramses' cartouches on the door jambs **[c]**). Where the *Book of Gates* reaches the Hall of Osiris **[d]**, a flame-breathing snake and catfish-headed gods infest the *Book of Caverns* **[e]**. As Re's barque approaches the Seventh Gate, beyond which twelve gods hold a rope festooned with whips and heads **[f]**, the *Book of Caverns* depicts a procession of *ka* figures **[g]**. From here on, the astronomical ceiling features an attenuated sky-goddess and the *Book of Day and Night*.

The eighth and ninth divisions of the *Book of Gates* **[h]** and fifth division of the *Book of Caverns* **[i]** decorate the next chamber, originally a vestibule to the hall beyond, which marked the limits of Ramses V's tomb. This contains the concluding sections of the *Book of Gates* **[j]**, the seventh division of the *Book of Caverns* **[k]** and a summary of the world's creation **[l]**. The rear wall also features a scene of Ramses VI making offerings and libations to Osiris. On the pillars, he makes offerings to Khonsu, Amun-Re, Meretseger, Ptah-Sokar, Ptah and Re-Herakhte **[m]**.

The descent to the next corridor is guarded by winged serpents representing the goddesses Nekhbet and Neith (left), Meretseger and Selket (right). On the corridor walls appear the introductory **[n]** and middle sections **[o]** of the *Book of Amduat*; on the ceiling, extracts from the *Books of Re* and the *Book of Day and Night*. Scenes in the next corridor relate the fourth and fifth **[p]** and eighth to eleventh **[q]** chapters of the *Book of Amduat*. The small vestibule beyond contains texts from the *Book of Coming Forth by Day*, including the "negative confession" **[r]**. On the ceiling, Ramses sails the barques of Day and Night across the first register, while Osiris rises from his bier in the second.

Lovely back-to-back versions of the *Book of Day* and *Book of Night* adorn the ceiling of Ramses VI's burial chamber, where his image makes offerings at either end of one wall **[s]**. The rear **[t]** and right-hand walls carry portions of the *Book of Aker*, named after the earth-god of the underworld who fettered the coils of Apopis, safeguarding Re's passage. Incarnated as a ram-headed beetle, the sun-god is drawn across the heavens in his divine barque **[u]**.

The king's black granite **sarcophagus** was smashed open by treasure hunters in antiquity, and his mummy left so badly damaged that the priests had to pin the body to a board to provide the remains with a decent burial in another tomb.

Tomb of Merneptah (#8)

Merneptah (1236–1217 or 1213–1203 BC), the fourteenth son of Ramses II, didn't become pharaoh until his 50s, having outlived thirteen brothers with prior claims on the throne. On the evidence of his mummy, he was afflicted by arthritis and hardening of the arteries, and underwent dental surgery in old age. Many scholars hold, on the strength of his "Israel Stele" at Karnak and the identification of his father as the Pharaoh of the Oppression, that Merneptah was the Pharaoh of the Exodus (although this is disputed by Rohl; see p.601).

Like other tombs of the XIX Dynasty, his descends in corridors, with a total length of about 80m. In the first corridor, Merneptah is welcomed by Re-Herakhte and Khepri **[a]**, the *Litany of Re* **[b]** unfolds opposite the sixteen avatars of Osiris **[c]**, Re's barque is pulled through the underworld **[d]**, and Nekhebkau leads his soul towards Anubis **[e]**. Beyond a pit watched by Thoth and

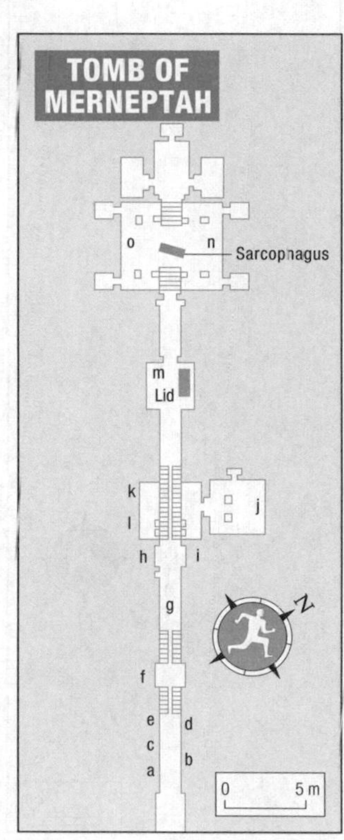

Anubis [f], another corridor decorated with the *Book of Amduat* [g] leads to an antechamber with images of Osiris and Nephthys [h], and Merneptah as Imutef [i].

The next hall is a false burial chamber (a trick that seldom fooled robbers) decorated with hymns to Osiris [j] and scenes from the *Book of Gates*. Notice the binding of the Serpents of Chaos [k], a tug-of-war over a "rope" of human souls [l], and the Osirian avatars above the lintel. The final corridors are largely bare, but for the outer **lid** of Merneptah's sarcophagus – left there by thieves – and the faint image of a monkey [m].

In the real burial chamber, the gods voyage through the night across the ceiling, while murals show the metamorphosis of Khepri into Re, encircled by bird-men requesting the deceased's *ba* (soul) [n], and Khnum piloting a boat with the pharaoh's mummy floating above [o]. There is a carving of the sky-goddess Nut inside Merneptah's massive granite **sarcophagus**.

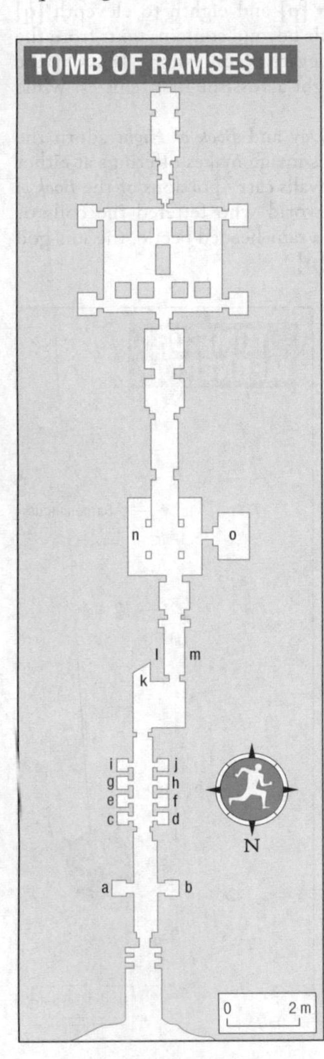

Tomb of Ramses III (#11)

The grandest of the Ramessid tombs is that of **Ramses III**. His 31-year reign (1198–1166 or 1184–1154 BC) marked the heyday of the XX Dynasty, whose power declined under the later Ramessids. Like his temple at Medinet Habu, the tomb harks back to the earlier glories of the New Kingdom. Uniquely for royal tombs, its colourful sunk-reliefs include scenes of everyday life. From another vignette derives its popular name, the Tomb of the Harpists.

Off the entrance corridors lie ten side chambers, originally used to store funerary objects. Within the first pair are fragmentary scenes of butchery, cooking and baking [a], and ships setting sail, those with furled sails bound downriver [b]. Next, Hapy blesses grain-gods and propitiates snake-headed Napret, with her escort of aproned *uraei* [c]. The bull of Meri (right) and the cow of Hesi (left) coexist with armoury scenes [d], while hermaphrodite deities bring offerings [e] to a treasury [f]. Ramses owns cattle and minerals [g], and from his boat inspects peasants working in the Fields of Yaru [h]. In a famous scene, two harpists sing to Shu and Atum, while Harsomtus and Anhor greet the king; the lyrics of the song cover the entrance wall [i]. The twelve forms of Osiris [j] are possibly linked to the twelve divisions of the night.

The dead-end tunnel [k] shows where diggers accidentally broke into a neighbouring tomb, at which point the original builder, Pharaoh Sethnakht, abandoned it and appropriated Tawsert's (see p.311). When construction resumed under Ramses, the tomb's axis was shifted west. The corridor has scenes from the fourth [l] and fifth [m] hours of the *Book of Amduat*. Part of the *Book of Gates* specifies four races of men: Egyptians, Asiatics, Negroes and Libyans (along the bottom) [n]. On the facing wall, the pinioned serpent Apopis is forced to disgorge the heads of his victims, in the fifth chapter of the *Book of Gates*. In the side room [o] are scenes from the *Book of Amduat*. The rest of the tomb has been barred since its ceiling fell down. Ramses III's mummy (in the Cairo Museum) was the model for Boris Karloff's figure in the 1930s film *The Mummy*.

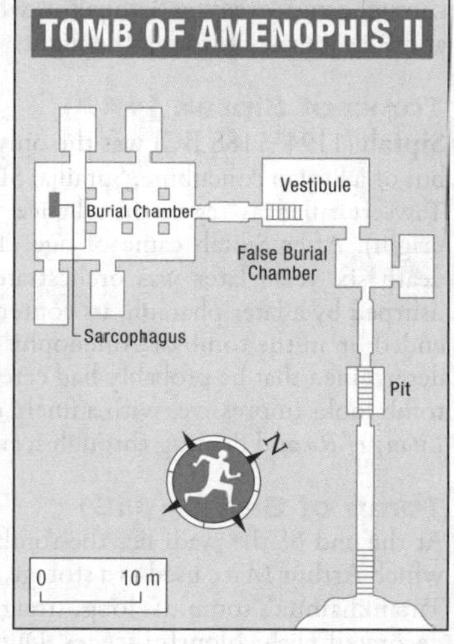

Tomb of Amenophis II (#35)

One of the deepest tombs in the valley lies at the head of the wadi beyond Horemheb's tomb. Built for **Amenophis II** (1427–1400 BC) midway through the XVIII Dynasty, it has more than ninety steps and gets hotter and stuffier with each lower level. When the tomb was discovered in 1898, the body of the king was still in its sarcophagus and nine other royal mummies were found stashed in another chamber. The tomb's **defences** included a deep pit (now bridged) and a false burial chamber to distract robbers from the lower levels (which would have been sealed up and disguised).

From a pillared vestibule, steps descend into the huge chamber. On its six square pillars, Amenophis is embraced and offered ankhs by various gods. Beneath a star-spangled ceiling, the walls are painted pale beige and inscribed with the entire *Book of Amduat*, like a continuous scroll of papyrus. Notice the preliminary pen sketches to the left of the left-hand niche. When found in his quartzite sarcophagus (still *in situ*), the king's mummy had a floral garland around its neck. The second chamber on the right served as a **cache** for the mummies of Tuthmosis IV, Merneptah, Seti II, Ramses V and VI and Queen Tiy, after their original tombs proved insecure.

In 2006 Joann Fletcher rediscovered three mummies that had been catalogued, sealed up and forgotten in 1898. She believes that one might be the mummy of Akhenaten's queen, **Nefertiti**; a theory other Egyptologists dismiss as wishful thinking.

Tomb of Tawsert/Sethnakht (#14)

Located en route to Seti II's tomb, this one is unusual for having two burial chambers. It originally held the mummy of Seti's wife, Queen **Tawsert**, but was usurped by Pharaoh **Sethnakht** (c.1200–1185 BC) after his own tomb (now Ramses III's) ran into difficulties. In the first corridor you find Sethnakht making offerings to Horus and Isis, and Osiris enshrined. Further on, a ram-headed god with a knife is followed by Anubis and Wepwawet. Texts from the *Book of the Dead* cover what was meant to be Tawsert's tomb chamber beyond which steps lead down towards Sethnakht's vault.

At the bottom of the stairs, the pharaoh's soul attains harmony with Maat, cherishing the Papyrus and Lotus of the Two Lands, while Anubis embalms his mummy in a side chamber further on. A hall of texts from the *Book of Caverns* and the Opening of the Mouth ceremony precedes the burial chamber, whose pillars show the gods greeting Sethnakht, while the walls depict the resurrection of Osiris and Re's journey through the night.

Tomb of Siptah (#47)

Siptah (1194–1188 BC) was the only son of Seti II, born not of Queen Tawsert, but of a Syrian concubine, Sutailja. Since he was only a boy, with an atrophied leg, Tawsert ruled as regent in alliance with an official named Bay (also of Syrian origin). After Siptah came of age, Tawsert married him; some believe that his death six years later was orchestrated by Tawsert and Bay. Siptah's tomb was usurped by a later pharaoh, its contents smashed up in antiquity, and his mummy ended up in the tomb of Amenophis II. There it was found in 1905, when it was determined that he probably had cerebral palsy or polio as an infant. However, his tomb looks impressive, with a finely dressed Siptah mingling with the gods in the *Litany of Ra* and floating through scenes from the *Book of Amduat*.

Tomb of Seti II (#15)

At the end of the wadi lies the tomb of **Seti II** (1216–1210 or 1200–1194 BC), which Arthur Mace used as a storage and restoration area during the excavation of Tutankhamun's tomb. Its long, straight corridors are typical of the XIX Dynasty, decorated with colourful scenes. Due to Seti's abrupt demise, however, there was only time to carve sunk-reliefs near the entrance, and the rest was hastily filled in with paintings or outline drawings. The king's mummy was later hidden in tomb #35 and replaced by that of an anonymous dignitary, which was plundered by thieves, who left only the sarcophagus lid. His mummy indicates that he suffered from arthritis, but had good teeth, which was unusual for that time.

Tomb of Tuthmosis III (#34)

Likewise secreted in a separate wadi, high up in a cleft, the tomb of **Tuthmosis III** (1479–1425 BC) is one of the oldest in the valley. Its concealment and (futile) defences make this tomb especially interesting, though some are disappointed by its artwork. Having ascended a wooden stairway to the cleft, you descend through several levels, crossing a pit by footbridge to reach a vestibule. The walls depict 741 deities as stick figures, in imitation of the format used on papyrus texts from the Middle Kingdom onwards, which was favoured for murals early in the New Kingdom. Reduced to their essentials, the ramps and shafts that led into the underworld, and Khepri's role in pulling Re's barque, are clearly visible.

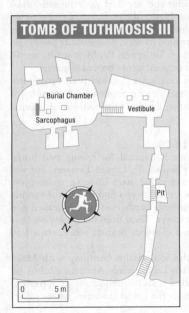

The unusual rounded burial chamber is also decorated with outline figures and symbols. Although the yellow background simulates aged papyrus, the texts were only painted after Tuthmosis had been laid to rest; there's a crossed-out mistake on the "instruction" fresco.

Elsewhere you'll notice double images (as at Abu Simbel), believed by some

Egyptian temple architecture

Two types of temple were built in Egypt from the earliest times. Mortuary temples were devoted to the worship of a dead king, whereas cult temples were dedicated to the principal god or goddess of a region, whose effigy was honoured with daily rituals and periodically taken to visit its divine spouse in another temple. Most temples embody centuries of work by successive kings, some of whom added major sections while others merely decorated a wall or carved their name on another pharaoh's statue, usurping it for their own glory.

Pylons at Edfu ▲

Hypostyle Hall at Karnak ▼

Temple layout

The general form and layout of temples hardly changed over millennia. Most temples were surrounded by high mud-brick **enclosure walls** (still intact at Karnak and Medinet Habu) which defined the holy precincts. Generally inaccessible to commoners, these contained priestly residences, storehouses and a **Sacred Lake** for ritual ablutions. In Greco-Roman times, there was also a **Birth House** or *mamissi* containing scenes asserting the king's divine ancestry, while at certain "healing" temples – notably Dendara and Karnak – ordinary folk could submit prayers to **Chapels of the Hearing Ear** by the outer rear wall.

Entering the temple proper meant passing through massive stone **pylons**, whose facades bore giant reliefs of the pharaoh making offerings to the gods and smiting Egypt's foes (depicted begging for mercy or with their amputated hands and genitals being tallied by royal scribes). Some temples also had **obelisks** with tips sheathed in gold or electrum (an alloy of gold and silver), guardian **colossi** representing a pharaoh or a deity, and open **courts** flanked with **colonnades** of Osiride pillars.

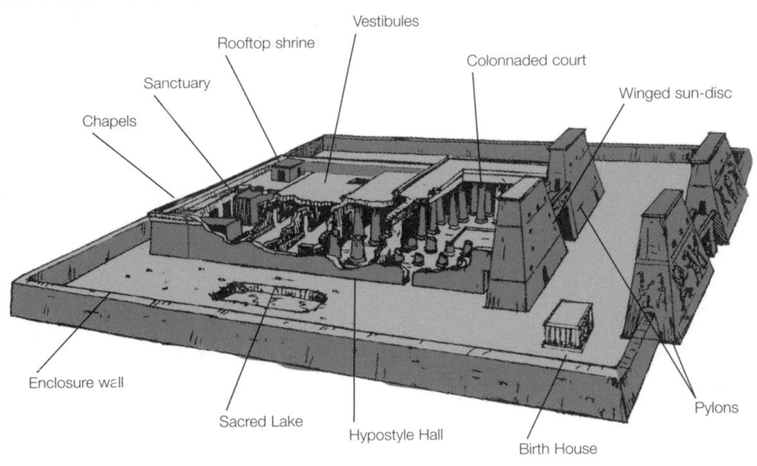

Another pylon marked the transition to the **Hypostyle Hall**, whose forest of columns was meant to resemble a papyrus thicket. Beyond lay a series of **vestibules**, climaxing in the **sanctuary** where the deity's idol and gilded boat-shaped shrine, or barque, reposed.

Some temples had a **rooftop shrine** for an annual ritual celebrating the resurrection of Osiris, whose idol was carried to the roof to be touched by the sun at dawn. The best preserved shrine is at Dendara, which depicts Isis restoring Osiris to life by copulating with his mummy.

Decoration

As in Ancient Greece and Rome, temples were whitewashed and painted all over, looking far gaudier than today, when a bit of remaining **colour** makes an exciting change from monochrome masonry. Virtually every wall is covered in **reliefs,** either carved proud (bas-reliefs, the most delicate and time-consuming method), recessed into the surface (sunk-reliefs) or simply incised (the quickest form to execute) in rows called "registers".

Hieroglyphs and **cartouches** (ovoid frames, each containing a pharaoh's name) are carved everywhere, lauding whoever founded or enlarged the temple, the rituals of its consecration or the myth of its deity. All have been sources of information ever since Champollion deciphered the Rosetta Stone and showed how to read hieroglyphics.

Imagery often refers to the union of the Two Lands – the Nile Valley and its Delta – represented by the vulture-goddess Nekhbet and the cobra-goddess Wadjet combined with a sun-disc on the lintels of doorways; by their heraldic plants, the sedge and lotus; and by the ribbed Djed pillar, symbolizing stability.

▲ Relief of Ramses II, Temple of Seti I, Abydos

▲ Winged sun-disc on a doorway, Medinet Habu

▼ Astronomical ceiling at Dendara

Column with composite (mixed-style) capital ▲

Hathor-headed pillar, Dendara ▼

Deir el-Bahri: mortuary temple of Queen Hatshepsut ▼

Some Ptolemaic temples featu[re] **astronomical ceilings** combining ancient Egyptian and Babylonian cosmology, with the sky-goddess Nut swallowing and giving birth to the sun, planets and stars juxtaposed with bulls, scorpions and other zodiac symbols. The finest example is in the Hypostyle Hall at Dendara.

Pillars and columns were both structurally essential and boldly decorative. Square-sectioned **pillars** were faced with a statue of the pharaoh as a god (usually Osiris, hence the term Osiride pillars) or crowned with the head of the goddess Hathor (occasionally with a cow's face, but more often with cow's ears). **Columns** derived from plant forms, with different permutations of shafts and capitals. Palm columns had a plain shaft and leafy capital, papyrus columns chevron markings and an open (flowering) or closed bud capital, with a shaft sometimes resembling a bundle of stems.

Top five temples

▸▸ **Karnak** Its pylons and Great Hypostyle Hall are on an epic scale, reflecting the supremacy of the cult of Amun during the New Kingdom. See p.283

▸▸ **Dendara** The temple's magnificent astronomical ceiling has been restored to its original bright colours, unseen for centuries. See p.257

▸▸ **Deir el-Bahri** Overhung by sheer cliffs, Queen Hatshepsut's temple is almost Modernist in its linear simplicity. See p.314

▸▸ **Abydos** Seti I's mortuary temple contains some of the finest bas-reliefs from the New Kingdom, retaining much of their original colours. See p.252

▸▸ **Abu Simbel** This rock-hewn sun-temple is a monument to unabashed egoism, dominated by four colossi of Ramses II. See p.370

imagery in the burial ch... typical nobles' vignette of ... here the ... *Amduat* is ... deceased spearing fishes and birds. Given ... distance by road off the main ... is clearly signposted), you can ... to the Valley of the Kings (the Western Valley ... are sold at the entrance to the W... get there by car or with a trail bike – tickets ... of the Kings.

Deir el-Bahri

Of all the sites on the west bank, none can match the breathtaking panache of **Deir el-Bahri**. Set amid a vast natural amphitheatre in the Theban Hills, the temple rises in imposing terraces, the shadowed vertical... of its colonnades drawing power from the massive crags overhead. Its great ramps and courts look modern in their stark simplicity, but in ancient times would have been softened and perfumed by gardens of fragrant trees. The reliefs that cover its colonnades and chapels bespeak of an extraordinary woman who undertook the most famous voyage in Ancient Egyptian history.

Deir el-Bahri ("Northern Monastery") is the Arabic name for the **Mortuary Temple of Hatshepsut** (pronounced "Hat-Cheap-Suit"), the only woman ever to reign over Ancient Egypt as pharaoh (1503–1482 or 1473–1458 BC). A daughter of Tuthmosis I, married to his successor Tuthmosis II, Hatshepsut was widowed before she could bear a son. Rather than accept relegation in favour of a secondary wife who had produced an heir, Hatshepsut made herself co-regent to the young Tuthmosis III and soon assumed absolute power.

To legitimize her position, she was depicted in masculine form, wearing a pharaoh's kilt and beard; yet her authority ultimately depended on personal willpower and the devotion of her favourite courtier, Senenmut, who rose from humble birth to the stewardship of Amun's estates, before falling from grace for reasons unknown. When Tuthmosis III came into his inheritance after her death, he defaced Hatshepsut's cartouches and images, consigning her memory to oblivion until her deeds were rediscovered by archeologists.

Tragically, in November 1997 Deir el-Bahri made headlines when 58 tourists and four guards were shot or stabbed to death by Islamist terrorists on the temple's Middle Terrace. The day is vividly remembered on the west bank, ... the donkey guides who witnessed the **massacre** from the clifftop ...

Tickets (see p.297) are sold at a kiosk just outside th... Beyond is a **visitors' centre** (free) featuring a scale mo... the neighbouring mortuary temples of Mentuhotep ... largely demolished). From here you can walk or ... 300m to the temple. A **Sound and Light** ... inaugurated in 2010.

…convinced that it actually is Ra…

T… …shef (#19)

Site… …om-visited tomb of **Monthuhirkhopshef** casts light … …his case, a son of Ramses IX, named "The Arm of Mont… …rkhopshef died in his teens – before his father – for he wea… …d-g… …sidelock of youth, a finely pleated linen skirt and elaborat… …e-up, as h… makes offerings to deities in the entrance corridor of his tomb. Eye make-up was worn by both sexes in Ancient Egypt; it's thought that some of the ingredients helped to prevent eye diseases such as glaucoma.

Tomb of Tiy or Smenkhkare (#55)

Identifying mummies isn't easy if the tomb was left undecorated and later looted – or the excavation was botched. The tomb designated **KV55** has been a conundrum ever since Theodore Davis failed to record its contents before removing the decrepit mummy in 1907, which he attributed to **Queen Tiy** – the wife of Amenophis III – due to its pelvic shape and "feminine" position (left arm bound across the chest, right arm alongside the body), and a gilded panel depicting her with Akhenaten. Later forensic analysis identified the bones as those of a man under 26 with signs of hydrocephalus, which seemingly fitted **Akhenaten**, until another examination in 2000 identified a man no older than his early twenties with a skull similar to Tutankhamun's, which many think was his mysterious predecessor, **Smenkhkare.** Recent DNA analysis has confirmed a familial relationship between the mystery man and Tutankhamun, but the riddle of his identity is still unsolved.

The Western Valley

A neglected offshoot of the Valley of the Kings, the **Western Valley** (Biban el-Gurud) contains only four tombs (two of them royal), of which just one is open. …**Tomb of Ay** (#23) was built for Tutankhamun's successor, who had earlier …ten's vizier and prepared himself a tomb at Tell el-Amarna (see …the Western Valley is notable for the blend of royal and noble

Hatshepsut's temple

Hatshepsut called her temple **Djeser Djeseru**, the "Splendour of Splendours". In ancient times an avenue of sphinxes probably ran from the Nile to its **Lower Terrace**, which was planted with myrrh trees and cooled by fountains (the stumps of two 3500-year-old trees remain near the final barrier). At the top and bottom of the ramp to the next level were carved pairs of lions (one of each is still visible). Before ascending the ramp, check out its flanking **colonnades**, whose reliefs were defaced by Tuthmosis III, and later by Akhenaten. While Hatshepsut's image remains obliterated, those of Amun were restored after the Theban counter-revolution. Behind the northern colonnade (right of the ramp) can be seen a cow-herd, wildfowl and a papyrus swamp; reliefs in the southern (left) colonnade show the transport by river of two obelisks from Aswan – doubtless the pair that Hatshepsut erected at Karnak.

The **Middle Terrace** once also boasted myrrh trees, which Hatshepsut personally acquired from the Land of Punt in a famous expedition that's depicted along one of the square-pillared colonnades flanking the ramp to the uppermost level.

The Birth and Punt colonnades

To the right of the ramp is the so-called **Birth Colonnade**, whose faint reliefs assert Hatshepsut's divine parentage. Starting from nearest the ramp, its rear walls show Amun (in the guise of Tuthmosis I) and her mother Queen Ahmosis (seated on a couch), their knees touching. Next, bizarre deities lead the queen into the birth chamber, where the god Khnum fashions Hatshepsut and her *ka* (both represented as boys) on his potter's wheel. Her birth is attended by Bes and the frog deity Heqet; goddesses nurse her, while Thoth records details of her reign. The sensitive expressions and delicate modelling convey a sincerity that transcends mere political expediency.

At the far end of the colonnade, steps lead down into a **Chapel of Anubis** with fluted columns and colourful murals. Tuthmosis III and a falcon-headed sun-god appear over the niche to the right; a yellow-skinned Hathor on the facing wall; offerings by Hatshepsut and Tuthmosis to Anubis on the other walls. As elsewhere, the images of Hatshepsut were defaced after her death by order of Tuthmosis. Notice the friezes of cobras in the central, barrel-vaulted shrine.

On the other side of the ramp is the famous **Punt Colonnade**, relating Hatshepsut's journey to that land (thought to be modern-day Somalia). Though others had visited Punt to obtain precious myrrh for temple incense, Hatshepsut sought living trees to plant outside her temple. Alas, the faintness of the reliefs (behind a guard-rail) makes it difficult to follow the story as it unfolds (left to right). The Egyptian flotilla sails from the Red Sea Coast, to be welcomed by the king of Punt and his wife. In exchange for metal axes and other goods, the Egyptians depart with myrrh trees and resin, ebony, ivory and panther skins; baboons play in the ships' rigging. Back home, the spoils are dedicated to Amun and the precious myrrh trees bedded in the temple gardens.

The Punt Colonnade leads into a larger **Chapel of Hathor**, whose face and sistrum (sacred rattle) form the capitals of the square pillars. In the first, roofless, pillared chamber, the goddess appears in her bovine and human forms, and suckles Hatshepsut (whose image has not been defaced here) on the left-hand wall. The next chamber features delicate reliefs of festival processions (still quite freshly coloured) on the right-hand wall. Peering into the gated sanctuary, you can just about make out another intact Hatshepsut worshipping the divine cow (left), and an alcove (right) containing a **portrait of Senenmut**, which would have been hidden when the doors were open. Apocryphally, it was this claim on the pharaoh's temple that caused his downfall. After fifteen years of closeness to

Hatshepsut and her daughter Neferure (evinced by a statue in the Cairo Museum, which some regard as proof of paternity), Senenmut abruptly vanished from the records late in her reign. When archeologists excavated the sanctuary in the early twentieth century they found it stacked with baskets full of wooden penises, seemingly used in fertility rituals.

The Upper Terrace

Reached by a ramp with falcon statues at the bottom, the **Upper Terrace** has emerged from decades of research and restoration work by Polish and Egyptian teams. Eight giant statues of Osiris front its portico and a red granite portal into a courtyard flanked by colonnades and sanctuaries. Bodyguards and oarsmen rowing the royal barque are depicted on the inside wall to the left as you enter. On the far wall are eight niches for votive statues, carved with hieroglyphs that rival the delicacy of Seti's reliefs at Abydos.

You can peep into (but not enter) the **Sanctuary of Amun**, dug into the cliff aligned towards Hatshepsut's tomb in the Valley of the Kings on the other side of the mountain. In Ptolemaic times the sanctuary was extended and dedicated to Imhotep and Amenhotep, the quasi-divine counsellors of Zoser and Amenophis III. Beneath it lies another burial chamber for Hatshepsut, presumably favoured over her pro forma tomb in the Valley of the Kings, since it was dug at a later date.

Other sites

From the heights of Hatshepsut's temple you can gaze southwards over the ruins of two similar edifices. The **Mortuary Temple of Tuthmosis III** was long ago destroyed by a landslide, but a painted relief excavated here can be seen in the Luxor Museum; more remains of the far older **Temple of Mentuhotpe II**, the first pharaoh to choose burial in Thebes (XI Dynasty). Unlike his XVIII Dynasty imitators, Mentuhotpe was actually buried in his mortuary temple; his funerary statue is now exhibited in the Cairo Museum.

Whereas Mentuhotpe's remains weren't discovered till modern times, many of the New Kingdom royal tombs were despoiled soon after their burial in the Valley of the Kings. Towards the end of the XXI Dynasty, the priests hid forty mummies in a **secret cache** in a hollow to the south above Mentuhotpe's temple, which the villagers of Gurna found in 1875 and quietly sold off for years until rumbled by the authorities, who forced them to reveal the cache's location. Amongst the mummies recovered were Amenophis I, Tuthmosis II and III, Seti I and Ramses II and III. As the steamer bore them downriver to Cairo, villagers lined the banks, wailing in sorrow or firing rifles in homage – a haunting scene in Shady Abdel Salem's film *The Mummy*, a classic of Egyptian cinema (1975).

How much may still lie undiscovered is suggested by the **Tomb of Montemhat**, mayor of Thebes under Amenophis II. Presently being excavated, it has a courtyard as big as a tennis court, flanked by giant carvings of heraldic plants, visible 20m beneath the desert's surface – be careful peering over the edge of the pit. You can see a long underground ramp leading to the tomb beside the *tuf-tuf* terminus of Hatshepsut's temple.

The Asasif Tombs

Midway between Deir el-Bahri and the Tombs of the Nobles lies a burial ground known as the **Asasif Tombs**, currently being studied by several archeological teams. While some of its 35 tomb chapels date from the XVIII Dynasty, the majority are from the Late Period (XXV–XXVI Dynasty), when Thebes was ruled by Nubian kings, and then from the Delta. **Tickets** for these tombs are sold at the Deir el-Bahri ticket office.

The most likely to be open is the **Tomb of Pabasa (#279)**, the steward to a Divine Votaress of Amun during the XXVI Dynasty. His tomb reflects the Saïte Dynasty obsession with the Old Kingdom, having a similar design to tombs at Saqqara. Its massive gateway leads into a pillared court with scenes of hunting, fishing and viticulture (note the bee-keeping scene on the central column). A funeral procession and the voyage to Abydos appear in the vestibule.

Also worth noting is the **Tomb of Kheru-ef (#192)**, a steward of Queen Tiy during the Amarna period. His scenes depict a Jubilee Festival, Tiy and Amenophis III, musicians, dancers and playful animals – as lyrical as those in Ramose's tomb (see p.318).

The Tombs of the Nobles

The **Tombs of the Nobles** are a study in contrasts to their royal counterparts. Whereas royalty favoured concealed tombs in secluded valleys, Theban nobles and high officials were ostentatiously interred in the limestone foothills overlooking the great funerary temples of their masters. The pharaohs' tombs were sealed and guarded; the nobles' were left open, for their descendants to make funerary offerings. Whereas royal tombs are filled with scenes of judgement and resurrection, the nobles' chosen artwork dwells on earthly life and its continuation in the hereafter. Given more freedom of expression, the artists excelled themselves with vivid **paintings** on stucco (the inferior limestone on this side of the hills militates against carved reliefs).

The **tombs' layout** marks a further evolution in funerary architecture since the Middle Kingdom tombs of Beni Hassan. Most are entered via a courtyard, with a transverse hall preceding the burial shrine with its niche containing an effigy of the deceased (or statues of his entire family). Strictly speaking, they are tomb chapels rather than tombs, since the graves themselves lie at the bottom of a shaft (usually inaccessible).

All the tombs open to visitors cluster in the locality once occupied by the village of Old Gurna, where they're divided into four groups (each requiring a separate ticket from the main ticket office), namely: **Rekhmire and Sennofer**; **Ramose, Userhat and Khaemhat**; **Nakht and Menna**; and **Khonsu, Userhet and Benia**. The first two lie furthest west and back from the road; the next trio downhill towards the Ramesseum; and the last two sets of tombs to the northeast, closer to Deir el-Bahri.

As visiting all the tombs would take two hours or so, most people limit themselves to a single group or the highlights from each (marked ★ in the accounts following).

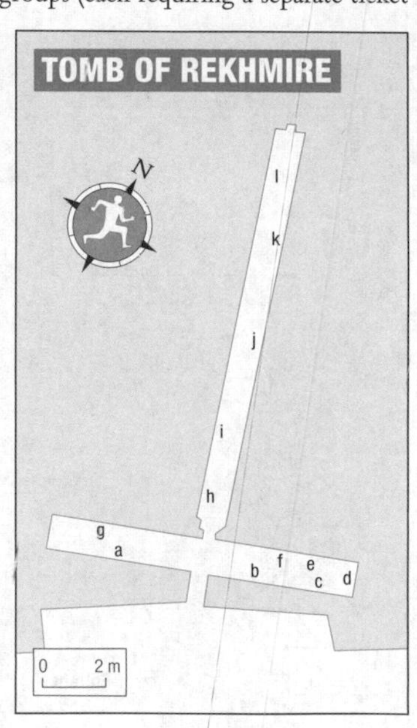

Tomb of Rekhmire (#100)*

Located off to the right of a mosque, the richly decorated tomb of **Rekhmire** casts light on statecraft and foreign policy under Tuthmosis III and Amenophis II, whom Rekhmire served as vizier. The badly damaged murals in its transverse hall show him collecting taxes from Upper **[a]** and Lower **[b]** Egypt, and inspecting temple workshops, charioteers and agricultural work [c]. Around the corner from his ancestors [d], grapes are trod in large tubs and the juice is strained and stored in jars [e].

Along the rear wall are depicted a desert hunt [f] and a famous scene of Rekhmire receiving tributes from foreign lands [g]. Among the gifts shown are vases from Crete and the Aegean Islands (fourth row); a giraffe, monkeys and elephant tusks from Punt and Nubia (third row); and chariots and horses from Syria (second row).

Growing in height as it recedes towards the false door at the back, the long corridor is decorated with scenes of work and daily life. Slaves store grain in silos [h], whence it was later disbursed as wages to armourers, carpenters, sculptors and other state-employed craftsmen [i]. An idealized banqueting scene with female musicians [j] merges into an afterworld with a lake and trees [k]. Also note Rekhmire's funeral procession and offerings to sustain him in the afterlife [l].

Tomb of Sennofer (#96)

From Rekhmire's tomb, slog 50m uphill to the left to find another colourful tomb, in better condition. Entered by a low, twisting stairway, the tomb of **Sennofer** is known as the "Tomb of Vines" after the grapes and vines painted on the textured ceiling of the antechamber. As mayor of Thebes and overseer of Amun's estates under Amenophis II, Sennofer had local viticulture among his responsibilities. The walls of the burial shrine depict his funeral procession (left), voyage to Abydos (back, right) and mummified sojourn with Anubis (right). Its square pillars bear images of Hathor, whose eyes follow you around the room. A small tree-goddess appears on the inner side of the rear left-hand pillar.

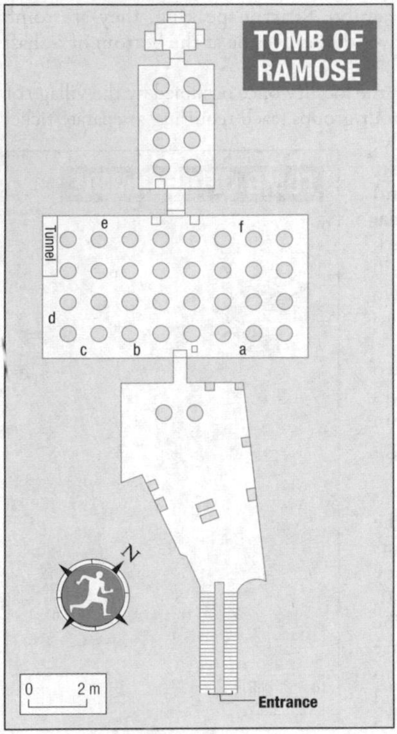

Tomb of Ramose (#55)*

Down a dirt road to the southeast lies the tomb of **Ramose**, who was vizier and governor of Thebes immediately before and after the Amarna revolution. His spacious tomb captures the moment of transition from Amun- to Aten-worship, featuring both classical and Amarna-style reliefs, the latter unfinished since Ramose followed Akhenaten to his new capital. Besides its superb reliefs, the tomb is notable for retaining its courtyard – originally a feature of all these tombs.

Along the entrance wall of its pillared hall are lovely carvings that reflect the mellowing of classicism during the reign of Amenophis III, Akhenaten's father. Predictable scenes of Ramose and his wife [a],

Amenophis III and Queen Tiy [b] making offerings come alive thanks to the exquisite rendering of the major figures, carried over to their feasting friends and relatives [c]. The sinuous swaying of mourners likewise imparts lyricism to the conventional, painted funerary scene [d], where Ramose, wife and priests worship Osiris.

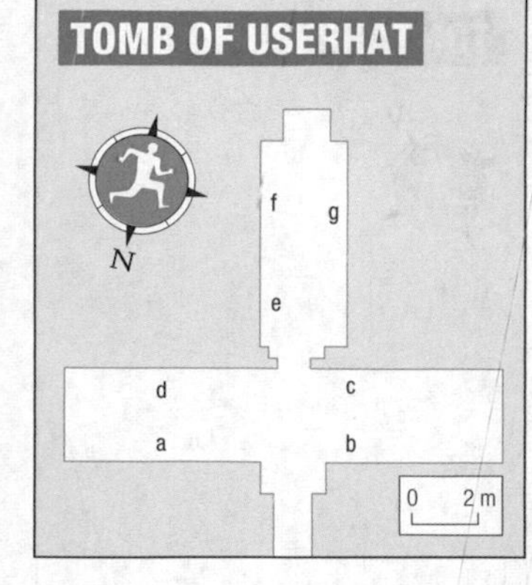

The onset of Aten-worship and the Amarna style is evident in the reliefs at the back, despite their battered condition. Those on the left [e] were carved before Amenophis IV changed his name to Akhenaten and espoused Aten-worship, so the pharaoh sits beneath a canopy with Maat, the goddess of truth, receiving flowers from Ramose. (At the far end, note the red grid and black outlined figures by which the artist transferred his design to the wall before relief-cutting took place.) However, the corresponding scene [f] depicts the pharaoh as Akhenaten, standing with Nefertiti at their palace window, bathed in the Aten's rays. Ramose is sketched in below, accepting their gift of a golden chain; his physiognomy is distinctly Amarnan, but rather less exaggerated than the royal couple's (see p.232).

Tomb of Userhat (#56)

Immediately south of Ramose's tomb lies that of **Userhat**, a royal scribe and tutor in the reign of Amenophis II. Although some of the figures were destroyed by early Christian hermits who occupied the shrine, what remains is freshly coloured, with unusual pink tones. The tomb is also interesting in that it's still illuminated by means of a mirror reflecting sunlight inside, just as it was when the artists decorated the tomb.

Along the entrance wall of the antechamber are scenes of wine-making, harvesting, herding and branding cattle, collecting grain for the royal storehouse [a], and the customary offerings scenes [b]. On the rear wall are reliefs of baking, assaying gold dust, and – lower down – a barber trimming customers beneath a tree [c]. The funerary feast scene [d] was extensively damaged by hermits, particularly the female figures. The inner hall contains paintings of Userhat hunting gazelles, hares and jackals from a chariot in the desert [e]; fowling and fishing amid the reeds [f]; and funerary scenes [g]. In a niche at the end is a headless statue of the deceased's wife.

Tomb of Khaemhat (#57)

Next door is the tomb of **Khaemhat**, royal scribe and inspector of granaries under Amenophis III, which is reached via a forecourt off which two other tombs, now locked, once led. Flanking its doorway outside are battered reliefs of Khaemhat worshipping Re, and the complete set of instruments for the Opening of the Mouth ceremony (right). In the transverse antechamber with its red and black patterned ceiling, the best reliefs are on the left as you enter. Although Renenet the snake-headed harvest-goddess has almost vanished, a scene of grain boats docking at Thebes harbour is still visible nearer the niche containing statues of Khaemhat and Imhotep. In the bottom row to the left of the door into the corridor, Hathor breastfeeds a boy-king, surrounded by sacred cows.

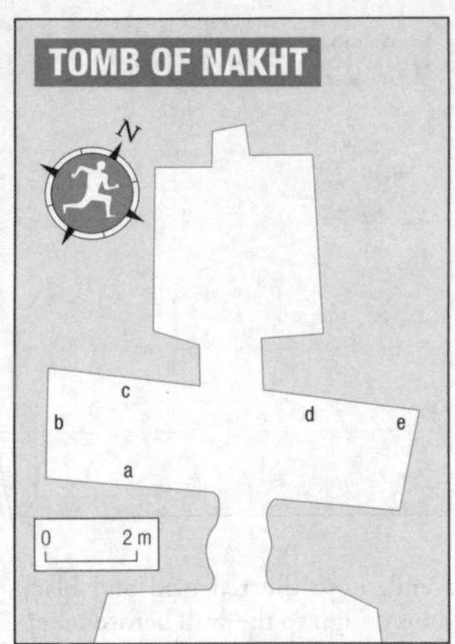

Fishing, fowling and family scenes decorate the right-hand wall of the corridor, leading to a triple-niched chapel containing seated statues of Khaemhat and his family.

Tomb of Nakht (#52)*

Northeast of Ramose's tomb lies the burial place of **Nakht**, whose antechamber contains a small museum with drawings of the reliefs (which are covered in glass) and a replica of Nakht's funerary statue, which was lost at sea en route to America in 1917. Nakht was the overseer of Amun's vineyards and granaries under Tuthmosis IV, and the royal astronomer, but stargazing does not feature among the activities depicted in his tomb. The only decorated section is the transverse antechamber, whose ceiling is painted to resemble woven mats, with a geometric frieze running above the brilliantly coloured murals.

To one side, Nakht supervises the harvest in a scene replete with vivid details **[a]**. In the bottom register, one farmer fells a tree, while another swigs from a waterskin; of the two women gleaning in the row above, one is missing an arm. Beyond a stele relating Nakht's life **[b]** is the famous banqueting scene **[c]**, where sinuous dancers and a blind harpist entertain friends of the deceased, who sits beside his wife, Tawi, with a cat scoffing a fish beneath his chair; sadly, their figures have been erased.

The defacement of Nakht's image and Amun's name is usually ascribed to Amarna iconoclasm, but the gouging out of his eyes and throwing sticks in the hunting scene **[d]** suggests a personal animus. Happily, this has not extended to the images in the corner **[e]**, where peasants tread grapes in vats, and birds are caught in clap-nets and hung for curing (below). The plain inner chamber has a false door painted to resemble Aswan granite, and a deep shaft leading to the (inaccessible) burial chamber.

Tomb of Menna (#69)

More scenes of rural life decorate the nearby tomb of **Menna**, an XVIII Dynasty inspector of estates. Accompanied by his wife and daughter, Menna worships the sun in the entrance passage. In the left wing of the first chamber, he supervises field labour (notice the two girls pulling each other's hair, near the far end of the third row), feasts and makes offerings with his wife. Across the way they participate in ceremonies with Anubis, Osiris, Re and Hathor. Though chiefly decorated with mourning and burial scenes, the inner chamber also features a spot of hunting and fishing, vividly depicted on the right-hand wall. The niche at the end contains the legs of Menna's votive statue.

Tombs of Khonsu, Userhet and Benia

This trio of small tombs near those of Nakht and Menna was opened to the public in 1992. The themes are standard, with scenes of offerings, hunting, fishing and funerary rites. In the tomb of Userhet (not to be confused with the Userhat in tomb #56), the guard may produce a mummified head for baksheesh.

Khoka Tombs

Set apart from the others, the **Khoka** (or, as locals say, "Hookah") tombs were built for a trio of New Kingdom officials. **Neferonpet** (known as Kenro) was a treasury scribe; the tomb's inner chamber depicts him assessing deliveries of gold and food, and the work of sculptors and weavers. The golden-yellow, red and blue murals, the brightly patterned ceilings and the votive statues of the deceased and his wives (badly disfigured) are also characteristic of the tomb of **Nefersekheru**, next door. Here, the wives enjoy greater prominence, flanking Nefersekheru pictorially (to the right as you enter) and sculpturally (in niches), and known to posterity as Maatmou, Sekhemui and Nefertari. Their mummies were buried in a shaft off the rear corridor, which leads into the adjacent tomb of Dhutmosi (now inaccessible).

Tombs of Roy and Shuroy

These two tombs are on the edge of Dra' Abul Naga, just over 1km from the Khoka Tombs by road. You can get here by pick-up heading towards El-Jebannah; get off when you see a billboard with Mubarak's face and follow the signposted slip-road beyond it to the left.

The colours in both tombs are remarkably fresh. High priest **Roy** from the time of Horemheb has a small rectangular tomb (#255), whose scenes of wailing mourners, sacrificial bulls and funerary offerings are offset by a ceiling checkered with yellow, red, black and white crosses. His near namesake **Shuroy** was a brazier-bearer at Amun's temple during the XIX Dynasty and has a larger T-shaped tomb (#13). Here, the murals are fragmentary or merely sketched in, though there's a fine frieze of dwarfs along the top of the wall to the left inside the transverse hall.

The Ramesseum

The **Ramesseum** or mortuary temple of Ramses II was built to awe the pharaoh's subjects, perpetuate his existence in the afterlife and forever link him to Amun-United-with-Eternity (one of Amun's many avatars). Had it remained intact, the Ramesseum would doubtless match his great sun temple of Abu Simbel for monumental grandeur and unabashed self-glorification. But by siting it beside an earlier temple on land that was annually inundated, Ramses unwittingly ensured the ruination of his monument; its toppled colossi would later mock his presumption, inspiring Shelley's sonnet *Ozymandias*.

Nineteenth-century writers knew the ruins as the Memnonium. Their present name only caught on late in the nineteenth century, by which time the Ramesseum had been plundered for statuary – not least the seven-tonne head of one of its fallen colossi, now in the British Museum. Its devastation lends romance to the conventional architecture, infusing it with pathos.

Half an hour suffices to see the famous colossi and the best reliefs, but you may care to linger. The nearby *Ramesseum Resthouse* sells cold drinks and hot meals; the owner's grandfather, Sheikh Hussein Abdul, was a teaboy at Carter's excavation in 1922 and photographed wearing a jewelled collar from Tut's tomb. Remember to buy a **ticket** for the site at the main ticket office before you come here.

The site

Like other mortuary temples in the Theban Necropolis, the Ramesseum faces towards the Nile and was originally entered via its **First Pylon**. Wrecked by the earthquake that felled the colossi, it stands marooned in the scrub beyond a depression that was once the **First Court**. Today, you enter the temple via its **Second Court**, to be confronted by the awesome **fallen colossus of Ramses II**. This

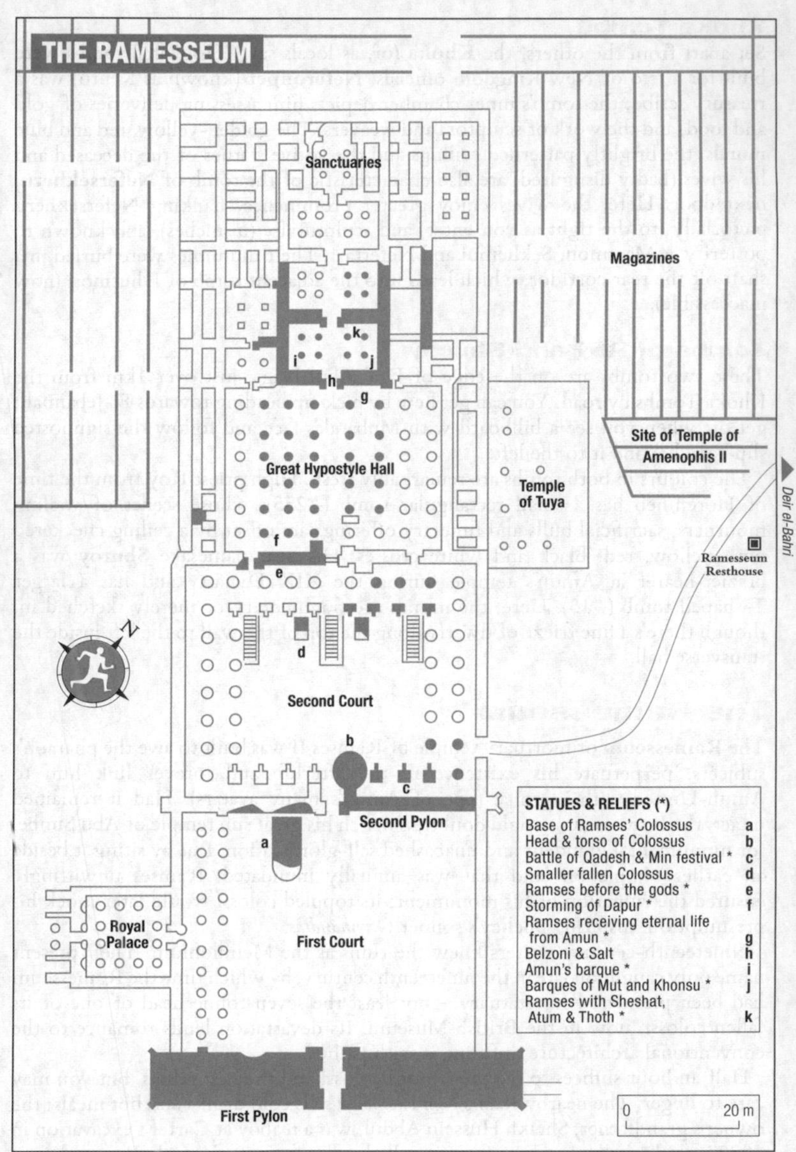

seated megalith once towered over the stairs from the first into the second court [a]; over 18m tall and weighing about 1000 tons, it was only surpassed by the Colossi of Memnon thanks to their pedestals. When it toppled some time after the first century AD, its upper half smashed through the Second Pylon into the court, where its head and torso lie today [b], measuring 7m across the shoulders; the cartouche on its bicep reads: "Ruler of Rulers". In the lower court are other fragments, notably feet and hands.

Behind the chunky Osirian pillars rises what's left of the **Second Pylon**, whose inner face bears scenes from the second Battle of Qadesh, surmounted by a register depicting the festival of the harvest-god Min **[c]**. At the far end of the second courtyard, where three stairways rise to meet a colonnaded portico, is a **smaller fallen colossus** of Ramses **[d]**, more fragmented, though its face has suffered merely nasal damage. Originally there were two colossi, but the other – dubbed the "Young Memnon" – was seized for Britain in 1816 by the treasure-hunter Belzoni. The name "Ozymandias" arose from the Ancient Greeks' misreading of one of the king's many titles, User-Maat-Re.

Beyond here, the core of the Ramesseum is substantially intact. The first set of reliefs worth noting occurs on the front wall of the **portico**, between the central and left-hand doorways **[e]**. Above a bottom row depicting eleven of his sons, Ramses appears with Atum and Mont (who holds the hieroglyph for "life" to his nose), and kneels before the Theban Triad (right) while Thoth inscribes his name on a palm frond (centre). The top register shows him sacrificing to Ptah and making offerings to Min, whose outsize erection is decorously termed "ithyphallic" by Egyptologists.

The **Great Hypostyle Hall** had 48 columns, of which 29 are still standing. The taller ones flanking the central aisle have papyrus shafts and turquoise, yellow and white lotus capitals, while the lower side columns have papyrus-bud capitals. On the wall as you come in, reliefs depict Egyptian troops storming the Hittite city of Dapur, using shields to protect themselves from arrows and stones **[f]**. At the back of the hall, incised reliefs **[g]** show lion-headed Sekhmet (far right) presenting Ramses to an enthroned Amun, who gives him the breath of eternal life from an ankh; along the bottom are depicted some of the king's hundred sons. Notice the names of Belzoni and his patron, the British consul Henry Salt, carved on the right-hand door jamb **[h]**.

Beyond this lie two **smaller Hypostyle Halls**. The first retains its astronomical ceiling, featuring the oldest known twelve-month calendar (whether lunar or solar months is debatable). Notice the barques of Amun, Mut and Khonsu (**[i]** & **[j]**), and the scene of Ramses beneath the persea tree with Atum, Sheshat and Thoth **[k]**. The ruined **sanctuaries** were presumably dedicated to Amun, Ramses the god and his glorious ancestors.

The whole complex is surrounded by mud-brick **magazines** that once covered about three times the area of the temple and included workshops, storerooms and servants' quarters, that have survived far better than the **royal palace** and **Temple of Tuya** that once adjoined the temple, of which only stumps of walls and columns remain. Nearby, the Italian mission is excavating the remains of the **Temple of Amenophis II**.

Other mortuary temples

In ancient times, the Ramesseum was one of half a dozen mortuary temples ranged along the edge of the flood plain with no regard for chronological order. The **Temple of Merneptah**, built by Ramses' thirteenth or fourteenth son, lies just southwest of the Ramesseum, intruding onto the edges of, and reusing masonry from, the vast complex of Amenophis III that once spread to the Colossi of Memnon. The site consists of fragments of the temple, placed in their original positions and supported by modern stonework; its entrance (reached by walking past the *Marsam Hotel*) represents the original position of the first pylon. An informative **museum** exhibits stone-carvings from the site (forty percent of them originally belonging to Amenophis III's temple or Deir el-Bahri). Further in to the left stands a copy of the famous **Israel Stele** also replicated at Karnak (see p.290). Guards can unlock another section, containing the remains of a monumental gateway from Amenophis III's temple, clearly reused to build Merneptah's edifice.

While nothing remains of the temples of Tuthmosis IV, Tuthmosis II, Ay and Horemheb that once extended towards Medinet Habu, there is a substantial **Temple of Seti I** near the village of Gurna Ta'rif (accessible by pick-ups from Gezira). This is the only temple in Egypt where the future Ramses II is depicted as a prince, wearing a tiger-skin tunic and kneeling before his father, Seti. Again, you must buy a ticket in advance at the main ticket office.

Deir el-Medina: the Workers' Village

Deir el-Medina, the **Workers' Village**, housed the masons, painters and sculptors who created the royal tombs in the Valley of the Kings. Because many were literate and left records on papyrus or *ostraca*, we know such details as who feuded with whom, their sex lives and labour disputes. As state employees, they were supposed to receive fortnightly supplies of foodstuffs and beer, but when these failed to arrive (as often happened during the ramshackle XX Dynasty), the workers downed tools, staged sit-ins at Medinet Habu, or demonstrated in Luxor.

Normally they worked an eight-hour day, sleeping in huts near the tombs during their ten-day shift before returning to their families at Deir el-Medina. In their spare time craftsmen worked for private clients or collaborated on their own tombs, built beneath man-size pyramids. Their own murals appropriated imagery from royal and noble tombs, which was parodied in the famous *Satirical Papyrus*, showing animals judging souls, collecting taxes and playing *senet* (an Ancient Egyptian board game), and humans having sex.

Anyone taking the donkey trail to the Valley of the Kings can get a fine **overview** of the village from the hillside – but the real attraction is its tombs. Visitors should bear in mind that the Deir el-Medina **ticket** (#6) doesn't cover the tomb of Peshedu, which needs a separate ticket (#11) – both available only from the main ticket office. You can easily walk to Deir el-Medina from the main road; it's also feasible to do so from the Valley of the Queens or Medinet Habu.

The nearest pyramid to the entrance marks the **Tomb of Sennedjem** (or Sennutem), whose vaulted burial chamber is reached by steep flights of steps and two antechambers. Its colourful murals feature ithyphallic baboons (right end wall), Osiris and the Fields of Yaru, and Anubis ministering to Sennedjem's mummy (facing wall, far left). The **Tomb of Ankherha** (#359) has a similar design; on the left wall of the burial chamber, Ankherha appears with Wepwawet and Khepri; Anubis breathes life into his mummy; his wife adores Horus as a falcon; and his naked daughters make libations. In the **Tomb of Peshedu** (#3), one can see the deceased praying beneath the tree of regeneration, below which flow the waters of the Amuntit, the "Hidden Region" where souls were judged. Unusually for Deir el-Medina, the **Tomb of Iphy** (#217) eschews ceremonial scenes and deities for tableaux from everyday life. The **Tomb of Iri Nefer** (#219) isn't officially open, but can be seen for baksheesh.

Near the village stands a **Ptolemaic temple** dedicated to Maat and Hathor, whose head adorns the pillars between the outer court and naos. Each of its three shrines is decorated with scenes from the *Book of the Dead*. Early in the Christian era, the temple and the workers' village were occupied by monks – hence the site's Arabic name of Deir el-Medina ("Monastery of the Town").

The Valley of the Queens

The **Valley of the Queens** is something of a misnomer, for it also contains the tombs of high officials (who were interred here long before the first queen was buried in this valley during the XIX Dynasty) and royal children. Princes were educated by priests and scribes, taught swimming, riding and shooting by officers, and finally apprenticed to military commands around the age of 12. Less is known about the schooling of princesses, but several queens were evidently well versed in statecraft and architecture.

Originally named the "Place of Beauty", but now known in Arabic as Biban el-Harem ("Gates of the Harem"), the valley contains nearly eighty tombs, most of which are basically just pits in the ground. Although the finest murals rival those in the Valley of the Kings for artistry, many have been corroded by salt deposits or badly vandalized, and the **tomb of Nefertari** is so fragile that it is only accessible to VIP groups and clients of Ancient World Tours (see p.31). **Tickets** for the other tombs are sold at the entrance to the valley; it takes fifteen minutes to walk there from Deir el-Medina or the main ticket office.

Tomb of Amunhirkhepshef (#55)

After Nefertari's, the best tomb in the valley belongs to **Amunhirkhepshef**, a son of Ramses III who accompanied his father on campaigns and perhaps died in battle at the age of 9. He is shown wearing the royal sidelock of youth, in lustrous murals where Ramses conducts him through funerary rituals, past the Keepers of the Gates, to an unfinished burial chamber containing a granite sarcophagus. A glass case displays a mummified foetus that his mother aborted through grief at Amunhirkhepshef's death, and entombed with her son.

Tomb of Queen Titi (#52)

Sited along the well-trodden route to Amunhirkhepshef's tomb, this cruciform structure was commissioned by **Queen Titi**, wife of one of the Ramessid pharaohs of the XX Dynasty. A winged Maat kneels in the corridor (where Titi appears before Thoth, Ptah and the sons of Horus) and guards the entrance to the burial chamber with Neith (left) and Selket (right).

The burial chamber itself boasts jackal, lion and baboon guardians, plus three side chambers, the finest being the one to the right. Here, Hathor emerges from between the mountains of east and west in her bovine form, while the tree-goddess pours Nile water to rejuvenate Titi, who reposes on a cushion across the room. Sadly, most of these murals are faded or damaged.

Tomb of Prince Khaemweset (#44)

This colourfully painted tomb is reached via a separate path. **Prince Khaemweset** was one of several sons of Ramses III who died in a smallpox epidemic, and the murals in his tomb give precedence to images of Ramses, making offerings in the entrance corridor and worshipping funerary deities in the side chambers. In the second corridor, decorated with the *Book of Gates*, Ramses leads Khaemweset past the fearsome guardians of the Netherworld to the Fields of Yaru, bearing witness for him before Osiris and Horus in the burial chamber. Notice the four sons of Horus on the lotus blossom.

Medinet Habu

Medinet Habu ("Habu's Town") is the Arabic name for the gigantic **Mortuary Temple of Ramses III**, a structure second only to Karnak in size and complexity, and better preserved in its entirety. Modelled on the Ramesseum of his illustrious ancestor, Ramses II, this XX Dynasty extravaganza deserves more attention than it usually gets, being the last stop on most tourists' itineraries. Its massive enclosure walls sheltered the entire population of Thebes during the Libyan invasions of the late XX Dynasty and for centuries afterwards protected the Coptic town of Djeme, built within the great temple.

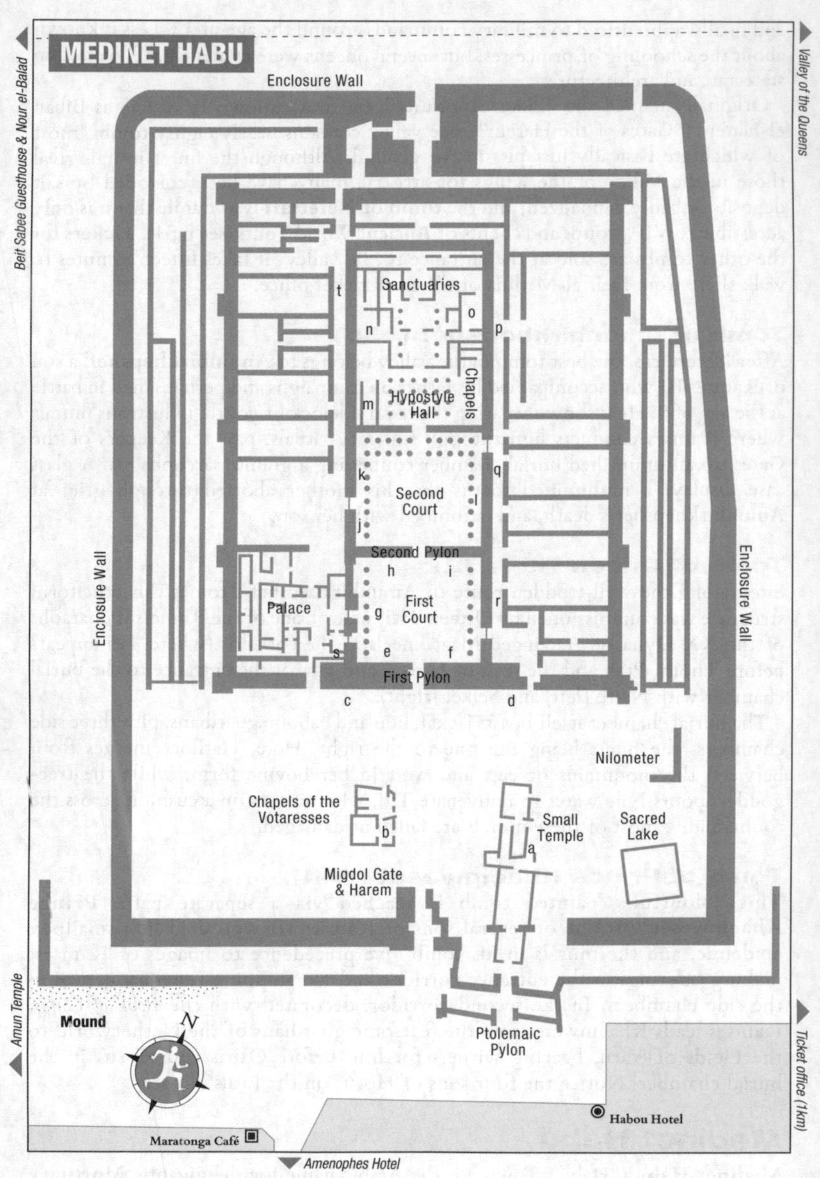

The temple precincts

The entire complex was originally surrounded by mud-brick **enclosure walls**, sections of which rise at intervals from the plain. Its front facade is quite asymmetrical, with a jutting **Ptolemaic Pylon** whose winged sun-disc glows with colour since its recent restoration, overshadowing the entrance to the temple precincts. This **Migdol Gate** is named after the Syrian fortress that so impressed Ramses with its lofty gatehouse that he built one for his own temple, and often relaxed with his **harem** in a suite above the gate (inaccessible), decorated with reliefs of dancers in slinky lingerie. Here, a secondary wife hatched a harem conspiracy to murder him during the Optet festival, so that her son could inherit – but the conspirators were discovered and forced to commit suicide. The two grey-green diorite statues of Sekhmet by the gate's entrance may have served to transmit the prayers of pilgrims to Amun, who "dwelt" within the temple.

To the north stands the **Small Temple**, reputedly where the primeval mound arose from the waters of Chaos, preceding the creator-god Re-Atum of the Hermopolitan Ogdoad. The existing structure was built and partly decorated by Hatshepsut, whose cartouches and images were erased by Tuthmosis III. Akhenaten did likewise to those of Amun, but Horemheb and Seti replaced them. Some defaced reliefs **[a]** show Tuthmosis presiding over the foundation ceremonies, "stretching the cord" before the goddess Seshat, "scattering the gypsum" and then "hacking the earth" before a priapic Min.

Whereas the Small Temple antedates Ramses' work by three centuries, the **Chapels of the Votaresses** are Late Period additions. Several date from the XXV Dynasty of Nubian kings, who appointed these high priestesses of Amun and de facto governors of Thebes. The best reliefs are in the forecourt **[b]** and shrine of Amenirdis, sister of King Shabaka, whose alabaster funerary statue is now in the Cairo Museum. Ironically, these chapels remained objects of veneration long after Ramses' temple had been abandoned. Notice the granite altars for offerings.

In the right-hand corner of the enclosure are the remains of a **Sacred Lake** where childless local women came to bathe at night and pray to Isis for conception.

Entering the Mortuary Temple of Ramses III

Like Deir el-Bahri and the Ramesseum, this mortuary temple was a focus for the pharaoh's cult, linking him to Amun-United-with-Eternity. The effigies of Amun, Mut and Khonsu paid an annual visit during the Festival of the Valley, while other deities permanently resided in its shrines, and Ramses himself often dwelt in the adjacent palace. Aside from its lack of freestanding colossi, the sandstone temple gives a good idea of how the Ramesseum must have looked before it collapsed.

Had it not lost its cornice and one corner, the **First Pylon** would match Luxor Temple's in size. For baksheesh, a guard may unlock a stairway to the top, which offers a panoramic view of the temple, Theban Hills and Nile Valley. Reliefs on the outer walls (copied from the Ramesseum) show Ramses smiting Nubians **[c]** and Syrians **[d]**, though he never warred with either. Those on the inner wall relate genuine campaigns with Ramessid hyperbole. An outsized Ramses scatters hordes of Libyans in his chariot **[e]**. Afterwards, scribes tally the severed hands and genitals of dead foes (third row from the bottom) **[f]**.

Until the nineteenth century, the ruined houses of Coptic Djeme filled the **First Court**, now cleared to reveal its flanking columns. Those on the right bear chunky Osiride statues of the king, attended by knee-high queens. The other side of the court abuts the royal palace (now ruined and entered from outside). In the middle of this wall was a Window of Appearances **[g]** flanked by sunk-reliefs of prisoners, whence the king rewarded loyal commanders with golden collars. Yet more scenes of triumph cover the outside of the **Second Pylon**, where Ramses leads three rows of prisoners to Amun and Mut **[h]** (those in the lowest row are Philistines) and a long inscription lauds his victories in Asia Minor **[i]**. The vultures on the ceiling of the pylon's gateway are still coloured.

Halls and sanctuaries

During Coptic times most of the Osirian pillars were removed to make room for a church, and a thick layer of mud was plastered over the reliefs in the **Second**

Court. Now uncovered, these depict the annual festivals of Min **[j]** and Sokar **[k]**, with processions of priests and dancers accompanying the royal palanquin. Elsewhere, the events of Ramses' fifth regnal year are related in a long text lower down the wall **[l]**. The lotus-bud columns of the rear arcade are coloured blue, red and turquoise.

The now-roofless **Hypostyle Hall**, beyond, once had a raised central aisle like the Great Hall at Karnak, and still has some brightly coloured pillars at the back. To the right lie five **chapels** dedicated to Ramses, his XIX Dynasty namesake, Ptah, Osiris and Sokar. On the opposite side are several (locked) treasure chambers whose reliefs show the weighing of myrrh, gold, lapis lazuli and other valuables bestowed upon the temple **[m]** – also visible on the outer walls.

Beyond this lie two **smaller halls** with rooms leading off. To the left of the first hall is the funerary chamber of Ramses III **[n]**; notice the lion-headed deity on the right-hand wall. The other side – open to the sky – featured an altar to Re. On the lintels that once supported the roof **[o]**, Ramses and several baboons worship Re's barque. The central aisle of the next level is flanked by red granite statues of Ramses with Maat or Thoth. At the back are three **sanctuaries** dedicated to the Theban Triad of Mut (left), Amun (centre) and Khonsu (right).

Along the outer walls

Some of the best reliefs at Medinet Habu are on the **outer walls** of the temple, involving a fair slog over broken ground. As most are quite faint, they're best viewed early or late in the day, when shadows reveal details obscured at midday. The famous **battle reliefs of Ramses II** run along the temple's northern wall, starting from the back. Although you'll encounter the last or middle scenes first, we've listed them in chronological order, as Ramses intended them to be seen. The first section **[p]** depicts the invasion of land-hungry Libyans, early in his reign. In the vanguard of the battle are Ramses, a lion, and the standard of Amun. Afterwards, scribes count limbs and genitals to assess each soldier's reward in gold or land. Yet despite this victory, Ramses was soon beleaguered on two fronts, as the Libyans joined with the Sea Peoples (Sardinians, Philistines and Cretans) in a concerted invasion of the Nile Delta. A giant Ramses fires arrows into a melee of grappling ships, in the only Egyptian relief of a sea battle **[q]**. A third invasion by the Libyans **[r]** was also thwarted, but their descendants would eventually triumph and rule Egypt as the XXIII and XXIV dynasties.

On the other side of the temple behind the First Pylon is a dramatic relief of Ramses hunting antelopes in the desert and impaling wild bulls in a marsh **[s]**, near a ruined **Palace** where he resided during visits. A calendar of festivals appears at the far end of the temple **[t]**, which is surrounded on three sides by mud-brick **storehouses**, eroded into worm-like shapes.

Other sites on the west bank

The village of **NAG LOHLAH** beside Medinet Habu will be familiar to readers of Richard Critchfield's *Shahhat* as the birthplace of its eponymous hero and the irascible Hagg Ali, owner of the *Habou Hotel* (which still exists, though Hagg is deceased). Most families have one foot in tourism and the other in farming, so that one finances the other as fortune allows. While Medinet Habu brings customers to their doorsteps – the *Maratonga Café* is ideal for cooling off – few visitors realise there's also an **Amun Temple** in someone's backyard (no set hours; baksheesh expected). Though small and knocked about, its reliefs retain some of the white background that has faded in other temples.

Monastery of St Tawdros

If it's not too hot, the **Monastery of St Tawdros** in the desert beyond Medinet Habu makes an interesting excursion. You can walk here from Medinat Habu in about twenty minutes, or cycle; even better, go riding in time for sunset. Be sure to cover your head and bring plenty of water; the unpaved track from Medinet Habu to the French House is easy going, but has no shade at all.

Roughly 200m right off the track into the desert, the monastery is easily identified by its beehive domes. Pharaonic, Greek and Roman masonry is incorporated into the low-vaulted church, whose shrines are dedicated to the Coptic martyrs Tawdros, Elkladius and Foktor. Tawdros (295–306 AD) was a leader in the Roman army before his conversion to Christianity, hence the monastery's alternative name, El Muharrib ("The Warrior"). The day of his martyrdom (January 20) and Easter see crowds of Copts descending on the monastery, but at other times the nuns who live here receive few visitors and seem pleased if anyone rings the bell.

Esna

Small-town life and ancient stone are boldly juxtaposed at **ESNA**, on the west bank of the Nile 54km south of Luxor and 155km north of Aswan. A huge pit in the centre of Esna exposes part of the **Temple of Khnum**, but some visitors are disappointed by what they find: the only part to have been excavated is the Hypostyle Hall, whose somewhat inferior reliefs detract from the forest of columns and lofty astronomical ceiling. Nowadays, you have to be really committed if you want to see Esna's temple, as there are no organized excursions to it.

Visible just north of Esna are two **barrages** that act as bridges over the Nile, with **locks** to allow vessels to pass through. Now that few cruise boats moor on Esna's Corniche, salesmen wait at the locks to throw their wares on to the decks for sunbathing tourists to buy.

The Temple of Khnum

When Amelia Edwards visited Esna, the **Temple of Khnum** (daily: summer 7am–5pm; winter 7am–4pm; £E20) was "buried to the chin in the accumulated rubbish of a score of centuries" and built over with houses. To minimize their destruction, only a portion was excavated in the 1860s. Now 10m below ground level, the temple resembles a pharaonic Fort Knox, its boxy mass fronted by six columns rising from a screen, the open space above them covered with wire mesh to discourage nesting birds.

Arriving in Esna by bus, you can head to the temple by *calèche* (£E15) or pick-up (£E1) on the main road near the bus station, or walk there in about twenty minutes. The easiest way is to do this is to follow the Corniche south past

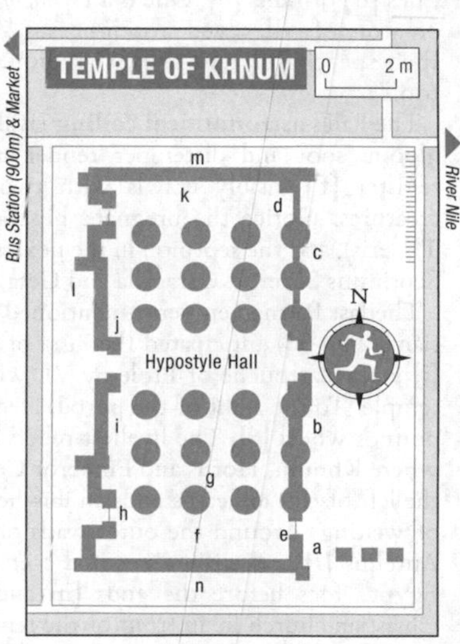

Khnum and Hapy

▲ Khnum

In Upper Egypt, **Khnum** was originally the ram-headed creator-god who moulded man on a potter's wheel, and the guardian of the Nile's source (which myth was assigned to the caves just beyond the First Cataract, although the Ancient Egyptians must have known better). Later, however, Khnum was demoted to an underling of Amun-Re and shared his role as river deity with **Hapy**, god of the Nile in flood, who was also believed to dwell in an island cavern near the First Cataract. Shown with a blue-green body and a female breast, wearing a crown of lotus or sedge (the heraldic plants of Upper and Lower Egypt), he should not be confused with Horus's son, Hapi, the ape-headed deity of canopic jars.

▲ Hapy

the *dahabiya* moorings and some old *mashrabiya*'d houses, until you catch sight of a riverside kiosk housing the temple's **ticket office,** from which a covered tourist bazaar leads directly to the temple.

The site

The temple, a Ptolemaic-Roman replacement for a much older structure dedicated to the ram-headed creator-god of ancient myth, faced eastwards and probably rivalled Edfu's for size. Since what you see is merely the Roman section (dating from the first century AD), the **facade** bears the cartouches of Claudius **[a]**, Titus **[b]** and Vespasian **[c]**, and the battered sun-disc above the entrance is flanked by votive inscriptions to these emperors.

As you enter the lofty **Hypostyle Hall**, your eyes are drawn upwards by a forest of columns that bud and flower in variegated capitals. Their shafts are covered with festival texts (now defaced) or hieroglyphs in the form of crocodiles **[d]** or rams **[e]**. One is a *Hymn of Creation* that acknowledges Khnum as the creator of all, even foreigners: "All are formed on his potter's wheel, their speech different in every region… but the lord of the wheel is their father too."

The hall's **astronomical ceiling** rivals Dendara's for finesse and complexity, but gloom, soot and distemper render much indiscernible. However, the zodiac register **[f]** visibly crawls with two-headed snakes, winged dogs and other creatures. Notice the pregnant hippo-goddess Tweri (whom the Greeks called Thoeris), and the scorpion in the next aisle **[g]**. Registers on the walls below show Septimius Severus, Caracalla and Geta before the gods.

The last Roman emperor mentioned is Decius **[h]**, whose persecution of Christians (249–51) anticipated the "Era of Martyrs" under Diocletian. Further along **[i]** is the cartouche of Ptolemy VI, whose father began the construction of Esna temple. To the right of the portal, Decius makes offerings to Khnum, including a potter's wheel **[j]**. The liveliest reliefs are near the foot of the northern wall **[k]**, where Khnum, Horus and Emperor Commodus net fish and malignant spirits. To the left of this tableau stands an ibis-headed Thoth; to the right, Sheshat, goddess of writing. Around the outer walls of the temple are texts dedicated to Marcus Aurelius **[l]** and stiffly executed scenes of Titus, Domitian and Trajan smiting Egypt's foes before the gods **[m** and **n]**. Several stone blocks from an early Christian church lie in front of the temple.

Practicalities

Sadly for the local economy tourism tends to bypass Esna, as most **cruise boats** merely pass through the locks, while travellers on **feluccas** from Aswan disembark short of Esna to drive directly to Luxor, and hotels in Aswan and Luxor no longer feature it on day excursions to Edfu and Kom Ombo. If you're still determined, expect to pay about £E200–300 for a four-seater taxi from Luxor.

Getting here by **train** is awkward, as the station is on the east bank of the Nile, far from the temple (£E20 by taxi), and not all trains stop at Esna anyway. **Buses** are handier, with four a day from Luxor and Aswan, which drop you in the centre of town, just under 1km from the temple.

The **tourist police** are near the temple ticket booth, with a **bank** and a **post office** further north along the Corniche. A humble place on the corner by the temple serves **meals**, and street food is sold in the souk.

Edfu and around

Situated on the west bank of the Nile, roughly equidistant from Luxor (115km) and Aswan (105km), the provincial town of **EDFU** boasts the best-preserved **cult temple** in Egypt, dedicated to the falcon-headed god **Horus**. Though actually built in the Ptolemaic era, this mammoth edifice respects all the canons of pharaonic architecture, giving an excellent idea of how most temples once looked. In terms of sheer monumental grandeur, it ranks alongside Karnak and Deir el-Bahri as one of the finest sites in the Nile Valley. A must-see for tourists (and on every cruise boat or felucca itinerary), it has saved Edfu from the fate of Esna.

Practicalities

Edfu is most easily reached on minibus **excursions** arranged by hotels in Aswan (see p.356), in tandem with Kom Ombo and ending up in Luxor; the cost per person (£E65–85) doesn't include admission tickets. Far fewer tourists want to do this trip in the opposite direction, making it more expensive if you start from Luxor, where you might have to pay £E250 to hire a taxi. Otherwise, the only alternative is to use public transport.

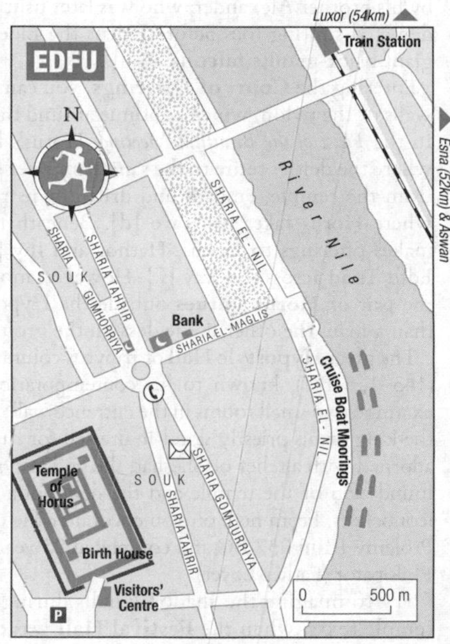

The **train station** is on the east bank of the Nile, 4km from the temple. **Buses** travelling between Aswan and Luxor drop passengers either there or on the highway, from where you'll need to catch a covered pick-up to the bridge and then another into town (each costs 50pt), or rent one for the entire journey to the main square (about £E5), ten minutes' walk from the temple. Arriving by river is a different story, as **cruise boats** moor within a *calèche*-ride of the temple, and passengers disembarking from **feluccas** are invariably driven to the temple by minibus.

However you arrive in Edfu, the temple is approached via a fenced-off security zone with a single sunken access road overlooked by gun-towers, which have abolished the previous proximity of houses overlooking the temple, creating a sterile tourist zone with a bazaar and a lacklustre **visitors' centre** that mainly functions as a toilet. **Tickets** for the site (daily: summer 7am–7pm; winter 7am–8pm; £E50) are sold from a kiosk in the car park.

The Temple of Horus

The **Temple of Horus** lay buried to its lintels until the 1860s, when Auguste Mariette cleared the main building; a splendid drawing by David Roberts shows the courtyard full of sand and peasant houses built atop the Hypostyle Hall. Yet the mammoth task of excavation was nothing compared to the temple's construction, which outlasted six Ptolemies, the final touches being added by the twelfth ruler of that dynasty. The reliefs and **inscriptions** on the walls include the myth of the struggle between Horus and Seth and an account of the temple's foundation-rituals, known to Egyptologists as the Edfu texts. You can read them *in situ* using Dieter Kurth's annotated text, *Edfu Temple: A Guide by an Ancient Egyptian Priest* (see "Books" in Contexts).

Visitors approach the temple as the ancients did, passing through high mud-brick **enclosure walls** and a **Pro-Pylon** (now ruined). Off to the left, the colonnaded **Birth House** was a focus for the annual Coronation Festival re-enacting the divine birth of Horus and the reigning pharaoh. Don't miss the reliefs of Horus being suckled by Isis, both as a baby (low down on the rear wall) and as a young man (on the facing columns) **[a]**.

The temple **pylon** was erected by Ptolemy IX before he was ousted from power by his brother Alexander, who was later usurped by another ruler, Neos Dionysos, depicted smiting foes before Horus the Elder **[b]**. Its gateway is fronted by two giant black-granite **falcons**.

Entering the **Court of Offerings**, you can study the festival reliefs on the inner walls of the pylon, which continue around the court along the bottom of the wall. In the *Feast of the Beautiful Meeting*, Horus's barque tows Hathor's to the temple, where the deities retire to the sanctuary after suitable rituals **[c]**. Later they emerge from the temple, embark and drift downstream to the edge of the Edfu nome, where Horus takes his leave **[d]**. Beneath the western colonnade, Ptolemy IX makes offerings to Horus, Hathor and Ihy **[e]**; his successor appears before the Edfu Triad across the way **[f]**. However, most visitors are content to photograph the pair of **Horus statues** outside the Hypostyle Hall. One hawk stands higher than a man, the other lies legless on the ground.

The great **Hypostyle Hall** of papyrus columns dates from the reign of Ptolemy VII (145–116 BC), known to his contemporaries as "Fatty". With a torch, you can examine two small rooms in the entrance wall: the Chamber of Consecrations, where the king or his priestly stand-in dressed for rituals **[g]**; and a Library of sacred texts adorned with a relief of Sheshat, the goddess of writing **[h]**. The reliefs showing the foundation of the temple and the deification of Horus **[i]** have been mutilated by iconoclasts. From here on you encounter the oldest section of the temple, begun by Ptolemy III in 237 BC and completed 25 years later by his son, who styled himself Philopator (Father Lover).

Try to imagine the shadowy halls during the annual festivals rhapsodized in temple texts, when the **Festival Hall** was decorated with faïence, strewn with

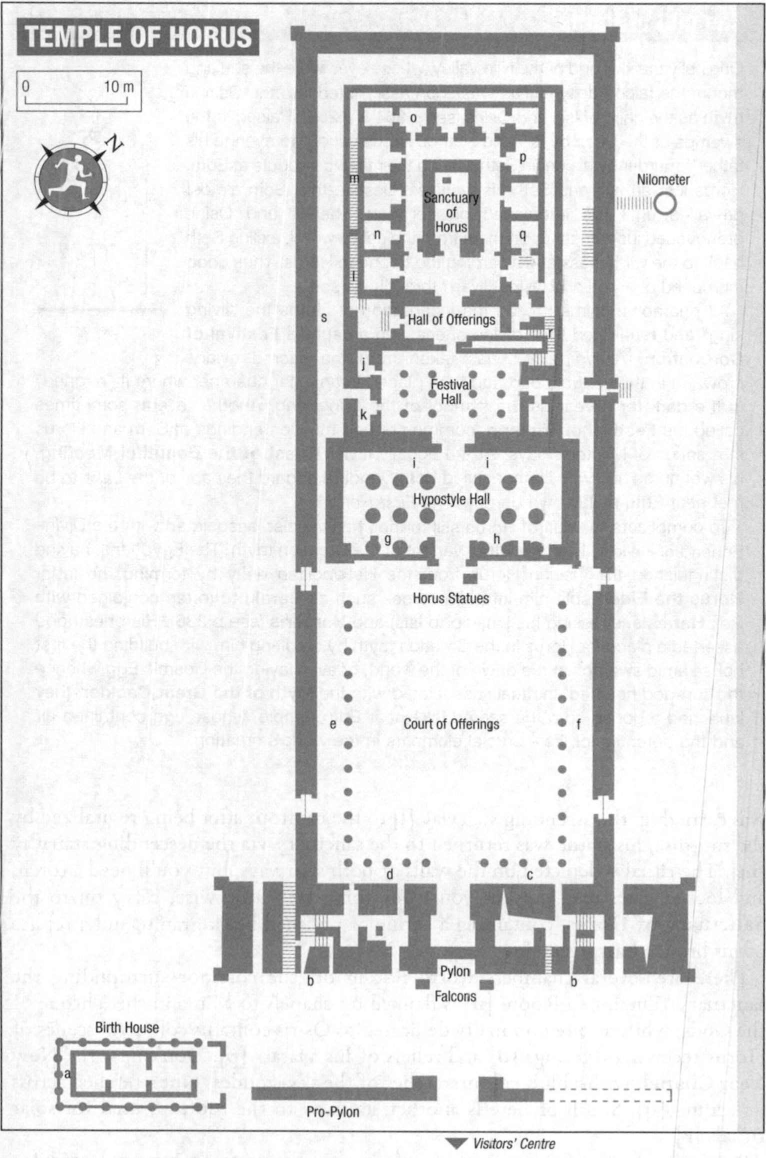

flowers and herbs and perfumed by myrrh. Incense and unguents were blended according to recipes inscribed on the walls of the Laboratory **[j]**. Nonperishable offerings were stored in the room next door **[k]**, while libations, fruit and sacrificial animals were brought in through a passageway connected to the outside world.

The sacred barques of Horus and Hathor appear in glorious detail on either side of the doorway into the **Hall of Offerings**. During the New Year Festival, Horus

The cult of Horus

▲ Horus

Originally the sky-god of the Nile Valley, whose eyes were the sun and moon, the falcon deity **Horus** was soon assimilated into the Osirian myth as the child of Isis and Osiris (see p.364 & p.255). Raised in the swamps of the Delta by Isis and Hathor, Horus set out to avenge his father's murder by his uncle Seth. During their titanic struggle at Edfu, Horus lost an eye and Seth his testicles. Despite this, Seth almost prevailed until Isis intervened on her son's behalf and Osiris pronounced judgement upon them from the netherworld, exiling Seth back to the wilderness and awarding the throne to Horus. Thus good triumphed over evil and Osiris "lived" through his son.

All pharaohs claimed to be the incarnation of Horus the "living king" and reaffirmed their divine oneness in an annual **Festival of Coronation**. A live falcon was taken from the sacred aviary, crowned in the central court and then placed in an inner chamber where it "reigned" in the dark for a year as the symbol of the living king. Another event, sometimes called the **Festival of Triumph**, commemorated the Contendings of Seth and Horus in a series of Mystery Plays. At the equally lavish **Feast of the Beautiful Meeting**, his wet nurse and wife Hathor sailed from Dendara aboard the *Lady of the Lake* to be met near Edfu by his own barque, *The First Horus*.

To complicate the cult of Horus still further, he was also associated with the Divine Ennead of Heliopolis and another variant of the Creation myth. The Egyptians, having distinguished the Osirian Horus from the Heliopolitan deity by terming the latter **Horus the Elder**, split him into archetypes such as **Herakhte** (often conjoined with Re), **Hariesis** (stressing his kinship to Isis) and **Haroeris** (see p.336). His priesthood asserted a place for Horus in the Creation myth by crediting him with building the first house amid swamps at the dawn of the world, or even laying the Cosmic Egg whence the sun-god hatched. In rituals associated with the **Myth of the Great Cackler**, they launched a goose onto the sacred lake near Edfu temple, whose egg contained air and the potential for life – crucial elements in the world's creation.

was carried up the ascending stairway **[l]** to the rooftop; after being revitalized by the sun-disc, his statue was returned to the sanctuary via the descending stairway **[m]**. The ritual is depicted on the walls of both stairways, but you'll need a torch, and locked gates may prevent you from going far. Otherwise, carry on to the **Sanctuary of Horus**, containing a shrine of polished black granite and a replica of his bronze **barque shrine**.

There are several chambers worth noting off the corridor surrounding the sanctuary. The Linen Room **[n]** is flanked by chapels to Min and the Throne of the Gods, while a suite nominally dedicated to Osiris contains colourful scenes of Horus receiving offerings **[o]** and reliefs of his avatars **[p]**. Don't miss the **New Year Chapel**, with a blue-coloured relief of the sky-goddess Nut stretched across its ceiling **[q]**. South of here is another stairway to the rooftop, used for solar rituals **[r]**.

Returning to the Festival Hall, you can gain access to an external corridor running between the inner and outer walls, where the priesthood tallied tithes assessed on the basis of readings from the temple's own **Nilometer** (accessible by a passage in the temple's pylon). On the other side of the temple are tableaux from the Triumph of Horus over Seth, depicting Mystery Plays in which Seth was cast as a hippopotamus, lurking beneath his brother's boat **[s]**. At the end of the play, the priests cut up and ate a hippo-shaped cake, to destroy Seth completely.

El-Kab, Kom al-Ahmar and Silsilah

Fifteen kilometres downriver from Edfu, the east bank road between Luxor and Kom Ombo passes the site known as **EL-KAB**, once the ancient city of Nekheb, dedicated to the vulture-goddess of Upper Egypt, whose ruins are less spectacular than other temple sites. Tickets are sold from a kiosk by the highway, which bisects the site. Buses from Aswan or Luxor can drop you here on request, but getting a ride out later could be difficult. If you happen to be aboard a felucca or *dahabiya*, ask to be let ashore to visit.

The most conspicuous part of the site (daily 7am–5pm; £E30) lies towards the Nile, where the vast mud-brick **walls** that once enclosed the city stand, along with the conjoined **temples** of Nekhbet and Thoth, now reduced to stumps of painted columns and a series of **crypts** (notable for a scene of baboons dancing to the rituals of Mut). Across the road and up the slope from the ticket office, other ruins are scattered eastwards across the desert. Of the **tombs** dug into the nearest ridge of hills, the best preserved is that of **Daheri**, royal scribe and tutor, and son of Tuthmosis I, which features ranks of lotus-sniffers and field workers. Next door are the tombs of commander **Ahmose**, who took part in the war to expel the Hyksos from Egypt and left a long account of his bravery; **Setau**, high priest of Nekhbet; and superintendent **Renini**.

On the far side of the Nile lies another site – **off-limits** to tourists – known as **Kom Al-Ahmar** (Red Mound), which the ancient Egyptians called Nekhen and the Greeks **Hierakonopolis** (City of the Falcon). As its names suggest, the city was closely associated with Horus and an earlier, local falcon-god, Nekheny. It flourished during the late Predynastic and early dynastic periods (c.4000–2686 BC) and may have been the first administrative capital of the Two Lands, judging by such famous artefacts as the Palette of Narmer and the Scorpion Macehead. News of current excavations appears on Ⓦwww.hierakonopolis.org and www.archaeology.org.

Travelling this way **by river**, you'll pass a succession of ancient quarries. At **Silsilah** the river is constricted by sheer cliffs and the bedrock changes from Egyptian limestone to Nubian sandstone; its ancient name, Khenu ("Place of Rowing"), suggests that rapids once existed here. Feluccas and *dahabiyas* moor to let passengers explore the **quarries** on the east bank, reached by a defile down which cut stones were dragged. Across the Nile are 32 rock-hewn **shrines** (daily 7am–5pm; £E25) dedicated to officials, priests, and pharaohs **Merneptah** and **Horemheb** – spotlit at night for the benefit of passing cruise boats. Silsilah is accessible **by car** (£E400) from Luxor using backroads known to Haggag at the *Restaurant Mohammed* (see p.299).

Kom Ombo

Many of the Nubians displaced by Lake Nasser have settled around the town of **KOM OMBO**. In ancient times this stood at the crossroads of the caravan route from Nubia and trails from the gold mines of the Eastern Desert; under Ptolemy VI (180–145 BC), it became the capital of the Ombos nome and a training depot for African war elephants, which the Ptolemies required to fight the pachyderms of the Seleucid Empire.

In 2007 Belgian archeologists discovered what may be Egypt's **oldest rock art**, on boulders in the village of **Qurta**, outside Kom Ombo. Provisionally dated to 15,000 years ago (like the famous Lascaux Caves in France), the painted carvings of cattle, gazelles, hippos, fish, and humans with exaggerated buttocks are sure to be off-limits for the foreseeable future, and Kom Ombo remains far better known for its Ptolemaic **Temple of Haroeris and Sobek**. Unlike other temples in the valley, this still stands beside the Nile, making the approach by river one of the highlights of a cruise.

Practicalities

Kom Ombo lies along the east-bank road between Luxor (170km) and Aswan (45km), roughly 60km south of Edfu. Since the temple is 4km south of town, it's best to travel here directly on a minibus **excursion** from Aswan (see p.356) or wherever your felucca moors (see p.251), or to arrive on a cruise boat which docks nearby. Getting here by **public transport** is a hassle; buses from Aswan can drop you at the signposted turn-off before town, from where you can walk or hitch 1700m to the temple; the train station is even further away. As at other sites, a security zone-cum-tourist bazaar separates the temple from everyday life. Here you can eat in the shady *Rural Home* **cafeteria**, offering henna-tattooing and other diversions for children.

The Temple of Haroeris and Sobek

The **Temple of Haroeris and Sobek** (daily: summer 7am–5pm; winter 7am–4pm; £E30) stands on a low promontory near a bend in the river whose sandbanks were a basking place for crocodiles in ancient times. This proximity to the Nile has both preserved and damaged the site, covering the temple with sand which protected it from Coptic iconoclasts, but also washing away its pylon and forecourt. What remains was aptly described by Amelia Edwards as a "magnificent torso"; truncated and roofless yet still imposing.

Its defining characteristic is its bisymmetry, with twin entrances and sanctuaries, and halls nominally divided down the middle. The left side is dedicated to the falcon-headed Haroeris, the "Good Doctor" (a form of Horus the Elder) and his consort Ta-Sent-Nefer, the "Good Sister" (an aspect of Hathor). The crocodile-god Sobek (here identified with the sun as Sobek-Re), his wife (another form of Hathor) and their son Khonsu-Hor are honoured on the right side of the temple.

Approaching it by road, you first sight the **Gate of Neos Dionysos**. Its provenance is obscure, as scholars disagree over the number, order and dates of the various Ptolemies, each of whom adopted a title such as Soter (Saviour), Euergetes (Benefactor) or Philometor (Mother Lover). Some identify Neos Dionysos as Ptolemy XII, others as Ptolemy XIII, but all agree that he fathered the great Cleopatra and was nicknamed "The Bastard".

The facade and Hypostyle Halls

With the forecourt (added by Emperor Trajan in 14 AD) reduced to low walls and stumps of pillars, your eyes are drawn to the **facade** of the Hypostyle Hall, whose surviving columns burst in floral capitals beneath a chunk of cavetto cornice bearing a winged sun-disc and twin *uraei* above each portal, their colours still vivid. Bas-reliefs on the outer wall show Neos Dionysos being purified by Thoth and Horus **[a]**, and yet again in the presence of Sobek, whose face has been chiselled away **[b]**.

Wandering amid the thicket of columns inside the **outer Hypostyle Hall**, notice the heraldic lily of Upper Egypt or the papyrus symbol of the Delta carved on their bases. On the inner wall of the facade are splendid carvings of Neos Dionysos's coronation before Haroeris, Sobek, Wadjet and Nekhbet (the goddesses of the north and south) **[c]**, and his appearance before Isis, Horus the Elder and a lion-headed deity **[d]**. Neos Dionysos makes offerings to the same deities at the back of the hall, whose right side retains much of its roof, decorated with flying vultures.

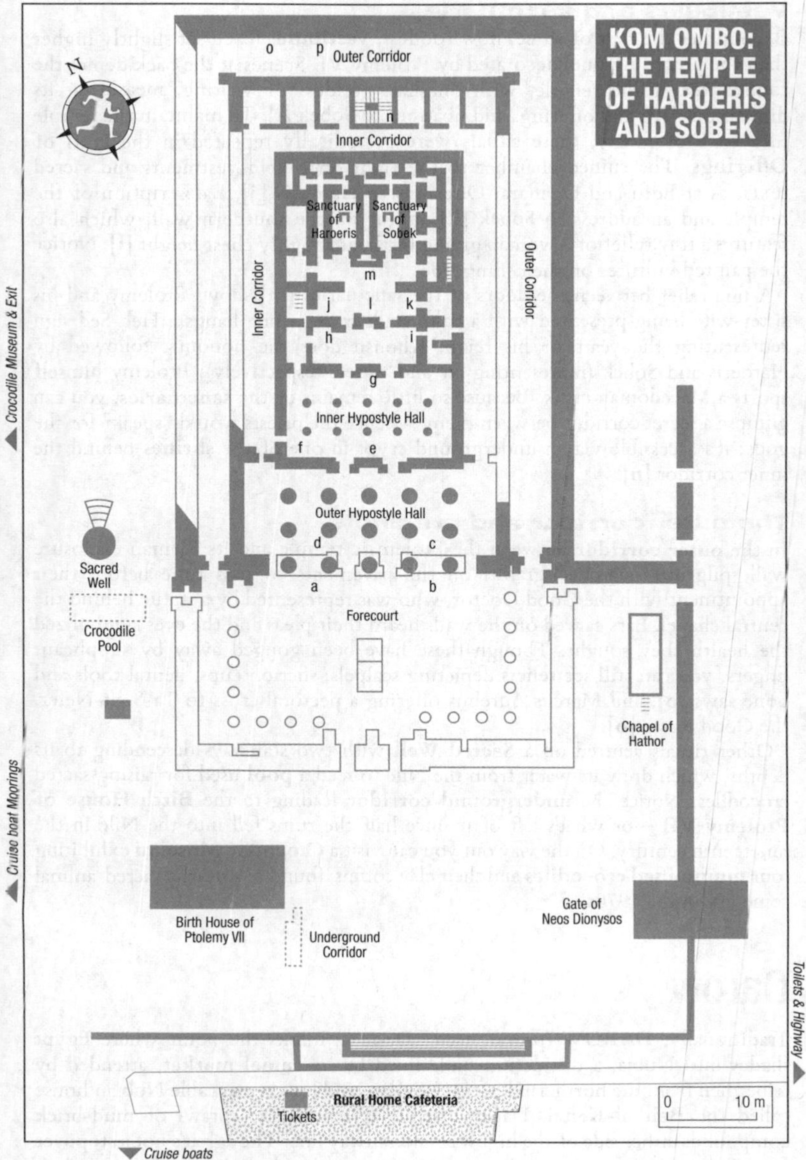

Entering the older, **inner Hypostyle Hall**, you'll find a relief of Sobek in his reptilian form between the portals **[e]**. Ptolemy II receives the *hps* (sword of victory) from Haroeris (accompanied by his sister Cleopatra and his wife of the same name) in the southwest corner of the hall **[f]** and makes offerings to gods on the shafts of the pillars, while his elder brother does likewise to Haroeris at the back of the hall, where a list of temple deities and festivals appears between the doors **[g]**.

Vestibules and sanctuaries

Beyond lies the first of three, now roofless, **vestibules** (each set slightly higher than the preceding one) decorated by Ptolemy VI. Scenes at the back depict the foundation of the temple, with Sheshat, goddess of writing, measuring its dimensions **[h]**; and offerings and libations to Sobek **[i]**. To maintain the temple in a state of purity, these rituals were periodically repeated in the **Hall of Offerings**. The ruined chamber to the right once held vestments and sacred texts, as at Edfu and Dendara. Offerings to Haroeris **[j]**, a description of the temple and an address to Sobek **[k]** appear on the southern wall, which also features a tiny relief of a woman giving birth, at roughly chest height **[l]**. Notice the painted vultures on the ceiling, too.

A fine relief between the doors of the sanctuaries **[m]** shows Ptolemy and his sister-wife being presented with a palm stalk from which hangs a Heb-Sed sign representing the years of his reign. Khonsu does the honours, followed by Haroeris and Sobek (representing air and water, respectively); Ptolemy himself sports a Macedonian cloak. Because so little remains of the **sanctuaries**, you can glimpse a secret corridor between them, whence the priests would "speak" for the gods; it's accessible via an underground crypt in one of the **shrines** behind the inner corridor **[n]**.

The outer corridor and precincts

In the **outer corridor** between the Ptolemaic temple and its Roman enclosure wall, pilgrims scratched graffiti on the pavements to pass time before their appointment with the Good Doctor, who was represented by a statue behind the central chapel. Ears carved on the walls heard their pleas and the eyes symbolized the health they sought. Though these have been gouged away by supplicant fingers, you can still see reliefs depicting scalpels, suction cups, dental tools and bone saws **[o]**, and Marcus Aurelius offering a pectoral cross to Ta-Sent-Nefer, the Good Sister **[o]**.

Other rituals centred on a **Sacred Well** with two stairways descending to its depths, which drew its water from the Nile to feed a **pool** used for raising sacred crocodiles. Notice the **underground corridor** leading to the **Birth House of Ptolemy VII** – or what's left of it since half the ruins fell into the Nile in the nineteenth century. On the way out you can visit a **Crocodile Museum** exhibiting four **mummified crocodiles** and their clay coffins, found in a nearby sacred-animal cemetery in the 1970s.

Darow

Traditionally, **DAROW** (pronounced "De-*rao*") marks the point where Egypt shades into Nubia, a distinction underlined by its **camel market**, attended by tribesmen from the northern deserts of Sudan, and by a remarkable Nubian house called the **Beit al-Kenzi**. Darow itself is a ramshackle sprawl of mud-brick compounds either side of the highway and railway line. Though it's not a stopover for minibus excursions from Aswan or Luxor, **getting here** is straightforward, as almost all trains except sleepers call here, and feluccas sailing this far downriver from Aswan usually allow passengers a visit ashore.

Darow Camel Market

The **Camel Market** (Souk el-Gamal) happens every Tuesday throughout the year, and maybe also on Sundays or Mondays over winter. Although hours (7am–2pm) remain constant, with activities winding down after 11am, the location of the market changes seasonally. Over winter, it's often held in two dusty compounds on the eastern outskirts of Darow (fifteen minutes' walk from the main intersection). During summer, it may take place on the other side of town beyond the vegetable and poultry souk – just follow the crowds. The giveaway is truckloads of camels bumping hither and thither along a dusty lane.

At the end you'll find hundreds of camels with their forelegs hobbled in the traditional manner, and drovers and buyers drinking tea and smoking *sheeshas* beneath awnings. As the principal camel market between Dongola and Cairo, Darow is a good place to do business. The camels spend two days in quarantine before being sold to *fellaheen* who need a beast of burden, or merchants who plan to sell the camels for a profit at Cairo's Birqesh market. Many are destined to end up on the dinner tables of the poor.

The Souk el-Gamal coincides with a **livestock market** where donkeys, sheep and cows jostle for space with people and trucks. In summer the two markets are often held side by side, with **handicrafts** (as well as saddlery) also sometimes sold at the camel market throughout the winter.

Beit al-Kenzi

A cooler attraction is the **Beit al-Kenzi** – a fabulous house in the traditional Nubian style, built of mud-bricks and dom palms, with beehive domes, inner courtyards and spacious rooms divided by reed-lattice partitions, to allow air to circulate. Built in 1912 by the grandfather of its present occupant so that his descendants would retain something of the ancestral village that was sacrificed to the first Aswan Dam, its owner, Aid Mohammed Hassanein, is happy to show visitors around. The house is beside the Gar Rasoul Mosque on Sharia al-Kunuz; turn right outside the train station, walk along the road and head left to find it.

Aswan and around

Egypt's southernmost city and ancient frontier town has the loveliest setting on the Nile. At **ASWAN** the deserts close in on the river, confining its sparkling blue between smooth amber sand and rugged extrusions of granite bedrock. Lateen-sailed feluccas glide past the ancient ruins and gargantuan rocks of Elephantine Island, palms and tropical shrubs softening the islands and embankments till intense blue skies fade into soft-focus dusks.

Although its own monuments are insignificant compared to Luxor's, Aswan is the base for **excursions** to the **temples of Philae and Kabasha**, near the great dams beyond the First Cataract, and the Sun Temple of Ramses II at **Abu Simbel**, far to the south. It is also the best starting point for excursions to Darow Camel Market, and the temples of Kom Ombo and Edfu, between Aswan and Luxor. Though Kom Ombo and Edfu are easier to reach by road, the classic approach is to travel downriver by felucca, experiencing the Nile's moods and scenery as travellers have for millennia – or on a luxurious cruise. The ins-and-outs of **felucca journeys**, **dahabiyas** and **Nile cruises** are described on pp.250–252, p.249 and p.248. Aswan itself is laid-back to the point of torpor, with a local **tourism** scene essentially similar to Luxor's but far less dynamic.

Situated near the Tropic of Cancer, Aswan is hot and dry nearly all the time, with average daily temperatures ranging from a delicious 23–30°C in the winter to a searing 38–54°C over summer. In late January and early February, hordes of Egyptians visit Aswan, block-booking hotels and seats on trains from Luxor and Cairo. Late autumn and spring are the perfect times to visit, being less crowded than the peak winter period, yet not so enervating as summer (May–Oct), when long siestas, cold showers and air conditioning are essential and nocturnal power cuts not only deprive you of cooling and lighting, but mean that food may go bad in fridges overnight.

Some history

Elephantine Island – opposite modern Aswan in the Nile – has been settled since remotest antiquity, and its fortress-town of Yebu became the border post between Egypt and Nubia early in the Old Kingdom. Local governors, or "Guardians of the Southern Gates", were responsible for border security and trade with Nubia, for huge quarries for fine red granite, and mining of amethysts, quartzite, copper, tin and malachite in the desert hinterland. Military outposts further south could summon help from the Yebu garrison by signal fires and an Egyptian fleet patrolled the river between the First and Second Cataracts.

Besides this, Yebu was an important cult centre, for the Egyptians believed that the Nile welled up from subterranean caverns at the **First Cataract**, just upriver (see p.356). Its local **deities** were Hapy and Satet, god of the Nile flood and goddess of its fertility, though the region's largest temple honoured Khnum, the provincial deity (see p.330).

During settled periods, the vast trade in ivory, slaves, gold, silver, incense, exotic animal skins and feathers spawned a **market town** on the east bank, but the island

Nubia and the Nubians

Nubia and Egypt have been neighbours since time immemorial. The Egyptians called Nubia Ta-Seti (Land of the Bow), after the weapons for which the Nubians were renowned, while its modern name is thought to derive from *nbw*, the ancient word for gold, which was mined there until Greco-Roman times.

A Nilotic people living between the First and Sixth Cataracts of the Nile (roughly from Aswan to Khartoum) may have been the forerunners of Egypt's civilization. Archeologists have found exquisite figurines predating prehistoric finds in Egypt by three thousand years, and the **world's oldest solar calendar** of standing stones, dating from around 6000 BC, at **Nabta Playa**, 100km from Abu Simbel. Pharaonic and ancient Nubian civilization evolved in similar ways until 3500 BC, when Egypt's unification raised the Old Kingdom to a level from which it could exploit Nubia as a source of **mineral wealth**, exotic goods and **slaves**. The onset of the Middle Kingdom saw the annexation of Lower Nubia – the land between the First and Second Cataracts – while under the New Kingdom, Nubia was ruled by a viceroy entitled the King's Son of **Kush**. It was only at the end of the Third Intermediate Period that Nubia got its own back, as the local rulers of **Napata** took advantage of Egypt's disunity to invade and establish their own **Kushite Dynasty** of pharaohs (747–656 BC), who reigned until the Assyrian invasion of Egypt in 671 BC.

Reconsolidating itself beyond the Fourth Cataract, the Kushite **Kingdom of Meröe** marked the apogee of Nubian civilization, building remarkable **pyramids** and maintaining relations with the Ptolemies, but angering the Romans, who occupied Lower Nubia from 23–272 AD. Before withdrawing, they invited warriors called the **Nobatae** (perhaps Nuba from the Red Sea Hills of Sudan) to fill the vacuum, hastening the decline of Meröe. In the seventh century the Nobatae were converted to Christianity by monks from Aswan's Monastery of St Simeon, and later became the main bulwark against attacks by the Islamic rulers of Egypt during the Fatimid era, until in 1315 the last Christian king was replaced by a Muslim one and most of the population accepted Islam.

Egypt's rulers made little attempt to control Nubia so long as it supplied the ivory and exotica they prized, until **Mohammed Ali** visited devastation on Nubia when he remained paramount throughout classical times, when it was known by its Greek appellation, **Seyene**. The Alexandrian geographer **Eratosthenes** (276–196 BC) heard of a local well into which the sun's rays fell perpendicularly at midday on the summer solstice, leaving no shadow; from this he deduced that Seyene lay on the Tropic of Cancer, concluded that the world was round and calculated its diameter with nearly modern accuracy – being only 80km out. (Since that time, the Tropic of Cancer has moved further south.)

The potency of the **cult of Isis** at nearby **Philae** (see p.364) made this one of the last parts of Egypt to be affected by **Christianity**, but once converted it became a stronghold of the faith. From their desert Monastery of St Simeon, monks made forays into Nubia, eventually converting the local Nobatae, who returned the favour by helping them to resist Islamic rule until finally subjugated by Salah al-Din. However, Bedouin raiders persisted through to 1517, when Sultan Selim garrisoned an entire army here, by which time the town's name had changed from Coptic Sawan to its present form, and the population had embraced **Islam**.

During the nineteenth century Aswan was the base for the conquest of Sudan and the defeat of the Mahadist Uprising (1881–98) by Anglo-Egyptian forces. As British influence grew, it also became the favourite **winter resort** of rich, ailing Europeans, who flocked to Aswan for its dry heat and therapeutic hot sands, luxurious hotels and stunning scenery. Its final transformation into the Aswan of

sent his son to enslave its male population as cannon fodder for his new army. Resentment smouldered through the reigns of the khedives, drawing in the **British**, who began by supporting khedival forces and ended up underwriting an Anglo-Egyptian government in 1899, when the border between Egypt and Sudan was drawn 40km north of Wadi Halfa and Nubia was divided, yet again.

Meanwhile, the **Nubians** remained true to their ancestral homeland and traditional life centred round **villages** of extended families (each with its own compound of domed houses), living by farming the verges of the river, fishing, and transporting trade goods. Socially and spiritually, the Nile formed the basis of their existence; villages celebrated births, weddings and circumcision ceremonies with Nile rituals.

This way of life – which had existed pretty much unchanged for five millennia – was shattered by the **Aswan Dams**. The first dam, built in 1902, forced the Nubians to move onto higher, unfertile ground; many menfolk left for Cairo, sending back remittances to keep the villages going. With construction of the High Dam, the Nubians' traditional homeland was entirely submerged, displacing the entire 800,000-strong community, around half of whom moved north, settling around Aswan and Kom Ombo. Meanwhile the **ancient monuments** of Nubia were moved to higher ground or foreign museums, under a huge project co-ordinated by UNESCO.

In Egypt, **Nubians took advantage** of higher education and business opportunities to make their mark in government, commerce or tourism. Remarkably, the community has maintained its cultural identity, with the resettled villages in Upper Egypt (which took their old names) acting as guardians of tradition and hopes of settling the shores of Lake Nasser.

The Nubian **language** is still spoken, but not written; its linguistic ancestor Old Nubian was recorded in a modified Greek alphabet which some scholars maintain has 26 letters, others 30. Among **websites** devoted to Nubian history and culture are Ⓦwww.homestead.com/wysinger/nubians.html (for prehistory and the Meröe pyramids), Ⓦwww.thenubian.net (for cultural commentaries) and Ⓦwww.napata.org (with recordings of spoken Nubian, contemporary and traditional music).

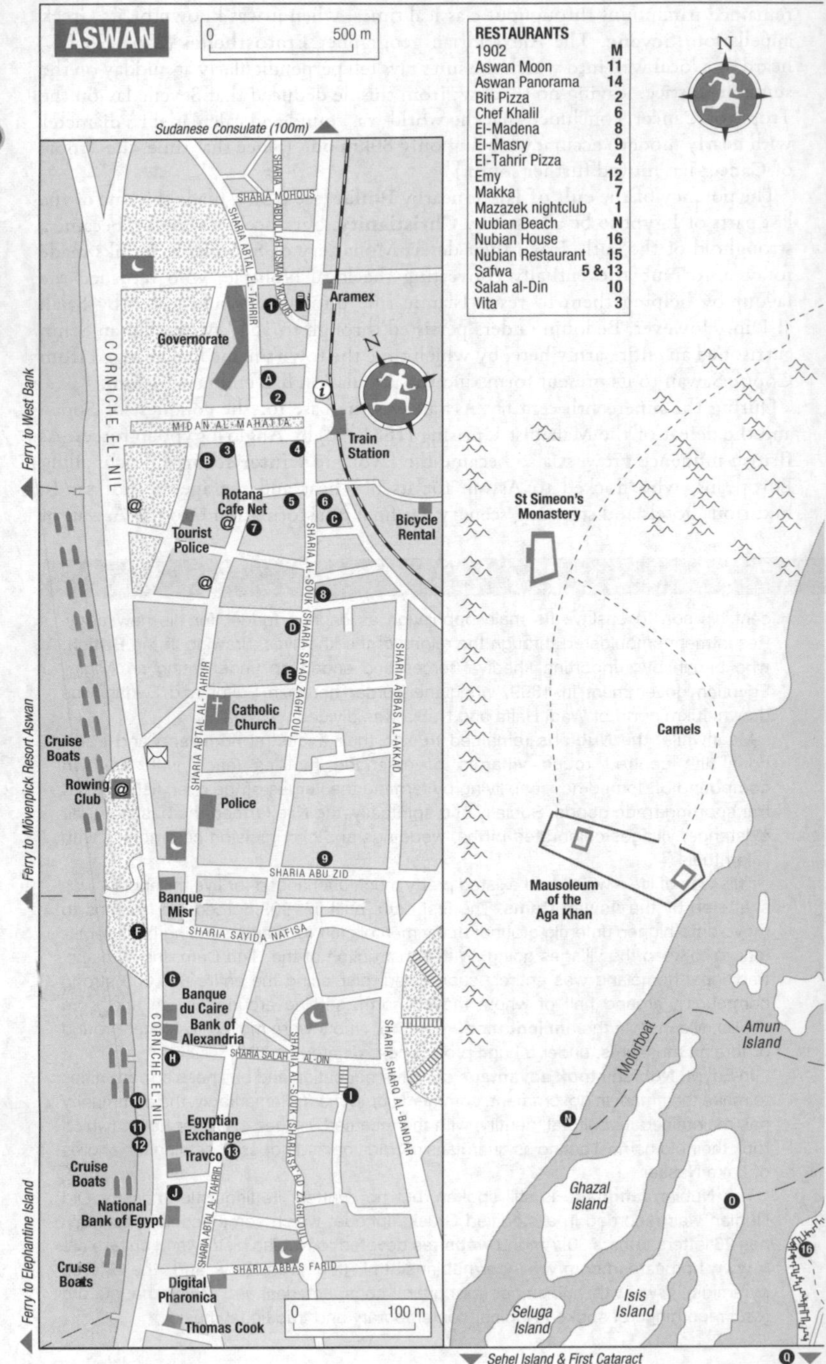
ASWAN
0 500 m
RESTAURANTS
1902 M
Aswan Moon 11
Aswan Panorama 14
Biti Pizza 2
Chef Khalil 6
El-Madena 8
El-Masry 9
El-Tahrir Pizza 4
Emy 12
Makka 7
Mazazek nightclub 1
Nubian Beach N
Nubian House 16
Nubian Restaurant 15
Safwa 5 & 13
Salah al-Din 10
Vita 3
N
Sudanese Consulate (100m)
SHARIA MOHOUS
SHARIA ABDULLAH OSMAN YACOUB
SHARIA ABTAL EL-TAHRIR
Aramex
Governorate
CORNICHE EL-NIL
MIDAN AL-MAHATTA
Train Station
Rotana Cafe Net
Tourist Police
Bicycle Rental
St Simeon's Monastery
SHARIA AL-SOUK (SHARIA SA'AD ZAGHLOUL)
SHARIA ABBAS AL-AKKAD
Catholic Church
Cruise Boats
Rowing Club
Police
Camels
SHARIA ABU ZID
Banque Misr
Mausoleum of the Aga Khan
SHARIA SAYIDA NAFISA
Banque du Caire
Bank of Alexandria
SHARIA SALAH AL-DIN
SHARIA SHARQ AL-BANDAR
Motorboat
Amun Island
Egyptian Exchange
Travco
Ghazal Island
National Bank of Egypt
SHARIA ABBAS FARID
Digital Pharonica
Isis Island
Seluga Island
0 100 m
Thomas Cook
Ferry to West Bank
Ferry to Mövenpick Resort Aswan
Ferry to Elephantine Island
Sehel Island & First Cataract

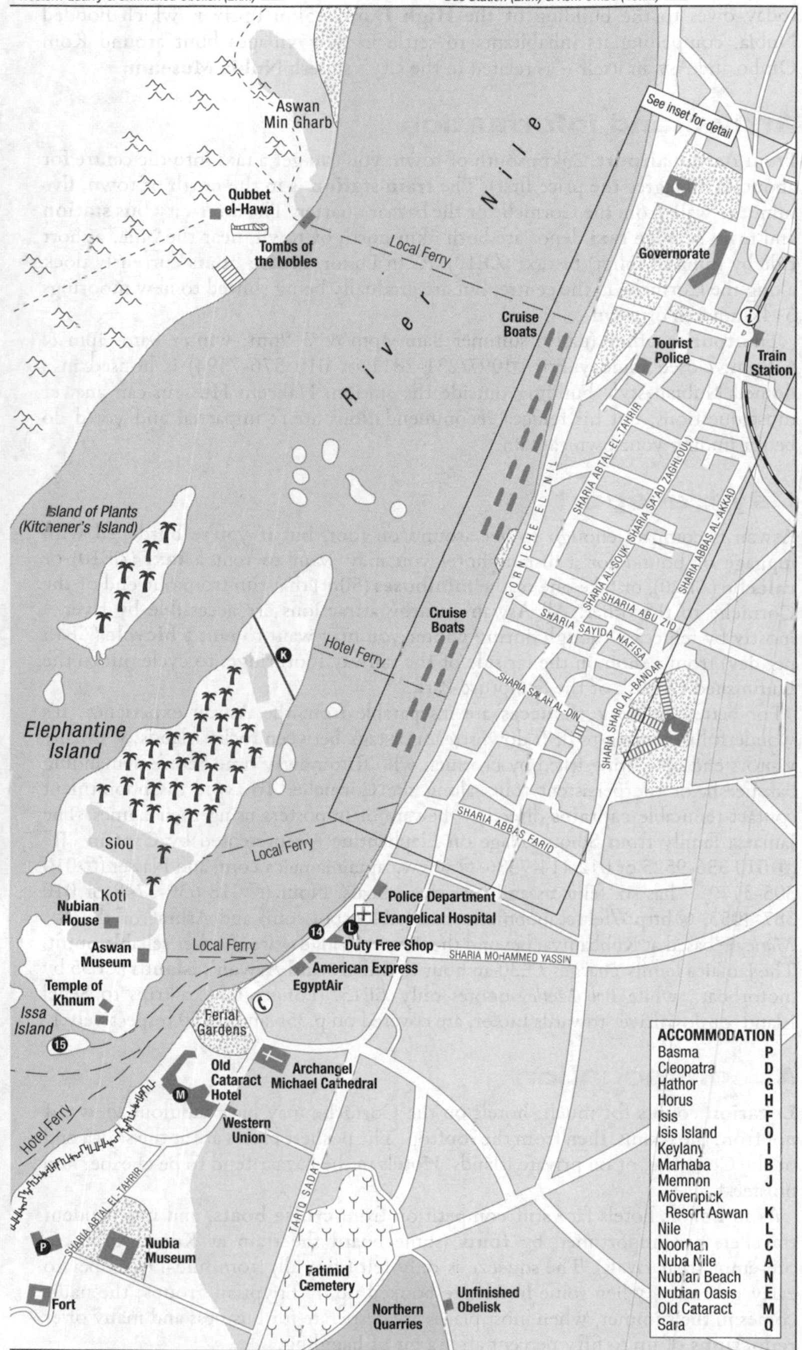
Western Quarry & Unfinished Obelisk (2km)
Bus Station (2km) & Kom Ombo (45km)
Aswan Min Gharb
See inset for detail
River Nile
Qubbet el-Hawa
Tombs of the Nobles
Local Ferry
Governorate
Cruise Boats
Tourist Police
Train Station
Island of Plants (Kitchener's Island)
Corniche El-Nil
Sharia Abtal El-Tahrir
Sharia Sa'ad Zaghloul
Sharia Abbas Al-Akkad
Sharia Al-Souk
Sharia Abu Zid
Sharia Sayida Nafisa
Sharia Sharq Al-Bandar
Sharia Salah Al-Din
Sharia Abbas Farid
Hotel Ferry
Elephantine Island
Siou
Koti
Nubian House
Aswan Museum
Temple of Khnum
Issa Island
Police Department
Evangelical Hospital
Duty Free Shop
Sharia Mohammed Yassin
American Express
EgyptAir
Ferial Gardens
Old Cataract Hotel
Archangel Michael Cathedral
Western Union
Sharia Abtal El-Tahrir
Tariq Sadat
Nubia Museum
Fort
Fatimid Cemetery
Northern Quarries
Unfinished Obelisk
Hospitals, Sculpture Park, Aswan Dams & Abu Simbel
ACCOMMODATION
Basma P
Cleopatra D
Hathor G
Horus H
Isis F
Isis Island O
Keylany I
Marhaba B
Memnon J
Mövenpick Resort Aswan K
Nile L
Noorhan C
Nuba Nile A
Nubian Beach N
Nubian Oasis E
Old Cataract M
Sara Q

today owes to the building of the **High Dam**, 15km upriver, which flooded Nubia, compelling its inhabitants to settle in new villages built around Kom Ombo and Aswan itself – as related in the city's superb **Nubia Museum**.

Arrival and information

From **Aswan airport**, 23km south of town, you can get a taxi into the centre for about £E50 (agree the price first). The **train station** is in the north of town, five minutes' walk from the Corniche or the bazaar quarter. The inter-city **bus station** and main **service taxi** depot are both 3km north of town, near the Nile, a short ride by minibus (50pt) or taxi (£E10). As in Luxor, **cruise boats** currently dock along the Corniche in the centre, but are gradually being shifted to new moorings 3–4km north of town.

The **tourist office** (daily: summer 8am–3pm & 7–9pm; winter 8am–3pm & 6–8pm; closed midday Fri; ⓣ097/231-2811 or 010 576-7594) is housed in a domed Nubian-style building outside the station. Hakeem Hussein can answer most questions, but his felucca recommendations aren't impartial and you'd do better finding your own captain.

City transport

Aswan is compact enough to get around on foot, but if you're burdened with luggage or bound for a distant hotel you may want to rent a **taxi** (£E10) or **calèche** (£E20), or take one of the **minibuses** (50pt) that run from one end of the Corniche to the other. All Aswan's nearby attractions are accessible by river – mostly by felucca – though during winter you may want to rent a **bicycle** (£E15 per day) from a shop on the far side of the railway footbridge, to cycle out to the Unfinished Obelisk or the Sculpture Park.

For better or worse, **feluccas** are inseparable from the Aswan experience. It's wonderfully relaxing to drift downstream or tack between rocky islands; yet many visitors end up getting irked by boatmen who fritter away time before demanding baksheesh, or the persistent touts along the Corniche. To avoid disappointment contact reputable **captains** directly – beware of imposters using their names. The Jamaica family from Sihou village on Elephantine – represented by Captain "JJ" (ⓣ010 356-9525 or 012 414-7386, ⓦwww.captainjamaica.com) and Nasser (ⓣ010 505-3179) – has six feluccas and two motorboats. Nour (ⓣ018 639-3748 or 010 387-4053, ⓦhttp://feluccabobmarleyfamily.blogspot.com) and Ashraf of the *Bob Marley* – based at Kubbaniya, beyond the Aswan Bridge – are another reliable outfit. The Jamaica family charges £E30 an hour to **sail around Aswan's islands** (£E35 by motorboat), while *Bob Marley* quotes only £E15. (Longer felucca trips to Sehel Island, or downriver towards Luxor, are covered on p.356 and p.250 respectively.)

Accommodation

Location counts for much: hotels on the Corniche may have fabulous views, if not from the rooms, then from the rooftop. The poshest places are at the south end of the Corniche, or on private islands. Hotels in the bazaar tend to be cheaper and noisier.

As in Luxor, hotels face stiff competition from **cruise boats**, and independent travellers are importuned by **touts** (some board the train at Kom Ombo, to pre-empt their rivals). The squeeze is only felt (if at all) from mid-December to early February, when some hotels are booked up by Egyptian groups; the nadir comes in the summer, when most places are desperate for business and many offer **reductions** of up to fifty percent after a bit of haggling.

In many budget hotels guests are subjected to **pressure** to sign up for minibus or felucca trips. Such excursions can be an economical way to see the sites, but don't be railroaded into a hasty decision.

Along the Corniche

Hathor ⓣ097/231-4580, ⓦwww.hathorhotel.com. Midway along the Corniche, the *Hathor* has en-suite a/c rooms of varying sizes – some facing the Nile, others gloomy – and a rooftop with a small pool, sunloungers and splendid Nile views. Used by Amigo Tours clients (see p.217). BB ❷

Horus ⓣ097/231-3313. Reached by private lift from a passage, it has clean, slightly shabby Nile-facing rooms with fans and tiny bathrooms; the ones at the back are much tattier. Their bar-restaurant and rooftop have great views, and there's a sound-proofed nightclub. BB ❷

Isis ⓣ097/231-5100, ⓦwww.pyramisaegypt.com. Right beside the Nile midway along the Corniche, this mini-resort has faded a/c bungalows in a small garden with a pool facing Elephantine Island, and an Italian restaurant. BB ❼

Marhaba ⓣ097/233-0102, ⓦwww.marhaba-aswan.com. Aptly named "Welcome", this mock-pharaonic three-star is certainly inviting, with friendly staff, a generous buffet breakfast and fabulous views from its rooftop. The nicely decorated a/c rooms have satellite TV, splendid bathrooms and Nile views. BB ❼

Memnon ⓣ097/230-0483. Also used by Amigo Tours, this aged hotel has one renovated floor and a shallow pool on its shadeless rooftop. Reception on the third floor, reached by a private lift. BB ❷

Nile ⓣ097/231-4222, ⓦwww.nilehotel-aswan.com. Sited near the end of the Corniche near EgyptAir, its spotless, spacious a/c rooms have Nile views, satellite TV and fridges. Wi-fi (£E30/day) and book exchange. BB ❺

Old Cataract ⓣ097/231-6000, ⓦwww.sofitel.com. Set on an outcrop overlooking the river, with a huge garden behind, this Edwardian pile takes you back to the days of Agatha Christie (parts of *Death on the Nile* were filmed here). Closed for refurbishment at the time of writing, it should offer top-class service once it reopens, with rates ranging from around $200 for a garden-view room up to $1500 for a deluxe suite. ❽

Around the bazaar and the train station

Cleopatra Sharia al-Souk ⓣ097/231-4001, ⓔcleopatra hotel_aswan@yahoo.com. Centrally located, with clean a/c en-suite rooms with fridges and TV, a swimming pool on its shadeless rooftop, and a swanky coffee-shop, the three-star *Cleopatra* is popular with tour groups. Accepts Visa. BB ❹

Keylany Sharia Keylany ⓣ097/231-7332 or 010 072-4270, ⓦwww.keylanyhotel.com. Set in a quiet backstreet, this friendly, well-run hotel has rooms with fans, a/c, fridges and safes; free wi-fi, a pool table, a hydro-massage spa, and an attractive rooftop with a tiny pool, where pancakes are served for breakfast and Colmbian coffee brewed to order. Accepts Visa and MasterCard. BB ❸

Noorhan Off Sharia al-Souk ⓣ097/231-6069. Five minutes' walk from the station, this much-hustled place has cleanish rooms with dirty shared bathrooms; it's worth paying £E5–10 extra for an en-suite a/c room. Breakfast not included. There's an internet café next door. ❶

Nuba Nile Off Midan al-Mahatta ⓣ097/231-3353. The best option near the station, family-run and ultra clean, with a small swimming pool, wi-fi (£E4/hr) and computer rental (£E7/hr). Rooms come in all shapes and sizes – ask to see a few before choosing. All have a/c, bath tubs and fridges. BB ❸

Nubian Oasis Off Sharia al-Souk ⓣ097/231-2123 or 012 490-8634, ⓔnubianoasis_hotel_aswan@hotmail.com. A 1960s' high-rise with shabby rooms with fans or a/c (bathroom £E5-10 extra) and erratic hot water, whose popularity with backpackers owes to its low rates, its laid-back rooftop, and manager Ahmed ("Aco"), who can arrange anything. BB ❶

Elephantine and Isis islands

Isis Island ⓣ097/231-7400, ⓦwww.pyramisaegypt.com. Owned by President Mubarak's elder son, this five-star colossus was built beside a nature reserve containing the only primordial Nilotic vegetation left in Egypt. It has rooms and chalets, two pools, a health club, mini-golf, a kids' zoo, and free wi-fi in the lobby. Reached by a 24hr launch from the docks near EgyptAir. Takes Visa and MasterCard. BB ❽

Mövenpick Resort Aswan ⓣ097/230-3455, ⓦwww.movenpick-hotels.com. Though it blights Elephantine, the hotel's gardens and views are lovely, and the pool and spa worthy of its five-star rating. Double rooms from $150, suites from $210. Reached by a 24hr ferry from near the *Isis Hotel*. ❼

Elsewhere

Basma On the hillside above the *Old Cataract Hotel* ⓣ097/231-0901,

ⓦ www.basmahotel.com. This four-star complex has a large heated pool and a garden terrace with stunning views of Elephantine, but is best avoided during the sculpture symposium (see p.355) due to the noise outside. Disabled access. Free bus from the *Isis* every hour. BB ❽

Nubian Beach On the west bank, opposite Ghazal Island ⓣ 012 169-9145. If getting close to nature appeals, this "ethnic" Nubian house beside the Nile out towards the First Cataract offers river bathing, sand saunas (see p.354), and simple rooms with fans on a half- or full-board basis. Call to arrange a boat (£E10) to collect you in Aswan. ❺

Sara On a clifftop 2km beyond the Nubia Museum ⓣ 097/232-7234, ⓦ www.sarahotel-aswan.com. Equally remote, this restful hotel has stunning views over the First Cataract and the Western Desert, a pool overlooking the Nile, clean rooms with satellite TV, and a free hourly shuttle bus into town. BB ❻

The Town

Although Aswan's **Corniche** follows the river bank for more than 4km, most things worth noting lie along the 1500-metre stretch between the Rowing Club and **Ferial Gardens,** where the road swings inland past the *Old Cataract Hotel* and uphill to the **Nubia Museum**. Otherwise, the main focus of interest is **Sharia al-Souk**, the **bazaar** that runs two to three blocks inland all the way from the train station down to Sharia Abbas Farid, roughly paralleled by **Sharia Abtal al-Tahrir**, which is far less touristy; lined with grocers' stores, bakeries and cafés, it gets leafier by the colonial-style police station near Sharia Abu Zid, the main intersection leading to the Nile. Beyond this it shrinks to a narrow backstreet before transforming itself into the avenue to the Nubia Museum. Note that not all the streets off the bazaar appear on our map of town, and some areas are still being demolished to create wider roads.

The bazaar and Corniche

Aswan's **bazaar** is renowned as the best in Egypt outside Cairo, but – as in Luxor – its ambience has been diminished by a makeover that has left it more touristy than authentically local. Souvenirs, jewellery, basketwork and piles of spices start to vie for attention a few blocks from the train station, all the way down to Sharia Saiyida

▲ Souvenir vendors in Aswan's bazaar

Nafisa, beyond which fruit and veg sellers, ironmongers and other merchants appear. Popular buys include colourful **Nubian skullcaps** and long scarves; heavier, woven **shawls**; or **baskets** and **trays**, some semi-antique and others new. **Galabiyyas** and embroidered Nubian robes can be bought off the peg or tailored to order; try Abu Shmeil on Sharia al-Souk, near the corner of Sharia Abu Zid. For contemporary and antique Bedouin and Nubian **jewellery**, check out the Butterfly Bazaar at 208 Sharia al-Souk. Pyramids or baskets of **spices** and dyes are another eye-catching feature; dried **hibiscus** (used to make *karkaday*), indigo dye and what is labelled as "saffron" are common tourist purchases. Aswan is also famous for its peanuts and its **henna** powder, sold in different grades.

Aswan's **Corniche** is the finest in Egypt, less for its architecture than for the superb vista of Elephantine Island, and feluccas gliding over the water like quill pens across papyrus, with the tawny wastes of the Western Desert on the far bank. If the view from riverside restaurants is spoilt by diesel-belching cruise boats moored alongside, you can enjoy the sunset from the rockbound **Ferial Gardens** (daily 9am–11pm; £E5) or the terrace of the **Old Cataract Hotel** (once it reopens), which afford a sublime view of the southern end of **Elephantine Island** and the smaller islands beyond.

The Nubia Museum

Aswan's **Nubia Museum** (daily 9am–9pm; Ramadan 9am–3pm; £E50) has been widely acclaimed, delighting its sponsors, UNESCO, and posthumously crowning the career of its architect, Mohammed al-Hakim. Opened in 1998, it's housed in an impressive modern building, loosely based on traditional Nubian architecture and faced in limestone, surrounded by landscaped grounds. It displays some five thousand artefacts, excellently organized and clearly labelled in English, making it a "must see" introduction to the history and culture of the Nubians; for a preview check out Ⓦ www.numibia.net/nubia.

At the entrance to the main hall, a scale model of the Nile Valley shows the magnitude of the Nilotic civilizations and their architectural achievements. The exhibits lead you from prehistory through the kingdoms of Kush and Meröe into Christian and Islamic eras, until the drowning of Nubia beneath Lake Nasser and the salvage of its ancient monuments. Among the highlights are a quartzite statue of a Kushite priest of Amun, an eight-metre-high Ramses II, horse-armour from the Ballana tombs and frescoes from the Coptic churches of Nubia. There are also life-size models of traditional Nubian houses and photographs of the mud-brick fortresses, churches and cemeteries that were abandoned to the rising waters of Lake Nasser as the temples were moved to higher land.

In the grounds are further monuments and exhibits, including the mausoleum of 77 *wali* (sheikhs), a traditional Nubian house, and a cave containing prehistoric rock art removed from now inundated areas. An artificial watercourse runs through the corner of the grounds nearest the main road, attractively spotlit at night.The museum is about 500m uphill beyond the *Old Cataract Hotel*, about thirty minutes' walk from the town centre (£E10 by taxi). If you've still got some energy after the museum, you can trek uphill past the *Basma Hotel* to find a derelict mud-brick **fort** with a watchtower, built in Mohammed Ali's time (now off-limits as a military zone), and a vantage point overlooking the Fatimid Cemetery (see below).

The Fatimid Cemetery, the Unfinished Obelisk and the Sculpture Park

Other sites on Aswan's outskirts are best reached by taxi. During winter you might consider cycling there, or even walk down from the Nubia Museum to the Fatimid Cemetery and on to the Unfinished Obelisk. The **Fatimid Cemetery** (daily 24hr;

free) is a dusty sprawl of mud-brick tombs ranging from simple enclosures to complex domed cubes. While not as grand as the mausolea in Cairo's Cities of the Dead – or inhabited by squatters – they're an eerie sight. You can walk through the cemetery to emerge on the road to the Northern Quarries.

The **Northern Quarries** (daily 8am–4pm; £E30) are the best-known of the many quarrying sites in the hills south of Aswan, which supplied the Ancient Egyptians with fine red granite for their temples and colossi. Its fame derives from a gigantic **Unfinished Obelisk**, roughly dressed and nearly cut free from the bedrock, before being abandoned after a flaw in the stone was discovered. Had it been finished, the obelisk would have weighed 1168 tons and stood nearly 42m high. It's reckoned that this was the intended mate for the so-called Lateran Obelisk in Rome, which originally stood before the temple of Tuthmosis III at Karnak and is still credited as being the largest obelisk in the world. From chisel marks and discarded tools, archeologists have been able to deduce pharaonic quarrying techniques, such as soaking wooden wedges to split fissures, and using quartz sand slurry as an abrasive. A visitors' trail runs through the quarries past some **pictographs** of dolphins and ostriches, painted by ancient quarry workers.

While it's just about feasible to walk to the Northern Quarries, you definitely need wheels to reach the **Sculpture Park** near the **Southern Quarries** out towards the Old Dam. The park displays sculptures by artists attending Aswan's international Sculpture Symposium (see p.355); besides their variety and imaginativeness, the park enjoys a wonderful **view**, especially at sunset. Be sure to get a taxi whose driver knows what you mean by "*El Mathaf el-Maftouh*" and a rough idea of the route (about thirty minutes' journey). Take the road for the Old Dam, but turn off onto an uphill road rather than towards the Shellal docks (for ferries to Philae). Continue until you reach the top; the sculptures are on the right, the quarries to the left.

While minibus excursions to Abu Simbel often visit the Unfinished Obelisk on the way back to Aswan, you'll need to hire a private **taxi** for a few hours to cover all three sites in one trip (£E60–70).

Elephantine Island

Elephantine Island takes its name from the huge black **rocks** clustered around its southern end, which resemble a herd of pachyderms bathing in the river. From a felucca you can see cartouches and Predynastic inscriptions carved on the rock faces, which are too sheer to view from the island. Elephantine's spectacular beauty is marred only by the towering *Mövenpick Resort Aswan*, reached by its own private ferry and cut off from the rest of the island by a lofty fence. (An even larger hotel lies abandoned at the far end of the island, after investors pulled out.)

Further south, two **Nubian villages** – **Siou** and **Koti** – nestle amid lush palm groves, their houses painted sky-blue, pink or yellow and often decorated with hajj scenes. Chickens peck in the dust and goats chew garbage in mud-brick alleys twisting past walled gardens, where the only concession to tourism is a signposted **Nubian House,** whose owner sells tea and handicrafts and arranges henna-painting (see p.354). Simple motor-launches serving as public **ferries** (every 15min 6am–11pm; £E1) sail to Elephantine from the landing stages near Thomas Cook and EgyptAir (boats from the latter dock conveniently close to the Aswan Museum) – or you can get here by felucca or private motor-launch (about £E5).

The Aswan Musuem

The small **Aswan Museum** (daily: summer 7am–5pm; winter 7am–4pm; £E30, ticket also valid for the Nilometer and ruins further south) casts light on the island's past, when its southern end was occupied by the town of Yebu or Abu (meaning both "elephant" and "ivory" in the Ancient Egyptian language). Most of the museum's best exhibits have been moved to the Nubia Museum, but a mummified gazelle and jewellery found at the island's Temple of Satet are worth a look, as is the **Annexe**, whose highlights include a life-size granite statue of a seated Tuthmosis III, a colobus monkey embracing a pillar, and a pre-nuptial agreement from the reign of Nectanebo II. The museum was originally the villa of Sir William Willcocks, who designed the first Aswan Dam, and is set amid fragrant subtropical **gardens**. Come back and enjoy them once you've visited the Nilometer and the ruins of Yebu.

The Nilometers

In ancient times the Nilometers at Aswan were the first to measure the river's rise, enabling priests to calculate the height of the inundation, crop yields over the next year and the rate of taxation (which peasants paid in kind). There are two on the island, built at the tail end of pharaonic civilization but based on far older practice and used for centuries afterwards.

The easier to find is the **Nilometer of the Satet Temple**, by the riverside; ninety enclosed rock-cut steps lead down to a square shaft with walls graduated in Arabic, Roman and pharaonic numerals, reflecting its usage in ancient times and during the late nineteenth century. To get there from the museum, follow the path southwards for 300m to find a sycamore tree (the pharaonic symbol of the tree-goddess, associated with Nut and Hathor), which shades the structure. Should you approach it by river, notice the rock embankments to the south, which bear **inscriptions** from the reigns of Tuthmosis III, Amenophis III and the XXVI Dynasty ruler Psammetichus II.

The **Nilometer of the Temple of Khnum** is further inland amid the remains of Yebu. Built in the XXVI Dynasty, it consists of stairs leading down to what was probably a basin for measuring the Nile's maximum level; a scale is etched by the stairs at the northern end.

The ruins of Yebu

The southern end of the island is littered with the **ruins** of the ancient town, which covered nearly two square kilometres by Ptolemaic times. You can follow a trail from the Aswan Museum past numbered plaques identifying structures excavated or reconstructed by German and Swiss archeological teams working on Elephantine. The German mission's excellent guidebook, *Elephantine: The Ancient Town*, describes its 4400-year history and monuments.

A massive platform and foundation blocks (#6, #12 and #13) mark the site of the **Temple of Khnum**, god of the Aswan nome. The temple was founded in the Old Kingdom but entirely rebuilt during the XXX Dynasty. On its north side are the remains of pillars painted by the Romans, and Greek inscriptions; to the west stands the imposing gateway added by Alexander II, shown here worshipping Khnum.

Immediately to the north lies a Greco-Roman **Necropolis of Sacred Rams** (#11), unearthed in 1906, while further northwest stands the small **Temple of Hekayib**, a VI Dynasty nomarch buried in the Tombs of the Nobles (see p.351) who was later deified; the stelae and inscriptions found here by Labib Habachi in 1946 revealed much about Aswan during the Middle Kingdom.

Due east lies a **Temple of Satet** where excavations continue to produce discoveries. Built by Queen Hatshepsut around 1490 BC, it was the last of more than thirty such temples on this site, dating back four millennia, dedicated to the goddess who incarnated the fertile aspect of the inundation. Beneath the temples, German archeologists have found a shaft leading 19m into the granite bedrock, where a natural **whirl hole** is thought to have amplified the sounds of the rising water table (the first indication of the life-giving annual flood) and was revered as the "Voice of the Nile". Although the High Dam has since silenced its voice, a half-buried statue near the temple still draws new brides and barren women longing for the gift of fertility.

To the southwest of Khnum's temple, the layered **remains of ancient houses** have yielded Aramaic papyri attesting to a sizeable **Jewish colony** on Elephantine in the sixth century BC. A military order by Darius II permitting the Yebu garrison to observe Passover in 419 BC suggests that they defended the southernmost border of the Persian empire. Although nothing remains of their temple to Yahweh, the Germans used leftover blocks from Kalabsha (see p.365) to reconstruct a **Ptolemaic sanctuary** with decorations added by the Nubian Pharaoh Arkamani in the third century BC, at the southern tip of the island.

The other islands

On the far side of Elephantine, almost hidden from the town by its bulk, the **Island of Plants** (Geziret an-Nabatat) is still commonly referred to by tourists as "**Kitchener's Island**". Presented with the island in gratitude for his military exploits in Sudan, Consul-General Kitchener indulged his passion for exotic flora, importing shrubs and seeds from as far afield as India and Malaysia. Today this island-wide **botanical garden** (daily 7am–sunset, 5/6pm in summer; £E10) is a lovely place to spend a quiet afternoon (except on Fridays), with lots of **birdlife**. The island is accessible by rowing boat or felucca from the west bank or Elephantine for £E10.

The craggy strait between Elephantine and Amun islands looks its best from a felucca. If you're not already waterborne, the surrounding coves are frequented by lads who'll happily sail you to any of the islands or the west bank. The hotel on **Isis Island** is accessible by private ferry from a signposted landing stage across the road from EgyptAir. Just north of this is another jetty used by boats to **Issa Island** – whose *Nubian Restaurant* has a huge palm garden for sitting out in the summer – and to the *Nubian Beach* on the west bank of the river (see p.353 for details of both).

The west bank

The main sights on the **west bank** of the river are the **Mausoleum of the Aga Khan** (only visible from outside) and the desert **Monastery of St Simeon**. Unless you're prepared to hike for more than 2km across the hills, the more northerly **Tombs of the Nobles** are best visited as a separate excursion, like the **Western Quarry** and its **Unfinished Obelisk**, which can only be reached by camel.

The Aga Khan's Mausoleum

Just uphill from the embankment is a walled estate with a riverside garden and a stairway ascending the hillside to the domed **Mausoleum of the Aga Khan**. Its marble sarcophagus enshrines Aga Khan III, the 48th Imam of the Isma'ili sect of Shiite Muslims, who was weighed in jewels for his diamond jubilee in 1945. Initially drawn to Aswan by its climate and hot sands, which relieved his rheumatism, he fell in love with its beauty, built a villa and spent every winter here till his death in 1957. Until she was buried beside him in 2000, his widow ensured that a fresh red rose was placed on his sarcophagus every day; legend has it that when none was available in Egypt, a rose was flown in by private plane from Paris on six successive days. The compound has been **closed** since her death but remains an imposing sight.

The Monastery of St Simeon

Unless you walk across the desert from the Tombs of the Nobles (see below), the ruined **Monastery of St Simeon** (Deir Anba Samaan; daily: summer 7am–4pm; winter 7am–5pm; £E25) must be approached from the valley below. You can either scramble uphill through soft sand (30min) or negotiate hiring a **camel** near the landing stage (£E30–35 for an hour; tell the driver beforehand if you want to stay longer), but either way, bring water.

Founded in the seventh century and rebuilt in the tenth, the fortress-like monastery was originally dedicated to Anba Hadra, a local saint who encountered a funeral procession the day after his wedding and decided to renounce the world for a hermit's cave before the marriage was consummated. From here, monks made evangelical forays into Nubia, where they converted the Nobatae to Christianity. After the Muslim conquest, the Nobatae used the monastery as a base during their incursions into Egypt, until Salah al-Din had it wrecked in 1173.

One of the custodians will show you around the complex, whose now-roofless **Basilica** bears traces of frescoes of the Apostles, their faces scratched out by Muslim iconoclasts. In a nearby chamber with a font is the place where St Simeon used to stand sleeplessly reading the Bible, with his beard tied to the ceiling so as to deliver a painful tug if he nodded off. The central **Keep** has room for three hundred monks sleeping five to a cell; graffiti left by Muslim pilgrims who camped here en route to Mecca can be seen in the last room on the right.

The Tombs of the Nobles

Relatively few tourists bother with the **Tombs of the Nobles** (daily: summer 7am–4pm; winter 7am–5pm; £E30) hewn into the hillside further up the west bank, whose artwork has an immediacy and concern for everyday life that makes a refreshing change from royal art. If you're curious, **local ferries** ply between the station end of the Corniche and the landing stage of the west bank village of **Aswan Min Gharb** (every 30min 6am–11pm; £E1). To combine a visit with the monastery and mausoleum, start early at the tombs, then ascend to the domed hilltop Muslim shrine known as **Qubbet el-Hawa** (Tomb of the Wind), and walk across the desert to St Simeon's (45min).

The Tombs of the Nobles lie at different heights (**Old and Middle Kingdom** ones uppermost, **Roman** tombs nearest the waterline), and are numbered in ascending order from south to north. Taking the path up from the ticket kiosk, you reach the high-numbered ones first.

Tomb of Sirenput I (#36)

Turn right at the top of the steps and follow the path downhill around the cliffside to find the tomb of **Sirenput I**, overseer of the priests of Khnum and Satet and Guardian of the South during the XII Dynasty. The six pillars of its vestibule bear portraits and biographical texts. On the left-hand wall he watches bulls fighting and spears fish from a papyrus raft, accompanied by his sandal-bearer, sons and dog. On the opposite wall he's portrayed with his mutt and bow-carrier, and also sitting above them in a garden with his mother, wife and daughters, being entertained by singers; the lower register shows three men gambling. Among the badly damaged murals in the hall beyond, you can just discern fowlers with a net (on the lower right wall), a hieroglyphic biography (left), and a marsh-hunting scene (centre). Beyond lies a chapel with a false door set into the rear niche; the corridor to the left leads to the burial chamber.

Tombs of Pepi-Nakht (#35) and Harkhuf (#34)

To reach the other tombs from Sirenput I, return to the top of the steps and follow the path southwards. Among a cluster of tombs to the left of the steps are two rooms ascribed to Hekayib (whose cult temple stands on Elephantine), called here by his other name, **Pepi-Nakht**. As overseer of foreign troops during the long reign of Pepi II (VI Dynasty), he led colonial campaigns in Asia and Nubia, which are related on either side of the door of the left-hand room.

A bit further south is the tomb of **Harkhuf** (#34), who held the same position under Pepi I, Merenre and Pepi II. An eroded biography inside the entrance relates his three trading expeditions into Nubia, including a letter from the eight-year-old Pepi II, urging Harkhuf to bring back safely a "dancing dwarf from the land of spirits" (thought to be a pygmy from Equatorial Africa), whom Pepi desired to see "more than the gifts of Sinai or Punt". The tiny hieroglyphic figure of a pygmy appears several times in the text.

Tombs of Sirenput II (#31)

The largest, best-preserved tomb belongs to **Sirenput II**, who held the same offices as his father under Amenemhat II, during the apogee of the Middle Kingdom. Beyond its vestibule (with an offerings slab between the second and third pillars on the right) lies a corridor with six niches containing Osirian statues of Sirenput, still vividly coloured like his portraits on the four pillars of the chapel, where the artist's grid lines are visible in places. Best of all is the recess at the back, where Sirenput appears with his wife and son (left), attends his seated mother in a garden (right), and receives flowers from his son (centre). Notice the elephant in the upper left corner of this tableau.

Tombs of Mekhu (#25) and Sabni (#26)

At the top of the double ramps ascending the hillside (up which sarcophagi were dragged) are the adjacent tombs of a father and son, which are interesting for their monumentality – a large vestibule with three rows of rough-hewn pillars, flanked by niches and burial chambers – and for their story. After his father **Mekhu** was killed in Nubia, **Sabni** mounted a punitive expedition that recovered the body. As a sign of respect, Pepi II sent his own embalmers to mummify the corpse; Sabni travelled to Memphis to personally express his thanks with gifts, as related by an inscription at the entrance to his tomb.

The Western Quarry

The ancient **Western Quarry** in the desert behind the Tombs of the Nobles is harshly evocative of the effort to supply stone for pharaonic monuments. Huge blocks were prised from the sandstone of Jebel Simaan and dragged on rollers towards the Nile for shipment downriver; the stone for the Colossi of Memnon may have come from here. An **Unfinished Obelisk** with hieroglyphs extolling Seti I was abandoned by the wayside after a flaw in the rock was discovered. This desolate site is seldom visited (beware of snakes) and can only be reached **by camel** with a guide from the ferry landing by the tombs (for £E50–60); the ride takes half an hour each way. If that seems too arduous, another unfinished obelisk south of Aswan is easier to reach (see p.348).

Eating and drinking

Eating out in Aswan offers the pleasures of fresh fish and Nubian dishes such as okra in spicy tomato sauce, in riverside **restaurants** that are great on balmy nights but empty when it's cold. The bazaar is good for **street food**, with *fuul* and sandwiches sold near the station end of the street, and fruit and nuts on every corner.

All the Corniche places are **open** till around midnight (later if there is custom); cafés in the bazaar may close an hour or two earlier, or stay open till the small hours. Phone numbers are only given where **reservations** are advisable. Unless stated otherwise, **alcohol** is not available.

Restaurants, cafés and bars

1902 Restaurant *Old Cataract Hotel*, Corniche el-Nil. When the hotel reopens, this looks set to offer haute cuisine similar to that at the *1896 Restaurant* in Luxor's *Sofitel Winter Palace* (see p.276), with a dress code in keeping with its palatial colonial decor.

Aswan Moon Corniche el-Nil, near the *Horus Hotel*. A spacious floating restaurant hung with colourful tent fabric, serving fish, chicken, vegetable dishes, pizzas and pasta dishes (£E25–45 plus tax). Try *douad basha*, meatballs in tomato sauce, in an earthenware pot.

Aswan Panorama Corniche el-Nil, near the duty-free shop. Another riverside place, which was closed for refurbishment at the time of writing. If past form is anything to go by, its menu and prices should be similar to the *Aswan Moon*'s once it reopens.

Biti Pizza Midan al-Mahatta. Tourists are given an English menu of Western-style pizzas (£E38) rather than an Arabic one with more combinations, including *fiteer*, which they only serve after 3pm. The upstairs dining rooms are a/c, with a view of the square.

Chef Khalil Sharia al-Souk. This small a/c café near the train station offers delicious fresh crab (£E35), shrimp (£E50), sea bream (£E40), sea-bass (£E40) and lobster (£E100), all served with rice, salad and *tahina*. It's worth waiting for a table.

El-Madena Sharia al-Souk. A share-a-table diner with set meals (£E35–40) of liver, chicken or kebab with salad, *tahina*, vegetable stew, rice and bread.

El-Masry Sharia Abu Zid. This simple, clean a/c restaurant serves set meals (£E37–47) based around fish, kebab, pigeon or stuffed courgettes, with a rapid turnover of Egyptian clients that ensures that the food is always fresh.

El-Tahrir Pizza Midan al-Mahatta. A cheery, inexpensive rival to *Biti* offering sweet *fiteer* as well as savoury ones (£E20–25) and Western-style pizzas (£E30), plus Egyptian desserts such as *muhalabiyya*, *basboosa* and *Um Ali* (unusually served cold, though you can ask for it hot).

Emy Corniche el-Nil. A haunt for felucca captains and expats, *Emy* (pronounced "Ee-me") has a double-decker boat section with views of Elephantine Island, and an enclosed part that's cooler in summer. Meals £E15–40, plus Egyptian beer and wine, as cheap as you'll find in Aswan.

Makka Sharia Abtal al-Tahrir. Highly rated by locals yet seldom visited by tourists, it serves both meat and fish dishes with salad, rice, *tahina* and vegetables, at similar prices to *El-Masry* (see above).

Nubian Beach On the west bank opposite Ghazal Island ☎012 169-9145. For £E70 per person, you can enjoy a full Nubian meal at this rustic riverside bathing spot (see p.354), with a motorboat pick-up and transport back to Aswan. Try their Nubian coffee, spiced with ginger, cardomam and nutmeg. Call ahead to order a boat.

Nubian House Uphill from the *Basma Hotel* ☎097/236-6226. Not to be confused with the *Nubian House* on Elephantine or the *Nubian Restaurant* on Issa Island, this place is only open during the tourist season, when it's worth a taxi ride (£E10) for its amazing views over Elephantine Island and the First Cataract, its Nubian meals (£E35–50) and occasional folklore shows with music. Phone to check what's on.

Nubian Restaurant Issa Island ☎097/230-2465. Geared towards tour groups, for whom a buffet and folk show are laid on, it's lacklustre at other times, though its palm garden is a delightful place to relax over a *sheesha* on summer evenings. Free boat from the dock opposite EgyptAir.

Safwa Off Sharia al-Souk. A two-storey *kushari* diner that also does "quiches" of macaroni with meat, and *muhalabiyya* for dessert. There's a smaller branch near the southern end of Sharia Abtal al-Tahrir, inland from the *Memnon Hotel*.

Salah al-Din Corniche el-Nil. Alongside the *Aswan Moon*, this multi-level restaurant offers a slightly wider menu than its Corniche rivals, with veal piccata (£E35), stuffed pigeon (£E31) and beef curry (£E35) plus Egyptian beer (£E12) and wine (£E25 a glass). Like *Emy*, it's a hang-out for felucca captains.

Vita Midan al-Mahatta. An ice-cream parlour boasting twenty flavours, of which a dozen are available at any time. They taste great, despite being short on cream.

Activities

Some hotels let non-residents use their **swimming pools**: *Cleopatra* is cheapest (£E20); *Isis Island* has both heated and cold pools (£E100, including use of a pool cabin and £E50 worth of drinks). Though local boys bathe **in the Nile**, tourists seldom do for fear of bilharzia, which is a problem near the riverbanks and islands that impede the water's fast flow. If you're still keen, there are some lovely bathing spots out at the First Cataract or the *Nubian Beach* opposite Ghazal Island (see p.346).

While felucca trips are the main outdoor activity, **birdwatchers** can have a field day under the guidance of ornithologist Mohammed Orabi (Ⓣ012 324-0132), who owns his own boat for getting up close to waterfowl and other nesting species. More traditional Aswani diversions include **promenading** along the Corniche, meeting friends in riverside **restaurants** and listening to Nubian **music**. Most tourists spend their days sightseeing, and when not attending the **Sound and Light Show at Philae** (see p.361) usually opt for an early night.

Music and dancing

Nubian music ranges from traditional village songs backed by drums and handclapping to urban sounds reflecting the influence of jazz, funk, trance or even classical music. The one thing that all these forms have in common is that they're sung in Nubian. While famous abroad thanks to the late masters Ali Hassan Kuban and Hamza al-Din, in Egypt Nubian music isn't widely popular outside the far south. Nubian CDs and cassettes are sold in Aswan, but contemporary Nubian stars seldom hold public concerts here. As with the jobbing musicians who sometimes play in the Ferial Gardens or the Corniche-side parks at the northern end of town, their main income derives from performing at weddings or other private functions.

Nubian weddings are celebrated on a lavish scale, with musicians costing as much as £E30,000. The bridegroom recoups the expense by inviting hundreds of guests and charging them £E20 each, which makes summer – the wedding season – an expensive time for locals. As guests from foreign lands are held to be auspicious, tourists are often invited to attend weddings in the villages around Aswan.

Nubian music is often accompanied by stick-dancing and other folk dances, which can be seen at venues that lay on a **folklore show** (often with a whirling dervish thrown in for good measure); try the *Nubian House* overlooking the First Cataract, the *Nubian Restaurant* on Issa Island (see p.353 for details of both) or the *Kenzi House* on Sehel Island (see p.356). Events are organized for tour groups or if enough people are interested. The cost (£E50–75 per person) includes food, entertainment and transport by boat if required. If you're craving some excitement, there's **bellydancing** at two venues (midnight–5am): the fifth-floor nightclub in the *Horus Hotel* on the Corniche, and the basement *Mazazek* club beside the *Queen Noorhan Hotel*, two blocks north of the station. Alternatively, the *Isis Island* hosts an "Oriental" **band** from 7–10pm nightly.

Henna designs and spas

Elaborate **designs in henna** on the hands and feet of brides are a feature of Nubian culture. Foreign women can be "tattooed" by Madame Rahmat (Ⓣ097/230-1465) at her home, or by local women at the *Nubian House* (Ⓣ097/232-6226) on Elephantine; men wanting designs must go to guys in the bazaar such as Mahmoud Wahish (Ⓣ097/230-2651). Expect to pay £E30–60, depending on the size and complexity of the design. Another beauty treatment is "**sugaring**" – a traditional form of waxing using syrup; the *Keylany Hotel* offers a full-body exfoliation for £E120.

The *Mövenpick Resort Aswan* has various **spa** packages including the use of its sauna, gym and steam bath, massages, immersion in **hot sand** (good for arthritis and rheumatism) and a whirlpool bath. Similar facilities are available at the *Isis Island* resort; contact either hotel for details. You can also get "sand saunas" in the rustic setting of the *Nubian Beach* (see below) for £E70, including a boat there and back.

In Aswan itself, various kinds of **massage** (from €10–18) are available at the *Keylany*, *Marhaba* and *Nuba Nile* hotels; the *Keylany* even offers hydro-massage (£E30/hr).

Festivals

Aswan's main event is an international **Sculpture Symposium** running from mid-January to mid-March, when you can see sculptors at work on the terrace of the *Basma Hotel*, before their creations are sent to the Sculpture Park (see p.348). On **Aswan Day** (January 15), the Corniche witnesses a good-natured parade of civic and military hardware: fire engines and ambulances follow jeep-loads of perspiring frogmen and rubber-suited decontamination troops.

Listings

American Express Corniche el-Nil (daily except Fri 9am–5pm) ⓣ097/230-6983, ⓦwww.amexfranchise.com. Will exchange currency and travellers' cheques, hold client mail and organize travel.

Banks and exchange The Egyptian Exchange (daily 8am–8pm) offers slightly better rates than most banks along the Corniche, where you'll find ATMs outside Banque Misr, Banque du Caire, Bank of Alexandria and the National Bank of Egypt.

Books The Nubia chainstore stocks Egyptology, AUC titles, picture books, repro vintage photos, CDs and foreign novels, with branches on Sharia al-Souk (daily 9am–midnight), beside the Rowing Club on the Corniche (daily 8am–11pm) and by the Unfinished Obelisk (daily 7am–4pm).

Duty Free Southern end of the Corniche (daily 9am–2pm & 6–10pm). The only retail outlet in Aswan selling alcohol: you'll need to show your passport to buy imported booze, which must be paid for in hard currency; Egyptian wine, beer and spirits also sold. Takes Diners Club cards.

EgyptAir On the Corniche (daily 8am–8pm; ⓣ097/231-5000) and at the airport (ⓣ097/248-0568).

Hospitals The Evangelical Hospital off the Corniche (ⓣ097/230-7176) is okay for a consultation (Mon–Sat 7am–noon & 4–6pm), but for serious problems you're better off at the Ta'mim (Insurance) Hospital (ⓣ097/231-5112) or Mubarak Military Hospital (ⓣ097/231-7985), both on Tariq Sadat. Aswan's tourist office can recommend doctors or dentists.

Internet The Rowing Club on the Corniche, Rotana Café Net on Sharia Abtal al-Tahrir, and Casper beside the *Noorhan Hotel*, all charge £E5 per hour and are open till midnight or later.

Photography You can burn photos onto a CD (£E25) or DVD (£E50) at the *Keylany Hotel* or Digital Pharonica on Sharia Abbas Farid.

Police The Tourist Police (ⓣ097/231-6436) are based near the Corniche beside Misr Travel, with a branch in the train station; both are open round the clock. For serious cases, contact the chief (ⓣ097/231-4393).

Post Main post office on the Corniche (8am–2pm, closed Fri). Aramex, north of the tourist office, is a reliable courier firm (ⓣ097/232-9993; 8am–5pm, closed Fri).

Thomas Cook On the Corniche (daily 8am–2pm & 5–8pm; ⓣ097/230-4011). Changes money, sells cheques and arranges private tours to Abu Simbel.

Visa extensions The passport office (Mon–Thurs & Sun 8am–2pm & 6–8pm; ⓣ097/231-7006) is in the Police Department on the Corniche. Use the side entrance to the north and head for the second floor; you'll need a photocopy of your passport details and one photo.

Western Union Outside the *Old Cataract* (8.30am–10pm, Fri 3–10pm ⓣ097/230-0941).

Excursions from Aswan

Aswan is a base for **excursions** to many sites, some also accessible from Luxor. Many visitors cram the highlights into two long day-trips: south to Abu Simbel and Philae, returning to Aswan; and north to Kom Ombo and Edfu, finishing in Luxor. Most independent travellers go in **minibuses** arranged by Aswan's budget hotels, but you don't need to be a guest to join one, as Ahmed at the *Nubian Oasis Hotel* (ⓣ012 490-8634, ⓔA-ACO-Aswan@hotmail.com) acts as a consolidator, collecting clients from all over. Seating may be cramped and the air-conditioning faulty, but this method is far cheaper than hiring a **private taxi** through Thomas Cook, American Express or any other travel agency. Details of **Nile trips** from Aswan are covered on pp.248–252.

All tourist traffic to **Abu Simbel** travels in a **convoy** leaving Aswan at 4am – which means rising at 3am to eat breakfast, and travelling the first three hours in darkness – but this is prefereable to joining the second convoy at 11am, which completes the entire trip in the full heat of day. The only reason to take a public bus (see p.357) is to travel outside of convoy hours or stay overnight at Abu Simbel. Alternatively – and more expensively – you can get there by **flying** (see p.357), or on a four-day **cruise on Lake Nasser** departing from the High Dam (see box, p.360).

Hotels offer a choice between the "short trip" to Abu Simbel only (9hr; £E60–70 per person), and the "long trip" (12hr; £E70–90), which also visits **Philae Island** with its lovely Temple of Isis, and the **Unfinished Obelisk** outside Aswan, on the way back. Neither price includes admission tickets to the sites. Any other itinerary will have to be a one-off excursion by taxi: Ahmed at the *Nubian Oasis* charges £E90 for a round-trip to **Kalabsha Temple** by taxi (for up to four people).

The other main excursion takes in the temples of **Kom Ombo** and **Edfu**, between Aswan and Luxor, stopping for an hour at each site and then carrying on to Luxor. Again, the minibuses may be cramped, and you might be asked to switch vehicles mid-route to accommodate passengers who've come up by felucca. This excursion costs £E65–85 per person booked through a low-budget hotel, but you can do it for as little as £E45 by booking it with minibus drivers such as Ali (Ⓣ012 106-5771), who shuttles between Aswan and Luxor and back every day. Alternatively, you could visit Kom Ombo and Edfu by felucca or a cruise boat.

For accounts of the Aswan Dams, Philae, Kalabsha Temple and Abu Simbel, see the subsequent sections.

Sehel Island and the First Cataract

Travellers enamoured of felucca journeys should visit **Sehel Island**, 4km upriver from Aswan. Captain Nour of the *Bob Marley* (see p.344) offers a full day's trip with lunch and a tour of the island (£E150 for two people; £E250 for more), while Ahmed at the *Nubian Oasis* (see p.355) can arrange a visit by motorboat (£E150). Bring swimming gear, water and a hat, and come well shod: although the river is cool, the rocks and sand are scorchingly hot. En route, look out for the bougainvillea-festooned villa of the pop star Mohammed Mounir, on the east bank of the river.

Landing on Sehel you may be mobbed by kids wanting to take you to a **Nubian village** where the **Kenzi House** offers **music** and **meals** by arrangement with Gelal Mohammed Hassan (Ⓣ012 415-4902). Kids are also keen to lead you to the "ruins", two hills of fenced-off jumbled boulders that dominate the island (daily: summer 7am–5pm, winter 7am–4pm; £E65). Here are over 250 **inscriptions** from the Middle Kingdom until Ptolemaic times. Most record expeditions beyond the First Cataract or prayers of gratitude for their safe return, but atop the eastern hill you'll find a Ptolemaic **Famine Stele** (#81). Backdated to the reign of Zoser, it relates how he ended a seven-year famine during the III Dynasty by placating Khnum, god of the cataract, with a new temple on Sehel and the return of lands confiscated from his cult centre at Esna, which had provoked Khnum to withhold the inundation.

The summit provides a superb view of the **First Cataract**, a lush, cliff-bound stretch of river divided into channels by outcrops of granite. Before the Aswan Dams, the waters foamed and roiled, making the cataract a fearsome obstacle to upriver travel. In ancient times it was credited as being the source of the Nile (which was believed to flow south into Nubia as well as north through Egypt) and the abode of the deity who controlled the inundation (either Hapy or Khnum, or both working in tandem). The foaming waters were thought to well up from a subterranean cavern where the Nile-god dwelt. Offerings continued to be made at Sehel even after the cavern's putative location shifted to Biga Island during the Late Period or Ptolemaic times (see "Philae", p.362).

Moving on from Aswan

Anyone moving on by **train** should be aware that staff at the station will try to browbeat tourists into using a single first-class service at 6.45pm – which costs £E165 whether you're going to **Luxor** or **Cairo** – or the even pricier Abela sleepers (see p.282) that leave at 5pm, 7pm and 8.45pm. In fact, you can travel on five or six other first- and second-class trains by bluffing your way past the security check (say you have to catch a flight home), boarding a carriage and paying the ticket collector the fare plus a £E6 surcharge. Seat reservations are only mandatory on Abela trains.

Many tourists kill two birds with one stone by taking a **minibus** excursion to Kom Ombo and Edfu (see p.356) that continues on to Luxor; baggage can be carried on the roof rack. This is far easier than trying to reach either temple by public transport. Getting information about **buses** to Abu Simbel (see p.371) or **Mersa Alam** (5hr) on the Red Sea usually entails a trip to the bus station, which can be reached by taxi (£E10) or by minibus (50pt) from the Corniche. About the only reliably scheduled buses are the Superjets to Luxor (3hr), **Hurghada** (7hr), **Suez** (12hr) and **Cairo** (13hr), leaving at 6am and 3.30pm.

EgyptAir flies from Aswan to **Luxor** (daily; 45min), **Cairo** (daily; 1hr 30min) and **Abu Simbel** (twice daily; 30min). Abu Simbel is usually visited on a day-return ticket that includes transfers between the temple and the airport; if you wish to stay there, you must take the later flight.

For the truly adventurous, a weekly **ferry to Wadi Halfa in Sudan** leaves from the High Dam Dock in Lake Nasser on Monday afternoon, arriving 24 hours later. Put your name on the waiting list at the Nile River Transport Corporation (Ⓣ097/230-3348) in the arcade behind the Tourist Police before applying for a Sudanese **visa** at their consulate (daily except Fri 9am–4pm Ⓣ097/230-7231) ten minutes' walk north from the train station. One-way first- (£E450) and second-class (£E350) fares include meals, but you may wish to bring your own food. From Wadi Halfa, it's fifty hours by train to Sudan's capital, Khartoum.

The Aswan Dams

The **Aswan Dams** attest that Egypt's fundamental dilemma is more intractable than suggested by John Gunther's pithy diagnosis: "Make more land. Make fewer people. Either solution would alleviate the problem, but neither is easy." Although each dam has brought large areas under cultivation, boosted agricultural productivity and provided hydroelectricity for industry, the gains have been eroded by a population explosion – impelling Egypt to undertake yet more ambitious irrigation projects.

Ever conscious of the dams' significance, Egyptians are inclined to view them as a tourist attraction, whereas most foreigners simply regard the edifices as a route to the temples of Abu Simbel, Philae and Kalabsha, which were reassembled on higher ground following the construction of the High Dam. Views from the top of the dams are spectacular, though.

The Old Dam

Just upriver from the First Cataract stands the old **Aswan Dam**, built by the British (1898–1902) and subsequently twice raised to increase its capacity. Once the largest dam in the world, it stands 50m tall, 2km long, 30m thick at the base and 11m at the top. Now that its storage and irrigation functions have been taken over by the High Dam, the dam chiefly serves to generate hydroelectricity for the nearby fertilizer

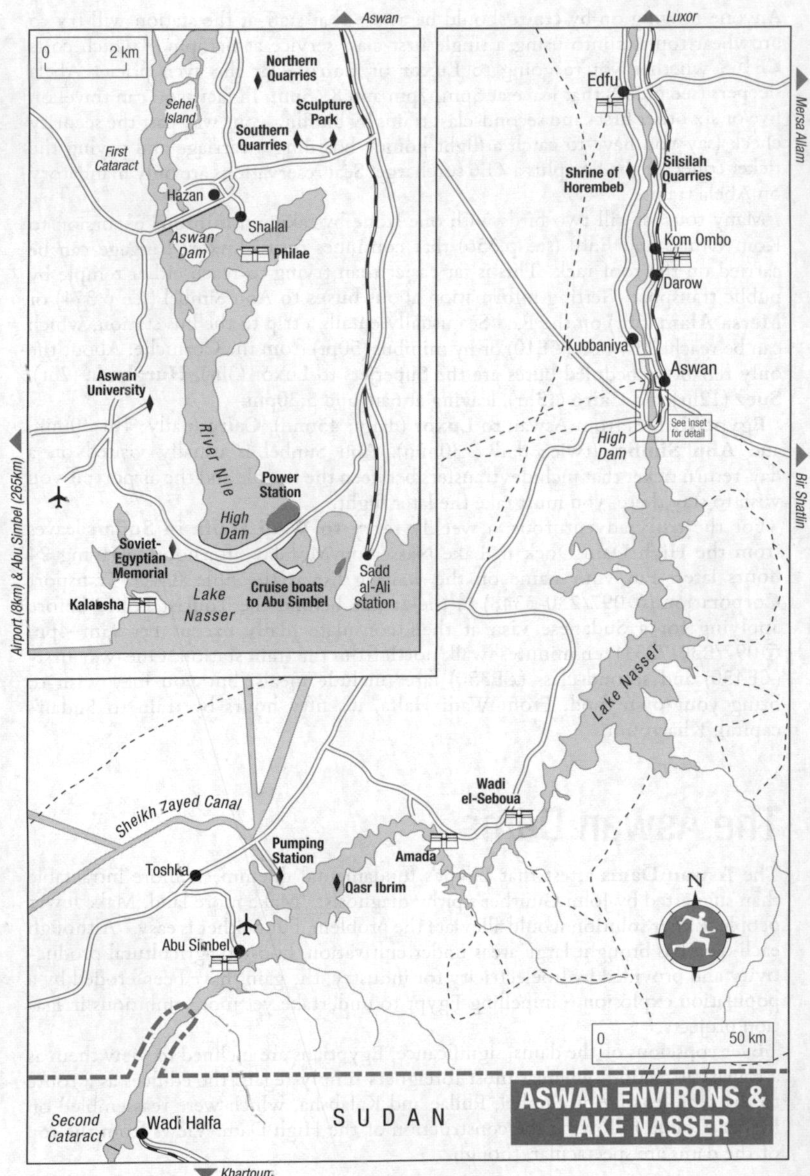

factory. Driving across, you'll notice the 180 sluice gates that used to be opened during the inundation and then gradually closed as the river level dropped, preserving a semi-natural flood cycle. **Philae** is visible among the islands to the south of the dam. Near the eastern end of the dam lies a residential colony for hydro-engineers, called **Hazan**, where colonial villas nestle amid verdant gardens.

The High Dam

By 1952 it was apparent that the Aswan Dam could no longer satisfy Egypt's needs nor guarantee security from famine. Nasser pledged to build a new **High Dam** (Al-Sadd al-Ali) 6km upstream, which would secure Egypt's future, power new industries and bring electricity to every village. When the World Bank reneged on its promised loan under pressure from the US, Nasser nationalized the Suez Canal to generate revenue for the project and turned to the Soviet Union for help. The dam's construction (1960–71) outlasted his lifetime and the era of Soviet–Egyptian collaboration.

The most visible consequence of the High Dam is **Lake Nasser**, which backs up for over 500km, well into Sudan. Over 180m deep in places, with a surface area of 6000 square kilometres, the lake is the world's largest reservoir, and seems more like an inland sea. Since a dam burst would wash most of Egypt's population into the Mediterranean, its security is paramount. The surrounding hills bristle with radar installations and anti-aircraft missiles.

Environmental consequences

As Lake Nasser rose behind the High Dam, flooding ancient Nubia, an international effort ensured that mud-brick fortresses and burial grounds were excavated and photographed, before being abandoned to the rising waters. Half a dozen temples and tombs were salvaged to be reassembled on higher ground or in foreign museums. Since then, however, many temples in Upper Egypt have been affected by damp and salt encrustation, blamed on the rising water table and greater humidity.

Although the human, cultural and environmental costs are still being evaluated, the dam has delivered most of its promised **benefits**. Egypt has been able to convert 3000 square kilometres of cultivated land from the ancient basin system of irrigation to perennial irrigation – doubling or tripling the number of harvests – and to reclaim more than 4200 square kilometres of desert. The dam's turbines have powered a thirty percent expansion of industrial capacity; fishing and tourism on Lake Nasser have developed into profitable industries, and the new Toshka pumping station and the Sheikh Zayed Canal are set to turn more desert into farmland as the **Toshka Project** progresses (see box, p.374).

While the main losers have been the **Nubians**, whose homeland was submerged by the lake (see p.340), other environmental consequences are still being assessed. Evaporation from the lake has caused haze, clouds and even rainfall over previously arid regions and the water table has risen. Because the dam traps the silt that once renewed Egypt's fields, farmers now rely on chemical fertilizers, and the soil salinity caused by perennial irrigation can only be prevented by extensive drainage projects, which create breeding grounds for mosquitoes and bilharzia-carrying snails. And with no silty deposits to replenish it, the Delta coastline is being eroded by the Mediterranean.

Others fear international conflicts over water resources in the future. When Ethiopia commissioned a study on damming the Abbai River (the source of the Blue Nile), Cairo warned that any reduction of Egypt's quota of Nile water, fixed by treaty at 59 billion cubic metres annually, would be seen as a threat to national security, and that Egypt would, in fact, need a larger share in the future.

Cruises and fishing safaris on Lake Nasser

Cruise boats began operating on the lake in 1993 thanks to Mustafa al-Guindi, a Cairo-born Nubian who launched the opulent *Eugénie* and *Qasr Ibrim*. There are now five more boats run by different companies, mostly with five-star ratings. Each follows a similar **schedule**, departing from the High Dam (four days) or Abu Simbel (three days), taking in the otherwise inaccessible sites of **Wadi el-Seboua**, **Amada** and **Qasr Ibrim** (see pp.367–370) plus **Abu Simbel** and **Kalabsha** temples. Most passengers book through companies abroad, but trips can also be arranged in Egypt, sometimes at short notice. Rates are lowest in the summer, highest over Christmas/New Year and Easter.

Besides antiquities, Lake Nasser is renowned for its **fishing** – for **Nile perch** (the largest caught weighed 176kg, just short of the world record), huge **tilapia**, piranha-like **tigerfish** and eighteen kinds of **giant catfish**. After tilapia (at the bottom of the food chain) spawns in mid-March, perch and catfish thrive in depths of up to 6m till late September, after which big fish are caught in deeper water until February by trolling over submerged promontories or islands, and by shore- or fly-fishing from March to July. The best fishing grounds are in the north of the lake – beyond Amada the fish get eaten by crocodiles. Anglers base themselves on mother ships and fish in twos or threes off smaller boats. Fishing packages include meals, soft drinks and transfers from Aswan in the price; specialist rods can be hired if needed.

Cruises

Eugénie Ⓦwww.eugenie.com.eg. Managed by Belle Époque Travel in Cairo and named after the empress who opened the Suez Canal, this magnificent boat is modelled on a khedival hunting lodge, with a Turkish steam bath, French *haute cuisine*, cocktails and classical music at Abu Simbel to please its guests.

Nubian Sea Its 70 cabins and pool are nothing special, but the buffet meals are superior to all the boats on Lake Nasser except the *Eugénie* and *Qasr Ibrim*. Cruises sold abroad by Thomson and Voyages Jules Verne (including flights), and by Memphis Tours in Egypt (four days €320–495).

Prince Abbas Operated by the *Mövenpick* company, this has 55 cabins, billiards, a mini gym, jacuzzi and a plunge pool on the sundeck. Packages sold by Travel in Style (in the US) and Longwood Holidays (in the UK); cruise-only deals by Memphis Tours in Egypt (from €110–250).

Qasr Ibrim Ⓦwww.kasribrim.com.eg. With its lavish 1930s Art Deco interiors and *haute cuisine*, this boat is as grand as the *Eugénie*, and likewise managed by Belle Époque Travel in Cairo.

Queen Abu Simbel Ⓦnaggar.4mg.com. Run by Naggar Travel in Cairo, it features a sauna, jacuzzi and Turkish bath, billiards and bridge.

Jaz Omar Khayam and **Tania** Ⓦwww.travcotravel.com. Marketed in Egypt by Travco, the *Jaz Omar Khayam* is comparable to other five-star boats, while the four-star *Tania* is less fancy. You can buy tickets on the spot from Travco's office in Aswan (Ⓣ097/233-3257).

Fishing safaris

African Angler Ⓣ097/230-9748 or 012 749-1892, Ⓔenquiries@african-angler.net. Former Kenyan safari guide Tim Bailey organizes one-, six- or thirteen-day fishing trips, marketed in Britain through Tailor Made Holidays.

Lake Nasser Adventure Ⓦnilefishing.com. Nubian fisherman Nekrashi (Ⓣ012 350-3825, satellite phone Ⓣ+88216 333 601 38) and his partner Steven (Ⓣ012 104-0255 or Ⓣ+88216 333 601 04) have three mother ships on the lake almost all year round. Prices depend on the time of year.

Miskaa Ⓣ012 367-1705, Ⓦwww.miskaa.com. Another local safari outfit with eight small boats and mother ships, which also offers crocodile-watching on Lake Nasser.

Visiting the High Dam

Many tours to Abu Simbel from Aswan drive across the High Dam, which is only 13km from the city and can be crossed anytime between 7am and 5pm. However, they seldom stop there as this renders all passengers liable to a £E20 sightseeing **fee**. Along the western approach stands the **Soviet-Egyptian Memorial**, a giant lotus-blossom tower built to symbolize their collaboration and the dam's benefits, as depicted in heroic, Socialist Realist bas-reliefs. A lofty **observation deck**, reached by elevator, allows four people at a time to see how the dam's concrete is crumbling and be stricken by vertigo. Off the road at the east end of the dam is a **visitors' pavilion** (daily 7am–5pm), which the curator will unlock for baksheesh. Exhibits include a fifteen-metre-high model of the dam, plans for its construction (in Russian and Arabic), and a photo narrative of the relocation of Abu Simbel.

Some drivers risk stopping midway across the dam to allow passengers a brief look. From this vantage point the dam's height (111m) is masked by the cantilever, but its length (3830m) and width at the top (40m) and base (980m) are impressive. From the southern side of the dam you can gaze across Lake Nasser to Kalabsha Temple. The **view** northwards includes the huge 2100-megawatt power station on the east bank and the channels through which water is routed into the Nile, rushing out amid clouds of mist, sometimes crowned by a rainbow. **Philae** lies among the cluster of islands further downriver.

Philae

The island of **PHILAE** and its **Temple of Isis** have bewitched visitors since Ptolemaic times, when most of the complex was constructed. The devout and curious were drawn here by a cult that flourished throughout the Roman Empire well into the Christian era. Although the first Europeans to "rediscover" Philae in the eighteenth century could only marvel at it from a distance after their attempts to land were "met with howls, threats and eventually the spears of the natives living in the ruins", subsequent visitors revelled in this mirage from antiquity.

After the building of the first Aswan Dam, rising waters lapped and surged about the temple, submerging it for half the year, when tourists would admire its shadowy presence beneath the translucent water. However, once it became apparent that the new High Dam would submerge Philae forever, UNESCO and the Egyptian authorities organized a massive operation (1972–80) to **relocate** its temples on nearby **Aglika Island**, which was landscaped to match the original site. The new Philae is magnificently set amid volcanic outcrops, like a jewel in the royal blue lake, but no longer faces Biga Island, sacred to Osiris.

Most people visit Philae on **tours from Aswan** (see p.356), which is the only easy way of getting there and back. Minibuses drop you at the **Shallal** motorboat dock, 2km from the eastern end of the Old Dam, where you can buy site **tickets** (daily: winter 7am–4pm; summer 7am–5pm; £E50) and a ticket (£E10) for a **motorboat** to the island; the boatman expects baksheesh if you linger more than an hour.

Philae's **Sound and Light Show** is better than the one at Karnak. There are two or three performances nightly; check the schedules at Aswan's tourist office. As at Karnak, the show consists of an hour-long tour through the ruins, whose floodlit forms are more impressive than the melodramatic soundtrack. **Tickets** (£E75; no student reductions) are sold at the dockside just before the first show begins. You'll need to rent a **taxi** from Aswan to take you there and back; expect to pay £E50–60 for a four-seater cab (including waiting time), plus the cost of the motorboat ride there and back.

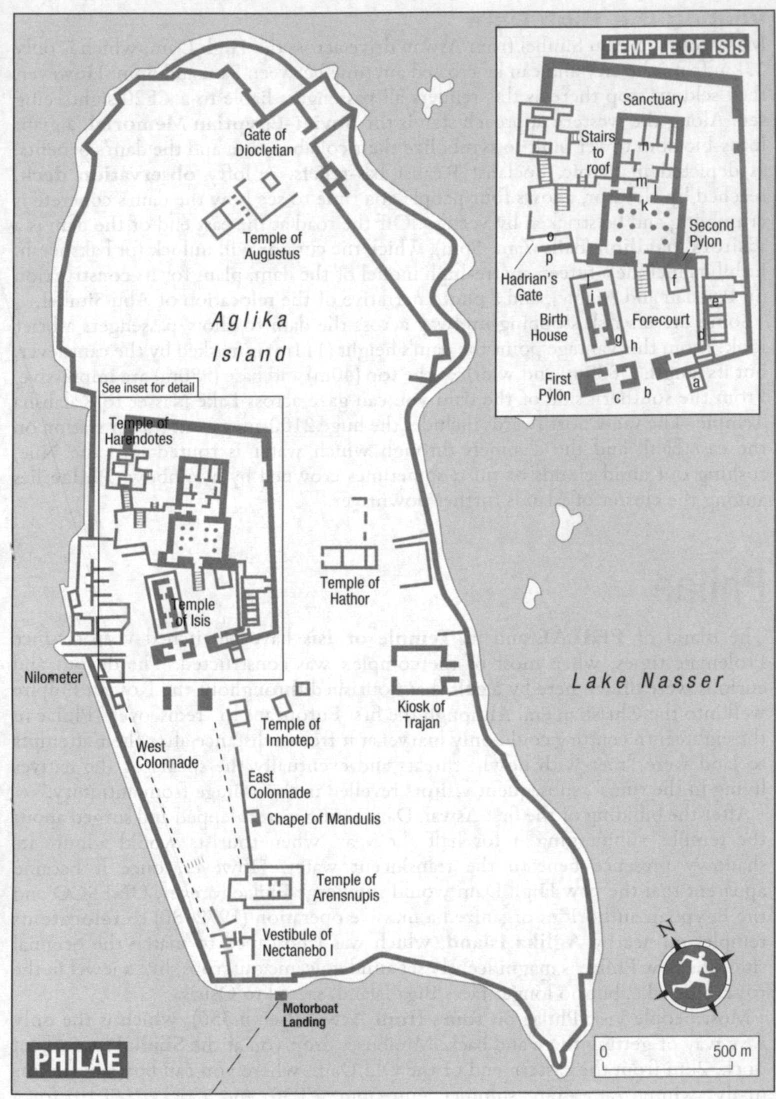

The Temple of Isis

Philae's cult status dates back to the New Kingdom, when Biga Island was identified as one of the burial places of Osiris – and the first piece of land to emerge from the primordial waters of Chaos. Since Biga was forbidden to all but the priesthood, however, public festivities centred upon neighbouring **Philae**, which was known originally as the "Island from the Time of Re".

Excluding a few remains from the Late Period, the existing **Temple of Isis** was constructed over some eight hundred years by Ptolemaic and Roman rulers who sought to identify themselves with the Osirian myth and the cult of Isis. An exquisite fusion of ancient Egyptian and Greco-Roman architecture, the temple complex harmonizes perfectly with its setting, sculpted pillars and pylons gleaming white or mellow gold against Mediterranean-blue water and black Nilotic rock.

Approaching the temple

Motorboats land near at the southern end of the island. In ancient times, on the original Philae, visitors ascended a double stairway to the **Vestibule of Nectanebo** at the entrance to the temple precincts. Erected by a XXX Dynasty pharaoh in honour of his "Mother Isis", this was the prototype for the graceful kiosks of the Ptolemaic and Roman era. Notice the double capitals on the remaining columns, traditional flower shapes topped with sistrum-Hathor squares that supported the architrave. The screens that once formed the walls are crowned with cavetto cornices and rows of *uraeus* serpents, a motif dating back to Zoser's complex at Saqqara, nearly three thousand years earlier.

Beyond the vestibule stretches an elongated trapezoidal courtyard flanked by colonnades. The **West Colonnade** is the better preserved, with finely carved capitals, each slightly different. The windows in the wall behind once faced Biga, the island of Osiris; the one opposite the first two columns is topped by a relief of Nero offering two eyes to Horus and Isis. The plainer, unfinished **East Colonnade** abuts a succession of ruined structures. Past the foundations of the **Temple of Arensnupis** (worshipped as the "Good Companion of Isis" in the Late Period) lies a ruined **Chapel of Mandulis**, the Nubian god of Kalabsha. Near the First Pylon, an unfinished **Temple of Imhotep** honours the philosopher-physician who designed Zoser's Step Pyramid and was later deified as a god of healing. Its forecourt walls show Khnum, Satis, Anukis, Isis and Osiris, and Ptolemy IV before Imhotep.

The Pylons and Forecourt

The lofty **First Pylon** was built by Neos Dionysos (Ptolemy XII), who smites enemies in the approved fashion at either corner, watched by Isis, Horus and Hathor. Set at right angles to the pylon, the Gate of Ptolemy II **[a]** is probably a remnant of an earlier temple. The pylon's main portal **[b]** is still older (dating from the reign of Nectanebo II) and was formerly flanked by two granite obelisks; now only two **stone lions** remain. Inside the portal are inscriptions by Napoleon's troops, commemorating their victory over the Mamlukes in 1799. The smaller door in the western section of the pylon leads through to the Birth House and was used for rituals; the entrance depicts the personified deities of Nubia and the usual Egyptian pantheon **[c]**. On the back of the pylon are scenes of priests carrying Isis's barque.

Emerging into the **Forecourt**, most visitors make a beeline for the Birth House or the Second Pylon, overlooking the colonnade to the east. Here, reliefs behind the stylish plant columns show the king performing rituals such as dragging the barque of Sokar **[d]**. A series of doors lead into six rooms which probably had a service function; one of them, dubbed the Library **[e]**, features Thoth in his ibis and baboon forms, Maat, lion-headed Tefnut and Sheshat, the goddess of writing. At the northern end stands a ruined chapel **[f]**, which the Romans erected in front of a granite outcrop that was smoothed into a stele under Ptolemy IV and related his gift of lands to the temple.

Set at an angle to its forerunner, the **Second Pylon** changes the axis of the temple. A large relief on the right tower shows Neos Dionysos placing sacrifices before Horus and Hathor; in a smaller scene above he presents a wreath to Horus and Nephthys, offers incense and anoints an altar before Osiris, Isis and Horus. Similar scenes on the other tower have been defaced by early Christians, who

The cult of Isis

▲ Isis

Of all the cults of ancient Egypt, none endured longer or spread further than the worship of the goddess **Isis**. As the consort of Osiris, she civilized the world by instituting marriage and teaching women the domestic arts. As an enchantress, she collected the dismembered fragments of his body and briefly revived him to conceive a son, Horus, using her magic to help him defeat the evil Seth and restore the divine order. As pharaohs identified themselves with Horus, the living king, so Isis was their divine mother – a role which inevitably associated her with Hathor, the two goddesses being conflated in the Late Period. By this time Isis was the Great Mother of All Gods and Nature, Goddess of Ten Thousand Names, of women, purity and sexuality.

By a process of identification with other goddesses around the Mediterranean, **Isis-worship** eventually spread throughout the Roman empire (the westernmost Iseum or cult temple extant is in Hungary). The nurturing, forgiving, loving Isis was Christianity's chief rival between the third and fifth centuries. Many scholars believe that the cult of the Virgin Mary was Christianity's attempt to wean converts away from Isis; early Coptic art identifies one with the other, Horus with Jesus, and the Christian cross with the pharaonic ankh.

executed the paintings in the upper right-hand corner of the pylon passageway, leading into the temple proper.

The Birth House

The western side of the forecourt is dominated by the colonnaded **Birth House** of Ptolemy IV, which linked his ancestry to Horus and Osiris. Most of the exterior reliefs were added in Roman times, which is why Emperor Augustus shadows Buto, goddess of the north, as she plays a harp before the young, naked Horus and his mother at one end of the central register, behind the Hathor-headed colonnade **[g]**. Further south and higher up, the Roman reliefs overlie inscriptions in hieroglyphs and demotic characters that partly duplicate those on the Rosetta Stone **[h]**. Inside, a columned forecourt and two vestibules precede the sanctuary, which contains the finest scenes **[i]**. Although iconoclasts have defaced the goddess suckling the child-pharaoh on the left-hand wall, you can see Isis giving birth to Horus in the marshes at the bottom of the rear wall. Around the back of the sanctuary behind the northern colonnade is a corresponding scene of Isis nursing Horus in the swamp **[j]**.

Inside the Temple of Isis

Immediately behind the Second Pylon lies a small open court that was originally separated from the **Hypostyle Hall** by a screen wall, now destroyed. A lovely drawing by David Roberts shows this "Grand Portico" in its rich original colours: the flowering capitals are in shades of green with yellow flowers and blue buds; crimson and golden winged sun-discs are seen flying down the central aisle of the ceiling, which elsewhere bears astronomical reliefs. The unpainted walls and column shafts show the hall's builder, Ptolemy VII Euergetes II, sacrificing to various deities. After the emperor Justinian forbade the celebration of Isis rituals at Philae in 550 AD, Copts used the hall for services and chiselled crosses into the walls. On the left-hand jamb of the portal **[k]** into the vestibule beyond, a piece of Roman graffiti asserts *B Mure stultus est* ("B Mure is stupid").

As at other temples, the **vestibules** get lower and darker as you approach the sanctuary. By a doorway **[l]** to the right of the first vestibule, a Greek inscription records the "cleansing" of this pagan structure under Bishop Theodorus, during the reign of Justinian. On the other side of the vestibule is a room giving access to the **stairs** to the roof (see below). The next vestibule has an interesting scene flanking the portal at the back **[m]**, where the king offers a sistrum (left) and wine (right) to Isis and Harpocrates (Child Horus). On the left-hand door jamb, he leaves offerings to Min, a basket to Sekhmet and wine to Osiris, with the sacred bull and seven cows in the background. In the partially ruined transverse vestibule, the king offers necklaces, wine and eye paint to Osiris, Isis, Hathor and Nephthys, outside the sanctuary **[n]**.

Dimly lit by two apertures in the roof, the **sanctuary** contains a stone pedestal dedicated by Ptolemy III and his wife Berenice, which once supported the goddess's barque. On the left wall, the pharaoh faces Isis, whose wings protectively enfold Osiris. Across the room, an enthroned Isis suckles the infant Horus (above) and stands to suckle a young pharaoh (below, now defaced). The other rooms, used for rites or storage, contain reliefs of goddesses with Nubian features.

Hadrian's Gate

By leaving the temple through the western door of the first vestibule you'll emerge near **Hadrian's Gate**, set into the girdle wall that once encircled Philae Island. Flanking your approach are two walls from a bygone vestibule, decorated with notable reliefs. The right-hand wall **[o]** depicts the origin of the Nile, whose twin streams are poured forth by Hapy the Nile-god from his cave beneath Biga Island, atop which perches a falcon. To the right of this, Isis, Nephthys and others adore the young falcon as he rises from a marsh.

Above the door in the opposite wall **[p]**, Isis and Nephthys present the dual crowns to Horus, whose name is inscribed on a palm stalk by Sheshat (right) and Thoth (left). Below, Isis watches a crocodile drag the corpse of Osiris to a rocky promontory (presumably Biga). Around the gate itself, Hadrian appears before the gods (above the lintel) and the door jambs bear the fetishes of Abydos (left) and Osiris (right). At the top of the wall, Marcus Aurelius stands before Isis and Osiris; below he offers Isis grapes and flowers.

North of the gateway lie the foundations of the **Temple of Harendotes** (an aspect of Horus), built by the emperor Claudius.

Elsewhere on the island

To complete the cast of deities involved in the Osirian myth, a small **Temple of Hathor** was erected to the east of the main complex – really only notable for a relief of musicians, among whom the god Bes plays a harp. More eye-catching and virtually the symbol of Philae is the graceful open-topped **Kiosk of Trajan**, nicknamed the "Pharaoh's Bedstead". Removed from its watery grave by a team of British navy divers, the reconstructed kiosk juxtaposes variegated floral columns with a severely classical superstructure; only two of the screen wall panels bear reliefs.

Kalabsha

The hulking **Temple of Kalabsha** broods beside Lake Nasser near the western end of the High Dam, marooned on an island or strung out on a promontory, depending on the water level. Between the site and the dam lies a graveyard of boats and fishy remains, enhancing its mood of desolation. The main temple originally came from Talmis (later known as Kalabsha), 50km to the south of Aswan; in a German-financed operation, it was cut into 13,000 blocks and reassembled here in 1970, together with other monuments from Nubia. Strictly speaking, "Kalabsha" refers to the original site rather than the temple itself, which is named after the god Mandulis, and has no historic connection with two smaller monuments in the vicinity, relocated here from other sites in Nubia.

Taxis are the only way of getting to Kalabsha and back; Ahmed at the *Nubian Oasis Hotel* (p.355) can arrange a trip for up to four people for £E90. When the water level is low you can walk across a causeway to Kalabsha; otherwise, you can find a **motorboat** on the western side of the High Dam (about £E40 for the return trip with an hour's waiting time). Tickets for the **site** (daily: summer 7am–5pm; winter 7am–4pm; £E35) are sold at the temple itself.

The Temple of Mandulis

The **Temple of Mandulis** is a Ptolemaic-Roman version of an earlier XVIII Dynasty edifice dedicated to the Nubian fertility god Marul, whom the Greeks called Mandulis.

By Ptolemaic times, Egypt's Nubian empire was a token one, dependent on the goodwill of the powerful kingdom of Napata ruled from Meröe near the Fourth Cataract, about 400km south of Abu Simbel. Having briefly restored old-style imperialism, the Romans abandoned most of Nubia during the reign of Diocletian, falling back on deals with local rulers to safeguard Egypt's southern border. As the linchpin of the last imperial town south of Aswan, the temple bears witness to this patronage and the kingdoms that succeeded the Napatan state, which disintegrated under the onslaught of marauding Blemmye (c.550 AD), a group of nomadic tribes who were perhaps the ancestors of the modern Beja.

Approaching the sandstone temple from behind, you miss the dramatic effect of the great stone **causeway** from the water's edge, used by pilgrims in the days when Kalabsha was a healing temple, like Edfu and Dendara. For reasons unknown, its chunky **pylon** is skewed at a slight angle to the temple, a blemish rectified by having a trapezoidal **courtyard** whose pillars are set closer together along the shorter, southern side.

The first batch of reliefs worth a mention occurs on the **facade** of the Hypostyle Hall at the back of the court. While Horus and Thoth anoint the king with holy water in a conventional scene to the left of the portal, the right-hand wall bears a decree excluding swineherds and their pigs from the temple (issued in 249 AD); a large relief of a horseman in Roman dress receiving a wreath from the winged Victory; and a text in poor Greek lauding Siklo, the Christian king of the Nobatae, for repulsing the Blemmye.

The now roofless **Hypostyle Hall** has some interesting reliefs along the rear wall. Left of the portal, a Ptolemaic king offers crowns to Horus and Mandulis, while Amenhotep II (founder of the XVIII Dynasty temple) presents a libation to Mandulis and Min. Across the way, a nameless king slays a foe before Horus, Shu and Tefnet.

Within the **vestibules** beyond, look for figures personifying the Egyptian nomes, below a scene of the king offering a field to Isis and Mandulis and wine to Osiris (near the stairs off the outer vestibule); and a rare appearance by the deified sage Imhotep (low down on the left-hand wall of the inner vestibule).

The **Sanctuary** is similar in size to the vestibules and, like them, once had two columns. Along its back wall you can identify (from left to right) the emperor offering lotuses to Isis and the young Horus, and milk to Mandulis and Wadjet; then incense to the former duo and lotuses to the latter. Although the god's cult statue has vanished, Mandulis still appears at either end of the scene covering the temple's **rear wall**: in his royal form, with a pharaonic crown, sceptre and ankh sign (right); and as a god whose ram's-horn crown is surmounted by a solar disc, *uraeus* and ostrich plumes (left).

From the *pronaos*, you may be able to ascend a stairway to the **roof**, which features an abbreviated version of the Osirian shrines found at other complexes. The **view** of Lake Nasser and the High Dam, over the temple courtyards, is amazing. A passageway between the temple and its enclosure wall leads to a well-preserved **Nilometer**.

The Kiosk of Qertassi and Beit al-Wali

Re-erected near the lakeside at the same time as Kalabsha Temple, the **Kiosk of Qertassi** resembles a knocked-about copy of the "Pharaoh's Bedstead" at Philae, but actually came from another ancient settlement, 40km south of Aswan. Aside from its fine views of Lake Nasser, this Ptolemaic-Roman edifice is chiefly notable for two surviving Hathor-headed columns, which make the goddess look more feline than bovine. In the forecourt, notice the women pleading for mercy as Ramses seizes their menfolk, and the Nubians paying tribute in the form of gold, ivory, leopard skins, feathers, and even an ostrich.

The oldest monumental relic from Nile-inundated Nubia is a temple dug into the hillside behind Kalabsha Temple. Originally hewn under Ramses II, who left his mark throughout Nubia, this cruciform rock-cut structure is known by its Arabic name, **Beit al-Wali** (House of the Holy Man). The weathered reliefs flanking its narrow court depict the pharaoh's victories over Nubians and Ethiopians (left), Libyans and Asiatics (right). By contrast, scenes in the transverse hall are well preserved and brightly coloured. Here, Ramses makes offerings before Isis, Horus and the Aswan Triad (Hapy, Satet and Khnum), and is suckled by goddesses inside the sanctuary, whose niche contains a mutilated cult statue of three deities.

Wadi el-Seboua, Amada and Qasr Ibrim

At the time of writing, the three reconstructed sites known as **Wadi el-Seboua**, **Amada** and **Qasr Ibrim** can only be seen while **cruising on Lake Nasser** (detailed in the box on p.360), but spur roads to Wadi el-Seboua and Amada have been built, so access might improve if security restrictions are eased. Meanwhile, cruise boats provide their passengers with motorboat rides to Wadi el-Seboua and Amada, moor tantalizingly close to Qasr Ibrim (where you can't land), and start or end their tours at Abu Simbel or Kalabsha.

Wadi el-Seboua

Cruise boats departing from the High Dam must sail nearly half the length of Lake Nasser before they reach **Wadi el-Seboua**. They usually moor here after dark for passengers to enjoy an awesome floodlit vista of three temples, joined by what appears to be a long processional avenue, which is revealed next morning to be a track across a desert of tan-coloured sand and grey rocks. The landscape is dotted with a few bits of grass and a half-submerged crane that was used to transport the main temple from its original location, 4km away. **Admission** to the site costs £E45.

Wadi el-Seboua means "Valley of the Lions" in Arabic and refers to the **avenue of sphinxes** leading to the **temple** of that name. It was built during the reign of

Ramses II by his viceroy of Kush, Setau, using Libyan prisoners of war, who also worked on Abu Simbel. Like Abu Simbel, it was dedicated to Amun-Re, Re-Herakhte and the deified pharaoh, whose role as a conqueror is emphasized by images of Libyan and Asiatic captives carved on the pedestals of the statues of the king that flank its gateway. In the second court, the human-headed sphinxes give way to falcon-headed ones, representing the four forms of Horus.

Beyond the temple **pylon** is an **open court** with columns fronted by Osirian statues of Ramses, notable for their thick legs. Scholars disagree whether this reflected his physique or was merely to make him look stronger, but this feature occurs on all statues of Ramses, whose virility is further attested to by images of his numerous progeny (53 princes and 54 princesses) below the offering scenes on the walls. The remainder of the temple is cut from rock and once served as a Christian church; its **reliefs** retain much of their scarlet, white and yellow paint due to being covered by plaster for centuries. The best-preserved ones are in the transverse vestibule, including an unusual portrayal of Hathor with a woman's body and a cow's head. You can also see Ramses making offerings to his own sphinx, above and behind the doorway into the sanctuary, where a votive niche contains remnants of the Christian murals that once covered the walls, resulting in a surreal tableau of Ramses offering flowers to St Peter.

Temple of Dakka

From Wadi el-Seboua, passengers can walk or ride a camel (£E50) 1500m across the desert to the hilltop **Temple of Dakka** that once stood 40km north of its present site. Its most striking feature is an elegant freestanding **pylon**, which is over 12m tall; visitors are sometimes allowed to climb it, which affords them a fantastic view of the area. There isn't much carving on the walls but the gateway is crowned by a winged sun-disc, and on its left-hand side is graffiti in Meröitic script thought to have been left by Nubian soldiers, retreating from Aswan in 23 AD.

The temple itself was started by **Arkamani**, one of the rulers (218–200 BC) of the Kingdom of Meröe – which at that time controlled Lower Nubia – and was added to by his contemporary, **Ptolemy IV**, and decorated by later Ptolemies. You can see the Hellenistic influence in the composite capitals (combining Greek and Egyptian forms) and scenes in the *pronaos*, where Isis sports big breasts in the Greek style. Also notice the four sacred cobras, carved in the corners of the entrance wall. On many of the reliefs in the temple the king performing the rituals is simply identified by a cartouche reading "Pharaoh", as the masons didn't know who was in power at the time in Alexandria, or didn't want to inscribe the name of a Ptolemy who wouldn't be on the throne for long – though this wasn't the case for Ptolemy IV and his sister-wife Arsinöe, who are shown offering a Maat (truth) figure to Thoth and Wepset on the lintel of the doorway into the vestibule.

At the back of the vestibule is a passageway and stairs leading to the **roof**, which affords a stunning view, while beyond lies the **Chapel of Arkamani** that originally served as the temple's sanctuary. Here, Arkamani makes offerings to the gods beneath a frieze of his cartouche interspersed with falcons and ibises, while on the rear wall is an interesting relief of Thoth as an ape adoring Tefnut, who is shown as a lioness. A baboon worshipping a lion can also be seen in the side-passage leading off the chapel, while another ape consorts with a cow beneath a persea tree low down in the near right-hand corner of the sanctuary, which was built and decorated under the Roman emperors Augustus and Tiberius. On leaving the temple, walk around the east wall to see a **waterspout** in the shape of a lion's head.

Temple of Maharraqa

A short way downhill back towards the shore stands the small **Temple of Maharraqa**, taken from a site 50km north of its present location, which was the southern frontier of Egypt in Greco-Roman times. Its floral capitals and reliefs were left unfinished – in some places only roughly sketched in reddish-brown paint. The temple's most interesting feature, leading up to the roof, is the **spiral staircase**, the only one known in an Ancient Egyptian building. The temple was probably dedicated to Seraphis.

Amada

Beyond Wadi el-Seboua, Lake Nasser describes an S-shaped curve that takes it past another set of temples in one of the loveliest parts of Nubia, where the rocky desert shoreline is fringed with acacia scrub. Cruise passengers are ferried to **Amada** here by motorboat, and all three monuments are covered by one **ticket** (£E45). Bring a **torch** for examining the reliefs inside the temples.

Temple of Amada

The site is named after the **Temple of Amada**, which is the oldest surviving structure on Lake Nasser and contains some of the finest relief-carving to be seen on any of the Nubian monuments. It was built by the XVIII Dynasty pharaohs Tuthmosis III, Amenophis II and Tuthmosis IV, and restored and decorated during the XIX Dynasty. Like most of the Nubian temples, it was dedicated to Amun-Re and Re-Herakhte, who appear with various pharaohs in the usual offerings scenes.

For archeologists, the temple is particularly interesting for two historic **inscriptions**: the first, carved on a stele on the left side of the entrance, describes the Libyan invasion of Egypt in the fourth year (1232 BC) of Merneptah's reign; while the other, on the back wall of the sanctuary, dates from the second year (1423 BC) of Amenophis II's reign, and relates how he dealt with seven leaders of a revolt in Syria, whose heads and limbs were hung on the gates of Thebes as a warning to other would-be rebels.

When Amelia Edwards visited Amada in 1873 she found the temple "half-choked" with sand; judging by the **camels** drawn by Bedouin and pilgrims on the cornice of the facade, it was buried so in medieval times. The inner part of the temple consists of a vestibule and sanctuary with a small cult-chamber on either side, whose **reliefs** are as lapidary as any produced during the XVIII Dynasty. The ones in the right-hand room depict the foundation and consecration of the temple; Tuthmosis III and Amenophis II make offerings to the gods in the other chamber.

Temple of Derr

A few minutes' walk from Amada is the smaller **Temple of Derr**, once located on the east bank of the Nile (the only one in Nubia on that side of the river). With its gateway gone and its pillared forehall reduced to stumps, the temple now confronts visitors with a rugged portico featuring four square pillars and statues of Ramses II only roughed-out up to waist-level. The interior of the temple was entirely hewn from rock, with few straight lines or right angles, and its sunk-reliefs finished in stucco with painted details. On the side walls of the pillared hall, Re-Herakhte's sacred barque is carried in a procession on the shoulders of priests, as Ramses walks alongside wearing a leopard-skin cloak; the white background and the yellow of the barque and cloak are still visible. More colours survive on the walls of the sanctuary, where Ramses burns incense and pours a libation to the barque before annointing Re-Herakhte with his little finger (right). At the back, the four cult-statues that originally represented Ramses, Amun-Re, Re-Herakhte and Ptah were hacked away by Christian iconoclasts.

Tomb of Pennut

Leaving Derr temple, it's worth hurrying on ahead to get to the **Tomb of Pennut**, as it's only large enough to hold a few people. Pennut (or Penne) was a high official in Lower Nubia during the reign of Ramses VI, whose tomb was originally dug into a hillside at Aniba, 40km south of its present site. Sunk-reliefs in the rectangular offerings chamber show Pennut and his wife before the gods, mourners at his funeral, and Pennut worshipping the cow-goddess Hathor in the Western Mountains. As you leave the tomb, its custodian delves into a bucket to extract a baby **crocodile**, which he offers to tourists for a photo opportunity. The shallows of Lake Nasser beyond Amada are home to many crocodiles and monitor lizards, but they avoid spots frequented by tourists.

Qasr Ibrim

Qasr Ibrim – the last stop on the cruise before Abu Simbel – is unique for being the only one of the Nubian sites to remain *in situ*, albeit nowadays on an island rather than the summit of a hill. This continuity has allowed the Egypt Exploration Society to carry out **excavations** every two years since 1961 and establish that Qasr Ibrim was occupied throughout successive periods from the late New Kingdom until the early nineteenth century, when it was inhabited by Bosnian mercenaries of the Ottoman empire, who married into the local Nubian community. Before the Bosnians' arrival in the sixteenth century, Qasr Ibrim was one of the last redoubts of Christianity in Lower Nubia, as it had previously been the last area to forsake paganism, abandoning the worship of Isis two hundred years after the rest of Egypt.

A ruined sandstone **cathedral** dating back to the eighth century overlies a temple of Isis built by the Nubian XXV Dynasty pharaoh Taharka; as many as six temples once existed here. The cathedral's broken vaults rise amid a muddle of dry-stone and cut-masonry walls, riddled with portals, niches and cavities, attesting to the age and complexity of the site. Due to its fragility and the ongoing excavations, tourists are not allowed to land here, but boats moor so close to the shore that the ruins can easily be seen, or closely examined with **binoculars**.

Abu Simbel

The great **Sun Temple** of **Abu Simbel** (literally "Father of the Ear of Corn") epitomizes the monumentalism of the New Kingdom during its imperial heyday, when Ramses II (1304–1237 or 1279–1213 BC) waged colonial wars from the Beka'a Valley in Lebanon to the Fourth Cataract. To impress his power and majesty on the Nubians, Ramses had four gigantic statues of himself hewn from the mountainside, whence his unblinking stare confronted travellers as they entered Egypt from Africa. The temple he built here was precisely oriented so that the sun's rays reached deep into the mountain to illuminate its sanctuary on his birthday and the anniversary of his coronation. The deified pharaoh physically overshadows the sun-god **Re-Herakhte**, to whom the temple is nominally dedicated, just as his queen, **Nefertari**, sidelines **Hathor** in a neighbouring edifice, also hewn into the mountain.

The first European to see Abu Simbel since antiquity was the Swiss explorer Burckhardt, who found the temples almost completely buried by sand drifts in 1813. Although Belzoni later managed to clear an entrance, lack of treasure discouraged further efforts and the site was soon reburied in sand – a process repeated throughout the nineteenth century. Finally cleared, the temple became the scenic highlight of Thomas Cook's Nile cruises.

It was the prospect of losing Abu Simbel to Lake Nasser that impelled UNESCO to organize the **salvage** of Nubian monuments in the 1960s. Behind the temporary protection of a coffer dam, Abu Simbel's brittle sandstone was stabilized by injections of synthetic resin and then hand-sawn into 1041 blocks weighing up to thirty tons apiece. Two years after the first block was cut, Abu Simbel was reassembled 210m behind (and 61m above) its original site, a false mountain being constructed to match the former setting. The whole operation (from 1964 to 1968) cost $40 million.

Visiting Abu Simbel

Abu Simbel lies on the west bank of Lake Nasser, 280km south of Aswan and 40km north of the Sudanese border. A road runs here from Aswan, used by tourist vehicles travelling in a convoy, and public buses at other times. The site can also be reached by air or water – notably on the **luxury cruises** (p.360) that also visit other sites on Lake Nasser (see Wadi el-Seboua, Amada and Qasr Ibrim, on pp.367–370). Although most tourists visit Abu Simbel on a **day-trip** from Aswan, it's quite feasible to spend a night in Abu Simbel town, to enjoy its laid-back ambience or Nubian music at *Eskaleh* (see below).

From Aswan, Thomas Cook offers daily **excursions** by private taxi (£E1200 for two people, including site tickets), while budget hotels pack trippers into minibuses for £E65–90 per head (excluding tickets). The **convoy** leaves at 4am, arrives at Abu Simbel three and a half hours later, and starts the return journey at 10am. This schedule makes sense given the heat of the desert, but means that hundreds of tourists arrive at the same time, packing out the temples. If you want to enjoy them in privacy and stay longer at Abu Simbel, there are two public **buses** (4hr; £E25) a day from Aswan, which start the return journey from outside the *Wadi El Nile* café on Abu Simbel's main drag.For those with more cash, **flying** saves time and provides a unique view of Lake Nasser and Abu Simbel. EgyptAir flights from Aswan and Luxor are scheduled according to demand, with at least two flights daily, more during peak times. Most people opt for a same-day return flight from Aswan (£E590, including airport transfers); if you want to stay overnight you are obliged to use the 11.15am flight. For those with more time and money, a luxury **cruise** to Abu Simbel is the best way to appreciate Lake Nasser and see the temples as the pharaohs did (see p.360 for details).

Cruise-boat passengers provide most of the audience at the nightly **Sound and Light Show** (£E75; no student discount; Ⓦ www.soundandlight.com.eg), starting at 7pm and 8pm in the winter and one hour later in summer. Don't worry about which language the show is in, as they provide headphones for simultaneous translation and, in any case, the images projected onto the temple facades are more arresting than the soundtrack. Tickets are sold at the temple ticket office.

Abu Simbel town

The new town of **ABU SIMBEL** looks a desolate place as you roll in past the airport, but once beyond the main intersection it becomes quite picturesque as it straggles around rocky headlands dotted with beehive-domed houses and crimson oleander bushes. From the junction with its row of **cafés**, you can follow the main road as it curves around towards the temple, 1km away. This takes you past a **telephone office** and three **banks** with ATMs (closed Fri & Sat), followed by a **post office** with the **tourist police** around the corner, before you pass the town council and reach the souvenir arcade that precedes the visitors' centre and ticket office for the temples – about fifteen minutes' walk in all, or £E5 by taxi.

Accommodation

Few tourists stay at Abu Simbel, where the choice of hotels is limited and prices are high – but some may find the opportunity to savour the temples without

Birdwatching at Abu Simbel

Due to its location on a large body of water surrounded by desert, near the Tropic of Cancer, Abu Simbel sustains both indigenous African and migrant species of birds. Among the rarer species are pink-backed pelicans, yellow-billed storks, long-tailed cormorants, African skimmers and pied wagtails, and pink-headed doves. While serious twitchers will haunt the coves with binoculars, casual bird-spotters can see quite a few dazzling birds in the grounds of the visitors' centre or the *Eskaleh* and *Seti Abu Simbel* hotels. The best time for bird-watching is during the **breeding season** in late January/early February. Mohammed Orabi from Aswan (Ⓣ012 324-0132) is a recommended bird-watching **guide**.

hordes of other tourists around irresistible, and the Nubian music scene at *Eskaleh* is another lure.

Abu Simbel Village Ⓣ097/340-0092. Sited 200m from the main junction in the opposite direction from the temples, this compound of domed rooms is the cheapest place to stay but hardly anyone does. BB ❷

Eskaleh Ⓣ012 368-0521, Ⓦwww.eskaleh.110mb.com. Some 20 minutes' walk from the temples, overlooking a creek to the northwest of town, this comfy Nubian-style ecolodge has a unique vibe conjured up by its musician owner Fikry Kachif. Some complain of rip-off exchange rates and taxi fares to the temples – but on balance it's still the best option, with a great restaurant, free wi-fi and a library. ❻

Nefertari No phone. Some 15 minutes' walk beyond the *Abu Simbel Village*, on a promontory outside town, this ex-government hotel is basic (don't believe its three-star rating on the web) and way overpriced, with only its wonderful view of Lake Nasser to commend it. ❹

Seti Abu Simbel Ⓣ097/340-0720, Ⓦwww.setifirst.com. Closest to the temples, with a stunning view of Lake Nasser from its lush garden and three swimming pools, this nominally priced five-star resort is let down by its faded a/c chalets, lacklustre restaurant and surly staff. BB ❼

Eating, drinking and nightlife

Eating out is likewise limited, with *Eskaleh* the best option, serving tasty meals of produce from their own organic garden – prices are vague but expect to pay from £E60 for a full lunch or dinner. In theory, the *Seti Abu Simbel* offers a more elaborate buffet breakfast (£E60), lunch (£E100) and dinner (£E130), but this may depend on how full the hotel is – though you can rely on them to sell **alcohol**. For cheaper eats, check out *Toya* on the road to the temples, which serves breakfast and simple meals for £E20–30. The *Wady El Nile* and other cafés on the main street are fine for tea and *sheesha*, but their food may not be fresh. As for **nightlife**, Fikry's Nubian jam sessions at *Eskaleh*, and the still more laid-back, gay-oriented scene at the *Nubian Village* higher up the hill, are the only game in town.

The Sun Temple of Ramses II

Having checked out the **Visitors' Centre**, which relates how the temples were moved to their present location, visitors walk around the hill to be confronted by the great **Sun Temple** (daily: summer 6am–6pm; winter 6am–5pm, later if planes land in the evening; £E80), seemingly hewn from the cliffs overlooking Lake Nasser. Its impact is perhaps a little diminished by familiarity (the temple has been depicted on everything from T-shirts to £E1 notes): the technicolour contrast between red rockscape and aquamarine water is more startling than the clean-swept facade, which looks less dramatic than the sand-choked Abu Simbel of nineteenth-century engravings. For all the meticulous reconstruction and landscaping, too, it's hard not to sense its artificiality…but gradually the temple's presence asserts itself, and your mind boggles at its audacious conception, the logistics of constructing and moving it, and the unabashed megalomania of its founder.

The colossi and facade

Although Re-Herakhte, Amun-Re and Ptah are also carved on the facade as patron deities, they're clearly secondary to Ramses II, who ruled for 67 years, dying at the age of 96, having sired scores of sons, most of whom predeceased him. The temple facade is dominated by four enthroned **Colossi of Ramses II**, whose twenty-metre height surpasses the Colossi of Memnon at Thebes (though one lost its upper half following an earthquake in 27 BC). Their feet and legs are crudely executed but the torsos and heads are finely carved, and the face of the left-hand figure quite beautiful. Between them stand figures of the royal family, dwarfed by Ramses' knees. To the left of the headless colossus is the pharaoh's mother, Muttuy; Queen Nefertari stands on the right of the colossus, Prince Amunhirkhepshef between its legs. On its right calf, an inscription records that Greek mercenaries participated in the Nubian campaign of the Saïte king Psammetichus II (c.590 BC).

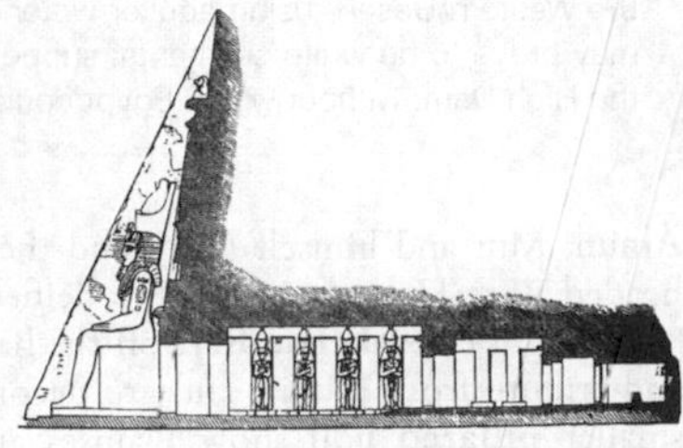
▲ Cross-section of the Sun Temple

The **facade** is otherwise embellished with a niche-bound statue of **Re-Herakhte**, holding a sceptre and a figure of Maat. This composition is a pictorial play of words on Ramses' prenomen, User-Maat-Re, so the flanking sunk-reliefs of the king presenting the god with images of Maat actually signify Ramses honouring his deified self. Crowning the facade is a corvetto cornice surmounted by baboons worshipping the rising sun. On the sides of the colossal thrones flanking the temple entrance, twin Nile-gods entwine the heraldic papyrus and sedge around the hieroglyph "to unite", with the rows of captives beneath them divided between north and south, Asiatics on the right-hand throne and Nubians on its left-hand counterpart.

The Hypostyle Hall and Sanctuary

This schematic division reappears in the lofty rock-cut **Hypostyle Hall**, flanked on either side by four pillars fronted by ten-metre-high statues of Ramses in the Osiris position, carrying the crook and flail (the best is the end figure on the right). Beneath a ceiling painted with flying vultures, the walls crawl with scenes from his campaigns, from Syria to Nubia. On the entrance walls, Ramses slaughters Hittite and Nubian captives before Amun-Re (left) and Re-Herakhte (right), accompanied by his eight sons or nine daughters, and his *ka*. But the most dramatic **reliefs** are found on the side walls (all directions here are as if you're facing the back of the temple).

The right-hand wall depicts the **Battle of Qadesh** on the River Orontes (1300 BC), starting from the back of the hall. Here you see Ramses' army marching on Qadesh, followed by their encampment, ringed by shields. Acting on disinformation tortured out of enemy spies, Ramses prepares to attack the city and summons his reserve divisions down from the heights. The waiting Hittites ford the river, charge one division and scatter another to surround the king, who single-handedly cuts his way out of the trap. The final scene claims an unqualified Egyptian triumph, even though Ramses failed to take the city. Notwithstanding this, the opposite wall portrays him storming a Syrian fortress in his chariot (note the double arm, which some regard as an attempt at animation), lancing a Libyan and returning with fettered Nubians. Along the rear wall, he presents them to

The Toshka and East Oweinat irrigation projects

Inaugurated by President Mubarak in 1997, the **Toshka Project** is a twenty-year venture whose goal is to cultivate 5700 square kilometres of desert northwest of Abu Simbel, and settle six million people there. The alluvial soil is potentially fertile and experimental farms have already grown cotton, watermelons, grapes and wheat. To irrigate the land, $1 billion has been spent on creating the world's largest **pumping station** to extract five billion cubic metres of water from Lake Nasser annually, and digging the **Sheikh Zayed Canal**, named after the president of the United Arab Emirates (a big investor). The main canal (completed in 2002) is 50km long, 30m wide and 6m deep; work is now underway on four branch canals totaling 159km in length, and a network of roads links Toshka to another irrigation project at **East Oweinat** in the Western Desert, using aquifer water (see p.433). Critics fear that these projects may prove to be white elephants; supporters retort that the same was once said of the High Dam, without which Egypt could not sustain itself today.

Amun, Mut and himself (left), and the captured Hittites to Re-Herakhte, lion-headed Wert-Hekew and his own deified personage (right).

The eight **lateral chambers** off the hall were probably used to store cult objects and tribute from Nubia, and are decorated with offering scenes. Reliefs in the smaller **pillared hall** show Ramses and Nefertari offering incense before the shrine and barque of Amun-Re (left) and Re-Herakhte (right).

Walk through one of the doors at the back, cross the transverse vestibule and head for the central **Sanctuary**. Originally encased in gold, its four (now mutilated) cult statues wait to be touched by the sun's rays at dawn on February 22 and October 22. February 21 was Ramses' birthday and October 21 his coronation date, but the relocation of Abu Simbel has changed the timing of these **solar events** by one day. Perhaps significantly, the figure of Ptah "the Hidden One" (on the far left) is situated so that it alone remains in darkness when the sun illuminates Amun-Re, Re-Herakhte and Ramses the god. Before them is a stone block where the sacred barque once rested.

The Hathor Temple of Queen Nefertari

A little further north of the Sun Temple stands the smaller rock-hewn **Temple of Queen Nefertari**, identified here with the goddess Hathor, who was wife to the sun-god during his day's passage and mother to his rebirth at dawn. As with Ramses' temple, the rock-hewn facade imitates a receding pylon (whose corvetto cornice has fallen), its plane accentuated by a series of rising buttresses separating six **colossal statues of Ramses and Nefertari** (each over 9m tall), which seem to emerge from the rock. Each is accompanied by two smaller figures of their children, who stand knee-high in the shadows. A frieze of cobras protects the door into the temple, which is simpler in plan than Ramses', having but one columned hall and vestibule, and only two lateral chambers; it runs 24m into the hillside.

The best **reliefs** are in the hall with square, Hathor-headed pillars whose sides show the royal couple mingling with deities. On the entrance wall Nefertari watches Ramses slay Egypt's enemies; on the side walls she participates in rituals as his equal, appearing before Anuket (left) and Hathor (right). In the transverse vestibule beyond, the portal of the sanctuary is flanked by scenes of the royal couple offering wine and flowers to Amun-Re and Horus (left), Re-Herakhte, Khnum, Satet and Anuket (right). The **Sanctuary** niche contains a ruined cow-statue of Hathor, above which vultures guard Nefertari's cartouches. On the side walls, she offers incense to Mut and Hathor (left), while Ramses worships his own image and that of Nefertari (right).

3

The Western Desert Oases

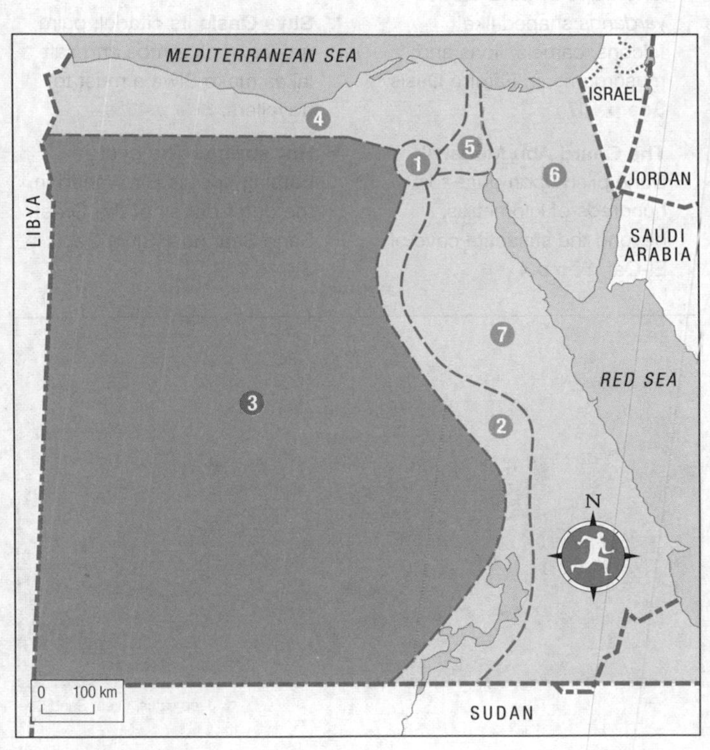

CHAPTER 3

Highlights

✱ **Jeep safaris** Whether you spend a night in the White Desert, or two weeks in the Great Sand Sea and the Gilf Kebir, you'll never forget the experience. See p.379

✱ **Birdwatching** Senegal coucals, kestrels, kites and herons are among the many species at Wadi Rayan. See p.391

✱ **White Desert** A surreal landscape of wind-eroded *yardangs* shaped like falcons, camels, lions and mushrooms, in Farafra Oasis. See p.407

✱ **The Ghard Abu Muharrik** Dune piled upon dune for hundreds of kilometres, beyond the stalactite cave of El-Qaf. See p.411

✱ **Al-Qasr** This fantastic labyrinth of mud-brick dwellings dating back to the tenth century is one of several once-fortified qasr villages in Dakhla Oasis. See p.418

✱ **Prehistoric rock art** *The English Patient* cast a spotlight on the Cave of the Swimmers in the remote Gilf Kebir, and there are many other sites at Jebel Uwaynat. See p.433

✱ **Siwa Oasis** Its citadel, palm groves, rock tombs and salt lakes make Siwa a must for travellers. See p.438

✱ **Hot springs** The best bathing spot is Bir Wahed in the outer dunes of the Great Sand Sea, near Siwa Oasis. See p.449

▲ Jeep safari, Great Sand Sea

The Western Desert Oases

For the Ancient Egyptians civilization began and ended with the Nile Valley and the Delta, known as the "Black Land" for the colour of its rich alluvial deposits. Beyond lay the "Red Land" or desert, whose significance was either practical or mystical. East of the Nile it held mineral wealth and routes to the Red Sea Coast; west of the river lay the Kingdom of Osiris, Lord of the Dead – the deceased were said to "go west" to meet him. But once it was realized that human settlements existed out there, Egypt's rulers had to reckon with the **Western Desert Oases** as sources of exotic commodities and potential staging posts for invaders. Though linked to the civilization of the Nile Valley since antiquity, they have always been different – and remain so.

Siwa Oasis, far out near the Libyan border, is the most striking example: its people speak another language and have customs unknown in the rest of Egypt. Its ruined citadels, lush palm groves, limpid pools and golden sand dunes epitomize the allure of the oases. The four "inner" oases of **Bahariya**, **Farafra**, **Dakhla** and **Kharga** lie on the "**Great Desert Circuit**" that begins in Cairo or Assyut – a Long March through the New Valley Governorate, where modernization has affected each oasis to a greater or lesser extent. While Bahariya and Farafra remain basically desert villages, living off their traditional crops of dates and olives, Dakhla and Kharga have spawned full-blown modern towns. The appeal of the latter two is stronger in the journeying – across hundreds of miles of awesome barrenness, most of it gravel pans rather than pure "sand desert".

Much nearer to Cairo (and suitable for day excursions) are two quasi-oases: the Fayoum and Wadi Natrun. The **Fayoum** is more akin to the Nile Valley than the Western Desert, with many ancient ruins to prove its importance since the Middle Kingdom. Though a popular holiday spot for Cairenes, it doesn't attract many foreign tourists except for hunters and ornithologists. **Wadi Natrun** is significant mainly for its Coptic monasteries, which draw hordes of Egyptian pilgrims but, again, comparatively few foreigners go there.

The desert

Much of the fascination of this region lies in the desert itself – vast tracts of which was once savanna, before being reduced to its current state by overgrazing by Stone Age pastoralists and climate change. The **Western Desert**, which covers

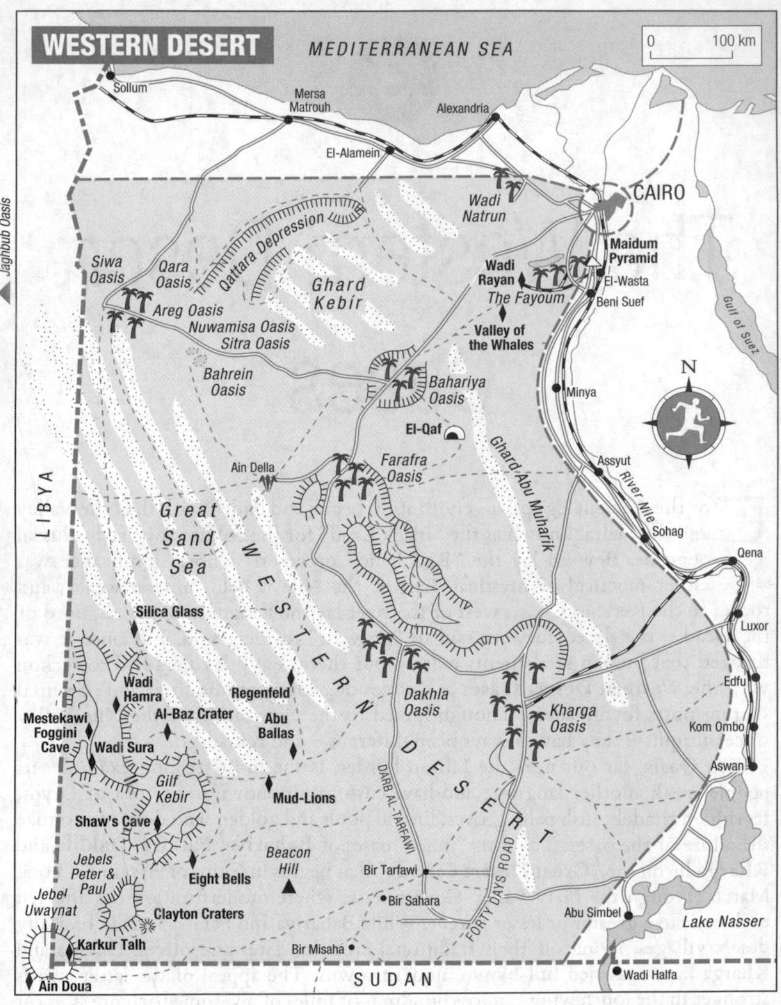

681,000 square kilometres (over two-thirds of Egypt's total area), is merely one part of the Sahara belt across northern Africa: its anomalous name was bestowed by British cartographers who viewed it from the perspective of the Nile – and, to complicate matters further, designated its southern reaches and parts of northwestern Sudan as the "Libyan Desert". Aside from the oases, its most striking features are the **Qattara Depression**, the lowest point in Africa, and the **Great Sand Sea** along the Libyan border, an awesome ocean of dunes that once swallowed up a whole army (see p.412). Further south, the **Gilf Kebir** and **Jebel Uwaynat** feature some of the most magnificent prehistoric rock art in Egypt, and were the setting for the events in the book and film *The English Patient*.

All the **practicalities** of visiting the oases (including the best times to go) are detailed under the respective entries in this chapter. The most comprehensive source of historical, ethnographic and geographical **information** is Cassandra

Vivian's *The Western Desert of Egypt: An Explorer's Handbook* (updated in 2009). A laminated colour *Map of the Western Desert Oases* (published by Geodia) is the next best thing, if you don't find free **maps** of the White Desert and the Gilf Kebir at the White Desert National Park ticket office or bookshops in Cairo or Bahariya.

Desert safaris

Organized desert safaris are the easiest, and often the only, way to reach some of the finest sites in and beyond the oases. There are **local operators** in all the oases, whose contact details appear in the text. As more are based in **Bahariya** (see p.403) than anywhere else, this is the best place to arrange safaris at short notice, particularly to the White Desert. Longer trips (4–19 days) to remoter sites such as the Great Sand Sea, the Gilf Kebir or Jebel Uwaynat must be booked at least a month ahead and are generally restricted to spring and autumn, due to the bureaucracy involved and the extremes of climate in this region.

Sadly, some safari outfits fail to respect the **environment**, leaving rubbish behind or encouraging tourists to remove flint arrowheads or spray water on rock paintings so that they look clearer in photos. All those we recommend below have good environmental credentials and can be booked in advance from Cairo or from abroad.

Ancient World Tours ⓦ www.ancient.co.uk. This British firm specializing in archeological travel does a fourteen-day safari featuring the Gilf Kebir, the Great Sand Sea and Ain Della (£2585), and a thirteen-day grand tour of all the oases (£2364). Flights from Britain and hotels in Cairo and/or Luxor are included in the price.

Dunes

Though gravel plains, limestone pans and scarps account for sixty percent of Egypt's Western Desert, it is **dunes** that captivate the imagination. Lifeless yet restless, they shift and reproduce, burying palm groves, roads and railways in their unstoppable advance. Their shape is determined by prevailing winds, local geology and whatever moisture or vegetation exists. Where sand is relatively scarce and small obstructions are common, windblown particles form **crescent-shaped** *barchan* dunes, which advance horns first, moving over obstacles without altering their height. Baby dunes are formed downwind of the horns, which produces parallel lines of *barchans* with flat corridors between them, advancing up to 20m each year. *Barchans* can grow as high as 95m, extend for 375m, and weigh up to 450 million kilos. However, their mass is nothing compared to **parallel straight dunes**, or *seif* dunes (from the Arabic word for "sword"); some in the Great Sand Sea are 140km long. Formed by a unidirectional wind, they have slipfaces on both sides and a wavy, knife-edged crest along the top. When *seif* dunes fall over an escarpment they reform at the bottom as crescent dunes, which is why *barchans* are the prevailing form in Dakhla and Kharga. Occasionally, they pile one on top of another to create mountainous **whalebacks** or mega-*barchans*. *Seif* and whaleback dunes can combine to form huge **sand seas** or *ergs*. Egypt's Great Sand Sea extends from Siwa Oasis to the Gilf Kebir and far into Libya, where it merges with the Calanscio Sand Sea. When the wind direction alters constantly, it can even form **star-shaped** dunes. These are rare in Egypt, but one has been recorded at Wadi al-Bakht in the Gilf Kebir. Another type of formation is the flat, hard-packed **sand-sheet**, found in the Darb al-Arba'in Desert.

Much of the science of dune formation was discovered by the explorer Ralph Bagnold, whose classic book *The Physics of Blown Sand and Desert Dunes* (1939) later helped NASA to interpret data from its Martian space probes. The book was written with the benefit of five years' experimentation with a home-made wind tunnel and builder's sand; after his desert journeys of the 1920s, Bagnold felt "it was really just exploring in another form".

Travel permits

Several near-fatal incidents in remote areas have prompted tighter controls on travelling in the "deep desert", which Egyptian Military Intelligence takes to mean everywhere west of the highway between Bahariya, Farafra, Dakhla and Kharga – namely between Bahariya and Siwa, to Ain Della, the Great Sand Sea or the Gilf Kebir – but not sites east of the highway, such as the White Desert or El-Qaf.

Permits for 24 hours ($5 per person; $100 for ten or more; plus a fee of £E10 per person) can only be used to travel by day **between Siwa and Bahariya** (without leaving the road), or to **Ain Della and the Hidden Valley**. Doing either with a safari operator means they'll handle the paperwork; otherwise you'll need to submit a photocopy of your passport and visa (plus your licence and insurance if you're driving) to NGOs in Bahariya (see p.398) or Siwa (p.442), which will process them in 24 hours (except on Fri & Sat). Only **registered travel agencies** can apply for overnight or multi-day permits for off-road travel between Siwa and Bahariya ($10 per person daily) or to the Gilf Kebir (€20 per person daily). Expect to pay a surcharge if your safari outfit uses a partner agency to apply on its behalf, and allow a month for the application to be processed.

Badawiya Expedition ⓦwww.badawiya.com. Based in Farafra (see p.408) and Dakhla (p.417), but tours start from Cairo. Camel treks in the White Desert and jeep safaris to the Mestakawi-Foggini Cave, Karkur Talh and the Silica Glass area (€120 per person per day).

Dabuka Expeditions ⓦwww.dabuka.de. This German-based company runs safaris in Libya, Sudan, Tunisia and Jordan as well as Egypt, where they retrace the routes taken by early explorers and run a three-day desert driving course.

Egypt Off-Road ⓦwww.egyptoffroad.com. Peter Gaballa runs fourteen-day expeditions to the Gilf paired with Uwaynat or the Sand Sea, plus three-day desert driving courses, outside Cairo. Peter speaks English, French, German and Arabic.

Fliegel Jerzerniczky Expeditions ⓦwww.fjexpeditions.com. In the tradition of Almássy, this Hungarian company, run by Sahara expert András Zboray, mounts four or five expeditions a year to the Gilf and Uwaynat, sometimes venturing into Libya or Sudan. András speaks English and German.

Hisham Nessim ⓦwww.raid4x4egypt.com. Rally driver and owner of the *AquaSun* hotels in Farafra and Sinai, his programmes include visiting a meteorite crater discovered in 2005, searching for the Lost Army of Cambyses, and three different safaris to Uwaynat, the remotest point in Egypt.

Pan Arab Tours ⓦwww.panarabtours.com. A highly experienced Cairo-based agency, offering 4WD tours of the oases and tailor-made safaris to the Gilf, Uwaynat, the Sand Sea, and the Qattara Depression.

Zarzora Expedition ⓦwww.zarzora.com. Former Border Guards colonel Ahmed Mestekawi runs a nineteen-day safari to the Gilf, Uwaynat and the Clayton Craters, including the prehistoric rock-art cave that he discovered in 2002.

Wadi Natrun

The quasi-oasis of **Wadi Natrun**, just off the Desert Road between Cairo and Alexandria, takes its name – and oasis stature – from deposits of natron salts, the main ingredient in ancient mummifications. Wadi Natrun's most enduring legacy, however, is its **monasteries**, which date back to the dawn of Christian monasticism, and have provided spiritual leadership for Egypt's Copts for the last 1500 years. Their fortified exteriors, necessary in centuries past to resist Bedouin raiders, cloak what are today very forward-looking, purposeful monastic establishments.

In the 1950s, model villages, olive groves and vineyards were planted here to reclaim 25,000 hectares of land from the desert, a project initially financed by the sale of King Farouk's stamp collection. After decades of patient labour, palms, flowers and hothouse vegetables now grow beside the **Desert Road** to Alex. Not far beyond Giza you'll pass the glass pyramids of **Media City**, a science park-cum-studio that embodies Egypt's high-tech aspirations for the future. On the other side of the highway, motels have sprung up around the turn-off for Wadi Natrun, which runs via the township of **Bir Hooker** (aka "Wadi Natrun City") into the Natrun Valley.

Getting here

The monasteries are most easily reached from Cairo or Alexandria by **taxi** (£E200–300 depending on how many you visit). West Delta **buses** (hourly 6.30am–6.30pm) from Cairo's Turgoman station or Alex's Moharrem Bey terminal run to Bir Hooker, and **service taxis** from Cairo (Aboud terminal) or Alex (Moharrem Bey) run to the **Wadi Natrun Resthouse** at km 105 on the Desert Road, from where you should be able to hire a taxi to tour the monasteries for about £E25 an hour, or hope to be offered a lift by the busloads of Coptic pilgrims that come this way on Fridays, Sundays and public holidays. Alternatively, you could join a **tour** with Holy Family Egypt (Ⓦwww.holyfamilyegypt.com), a Dutch-Egyptian travel agency that can accommodate individuals on its group tours by prior arrangement.

The monasteries of Wadi Natrun

Christian monasticism was born in Egypt's Eastern Desert, where the first Christian hermits sought to emulate St Anthony, forming rude communities; however, it was at Wadi Natrun that their rules and power were forged, during the persecution of Christians in urban areas under Emperor Diocletian. Several thousand **monks** and hermits were living here by the middle of the fourth century, harbouring bitter grudges against paganism, scores which they settled after Christianity was made the state religion in 330 by sacking the temples and library and murdering scholars in Alexandria. The Muslim conquest and Bedouin raids encouraged a siege mentality among the monks, who often lapsed into idle dependence on monastic serfs. Nineteenth-century foreign visitors unanimously

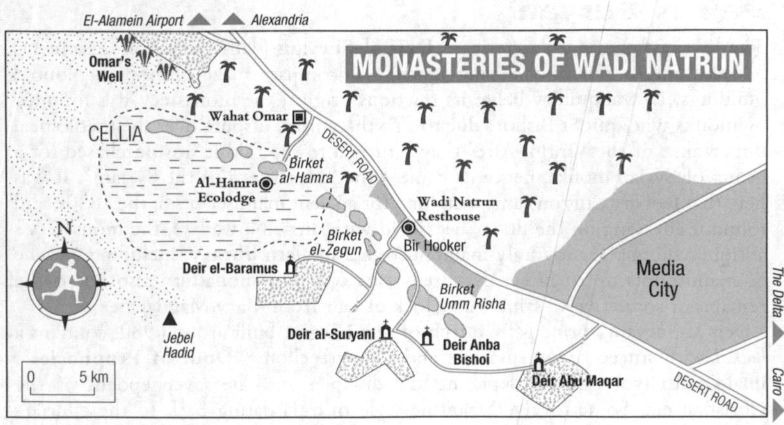

described them as slothful, dirty, bigoted and ignorant – the antithesis of the monks here today.

The four **Wadi Natrun monasteries** have all been totally ruined and rebuilt at least once since their foundation during the fourth century; most of what you see dates from the eighth century onwards. Each has a high wall surrounding one or more churches, a central keep entered via a drawbridge, containing a bakery, storerooms and wells, enabling the monks to withstand siege, and diverse associated chapels. Their low doorways compel visitors to humbly stoop upon entry (don't forget to remove your shoes outside). Their **churches** – like all Coptic chapels – are divided into three sections. The *haikal* (sanctuary) containing the altar lies behind the iconostasis, an inlaid or curtained screen, which you can peer through with your escort's consent. In front of this is the choir, reserved for Coptic Christians, and then the nave, consisting of two parts. *Catechumens* (those preparing to convert) stand nearest the choir, while sinners (known as "weepers") were formerly relegated to the back.

Practicalities

Visiting hours vary from monastery to monastery, as does the extent to which each closes during the Coptic **Lents** or periods of fasting (from June 27–July 10; August 7–21; Nov 25–Jan 6) – only Deir Anba Bishoi is open every day of the year. You can check if Deir al-Suryani (Ⓣ02/591-4448) or Deir el-Baramus (Ⓣ02/592-2775) are open by phoning their Cairo "residences". Deir Abu Maqar will only admit those with a letter of introduction from the Coptic Patriarchate in Cairo (next to the Cathedral of St Mark, 222 Sharia Ramses, Abbassiya; Ⓣ02/282-5374) or Alexandria (in the Cathedral of St Mark on Sharia al-Kineesa al-Kobtiyya; Ⓣ03/483-5522). Fridays, Sundays and public holidays see the monasteries crowded with Coptic pilgrims – good for hitching a lift but not the most tranquil times to visit.

While men can sleep at Deir Anba Bishoi, Deir al-Suryani or Deir al-Baramus (whose lodgings are the least spartan of the three) with written permission from the Patriarchate, the chief reason for **staying** is to explore the wildlife around Birket al-Hamra, where the *Al-Hamra Ecolodge* (Ⓣ02/705-3081 or 010 388-2001; ④) has chalets or rooms on a B&B or half-board basis. To get there, turn off 100m before the *Wahat Omar* **restaurant** at km 112 on the Desert Road, and follow the signs. *Wahat Omar* serves tasty Egyptian and Italian dishes, with an adjacent mini-zoo to entertain kids.

Deir al-Suryani

The loveliest of the monasteries is **Deir al-Suryani** (daily 9am–6pm except Fri 3–6pm; Sat & Sun only during Lents) – a compact maze of honey-coloured buildings. Its tranquillity belies its fractious origins; the monastery was founded by monks who quit St Bishoi's due to a sixth-century dispute over the theological importance of the Virgin. After they returned to the fold it was purchased for a group of Syrian monks, hence its name – the "Monastery of the Syrians". It was here that Robert Curzon came searching for ancient manuscripts in the 1830s, and found them lying on the floor "begrimed with dirt". Nowadays, the monastery's antique volumes are lovingly maintained in a modern **library**, including a cache of manuscripts up to fifteen hundred years old. The monastery also boasts the remains of some twelve saints and a lock of hair from Mary Magdalene.

Deir al-Suryani's principal **Church of the Virgin**, built around 980, contains a *haikal* with stucco ornamentation, and a superb ebony **"Door of Prophecies"**, inlaid with ivory panels depicting the disciples and the seven epochs of the Christian era. Some lovely Byzantine-style **murals** dating back to the church's

▲ Deir al-Suryani, Wadi Natrun

foundation have been uncovered by restorers. A dark passageway at the back of the church leads to the **cave** where St Bishoi tied his hair to a chain hanging from the ceiling to prevent himself sleeping for four days, until a vision of Christ appeared. The marble basin in the nave is used by the abbot to wash the feet of twelve monks on Maundy Thursday, emulating Christ's act during Passion Week.

Outside, the large **tamarind tree** enclosed by walls is said to have grown from the staff of St Emphram, who, as a monk, thrust it into the earth after his fellows criticized it as a worldly affectation. As Coptic pope, he established cordial relations with the Fatimid caliph in 997.

Deir Anba Bishoi

Deir Anba Bishoi (daily: summer 7am–8pm; winter 7am–6pm) is the largest of the four monasteries. Over 150 monks and novices live here, and the monastery receives a constant stream of pilgrims. The legend of **St Bishoi** suggests he was one of the earliest monks at Wadi Natrun. An angel told the saint's mother that he was chosen to do God's work even before his birth in 320; two decades later he moved here to study under St Bemoi alongside John "the Short". Since Bishoi's death in 417 his body has reportedly remained uncorrupted within its casket, which is carried in procession around the church every year on July 17. Next to him lies Paul of Tammuh, who was revered for committing suicide seven times.

St Bishoi's is the oldest of the five **churches** in the monastery, its *haikals* dating from the fourth, ninth and tenth centuries. The **keep**, built three to four hundred years later, has chapels at ground level (around the back) and on the second storey, one floor above its drawbridge. There's also a fifth-century **well** where Berber tribesmen washed their swords after massacring the 49 Martyrs of Deir Abu Maqar (see p.384).The multi-domed building furthest from the entrance is the **residence of Shenouda III**, the Coptic pope, who uses it as an occasional retreat and sometimes ostentatiously secludes himself here to protest at the mistreatment of Copts.

Deir Abu Maqar

Enclosed by a circular wall ten metres high, **Deir Abu Maqar** requires visitors (with the requisite letter of introduction; see p.382) to pull a bell rope; in times past, two giant millstones stood ready to be rolled across to buttress the door against raiders. Its founder, **St Makarius**, died in 390 "after sixty years of austerities in various deserts", the last twenty of which were spent in a hermit's cell at Wadi Natrun. A rigorous faster, his only indulgence was a raw cabbage leaf for Sunday lunch.

Over the centuries, thirty Coptic patriarchs have come from the monastery; many are buried here, together with the 49 Martyrs killed by Berbers in 444. In 1978, monks discovered what they believed to be the **head of John the Baptist**; however, this is also claimed to be held in Venice, Aleppo and Damascus. Since its nadir in 1969, when only six monks lived here, the monastery has acquired over a hundred brethren, a modern printing press and a farm employing six hundred workers. The monks have mastered pinpoint irrigation systems and bovine embryo transplant technology in an effort to meet their abbot's goal of feeding a thousand laypersons per monk.

Deir el-Baramus

Deir el-Baramus (Fri–Sun 9am–5pm; closed during Lents) is likewise surrounded by orchards and fields. The monastery was founded by St Makarius in 340, making it the oldest of the four that remain in Wadi Natrun, and has eighty monks and novices, one of whom will show you around. Visitors are greeted outside by a picture of St Moses the Black, a Nubian robber who became a monk under the influence of St Isidore. The monastery's name derives from the Coptic Pe Romios ("House of the Romans"), referring to Maximus and Domidus, two sons of the Roman Emperor Valentinus who died from excessive fasting; the younger one was only 19 years old. Their bodies are reputedly buried in a crypt below the **Church of the Virgin**, whose principal altar is only used once a day, since Mary's womb begot but one child. The relics of Moses and Isidore are encased in glass; pilgrims drop petitions into the bier.

Restoration work has revealed layers of medieval **frescoes** in the nave, the western end of which incorporates a fourth-century **pillar** with Syriac inscriptions. It was behind here that St Arsanious prayed with a pebble in his mouth, grudging every word that he spoke (including a statement to that effect). The ninth-century church, with belfries of unequal height (symbolizing the respective ages of Maximus and Domidus), shares a vine-laden courtyard with a **keep** and four other churches.

Birket al-Hamra

Beyond Deir al-Baramus are numerous **salt lakes** rimmed by crusts of **natron**, a mixture of sodium carbonate and sodium bicarbonate, which the Ancient Egyptians used for dehydrating bodies and making glass. **Birket al-Hamra** ("Red Lake") is magenta-hued and highly saline, with a "miraculous" sweetwater **spring** in the middle – Copts believe that the Virgin Mary quenched her thirst here. You can wade out to the spring (enclosed by an iron well) and taste it for yourself; the mud on the lake-bed is reputedly good for various afflictions.

The local *Al-Hamra Ecolodge* (see p.382) can arrange **horseriding**, **camel trekking** and **birdwatching** (look out for spur-winged plovers, crested larks, jacksnipes and sandpipers). The lakes harbour Egypt's last surviving wild **papyrus**, a dwarf subspecies of the plant that once flourished throughout the Nile Valley, but gradually became extinct; the last large papyrus (which could reach 6m) was found in the Delta in the mid-nineteenth century. Today it exists only on plantations, thanks to Dr Rageb (see p.196), who rediscovered the lost technique of making papyrus paper. There are also **petrified mangroves** from the Eocene Period – thick, fallen trunks, rather than the petrified roots found at the Valley of the Whales (see p.391).

The Fayoum

Likened in Egyptian tradition to a bud on the stem of the Nile and an "earthly paradise" in the desert, the **Fayoum** depends on river water – not springs or wells, like a true oasis. The water is distributed by a system of canals going back to ancient times, through palm groves and orchards, to flow into Lake Qaroun. The governorate capital, Fayoum City, is less alluring than the **antiquities** and **birdlife** on the Fayoum's periphery, which mostly require a car to reach them (or a lot of effort by public transport). Now that only organized groups may enter the **Valley of the Whales**, perhaps the best option is a **safari** out of Cairo, combining a few Fayoum highlights with other Western Desert locations. Minamar Travel (Ⓣ02/251-3803, Ⓦwww.minamar.com) does a five-day safari to Qasr Qaroun, Wadi Rayan, the Valley of the Whales, El-Qaf (see p.411), the White Desert (p.406) and Bahariya Oasis (p.397) for €260–340 per person. Marzouk Desert Cruisers (Ⓣ02/258-8083, Ⓦwww.marzouk-dc.com) covers the same, minus El-Qaf, in six days. Alternatively, you could visit the Valley of the Whales on a safari out of Bahariya, using a local outfit (see p.403).

Getting here

The highway **from Cairo** to the Fayoum starts near the Pyramids of Giza, whose silhouettes sink below the horizon as the road gains a barren plateau dotted with army bases, then (76km later) reaches the edge of the Fayoum depression. Here, you'll pass the Ptolemaic-Roman site of Kom Oshim (on the left) before you sight Lake Qaroun and cruise down through Sinnuris into Fayoum City, driving past the Obelisk of Senusret I.

Buses from Cairo's Aboud (every 15min 6am–8pm) and El Moneeb (every 30min 6am–7pm) terminals do the one-hundred-kilometre journey in two to three hours. **Service taxis** from Midan Orabi, Midan Ramses, Midan Giza or El Moneeb run almost nonstop from early morning to late at night, reaching Fayoum City in about two hours – a high-speed ride that's not for the fainthearted. From the Nile Valley, half-hourly buses or service taxis **from Beni Suef** take an hour or so to reach Fayoum City.

Fayoum City

A kind of pocket-size version of Cairo, with the Bahr Yussef canal in the role of the Nile, **FAYOUM CITY** makes a grab at the wallets of middle-class Cairenes who come to bask beside Lake Qaroun during summertime. The few foreigners that venture here tend to be whisked through in buses and remain immured in

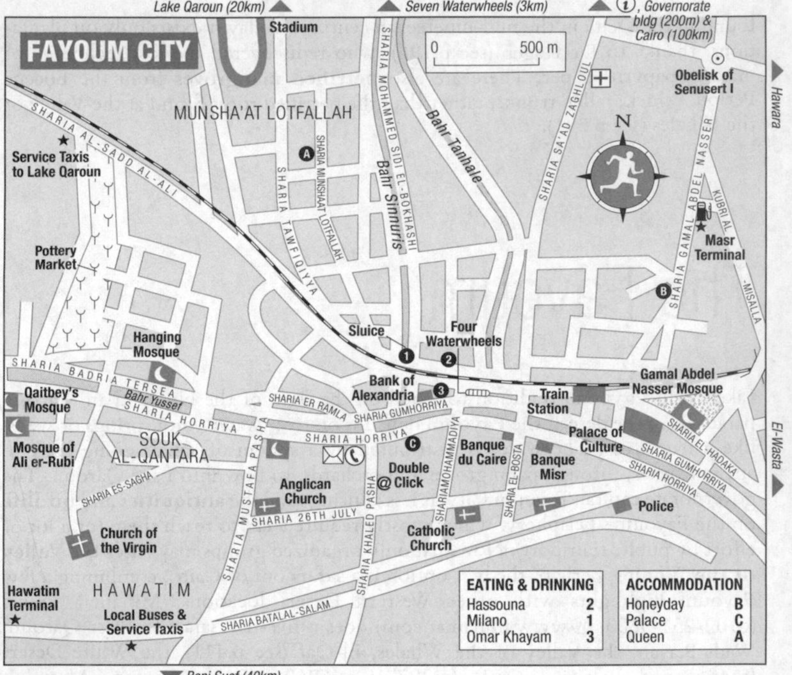

hotels, so independent travellers draw attention – especially women. On the plus side, the city has an authentic **souk**, three venerable **mosques** and two colourful **moulids** (see box, opposite), and serves as the jumping-off point for almost everywhere you might consider visiting in the oasis. Though officially named **Medinet el-Fayoum**, the city is known colloquially as El-Fayoum or Fayoum. The word "Fayoum" probably derives from Phiom, the Coptic word for "sea", although folklore attributes it to the pharaoh's praise of the Bahr Yussef: "This is the work of a thousand days" (*alf youm*).

Arrival and information

Trains from Cairo terminate at the **station** in the centre of town, while buses and service taxis end up at the **Masr** depot on Sharia Gamal Abdel Nasser (£E5 by taxi to or from the centre). Coming from Beni Suef you arrive at the **Hawatim** depot south of the old town – a taxi shouldn't cost over £E15, or #1, #2, #3 and #7 minibuses to the downtown area (*wust al balad*) cost only 50pt.

With the Bahr Yussef canal facilitating **orientation,** everything of interest downtown can be reached on foot. North of the centre, the **tourist office** (daily 9.30am–3pm; ⓣ084/634-2313 or 010 543-4726) in the Governorate Building can organize a guide and a taxi for excursions to sites on the Fayoum's periphery (see p.389). On checking into a hotel, you'll be assigned a minder from the **tourist police** (ⓣ084/630-7298), who'll accompany you around or outside the city. They probably won't speak English but if you can muster a little Arabic they might prove helpful rather than a hindrance.

You can **change money** at any of the banks beside the Bahr Yussef (all have ATMs) or the Forex bureau near the corner of Sharia er-Ramla. The main **post office** (daily except Fri & Sat 8am–2pm) and 24-hour **telephone** exchange are on the south side of the canal, off which is DoubleClick **Internet** (daily 10am–7am) on Sharia Khaled Pasha. Patients at the **hospital** on Sharia Sa'ad Zaghloul must pay cash up front.

Accommodation

Outside of Er-Rubi's festival (see box below), there shouldn't be any difficulty finding a room in town, though none of the hotels is great. You may well prefer to stay out near Lake Qaroun, at Shakshuk or Tunis (see map, p.390), where the ambience is better.

Fayoum City

Honeyday 105 Sharia Gamal Abdel Nasser ⓣ&ⓕ 084/634-0105. Near Masr bus depot, this high-rise hotel (whose name is pronounced "honey-die") has attractive a/c rooms with TV and fridge, a restaurant and a sleazy bar. BB ❸

Palace Sharia Horriya ⓣ 084/631-1222. Look out for the sign facing the Bahr Yussef; the entrance is an alleyway, behind some kiosks. Its rooms are clean and have optional baths and a/c and the manager speaks English. ❷

Queen Sharia Munsha'at Lotfallah ⓣ 084/634-6819. Spacious en-suite rooms with satellite TV (a/c costs extra) in a quiet neighbourhood, 15min walk from the centre. BB ❹

Shakshuk

Helnan Auberge Fayoum ⓣ 084/698-1200, ⓦ www.helnan.com. Though only its first-floor rooms can justly claim to have a lake view, this historic hotel's swimming pool and vestiges of 1940s class may lull you into overlooking its shortcomings as a four-star establishment. Amenities include a restaurant; billiards and internet. Takes Diners Club, MasterCard and Visa. BB ❼

New Panorama Village ⓣ 084/683-0746. Nearer to Shakshuk, this lakeside three-star cluster of a/c chalets has a small pool and a restaurant (no alcohol served). BB ❻

Tunis

Zad al-Mosafer ⓣ 084/682-0180 or 010 639-5590. Run by ex-journalist Abdu Gobair, this charming eco-friendly rustic guesthouse has cosy rooms, a small pool and a playground, serves tasty organic meals, and can organize birdwatching or camel rides. ❺

The City

Fayoum City's most central landmark is the four large wooden **waterwheels**, groaning away near the confluence of two canals. The Fayoum has about two hundred such waterwheels, introduced by Ptolemaic engineers in the third century BC. Because Nile water enters the sloping Fayoum depression at its highest point, gravity does half the work of distribution, and the current is strong enough to power the waterwheels for lifting irrigation water. During January the whole system is allowed to dry out for maintenance; the waterwheels have a working life of ten years if properly tarred and maintained.

Coptic and Muslim folklore ascribes the **Bahr Yussef** (River of Joseph) to its Biblical namesake, who's believed to have been the pharaoh's vizier and minister

Fayoumi festivals

It's worth visiting Fayoum City simply for its **festivals,** as many local farmers do. Hotels overflow during **Ali er-Rubi's moulid** in Sha'ban (the eighth month in the Muslim calendar), when the alleys around his mosque are crammed with stalls selling sugar dolls and horsemen, and all kinds of amusements can be tried, while the devout perform *zikrs* in the courtyard. The other big occasion is the "viewing" (*er-ruyeh*) of the new moon that heralds **Ramadan**. This calls for a huge procession from the Gamal Abdel Nasser Mosque: a parade of carnival floats represents the different professions (it's headed by the security forces, imams and sheikhs), and bombards spectators with "lucky" prayer leaflets.

for public works. Originally a natural waterway branching off the Nile near Beni Suef, it was regulated from the XII Dynasty onwards, and now draws water from the Nile at Dairut, nearly 300km further south. Baskets, pots and other **handicrafts** are sold on the north bank of the Bahr Yussef near the four waterwheels.

Walking west alongside the canal and crossing the fourth bridge from the four waterwheels you can follow a street with a wooden roof into the **Souk al-Qantara**, a labyrinth of tiny shops selling copperware and spices, grain and pulses, clothing and other goods. **Sharia es-Sagha**, the Street of Goldsmiths, is crammed with jewellers' shops, mostly owned by Christians, whose churches are ranged along Sharia 26th July. The oldest is the **Church of the Virgin**, dating from the 1830s, which contains an altar dedicated to the local saint Anba Abram (1829–1912), who was reputedly able to transport himself across distances in a miraculous fashion.

Near the souk you'll also find three historic mosques. The **Mosque of Ali er-Rubi** is dedicated to a local sheikh whose renown among the Fayoumis eclipses even Anba Abram's. His mausoleum, down some steps from the courtyard, is surrounded by an enormous *darih* or carved box-frame, and people muttering supplications. Further west beside the canal, the **Mosque of Qaitbey** is the oldest in the Fayoum, built (or perhaps restored) by the Mamluke Sultan Qaitbey (see p.135), who was also responsible for building the twin-arched **bridge** nearby.

Crossing this, you can head along the riverside to find the **Hanging Mosque**, so called because its north frontage is upheld by five arches, once occupied by workshops. Further north, backstreets near the Muslim cemetery host a Tuesday **pottery market** for red, pink or unglazed pots made at the village of Nazla, and a Friday morning **farmers market**.

East of the train station, the **Palace of Culture** is Fayoum City's modernist landmark, an inverted pyramid housing a cinema, theatre and library. Behind it stands the **Gamal Abdel Nasser Mosque**, one of many that Nasser had built in provincial towns in the 1960s, and which bear his name.

For a pleasant half-hour's walk in the morning or evening, follow the right bank of the Bahr Sinnuris northwards out of town for 3km to reach the **Seven Waterwheels** (not to be confused with the four in the centre). First comes a single wheel near a farm; slightly further on, a quartet revolves against a backdrop of mango trees and palms; the final pair is a little way on, near a crude bridge.

Entering or leaving town by the Cairo road, you'll pass the thirteen-metre-high red-granite **Obelisk of Senusret I**, the only obelisk in Egypt to have a rounded tip. Senusret was the second king of the XII Dynasty, who displayed a special fondness for the Fayoum and was the first to regard it as more than just a hunting ground.

Eating and drinking

Don't expect any fancy **restaurants** in Fayoum City – the closest you'll get is the one in the *Queen Hotel*, which is nicely decorated and has a longish menu. *Hassouna*, on Sharia Al-Sadd al-Ali, is one of a few local cafés signposted in English, serving *shawarma*, *fuul*, *taamiya* and grilled chicken, to eat in or take away. Further along, by the Bahr Sinnuris, *Milano* is the place for freshly squeezed juices, ice cream and crème caramel, while *Omar Khayam*, across the road from *Hassouna*, is a vintage teahouse with a pleasant shady garden; try the cold *sahleb*, which comes topped with slices of banana. The only place selling **alcohol** (local beer and spirits) is the bar in the *Honeyday Hotel*, frequented by prostitutes.

Around the oasis

Lake Qaroun is readily accessible from Fayoum City, but reaching **Wadi Rayan** or the seldom-visited **ancient sites** on the edge of the oasis is trickier, so don't undertake a trip without adequate water and food for the day. The **tourist police** will probably insist that you take a taxi and be accompanied by a plainclothes escort, unless you engage a **guide** through the tourist office (about £E300 for a full day, including the taxi) – but we've noted public transport where it exists, just in case using it is permitted.

Lake Qaroun

Short of tankers gliding between the sandbanks of the Suez Canal, Egypt has no weirder juxtaposition of water and desert than **Lake Qaroun** (Birket Qaroun), where fishing boats bob against a backdrop of arid hills and the immensity of the Western Desert. Known to locals as "The Pond" (El-Birka), the lake's name may derive from the horn (*qorn*)-shaped peak on an island in the middle, but Fayoumis believe that it's named after a character in the Koran, who was swallowed up by the earth as a punishment for being "exultant in his riches". The lake is favoured as a **bathing resort** despite its beach of broken shells and saline gunk. The "season" runs year-round, but from January to April it's too cold to swim.

Since 2005 the shore has been embanked against flooding; in 2009 civil defence workers just managed to save the *Helnan Auberge Fayoum*, a hotel that was once King Farouk's hunting lodge, where Allied and Arab leaders met after World War II to carve up the Middle East. With binoculars, you can observe the lake's prolific **birdlife**: 88 species, including flamingoes, which have a colony on **Horn Island** (Geziret el-Qorn). You can hire a fisherman's **boat** near the *Auberge* or *New Panorama Village*, to enjoy the view from the water.

The lake itself covers 214 square kilometres, a fraction of its size when the Nile first broke into the Fayoum depression, forming a lake 40m above the current level, which Ancient Egyptian mythology identified with the waters of chaos and primeval life. Although the Middle Kingdom emerged at nearby Herakleopolis, it wasn't until Pharaoh Amenemhat I moved his capital to Lisht that the Fayoum became important. He had canals dug and the channel to the Nile deepened, draining parts for agriculture and submerging a greater area with what the ancients called **Lake Moeris**. It was this that the Ptolemies lowered to reclaim land for their settlements, whose decline by the end of the Roman period matched the lake's drop to 36m below sea level – it has since dropped a further eleven metres.

Sobek and Crocodilopolis

The Fayoum's ancient capital, **Crocodilopolis** (later renamed Arsinoë after Ptolemy II's sister-wife), was the centre of the **crocodile cult** supposedly began by Pharaoh Menes, the legendary unifier of Upper and Lower Egypt, whose life was saved by a croc while he was hunting in the Fayoum marshes. The crocodile deity, **Sobek**, was particularly favoured by Middle Kingdom rulers and assumed national prominence after being identified with Re (as Sobek-Re) and Horus. Sobek was variously depicted as a hawk-headed crocodile or in reptilian form with Amun's crown of feathers and ram's horns. At the Sacred Lake of Crocodilopolis, reptiles were fed and worshipped, and even adorned with jewellery, by the priests of Sobek. Today, nothing remains of the ancient city, north of the modern capital.

▲ Sobek

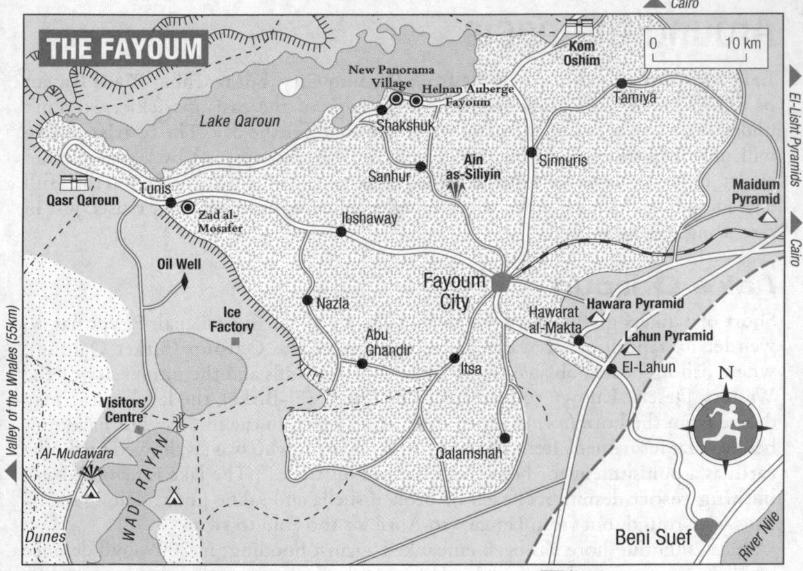

Practicalities

If the police allow it, Lake Qaroun is also accessible by **service taxi** from the depot on Sharia Sadd al-Ali to the industrial town of Shakshuk. Depending on which route it takes, you'll pass the lakeside east or west of town, and can get off wherever looks promising. Cairenes come to stay at the **hotels** (see p.387) and villas spreading out along the road that ultimately leads to Qasr Qaroun and Wadi Rayan. If you've got a car, keep going, since local women and children pester you remorselessly for baksheesh. Of the lakeside **eating** spots, the *Café Gabal el-Zinah*, 1km east of the *Auberge*, serves meals of fish or duck from the lake and has children's play areas, while the *Auberge* has a similar menu with silver service and alcohol.

Qasr Qaroun and Tunis

According to local legend, the miser who was punished by Allah stashed his treasure in **QASR QAROUN** (daily 9am–4pm; £E25). Not a palace as its Arabic name (pronounced 'asr 'aroun) suggests, Qasr is actually a Ptolemaic **temple**, outwardly plain but inwardly labyrinthine and riddled with holes dug by treasure-hunters. You'll need a torch to explore its warren of chambers, stairs and passageways at different levels; beware of scorpions, bats, snakes and lizards – the last resemble miniature crocodiles, as befits a temple dedicated to Sobek. Round about are the **ruins of Dionysias**, a Ptolemaic-Roman town believed to have been abandoned when the lake shrank (it's now 45 minutes' walk away). West of the temple is an even more ruinous **fortress**, constructed during the reign of Diocletian against the Blemmye (an indication of how far north these Nubian raiders went).

Located on the northwestern rim of the oasis, 45km from Fayoum City, Qasr can be reached by taking a service taxi to Shakshuk, and then another to the village of Qaroun, but it's easier to hire a car to visit the site in conjunction with Wadi Rayan. En route you'll pass through **TUNIS**, a hilltop farming village turned **artists'**

colony. In 1990 the Swiss potter Evelyne Porret founded a **pottery school** (ⓣ084/682-0405) for local children; former students Abdel Sattar (ⓣ084/682-0827) and Rawaya Abdel Kader Salem (ⓣ084/682-0911) now have their own **workshops**, viewable by appointment, like the school itself. In January, Mohammed Abla's **Fayoum Art Centre** (ⓣ012 338-2810, ⓦwww.ablamuseum.com) runs six-week **courses**, ranging from sculpture to printmaking. Participation is free but there's a daily charge of €20 for **staying** at the nearby *Zad al-Mosafer* (see p.387).

Wadi Rayan and the Valley of the Whales

Wadi Rayan is a separate depression 15km outside the oasis, which has become a man-made wildlife haven and beauty spot. The idea of piping excess water from the Fayoum into the wadi was first mooted by the British but only put into practice in 1966, when three lakes and a waterfall were created, vegetation flourished and the area became a major nesting ground for birds. It is now a **nature reserve** (daily 8.30am–5pm) harbouring the world's sole known population of slender-horned gazelles, eight other species of mammals, thirteen species of resident birds and 26 migrant and vagrant ones – not to mention the unique fossils in the **Valley of the Whales**, further into the desert, a zone under special protection.

No public transport goes anywhere near Wadi Rayan; a **taxi** costs about £E250 from Fayoum City, £E100–150 from Shakshuk. Leaving the lakeside road at a signposted turning and following it to the entrance gate, you're charged an **admission fee** of $5 plus £E5 for the vehicle. The open desert beyond gets sandier the closer you get to the azure **lakes**, where a track leads to the **waterfalls** (*shallalat*). The only ones in Egypt, they've appeared in countless videos and films despite being only a few metres high. Hordes of visitors descend on Fridays and holidays, to sunbathe and play ghettoblasters on the beach, which has several cafés. The lake is too saline for swimming, but **boating** is popular.

Beyond the car park a well-designed **Visitors Centre** (daily 11am–3.30pm; free) covers the wildlife, geology and prehistory of Wadi Rayan. About 10km on, the road passes a hill known as **Al-Mudawara**, which you can hike up for a spectacular **view** of the reed-fringed lake and desert scarp beyond. Soon afterwards is the turn-off for the Valley of the Whales, followed by a signposted turning to a **birdwatching** site by the shore. Besides the ubiquitous cattle egrets, grey herons and little bitterns, there are hard-to-spot wagtails, skylarks, kestrels, kites and Senegal coucals.

Further on, magnificent *seif* **dunes** 30m high parallel an inlet fringed by tamarisks, with three sulphur **springs** nearby. Thereafter, the road crosses a boring stretch of desert to return to the oasis. All of this route can be done in a 2WD car, unlike the 50km to the Valley of the Whales whose paved stretch of road (38km) may be blocked by windblown sand.

By arrangement with the park administration (ⓣ084/683-0535, ⓔwadielrayan @parksegypt.com), visitors can **camp** at designated spots near Al-Mudawara, on the lake's western shore, and at the entrance to the Valley of the Whales. No tents or sleeping bags are available; the nearest proper lodgings are in Tunis (see above).

The Valley of the Whales

Since being declared a World Heritage site in 2005 – and a scandal over Belgian diplomats who pulverised a fossil with their jeep – access to the **Valley of the Whales** (Wadi al-Hitan) has been limited to organized **tours** (see p.385) whose vehicles are restricted to marked tracks, with walking trails in between the fossilized remains. The unique **fossils** consist of amphibious mammals deposited by the swirling waters, and marine life stranded when the sea receded 40 million years ago; today they have fallen from (or remain embedded in) hillocks shaped like giant whelks or filigreed slugs, part of the Qasr es-Sagha Formation created by the ancient Tethys Sea.

In 1877, geologist George Schweinfurth found two hundred fossilized skeletons of what he believed was a reptile named Basilosaurus ("King Lizard"), later reclassified as a seven-tonne mammal with a slender body 18m long, and small but fully developed hind feet. It's thought that this **zeuglodon** was a dead-end in the evolution of whales that began when some land mammals migrated into the sea, and that another shark-eating creature, **dorudon** ("spear-toothed"), may be the ancestor of modern whales. New skeletons are being discovered all the time – over five hundred have been logged – and there are fossilized **mangrove roots** from a time when the valley resembled the Florida Everglades. A **Visitors Centre** is due in the future.

Kom Oshim (ancient Karanis)

The most accessible of the ancient sites in the Fayoum is **Kom Oshim** (daily 9am–4pm), 30km northeast of Fayoum City, where the Cairo road descends into the depression. Ask a bus or taxi driver to drop you at Mathaf Kom Oshim, the small **museum** by the road, where admission **tickets** are sold (£E10 for the museum; £E25 for the site). Its curator speaks good English and is keen to explain details. Pottery and glassware, terracotta figures used for modelling hairstyles and two lifelike "Fayoum portraits" (see p.102) convey the wealth and sophistication of the ancient farming town whose ruins lie atop a huge mound rising 12m above the surrounding plain.

The **ruins of Karanis** show the layout of this Ptolemaic-Roman town, founded by Greek mercenaries and their camp followers during the third century BC, which had a population of three thousand or so until the fifth century AD. Although the mud-brick houses have been reduced to low walls, two stone **temples** are better preserved. The larger one was built towards the end of the first century BC and dedicated to two local crocodile gods; priests kept a live crocodile in the sanctuary, feeding it on raw meat and honey-cakes.

To return to Fayoum or Cairo, flag down any passing bus or service taxi – though it may be a while before one with a vacant seat comes by.

Pyramids around the Fayoum

The Fayoum is associated with four separate **pyramid sites** on its eastern periphery. By far the finest is **Maidum**, with its dramatic-looking "Collapsed Pyramid" that marks an evolutionary step between the pyramids at Saqqara and Giza. **Hawara** and **Lahun** are less spectacular relics from the XII Dynasty, which governed Egypt – and ordered the waterworks that transformed the Fayoum – from its capital Itj-tway (Seizer of the Two Lands), near **El-Lisht**, where the dynasty's founder Amenemhat I built his own pyramid, the least interesting and accessible of the four, and not covered here.

Maidum Pyramid

Although beyond the limits of the Fayoum, the **"Collapsed Pyramid" of Maidum** (daily 8am–4pm; £E35) can be reached from there, or from Cairo by taking an early-morning train to El-Wasta (1hr 30min), and then a service taxi to the village of Maidum (15min). From the far end of the village it's a short walk across the fields and two canals into the desert; the pyramid is visible from the Nile Valley road, and during the last stage of the train journey. Tickets include admission to two mastabas and a ruined mortuary temple. Ask to see them or you won't get into either.

▲ The "Collapsed Pyramid" of Maidum

The pyramid rises in sheer-walled tiers above mounds of debris: a vision almost as dramatic as the act of getting inside used to be, when "visitors had to hang by their hands from the ledge above and drop into the entry guided by a guard". Nowadays you climb a thirty-metre stairway on the north side, descend 75m to the bedrock by a steep passageway and then ascend to the airless **burial chamber** (bring a torch).

Archeologists ascribe the pyramid to **Snofru** (see p.181) or to his father **Huni** (2637–2613 BC), whose partisans argue that Snofru built the Red and Bent pyramids at Dahshur, and would therefore not have needed a third repository for his *ka*. A contrary theory is that Maidum was started by Snofru as a step pyramid (like Zoser's at Saqqara) and later given an outer shell to make it a "true" pyramid – but the design was faulty, distributing stresses outwards rather than inwards, so that its own mass blew the pyramid apart. This theory postulates that Snofru had already embarked on another pyramid at Dahshur, whose angle was hastily reduced (hence the Bent Pyramid), and that the Red Pyramid was a final attempt to get things right (see p.182).

Round about the pyramid are several mastabas reduced to ruinous lumps, where the exquisite "Maidum Geese" frieze and the famous statue of Snofru's son Rahotep and his wife Nofret were found (both are now in the Cairo Museum). **Mastaba #17** can be entered by descending a 47-metre-long corridor and a makeshift ladder to the burial chamber, whose sarcophagus is larger than the chamber's entrance – presumably another shaft exists but has yet to be discovered.

Hawara Pyramid

Hawara ("Great Mansion") may have stood on the shores of Lake Moeris when it was built during the XII Dynasty, and later became the finishing point of a one-hundred-kilometre **desert endurance race** (Ⓦwww.egyptianmarathon.com) instituted by Pharaoh Taharqa (690 BC) to train his troops, and revived as an event in 2001. Other than during the race, held every November, Hawara gets few visitors, for its 54-metre-high **Pyramid of Amenemhat III** (daily 8am–4pm; £E35) has degenerated into a mud-brick mound since its limestone casing was removed in antiquity. Unlike most pyramids, its entrance was on the south side: one of many ruses devised to foil tomb-robbers. Alas, due to rising ground water, you can't go inside to examine such ingenious features as the stone portcullises that sealed the corridor or the roof block that was lowered into place once the sarcophagus was in the burial chamber, both operated by sand. None of them saved the body of the pharaoh from being looted and burned; his sarcophagus was later stashed alongside that of his daughter, to be found intact with her treasures in 1956.

To the south, towards and beyond the canal, a few column stumps and masses of limestone chippings mark the site of the fabled **Labyrinth**, which Herodotus described as containing over three thousand chambers hewn from a single rock. Most archeologists think that it was Amenemhat III's mortuary temple, although Rohl argues that it may have been an eternal representation of the bureaucracy and waterworks that Joseph devised to prepare Egypt for the seven years of famine foretold by the pharaoh's dream (Genesis 41:1–4).

During the early excavations at Hawara in the nineteenth century, Petrie unearthed 146 brilliantly naturalistic **"Fayoum Portraits"** (see p.102) in the Roman cemetery to the north of the pyramid.

Buses running between Fayoum City and Beni Suef (see p.220) pass through **Hawarat al-Makta**, where you cross the Bahr Yussef by a bridge, turn right at the T-junction beyond the village and walk on until the pyramid appears. From its summit (easily reached by climbing the southwest corner) you should be able to see the Lahun Pyramid on the southeastern horizon.

Lahun Pyramid

Ten kilometres beyond Hawara, the incoming Nile waters pass through **El-Lahun**, where modern sluices stand just north of the **Qantara of Sultan Qaitbey**, the thirteenth-century equivalent of the regulators installed by Amenemhat III. Lahun gets its name from the ancient Egyptian Le-hone ("Mouth of the Lake"), and gives it to the Pyramid of Senusret II sited 5km away. Most of the service taxis from the Hawatim depot to El-Lahun stop where the track leaves the main road; it's well over an hour's walk to the pyramids from there. Part of the route follows a massive **embankment** thought to have been part of Amenemhat I's original barrage to divert water into the Fayoum. It ends at the desert's edge, where visitors buy an admission ticket for the site and pick up a police escort to walk the final kilometre to the pyramid.

Built seven or eight centuries after the pyramids at Giza, the **Pyramid of Senusret II** (daily 8am–4pm; £E35) employed a new and different technique, devised by the architect Anupy. The core consists of a rock knoll on which limestone pillars were based, providing the framework for the mud-brick overlay, which was finally encased in stone. The removal of its casing left the mud-brick pyramid exposed to the elements, which eroded it into its present mess. When Petrie entered the pyramid and found Senusret's sarcophagus, it had been looted long ago; however, Brunton discovered the jewellery of Princess Sat-hathor, which is now divided between Cairo's Antiquities Museum (room 4) and the Metropolitan Museum of Art in New York.

Senusret II (1897–1878 or 1880–1874 BC), Amenemhat III's grandfather, ordered eight rock-cut mastabas for his family to the north of his pyramid; east of them is the shapeless so-called **Queen's Pyramid**, apparently lacking any tomb. In 2009 the discovery of a coffin and artefacts from the II Dynasty showed that Lahun was used for burials a thousand years earlier than hitherto reckoned.

The Great Desert Circuit

The **Great Desert Circuit** is one of the finest journeys Egypt has to offer. Starting from Cairo, Luxor or Assyut, it runs for over 1000km through a desert landscape pocked by dunes and lofty escarpments. En route, amid wind-eroded depressions, **four oases** are sustained: Bahariya, Farafra, Dakhla and Kharga. Unlike Siwa, these "inner oases" have been almost continuously under the control of the Nile Valley since the Middle Kingdom, ruled by the pharaohs, Persians, Romans, Mamlukes, Turks and British, who've left behind temples, tombs, forts, mosques and roads. Since Nasser's time, an ambitious development programme known as the **New Valley** (see box below) has transformed the oases, though this has now slowed.

Although each oasis has a central focus, the differences between them are as marked as their similarities. **Bahariya** and **Farafra** both score highly on their hot springs and palm groves, but Bahariya is influenced by Cairene ways and a major centre for **desert safaris**, whereas Farafra is more rural and traditional. In **Dakhla** and **Kharga** the modern centres are less appealing than the ancient ruins and villages on their peripheries, redolent of historic links with the Nile Valley or caravan routes from Sudan. Staying overnight in the haunting **White Desert** between Bahariya and Farafra is a must; while for those with more time and money there are safaris to remoter sites like the **El-Qaf** stalactite cave, or the uninhabited oases along the desolate road to **Siwa Oasis**, which allows die-hard travellers to visit all the Western Desert oases in a mega-circuit of over 1400km.

Relying on **public transport**, it's likely to take the best part of a week to visit all four New Valley oases. If you only have a few days, Bahariya and Farafra are the obvious destinations to aim for from Cairo; starting from Luxor and travelling in the opposite direction, if you're pushed for time it would make sense to ride straight on to Dakhla rather than stop in Kharga. But it would be a shame to rush the oases, when lazing around is part of their appeal.

Visiting the oases

While it's possible to tour the oases in comfort, don't expect to find many fancy restaurants or bright lights – though you can look forward to Bedouin parties

The New Valley

The four "Great Desert Circuit" oases are situated along a dead, prehistoric branch of the Nile, and depend on springs and wells tapping a great subterranean aquifer. In 1958 Nasser's government unveiled plans to exploit this, irrigate the desert, and relocate landless peasants from the overcrowded Nile Valley and Delta to the "**New Valley**" (El-Wadi el-Jedid). From this emerged a New Valley Governorate to run Kharga, Dakhla and Farafra oases, in collaboration with the 6th October Governorate, which administers Bahariya Oasis. Since work began in the 1970s doubts have surfaced about the aquifier, which was previously thought to be replenished by underground seepage from Lake Chad and Equatorial Africa but is now believed to be finite. The water-table has fallen dramatically in all the oases except Siwa; boreholes must be deeper and the groundwater pumped to the surface is hotter. Although the government has initiated **new projects** to bring Nile water to Kharga Oasis by the **Sheikh Zayed Canal** and exploit the groundwater beneath the desert at **East Oweinat**, many of the new settlements are still half empty, and advertisements urging farmers to settle there no longer appear on television.

round the campfire. All the oases have a range of **accommodation**, from chic ecolodges or air-conditioned "Bedouin villages", to thatched huts on the edge of the desert. Most double as safari operators, offering tours of other oases as well as their own. Getting around using public **transport** is manageable, but you'll need to take a few jeep trips to get the best from the oases. Always keep your **passport** handy in case the police want to see it at checkpoints. There are **banks** in the "capitals" of Bahariya, Dakhla and Kharga oases, though only the last two have ATMs and it's wise to bring some cash in case the server goes down.

Broadly speaking, the oases share the **climate** of Nile Valley towns on the same latitude – Bahariya is like Minya, and Kharga like Luxor – but the air is fresher (although the dust sometimes causes swollen sinuses). Winter is mild by day and near freezing at night (bring a sleeping bag); in summer temperatures can soar to 50°C at midday and hover in the 20°s after dark. Spring and autumn are the **best times** to visit the oases, with the orchards in bloom or being harvested and enough fellow travellers around to make sharing costs easy.

Tourism is in the hands of local officials and entrepreneurs whose competence and honesty varies. While it pays to check out different sources and compare what they're offering, don't let over-suspicion sour things, since you really need local help to get the best from the oases and will have to strike a deal with somebody in the end.

Visitors should respect local values by dressing modestly and observing the conventions on bathing in **outdoor springs** (mostly keyhole-shaped concrete tanks fed by water pumped up from below). The ones nearest town are always used by local men; if women bathe there, it is only after dark, never when males are present, and only fully covered by a *galabiyya*. Tourists can avoid these restrictions by bathing in more isolated spots, but most **women** cover up anyway. Women on their own should beware of entering palm groves or gardens – behaving thus is regarded here as an invitation to sex.

Transport to the oases

You can begin the Great Desert Circuit at either end. Starting **from Cairo**, you should book seats a day beforehand at the Cairo Gateway (formerly known as the Turgoman garage) in Bulaq (see p.210) for buses to Bahariya (5–6hr), Farafra (8–10hr) or Dakhla (13hr). Kharga oasis (7–8hr; £E40–55) is served by overnight buses routed via the Desert Road that parallels the Nile Valley, some of which run on to Dakhla. All Upper Egypt and Superjet buses running both routes have air conditioning, but whether it works is another matter. Or you could arrange a taxi or minibus transfer from anywhere in Cairo to Bahariya through Eden Garden Camp (see p.400).

If you fancy **flying** over the Western Desert and embarking on the Circuit at its southern end, an Egyptian petroleum company operates weekly flights from Cairo airport's Terminal 2 to Dakhla (Thurs 8am; 45min) and Kharga (Wed 8am; 1hr). Tickets are sold in Cairo at 45 Akfit al-Mahdi, off Sharia Al-Azhar (Ⓣ02/392-1674 or 012 646-7705); a one-way ticket costs £E500.

Kharga is only two hours' drive **from Luxor,** where some hotels can arrange a **car** (£E350–500) and safaris as far the White Desert (see p.282). Or you can ask guys in the oases to collect you: Mohsen from Kharga (p.426) will drive you there (£E400) or to Dakhla (£E700), stopping at temples and villages en route; while the *Anwar Hotel* (p.413) quotes £E600 to drive you straight to Dakhla. There is no longer a weekly train from Luxor, the tracks having been covered by dunes, like the British-built railway to the Nile Valley a century earlier. Kharga is also accessible **from Assyut** in Middle Egypt, by bus or service taxi (4–5hr).

Travellers hoping to combine the Great Desert Circuit with **Siwa** should consult Siwa's tourist office (p.441) or the NGO Desert Lover in Bahariya (p.398) to ascertain the situation regarding **permits**. Currently, the paperwork is easy to fix in either oasis, but this can change at short notice. Finding enough people to share the cost of a **car** (at least £E1200) is another issue, particularly off-season when there are few travellers in the oases. In any case, vehicles are obliged to travel in a convoy escorted by an army officer and equipped with a satellite phone.

Bahariya Oasis

Bahariya Oasis is the smallest of the four depressions, only 94km long and 42km wide. In the Late Cretaceous era, 94 million years ago, the environment resembled the Florida Everglades, with mangrove swamps inhabited by dinosaurs such as the plant-eating paralititan and the carnivorous carcharodontosaurus, whose bones have been found at Jebel el-Dist and Jebel el-Fagga. The oasis is known to have been under pharaonic control by the Middle Kingdom, when it exported wine to the Nile Valley. During the Late Period, Bahariya thrived as an artery between Egypt and Libya, while throughout Islamic times, Arab armies, merchants and pilgrims passed through. Today, it is tourists who come here to enjoy the hot springs and palm groves, or undertake safaris into the dunes and rock formations of the Western Desert.

Although Bahariya covers 1200 square kilometres, less than one percent is actually cultivated, with date palms, olive and fruit trees, vegetables, rice and corn. Ominously, where groundwater was once tapped at a depth of 30m, they must now bore 1000m underground; fruit trees have suffered from being irrigated by hotter water, raising fears for Bahariya's future sustainability.

The **journey from Cairo** (360km) begins with the Pyramids of Giza visible as you enter the Western Desert. Not long afterwards you'll pass **6th October City**, one of the high-rise satellite cities meant to reduce Cairo's congestion. To relieve the tedium of traversing flat, featureless desert, vehicles stop at a grubby halfway **resthouse**. Soon after entering Bahariya Oasis the road passes a track to the outlying settlement of El-Harra, and subsequent side roads to the villages of Mandisha and Agouz. Don't get off if the bus calls at any of these places – wait for the end of the line at the oasis "capital", **Bawiti**. The oasis comes under the 6th October governorate and shares its telephone prefix.

Bawiti

BAWITI harbours a picturesque nucleus of old houses on a ridge overlooking luxuriant palm groves, but that's not what you see on arrival. The lower ground beside the Cairo–Farafra road is littered with half-finished New Valley projects, disrupting donkey traffic but not the ramshackle shops and cafés that enliven Bawiti's **main street**, Sharia Masr/Sharia Gamal Abdel Nasser. Buses from Cairo or Farafra drop you right in the centre, where you'll immediately be besieged by **touts** who'll try to get you to stay at their place (not all hotels or campgrounds use them). Your choice of lodgings may well determine which safari outfit you go with (see p.403), so consider the options well beforehand.

Arrival and information

Arriving by bus, you'll be dropped near the low-key **tourist office** in the Government Building (daily except Fri 8.30am–2pm, Nov–April also 7–8pm; ⓣ02/3847-3039 or 012 373-6567, ⓔmohamed_kader26@hotmail.com), where

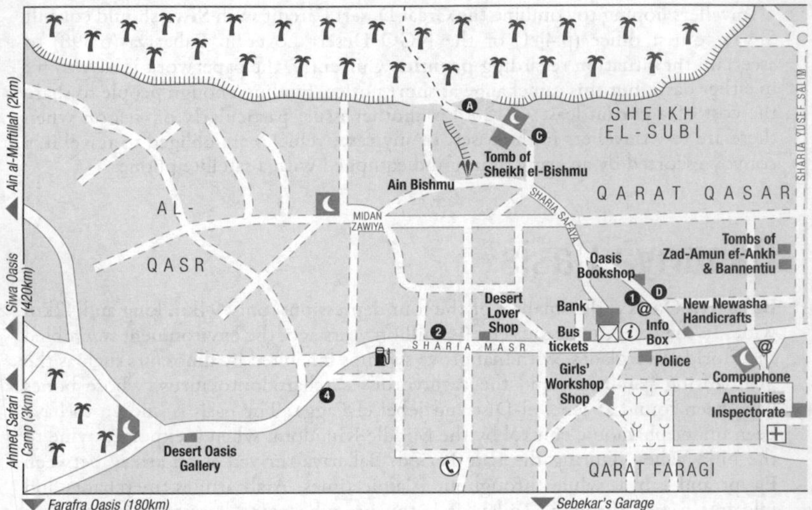

Mohammed Abdel Kader is an alternative source of information to local safari outfits (see p.403), though no less self-interested.

The same goes for **Desert Lover** (☎02/3847-3439 or 014 198-5905, Ⓦwww.bahariyaoasis-ngo.org), an NGO that handles applications for 24-hour travel permits (see box, p.380), mounts desert clean-ups and runs a handicrafts shop in the bazaar. Applications are currently received at Compuphone, 500m east along the main drag (see below), but may be dealt with at their shop in the future. Bahariya's **tourist police** (daily 24hr; ☎02/3848-2900) will record your nationality at their checkpoints, but are otherwise irrelevant.

The National Bank for Development (Mon–Thurs & Sun 8am–2pm) behind the post office can change **money,** but hasn't yet an ATM. When it's closed, Peter Wirth at the *International Hot Spring Hotel* changes money. The **post office** (daily except Fri 8am–2pm) is around the corner from two **internet** kiosks, InfoBox and M&N Internet (both 9am–2pm & 5–10pm). Compuphone (daily 9am–1pm & 2pm–midnight), on Sharia Gamal Abdel Nasser, can burn digital photos onto CDs. There's a **telephone** office (daily 8am–midnight) off the main drag. Bawiti has two **pharmacies** and a **hospital** (☎02/3847-2390), but you'd be better off travelling to Cairo if there's a serious problem.

Accommodation

Hotels and campgrounds cater for every taste and budget and are rarely full, so it's a buyers' market. Decide whether you want desert seclusion or the "facilities" of Bawiti close at hand, and what kind of scene you fancy in the evenings. While locals make music and party on some of the campgrounds, the hotels tend to be devoid of nightlife. Also, most campgrounds will provide free transport out from town, and usually into town too, while for some of the hotels you might have to rely on taxis or rent a bicycle.

The term **campground** doesn't refer to somewhere you pitch a tent (though you can), but to a place that rents palm-thatch or mud-brick huts with sleeping platforms and mattresses – or proper rooms with beds and showers on the fancier sites. Most can rustle up a meal even if they lack a restaurant. If you're staying a long time or coming with your family, consider renting a three-bedroom **flat** in

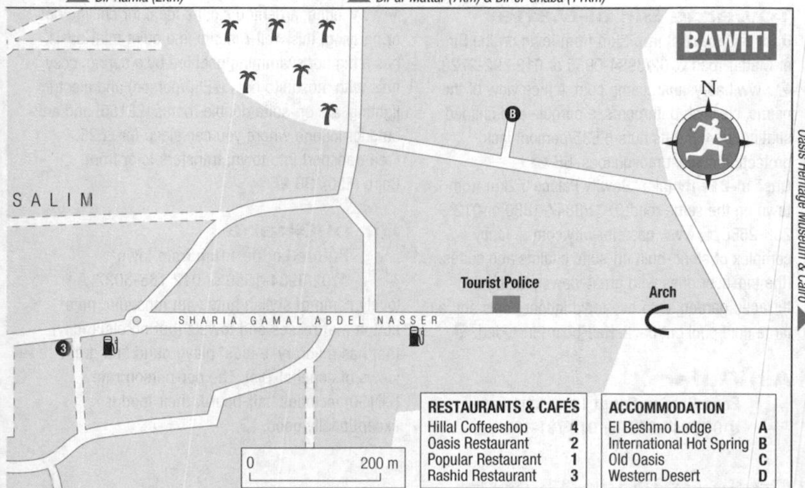

the village of Agouz, 2km from Bawiti, for £E100 a night: contact Yehiya Kandil for details (ⓣ02/3849-6754 or 012 321-6790, ⓔyahiakandil@yahoo.de).

For locations of places reviewed outside Bawiti, see the Bahariya oasis map on p.405.

Bawiti

El Beshmo Lodge Ain Bishmu ⓣ02/3847-3500, ⓦwww.beshmolodge.com. Located on a ridge overlooking Bawiti's palm groves, it has cosy en-suite rooms, a tepid spring-fed pool, and a restaurant, but no garden to speak of. BB ❸

International Hot Spring On the edge of town ⓣ&ⓕ02/3847-2322 or ⓣ012 321-2179, ⓦwww.whitedeserttours.com. This comfy German-managed spa hotel offers an indoor thermal pool, gym, sauna, and massage. It has a playground, restaurant and bar, plus a palm tree growing out of a deep hole in the ground. Rates include half-board (children under 5 free, 50% off for under-12s). ❼

Old Oases Ain Bishmu ⓣ02/3847-3028 or 012 232-4425, ⓦwww.oldoasissafari.4t.com. Sharing the same view as the *El Beshmo Lodge*, this has en-suite rooms linked by walkways, table tennis, a warm spring-fed pool and a luxuriant garden. A/c costs £E60 extra. BB ❸

Western Desert Sharia Safaya ⓣ02/3847-1600 or 012 433-6015, ⓦwww.westerndeserthotel.com. Right in the centre, this well-run hotel has en-suite rooms with fans or a/c, satellite TV and balcony, internet access, billiards and a rooftop with panoramic views of Bawiti. BB ❹

Agouz and the Black Mountain

Bedouin Village Agouz, 2km from Bawiti ⓣ02/3849-6811. Behind the school, 200m from the highway, this mostly shadeless campground has small clean rooms with fans and bathrooms (£E50 per person), mud huts (£E15 per person) and a pergola for occasional parties. BB ❶

Oasis Panorama 2km from town, halfway up the Black Mountain ⓣ02/3847-3354, ⓦwww.oasispanorama.net Resembling a beach hotel whose sea has receded, its en-suite rooms have a/c and mosquito nets, but the garden is shadeless and neglected, and it lacks atmosphere. BB ❸

Palm Village Between Agouz and Zabu, 5km from town ⓣ02/3849-6272 or 012 468-1024. A bit lifeless but nicely laid out, with large a/c rooms, luxurious suites, horseriding (£E60/hr), billiards and fine views of the Black Mountain. BB ❻

Tibniya

Ahmed Safari Camp 4km from town ⓣ02/3847-1414 or 012 492-5563, ⓦwww.ahmedsafaricamp.com. Close to Alexander's Temple but otherwise remote, it mainly caters to overland adventure groups, offering en-suite rooms with fans or a/c (£E50 extra), table tennis, billiards, and a small menagerie to amuse kids. BB ❷

Towards Bir al-Mattar

Badr's Sahara Camp 3km from town on the Bir al-Mattar road ⓣ02/3984-0955 or 012 792-2728, ⓦwww.badrysaharacamp.com. A nice view of the palms, cleanish bathrooms, a pergola and shaded seating area, but its huts (£E35/person) lack protection against mosquitoes. BB ❷

Qasr el-Bawity (aka "Bawity Palace") 2km from town on the same road ⓣ02/3847-1880 or 012 258-2586, ⓦwww.qasrelbawity.com. A fancy complex of stone-built en-suite chalets and suites (the top-floor ones with great views), facing a terraced garden, with two tepid indoor pools and a large cold pool out back. Half-board included. ❺

Ain Gufar

Eden Garden Camp 10km from Bawiti ⓣ02/3847-3727 or 012 731-1876, ⓦwww.edengardentours.com. Ideal for chilling out or partying, this well-run site in a quiet mini-oasis has a big hot swimming pool fed by a spring, cosy huts with mosquito nets (£E50/person) and electric lighting, a/c en-suite double rooms (£E150) and an outdoor lounge where you can sleep for £E25. Free transport into town; transfers to or from Cairo (€50). BB ❷

Bir el-Ghaba

Nature Lodge 11km from town ⓣ02/3984-1550 or 012 165-3037. A lovely camp of stylish huts with mosquito nets, cotton mattresses and towels (but no electricity), that has a library, a kids' playground and great views of Jebel el-Dist. The per-person rate (£E150) includes half-board; their food is exceptionally good. ❺

Oasis Heritage Museum

Bawiti's most visible "sight" is the **Oasis Heritage Museum** created by Mahmoud Eed, a self-taught sculptor inspired by Badr in Farafra (see p.409). Both artists portray a way of life that's almost disappeared in the oases, for the men at least, whose job it once was to hunt gazelles and weave mats (women's roles haven't changed so much). There's also a rather sad **Reptile Collection** (£E10) of lizards, snakes and hedgehogs, captured in the desert. You can't miss the museum, 1km beyond the town limits; a hilltop stockade with a pigeon tower and beehive domes, signposted *Camel Camp*. Mahmoud can usually be found at the museum or contacted by phone (ⓣ02/3847-3666 or 012 710-7965).

Antiquities Inspectorate

The unobtrusive **Antiquities Inspectorate** near the hospital displays three **mummies** from the huge cache found outside Bawiti. All are encased in gilded and painted *cartonage* (linen pasteboard) and have sculpted stucco masks, two of them gilded – hence their sobriquet "The Golden Mummies". Poignantly, the child was buried with its parents, and the female mummy had its head inclined towards her husband's. Her "chest plate" is sculpted with tiny triangular breasts – a funerary fashion in Greco-Roman times. In this era mummification was often perfunctory, as you can see from the sad, natron-soaked bundle that was once a child. Almost all the mummies removed from the earth have deteriorated – some previously on display here are no longer fit to be shown.

The tombs

From the Antiquities office you can walk downhill and cross the main road to reach **Qarat Qasr Salim**, a dusty ridge harbouring two tombs opened to the public in the 1990s (four more have since been found but aren't yet accessible). Both belonged to local merchants of the XXVI Dynasty, whose wealth enabled them to construct **tombs** of a kind previously reserved for high officials. That of **Zad-Amun ef-Ankh**, Bahariya's governor in the reign of the XXVI Dynasty pharaoh Amasis, is sunk in a steep-sided pit; its hall has rounded pillars (unusual for Bahariya) and is decorated with deities (notice the people bringing gifts, to the left), painted in ochre, brown and black upon a white background. He was buried in an alabaster sarcophagus enclosed within a limestone one, which are thought to have been quarried near Tell el-Amarna and Giza, shipped along the Nile and then

Bawiti's Antiquities Trail

All the **antiquities** open to the public (the tombs of Zad-Amun ef-Ankh and Bannentiu; the Temple of Alexander and the chapels of Ain al-Muftillah) are covered by a single **ticket** (£E45) sold at a kiosk downhill from the Antiquities Inspectorate in the centre of town, which includes admission to its makeshift **museum,** displaying three of the famous "Golden Mummies". Since Ain al-Muftillah and Alexander's Temple are several kilometres outside Bawiti, you'll need private transport to realise the full value of your ticket.

dragged 200km overland to Bawiti. Nearby is the tomb of his son, **Bannentiu**, at the bottom of a ten-metre shaft – mind your head on the steel grating and the low entrance to its votive hall. Here the pillars are square and the murals are in brick red, golden yellow, pale blue and black upon white, and some of the deities have only been sketched in, but there's a fine solar barque at the back, and the embalming process is shown on the right-hand wall.

Bawiti's old quarter, Ain Bishmu and Al-Qasr

Bawiti's **old quarter** is in the centre of town, a huddle of mud-brick homes and mausolea flanking a main street where elders sit and gossip on mastabas. To appreciate its commanding position, follow the alley winding off to **Ain Bishmu**, a craggy fissure in the bedrock where a spring was hewn in Roman times, gushing hot water (35°C) into a natural basin, to flow into the **palm groves** below. Sadly, the ravine is now disfigured by a pumping station, although the hotels that have been built here try not to mar the breathtaking view of the palm groves. The gardens look especially lovely spangled with apricot blossom in spring. Nearby is the dovecote-shaped **Tomb of Sheikh el-Bishmu**.

The old quarter's main street runs into **Al-Qasr**, an older village built directly over the capital of the oasis in pharaonic times and continuously inhabited since then – though many of the houses are now abandoned or used as livestock pens. Narrow alleys snake past secretive courtyards and walled gardens, abruptly ending or joining up with other lanes – making it easy to go astray. Some of the houses incorporate stones from a bygone XXVI Dynasty temple, and a Roman triumphal arch that survived until the mid-nineteenth century.

Ain al-Muftillah and the Temple of Alexander

The ancient town once extended 3km to **Ain al-Muftillah**, a spring that's nowadays almost lost on the outskirts of the desert. It's feasible to cycle but better to get there by car, as the route is not signposted or easy to explain. Look out for a barbed wire enclosure containing four **ruined chapels** excavated by Steindorff and Fakhry. Built during the XXVI Dynasty, they don't conform to the canons of temple architecture and are built of local sandstone, streaked with ochre and sienna, which makes them look unusually colourful but liable to flake. One of the temples was dedicated to Bes, the patron deity of musicians and dancers, but all that remains of his image is a foot and a tail (though Bawiti's museum has a fine statue). By crossing the rise and a dune beyond, you can enjoy a **panoramic view** of Al-Qasr, Bawiti, and the springs and mountains described below.

Further out in the locality of Tibniya, ask at *Ahmed Safari Camp* for directions to the **Temple of Alexander**, 400m away via a track. Built of the same stone as the chapels, its reliefs have suffered from being sandblasted by the wind for centuries, obliging the SCA to recreate the face and cartouche of Alexander the Great that archeologists recorded in the 1930s. This is (or was) the only temple in Egypt to bear Alexander's figure and cartouche, and it is thought to have been founded by Alexander when he passed through the oasis en route from Siwa to Memphis.

Valley of the Golden Mummies

In 1996, a donkey owned by one of the guards at Alexander's Temple stumbled into a hole in the desert, thus alerting its master to what turned out to be the largest cache of mummies ever found in Egypt. Surveys have since shown that the necropolis covers ten square kilometres and may contain ten thousand mummies, stacked in family vaults – hundreds have been found so far. Whereas most are simply wrapped in linen, others are in terracotta coffins adorned with human faces, their bodies covered in gilded *cartonage* and their faces with stucco masks. These **Golden Mummies** caught the imagination of the public, and TV networks have paid millions of dollars to film the opening of a series of burial chambers. The main **excavation** site at "Kilo Setta" (km 6) is off-limits without a permit from the SCA – granted only to a select few tour operators.

Handicrafts, natural healing and massage

Despite a living crafts tradition in the oasis, Bawiti's **handicrafts shops** give more space to things made elsewhere than to homegrown products – with the honourable exceptions of the Girls' Workshop Shop (daily except Fri 10am–1pm), near the cemetery on Qarat al-Faragi, and the Desert Lover shop on Sharia Masr (daily 9am–1pm & 3–9pm). For naïve paintings and sculptures, visit the Desert Oasis Gallery (no set hours) beyond the bazaar. The Oasis Bookshop (daily 9am–8pm) near the *Western Desert Hotel* sells photo books, prints and posters of the oases.

Meditation groups are a lucrative sideline for local safari outfits like Khalifa Expedition, working with companies such as Energies of Egypt (ⓦwww.hiddenegypt.com) and The Lightweaver (ⓦthelightweaver.org), and drawing clients from Europe. Additionally, several hotels offer **natural healing** to their guests: the *International Hot Spring* (see p.399) has a range of **massage** treatments (£E200 per hour).

Eating, drinking and nightlife

Hot **meals** can be had at most hotels and campgrounds – *Nature Lodge* has the best cuisine, which non-residents can enjoy for £E50 by phoning a few hours ahead. Few visitors leave Bawiti without sampling the *Popular Restaurant* (daily 6am–10pm) – otherwise known as *Bayoumi's* after its genial owner – which cooks one set meal a day of soup, vegetable stew, lamb, rice and salad, and sells beer. On Sharia Masr, in the bazaar, the *Oasis Restaurant* does grilled chicken, *fuul* and *taamiya*, while the *Rashid* out towards the other end of the main drag is better for desserts and *sheeshas*. In the bazaar are more tea and *sheesha* dens, including the *Hillal Coffeeshop* which doubles as a bus stop.

Compared to other oases, **alcohol** is rife. Most campgrounds don't mind you consuming takeaway beer (£E15) from the *Popular Restaurant* even if they sell it themselves. Guests at the *International Hot Spring* can enjoy *Peter's Bar* – serving local wine (£E80 a bottle), imported spirits (£E30 a shot) and a vodka, watermelon and lime cocktail (£E25) – open to non-residents by arrangement only.

Night-time entertainment consists of **Bedouin parties** held in a tent or round a fire. Most campgrounds will stage a party whenever a tour group arrives or guests request one. You don't need to be staying at *Eden Garden Camp* to order a fantastic **BBQ and pool-party** (for £E50 a head; beer, wine and spirits cost extra). The singing, drumming and dancing are intoxicating even without booze or hashish.

Desert safaris from Bahariya

Bawiti is the main departure point for **safaris** in the Western Desert, ranging from forays into Farafra's White Desert to long-range expeditions to the remote Gilf Kebir. For **overnight** trips to the White Desert, most safaris leave Bahariya in the morning, to visit the Black Desert and Crystal Mountain before reaching the White Desert to set up camp by nightfall. Most trips are priced on the basis of four passengers; some outfits quote group rates and others per person. Safaris can also be organized from Farafra (see p.407 for details), but tend to be pricier, as there's far less competition.

Price shouldn't be the only consideration when **choosing a guide**: the farther off-road you go into the desert the more vital their competence becomes. If someone promises the White Desert overnight for only £E100 per person, your vehicle, driver or food might well be second-rate, but the situation won't be as bad as on an off-road trip to Dakhla. Any safari should provide at least one jeep as logistical support for the car carrying tourists. In the case of **camel treks**, the supply-car stays out of sight and only appears to set up camp, as trekkers alternate between riding and walking. Off-road trips to Siwa or Dakhla – never mind the Gilf Kebir or the Great Sand Sea – require guides who've memorized the terrain from experience and aren't merely dependent on navigating by **GPS** waypoints.

See the box on p.380 regarding **permits** for travel between Bahariya and Siwa or to visit "deep desert" locations. Permits are not required for the White Desert or El-Qaf, or travel off-road between Bahariya and Dakhla.

Safari operators

Yehiya Abdallah ⓣ018 771-0511, ⓔyahyaoasis@hotmail.com. "Yuyu" specializes in off-road trips to the White Desert and Dakhla Oasis, camel trekking, and sandboarding at Bir Qarawein (see p.412).

Mahmoud Bahr ⓔtiger84@yahoo.com. Mahmoud does trips to Siwa (£E1200 for four people; £E1400 off-road) and a three-day safari featuring Ain Della and the White Desert (for €75 per person per day). He's also a great dancer at Bedouin parties.

Desert Ship Safari ⓣ02/3849-6754 or ⓣ012 321-6790, ⓦwww.desertshipsafari.com. Yehiya Kandil is an expert guide and driver who can take you anywhere from El-Qaf to the Gilf Kebir by jeep (€50–120 per person per day), or arrange camel trekking (minimum four people).

Eden Garden Tours ⓣ02/3847-3727 or 012 731-1876, ⓦwww.edengardentours.com. Talat Mulah at *Eden Garden Camp* organizes off-road tours throughout the Western Desert (€50 per person per day; €120 for the Gilf), camel treks and walking tours, with great music and faultless logistics. Minibus transfers (€50) to/from Cairo by arrangement.

Hamada Hamedtay ⓣ02/3847-1747 or 012 731-9512, ⓦwww.bahariyaexpedition.com. A well-regarded guide and driver, Hamada runs safaris to the Gilf, the Great Sand Sea, El-Qaf, the Valley of the Whales and the White Desert.

Khaled Kandeel ⓣ02/847-2835 or 012 716-0782, ⓔwestern_desert2000@yahoo.com. Safaris to El-Qaf, the Valley of the Whales or Bir Dikkur, for €120 per day (shared between four people).

Khalifa Expedition ⓣ012 321-5445, ⓦwww.khalifaexpedition.com. Khaled and Rose-Maria do jeep safaris to the Gilf, the Great Sand Sea and El-Qaf, camel trekking and meditation in the White Desert and painting tours to Ain Um Dabadib in Kharga Oasis.

Ashraf Lotfi ⓣ012 165-3037, ⓔnaturelodge@hotmail.com. From *Nature Lodge*, Ashraf leads jeep, camel or walking tours, and expeditions as far as the Gilf. The food provided on his safaris is especially good.

Old Oasis Safari ⓣ02/3847-3038 or 012 232-4425, ⓦwww.oldoasissafari.4t.com. The White Desert by day (£E500 group-rate without food) or overnight (£E750 including meals), El-Qaf (£E300 per person per day) and the Gilf (from €120 per person per day).

Samy Mansour ⓣ02/3849-7260 or 012 368-2070, ⓔsamy_ba@hotmail.com. From the Bedouin family that owns all the camels in Bahariya, Samy leads camel and walking tours for £E150 per person per day. He doesn't speak much English, but Ashraf Lotfi (see above) can facilitate contact.

Mohammed Senussi ⓣ02/3847-3439 or 012 224-8570, ⓔaisha_kosa@yahoo.de. Bahariya's most experienced guide and driver, "Kosa" can take you anywhere in the Western Desert, and often guides others' expeditions to the Gilf Kebir.

Western Desert Safari ①&Ⓕ 02/3847-1800 or 012 433-6015, Ⓦ www.westerndeserthotel.com. The only guide who knows the location of the mysterious Sand Volcano (see p.411), Samir also does El-Qaf, Wadi Rayan, and other destinations.

White Desert Tours ① 02/3847-2322 or 012 736-9493, Ⓦ www.whitedeserttours.com. Peter Wirth guides self-drive and tailor-made jeep safaris all over the Western Desert, and motorbike tours by arrangement. Peter speaks English and German, and his wife, Miharu, speaks Japanese.

Zaki Mohammed Zaki ① 012 963-9098, Ⓔ desert_wolf642@yahoo.com. The "Desert Wolf" offers a night in the White Desert (£E200/person) or camel trekking in Bahariya and Farafra (€60 per person per day).

Around the oasis

If they're not busy taking people to the White Desert, some safari operators may do **half-day tours** of the oasis, visiting the Black Mountain, Jebel el-Dist and Bir el-Ghaba to the northeast of Bawiti. Priced per jeep (four or five passengers), trips costs around £E300. Alternatively, you could **rent a bicycle** for £E25 a day from New Newasha Handicrafts and cycle out to Bir el-Ghaba – about 25km round-trip – or settle for exploring the palm groves, springs and villages nearer town.

Northeast of Bawiti

The nearest spring to Bawiti is **Bir Ramla**, a nice two-kilometre walk from Bawiti past palm and fruit orchards, but too hot (45°C) for most and quite public. Men can bathe here in shorts, women only at night, in full-length opaque clothing. Similar rules apply to **Bir el-Negba**, 1km further on. More distantly, **Bir al-Mattar** has become too hot to bathe in, and the spring out at **Bir el-Ghaba** (Well of the Forest) has dried up, yet it's worth visiting purely for the scenery, with palm and eucalyptus groves yielding to scrub and tawny mountains in the near distance.

Jebel el-Dist ("Mountain of the Pot") is more accurately described by guides as "Pyramid Mountain", and the ever-changing play of light across it has inspired another name, "Magic Mountain". Its **dinosaur beds** have been picked bare, but the fields and acacia groves towards Bir el-Ghaba abound in insects and **birdlife**. You'll also see **camels** belonging to a Bedouin family that goes walkabout in the desert in July, when the oasis is plagued by camel-ticks.

En route to all these sites you'll pass the aptly named **Black Mountain**, whose dolomite and basalt mass is crowned by a ruined look-out post used by Captain Williams to monitor the Senussi in 1916, for which it is nicknamed Jebel el-Ingleez, the "English Mountain". Most of the inhabited parts of the oasis are visible from its summit, whose rocks have an oddly sticky texture and smell faintly of biscuits.

East of Bawiti

Most tourists pay little heed to the **villages** outside Bawiti, whose people are friendly and hospitable. It's feasible to walk to **AGOUZ**, only 2km from town, off the Cairo highway. Agouz is reputedly inhabited by the descendants of families banished from Siwa Oasis for the loose morals of their womenfolk, but they would rather forget this slur on their ancestors. Following the link road towards **Mandisha**, you'll pass a field of dunes that threatens neighbouring **Zabu**, where houses and palm groves have been drowned in sand. Behind the gardens at the back of the village, facing towards the escarpment, you can follow a track into a canebrake to find **Qasr el-Zabu** – a giant sandstone boulder where Libyan nomads and other travellers have carved **inscriptions** since the twelfth century. Besides petroglyphs and sun symbols, you can see horses, a charioteer, a woman with her arms akimbo, and the name of the explorer Hyde.

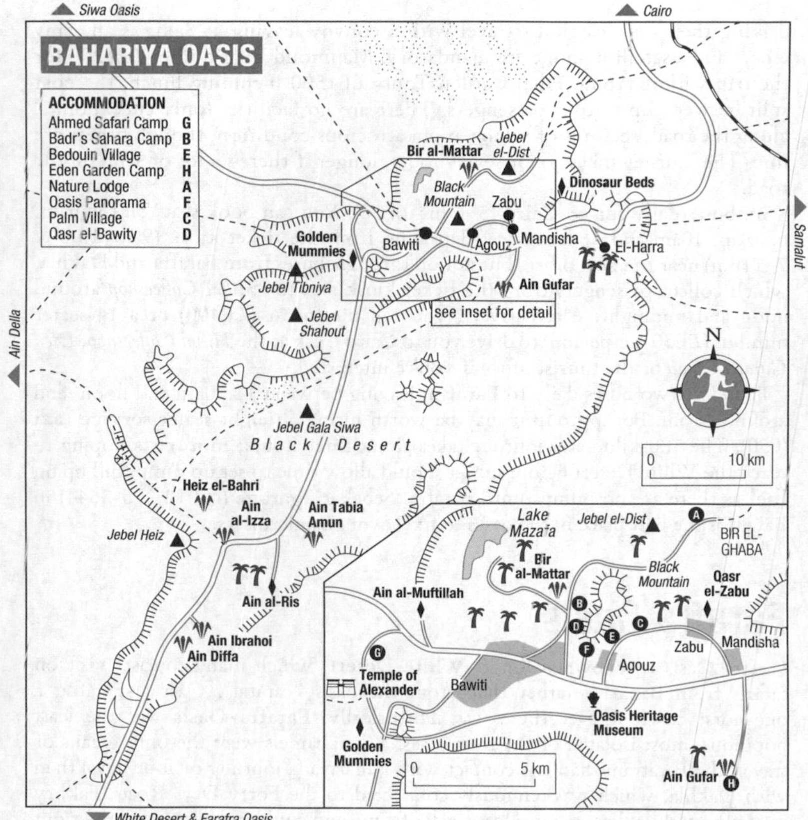

South of Bawiti

The southern part of the oasis is generally seen by tourists bound for the White Desert on 4WD safaris. While some make a cursory detour off-road into the **Black Desert** (Sahara Souda) of charred outcrops and table-top rocks, others swing around the far side of **Jebel Gala Siwa** to see a lovely **dune** that has formed in the lee of the escarpment – ideal for **sandboarding**. These tours sometimes stop for lunch at **Heiz el-Bahri**, where tamarisk-mounds and palms surround a cold spring, one of several fertile enclaves in the locality called El-Heiz. Sticking to the highway, instead, you may notice a white **tomb** in the desert roughly 30km from Bawiti: a monument to Swiss René Michel, a pioneer of tourism to Bahariya, who died here from heatstroke in 1986. At km 56 are a checkpoint and the *Oasis Cafeteria*.

The Bahariya and Farafra depressions are separated by a limestone **escarpment** where gigantic drifts of sand flank the road as it traverses the **Naqb es-Sillum** (Pass of the Stairs), and two microwave masts relay signals between the oases (there's a first-aid post with an ambulance by the mast nearest Bahariya). From here on, many safari groups head off-road to reach Agabat and the White Desert, as described under Farafra Oasis (see p.406).

Moving on from Bahariya

To travel the 420km partly surfaced **road to Siwa Oasis** requires a 24-hour **permit** from the NGO Desert Lover (see p.398 and the box, p.380). Anyone driving their own car must travel with a convoy leaving at 8am, as an army escort and a satellite phone are mandatory. Mahmoud Bahr quotes £E1200 for the trip without food, Eden Garden Tours £E1500 including lunch, the **cost** split between up to four passengers. There are no facilities (only checkpoints) along the road, sections of which are in atrocious condition, though others are fine. The journey takes six or seven hours, longer if there's a lot of sand on the road.

Six buses daily run to **Cairo** (5–6 hr; £E30). You can book seats on the 6am, 6.30am, 10am and 3pm services departing from the ticket kiosk (9am–1pm & 7–11pm) near the post office, but not on through-buses from Farafra and Dakhla, which collect passengers from the ticket kiosk and the *Hillal Coffeeshop* around noon and midnight. Alternatively, you can hire a car (£E400) or a 14-seater minibus (£E30 per person) to drive you to Cairo – ask at the *Hillal Coffeeshop*, *Eden Garden Camp* or the tourist office if you're interested.

There are two buses daily to **Farafra**, leaving between 11.30am and noon, and around 11pm. For a group it may be worth hiring an eight-seater **service taxi** (€50). The 180-kilometre journey takes about three hours; **motorists** hoping to reach the White Desert before sunset should allow time to set up camp. Fill up on **fuel** as there are no pumps until Farafra. Sebekar's **garage** (Ⓣ012 275-2644) in Bawiti is the best place in the oases to fix Toyota Landcruisers.

Farafra Oasis

Farafra Oasis is renowned for its **White Desert**, which many tourists visit on safaris from Bahariya rather than from the oasis "capital", Qasr al-Farafra, a one-horse town if ever there was. Historically, **Farafra Oasis** was the least populous, most isolated of the four oases. When camels were the only means of travel, the Farafranis had less contact with Bahariya (a journey of four days) than with Dakhla, which was tenuously connected to the Forty Days Road. Fakhry relates how the villagers once lost track of time and could only ascertain the right day for Friday prayers by sending a rider to Dakhla.

Qasr al-Farafra was the only village in the oasis before the New Valley scheme seeded a dozen hamlets across the depression, now inhabited by fifteen thousand settlers from the Assyut region or the Delta. Qasr has remained a tight-knit community of four extended families and is noted for its piety, apparent during Ramadan, when the mosque overflows with robed imams and sheikhs. Compared to Bahariya few people are involved in **tourism** so there's almost no hustling – but little to do at night either. Farafra is the sleepiest of all the oases and few tourists stay longer than a night in Qasr.

Crystal Mountain, Agabat and the White Desert

Coming from Bahariya, you'll enjoy a succession of fantastic views as you enter the Farafra depression, where safaris halt to pay admission fees to the White Desert National Park (see "Practicalities") and let passengers admire the **Crystal Mountain** (Jebel al-Izaz), a shiny quartz ridge with a human-high natural arch through the middle, which is why locals call it Hagar al-Makhrum, the "Rock with a Hole". At this point 4WDs may turn off onto the so-called **English Track** into the White Desert, or continue along the highway, descending the Naqb es-Sillum past the landmark **Twin Peaks** on your left, followed by Agabat.

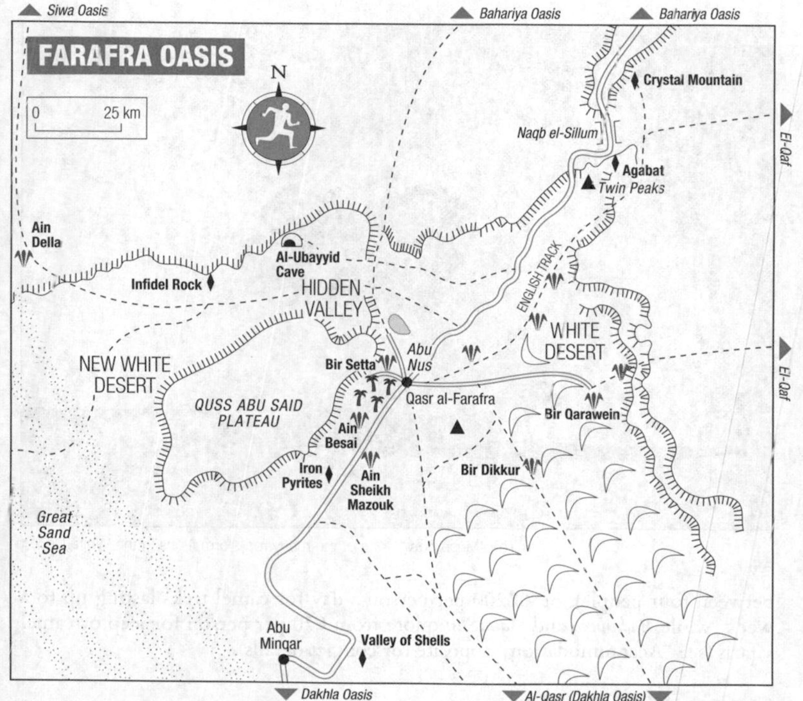

Agabat (Wonders) is the local name given to scores of rock sugarloaves surrounded by soft sand and powdered chalk, which some older people call *Akabat* (Difficult), for the sand can easily entrap vehicles that try to reach it from the highway – though a steep off-road descent is possible just after Twin Peaks.

This spectacularly rugged terrain merges into the famous **White Desert** (Sahara el-Beida) on either side of the highway. Here, the wind has eroded chalk monoliths into surreal forms resembling skulls, ostriches, hawks, camels, mushrooms and leopards, looming above a dusty pan strewn with shells, crystals and iron pyrites shaped like sea urchins or twigs. The chalk *yardangs* glint pale gold in the midday sun, turn violet and pink around sunset, and resemble icebergs or snowdrifts by moonlight – while **gazelles** may be glimpsed at daybreak as they forage for a few hours.

Practicalities

Covering 3010 square kilometres on both sides of the highway, the White Desert National Park levies a **fee** of $5 per person and $5 per car to enter, plus £E10 to camp overnight. To protect the landscape, cars are restricted to four trails with designated **camping** spots (shown on a leaflet available from the ticket office). Keep **safety** in mind nonetheless: several tourists have got lost and nearly died in the White Desert. Don't wander far from camp at night – it's easy to get disoriented by the *yardangs*.

Although the White Desert is in Farafra Oasis, many tourists visit it with safari outfits from Bahariya (see p.403), whose excursions are competitive, with the scenic bonus of the Black Desert and Naqb es-Sillum en route. In Farafra, the *Sunrise* and *El-Waha* hotels charge £E600 for a night in the White Desert (split

▲ The "Mushroom"– one of the many rock formations in the White Desert

between four people), or £E200 per person a day for camel treks lasting up to a week, while *Badawiya* and *AquaSun* quote from €70 per person for jeep or camel safaris (see "Accommodation" opposite for contact details).

Qasr al-Farafra

The low ground in **QASR AL-FARAFRA** has been colonized by modern infrastructure, which obscures the view of the hilltop village, backing onto palm groves. Even there modernization is apparent, with austerely beautiful old mud-brick houses topped by flowing pediments or crenellations being superseded by breeze-block homes with proper bathrooms. Though Qasr's population has shot up to five thousand in the last twenty years due to better healthcare, its shops and market are still meagre and frugality is the order of the day, despite a few wealthy locals who've built villas on the edge of town.

Arrival and information

While a triumphal arch welcomes traffic from Dakhla, buses from Bahariya pass the *Sunrise* and *Badawiya hotels* on the outskirts before dropping passengers at the fuel station and shops down the road. On **arrival**, local police may enquire about your nationality, but shouldn't trouble you after that. The **post office** (daily 8.30am–2.30pm) and **telephone exchange** (24hr) are behind the Town Council, and a last-resort **hospital** (Ⓣ092/751-0047) out past the *Badawiya*. In the absence of a bank, you may be able to change small amounts of **cash** at the hotels.

As there isn't a tourist office, visitors rely on hotels and safari operators for **information**, with the Ali family being the main players: Atif Ali manages the *Badawiya* hotel; Hamdy Ali leads Badawiya Expedition and Sa'ad runs its Cairo office; while their artist brother Badr has a local museum and gallery.

Accommodation

Your choice of accommodation may decide which safari operator you travel with (or vice versa), as the hotels expect their guests to sign up for safaris, and regard it as bad form for them to go elsewhere.

AquaSun Bir Setta, 6km from town ⓣ&ⓕ 02/3337-2898 or ⓣ 010 667-8099, ⓦ www.aquasunhotels.com. This quiet, remote hotel has a/c chalets with satellite TV, a warm spring-fed indoor pool (phone ahead to request that it's cleaned), and a safari outfit (ⓦ www.raid4x4egypt.com) run by rally driver Hisham Nessim (see p.380). Half-board included. ⑤

Badawiya ⓣ 092/751-0060 or 012 214-8343, ⓦ www.badawiya.com. Located on the edge of town, this desert-palace-style complex has split-level rooms with raised beds and mosquito nets, suites (€55), a big spring-fed pool, Qasr's best restaurant, a major safari outfit (see p.380) and a sister-hotel in Dakhla Oasis (p.415). BB ④

El-Waha ⓣ 012 720-0387, ⓔ wahafarafra@yahoo.com. This small hotel near Badr's Museum has basic rooms, some with bathrooms (£E15 extra) – from such modest beginnings its owners have financed the *Sunrise*. BB ②

Sunrise ⓣ 012 291-0878. Fancier than the *El-Waha* and cheaper than the *Badawiya*, it has cosy domed en-suite rooms with mosquito nets and Farafra's only low-budget safari outfit. BB ③

The village

Behind the school you'll find **Badr's Museum** (no set hours; £E10), the creation of a self-taught artist who has exhibited in Germany, France and Britain. His museum resembles a Disneyfied desert mansion, with reliefs of camels and farmers decorating its walls, and an antique wooden lock on the door. Its dozen-odd rooms exhibit Badr's rustic sculptures and surreal paintings, stuffed wildlife, weird fossils

and pyrites. Here, "Mr Socks" sells handknitted camel-hair mittens, hats and thick woolly socks, for those cold desert nights.

Otherwise, you can investigate the mud-brick **fortress** (*qasr*) that gives the village its name (though the full title isn't used in everyday speech). Until early in the twentieth century, Farafranis would retreat inside when invaders came; each family had a designated room, where, during normal times, provisions were stored and guarded by a watchman. Damaged by heavy rainfall, the fortress began to crumble in the 1950s; the less damaged parts are home to a few families, and blend into the surrounding houses.

You can also wander around the **palm groves** behind the village, which look especially lovely before sunset. They are divided into walled gardens planted with olive and fruit trees as well as date palms (whose branches are used to fence the land). You can walk the paths freely, but shouldn't enter the gardens uninvited; for single women to do so is regarded as provocative. Likewise, avert your eyes from the **men's bathhouse** on the edge of the village, where youths splash around in a concrete tank fed by a pipe gushing warm water. Foreigners are expected to bathe at other springs.

Come nightfall, there's little to do but hang out in teahouses or maybe wallow in the hot spring at Bir Setta (see below), unless you happen to chance upon a *zikr* in somebody's home. **Zikrs** play an important role in the religious and social life of Farafra; foreigners of both sexes are welcome, providing they respect that they are guests at a religious ritual, not spectators at a tourist attraction – which means modest dress and behaviour.

Local excursions

Besides the White Desert, there are other beauty spots around Farafra. **Bir Setta** is a concrete tank of sulphurous hot water that's good for wallowing but stains clothes brown. Three kilometres away, the turquoise lake of **Abu Nus** has only formed in the last ten years, but draws all kinds of wildlife. Further afield are Ain Besai, a cold pool beside the rock tombs and chapels of a settlement abandoned in Christian times; the small, uninhabited oasis of **Ain el-Tanien**; and **Ain Sheikh Mazouk**, a hot sulphur spring feeding a tank where local men bathe. While Bir Setta is accessible by taxi from town, and Ain Sheikh Mazouk is close enough to the highway to be reached by bus, the others require a jeep. This is also true of two sites of geological interest, namely an area of desert (known to safari guides) strewn with flower-shaped iron pyrites, and the **Valley of Shells** (Wadi el-Khawaka) out towards Abu Minqar. All these sites can be explored on jeep or camel safaris organized by Farafra's hotels for the same rates as their trips to the White Desert.

Eating and drinking

It doesn't take long to sample the culinary delights of Farafra. *Badawiya's* dining room serves freshly made pasta dishes, *kofta*, kebab and salads using organic vegetables from the hotel's farm; a meal costs £E30–80. *AquaSun*'s restaurant is hardly a convenient option, being out of town; its menu is much the same as *Badawiya*'s, anyway. In town, humbler **restaurants** serve simple meals until 7pm: omelette, *fuul* or liver at the *Mushroom Coffee Shop*; grilled chicken at the *El Waha* or *Hussein*; and spicy kebabs at the *Samir* (ask the price first). For *sheeshas,* tea or coffee, there are a few joints (one of which doubles as a bus stop) among the shops on the main street, where you'll also find a **bakery**. Nowhere in Farafra sells **alcohol** and only one shop (at the far end) stocks cigarettes.

Moving on from Farafra

Buses to Bahariya (2–3hr; £E20) and **Cairo** (8–10hr; £E40) leave around 10am and 10pm daily, with an extra bus to Cairo on Monday, Wednesday and Friday at 9am. You buy tickets on board and there's usually no problem getting a seat, but be sure to arrive in good time. Otherwise, there's a chance of **minibuses** to Bahariya, or lifts from cars that have just deposited tourists after a night in the White Desert.

Buses to Dakhla Oasis (4hr; £E20) leave between 1pm and 2pm and 1am and 2am. Minibuses also cover the route, once or twice a day. In a fully-loaded vehicle, passengers pay about £E20 each. If you're planning to do this, spread the word so drivers know that you're interested. Buses both ways can be flagged down outside the *Badawiya Hotel* (the police there will do it for you) and also stop at the teahouse among the shops in town for a few minutes.

El-Qaf and the Ghard Abu Muharrik

Some safari operators in Farafra and Bahariya run trips to **El-Qaf** – also known as Gara or Djara – a remote **stalactite cave** near the great sand barrier of the Ghard Abu Muharrik. Though known to Bedouin long before it was "discovered" by Gerhard Rohlfs in 1873, its whereabouts were forgotten until it was rediscovered by Carlo Bergmann in 1989. Archeologists have found stone arrowheads and knives predating similar tools in the Nile Valley by 500 years, suggesting that Neolithic technology originated in the desert. The cave was formed some 100,000 years ago but its limestone formations stopped growing when the rains ceased about 5000 BC. Since then it has filled with sand to a depth of 150m – what's visible today is a fraction of its totality. Some of the pure white stalactites and veil-formations are six metres tall; each one resonates with a different note if gently tapped at its point. Bring lighting – the cave isn't lit by electricity.

Equally impressive is the **Ghard Abu Muharrik** or "Dune with an Engine", which passes within 20km of El-Qaf on its way to Kharga Oasis. As Abu Muharrik consists of three stretches 100–125km long, separated by high, rocky ground, pedants dismiss its claim to be the longest dune in Africa, but it's still an awesome sight, dune piled upon dune from horizon to horizon. You can visit it after spending the night at El-Qaf, which is six or seven hours, drive from Bahariya or Farafra, though many safaris combine it with the White Desert and other localities over several days. Samir from Western Desert Safari in Bahariya (see p.404) has discovered what he calls a **Sand Volcano**, where sand blows up from a subterranean fissure – a phenomenon that has yet to be explained, that can only be seen on his tours.

The Hidden Valley and Ain Della

The far reaches of the Farafra depression can now be explored as an add-on to White Desert safaris, using a 24-hour **permit** obtained in Qasr al-Farafra or Bawiti – though few outfits offer it as an option or even know the way to the **Hidden Valley** behind the Qus Abu Said Plateau. A terrain similar to the White Desert on the other side of the highway but with volcanic massifs too, it even has stalactites in the **Al-Ubayyid Cave** – a miniature El-Qaf. Further on stands the **Infidel Rock**, an anthropomorphic rock formation that locals believe marks the last known location of the fabled Lost Army of Cambyses (see box, p.412). Huge chalk *inselbergs* dominate the plain beyond, which local guides have dubbed the **New White Desert**.

Until quite recently this whole area was off-limits due to the proximity of **Ain Della** ("Spring of the Shade"), which has played an epic part in the history of the Western Desert as the last waterhole before the Great Sand Sea. Used by raiders and smugglers since antiquity, explorers in the 1920s and 1930s, and the Long Range Desert Group in World War II, it now has a garrison of Border Guards that chases smugglers using 4WD instead of camels, as in the days of the Frontier Camel Corps.

The Lost Army of Cambyses

One of the most famous tales in the *Histories* of Herodotus is of the Persian conqueror **Cambyses** (525–522 BC), son of Cyrus the Great, who sent an army across the desert to destroy the Siwan Oracle. According to Herodotus, the 50,000-strong **army** marched from Thebes (Luxor) for seven days to an "oasis", and thence towards Siwa – which leaves room for doubt as to whether the oasis was Kharga or Farafra. Depending on which you favour, their last watering hole was Ain Amur or Ain Della, beyond which the army ran out of water and perished in the Great Sand Sea after a sandstorm scattered and buried the weakened troops. Some ascribe this disaster to the Persians miscalculating their longitude; others blame their ignorance of the environment. The mystery of where the **Lost Army** disappeared tantalized explorers such as Almássy (see p.435), who claimed to have found the site but never disclosed its location. In 2001, an Egyptian professor announced he had found it after discovering bronze arrowheads and human skeletons north of the Al-Ubayyid Cave, but failed to convince anyone; in 2010, two Italians claimed to have found Persian armour, but were denied permission to excavate. Others theorize that the army numbered far less than 50,000 (Persian sources routinely overestimated the size of armies), perhaps no larger than five thousand soldiers.

The road to Dakhla

Relatively few vehicles follow the 310-kilometre road **between Farafra and Dakhla Oasis**. Once you're past Ain Sheikh Mazouk, the desert shifts from white stone to gravel and sand until you reach **Abu Minqar** (Father of the Beak). A green smudge in the wilderness, where wells have been sunk and houses built in an effort to attract settlers, it is the westernmost point on the Great Desert Circuit, and an obligatory tea-stop. Beyond lie more gravel pans, where golden orioles flit across the highway as it veers towards the escarpment that delineates Dakhla Oasis, where you'll pass through Al-Qasr and Mut Talatta before reaching Mut, Dakhla's main centre.

Off-road to Dakhla Oasis

If you've got time to spare, this is an amazing journey that deserves several days, with constantly varying scenery. A paved road starting in Qasr al-Farafra runs out to **Bir Qarawein**, whose ancient well has now been supplemented by boreholes, allowing watermelons to be grown among dunes that are perfect for **sandboarding**. By turning off the road halfway to Qarawein, you can follow a track to the sweet-water spring of **Bir Dikkur**, marked by two palms and a camel's skeleton, and into the **dune lanes** that advance in a southeasterly direction. Some have trees protruding from their crests, where the dunes have buried whole palm groves on their relentless march towards Dakhla. Further on lie the **Black Valley**, whose floor is covered in iron pyrites, and the **Marble Labyrinth**, whose sharp stones are equally hard on tyres. Mobile phones don't work beyond Bir Dikkur. The route ends with a steep **descent** from the plateau to Al-Qasr (see p.418) in Dakhla.

Dakhla Oasis

Verdant cultivated areas and a great wall of rose-hued rock across the northern horizon make a feast for the eyes in **Dakhla Oasis**. Partitioned by dunes into more or less irrigated, fertile enclaves, the oasis supports 75,000 people living in fourteen settlements strung out along the Farafra and Kharga roads. Although it's the outlying sites that hold most attraction, the majority of travellers base themselves in or near **Mut**, Dakhla's "capital". Minibuses between Mut and the villages enable you to see how the Dakhlans have reclaimed land, planted new crops, and generally made the best of New Valley developments.

Most **villages** have spread down from their original hilltop maze of medieval houses and covered streets, into a roadside straggle of breeze-block houses, schools and other public buildings. Besides Islamic architecture, Dakhla has pharaonic, Roman and Coptic antiquities, dunes, palm groves and hot springs to explore.

Mut

Dakhla's capital, **MUT** (pronounced "moot"), was branded a miserable-looking place by travellers early in the nineteenth century, but it has come on apace since the 1950s, as the Dakhlans have subverted or embraced planned modernity according to their needs and tastes. The architect of Mut's already crumbling low-rise flats is unlikely to have foreseen their balconies being converted into extra rooms or pigeon coops, and the four-lane Sharia al-Wadi that snakes through town carries more cyclists than cars.

Arrival and information

Arriving by bus you can get off at Midan Tahrir (rather than Midan Gam'a, where buses terminate), 250m from Mut's **tourist office** (daily 8am–2pm, and maybe 6–9pm; ⓣ092/782-1686 or 012 179-6467, ⓔdesertlord@hotmail.com). Omar Ahmed is knowledgeable and helpful; organizing excursions to the fury of local **safari operators** Nasser (who owns the *Nasser Hotel & Camp* in Sheikh Wali and whose brothers own the *Ahmed Hamdy*, *Hamdy* and *Abu Mohammed* restaurants) and the guys at the *Anwar Hotel* – who complain of him demanding kick-backs from taxi drivers. Larger safari outfits like Badawiya, Zarzora and Dabuka (see p.380) are also represented in Dakhla. All are useful sources of **information**, bearing in mind that they'll try to persuade you to sign up for an excursion.

Mut's Banque Misr (daily except Fri 8am–2pm) has an ATM and changes **money**. Menatel card-phones all over town can be used for international calls if you can't be bothered to queue at the **telephone exchange** on Sharia es-Salam (24hr). There are **post offices** on Midan Gam'a and beside the telephone exchange (daily except Fri 8am–2pm), and **internet** access at the *Abu Mohammed Restaurant* (£E15 per hour), the *El-Forsan Hotel* (£E10 per hour) and MDO Net (£E10 per hour).

Mut's Central **hospital** (ⓣ092/782-1555) is well equipped by the standards of the Western Desert, located 1500m from Midan Tahrir along Sharia Mut-Balat, past the **police** (ⓣ092/782-1500) and Government Building, with fuel stations and car repair shops further along the road.

Accommodation

Dakhla offers a wide range of **accommodation** – less so in Mut itself than out at Mut Talatta springs (see p.418) or further afield in Sheikh Wali (p.420), El-Douhous (p.418), Al-Qasr (p.418), off the road between Rashda and Budkulu (p.418) or out at Bir el-Gabel (p.418). All except the last two are readily accessible by minibus; their locations are shown on the map on p.417. The **water** supply is cut off in Mut (but not elsewhere) at 10pm.

Mut

Anwar Sharia es-Salam ⓣ092/782-0070 or 018 327-8732. The only hotel in Mut running its own safaris and minibuses to Luxor, its clean-ish rooms have fans or a/c and shared bathrooms. ❷

El-Forsan Sharia al-Wadi ⓣ092/782-1343, ⓦwww.elforsanhotel.com. Decent rooms with fans (en suite costs £E50 more) and larger, airless bungalows out back. The hotel has internet access, a hilltop garden and coffeeshop with a view of Old Mut. ❶

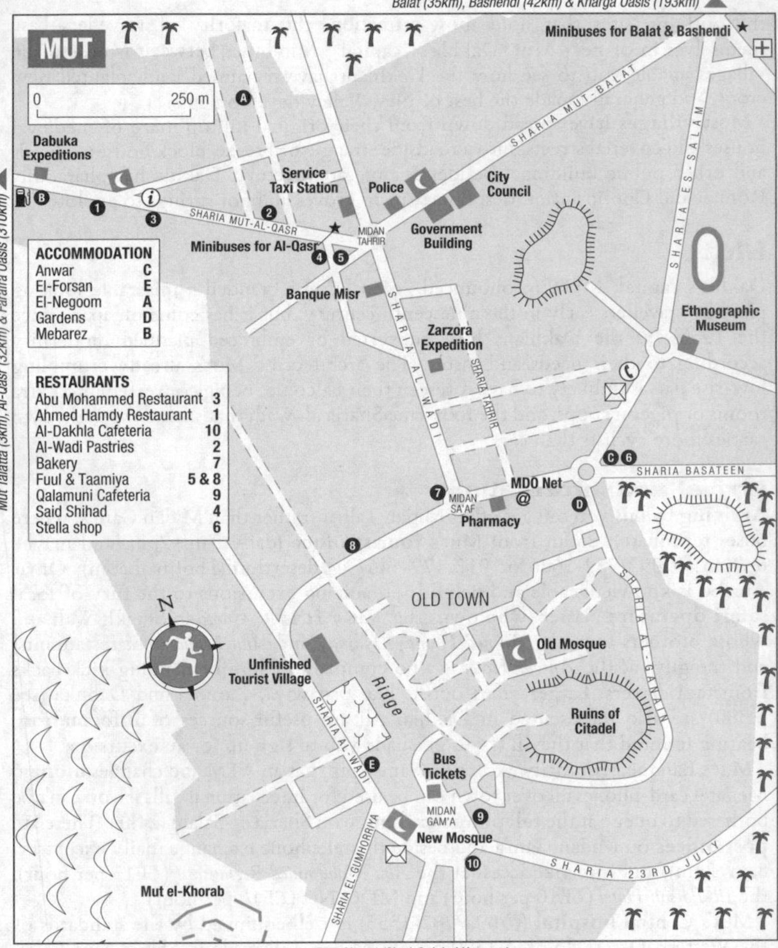

El-Negoom A few blocks behind the tourist office ⓣ092/782-0014, ⓕ782-3084. Quiet, clean and welcoming, with a large garden and patio. Most rooms have a/c, phones and en-suite facilities, or share a bathroom and a TV lounge with two other rooms. BB ③

Gardens Sharia Al-Ganain ⓣ092/782-1577. As cheap as you'll find in Dakhla, this very shabby, friendly hotel has small rooms with fans and lumpy beds (only £E16 for a double; £E25 with shower), and a dusty palm garden. ①

Mebarez Sharia Mut-Al-Qasr ⓣ092/782-1524, ⓔmebareztouristhotel@hotmail.com. Popular with safari groups, it has en-suite a/c rooms with soft beds, fridges and satellite TV. Staff are grumpy however, and guests should phone ahead to ask them to fill the tepid spring-fed pool out back. BB ③

Mut Talatta

Sol y Mar Mut Inn 3km from Mut ⓣ092/792-7982, ⓦwww.solymar.com. With its dinky en-suite chalets around a large spring-fed hot pool where alcohol is served, this place is nice but a bit overpriced – you'd do better staying elsewhere and paying £E10 to use its pool. Rates include half-board. ⑥

Sheikh Wali

Nasser Hotel & Camp 5km from Mut ⓣ092/782-2727 or 010 682-6467. Basic rooms with fans and shared bathrooms, beneath a lukewarm rooftop pool fed by spring-water. Travellers pay £E30 each or £E25 to pitch a tent in the yard. Nasser offers jeep and camel safaris, and natural healing. BB ❷

El-Douhous

El-Douhous Village 8km from Mut ⓣ092/785-0480 or 010 644-5154, ⓦwww.dakhlabedouins.com. A Disneyesque hilltop complex of en-suite rooms (£E120 for a double), domed a/c chalets with fridges, and basic reed huts (double £E50). Its Bedouin owner Hagg Abd El Hameed organizes safaris around Dakhla Oasis and the White Desert, and extended camel treks to Siwa (see p.438). BB ❶

Between Rashda and Budkhulu

Al Tarfa Desert Sanctuary 17km from Mut ⓣ092/910-5007, ⓦwww.altarfalodge.com. Favoured by the likes of Robert De Niro and managed by retired explorer Wael Abed, this gorgeous deluxe ecolodge has 20 individually-styled suites and rooms set far apart for privacy, a sauna, hammam, gym, massage, indoor and outdoor pools. Horse- and camel-rides (€15) arranged. Rates include a daily guided walk, use of the spa, and full board (excluding alcohol). ❾

Bir el-Gabal

Badawiya Dakhla 31km from Mut ⓣ092/772-7451, ⓦwww.badawiya.com. Built around a bleak hill beside the highway, this latest venture by the Ali family from Farafra (see p.408) has en-suite chalets with a/c, fridges and kingsize beds, and a swimming pool with fine views of the desert. ❻

Bir el-Gabal Camp 37km from Mut ⓣ012 106-8227. Out towards the escarpment, it has simple rooms with fans sharing bathrooms, naturally cooled en-suite ones for £E40 more, and a warm plunge pool nearby. You can arrange camel treks here or rent a bike (£E15/day) to explore Al-Qasr. BB ❷

Al-Qasr

Al-Qasr Resthouse 32km from Mut ⓣ092/772-6013 or 012 106-8227. Flyblown yet friendly, with triple-bed dorms sharing a bathroom, it's favoured by long-stay travellers who like its rock-bottom prices and proximity to Al-Qasr's old town. Under the same management as *Bir el-Gabal Camp*. ❶

Desert Lodge 33km from Mut ⓣ092/772-7602, ⓦwww.desertlodge.net. Set on a barren hilltop behind Old Qasr, it has ravishing desert views, internet, a library and classes in yoga, Arabic and calligraphy – all very classy, but its staff could be a lot more welcoming. BB ❻

The Town

With its low-rise blocks and wide streets, the **New Town** which compromises most of present-day Mut presumably once looked good on a drawing board. Sharia al-Wadi runs past **Hassan Fathy**'s pioneering design for a **tourist village**, signposted as a national monument (never finished, it later inspired similar complexes all over Egypt), but there are no directions to the **Old Town** behind the ridge. Mut originated as a hilltop *qasr* or **citadel**, divided into quarters separated by gates that were locked at night. Though the summit is in ruins, the lanes below are still bustling with life and fun to explore (though perhaps not for women on their own). You can enter from the north and exit on to Midan Gam'a, using the Old and New **mosques** as landmarks. **Midan Gam'a** used to be the hub of social life but is pretty sleepy nowadays, despite its role as a bus and service taxi terminus.

Off to the south you can glimpse the remains of **Mut el-Khorab** ("Mut the Ruined"), an ancient city dedicated to the Theban goddess Mut. Fennec foxes dwell in burrows in the sides of pits left by treasure-hunters, emerging to hunt at dusk, and can be seen on the way back from enjoying the sunset over the **dunes** that rise beyond the fields. This is the most accessible dune field in Dakhla, but not the finest.

By arrangement with the tourist office, you can visit Mut's **Ethnographic Museum** (£E3), ordered like a family dwelling, with household objects on the walls and a complex wooden lock on the palm-log door. Its seven rooms contain clay figures posed in scenes from village life, by the Khargan artist Mabrouk. Preparing the bride and celebrating the pilgrim's return from Mecca are two scenes that remain part of oasis life today.

Natural healing

As in Bahariya, there's a niche market in **natural healing** and spiritual tourism. Nasser and his wife at Sheikh Wali offer massage, herbal medicine and Islamic prayers and charms for diverse afflictions. The *Anwar* hotel can arrange bathing at hot springs and a "hot sand spa" for £E300 per person (including meals, transport and lodging), while guests at the *Al Tarfa Desert Sanctuary* can enjoy Turkish, Finnish, Japanese and Thai spa and massage treatments (see "Accommodation"). Or you can simply head out to Mut Talatta, to wallow in their hot pool for only £E10.

Eating and drinking

Most **restaurants** in Mut offer similar menus of soup, pasta or rice, vegetable stew, chicken, or *kofta*, for £E20–35 all in. The *Abu Mohammed* restaurant on Sharia Mut-Al-Qasr comes in just ahead of the nearby *Ahmed Hamdy,* while *Said Shihad* tops both with its spicy lamb kebabs. The *Qalamuni Cafeteria* on Midan Gam'a does a few dishes, too, unlike the nearby *Al-Dakhla*, which just serves drinks. Otherwise, you can buy *fuul* and *taamiya* off Midan Tahrir and on Sharia al-Wadi; hot rolls from the **bakery** on Midan Sa'af; fruit at the **market** on Tahrir; or freshly-baked *fiteer* (sweet, or with cheese if you bring some along) at *Al-Wadi Pastries* on Sharia Mut-Al-Qasr. **Beer** is only available at the Stella shop on Sharia Basateen (for £E15; open in the evening) and the *Abu Mohammed* restaurant (for £E20) – though you can enjoy a beer (£E19) or a bottle of wine (£E115) around the hot pool at Mut Talatta (see p.418).

Moving on from Mut

Upper Egypt **buses** leave Mut for **Kharga** (3hr; £E12–15) daily at 6am, 7pm, 8pm and 10pm, continuing on to **Assyut** (8hr; £E24). For **Farafra** (4hr; £E17), **Bahariya** (6hr; £E30) and **Cairo** (13hr; £E50–60) the bus departs at 6am and 5pm. There are also a/c Superjet buses to Cairo (13hr; £E70) at 7pm and 8pm daily, routed via Kharga and Assyut. Tickets to Cairo should be purchased the day before. All buses leave from Midan Gam'a, where tickets are sold; by buying them the day before you can board at Midan Tahrir or Al-Qasr if it's easier. **Minibuses** and **service taxis** also run from Midan Gam'a to the other New Valley oases and charge similar rates to the buses providing they are full. The *Anwar* hotel can arrange a car (£E600) or minivan (£E1000) to **Luxor** (10hr). Before leaving Mut, **motorists** should fill up with fuel, as there's no more petrol until Kharga or Farafra. A weekly **flight** to **Cairo**, operated by a petroleum company, departs at 4pm on Tuesday. Tickets (£E500 one-way) are sold in the Government Building near Midan Tahrir; contact Kemal Safina (☎092/782-1514 or 016 034-3158).

Around the oasis

Transport around Dakhla is hit and miss, depending on your destination. **Taxis** are the priciest option – bargain hard if you want the driver to wait at sites and then return to Mut, or try Omar at the tourist office, who can fix a taxi with no hassle, or a **minibus** or **4WD**, with driver.

Public transport consists of green-and-white **minibuses**, running out towards both ends of the oasis. Minibuses to Al-Qasr (£E1.50–2) and other western villages pick up passengers near the corner of the Al-Qasr road and Midan Tahrir, while vehicles for Balat (£E2) leave from a depot beyond the hospital. Between 2 and 3pm, you're unlikely to get a ride as all the minibuses are full of schoolkids travelling home.

Local farmers get around in covered **pick-ups**, which usually charge minibus rates, though you may get a free lift or, conversely, be expected to pay "special"

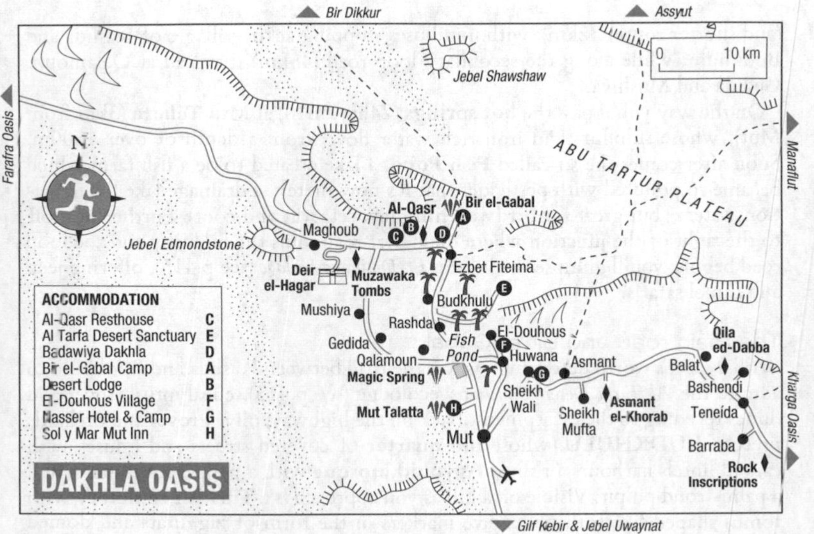

rates. Cycling is feasible in winter and **bikes** can be rented from the *Abu Mohammed* restaurant or *Gardens* hotel for £E15 a day. You need to be fit, though, since visiting outlying villages will involve a round trip of at least 60km.

As some places are hard to reach, and it takes local knowledge of natural beauty spots to get the best from Dakhla, organized **excursions** can be a good idea. Omar at the tourist office can arrange half-day trips either to the east or the west (£E150 for the car) or a full day-trip to both (£E300; £E500 by 4WD), focusing on local antiquities. Other tours combine Al-Qasr with the Magic Spring and dunes. The *Abu Mohammed* restaurant quotes £E120 per person for a day-trip also featuring the Muzawaka Tombs and Qalamoun; for a similar trip ending at an old Islamic cemetery near the escarpment the *Anwar* hotel asks £E100 – as they do for an **overnight** trip by jeep or camel (minimum three people; meals included).

The Bedouin at *El-Douhous Village* (see p.415) offer overnight jeep trips (£E150 per person), **camel trekking** in the **White Desert** (£E300 per person per day for a minimum of seven people) and a one-month trek to **Siwa Oasis** (£E400 per person daily; minimum three people). Safaris to the **Gilf Kebir** (from €120 per person daily) are the preserve of Badawiya Expedition at the *Badawiya Dakhla* hotel (see p.415), Zarzora Expedition (5 Sharia Tahrir ⓣ092/782-2860) and Dabuka Expeditions (Sharia Mut–Al-Qasr ⓣ092/782-4045) in Mut (see map, p.414).

North of Mut

Most visitors are initially drawn to the western part of the oasis by the village of **Al-Qasr**, which is deservedly renowned for its old town, an abandoned enclave of medieval mud-brick architecture. The **Muzawaka Tombs** are also within striking distance, as is the restored Roman temple of **Deir al-Hagar**, which lies further from the main road. To cover more ground than this requires days to spare or private transport. Shop around the various safari operators in Mut for trips to other villages, or **springs** and **dunes** you can reach by camel at sunset (staying overnight if desired).

There are two **routes** to Al-Qasr via different villages, so, if you can, it's worth following one out and the other one back. Most traffic leaves Mut by the main road (and shorter route; 32km), with minibuses stopping at the villages of Rashda and Budkhulu; while along the secondary loop road (45km) they call at Qalamoun, Gedida and Mushiya.

On the way you'll pass the **hot springs** (24hr; £E10) at **Mut Talatta** (3km from Mut), whose sulphur- and iron-rich water flows from a depth of over 1000m. Soon after comes the so-called **Fish Pond**, a lake created to be a fish farm which became so polluted with pesticides that it's now merely a drainage lake for irrigation water – but great for **birdwatching** (avocet, stilt and coot). Further out, off to the right of the junction where the desert road joins the highway and the loop road begins, you'll glimpse the hilltop *El-Douhous Village* (see p.415), offering jeep and camel safaris.

The main road and Bir el-Gabal

With a car it's worth detouring east off the road between Rashda and Budkhulu to admire the *Al Tarfa Desert Sanctuary* ecolodge (see p.415), eucalyptus groves and dunes receding to the escarpment. Back on the highway, olive groves and orchards precede **BUDKHULU**, whose **old quarter** of covered streets and houses with carved lintels harbours a ruined **Ayyubid mosque** with a pepperpot minaret and a palm-frond pulpit. Visible on a hill as you approach is a **Turkish cemetery** with tombs shaped like bathtubs, grave markers in the form of ziggurats and domed shrines: the freshly painted one belongs to a revered local sheikh, Tawfiq Abdel Aziz.

Shortly before Al-Qasr, the *Badawiya Dakhla* hotel (see p.415) is an eyesore marking the turning off the highway that leads to **Bir el-Gabal** (6km) on the desert's edge. Here, *Bir el-Gabal Camp* (see p.415) organizes camel trekking and rents bicycles – making it a feasible base for visiting Al-Qasr – and a villa owned by a German woman hosts **meditation** courses.

The loop road

Tourists are often taken to bathe at the **Magic Spring**, a warm, deep waterhole fringed by palms, that's so-named by tour guides because bubbles rising up from below make it impossible to touch the bottom. The spring is just off the **loop road** to Al-Qasr, which links three villages interspersed by stagnant pools and desert. **QALAMOUN** dates back to pharaonic times, and many families are descended from Mamluke and Turkish officials once stationed here. Shortly before reaching **Mushiya**, the road passes **Bir Mushiya**, a keyhole-shaped tank fed by a tepid spring, where tourists are also taken to bathe. The loop road joins the highway opposite a golden **dune field**. Originating as longitudinal dunes on the plateau above the escarpment, they cascade down the cliff to reform as crescent dunes below, and continue their way southwards. Tourists are brought here by jeep or camel to enjoy rolling down the dunes and to take in the view at sunset.

Al-Qasr

AL-QASR (or Al-'Asr, as locals say) is a must – an amazing Islamic settlement built upon Roman foundations, that may be the longest continually inhabited site in the oasis and was indubitably Dakhla's medieval capital. Three or four families still live in the mud-brick old town crowning a ridge above palm groves and a salt lake, set back from New Qasr beside the highway. The "border" is marked by **handicrafts** sellers beside the New Mosque and a **tour centre** (daily 9am–5pm) where you can pick up a guide to lead you around and unlock houses and workshops. Pay him at the end – £E10 per group seems fair.

Beyond the twelfth-century **Nasr el-Din Mosque**, whose 21-metre-high **minaret** has a "pepperpot" finial typical of Ayyubid architecture, you enter a maze of high-walled alleyways and gloomy **covered passages**. Many of the houses here have acacia-wood **lintels** whose cursive or Kufic inscriptions name the builders or occupants (the oldest dates from 1518): look out for **doorways** with Pharaonic stonework and arabesque carvings, **archways** with *ablaq* brickwork, and a **frieze** painted in one of the passageways. Near the **House of Abu Nafir** – built over a Ptolemaic temple, with hieroglyphics on its door jambs – is a donkey-powered **grain-mill**.

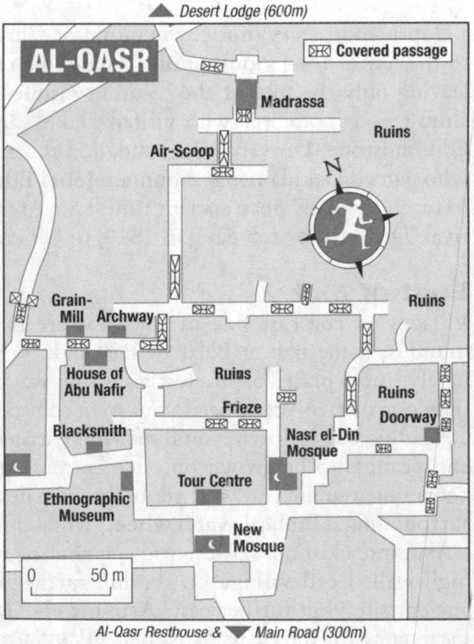

Another interesting feature is the rooftop *mala'af* or **air-scoop**, incorporated into an especially long T-shaped passage to convey breezes into the labyrinth. Beyond here is a tenth-century **madrassa** (school and court), featuring painted *liwans*, niches for legal texts, cells for felons, and a beam above the door for whippings. The maze of alleyways also harbours a restored **blacksmith**'s forge and an antique **waterwheel** (*saqqiya*). For more information on these and other facets of the old way of life, check out the **Ethnographic Museum** (daily 10am–5pm; £E5) near the tour centre, founded by the anthropologist Aliya Hussein and containing artefacts and photos from all of the oases in the Western Desert.

If you fancy **staying** there's the *Al-Qasr Resthouse* beside the main road, or the *Desert Lodge* on a hill behind the old town (see p.415 for details). Both serve **meals**.

The Muzawaka Tombs

Five kilometres west along the highway from Al-Qasr, a signpost indicates the track to the **Muzawaka Tombs**, a twenty-minute walk or a slow drive through the silent desert, past rock buttes gouged with empty tombs. Of the three hundred or so recorded by Egyptologist Ahmed Fakhry in 1972, two deserve his exclamation "Muza!" (Decorations), from which their name derives. Both have been **closed** for years as restoring their murals has proved far harder than anticipated – but tour groups often come here anyway to see the eerie-looking site and peer into a tomb full of leathery embalmed corpses (baksheesh expected).

Deir al-Hagar

Unless you've chartered a taxi, getting to **Deir al-Hagar** (daily 8am–sunset; £E25) demands commitment. A kilometre beyond the Muzawaka turning off the highway, an unmarked road runs south past some Roman ruins to a small, colourfully painted village (1km); beyond here a track crosses a ridge, whereupon the temple becomes visible on the right. Notwithstanding its Arabic name, "Stone Monastery", Deir al-Hagar is actually a Roman temple dedicated to the Theban Triad and the god of the oasis, Seth. Its sandstone Hypostyle Hall, sanctuary and brick enclosure wall were built in the first century AD, under emperors Nero, Vespasian, Titus and Domitian (whose cartouches can be seen) and later served as a Coptic monastery (notice the mural of Christ, the lion and the lamb, in a niche to the left of the pylon), until a huge dune consumed it, collapsing the roof and leaving only the tops of the columns visible. One is inscribed with the names of almost every explorer who visited Dakhla in the nineteenth century, including Edmondstone, Drovetti, Cailliaud, and the entire Rohlfs expedition. It was they who named Dakhla's only mountain **Jebel Edmondstone**, after the first European to reach the oasis since ancient times; Sir Archibald Edmondstone beat his French rival, Drovetti, by ten days, in 1819, to "discover" it in the name of England.

East of Mut

Villages on the east side of the oasis are more or less accessible from Mut by minibus; some halt at Balat or Bashendi, others go as far as Teneida. Unfortunately, most places of interest are some way off the main road, so to visit more than one or two you'll need your own transport.

Heading out of town, you'll see where irrigation canals have enabled wheat, rice and peanuts to be grown on once barren land. **Sheikh Wali** is on the verge of becoming a suburb of Mut, yet backs onto desert, with olive groves and goat-pens surrounding a Biblical **waterwheel**, while dunes swell in the distance.

Asmant, 6km on, has the usual sprawl of modern buildings by the road and a high-walled **old village** on the hill further back, which lend their name to an ancient site 9km further east. **Asmant el-Khorab** ("Asmant the Ruined") is the local name for the **ruins of Kellis**, a Roman and Coptic town inhabited for seven centuries, whose temples and churches mark the shift from pagan Rome to Byzantine Christianity; one of the **churches** dates back to the end of the first century AD. The Dakhla Oasis Project has unearthed the remains of aqueducts, farmhouses and tombs, including 34 mummies and wooden codices, casting light on religion and daily life in the third century AD. The site is **off-limits** while excavations continue.

Balat and Qila ed-Dabba

After the stretch of desert beyond Asmant one welcomes the casuarina-tree-lined road through **BALAT**, whose teahouse is a *de facto* bus stop. Cross the road to explore the old village beyond the TV mast, with its 300-year-old **mosque** upheld by palm-trunks, and a maze of twisting **covered streets** that protect the villagers from sun and sandstorms and once prevented invaders from entering on horseback. Painted oxblood, salmon, terracotta or pale blue, with carved lintels and wooden peg-locks, its mud-brick **houses** are only slightly less impressive than the ones in Al-Qasr, with many still inhabited. Although the oldest dates from Mamluke times, Balat was a town and a governors' seat (its name means "Palace of the Lord") way back in the Old Kingdom, when it prospered through trade with Kush (ancient Nubia).

There's proof of this in Balat's ancient necropolis, known to the locals as **Qila ed-Dabba**, where five mud-brick *mastabas*, once clad in limestone but long ago reduced to lumps, mark the **tombs of VI Dynasty governors**. In 1986, French archeologists discovered an intact one from the reign of Pepi II (2292–2203 BC) by excavating a deep pit to expose the burial chamber (daily 8am–sunset; £E25). Its painted reliefs are faint, but you can see the governor, Khentika, his wife and son; people ploughing, driving cattle and sailing boats. The ticket is also valid for the ruins at **Ain Asil**, 1500m east of the necropolis, where a fortress and farming community whose name meant "Our Root is Lasting in the Oasis" existed from the Old Kingdom until Ptolemaic times. Both sites are reached by a track 100m east of Balat's teahouse, and from Ain Asil a back road continues to Bashendi – about 5km in all.

Bashendi

Minibuses either terminate at or pass the turning for the village of **BASHENDI**, 2km off the main road. Its name derives from Pasha Hindi, a medieval sheikh who is buried in the local cemetery, which dates back to Roman times. Tombs form the foundations of many of the houses, which are painted pale blue or buttercup yellow with floral friezes and hajj scenes, merging into the ground in graceful curves. The cemetery is at the back, where the desert begins. Empty sarcophagi separate the domed tomb of Pasha Hindi from the square **Tomb of Kitnes**. While both structures are of Roman origin, the latter still retains its original funerary reliefs, depicting Kitnes meeting the desert-gods Min, Seth and Shu. Its key is held by a villager who can be fetched, but since admission costs £E25, you might settle for viewing its pharaonic lintels.

Teneida and the road to Kharga

TENEIDA, on the eastern edge of the oasis, is a modern affair centred on a leafy square, whose only "sight" is a **cemetery** with weird tombstones resembling tiny houses. With a car, you can press on to see some **rock inscriptions** off the highway 10km beyond Teneida. The carvings include an ostrich at the base of the sandstone outcrop beside the road, while beyond some fields another rock shaped like a seated camel is covered in prehistoric and Bedouin drawings of giraffes, camels and hunters, as well as the name of Jarvis (British governor of Dakhla and Kharga in the 1930s) and many other visitors.

Beyond the last flourish of greenery, wind-sculpted rocks give way to dun table-tops and gravelly sand, persisting for most of the way from Dakhla to Kharga (193km). Following the Darb el-Ghabari or "Dust Road", the modern road skirts the phosphate-rich Abu Tartur Plateau that separates the two depressions. The appearance of a phosphates factory 45km outside Kharga alerts you for a treat to follow. Golden **dunes** march across the depression, burying lines of telegraph poles and encroaching on the highway. Villagers faced with their advance have been known to add an extra storey to their house, live there while the dune consumes the ground floor and move back downstairs once it has passed on. These dunes are outstretched fingers of the **Ghard Abu Muharrik** (see p.411), of the type known as "whalebacked".

Kharga Oasis

Despite being the nearest of the oases to Luxor and the New Valley's capital, **Kharga Oasis** gets far fewer tourists than the others. **El-Kharga** is a 1970s metropolis of sixty thousand people with adequate facilities and a decent museum, but otherwise dull. While the oasis contains many ancient sites, most are only accessible by car, and the local police insist on accompanying tourists everywhere in town, even radioing HQ for permission before letting them step outside their hotel – which hardly makes for a comfortable atmosphere.

Submerged by the sea aeons ago, leaving fossils on the high plateau, the Kharga depression is hemmed in by 350-foot-high cliffs, with belts of dunes advancing across the oasis. It's thought that there were no dunes in Kharga during Roman times; myth has it that they erected a brass cow on the escarpment, which swallowed up the sand. Historically, Kharga's importance is due to the desert trade routes that converged on the oasis, notably the **Forty Days Road** (see p.430). Deserted Roman forts and villages that claim descent from Mamluke soldiers attest to centuries of firm control by Egypt's rulers, who have used

Kharga as a place of exile since antiquity. Today, Islamists are incarcerated in the tuberculosis-ridden **Kharga Prison** (visible from the highway as one enters the oasis from the north).

Kharga is also seen by some as a portent that the New Valley spells ruin for the oases. The influx of *fellaheen* from the Nile Valley has changed agricultural practices; **rice** cultivation has proved more water-intensive than expected, depleting aquifers and turning land saline – leading to strict limits on its production.

It's indicative of the mixed antecedents of its citizens that the **name** Kharga may be pronounced "Harga" or "Harjah", depending on who's talking. Both the oasis and its capital are called Kharga; we've used the prefix "El-" to refer to the city.

El-Kharga

As the capital of the New Valley Governorate (comprising Kharga, Dakhla and Farafra oases), **EL-KHARGA** has grown into a sprawl of mid-rise buildings and highways, with the only reminder of its romantic oasis-town origins being the souk and lush palm groves. Banks and government buildings line the wide **Sharia Gamal Abdel Nasser**, which is too long and monotonous for pleasant walking, despite its ornamental obelisks, arches and shrubs. But **getting around** is easy, with green-and-white minibuses shuttling along Sharia Gamal Abdel Nasser, between Midan Showla and the Mabrouk Fountain, at either end of town (50pt–£E1 fare). The only impediment to one's freedom of movement is the police – though they'll agree to withdraw their plainclothes **escort** if you write a letter stating that you don't need one.

Arrival and information

Arriving by bus, it makes sense to decide on a hotel and get dropped off at the nearest point, rather than riding on to the bus station off Midan Basateen. At the **tourist office,** by the Mabrouk Fountain on Sharia Gamal Abdel Nasser (Mon–Thurs & Sun 8.30am–2pm and maybe 4–10pm; ⓣ092/792-1206 or 010 180-6127), Mohsen speaks good English and offers tours of the oasis (see p.426). The **tourist police** (ⓣ092/792-1367; 24hr) are next door to the tourist office, with the regular **police** across the road.

You can change **money** at the Banque du Caire (which has an ATM) and Banque Misr (both daily except Fri 8.30am–2.30pm & 5.30–8pm). The **telephone** exchange (24hr) and main **post office** (daily except Fri 8am–2.30pm) are both on Midan Abdel Moneem Riad, with several **internet** cafes in a block's radius of Midan Basateen. The private Al-Salam **hospital** opposite the Museum of the New Valley is better than the public one on Sharia el-Nabawy, where there are also several **pharmacies**.

Accommodation

There's no problem with finding accommodation in El-Kharga, though it's not always great value. Staying outside town is feasible with a car but somewhat awkward if you're relying on local transport, although two options are actually within walking distance of temples (see the map on p.426 for locations).

El-Kharga

Dar Al-Bayda Off Midan Showla ⓣ092/792-1717. Recently redecorated in lurid colours, this hotel is handy for the service taxi station but noisy. Most rooms have TV and fans, some have baths; internet in the lobby. BB ❷

El-Kharga Oasis Sharia Aref ⓣ092/792-4940. Large a/c rooms with soft beds, bathrooms, and balconies overlooking a huge palm garden (where you can pitch a tent for £E25) – it sounds great, but the hotel is always weirdly empty and the garden is rife with mosquitoes. BB ❷

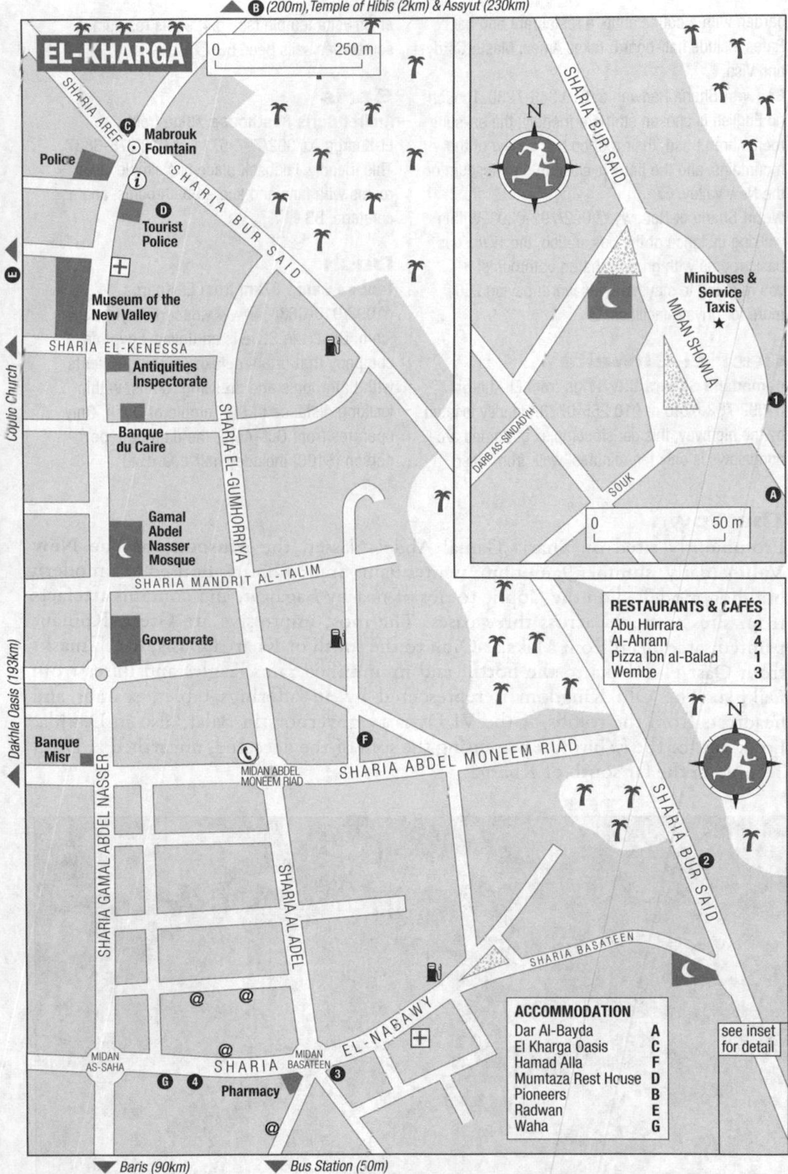

Hamad Alla Off Sharia Abdel Moneem Riad ⓣ092/792-0638. On a quiet backstreet, this small, dark place has rooms with soft beds; some have bathrooms, a/c, fridges, TV, heaters and balconies. Ask to see a few before deciding. BB ❷

Mumtaza Rest House A government resthouse behind the tourist office (which handles reservations), with four carpeted chalets (fan or a/c) sleeping up to nine people in dorms (£E25 per bed), plus TV, bath and phone. ❶

Pioneers ⓣ092/792-9751, ⓦwww.solymar.com. Out towards the Temple of Hibis, Kharga's fanciest hotel has a/c rooms with satellite TV around a large swimming pool, a lush garden with a coffee shop, a restaurant and bar. Rates include half-board. Takes Amex, MasterCard and Visa. 7

Radwan Sharia Radwan ⓣ010 345-7230. Though no English is spoken staff are friendly, the en-suite rooms aren't bad, their rooftop has a view of the mountains, and the hotel is close to the Museum of the New Valley. 2

Waha Sharia el-Nabawy ⓣ092/792-0393. Within walking distance of the bus station, the *Waha* has basic rooms with grungy shared bathrooms; if you're going to stay here, it's worth paying £E6 more for private facilities. 1

Qasr el-Ghweita

Hamadalla Sahara City 17km from El-Kharga ⓣ092/762-0240 or 010 255-0773. Handily located by the highway, this garish complex of domed a/c bungalows is only ten minutes' walk from Qasr el-Ghweita temple (see p.429). Its restaurant sometimes sells beer. BB 3

Baris

Amiret Baris Resthouse 70km from El-Kharga ⓣ092/797-5711 or 012 376-6837. This friendly, laidback place has simple clean rooms with fans and shared bathrooms, and a cafeteria. BB 2

Dush

Tabuna Camp 87km from El-Kharga ⓣ092/910-0688, ⓦwww.desertinstyle-egypt.com. Desert in Style is an Italian-Egyptian company that offers deluxe camping in tents with bathrooms and dressing rooms, within walking distance of the Temple of Dush. Only operates from Oct–April; the daily rate per person ($100) includes half-board. 8

The Town

Prominently sited on Sharia Gamal Abdel Nasser, the **Museum of the New Valley** (daily: summer 9am–6pm; winter 9am–5pm; £E30) is housed in a modern building modelled on the Coptic tombs of nearby Bagawat, and contains artefacts from sites scattered across three oases. The most impressive are Greco-Roman: painted sarcophagi from Maks al-Qibli to the south of Kharga Oasis; death masks from Qasr el-Labeka to the north; and mummified rams, eagles and ibises from Dakhla. The Old Kingdom is represented by an offerings tablet, scarabs and headrests from the tombs of the VI Dynasty governors in Balat, also in Dakhla. Look out for the *ba* birds, representing the soul of the deceased, unearthed at Dush Temple in the far south of Kharga.

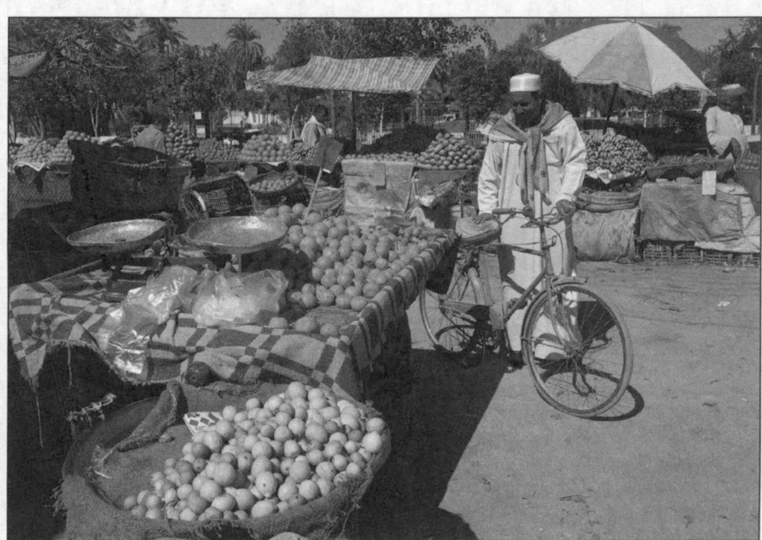

▲ The souk in El-Kharga

While in the vicinity, check out the (dry) **Mabrouk Fountain**, just up the road at the main junction, created by a local artist in three days. Its lusty figures symbolize Mother Egypt dragging her unwilling child (the oases) towards its destiny.

Aside from the **Gamal Abdel Nasser Mosque** and a **Coptic Church** located off the high road, there's nothing else to see until you reach the lower town (take a minibus, rather than walk the 2–3km), centred on **Midan Showla**. A lively **souk** runs off into an old quarter of mud houses painted apricot or azure and daubed with the Hand of Fatima. Turn right at the first crossroads and then left to find the **Darb as-Sindadyh**, a dark, serpentine alley roofed with palm trunks, which once extended over 4km; only the initial renovated stretch remains nowadays.

Though El-Kharga is no longer encircled by **palm groves**, they still flourish beyond Sharia Bur Said, and dates play an important part in the social calendar. **City Day** (Oct 3) celebrates the beginning of the date harvest with a parade of floats along Sharia Gamal Abdel Nasser, and the marriage season is also timed to coincide with the flowering of the date crop (from July until harvest time).

Eating, drinking and swimming

The *Pioneers Hotel* **restaurant** features a buffet supper (€10) when tour groups are staying, and otherwise offers an à la carte menu of continental and Egyptian dishes. You can eat well for £E70 (excluding drinks). Other hotels offer variations on a three-course meal (£E30–50) of soup, chicken, rice and salad, as do *Wembe* on Midan Basateen and the *Al-Ahram* café on Sharia el-Nabawy, which sometimes also has *firik* (roasted green wheat served like rice or used as stuffing for chicken). *Abu Hurrara* on Sharia Bur Said is the best place for kebab or *kofta*. Alternatively, you can enjoy delicious thin-crust pizza or sweet *fiteer* at *Pizza Ibn al-Balad* on Midan Showla (open daily 7–11pm).

If you want to drink **alcohol,** the bar at the *Pioneers* stocks Egyptian beer (£E22), domestic (£E125) or imported (£E380) wine and spirits (£E38–60); the *El-Kharga* hotel sells Egyptian wine (£E80) and the *Hamad Alla* sometimes has beer. Since the *Pioneers* also serves the best food in town, you may be tempted to spend the day chilling out by its **swimming pool** (£E50 per person for non-residents).

Moving on from El-Kharga

Buses to Cairo (7–8 hr; £E50–60) leave the terminal off Midan Basateen at 9pm, 10pm and 11pm, taking the Desert Road that bypasses the Nile Valley. On moonlit nights, try to get a seat on the left of the bus to see the magnificent escarpment en route to Assyut. It's almost worth travelling to Assyut (4–5 hr; £E20) by day just for the view; buses depart at 6am, 7am and 11am. Buses to Dakhla (£E15) at 5am, 2pm and 11pm are supplemented by **service taxis** from Midan Showla (your best bet is before 10am or just after 2pm). Alternatively, Mohsen at the tourist office will take up to three people in his **car** to Dakhla for £E300, visiting Teneida, Bashendi and Balat (see p.420) en route. He'll even drive one or two people to Farafra or Bahariya with stopovers en route, for €50 per person per day.

There are no buses or service taxis along the **road to Luxor** (275km) which leaves the oasis at Baghdad (see p.429), but Mohsen will drive up to three people for £E400, and taxi drivers on Midan Showla charge £E400–500. The road is excellent and the journey takes only two hours. There are two first-aid stations with water, but no fuel, en route. The road meets the Nile Valley at Riziq, 15km south of Luxor.

As in Dakhla, there's a weekly **flight to Cairo** (Wed 4pm; £E500 one-way) operated by an oil company. Tickets are sold in the Governorate building (Ⓣ092/793-6900).

Around the oasis

The size of the oasis, its minimal public transport and the remoteness of many sites means that you really need a car (if not a guide) to experience all that it has to offer. Mohsen at the tourist office (ⓣ012 686-6299 or 010 180-6127, ⓔmohsen_dl@yahoo.com) or Mahmoud Youssef of the New Valley Museum (ⓣ092/793-4716 or 019 451-2733) will drive up to three passengers on tours (priced per group). Mohsen does day-long **tours** of Bagawat, Ed-Deir, Qasr al-Ghweita and Qasr al-Zayan ($30), and half-day trips to Qasr el-Labeka (€60) or Ain Um Dabadib (€150). Mahmoud asks €300 a day for a two-day grand tour of all the sites from Ain Um Dabadib in the north to Dush in the far south – or will guide people with their own 4WD for €150. A 2WD car should be able to reach

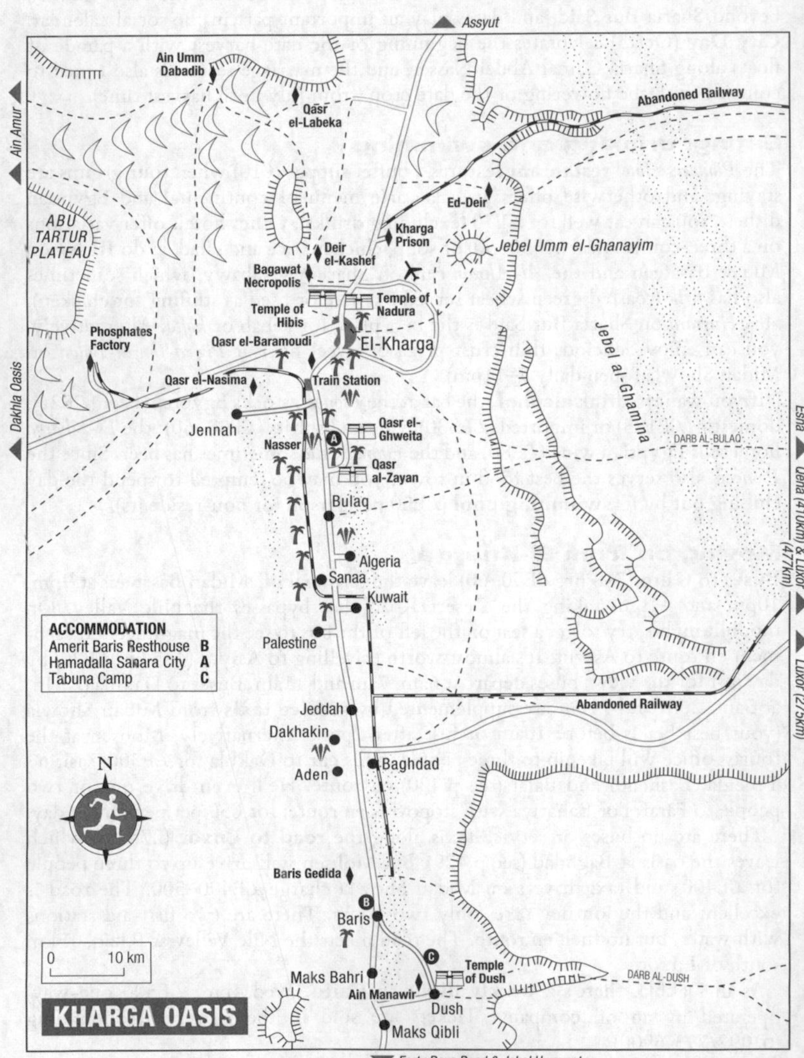

most places using spur-roads or well-worn tracks – only Ain Um Dabadib definitely needs 4WD.

North of El-Kharga

Three of the oasis' most evocative monuments lie just a few miles north of El-Kharga. The **Temple of Hibis** can be admired, juxtaposed against the **Bagawat Necropolis**, one of the oldest Christian cemeteries in Egypt, itself backed by an imposing ruined monastery, **Deir el-Kashef**. Further north, the depression is littered with ruins of ancient towns, forts, tunnels and other feats of Roman engineering waiting to be explored – however sites such as **Ed-Deir**, **Qasr el-Labeka** and **Ain Um Dabadib** are difficult to reach and require a guide (see p.426).

The Temple of Hibis

Although you can get here by catching a minibus from Midan Showla bound for El-Munira and asking to be dropped at *el-ma'abad* (the temple), it's fun to walk from the Mabrouk Fountain (2km) if the weather isn't too hot. En route, you'll catch sight of the ruined Ptolemaic **Temple of Nadura** atop a low hill in the desert to your right: its eroded sandstone wall and pronaos aren't worth the trek up to the top, though the view is.

Further on you'll come upon the **Temple of Hibis** (daily: summer 8am–6pm; winter 7am–5pm; £E60), the largest temple in all the oases, began in the reign of the Saïte ruler Psammetichus II (595–589 BC), and completed by the Persian emperor Darius I (521–486 BC). Recently reconstructed after a $20 million conservation fiasco (during which the temple was dismantled to move it to higher ground, only for engineers to decide that a drainage system was a better solution to the rising groundwater that was undermining its foundations), it features a **crypt** containing reliefs of dolphins, and graffiti by Francis Catherwood, later famous for discovering Mayan temples in Central America.

The vegetation roundabout covers the site of ancient Hibis, an XVIII Dynasty settlement that prospered under the Saïtes, Persians and Ptolemies. Here you'll find a **kiosk** selling tickets for Bagawat and Deir el-Kashef (daily: summer 8am–6pm; winter 7am–5pm; £E25 for both sites).

The Bagawat Necropolis

The hilltop **Bagawat Necropolis** consists of 263 mud-brick chapels, used for Christian burials between the third and seventh centuries – latterly by followers of Bishop Nestorius, exiled to Kharga for heresy. The chapels embody diverse forms of mud-brick vaulting or Roman-influenced portals, but are best known for their Coptic murals. Adam and Eve, Noah's Ark, Abraham and Isaac populate the dome of the **Chapel of Peace**, while Roman-looking pharaonic troops pursue the Jews, led by Moses, out of Egypt, in the **Chapel of the Exodus**. Flowery motifs and doves of peace can be seen inside **Tomb #25**, one of three adjacent family vaults on the ridge. The scenes are crudely executed but full of life and vividly coloured.

Deir el-Kashef

From the ticket kiosk, a track runs behind the hill, past an archeologists' resthouse and rows of rock-cut tombs, to reach the dramatic ruins of **Deir el-Kashef**, the Monastery of the Tax Collector. Named after a Mamluke governor, Mustafa, the five-storey monastery once housed hermits and travellers in its vaulted cells, and still commands a view of the point where the Darb al-Ghabari from Dakhla crossed the Forty Days Road. In the valley below you can see the ruins of a small **church** or hermitage, with Greek texts on the walls of the nave and the tiny cells where the monks slept.

Other sights

For those with a sturdy car or dirt-bike and a local guide, there are many other sites to explore. A track from Bagawat skirts the foothills of the bat- and snake-infested **Jebel el-Teir** (Bird Mountain), whose wadis contain prehistoric, pharaonic and Coptic **inscriptions**. More intriguing are feats of ancient engineering nearer the escarpment. Here are **Roman fortresses** that once guarded, taxed and sheltered caravans on the road to Assyut – invariably sited near springs, either natural or man-made. Kharga has numerous **underground aqueducts** known as *manafis*, that drew on ground water like the *qanats* of ancient Persia (Ahmed Fakhry suggests that the system originated under Persian rule).

Qasr el-Labeka is reached via a spur-road off the highway that turns into a sandy track leading to a tiny oasis, where a farmer has cleared out the *manafi* to irrigate palms and plots. If you don't mind getting your feet wet, the shaft is narrow but tall enough to venture into. The vertical shafts allowing access from the surface give their name to such aqueducts (*manafi* means "shaft"). You can tell where water lies near the surface from the scrub or palm trees on the plain beyond. Ruined houses and a temple lie half-buried in the sand, with the fortress looming from a crag. Its twelve-metre walls enclose sand-choked chambers and the rear gate overlooks a palm grove. If Labeka's Arabic name "Palm-wine Fort" signifies anything, it wasn't the worst posting for a legionary.

Although **Ain Um Dabadib** is only 18km from Labeka, cars may have to backtrack as far as El-Kharga to find a corridor through the dunes. The site covers more than two hundred square kilometres and includes a ruined fortress, churches and tombs, but is most remarkable for its four underground aqueducts, with access shafts every 20m; the deepest is 53m underground; the longest runs for 4.6km. When one of the *manafis* was cleared in the 1900s, water began to flow again. Now choked with sand and inhabited by snakes, scorpions and bats, they are risky to explore.

Further west, beyond the limits of the Kharga depression, the totally isolated, windblown spring of **Ain Amur** is situated 200m up the cliffs of the Abu Tartur Plateau. At 525m above sea level, this is the highest spring in the Western Desert, fed by aquifers in the escarpment; some believe that it was the last watering hole of the legendary Lost Army of Cambyses (see box, p.412). Travel to Ain Amur requires **permission** and a recognized guide such as Mohsen or Mahmoud (see p.426).

Far across the oasis near the eastern scarp wall, **Ed-Deir** once guarded the shortest camel route to the Nile. The fort lies 1km beyond the end of a track starting near Munira (the checkpoint on the road as you enter Kharga Oasis from the north); you must walk over the dunes at the end. Built in the reign of Diocletian, its twelve rounded towers are connected by a gallery and the surviving rooms covered in **graffiti** drawn by generations of soldiers. The **abandoned railway** in the distance was built by the British in 1906–08. Trips to Ed-Deir don't require permission.

South towards Baris

Exploring the **southern spur** of the oasis means flitting between sites off a highway. It's possible to negotiate with pick-up or **taxi** drivers on Midan Showla, who may agree to take you to the temples of Qasr el-Ghweita, Qasr al-Zayan and Dush for £E200–300. Buses to Baris can drop you at the turn-off for Qasr el-Ghweita or Qasr al-Zayan – which are only 5km apart – but to visit Dush as well means staying overnight in Baris or Dush (see p.424 for details). **Buses**

(2hr; £E5) leave El-Kharga at 6am and 9am, begining the return journey from Baris at 3pm and 5pm; **minibuses** also cover the route at irregular intervals.

Five kilometres south of town you'll pass Kharga's extravagantly-marbled **train station**, moribund since the railway line to Luxor was abandoned to the desert sands in 2008.

Excavations, dunes and springs

Mahmoud Youssef (see p.426) in El-Kharga will know about the ongoing **excavations** at two sites a few kilometres from the station and may be able to arrange a visit in the future. **Qasr al-Baramoudi** is a Roman fort with an oven-shaped pigeon tower, which once supplied the garrison with fowl. Such towers have been used in Egypt since antiquity and are still seen in the Nile Valley, but this is exceptional for being Roman and incorporated into military architecture. For reasons known to the architects, another fortress in the locality – **Qasr al-Nasima** – was equipped with an underground shaft for birds to roost in.

Further south and also off the highway, the village of **Jennah** backs onto a field of **dunes**, which tourists can admire at sunset before enjoying a soak in one of the **hot springs** in the palm groves on the far side of the highway, which vary in temperature up to 45°C. Usually the final stop on day-tours of the oasis, they're also visited by safari groups from Luxor en route to Dakhla Oasis, who usually **stay** at *Hamadalla Sahara City* (see p.424).

Qasr el-Ghweita and Qasr al-Zayan

Visible from behind *Hamadalla Sahara City*, **Qasr el-Ghweita** (daily: summer 8am–6pm; winter 7am–5pm; £E25) is a fortified hilltop temple from the Late Period, with a commanding view of the area, which was intensively farmed in ancient times. Its ten-metre-high walls enclose a sandstone temple dedicated to the Theban Triad, built by Darius I on the site of an older shrine; the Hypostyle Hall contains scenes of Hapy the Nile-god holding symbols of the nomes of Upper and Lower Egypt.

The spur-road continues 5km south to **Qasr al-Zayan** (daily: summer 8am–6pm; winter 7am–5pm; £E25), a Ptolemaic-Roman temple that lends its name to a village built over the ancient town of Tkhonemyris. This proximity to daily life helps you imagine it as a bustling settlement in antiquity. As at Qasr el-Ghweita, the temple is enclosed within a mud-brick fortress, together with living quarters for the garrison, a cistern and a bakery. The plain hereabouts is 18m below sea level, the lowest point in Kharga Oasis.

Returning to the highway, the next settlement, **Bulaq**, consists of a picturesque old village to the west and a larger modern one to the east. Its **hot springs** are visible immediately before you enter town, on the right. Bulaq is followed by a string of New Valley settlements founded in the 1980s, named Algeria, Kuwait, Palestine, Baghdad and Aden in a gesture of Arab solidarity. The **checkpoint** at the start of the **road to Luxor** (275km), near Baghdad, closes at 4pm.

Baris and beyond

Seventy kilometres south of El-Kharga, the township of **BARIS** (pronounced "Bar-ees") is named after the French capital, though its foraging goats and unpaved streets make a mockery of a billboard welcoming visitors to "Paris". Two kilometres before town, you'll pass the abandoned village of **Baris Gedida** (New Baris), begun in the early 1960s by architect Hassan Fathy and based on the principles of traditional oasis architecture, including wind shafts to cool the marketplace. Alas, work was halted by the Six Day War of 1967 and never

The Forty Days Road

Of all the trade routes between North Africa and the tropical south, the **Forty Days Road** (Darb al-Arba'in) was the one most involved in **slavery** – the only business profitable enough to justify the risks and rigours of the thousand-mile journey. The slaves, purchased at the Dongola slave market or kidnapped by the fierce desert tribes, were assembled at **Kobbé**, a town (no longer existing) 60km northwest of El-Fasher, the capital of Sudan's Darfur Province, once an independent kingdom.

After a few days' march from Kobbé, the slaves were unchained from their yokes, for there was no way to escape. With no permanent water source until Bir Natrun, 530km away, they could only survive on the ox skins of water that burdened the camels. While human losses were erased by the sands, the road gained definition from its Bactrian casualties; a 1946 survey of northwestern Sudan noted "a track about one mile wide marked with white camel bones".

Egyptian customs posts taxed caravans arriving in **Kharga Oasis**, the last stage before their ultimate destination, Assyut. As the caravans approached, small boys were hidden in empty water skins to evade tax, but officials would beat them to thwart this ploy. Traffic along the Forty Days Road ended in 1884, after the rise of the Dervish Empire in Sudan closed the border; by the time it reopened, slavery had been prohibited in Egypt. Today, a new form of human trafficking is flourishing in the **Darb al-Arba'in Desert**: smuggling refugees from war-torn Darfur and Somalia into Libya, via the remotest corner of Egypt (see p.437).

resumed, so the initial settlers soon drifted away. Today, old Baris is set to develop further once the **Sheikh Zayed Canal** – drawing water from Lake Nasser (see p.374) – reaches Kharga, entering the depression at Baris; at the time of writing it had 80km to go.

Accommodation and **meals** are available at the laidback *Amiret Baris Resthouse* (see p.424), beside the garage opposite the radio mast. Its staff can arrange **camel trips**, or a **pick-up** to take you to the Temple of Dush, 17km away (about £E30 round trip including waiting time), via a spur road leaving Baris by the radio mast.

Dush has been excavated since 1976 by the Institut Français d'Archéologie Oriental (IFAO), which is currently studying **Ain Manawir**, three deep subterranean aqueducts that once supplied water to **Kysis**, a trading community straddling the Darb al-Dush to the Nile Valley, safeguarded with a hilltop Roman **fortress**. Its mud-brick walls are six metres high, with four or five storeys below ground.

Abutting this, the **Temple of Dush** (daily: summer 8am–6pm; winter 7am–5pm; £E25) was built by Domitian and enlarged by Hadrian and Trajan, who added a monumental gateway. Reputedly once sheathed in gold, it is covered in dedications to the last two emperors, and the gateway in **graffiti** by Cailliaud and other nineteenth-century travellers. "Dush" is believed to derive from Kush, the name of the ancient Nubian kingdom.

From October to April visitors will find the IFAO mission in residence near the temple, and also the deluxe *Tabuna Camp*, an idyllic place to **stay** if you can afford it (see p.424).

From Dush, it's 32km by road to **MAKS BAHRI** (Customs North), a village that once lived off the infamous **Forty Days Road** (see box above), taxing each slave that entered the oasis, selling supplies and pandering to the slavemasters. Caravans going in the other direction were taxed at **MAKS QIBLI** (Customs South), where you can see a small mud-brick fort, the **Tabid el-Darawish**, built by the British after the Dervish invasion of 1893. Nowadays, the Forty Days Road has been paved as far south as Bir Tafarwi, to link up with the agricultural project at East Oweinat, but cars can't go beyond the **checkpoint** 5km south of Maks Qibli without a permit (see box, p.380).

The Gilf Kebir and the Great Sand Sea

Egypt's final frontier is the vast wilderness of the **Great Sand Sea** and the **Uwaynat Desert**, dominated by the huge plateau of the **Gilf Kebir**. Riven by wadis draining into lakes that dried out thousands of years ago, with colossal dunes leapfrogging each other to climb the 1000-metre-high escarpment, the Gilf is the closest environment on earth to the surface of Mars and has been studied by NASA since the 1970s. More recently, this obscure corner of Egypt was thrust into the limelight by the book and film *The English Patient*, dwelling on the exploits of the explorer László Almássy and his discovery of the **Cave of the Swimmers** at **Wadi Sura**. This magnificent example of **prehistoric rock art** is only one of thousands of engravings, drawings or paintings in the *wadis* of the Gilf Kebir and **Jebel Uwaynat**, a massif straddling the borders of Egypt, Libya and Sudan. Their depictions of giraffes, ostriches, lions and cattle – and people hunting and swimming – suggests what the environment was like before the decisive shift from savanna to desert occurred at the end of the Holocene wet period, around 5000 BC.

Since then, the Uwaynat Desert has become the **driest desert on earth**, with an aridity index of 200 (meaning that the solar energy received could evaporate 200 times the amount of precipitation received). Rainfall is less than a millimetre a year, and may fall only once a decade at Uwaynat and every five years on the Gilf. Barring a fluke rainfall such as allegedly saved Rohlfs in the Great Sand Sea, the nearest **water** supply is at least 500km away at Bir Tarfawi, where an experimental farm called East Oweinat draws on fossil water (trapped underground for millennia), and where the road to civilization begins. Beyond Bir Tarfawi there are only tracks or trackless desert: no fuel, food nor means of communication with the outside world (except by satphone); nor any people except survey or safari expeditions, smugglers and bandits.

The kidnapping of a safari group by Chadian rebels in 2008 was a wake-up call for the Egyptian authorities who had previously turned a blind eye to people being trafficked through Egypt into Libya and failed to anticipate that banditry in Darfur might over-spill the border. **Security** is now a consideration for anyone travelling this far south, so check your government's advice for travellers (Germany warns its citizens not to expect to be rescued at the state's expense).

The websites Ⓦ www.fjexpeditions.com, www.zarzora.com and www.khalifaexp.com feature extensive **photogalleries** of the Gilf and Uwaynat, and news of recently discovered rock art. For an in-depth focus on Saharan rock art and prehistory, subscribe to the journal *Sahara* (Ⓦ www.saharajournal.com).

Travel practicalities

While the outermost dunes of the Great Sand Sea are easily accessible from Siwa (see p.447), crossing the Sand Sea or travelling to the Gilf Kebir or Jebel Uwaynat entails a deep-desert safari whose cost may be prohibitive. Even if it isn't, you need to **reserve** perhaps six months ahead to be sure of getting a place; expeditions only run from February to March and September to November, when the temperature is tolerable. Even so, **discomfort** is inevitable: sand gets into every crevice of your body, there's no water to spare for washing, and you start to stink – like everybody else in the vehicle. Unless you're willing to rough it and muck in when needed, there's no point in coming at all. But if you do, you're sure to remember it for the rest of your life.

Safaris to the Uwaynat Desert are a major logistical effort. Don't think of going with fewer than three 4WD vehicles, or without a GPS set and satellite phone. Also essential is a **guide** who's done the trip enough times before to be confident; few use maps or GPS to chart the route, depending on their memory of landmarks. All expeditions need a multi-day permit from Military Intelligence (see p.380) and are accompanied by an **army escort** who reports their position each day by satphone. See p.380 and pp.403–404 for details of operators that specialize in the Gilf Kebir and Jebel Uwaynat.

Most safari outfits will take people in their own 4WDs providing they're able to handle the **driving**, which needs experience, skill and nerve. If you have doubts on any of these scores then you should come as a **passenger** and let the safari team handle all the work. Check that your travel **insurance** covers deep-desert journeys and what (if any) back-up exists in case of **emergencies**. Though the operator will supply meals, tents and bedding, you need to **bring** personal essentials such as sun block and skin cream and any luxuries like alcohol or cigarettes (the nearest supply is in Kharga or Dakhla oases). Binoculars are a must, too.

Approaches

There are two classic approaches to this corner of Egypt. One takes the Darb el-Tarfawi south from Dakhla Oasis and then a track to **Abu Ballas**, en route to the Gilf and then Uwaynat. The other assumes a more easterly starting point, from Kharga Oasis or even Aswan or Abu Simbel, and uses the Darb al-Arba'in – now paved as far south as Bir Kiseba – to reach **Bir Tarfawi**, from where the first motorized explorers approached Uwaynat in the mid-1920s, finding the desert easier to cross than they'd expected. Approaching the Gilf from the north was – and is – more difficult due to the Great Sand Sea, but some safaris do it, in which case Regenfeld is a mandatory stopover (see p.438).

From Dakhla

Abu Ballas (Father of Pots) is 240km from Dakhla, before the southeastern tip of the Great Sand Sea. Named by Prince Kemal el-Din in 1916, this hill is an ancient water cache strategically located between caravan trails and springs. Since 2000, German archeologists have excavated 27 way stations en route from Abu Ballas to the Gilf Kebir, seemingly part of a pharaonic trade route that may have led as far as Chad and possibly originated in Neolithic times.

Once there were hundreds of pots at Abu Ballas, each able to hold about thirty litres of water, some as old as the VI Dynasty, others stashed by Tebu nomads from the Libyan Desert to sustain their raids on Dakhla during Ottoman times. Eventually, men from Dakhla found the cache and smashed the pots; archeologists, explorers and tourists have removed most of the fragments, though a few remain photogenically posed. In the 1920s, geologist John Ball suggested that the "lost oasis" of Zerzura (see p.433) might actually be Abu Ballas and that the word *zerzura*, which is the Arabic name for a small black starling found in the Western Desert, might in this case refer to a *zir* or water jug. There is **rock art**, too, halfway up the southeast face: a cow suckling its calf, a bearded hunter and his dog chasing an antelope with a bow and arrows, and a man's profile. An hour's drive beyond Abu Ballas is a spectacular field of sedimentary *yardangs* resembling basking sea lions, dubbed the **Mud-Lions** (or Red Lions). Thereafter, dunes slope imperceptibly to the top of the plateau, impeding the way to the Gilf.

From Kharga

Depending on how far south you follow the Darb al-Arba'in and which roads you use, you may pass the ancient spring of **Bir Tarfawi**, in a depression surrounded by palms, acacias and tamarisks, once filled by two lakes ringed by Neolithic settlements. In 1981, Space Shuttle radar imaging revealed ancient riverbeds that convinced NASA scientist Farouk Al-Baz (see p.438) that fossil water lay beneath the desert. His hypothesis proved to be correct, for the government has dug wells and established experimental farms near Bir Tarfawi. Collectively named **East Oweinat** (the English spelling differentiates it from Jebel Uwaynat, far away and unrelated to the project), they consist of circular fields irrigated by giant sprinklers, where high-value crops are grown for export to France from an airstrip.

The Gilf Kebir

Named the **Gilf Kebir** (Great Barrier) by the first European to sight it, this 7770-square-kilometre plateau rises 1000m from the desert floor, an even more formidable obstacle than the Great Sand Sea. Aeons ago in the late Tertiary age, the Gilf was a watershed draining in all directions; its wadis were eroded by water and then by wind and sand over 100,000 years. The sheer cliffs on the south and southwest sides are the highest, while the northeasterly ones have been worn down by the Sand Sea. **Dunes** have filled up the valleys and are climbing one on top of another to reach the plateau at Lama Pass; white by the Sand Sea, or red around the middle of the plateau and its southern landmass. Despite being so arid, the top of the plateau gets just enough rainfall for hardy **flora and fauna** to survive: foxes, lizards, birds and butterflies, Roses of Jericho and acacia trees. Visitors may also find other surprises, too, like the wreck of a South African Air Force Blenheim bomber that turned up on the plateau in 2001.

For many visitors the Gilf's allure has more to do with its fantastic **prehistoric rock art** – at Wadi Sura, Wadi Abd el-Malik and other sites – or the romance attached to the **explorers** who "discovered" it (Tebu and Gor'an nomads were fully aware of it all along, since it was their ancestors who created it). Almássy gets all the limelight, naturally, but Michael Ondaatje's novel also mentions other explorers of the 1920s and 1930s, such as the Egyptian Prince Kemal el-Din, the Englishmen Ralph Bagnold, Douglas Newbold and Kennedy Shaw, and the Irishman Patrick Clayton. During World War II, they set up the Long Range Desert Group (LRDG) that wreaked havoc behind Italian and German lines, while their former comrade Almássy served on the other side with the Afrika Korps.

The "Zerzura" wadis

When Almássy and Lord Robert Clayton took three cars and a plane to the Gilf in February 1932, the aim of their **Zerzura Expedition** was to find the legendary lost oasis of that name, which had obsessed Western explorers for generations. Almássy was away visiting the Italians in Kufra when Clayton and Penderel flew over the northern Gilf and glimpsed "an acacia-dotted wadi" that they were unable to pinpoint on a map. After his return they made further flights and spotted two such wadis from the air, but couldn't locate them on foot. Almássy and Clayton believed that these were two of the three valleys mentioned by Wilkinson in his 1835 list of unknown sites that set the European search for Zerzura rolling. But fate intervened in their plans, for Clayton died of polio on a visit to England, followed within a month by the expedition's sponsor, Prince Kemal el-Din, leaving Almássy to seek new sponsors and Clayton's widow to continue her husband's quest independently (see box opposite).

Returning the following spring in cars with balloon tyres, Almássy's party explored **Wadi Abd el-Malik**, the longest of the deep fissures in the northern Gilf. They found lots of acacia trees and sites of Tebu encampments and a large cave with **drawings** of longhorn cattle, men, and a prehistoric dwelling. (Another grotto was later found by Bagnold, containing **paintings** of cattle and a dog.) It was a Tebu caravan guide who told Almássy the name of the wadi and its side-valley, **Wadi Talh** (Acacia Valley), and spoke of a third valley called Wadi Hamra. When asked if he knew of Zerzura, he replied: "Oh, those silly Arab people, they do not know anything; they call these three wadis in the Gilf, Zerzura, but we local people know their real names." Almássy was sure that they had found Zerzura.

In 2002, an expedition exploring a valley to the west of Wadi Abd el-Malik climbed down three small canyons and found the largest cave yet discovered in the Gilf. Co-named after the expedition's leader and sponsor, the **Mestakawi-Foggini Cave** contains a peerless array of prehistoric art: **paintings** of humans and animals, **engravings** of cattle and ibexes, and the ghostly blown-outlines of dozens of **hands**. Some safari outfits now feature the cave on their itineraries (see p.380).

Wadi Hamra (Red Valley), on the eastern side of the plateau, is another must-see, named for its gorgeous red dunes drifting down a black mountainside – a Martian landscape found nowhere else in Egypt. The sandstone rocks bear **engravings** of giraffes, oryx, ostriches, gazelles and Barbary sheep – the prey that hunter-gatherers killed with dogs, lassos, bows and arrows during the Early

▲ Rock art in the Mestekawi-Foggini cave

László Almássy – the real "English Patient"

While Michael Ondaatje's novel *The English Patient* and the subsequent Oscar-winning film rescued Almássy's name from obscurity, both texts took liberties with the truth to cast "Count Ladislaus de Almasy" as a romantic hero whose love for another man's wife sealed their fates and left him dying of burns in an Italian villa. The real story is rather different – not least because Almássy was, in fact, homosexual.

Born in 1895, in Hungary, **László Ede Almássy** learned to fly while at boarding school in England. During World War I he was a fighter ace and then an aide to the last Habsburg monarch (who once mistakenly called him "Count" – a title that stuck), serving as his driver during two farcical attempts to regain the throne in 1921. Almássy then became a salesman for the off-road-car manufacturers Steyr, for whom he won many races, and in 1926 took Steyrs into the desert on the first of his numerous Sahara expeditions, about which he wrote several books. The Bedouin called him Abu Ramleh – Father of the Sands.

In February 1932 he initiated the **Zerzura Expedition** to the Gilf Kebir, the first to combine cars with light aircraft. His co-explorers were **Lord Robert** and **Lady Dorothy Clayton-East-Clayton** (the fictional Geoffrey and Katherine Clifton), the Irish desert surveyor **Patrick Clayton** (no relation) and Squadron Leader **Penderel**. Unlike in fiction, Lord Clayton died of a sudden illness back home in England, and although his widow returned to the desert to continue searching for Zerzura, she didn't meet Almássy again or share his discovery of the Cave of Swimmers – nor did she perish there in 1939, but rather in a fall from her plane in England six years earlier. Thus the motive for Almássy's collaboration with the Germans in *The English Patient* is pure invention.

As a reserve officer in the Hungarian air force, Almássy could hardly refuse being posted to Rommel's **Afrika Korps**, which used his expertise as a spotter and his photos for their official handbook – to the fury of his old companions in Egypt, many of whom were now in the LRDG (see box, p.436). Thanks to the codebreakers of Bletchley Park, the British knew of Almássy's infiltration of two German spies into Egypt, whom he guided through the Gilf to Kharga Oasis in 1941. He later made amends by visiting Patrick Clayton in an Italian POW camp and getting him moved to a better one. Almássy himself wound up in a Soviet camp where he lost his teeth from scurvy, before a People's Court cleared him of being a Nazi sympathizer after testimony that he had sheltered Jewish neighbours in his flat in Budapest. His **final years** were spent in Africa, where he flew gliders and ran safaris. After catching dysentery in Egypt, he died in a clinic in Salzburg in 1951.

Holocene epoch (8000–6000/5000 BC). This rock art is centuries if not thousands of years older than the images in the Cave of the Swimmers. Wadi Hamra was found in 1931 by Patrick Clayton, who noted plenty of trees and Barbary sheep, while Almássy discovered that it led up to the Gilf plateau. During the war, he reputedly tried to persuade Rommel to land glider-troops on top of the Gilf and bring them down into Wadi Hamra.

Wadi Sura and the Cave of the Swimmers

Although *The English Patient* transposes the Cave of the Swimmers to Ain Doua at Jebel Uwaynat, it actually lies in **Wadi Sura**, where Almássy found it in 1933, with the Frobenius expedition that was searching for rock art at Uwaynat and in the western valleys of the Gilf that had been explored by Patrick Clayton two years earlier. Clayton's son believes that his father found the wadi and its other caves first, but it was Almássy's privilege to discover the Cave of the Swimmers and name the valley. The film, shot in Tunisia, took liberties by making the cave where

Katherine Clifton died a deep, convoluted passage: it is, in fact, a shallow hollow on the lip of the wadi, and shockingly exposed to the elements.

The **Cave of the Swimmers** harbours well over a hundred figures in diverse styles. The famous swimmers are 10cm long and painted in red, with small rounded heads on stalks, tadpole-shaped bodies and spidery arms and legs. Some are diving, implying that a lake once existed here (for which there's geological evidence). A second group of figures are depicted standing, with clumsy limbs, thick torsos and pea-shaped heads; hands only appear on the larger figures. Most are dark red, with bands of white around their ankles, wrists or waists, similar to the hunters at Karkur Talh. Still more intriguing are two yellow figures that seem to be stretching out their arms to welcome a third, smaller, red one, which may be a child and its parents. Cattle, giraffes, ostriches and dogs are also depicted on the walls.

Further along, the **Cave of the Archers** contains dark red and white figures of naked men clutching bows, some of them shooting at cattle – whose presence dates these pictures to the Cattle Period (5000–2500 BC) of North African rock art. Hans Winkler of the 1938 Monod expedition termed the style of the male figures "balanced exaggeration", for they all have wide shoulders and hips, tiny waists and tapering limbs; feet and hands are rarely shown, and heads often omitted too – unlike the spear-carrying hunters depicted in Karkur Talh at Jebel Uwaynat, which are otherwise similar in style.

On the sandy plain before the wadi a huge fallen boulder covers the **Giraffe Cave**, found by Clayton in 1931. Inside are giraffes, cattle and dogs painted in black or white.

Other wadis

The southern part of the Gilf is riddled with wadis, some easy to enter, others nearly impossible. **Wadi Mashi** (Walking Valley) gets its name because the mountains vanish and reappear as you approach, but has yet to yield any finds, unlike **Wadi Dayyiq** (Narrow Valley), where a large area is covered by stone-chippings left by prehistoric people manufacturing knives, blades and arrow-heads from hard rocks; or **Wadi al-Bakht**, where four **prehistoric settlements** have been found. It's thought that people lived here for centuries, hunting ostriches and raising cattle around the shores of a lake until it disappeared by 5200 BC.

The Long Range Desert Group (LRDG)

Founded by Ralph Bagnold in June 1940 to reconnoitre Axis forces and engage in "piracy on the high desert", the **Long Range Desert Group**'s motto was "Not by Strength, but Guile". Led by Bagnold and other prewar explorers such as Patrick Clayton, Kennedy Shaw and Douglas Newbold, it consisted mainly of New Zealanders, who soon learnt the arts of desert warfare. As with Special Forces ever since, the emphasis was on self-reliance and mobility. Each patrol took all it needed for a cross-desert journey of 1500 miles (which could be doubled by establishing a forward supply dump), in stripped-down Chevy trucks fitted with sand mats and channels (doubling as air markers for supply drops) and a sun compass invented by Bagnold. Patrols operated for up to eleven weeks as they espied convoys or delivered SAS commandos to attack airfields – in ten months, over four hundred planes were thus destroyed (more than the RAF managed). You can **read** about the LRDG's exploits in Bagnold's *Sand, Wind and War: Memoirs of a Desert Explorer*, Saul Kelly's *The Hunt for Zerzura*, Peter Clayton's *Desert Explorer* (about his father, Patrick), or on the LPDG Preservation Society's website ⓦwww.lrdg.org.

Jebel Uwaynat

On a map of North Africa, the ruler-straight borders of Libya, Egypt and Sudan intersect at **Jebel Uwaynat**, the highest point in the Libyan Desert. Surrounded by sand-sheets, it rises sheerly to 1898m above the desert floor and 600m above sea level, just high enough to attract a little rainfall, which percolates down to small pools or "springs" at its base (after which Uwaynat is named). The valleys here (called *karkurs*) are fertile if watered, sustaining communities from prehistoric times until the early 1930s; with **rock art** spanning thousands of years. In **Karkur Talh** (Acacia Valley), Hassanein Bey found engravings of lions, giraffes, ostriches, gazelles and cows on the rocks, and Shaw discovered ninety human figures drawn on the roof of a cave. These figures were lither than the hunters in the Cave of the Archers at Wadi Sura but otherwise similar, leading Winkler to conclude that both were the work of the ancient Tebu, who once ranged across the Sahara from their mountainous homeland of Tibesti, in Chad.

After the Italians occupied Kufra and placed an outpost at Uwaynat, the possibility that it could be an unguarded back door into Egypt during wartime occurred to both Bagnold and the Italian commander Lorenzini – but not to the HQ staff-wallahs who turned down Bagnold's proposal for car patrols along the frontier. It wasn't until Italy declared war in 1940 that Bagnold was authorized to set up long-range patrols to monitor any activity. In the event, the Italians never tried anything so bold, but Almássy later slipped through from Kufra via Uwaynat and the Gilf, to guide two German spies as far as Kharga Oasis, before returning to Libya. Today, an outpost of **Border Guards** at Karkur Talh has the task of securing Egypt's back door, while Libya has deployed forces along its side of the border.

Nor is it just prehistory that has been preserved, for in 1991 a World War II ammunition truck was found in the desert to the east of Wadi Dayyiq. After being refuelled it started, and is now in the war museum at El-Alamein (see p.488). There are relics of the **Long Range Desert Group** (see box opposite) all over the region, from a Ford lorry and a GM stake-bed truck 10km southeast of the Gilf's southern tip, to hundreds of metal petrol cans with the Shell logo, laid out to form route markers. An evocative example is the **abandoned aerodrome** with a landing strip marked by concentric rings of petrol cans, near the wadi known as **Eight Bells**. This cluster of hills and depressions is the result of a vast prehistoric drainage system which carried water south into an even larger one that fed a super-lake stretching from Lake Chad to within 600km of the Gilf Kebir. The southern Gilf is broken up by **Wadi Wassa** (Wide Valley), another ancient drainage valley with dozens of side wadis, islands, and a wrecked LRDG Chevy. On the col that divides Wadi Wassa from **Wadi Faragh** (Empty Valley), Shaw found a cave containing engravings of cows and more ancient giraffes, henceforth shown on maps as **Shaw's Cave**.

Wadi Faragh emerges on a plain of hard-packed sand that serves as a natural highway for trucks **smuggling** people into Libya through the gap between the Gilf and Uwaynat. It's here that an army escort is most appreciated, even though smugglers tend to keep a distance in the event of encountering safari groups.

Where the trail rounds the Gilf's southern tip, Almássy erected a simple **Monument to Prince Kemal el-Din** to commemorate the prince's expeditions to Uwaynat, the Gilf and Merga Oasis, using caterpillar-tracked Citröens. Safaris carrying on to Uwaynat (see box) pass the **Clayton Craters**, twenty in number and up to 1km across with rims rising 30m from the desert floor, which some ascribe to meteor strikes like the Al-Baz Crater and silica glass in the Great Sand Sea (see p.438), and others to volcanic activity.

The Great Sand Sea

Between the Gilf Kebir and Siwa Oasis lie 72,000 square kilometres of dune fields that the explorer Gerhard Rohlfs named the **Great Sand Sea** (Bahr er-Raml in Arabic). Although its general existence was known at the time of Herodotus, the extent to which it stretched southwards wasn't realized until the **Rohlfs expedition** of 1874 headed west from Dakhla, bound for Kufra Oasis in Libya. With seventeen camels bearing water, they soon met the *erg*'s outermost ranges: "an ocean" of sand-waves over 100m high, ranked 2–4km apart. Rohlfs estimated that their camels could scale six dunes and advance 20km westwards on the first and second days, but that their endurance would rapidly diminish thereafter, so with no prospect of water or an end to the dunes they were forced to turn north-northwest and follow the dune lanes towards Siwa.

By the eighteenth day the expedition could no longer water every camel and the animals began dying. Then, according to the English version of his adventures, there was torrential rainfall in a spot where barely a drop falls for years, saving their lives and replenishing their water supply. Rohlfs called the spot **Regenfeld** (Rainfield) and marked it with a cairn before he left, wondering "Will ever man's foot tread this place again?" However, in the German edition of his book, *Drei Monate in der libyschen Wüste*, Rohlfs described a smaller expedition with no hint of supply problems – and whether or not a miraculous rainfall really saved their lives, Regenfeld has since been visited by scores of explorers and tourists.

Visiting the Great Sand Sea

Today, tourists can cross the Sand Sea on deep-desert safaris from Bahariya or Farafra (see p.397 & p.406). Most itineraries feature Regenfeld and an area of desert strewn with pale green deposits of translucent **silica glass** – a material known to the Ancient Egyptians, for it was from this that the scarab on Tutankhamun's funerary pectoral cross was carved. The deposits are thought to have originated in a prehistoric meteorite strike, whose impact fused sand into glass. Ground zero may have been the four-kilometre-wide **Al-Baz Crater**, 150km southeast of the silica glass region (named after its Egyptian-American discoverer, Farouk Al-Baz, a pioneer in using satellites to search for water in arid areas).

If you can't afford a safari into the heart of the Sand Sea, a **brief excursion** from Siwa Oasis to **Bir Wahed** (see p.449) is enough to experience the utter desolation and colossal size of its dunes.

Siwa Oasis

Isolated by hundreds of kilometres of desert, **Siwa Oasis** remained virtually independent from Egypt until the late nineteenth century, sustaining a unique culture. Yet despite – or because of – its isolation, outsiders have been drawn here since antiquity. The legendary Army of Cambyses was heading this way when it disappeared into a sandstorm; Alexander the Great journeyed here to consult the famous Oracle of Amun; and Arabic tales of Santariyah (as the oasis was known) were common currency into the nineteenth century. In modern times, Siwa has received visits from kings and presidents, anthropologists and generals. Tourism only really began in the mid-1980s but has gathered steam since then.

The oasis offers all you could ask for in the way of desert **beauty spots**: thick palm groves clustered around freshwater springs and salt lakes; rugged massifs and enormous dunes. Equally impressive are the **ruins** of Shali and Aghurmi, labyrinthine mud-built towns that once protected the Siwans from desert raiders. Scattered around the oasis are ruined **temples** that attest to Siwa's fame and prosperity during Greco-Roman times. Visitors are also fascinated by **Siwan culture** and how it is reacting to outside influences like TV, schooling and tourism. Nowadays, it is mostly only older women who wear the traditional costume, silver jewellery and complex hair-braids; younger wives and unmarried women dress much the same as their counterparts in the Nile Valley. But the Siwans still observe their own festivals and wedding customs; and among themselves they speak Siwi, a Berber tongue. Though things are changing, the Siwans remain sure of their identity and are determined to maintain it.

Some history

Beyond the fact that it sustained hunter-gatherers in Paleolithic times, little is known about Siwa Oasis before the XXVI Dynasty (672–525 BC), when the reputation of its **Oracle** spread throughout the Mediterranean world. Siwa's population seems to have been at risk from predatory desert tribes, so their first settlement was a fortified acropolis, about which Classical accounts reveal little about beyond its name, **Aghurmi**, and its position as a major caravan stop between Cyrenaica and Sudan. The Siwans are related to the Berbers of Algeria, Tunisia and Morocco, and their language is just a variant of the Berber tongues, so their society may have originally been matriarchal. Their later history is detailed in the *Siwan Manuscript*, whose whereabouts are a closely guarded secret. A century-old compilation of oral histories, it relates how Siwa's rulers considered poisoning the springs with mummies in order to thwart the Muslim conquest (date uncertain), and how Bedouin and Berber raids had reduced Aghurmi's population to a mere two hundred by the twelfth century AD.

Shali and Siwan society

Round about 1203, seven families quit Aghurmi to found a new settlement called **Shali** (the Town). Their menfolk are still honoured as the "forty ancestors", and these pioneering families were probably the most vigorous of the surviving Siwans. Later, newcomers from Libya settled in the oasis, giving rise to the enduring distinction between the "Westerners" and the original, more numerous "Easterners", whose historic feud began after they disagreed over the route of a causeway that both had undertaken to build across the salt lake of Birket Siwa. Nonetheless, both coexisted within a single town built of *kharsif*: a salt-impregnated mud which dries cement-hard, but melts during downpours – fortunately, it rains heavily here only every fifty years or so. Fearful of raiders, Shali's *agwad* (elders) forbade families to live outside the walls, so as the population increased the town could only expand upwards.

Siwan bachelors aged between 20 and 40 were obliged to sleep in caves outside town, guarding the fields – hence their nickname, *zaggalah* (club-bearers). Noted for their love of palm liquor, song and dance, they shocked outsiders with their open **homosexuality**. Gay marriages were forbidden by King Fouad in 1928, but continued in secret until the late 1940s. Today, Siwans emphatically assert that homosexuality no longer exists in the oasis – whatever may be said on the Ⓦ www.gayegypt.com – and palm liquor has now been superseded by *arak* made from dates.

Another feature of Shali was the tradition of violent **feuds** between the Westerners and Easterners, in which all able-bodied males were expected to participate. Originally ritualized, with parallel lines of combatants exchanging blows between sunrise and sunset while their womenfolk threw stones at cowards and shouted encouragement, feuds became far deadlier with the advent of firearms. Despite this, the Siwans immediately closed ranks against outsiders – Bedouin raiders, khedival taxmen or European explorers.

Egyptian and British control

Visitors of the eighteenth and nineteenth centuries regularly experienced Siwan **xenophobia**. "Whenever I quitted my apartment, it was to be assailed with stones and a torrent of abusive language", W.G. Browne wrote in 1762. Frédéric Cailliaud was permitted to visit the gardens and ruins in 1819, but the town remained barred to strangers until six hundred troops sent by Mohammed Ali compelled the oasis to recognize **Egyptian authority** in 1820.

Although the Siwans regularly revolted against their governor and defaulted on taxes (payable in dates), the oasis began to change. With the desert tribes suppressed, and Shali rendered unsafe by heavy rains, the *agwad* permitted families to settle outside the walls. From the 1850s onwards the great reformist preacher Mohammed Ibn Ali al-Senussi cast a spell over the desert peoples from Jaghbub Oasis just over the border, and Siwa – the site of his first *zawiya* – supported **Senussi** resistance to the Italian conquest of Libya (1912–30), until it became clear that their Senussi "liberators" would not restore Siwan independence. Thus in 1917, British forces were "welcomed by the cheering Siwans, who declared their loyalty as they always did with every new victorious conqueror", as Fakhry put it.

Anglo-Egyptian control of Siwa was maintained by the Frontier Camel Corps and Light Car Patrols. Agricultural advisors, a school and an orthodox imam were introduced following King Fouad's visit to the oasis in 1928. When the British withdrew as the Italians advanced across North Africa in 1942, the Siwans accepted Axis **occupation** with equal resignation. Unlike Rommel, who made a favourable impression during his flying visit, King Farouk dismayed the Siwans by wearing shorts and asking if they "still practised a certain vice" when he visited the oasis in 1945.

Modern Siwa

Paradoxical as it sounds, Siwa's biggest problem is an excess of water, which gushes from springs and drains into salt lakes, increasing their volume and salinity. Smelly, mosquito-infested ponds all over town attest that the **water table** lies only twenty centimetres underground. The water supply is saline or sandy, so residents have to collect water from springs by donkey. Foreign engineers are installing a drainage system and a water-purification plant at Dakhrour, outside town, but it will be some years before they're finished.

While Egyptian military bases exist here on sufferance, Siwans have welcomed developments in healthcare, education and communications. The road to Matrouh (completed in 1984) has encouraged exports of dates and olives, and tourism to the oasis, and in the 1990s the **economy** was boosted by factories producing olive oil, mineral water and carpets. More recently, some five hundred Siwan **women** have been stitching traditional embroidery for an Italian couture house, earning twice the average Siwan wage for an agricultural labourer: the unmarried ones have saved so much money that they can be choosy about taking a husband.

Meanwhile, the Siwans' desire for breeze-block houses or low-rise flats with proper bathrooms rather than the traditional dusty mud-brick dwellings has alarmed conservationists. Britain's Prince Charles is among the VIPs backing the

Friends of Siwa Association, a conservationist body set up by **Mounir Nematalla** (see p.450). Many locals regard the Friends of Siwa as a scam to embezzle donations, and resent Nematalla for expropriating part of Shali for his own profit, but no one doubts his energy or friends in high places.

Siwans remain deeply conservative in matters of **dress** and **behaviour**. The tourist office asks visitors to refrain from public displays of affection, and women to keep their arms and legs covered – especially when bathing in pools. Women should also avoid wandering alone in places with few people around. Local people are generally more reserved than Egyptians, and invitations home are less common.

Visiting Siwa

The **best time** to come is during spring or autumn, when the Siwans hold festivals and the days are pleasantly warm. In winter, windless days can be nice, but nights – and gales – are chilling. From May onwards, rising temperatures keep people indoors between 11am and 7pm, and the nights are sultry and mosquito-ridden. Even when the **climate** is mild you'll probably feel like taking a midday siesta or a swim.

Unless you sign up with a deep-desert safari that reaches Siwa by the Great Sand Sea or the Qattara Depression there are only two possible **approaches**: by a permit-only road from Bahariya Oasis (see p.405) or the highway that runs inland from the Mediterranean Coast at Mersa Matrouh, used by **buses**. The 8pm bus (£E55) from Cairo's Turgoman terminal takes nine hours to reach Siwa via the desert road to El-Alamein, so there's no need to start your journey at Alexandria's Moharrem Bey terminal (see p.483) or interrupt it at Matrouh (see box, p.486) unless you want to.

The three-hundred-kilometre journey from Matrouh to Siwa takes four hours by car or bus, with the Siwa road turning off the highway 20km west of Matrouh, at a checkpoint. Soon after, mobile phones cease to function until you reach a **resthouse** known as **Bir Nous** (Halfway Well), selling tea, soup and soft drinks. Its toilets are the nearest you get to the horrors of this route before the road was built.

Siwa Town

Most visitors rate **SIWA TOWN** and the pools, rocks and ruins around as the oasis's main attractions, and not many bother to visit the outlying villages. Siwa Town has grown as its population has risen to 25,000 (at least one thousand of them from outside the oasis), and people have moved into modern housing, forsaking traditional mud-brick dwellings – just as their ancestors had previously abandoned the fortified hilltop city of **Shali**, whose ruins overlook the modern town. A triumphal arch and broad roads debouch onto a central market area, but the town slips away into a maze of alleyways, and loses itself amid the encircling palms.

Arrival and information

Siwa's **tourist office** (summer daily 9am–2.30pm & 7–10pm, Fri 11am–1pm; winter daily except Fri 9am–2.30pm & 5–8pm; Ⓣ&Ⓕ046/460-1338 or 010 546-1992, Ⓔmahdi_hweiti@yahoo.com) is in the north of the town, near the bus station. It's run by English-speaking Mahdi Hweiti, a native Siwan who knows everything about the oasis and can arrange trips to outlying villages. Should you have any trouble in Siwa, go to him rather than the police.

There's a **pharmacy** near the centre and a grungy public **hospital** on the outskirts. Women patients will fare better at the Mother and Child Clinic opposite

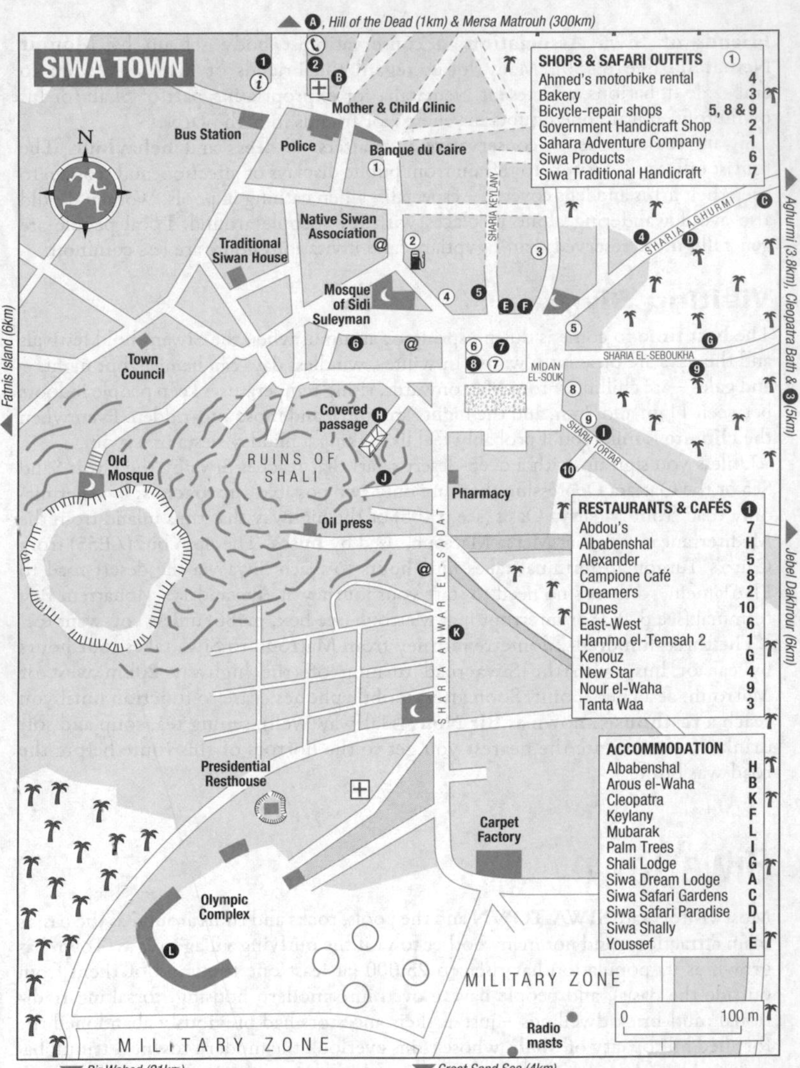

the tourist office. The **police** (☎046/460-1008) are next door to the **Banque du Caire** (Mon–Thurs & Sun 8.30am–2pm & 5–8pm, Fri & Sat 8–11am & 5–8pm), which has an ATM. The most reliable **internet** cafe is Desert Net in the block of flats across the first-floor landing from the **Native Siwan Association** NGO (☎046/460-2110, Ⓦwww.siwaegypt.com), which issues 24-hour permits for travel to Bir Wahed (see p.449) or Bahariya Oasis (p.452).

Accommodation

Siwa has both low-budget and upmarket **hotels**, including two lakeside ecolodges beside Birket Siwa, 16km from town. While it's worth reserving ahead if you're fussy about where you stay, the only time it's essential to do so is during Siwan festivals, when tour groups block-book hotels. On the whole, though, it's safe to assume that you'll find a bed. People wanting their own space can rent **apartments** in the centre (£E800–1000 per month) through Mahdi at the tourist office. Places out of town are marked on the map of Siwa Oasis on p.448.

Siwa Town

Albabenshal Off Midan el-Souk ⓣ046/460-2399, ⓦwww.siwa.com. Named the "Door of the Country" in Siwi, this austerely lovely "heritage lodge" occupies several old houses at the base of Shali. Built of *kharsif* and salt-slabs like *Adrère Amellal* (see below), its rooftop restaurant has wonderful views. With only eleven rooms, reservations are essential. ⑤

Arous al-Waha Opposite the tourist office ⓣ046/460-0028. A state-owned hotel whose Arabic name means "Bride of the Oasis", it has worn but clean rooms with fans, shower-cabins and fridges. ②

Cleopatra Sharia Anwar el-Sadat ⓣ&ⓕ046/460-0421, ⓦwww.cleopatra-siwa.net. Simple rooms, some with toilet, balcony and fan; those in the quieter "chalet" block (£E45) have all three, but are plagued by mosquitoes. ①

Keylany Midan el-Souk ⓣ046/460-0415 or 012 403-9218. Guests lured by its shaded rooftop café later discover the downside of bedbugs and noise from the bazaar. ①

Mubarak In the Olympic complex ⓣ046/460-0883, ⓕ460-0884. Its antiseptic a/c rooms with satellite TV and fridge, chalets with lounges, lavish VIP suites, and jacuzzi and sauna for guests find few takers. BB ④

Palm Trees Off Midan el-Souk ⓣ046/460-1703 or 012 104-6652. Popular for its lovely but mosquito-ridden palm garden and quiet, central location, it has basic rooms with fans (a bathroom costs £E10 extra) and an erratic water supply in the main block, and a/c chalets (£E140) out back. ①

Shali Lodge Sharia el-Seboukha ⓣ046/460-1299, ⓔinfo@eqi.com.eg. A bijou hotel built of *kharsif* and palm-logs in the traditional oasis style, with palm trees growing up through the floor of its rooftop restaurant, *Shali Lodge* was the prototype for *Albabenshal* and *Adrère Amellal* and comes under the same management. ⑤

Siwa Dream Lodge Near the Hill of the Dead ⓣ046/921-0315 or 010 099-9255, ⓦwww.siwadreamlodgehotel.com. Existing in splendid isolation 15min walk from town, it has domed bungalows around a pool and cafeteria with Bedouin-style trimmings. BB ④

Siwa Safari Gardens Sharia Aghurmi ⓣ046/460-2801, ⓦwww.siwagardens.com. Domed en-suite chalets in a palm grove with a spring-fed pool, outside town but only a 5min walk from the centre. Rates include half-board. ⑤

Siwa Safari Paradise Sharia Aghurmi ⓣ046/460-1590, ⓦwww.siwaparadise.com. A mini-tourist village of a/c rooms with fridges and satellite TV (€75), and bungalows with fan, heater and TV (€60) around a large cold spring pool for swimming. Rates include half-board. ⑥

Siwa Shally Off Sharia Anwar el-Sadat ⓣ046/460-1203. Tiny and tidy, with awesome views of Shali from its rooftop; all rooms have fans, and some baths, and balconies overlooking Shali, almost on its doorstep. ①

Youssef Midan el-Souk ⓣ046/460-2565. Central, noisy and cheap, its rooms are pretty basic (en suite costs £E10 extra), but guests can use the kitchen and the view of town from its rooftop is great. ①

East of town: Jebel Dakhrour

Qasr el-Zeytuna 3.5km from town ⓣ012 222-4209. Spacious en-suite rooms backing on to a garden and palm grove with a view of the Sand Sea, to the west of Dakhrour. ④

Siwa Shali Resort 5km from town ⓣ046/921-0064, ⓦwww.siwashaliresort.com. Mainly used by Italian tour groups, this slick *kharsif*-style complex of a/c rooms boasts a 200m-long serpentine pool, a Turkish bath, billiards, a piano and a desert library. Half-board included. ⑦

Tala Ranch 10km from town ⓣ010 588-6003, ⓦwww.talaranch-hotel.com. To get close to the desert, stay at this boutique Bedouin residence beside the Sand Sea, run by Sherif Fahmy and his Kuwaiti wife Siham. It has six stylish rooms, an archery range, camels to ride, and a Bedouin tent where delicious meals are served. BB ⑦

West of town: Birket Siwa

Adrère Amellal (aka the *Ecolodge*) 16km from town ⓣ010 166-2729, ⓦwww.adrereamellal.net. An amazing mud-brick complex with superb views over the lake, a huge pool and palm garden, and candle-lit rooms encrusted with salt-crystals (see p.450). The guest-rate (single $336; double $448) includes unlimited meals prepared from organic ingredients, a 24hr bar, and horseriding. ⑨

Taziry 15km from town ⓣ02/3337-0842, ⓦwww.taziry.com. Around the lake from *Adrère Amellal*, this hotel (whose name means "Moon" in Siwi) is similar in style, though on a smaller scale and with less greenery around its lakeside pool. Tranquillity assured; no electricity, internet or mobile phones. Rates include full-board. ⑧

The Town

The **ruins of Shali**, looming above the centre and floodlit in the evening, are a standing invitation to explore. Until the 1890s, this hermetic labyrinth attained a height of over 60m, with many levels of chambers, passages and granaries, whose remains cover the entire saddle of rock below Siwa's **Old Mosque**. Built in 1203, its crooked minaret is said to have been the last one in Egypt where the muezzin still shouted out the call to prayer without the benefit of a loudspeaker. From vantage points in Shali you can see the whole modern town, its palm groves, the salt lakes and table-top rocks beyond. Shali's main entrance is beside the **Albabenshal** hotel, seamlessly grafted onto its fortified walls. Many locals are miffed by Nematalla's expropriation of a listed monument, but not the Friends of Siwa Association (see p.441). Behind the hill is a donkey-driven **oil-press**, only used in December and January, which dates back centuries. You may hear a **blacksmith** plying his trade among the abandoned houses used as stables.

Siwan festivals

Siwan festivals represent the most public side of a largely private culture, so it's worth attending one. As many Egyptians enjoy going to them, it's wise to reserve a room well in advance and get there several days early, as buses to the oasis fill up nearer the time.

The largest, most famous is **Siayha**, when ten thoudand Siwans gather at Jebel Dakhrour to celebrate the date harvest with three days of festivities. Quarrels are resolved, friendships renewed, and everyone partakes of a huge feast after the noon prayer, blessed by a sheikh from Sidi Barrani. Many foreigners come too, and are made welcome – though women should keep a respectful distance from the circles of men performing Sufi *zikrs*. Siayha occurs during the period of the full moon in October, unless this coincides with Ramadan, in which case it's postponed until November.

A smaller festival after the corn harvest in late summer is also rooted in Sufism. Known in Siwi as the **Moulid at-Tagmigra**, it honours Siwa's patron sheikh, Sidi Suleyman, with *zikrs* outside his tomb, attached to the mosque bearing his name. Tourists may attend if they dress and behave appropriately; women must cover their hair. Siwans still tell tales about Sidi Suleyman, whose miraculous powers were manifest even before he was born, for when his pregnant mother craved fish a pigeon dropped a fully cooked one at her feet. He is also said to have once conjured up a sandstorm to bury an army of Tebu raiders.

Ashura, on the tenth of Moharram (the first month in the Islamic calendar) was once Siwa's principal feast but is nowadays chiefly an event for children, who decorate their homes with palm stalks soaked in olive oil and burn them at sunset, singing while the town is illuminated by torchlight. Afterwards the children go from house to house exchanging presents.

Local kids are also involved in creating the installations for the **Siwan Art Project**, an event which has seen thousands of kites set ablaze on Dakhrour and a "Ship of Siwa" launched on Birket Zeitun. Staged every odd-numbered year, the Art Project (featured on ⓦwww.siwa.com) is another initiative by Nematalla, who also hosts four days of **classical music concerts** by world-class artists at *Adrère Amellal* in late October. Tickets for this exclusive event are available from Philippe de Malherbe (ⓔp.demalherbe@wanadoo.fr).

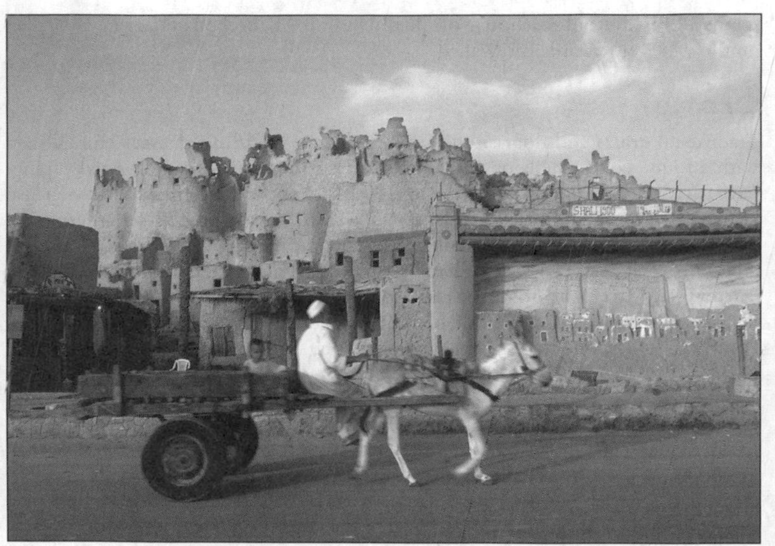

▲ Siwa town

Another peek into the past is afforded by the **Traditional Siwan House** (Mon–Thurs & Sun 9am–2pm; £E5), set up by a Canadian diplomat's wife who feared that few such mud-brick dwellings would survive. A veritable museum of traditional dress, jewellery and toys, it can help you distinguish antiques from replicas in the handicrafts shops near the **market** on Midan el-Souk, which is busiest on Fridays, when villagers come in to buy and sell. The other focus of life is the **Mosque of Sidi Suleyman**, built by King Fouad next to the whitewashed **tomb** of Siwa's patron sheikh (see box opposite).

By following the Mersa Matrouh road out of town and then bearing right, you'll reach the unmistakable Jebel al-Mawta, or **Hill of the Dead** (daily 9am–5pm; £E25). Among scores of XXVI Dynasty and Ptolemaic tombs reused by the Romans, who cut *loculi* for their own burials, four locked ones still retain murals or inscriptions. The custodian might let you climb the hill to enjoy the view without paying but you need a ticket to enter the tombs. In the **Tomb of Si-Amun**, murals depict a bearded, Greek-looking merchant and his family worshipping Egyptian deities, sadly vandalized by British soldiers after the tomb's discovery in 1940, when the Siwans dug into the necropolis to escape air raids and also found the **Tomb of Mesu-Isis**. Another third-century BC creation, this was used for two burials, although the decorators never got far beyond the entrance. Whereas Si-Amun's tomb bespeaks of Cyrenaic influence, the **Tomb of the Crocodile** reflects Siwa's longstanding ties to the Fayoum, where the crocodile cult flourished – with a dash of Hellenistic style in the painting of gazelles nibbling at a tree. The battered XXVI Dynasty **Tomb of Niperpathot** has a tiny burial chamber covered with red inscriptions. The curator can unlock other, unpainted tombs to show you **mummies** found at the Hill of the Dead.

Lastly, there's Siwa's incongruously pink and empty **Olympic complex**, built within an army base to the south of town. With seating for twenty thousand, it could accommodate most of the population of the oasis, but is only utilized by a few officers, as it awaits its place in Egypt's bid to host the Olympic Games some time in the future. The complex incorporates the *Mubarak Hotel*; on an outcrop stands a **Presidential resthouse** originally built for King Fouad. Both can be seen on the way out towards Bir Wahed.

Crafts

Traditional **crafts** still flourish in Siwa. Authentic **wedding dresses** embellished with antique coins, shells or beads, and black **robes** with orange or red piping, have narrower braiding than the versions made for the tourist market. Women also weave **carpets** and all sorts of **baskets** made from palm-fronds. The largest is the *tghara*, used for storing bread; smaller kinds include the red and green silk-tasselled *nedibash* or platters like the *tarkamt*, used for serving sweets. They also mould **pottery** and fire it at home in bread-ovens: robust cooking and storage pots, delicate oil lamps, and a kind of baptismal crucible called the *shamadan en sebaa*. Popular buys include the *adjra*, used for washing hands, and *timjamait*, or incense burners.

Unlike the gold-loving Egyptians, Siwans have traditionally preferred **silver jewellery**, which served as bullion assets for a people mistrustful of banks and paper money. The designs are uniquely Siwan, influenced by Berber rather than Egyptian heritage. Local silversmiths once produced most of it, but in modern times it has largely come from Khan el-Khalili. Broad silver bracelets and oval rings wrought with geometric designs are the most popular items with visitors, while *Al-Salhat*, with its six pendants hung from silver and coral beads, is the easiest type of necklace to identify. You'll also recognize the *tiyalaqan*, a mass of chains tipped with bells, suspended from huge crescents; and an ornament for the head consisting of silver hoops and bells suspended from matching chunks of bullion, called a *qasas*.

The Government Handicraft Shop (daily except Fri & Sat 9am–4pm) opposite Sidi Suleyman's mosque sells stuff at fixed prices, providing a benchmark for haggling at the private **shops** that have mushroomed around Midan el-Souk. Siwa Traditional Handicraft is a good place to start.

Eating and drinking

As the oases go, Siwa is good for eating, with several **restaurants** whose ambience is quite chic, and a number of cafés where you can eat well for under £E60. Providing there are customers, all are open till around midnight. Tea-houses and coffeeshops keep similar hours.

Alcohol is only available at the *Taghaghien Touristic Camp,* signposted off the road beside Birket Siwa (which charges non-residents £E10 entry and sells lukewarm Sakkara beer and Egyptian wine), or to residents of *Adrère Amellal*, who can consume unlimited imported liquor. The **shops** on Midan el-Souk are well supplied with canned goods, sweets, juices and bottled water, with fresh bread available at the **bakery**, while the **market** stocks seasonal vegetables, dates and olives galore, which you can sample before buying. Look out for the sweets made from dates stuffed with chocolate or almonds, at Siwa Products.

Abdou's Midan el-Souk. This outdoor café is the place for breakfast, pizzas (£E25–40), *shish tawook* and people-watching, acting as the informal hub of tourism in Siwa.

Albabenshal Midan el-Souk. A romantic, moodily lit rooftop restaurant with stunning views of Shali, but the cooking doesn't live up to the setting, and you can eat better elsewhere for half the price.

Alexander Sharia Keylany. Just off the main square, it serves similar fare to *Abdou's* plus a few curry dishes of dubious authenticity.

Campione Café Midan el-Souk. This tiny corner-stand in the bazaar serves genuine Italian espresso, prepared any way you like it.

Dreamers Near the tourist office. A lively hang-out with reggae music and fresh juices, that sometimes serves snacks.

Dunes Off Sharia Tortar. Serves tasty chicken biryani and grilled meats in a garden setting, near the *Palm Trees* hotel.

East-West Midan el-Souk. Named after the rival clans of Shali, this is a cut-price competitor to *Abdou's* and *Alexander*.

Hammo el-Temsah 2 By the tourist office. An offshoot of a well-known restaurant in Mersa Matrouh – from where seafood is trucked in daily – it serves delicious combo platters of grilled tilapia, squid or shrimp, salads and dips (£E30–60).

Kenouz *Shali Lodge*. The chef's repertoire includes spicy and sweet-and-sour dishes as well as Egyptian staples, pizzas, and stuffed goat, lamb or turkey by special order.

New Star Sharia Aghurmi. Candle-lit tables beneath the palms, a short walk from the bazaar down a country lane.

Nour el-Waha Sharia el-Seboukha. Off another lane near the centre, the "Light of the Oasis" has backgammon, dominoes, *kofta* and kebabs.

Tanta Waa Cleopatra's Bath. You can't get more laidback than this funky haven, with hammocks and *sheeshas*. Their menu features salads, meat and pasta dishes; the lasagne alone is worth the journey.

Moving on from Siwa

Buses leave from a depot near the tourist office, where you should buy tickets the night before to be sure of getting a seat on the morning services. Daily buses to **Alexandria** (9hr; £E35) depart at 7am, 10am and 8pm; the latter runs on to **Cairo** (12hr; £E55), where it terminates at Midan Ataba. All call at **Mersa Matrouh** (4–5hr; £E15), where other buses, leaving Siwa at 1pm and 10pm, terminate. There's usually also a **minivan** to Matrouh (£E15) in the afternoon, leaving from the Sidi Suleyman mosque.

Travelling to **Bahariya Oasis** (420km) currently takes seven or eight hours, depending on how much sand has blown across the road. A **permit** is required (see below) and vehicles usually travel in a **convoy** (see p.452). Those planning to **drive** themselves will need a 4WD with ample fuel and water, and must register their licence number when getting a permit. Tourists hoping to split the cost of a **ride** can advertise for fellow travellers at the tourist office or the Native Siwan Association. A car costs at least £E1400; to travel straight on **to the White Desert** in Farafra Oasis and camp there, around £E2600 (including meals).

Around Siwa Oasis

Although the **Siwa Oasis** depression is some 82km long and up to 28km wide, cultivated areas amount to less than two thousand acres and the total population is only 25,000; in some areas both population and cultivation have diminished since salination turned ancient gardens into barren *kharsif*. Nearer town, dense **palm groves** and wiry olive trees are carefully tended in mud- and palm-leaf-walled gardens. Siwa has over 300,000 palm trees, each yielding about ninety kilos of dates a year and requiring some thirty litres of water every day.

Palms form the backdrop to most places you're likely to visit, especially **pools** or **baths**. The nearer sites can be reached by bicycle, donkey *caretta* or on foot; just time your visit to avoid travelling in the hottest part of day. **Bicycles** are best rented from bike-repair shops rather than hotels or handicraft shops (£E15 a day). Ahmed's shop, near the garage, and the *Palm Trees* hotel rent **motorbikes** (£E120).

Though most of the oasis is freely accessible you need a 24-hour **permit** from the Native Siwan Association (p.442) to visit Bir Wahed, Shiatta or Qara Oasis, or use the road to Bahariya. In each case there's a fee of $5 for the permit plus £E12 per individual (or £E50 per person in total). Your safari operator can arrange it a day before (Fri & Sat excepted), given a photocopy of your passport.

Shop around for **excursions**; the tourist office may be able to arrange trips to certain places more cheaply than **safari operators** based at hotels, shops or

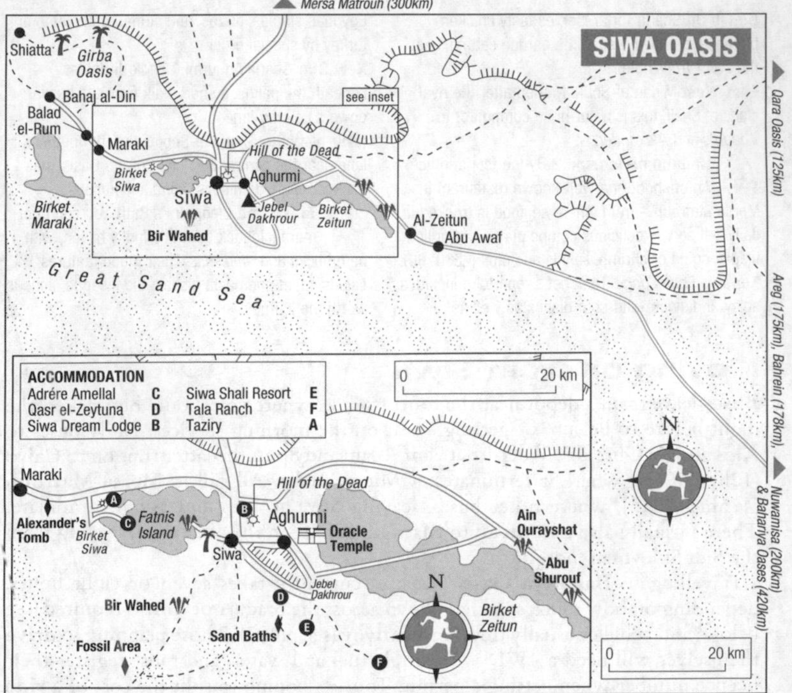

restaurants. Among those worth asking for a quote are the *Keylany* and *Palm Trees* hotels, Fathy Abdallah (☎010 656-6518) at *Abdou's Restaurant*, and Aloush (☎010 543-5455) at the *Nour el-Waha* restaurant. Jeep safaris are the rule in Siwa, **camel-trekking** having been only recently introduced by Sherif Fahmy at *Tala Ranch*, who charges £E150 for a half-day or £E350 for a full day's trekking and camping overnight. The Safari Adventure Company near Siwa's bank has a wide range of **equipment** for rent, from sleeping bags to dune-surfing boards.

Aghurmi and Jebel Dakhrour

Being too far to walk in the heat, it's best to hire a donkey *caretta* with a guide to ensure that you won't go astray on umarked roads and tracks. Agree on a price beforehand; a two-hour circuit of the Oracle Temple, the Tamusi Bath and Jebel Dakhrour should cost about £E30 for up to three people.

The road to Aghurmi begins at Siwa's main square and runs through the palm groves for 4km (a nice hour's walk if you're not going much further). Keep going straight on past the crossroads and the modern village of **AGHURMI** appears shortly before the hill where the ancient Siwans built their first fortified settlement (daily 9am–5pm; £E25). Raised 12m above the plain and entered by a single gateway, it had its own well, making it impervious to sieges. It is signposted as the "Alexander Crowning Hall" for it was here that the Siwan Oracle reposed in antiquity. You can enter the **Oracle Temple** and enjoy a superb **view** encompassing two salt lakes, Dakhrour and Siwa Town in the distance, and a great mass of palms.

Fakhry dates the temple to the reign of Amasis the Drunkard (570–526 BC) but reckons it evolved from an older site dedicated to Amun-Re, which others have attributed to the ram-headed Libyan god Ammon. Its history is subsequently documented: a Persian army sent to destroy it was obliterated by the desert; emissaries sent by Cimon of Athens were told of his death as it happened; and Lysander tried bribery to win the oracle's endorsement of his claim to the Spartan throne.

But the most famous petitioner was **Alexander the Great**. Having liberated Egypt from its hated Persian rulers and ordered the creation of a city on the Mediterranean, he hurried to Siwa in 331 BC. It's thought that he sought confirmation that he was the son of Zeus (whom the Greeks identified with Amun), but the oracle's reply – whispered by a priest through an aperture in the wall of the sanctuary – is unrecorded, and Alexander kept it secret unto his death in Asia eight years later. Despite his personal wish to be buried near the oracle, he was probably interred in Alexandria, the capital he never saw – though two Greeks once claimed to have found his tomb in Siwa (see p.450).

In ancient times the Oracle Temple was linked by a ritual causeway to the **Temple of Amun** known locally as "Um Ubayda" (signposted further along the road). It was probably founded by Nectanebo II (360–343 BC), who also rebuilt the Temple of Hibis at Kharga Oasis. A painted bas-reliefed wall and giant blocks of rubble are all that remain of this once-substantial XXX Dynasty creation after it was dynamited by a treasure-hunting governor in 1897.

Follow the path on to reach Ain Juba, known to tourists as the **Cleopatra Bath**, a deep circular pool of gently bubbling spring water where local men bathe (there are changing rooms behind the *Tanta Waa* café). Being fully visible to anyone passing along the trail, it's not a place where women can comfortably swim, and many prefer the **Tamusi Bath**, secluded 150m back along the path. *Ali's Garden* here serves tea and *sheeshas*, and by arrangement can offer special meals or host parties.

Heading on from the Cleopatra Bath, bear left at the fork and take the first path on the right. A ten-minute walk through clover fields and groves of palms will bring you out in the desert near **Jebel Dakhrour**. This rugged massif is the site for the Siayha **festival** and affords stunning **views** from its summit. In contrast to the verdant oasis and the silvery salt lake, the southern horizon presents a desolate vista of crescent dunes and blackened mesas: the edge of the Great Sand Sea.

The hot sand at Dakhrour is good for arthritis, rheumatism and spinal problems; sufferers come to be buried up to their necks over three to five days during the summer months. Twenty-minute sessions in the **sand baths** are interspersed by sips of medicinal tea to induce sweating, and hours of rest: a day's treatment costs £E150, including the use of a tent. Don't bring any valuables – thefts have been reported.

Bir Wahed

One of the best excursions on offer is into the outer dunes of the Great Sand Sea, to **Bir Wahed**, 12km southwest of town. It's a magical spot, a **hot pool** the size of a large jacuzzi, into which sulphurous water gushes; the run-off irrigates a garden around the pool. To soak up to your chest, puffing a *sheesha*, while the sun sets over the dunes all around, is a fantastic experience. Women may wear bathing costumes without offending any locals. You can climb outcrops or hunt for **fossils** in the vicinity, and on the way there or back you can plunge into a deep, jade-green **cold pool**, or sand-surf or roll down the sides of huge knife-edged dunes. The only downside is that mosquitoes are awful from dusk till dawn.

Most tourists visit Bir Wahed on a 4WD **excursion** with local safari outfits. Expect to pay £E100–120 per person for a daytime visit, £E120–150 for an overnight stay, including supper and breakfast, blankets and tents – but not the obligatory **permit**, which costs extra (see p.447). If you're driving yourself, a guide is also mandatory.

Fatnis Island and Birket Siwa

Another popular destination is "Fantasy" or **Fatnis Island**, on the salt lake of Birket Siwa, 6km west of town. An easy bike ride, it can also be reached by *caretta* (£E15–25) or on foot (1hr). Take the road out past the town council, then the left-hand road at the first fork. En route you'll pass the Abu Alif Bath, where farmhands wash; beyond the palm groves, follow a causeway across salt-encrusted pans onto Fatnis, where palms surround a large circular tiled **pool**, fed by fresh water welling up from clefts in the rock 15m below. There's a stall selling tea and *sheeshas*.

Actually, Fatnis is no longer an island; the **Birket Siwa** has receded and a barrage now divides it into a drainage reservoir and an intensely saline remnant which blackens the surrounding vegetation. Despite its faintly acrid smell the lake looks beautiful, with sculpted table-tops on the western horizon. The largest was bestowed the name **Jebel Beida** (White Mountain) by British cartographers; the Siwans call it Adrère Amellal in their own language, while Egyptians know it as Sidi Jaffar.

On the far side of this is the extraordinary **Adrère Amellal** ecolodge, a vast, fantasy *qasr*-style hotel entirely built of *kharsif*, palm logs and salt slabs (used instead of glass). The brainchild of Cairene environmental engineer Mounir Nematalla, the ecolodge is designed to save energy and water and recycle waste products on its organic farm. Since it often has no guests at all, they don't mind the odd visitor looking around providing you get written permission from the *Shali Lodge* in town first. Further round the lake is the similar but smaller *Taziry* hotel. Both are reached by a spur road off the route to Maraki, which turns off the Mersa Matrouh highway 1km north of town. It's rather far to cycle (16km) so you'll need to take a car (£E50 return), or you could include it as a stopover on excursions to Maraki (see p.451).

Maraki and Shiatta

MARAKI is the collective name for several **villages** at the western end of the depression, separated from the main oasis by a rocky desert riddled with caves and tombs, with a salt lake beyond. Intensively cultivated from Roman times until the fifteenth century, Maraki is now mostly used for grazing by the **Bedouin** Al-Shihaybat tribe. Buildings here are quite new, as the old settlements were destroyed by the deluge of 1982, which forced residents to shelter in caves at **Balad el-Rum** (Town of the Romans). In 1991, Maraki made news when Liana and Manos Souvaltzi announced their discovery of the **"Tomb of Alexander the Great"** beneath a ruined **Doric temple** near Balad el-Rum. Having endorsed their claim, the SCA backed off after the Greeks failed to refute criticism that they'd misread vital inscriptions; revoked their licence and moved all the stones to a depository.

To travel beyond the checkpoint at Bahaj al-Din requires a **permit** (see p.447). Here a track runs off to **Girba Oasis**, occupied by Bedouin from the settlement of **SHIATTA** and a detachment of Border Guards. For decades this was a halt on the Masrab el-Ikhwan (Road of the Brotherhood) from Jaghbub Oasis in Libya, whereby Senussi preachers reached the Western Desert oases. (*Masrab* is the Siwan word for a camel route, called a *darb* in other oases.) Shiatta's salt **spring** is thought to be the remnant of a lake that once spread towards Aghurmi, where **fossils** of fifty-million-year-old crocodiles have recently been discovered.

A full day's **excursion** to Maraki, Balad el-Rum and Shiatta can be arranged by the tourist office (£E160 for two or three people) or hotels such as the *Palm Trees* (£E700 for four; £E800 including Bir Wahed on the way back).

Around Birket Zeitun

The largest salt lake in the oasis, **Birket Zeitun** is visible from Jebel Dakhrour, from where a **causeway** crosses acres of mud, attesting to the lake's slow recession. Only the far shore is inhabited, with villages that flourished in Roman times before centuries of slow decline set in. The lake's increasing salinity is both the cause and result of depopulation: as fewer irrigation works are maintained, more of the warm water from the **Ain Qurayshat** spring flows unused into the lake, crystallizing mineral salts as it evaporates. The source is enclosed by an industrial-sized concrete tank where you can bathe – but beware of underwater ledges.

Better bathing can be found 35km southeast of Siwa Town at **ABU SHUROUF**, where there's a large kidney-shaped pool of cool, clear, azure water with bug-eyed fishes swimming about, opposite the Hayat mineral water bottling plant. The village beyond is remarkable for harbouring all the female **donkeys** in the oasis, which are kept and mated here. In Siwan parlance, "Have you been to Abu Shurouf?" is a euphemism for "Have you had sex?"

Further out along the lake, **AL-ZEITUN** was once a model Senussi village tending the richest gardens in the oasis, until it was abandoned after an Italian bombing raid in 1940. Near the far end is a smoke-blackened kiosk-**temple** where the locals once sheltered from bombs. Hundreds of **Roman tombs** riddle the hills been Al-Zeitun and **Ain Safi,** the last hamlet in the oasis before the Darb Siwa to Bahariya Oasis enters the deep desert (see p.452).

A half-day **tour** of these sites can be arranged through Siwa's tourist office (£E50 each for two or three people) or the *Palm Trees* hotel (£E120 per person, including lunch).

Qara Oasis and the Qattara Depression

If you're seriously into desert travel, **Qara Oasis** has a compelling fascination. The smallest and poorest of the oases, populated by the descendants of runaway slaves, it has been described as "Siwa yesterday". Visitors are so rare that the villagers turn out to welcome them and serve a meal in their honour. Until flooding rendered it unsafe in 1982, the Qarawis occupied a Shali-like labyrinth atop "a solitary white mushroom of rock", edged by a "high smooth wall, impregnable to raiders, with one black tunnel for a street". Now, most families live in new houses on the plain.

The shortest **route** from Siwa to Qara is the Masrab Khidda (125km), whose featureless mud flats make it essential to have someone who knows the way. Alternatively, you can head north towards Mersa Matrouh and turn off at the checkpoint just before the Bir Nous resthouse, onto a dirt road. Though not often in demand, Siwa's tourist office can arrange a day-**excursion** to Qara for about £E600. You'll need a **permit** (see p.447).

Northeast of Qara the land plummets into the **Qattara Depression**, which is seven times the size of all the Western Desert oases combined and, at 60–134m below sea level, the lowest point in Africa. Planners have long dreamed of piping water 38km from the Mediterranean to the depression, utilizing the fall in height to generate hydroelectricity and run desalination plants and irrigation systems, but all attempts have foundered through lack of capital. There is, however, exploration for **oil** at many points in the desert between Qattara and Mersa Matrouh, hence the upgraded tracks that crisscross the wilderness.

Siwa to Bahariya

The ancient Darb Siwa caravan route to Bahariya Oasis (420km) has been upgraded to a proper **road** for some 300km, with the rest due to be finished by 2012. Six **checkpoints** en route provide assurance that vehicles which break down will be missed, but otherwise there are no sources of water, nor any fuel – and mobile phones are beyond signal range. All travellers require a day-permit (see p.447) and must travel with an army escort and a satphone, which usually means joining a **convoy** leaving at 7am, from out near Siwa's carpet factory.

If you're hiring someone to drive you from Siwa (see p.447), bear in mind that the quoted rate is for a nonstop journey, bypassing all the uninhabited oases off the road, whose beauty can only be appreciated on excursions requiring an **overnight** permit (see p.380), arranged through a licensed safari company.

Areg Oasis, 175km from Siwa, is surrounded by striated chalk buttes which look like giant brioches that have sat in the oven too long. Regarded as a haunt of bandits by nineteenth-century travellers, its cliffs are riddled with **tombs**. A tablet from Alexandria records that the population of Siwa, Bahrein and other now-deserted oases numbered 400,000 in Persian times.

Bahrein Oasis – named after its two azure salt lakes – is awash with custard-coloured sand, hemmed in by croissant-shaped buttes riddled with Greco-Roman **tombs**. Seductive as they look, the **salt lakes** are surrounded by mushy sand and salt crusts that can trap unwary vehicles, and if safari groups camp here they do so in the palm groves on the far side, away from the mosquitoes and protected from sandstorms.

Nuwamisa Oasis looks equally lovely, with a salt lake rimmed by palms and crescent cliffs – but its name, "Oasis of the Mosquitoes", is all too true. Millions of **mosquitoes** swarm as soon as the sun goes down making camping a nightmare even if you're all zipped up in your tent. Safaris prefer to camp in **Sitra Oasis**, which isn't so badly infested and used to be a watering hole for Bedouin smugglers bringing hashish into Egypt. During the last 45km of the journey to Bahariya the road skirts the **Ghard Kebir** (Great Dunes), voyaging south from the Qattara Depression, destined to arrive in Bahariya in a few hundred years.

Alexandria, the Mediterranean coast and the Delta

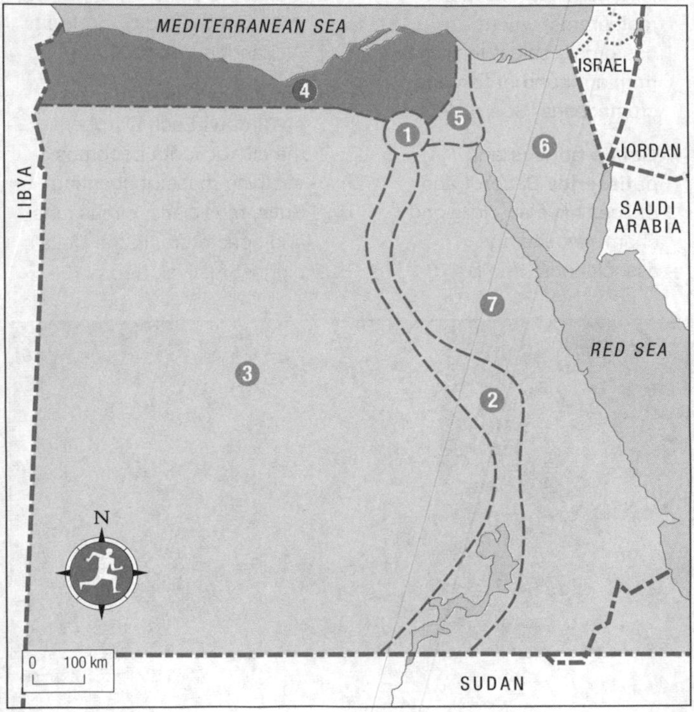

MEDITERRANEAN SEA
ISRAEL
JORDAN
LIBYA
SAUDI ARABIA
RED SEA
SUDAN
N
0 100 km

CHAPTER 4

Highlights

* **Bibliotheca Alexandrina** The city's library is a stunning example of contemporary architecture, aimed at reviving the legendary "Mother Library" of antiquity. See p.472

* **Catacombs of Kom es-Shoqafa** This eerie subterranean Roman necropolis is full of bizarre carvings, with a dining room for mourners. See p.473

* **Fresh seafood** Alexandria is famous for its seafood restaurants, where customers select their meal from a mound of fish and crustaceans. See p.477

* **Coffee houses and patisseries** *Baudrot* and *Délices* have an old-world charm and literary associations. See p.478

* **Diving** Explore the remains of Cleopatra's Palace, Napoleonic warships and World War II aircraft in the waters off Alexandria. See p.481

* **El-Alamein** The war museum and cemeteries are stark reminders of the decisive battle in 1942. See p.485

* **Rosetta** This town has been busy restoring its legacy of Ottoman mansions built in the distinctive Delta style, making it a worthwhile day trip from Alexandria See p.490

* **Moulid of Saiyid Ahmed el-Bedawi** Each October, the city of Tanta becomes a seething mass of chanting Sufis, musicians, circus acts and spectators, in the Delta's biggest festival. See p.494

▲ The Bibliotheca Alexandrina

4

Alexandria, the Mediterranean coast and the Delta

Egypt's second city, **Alexandria** was once a lodestar throughout the ancient world, its lighthouse and library beacons of enlightenment, its rulers synonymous with splendour and depravity. A unique fusion of Hellenistic, Levantine, Egyptian, Jewish and European cultures, its cosmopolitanism took a heavy knock in the Nasser era and has since been diluted further by an influx of provincial Egyptians who deplore its tradition of mixed marriages and cultural curiosity. To those of a nostalgic bent it is the "Capital of Memory", rich in literary and historical associations nurtured by Lawrence Durrell, E.M. Forster and Constantine Cavafy. If Alexandria's monuments are a pale shadow of its ancient glory, its new Library and cultural vigour show that the city is still a force to be reckoned with.

For Ancient Egyptians, the **Mediterranean coast** marked the edge of the "Great Green", the measureless sea that formed the limits of the known world. Life and civilization meant the Nile Valley and the Delta – an outlook that still seems to linger in the country's subconscious. For, despite the white beaches, craggy headlands and turquoise sea that stretch for some 500km, much of the Egyptian Med is eerily vacant and underpopulated. Aside from a score of resorts that mainly cater to Egyptians, the only place of note is the World War II battlefield of **El-Alamein**, where the Western Desert campaign was decided.

While the coast's significance has been fleeting and Alexandria is a relative latecomer to the stage of Egyptian history, the Nile **Delta** was one of the Two Lands of Ancient Egypt and remains the archetypal heartland of the nation. Though seldom acknowledged in political science textbooks, Egypt is ruled by elites from Cairo, Alexandria and the Delta province of Menoufiya (birthplace of presidents Sadat and Mubarak). As the home of Egypt's cotton industry, its textile workers are the most unionized and militant section of the working class. While its attractions are limited to the Ottoman mansions of **Rosetta**, moulids at **Tanta** and **Damanhur** and ruins at **Bubastis** and **Avaris**, the Delta is the "real Egypt", without any concessions to tourism.

As for the **weather**, the Mediterranean coast gets hotter and drier the further west you travel, but in winter Alexandria can be cold and windy with torrential downpours and waves crashing over the Corniche, and the Delta experiences showers. The Mediterranean Sea doesn't become warm enough for **swimming** till June, but you can be pretty sure of continuous sunshine from April until November.

Alexandria

Alexandria, princess and whore. The royal city and the *anus mundi*.

Lawrence Durrell, *The Alexandria Quartet*

A hybrid city dubbed the "Capital of Memory" by Durrell, **ALEXANDRIA** (El-Iskandariya in Arabic) turns its back on the rest of Egypt and faces the Mediterranean, as if contemplating its glorious past. One of the great cities of antiquity, Alex slumbered for 1300 years until it was revived by Mohammed Ali and transformed by Europeans, who gave the city its present shape and made it synonymous with cosmopolitanism and decadence. This era came to an end in the 1950s with the mass flight of non-Egyptians and a short-lived dose of revolutionary puritanism, but Alexandria's beaches, restaurants and breezy climate still attract hordes of Cairenes during the summer, while its jaded historical and literary mystique remains appealing to foreigners.

Alex is easily reached **from Cairo**, with a choice of train, bus, service taxi or plane. Buses and service taxis offer two routes, travelling by the verdant Desert Road past the turn-off for Wadi Natrun (whose monasteries are covered in Chapter 3), or by the hazardous, congested Delta Road, which is much slower, though the distance is roughly similar (about 225km).

The best **buses**, which do the journey in three hours, are operated by Superjet from outside Cairo's *Ramses Hilton* hotel; slightly cheaper and less comfortable services, run by the West Delta bus company, leave from the Turgoman Garage and the Aboud Terminal. The fastest **trains**, a/c Spanish and Turbini services, both leave three times daily and take just over two hours. There is also the so-called French service that has nine daily departures, takes thirty minutes longer and costs thirty percent less. **Service taxis** do the run in about three hours; in Cairo both car- and minibus-taxis cluster outside Ramses Station and at the Aboud Terminal, their drivers bawling "Iskandariya! Iskandariya!". **Flying** from Cairo (50min) won't save you any time once you take getting to and from the airports into account. For full details of bus, train, taxi and flight schedules and terminals, see pp.209–212.

Some history

When **Alexander the Great** wrested Egypt from the Persian Empire in 332 BC at the age of 25, he decided against Memphis, the ancient capital, in favour of building a new city linked by sea to his Macedonian homeland. Choosing a site near the fishing village of **Rhakotis**, where two limestone spurs formed a natural harbour, he gave orders to his architect, Deinocrates, before travelling on to Siwa and thence to Asia, where he died eight years later. His corpse was subsequently returned to Egypt, where the priests refused burial at Memphis; its final resting place remains a mystery.

Thereafter Alexander's empire was divided amongst his Macedonian generals, one of whom took Egypt and adopted the title Ptolemy I Soter, founding a dynasty (305–30 BC). Avid promoters of Hellenistic culture, the **Ptolemies** made Alexandria an intellectual powerhouse: among its scholars were Euclid, the "father of geometry", and Eratosthenes, who accurately determined the circumference and diameter of the earth. Alexandria's great lighthouse, the **Pharos**, was literally and metaphorically a beacon, rivalled in fame only by the city's library, the **Bibliotheca Alexandrina** – the foremost centre of learning in the ancient world.

While the first three Ptolemies were energetic and enlightened, the later members of the dynasty are remembered as decadent and dissolute – perhaps due to their brother-sister marriages, in emulation of the pharaohs and gods of Ancient Egypt – and relied on Rome to maintain their position. Even the bold **Cleopatra VII** (51–30 BC) came unstuck after her lover, Julius Caesar, was murdered, and his successor in Rome (and her bed), Mark Antony, was defeated by Octavian. The latter hated her and so detested Cleopatra's capital at Alexandria that he banned Roman citizens from entering Egypt on the pretext that its religious orgies were morally corrupting.

Roman rule and Arab conquest

Whereas Alexandria's Egyptians and Greeks had previously respected one another's deities and even syncretized them into a common cult (the worship of Serapis), religious conflicts developed under **Roman rule** (30 BC–313 AD). The empire regarded Christianity, which was supposedly introduced by St Mark in 45 AD, as subversive, and the persecution of Christians from 250 AD onwards reached a bloody apogee under Emperor Diocletian, when the Copts maintain that 144,000 believers were martyred. (The Coptic Church dates its chronology from 284 AD, the "Era of Martyrs", rather than Christ's birth.)

After the emperor Constantine made **Christianity** the state religion, a new controversy arose over the nature of Christ, the theological subtleties of which essentially masked a political rebellion by Egyptian **Copts** against Byzantine (ie Greek) authority. In Alexandria, the Coptic patriarch became supreme and his monks waged war against paganism, sacking the Serapis Temple and library in 391 and murdering the female scholar Hypatia in 415.

Local hatred of Byzantium disposed the Alexandrians to welcome the **Arab conquest** (641), whose commander, Amr, described the city as containing "4000 palaces, 4000 baths, 400 theatres, 1200 greengrocers and 40,000 Jews". But while the Arabs incorporated elements of Alexandrian learning into their own civilization, they cared little for the city itself. Owing to neglect and the silting up of the waterways that connected it to the Nile, Alexandria inexorably declined over the next millennium, so that when Napoleon's expeditionary force arrived in 1798, they found a mere fishing village with four thousand inhabitants.

From Mohammed Ali to modern times

Alexandria's **revival** sprang from Mohammed Ali Pasha's desire to make Egypt a commercial and maritime power. The Mahmudiya Canal, finished in 1820, once again linked Alexandria to the Nile, while a harbour, docks and arsenal were created. European merchants erected mansions and warehouses, building outwards from the Place des Consuls (modern-day Midan Tahrir), and the city's population soared to 230,000. Nationalist resentment of foreign influence fired the **Orabi revolt** of 1882, in retaliation for which British warships shelled the city. Yet such was Alexandria's vitality and commercial importance that it quickly recovered; the next five decades were a Belle Époque that even two world wars only briefly disturbed.

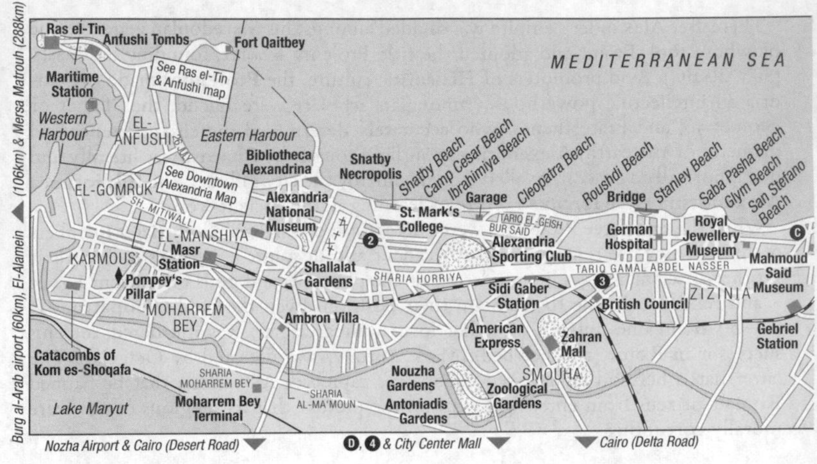

But the era of European supremacy was nearing its end, as anti-British riots expressed rising **nationalism**. The **revolution** that forced King Farouk to sail into exile in 1952 didn't seriously affect the "foreign" community (many of whom had lived here for generations) until the Anglo-French-Israeli assault on Egypt during the Suez Crisis of 1956, following which Nasser expelled all French and British citizens and nationalized foreign businesses, forcing a hundred thousand non-Egyptians to emigrate. Institutions, street names and businesses were Egyptianized, and the custom of moving the seat of government to Alexandria during the hot summer months was ended.

Though "old" Alexandrians regret the **changes** since Suez, Durrell's complaint that they rendered Alexandria "depressing beyond endurance" is unjustified. Egypt's second city (pop. 5,500,000) has become more Egyptian and less patrician, but it doesn't lack subtlety or vitality. Alexandrians whose families have lived here for generations are proud of their multi-ethnic heritage (marriages between Copts and Muslims aren't unknown even today) and their openness to new ideas and influences – it's no coincidence that the first blogger to be jailed in Egypt was an Alexandrian.

This liberal tradition is countered by demographics. Over one million incomers from the Delta and Upper Egypt brought ingrained habits of bigotry and vendettas with them. As the city's infrastructure buckled under the strain and the Muslim Brotherhood grew bolder, tension mounted – erupting in 2006, when a knife attack by a "deranged" Muslim at a Coptic church was followed by three days of sectarian rioting. Fearing that Alexandria was sliding out of control, Mubarak appointed Adel Labib as city governor to turn things around as he had in Qena (see p.262). Since then, improvements in public services have restored peoples' faith in the city's viability and hopes of it flourishing in the future.

Arrival, orientation and information

West Delta and Superjet **buses** drop passengers at the vast **Moharrem Bey** terminal on the city's outskirts, from where you can reach the centre by taxi (£E15) or a minibus (£E1.25) to the Tomb of the Unknown Soldier by the Corniche. Trains from Cairo usually stop at Sidi Gaber Station (east of the centre)

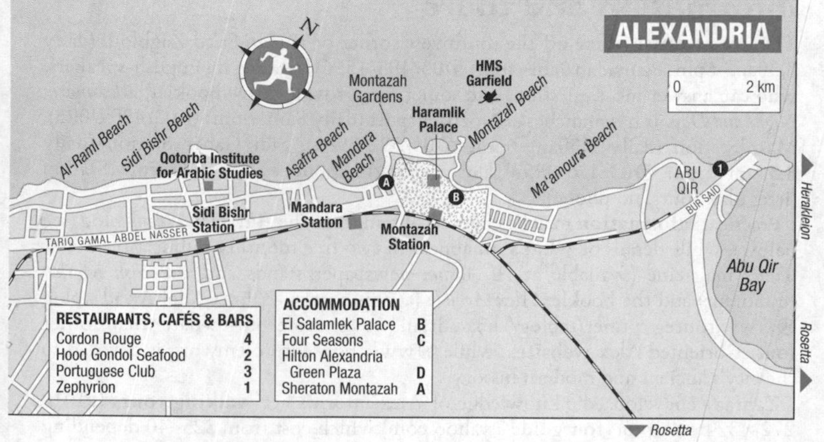

before terminating at **Masr Station**, about 1km south of downtown Midan Sa'ad Zaghloul, which you can reach by walking up Sharia Nabi Daniel (10–15min). **Service taxis** are likely to wind up on **Midan el-Gumhorriya**, outside Masr Station, but might terminate at the Moharrem Bey depot or even El-Agami – be sure to ask at the start of your journey.

Alexandria is served by three **airports**. EgyptAir uses **Nozha**, 5km south of the city, as a stopover on some flights to Europe; other airlines use the new international terminals at **Al-Alamein** or **Burg al-Arab** airport, respectively 130km and 60km from Alex. Public **transport** is limited to bus #555 (scheduled to coincide with flight arrivals and departures; £E10) from Burg al-Arab to Midan Sa'ad Zaghloul. A **taxi** to Alex from Al-Alamein airport costs £E200–300, from Burg al-Arab £E150, from Nozha £E30–50.

Mediterranean **cruise boats** dock at the **Maritime Station** in the Western Harbour, access to which is restricted, so that taxis can only be hailed (or drop) outside the perimeter; passengers are taken on excursions into the centre by coach.

Orientation and maps

Alexandria runs along the Mediterranean for 20km without ever venturing more than 8km inland – a true waterfront city. Its great **Corniche** sweeps around the **Eastern Harbour** and along the coast past a string of city **beaches** to **Montazah** and **Ma'amoura**, burning out before the final beach at **Abu Qir**. In the opposite direction, you need to get past the industrial zone of **Al-Max** to reach the western beaches of **Hannoville** and **El-Agami**. Most foreign tourists frequent the downtown quarter of **El-Manshiya** (see map, p.464), where many of restaurants and hotels are within a few blocks either side, or inland, of **Midan Sa'ad Zaghloul**.

The Corniche (and breezes blowing inland) make basic orientation quite simple, but the finer points can still be awkward and even the latest **map** – *Alexandria Key* (£E25 from local bookshops, see p.482) – doesn't show every backstreet in the centre. **Street names** are also problematic, for signs don't always square with the latest official designation or popular usage. In the downtown area, most of the signs are in English or Arabic, and people may use either when giving directions. A historical map of *Archeological Sites of Alexandria*, published by the Alexandria Preservation Trust, is on sale at bookshops.

Information and tours

The main **tourist office** off the southwest corner of Midan Sa'ad Zaghloul (daily 8.30am–6pm; Ramadan 9am–4pm; ⓣ03/485-1556) is staffed by English-speakers, who can answer most questions and sometimes provide a free booklet, *Alexandria Night and Day*. It has branches at Nozha airport (daily 8am–8pm; ⓣ03/420-7023), Masr Station (daily 8.30am–6pm; ⓣ03/392-5985), Sidi Gaber Station (daily 8.30am–3pm; ⓣ03/426-3953) and a part-time one at the Maritime Station (irregular hours, no phone).

Practical **information** may be easier to obtain from the *Alexandria News* blog (see below), while details of **what's on** appear in two free monthly publications: *Alex Times* magazine (available at *Al-Ahram* newspaper stands and the *Fish Market* restaurant) and the booklet *Alex Agenda* (at top hotels). Zahraa Adel Awad's blog ⓦwww.touregypt.net/teblog/alexandrianews is more up-to-date than other tourist-oriented Alex **websites**, while ⓦwww.houseofptolemy.org is devoted to the city's ancient and modern history.

Zahraa's encyclopaedic knowledge of Alex informs her **walking tours** (ⓣ010 272-4324; ⓔegypt_tourguide@yahoo.com) which cost from $25–40 depending on the size of the group and the tour's duration (normally 4hr). Her Roots Tour – aimed at people with ancestral ties to the city – can be tailored to personal wishes (such as finding the house where your grandparents once lived), while other tours are devoted to Durrell, Cavafy and E.M. Forster, or Italianate or Art Deco architecture.

City transport

Downtown is compact enough to walk around, and along the Corniche to Fort Qaitbey makes a healthy constitutional (35–50min). However, you really need transport to reach other outlying areas. The main downtown terminals are **Ramleh** tram station; the square outside Masr Station, **Midan el-Gumhorriya**; and the Tomb of the Unknown Soldier between **Midan Orabi** and the Corniche. Minibuses running along the Corniche can be boarded from the seafront side of both Midan Orabi and Sa'ad Zaghloul.

Trams, buses and minibuses

Trams run from 5.30am to 1am, with fares of 50pt or 75pt. Destinations and route numbers are in Arabic only, but you can get an idea from the vehicle's livery where it's heading: trams between Ramleh and Ras el-Tin (to the west) are painted yellow with a red or blue trim; trams between Ramleh and points east (all of which stop at the Sporting Club), blue and white. On trams with three carriages, the middle one is reserved for women. Over summer, a 1936-vintage wooden tram (£E1) runs from Ramleh out to Zizinia (between Glym and Stanley).

Buses (£E1–2) are also numbered in Arabic and keep similar schedules to the trams, but are faster, with passengers boarding on the run between Sa'ad Zaghloul, Tahrir and El-Gumhorriya squares. Vehicles are crowded, except on the red double-decker buses found on some routes, which charge £E3. **Minibuses** offer seating-only rides on many of the same routes, with fares ranging from £E1.25–2.

Taxis, calèches and car rental

Alex's black-and-yellow **taxis** never use meters and will charge whatever they can get away with (especially going to Masr Station or any other departure point). You

Useful public transport services in Alexandria

Trams	
#1 & #2 (yellow)	Ramleh to Victoria (near Sidi Bishr), via the Sporting Club and the Roushdi district
#2 (blue)	Ramleh to Victoria, via the Sporting Club and Roushdi
#15 (yellow)	Ramleh to Ras el-Tin, via El-Gomruk and El-Anfushi (near Fort Qaitbey)
#16	Midan Orabi (Unknown Soldier) to Pompey's Pillar and the Catacombs
Buses	
#3	Ramleh to Hannoville (El-Agami), via the Corniche
#11	Ras el-Tin to Ma'amoura, via the Corniche
#12	Midan Khartoum to Hannoville, via the Corniche
#555	Midan Sa'ad Zaghloul to Burg al-Arab airport
Minibuses	
#1	Midan Sa'ad Zaghloul to the Sidi Gaber station and Sidi Bishr
#2	Ramleh to Hannoville
#3	Ramleh west to Abu Talaat (beyond El-Agami)
#11	Ras el-Tin to Montazah and Ma'amoura, via the Corniche
#260	Anfushi to Abu Qir
#739	Ras el-Tin to Sidi Bishr, via the Corniche
#751	Moharrem Bey to Bitash
#765	Masr Station to Hannoville (El-Agami)
#766	Ras el-Tin to Abu Qir, via Sidi Gaber and the Corniche from Shatby onwards
#768	Masr Station to Ma'amoura, inland

should pay about £E5 for a ride across downtown (say, to Shatby Beach), and £E30 for a trip all the way east to Montazah Beach. There are also rarely seen "City Taxis" (silver-grey Toyota Corollas) with meters, which can be booked on freephone ⓣ0800 999-9999.

Horse-drawn carriages solicit passengers with cries of "*calèche, calèche*" outside Masr Station and along the Corniche. You'll have to negotiate a price – reckon on about £E50 an hour.

With driving in the city so crazy, **renting a car** only makes sense to visit El-Alamein and the Monastery of St Mina, west of Alexandria (see pp.484–489). For self-drive rental, Avis in the *Hotel Cecil* (ⓣ03/485-7400) charges $45 per day for a Toyota or Hyundai, including 100km of mileage. For hiring a car with an English-speaking **driver**, you're better off going to Thomas Cook on Midan Ramleh, whose price for a full day's tour of El-Alamein and St Mina (£E380) is far cheaper than Avis (£E660).

Accommodation

A sea view is a big plus, and hotels charge accordingly. One drawback that only later becomes apparent is **tram noise** – basically, you either learn to live with it or move further inland. **Reservations** are essential in high season, and the **price codes** quoted below refer to rooms without a sea view. The downtown hotels are all marked on the map on pp.464–465. If you don't mind being out of the centre, there are **upmarket hotels** at San Stefano and Montazah (see p.476) or out near the malls on Alexandria's southern edge. Look for discount rates online.

Downtown

Acropole 27 Sharia Gamil el-Din Yassin, fourth floor ⓣ03/480-5980 or 010 376-6647, ⓔacropole_hotel@yahoo.com. Very central and within earshot of the trams, this old-fashioned hotel is smartening itself up. It's worth paying £E40 extra for an en-suite room with a balcony and a sea view; other rooms sharing bathrooms have a wash basin. BB ❷

Cecil 16 Midan Sa'ad Zaghloul ⓣ03/447-7173, ⓦwww.sofitel.com. Dead central, with fab views of the Eastern Harbour, the *Cecil* is an Alexandrian institution. Durrell, Churchill, Noël Coward and Josephine Baker head the list of former guests, but modernization and *Sofitel* management have dispelled the old ambience. Regular rooms are cosy and a/c but nothing special. You'll pay €30 extra for a sea view; a grand corner suite costs €280. Takes Amex, MC and Visa. BB ❽

Crillon 5 Sharia Adib Ishtak ⓣ03/480-0330. The best-preserved of Alex's prewar *pensions* has a lobby full of stuffed birds and Art Deco rooms with sea-view balconies and spotless shared bathrooms on the third floor; don't bother with the smaller en-suite rooms upstairs. Half board obligatory in high season. BB ❸

Egypt 1 Sharia Degla ⓣ03/481-4483, ⓔegypt_hotel_alx@yahoo.com. Just off Midan Ramleh, smack in the centre, this third-floor hotel's columned lobby raises expectations that its a/c en-suite rooms with TV and fridges don't quite deliver; even with free wi-fi it's a bit overpriced. BB ❺

Metropole 52 Sharia Sa'ad Zaghloul ⓣ03/486-1467 ⓦwww.paradiseinnegypt.com. Likewise just off Ramleh, this ornate 1900s hotel has bags of character. All rooms have a/c; the suites are furnished with antiques and have jacuzzis. It's worth paying $40 extra for a sea view. Takes Amex, DC, MC and Visa cards. BB ❻

New Capri 23 Sharia Minaa es-Sharqiya ⓣ03/480-9310, ⓕ03/480-9703. On the eighth floor above the tourist office, this renovated 1930s *pension* has kitsch Arabesque touches, billiards, a library, free internet and a buffet breakfast. Ask for a room with a balcony and Corniche view. BB ❸

Nile Excelsior 16 Sharia al-Bursa al-Qadima, second floor ⓣ03/480-0799. Just up the road from the *Spitfire Bar* (see p.479), this old-fashioned hotel has smallish, clean, comfortable en-suite rooms, but lacks the panache of the neighbouring *Swiss Canal* (see below). BB ❸

Swiss Canal 14 Sharia al-Bursa al-Qadima ⓣ03/480-8373. Named after the Suez Canal (according its Egyptian pronunciation), this invitingly bright hotel has an Art Deco foyer and spacious en-suite rooms with soft beds, fridge, TV, fans or a/c (£E13 extra), painted pink throughout. ❷

Triomphe 26 Sharia Gamil el-Din Yassin, 5th floor ⓣ03/480-7585. Attractively kitsch, with some rooms en-suite (£E20 extra) but no sea views, this is another good low-budget option. ❷

Union 164 Sharia 26 July, 5th floor ⓣ03/480-7312. This Art Deco hotel on the Corniche has a lounge facing the Eastern Harbour. It's worth paying £E10 more for a room with a sea view and private bathroom. ❸

Windsor Palace 17 Sharia ash-Shohada ⓣ03/480-8123, ⓦwww.paradiseinnegypt.com. An Edwardian hotel with a soothing green and gold decor, whose management routinely overbooks and then tries to palm guests off onto its sister hotel way out in Ma'amoura. BB ❼

Outside the centre

El Salamlek Palace Montazah Gardens, 30–40min by taxi from the city centre ⓣ03/547-7999, ⓦwww.sangiovanni.com. Built by Khedive Abbas II for his Austrian mistress, this bijou hunting lodge in the grounds of the royal palace has gorgeous suites ($1980) but other rooms are showing their age, and poor service and snooty staff take the shine off its swanky restaurant, private beach and casino (open to non-residents with passports). All major cards. BB ❼

Four Seasons San Stefano, 20min by taxi from the centre ⓣ03/581-8000, ⓦwww.fourseasons.com/alexandria. Setting new standards for luxury in Alex, this marbled five-star behemoth has balconies, CD players, LCD screens and deep tubs in all its rooms (from $490); a wellness spa, a private beach and marina, and an infinity pool overlooking the Med. ❾

Hilton Alexandria Green Plaza 14th of May Bridge, Smouha, 20min by taxi from the city centre ⓣ03/420-9120, ⓦwww.hilton.com. With its five-star amenities and the Green Plaza Mall on its doorstep, who cares if you're beside a motorway on the city's edge? All major cards. BB ❼

Sheraton Montazah On a busy junction outside the Montazah Gardens ⓣ03/548-0550, ⓦwww.sheratonmontazah.com. Its sea views are the main attraction of this concrete tower, whose facilities are less elaborate than at the *Hilton*, never mind the *Four Seasons*. BB ❽

The City

Alex encourages nostalgia trips and random exploration, if only because the "sights" are limited and chance incidents often more revealing. Don't be afraid of following your nose and deviating from the usual itineraries, which could be completed in a day or so if you focus on the city's monumental **highlights**. The **Roman Theatre** and **Villa of Birds at Kom el-Dikka** and the spooky **Catacombs of Kom es-Shoqafa** are musts, as is the city's magnificent new **library** and **Alexandria National Museum**, exhibiting statues and other artefacts dredged from ancient cities on the seabed. If you also want to savour the ambience and literary mystique of the former European and "native" quarters, allow two or three days.

South and east of Midan Sa'ad Zaghloul

Since E.M. Forster wrote his guide to Alexandria in 1922, the city's centre has shifted eastwards from the former Place Mohammed Ali (now Midan Tahrir) to the seafront **Midan Sa'ad Zaghloul**, a square named after the nationalist leader (1860–1927) whose **statue** gazes towards the Mediterranean. His deportation by the British to Malta provoked nationwide rioting in 1919 and guaranteed Zaghloul a hero's return, though the independence he sought was denied for another generation. Zaghloul is referred to as "the Pasha" in Naguib Mahfouz's Alexandrian novel, *Miramar*.

With no trace of the Caesareum that stood here in ancient times (see below), the square today looks post-colonial; decrepit edifices that could have been lifted from Naples or Athens overshadow the tourist office. The dominant building is the pseudo-Moorish **Hotel Cecil**, where British Intelligence hatched the El-Alamein deception plan from a suite on the first floor. No longer the decadent and moribund establishment of *The Alexandria Quartet*, it now belongs to the *Sofitel* chain.

A similar mystique once attended Alexandria's **patisseries**, of which there are a handful in the vicinity. *Délices*, established in 1922, is a tearoom with two long halls whose French name belies the fact that it was originally owned by Greeks, like the *Trianon* (where the poet Cavafy worked as a clerk for the First Circle of Irrigation on the floor above and scenes from the British war movie *Ice Cold in Alex* were filmed), and *Athineos* on Midan Ramleh (see p.478 for reviews of these and other patisseries). The *Trianon* stands just behind the former site of **Cleopatra's Needles**, two giant obelisks that once marked the entrance to the Caesareum (see below). Both were removed in the 1870s, to be re-erected on London's Embankment and in New York's Central Park. Their popular name is a misnomer, for they originated at Heliopolis fourteen centuries earlier, and were moved to Alexandria fifteen years after Cleopatra's death.

Along Sharia Nabi Daniel

Starting as an inconspicuous backstreet beside the tourist office, **Sharia Nabi Daniel** grows wider as it runs south along the route of the ancient **Street of the Soma**. Paved in marble and flanked by marble colonnades, this dazzled the Arabs in 641 even though its finest buildings had already vanished. Before its destruction by feuding Christians in the fourth century, the north end of the street was crowned by the **Caesareum**, a temple begun by Cleopatra for Antony, which Octavian completed and dedicated to himself.

A short way down Nabi Daniel, high wrought-iron gates and police guard the **Eliyahu Ha-Navi Synagogue**, entered via an alley to the north (admission may be possible from 9am–2pm except on Fri & Sat; bring your passport and pretend

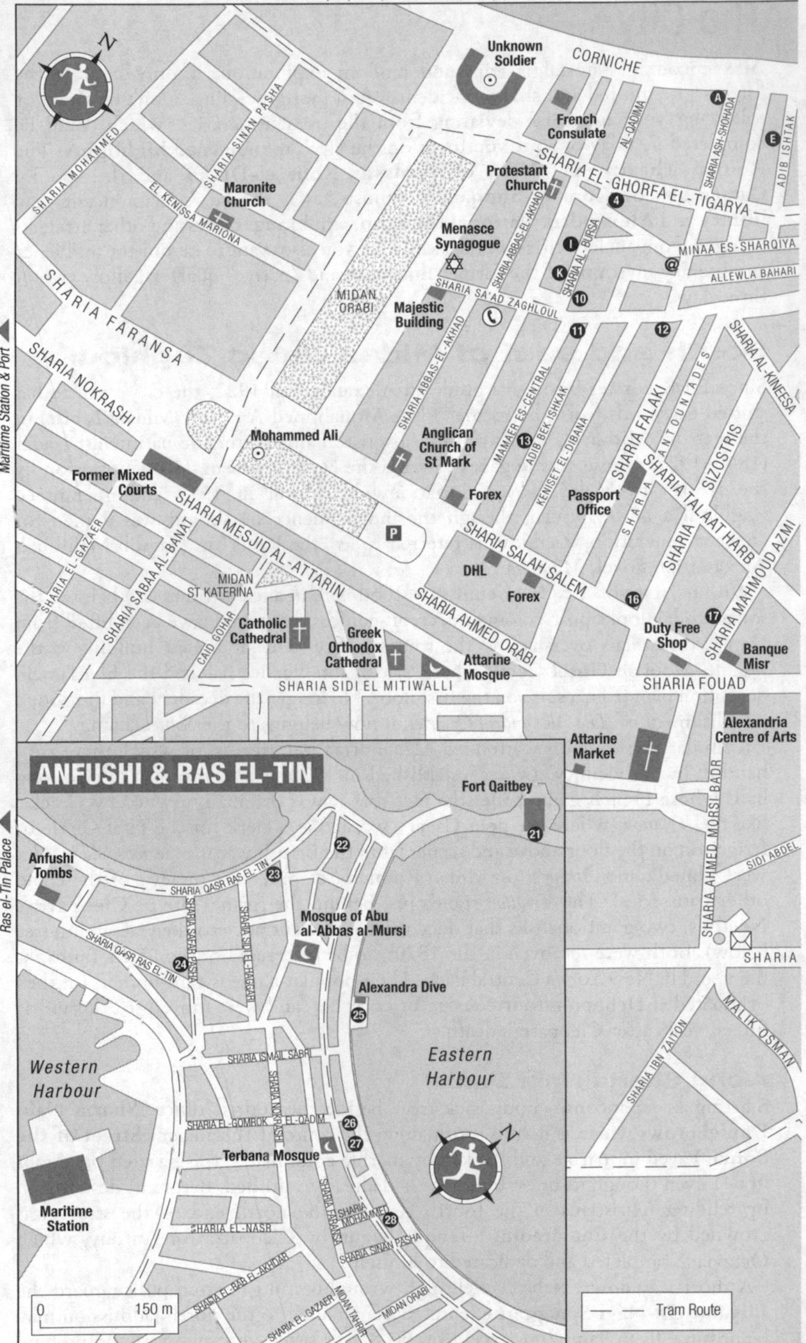
Al-Mursi Mosque (900m)
Fort Qaitbey (1.5km)
Maritime Station & Port
Ras el-Tin Palace
Pompey's Pillar & The Catacombs
Unknown Soldier
CORNICHE
French Consulate
Protestant Church
SHARIA EL-GHORFA EL-TIGARYA
Maronite Church
Menasce Synagogue
MIDAN ORABI
Majestic Building
SHARIA SA'AD ZAGHLOUL
SHARIA FARANSA
SHARIA NOKRASHI
Mohammed Ali
Anglican Church of St Mark
Former Mixed Courts
Forex
Passport Office
SHARIA SALAH SALEM
DHL
SHARIA MESJID AL-ATTARIN
MIDAN ST KATERINA
Catholic Cathedral
Greek Orthodox Cathedral
Attarine Mosque
SHARIA AHMED ORABI
Duty Free Shop
Banque Misr
SHARIA SIDI EL MITIWALLI
SHARIA FOUAD
Alexandria Centre of Arts
Attarine Market
ANFUSHI & RAS EL-TIN
Fort Qaitbey
Anfushi Tombs
SHARIA QASR RAS EL-TIN
Mosque of Abu al-Abbas al-Mursi
Alexandra Dive
Eastern Harbour
Western Harbour
SHARIA ISMAIL SABRI
SHARIA EL-GOMROK EL-QADIM
Terbana Mosque
Maritime Station
SHARIA EL-NASR
SHARIA SINAN PASHA
0
150 m
Tram Route

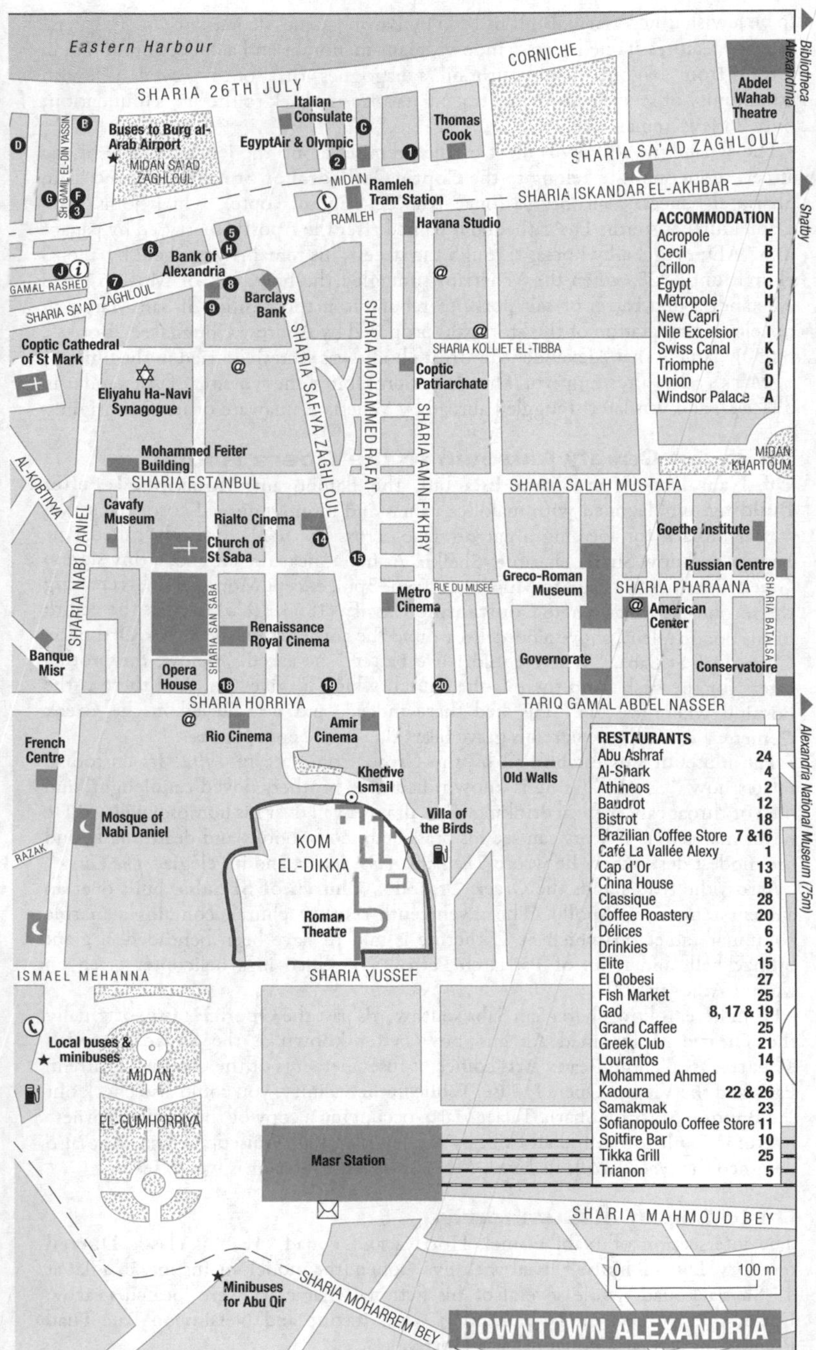
Eastern Harbour
CORNICHE
SHARIA 26TH JULY
Italian Consulate
Thomas Cook
Abdel Wahab Theatre
Bibliotheca Alexandrina
Buses to Burg al-Arab Airport
MIDAN SA'AD ZAGHLOUL
SH GAMIL EL-DIN YASSIN
EgyptAir & Olympic
SHARIA SA'AD ZAGHLOUL
MIDAN
Ramleh Tram Station
RAMLEH
SHARIA ISKANDAR EL-AKHBAR
Shatby
Havana Studio
Bank of Alexandria
GAMAL RASHED
Barclays Bank
Coptic Cathedral of St Mark
SHARIA KOLLIET EL-TIBBA
Coptic Patriarchate
Eliyahu Ha-Navi Synagogue
SHARIA SAFIYA ZAGHLOUL
SHARIA MOHAMMED RAFAT
SHARIA AMIN FIKHRY
Mohammed Feiter Building
MIDAN KHARTOUM
SHARIA ESTANBUL
SHARIA SALAH MUSTAFA
AL-KOBTIYA
Cavafy Museum
Rialto Cinema
Church of St Saba
Goethe Institute
Russian Centre
SHARIA NABI DANIEL
RUE DU MUSEE
Greco-Roman Museum
SHARIA PHARAANA
SHARIA BATALSA
Metro Cinema
American Center
SHARIA SAN SABA
Renaissance Royal Cinema
Banque Misr
Opera House
Governorate
Conservatoire
SHARIA HORRIYA
TARIQ GAMAL ABDEL NASSER
Alexandria National Museum (75m)
French Centre
Rio Cinema
Amir Cinema
Khedive Ismail
Old Walls
Mosque of Nabi Daniel
Villa of the Birds
RAZAK
KOM EL-DIKKA
Roman Theatre
ISMAEL MEHANNA
SHARIA YUSSEF
Local buses & minibuses
MIDAN EL-GUMHORRIYA
Masr Station
SHARIA MAHMOUD BEY
0 100 m
Minibuses for Abu Qir
SHARIA MOHARREM BEY
DOWNTOWN ALEXANDRIA
Durrell's House (3km)
ACCOMMODATION
Acropole F
Cecil B
Crillon E
Egypt C
Metropole H
New Capri J
Nile Excelsior I
Swiss Canal K
Triomphe G
Union D
Windsor Palace A
RESTAURANTS
Abu Ashraf 24
Al-Shark 4
Athineos 2
Baudrot 12
Bistrot 18
Brazilian Coffee Store 7 &16
Café La Vallée Alexy 1
Cap d'Or 13
China House B
Classique 28
Coffee Roastery 20
Délices 6
Drinkies 3
Elite 15
El Qobesi 27
Fish Market 25
Gad 8, 17 & 19
Grand Caffee 25
Greek Club 21
Lourantos 14
Mohammed Ahmed 9
Kadoura 22 & 26
Samakmak 23
Sofianopoulo Coffee Store 11
Spitfire Bar 10
Tikka Grill 25
Trianon 5

to be Jewish if necessary). Built in 1885 by Baron Jacques de Menasce, its Italianate interior features stained-glass windows, giant menorahs and a collection of Torah scrolls from bygone neighbourhood synagogues that once served a Jewish community of seventy thousand, tracing its ancestry back to the city's foundation; only 26 Jews remain today.

The synagogue still owns most of the premises along the left-hand side of the street; those opposite belong to the **Coptic Cathedral of St Mark**, entered from Sharia al-Kineesa al-Kobtiyya (once Rue de l'Eglise Copte), which joins Nabi Daniel further south. The cathedral is named after the Apostle martyred by pagans in 67 AD; dragged by horses through the streets, his remains were held by a local church until 828, when the Venetians smuggled the body out of Muslim-ruled Alexandria in a barrel of salt pork, to rebury it at the Basilica di San Marco. A novel reinterpretation of this story was proposed by Andrew Chugg (see "Books", p.630), namely that Alexander the Great's body was secretly buried in the guise of St Mark's relics after Emperor Theodosius prohibited the worship of Alexander in 391 AD, and was later smuggled abroad by Venetians unaware of its true origin.

From the Cavafy Museum to the Opera House

Off Nabi Daniel on Sharia Estanbul, the flamboyant **Mohammed Feiter Building**, emblazoned with majolica panels and monogrammed coronets, serves as a landmark for locating a narrow lane across the road, formerly called Rue Lepsius and now Sharia Sharm el-Sheikh. At no. 4, near the far end, a tiny sign in Greek identifies the **Cavafy Museum** (10am–3pm, except Mon; £E15), recreating the second-floor flat where **Constantine Cavafy** (1863–1933) lived at the zenith of his poetic talent, above a bordello around the corner from the Greek Orthodox Church of St Saba. "Where could I live better?" he asked. "Below, the brothel caters for the flesh. And there is the church which forgives sin. And there is the hospital where we die." He died there indeed, and was buried in the Greek Cemetery at Shatby, where his grave bears the simple epitaph, *Poet*.

The museum was established by the Greek Consulate in 1992. Its custodian relates how "Cavafis" (as he is known) had nine brothers, loved candlelight, and died of throat cancer from drinking – but draws a veil over his homosexuality ("He never married"). Visitors can see his brass bed, icons, books and death mask, and the modest desk where he wrote *The Barbarians*, *Ithaca*, and his elegiac *The City*.

Across the road stands the Greek Orthodox **Church of St Saba**, built over an ancient temple of Apollo. The seventeenth-century church contains a marble columnar tablet on which St Catherine is said to have been beheaded, a giant bronze bell, and relics of Patriarch Petros VII, killed in a helicopter crash on Mount Athos in 2004.

From here, follow Sharia San Saba southwards past the **Opera House**, originally the Theatre Mohammed Ali and now better known as the **Sayed Darwish Theatre**. A splendid Beaux Arts edifice, it fuses elements of the Odéon Théâtre in Paris and the Vienna Opera House. While in the vicinity, you could also check out the **Banque Masr** on Sharia Talaat Harb, occupying a copy of the Palazzo Farnese in Rome, built for an Italian bank by the Jewish fascist Guiseppe Loria (who also designed the *Hotel Cecil*); its lavish Moorish-Gothic interior is worth seeing.

On to Midan el-Gumhorriya

The intersection of Nabi Daniel, Horriya and Fouad streets is classic **Durrell** territory. Durrell himself lived with Eve Cohen (the model for Justine) in a flat at 40 Sharia Fouad, while several of his fictional characters were located nearby: Darley and Pombal on Nabi Daniel; Clea, Justine and Nessim on Rue Fuad Premier (now Sharia Fouad/Sharia Horriya).

The junction lies near the crossroads of ancient Alexandria, whose east–west axis, the **Canopic Way**, was lined by marble colonnades extending all the way from the Gate of the Sun, where visitors entered the city. Many scholars believe that this crossroads was the site of the **Mouseion** ("Shrine of the Muses"), an institution from which our word "museum" derives. Founded by Ptolemy I Soter (323–282 BC), it incorporated lecture halls, laboratories, observatories, and the legendary "Mother" Library (see p.472).

Across the way stood the **Soma** (meaning "dead body"), a temple where Alexander the Great was entombed alongside several Ptolemies. Alexander reposed in a gold sarcophagus until Ptolemy IX melted it down to mint coins during a crisis, but his body remained on view long after the dynasty had fallen. The victorious Octavian paid his respects to Alexandria's founder but disdained his heirs, stating "I wished to see a king, I did not wish to see corpses." According to one chronicler, Octavian accidentally broke Alexander's nose while bending to kiss the dead conqueror.

What happened to Alexander's body later remains a mystery. Some scholars believe that the Romans reburied him outside the Royal Quarter, in what is now Shatby, where the Christian cemeteries are today (see p.474). Reports from Mohammed Ali's time suggesting that Alexander's tomb lay deep beneath the nineteenth-century **Mosque of Nabi Daniel** (whose crypt holds the remains of the Sufi sheikh Mohammed Danyal al-Maridi) have impelled several excavations. The most recent suggests that the mosque does indeed rest on the site of a Roman temple, but further digging has been vetoed by the religious authorities.

Sharia Nabi Daniel ends at **Midan el-Gumhorriya**, a seething mass of bus and taxi ranks outside the neo-Baroque **Masr Station**, designed by a Greek and an Italian in 1927. You can beat a retreat into the Roman Theatre at Kom el-Dikka off Sharia Yussef.

Kom el-Dikka

In 1959, Polish archeologists searching for Alexander's tomb beneath the Turkish fort and slums on **Kom el-Dikka** ("Mound of Rubble") found a stratum of Roman remains (daily 9am–4.30pm; Ramadan until 3pm; £E20). During Ptolemaic times this was the Park of Pan, a hilly pleasure garden with a limestone summit carved into the shape of a pine cone. The elegant **Roman Theatre** has marble seating for seven to eight hundred, cruder galleries for the plebs, and a forecourt with two patches of mosaic flooring. In Byzantine times, gladiatorial games were superseded by chariot races. Along the northern side of the theatre's portico are thirteen auditoria that might have been part of Alexandria's ancient **university**, with an annual enrolment of five thousand students.

A separate ticket, sold at the main entrance, entitles you to enter the **Villa of Birds** (£E15) – so called because of its mosaic floors, depicting nine different species of birds (and a panther). En route to the villa you'll pass a laboratory for cleaning antiques, with assorted masonry recently dredged from the sea bed laid outside.

Sharia Safiya Zaghloul and the Quartier Grec

Exiting Kom el-Dikka and turning northwards round the corner of the site, you'll come to a **statue of Khedive Ismail** that once stood by the Corniche. It was removed in 1956 when he became reviled by nationalists as a dupe of colonialism, and has only now been granted a permanent home here. From the statue, cross over Sharia Horriya and head north along **Sharia Safiya Zaghloul**. In Cavafy's day this was called the Rue Missala and known for its billiard halls and rent boys; today it is named after the wife of the nationalist leader and noted for its shops and cinemas. The turning just beyond the Metro Cinema leads to the heart of what was once the **Quartier Grec**, or Greek Quarter, one of five urban zones allotted to different ethnic groups by Mohammed Ali that became as rich and cosmopolitan as Alexandria itself. Many of its villas now house **cultural centres** (see p.482), along Sharia Batalsa (still identified by its old name of Rue des Ptolémées) and Sharia Phara'ana (signed Rue des Pharaons), including the American Center, previously owned by philanthropist and Zionist Georges Menasce.

The Greek Quarter's most famous building, however, is the **Greco-Roman Museum**, whose Classical facade by Leopold Deitrich Bey (1892) is visible at the far end of Rue du Musée. Formerly home to Egypt's best collection of Classical antiquities, the museum is closed until 2012, pending the construction of a second floor; meanwhile its antiquities are on loan abroad and the Alexandria National Museum has been making all the running in revealing new-found Greco-Roman artefacts.

The Alexandria National Museum

Back on Sharia Horriya (aka Tariq Gamal Abdel Nasser), head east beyond the governorate, passing en route a stratified section of the **old walls** behind some houses in an alley, to reach the impressive **Alexandria National Museum** (daily 9am–4pm; £E35) near the corner of Midan Khartoum. Occupying an Italianate mansion once owned by a wood merchant, it displays some of the amazing archeological finds made during the past decade. Artfully lit and with English labelling, the museum also has an impressive art and history bookshop.

On the ground floor, pride of place is afforded to Hellenistic artefacts from **Herakleion** and **Canopus** (see p.477). A diorite sphinx, a priest of Isis carrying a Canopic jar and a statue of the goddess share the spotlight with a granite stele of Nectanebo II that once stood at the mouth of the Canopic branch (see p.477) of the Nile. From **ancient Alexandria** come an effigy of Emperor Caracalla in pharaonic headgear, a **mosaic** of Medusa found beneath the Diana Cinema, a marble hand from an unknown colossus and the **head of Briniky**, the wife of Ptolemy II. The latest exhibit is a marble statue of a naked warrior, presumed to represent **Alexander the Great**, which was found beneath the Shallalat Gardens in 2009.

Upstairs, splendid mother-of-pearl-inlaid doors and *mashrabiyas* precede **Coptic** stelae and friezes carved with lions, sheep or grapevines, followed by icons, priestly garments and accoutrements. The **Islamic** artefacts include sashes and capes of Persian or Turkish origin, gold coins minted under the Fatimid and Byzantine empires, and Mamluke and Ottoman weaponry. A final room upstairs entitled "Alexandria in the Twenty-First Century" juxtaposes photos of colonial street scenes and a satellite view of the city with tableware, jewellery and medals from King Farouk's collection. Look out for the life-size silver fish with a flexible body.

Around Midan Orabi and Midan Tahrir

The old heart of "European" Alexandria lies less than 500m west of Midan Sa'ad Zaghloul, a short walk along **Sharia Sa'ad Zaghloul**, which starts as a busy shopping street aglow with neon, and ends as a shadowy alley. Along the way you can see traces of the past in Art Deco frontages and faded plaques bearing Greek, French or Armenian names, and stop at atmospheric coffee-houses or bars for refreshment (see pp.477–479). At the far end you'll find the **Majestic Building** where E.M. Forster stayed when it was a hotel, across the road from the derelict **Menasce Synagogue**, a relic of the area's social complexion a century ago, like the German **Protestant Church** on Sharia el-Akkad el-Boustra.

Emerging onto **Midan Orabi**, you'll see a Neoclassical **Monument of the Unknown Soldier** facing the seafront, where a naval guard of honour is changed every hour on the hour. No trace remains of the French Gardens where expatriates once strolled among the acacia trees and shrubs, just off "Frank Square", the European city's social hub. Originally the Place des Consuls, it was renamed in honour of **Mohammed Ali**, whose equestrian **statue** (by Jacques Mart; 1868) rears outside the former **Mixed Courts**, where foreigners were once tried under their own jurisprudence rather than Egyptian law. After the Orabi Revolt of 1882, rebels were shot and buried here by British forces. Not surprisingly, its name was changed to Liberation Square – **Midan Tahrir** – following the Revolution. It was here, on the fourth anniversary of King Farouk's abdication, that Nasser delivered a three-hour speech broadcast live on national radio, climaxing in the announcement that Egypt had taken possession of the Suez Canal; the repetition of the name "Lesseps" earlier in his peroration was actually the codeword for the operation to begin.

A parking lot marks the site of the Stock Exchange that once stood on the corner of Rue Chérif Pacha, the Bond Street of Alexandria (as the British conceived it) and Cavafy's birthplace. Now **Sharia Salah Salem**, the street is less chic than in colonial times, but still the place to find **antiques** and **jewellery**. Further along on the left, the building at 2 Sharia Mahmoud Azmi is associated with Durrell (who worked at a propaganda bureau here in 1942) and the **Al-Fayeds**, who founded their first trading company here (its sign remains) and went on to become international business moguls – a far cry from their impoverished childhood in Anfushi.

The parallel **Sharia Mesjid al-Attarin** is named after the fourteenth-century **Attarine Mosque** that stands on the site of the fourth-century Church of St Athanasius, from which Napoleon's forces removed a seven-ton sarcophagus, thought to be Alexander's but later attributed to Nectanebo I. The neighbouring **Greek Orthodox** and **Catholic cathedrals** are the heart of their respective communities, while the lane running between Sidi el Mitiwalli and Ahmed Morsi Badr streets harbours the **Attarine antique market**, an intriguing place to browse.

Northwest of Tahrir, grandiose edifices give way to **souks** spreading off **Sharia Nokrashi** – heaving with fruit and vegetable stalls, butchers and hardware stores – and **Sharia Faransa** (French Street), devoted to clothes and dressmaking materials. Before the revolution, Nokrashi was notorious for its child bordellos. In *The Alexandria Quartet*, Justine sought her kidnapped daughter here, the diplomat Mountolive was mauled by child prostitutes, and Scobie (modelled on "Bimbashi" McPherson, the paedophile head of the prewar British secret police) killed his neighbours with moonshine whisky.

Anfushi, Fort Qaitbey and the Pharos

Although the **Eastern Harbour** is no longer the busy port of ancient times, its graceful curve is definitely appealing. As it sweeps around towards Qaitbey's Fort, bureaucratic monoliths from the last decades of the twentieth century give way to stately palms and weathered colonial mansions, likened by Michael Palin to "Cannes with acne". Walking at least some of the way along the Corniche is highly recommended, but you may wish to use minibuses or trams for longer distances.

In ancient times, a seven-league dike – the **Heptastadion** – connected Alexandria with Pharos, then an island. Allowed to silt up after the Arab conquest, the causeway gradually turned into a peninsula that the newcomers built over, creating the **Anfushi** quarter (or El-Anfushi). Its Ottoman mosques, *mashrabiya*'d houses and bustling streetlife makes Anfushi ripe for exploration. Tram #15 runs one block inland from the Corniche, passing all the major landmarks.

The seventeenth-century **Terbana Mosque** incorporates a public drinking fountain and numerous antique columns; a huge pair with Corinthian capitals supports the minaret. Further north, the **Mosque of Abu al-Abbas al-Mursi** honours the patron saint of local fishermen and sailors, a thirteenth-century

Andalusian sheikh. The existing structure was built in 1938 by an Italian architect, Mario Kossi, but its keel-arched panels, elaborately carved domes and cornices look as old as the sixteenth-century original.

Fort Qaitbey and the Pharos

One tram stop after Al-Mursi's mosque, take a short walk past the fishing port and **shipbuilding** yard full of brightly painted wooden boats, and you'll come to the promontory bearing Sultan Qaitbey's fort and the **Alexandra Yacht Club**, which holds an annual regatta in October. **Fort Qaitbey** (daily 9am–2pm; £E25) is an Alexandrian landmark, a doughty citadel buffeted by wind-borne spray, its flag forever rippling. Built during the 1480s and later beefed up by Mohammed Ali, it commands great views of the city and the spume-flecked Mediterranean. Within the restored keep there's a mosque whose minaret was blown away by the British in 1882.

The fort is thought to incorporate masonry from the legendary **Pharos** – Ancient Alexandria's lighthouse – which once stood just offshore. One of the Seven Wonders of the ancient world, the Pharos transcended its practical role as a navigational aid and early-warning system, becoming synonymous with the city itself. A combination of aesthetic beauty and technological audacity, it exceeded 125m – perhaps even 150m – in height, including the statue of Zeus at its summit.

Possibly conceived by Alexander himself, the Pharos took twelve years to build under the direction of an Asiatic Greek, Sostratus, and was completed in 283 BC. Its square base contained three hundred rooms, that, according to legend, once housed the seventy rabbis who translated the Hebrew scriptures into Greek, and perhaps also machinery for hauling fuel up to the lantern in the cylindrical third storey, whose light is thought to have been visible 56km away. Some chroniclers also mention a "mirror" that enabled the lighthouse keepers to observe ships far out at sea; a form of lens (whose secret was lost) has been postulated.

Around 700 AD the lantern collapsed, or was demolished by a treasure-hunting caliph; the base survived unscathed and Ibn Tulun restored the second level, until an earthquake in 1303 reduced the whole structure to rubble. The northwest

▲ Artist's impression of the Pharos

section of the fort's enclosure walls incorporates some huge red-granite pillars that might have been part of the Pharos.

Divers from the Centre d'Etudes Alexandrines have located over 2500 stone objects **underwater** at depths of 6–8m, including the head of a colossus of Ptolemy as pharaoh, and the base of an obelisk inscribed to Seti I, which have been brought to the surface; and several **monoliths**, weighing 50–70 tonnes apiece and embedded in the rock by the impact of their fall, that can only have belonged to the lighthouse. Five hundred metres offshore **wrecks** of Greek and Roman trading vessels laden with amphorae of wine and fish sauce have been found, and over fifty **anchors** of all eras – more pieces in the mosaic picture of ancient Alexandria that's emerging from surveys of the Eastern Harbour (see below). See p.481 for details of **diving** in the harbour.

Ras el-Tin and the Western Harbour

Tram #15 runs on to the **Ras el-Tin** ("Cape of Figs") quarter, where you can alight at Sharia Ras el-Tin to find the rock-cut **Anfushi Tombs** (daily 9am–4.30pm; £E20), uncovered in 1901. Sited in pairs around a staircase, the four tombs are painted to simulate costly alabaster or marble and belonged to third-century BC Greek Alexandrians who adopted Ancient Egyptian funerary practices. The right-hand set has pictures of Egyptian gods, warships and feluccas; a Greek workman has also immortalized his mate's virtues in graffiti.

It's possible that the necropolis extends beneath the gardens of **Ras el-Tin Palace**, overlooking the Western Harbour. The palace was built for Mohammed Ali, its audience hall sited so that he could watch his new fleet at anchor while reclining on his divan. Rebuilt and turned into the summer seat of government under Fouad I, it witnessed King Farouk's abdication on July 26, 1952, and is now off-limits as a presidential residence.

The **Western Harbour** has been Egypt's main port and naval base since the mid-nineteenth century, and witnessed the boldest Italian commando raid of World War II. On December 18, 1941, three manned torpedoes penetrated the harbour to lay charges beneath the battleships *HMS Valiant* and *HMS Queen Elizabeth*. The British pretended that the ships were still afloat when their hulls were resting on the sea bed.

On the way back you could enjoy lunch at one of the many **fish restaurants** on Sharia Safar Pasha (between Ras el-Tin and Anfushi) or along the Corniche (see p.478).

The submerged Royal Quarters

The opposite jaw of the Eastern Harbour is formed by a narrow promontory called **Silsileh** ("the Chain"), that's occupied by the navy and out of bounds. Aside from being the site of Naguib Mahfouz's fictional *Pension Miramar*, its interest lies in the **underwater** discoveries made since 1996 by Franck Goddio and his team, whose survey of the seabed five metres down has revealed extensive submerged **ruins**, including granite columns, votive statues, sphinxes, pavements, ceramics and a pier from the **ancient Royal Quarters** of Alexandria. Samples of their salvage can be seen on Goddio's website, Ⓦ www.underwaterdiscovery.org.

Goddio was quick to claim that they had found the site of **Cleopatra's palace** on the island of Antirrhodos (where she met her death), which had been plunged into the sea by an earthquake and a tsunami in 365 AD – an assertion questioned by archeologists until he found inscriptions verifying his claim. The SCA is keen on creating the world's first underwater museum – with Plexiglas tunnels that would allow visitors to stroll below the surface; a feasibility study is now underway.

Meanwhile you can investigate the ruins by **diving**, with visibility at its best (from 7–20 metres) from April to June and October to December. As well as seven or eight sphinxes (one of these is 5m long), a giant obelisk and numerous columns, divers can see the wreck of a British **Beaufort bomber** that narrowly missed crashing into the *Hotel Cecil* in 1942; the pilot's flight mask is fused into the rock. Contact Alexandra Dive (see p.481) for all arrangements.

The Bibliotheca Alexandrina

On the mainland beyond Silsileh, another wonder of antiquity has been resurrected in a new form. The **Bibliotheca Alexandrina** (Sat–Thurs 11am–7pm, Fri 3–7pm; Ⓦ www.bibalex.org) resembles a giant discus embedded in the ground at an angle, representing a second sun rising beside the Mediterranean. Pictograms, hieroglyphs and letters from every alphabet are carved on its exterior, evoking the diversity of knowledge embodied in the ancient library and the aspirations of the new one. Seventeen years in the building at a cost of $355 million, the library was controversial even before its inauguration in 2002 (when an exhibition of books from every nation featured the *Protocols of the Elders of Zion* as Israel's entry), but no one doubts its impact on the city's cultural scene or its must-see status with tourists. Its stunning architecture (by a Norwegian-Austrian team) is matched by the diversity of **events** at the **Cultural Centre** in the block opposite the entrance to the library – see the website for what's on. The library's *Hilton* **café** is a popular meeting spot.

Visiting the library

On the inland side facing Sharia Bur Said, a **colossus of Ptolemy II** dredged from the Eastern Harbour watches over a cloakroom where all bags must be checked in, and kiosks selling **tickets** for the library (£E10; no children under 6) or a combo ticket (£E45; no student discount) that also covers two museums inside it, individual tickets for which (£E20 each) are sold on the spot. **Photography** is permitted in the Antiquities Museums (£E20, no flashes; video £E150), but not in the library itself. You can join a free **tour** in English (every 45min) just inside the entrance, or wander at will through the vast **reading area** – a stunning

Ancient Alexandria's library

Founded shortly after the city itself, on the advice of Ptolemy I's counsellor Demetrius of Phalerum, in antiquity Alexandria's library stood beside the Mouseion in the heart of the city (see p.467). Dedicated to "the writings of all nations", it welcomed scholars and philosophers and supported research and debates. By law, all ships docking at Alexandria were obliged to allow any scrolls on board to be copied, if they were of interest. By the mid-first century BC it held 532,800 manuscripts (all catalogued by the Head Librarian, Callimachus), and later spawned a subsidiary attached to the **Temple of Serapis**; the two were known as the "**Mother**" and "**Daughter**" **libraries**, and together contained perhaps 700,000 scrolls (equivalent to about 100,000 printed books today).

As many as 40,000 (or even 400,000) were burned during Julius Caesar's assault on the city in 48 BC, when he supported Cleopatra against her brother Ptolemy XIII; as compensation, Mark Antony gave her the entire contents of the Pergamum Library in Anatolia (200,000 scrolls). But it was Christian mobs that destroyed this vast storehouse of "pagan" knowledge, torching the Mother Library in 293 and the Daughter Library in 391, though medieval Europe later mythologized its destruction as proof of Arab barbarism. An apocryphal tale had the Muslim leader Amr pronouncing: "If these writings of the Greeks agree with the Koran they are useless, and need not be preserved; if they disagree, they are pernicious, and ought to be destroyed."

cascade of levels upheld by stainless-steel pillars suggestive of the columns in pharaonic temples.

Maps, engravings and photos in the **Impressions of Alexandria** exhibit show how the city has evolved since antiquity and its ruination by the British in 1882. A fine **Antiquities Museum** in the basement displays a giant head of Serapis, a black basalt Isis salvaged from Herakleion, and two mosaic floors unearthed during the building of the library, one depicting a dog beside a brass cup, the other a gladiator locked in combat. Ancient scrolls and tomes can be seen in the **Manuscripts Museum** on the entrance level. Lastly there's the **Planetarium**, a Death Star-like spheroid on the plaza facing the sea, screening IMAX science movies for children.

Pompey's Pillar and the Catacombs

The poor **Karmous quarter** in the southwest of the city contains two of Alex's best-known ancient monuments. Pompey's Pillar can be reached by taxi (£E30) or tram #16 from Midan Orabi. From there you can either ride the tram or walk on to the Catacombs of Kom es-Shoqafa. The pillar becomes visible as the tram passes the Muslim cemetery bordered by Sharia Amoud el-Sawary.

Towering 25m above a limestone ridge, the red-granite column known as **Pompey's Pillar** was actually raised to honour the Roman emperor Diocletian, who threatened to massacre Alexandria's populace "until their blood reached his horse's knees", but desisted when his mount slipped and bloodied itself prematurely. It may have come from the **Temple of Serapis** that once stood nearby, housing Cleopatra's "Daughter Library" of 42,800 texts, which outlived the Mother Library by almost a century, only to be destroyed by Christian mobs in 391 AD. All that remain are three subterranean galleries where the sacred Apis bulls were interred (see "Saqqara", p.178), a Nilometer and some underground cisterns – making the **site** (daily 9am–4.30pm, Ramadan 9am–3pm; £E35) pretty disappointing considering what used to exist here.

The Catacombs of Kom es-Shoqafa

Happily, the same isn't true of the **Catacombs of Kom es-Shoqafa** (daily 9am–4.30pm, Ramadan until 3pm; £E35), whose prosaic Arabic name, "Mound of Shards", hardly does justice to their wonderful amalgam of spookiness and kitsch. To get here, turn right around the corner after leaving Pompey's Pillar and follow the road straight on for five minutes; the entrance to the catacombs is on the left 150m beyond a square. Cameras must be left here, as photography is not allowed inside.

The catacombs were discovered in 1900 when a donkey disappeared through the ground. Hewn 35m into solid rock, the triple-level complex is reached via a spiral stairway, past the shaft down which bodies were lowered. From the vestibule with its scalloped niches, you can squeeze through a fissure into a lofty **hall** riddled with *loculi*, or family burial niches. Scholars named it the Hall of Caracalla after the Roman emperor who massacred Alexandrian youths at a review in 215 AD. Relatives toasted the dead from stone couches in the **Triclinium**, where the first archeologists to enter the chamber found wine jars and tableware.

In the **Central Tomb** downstairs–whose vestibule is guarded by reliefs of bearded serpents with Medusa-headed shields – you'll find muscle-bound statues of Sobek and Anubis wearing Roman armour, dating from the second century AD when "the old faiths began to merge and melt" (Forster). Water has flooded the **Goddess Nemesis Hall** (still accessible) and submerged the lowest level, hastening the catacombs' decay. For more information, buy Jean-Yves

Empereur's excellently illustrated *A Short Guide to the Catacombs of Kom es-Shoqafa*, available at the site.

Moharrem Bey, Bab Sharq and Smouha

East of Karmous, **Moharrem Bey** is a once-affluent suburb that grew up in the mid-nineteenth century after the completion of the **Mahmudiya Canal**, dug on the orders of Mohammed Ali at a cost of twenty thousand lives. Once home to Alexandria's mercantile elite, its mansions have become slums since the 1950s, but aficionados of **Durrell** will wish to see the **Ambron Villa** where he and Eve rented the top floor in 1943–44; *Prospero's Cell* and *The Dark Labyrinth* were written in the corner tower. Though now a listed building the villa has been allowed to decay and developers have built flats in the garden where the painter Gilda Ambron shared a studio with their neighbour, Clea Badaro, who inspired the character Cleo in *The Alexandria Quartet*. If you want to visit, get someone to write the address (19 Sharia al-Ma'amoun) in Arabic to show to your taxi driver (£E15–20 one-way).

Bab Sharq

Nearer El-Manshiya, the affluent **Bab Sharq** district can be easily approached from the Quartier Grec (see p.468) or en route to the Corniche beaches (see opposite). Its nexus is **Midan Khartoum**, an L-shaped park whose Ptolemaic **column** (erected to celebrate Britain's recapture of Khartoum in 1898) is a local landmark at the junction of Sharia Horriya and the Sharia Canal El Suez.

Flanking this, the hilly **Shallalat Gardens** are ablaze with scarlet flame trees in summer. Their nineteenth-century designer utilized remnants of the Arab city walls and a canal to create rockeries and ornamental ponds. Here, E.M. Forster had his first date with Mohammed el-Adl, a tram conductor whom he met at Ramleh in the winter of 1916–17. The racial, class and sexual barriers that their relationship challenged underlie the finale of *A Passage to India*, which Forster was struggling with when he learned of Mohammed's death in 1922. Near the northwest corner of the Gardens is the **Ibn el-Nabih Cistern** (dawn–dusk; free), its three levels upheld by antique columns from older structures.

Beyond Sharia Canal El Suez lies a sprawling necropolis of **cemeteries** consecrated to diverse faiths, full of lavish mausolea and sculptures. Though most date from the nineteenth or twentieth centuries, burials have occurred here since ancient times. An **alabaster antechamber** near the road that bisects the necropolis is believed by some to be part of a tumulus that might once have contained Alexander the Great's tomb (off-limits).

Smouha

The **Smouha** district in the southern suburbs is a magnet for wealthy Alexandrians, thanks to the **Zahran and Smouha Malls**, 300–400m from Sidi Gaber Station, and the **Green Plaza Mall** and **City Center** superstore (run by the French chain Carrefour), out by the 14th May Bridge. The district is named after the Baghdad-born Jewish architect Joseph Smouha, whose Smouha City (as it was originally called) was the local equivalent of Cairo's Heliopolis, a modern suburb for the upper-middle classes. Though all the "foreigners" were dispossessed by Nasser, their legacies – and names – survive in present-day Alexandria.

Embellished with Classical statuary, the **Antoniadis Gardens** (daily 9am–3pm; £E3) were once the private grounds of a wealthy Greek family and now host opera concerts over summer. Nearby are the **Zoological Gardens** (same hours; £E3) and **Nouzha Gardens** (same hours; £E1), laid out under Khedive Ismail. In ancient times, this was a residential suburb inhabited by the likes of Callimachus (310–240 BC), the Head Librarian of the Bibliotheca Alexandrina.

Corniche beaches

Alexandria's beaches are an overworked asset. Hardly a square metre of sand goes unclaimed during high season, when millions of Egyptians descend on the city. Before June the beaches furthest out are relatively uncrowded, except on Fridays, Saturdays and public holidays. Their popularity doesn't imply a Western-style beach culture; women bathers wade into the sea fully clad, except at Venezia beach at Montazah (see p.476).

The chief attractions on land are the **Royal Jewellery Museum** in Glym (if it's reopened), the **Mahmoud Said Museum** in San Stefano and the extensive grounds of the **Montazah** palace, further along the coast. Many visitors go beyond to **Abu Qir** for its seafood (though you can eat just as well closer in to Alexandria) or to go **wreck-diving**.

Shatby to Stanley

The district known as **Shatby** (or Chatby) is overshadowed by **St Mark's College**, a massive, red-brick, neo-Baroque edifice whose dome is visible from afar. Founded to educate the city's Christian elite, it now forms part of Alexandria University. On the far side of Sharia Bur Said is the grandly named **Shatby Necropolis** (daily 9am–4.30pm; Ramadan 9am–3pm; £E15), a small pit exposing some rock-cut ossuaries and sarcophagi from the third century BC. The adjacent **Camp Cesar** looks no grander for its association with Julius Caesar (who camped here during the battle that left Cleopatra at his mercy), while neighbouring **Ibrahimiya** was the birthplace of Hitler's deputy Führer, Rudolf Hess.

Shortly before Cleopatra beach, tram #2 turns further inland, passing through the **Bacos** quarter where Gamal Abdel Nasser was born on January 15, 1918. Tram #1 runs closer to **Cleopatra** beach, which has no connection with the lady herself, although the nearby **Roushdi** district was the site of Nikopolis, which Octavian founded because he hated living in Alexandria. Today, Roushdi is the centre of expat life but a vestige of its origins remains in the form of the

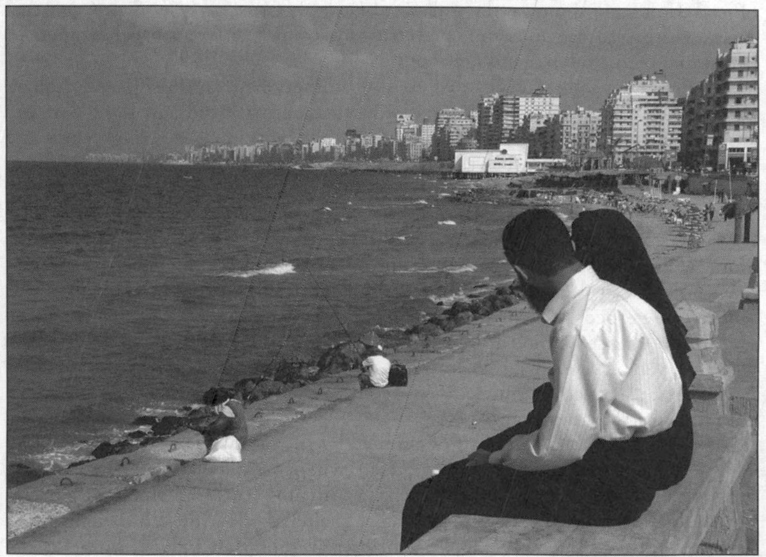

▲ A view of the Corniche

Mustafa Kamel Necropolis (daily 9am–4.30pm; £E15). Its four tombs, discovered in 1933, date from the second century BC; two are upheld by Doric columns and one contains a mural of a horseman. To get here, catch tram #2 from Ramleh to Roushdi tram station and walk towards the Corniche along Sharia al-Mo'asker al-Romani.

Travelling along the Corniche, you'll cross the **Stanley Bridge**, whose suspension towers mimic the Turko-Florentine architecture at Montazah. From the bridge, which takes only eastbound traffic, you can see Stanley Bay's tiers of concrete sun terraces and bathing cabins, built by the British in the 1920s.

The Royal Jewellery Museum

Due to reopen in 2010, the **Royal Jewellery Museum** (daily 9am–4.30pm; £E35) at 27 Sharia Ahmed Yehia is three blocks in from the Corniche, a short walk from the El-Fenoun el-Gamilia or Qasr el-Safa stops on the #2 tram line. The museum is housed in a mansion built for Mohammed Ali's granddaughter Princess Fatima el-Zaharaa and her husband, that's as splendidly vulgar as the treasures on display. Among the highlights are Mohammed Ali's diamond-inlaid snuffbox, King Farouk's gold chess set, a platinum crown with 2159 diamonds, and his diamond-studded gardening tools. The gallery downstairs is lined with stained-glass cameos of courtly love in eighteenth-century France, while images of Provençal farmers, milkmaids and food decorate the service corridors. Upstairs are the wildest his 'n' hers bathrooms – hers with tiled murals of nymphs bathing in a waterfall, his with scenes of Côte d'Azur fishermen.

The Mahmoud Said Museum

Another treat in this part of town is the **Mahmoud Said Museum** (daily except Mon 10am–6pm; £E10), on Sharia Mahmoud Said Pasha: take tram #1 or #2 to Gianaclis (the stop after the Jewellery Museum), cross the tracks, head up the steps to the raised road and turn right. A judge who painted as a hobby, Mahmoud Said (1897–1964) was the first Egyptian artist to receive a state prize, yet he disliked official commissions such as the wall-sized *Inaugural Ceremony of the Suez Canal* that greets visitors to the museum, preferring to paint pensive, sensual women or landscapes of Alexandria and Lebanon.

Upstairs, six rooms are devoted to the brothers Seif (1906–79) and Adham (1908–59) Wanly, who founded the first Egyptian artists' studio in 1942. Seif was an Expressionist who depicted such bourgeois delights as casinos, nightclubs and horse-racing, while Adham was into Cubism, abstraction and Socialist Realism, producing such polemical works as *Hunger* and *Palestine*.

Montazah

Some 16km kilometres east of the centre, **Montazah** is a former royal retreat that's now the city's pleasure ground (daily 24hr; £E6), distinguished by its well-tended flowerbeds, a clock tower, and the flamboyant Turko-Florentine **Haramlik Palace** (closed to the public). Commissioned by King Fouad, the palace served as a Red Cross hospital during World War I; it was here that E.M. Forster worked as a nurse. Restored by Sadat, the palace is now a presidential residence and guesthouse.

The largest of Montazah's bays is rimmed by the sandy **Venezia Beach** (£E50 admission with a beach chair and umbrella), where dress standards for women are fairly relaxed. A promontory ending in an ornate "Turkish" **Belvedere** and a **lighthouse** encloses the bay, providing a sheltered spot for **windsurfing** and **snorkelling** in summer. Inland, the smaller **El Salamlek Palace,** built for the Austrian mistress of Khedive Abbas, is now a luxury hotel (see p.462).

Canopus, Abu Qir and Herakleion

Further east, **Ma'amoura** is a private enclave of holiday flats and villas, followed by a row of naval bases occupying the ancient site of **Canopus** – a once-great Delta city which flourished when a branch of the Nile reached the sea by the nearby "Canopic Mouth". Myth has it that Canopus was founded by a Greek navigator returning from the Trojan Wars, whom the locals later worshipped in the form of a jar with a human head – hence the term Canopic jars, bestowed on similar receptacles used to preserve mummies' viscera.

In 2004 marine archeologists found life-size statues of Ptolemaic rulers and thousands of bronze pots and incense burners on the sea bed off Canopus, together with the wreck of **HMS Garfield**, sunk by a German U-boat in 1917. The wreck can be dived in conjunction with two underwater sites off the coast of **Abu Qir** (pronounced Abu Ear), where, in 1798, Admiral Nelson destroyed the French fleet in the so-called Battle of the Nile. In 1998–99, divers found the **wrecks** of the French flagship **L'Orient**, the **Sérieuse** and **Artémise** 8km offshore.

Two years later they discovered the ruins of **Herakleion**, a fabled ancient entrepôt that fell into the sea 1300 years ago. Buried by sediment 23–30m underwater, its identity was confirmed by a stele inscribed with the city's name and part of a temple seen by Herodotus in the fifth century BC. **Diving** at these sites is a fantastic experience that Alexandra Dive (see p.481) can organize, though the bureaucracy involved requires two to four days' notice and at least four paying customers (or fewer willing to pay more) on each trip.

Eating and drinking

Alexandria can't match Cairo for culinary variety, but it beats the capital when it comes to **seafood restaurants,** where fish and crustaceans are laid out for diners to select their own, priced per kilo (grey mullet from £E50; clams from £E55; sea bass from £E75; crab from £E60; jumbo shrimp from £E170). When these pall you can always fall back on Egyptian favourites like *shawarmas*, pizzas, *fuul* and falafel. **Coffee houses**, too, are an Alex speciality, and there are some good **bars** if you know where to look.

Downtown venues appear on the map on p.464, but there are also some recommendations further out (marked on the city plan on p.458).

Cafés and restaurants

The following establishments more or less represent the culinary and budgetary spectrum. Unless stated otherwise, credit cards are not accepted.

Downtown

Al-Shark Sharia al-Bursa al-Qadima. Serves kebab by the kilo and traditional Egyptian dishes such as *fatta* with mutton, rice with gizzards, or baked macaroni (£E10–30), to eat indoors or take away.

Café La Vallé Alexy Midan Ramleh. A cheery new café offering fresh juices (£E12), club sandwiches (£E19), grilled calamari (£E32), shrimp curry (£E61) and beef *fajitas* (£E42). Daily 9am–2am.

China House *Hotel Cecil*, Midan Sa'ad Zaghloul ☎03/487-7173. Nobody ever came to Alex to eat Chinese food, but if you're hankering for some, the chicken dumplings or grilled beef with garlic sauce are the best dishes on the menu (£E20–80). Serves alcohol; takes cards. Daily 1–11.30pm.

Gad Sharia Horriya, Sharia Mahmoud Azmi and Sharia Sa'ad Zaghloul. Three branches of the popular Egyptian chain, selling takeaway kebab, *kofta*, *shawarma*, *fuul* and shrimp sandwiches, all freshly prepared and costing under £E10 – ideal for a quick snack. Daily 24hr.

Mohammed Ahmed 17 Sharia Shakor Pasha, off Sa'ad Zaghloul. One of the cheapest places for a takeaway or a meal on the run, it serves tasty *fuul*, falafel, and other vegetarian dishes (£E3–10). Daily 6am–1am.

Anfushi and Ras el-Tin

Abu Ashraf 28 Sharia Safar Pasha. Accessible by tram #15, this street is full of fish and kebab restaurants, tempting passers-by with their outdoor grills. *Abu Ashraf* is devoted to seafood, which is always excellent. Try the seabass stuffed with garlic and herbs or the creamy shrimp *kishk* (casserole); dishes cost from £E40–70. Daily 24hr.

Fish Market Sharia 26th July ⓣ03/480-5119. Sited above the *Tikka Grill*, this posh seafood restaurant has a/c and a wonderful view of the harbour. The mandatory salad platter (£E10 per person) is a meal in itself; wine and beer are available, though not listed on the menu. Takes Diners' Club, MasterCard and Visa. Daily 12.30am–2pm.

Grand Caffee Sharia 26th July. An off shoot of the *Fish Market* and *Tikka Grill*, with indoor and outdoor seating, offering milkshakes (£E15), ice cream (£E14–15), Caesar salad (£E30) and pizzas (£E16–23). Daily 9am–2am.

Greek Club Sharia Qasr Qaitbey. A great place to tuck into grilled squid or fish, *mezze* or moussaka (£E20–35), with spacious rooms and a large terrace that catches the afternoon breeze from the harbour. There's a £E6 admission charge. Daily noon–11pm.

Kadoura Sharia Bairam el-Tonsi and Sharia 26th July. An Alexandrian institution, *Kadoura* (pronounced Adoura) is devoted to seafood; all orders come with salad, rice and dips. Meals (£E50–70) are served at tables in the street in the scruffy "old" *Kadoura* in Anfushi; the new branch on the Corniche has air conditioning and indoor seating. Daily noon–midnight.

Samakmak 42 Sharia Qasr Ras el-Tin ⓣ03/481-1560. Owned by retired belly-dancer Zizi Salem, this upscale fish place is renowned for its crab *tageen*, crayfish, and spaghetti with clams (£E40–100). In the summer you can eat outdoors in a large tent. Daily noon–midnight.

Tikka Grill Underneath the *Fish Market* ⓣ03/480-5114. More Levantine than Indian – its menu ranges from veal piccata (£E55) to marinated spicy chicken (£E39) – but nonetheless recommended for its silver service and delicious *puris*. Serves alcohol. Daily 1pm–1am.

Further out

Cordon Rouge Green Plaza Mall, 14th May Bridge, Smouha. This slick, Mediterranean-style restaurant-cum-bar is popular with locals and expats, with a menu featuring pasta, salads, grills (£E50–100) and cocktails, and a DJ on Thursday nights. Daily noon–2am.

Hood Gondol Seafood Corner of Sharia Omar Lofty and Sharia Mohammed Motwe. Located near the Bibliotheca Alexandrina (ask any local for directions), this eatery does a massive plate of mixed seafood for a paltry £E35. Little English spoken, nor any menu; just point to the seafood display and find yourself a seat. Daily noon–11pm.

Zephyrion Abu Qir beach. Fronted by a cactus garden, *Zephyrion* (Greek for "sea breeze") is the most identifiable of Abu Qir's seafood spots (some simply tables on the beach) and serves alcohol. A meal will set you back around £E70. Daily noon–midnight.

Coffee houses, patisseries and juice bars

Before the Revolution, Alexandria's **coffee houses** and **patisseries** were the hub of bourgeois society. Artists, writers and socialites mingled and pursued affairs in such salons as *Athineos*, *Trianon* and *Pastroudis*. Since then some have closed and others depend on tourists or a loyal, dwindling clientele of elderly Egyptian gentlemen. Younger Alexandrians prefer modern, Western-style places like *Bistrot* and *Coffee Roastery* or the terraced cafés in the Green Plaza Mall and other malls in Smouha (see p.474). For nocturnal types, there are **24-hour** coffee shops in the *Cecil* and *Montazah Sheraton* hotels.

Downtown

Athineos Midan Ramleh. Take a look inside, but don't eat here; its cakes are as flyblown as its Classical motifs and mirrors, and the service is awful. Daily 8am–midnight.

Baudrot 23 Sharia Sa'ad Zaghloul. Not the original *Baudrot* where Durrell first met Eve Cohen, but it looks the part, with a dark-panelled salon and a vine-trellised inner courtyard, serving cakes, coffee and sandwiches. Daily 8am–midnight.

Bistrot 6 Sharia Fouad. One of the new breed of cafés, serving salads, sandwiches, tasty pasta dishes (£E25–35) and fresh juices, with a pastry corner for breakfast and a shady terrace frequented by courting couples. Daily 9am–10pm.

Brazilian Coffee Store Corner of Nabi Daniel and Sa'ad Zaghloul, near the tourist office. Slightly less atmospheric since they refurbished it and installed seating upstairs, this popular breakfast spot has an antique coffee mill and a glass map of Brazil from 1929. There's another branch like a 1950s diner, on the corner of Sharia Salah Salem and Sharia Sizostris. Both daily 6.30am–midnight.

Coffee Roastery 48 Sharia Fouad ⓣ03/483-4363. Come for the preppy MTV ambience and karaoke (Wed from 9.30pm; reservation required), as well as great smoothies and non-alcoholic cocktails, though the *fajitas*, salads and melts are disappointing. Daily 7.30am–1am.

Délices Between Midan and Sharia Sa'ad Zaghloul. A spacious, elegant air-conditioned tearoom serving a decent Continental breakfast, delicious cakes, savouries, soft drinks and beer (which must be drunk indoors), with tables outside when the weather is fine. Daily 7am–11pm.

Sofianopoulo Coffee Store 18 Sharia Sa'ad Zaghloul. A vintage stand-up coffee shop furnished with silver grinders and allegorical statues, with a small sit-down annexe next door. Great cappuccino and croissants. Daily 9am–11pm.

Trianon Corner of Sa'ad Zaghloul and Ramleh. Though it still does a good Continental breakfast and lets customers linger for ages, this historic venue's once impressive decor has gone to seed and its restaurant is best avoided. Daily 7am–midnight.

Further out

Classique 60 Sharia 26th July. This air-conditioned patisserie has a sumptuous array of European gateaux and Middle Eastern pastries, and is non-smoking throughout. Daily 10am–11pm.

El Qobesi Sharia 26th July. Serving wonderful mango juice in chilled glasses, it has no sign in English but you can't miss the hundreds of mangoes stacked outside, nor the fairy-lit palm trees after dark. Daily 24hr.

Drinking

Although Alex is the centre of Egypt's wine and spirits industry (the vineyards are at Gianaclis, near Lake Maryut), **bars** have a low profile. *Monty's Bar* (daily 6pm–2am) in the *Hotel Cecil* is an anodyne place to sip beer or cocktails; if you're going to pay top prices, the *Fouad Bar* (daily 11am–4am) in the *El Salamlek Palace Hotel* at Montazah is plusher, with piano music in the evenings (smart dress required). But foreign residents and local drinkers tend to gather at the more characterful watering holes detailed below, where prices are lower. If you just want to buy booze, Drinkies (noon–midnight except Fri and Muslim holidays) on the corner of Sharia Gamil el-Din Yassin and Sharia el-Ghorfa el-Tigarya sells local wine and spirits and imported beer and alcopops; other foreign brands can be purchased within 48 hours of arrival in Egypt at the **duty-free shop**, 31 Sharia Salah Salem (daily 11am–10pm; Ramadan 11am–2pm & 8–10pm), which accepts US dollars, sterling, euros or Visa cards only. All the places below are marked on the map on pp.464–465 unless stated otherwise.

Cap d'Or (aka *Sheikh Ali*) 4 Sharia Adib Bek Ishtak, off Sharia Sa'ad Zaghloul. A real slice of old Alex, furnished with Art Nouveau mouldings and engraved mirrors, where bohemians and expats rub shoulders over grilled sardines and bottles of whisky or tequila. It has a friendly atmosphere, and is popular with the gay community after midnight, when there may be live *oud* (lute) music. A seafood and salad meal with a beer costs about £E65. Daily 10am–3am.

Elite 43 Sharia Safiya Zaghloul. Closed for a refit at the time of writing, this simple blue-painted extension to the restaurant of the same name (the food is awful) is a place to meet people and find out what's happening on Alexandria's cultural scene.

Portuguese Club (*Nady Portugali*) 42 Sharia Abd el-Qader Ragab, Roushdi ⓣ03/542-7599. A country club-cum-singles' bar frequented by expats, with pool or darts competitions (Tues), a disco (Thurs) and monthly party nights. Located 3km from the centre, off Tariq Gamal Abdel Nasser; catch tram #2 to the Egyptian-American Center and walk two blocks inland to find the first side street off Sharia Kafr Abdou – which is the name to give if you take a taxi (£E10). There's no sign outside the club. Daily 3pm till the last customer leaves; open for breakfast from 10am on Fri.

Spitfire Bar 7 Sharia al-Bursa al-Qadima. Small hangout covered in stickers from oil companies, warships and overland travel groups (the kind of foreigners that frequent the place), with 70s rock music and TV sports. Mon–Sat noon–1am.

Entertainment and activities

Thursday and Friday are the big nights out in Alex, but there's something happening all week. Several hotel **nightclubs** offer **bellydancing** and/or a Russian Show and DJ. It's wise to phone ahead and book a table at the *El Salamlek Palace,* which has a nightly programme (11pm–1am) in the summer. In the centre, the *Hotel Cecil*'s nightclub (daily except Fri & Wed midnight–4am) has two or three bellydancers (minimum charge £E75 per person). A sleazier, more raucous nightclub is *Lourantos* at 44 Sharia Safiya Zaghloul (Ⓣ03/483-3576), best visited with an Egyptian friend to get past the doorman who might claim there's an entry charge (there isn't one), or to argue if they try to add it to your bill. The dancing starts at midnight and runs through till dawn if enough patrons are still paying.

Though most four- and five-star hotels have **discos**, they're moribund outside of summer. All of them, aside from the *Sheraton*'s, restrict entry to mixed-sex groups, so if you're on your own, hang out at the *Portuguese Club* (see p.479) until a decent-sized group of people there decides to go dancing and tag along. If you prefer **karaoke**, there's a Wednesday-night bash at the *Coffee Roastery* (see p.479), though without any alcohol to loosen inhibitions.

Arts and festivals

After decades in the doldrums, Alexandria's cultural scene has seen a renaissance. The library is naturally at the forefront, but money has also been spent on the city's historic opera house and other venues. The tourist office has details of their monthly programmes, also advertised *in situ* and at the *Elite* restaurant (see p.479).

The Cultural Centre at the **Bibliotheca Alexandrina** (see p.472) stages **classical music** (Arabic as well as European), modern **dance** and **drama** (tickets £E10–20), and art house movies (free). Larger orchestral works and **ballet** are performed at the **Opera House** off Sharia Horriya (see p.466; Ⓣ03/486-5106). A few blocks west of the opera, the **Alexandria Centre of Arts** (Ⓣ03/495-6633) hosts concerts by musicians from Egypt and abroad. Another, smaller venue for music is the **Conservatoire de Musique d'Alexandrie** at 90 Sharia Horriya (Ⓣ03/487-5086). Over summer, **operas** are also staged in the **Antoniadis Gardens** (see p.474). The most "alternative" venue is **Garage** in Sidi Gaber (Ⓣ03/544-3246, Ⓔtfetouh@yatfund.org), putting on performances by local and foreign youth theatre groups, in the former garage of the Jesuit Centre at 298 Sharia Bur Said (see map, p.458).

In August you can see **folk dances** by the Rida Troupe (Ballet Rida) or the National Troupe (El-Fir'a el-Qawmiyya) at the outdoor **Abdel Wahab Theatre** (Ⓣ03/486-3637), on the Corniche east of Midan Ramleh. During summer there's also a **circus** (Ⓣ03/591-3795), which sets up at St Mark's College in Shatby: check performance times with the tourist office.

Other events include the two-week **Alexandria Biennial**, an exhibition of art from Mediterranean countries staged in October in odd-numbered years, and two annual sporting festivals: an **International Yachting Regatta** off the Eastern Harbour and an **International Marathon** along the Corniche from Ras el-Tin to Montazah, both staged in October.

During Ramadan, Alex revels in five **moulids** over five consecutive weeks, starting with *zikrs* outside the Mosque of Al-Mursi. The day after its "big night", the action shifts to Sidi Gaber's mosque, then Sidi Bishr's; these are followed by the moulids of Sidi Kamal and Sidi Mohammed al-Rahhal. And should you happen to be here over **New Year**, beware the blizzard of crockery that Alexandrians throw out of their windows at midnight.

Film

Each September, Alexandria's **International Film Festival** gives Egyptians a rare opportunity to see foreign movies in an uncensored state: the Convention Hall en route to the library is the main venue, but every cinema in town screens a small selection. Film-going is popular throughout the year, with extra screenings at all **cinemas** during Ramadan. Downtown, the three-screen Royal Renaissance (ⓣ03/485-5725) by the Opera House and the six-screen Amir (ⓣ03/391-7972) on the corner of Sharia Horriya and Safiya Zaghloul screen English-language films you might have seen last year. Out in Smouha (25 minutes by taxi), the six-screen Green Plaza Mall Cineplex (ⓣ03/532-5745), the five-screen Osman Group Cinema (ⓣ03/424-5897) in Smouha Mall and the seven-screen Renaissance City Center (ⓣ03/397-0156) in the City Center Mall vie to show the latest Hollywood blockbusters, while the eight-screen Renaissance San Stefano (ⓣ03/490-0056) in the mall behind the *Four Seasons Hotel* is currently the "in" spot for young Alexandrians.

Diving and fishing

For those qualified to go **diving**, there are many **ancient ruins and wrecks** to be seen five to eighteen metres beneath the waters around Alexandria. Few other cities boast such a wealth of historic underwater sites, with blocks from the Pharos littering the sea bed near Qaitbey's fort, and Roman trading vessels lying 500m offshore. Some eleven thousand artefacts and pieces of masonry remain from what was once the Royal Quarter in the Eastern Harbour, while Napoleonic wrecks and an ancient port lie beneath Abu Qir Bay.

Visibility in the Eastern Harbour declines as the water gets warmer, whereas other, less sheltered sites are best dived in the summer, when the sea is calm. **Alexandra Dive** (ⓣ03/483-2045 or 014 261-1115, ⓦwww.alexandra-dive.com), beside the *Tikka Grill* on the Corniche, can usually forecast conditions for the next 24 hours, and offers diving at two sites for €85 per person (including lunch and the fee to Underwater Archeology Department; equipment costs €15 extra). As the Pharos and Cleopatra's palace are only 5–8m underwater, even uncertified divers may be accepted if they can pass a try-out – whereas the wrecks and ruins at Abu Qir demand more than open-water experience. Unfortunately, their "buddy" system doesn't always work as well as it should.

The same outfit also offers two-hour **snorkelling** (€25 per person) and **fishing** (€30 per person) trips for a minimum of ten people, and PADI open-water **courses** (€280).

Listings

Airlines EgyptAir, 19 Midan Ramleh (ⓣ03/486-0778); Air France, 6 Sharia Horriya (ⓣ03/486-8547); British Airways, Burg al-Arab airport (ⓣ03/459-2834); Lufthansa, 6 Sharia Talaat Harb (ⓣ03/486-2607). Most other airlines are represented by travel agents.

American Express El-Saladya Building, Sharia 14 Mai (ⓣ03/420-1050). Based in a travel agent out in Smouha, it's a nuisance to reach. Daily except Fri & Sat 9am–5pm.

Arabic courses Qortoba Institute for Arabic Studies, on the corner of Mohammed Nabeel Hamdy and Khalid Ibn Walid sts, Miami (ⓣ03/556-2959 or 010 584-3483, ⓦwww.qortoba.net), offers one-on-one tuition for €4–4.50/hr and can arrange for student accommodation (from €65/month) or flat rental (from €170/month) nearby, to avoid you having to slog across town for lessons.

Banks Barclays, corner of Sharia Sa'ad Zaghloul and Sharia Safiya Zaghloul; Bank of Alexandria,

59 Sharia Sa'ad Zaghloul, 23 Sharia Talaat Harb and 26 Sharia Salah Salem; National Bank of Egypt in the *Montazah Sheraton* and *Cecil* hotels; HSBC, 47 Sharia Sultan Hussein; Banque Misr, 1 Sharia Talaat Harb, all have ATMs. There are better rates of exchange at the Forex bureaux on Midan Ramleh and Sharia Salah Salem.

Bookshops The best for non-fiction and novels in English are Dar el-Mustaqbal, 32 Sharia Safiya Zaghloul (Mon–Thurs & Sat 9am–4pm, Sun 9am–1pm); Al-Ahram, on the corner of Sharia Horriya and Talaat Harb (Mon–Thurs & Sat 9am–4pm, Sun 9am–1.30pm); and in the Alexandria National Museum (see p.468). Foreign newspapers are sold outside Ramleh telephone exchange and the *Metropole Hotel*.

Consulates Ireland, 55 Sharia Sultan Hussein (☎03/485-2672; Mon–Thurs & Sun 8am–1pm); UK, 3 Sharia Mena, Roushdi (☎03/546-7001; Mon–Thurs & Sun 8am–1pm); USA, 3 Sharia Phara'ana (☎02/486-1009; Mon–Thurs & Sun 9am–3pm). Australia, New Zealand and Canada have no consular representation; for other consulates, ask at the tourist office.

Cultural centres American Center, 3 Sharia Phara'ana (☎03/486-1009, Ⓦhttp://cairo.usembassy.gov/acalex/index.htm Mon–Thurs & Sun 10am–4pm); British Council, 11 Sharia Mahmoud El Ela, Roushdi (☎03/545-6512, Ⓦwww.britishcouncil.org.eg; daily except Fri 11am–7pm); French Centre, 30 Sharia Nabi Daniel (☎03/391-8952, Ⓦwww.alexfrance.org.eg; daily except Fri & Sat 9am–noon & 5–7.30pm); Goethe Institute, 10 Sharia al-Batalssa (☎03/484-9870, Ⓦwww.goethe.de/Alexandria (site in German/Arabic only); Mon–Thurs 9am–1pm, Sun 9am–2pm); Russian Centre, 5 Sharia Batalsa (☎03/486-5645; Mon–Thurs & Sun 10am–1pm & 5–8pm).

Dentist Alexandria Dental Centre, 321 Sharia Abu Qir, Cleopatra (☎03/427-7790).

DHL 9 Sharia Salah Salem (daily except Fri 9am–5pm; ☎03/485-1911).

Hospitals The German (Al-Almani) Hospital, 56 Sharia Abdel Salaam Aref, Saba Pasha (☎03/584-1806), and the International Hospital, 20 Sharia Beha al-Din, Smouha (☎03/420-7427) are both well equipped, with English-speaking doctors.

International calls There are Menatel booths all over town. The 24hr exchange on Midan Ramleh has direct-dial phones and sells phonecards; the exchanges on Midan el-Gumhorriya and Sharia Sa'ad Zaghloul (both daily 8am–11pm) work on the pre-booking system.

Internet Cyber cafés come and go, but try looking at 10 Sharia ash-Shohada (daily 9.30am–2am), 18 Sharia Kolliet el-Tibba (Sat–Thurs 8am–1am & Fri 3pm–1am), or Sharia Dr Hassan Fadaly, off Safiya Zaghloul (Mon–Sat 11am–11pm), downtown. Most charge £E2–4/hr.

Passport office To renew your visa, go to kiosk #6 on the first floor of 25 Sharia Talaat Harb (☎03/482-7873; Mon–Thurs 8.30am–2pm, Fri 10am–2pm, Sat & Sun 9–11am), with one photo and a copy of the relevant pages of your passport (there's a photocopier on the street outside). No applications accepted after noon.

Pharmacies Khalil, on Sharia el-Ghorfa el-Tigarya, off Midan Sa'ad Zaghloul (Mon–Sat 9am–10pm, Sun 10am–10pm; ☎03/480-6710), plus others on Midan Ramleh, Safiya Zaghloul and Nabi Daniel sts.

Photography The Havana Studio on Ramleh (daily 4–10pm) can burn digital images onto a CD, while Kodak Express (36 Sharia Safiya Zaghloul) sells memory cards for digital cameras and can print digital photos.

Post offices Midan Ramleh (daily 8am–3pm), Sharia el-Ghorfa el-Tigarya (same hours) and Masr Station (daily 8am–5pm). Express Mail Service is open till 2pm at all the main post offices.

Thomas Cook 15 Midan Sa'ad Zaghloul (☎03/487-5118, Ⓦwww.thomascook.com.eg) Cashes and sells travellers' cheques, and deals with stolen ones. Daily 8am–5pm.

Tourist police Above the tourist office (☎03/485-0507), in the Maritime Station (no phone) and at the entrance to Montazah gardens (☎03/547-5025). All except the last are open 24hr.

Western Union 73 Sharia Horriya (☎03/492-0900) and 281 Sharia Gamal Abdel Nasser (☎03/420-1148); both daily 8.30am –10pm.

Moving on

Many of the places featured in the remainder of this chapter can be reached from Alexandria by public transport, making **day excursions** to Rosetta and Tanta in the Delta easy; despite being nearer, El-Alamein and the Monastery of Abu Mina are awkward unless you hire a taxi, while the Monasteries of Wadi Natrun (see p.381) require a taxi at least part of the way.

Rail services between Alex and Cairo are detailed on p.209. At **Masr Station**, tickets for first and second class air-conditioned trains are sold from the office beside the tourist information booth on platform one, while ordinary second class and third class tickets are sold in the front hall. Services to Tanta and Cairo can also be boarded at **Sidi Gaber Station**.

Buses

All buses depart from the **Moharrem Bey Terminal** (aka el-Mo'gaf Jeddid) on the southern outskirts (£E15 by taxi from the centre). West Delta has **ticket offices** on the corner of Midan Sa'ad Zaghloul and Sharia el-Ghorfa el-Tigarya (ⓣ03/480-9685), downtown; near Sidi Gaber Station (ⓣ03/520-6701) and at Moharrem Bey (ⓣ03/363-3993). Superjet has offices only at Moharrem Bey (ⓣ03/363-3552) and Sidi Gaber (ⓣ03/543-5222). From 5.30am till 1am, both run a/c services to **Cairo** (£E25–35) and its airport (£E35–50) every half-hour. West Delta buses to **Siwa Oasis** (£E33–35) leave Alex at 8.30am, 11am, 2pm and 10pm. You can travel there directly – a ten-hour journey that makes it wise to catch the early morning bus – or go as far as Mersa Matrouh, stay overnight and carry on to Siwa next day. Hourly West Delta buses to **El-Alamein** (£E15) and **Mersa Matrouh** (£E20–33) run all year, augmented by Superjet (8am & 9am; £E35) in the summer. Many run on to **Sollum** (£E20), though if you're travelling to Libya it's easier to take an international bus from Cairo to Tripoli (see p.211).

Other destinations include **Port Said** (Superjet 7.30am; £E25; West Delta 6am, 8am, 11am, 2.30pm, 4pm, 6pm & 7pm; £E20–25); **Ismailiya** (West Delta 7am & 2.30pm; £E25); **Hurghada** (Superjet 8pm; £E95; West Delta (9am & 6.30pm; £E85–100); **Sharm el-Sheikh** (Superjet 9pm; £E110; West Delta 9pm; £E85); **Tanta** (West Delta hourly 6am–6pm; £E10) and **Zagazig** (West Delta 8am, 9am & 2pm; £E17).

Service taxis

Moharrem Bey is also the departure point for Peugeots, minibuses and minivans to Cairo, the Wadi Natrun resthouse, the Monastery of Abu Mina, El-Alamein, Mersa Matrouh, Port Said, Rosetta, Tanta and Zagazig. Listen for the drivers shouting out destinations, or ask for directions to the right clump of service taxis.

The Mediterranean coast

Egypt's five-hundred-kilometre-long **Mediterranean coast** (known as Al-Sahel) has beautiful beaches and sparkling sea all the way to Libya. However, many stretches are still mined from World War II or off-limits due to military bases, while all the most accessible sites have been colonized by holiday villages catering mainly to Egyptians, whose beach culture is so different from Westerners' that most foreigners prefer the Sinai and Red Sea resorts. Travelling between Alexandria and the World War II battlefield of **El-Alamein**, you'll pass a slew of **resorts** reserved for elite sections of Egyptian society such as the army, navy and diplomatic corps, and others open to anyone who can afford to stay, though for independent travellers they're simply blights on the landscape which make the colonial-era beach resort of **El-Agami** (20km from downtown Alexandria and now a commuter suburb) seem historic by

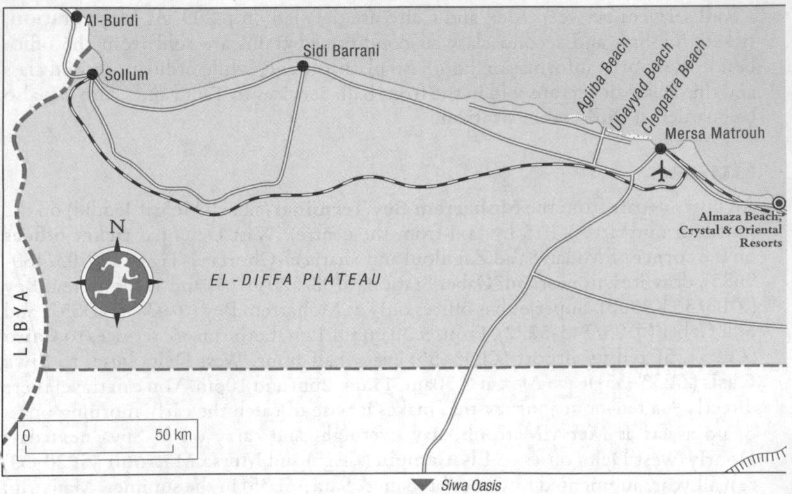

comparison. With the ancient lighthouse at Abu Sir and the ruins of Taposiris Magna off-limits, the only accessible "sight" is the Coptic **Monastery of Abu Mina**, 15km inland of the highway midway between Alexandria and El-Alamein.

The Monastery of Abu Mina

If you're hiring a car to visit El-Alamein, consider a side-trip to the Coptic **Monastery of Abu Mina**, which can also be reached from Alexandria by minibus from the Moharrem Bey Terminal. Deir Mari Mina, as it's known

Taposiris Magna and the search for Cleopatra's tomb

Thirty kilometres beyond El-Agami the highway passes a site called **Abu Sir**, better known to archeologists by its Roman name, **Taposiris Magna**. This ancient **city** – which the Egyptians called Per Usiri ("Dwelling of Osiris") and the Greeks Busiris – had one port on the Mediterranean and another on Lake Maryut. In Roman times the Maryut region was a major source of grain, shipped to Italy to placate the potentially riotous plebs in Rome. A chain of lighthouses from Alexandria to Cyrenaica (Libya) warned sailors of the abrupt change from sea to sand along a coastline devoid of landmarks. While Alexandria's Pharos has disappeared, archeologists have gleaned clues to its shape from the sole surviving **lighthouse** in the chain, at Abu Sir – which most believe was a one-tenth scale replica of the Pharos.

Today, both the lighthouse and Taposiris Magna are off-limits while the SCA conducts excavations in search of the **tomb of Cleopatra and Mark Antony**. The Dominican scholar Kathleen Martinez believes it lies beneath the city's Temple of Osiris, having found the mummies of ten nobles just outside, and coins bearing Cleopatra's face and an alabaster mask with a cleft chin similar to portraits of Antony within the temple precincts. Her belief is also founded on the historian Plutarch's assertion that Octavian allowed the couple to be buried together after their respective suicides in 30 BC. If Martinez is right and finds their mummies, it will be the greatest discovery since Tutankhamun's tomb.

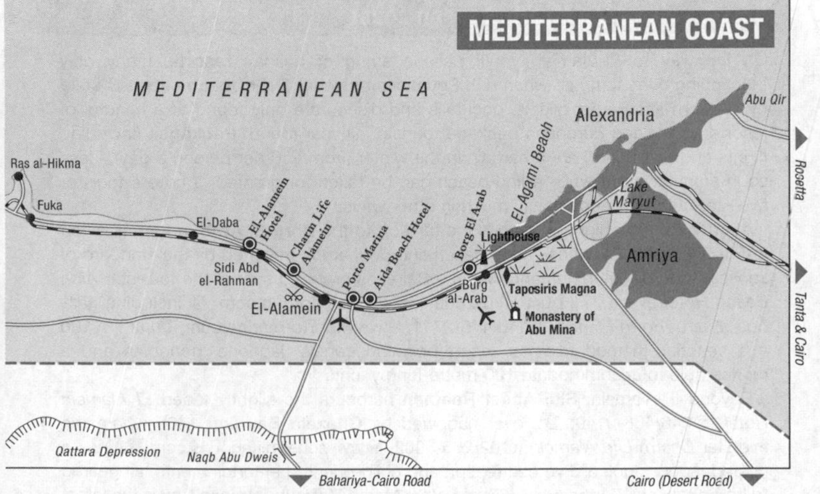

locally, honours **St Menas**, an Egyptian-born Roman legionary who was martyred in Asia Minor in 296 after refusing to renounce Christ. His ashes were buried here when the camel that was taking them home refused to go any further. Miraculous events on the spot persuaded others to exhume Menas in 350 and build a church over his grave, later enclosed within a huge basilica. A wealthy **pilgrim city** grew up as camel trains spread his fame (Menas is depicted between two camels), and "holy" water from local springs was exported throughout Christendom. But when these dried up in the twelfth century, the city was abandoned – its extensive **ruins** are on UNESCO's Endangered World Heritage list.

While its belfry towers are visible from far away, high walls enclose the concrete buildings of the modern monastery, erected in 1959. Its **cathedral** is adorned with Italian marble, black and rose Aswan granite, and stained glass. Busloads of pilgrims arrive daily, particularly on November 11, **St Menas's Day**, when the cathedral overflows. In addition to Menas, the crypt houses the body of Pope Kyrillos VI (1959–71), whom Copts regard as a saint, writing petitions on his marble grave.

El-Alamein

Before Alamein we never had a victory. After Alamein we never had a defeat.

Winston Churchill, *The Hinge of Fate*

The utterly misnamed "city" of **EL-ALAMEIN** squats on a dusty plain 106km west of Alexandria, situated along a spur road that turns inland from the coastal highway. Anyone driving past could blink and see nothing except construction debris until they pass the Italian War Cemetery 9km down the highway. Still, El-Alamein ("Two Worlds") is an apt name for a place that witnessed the turning point of the North African campaign, determining the fate of Egypt and Britain's empire. When the Afrika Korps came within 111km of Alexandria on July 1, 1942, control of Egypt, Middle Eastern oil and the Canal route to India seemed about to be wrested from the Allied powers by Germany and Italy. Instead, at

Resorts along the Mediterranean coast

On the way to El-Alamein you'll pass a string of holiday **resorts**, many only functioning over summer, when rich Egyptians move in. Their **beach scene** is staid by Western standards; bikinis, cocktails and discos are only found at a handful of resorts also taking European package tourists, all year round. **Packages** (including flights and half-board) are a bargain in the winter (from €50 per person a day) – less so in summer – but while a fine beach can be taken for granted, a hotel's four- or five-star rating may not signify much in other ways.

At km 52 on the highway there's the turn-off to the **Borg El Arab, a** former *Hilton* (ⓣ03/374-0730; ⑦), whose huge beach and pool aren't matched by the standard of service, food or entertainment. Wealthy Cairenes prefer to stay at the four-star *Aida Beach Hotel* at km 77 (ⓣ046/410-2802, ⓦwww.aidagroup.com; ⑧ including half-board) or at *Porto Marina* (ⓣ046/445-2711, ⓦwww.porto-marina.com; ⑧) at km 100 – a Venetian-themed five-star resort boasting canals, lagoons, gondolas and a marina able to accommodate 100-metre-long yachts.

Beyond El-Alamein, **Sidi Abdel Rahman** harbours the slightly faded *El Alamein Hotel* (ⓣ046/468-0140; ⑧), overshadowed by **Ghazala Bay** (km 140), where the five-star *Charm Life Alamein* (ⓣ02/266-8902, ⓦwww.charmlifehotels.com; ⑦) has a heated indoor pool; a **dive** centre, spa and child-oriented entertainments, all geared to Italian tourists. Further west, 37km before Mersa Matrouh, **Almaza Bay** is the latest mega-development, with a splendid beach and **spa** shared by the *Almaza Beach* (ⓣ046/436-0000, ⓔalmaza@jaz.travel; ⑦), *Crystal* (ⓣ046/436-0020, ⓔcrystal@jaz.travel; ⑦) and *Oriental* resorts (ⓣ046/436-0030, ⓔoriental@jaz.travel; ⑦).

The Mediterranean governorate capital, **Mersa Matrouh,** is also a summer resort, but its beach scene is ultra-conservative and the few Westerners that come here do so off-season, en route between Alex and Siwa (see p.483). Though Matrouh's beaches are small, there's the vast **Ubayyad Beach** and a stunningly beautiful cove at **Agiiba Beach**, 14km and 24km west of town. Visitors can stay at the *Arous el-Bahr* (ⓣ046/493-4420; ⑥) or *Reem* (ⓣ046/493-3605; ⑤) on the Corniche, or the *Lido* (ⓣ046/493-2248; ⑤) two blocks inland, and eat delicious seafood at the *Hammo al-Temsah Fish* or *Abu al-Araby* restaurants on Sharia Tahrir. Matrouh's bus station is 3km from the centre (£E10 by taxi or 50pt by minibus).

El-Alamein, the Allied Eighth Army held, and then drove the Axis forces back, to ultimate defeat in Tunisia. Some eleven thousand soldiers were killed and seventy thousand wounded at El-Alamein alone; total casualties for the North African campaign (Sept 1940–March 1943) exceeded one hundred thousand. Travellers who wish to pay their respects to the dead or have an interest in military history should find the **cemeteries** and the **war museum** worth the effort of getting there.

The easiest way is by **renting a car** with a driver, through Thomas Cook in Alex for £E380 (see p.461); alternatively, you may be able to charter a **taxi** for £E250–350, depending on your bargaining skills. Though comparatively expensive, a car enables you to reach the far-flung cemeteries and leave El-Alamein without difficulty – a major advantage over public transport. Hourly West Delta **buses** from Alex to Matrouh can drop you at the police checkpoint by the turn-off for the Allied War Cemetery, or 1km further west along the highway, closer to the War Museum (see below). The other way is to catch a **minibus** (£E8–10) from the Moharrem Bey terminal in Alex.

While getting there is straightforward enough, leaving can be harder. Basically, you walk back to the highway and flag down any bus or minibus heading in the right direction – but ensure they're going all the way to your destination. Vehicles heading towards Mersa Matrouh may turn off the highway to settlements from which there is no onward transport except for private taxis, while most minibuses heading in the direction of Alexandria actually terminate at the industrial satellite-city of Amriya (from where it's £E15 by taxi or 50pt by minibus to downtown Alex).

The War Museum, cemeteries and battlefield

While you can be sure of finding all the **cemeteries** open (daily: summer 8am–5pm; winter & Ramadan 9am–3pm), it's worth phoning ahead to check about the museum (Ⓣ046/410-0031), as it closes now and again for some reason or another. All the Allied memorials lie beside a spur road off the highway, which begins just after the turn-off for the Qattara Depression (see p.451). First comes the **Greek Memorial**, followed 400m later by the **South African Memorial**, and then the **Allied War Cemetery** secluded on the reverse slope of a hill. Planted with trees and flowers, it is a tranquil site for the graves of 7367 Allied soldiers (815 of them nameless, only "known unto God"), with memorial cloisters listing the names of 11,945 others whose bodies were never found. Though over half were Britons, the dead include Australians, New Zealanders, Indians, Malays, Melanesians, Africans, Canadians, French, Greeks and Poles. If you want to find a particular headstone, the Commonwealth War Graves Commission (Ⓦwww.cwgc.org) in London can tell you exactly where to look. Walking down to the cemetery, you'll pass the **Australian Memorial**, honouring the 9th Australian Division that stormed Point 29 and Thompson's Post during the penultimate phase of the Third Battle.

If you're coming by bus or service taxi, you're likely to be dropped further west along the highway, where a Sherman tank (not of World War II vintage, but captured from the Israelis) near a gas station marks the start of an uphill turn-off leading to the museum (El Mathaf in Arabic). Follow this to a T-junction and turn left; the **War Museum** is 200m ahead (daily: summer 9am–5pm; winter & Ramadan 9am–4pm; £E15), past a telephone exchange. Well presented, the museum has photos and models conveying the harsh conditions in the field. Notice

▲ Tanks at El-Alamein's War Museum

The Battle of El-Alamein

Rather than the single, decisive clash of arms that many people imagine, the Battle of El-Alamein consisted of three savage bouts of mechanized warfare separated by relative lulls over a period of five months (July–Nov) in 1942. In the **First Battle** of El-Alamein, the **Afrika Korps**' advance was stymied by lack of fuel and munitions and stiff Allied resistance organized by General Auchinleck. Once resupplied, however, Field Marshal Erwin **Rommel** was able to press the advantage with 88-millimetre cannons that outranged the Allies' guns, as well as faster, better-armoured tanks, used with an élan that earned him the title "the Desert Fox".

In August, General Bernard **Montgomery** ("Monty") took over the Allied **Eighth Army**, vowing that it would retreat no further. He negated his army's weaknesses by siting its tanks "hull down" in pits with only their gun turrets above ground, protecting them until the Panzers came within range. Aware that the Allies were being resupplied, Rommel attacked the Alam Halfa Ridge in the **Second Battle** of El-Alamein (Aug 31 to Sept 6). Repulsed with heavy losses and desperately short of fuel, the Afrika Korps withdrew behind a field of five hundred thousand landmines. Monty patiently reorganized his forces, resisting pressure from his superiors to attack until he had amassed one thousand tanks. A stage illusionist, Jasper Maskelyne, concealed them in the desert and constructed fake tank parks as part of an elaborate deception plan to mislead Rommel as to where and when the Eighth Army's main offensive would occur.

Shortly after nightfall on October 23, Monty launched the **Third Battle** of El-Alamein with a barrage of 744 guns that was heard in Alexandria. Having cracked the Nazi Enigma code, the Allies knew that Rommel was convalescing in Italy; when the Eighth Army punched a corridor through the minefields of the central front on October 23, the Germans were taken unawares. Rommel managed to return two days later, but was obliged to concentrate his mobile units further north, stranding four Italian divisions in the south. The Allies had established a commanding position at Kidney Ridge, from where Monty launched the decisive strike on November 2, leaving Rommel with only 35 operational tanks by the end of the day. On November 5 the Eighth Army broke out and surged westwards; the Afrika Korps fought rearguard actions back through Libya until its inevitable surrender six months later.

the section on Almássy (of *The English Patient*; see p.435) and his role in guiding two German spies through the desert. Outside are two dozen tanks, cannons and trucks, including a lorry belonging to the Long Range Desert Group (see p.437) that was found in the desert in 1991. There's also a restored **Command Bunker** that was used by Monty during the battle, which you'll have to ask a guide to unlock.

On the highway west of El-Alamein is a **plaque** marking the furthest point of the Axis advance, which asserts: *Manco la Fortuna, Non il Valore* ("Lacking Fortune, Not Valour"), *1.7.1942, Alessandria 111km*. Further out you'll glimpse the **German Cemetery**, a squat octagonal ossuary housing the remains of 4280 soldiers and overlooking the sea from a peninsula to the north. An elegant white tower marks the **Italian Cemetery**, 3km further along the highway, which contains a small museum, and a chapel dedicated to the 42,800 Italian soldiers, sailors and airmen who died during the campaign. Do not wander around between these cemeteries; while the grounds themselves have been cleared, the intervening strips of land are still mined.

The **battlefield** itself is generally far too dangerous to explore, due to the **minefields** laid by both sides. A staggering 17.2 million landmines are estimated to remain in the Western Desert, which still kill and maim local Bedouin to this day. Germany, Britain and Italy have always rejected Egyptian and Libyan demands that they fund mine clearance programmes – the current excuse is that Egypt hasn't signed up to the Ottawa Convention banning the manufacture of mines. Although a few Bedouin with 4WDs are prepared to take people to such strategic strongpoints as **Kidney Ridge** (which the 51st Highland Division was disconcerted to find was actually a depression, leaving them exposed to enemy fire) and **Tell el-Issa** (stormed by the Australians), you would be foolish to rely on assurances that they know safe routes through the minefields.

The Delta

The Nile **Delta** is Egypt's most fertile and (barring Cairo) its most heavily populated region – nearly half the people in Egypt live here, and despite the lack of ancient sites, a scoot around the Delta on service taxis and third-class trains gives a feel for today's Egypt in a way that visits to tombs and temples do not. Although several pharaonic dynasties arose and ruled from this region – Lower Egypt – little of their capitals remain beyond mounds of debris known as *tell* or *kom*. The pharaohs themselves plundered older sites of sculptures and masonry, and with a yearly rainfall of nearly 20cm (the highest in Egypt) and an annual inundation by the Nile that coated the land in silt, mud-brick structures were soon eroded or swept away. More recently, farmers have furthered the cycle of destruction by digging the mounds for a nitrate-enriched soil called *sebakh*, used for fertilizer; several sites catalogued by nineteenth-century archeologists have now all but vanished. On those that remain, there's good information at Ⓦegyptsites.wordpress.com/category/delta.

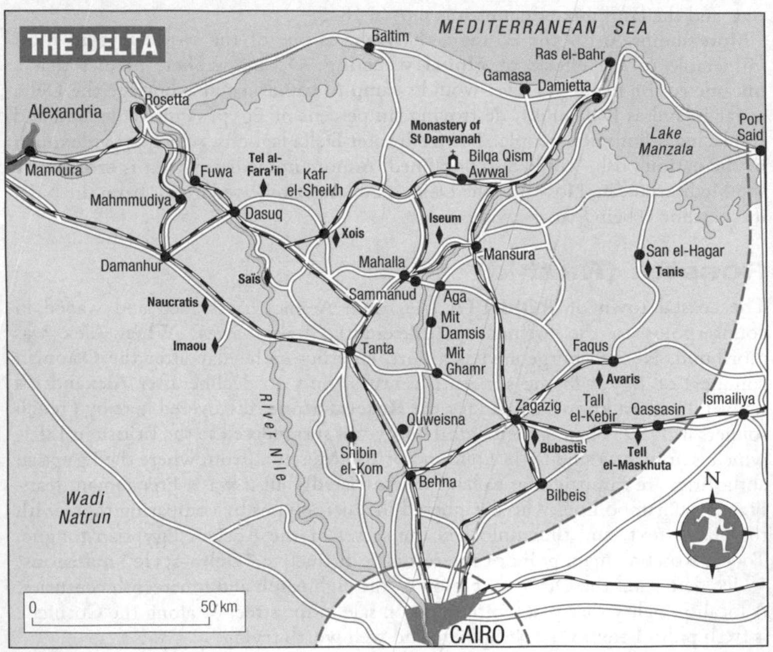

Getting around the Delta

For many places in the Delta, day-trips from Cairo, Alexandria or Port Said are more feasible than overnight stays. From Cairo, **buses and service taxis** to all parts of the Delta leave from Aboud terminal in Shubra (see p.211); some service taxis also depart from outside Ramses train station, but these leave town by a more roundabout route and end up taking longer. Trains are OK for reaching major towns, but service taxis are the easiest way to **get around**. Renting a car isn't necessarily a good idea: it's easy to have accidents on the busy Delta roads, and the unsurfaced ones are legally off-limits to foreign drivers – a hangover from 1960s spy-phobia. Should the police decide to make a fuss, you could conceivably spend a night in jail.

Rosetta is a charming little town, with a special architecture of its own, but the main cities of the Delta, including **Mahalla**, **Tanta** and **Damietta**, are of interest not so much for any sights or attractions, as because they do not have any, and thus represent a chance to see the ordinary, workaday "real" Egypt which usually escapes most tourists. The Delta also abounds in **moulids** (popular festivals), the largest of which draw crowds of over a million. Companies of *mawladiya* (moulid people) run stalls and rides, Sufi *tariqas* perform their *zikrs*, people camp outdoors, and music blares into the small hours. Smaller, rural moulids tend to be heavier on the practical devotion, with people bringing their children or livestock for blessing, or the sick to be cured.

The Delta's other main attraction is its flat, intensely green **landscape**, riven by waterways where feluccas glide past mud-brick villages and wallowing buffalo. The northern **lakes** are a wintering ground for **birdlife** – in ancient times, wealthy Egyptians enjoyed going fowling in the reeds, using throwing sticks and hunting cats; their modern-day counterparts employ shotguns. The Delta is also still a habitat for wildcats and pygmy white-toothed shrews, but boars have been driven out, and the last hippopotamus was shot in 1815.

More sombrely for the ecology, the Delta is one of the world regions most vulnerable to the effects of **global warming**. Oceanographers predict that a one-metre rise in the sea level would swamp Alexandria and submerge the Delta as far inland as Damanhur, destroying six percent of Egypt's cultivable land and displacing 3.3 million people. The freshwater Delta lagoons, which provide much of the nation's fish, would also be ruined. A more immediate threat is **erosion** by the Mediterranean. Now that the Delta is no longer renewed by silt from the Nile, its coastline is being worn away.

Rosetta (Rashid)

The coastal town of **ROSETTA** (*Rashid* in Arabic) has waxed and waned in counterpoint to the fortunes of Alexandria, 65km away. When Alex was moribund, Rosetta burgeoned as a port, entering its heyday after the Ottoman conquest of Egypt in the sixteenth century, only to decline after Alexandria's revival. It is best known abroad for the **Rosetta Stone**, discovered here by French soldiers in 1799. Their archeological booty was surrendered to the British in 1801, which is how it wound up in London's British Museum (from where the Egyptian authorities are campaigning to have it repatriated), but it was a Frenchman, Jean-François Champollion, who deciphered the hieroglyphs by comparing them with the Greek text, and thus unlocked the secret of the Ancient Egyptian tongue. Today, Rosetta's main point of interest is its distinctive **"Delta-style" mansions**, which date from the Ottoman period of the eighteenth and nineteenth centuries. A local speciality that you'll often find on sale in the street or along the Corniche is fresh **palm heart**, very cheap here and well worth trying.

Around mid-November, the chain of festivals that started in Tanta the previous month (see p.494) should reach Rosetta. Don't despair if you come a few weeks earlier, since similar **moulids** occur at Fuwa, Mahmudiya and Dasuq, further inland. Salted fish (*fisikh*) and hummus are the traditional snacks at these events.

Getting there

The quickest way to reach the town is by **service taxi** (1hr) from Alexandria's Midan el-Gumhorriya. There are also nine **trains** a day from Alex (2hr). From Cairo, there is no direct transport, and the best way to get here is by bus or service taxi to Damanhur (2hr), from where you can take another service taxi to Rosetta (1hr 15min). If you get to Damanhur by train, you'll then need to take a cab (£E2) to the bus and *servees* station for your onward connection. There are no direct train services between Rosetta and Dasuq, Damanhur, Tanta or Cairo.

The Town

Many of the Ottoman Delta-style mansions have been (or are being) restored, their hallmarks being pointed brickwork (usually emphasized by white or red paint), inset beams and carved lintels, and a profusion of *mashrabiya*-work. Some also incorporate ancient columns. Though the restored mansions look great from the outside, most are not currently open to the public. To find out what's open, go to **Abu Shahim Mill** (see p.492), where they'll sell you a ticket which covers the mill, the **Hammam Azouz** bathhouse (see p.493) and whichever of the mansions is currently open (usually only one, but sometimes none at all). Alternatively, the caretakers at certain restored mansions may be on hand, and may allow you in to have a look. Our map shows the locations of the most interesting houses, not all of which are described individually in the text, but which make a good basis for exploring the town.

The places of interest start almost opposite the service taxi station, on Sharia Azouz Sama; you'll see some fine Delta-style houses, all dating from the eighteenth century. **Kohiya House** stands next to the fine **Al-Araby Mosque**. Two doors further on stand the trio of **Ramadan House, Maharem House** and **Al-Gamal House**, with **Abouhoum House** just across the street.

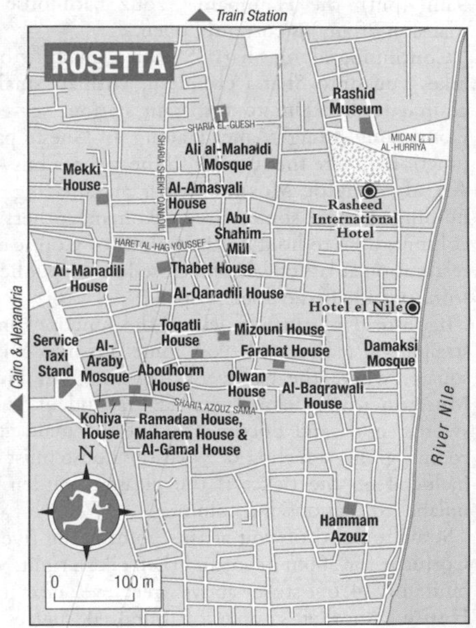

Further examples of Rosetta's Delta-style architecture (including **Thabet House**, one of the oldest of the Delta-style houses, built in 1709, and **Al-Manadili House**, whose portico is supported by two ancient columns of pharaonic or Greco-Roman origin) lie on, or just off, Sharia Sheikh Qanadili, which runs north from Azouz Sama, parallel to the river. It's the second turning on your left past Beit Abouhoum, and leads to **Al-Amasyali House**, whose upstairs reception room are ennobled by a superb wooden

▲ Part of the facade of Ramadan House

ceiling and mother-of-pearl-inlaid *mashrabiyas*. Like the **Abu Shahim Mill** next door, it was built around 1808 for the Turkish Agha, Ali al-Topgi, who bequeathed them both to his servant Al-Amasyali. The mill, with its huge wooden grinders and delicately pointed keyhole arches, is open to the public, and it is here that you can buy a £E15 ticket (£E8 for students) allowing you to visit the mill (daily 9am–4pm), the Hammam Azouz bathhouse (see opposite), and whichever mansion (if any) is currently open.

Continuing along Sharia Sheikh Qanadili from here, a right turn after 100m takes you onto Sharia el-Guesh, with its small church. A left just before the church leads 500m to the train station, served by nine daily trains to Alex. Continuing straight ahead along El-Guesh past the church, you come to a junction, where the turning to the right, a busy market street, takes you past the **Ali al-Mahaldi Mosque**, with an amazing miscellany of pilfered columns holding it up, some Greco-Roman, others looking suspiciously like the columns used to hold up the pulpits of Coptic churches. The Mosque was under restoration at last check, and closed to the public, though you can see the columns from outside if the door is open.

If, instead of turning left at the junction on Sharia el-Guesh, you continue straight on (eastwards), you come out into Midan al-Hurriya, the town's main square, where the eighteenth-century **Kili House** contains the small **Rashid Museum** (daily 9am–4pm; £E15, students £E8). Exhibits include some old swords, guns and documents, but the main attraction is the restored upstairs rooms, giving a feeling of what the house must have been like in its heyday. Also included on the ticket is the pleasant garden opposite, decorated with a few unlabelled cannons and columns.

Straight ahead of you at this point is the river, and if you continue along the Corniche for 300m or so, and then take a right, you'll find the **Damaksi Mosque**, built in 1714, one storey above street level, next to another mansion, **Al-Baqrawali House**. Another couple of hundred metres south is a nineteenth-century bathhouse, **Hammam Azouz** (daily 9am–4pm; tickets from Abu Shahim Mill, see p.491), whose interior, with its marble floors and fountains, has been lovingly restored, enabling you to see a fine example of a traditional bathhouse, though it is not in use today.

Seven kilometres north of town is the **Fort of Qaitbey** (daily 9am–4pm, Ramadan 9am–3pm; £E15, students £E8). Built in 1479 to guard the mouth of the Nile and protect Egypt's spice trade against any predatory maritime power, it was later reinforced by the French, whose use of masonry imported from Upper Egypt led to the discovery of the Rosetta Stone. The fort can be reached from town by green-and-white taxi (£E5) or fishing boat (£E50 after bargaining), or you can head 500m north along the Corniche, to the point where it does a bend, and pick up a service taxi from there (£E1). For an alternative river trip, you can visit the tranquil old **Mosque of Abu Mandar**, 5km south of Rosetta; taxi-boats leave from the docks near Midan al-Horriya – expect to pay £E20–30 after haggling.

Rosetta's best **hotel** is the *Rasheed International* on the south side of the park south of Midan al-Horriya (ⓣ045/293-4399, ⓔrasheedhotel@yahoo.com; BB ❸), which is great value with a/c en-suite rooms, some giving views over Midan al-Horriya or the river, while its **restaurant** offers the best eating in town. For budgeteers, the *Hotel el Nile*, 300m south of Midan al-Horriya on the Corniche (ⓣ045/292-2382; ❶), is very simple, with rather hard mattresses and shared bathrooms, but it's decent enough, and some rooms have balconies overlooking the river. For cheap eats, your best bet is the slew of places opposite the service taxi stand.

Damanhur and around

Most of the land between Alex and Tanta is given over to **cotton**, Egypt's major cash crop, whose intensive cultivation began under Mohammed Ali. Hardly surprising, then, that local towns are heavily into textiles, particularly the Beheira governorate capital, **DAMANHUR**, once Tmn-Hor, the City of Horus, the main **transport** hub for the Western Delta. It has regular trains to Cairo and Tanta, or to Alex, plus service taxis to all those places and to Rosetta or Dasuq (change there for Kafr el-Sheikh) from its new bus and *servees* station (£E2 by cab from the train station).

Damanhur is rather drab, but blossoms during its festival, **Moulid of Sheikh Abu Rish**, held in late October and early November, when turbaned Sufis perform *zikrs* and *munshids* to enthusiastic crowds. This occurs a week after Dasuq's moulid (see below); with venues so close together, the *mawladiya* (moulid people) can easily move on to the next event: barbers, circumcisers and all.

Egypt's only **Jewish moulid**, held over two days in January, is a very different scene. The shrine of **Abu Khatzeira** ("Father of the Mat"), a nineteenth-century mystic, has often been suspended in recent years, and when it *is* held, it is cordoned off by security police who rigorously exclude non-Jewish Egyptians, fearing a terrorist attack. Within the cordon a few thousand mostly French or Israeli visitors bring sick relatives or bottled water to be blessed, and "bid" for the key to Abu Khatzeira's shrine; the money raised supports its upkeep.

Two moulids: Dasuq and Fuwa

A week or so after Tanta's festival (see p.494), and a week before Damanhur's (see above) the agricultural town of **Dasuq** (the "q" usually pronounced as a glottal stop) holds the **Moulid of Ibrahim al-Dasuqi** (starting Oct 10), drawing almost as many people. Al-Dasuqi (1246–88) was the only native-born Egyptian to found a major Sufi order, the Burhamiya, whose chosen colour is green: the other brotherhoods originated abroad, or were started here by foreigners.

Should you decide to attend the eight-day event, Dasuq is probably easiest to reach from Damanhur by bus or service taxi. You can also get to it by service taxi from Kafr el-Sheikh or Rosetta. Service taxis from Dasuq also serve **Fuwa**, 13km northwest, where another **festival** occurs in late October or early November.

Tanta

A bustling industrial city (Egypt's fifth-largest), **TANTA** marks the end of the cotton harvest in October with Egypt's largest festival, the **Moulid of Saiyid Ahmed el-Bedawi**, when its population jumps from 430,000 to nearly three million as visitors pour in from the Delta villages, other parts of Egypt and the Arab world. The moulid honours the founder of one of Egypt's largest Sufi brotherhoods. Born in Fez in Morocco in 1199, **Saiyid Ahmed el-Bedawi** was sent to Tanta in 1234 by the Iraqi Rifaiyah order, and later established his own *tariqa* ("brotherhood"), the Ahmediya. Streets and squares fill with tents and stalls for the moulid, thousands camp out amidst heaps of blankets and cooking pots among the music and chanting, vendors and devotees, Sufi *zikrs*, even a circus with tigers and a levitation act. Events focus on the triple-domed, Ottoman-style **mosque** wherein Bedawi and a lesser sheikh, Abd el-Al, are buried, which is located some 300m east of the railway station. The climax to the eight-day festival occurs on a Friday, when the Ahmediya – whose banners and turbans are red – parade with drums behind their mounted sheikh. If you attend the moulid, it is best to leave your valuables somewhere safe: pickpocketing is rife and people quite often suffer injuries from crushing or fist-fights in the dense crowds.

Tanta is known for its roasted chickpeas (*hummus* in Arabic, though it does not necessarily mean that they are mashed with garlic and tahini). They can be bought at any of the multitude of sweet shops surrounding the mosque.

Practicalities

With regular trains and service taxis from Alex and Cairo running from early morning till nigh on midnight, it's easy to come to Tanta on a day-trip, but if you want **to stay** here during the moulid, you'll need to book a room as far in advance as possible. The *New Arafa Hotel* on Midan al-Mahata, almost opposite the train station (Ⓣ040/340-5040, Ⓕ335-7080; BB ❺), is conveniently located and has good-sized rooms equipped with a/c, TV and a minibar. The cheaper *Green House Hotel* on Sharia el-Borsa, off Midan el-Gomhurriya, about 600m east of the station (Ⓣ040/333-0761 or 2, Ⓕ333-0320; BB ❹), has similar facilities but smaller rooms and is not quite as comfortable, though its friendly staff can organize most things for you on request. On Midan el-Gomhurriya, opposite the street leading to the *Green House*, the Ahli United **Bank** changes money and has an ATM.

From the handsome railway station in the city centre, there are twelve air-conditioned **train** services a day to Benha, Cairo, Damanhur and Alexandria, plus innumerable slow ones to the above destinations, as well as six to Mansura (1hr 15min) and three to Damietta (2hr 35min), but only two to Zagazig (2hr 10min). Regular buses to Cairo's Aboud terminal (half-hourly 6am–10pm; 1hr 30min) leave from **Gomla bus station**, 2km north of the city centre, where you will also find buses to Damanhur and Alexandria (hourly 7am–7pm), and to Port Said (3 daily), and Suez (3 daily), plus service taxis to Cairo (1hr 15min), Damanhur (1hr) and Alex (2hr 15min). Buses to Mahalla el-Kubra leave every fifteen minutes from **Mura Shaha station**, where you will also find service taxis to Mahalla (30min), Sammanud (40min), Mansura (1hr), Ismailiya (2hr) and Zagazig (1hr). Service taxis to Kafr el-Sheikh (1hr) leave from a place called Staad, between Mura Shaha and the city centre. All of these depots are connected with each other and with the train station by regular service taxi microbuses (40pt), or by taxi (£E2–3).

Around Tanta

There are **ancient sites** around Tanta but you'd have to be an enthusiast to seek them out. They aren't served by public transport so, unless you have your own vehicle, you'll need to hire a private taxi. The most important town in the area is **MAHALLA** (el-Mahalla el-Kubra, to give it its full title), Egypt's fourth largest city and a big textile centre, located 24km northeast of Tanta. Egypt's cotton industry is one of the few in the country with relatively strong unionization, and the failure of wages to keep up with inflation was highlighted by an April 2008 textile workers' strike, supported by opposition activists nationwide. This led to riots when the government banned all protests and attempted to quell them by force. Police used live ammunition against the demonstrators and killed at least three people including a schoolboy. Forty-nine protestors were charged with offences arising from the riots, and many were tortured by police (common practice in Egypt for political crimes) before getting sentences of three to five years in prison. Mahalla's top **hotel** is the two-star *Omar Khayyam* on Midan Setta w'Ashreen Yulyu (23rd July Square), 300m north of the train station along 23rd July Street, aka Sharia al-Bahr (Ⓣ040/223-4866, Ⓕ223-4299; BB ❸), which is good-value, clean and well-kept, with a choice of smaller rooms with shared bathrooms or larger en-suite rooms with a/c. Service taxis to Mansura, Damietta and Alexandria, along with frequent local buses to Tanta, leave from a depot near the train station (400m up Sharia Talaat Harb from the *Omar Khayyam*), while intercity buses, and service taxis for Tanta and Cairo, leave from Midan ash-Shur, nearly a kilometre south of the *Omar Khayyam* on 23rd July Street, by a clock in the form of the Eiffel Tower.

Places worth seeing around Mahalla include the riverside town – almost a suburb, these days – of **SAMMANUD**, where the Holy Family are believed to have stayed during their sojourn in Egypt. Immediately west of the Sammanud taxi depot in Mahalla, near the hospital, a large mound and a scattering of red and black granite blocks mark the site of the Temple of Onuris-Shu, rebuilt by Nectanebo II (360–343 BC) to grace **Tjeboutjes**, the capital of the Twelfth Nome. Nectanebo, the last XXX Dynasty pharaoh, was also the last ruler of Egypt until Nasser who wasn't foreign or of foreign origin. Another city, **Busiris**, occupied a bluff overlooking the river further south, along the road out of Sammanud. However, part of a XXVI Dynasty basalt statue and fragments of a monumental gateway are all that remain of this reputed birthplace of Osiris.

Northeast of Tanta, **Tell el-Fara'in** ("Mound of the Pharaohs"), is a long *tel* on the edge of marshes north of the village of Ibtu, itself 5km north off the Dasuq–Kafr el-Sheikh road, appears on maps as **Buto**, the Greek name for a dual city known to the Ancient Egyptians as *Pr-Wadjet*. **Wadjet**, the cobra-goddess of Lower Egypt was worshipped in one half of the city, known as Dep. The other half, Pe, was dedicated to Djbut, the heron-god, later supplanted by Horus. The site has a *kom* at each end, with a Temple of Wadjet in the middle, but nothing of great significance to an untrained eye. For more on Tell el-Fara'in, go to Ⓦegyptsites.wordpress.com//category/delta and click on "Tell el-Fara'in".

Nothing but a few pits and blocks of masonry remains of the once great city of **Saïs**, near the modern village of **Sa el-Hagar**, beside the Rosetta branch of the Nile. Founded at the dawn of Egyptian history, it was always associated with the goddess of war and hunting, **Neith**, identified by the Greeks with their goddess Athena. The city became Egypt's capital during the **Saïte Period**, under the XXVI dynasty (664–525 BC).

Zagazig

The charmingly named **ZAGAZIG** (usually pronounced "Za'a'zi") was founded in 1830, and is actually a grimy industrial town. **Ahmed Orabi** (1839–1911), leader of the 1882 revolt against British rule, was born here, and has a statue outside the station. Zagazig is the source of most of the **papyruses** sold in tourist shops throughout Egypt, which are manufactured in sweatshops and sold to dealers for as little as £E3–4 apiece. From a tourist's standpoint, its attractions are the **Moulid of Abu Khalil**, held outside the main mosque during the month of Shawwal (currently Oct or Nov), and the paltry ruins of Bubastis.

Zagazig is accessible from Cairo's Aboud terminal by **bus** (every 20min; 1hr 30min) or **service taxi** (1hr 15min); coming back, service taxis for Cairo leave from just by the railway station. To find the main bus station, cross the tracks via the pedestrian underpass, then turn left, alongside the railway, and it's 200m ahead on the right. Buses serve Cairo (half-hourly; 1hr 30min), Alexandria (3 daily; 3hr 30min), Port Said (1 daily; 4hr), Ismailiya (3 daily; 2hr) and Suez (4 daily; 4hr). Service taxis for Ismailiya and Port Said leave from the Ismailiya *servees* station, 5km from the town centre, while buses and service taxis for Tanta, Mansura and Faqus leave from the Mansura bus station, about 3km from the centre; both are served by microbus (35pt) from outside the train station. **Trains** from Zagazig serve Cairo (13 daily; 1hr 40min), Ismailiya (9 daily; 1hr 20min), Mansura (1 daily; 1hr 35min) and Port Said (8 daily; 2hr 35min).

There's a cheap and basic **hotel**, the *Opera* off the square **in front of** the train station (sign in Arabic only, entrance down a side alley; ⓣ055/230-3718; ❶). For something a little bit classier, try the three-star *Marina* at 58 Sharia Gamal Abdel Nasser, near al-Fatr Mosque (ⓣ055/231-3934; BB ❹).

Bubastis

To reach the site of **Bubastis** (*Bubasta* in Arabic; daily 8am–4pm; £E20, students £E15), take the underpass on the left-hand side of the station and continue straight ahead (southeast) along Sharia Farouq for just under a kilometre, either on foot, or by microbus from the beginning of Farouq (35pt), or by taxi (£E1.50). The site is about 100m to your right at the end of the street. Take your passport and expect a grilling on entry from the guards, who are not used to foreign visitors, and may follow you around the site. There's little to see beyond the few displayed artefacts but archeologists have found Old and New Kingdom cemeteries and vaulted catacombs full of feline mummies, and the city was known to the Ancient Egyptians as *Pr-Bastet* ("House of Bastet"), after the cat-goddess (see box opposite) whom they honoured with licentious festivals. Fifth-century BC Greek historian Herodotus said that its 700,000 revellers consumed more wine than "during the whole of the rest of the year", and described how the city lay on raised ground encircling a canal-girt temple, "the most pleasing to look at" in all of Egypt. Begun by the VI Dynasty pyramid-builders, Bubastis reached its apogee after its rulers established the XXII Dynasty in 945 BC, though the capital at this time was probably still Tanis (see p.498).

Bastet

The feline goddess **Bastet** was originally depicted as a lioness, her head surmounted by a solar disc and *uraeus* serpent. As the daughter of Re, she was associated with the destructive force of the sun-god's eye. This aggressive side of Bastet can be seen in texts and reliefs describing the pharaoh in battle. Her epithet, "Lady of Asheru", also linked her to the goddess Mut at Karnak, where temple reliefs show the pharaoh running ritual races in front of Bastet.

After about 1000 BC, however, this aspect of Bastet became subsumed by Sekhmet (see p.291), and the goddess herself was portrayed more commonly as a cat, often with a brood of kittens, and carrying a sacred rattle. The *Coffin Texts* of the Middle Kingdom frequently invoke her protection as the first-born daughter of Atum (another aspect of the sun-god). In return, the Egyptians venerated cats and mummified them at several sites, including Bubastis and Memphis. It was even a capital offence to kill a cat in ancient Egypt, and when people's pet cats died, they were accorded funerary rites like those given to humans.

The Greeks later identified Bastet with Artemis, the Virgin Hunter, who was believed to be able to transform herself into a cat. The Egyptian association with cats remained strong even after the arrival of Christianity, and it was from Egypt that cats are thought to have arrived in Europe during or before the fourth century AD.

Tanis, Avaris and the "Land of Goshen"

According to the Bible (Genesis 47:27), the ancient Israelites lived in a land called **Goshen** and (Exodus 1:11) toiled as slaves there, building "treasure cities" called Pithom and Raamses, before Moses led them out of Egypt to the Promised Land. Victorian archeologists strove to uncover these biblical locations, some shrewdly plugging the biblical connection to raise money for digs. Pithom may have been **Tell el-Maskhuta**, an enormous *kom* off the road between Zagazig and Ismailiya, while Raamses has usually been identified as **Pi-Ramses**, the royal city of the XIX Dynasty pharaoh Ramses II – which is why his successor, Merneptah, regularly gets fingered as the pharaoh of the Exodus. In the 1930s, French archeologist Pierre Montet discovered Tanis, and suggested that this was Pi-Ramses, but work by Austrian archeologist Manfred Bietak in the 1960s showed that in fact Pi-Ramses centred on the modern-day village of **Qantir**, and extended to the nearby site of Avaris.

Avaris had previously been the capital of the **Hyksos** (XV Dynasty), whose name derives from *hekau-khasut* ("princes of foreign lands"). The Hyksos rulers had Semitic names, but in 1991, **Minoan-style frescoes** were unearthed at a Hyksos-era palace on the western edge of the site, evincing strong links with the Minoan civilization of Crete, though most still believe that the Hyksos originated in Palestine or Syria. But Avaris existed long before the Hyksos invasion, and before finding the frescoes, Bietak's team excavated what had been a hilly residential quarter, uncovering grave goods which suggested that the bulk of the population originated from Palestine and Syria. This lay above a stratum of evidence for an older, more sophisticated community of non-Egyptians, where 65 percent of the burials were of children below the age of two. David Rohl (see p.601) argues that this represents the **Israelites** during their sojourn in Egypt and the culling of their male newborn by the "pharaoh who did not know Joseph" (Exodus 1:8), and that the Exodus occurred during the XIII Dynasty rather than the New Kingdom, as biblical scholars believe. The main archeological site at Avaris is **Tell ed-Daba**, 7km from Faqus, but it is not open to tourists. For further information on the site, see Ⓦ egyptsites.wordpress.com/category/delta (click on

"Tell el-Dab'a"), and the official website of the Austrian excavation team at Ⓦwww.auaris.at, which includes a map of the area.

Tanis

The Delta's most impressive archeological site is a huge *kom* near the village of **San el-Hagar** ("San of the Stones"), 167km northeast of Zagazig and best known by its Greek name, **TANIS**, though it was called *Zoan* in the Bible (Numbers 13:22; Isaiah 19:11 and 13, and 30:4; Ezekiel 30:14), and known to the Ancient Egyptians as *Djanet*. In *Raiders of the Lost Ark*, it is here that Indiana Jones uncovers the Ark of the Covenant. The ruins aren't all that impressive in themselves and few tourists come here, so you'll have the site pretty much to yourself.

Originally identified by archeologists with Avaris, the capital of the Hyksos, or the much later city of Pi-Ramses, Tanis is now thought to have come into existence long afterwards, during the Third Intermediate Period (1070–664 BC). The **site** looks as if the huge Ramessid **Temple of Amun** was shattered by a giant's hammer, scattering chunks of masonry and fragments of statues everywhere. Confusingly for scholars, the founders of Tanis plundered masonry from cities all over the Delta (some predating the Hyksos, who had earlier usurped it). In 1939, Pierre Montet discovered the **tombs of Psusennes II and Osorkon II**, containing the "Treasure of Tanis", which is now in the Cairo Museum. Perplexingly, it was soon noted that the tomb of the XXI Dynasty ruler Psusennes seems to have been built *after* that of Osorkon, who is supposed to have lived well over a century later, during the XXII Dynasty. In his book *A Test of Time* (see p.631), British Egyptologist David Rohl (see p.600) argues that the two dynasties were actually contemporary, and that by assuming that they were sequential, archeologists have overestimated the duration of the Third Intermediate Period by at least 140 years – thus distorting the whole chronology of Ancient Egypt, but Rohl's views are highly controversial, and not accepted by most egyptologists.

While the site at Tanis can be wandered at will, **getting there** is awkward. The best jumping-off point is **Faqus**, 37km to the south, which can be reached by service taxi from Ismailiya, Cairo or Zagazig, by bus from Zagazig or from Cairo's Aboud terminal (hourly 9.15am–7pm; 2hr). From Faqus, you can catch a local bus or service taxi to San el-Hagar, or hire a private taxi for the round trip.

Mansura

MANSURA was founded as the camp of Sultan al-Kamil's army during the 1218–21 siege of Damietta, though its name ("The Victorious") was a premature boast, since the Crusaders reoccupied Damietta in 1247. Weakened by cancer and tuberculosis, Sultan Ayyub was unable to dislodge them, and died here in 1249 – a fact concealed by his widow, Shagar al-Durr, who issued orders in Ayyub's name, buying time until his heir could return from Iraq. Encouraged by the Mamlukes' withdrawal, France's Louis IX (later canonized as Saint Louis) led a sortie against the enemy camp, slaying their general in his bath. But with victory in sight, the Crusaders were struck by food poisoning after eating fish deliberately fed on corpses by the townspeople of Damietta, just before a devastating counterattack launched by Beybars the Crossbowman. Louis was captured and ransomed for Damietta's return, and later died in Tunisia while engaged on yet another ill-fated crusade.

The medieval house where Louis was imprisoned, Beit Ibn Luqman, is now the **Mansura National Museum** (closed for renovation at last check, until 2010, but previously daily except Mon 8am–6pm; £E3). It is located on Sharia Bur Said, 50m up from the Corniche, next to a large mosque. As well as the room where

Louis was held prisoner, the museum has a hall of artworks portraying the events and characters of the defence of Mansura, most notably a wonderful tableau by Abdel Aziz Darwish in which a tired crusader knight is about to have his head hewn off by an Egyptian soldier, while one to his left holds aloft a severed head, and one to his right is busy throttling a crusader with his bare hands. There are also some swords and pieces of armour from the battle.

The rest of the town is mostly modern, with tree-lined avenues, a university, and a central mosque whose twin minarets are visible from far away. For outsiders, the town's most interesting feature is its delicious buffalo-milk **ice cream**, which can be sampled at the sweet shops on Sharia el-Habasy, a couple of blocks west of Sharia Bur Said.

Practicalities

Buses to Cairo (every 30 minutes; 2hr) and Zagazig (every 30 minutes; 1hr 30min) run from the international bus station, 500m east of the train station down Sharia Gamal el-Din el-Afghani at the junction with Sharia el-Guesh. Buses from here also serve Sinai and the Canal Zone, with six a day to Sharm el-Sheikh (7hr) and six to Suez (3hr 30min). Service taxis to Zagazig and Cairo leave from a station 1km further to the southeast. For Tanta, Alexandria, Mahalla el-Kubra, Kufr el-Sheikh, Damietta and Port Said, service taxis run from Talkha station across the river (25pt by microbus from across the bridge opposite the end of Sharia Bur Said). **Trains** from Mansura are all pretty slow, serving Cairo (5 daily; 2hr 15min–3hr 05min), Damietta (4 daily; 1hr 30min), Tanta (7 daily; 1hr) and Mahalla (8 daily; 35–55min).

Mansura's top **hotel** is the *Marshal el-Gezirah*, 2km west of the town centre on the Corniche (Ⓣ050/221-3001; BB ❺), but the slightly more modest two-star *Marshal Hotel* opposite the station on Midan Oum Kalthoum (Ⓣ050/233-3920; BB ❸) is more conveniently located and excellent value, with a/c carpeted rooms – ask for a big one, as they all cost the same – and a café and pastry shop downstairs.

Mit Damsis

The Coptic **Moulid of St George** (Aug 2–28) is held at the village of **Mit Damsis** near the Damietta branch of the Nile on the Mit Ghamr–Aga road between Zagazig and Mansoura. The moulid is notable primarily for its **exorcisms**. Copts attribute demonic possession to improper baptism or deliberate curses, and specially trained priests bully and coax the *afrit* ("demon") to leave through its victim's fingers or toes rather than via the eyes, which is believed to cause blindness. Because the moulid is well attended, there's a fair chance of lifts along the seven-kilometre track that turns west off the main road, 15km south of Aga. Mit Damsis rarely appears on maps; don't confuse it with Damas, which does.

Damietta (Dumyat)

Sited near the mouth of the eastern branch of the Nile, the port city of **DAMIETTA** became prosperous in medieval times, through its trade in coffee, linen, dates and oil. However, it was always wide open to seaborne invasions and was seized by the Crusaders in 1167–68 and 1218–21, on the latter occasion accompanied by St Francis of Assisi – who ignorantly imagined that the Sultan al-Kamil knew nothing of Christianity, although he numbered Copts amongst his advisors. In 1247, the townspeople managed to get rid of the Crusaders by selling them fish fed on rotting corpses (see opposite). With the opening of the Suez Canal, Damietta had to reorient its trade towards Port Said, some 70km east; nowadays it's a thriving port city known as a centre for the manufacture of furniture, which is the local cottage industry.

Damietta offers the chance to see the "real Egypt", far from any major tourist sights, and most foreigners who stay here simply use it as a base for **birdwatching** on **Lake Manzala**, Egypt's most important wetland habitat, where winter is the best time to see herons (*balashon* to locals), spoonbills (*midwas*), pelicans (*begga*) and flamingoes (*basharus*). The lake's average depth is 1.3m, and only the northern part is navigable, in flat-bottomed boats; you'll need to find a boatman who will agree to punt you through the reeds. Pollution and encroachment by farmland and fish farms are nowadays severely threatening the lake's continued existence.

There are several modest **hotels** in Damietta, including the three-star *Soliman Inn* at 5 Sharia el-Gala', 100m off the Corniche (Ⓣ057/376-050, Ⓕ377-050; BB ❺), with a/c, TV and fridge in every room, and the less well-equipped but friendly and comfortable *El Manshy*, just off el-Gala' at 5 Sharia el-Nokrashy (Ⓣ057/323-308; BB ❸), which also has a decent restaurant. As for **transport**, Damietta is linked by rail to Mansura, Tanta, Zagazig, Alex and Cairo, and by hourly buses (6am–5pm) or service taxis to Mansura and Cairo.

5

The Canal Zone

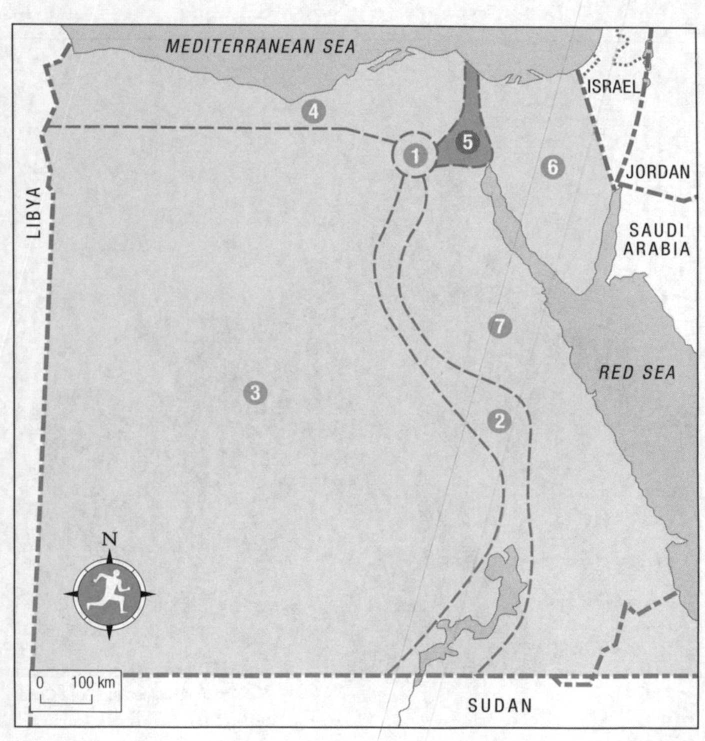

CHAPTER 5 Highlights

* **Ship-watching on the Suez Canal** International ferries are among the many giant ships that ply the Canal, still a crucial trade link between the West and the East. See p.508
* **Ismailiya** This European-style garden city was constructed for the builders of the Canal. See p.509
* **Limbo Festival** Not what you might assume, this is a doll-burning festival, held annually in Ismailiya a week after Easter. See p.512
* **Colonial architecture** Port Said's crumbling but atmospheric townhouses highlight the city's French, British and Italian influences. See p.512
* **Mediterranean air** The fresh sea breeze, shopping and pleasant street cafés are a particular attraction of Port Said. See p.515

▲ A ship navigates the Suez Canal

5

The Canal Zone

Once feted as a triumph of nineteenth-century engineering and regarded as the linchpin of Britain's empire, the **Suez Canal** nowadays seems as Joseph Conrad described it: "a dismal but profitable ditch", connecting the Red Sea and the Mediterranean. Except around the harbour mouths or where ships are glimpsed between sandbanks, it's a pretty dull waterway relieved only by the Canal cities of Port Said and Ismailiya.

Foreigners generally unfairly overlook both cities, prejudging them on the basis of **Suez**, a neglected and untidy place but a vital transport nexus between Cairo, the Sinai and the Red Sea Coast. The Canal scarcely impinges on the leafy, villa-lined streets of **Ismailiya**, once the residence of the Suez Canal Company's European staff and now a popular honeymoon destination for Egyptians. By contrast, with its evocative waterfront, beaches and duty-free shopping, **Port Said** feels like Alexandria minus its cultural baggage – and a place that's somehow more authentic as a maritime city.

Several trains serve the Suez Canal towns daily **from Cairo**, but the carriages are grimy and it's better to head here by bus or service taxi, which also represent your options if you're starting **from Alexandria**. **From Hurghada**, you can reach Suez by bus, but if you intend to head on to Sinai the same day, aim to arrive in Suez by noon to be sure of getting an onward connection – frequent between Suez, Ismailiya and Port Said. Drivers should note that stretches of the canal are **off-limits** and stick to main routes to avoid questioning by the military.

Heading on to **south Sinai** by road, you'll cross the canal via either the **Ahmed Hamdi Tunnel** (12km north of Suez) or the **car ferry** 7km north of Ismailiya. Destinations in **north Sinai** are served by a passenger ferry, at **Qantara**, and the nearby 4.1-kilometre **Ferdan Suspension Bridge**. A couple of kilometres south is the **Ferdan Railway Bridge**, built on the site of an old track hastily constructed to transport army troops to Gaza during World War I, but dismantled by the Israelis in 1968. The world's largest retractable bridge, with a span of 340m, it was devised in the late 1990s, when a rail network running the Orient Express was planned, linking Egypt to Turkey and Europe via Palestine, Israel and Lebanon. This has since been put on hold, but you can still see the bridge – which sits alongside the canal when not in use – closing daily from 9am to 11am and again from 9pm to 1am, a process which takes twenty minutes, to allow trains and cars to cross the canal.

The Canal's history

The **first attempts** to connect the Red Sea and the Mediterranean are usually attributed to Necho II (610–595 BC). However, it was Persian emperor **Darius**, around 500 BC, who completed the region's first canal, linking the Red Sea and

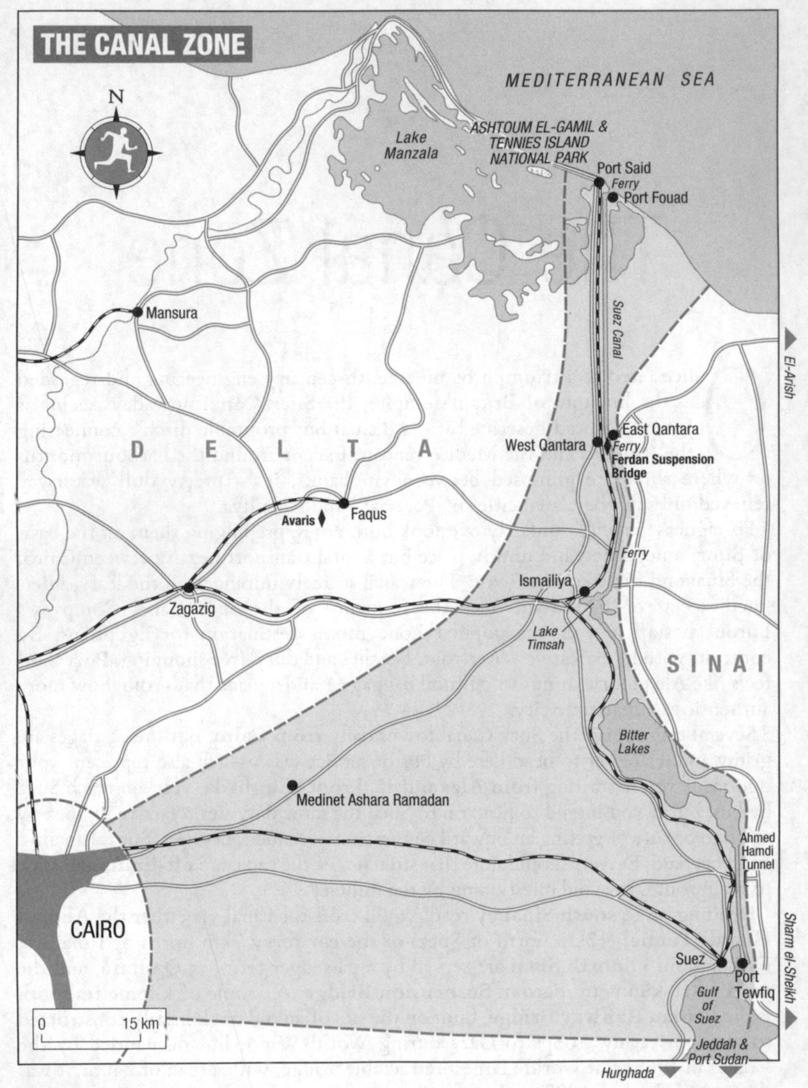

the Great Bitter Lake, from where an older waterway connected with Bubastis on the Nile and from there to the Mediterranean. Refined by the Ptolemies and Trajan, these waterways were restored by **Amr,** following the Muslim conquest, and used for shipping corn to Arabia until the eighth century, when they were deliberately abandoned to starve out rebels in Medina.

The idea of a direct Red Sea-Mediterranean canal was first mooted – then vetoed – by Napoleon's engineers, who miscalculated a difference of ten metres between the two sea levels. The later discovery of this error encouraged junior French consul **Ferdinand de Lesseps** to present his own plan to Said Pasha, who approved it despite British objections.

Work began in 1859 and continued throughout the reign of Said's successor, Ismail, who went bankrupt attempting to finance his £19 million sterling investment. In 1875, he was forced to sell his shares to Britain – swooping before France could make an offer – for £4 million sterling. When the Canal opened in 1888, its vast profits went abroad with the **Suez Canal Company**, while two world wars transformed the **Canal Zone** into the world's largest military base.

In the wake of World War II, guerrilla attacks in the Zone led to the British assault on Ismailiya's police barracks, sparking Cairo's "Black Saturday" (see p.104). After the 1952 Revolution, Egypt demanded the British army's withdrawal and a greater share of the Canal's revenue, and when the West refused to make loans to finance the Aswan High Dam, Nasser announced the Canal's **nationalization** (July 26, 1956). Britain and France agreed to use Israel's advance into Sinai that October as a pretext for "safeguarding" the Canal by bombarding and invading its cities. But by standing firm and appealing to outraged world opinion, Nasser emerged victorious from the **Suez Crisis**.

The **1967 War** with Israel, and the subsequent "War of Attrition", led to the closure of the Canal until 1969. The Egyptians then stormed the Israeli-fortified Bar-Lev Line along the Canal's east bank during the 1973 **10th Ramadan/Yom Kippur** war. Although the Canal was reopened in 1975, both sides remained dug in on opposite banks until 1982, when Israel withdrew from Sinai.

Suez

Unlike Port Said and Ismailiya, **SUEZ** (Es-Suweis in Arabic) has a history long predating the Canal, going back to Ptolemaic Klysma. As Arabic Qulzum, the port prospered from the spice trade and pilgrimages to Mecca throughout medieval times, remaining a walled city until the eighteenth century. The Canal brought modernization and revenues, later augmented by the discovery of oil in the Gulf of Suez, though the city was later devastated during the wars with Israel. Today most of Suez's 490,000 inhabitants live in prefabricated estates or the patched-up remnants of older quarters, while noxious petrochemical refineries, cement and fertiliser plants ring the outskirts. For visitors, there is a distinct lack of things to do in the city. Though local people are friendly, modest dress is advised.

Arrival and information

Buses and service taxis arrive at Suez's **Arba'in Terminal** (Ⓣ062/322-0753) on the Cairo road on the outskirts of the city; from here you can take a taxi (£E10) or microbus (50pt) into the centre. The **train station** is 1500m west of the city centre's Arba'in Market (50pt by minibus).

Suez Canal facts and figures

The 163km long Suez Canal, the world's third longest, generally handles up to fifty ships a day (though its full capacity is seventy-five) with an average transit time of fifteen hours. During its closure in the early 1970s, supertankers were built to travel around Africa – and proved too large to pass through Suez once it reopened. The Canal was subsequently widened in places, but is still not wide enough for continuous bi-directional traffic. In 2008–09, the canal earned a record $5.11 billion, but the subsequent fail in global trade means this may not be matched for some time to come. For more, see Ⓦwww.suezcanal.com.

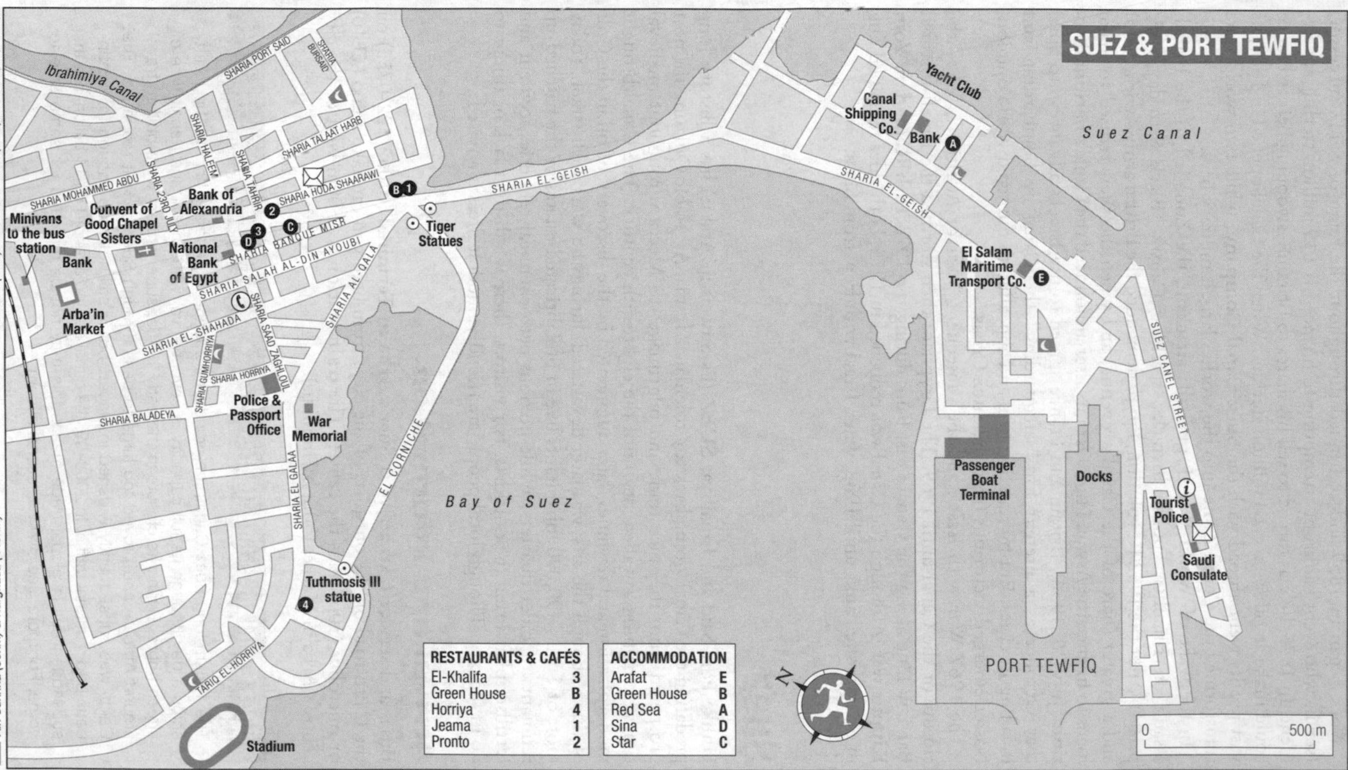
SUEZ & PORT TEWFIQ
Suez Canal
Bay of Suez
PORT TEWFIQ
Ibrahimiya Canal
Yacht Club
Canal Shipping Co.
Bank
El Salam Maritime Transport Co.
Passenger Boat Terminal
Docks
Tourist Police
Saudi Consulate
SUEZ CANEL STREET
SHARIA EL-GEISH
Tiger Statues
EL CORNICHE
Tuthmosis III statue
Stadium
TARIQ EL-HORRIYA
SHARIA EL GALAA
War Memorial
Police & Passport Office
SHARIA SAAD ZAGHLOUL
SHARIA HORRIYA
SHARIA GUMHORRIYA
SHARIA BALADEYA
SHARIA EL-SHAHADA
SHARIA SALAH AL-DIN AYOUBI
SHARIA AL-QALA
SHARIA BANQUE MISR
SHARIA HODA SHAARAWI
SHARIA TALAAT HARB
SHARIA BURSAID
SHARIA PORT SAID
SHARIA TAHRIR
SHARIA HALEEM
SHARIA 23RD JULY
SHARIA MOHAMMED ABDU
Bank of Alexandria
National Bank of Egypt
Convent of Good Chapel Sisters
Bank
Arba'in Market
Minivans to the bus station
Bus Station (2km) & Ismailiya (87km)
Train Station (1km)
Ain Sukhna (60km) & Hurghada (445km)
RESTAURANTS & CAFÉS
El-Khalifa 3
Green House B
Horriya 4
Jeama 1
Pronto 2
ACCOMMODATION
Arafat E
Green House B
Red Sea A
Sina D
Star C
N
0
500 m

The **tourist office** (officially Mon–Wed & Sun 8am–8pm, though it doesn't always keep to these times; ⓣ062/333-1141) and **tourist police** (24hr; ⓣ062/333-3543) are way out on the edge of **Port Tewfiq** (Bur Tewfiq in Arabic) on Suez Canal Street; you can catch a minibus out along Sharia el-Geish as far as the Passenger Terminal.

You can **change money** at the Bank of Alexandria on Sharia el-Geish (Sun–Thurs: summer 9am–2pm & 5–8pm; winter 8am–2pm & 6–9pm); the National Bank of Egypt on Sharia Sa'ad Zaghloul (Sun–Thurs 8.30am–2pm & 5–8pm); the Banque du Caire in Port Tewfiq (Sun–Thurs & Sat 8.30am–2pm & 5–8pm), or the Al Zahabeh Exchange on Sharia el-Geish (Sun–Thurs 8am–2pm & 6–10pm); there are also private exchanges in the souk. For ATMs, head to Sharia el-Geish. There are post offices in Port Tewfiq and on Sharia Hoda Sharawi, in the centre of town (both daily except Fri 8am–3pm), and you can make international calls from the **telephone exchange** (daily 8am–midnight) on the corner of Sa'ad Zaghloul and El-Shahada.

Visa extensions can be made at the **passport office** (daily except Fri 8am–2pm) inside **police** headquarters on Sharia Horriya; as always, arrive early with your passport and photo, a pen, something to read and a sense of humour.

Accommodation

Outside the hajj season, **finding a room** in Suez should be easy, though none of the hotels is anything to write home about and most are overpriced.

Arafat Hotel Off Sharia el-Geish, Port Tewfiq ⓣ062/333-8355. The only budget option in the port area, *Arafat* has small and clean if tatty rooms with balconies and fans; some also have bathrooms. The manager has information about passenger ships for Saudi Arabia and beyond. ❷

Green House Hotel Corner of Sharia el-Geish and El Nabi Mousa St ⓣ062/333-1553, ⓔgreen-house@hotmail.com. Suez's smartest hotel has straightforward, comfortable en suites with a/c, TV and baths; some also have gulf views. Perks include a swimming pool, a very good restaurant and coffee shop, and 24 hr room service. It's popular, so book ahead. BB ❺–❻

Red Sea Hotel 13 Sharia Riad, Port Tewfiq ⓣ062/319-0190, ⓔinfo@redseahotel.com. Although the a/c rooms with bath, phone, balcony and TV are a bit cramped, they are a good alternative if the *Green House* is full. The sixth-floor *Mermaid Restaurant* has great views of the canal. BB ❺–❻

Sina 21 Sharia Banque Misr ⓣ062/333-4181. If money is tight, the centrally-located *Sina* has inexpensive digs with shared or private facilities and fans. It's a bit shabby, with lots of peeling paint, but ok for a night. The nearby *Star*, at no.17, is similar. ❶

The City

Downtown Suez is easily accessible by microbus (50pt) or taxi (£E10) from the bus terminal. The main street, **Sharia el-Geish**, is a two-kilometre-long swath where cruising minibuses drop and collect passengers along the way to Port Tewfiq. Dusty palms and decrepit colonial-era buildings (including several churches) are followed by a strip of hotels, restaurants and currency exchanges. The **Convent of the Good Chapel Sisters** is an imposing colonial-style building given to the international sisterhood in 1872 by the Suez Canal Company after one of its directors recovered from a mystery illness while in their care. A decline in their numbers led the nuns to give their chapel over to the Coptic church, but they still run a primary school and a dispensary for the poor.

The backstreets to the south of El-Geish harbour cheap cafés, while **Sharia Sa'ad Zaghloul** runs past consulates and a fun park towards the governorate. North of El-Geish, a tawdry souk overflows along **Sharia Haleem**, presaging a quarter of workshops and chandlers, crumbling century-old apartments with wooden balconies interspersed with modern government-built low-rises. There's a better **bazaar** to the northwest in Arba'in.

An imposing statue of the pharaoh Tuthmosis III stands at the western end of El Corniche, which overlooks the Bay of Suez; meanwhile, on either side of the road at the eastern entrance, you'll see statues of two tigers growling and crouching as if ready to pounce. Signifying strength, they were built to guide ships through the canal. Similar tiger statues, destroyed by the Israelis in the 1967 war, originally stood on either side of the canal's entrance.

The premier Suez activity is, of course, to take a trip to the port area to look at the enormous freighters and supertankers on the Canal. Don't be tempted to take photographs, however; it's illegal, and there are security officers stationed in the area. In spring, migratory **birds of prey** (including Griffon vultures and eagles) make an arresting sight.

Eating and drinking

Eating options in Suez are very limited. Your best bet for seafood is the bustling *El-Khalifa* (☎064/333-7303) at 320 Sharia el-Geish: there's no menu; just wait for the friendly proprietor to bring out a platter of fish and simply point to what looks best. They often have *umm el-khaloul*, the popular local shellfish, on offer, though in hot weather avoid it if it looks as though it might have been left standing around. In the streets behind the restaurant you'll find a few simple shops selling snacks and fresh juices. Another good choice for simple fish dishes is the *Dolphin* restaurant on Tariq El-Horiya, and for pizzas, burgers and sandwiches (each around £E20), check out *Pronto*, a red and white canteen on Sharia el-Geish. The best restaurant in town is at the *Green House Hotel*, a swanky dining room with excellent service and a continental menu. Try the good fish kebabs, from around £E35, and finish off with one of the decadent cream cakes.

Suez is a dry town, but for non-alcoholic beverages and sheesha, try the *Jeama* garden café next to the *Green House Hotel*, or the foyer coffee shop in the hotel itself.

Suez transport connections

Suez is mainly used by travellers as an interchange between Cairo, Sinai and Hurghada. The bus station has three ticket kiosks: one for **Cairo**, one for East Delta buses to **Sinai, Alexandria** and **the Delta**, and one for Upper Egypt buses to **Hurghada**, **Luxor** and **Aswan**. You will also find service taxis here heading to all major destinations, though fares vary widely according to demand.

- **Sinai** Most of the buses from Suez to Sinai start their journey in Cairo. There are seven buses daily from Suez to **Sharm el-Sheikh** (6–7hr). The 11am bus goes via Nuweiba and Dahab on the eastern coastal road and takes around three hours longer. There are another two buses to **Nuweiba** and **Taba** daily (3pm & 5pm; 5–6hr).
- **Ismailiya and Port Said** Buses and service taxis run frequently to Ismailiya (6am–6.30pm; 1hr–1hr 30min). There are also five daily buses to Port Said (7am, 9am, 11am, 12.15pm & 3.30pm; 2hr 30min–3hr).
- **Alexandria** There are four buses daily (7am, 9am, 2.30pm & 5pm); around 6hr; service taxis are a little quicker.
- **Cairo** Buses and service taxis leave every 30min (1hr 30min–2hr) throughout the day. There are also six daily trains (3–4hr).
- **Hurghada** 12–14 buses daily (6–7hr), most of which stop at the **Ain Sukhna** (1hr), not far from Suez. There are also frequent service taxis.
- **Upper Egypt** Buses leave for Luxor (8am, 2pm & 8pm; 8–10hr) and Aswan (5am, 11am & 5pm; 10–12hr).

Ismailiya

ISMAILIYA is popular with Egyptian tourists and honeymooners, who come to enjoy the beaches along Lake Timsah. While many might think that the place came into being with the building of the Suez Canal in 1862, historical research dates human settlement in the region to biblical times – the area is mentioned in the Bible itself. Today the city has a schizoid character, defined by the rail line that cuts across it. South of the tracks lies the European-style **garden city** built for foreign employees of the Suez Canal Company, which extends to the verdant banks of the Sweetwater Canal. Following careful restoration, its leafy boulevards and placid streets, lined with colonial villas, look almost as they must have done in the 1930s, with bilingual street signs nourishing the illusion that the British Empire has just popped indoors for a quick cocktail. North of the train tracks is another world of hastily constructed flats grafted onto long-standing **slums**, and a quarter financed by the Gulf Emirates that provides a *cordon sanitaire* for the wealthy suburb of **Nemrah Setta** (Number Six).

Ismailiya was the birthplace of the **Muslim Brotherhood**, (see p.616) and its founder Hassan el-Banna, who mounted a series of attacks against the British and an economic boycott in the Canal Zone. The British suspected the Brotherhood was being aided by elements in the Egyptian police, and on January 25, 1952, tried to disarm Ismailiya's main barracks – fifty officers were subsequently killed, sparking rioting in Cairo the following day, which became known as "Black Saturday".

Although Ismailiya can be reached from Cairo by train (6 daily; 3–5hr), buses or service taxis are quicker and leave frequently from the Turgoman Garage in **Cairo** (every 30min 6.30am–8.30pm; 2hr), stopping en route at the Almaza terminal in Heliopolis. The 120-kilometre desert road from Cairo to Ismailiya runs through two places worth noting. **Khanka** contains Egypt's main asylum for the criminally insane, which has made its name a popular synonym for "totally crazy". Further out, a spate of country clubs presages **Medinet Ashara Ramadan** (10th of Ramadan City), a satellite city for the new breed of Cairene commuters, complete with quasi-American suburban homes and steak houses.

Arrival and information

All buses and service taxis wind up at the **bus station** on the ring road outside Ismailiya, opposite the massive Suez Canal University building. From here take a taxi (£E5) or microbus (50pt) into the town centre. The old town's grid-plan and clearly named streets make **orientation** easy.

The **post office** (daily except Fri 9am–4pm) and the 24-hour **telephone exchange** are both just off Midan Orabi, while the **passport office** (daily except Fri 8am–2pm) is nearby on Midan Gumhorriya. You can **change money** at the Bank of Alexandria or the National Bank of Egypt – which takes Visa and MasterCard – both are just off Midan Orabi (both Mon–Thurs, Sat & Sun 8.30am–2pm & 5–8pm, Fri 8.30am–noon). There's an HSBC ATM outside Metro Supermarket on Sharia Sultan Hussein. For **internet** access, try Anosh Net (£E2/hr), just off Sharia Tahir.

Accommodation

While most of Ismailiya's accommodation has seen better days, the majority of places are safe, reasonably clean and inexpensive, and only really get busy during festivals and the summer season – May to September.

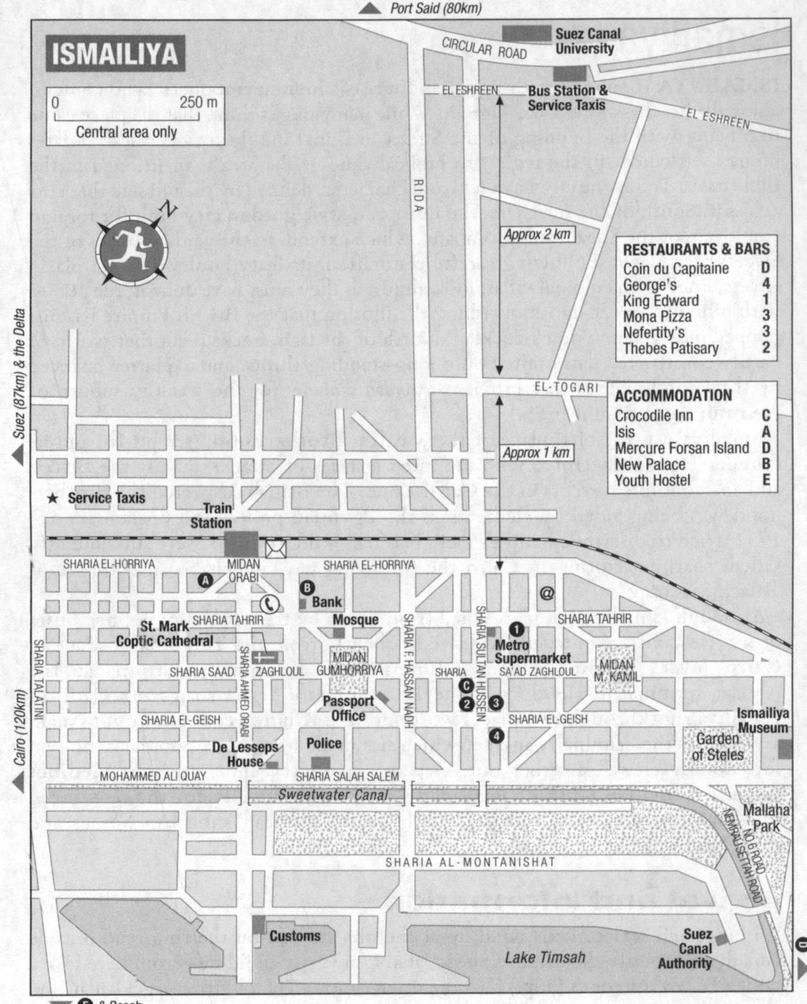

Crocodile Inn (also known as Timsah Hotel) 172 Sharia Sa'ad Zaghloul ⓣ064/391-2555, ⓕ391-2666. A fresh lick of paint has rejuvenated this central hotel, which has spacious, carpeted en suites with a/c, bath tubs and small balconies. BB 4

Isis Midan Orabi ⓣ064/392-2821. A monolith of a hotel, with a dust-covered facade, offering spartan but pretty clean rooms with fans for those on a budget. Staff are helpful and there are reductions for long-staying guests. 1

Mercure Forsan Island 2km east of town ⓣ064/391-6316, ⓦwww.mercure.com. Leafy four-star resort set in fifty acres of grounds with a lake. More than 100 minimalist a/c en suites and garden villas with satellite TV and minibar. Swimming pool and private beach with watersports, plus a bar. Good online discounts. BB 7

New Palace Midan Orabi ⓣ064/391-6327, ⓕ391-7761. A wonderfully pretentious nineteenth-century pile with a pink exterior, good value a/c rooms, satellite TV and private baths. Popular with honeymooners, so often full. BB 3

Youth Hostel Sharia Imhara Siyahi, 1km from the centre ⓣ064/392-2850, ⓦwww.hihostels.com. Overlooking Lake Timsah, with its own beach, this has a double, triple and six-bed rooms with private baths. It's just beyond the bridge on the left as you head south out of town. Dorm beds from £E15. BB 1.

The town and around

Shaded by pollarded trees, Ismailiya's carefully restored old town is a pleasure to explore; most of the sights can be reached on foot within ten minutes. Heading to the sights outside town, catch a service taxi from the turn-off near Mallaha Park.

Starting on Mohammed Ali Quay, first on the trail is the large, vaguely Swiss-looking **House of Ferdinand de Lesseps**, who lived here during the canal's construction. Disappointingly, you can only visit the interior if you're a VIP; it now serves as a private hotel for guests of the Suez Canal Authority. Lone visitors might chance a peek inside, however, if the rear gate is open. Books and photographs are scattered around de Lesseps' study, and the licence to dig the canal hangs on one of the walls, while his carriage stands outdoors, encased in glass.

A pleasant fifteen minutes' walk down the street from the de Lesseps' House, the **Ismailiya Museum** (Mon–Thurs, Sat & Sun 9am–4pm, Fri and during Ramadan 9.30am–noon & 1.15–4pm; £E15, students £E5) has four thousand Greco-Roman and pharaonic artefacts and an entire section devoted to the waterways of Ramses and Darius. Highlights include a lovely fourth-century mosaic depicting Phaedra, Dionysos, Eros and Hercules, and a beautiful collection of tiny glass vases for "preserving tears". Other sections cover the Canal in modern history, the Battle of Ismailiya and the "Crossing" of October 1973. A small sphinx stands guard outside.

With permission from the museum, you can also visit some plaques and obelisks from Ramses II's time in the **Garden of Steles** just to the west. It's nicer, however, to wander amid the five hundred acres of exotic shrubs and trees of **Mallaha Park** to the south, or to stroll alongside the shady **Sweetwater Canal** that was dug to provide fresh water for labourers building the Suez Canal. Previously, supplies had to be brought across the desert by camels, or shipped across Lake Manzala to Port Said.

Lake Timsah

Notwithstanding its name, which translates as "Crocodile Lake", **Lake Timsah** has several nice **beaches**. Get there by taking a taxi or walking 1km out along Sharia Talatini. You can dine outside near picturesque fishing boats, or pay £E10-30 to use the manicured lawns and beaches of the private resorts and clubs, though many of these places close outside high season. Wealthier citizens patronize the *Mercure Forsan Island* with its **waterskiing**, **windsurfing** and **tennis** facilities; you can use the beach and swimming pool here for a small fee.

Eating, nightlife and festivals

Ismailiya's dining options are adequate, if nothing special, though there is one gem. When the weather's fine, locals head to the fishing port on Lake Timsah to dine alfresco; it's worth the cost of a taxi (£E5) out along Sharia Talatini to eat fish straight from the lake. You might even try the local speciality, *umm el-khaloul* (see p.508). Otherwise, there are several decent restaurants clustered together in the centre. *George's*, a Greek place on Sharia Sultan Hussein dating back to 1950, has an illicit, speakeasy-feel, with dim lighting, white-shirted waiters and excellent steak, offal and seafood (mains £E50-60): try the meatballs in a tomato sauce. Alcohol is also served here – a Stella costs £E25. Across the street, *Nefertity's* offers inexpensive chicken, kebabs, pastas and a few seafood options (mains from £E25). *Mona Pizza* next door does reasonable pizzas. Head to *Thebes Patisary* diagonally opposite for dessert – cakes, pastries and ice cream are all served up.

The most popular **places to drink** are *King Edward*, 171 Sharia Tahrir (☎064/332-5451), an air-conditioned haunt favoured by expat engineers and serving continental and Egyptian food, the *Coin du Capitaine* bar at the *Mercure*

Forsan Island and *George's*; all attract an interesting crowd as the night wears on. The *Mercure* also has a nightly disco until 2am.

Festivals

Around Easter time, Ismailiya is a good place to witness the spring festival of **Sham el-Nessim**, when families picnic in the park between the Sweetwater Canal and Lake Timsah, vehicles are decorated with flowers and little girls compete for the coveted title of "Miss Strawberry". Even better is the **"Doll-Burning"** or **Limbo Festival**, held a week later. Its curious title refers to a hated nineteenth-century local governor – Limbo Bey – effigies of whom were torched by the citizenry. Ever since then, it has been customary to burn dolls resembling your pet hate: footballers are popular targets whenever Ismailiya's soccer club does poorly. The dolls are burned on the streets after dark.

Moving on

To get anywhere from Ismailiya, head back to the bus station. There are regular buses and service taxis to **Cairo** throughout the day (6.30am–8.30pm; 2hr–2hr 30min). For the **Sinai**, buses and service taxis leave throughout the day and night to **Sharm el-Sheikh** (6.30am–midnight; 7–8hr); those at 2.30pm and 11pm go on to Dahab (8-10hr). Service taxis also run to Rafah, if the border is open (see p.566). To get to the **Canal cities**, take any of the buses and service taxis that go regularly via Ismailiya and **Qantara** between **Port Said** (6.30am–6pm; 1hr–1hr 30min) and **Suez** (6.30am–6pm; 1hr–1hr 30min).

North of Ismailiya – Canal crossings

Seven kilometres north of Ismailiya, a **car ferry** crosses the canal more or less non-stop during daylight hours. Together with the Ahmed Hamdi Tunnel outside Suez, it used to carry almost all the traffic between mainland Egypt and Sinai until the opening of the Salaam (or Ferdan) Suspension Bridge in October 2001, which is now the most direct route from Cairo to Israel.

The only other crossing point is at **QANTARA**, 44km from Ismailiya and 80km from Port Said. As its name ("Bridge") suggests, this was the route used by pilgrims and armies to cross the marshy Isthmus of Suez before the canal was built. Since then, it has been spanned by pontoon bridges in wartime, but is now negotiated by a small passenger ferry, carrying locals, bikes and donkeys from one side of Qantara to the other. Most of the town is on the west bank, whose unpaved main drag has a busy souk and lines of service taxis going to Cairo and the Canal cities; the battered, poorly rebuilt houses are a reminder that armies clashed here in 1973.

Port Said

Founded at the start of the Canal excavations, **PORT SAID** (*Bur Said* in Arabic) was by the late nineteenth century an important port where all the major maritime powers had consulates. It was long synonymous with smuggling and vice, and the adventurer De Monfreid was amused by the Arab cafés where "native policemen as well as coolies" smoked hashish in back rooms, supplied by primly respectable Greeks. Nowadays, this bustling city of 540,000 remains an important harbour and fuelling station for ships passing through the Suez Canal. A faintly raffish atmosphere lingers and its timber-porched houses have something of the feel of New Orleans's French Quarter.

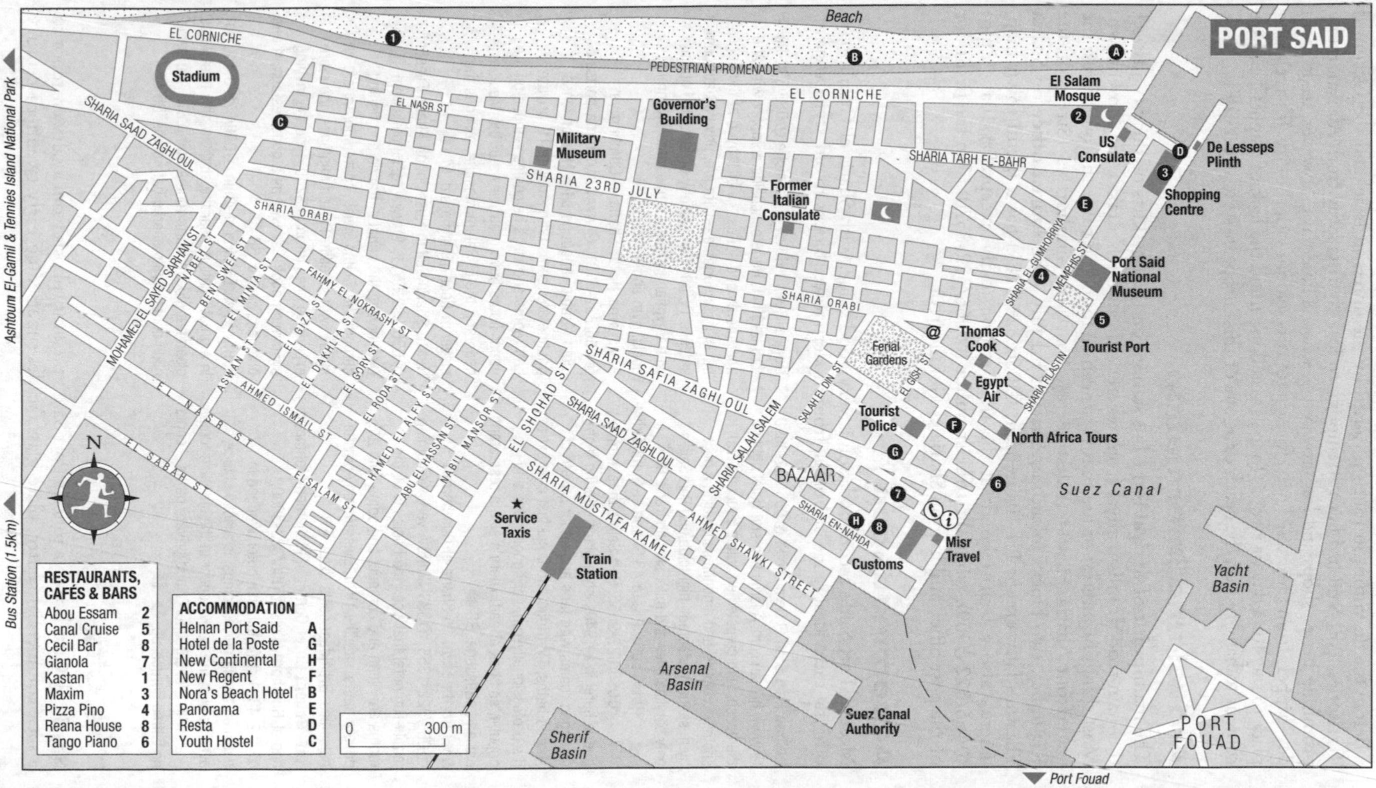

PORT SAID

RESTAURANTS, CAFÉS & BARS	
Abou Essam	2
Canal Cruise	5
Cecil Bar	8
Gianola	7
Kastan	1
Maxim	3
Pizza Pino	4
Reana House	8
Tango Piano	6

ACCOMMODATION	
Helnan Port Said	A
Hotel de la Poste	G
New Continental	H
New Regent	F
Nora's Beach Hotel	B
Panorama	E
Resta	D
Youth Hostel	C

Beach
EL CORNICHE
PEDESTRIAN PROMENADE
EL CORNICHE
Stadium
El Salam Mosque
US Consulate
De Lesseps Plinth
Shopping Centre
Governor's Building
Military Museum
Former Italian Consulate
Port Said National Museum
Tourist Port
Thomas Cook
Egypt Air
North Africa Tours
Tourist Police
Ferial Gardens
BAZAAR
Customs
Misr Travel
Suez Canal
Yacht Basin
PORT FOUAD
Port Fouad
Arsenal Basin
Sherif Basin
Suez Canal Authority
Train Station
Service Taxis
SHARIA SAAD ZAGHLOUL
EL NASR ST
SHARIA TARH EL-BAHR
SHARIA 23RD JULY
SHARIA ORABI
SHARIA ORABI
SHARIA EL-GUMHORRIYA
MEMPHIS ST
SHARIA FILASTIN
EL GISH ST
SALAH EL DIN ST
SHARIA SAFIA ZAGHLOUL
SHARIA SALAH SALEM
SHARIA SAAD ZAGHLOUL
SHARIA EN-NAHDA
AHMED SHAWKI STREET
SHARIA MUSTAFA KAMEL
EL SHOHAD ST
NABIL MANSOR ST
ABU EL HASSAN ST
HAMED EL ALFY ST
EL RODA ST
EL GORY ST
EL DAKHLIA ST
FAHMY EL NOKRASHY ST
EL GIZA ST
EL MINIA ST
BENI SWEF ST
NABEH ST
MOHAMED EL SAYED SARHAN ST
ASWAN ST
AHMED ISMAIL ST
EL NASR ST
EL SABAH ST
ELSALAM ST
N
0 300 m
Ashtoum El-Gamil & Tennies Island National Park
Bus Station (1.5km)

Before the downturn in tourism caused by the unrest in Israel and the Occupied Territories, Port Said had been attempting to lure tourists away from Alexandria by promising better shops and less crowded beaches. These days, however, aside from day-trippers from the cruise liners, foreign tourists seldom visit the city. It's a relaxing place to stay for a day or two, as long as you don't mind the lack of "sights", and are content to hang out on the beach or at one of the European-style street cafés.

Arrival and information

The main **point of arrival** is the bus station, on the outskirts of the city just off the main road from Ismailiya, from where you can catch a taxi (£E5) downtown. Most things of interest or use to tourists can be found on three thoroughfares: the waterfront Sharia Filastin (Palestine St); Sharia el-Gumhorriya (Street of the Republic), two blocks inland; or Sharia 23rd July. The **tourist office** on Sharia Filastin (daily except Fri 10am–5pm; ⓣ066/323-5289) has a useful town map. There's also a tourist booth at the train station (daily except Fri 10am–2pm; ⓣ066/322-3909), while the **tourist police** (ⓣ066/322-8570) is on the first floor of the post office building on Sharia el-Gumhorriya.

Accommodation

Most of Port Said's accommodation is very good value, with Sharia el-Gumhorriya offering the widest range of **hotels**, from modern tower blocks to old-style *pensions*.

Helnan Port Said El Corniche St ⓣ066/332-0890, ⓦwww.helnan.com. A large five-star hotel right on the beach, with carpeted en suites (around $250) in soothing colours, and amenities including a pool, gym, sauna, restaurant, nightclub and Port Said's only bowling alley and roller skating track. BB ❽

Hotel de la Poste 46 Sharia el-Gumhorriya ⓣ066/322-9655. Port Said's most atmospheric hotel is a 1940s-style place offering high-ceilinged rooms with fans and either private or shared baths; TV, fridge and breakfast cost extra. It's professionally-run, very good value and popular, so book ahead. There's also a restaurant, bar and patisserie. BB ❷

New Continental 30 Sharia el-Gumhorriya ⓣ066/322-1355, ⓕ333-8088. A very welcoming family-run hotel that does the basics well: the rooms are clean and compact and come with a/c, private baths, satellite TV, fridges and tiny private balconies. Breakfast costs extra. ❸

New Regent Hotel Corner of Mahamed Mahmoud and el-Gumhorriya sts ⓣ066/323-5000, ⓕ322-4891. This tall, thin hotel, wedged in between two larger buildings, is a solid choice, even though the brown decor in the smallish rooms – all with a/c, satellite TV and private baths – could do with a spruce-up. ❸–❹

Nora's Beach Hotel El Corniche ⓣ066/332-9834, ⓕ332-9841. Huge beachside complex with 200 apartments and suites – a bit frayed at the edges but still comfortable – with a/c, private bathroom, satellite TV, minibar, balcony or terrace. Popular with Egyptian families, it has three swimming pools, gym and disco. BB ❼

Panorama Hotel Sharia el-Gumhorriya ⓣ066/332-5101, ⓦwww.panorama-portsaid.com (Arabic-language site). No-nonsense, pristine a/c rooms with satellite TV, private bathrooms and large balconies – those on the upper floors have great views of the Mediterranean and the El Salam mosque, as does the eleventh-floor billiard room. ❸–❹

Resta Sharia Sultan Hussein, off Sharia Filastin ⓣ066/332-5511, ⓦwww.restahotels.com. Overlooking the canal entrance and fishing harbour, *Resta* has swish, contemporary a/c en suites with satellite TV and minibar – the more expensive ones (around $250) face the inviting swimming pool – as well as a good restaurant and business centre. BB ❽

Youth Hostel Sharia al-Amin ⓣ066/322-8702. Not in a great location, near the stadium, this hostel has clean but gloomy dorm rooms from £E15 and some plain doubles with shared bathrooms. BB ❶

The City

Sharia el-Gumhorriya reflects Port Said's metamorphosis from a salty entrepôt to a slick commercial centre, plate-glass facades superseding early twentieth-century balconies as the street progresses from the Arsenal Basin to Sharia 23rd July. The adjacent **bazaar quarter** ranges from humble stalls on Salah El Din Street to smart boutiques on Sharia en-Nahda and the junction between Sharia el-Gumhorriya and Sharia 23rd July.

The **Military Museum** on Sharia 23rd July (daily 9am–3pm; Fri opening hours are erratic; £E5) gives a strong sense of the Canal's embattled history. The 1956 Anglo-French-Israeli invasion is commemorated by lurid paintings and dioramas, while another room is dedicated to the October War of 1973.

Around 450m east is the former Italian consulate, once grand, now abandoned, which has an interesting World War I memorial dedicated to 22 Italian soldiers on its eastern wall. An inscription (in Italian) reads: "Empowered by civic pride, they all rushed to the call from the homeland and sacrificed their lives for Italy's glory. 1915–18." The **Port Said National Museum** on Sharia Filastin, a 15-minute walk east, has been closed for several years with no reopening date in sight.

South of here, head towards the bazaar area to see Port Said's dusty nineteenth-century European-style colonial houses, which although dilapidated remain wonderfully evocative. Memphis Street is a good place to start – the stand-out building is the glorious old Woolworths store. The area around Ahmed Shawki and Rue El Guesh streets, close to the Arsenal Basin, is also a good hunting ground. Sadly, with new constructions springing up constantly, these buildings may not last much longer.

From the Corniche you can watch the dozens of vessels at anchor in the Mediterranean waiting to go through the Canal. At the far end of the port area is a massive sandstone plinth that bore a huge **statue of de Lesseps**, before it was torn down following the 1952 Revolution. You can rent chairs and parasols or windbreakers for about £E10 on Port Said's shell-strewn **beach**.

Port Fouad

Founded as a suburb for Canal bureaucrats in 1927, **PORT FOUAD** is quieter than its sister city. Residents describe their daily commutes to Port Said as journeying between Asia and Africa; the battered ferry (every 10–15min) responsible offers an enjoyable ride, though it reeks of everything but intercontinental status. The suburb's decrepit but stylish **1930s architecture** can be appreciated by making a tour of its Art Deco flats, colonial villas and well-tended gardens.

Ashtoum El-Gamil and Tennies Island National Park

Seven kilometres west of Port Said, straddling the Damietta coastal road, the **Ashtoum el-Gamil and Tennies Island National Park** has been a small nature reserve since 1988. Covering roughly thirty square kilometres of inlets connecting the Mediterranean with Lake Manzala, it's a prime spot for birdwatching, particularly if you can find a boatman to take you through the reeds. Its dunes and lagoons are home to residents and winter migrants including flamingos, pelicans, kingfishers, plovers, spoonbills and ducks. There are no fees or permits to visit the area and if driving, you can just pull off the road.

Eating and drinking

Eating out in Port Said is enjoyable, as fresh seafood abounds and most places have tables outdoors, allowing you to savour the bustling street life. Sharia el-Gumhorriya has plenty of **patisseries** and **coffee houses** to relax in. If you fancy a dinner excursion up the Suez Canal, make a reservation on the **Canal Cruise** (Ⓣ066/334-5222 5pm, 7pm & 10pm; 1hr 30min; US$15 with soft drinks and snacks, US$30 including dinner) at the entrance to the tourist port on the waterfront near the now closed National Museum); schedules change, so check times at the booking office.

On the other hand, if your tastes run to old-style atmosphere and the company of aged Greeks, head for the spit-and-sawdust *Cecil Bar* beneath the *Reana House*. The bar, open till midnight or later and hidden behind tinted glass windows, is the only place in Port Said serving alcohol, other than the *Helnan* hotel restaurant.

Abou Essam El-Corniche St, diagonally opposite the *Helnan*. Excellent fish restaurant with good mezze and moderate prices. A full meal costs around £E40.

Gianola El-Gumhorriya, near the *New Continental* hotel. This stylish a/c coffee shop is ideal for breakfast, a sandwich – you can even get one with smoked salmon – or a hot drink. Sandwiches and snacks cost £E20-35.

Kastan El-Corniche St, towards the stadium. Large and very busy 24hr seafood and fish restaurant on the beach. Around £E60 for a full meal.

Maxim In the shopping centre on the corner of el-Gumhorriya and el-Corniche. With panoramic canal views and live music most evenings, this is a good place for seafood – with mains £E25–60, or steak, pasta and chicken options.

Pizza Pino On the corner of el-Gumhorriya and 23rd July sts. A busy Italian restaurant with an a/c dining area, quick service and sport and music videos on the TV. Chefs work nonstop in the open kitchen to produce a wide range of fairly authentic pizzas, pastas, grills and seafood dishes (mains from £E30), plus delicious ice creams including a banana split.

Reana House 5 Sharia el-Gumhorriya, diagonally across from the *New Continental* hotel. On the scruffy side, serving tasty Korean and Chinese food including vegetarian dishes, at reasonable prices. Open till midnight or later.

Tango Piano Sharia Filastin, just north of the main tourist office. Despite a distinct lack of tango music, this café with large windows facing the canal is a good spot for an inexpensive sandwich.

Listings

Currency exchange There are numerous private exchanges around Sharia en-Nahda, and the shopping malls at the northern end of Sharia el-Gumhorriya. Thomas Cook is at 43 Sharia el-Gumhorriya (daily 8am–5pm; ⓣ066/322-7559, ⓦwww.thomascookegypt.com). Most of the banks along Sharia el-Gumhorriya have ATMs that accept Visa and MasterCard.

Hospitals The best-equipped hospital is Al-Soliman, near the sports stadium (ⓣ066/333-1533). Emergencies can also be treated at the Al-Mabarrah (ⓣ066/322-0560) or El-Tadaman (ⓣ066/323-1790) hospitals.

Internet access Xpress, next to Ferial Gardens.

Pharmacy The 24 hour Hussein Pharmacy is on Sharia el-Gumhorriya (ⓣ066/333-9888) close to the *Hotel de la Poste*.

Post office The main branch (daily except Fri 9am–2pm) is near the southeast corner of Ferial Gardens.

Telephone exchange Near the tourist office on Sharia Filastin (24hr).

Travel agents Misr Travel, also near the tourist office on Sharia Filastin (ⓣ066/322-6610).

Visa extensions The passport office is in the governor's building on Sharia 23rd July (Thurs & Sat 8am–2pm).

Moving on

East Delta **buses** to Cairo or Alexandria, Superjet a/c services to Cairo's Turgoman Garage and buses to Ismailiya or the Delta all leave from the main bus station at the edge of town on the road to Ismailiya, about 3km from downtown. East Delta Bus Company (ⓣ066/322-7883) has daily buses to **Cairo** (1–2 an hour 7am–10pm; 3hr), **Alexandria** (7am, 11am, 3.30pm & 7pm; 3hr), **Ismailiya** (frequent 6.30am–6.30pm; 1hr–1hr 30min) and **Suez** (6am, 10am, 1pm & 4pm; 2hr 30min–3hr). For **Hurghada**, you have to catch a bus from Ismailiya, Suez or Cairo. Superjet (ⓣ066/321-1779) has two buses daily to Alexandria (7.25am & 6.15pm; 4hr; reserve a day in advance) and several throughout the day to Cairo (3hr). There are also six daily **trains** to Cairo (4hr), though it's more appealing to do the 220-kilometre journey by bus. Service taxis often provide the quickest connections within the Canal Zone. **EgyptAir** has an office on Sharia el-Gumhorriya (ⓣ066/322-0921), one block up from Thomas Cook.

6

Sinai

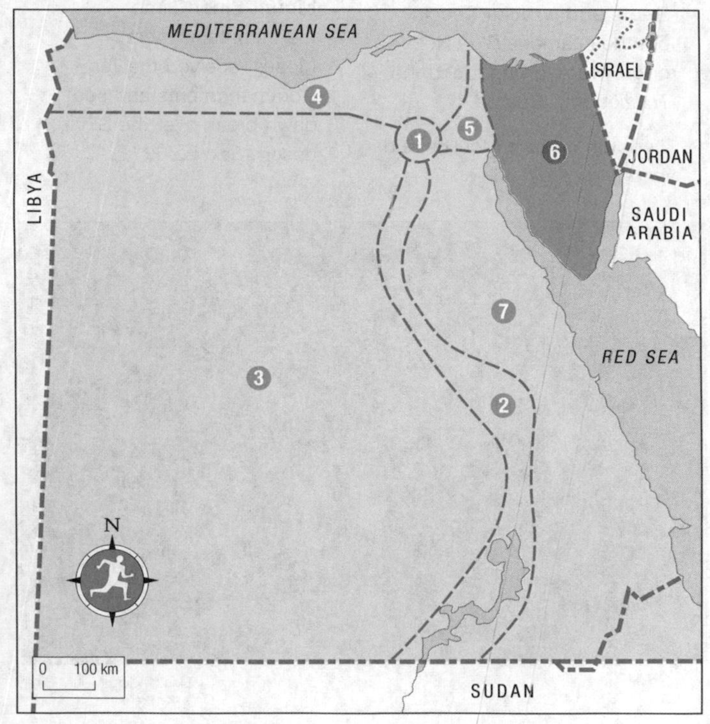
MEDITERRANEAN SEA
ISRAEL
JORDAN
SAUDI
ARABIA
LIBYA
RED SEA
SUDAN
N
0 100 km
4
1
5
6
7
3
2

CHAPTER 6

Highlights

* **Ras Mohammed** Egypt's first national park, sited at the tip of the Sinai peninsula, offers some world-class diving. See p.528
* **Na'ama Bay** Egypt's premier resort, its bars and clubs teem with hedonists by night. See p.535
* **Dahab** Chill out in Asilah, renowned for its diving, laid-back beach cafés and backpacker vibe. See p.542
* **Reefs and wrecks** Check out the infamous Blue Hole, or go wreck-diving round the *Thistlegorm*. See p.547
* **Bedouin culture** Moulids and weddings are held at full moon in the desert. See p.552
* **Desert safaris** Take a camel or jeep safari to secluded palm-fringed wadis with Bedouin hosts. See p.552
* **St Catherine's monastery** Built by Byzantine Empress Helena to commemorate the sight of the burning bush at the foot of Mount Sinai. See p.559
* **Mount Sinai** Climb the mountain where Moses received the Ten Commandments and see dawn break over the Sinai desert. See p.562

▲ Descending Mount Sinai

6

Sinai

The **Sinai** peninsula has been the gateway between Africa and Asia since time immemorial, and a battleground for millennia. Prized for its strategic position and mineral wealth, Sinai is also revered by disparate cultures as the site of God's revelation to Moses, the wanderings of Exodus and the flight of the Holy Family. As Burton Bernstein wrote, "It has been touched, in one way or another, by most of Western and Near Eastern history, both actual and mythic", being the supposed route by which the Israelites reached the Promised Land and Islam entered North Africa, then a theatre for Crusader-Muslim and Arab-Israeli conflicts, and finally transformed into an internationally monitored demilitarized zone.

Though mostly wilderness, Sinai looks far too dramatic – and beautiful – to be dismissed as "24,000 square miles of nothing". The interior of southern Sinai is an arid moonscape of jagged ranges harbouring **Mount Sinai** and **St Catherine's Monastery** – pilgrims climb from the site of the Burning Bush to the summit where God delivered the Ten Commandments. Further north, the vast **Wilderness of the Wanderings** resembles a Jackson Pollock canvas streaked with colour. The Sinai is also home to a remarkably high number of plants and wildlife; over sixty percent of Egypt's plant life thrives in this area, and 33 species are unique to it, including the world's smallest butterfly, the Sinai Baton Blue. Hyenas, ibex and the rabbit-like hyrax also inhabit the region. Venture into this "desert" on a jeep or **camel safari** and you will also find remote springs and lush oases, providing some insights into **Bedouin culture**. For an overview of safari destinations, see p.558.

Above all, the south has the lure of exquisite coral reefs and tropical fish in the **Gulf of Aqaba**, one of the finest **diving** and **snorkelling** grounds in the world; information on the best sites appears on p.526, and there's an introduction to the reefs and their denizens in the separate colour section. The beach resorts at **Sharm el-Sheikh** (which includes **Na'ama Bay**), **Dahab** and **Nuweiba** cater to every taste and budget. From Sharm el-Sheikh you can make expeditions to Egypt's deepest reefs and most diverse aquatic life at **Ras Mohammed**, a mini-peninsula at the southern tip of Sinai, and the **Tiran Strait**, scattered with the wrecks of ships that have floundered on the reefs of this narrow passageway connecting the Red Sea to the Gulf of Aqaba. Northwest of here, the **Gulf of Suez** pales by comparison with its eastern counterpart – though year-round winds make it a great destination for diehard windsurfers and kiteboarders, there are no reefs and few sites to interest the general visitor.

Sinai's **climate** is extreme. On the coast, daytime temperatures can reach 50°C (120°F) during summer, while nights are sultry or temperate depending on the prevailing wind. In the mountains, which receive occasional snowfall over

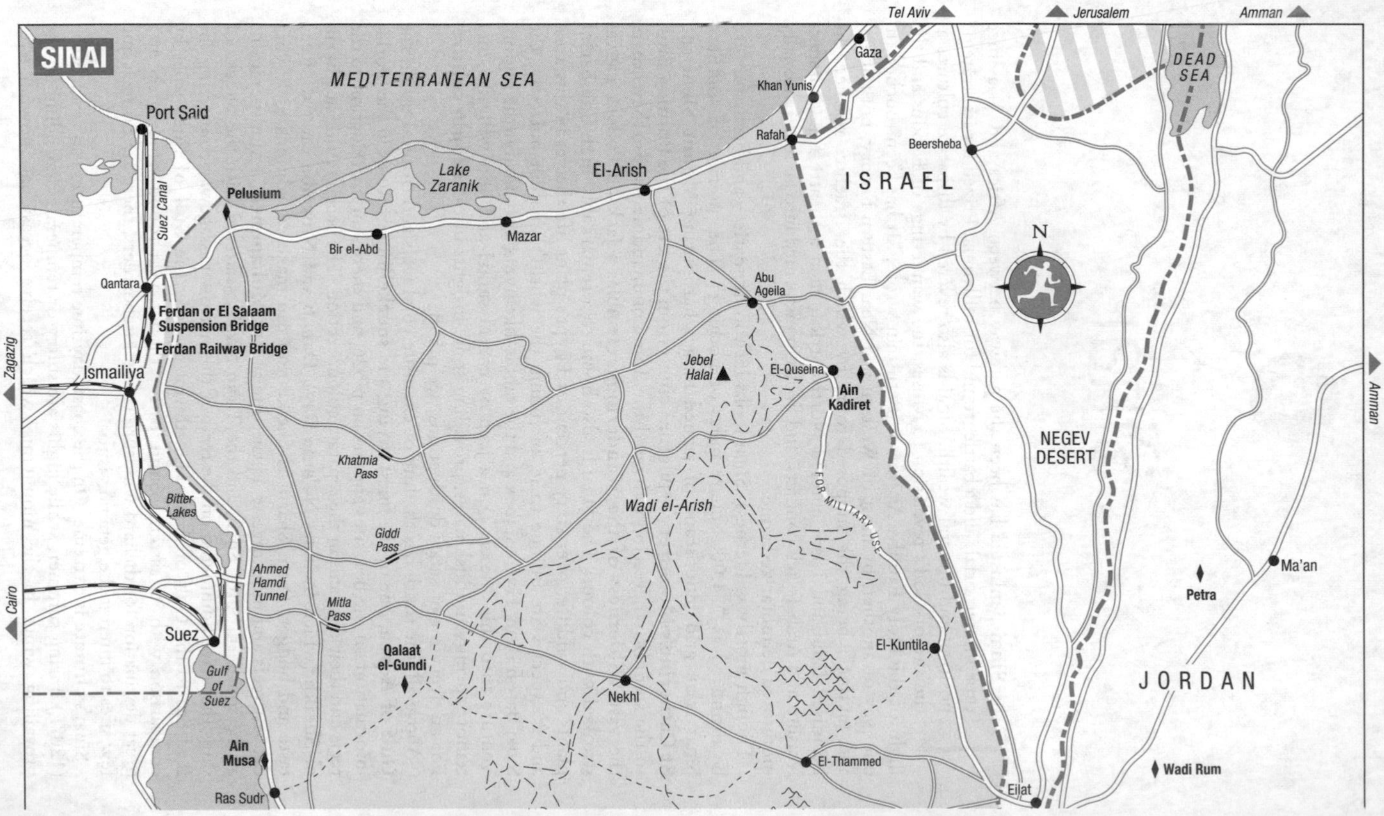

SINAI
MEDITERRANEAN SEA
Port Said
Suez Canal
Pelusium
Lake Zaranik
El-Arish
Mazar
Bir el-Abd
Qantara
Ferdan or El Salaam Suspension Bridge
Ferdan Railway Bridge
Zagazig
Ismailiya
Khatmia Pass
Bitter Lakes
Giddi Pass
Ahmed Hamdi Tunnel
Mitla Pass
Cairo
Suez
Gulf of Suez
Qalaat el-Gundi
Ain Musa
Ras Sudr
Tel Aviv
Jerusalem
Amman
Gaza
Khan Yunis
Rafah
Beersheba
ISRAEL
DEAD SEA
N
Abu Ageila
Jebel Halai
El-Quseina
Ain Kadiret
FOR MILITARY USE
Wadi el-Arish
NEGEV DESERT
Nekhl
El-Kuntila
El-Thammed
Eilat
Ma'an
Petra
JORDAN
Wadi Rum
Amman

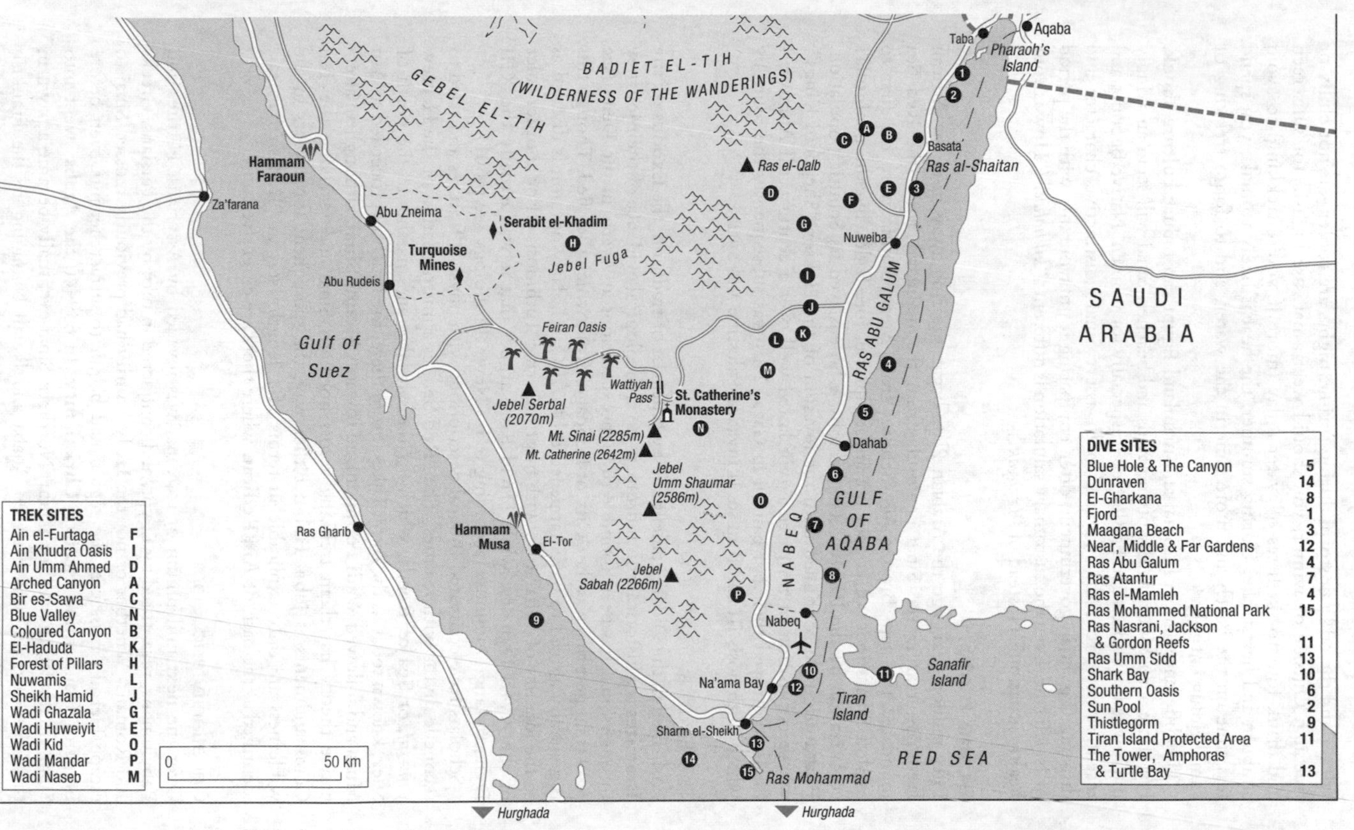
BADIET EL-TIH
(WILDERNESS OF THE WANDERINGS)
GEBEL EL-TIH
Taba
Aqaba
Pharaoh's Island
Basata
Ras al-Shaitan
Ras el-Qalb
Hammam Faraoun
Za'farana
Abu Zneima
Serabit el-Khadim
Turquoise Mines
Jebel Fuga
Abu Rudeis
Nuweiba
SAUDI ARABIA
RAS ABU GALUM
Gulf of Suez
Feiran Oasis
Wattiyah Pass
St. Catherine's Monastery
Jebel Serbal (2070m)
Mt. Sinai (2285m)
Mt. Catherine (2642m)
Jebel Umm Shaumar (2586m)
Dahab
GULF OF AQABA
NABEQ
Ras Gharib
Hammam Musa
El-Tor
Jebel Sabah (2266m)
Nabeq
Na'ama Bay
Sanafir Island
Tiran Island
Sharm el-Sheikh
Ras Mohammad
RED SEA
Hurghada
Hurghada
0 50 km
TREK SITES
Ain el-Furtaga F
Ain Khudra Oasis I
Ain Umm Ahmed D
Arched Canyon A
Bir es-Sawa C
Blue Valley N
Coloured Canyon B
El-Haduda K
Forest of Pillars H
Nuwamis L
Sheikh Hamid J
Wadi Ghazala G
Wadi Huweiyit E
Wadi Kid O
Wadi Mandar P
Wadi Naseb M
DIVE SITES
Blue Hole & The Canyon 5
Dunraven 14
El-Gharkana 8
Fjord 1
Maagana Beach 3
Near, Middle & Far Gardens 12
Ras Abu Galum 4
Ras Atantur 7
Ras el-Mamleh 4
Ras Mohammed National Park 15
Ras Nasrani, Jackson & Gordon Reefs 11
Ras Umm Sidd 13
Shark Bay 10
Southern Oasis 6
Sun Pool 2
Thistlegorm 9
Tiran Island Protected Area 11
The Tower, Amphoras & Turtle Bay 13

winter and the odd rainstorm during spring, nights are cooler – if not chilly or freezing. Outside of winter, you should wear a hat, use high-factor sunscreen and drink four to six litres of water a day (more if you're trekking) to avoid sunburn and heatstroke. During summer, the heat is likely to make you spend less time on the beach and more time in the water, and to forgo trekking or camel riding entirely.

The differences between Sinai and mainland Egypt can induce **culture shock**. For those accustomed to Egyptian towns and beaches, Sinai will seem amazingly uncrowded, laid-back and hassle-free – especially for women. Native Bedouin and recent settlers from the mainland both assert Sinai's distinctive character and disparage Egyptian government, often comparing it unfavourably with the period of Israeli rule. Even the customary salutation is different: "*kif halak*" ("How is your health/situation?") instead of "*izzayak*".

Some history

Fifty million years ago the Arabian Plate began shearing away from the African landmass, tearing the Sinai peninsula from the mainland while the Red Sea inundated the gap. Bronze Age Semites from Mesopotamia were the first to exploit Sinai's lodes of copper ore and turquoise, foreshadowing the peninsula's colonization by the III Dynasty pharaohs, who enslaved its Semitic population. **Pharaonic rule** continued until the invasion of the Hyksos "Shepherd Kings", whose occupation of northern Egypt lasted well over a century, till Ahmosis I finally destroyed their last bastion in Gaza. This was subsequently the route by which Tuthmosis III and Ramses II invaded Palestine and Syria.

The Exodus

Enshrined in the Old Testament and by centuries of tradition, the **Exodus of the Israelites** is a historical conundrum, as no archeological evidence of their journey through Sinai has been found – though excavations at Avaris in the Delta (see p.497) suggest this was the "City of Bondage" from which they fled. Though this is generally agreed to have happened c.1447 BC, scholarly opinion is divided as to the identity of "pharaoh", with most fingering Tuthmosis III or another ruler of the XVIII Dynasty, while David Rohl argues that it was actually the XIII Dynasty king Dudimose (according to his New Chronology see p.601).

Scholars have compared Biblical descriptions with physical features and tried to reconcile myths with realities. The "**Red Sea**" is a mistranslation of the Hebrew *yam-suf*, or **Sea of Reeds**, which fits the salt lakes and marshes to the north of Suez, known today as the Bitter Lakes. From there, the Israelites proceeded to **Ain Musa** and followed **Wadi Feiran** inland towards **Mount Sinai**, although an alternative theory has them trekking across northern Sinai and receiving the Ten Commandments at **Jebel Halal**. Either way, the subsequent forty years in the wilderness are only explicable in terms of a lengthy stay at "Kadesh Barnea", identified as the oasis of **Ain Kedirat**, where there are extensive ruins.

Christianity and Islam

Over the next millennium or so, Sinai was invaded by Assyrians, Hittites and Babylonians, recaptured by Egypt, and conquered in turn by the Persians, Greeks and Romans. Whether or not the **Holy Family** had previously crossed Sinai to escape Herod's massacre, the region had begun to attract hermits even before Emperor Constantine legalized **Christianity**. In 639–40 the **Arabs** swept into Sinai, fired with the zeal of **Islam**. Northern Sinai eventually became a pawn in the **Crusades**, the area between Aqaba and Rafah belonging to the Frankish Kingdom until its collapse at Acre. After the Crusades, the victorious Mamlukes reopened Sinai's trade routes but the peninsula remained Egypt's Achilles heel, as the Ottoman Turks and Mohammed Ali demonstrated with their conquests of 1517 and 1831.

Twentieth-century Sinai

Sinai's strategic importance increased with the completion of the **Suez Canal**, and in 1892 Britain compelled Turkey to cede it as a buffer zone. Backed by Germany, the Turks retook it in 1914. Anglo-Egyptian forces only dislodged them after a prolonged campaign.

During World War II Sinai saw little fighting, but the **creation of Israel** brought it back into the front line. In 1948 the Israelis repulsed Arab attacks from all sides and took the **Gaza Strip** and **El-Arish** before an armistice was signed, only withdrawing under British pressure. Nasser brought together British and Israeli interests by closing the Gulf of Aqaba to Israeli shipping and nationalizing the Suez Canal. Israel's advance into Sinai in October 1956 was the agreed pretext for Anglo-French intervention in the **Suez Crisis**; the three states, though militarily successful, were compelled to quit by international opposition, and UN peacekeeping forces established a buffer zone in Gaza and guaranteed free passage through the Gulf of Aqaba.

However, when Egypt ordered the UN to leave and resumed its blockade in 1967, Israel launched a pre-emptive strike and captured the entire peninsula, which it retained after the **Six Day War**. In the **October War of 1973**, Egypt broke into Sinai but then suffered a devastating counterattack across the Suez Canal.

US-sponsored peace negotiations culminated in President Sadat's historic visit to Jerusalem, the **Camp David Accords** and a peace treaty signed in 1979. Under its terms Israel evacuated all settlements founded during the occupation of Sinai and the territory reverted to Egypt. The phased transition was completed in 1982, except for the disputed enclave of Taba, finally resolved in 1989. The Multinational Force and Observers (**MFO**) based at Na'ama Bay monitors Sinai's demilitarized zones.

Tourism, introduced to Sinai by the Israelis, initially suffered from the handover, as the Camp David Accords forbade any development for five years. Since 1988, however, its recovery has shifted into overdrive. While the areas of Ras Mohammed, Abu Galum and Nabeq are protected by their status as nature reserves, the entire coastline north of Nuweiba, and from Sharm el-Sheikh to Nabeq National Park, is highly developed, with new resorts springing up all the time and innumerable charter flights from Europe into Sharm el-Sheikh.

The mercurial nature of Middle Eastern politics, however, means tourism along the Sinai coast is a fickle business. Unrest in the West Bank and Gaza has greatly slowed tourist traffic from Israel, while the 2004 **terrorist attacks** in Taba, with more attacks in Sharm el-Sheikh and Dahab in 2005 and 2006 respectively, have worsened the situation further. While tourists have flocked back to Sharm el-Sheikh and Dahab, the coast around Nuweiba and Taba is very quiet. The global recession is unlikely to improve matters.

Visiting Sinai

This guide divides the peninsula into three zones – the **gulf coasts of Suez and Aqaba**, the **interior** and **northern Sinai**, though the latter, for the time being, is largely inaccessible to travellers. Communications between the resorts along the coastal strip of the Gulf of Aqaba and the interior around St Catherine's are well established (these two areas make up the administrative region of South Sinai), but northern Sinai is effectively sundered from both. Transport to each zone **from mainland Egypt** is described at the start of each section, while the **approaches from Israel and Jordan** are covered in Basics (see p.28). You can visit part of the peninsula on a free **Sinai-only visa**, valid for two weeks and covering South Sinai only (for more, see p.60). If you wish to visit Ras Mohammed, other parts of Sinai's interior or mainland Egypt, you'll need a **regular visa**, which can be obtained upon arrival at Sharm el-Sheikh airport.

Most travellers find it easy to get around, as **buses** are relatively frequent and **service taxis** run to and from most resorts. Foreign **motorists** are restricted to main roads; **hitchhiking** is a dubious proposition unless your destination is nearby or you're certain of a ride all the way (or at least to somewhere with shade and buses). Women should *never* hitch alone.

Accommodation, costs and information

Accommodation ranges from costly all-inclusive holiday villages at Na'ama Bay to inexpensive "campgrounds" at Nuweiba – the latter consist of huts of stone, concrete, bamboo or palm leaves, and may or may not have electricity and bathrooms. Although tourism is a year-round business, there are peak periods when hotels charge higher prices and are liable to be full. To some extent this depends on the resort: Sharm el-Sheikh receives a surge of European package tourists over spring, autumn and Christmas. Also bear in mind **Egyptian holiday periods** (Dec 22–Feb 2, March 1–May 3 and July 19–Oct 31), when you should try to book in advance. **Tap water** is not drinkable in Sinai.

The **cost** of everyday items, meals and transport is higher in Sinai than elsewhere in Egypt, but still cheaper than in Israel or Europe. There are **banks** with ATMs in all the main resorts, while US dollars and euros can be used in many shops and most dive centres and hotels.

Serious divers or trekkers should acquire the 1:250,000 *Sinai Map of Attractions*, an English-language tourist map based on Israeli army surveys and sold at most resorts. For local information, pick up a copy of *H2O* (Ⓦwww.h2o-mag.com), a free quarterly **listings magazine** with a particular slant on diving; it's available in Sharm el-Sheikh hotels, but harder to find in Nuweiba and Dahab.

The gulf coasts

Sinai rises and tapers as the peninsula runs towards its southern apex, red rock meeting golden sand and deep blue water along two gulf coasts. Even the **Gulf of Suez**, as E.M. Forster noted, looks enticing from offshore – "an exquisite corridor of tinted mountains and radiant water" – though it's nowadays transformed after dark into a vision of Hades by the flaming plumes of oil rigs.

For most travellers, however, Suez is merely an interlude before the **Gulf of Aqaba**, whose amazing coral reefs and tropical fish have given rise to a number of popular resorts. The beach scene here is the best in Egypt, and many resorts can organize trips into the wild **interior**. Even from the beach, the view of the mountains of Sinai and Saudi Arabia is magnificent.

Diving

Much of the diving Sinai offers is easy to access and relatively sheltered from harsh winds and currents, making it a popular destination for those who have little or no experience. It's a cheap place to learn open-water diving and gain a PADI, BSAC or CMAS certificate, entitling you to dive anywhere in the world. The initial step is a five-day **open-water** course, starting at around €300–365 including equipment, plus €30–35 for the certificate. Most centres offer a supervised introductory dive (around €40–50), and some run Nitrox courses (around €180). Kids aged 8–10 years can try the PADI "**Bubble Maker**" course, (around €50), which includes a short two-metre dive in the coral close to the shore. At the other end of the skill spectrum, you can be trained as an **instructor** (around €800 for the 21-day dive-master course). If you're certified but haven't logged a dive in the past three months, you might have to take a "check dive" as a refresher before you can go on a sea trip.

The type of diving and the degree of experience required at each dive site are mainly determined by underwater topography and currents. Around Sharm the chief activity is **boat diving** (you enter the water offshore). Up the coast towards Dahab and Nuweiba this gives way to **shore diving**, where you wade or swim out to the reefs. **Liveaboards** (also called safari boats) allow you to spend days or weeks at sea, cruising the dive sites and shipwrecks of the north Red Sea around Ras Mohammed and the Tiran Strait (or the more southerly reefs beyond Hurghada). They also give access to less-visited sites out of "peak hours", and the chance to make up to five dives a day.

Boat trips to dive sites usually include tanks and weights; lunch on the boat is often extra (about £E50). **Dive packages** can be a good deal, costing around €260 for ten dives, with discounts sometimes available for advance or online bookings. Liveaboards can work out cheaper than staying in a hotel and buying a dive package separately, averaging around €100 per person per day, including full board. Where equipment rental isn't covered, count on an extra €25 or so per day. During quiet periods, bookings can be arranged at short notice (if you're interested in a liveaboard, try asking on the boat while it's at the marina), but to be sure of what you're getting it's best to book in advance (see p.533, p.537 & pp.547–548).

Choosing a dive centre

When **choosing a dive centre**, ask around and then stick to those setups that have been there the longest and have proper links with organizations like PADI. The Chamber of Diving and Watersports (Ⓦ www.cdws.travel) has a list of all legal dive centres in Sinai, as well as those that have been blacklisted. Though centres associated with big hotels are safer bets than outfits on their own, smart premises are less important than the **equipment**. If left lying about, chances are it'll also be poorly maintained. Also note the location of the compressor used to fill the tanks; if it's near a road or other source of pollution, you'll be breathing it in underwater. Ask to see a card proving the instructor is qualified to teach the course (PADI, BSAC or whatever), and not merely a dive master. Many dive centres offer courses not only in English but also in various European languages; linguistic misunderstandings can be dangerous, so you need an instructor who speaks your language well.

Finally, a number of Sinai dive centres charge an optional €1 per day levy on all divers to pay for the upkeep of the local hyperbaric chamber (see p.533).

Sinai dive sites

The following sites are all marked on the map at the start of this chapter.

Amphoras Between Ras Um Sidd and Na'ama Bay, this is named after a Turkish galleon laden with amphoras of mercury that lies on the reef (indeed the site is also known as "Mercury").

Blue Hole 8km north of Dahab. The challenge of this 107m-deep hole in the reef is to swim through a passage 60m down and come up the other side – highly risky even for expert divers. Even dive masters and instructors who have successfully passed through before have met their fate at the Blue Hole. You can safely snorkel around the rim of the hole.

Canyon Near the Blue Hole. A narrow reef crack, 50m deep and only for experienced divers.

Dunraven The *Dunraven* was a ship which, en route from Bombay to Newcastle, steered onto a reef in fine weather on April 25, 1873 and sank 25m almost completely upside down. Though its 25 crew escaped, the captain was found negligent (he fatuously remarked, "Twenty-five is my lucky number!").

El-Gharkana A luxuriant reef, offshore from mangroves and lagoons with rare waterfowl and flora. Part of the Nabeq protected area.

Fjord 10km south of Taba. A picturesque cleft with underwater reefs.

Gordon Reef Off the coast of Ras Nasrani, in the shipwreck-littered Tiran Strait, with sharks and strong currents. Not for beginners.

Jackson Reef A large reef between Tiran Island and the mainland, with a 70m drop-off, sharks and pelagic fish, and the shipwreck *Lara*. Strong currents; dangerous for beginners.

Maagana Beach 5–10km north of Nuweiba. The reef falls sheer around the "Devil's Head" to the north, getting shallower and less impressive further south.

Near, Middle and Far Gardens 1–5km north of Na'ama Bay. A series of lovely coral reefs, good for easy diving and snorkelling. The Near Gardens are within walking distance of Na'ama.

Pharaoh's Island Near Taba. There's superb underwater scenery, easy access by boat and a spectacular wall dive, but also strong currents; a diving guide is recommended.

Ras Abu Galum 50km south of Nuweiba. A 400-square-kilometre protected area with a deep virgin reef wall and great fish.

Ras Atantur Between Dahab and Nabeq. Colourful, abundant reef, with a shipwreck – the *Maria Schroeder* – 10km further south. Access by 4WD.

Ras el-Mamleh 20km south of Nuweiba. A slab of virgin reef wall on the northern edge of the Ras Abu Galum protected area. Access by 4WD or boat.

Ras Mohammed National Park 25km southwest of Sharm el-Sheikh. Wonderful corals, mangrove lagoons, anemone gardens and crevice pools, with shark reefs offshore. It's also the site of the *Yolanda* shipwreck (see below).

Ras Nasrani Sheer reef wall riddled with shark caves; the Light and the Point are notable spots. Large turtles are a common sight on the reef slope. Beware of sharks and strong currents. Not for inexperienced divers.

Ras Um Sidd Within walking distance of Sharm el-Sheikh at the north point of the harbour, this features exquisite fan corals and fish.

Shark Bay Colourful reef just off the beach of a small resort, 10km north of Na'ama Bay. Good for novices and experienced divers alike, and snorkellers.

Southern Oasis Gently sloping reef 7km to the south of Dahab, with easy diving and snorkelling.

Sun Pool 10–15km south of Taba. A gorgeous diving beach along a shallow reef extending as far north as the Fjord.

Thistlegorm Near El-Tor in the Gulf of Suez, this British ship, sunk by German bombers in 1941, was laden with rifles, uniforms, trucks and jeeps – and also packed full of ammunition, which exploded, ripping the ship apart and killing most of the crew. To this day, the rear decks are peeled back towards the bridge leaving many a diver wondering what exactly they are looking at. Tubeworms grow out of the bathtub in the captain's cabin and you can still see much of the armoured vehicles she was carrying. Discovered by Jacques Cousteau, it's a popular dive from Sharm el-Sheikh.

Tiran Island Protected Area An archipelago with over twenty dive sites, all amazing. Sharks and strong currents; only for experienced divers unless explicitly stated otherwise.

The Tower South of Na'ama Bay is this sheer reef pillar dropping 60m. Easy access from the beach and mild currents; good for novice divers.

Turtle Bay Between Ras Um Sidd and Amphoras, a shallow bay with turtles, easy to enjoy. Access is by boat.

Yolanda Off Ras Mohammed is this Cypriot freighter that struck a reef during a storm in 1981; its cargo includes a BMW and scores of porcelain lavatories.

Snorkelling

Snorkelling is also great fun and much cheaper than diving. **Gear** can be rented at most of Sinai's dive centres (€6-8 per day), but if you're planning to do a lot, it's cheaper to bring your own gear from home. Note that coral reefs and spiny urchins can rip unprotected feet to shreds; in all events you should only walk in designated "corridors" to protect the corals – if the water is too shallow to allow you to float above them. However cool the water may feel, the sun's rays can still burn exposed flesh, so always wear a T-shirt and use waterproof sunscreen.

Between Suez and Sharm el-Sheikh

There's little point stopping during the 338-kilometre journey between **Suez** and **Sharm el-Sheikh,** unless you've got private transport or are an avid windsurfer. Such attractions as exist along (or off) the route are otherwise awkward to reach, so most travellers pass them by. Although the resort of **Ras Sudr** is essentially an oil town, its proximity to Cairo (130km) means it is becoming popular with Cairenes as a weekend getaway, while its year-round wind draws windsurfers from further afield. Further south, and inland, the pharaonic ruins at **Serabit el-Khadim** are also starting to attract larger numbers of visitors. Beyond **El-Tor**, the area's administrative capital, there's little of interest until you reach **Ras Mohammed**.

Ras Sudr and Hammam Faraoun

Famed for the variety of seashells washed up on its beach, **RAS SUDR** (or Ras Sidr) is marred by a reeking oil refinery that doesn't seem to bother the middle-class Cairenes who patronize its holiday villages and **hotels**. The town itself has little more than some fly-blown **restaurants**, such as the *Manta Fish Market* next to the bus station, 300m south of the main road; a few shops and a cyber **café**, two blocks south of the main street.

This part of the coast is so windy it is often overlooked by travellers who seek the calmer reef-fringed shores of Sharm el-Sheikh, but the blemish-free beach and year-round cross-shore gusts make it a paradise for **windsurfers** and **kiteboarders**. Two resorts are both ideal for beginners, and can be reached by taxi from Ras Sudr's bus station. The *Ramada* (Ⓣ010/171-7844, Ⓦwww.ramada.com; ❼) 10km south of Ras Sudr has tidy chalets, some with kitchens, next to a wide sandy beach with restaurant, bar and minimarket; service can be slack. Lessons and equipment for windsurfing and kiteboarding can be organized through *Club Mistral* (Ⓦwww.club-mistral.com). *Moon Beach Retreat*, 40km south of Ras Sudr (Ⓣ069/340-1501, Ⓦwww.moonbeachretreat.com; ❼), has accommodation in adjoining a/c stone chalets; and sharing the same management is the newer *Green Hotel*, overlooking one of the lagoons, and with slightly smarter, pricier rooms than its neighbour. Boards and rigs can be hired, and there's also yoga instruction and mountain biking on offer.

Fifty-five kilometres south of Ras Sudr, a turn-off leads to **HAMMAM FARAOUN** ("Pharaoh's Bath"), several near-boiling **hot springs** which Arab folklore attributes to the pharaoh's struggles to extricate himself from the waves that engulfed his army as he chased the Israelites. Local Bedouin use the springs for curing rheumatism, and it is possible to bathe; a cave in the hill beside the shore leads into "the sauna", a warren of chambers awash with hot water, but it's more comfortable to bathe where the springs flow into the sea. There are plans to build a hotel nearby, but in the meantime the only option if you want to stay is to **camp**. You must inform the soldiers posted nearby, who enforce a ban on visiting the beach after 6pm.

Serabit el-Khadim and the turquoise mines

Built upon a 755-metre-high summit reached by a tortuous path, the rock-hewn temple known as **Serabit el-Khadim** is Sinai's only pharaonic temple, surrounded by some of the region's grandest scenery. Erected during the XII Dynasty, when turquoise mining in the area was at its peak, it is an enduring symbol of pharaonic power. Though Bedouin still glean some turquoise by low-tech methods, the amount that remains isn't worth the cost of industrial extraction.

Serabit el-Khadim is becoming a popular stop on **jeep safaris** from points south, via a track leading off the road from St Catherine's into **Wadi Mukattab** – the Valley of Inscriptions. There are dozens of hieroglyphic texts carved into the rocks, alongside Proto-Sinaitic **inscriptions** that continue into Wadi Maraghah, where ancient mine workings and stelae were damaged when the turquoise mines were revived by the British and before going bust in 1901. Most desert outfitters in Na'ama Bay, such as Sun 'n Fun (see p.537), can organize two- to three-day trips here for around $300.

El-Tor

There's little to see along the coastal highway besides a scattering of holiday resorts all the way to **EL-TOR** (or El-Tur), the administrative capital of South Sinai. The town itself is a mass of housing and construction sites, with a scattering of government buildings, and as with Ras Sudr, the main reason to come is for the **windsurfing and kiteboarding**. The only sight of note is the **Raithu Monastery**, commissioned by Byzantine emperor Justinian (527–565). Today it's home to a very hospitable Greek Orthodox order that will allow you to visit and look at the remaining old stones of the original monastery; knock on the door and ask nicely.

Most kiteboarders and windsurfers **stay** at the *Moses Bay Hotel* (T 069/377-4343, W www.oceansource.net; 6–7), 2km north of the centre on the coast. It's the most attractive hotel in the area, with en suite rooms with bath, a/c, satellite TV and a large sandy beach, as well as being home to the Oceansource windsurfing centre (W www.oceansource.net), renting out kite- and windsurfing boards and offering courses. Weekly hotel packages start from around €180 per person half-board. Otherwise there's the *Tur Sinai* (T 069/377-0059; 4), in a modern whitewashed building conveniently located next to the bus station and offering presentable rooms.

A couple of kilometres up the coast from *Moses Bay* are the **hot springs** of **Hammam Musa** (Moses's Bath; £E20), which lie in the shadow of the looming hill named after them. According to legend, Moses asked an elderly woman for a drink from the spring, but the woman refused him, so Moses called upon God to bless the water with therapeutic properties, making it unfit to drink. A path leading halfway up the hill affords spectacular views; facilities include changing rooms with towels and a cafeteria.

Ras Mohammed

At Sinai's southernmost tip is the not-to-be-missed **RAS MOHAMMED** peninsula, fringed with lagoons and reefs. Covering 480 square kilometres, it was declared a nature reserve in 1983, then Egypt's first marine **National Park** in 1989, and is home to a thousand-odd species of fish as well as 150 types of coral. Bordered to the west by the relatively shallow Gulf of Suez and to the east by the deep waters of the Gulf of Aqaba, it has strong currents, making the waters very rich in nutrients. The age of this amazing ecosystem is evinced by marine fossils in the bedrock dating back twenty million years; on the shoreline are newcomers only 75,000 years old. Though the area is chiefly one for **divers**, there are calmer reefs for **snorkellers** too. The park is also home to terrestrial species such as foxes, reptiles and migratory birds such as the white stork.

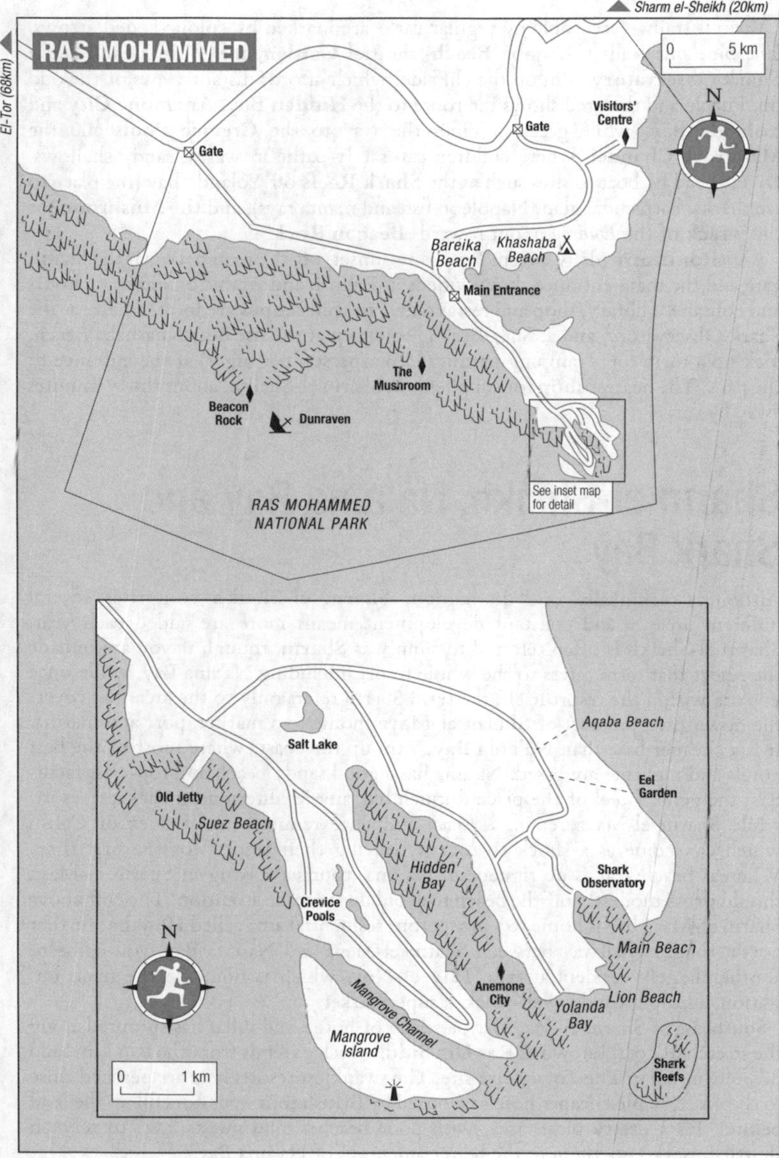

Just over ten percent of the national park is accessible to visitors from sunrise to sunset, but you will need a full Egyptian **visa** and not just a Sinai-only one (they check). The €5 is usually included in the cost of excursions by jeep or boat from Sharm el-Sheikh. Alternatively, if you just plan to snorkel you could charter a taxi (about £E200) or self-drive car for the day. There are two perimeter gates on the road between El-Tor and Sharm el-Sheikh, leading to a main entrance, whence it's 20km to the nearest reefs.

Various trails – accessible by regular car – are marked by colour-coded arrows. The blue one leads to **Aqaba Beach**, the **Eel Garden**, the **Main Beach** and a **Shark Observatory** 50m up the cliffside, which affords distant views of the odd fin. Purple and then red shows the route to the **Hidden Bay**, **Anemone City** and **Yolanda Bay**, while green signifies the way to the **Crevice Pools** and the **Mangrove Channel**, where children can safely bathe in warm, sandy shallows. Divers head by boat to sites such as the **Shark Reefs** off Yolanda Bay (the place to see sharks, barracuda, giant Napoleon fish and manta rays), and **the Mushroom** or the **wreck** of the *Dunraven*, out towards **Beacon Rock**.

A **visitor centre** (daily except Fri 10am–sunset) off the road between the Sharm gate and the main entrance shows videos in English and Arabic on alternate hours and contains a library, shop and restaurant. Free **telescopes** are located here, at the Shark Observatory, and at Suez Beach. To **camp** at the site near Khashaba Beach, pick up a form for a camping permit ($5 per person per night) at the entrance to the park. The nearest **shop** for supplies is in Sharm el-Sheikh, about thirty minutes away by car.

Sharm el-Sheikh, Na'ama Bay and Shark Bay

Although technically one destination, **Sharm el-Sheikh** comprises several different areas – and constant development means more are added each year. Sharm el-Sheikh is often referred to simply as **Sharm**, though if you are outside the resort that term refers to the whole resort, including Na'ama Bay, while once you are within the resort itself, the term Sharm refers only to the area that covers the downtown precinct of **Sharm el-Maya**, home to a market, port and marina. It is a cheaper base than **Na'ama Bay**, 7km up the coast, where most of the best hotels and nightlife are based. Na'ama has a good sandy beach and top-class facilities; the general feel of the place is much like any Mediterranean package resort, while Sharm el-Maya retains a *baladi* ambience reminiscent of Suez or Cairo, which can come as a shock to tourists leaving their resorts for the first time. Whereas beachwear is de rigueur in Na'ama, tourists staying in Sharm el-Maya should **dress** modestly off the beach to avoid unwelcome attention. The cliff above Sharm el-Maya bay is home to a prosperous residential area called **Hadaba**; further north, roughly halfway between Sharm el-Maya and Na'ama Bay, you come to another largely residential area, **Hay el-Nur,** which is home to the main bus station, a hospital and a well-stocked supermarket.

Southeast of Sharm el-Maya bay, a string of hotels and villas has sprouted along the stretch of coast known as **Ras Um Sidd**, which extends from the Ras Um Sidd dive site north to The Tower dive site. The swankiest resorts here are perched close to the coast, while cheaper hotels favoured by British tour operators fill up the land behind. It's a pretty bleak area, with poor beaches, and guests have to rely on shuttle buses to get them to the better amenities of Na'ama Bay.

Hotel development has not stopped at Na'ama Bay, and tourist villages, some up to a square kilometre in size, line the coast up to **Ras Nasrani** and even beyond to the borders of the **Nabeq** protected area. The once-beautiful and isolated retreat of **Shark Bay**, 8km north of Na'ama, is now swamped by large resorts – it still boasts a fine beach, however, and a view of Tiran Island.

Divers are not allowed to explore the reefs near Na'ama and Sharm el-Sheikh independently; all diving must be done with a guide, which in practical terms means sticking with trips run by the dive operators. All of the Sharm and Na'ama

Bay dive centres are members of the **South Sinai Association for Diving and Marine Activities** (Ⓣ069/366-0418, Ⓦwww.southsinai.org), which regulates and promotes the diving industry in the region and organizes regular clean-ups of the sea. Before signing up for any courses, ask where you'll be doing your training: the water in Sharm el-Maya is less pleasant than in Na'ama Bay thanks to the former's proximity to the marina.

Sharm and Na'ama Bay tragically hit the headlines on July 24, 2005, when a series of coordinated bomb attacks struck the resort, killing around eighty people and injuring more than two hundred. **Security measures** have been heightened since the attack, but travellers should always be vigilant.

Sharm el-Sheikh

A hunk of sterile buildings on a plateau commanding docks and other installations, **SHARM EL-SHEIKH** was developed by the Israelis after their capture of it in the 1967 war. Their main purpose was to thwart Egypt's blockade of the Tiran Strait and to control overland communications between the Aqaba and Suez coasts. Tourism was an afterthought – though an important one, helping to finance the Israeli occupation and settlements, which Egypt inherited between 1979 and 1982. Since then, Sharm's infrastructure seems to have expanded in fits and starts, without enhancing its appeal much. Despite some plush hotels and reams of propaganda about it being a slick resort, Sharm el-Sheikh is basically a **dormitory town** for the Egyptian workers who service neighbouring Na'ama Bay. Aside from package tourists conned by brochures, the only foreigners here are divers and a few backpackers who take advantage of its cheapish accommodation and commute into Na'ama Bay. Sharm has a beach, but its small bay doesn't match

ACCOMMODATION

Amar Sinai Egyptian Village	D	Hilton Sharm Waterfall Resort	H	Iberotel Palace	A	The Rock	B
Beach Albatros	E	Iberotel Club Fanara	J	New Tower Club	G	Tropicana Tivoli	C
				Ritz-Carlton	I	Youth Hostel	F

Na'ama's, and the seedy downtown area also detracts from the hotels' "luxury" pretensions. In its defence, however, **Sharm el-Maya** has some good restaurants and souvenir shops.

Sharm also has the **Dolphinella**, opposite the *Cliff Top Hotel* in Hadaba (Mon–Sat 10.30am–6pm), which puts on dolphin performances (3pm; £E150). In addition, throughout the day, you can swim with the dolphins for a hefty £E1200 for thirty minutes. However, the standards under which the animals are kept here have been the subject of a campaign by the pressure group Marine Connection (Ⓦ www.marineconnection.org), which views the keeping of dolphins in captivity with distaste.

Arrival, information and transport

East Delta and Superjet buses terminate at the Hay el-Nur **bus station** behind the Mobil station. The **port** where the catamaran arrives from Hurghada is 600m south of Sharm el-Maya. Sharm el-Sheikh **airport**, 10km north of Na'ama, is busy with charter flights from Europe, whose passengers are driven off to their resorts by bus; arriving on your own, you're dependent on taxis to get to Na'ama Bay or Sharm (£E25-40). The airport has an ATM and moneychanger.

Regular **minibuses** carry local workers between Sharm el-Maya and Na'ama (£E1–2 per person). You can flag them down at any point along the main road, but bear in mind you won't be sharing space with cosmopolitan Egyptian holidaymakers, so it's advisable to be modestly dressed. Private **taxis** demand around £E20 per carload.

The isolated and largely worthless **tourist office** (daily except Fri 9am–3pm; Ⓣ069/366-4721) is a couple of kilometres northeast of the main facilities of the Hadaba clifftop, where an arcade contains three **banks** (daily 8am–2pm & 6–8pm), a **post office** (daily except Fri 8am–3pm), and a **pharmacy** (daily 9am–3pm & 6–11pm). There's also a bank at *Iberotel Palace*. The Sharm International Hospital (Ⓣ069/366-0894; there's a good pharmacy next door too) and the Sharm Medical Centre (Ⓣ069/366-1744) are both in Hay el-Nur. The **police** (Ⓣ069/366-0415) and **tourist police** (Ⓣ069/366-0311), both open 24 hours, share a building near the arcade and beyond the mosque. Further inland is a 24-hour **telephone** exchange. Il Mercato in the clifftop area, away from the beach, is a sprawling shopping and entertainment complex with a Virgin Megastore, *Starbucks*, fast-food joints and restaurants.

Accommodation

The windswept **clifftop** area is the best place to look for mid-priced options.

Amar Sinai Egyptian Village Clifftop area Ⓣ069/366-2222, Ⓦwww.minasegypt.com. Eclectic hotel with over-the-top (and slightly camp) domes and arches, designed by its owner-in-residence. The a/c rooms with satellite TV, however, are undeniably attractive. It's very popular with British package tourists, and can be noisy. ❺

Beach Albatros On the cliff overlooking Sharm el-Maya, with access to the beach below via a very long staircase or lift Ⓣ069/366-3923, Ⓦwww.pickalbatros.com. Construction of the beach here involved infilling a stretch at the back of the reef, causing the latter's death. This hotel now has the best beach in this part of town, as well as a great view of the mountains and Ras Mohammed from the pool. Rates are all-inclusive. ❻

Hilton Sharm Waterfall Resort On the beach at Ras Um Sidd Ⓣ069/366-3232, Ⓦwww.hiltonworldresorts.com. *Hilton*'s most recent addition to Sharm has 400 large and understated a/c rooms with all the trimmings, no less than seven pools, an impressive waterfall feature and a small cable car to a small beach. ❼

Iberotel Club Fanara On the beach at Ras Um Sidd, next to the lighthouse Ⓣ069/366-3966, Ⓦwww.iberotel.com. Well-designed all-inclusive on one of the few good beaches (especially for snorkellers) in the area. Rooms have a/c, satellite TV, tiles and terraces, and many are geared towards families. Great service. ❼

Iberotel Palace Sharm el-Maya Ⓣ069/366-1111, Ⓦwww.iberotel.com. Attractive all-inclusive with more than 240 rooms featuring luxurious mod-cons (some even have bidets). There's a large section of beach, and lots of restaurants and sports facilities and a bank. Service is as good as at the *Fanara*. 7

Ritz-Carlton By the beach at Ras Um Sidd. ⓣ069/366-1919, ⓦwww.ritzcarlton.com. Trumpeted as the first *Ritz* in Africa, this huge resort has en suites with all the comfort and style you would expect from the international chain. There is a beach with direct access to a reef (good for snorkelling and diving, bad for swimming), two pools with a "river" and waterfall, and Italian, Middle Eastern and Japanese restaurants. 7

The Rock Clifftop area ⓣ069/366-1765, ⓔtherock@sinainet.com.eg. Neat and tidy rooms with balconies or patios, a/c and TV, plus a bar, pool and shuttle bus to the beach. Often gives suites to foreigners for the price of a standard room, making it good value. 4

Tropicana Tivoli Clifftop area ⓣ069/366-1381, ⓦwww.tropicanahotels.com. Straightforward hotel housing whitewashed a/c en suites with wooden furniture and boasting a decent pool, with a bar in the middle, and in-house masseurs. Runs a shuttle bus to its sister hotel in Na'ama Bay and the beach at Ras Um Sidd. Breakfast included. 5

Youth Hostel Clifftop area ⓣ069/366-0317, ⓦwww.hihostels.com. Small dorm rooms and cramped a/c doubles, and cleanish bathrooms. Facilities include a basketball and soccer court. May be full of young Egyptians or otherwise virtually empty. Breakfast included. Dorm beds from £E55, doubles 3

Diving and liveaboards

The majority of dive centres (generally daily 8.30am–6pm) are firmly attached to hotels, but most are happy to take non-guests for courses and daily boat diving. Dive boats set off at around 9am from the marina in Sharm el-Maya; most centres will collect you and drop you off again if necessary (crucial if you're marooned at one of the hotels on the cliff in Ras Um Sidd). Some of the dive centres listed below and on p.537 offer **liveaboards.** All the centres have offices in Hadaba, and set off from the marina in Sharm el-Maya.

In case of **diving emergencies**, contact Dr Adel Taher at the Hyperbaric Medical Centre near the Sharm el-Sheikh marina (ⓣ069/366-0922 or 012 212-4292). There is also a 24-hour emergency hotline (ⓣ012 333-1325) and a second decompression facility at the pyramid-shaped International Hospital in Hay el-Nur (ⓣ069/366-8094). Dive schools charge an optional €6 per diver for three weeks' cover allowing emergency use of the chambers. For more information on emergency diving support, visit ⓦwww.deco-international.com.

Dive centres

African Divers *Luna Sharm hotel* ⓣ069/366-4884, ⓦwww.africandiverssharm.com. PADI, CMAS, NAUI, SSI, French-speaking.

Colona Dive Club *Amar Sina*, Hadaba ⓣ069/366-3670, ⓦwww.colona.com. Caters primarily for Scandinavian clients. Liveaboards available. PADI Gold Palm resort, SSI, Nitrox.

Rasta Divers Ras Um Sidd ⓣ069/366-3328 or 012 213-3881 , ⓦwww.rastadivers.com. Rather exclusive, catering mostly to private groups. Liveaboards available. PADI, CMAS, SSI.

Liveaboards

King Snefro Boats ⓣ069/366-1202, ⓦwww.kingsnefro.de. Four boats and more than fifteen years' experience in the Red Sea. The cost, €80–120 per person per day, includes transfers and full board. Children under 7 go free and 7- to 12-year-olds are half price.

Sea Queen I, II and III ⓣ069/371-0506. Liveboards in opulent style.

Tornado Marine Fleet ⓦwww.tornadomarinefleet.com. Six boats offering week-long trips around the more popular dive sites and wrecks, from €1200.

Eating, drinking and nightlife

Aside from **eating and drinking** in hotels, Sharm el-Maya has its share of restaurants, cafés and *fuul* and *taamiya* stalls. The best **supermarket** in Sharm is Sheikh Abdullah's in Hay el-Nur.

For **drinking and nightlife**, head to the lively *Terrazzina* restaurant and bar (ⓦwww.terrazzina.com), which has beach parties every Friday, live music on Sundays and full moon events, plus decent food. *T2*, an offshoot of the *Tavern* English pub in Na'ama (see p.540), is next door to the *Rock Hotel* if you fancy a pint. Otherwise try the organized entertainment in the hotels, or catch a taxi to the clubs in Na'ama Bay.

Restaurants

Al-Fanar Ras Um Sidd Lighthouse ⓣ069/366-2218. The stunningly located and very romantic *Al-Fanar* is housed in a tent, dishes up excellent Italian food (mains £E50–160) and has a vast sea view taking in Ras Mohammed. It's also great for an evening drink and often has music nights.

Gazelle Fish In the main market. A good fish restaurant in which to grab a meal and take a break from the bustling market: a hefty mixed seafood platter will set you back £E80.

Melodies On the edge of the main market. Popular with Italian expats, this homely restaurant has a climbing plant-covered terrace and checked table cloths: the pasta dishes (£E40–50) are generally better than the pizzas.

Onions In the clifftop Il Mercato development. A modern a/c restaurant serving good-value sandwiches (including a "super Viagra" seafood-filled one, if you need perking up), pizzas, pastas and burgers for £E10–40.

Safsafa In the main market. Popular with tour groups, *Safsafa* serves up a good selection of fresh fish, seafood and mezze dishes. Mains £E30–80.

Sinai Star In the main market. Very similar menu and clientele to the neighbouring *Safsafa, Sinai Star* is a slightly more peaceful place to enjoy Sharm's seafood. Mains £E30–80.

Moving on from Sharm el-Sheikh

Sharm el-Sheikh is South Sinai's transport hub, with bus services to Cairo, the Canal Zone and most points in the peninsula, boats to Hurghada, and domestic **flights** to Cairo, tickets for which can be bought from EgyptAir in Sharm (daily 9am–2pm & 6–9pm; ⓣ069/366-1058).

All **buses** leave from the Hay el-Nur bus station (ⓣ069/366-0666). The Superjet buses leave for **Cairo** at 12.15pm, 1pm, 5pm and 11pm (7hr); you'll need to buy your ticket in advance in person at the bus station to be sure of getting a seat. These buses make fewer stops and tend to be quieter than the East Delta buses to Cairo (7-8 daily; 8hr), for which you have to reserve seats in person at the bus station in advance. The daily 9am service to **Taba** and **Nuweiba** stops at **Dahab** which can also be reached by around twelve other direct buses. Buses also run daily to the Canal cities of **Suez** (7 daily; 6–7hr) and **Ismailiya** (hourly; 7–8hr); as well as to **Luxor** (6am and 1pm) and **Alexandria** (9.15am). **Service taxis** serve Suez and Dahab, though other destinations can be negotiated. A taxi from the bus station to Na'ama or Sharm el-Sheikh should cost around £E25.

Finally, the ninety-minute **catamaran** trip from Sharm el-Sheikh to **Hurghada** departs on Saturdays, Tuesdays and Thursdays at 5pm, and Mondays at 6pm (adults £E250, children under 11 £E150, one-way; children under 3 free but they don't get a seat). Tickets can be bought at most of the hotels and travel agencies including Mena Tours (daily 10am–10pm except Fri from 1pm; ⓣ069/360-0190, ⓦwww.mena-tours.net) in Na'ama Bay's *Marriott Hotel*, or at Sharm el-Sheikh port one hour before departure.

Between Sharm and Na'ama

The fabulous array of **dive spots** around Sharm and Na'ama is the chief attraction of both resorts, offering endless scope for boat or shore diving. The most accessible site is **Ras Um Sidd**. The area is basically all coral reef without any natural sandy beaches – what sand there is has been imported by the hotels to create their own beaches, inevitably increasing the debris many divers now encounter underwater in this area.

From Ras Um Sidd, a paved road lined with holiday villages and hotels runs to **The Tower**, a fine diving beach colonized by the 120-room hotel, *New Tower Club* (ⓣ069/360-0231, ⓕ360-1237; ⑦) dominated by Italians but the beach café is a good place for people-watching. The real lure, however, is a huge **coral pillar** just offshore, which drops 60m into the depths.

It's easy to get to The Tower by taxi from either Sharm or Na'ama, but it is no longer possible to access most of the reefs between Ras Um Sidd and The Tower from land, as hotels along this stretch of coast now effectively block public access to the sea. Diving these reefs by boat, you come to (in order of appearance after Ras Um Sidd) Fiasco, Paradise, Turtle Bay, Pinky's Wall and Amphoras. **Turtle Bay** has sun-dappled water that's lovely to swim in, even if there are fewer **green turtles** than you'd hope.

Na'ama Bay

With its fine beach and upmarket facilities, **NA'AMA BAY** has transformed itself so rapidly that even the residents have trouble keeping up. A glitzy, over-developed tourist centre, with a vast array of fast-food joints, international restaurants and clubs, it is far from an authentic Egyptian experience. Nightlife and sunbathing are the main draws, though diving and snorkelling are popular too, with dive centres, hotels and malls being the only points of reference along the beachfront strip. The **beach** is divided into hotel-owned plots that are supposedly open to anyone providing they don't use the parasols or chairs – though hippy-looking types may be hassled and topless bathing is illegal. There are two public beaches (£E10), though they are no more than narrow unkempt strips squeezed in next to the *Novotel* and the *Hilton* beaches.

Arrival, transport and accommodation

For details of the airport, bus station and transport from Sharm, see p.532. Since the 2005 terrorist attack, Na'ama Bay's tourist area has been pedestrianized and

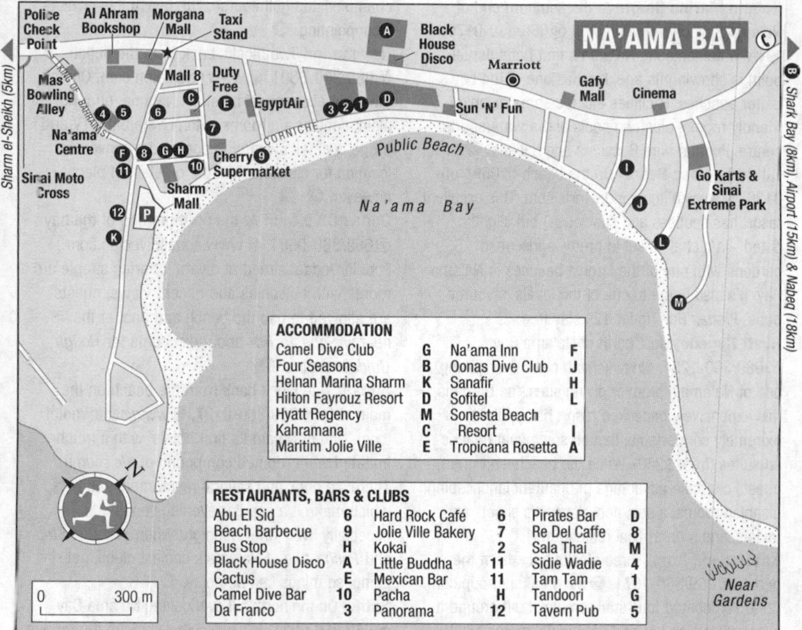

vehicles are no longer permitted south of the main coast road; King of Bahrain Street and the Corniche now have a piazza-style atmosphere, especially at night. To get a **taxi** you will have to walk beyond the large hotel complexes to the main road or along King of Bahrain Street to the police checkpoint at the junction with the main road. **Mopeds** to get around Na'ama are available for a negotiable $60 per day from Red Sea Star Sports Centre (Ⓣ012 407-7216), near the *Tam Tam* restaurant; they also rent **bicycles** (around £E30/hr).

Luxurious **holiday villages** featuring acres of marble floors and lush landscaped gardens are the norm in Na'ama Bay. Bargains can be had if you book a **package trip**, but make sure you're not shunted into one of the hotel "extensions", which often have a lower standard of accommodation and an awkward highway crossing to get to the sea. Rates include breakfast.

Camel Dive Club On the main strip one block back from the beach Ⓣ069/360-0700, Ⓦwww.cameldive.com. Attached to one of Na'ama's best dive centres is this well-designed hotel filled with trellis-style walls and climbing plants. Its a/c rooms have satellite TV, nice touches like tea/coffee making facilities and are arranged around the pool. There's a great Indian restaurant (see p.539) and rooftop bar (see p.540). Look out for online deals. 6

Four Seasons Ⓣ069/360-3555, Ⓦwww.fourseasons.com. Glitzy hotel designed for the jet set with stunning Arabian-style architecture. Expect six-star treatment and facilities such as a spa and a vast heated palm-shaded pool with underwater music. Rooms from $370. 9

Helnan Marina Sharm At the southern end of Na'ama Bay, on the main strip Ⓣ069/360-0170, Ⓦwww.helnan.com. Na'ama's first hotel (Israeli-built) is showing its age, but has one of the bay's better beaches. Facilities include some disabled-friendly rooms, plus two pools and a watersports centre. Popular with Russians and Italians. 7

Hilton Fayrouz Resort On the beach Ⓣ069/360-0136, Ⓦwww.hiltonworldresorts.com. This excellent resort has spotless and spacious – but slightly dated – a/c chalets set in pretty landscaped gardens with one of the largest beaches in Na'ama Bay. It's also home to one of the locals' favourite pubs, *Pirates Bar*. Under 12s stay free. 7

Hyatt Regency Just north of Na'ama Bay Ⓣ069/360-1234, Ⓦwww.hyatt.com. Overlooking one of Na'ama's premier diving sites, the Gardens, this expensively bedecked resort has opulent, extremely comfortable, though somewhat generic en suites (from $260). While the beach isn't great, guests can take advantage of beautiful landscaping, disabled rooms, a spa, non-allergenic sheets and towels, and a great Thai restaurant. 8

Kahramana Hotel Three blocks back from the beach Ⓣ069/360-1071, Ⓦwww.balbaagroup.com. Centrally located four-star complex built around a pool with a nice bar and pool table, rooms with small balconies and amiable staff. Popular with both Egyptian and foreign tourists. 7

Maritim Jolie Ville In the middle of Na'ama Ⓣ069/360-0100, Ⓦwww.jolieville-hotels.com. This hotel is so big it uses golf carts to shuttle occupants from one end of its immaculate grounds to the other. The tasteful 395 en suites have king-sized beds and flatscreen TVs ($310–360) – however, the cheapest ones are in the more basic extension over the road. It also boasts a popular beach bar and a casino. 9

Maritim Jolie Ville Golf and Resort 7km north of Na'ama Ⓣ069/360-3200, Ⓦwww.jolieville-hotels.com. Large and somewhat impersonal hotel with more than four hundred comfortable rooms, the best swimming pool in the area, a high-quality gym and health club, and of course an eighteen-hole championship golf course. The beach, however, is disappointing. 8

Na'ama Inn Two blocks back from the beach Ⓣ069/360-0801, Ⓦwww.naamainn.com. One of the most economical hotels in Na'ama, offering plain, angular a/c rooms with private bath, TV and fridge, a small swimming pool and a convenient location for clubbers. Not the quietest of places, however. 4–5

Oonas Dive Club At the northern end of the bay Ⓣ069/360-0581, Ⓦwww.oonasdiveclub.com. Popular lodge, aimed at divers, offering simple a/c rooms with balconies and decent views; guests are allowed to use the beach and pool at the nearby *Sonesta*. Ask about discounts for *Rough Guides* readers. 5

Sanafir One block back from the beach on the main strip Ⓣ069/360-0197, Ⓦwww.sanafirhotel.com. One of Na'ama's first hotels, with a much-imitated white-domed compound of a/c rooms. There's a pool, and several restaurants and bars, which make it a popular evening venue. It's especially lively after midnight when *The Bus Stop* and *Pacha*, two of Na'ama's coolest clubs, get going, so things can be noisy. 5–6

Sofitel On the north hill overlooking Na'ama Bay Ⓣ069/360-0081, Ⓦwww.sofitel.com. An impressive

Egypt's underwater world

For snorkellers and scuba divers the Red Sea and the Gulf of Aqaba are heaven-sent destinations. Thanks to their relative isolation from the Indian Ocean, they harbour numerous marine species found nowhere else on the planet, as well as many more common creatures, no less fascinating. The Red Sea's stable climate, shallow tides and exceptionally high salinity provide perfect conditions for unusually brilliant corals and sponges to flourish – a revelation if you have previously snorkelled in such places as Hawaii or the Caribbean, whose reefs will ever after seem dull by comparison.

Gorgonian fans ▲

Golden butterflyfish ▼

Parrotfish ▼

Red Sea reefs

Created by generations of minuscule polyps depositing their limestone exoskeletons on the remains of their ancestors, **coral reefs** can grow by 4–5cm a year. Besides **hard corals** such as brain and fire coral, which have a rigid outer skeleton, the Red Sea hosts an abundance of **soft corals**, including whip coral and sea fans; **gorgonian fans** can grow up to 2m across. Because most types of coral need a moderate amount of warm sunlight to flourish, the most spectacular formations are found within 30m of the surface.

Most **Red Sea** reefs are of the **fringing** type, with a shallow **lagoon** just offshore, whose warm water and rubble-strewn bottom attracts starfish and sea slugs; clams and sea urchins hide in crevices and schools of damselfish and butterflyfish flit about. Its seaward boundary is the reef flat, whose crest is usually a barren, rough-surfaced shelf, while deeper areas are rich in flora and fauna. Beyond is the coral-encrusted slope, leading to a **drop-off** like the edge of a cliff. Flatter areas may be dotted with coral pillars or knolls, attracting anthias, snappers and wrasses. Lower down, the coral is sparser, and you may find sandy terraces overgrown with seagrass, sustaining sea horses and pipefish. Beyond the drop-off lies open water.

Must-see species

Some of the Red Sea's most colourful and endearing species are easy to spot in the shallows, where the sunlight is brightest. Among the commonest are beak-mouthed **parrotfish**, jauntily striped **bufferflyfish**, and exotic-looking **pennantfish**, whose long dorsal fins diminish to filaments.

Wherever stinging anemones cling to the reef, you'll see **clownfish** (or anemone fish), immortalized in *Finding Nemo*. **Angelfish** are usually found close to the coral, singly or in pairs, while clouds of gold and vermillion anthias gather round coral heads and fans.

Slopes and fore reefs are the habitat of **snappers**, **goatfish** and **wrasses** (the largest of these, the Napoleon wrasse, can dwarf a person). In deeper waters you may see **sharks**, including whitetip reef sharks, grey reef sharks and (occasionally) scalloped hammerheads. Spotted reef **stingrays** are often seen on the sandy bottom.

Turtles, with their curious mixture of ugliness and grace, are among the most thrilling species to encounter underwater; the Red Sea has several species, including green turtles and hawksbill turtles. **Dolphin** encounters are much rarer, and those lucky enough to come across a pod of bottlenose or spinner dolphins are likely to count this among highlights of their trip.

▲ Clownfish

▲ Green turtle

▼ Crown jellyfish

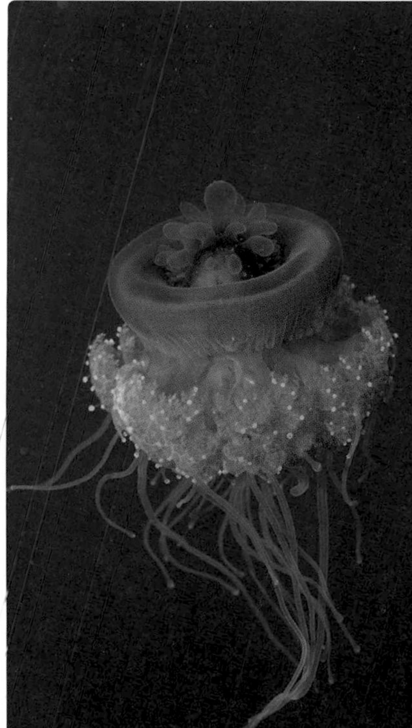

Dangers of the deep

Common sense and conservation-mindedness should keep you from **touching** any underwater flora or fauna, particularly coral, which can be extremely sharp and is easily damaged. It's also important to avoid aggravating any **potentially dangerous creatures** such as moray eels, which may bite when threatened, or stingrays, which can deliver a painful dose of venom. Certain times of the year see the arrival of hordes of **jellyfish**, contact with which can cause mild skin irritation. Very few Red Sea species behave aggressively towards people, though poisonous species to look out for include the spiny, bottom-dwelling **scorpion fish**, and the nocturnal **lionfish**, with its elaborate array of strikingly marked fins. The lethal **stonefish**, camouflaged as a gnarled rock, is harder to spot but fortunately rare.

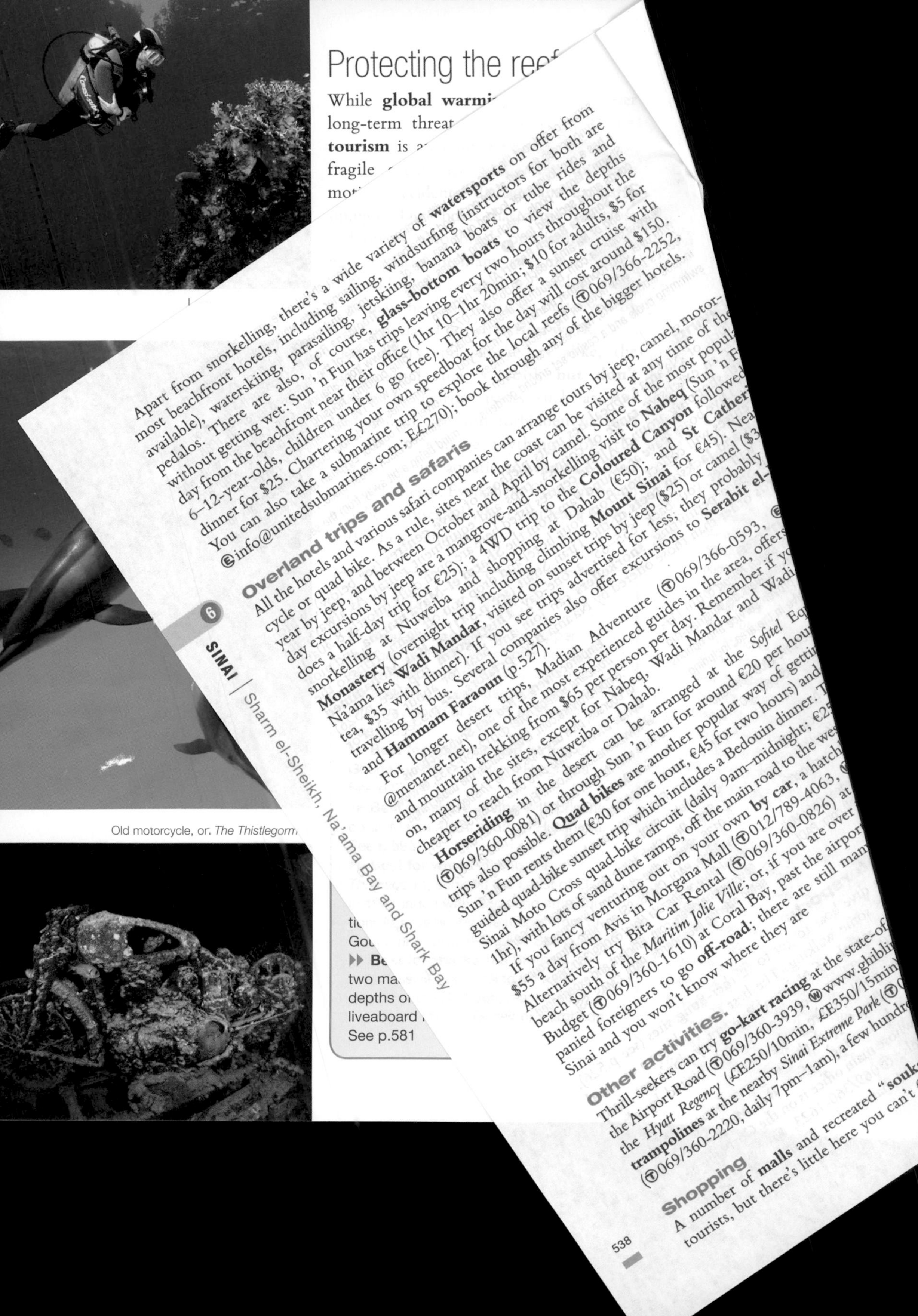

Protecting the ree[f]

While **global warmi**[ng] ... long-term threat ... **tourism** is ... fragile ... mot...

Old motorcycle, on *The Thistlegorm*

... **Be**... two ma... depths o... liveaboard ...

See p.581

Apart from snorkelling, there's a wide variety of **watersports** on offer from most beachfront hotels, including sailing, windsurfing (instructors for both are available), waterskiing, parasailing, jetskiing, banana boats or tube rides and pedalos. There are also, of course, **glass-bottom boats** to view the depths without getting wet: Sun 'n Fun has trips leaving every two hours throughout the day from the beachfront near their office (1hr 10–1hr 20min; $10 for adults, $5 for 6–12-year-olds, children under 6 go free). They also offer a sunset cruise with dinner for $25. Chartering your own speedboat for the day will cost around $150. You can also take a submarine trip to explore the local reefs (Ⓣ069/366-2252, Ⓔinfo@unitedsubmarines.com; E£270); book through any of the bigger hotels.

Overland trips and safaris

All the hotels and various safari companies can arrange tours by jeep, camel, motorcycle or quad bike. As a rule, sites near the coast can be visited at any time of the year by jeep, and between October and April by camel. Some of the most popul[ar] day excursions by jeep are a mangrove-and-snorkelling visit to **Nabeq** (Sun 'n F[un] does a half-day trip for €25); a 4WD trip to the **Coloured Canyon** followed [by] snorkelling at Nuweiba and shopping at Dahab (€50); and **St Cather**[ine's] **Monastery** (overnight trip including climbing **Mount Sinai** for €45). Nea[r] Na'ama lies **Wadi Mandar**, visited on sunset trips by jeep ($25) or camel ($3... tea, $35 with dinner). If you see trips advertised for less, they probably ... travelling by bus. Several companies also offer excursions to **Serabit el-**... and **Hammam Faraoun** (p.527).

For longer desert trips, Madian Adventure (Ⓣ069/366-0593, Ⓔ...@menanet.net), one of the most experienced guides in the area, offers ... and mountain trekking from $65 per person per day. Remember if yo[u] ... on, many of the sites, except for Nabeq, Wadi Mandar and Wadi ... cheaper to reach from Nuweiba or Dahab.

Horseriding in the desert can be arranged at the *Sofitel* Eq... (Ⓣ069/360-0081) or through Sun 'n Fun for around €20 per hou[r] ... trips also possible. **Quad bikes** are another popular way of gettin[g] ... Sun 'n Fun rents them (€30 for one hour, €45 for two hours) and ... guided quad-bike sunset trip which includes a Bedouin dinner. T... Sinai Moto Cross quad-bike circuit (daily 9am–midnight; €2... 1hr), with lots of sand dune ramps, off the main road to the wes[t] ...

If you fancy venturing out on your own **by car**, a hatch... $55 a day from Avis in Morgana Mall (Ⓣ012/789-4063, Ⓦ...). Alternatively try Bita Car Rental (Ⓣ069/360-0826) at ... beach south of the *Maritim Jolie Ville*; or, if you are over ... Budget (Ⓣ069/360-1610) at Coral Bay, past the airpor[t] ... panied foreigners to go **off-road**; there are still man[y] ... Sinai and you won't know where they are ...

Other activities

Thrill-seekers can try **go-kart racing** at the state-of-... the Airport Road (Ⓣ069/360-3939, Ⓦwww.ghibli...; E£250/10min, E£350/15min) ... the *Hyatt Regency* ..., a few hundre[d] ... **trampolines** at the nearby *Sinai Extreme Park* (Ⓣ0... (Ⓣ069/360-2220, daily 7pm–1am) ...

Shopping

A number of **malls** and recreated "**souks**" ... tourists, but there's little here you can't fi[nd] ...

The Panorama, a large thatched souk near the *Helnan Marina Sharm*, sells just about every Egyptian souvenir imaginable. A few interesting arts and crafts shops exist: try Aladdin at the *Camel Dive Club Hotel* and Bashayer, in Sharm Mall.

Eating

There are no really inexpensive places to eat in Na'ama. On the plus side, the quality of hotel cuisine is high, and ranges from Egyptian, Italian and seafood to Japanese, Indian and Thai. Prices tend to be higher along the **beach promenade** where every hotel offers at least one beachside restaurant, and along the lively inland King of Bahrain Street outside the *Sanafir* and *Camel Dive Club* hotels. Both these stretches are busy, with back-to-back bars and restaurant tables spilling out on to the street (several also have cooling water vapour machines, but the water used is not the cleanest). For **snacks, pastries and desserts**, head to the *Jolie Ville* bakery, at the northern end of the strip near *McDonald's*. Phone numbers have been included for restaurants where reservations are advisable.

Restaurants

Abu El Sid On the roof of the *Hard Rock Café*. As authentically Egyptian as you'll get in Na'ama, with an appealing rooftop dining area, carved wooden bar and innumerable lanterns. There are interesting specialities like pigeon stuffed with rice, rabbit with *molukhiyya* (Jew's mallow) and Circassian chicken. Mains around £E55.

Beach Barbeque Corniche, opposite *Jolie Ville*. Canopied restaurant right on the beach serving chargrilled steaks and seafood (plus interesting dishes like baked sea bass with squid, peppers, onions and coriander); the pizzas, however, are better elsewhere. Go for the mango cheesecake for dessert. Mains £E50–130.

Da Franco *Hotel Ghazala*, on the promenade between the *Maritim* and *Hilton*. Good wood-fired pizza (try the calzone) and pasta restaurant with reasonably priced main dishes (£E40–50). Staff, can be a little surly.

Kokai *Hotel Ghazala*, next to *Da Franco*. A Japanese restaurant with a pleasant terrace and teppanyaki chefs who will grill food at your table. Six maki rolls will set you back £E48, while the all-you-can-eat sushi buffet costs £E140.

Re Del Caffe Near entrance of Na'ama Centre. Small booth with authentic. Illy coffee – a cappuccino costs £E14 – plus crepes, non-alcoholic fruit cocktails and water pipes (the latter cost £E12–20).

Sala Thai *Hyatt Regency* ☎069/360-1234. Refined and suitably expensive Thai restaurant that's excellent for a special occasion – or if you just fancy a splurge. Expect to pay around £E200 per person for a meal.

Sidie Wadie Top floor, Na'ama Centre. Classy Moroccan joint with tagines, couscous, spicy harira soup and an interesting seafood pastilla (mains around £E90). Next door, sister restaurant *Fairuz* serves up good Lebanese food.

Tam Tam *Hotel Ghazala* ☎069/360-0155. Excellent Egyptian food – mezze, grilled meat and seafood and delectable sweets like Om Ali, a corn cake soaked in milk with raisins and coconut – and a breezy roof terrace with low tables, rugs and cushions to sit on. There's an Egyptian floor show three nights a week (see p.540). Mains £E55–85. Daily until 1am.

Tandoori *Camel Dive Club*. Some of Na'ama's best Indian food with plenty of veggie options, including *paneer jalfrezi* and tarka dhal, as well as – of course – tandoori meat dishes. Mains from £E25. Evenings only 6.30–11.30pm.

Drinking and nightlife

Alcoholic drinks are widely available, perhaps more so than anywhere else in Egypt, at European prices; the Corniche is lined with open-air bars attached to the resorts. The **duty-free shop** in front of the *Kahramana Hotel* (daily 11am–2pm & 6–11pm; shorter hours during Ramadan) sells cheap booze.

The *Sanafir* hotel is Na'ama's premier **nightspot**, with a variety of clubs, notably *Pacha* (see p.540). Its main competition is the *Hard Rock Café*, just round the corner from the main strip. Other worthwhile clubs include the *Black House Disco* at the *Rosetta*, and the *Cactus* at the *Jolie Ville*.

For a more Egyptian evening, the entire length of King of Bahrain Street is lined with **coffee shops** offering *sheeshas*. The top *sheesha* in town, however, can be had for £E10–20 at the outdoor café, the *Panorama,* with steps that climb up the hillside leading to private alcoves with tables, couches and great views. Most of the hotels offer Egyptian **floor shows**, but the best is at the *Tam Tam* restaurant, which holds an oriental dinner show featuring a lively team of dancers and musicians (Wed, Fri & Sun 7.30pm; £E148 including a full meal).

Na'ama Bay also has several **casinos**, including the *Casino Royale* at the *Jolie Ville*, and the Sinai Grand Casino at the *Sonesta*; take your passport.

Bars and clubs

Camel Dive Bar *Camel Dive Club*. A favourite starting point for the evening is this friendly affair, shaded by an awning. It's a good place to swap dive stories, watch a sports event on TV or listen to a DJ set.

Hard Rock Cafe Just around the corner from the main strip Ⓦ www.hardrock.com. An unmissable giant guitar marks the entrance to this restaurant, bar and club, which is unfeasibly popular, particularly with Europeans.

Little Buddha King of Bahrain St, Ⓦ www.littlebuddah-sharm.com. An offshoot of Paris's famous *Buddha Bar*, this slick lounge has low seats and equally low lighting, incense burning and a cutting-edge sound system. There's an enormous circular bar and dancefloor surrounding a downstairs dining area where Asian fusion food is served; a giant Buddha presides over the two storeys. Daily 1pm–3.30am.

Mexican Bar Next to the *Na'ama Inn*, under the cliff at the end of the main strip. A British hangout, with a giant statue of a Mexican man on the roof. Resident DJ from midnight. Daily 1pm–3am.

Pacha Ⓦ www.pachasharm.com and *Bus Stop* Both at the *Sanafir* hotel. Both venues feature swimming pools, foam parties, international DJs, regular Ministry of Sound and HedKandi nights, and podiums supporting professional dancers. Entry fees vary depending on the event, but expect to pay £E150–200. On Fridays, they also run *Echo Temple*, a desert venue at the foot of the Sinai mountains accommodating up to eight thousand people.

Pirates Bar In the *Hilton Fayrouz Resort*. A nautically themed venue popular with the expat dive crowd, and serves food. Happy hour 5.30–7.30pm.

Tavern Pub In a small mall behind the Na'ama Centre. One of the main hangouts for British divers, this starts out as a bar-restaurant (dishes include cottage pie and bacon butties) and later turns into a disco. There's karaoke every Thurs and Sat.

Listings

Banks and exchange Most hotels in Na'ama have banks (typically daily 8.30am–2pm & 6–9pm) or ATMs. The National Bank of Egypt has branches in the *Jolie Ville* and *Hilton*. You can get cash advances on Visa and MasterCard at Banque Misr (9am–1.30pm & 5–8pm) in the Sharm Mall. For changing cash, Swiss Exchange in Morgana Mall (daily 9am–midnight) may offer slightly better rates than the banks.

Books and newspapers Virgin Megastore at Il Mercato (see p.532) has the best selection of English-language books. Al Ahram Bookshop in Na'ama has a much smaller range (mainly Naguib Mahfouz and Agatha Christie titles). Vendors pushing carts along the beachfront and around town sell international magazines and newspapers.

Dentist Dr Hassan El Sharkawy, Sharm Dental Centre, Mall 8 Ⓣ 012 332-4160.

Doctor Dr Wael Habib, at the Mount Sinai Clinic in the *Jolie Ville* Ⓣ 069/360-0100. For diving emergencies, see p.533.

Hospitals The nearest hospitals are in Sharm El-Sheikh (see p.532).

Internet access Internet charges in Na'ama Bay are much higher than the rest of Egypt, at around £E30 per hour. There are cyber cafés every few metres around King of Bahrain Street.

Pharmacy Towa, in the Sharm Mall (daily 10am–1am; Ⓣ 069/360-0779), offers free home delivery. Another is Na'ama Bay Pharmacy (Ⓣ 069/366-0338). The best-stocked pharmacy is next to the hospital in Hay el-Nur.

Telephones If you don't fancy calling from a card phone, you can make calls from Sharm No. 2, opposite the entrance to the *Sheraton*, about 1km north of Na'ama Bay (daily 10am–10pm). Skype, offered at most internet cafés, is a much cheaper option.

Travel agents Thomas Cook, Gafy Mall (daily 9am–2pm & 6–8pm; Ⓣ 069/360-1809), offers the usual range of travel services, plus Visa cash advances. Mena Tours at the *Marriott*

(Ⓣ069/360-0190, Ⓦwww.menatours.com.eg) can organize tours and book tickets for the Hurghada catamaran.

Western Union At the DHL office in the *Rosetta* (Mon–Thurs & Sun 9am–9pm; Ⓣ&Ⓕ069/360-2222).

Shark Bay

Ten kilometres up the coast from Na'ama, **SHARK BAY** has been overwhelmed by numerous large holiday villages, and several others are on the way. But that hasn't deterred its many visitors, particularly the scores of daytrippers from Na'ama. Despite the bay's forbidding name (Beit el-Irsh, "House of the Shark" in Arabic), all the sharks have been scared away by divers, leaving a benign array of tropical fish and coral gardens just offshore, with deeper reefs and bigger fish further out. There's a £E10 charge to use the beach.

You can **stay** here at *Shark's Bay Umbi Diving & Camp* (Ⓣ069/360-0942, Ⓦwww.sharksbay.net; ❸–❹), a pleasant mix of bungalows, cabins and bamboo beach huts, some with a/c and en-suite bathrooms. It has its own private beach, jetty and a **dive centre** that runs boat trips to the Tiran Strait (day-dive €30–40; liveaboards €90 per day), while Bedouins who hang out there can arrange jeep safaris into the interior. Its restaurant and Bedouin café are quiet nightspots that close around midnight.

For a change of scene, head to the new Soho Square development (Ⓦwww.soho-sharm.com), near White Knights beach, between the *Savoy* and *Sierra* hotels, which has several restaurants (including the pricey but very good *L'Entrecote Steak House*), *Pangaea* nightclub, bowling alley, ice rink and (Africa's first) ice bar. The ten-minute taxi ride from Na'ama costs £E25–30.

The Tiran Strait and Nabeq

The headland of Ras Nasrani beyond Shark Bay marks the beginning of the **Tiran Strait**, where the waters of the Gulf of Suez flow into the deeper Gulf of Aqaba, swirling around islands and reefs. In 1992, the Tiran archipelago was declared a protected area, but there are no admission charges or facilities; the only access is by boat from Sharm el-Maya or Shark Bay. This is *not* an excursion for novice divers, as the sea can be extremely rough and chilling (bring high-calorie drinks and snacks to boost your energy).

Sharks, manta rays, barracuda and Napoleon fish are typical of the deepwater sites around the **islands of Tiran** and **Sanafir**, though there are also shallow reefs like the Small Lagoon and Hushasha. The multitude of **shipwrecks** in the Gulf is due to treacherous reefs and currents, insurance fraud, and Egypt's blockade of the strait in the 1960s. The **Jackson Reef** has a spectacular seventy-metre drop-off and the wreck of the *Lara* to investigate, while the **Gordon Reef** boasts the hulk of the *Lucila*. Two notable sites at **Ras Nasrani** are the **Light**, with a forty-metre drop-off and pelagic fish; and the **Point**, with a dazzling array of reef fish.

Nabeq

Beyond the mouth of the Gulf of Aqaba, a ninety-kilometre stretch of the coast as far north as Dahab City has been designated another protected area, named after the small oasis and **Bedouin village** of **NABEQ (or Nabq)**. As few dive boats come here from Na'ama, the **reefs** are quieter than at Tiran or Ras Mohammed, but anyone considering staying in Nabeq should bear in mind that it is much windier here than in Na'ama, that transport connections are limited to shuttle buses and that the beaches can be poor. Most visitors are on half-day trips to see Nabeq's mangrove forests – the most northerly in the world. **Mangroves** can filter salt from sea water and thus survive in tropical coastal areas. As sediment traps, they reduce erosion and provide a habitat for mating fish and migratory birds (in summer and autumn), acting as the ecological interface between the coast and the interior, whose flood-prone wadis sustain ibex, hyrax, foxes and other **wildlife**.

All approaches to Nabeq are best made by someone who knows the way; wander off the track and you might inadvertently encounter **mines** left over from Israeli-Egyptian wars, which killed a jeepload of tourists in 1995. Admission to the protected area costs €5; the only facilities are a **cafeteria** and visitors' centre (daily 8am–5pm).

One of the best of Nabeq's beachfront **hotels** is the *Radisson Blu* (Ⓣ069/371-0315, Ⓦwww.radissonblu.com; ❼), a luxurious resort 17km north of Na'ama, with six restaurants, three pools and a spa centre. Even better is the beautiful *Nubian Village* next door (Ⓣ069/371-0200, Ⓔnubian@link.net; full board ❼), designed to resemble a Nubian settlement, though it also has two pools, a nightclub, a spacious beach and a dive centre. Popular with Italians, it operates free shuttles to Na'ama.

Dahab and Asilah

Jagged mountains ranged inland of Na'ama Bay accompany the road 95km northwards, providing a magnificent backdrop for **Dahab**'s tawny beaches, from which its Arabic name – "gold" – derives. The resort divides into two localities: a cluster of holiday villages catering for affluent visitors, and the Bedouin settlement of **Asilah** 2.5km up the coast, where younger and independent travellers hang out in a kind of "Goa by the Red Sea" – though as Asilah moves upmarket, the distinction between them is blurring. In recent years aquatic pursuits have begun to be taken as seriously in Dahab as in Na'ama, and a third area north of Asilah, near the dive sites of the Canyon and Blue Hole, is tipped for development should tourist numbers rebound after the recent economic downturn.

Like Sharm and Taba before, Dahab's relaxed ambience was shattered when three **bombs** went off in Asilah at 7.30pm on April 24, 2006. They destroyed several restaurants, shops and a supermarket, and killed 23 people, with 60 injured. A month later a man wanted in connection with the bombings was shot dead in El-Arish. Today there is a noticeable **security presence**, with plain-clothes policemen and sniffer dogs. Whether you are on public or private transport, note that you will probably be asked to show your **passport** at checkpoints on leaving or entering Dahab.

Dahab City

Don't be discouraged by **DAHAB CITY**, the colony of municipal housing and government offices next to the holiday villages. The only reason to go there is to use its facilities: **petrol stations**, a **post office** and 24-hour **telephone exchange** (international calls with phonecards); a **supermarket** (daily 8am–10pm); and a **bank** with an ATM (Mon–Thurs & Sun 8.30am–2pm & 5–8pm, Sat 9am–2pm). The nearby *Swiss Inn Resort* has a bank that opens on Fridays (9am–noon & 6–9pm). The **tourist police** (Ⓣ069/364-0188) are located opposite the *Accor Coralia*, while the **hospital** (Ⓣ069/364-6208) is to the southeast of the bus station.

Most budget travellers arrive at Dahab City's East Delta **bus station** and then head straight onto Asilah; every bus is met by **taxis** and **pick-ups** charging £E5–10

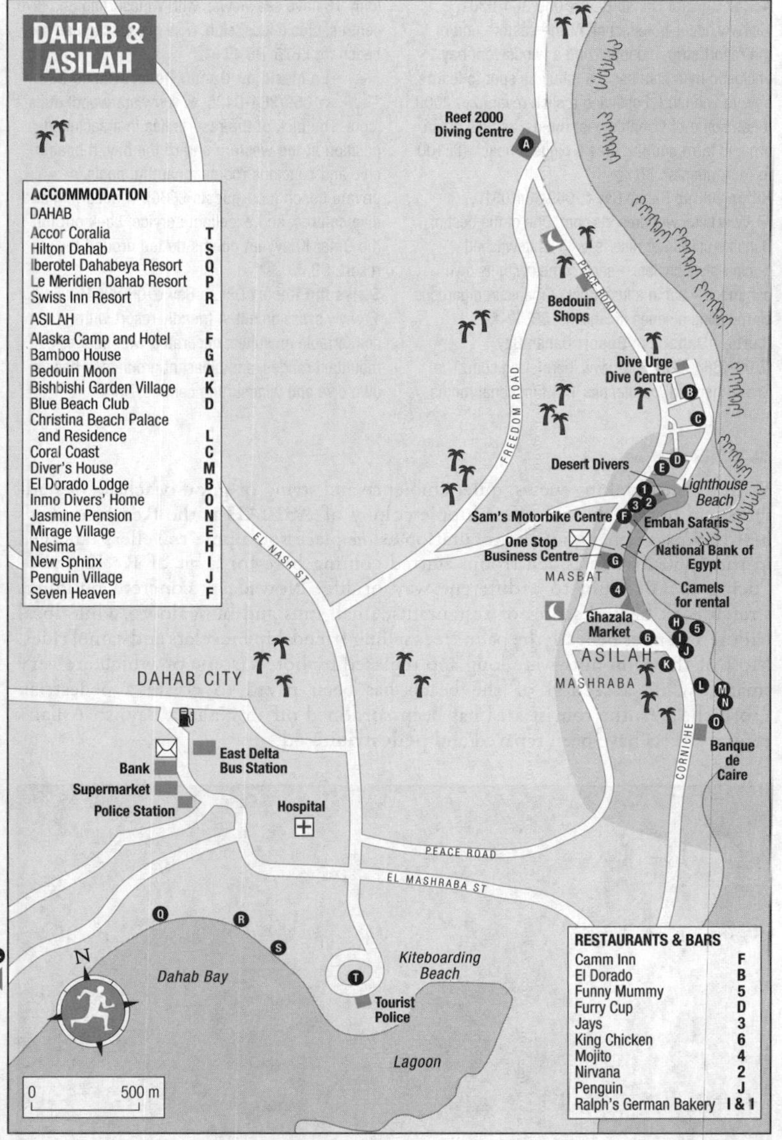

for a lift to Asilah, though you'll have to bargain. Few places are more than ten minutes' walk from the taxi drop-off point near the bridge in central Asilah.

Accommodation

The **holiday villages** around Dahab Bay are self-contained, with private beaches and access to a coral reef on the headland. They all arrange **shuttles** for their guests directly from Sharm el-Sheik Airport for around €30 each way.

Accor Coralia Dahab Bay ⓣ069/364-0301, ⓦwww.accor-hotels.com. At the eastern end of the resort strip, monopolizing a windswept bay enclosed by a sandbar – a fabulous spot to learn how to windsurf. Following a slick revamp in 2009, it has some of Dahab's best rooms, as well as an organic farm and the area's biggest beach (£E100 for non-guests). BB ❼

Hilton Dahab Dahab Bay ⓣ069/364-0310, ⓦwww.hiltonworldresorts.com. One of the best of Dahab's upmarket resorts, with whitewashed Nubian-style chalets – each comes with its own hammock – set in a lush tract of manicured gardens surrounding a series of lagoons. BB ❻–❼

Iberotel Dahabeya Resort Dahab Bay ⓣ069/364-1264, ⓦwww.iberotel-eg.com. The Greek-inspired *Iberotel* has 144 functional rooms (only 18 have sea views), with windsurfing and dive centres, plus a kids' club. Non-guests can use the beach for £E75. BB ❻–❼

Le Meridien Dahab Resort Dahab Bay ⓣ069/364-0425, ⓦwww.starwoodhotels.com. The pick of the resorts lies in a secluded position at the western end of the bay. It boasts chic and spacious rooms, beautiful pools, a private beach (non-guests £E80), windsurfing and dive centres, and excellent service. Look out for the Omar Khayyam poems dotted around the resort. BB ❼–❽

Swiss Inn Resort Dahab Bay ⓣ069/364-0054, ⓦwww.swissinn.net. A friendly resort with comfortable en suites, decorated with images of mountain ranges, and pleasant grounds. It has its own dive and windsurfing centres. BB ❼

Asilah

With its breathtaking views, quiet ambience and string of good beachside restaurants and hotels, the gentrified hippie colony of **ASILAH** is the Red Sea coast's best backpacker hangout. Its reputation as *the* place for hippie travellers emerged in the 1960s, when Israeli troops started coming here for a bit of R&R, introducing the Bedouin to a different way of life. Nowadays, concrete buildings stretch back behind scores of restaurants, small inns and bungalows, while local children wander beneath the palm trees selling friendship bracelets and camel rides. Most of the palm huts were long ago replaced by hotels (some of which are very smart), while a section of the beach has been paved to create a pedestrian "corniche". As the tourist area has been cordoned off in Na'ama Bay, so Asilah's central streets have been repaved and **pedestrianized**.

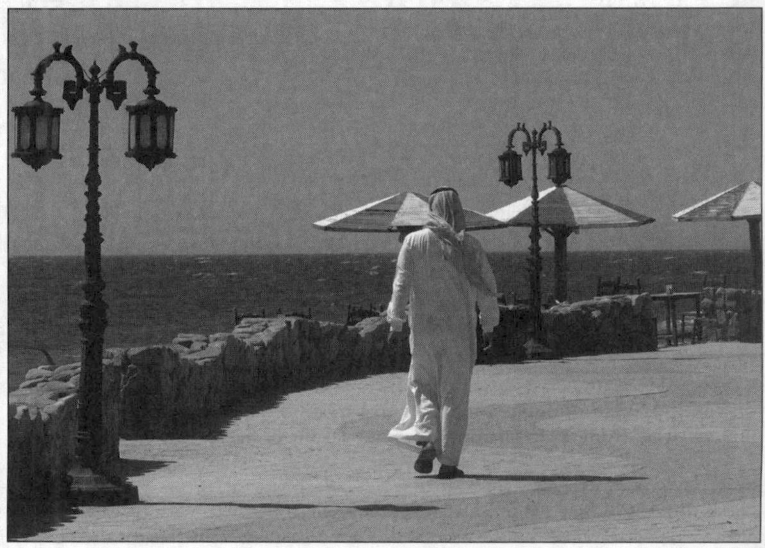

▲ Strolling on the Corniche, Asilah

Such is the lure of Asilah that visitors often stay longer than they'd expected, getting stuck in a daily routine of café life, or if they are more active, working at one of the dive centres. Given Asilah's reputation, it's important to stress the limitations on pure hedonism. Women can generally sunbathe here without any hassle, but **going topless** violates Egyptian law, and there are periodic crackdowns on **dope**. Finally, stick to bottled water to avoid the risk of **hepatitis** from contaminated cisterns; a dozen or so cases of infection occur every year.

Arrival and information

Arriving in Asilah, you'll be dropped at the parking lot in front of the **bridge** that divides **Masbat** to the north from **Mashraba** to the south. Both neighbourhoods extend for about a kilometre in each direction, strung out with restaurants and hotels along a pedestrian walkway, before petering out into the dust. **Lighthouse Beach**, at Masbat's northern headland, is the usual first stop for sunbathers and snorkellers (though don't expect a huge sandy expanse, for that you'll have to head down to Dahab Bay). The bridge itself has been rebuilt (it was the location of one of the bombs) and beneath it a tiled paddling pool has been laid out. **Bikes** can be rented from most of the dive centres (around £E10 per hour, £E40 per day).

There are a number of internet cafés (charging £E5-6/hr) up and down the walkway, some doubling as secondhand bookshops where for a small fee you can also swap books. Most usually have telephone (and Skype facilities), fax and photocopying facilities too. You can buy foreign newspapers and magazines from the vendor who sets up outside the centrally located Ghazala Market (rebuilt after one of the bombs went off outside) in the evenings. There are several ATMs, including one by Desert Divers and another outside Ghazala Market. Near *Christina Beach Palace* is a Banque du Caire (daily 9am–12.30pm & 6–9pm), which also has an ATM. The One Stop Business Centre at Bamboo House has safety deposit boxes, and you can buy stamps and post letters a couple of doors along at the shop close by simply called Post.

Accommodation

Asilah's accommodation ranges from simple, budget **campgrounds**, with basic concrete cells, and showers, sinks and toilets in the yard, to **hotels** with classy en suites, sea views and a/c. Factors to consider when choosing a campground are whether and when they have hot showers, how they're rigged up to deal with mosquitoes, and noise levels (especially anywhere near the main strip at Masbat).

Alaska Camp and Hotel Masbat ⓣ069/364-1004, ⓦwww.dahabescape.com. Extremely welcoming low-cost hotel with a relaxed vibe, Bedouin tent-style communal area and simple but super-clean rooms with private baths; the more expensive ones also have a/c and their own balconies. ❷–❸

Bamboo House Masbat ⓣ069/364-0263, ⓦwww.bamboohouse-dahab.com. A hotel with neat, modern a/c rooms with TV (though you'll have to pay more for one with sea views) and home to a popular café-bar. BB ❹

Bedouin Moon Hotel 3km north of Masbat ⓣ069/364-0695, ⓦwww.reef2000.com. Domed Arabic-style buildings with a choice of a/c and fan rooms – all are good, but some have been renovated, so ask to see a few. There's a pool and regular yoga sessions. Attached to the Reef 2000 dive club. ❸

Bishbishi Garden Village Mashraba ⓣ069/364-0727, ⓦwww.bishbishi.com. Operated by the indefatigable Jimmy, this popular backpacker hangout has a range of rooms from basic cells to a/c rooms with private bath. It's a good place to meet other travellers and organize a desert trek. ❶–❸

Blue Beach Club 200m north of Lighthouse Beach ⓣ069/364-0411, ⓦwww.bluebeachclub.com. Good-sized, stylish en suites with tiled floors and partial sea views, as well as a pool and beach area. Yoga, massage and horse-riding are all on offer, as is the opportunity for heavy drinking at the *Furry Cup* bar (see p.547). ❹

Christina Beach Palace and Residence Mashraba ⓣ069/364-0390, ⓦwww.christinahotels.com. A sophisticated hotel in two parts, one on the beach and another, less expensive older building on the main road. Both premises have very tasteful en suites in whitewashed blocks with domed ceilings. There's a good pool, but you pay extra for a/c. Service is excellent. *Christina Beach Palace* BB ⑤ *Christina Residence*, ④

Coral Coast 300m north of Lighthouse Beach ⓣ069/364-1195, ⓦwww.fantasearedsea.com. Away from the hustle of Masbat, this sizeable concrete hotel has a good selection of a/c en suites – all have balconies or terraces, but you have to pay more for ones with kettle, fridge and sea views. There's a small pool and a branch of Fantasea Divers. ④–⑤

Diver's House Tucked away in the south of Mashraba ⓣ069/364-0451, ⓦwww.divershouse.com. Rambling hotel with a variety of quirky rooms: the cabin-like room with huge domed ceiling or the a/c en suite with sea views are the ones to go for. Those at the back are best avoided. ②–③

El Dorado Lodge 350m north of Lighthouse Beach ⓣ069/364-1027, ⓦwww.eldoradodahab.com. Italian-run hotel with immaculate, recently refurbished a/c cabins, free from clutter; some also have toilet and shower. Own dive centre and an excellent restaurant (see below). ④–⑤

Inmo Divers' Home Mashraba ⓣ069/364-0370, ⓦwww.inmodivers.de. Run by a German-Egyptian couple, Inmo has simple rooms with shared baths aimed at backpackers and more comfortable a/c en suites with balconies and sea views. There are attractive bamboo walkways and communal areas, a pool, playground and dive centre. Arabic lessons available. ③–④

Jasmine Pension On the beach next to *Diver's House* ⓣ069/364-0852, ⓦwww.jasminepension.com. Small budget hotel right on the Corniche with a handful of tidy rooms – either a/c or fan – and a beachside café. ①–③

Mirage Village Near Lighthouse Beach ⓣ069/364-0341, ⓦwww.mirage.com.eg. Tucked away behind a walled compound, this has straightforward rooms with private bath set around a courtyard and a small private beach area. It's mosquito-free due to its windy position. The laid-back management organize regular fish barbecues. Rates are negotiable. ④

Nesima Mashraba ⓣ069/364-0320, ⓦwww.nesima-resort.com. Arguably the most beautiful hotel in Asilah, with a great pool and flower-filled pathways. The domed a/c rooms, though attractively furnished, are a little small and staff could be more welcoming. Massage (£E200/hr) options are on offer. ⑥

New Sphinx Mashraba ⓣ069/364-0032, ⓦwww.sphinx-hotels-dive.com. The rooms aren't as dramatic as the wonderfully over-the-top sphinx-shaped entrance, but have a touch of class with wrought-iron furnishings, a/c, private bath and TVs. There's a decent pool and a great restaurant, the *Funny Mummy*, right on the waterfront. BB ④

Penguin Village Mashraba ⓣ069/364-1047, ⓦwww.penguindahab.com. A popular backpacker haunt offering simple rooms with fan and shared or private bath, as well as a few smarter a/c en suites with sea views. Lots of activities, trips and inexpensive ways to pass the time on offer. ①–③

Seven Heaven Masbat ⓣ069/364-0080, ⓦwww.7heavenhotel.com. Economical option in a central location, between the bridge and Lighthouse Beach, drawing a regular stream of travellers, especially divers. The basic rooms are pretty worn, but clean and acceptable for a night or two. ①–②

Eating

A score of **restaurants** by the beach vie for customers. House, trance and chill-out music fills the air; floor cushions and posters reflect the mix of Bedouin and hippie influences. Cold drinks are always available, though not all places have alcohol licences, and you can sit around for hours without being required to eat.

Unless you splash out on lobster, you can eat quite well in Asilah for £E50–70 a meal, including drinks and dessert. Most places are open until midnight or later, though the choice of food diminishes after 9pm. There are also numerous **supermarkets** (generally daily 7.30am–midnight, though the Ghazala Market is open 24hr), **fruit stalls** and *taamiya* stands.

Camm Inn Masbat. The cane furniture and overgrown plants give this place the feel of a safari lodge, and its global menu demonstrates a touch more imagination than most, with the Malaysian dishes particular highlights. Mains £E20–70.

El Dorado 350m north of Lighthouse Beach. The best of Dahab's Italian restaurants, offering home-made thin-crust pizzas and delectable desserts like *affogato* and tiramisu ice cream. Mains £E40–75.

Funny Mummy Corniche. A traveller favourite with an attractive roof terrace festooned with twinkly lights, a large cushion- and low table-strewn area below, a wide-ranging food and drinks menu and sheesha pipes. Mains £E30–70.

Jays Masbat. Run by an Englishwoman, *Jays* is popular both for its menu – which includes Italian dishes, sandwiches, steaks and seafood, plus specials like banoffee pie – and its "no hassle policy", which means you won't be bothered by touts every time you walk by. Mains £E20–60.

King Chicken Mashraba. A modest eatery that's always busy with both locals and frugal travellers – you can get a chicken quarter, rice, salad, soup, bread and hummus for just £E15.

Nirvana Near Lighthouse Beach. A quality Indian restaurant with authentic curries, great nans and rotis, and plenty of vegetarian options. Mains £E20–50.

Penguin Corniche. Next door to *Funny Mummy*, the very similar – and equally popular – *Penguin* has a laid-back vibe, tasty food and great milkshakes. Mains £E30–70.

Ralph's German Bakery Mashraba. All manner of strudels, cakes, pastries, sandwiches and proper Lavazza coffee are on offer at this café, which has a second takeaway-only branch near Lighthouse Beach. Cakes £E10–20.

Drinking and nightlife

Unsurprisingly, **nightlife** centres on those hotels and restaurants serving alcohol. Both *Nesima* and the *New Sphinx* have popular bars, and *Funny Mummy* and *Penguin* are also hot spots. The main place for the diving set is the *Furry Cup* bar at the *Blue Beach Club* (happy hour 5–7pm); on Thurs there's an all-you-can-eat barbecue (£E50). *Mojito*, in Masbat, has good cocktails (£E30–40), movie nights, quizzes and salsa classes, plus DJs and live bands playing anything from jazz to hip hop. Women will feel comfortable here too. The nearby *Tota* bar – recognisable by its huge ship façade – was up for sale at the time of writing, but if it reopens it is likely to be worth a look too.

Diving, snorkelling and windsurfing

Shore diving is the norm in Dahab, with the reefs along the coast reached by pick-ups. The nicest reefs are to the north of Dahab Bay just past the lagoon; at Asilah the reefs are meagre, except for the area around the lighthouse, and much of the seabed is covered in rubbish. Experienced divers should look out for occasional free "trash dives", organized to clear the rubbish, mostly plastic bags blown into the sea, which sea turtles can mistake for jellyfish and choke on.

Most divers head 8km up the coast where you can find the Eel Garden, Canyon and Blue Hole dive sites, trips to which are arranged by most dive centres. The **Canyon** is a dark, narrow fissure that you reach from the shore by swimming along the reef and then diving to the edge of a coral wall. It can be frightening for inexperienced divers, as it sinks to a depth of 50m, but there's plenty to see at the top of the reef. Further north lies the notorious **Blue Hole**, which has claimed several lives (usually experienced divers who dive too deep for too long). This spectacular shaft in the reef plunges to 80m; the challenge involves descending 60m and swimming through a transverse passage to come up the other side. Divers who ascend too fast risk getting "bent"; inexperienced divers should not attempt this dive under any circumstances. Fortunately, the Hole can be enjoyed in safety by staying closer to the surface and working your way round to a dip in the reef known as the Bridge, which swarms with colourful fish and can even be viewed using snorkelling gear.

The main destination for day-long **dive safaris** is the Ras Abu Galum protected area, a thirty-kilometre stretch of coast with three diving beaches, accessible by jeep or camel (see p.549). **Naqb Shahin** is the closest to Dahab of the three, and has fantastic coral and gold fish, but the sea is very turbulent, so many divers prefer **Ras Abu Galum** or **Ras el-Mamleh**, further north. All three sites have deep virgin reefs with a rich variety of corals and fish. Sinai Divers offer an introductory beach dive for €35. Desert Divers do a one-day, two-dive trip by camel to Ras Abu Galum for €90. Fantasea runs trips to the *Thistlegorm* (see p.526) for €143.

While renting equipment is costlier here than in Na'ama, **diving courses** are generally cheaper. Competition means cut-price deals, especially when business is quiet, but you should keep a sense of perspective – the rockbottom outlets are unlikely to be rigorous about your safety. Stick to the long-established centres like Fantasea, Sinai Divers, Club Red and Desert Divers (the latter charges €270 for an open-water PADI course).

Dive centres

Club Red *Mohammed Aly Camp* ⓣ069/364-0380. ⓦwww.club-red.com. PADI.

Dahab Divers Lighthouse Beach ⓣ069/364-0381, ⓦwww.dahabdivers.com. PADI.

Desert Divers Masbat ⓣ069/364-0500, ⓦwww.desert-divers.com. PADI courses; also organizes desert or snorkelling safaris, yoga sessions in Ras Abu Galum and rock climbing.

Dive Urge Masbat ⓣ069/364-0957, ⓦwww.dive-urge.com. PADI.

Fantasea *Coral Coast Hotel* ⓣ069/364-1373, ⓦwww.fantaseadiving.net. PADI, SSI.

INMO Mashraba ⓣ069/364-0370, ⓦwww.inmodivers.de. PADI.

Mirage Divers *Mirage Village* ⓣ069/364-0341, ⓦwww.miragedivers.com. PADI.

Nesima Dive Centre *Nesima Hotel* ⓣ069/364-0320, ⓦwww.nesima-resort.com. PADI, BSAC.

Nirvana Dive Centre Near Lighthouse Beach ⓣ069/364-1261, ⓦwww.nirvanadivers.com. PADI, BSAC.

Planet Divers *Planet Oasis Hotel*, near Lighthouse Beach ⓣ069/364-1090, ⓦwww.planetdivers.com. PADI, CMAS, IANTD.

Red Sea Relax *Neptune Hotel*, just south of the footbridge between Mashbat and Mashraba ⓣ069/364-1309, ⓦwww.red-sea-relax.com. CMAS, SSI, PDIC.

Reef 2000 *Bedouin Moon Hotel* ⓣ069/364-0087, ⓦwww.reef2000.com. SSI.

Sinai Dive Club *Accor Coralia* ⓣ069/364-0465. PADI.

Sinai Divers *Hilton Dahab* ⓣ069/364-0100, ⓦwww.sinaidivers.com. PADI, CMAS, SSI

Sinai Divers Backpackers *Masbat* ⓣ069/364-1966, ⓦwww.sinaidivers.com. PADI.

Sub Sinai Mashraba ⓣ069/364-1317, ⓦwww.subsinai.com. PADI.

Free diving and snorkelling

Expert training in free diving – which is done on a single deep breath, without the aid of scuba gear – is available from Lotta Ericson of Freedive Dahab (ⓣ010 545-9916, ⓦwww.freedivedahab.com), who offers courses of one to three days' duration (€75 for a one-day session), the longest of which includes a trip to the Blue Hole. Most participants find they can hold their breath for up to four minutes after three days of training, enabling them to dive to 15m or deeper. As for **snorkelling**, for a more ambitious jaunt than just wading out from the shore, arrange an excursion to the Blue Hole (€10-15 for a half-day), which can be done through a number of operators, including Desert Divers.

Windsurfing

The wind blows at least two hundred days each year at Dahab, making it a haven for windsurfers and kiteboarders. Both the *Hilton* and the *Swiss Inn* have windsurfing centres and rent boards for about €17/$22 per hour. Kiteboarding is also popular and equipment can be rented from a Russian outfit, Go Dahab (ⓣ012 756-8358, ⓦwww.go-dahab.ru), at the lagoon near the *Iberotel Dahabeya Resort*. One-day introductory courses cost around $200, while equipment can be rented by experienced kitesurfers for around $60 for half a day.

Riding and safaris

If you fancy **riding** on the beach at Asilah, look out for the boys who rent out horses or camels (around £E50 per hour); they hang out by the restaurants on the beach near the palm trees in Masbat. Alternatively, the *Blue Beach Club* offers more organised rides down the beach for £E100 per hour; you can also do overnight trips into the desert and the mountains.

A more exciting option is to sign up for trips into the rugged interior, which can be organized at most campgrounds, through safari agencies, or by negotiating directly with guides. Itineraries and prices can vary widely so shop around. Some outfits, including Desert Divers, also organize rock-climbing trips (€45 for one day). Embah Safari near Lighthouse Beach (Ⓣ069/364-1690, Ⓦwww.embah.com) offers diving, camel or jeep safaris for around €40 per person per day, as well as excursions to St. Catherine's and the Coloured Canyon (around €30), and trips further afield to Petra in Jordan (€195 overnight) and Cairo (€100 overnight). Several companies, including Sam's Motorbike Centre to the north of the bridge and New Sphinx Safari, offer quad bike tours (£E180 for a 2hr trip) into the desert, and longer trips that including snorkelling at various spots along the coast. You can also hire motorbikes (around £E250 per day) from most of these places.

Ras Abu Galum

The coast between Dahab and Nuweiba is hidden from view as the road veers inland, but this remote area, the **Ras Abu Galum** Protectorate, harbours some of Sinai's richest wildlife. Access is limited to a coastal track (walking or camel only) from Dahab or an unpaved road (4WD) that branches off from the main road 20km short of Nuweiba. There are a couple of modest shops and restaurants, but it's wise to bring food and water if you plan on staying awhile. It is possible to walk from Dahab (Ras Abu Galum is approximately two hours from the Blue Hole) or you can rent a 4WD pick-up truck (around £E40). Some of the tour operators stop here on the way to the Blue Hole, but for more in-depth exploration, the eco-tourism outfit Centre for Sinai (Ⓣ010 666-0835, Ⓦwww.centre4sinai.com.eg), can introduce you to a Bedouin guide who organizes trips by jeep or camel.

Moving on from Dahab and Asilah

Buses leave from Dahab City's East Delta bus station (Ⓣ069/364-1808). There are around thirteen daily buses to **Sharm** (1hr 30min), and five to **Cairo** (7–8hr). Two daily buses (10am and 8.30pm) go to **Zagazig** (6–7hr) and **Ismailiya** (7–8hr). There are daily buses to **Nuweiba** at 10.30am, 4.30pm and 6.30pm (1hr–1hr 30min); the 10.30am bus continues on to Taba (3hr). Bus timetables are prone to change, so ask around for the latest information. There are no longer any direct buses to **St Catherine's**; see p.559 for details on how to get there. Shared taxis can be booked in advance at any of the safari agencies and at most camps and hotels; it's worth asking around, as prices can vary for the same trip.

Nuweiba and Tarabeen

Beautiful but desolate **NUWEIBA** is another resort on the Gulf of Aqaba, consisting of a **port** with nearby tourist complexes, followed 4km up the coast by **Nuweiba "City"**, an administrative and commercial centre grafted on to a former Israeli *moshav* (co-operative village). During the late 1970s, thousands of Israeli and Western backpackers flocked here to party and sleep on the beach – a heyday remembered fondly by shop and campground owners. Today tourism is at a virtual standstill and much of the year the campgrounds lie dormant. The beach is beautiful, but – with the exception of a few patches of privately-owned sand – covered with rubbish. For most travellers, Nuweiba serves primarily as a stepping stone for onward travel by bus to Eilat in Israel or by boat to Aqaba in Jordan. Nuweiba's neighbouring Bedouin settlement is called **TARABEEN**, after the local Bedouin tribe, and tends to attract younger travellers. Once there were more than twenty campgrounds and a numerous hotels on its wide and sandy beach, buzzing with restaurants and tourist bazaars; now the place is eerily empty, with only a few

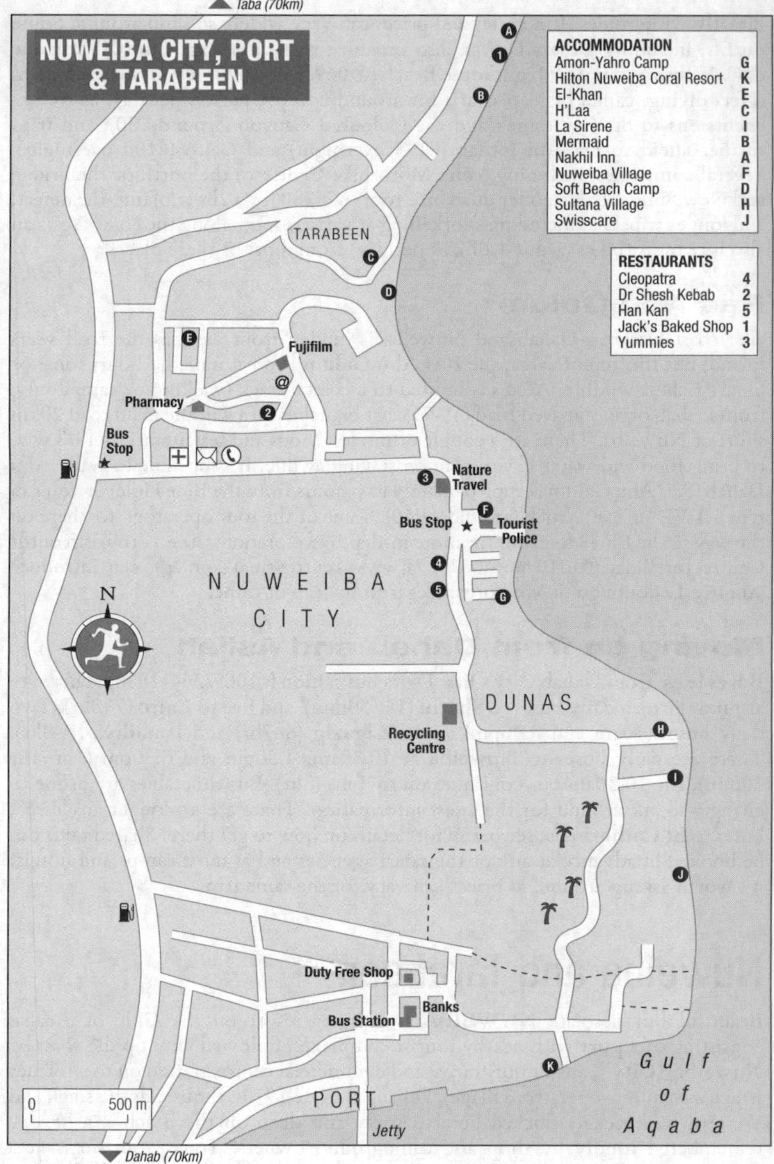

camps still functioning, though there are tentative signs that some travellers are starting to return.

Arrival and accommodation

Nuweiba's main **bus station** is at the port, though the Taba bus also stops on the highway close to Nuweiba City. **Taxis** charge £E15–20 from the port to Tarabeen, and £E5–10 from Nuweiba City to Tarabeen. You can walk from Nuweiba City to Tarabeen in twenty minutes along the beach; it takes slightly longer by road.

Accommodation is concentrated in three main locations: near the port, in Dunas along the beach south of Nuweiba City, and in Tarabeen, a couple of kilometres north. Tarabeen is the place to find cheap **campgrounds** (£E40–100), though these tend to come and go. Hotels generally include breakfast in the rate, but the campgrounds don't.

Amon-Yahro Camp The closest camp in Nuweiba to Dunas ⓣ069/350-0555, ⓦwww.amonyahro.net. The cheapest digs around are to be found at this tidy camp, right on the beach, which has wooden huts with mattresses (and nothing else) and clean shared facilities. It's run by Egyptologist Murad el Sayed, who takes visitors on reliable and informative trips into the desert. ❶

Hilton Nuweiba Coral Resort East of the port ⓣ069/352-0320, ⓦwww.hiltonworldresorts.com. Luxury holiday village with smart en suites, two heated pools, lots of sports facilities, including a dive centre, and a private beach. ❼

El-Khan East of the road between Nuweiba City and Tarabeen ⓣ069/350-0316, ⓔanis@sinai4you.com. Basic Bedouin-style camp offering simple low-cost accommodation and a restaurant. Though not on the beach, it is handy for late-night bus arrivals and can arrange camel and jeep safaris, and meditation retreats. ❷–❸

H'Laa Central Tarabeen ⓣ069/350-0679. Decent camp offering marine-coloured rooms with a/c, TV and – bizarrely – Disney rugs; it's somewhat nicer than what's on offer in neighbouring camps. Breakfast included. ❸

La Sirene Between Nuweiba City and the port ⓣ&ⓕ069/350-0701. On a lovely stretch of beach, but with the feel of a desert camp, *La Sirene* has sandy, off-white buildings bisected by stone walls containing a/c rooms with private bath, TV and colourful rugs. There's table tennis, billiards and table football facilities, plus a dive centre. ❹

Mermaid North Tarabeen ⓣ069/350-0871, ⓦwww.redsea-mermaid.com. A welcoming lodge with simple, good value en-suite rooms on a quiet stretch of private beach. The focal point is the restaurant, which serves a tasty mix of pastas, seafood and grills. Popular with Egyptian tourists. ❷–❹

Nakhil Inn North Tarabeen ⓣ069/350-0879, ⓦwww.nakhil-inn.com. Well-run, friendly camp with its own reef, private beach, dive centre and plenty of activities on offer. Choose between spacious en suites with French windows and split-level chalet-style rooms; both types are a/c and have nice features like kettles and fridge.

Nuweiba Village In the centre of Nuweiba ⓣ069/350-0401-3, ⓦwww.nuweibavillageresort.com. Snug a/c bungalows with TV set around neatly-tended gardens, plus a (sporadically open) disco, dive centre, a spacious pool area and a private beach with a suitably laid-back bar. ❹

Soft Beach Camp At the southern end of Tarabeen's main street ⓣ010 364-7586, ⓦwww.softbeachcamp.com. More than forty classic Sinai beach shacks – very basic octagonal huts with mattresses on the floor – as well as internet access, book exchange, restaurant and backpacker vibe. ❹

Sultana Village 2.5 km south of the *Nuweiba Village* ⓣ069/350-0490, ⓦwww.sultanavillage.net. Rustic stone huts with low ceilings, private baths and a/c – atmospheric, though possibly a little claustrophobic if you're tall. One of the sets of better beach bungalows in Dunas. ❸–❹

Swisscare 3km south of *Nuweiba Village* ⓣ069/352-0640, ⓦwww.swisscare-hotels.com. A pleasant resort with whitewashed villas, pool, range of restaurants and massage facilities. All the rooms are "suites", featuring a separate seating area, balcony or terrace, private bath and a/c. There's also the opportunity for horse or camel riding. ❺

Diving and snorkelling

Diving in Nuweiba is mostly from the shore thanks to a lack of jetties or safe anchorages. There are several shallow **reefs** offshore, the best of which is the **Stone House**, beyond the southern promontory. Though fine for **snorkelling**, they're not so great for **diving** unless you're a novice, so the divers that come here usually travel to Ras Abu Galum (p.549) or sites north of Nuweiba (see p.554). These trips can be arranged by any of Nuweiba's **dive centres**: for example, Emperor Divers at the *Hilton Nuweiba Coral Resort* (ⓣ069/352-0320, ⓦwww.emperordivers.com; PADI) has a jeep dive trip to Ras Mamlach for €87. Other dive centres include Diving Camp Nuweiba at *Nuweiba Village*

(Ⓣ069/350-0401-3, Ⓦwww.nuweibavillageresort.com; PADI, CMAS) and Scuba Divers at *La Sirene* (Ⓣ069/350-0705, Ⓦwww.scuba-divers.de; SSI).

Jeep and camel safaris

Local Bedouin guides offer a wide range of **camel or jeep safaris** into the interior, and these can be booked through any hotel or camp. Their duration depends on your destination and mode of transport; it usually takes two or three times as long by camel as it does by jeep.

Jeep safaris cost around $25 per day, camel trips around $35; both should include meals and the cost of registering the trip with the police. Drinking water may cost extra and be more expensive the further you get from shops, so it's wise to bring plenty along.

The nearest destinations are the palmy oasis of **Ain el-Furtaga** (which can be reached by regular car) and the colourful sandstone canyon of **Wadi Huweiyit** (by camel or 4WD). Slightly further north lies **Moyat el-Wishwashi**, a large rainwater catchment cistern hidden in a canyon between imposing boulders. All these sites can be reached by camel in a day. One of the most popular day jeep excursions is to the **Coloured Canyon** via a trail from Ain el-Furtaga. Its name comes from the vivid striations on the steep walls of the canyon, which is sheltered from the wind and eerily silent. Having got there by 4WD, you can hike through the canyon in either direction. Other destinations include **Wadi Ghazala**, with its dunes and acacia groves where gazelles may be glimpsed; **Ain Um Ahmed**, whose deep torrent fed by snow on the highest peaks of the Sinai shrinks to a stream as the seasons advance; the oasis of **Ain Khudra**, supposedly the Biblical Hazeroth, where Miriam was stricken with leprosy for criticizing Moses; and the beautiful – and relatively undiscovered by tourists – **Rainbow Canyon**.

Recommended **guides** include Anis Anisan at *El Khan* camp, who can arrange trips for small or large groups and will try to include a Bedouin wedding, camel race or a full moon *zwara* (traditional Bedouin meeting). The all-night **Bedouin weddings** are worth seeing as they provide a rare opportunity for young Bedouin men and women to mingle. Also recommended is Morad Said at *Amon-Yahro Camp*, an English- and German-speaking Egyptologist with plenty of insight into the Bedouin life. The *Habiba* camp, next to the *Amon-Yahro Camp* runs a camel riding school (Ⓦwww.sinai4you.com/crs) which offers a three-day camel experience (including half-board) for €355, teaching you to ride a camel and also how to feed it, and imparting an insight into desert survival from the Bedouin.

Eating, drinking and nightlife

As an established backpacker hangout, Tarabeen is home to a number of **budget cafés**, whose menus feature dishes such as pizza, pasta and pancakes. Nuweiba City has less to offer, though its shops are good for self-caterers. **Nightlife** boils down to an occasional disco in the *Nuweiba Village* hotel, or playing guitars, drums or backgammon and getting stoned at Tarabeen. If you want a beer, try the bars in the more upmarket hotels.

Restaurants

Cleopatra Nuweiba City, 220m south of *Nuweiba Village*. Egyptian restaurant serving good seafood, pizzas, pastas, *mezzes* and chicken dishes from £E20. Outside there's a fountain strung with drying shark and crustaceans; inside it's a mix of Ancient Egypt and maritime kitsch.

Dr Shesh Kebab In Nuweiba City's bazaar. A budget traveller favourite serving falafel, baba ganoush, pizza, spaghetti and seafood, as well as – of course – excellent kebabs. Mains E£10–30. The gracious Dr Shesh Kebab, as the owner styles himself, is usually around in the evenings, when he's happy to talk to tourists, offer travel advice and put you in contact with guides for a desert safari.

Han Kan Nuweiba City, close to *Nuweiba Village*. This Chinese-Korean restaurant seems somewhat out-of-place, but nevertheless serves up excellent food. Mains £E20–40.

Jack's Baked Shop Tarabeen, near *Nakhil Inn*. The American couple who run this wonderfully chilled-out restaurant produce delicious home-made pizzas, banana bread, cheese- and chocolate cakes (around £E10–20) and refreshing smoothies. Hours can drift by as you lounge on cushions, with a book in hand, listening to rock 'n' roll tracks.

Yummies Nuweiba City, just northwest of *Nuweiba Village*. Run by an Englishwoman, this café is full of tastes of Albion: fish and chips, shepherds pie, macaroni cheese and trifles, plus tea, coffee and beer. Mains £E20-50.

Listings

Banks and exchange There's a bank in the *Nuweiba Village* (daily except Fri 9am–1pm & 6–9pm), at the *Hilton*, and several in the port area with ATMs.

Doctor There is a doctor on call at the *Nuweiba Village*. Nuweiba hospital is poorly equipped, so head for Sharm el-Sheikh if you're seriously ill (see p.532).

Internet cafés Almostakbal (£E5/hr) on the main street.

Pharmacy Gasser, near *Dr Shesh Kebab* (☎069/350-0605; daily 10am–10pm).

Police Near the Town Council ☎069/350-0304; the tourist police (☎069/350-0231) are just outside the *Nuweiba Village*; both open 24hr.

Post office In the centre two blocks east of the bus stop (daily except Fri 9am–2pm).

Travel agent Nature Travel (☎069/350-0391, www.naturetravelegypt.com), near the Nuweiba Village, runs half-day trips to the Coloured Canyon ($30) and a full day-trip to St Catherine's ($50). It also runs trips to Petra and can book catamaran tickets (see box below).

Boats to Aqaba in Jordan

From Nuweiba's port (☎069/352-0427) you can catch a **ferry** or the **high-speed catamaran to Aqaba** in Jordan. Tickets are sold inside the port's entrance; you'll need to show your passport to go through the gates, and once inside you're not allowed to leave. Foreigners are assigned an official to guide them through customs and immigration and onto the boat. The office stops selling tickets about one hour before the ferries are scheduled to depart, so turn up a couple of hours early whichever service you want to travel on. There is a departure tax of £E50. The **ferry** leaves daily at 11am and 5pm (extra trips are sometimes put on during busy periods such as the hajj season) and takes three to five hours, depending on the weather. Foreigners must buy a first-class **ticket** ($35 one-way, payable in dollars); children under 2 go free, under 5s pay a quarter of the full fare, and under 12s half. During Ramadan or the hajj season, it's a definite advantage to have access to the first-class lounge, as the boat is crowded with Egyptian workers returning home or pilgrims bound for Mecca. The ferry also carries **vehicles** ($100). Don't be surprised if it leaves much later than scheduled. On boarding you'll be asked to hand over your passport, which will be returned at Aqaba customs or, if you go searching for it, on the boat. Tickets for the **catamaran** cost $75 one-way and are well worth the extra expense as this vessel is much more comfortable than the ferry and only takes an hour to Aqaba, though it doesn't take cars. Sailings are at 2pm (daily except Sat). Formalities are identical to those for the ferry. For both services, get to the port at least two hours in advance. **Jordanian visas** (valid for one month) are issued on board both the ferry and catamaran, or immediately after disembarkation; British, Canadian, US, Australian and New Zealand citizens shouldn't have any trouble getting one on the spot. Visa fees are around US$15 (payable in US dollars or dinars) but can cost more depending on nationality. Day-trips to Petra can be arranged through Nature Travel (see above): you can squeeze everything in for $230; a more comprehensive two-night visit costs $450. Prices include all transportation, departure tax, entry fees, guides and lunch; the latter also includes full board in a three-star hotel.

Moving on

Some intercity **buses** trundle through Nuweiba City, but the only sure way of getting a bus south is to take a taxi to the main bus station (Ⓣ069/352-0371) at the port. Buses leave daily – roughly – at 6.30am and 4pm for Dahab (1hr–1hr 30min) and Sharm el-Sheikh (3hr); periodically there's also a 10am–10.30am bus. Services to Cairo (7–8hr) go via Taba (1hr) and depart daily from the bus station at 9am, 1.30pm and 3pm, and five to ten minutes later from the bus stop on the highway near Nuweiba City. Schedules for all these services seem to change frequently, so it's important to check the situation on the ground. You might also find **service taxis** hanging around Tarabeen, bound for Taba, Dahab, Sharm el-Sheikh or St Catherine's. Service taxis also meet the arrival of the boats from Aqaba.

Between Nuweiba and Taba

The 70km of coastline between **Nuweiba** and the **Taba** border crossing into Israel was for a long while relatively untouched, scattered with just a few appealing low-key resorts. During the 1990s, these were joined by plenty of new holiday villages and a massive tourist development called **Taba Heights**. However, since September 11, 2001 many of these resorts have been virtually empty due to the dearth of Israeli visitors, with some closing down completely. Visitor numbers took a further knock after the events of October 7, 2004, when two massive car bombs destroyed a portion of the *Taba Hilton* hotel, killing 31 people and injuring more than 120. The attack coincided with a second bombing at Ras al-Shaitan that left three dead.

Time will tell if business will pick up again, but in the interim, independent travellers who venture this way will get long stretches of beautiful beaches more or less to themselves. The nicer places are signposted and may be visible from the highway, depending on the terrain. **Buses** can drop you at any point along the way if you ask the driver, but bear in mind that there are no **banks** until Taba, nor anywhere to buy **food** except the pricey resort restaurants.

The first spot worth noting is **MAAGANA BEACH**, whose southern end – called **Lami Beach** – begins 8km from Tarabeen. Though its reefs are quite shallow and unimpressive, the beach itself is nice, with public showers and toilets and striking rock formations. There's a **campground** with huts (❷) and a cafeteria frequented by Bedouin who run **camel and jeep trips** to Wadi Huweiyit (see p.552) and other sites. Two kilometres further on lies the picturesque headland of **RAS AL-SHAITAN**, where the **reef** drops off sharply to the north, making it ideal for shore diving and snorkelling. *Castle Beach Resort* (Ⓣ069/350-0926 or 012 220-6240; ❷) has **beach bungalows** with verandas, a decent restaurant, and a shop selling souvenirs. There is a good reef for divers, and you can **rent camels** and guides for excursions to Moyat el-Wishwashi (see p.552). Several other camps nearby have a variety of accommodation, including *Ras Satan* camp (Ⓣ010 525-9109, Ⓦwww.ras-satan.com; ❷), a basic place of huts with mattresses and colourful rugs run by the affable Ayash. He can put you in contact with guides who take three- to four-day camel trips to places such as Ain Hudra and Wadi Ghazala for around £E100 per person per day, or who will take you to a traditional village near Gebel Gunna in the St Catherine's Protectorate.

Another 2km along the coast is the new *Tango Beach Resort* (Ⓣ012 217-1478, Ⓦwww.tangobeachresort.com; ❺) with neat en-suite rooms set around an attractive mosaic pool. Buffet meals, evening floor shows, and wind- and kitesurfing are on offer. A further 8km up the coast is the upmarket beach resort of *Bawaki*

Basata

The trendiest resort in these parts is **Basata**, which lies by the headland of Ras el-Burqa. Created by the German-educated Sherif el-Ghamrawy, it is Egypt's most eco-friendly resort, with its own greenhouse, generator, bakery, desalination plant and school for local Bedouin children. Organic waste is fed to *Basata*'s donkeys, goats, pigeons and ducks, or used to fertilize the fruit and vegetables. Alcohol, drugs, television and loud music are forbidden lest they spoil the ambience, which is family-oriented with a New Age ethos. Such is *Basata*'s popularity that it's essential to **reserve ahead** (ⓣ069/350-0480, ⓦwww.basata.com; ❷–❹). There are a collection of simple huts and more comfortable chalets, or you can pitch a tent on the beach. Guests can sign up for **inland safaris** (around £E100 per person per day) or rent **snorkelling** gear, but divers aren't welcome. You'll either feel at home with *Basata*'s New Agers or find them unbearably cliquey.

(ⓣ069/350-0470, ⓦwww.bawaki.com; ❺), boasting air-conditioned bungalows with hot showers, a restaurant, bar and pool. It also has a few triple-bed huts. Rates are all-inclusive.

Just beyond *Bawaki*, there's more accommodation at **MAHASH**, which occupies a particularly fine stretch of white sandy beach with a cool breeze even on the hottest summer days. Camps here include *Yasmina*, *Ma'ayan* and *Eden*, with a small supermarket (all ❷).

Bir Swair and around

Five kilometres beyond *Basata* is *Club Aquasun* (ⓣ010 667-8099, ⓦwww.clubaquasun.com; ❹), a less eco-conscious mix of bungalows with air conditioning and bathrooms. The quiet sandy beach has a lovely **reef**, good for **snorkelling** and diving. **Jeep or camel trips** can also be arranged to Wadi Quseib and other destinations. A couple of kilometres further on is *Sallyland* (ⓣ069/353-0380, ⓦwww.sallylandresort.com; ❹–❺), a three-star hotel of little note except that it has one of the few **bars** in the area. Other similar newish hotels can be found along the coastal road, such as the *Sonesta* and *Safari Beach*.

Next is the Bedouin settlement of **BIR SWAIR**. Few of its camps survived the economic downturn, but *Alexandria* (ⓣ010 166-1042, ⓦwww.alexandriabeach.com; ❶) is up and running again: it has thatched bungalows with mattresses and mosquito nets, one of Sinai's nicest beaches, as well as friendly staff and atmosphere. Guests here can visit the Bedouin village behind the camps in the mountains; you will be graciously received with tea and hospitality, but it's a good idea to give them a few Egyptian pounds in return and, as ever, always ask before taking photographs.

Another great beach, 3km north of Taba Heights, is the **Sun Pool**, which begins with a gentle slope and then plunges as it nears the **Fjord**, a beautiful inlet in the hills by the shore.

Taba Heights

Eighteen kilometres south of Taba, the **TABA HEIGHTS** development (ⓦwww.tabaheights.com) covers 4.5 million square metres of land and boasts 5km of beach. Dubbed the "Red Sea Riviera", this huge resort complex is based around a "village", which features a casino, watersports, dive centre, restaurants, bars, cafés, shops, bazaars and a medical centre. The resort's luxurious **hotels** tend to be much cheaper if booked as part of a package. The newest addition is the striking green and orange *Intercontinental* (ⓣ069/358-0300, ⓦwww.intercontinental.com; ❼) with more than five hundred rooms around a man-made lake next to the beach, and surrounded by tropical gardens; amenities include a spa and indoor heated pool, a watersports centre and squash and tennis courts. Also here is the beautifully designed *Marriott* (Ⓣ069/358-0100, Ⓦwww.marriott.com; ❼), most of its rooms overlooking the Gulf of Aqaba, and featuring an excellent Arabian spa. The huge five-star *Hyatt Regency* (Ⓣ069/358-0234, Ⓦwww.taba.regency.hyatt.com; ❼) has six restaurants and bars, three pools, a private beach, kids' club, health centre, tennis courts, shuttle bus and car rental. The list of facilities is nearly as long at the slightly smaller *Sofitel* (Ⓣ069/358-0800, Ⓦwww.sofitel.com; ❼). A little less expensive than the rest is the all-inclusive *El Wekala Golf Resort* (Ⓣ069/360-1212, Ⓦwww.threecorners.com; ❼), which has smart rooms, three swimming pools, a spa and overlooks an eighteen-hole golf course, though the resort is a five-minute shuttle-bus ride from the beach. Though rates here include full board, guests can eat at other hotels using a "dine around" scheme.

Pharaoh's Island

Seven kilometres before Taba you'll see **Pharaoh's Island** (Gezirat Faraoun), known to Israelis as "Coral Island". Its barren rocks are crowned by the renovated ruins of a **crusader fort** built in 1115 to levy taxes on Arab merchants while ostensibly protecting pilgrims travelling between Jerusalem and St Catherine's Monastery. The fort was subsequently captured by Salah al-Din but abandoned by the Arabs in 1183. It is only 250m offshore, so can be admired from the mainland. Independent travellers who want to take a closer look will have to negotiate a boat trip from the *Salah al-Deen* hotel; see below). It costs £E20 to tour the fort, which retains several towers and passageways along with a large cistern. There's also an expensive cafeteria that only opens when there are lots of tourists around.

The main reason to come here, however, is to dive or snorkel in the maze of **reefs** off the northeastern tip of the island. As the currents are strong and the reefs labyrinthine, it's best to be accompanied by a guide; this can be arranged at the *Salah al-Deen* **hotel** by the road on the mainland, opposite the island (Ⓣ069/353-0340, Ⓔtabarsrt@gega.net; half-board ❹; under 12s stay free).

Taba and the border

Hugging the Gulf of Aqaba's northernmost reaches, the unassuming border town of **TABA** consists of little more than a handful of hotels, cafés, shops and a bus terminal. Its history, however, has been turbulent. Following its withdrawal from the Sinai, Israel claimed Taba lay outside the jurisdiction of the Camp David Accords, and demanded US$60 million compensation for its return to Egypt. It took ten years of bitter negotiations until international arbitration finally returned the town to Egypt in 1989. After a period of relative calm, Taba's peace was shattered on October 7, 2004 when a massive car bomb tore away a side of the *Hilton Taba Hotel*, killing 32 people. Now open again, the hotel and its *Nelson Village* annexe (Ⓣ069/353-0140, Ⓦwww.hiltonworldresorts.com; ❼) have all the usual resort features including bike hire, pool and watersports. That said, a better accommodation option is the newer *Tobya Boutique Hotel* (Ⓣ069/353-0275, Ⓦwww.tobyaboutiquehotel.com; ❼), on the highway 1km south of Taba. With a swimming pool, private beach and casino, this stylish complex is decked out in Egyptian-African themed hand-woven wool carpets, while the rooms are embellished with local crafts.

The East Delta **bus terminal** (Ⓣ069/353-0205) is a few hundred metres before the border. Daily services run from here to Nuweiba (1hr), Dahab (3hr), Sharm el-Sheikh (4hr) and Cairo (7hr); timetables are in a constant state of flux, so check the latest information on the ground. **Service taxis** operate to Tarabeen and Nuweiba, Dahab or Sharm el-Sheikh.

Crossing the border

The **border with Israel** is open 24 hours except during Yom Kippur and Eid el-Adha. Avoid crossing after mid-morning on a Friday or any time on Saturday, however, as most public transport and businesses in Israel shut down over *shabbat*. The whole process can be very quick, unless you get caught behind a large group. For details of entering Egypt at Taba, and entry and departure taxes, see p.28. Don't listen to any taxi drivers who tell you that you need to take a taxi to the East Delta terminal – it is less than five minutes' walk.

The Israelis issue free three-month **visas** to EU, US, Australian and New Zealand citizens. However, if you plan on travelling to Syria or other Arab countries that do not recognize Israel, ask immigration on both sides of the border to leave your passport unstamped. Travellers must walk across a no-man's land between the Egyptian and Israeli checkpoints; from the Israeli checkpoint you catch a shared taxi or a #15 bus the 10km into Eilat. If you need to **change money**, the exchange rate on the Egyptian side, at Bank Misr, which also has an ATM, is better than the Israeli bank where you pay your exit tax.

The interior

The **interior of Sinai** is a baking wilderness of jagged rocks, drifting sand and wind-scoured gravel pans, awesome in its desolation. Yet life flourishes around its isolated springs and water-holes, or whenever rain falls, renewing the vegetation across vast tracts of semi-desert. Hinterland settlements bestride medieval pilgrimage routes, which the Turks transformed from camel tracks into dirt roads, then the Egyptians and Israelis improved and fought over. Both sides also built and bombed the airstrips which the MFO now use to monitor the Sinai's demilitarized zones.

As a result, the only readily accessible part of the interior is **St Catherine's Monastery**, **Mount Sinai** and **Feiran Oasis**, although some other, smaller oases can be reached by jeep or camel from the Aqaba coast or St Catherine's (see below). That said, most buses from Cairo to Nuweiba traverse the **Wilderness of the Wanderings** via **Nekhl** and the **Mitla Pass**, allowing you to see something of the peninsula's interior. Because of the unexploded ordnance lying around, **independent motoring** is officially restricted outside the St Catherine's Feiran Oasis area.

Inland safaris and treks

Inland safaris range from half-day excursions to treks lasting up to two weeks. Travelling by **jeep** is obviously faster and makes few or no physical demands, but tends to distance you from the landscape. This is rarely the case if you travel by **camel**, which feels totally in keeping with the terrain. See "Riding" in Basics, p.50, for advice on posture and steering.

For those with more time and stamina, the most rewarding option is to go **trekking on foot**. Treks can be arranged at the village of St Catherine's (where you can also obtain maps for one-day walks in the area from the protectorate) or at certain points along the roads into the interior and also through many of the Bedouin who run trips from the coastal resorts. The list of destinations below should give an idea of what's on offer.

Practicalities depend on your destination and mode of travel. Day excursions from the coast can be made on a Sinai-only visa, but to travel for any longer or explore the High Mountain Region beyond the immediate vicinity of St Catherine's Monastery and Mount Sinai you must have a regular Egyptian visa. To climb mountains you must also have a **permit** from the police, which can be obtained by your Bedouin guide. It is illegal – and highly risky – to go trekking without a guide. To help you select destinations and plot routes, buy the 1:250,000 *Sinai Map of Attractions*. Other things to **bring** are listed in the "High Mountain Region and Feiran Oasis" section (p.564).

Finally, respect the landscape and leave it unspoiled.

Safari destinations

The following are all shown on the map on pp.520–521.

Ain el-Furtaga 16km from Nuweiba by road. Palmy oasis at the crossroads of trails to the Coloured Canyon, Wadi Ghazala and Ain Khudra Oasis.

Ain Khudra Oasis One of the loveliest oases in Sinai, it can be reached by hiking from the St Catherine's road, with help from local Bedouin, or from the south by 4WD.

Ain Kid Oasis 14km off the road between Sharm el-Sheikh and Dahab; reached via Wadi Kid, a red-walled canyon where a spring appears in rainy years. The oasis has a freshwater well.

Ain Um Ahmed Another beautiful oasis, accessible by 4WD or camel from Bir es-Sawa. Can serve as a base for climbing expeditions to Ras el-Qalb (see below).

Arched Canyon Sinuous gorge that's only accessible on foot; drop-off and pick-up by 4WD from Ain el-Furtaga or Bir es-Sawa.

Bir es-Sawa Small oasis with a spring issuing from a cave, beside the El-Thammed road.

Blue Valley 12km from St Catherine's. A canyon painted blue by a Belgian artist in 1978.

Coloured Canyon 17km north of Ain el-Furtaga. Two rainbow-hued canyons, great for walking or rock-climbing (no water). One of the most popular day-trips from Nuweiba.

El-Haduda The biggest sand dune in eastern Sinai, reached from Sheikh Hamid (see below).

Feiran Oasis Over twelve thousand palm trees, monastic remains, and access to Jebel Serbal. Wadi Feiran may have been the route taken by the Israelites to reach Mount Sinai.

Forest of Pillars A unique natural phenomenon of petrified tree stumps on the cliffs of Jebel el-Tih, 15km northeast of Serabit el-Khadim. Access by 4WD or camel only; guide essential.

Jebel Sabah A 2266m peak in southern Sinai, from which Saudi Arabia and mainland Egypt are visible on clear days. For experienced hikers only, with abundant food and water. Permit required.

Jebel Serbal Near Feiran Oasis, this is one of the loveliest mountains in Sinai, with ruined chapels lining the trail to the summit (2070m). No climbing skills needed, but guide and permit required.

Jebel Um Shaumar The second-highest peak in Sinai, whose summit (2586m) affords a view of the entire southern horn of the peninsula. Experienced climbers only. Permit required.

Nuwamis Prehistoric site with 5550-year-old graves and inscriptions 6km from Ain Khudra. Reached on foot (2hr 30min) from Sheikh Hamid, by appointment only.

Ras el-Qalb Isolated mountain (999m) associated in Bedouin folklore with the monster Ula. For climbers only; no water. Permit required.

Serabit el-Khadim Hilltop temple overlooking the Gulf of Suez, with ancient turquoise mines and inscriptions in the surrounding valleys; it's covered on p.527. Access by 4WD, then on foot.

Sheikh Hamid Bedouin settlement on the road to St Catherine's, 7km from the Dahab–Nuweiba road. This is the starting point for walking or camel treks to Ain Khudra, Nuwamis, El-Haduda, and remoter destinations (up to two weeks).

Wadi Ghazala Links Ain el-Furtaga and Ain Khudra Oasis. Acacia groves, dunes and gazelles.

Wadi Huweiyit North of Nuweiba. Colourful canyon with typical desert flora; easy hiking.

Wadi Mandar 40km north of Sharm el-Sheikh. Bedouin camel races occur here on January 1.

Wadi Naseb Runs down from Mount Catherine towards Dahab. The verdant upper reaches of the wadi are inhabited by Bedouin. 4WD essential.

St Catherine's Monastery and Mount Sinai

Venerated by Christians, Jews and Muslims as the site of God's revelation of the Ten Commandments, **Mount Sinai** overlooks the valley where Moses is said to have heard the Lord speaking from a burning bush.

The bush is now enshrined in **St Catherine's Monastery**, nestling in a valley at the foot of the Mount, surrounded by high walls and lush gardens. As tourists have followed pilgrims in ever greater numbers, the sacred mount has witnessed unseemly quarrels between Bedouin over the shrinking amount of sleeping space for the climbers at the peak, and the monastery itself shows signs of strain. Yet for most travellers it remains a compelling visit, while other seldom-visited peaks offer equally magnificent views if you're prepared to make the effort to reach them.

You can visit St Catherine's on **organized tours** from Na'ama Bay, Dahab, Nuweiba, Cairo, Hurghada or Eilat; travelling independently, however, is more difficult. There only a single public bus to St Catherine's Village – the 11.30am from Cairo's Abbassiya terminal via Feiran Oasis (around 7hr).

Bedouin Paths Camp in St Catherine's Village (Ⓣ018 966-2010, Ⓦwww.bedouinpaths.com) runs tourist buses between its camp and Dahab (£E40–45); you're not obliged to stay at the camp. Alternatively you can hire a taxi: from Dahab this should cost £E400 for the return journey and waiting time; from Nuweiba you should pay around £E100 less. Or you could take a **guided overnight trip** from Dahab or Sharm el-Sheikh, which includes a moonlit ascent of Mount Sinai, sleeping at the peak and returning to the monastery in the morning after sunrise.

All vehicles stop about 10km before the monastery at a petrol station/police checkpoint/ticket office for the St Catherine protectorate, where foreigners must purchase a **ticket** ($3) to enter the area.

▲ St Catherine's Monastery

The Bedouin of Sinai

The Bedouin community in St Catherine's – and throughout Sinai – is severely marginalised to the extent that the Egyptian government does not even collate official statistics on them. Few Bedouin work in the region's hotels, restaurants and travel agencies, and **guiding** is generally the only legal form of employment available. However, a few NGOs are working to improve the situation, including the **Community Foundation for South Sinai** (Ⓦwww.southsinaifoundation.org), which is based in St Catherine's and supports sustainable development, education, employment, health and conservation projects.

St Catherine's village

While the monastery and Mount Sinai are the focus of interest, most of the facilities of use to tourists are in the **village of St Catherine**, 3km away. Shared taxis provide **transport** between the two, charging £E5. The road terminates at the village's main square. On one side is an arcade containing a **bank** (Mon–Thurs & Sun 8.30am–2pm & 6–9pm; no ATM), several mini-supermarkets and a couple of restaurants; on the other side are the **tourist police** and a small and poorly equipped **hospital**. In the vicinity of the mosque are a **post office**, **telephone exchange** and the **bus station**. Fansina (daily 9.30am–3pm), opposite Safary Moonland Camp, is an EU-supported shop that sells handicrafts produced by local Bedouin women, including lovely bags, purses and cushion covers. There's a good value unnamed **restaurant** just uphill of the arcade – look out for the blue sign reading "Restaurant" and a collection of picnic tables; for £E25 you get chicken, rice, soup, bread and salad. A short walk downhill from the arcade takes you to *1Day* restaurant, which serves similar food, but is a bit smarter and more expensive.

For **short walks** in the area, guide maps can be purchased from the St Catherine Protectorate visitor centre and Bedouin museum (entry £E25) at the end of the road before the monastery. If you're planning to do any trekking in the High Mountain Region, ask locals to point you towards **El-Milga**, uphill past the main square of the village (about 150m northwest of the Co-op petrol station), where you'll find **Sheikh Mousa** (Ⓣ069/347-0457, Ⓦwww.sheikmousa.com), the chief of the Bedouin guides who lead expeditions. For more details, see "The High Mountain Region and Feiran Oasis", p.563.

Accommodation

Most people on tours arrive in the early hours to climb Mount Sinai and **catch the sunrise** before descending again. With night-time temperatures around 10°C during summer and near zero over winter (when frosts and snow aren't uncommon), a sleeping bag is essential if you plan to do this; you can also rent blankets on the summit. Note, however, that with so many people wanting to sleep out, there is often little room at the top and it's very uncomfortable, and you may have to sleep further down the mountain at Elijah's Hollow (see p.563) and complete the journey before sunrise.

Al-Karm Ecolodge Around 35km northeast of St Catherine's, near settlement of Sheikh Awad in Wadi Gharba Ⓣ010 132-4693, Ⓦwww.awayaway-sinai.net. Bedouin-owned and run camp with just six rooms in a wonderfully remote location (a 4WD is needed to get here; phone up for more detailed directions). It's run along environmentally-friendly lines: there are composting toilets and solar-powered showers, but no electricity. Hikes and cultural trips are on offer. ❷–❸

Bedouin Paths Camp 150m past the Co-op petrol station Ⓣ018 966-2010, Ⓦwww.bedouinpaths.com. Accommodation ranges from camping spots (£E10), simple dorms (£E20), rooms with proper beds, rugs and pink walls, and more comfortable en suites at this welcoming and popular lodge. There's a good restaurant, internet access and various activities on offer. ❷–❸

Catherine Plaza Just outside the village ⓣ069/347-0288, ⓦwww.catherineplaza.com. Large mid-range hotel offering comfy en suites with tubs, a/c and TV, plus an inviting pool, Chinese restaurant and billiards table. Rates are half-board. ❺

Daniela Village St Catherine's village ⓣ069/347-0379. *Daniela Village* is a bit dated but has neat and tidy rooms with a/c, TV and private bath. ❺

Desert Fox Camp 800m from the village, near the main intersection ⓣ069/347-0344 or 010 565-9399, ⓦhttp://foxsinai.net. This backpacker hangout is the cheapest place in the area, with basic stone cabins. If money is really tight, you can camp in the pleasant grounds (£E15). There's a restaurant, and sometimes live Bedouin music in the evenings. Ten percent of all online bookings goes to the Community Foundation for South Sinai (see box opposite). ❶

El Wadi El Mouqudus Between *Catherine Plaza* and *Daniela Village* ⓣ069/347-0225. Pleasant three-star rooms with a/c, fridge and TV, plus a swimming pool in summer. Service, however, is a bit erratic. B&B or half-board. ❹

Safary Moonland Camp and Hotel 500m from the village behind *Catherine Plaza* ⓣ018 658-4550, ⓔmnland2002@yahoo.com. The only budget place around where you can sleep on a bed rather than a mattress on the floor. Its doubles and triples (shared or private bath) are popular with backpackers and overlanders. ❷

St Catherine's Monastery Guesthouse Just outside the monastery walls ⓣ069/347-0353. Sheltered by the towering red cliffs of Mount Sinai, this hotel has a dramatic setting unmatched in the Sinai. The en-suite twin-bedded rooms are small and basic, though simple meals are included and the views are glorious. ❺

St Catherine Tourist Village By the main road, 500m from the monastery ⓣ010 489-7748, ⓔnasserenyen@yahoo.com. Made from local rock, this distinctive hotel has an impressive list of former guests, including President Mubarak and Jacques Chirac. The en suites are comfortable rather than flashy, with bath tubs, TV, a/c and mini seating areas. Half-board. ❺

The Monastery of St Catherine

The **Monastery of St Catherine** is a Greek Orthodox foundation. Its origins date back to 337 AD, when the Byzantine **Empress Helena** ordered the construction of a chapel around the putative **Burning Bush**, already a focus for hermits and pilgrimages. Since then, it has had cycles of expansion and decline, on occasion being totally deserted. Most of the monks today have come here from the monasteries of Mount Athos in Greece.

Visiting the monastery

The monastery is **open** to visitors from 9am till noon. It's officially closed on Fridays, Sundays and on all Greek Orthodox holidays, but will sometimes open from 11am to noon on these days, in order to accommodate tourist demands. There is no admission charge, but visitors must be modestly dressed.

You enter through a small gate in the northern wall near **Kléber's Tower** (named after the Napoleonic general who ordered its reconstruction) rather than the main portal facing west, which has a funnel that was used for pouring boiling oil onto attackers. Built of granite, 10–15m high and 2–3m thick, St Catherine's **walls** are essentially unchanged since Stephanos Ailisios designed them in the sixth century.

As you emerge from the passage, a right turn takes you past **Moses' Well**, where the then fugitive from Egypt met Zipporah, one of Jethro's seven daughters, whom he married at the age of 40. Walking the other way and around the corner, you'll see a thorny evergreen bush outgrowing an enclosure. This is the transplanted descendant of the **Burning Bush** whence God spoke to Moses: "Come now therefore, and I will send thee unto Pharaoh, that thou mayest bring forth my people the children of Israel out of Egypt" (Exodus 3:10). Sceptics may be swayed by the fact that it's the only bush of its kind in the entire peninsula and that all attempts to grow cuttings from it elsewhere have failed. The bush was moved to its present site when Helena's chapel was built over its roots, behind the apse of St Catherine's church. Nearby is the recently-revamped **Monastery Museum**

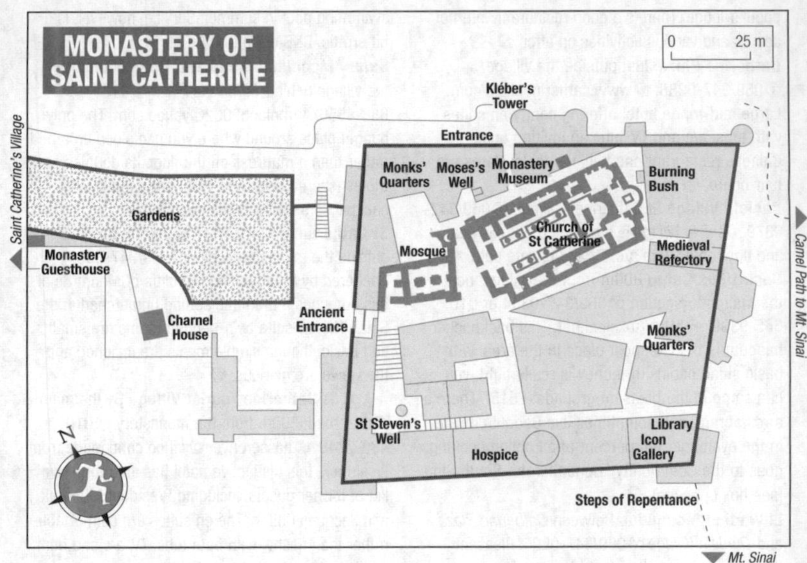

(£E25), which has Byzantine icons, crosses and chalices, reams of aged manuscripts, fragments of the world's oldest bible and other pieces from the library (see below). Exhibits are labelled in English and Arabic.

A granite basilica, **St Catherine's Church** was erected by Justinian between 542 and 551; the walls and pillars and the cedarwood doors between the narthex and nave are all original. Its twelve pillars – representing the months of the year and hung with icons of the saints venerated during each one – have ornately carved capitals, loaded with symbolism. At the far end, behind the iconostasis is the **Chapel of the Burning Bush**, only viewable by special dispensation. The narthex displays a selection of the monastery's vast collection of **icons**, running the gamut of Byzantine styles and techniques, from encaustic wax to tempera. The church's **bell** is rung 33 times to rouse the monks before dawn.

Other parts of the monastery are usually closed to laypersons. Among them are an eleventh-century **mosque**, added to placate Muslim rulers; a **library** of over three thousand manuscripts and five thousand books, surpassed only by the Vatican's; and a **refectory** with Gothic arches and Byzantine murals. You can usually enter the **charnel house**, however, which is heaped with monks' skeletons; the cemetery itself is small, so corpses have to be disinterred after a year and moved into the ossuary. The cadaver in vestments is Stephanos, a sixth-century guardian of one of the routes to the Mount.

Mount Sinai

While some archeologists question whether **Mount Sinai** was really the Biblical mountain where Moses received the Ten Commandments, it's hard not to agree with the nineteenth-century American explorer John Lloyd Stephens that "among all the stupendous works of Nature, not a place can be selected more fitting for the exhibition of Almighty power". Its loftiest peak, a craggy, sheer-faced massif of grey and red granite "like a vengeful dagger that was dipped in blood many ages ago", rises 2285m above sea level. Strictly speaking, it's only this that the Bedouin call Jebel Musa ("Mount Moses"), though the name is commonly applied to the whole massif. Some Biblical scholars reckon that Moses proclaimed the Commandments from Ras Safsafa, at the opposite end of the ridge, which overlooks a wide valley where the Israelites could have camped.

Walking to the summit

You have to hire a Bedouin guide (£E85) to climb the mountain; don't let them hurry you – do the climb at your own pace. The longer but easier route is via the switchback **camel path**, starting 50m behind the monastery. It's possible to rent a camel for most of the ascent from Bedouins hanging out at the foot of the mount (around £E50; 2hr), but it's really worth the effort of walking, which takes around two to three hours. You can stock up on water at the shops outside the monastery before setting off, and there are refreshment stalls along the way. Prices rise the higher you go, but restocking on the mountain saves you carrying extra weight right at the start. Bedouin entrepreneurs at the peak rent out blankets and mattresses for the night (£E5–10).

Beyond the cleft below the summit, the path is joined by the other route, known as the Sikket Saiyidna Musa ("Path of Our Lord Moses") or **Steps of Repentance**. Hewn by a penitent monk, the 3750 steps make a much steeper ascent from the monastery (1hr 30min), which is hell on the leg muscles; some of the steps are a metre high. Two buildings top the summit, a mosque and a Greek Orthodox church, both usually locked. Next to the mosque is the cave where God sheltered Moses: "I will put thee in a cleft of the rock, and will cover thee with my hand while I pass over" (Exodus 33:22). A little lower down the slope, a bunch of semi-permanent structures have sprung up, offering weary travellers a place to sleep.

Many people ascend by the camel path and descend by the steps. Start your ascent around 5pm (earlier during winter) to avoid the worst of the heat and arrive in time to watch the spellbinding sunset. With a torch, you could also climb the camel path (but not the steps) by night, though not during winter. Descending the steps, you'll enter a depression known as the Plain of Cypresses or **Elijah's Hollow**, where pilgrims pray and sing; a 500-year-old cypress tree stands here. This is also where Elijah is believed to have heard God's voice (I Kings 19:9–18) and hid from Jezebel, being fed by ravens. One of the two chapels is dedicated to him, the other to his successor, Elisha.

The High Mountain Region and Feiran Oasis

The area around St Catherine's is sometimes termed the **High Mountain Region**, as it contains numerous peaks over 2000m. Snow frequently covers the ground in winter and flash floods can occur year round. The scenery is fantastic, with phalanxes of serrated peaks looming above wadis full of tumbled boulders and wiry fruit trees. This harsh but beguiling land is the stamping ground of the Jebeliya and Aulad Said tribes, some of whom act as guides for **treks** on foot or by camel; the terrain is generally too rough for vehicles, even 4WDs. Foreigners are legally forbidden to embark on such expeditions without a Bedouin guide.

Trekking is possible in winter if you are prepared to put up with chilly nights and possible snow flurries; in the summer it's just a case of being fit enough to stand up to the heat. The main **starting point for treks is El-Milga village** near

St Catherine's (see p.560), where Sheikh Mousa will organize everything. An all-inclusive trek, including guide, food and transport, costs around €35 per day. You'll need comfortable hiking boots, warm clothes, a sleeping bag, sunglasses, sunscreen, lip salve, bug repellent, toilet paper and water purification tablets (unless you're willing to drink from springs). A good map of South Sinai (see p.524) and a compass are also useful.

Mount Catherine, Blue Valley and other walks

Egypt's highest peak, **Mount Catherine** (Jebel Katerina; 2642m), is roughly 6km south of Mount Sinai and can be reached on foot in five to six hours. The path starts behind St Catherine's village, running up the Wadi el-Leja on Mount Sinai's western flank, past the deserted Convent of the Forty and a Bedouin hamlet. Shortly afterwards the trail forks, the lower path winding off up a rubble-strewn canyon, Shagg Musa, which it eventually quits to ascend Mount Catherine – a straightforward but exhausting climb. On the summit are a chapel with water, two rooms for pilgrims to stay overnight, a meteorological station and **panoramic views**.

According to tradition, priests found **St Catherine's remains** here during the ninth or tenth century. Believers maintain she was born in 294 AD in Alexandria of a noble family, converted to Christianity and subsequently lambasted Emperor Maxentius for idolatry, confounding fifty philosophers who tried to shake her faith. Following an attempt to break her on a spiked wheel (hence Catherine wheels), which shattered at her touch, Maxentius had her beheaded; her remains were transported to Sinai by angels.

If climbing Mount Catherine seems too ambitious, consider visiting the **Blue Valley**, 5km southeast of the intersection of the roads to St Catherine's, Nuweiba and Feiran Oasis. You can do this as a day-trip from Dahab or in half a day from St Catherine's village by renting a jeep and guide. The canyon's name derives from a Belgian who in 1978 painted its rocks a deep blue in emulation of the Bulgarian artist Christo, who hung drapes across the Grand Canyon.

Longer treks

The two **four-day treks** outlined here give an idea of what can be done; other possibilities are mentioned under "Feiran Oasis" (see opposite). The **first trek**, starting off in **El-Milga**, begins by taking the path through the **Abu Giffa Pass** down into Wadi Tubug, passing walled gardens en route to Wadi Shagg, where you'll find Byzantine ruins and huge boulders. From there you proceed to an olive grove, where you spend the night. The next day you follow the trail through Wadi Gibal and climb one of two peaks offering magnificent views, before descending to Farash Rummana, a camping spot with showers. On the third day you strike north through a canyon to the water-holes of Galt al-Azraq, pushing on to camp at Farsh Um Sila or Farsh Tuweita. The final day begins with an easy hike down towards Wadi Tinya, before climbing Jebel Abbas Pasha (2383m), named after the paranoid ruler who built a palace there (now in ruins). You then follow a path down through the Zuweitun and Tubug valleys, back to Abu Giffa and El-Milga. If you want a more detailed account of the trek, track down a copy of Francis Gilbert and Samy Zabat's book, *A Walk in Sinai: St Catherine's to Al Galt Al Azraq*.

The **second trek** starts at **Abu Sila** village, 3km from El-Milga, where there are some rock inscriptions. You'll probably camp out near Bustan el-Birka's sweetwater spring. Day two involves descending into Wadi Nugra, below Jebel el-Banat, where you can bathe in pools fed by a twenty-metre-high waterfall.

You then press through Wadi Gharba to the tomb of Sheikh Awad, where the Aulad Gundi tribe holds an annual feast in his honour. Having spent the night here, you have a choice of three routes to Farsh Abu Tuweita, the final night's camping spot. On the fourth day you follow the same route as the final leg of the first hike.

Feiran Oasis

It's thought the ancient Israelites reached Mount Sinai by the same route that buses coming from the west use today, via Wadi Feiran and Wadi el-Sheikh. Travelling this road in the other direction, you might glimpse the **Tomb of Nabi Salah** near the **Watiyyah Pass**, where Bedouin converge for an annual **moulid** on the Prophet Mohammed's birthday. Beyond the pass lies El-Tafra, a small and dismal oasis village.

Roughly 60km from St Catherine's the road passes a huge walled garden marking the start of **FEIRAN OASIS**. A twisting, granite-walled valley of palms and tamarisks, the oasis belongs to the tribes of the Tawarah, who have houses and wells here. Feiran was the earliest Christian stronghold in the Sinai, with its own bishop and **convent**, ruined during the seventh century but now rebuilt. Further back in time, this was reputedly the Rephidim of the Amalakites, who denied its wells to the thirsty Israelites, causing them to curse Moses until he smote the Rock of Horeb with his staff, making water gush forth. Refreshed, they joined battle with the Amalakites the next day, inspired by the sight of Moses standing on a hilltop, believed to have been the conical one the Bedouin call **Jebel el-Tannuh**, with ruined chapels lining the track to its summit (1hr). Other **hiking** possibilities in the area include **Jebel el-Banat** (1510m), further north, and the highly challenging ascent of **Jebel Serbal** (2070m), south of the oasis.

As for finding a guide, make arrangements in El-Milga. Feiran Oasis lacks any **accommodation**, but you could probably camp out in the palm groves with local consent.

The Wilderness of the Wanderings

Separating the granite peaks of South Sinai from the sandy wastes of the north is a huge tableland of gravel plains and fissured limestone, riven by wadis: the **Wilderness of the Wanderings** (Badiet el-Tih). Life exists in this desert thanks to sporadic rainfall between mid-October and mid-April, which refills the cisterns that irrigate groves of palms and tamarisks. During Byzantine times, these cisterns sustained dozens of villages along the Sinai–Negev border; nowadays, the largest irrigated gardens are in Wadi Feiran and Wadi el-Arish.

Crossing the Wilderness via Nekhl and the Mitla Pass

The shortest route between Nuweiba and Cairo (470km; 6–7hr) crosses the great Wilderness via Nekhl and the Mitla Pass. The heat-hazed plateau is stupefyingly monotonous but contains several historic locations. The road from Nuweiba heads north to El-Thammed before cutting west across Wadi el-Arish. **NEKHL**, at the heart of the peninsula, has a **derelict castle** built by Sultan al-Ghuri in 1516. South of one of the wadi's many tributaries lies **Qalaat el-Gundi**, a **ruined fort** built by Salah al-Din; it can also be reached by a track from Ras Sudr on the Gulf of Suez. To the west, the road descends through the 480-metre-high **Mitla Pass**, one of three cleavages in the central plateau. The outcome of three Arab-Israeli conflicts was arguably determined here in some of the bloodiest **tank battles** in history.

Northern Sinai

While jagged mountains dominate the gulf coasts and interior of the peninsula, **northern Sinai** is awash with pale sand dunes. While the Israeli border crossing at Rafah – a divided and tense frontier town – is sporadically open, ongoing unrest means that travellers should use the Taba crossing. The only way to travel **between the Mediterranean and Aqaba coasts** is via Cairo and Suez. Roughly 40km along the road to El-Arish from Qantara you pass a turn-off for **PELUSIUM**, where parts of the pharaonic town and a **Roman amphitheatre** have been uncovered. You can visit (daily 9am–5pm), though you'll need a car and official permission from the local police station to tour the site. Travel is not advised to **El-Arish,** the site of two suicide bomb attacks in 2006 and more recently the scene of a major crackdown against Islamist militants by Egyptian security forces.

7

The Red Sea Coast

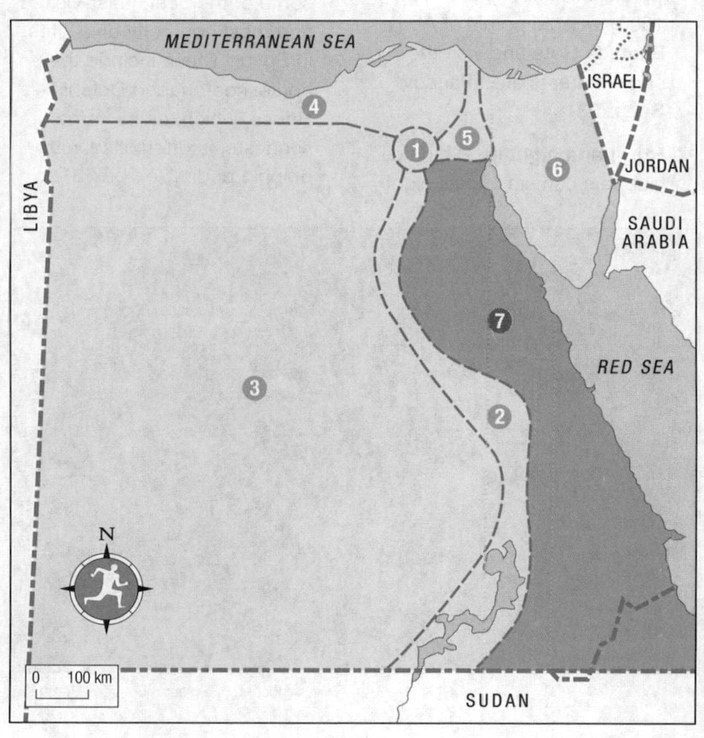

CHAPTER 7 Highlights

* **Red Sea monasteries** Deep in the desert, St Paul's and St Anthony's were the world's first monasteries, and still draw thousands of Copts from across Egypt each year. See p.569

* **Dive safaris** Hurghada is a good place to arrange diving trips or liveaboards, taking in the more remote reefs and wrecks of the south Red Sea. Observe moray eels at Careless Reef, explore the 1500-year-old corals at Abu Ramada Gota and visit the stunning reefs at El-Fanadir. See p.581

* **Hurghada nightlife** Die-hard clubbers can stay up all night at venues like *Ministry of Sound*, *HedKandi* and *Little Buddha*, which often play host to internationally-renowned DJs. See p.584

* **Red Sea Mountain excursions** Experience the wadis and Bedouin culture of the Red Sea Mountains, on camel or jeep safaris. See p.587

* **Mersa Alam** Camps and hotels here give access to some of the best, least-visited and most southerly dive sites in Egypt. These include the horseshoe-shaped Dolphin House, which, as its name suggests, is often filled with dolphin pods. See p.593

▲ A diver encounters a giant moray eel, Hurghada

7

The Red Sea Coast

An entrepôt since ancient times, the **Red Sea Coast,** stretching 1250km from Suez to the Sudanese border, was once a microcosm of half the world, as Muslim pilgrims from as far away as Central Asia sailed to Arabia from its ports. Though piracy and slavery ceased towards the end of the nineteenth century, smuggling still drew adventurers like Henri de Monfreid long after the Suez Canal had sapped the vitality of the Red Sea ports. Decades later, the coastline assumed new significance with the discovery of oil and its vulnerability to Israeli commando raids, which led to large areas being **mined** – one reason why tourism didn't arrive until the 1980s. Be aware that large areas of the coastline and many wadis are still mined: any area with barbed-wire fencing (however rusty) is suspect, and you should never wander off public beaches or into the desert without a guide.

Turquoise waves lap rocky headlands and windswept beaches along a coastline separated from the Nile Valley by the arid hills and mountains of the Eastern Desert, home to the **Red Sea monasteries**. While Cairenes appreciate the beaches at **Ain Sukhna**, south of Suez, the real lure consists of fabulous island reefs off the coasts of **Hurghada** – a bold and brash resort town – and the less touristy settlements of **Port Safaga**, **El-Quseir** and **Mersa Alam** to the south. The coast south of El-Quseir is subject to ambitious development plans and dive companies are also establishing bases along the southern coastline, and opening up "virgin" reefs to divers. A list of dive sites accessible from Hurghada appears on p.581, while sites further to the south are mentioned on p.589 and p.593.

The Red Sea monasteries

Secreted amid the arid Red Sea Hills, Egypt's oldest **monasteries** – dedicated to St Paul and St Anthony – trace their origins back to the infancy of Christian monasticism, observing rituals that have scarcely changed over sixteen centuries. You don't have to be religious to appreciate their tranquil atmosphere and imposing setting, however, and there's also scope for **birdwatching** in the vicinity.

Neither monastery is directly accessible by public transport, and a quick visit is impossible. If you feel OK about travelling with devout believers, it's best to join the **pilgrim tours** arranged from Cairo by the Coptic Patriarchate (22 Sharia Ramses, Abbassiya; ⓣ02/396-0025) or the YMCA (72 Sharia al-Gumhorriya, downtown; ⓣ02/591-7360). Coptic churches in Luxor or Hurghada may also run tours. Alternatively, chartering a **taxi** for the six- to eight-hour excursion should cost about £E500 from Suez, or £E800–900 from Cairo; taxis from Za'farana might do a four- to five-hour jaunt for around £E200. To drive from one monastery to the other (82km) takes about ninety minutes.

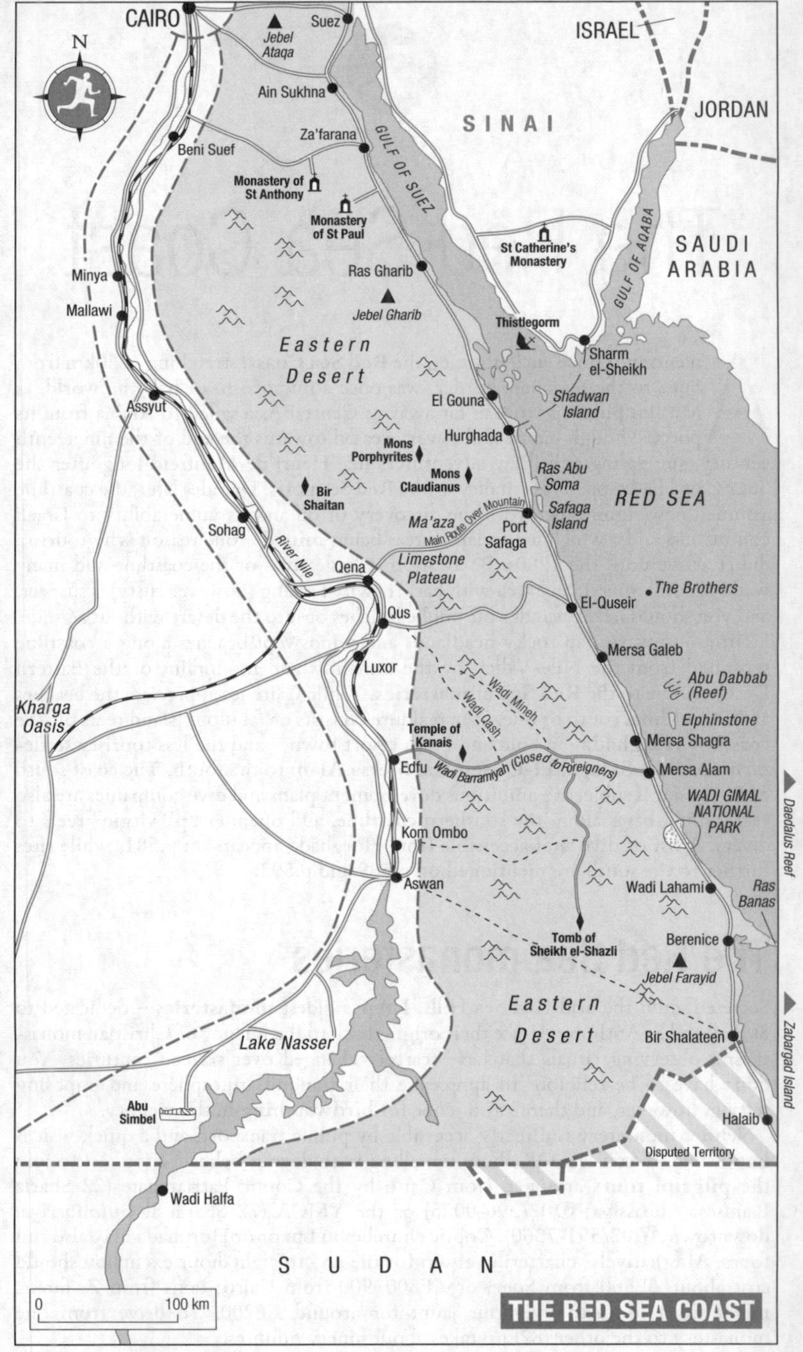
CAIRO
Suez
Jebel Ataqa
ISRAEL
N
Ain Sukhna
JORDAN
SINAI
Beni Suef
Za'farana
GULF OF SUEZ
Monastery of St Anthony
Monastery of St Paul
St Catherine's Monastery
SAUDI ARABIA
GULF OF AQABA
Ras Gharib
Minya
Mallawi
Jebel Gharib
Thistlegorm
Sharm el-Sheikh
Eastern Desert
El Gouna
Shadwan Island
Assyut
Hurghada
Mons Porphyrites
Mons Claudianus
Ras Abu Soma
Bir Shaitan
RED SEA
Safaga Island
Main Route Over Mountain
Ma'aza
Sohag
Port Safaga
River Nile
Qena
Limestone Plateau
The Brothers
El-Quseir
Qus
Mersa Galeb
Luxor
Wadi Mineh
Abu Dabbab (Reef)
Kharga Oasis
Wadi Qash
Elphinstone
Temple of Kanais
Mersa Shagra
Edfu
Wadi Barramiyah (Closed to Foreigners)
Mersa Alam
Daedalus Reef
WADI GIMAL NATIONAL PARK
Kom Ombo
Aswan
Wadi Lahami
Ras Banas
Tomb of Sheikh el-Shazli
Berenice
Jebel Farayid
Eastern Desert
Zabargad Island
Lake Nasser
Bir Shalateen
Abu Simbel
Halaib
Disputed Territory
Wadi Halfa
SUDAN
0
100 km
THE RED SEA COAST

The cheapest way to see the monasteries combines **public transport**, **hitching** and **walking**. Outside of the hottest months, this shouldn't be dangerous providing you bring ample water and minimal luggage. Any bus from Cairo or Suez to Hurghada can drop you at the **turn-off for St Paul's Monastery** (26km south of Za'farana, 152km south of Suez), recognizable by its plastic-roofed bus shelter. Young Copts alight here, confident of hitching to the monastery, 13km uphill, as there's a fair amount of traffic along the well-paved road. Another place to try to cadge a lift is the *Sahara Inn* motel's cafeteria (see p.573). Otherwise, you can approach St Anthony's Monastery via the service taxis running between Beni Suef and Za'farana. From the signposted turn-off 33km west of Za'farana, it's 15km uphill to the monastery, with some hitching prospects. It's also possible to hike between the two monasteries along a demanding trail across the top of the plateau; it's strongly recommended to engage a guide, which is easier to do at the Monastery of St Paul than at St Anthony.

Both monasteries are open daily from 9am to 5pm, but visitors are not permitted during Christmas or Lent. Both monasteries have dormitories (Ⓣ02/590-0218; you need written permission from the "residence" in Cairo to stay in them) and **cafeterias**, and St Paul's has a shop selling basic foodstuffs, but you might want to bring your own supplies. Smoking and drinking alcohol are forbidden here, and you should respect the monasteries' conventions on dress and behaviour.

The Monastery of St Anthony

West of Za'farana, a wide valley cleaves the Galala Plateau and sets the road on course for the Nile, 168km away. Called **Wadi Arraba**, its name derives from the carts that once delivered provisions to the monastery, though legend attributes it to the pharaoh's chariots that pursued the Israelites towards the Red Sea. Turning off the road and south into the hills, it's possible to spot the monastery sited beneath a dramatic ridge of cliffs, known as Mount Qalah.

Lofty walls with an interior catwalk surround the **Monastery of St Anthony**, whose lanes of two-storey dwellings, churches, mills and gardens of vines, olive and palms basically amount to a village. The community remains dependent on water from its **spring**, where Arab legend has it that Miriam, sister of Moses, bathed during the Exodus.

Some of the churches date from the early twentieth century and new ones are under construction. An English-speaking monk will give you a partial tour, though some areas are off-limits. Highlights include the **keep**, a soot-blackened **bakery** and a **library** of over 1700 manuscripts. The oldest of the five churches is dedicated to the monastery's namesake, who may be buried underneath it. Be sure not to miss the wall paintings, some of which date back to the seventh century and have been restored to their former glory. During Lent (when the gates are locked and deliveries are winched over the walls), monks celebrate the liturgy in the twelve-domed Church of St Luke, dating from 1776. A small **museum** details the monastery's history; next door is a well-stocked bookshop.

All of these buildings are recent compared to the monastery's foundation, shortly after Anthony's death in 356. A sojourn by St John the Short is all that's recorded of its early **history**, but an influx of refugees from Wadi Natrun, and then Melkite monks, occurred during the sixth and seventh centuries. Subsequently pillaged by Bedouin and razed by Nasr al-Dawla, the monastery was restored during the twelfth century by Coptic monks, from whose ranks several Ethiopian bishops were elected. After a murderous revolt by the monastery servants, it was reoccupied by Coptic, Syrian and Ethiopian monks. Today's permanent brethren are university graduates and ex-professionals – not unlike the kind of people drawn to monasticism in the fourth century AD. A typical day at the monastery begins at 4am, with two hours of prayer and hymns followed by communion and Mass, all before breakfast.

St Anthony's Cave

Early morning or late afternoon is the best time to ascend to **St Anthony's Cave** (*maghara*), 2km from, and 276m above, the monastery (bring water). After passing a sculpture of St Anthony carved into the mountain rock, you'll face 1200 steps (45min) up to the cave, but the stunning views from 680m above the Red Sea reward your effort. Technicolour wadis and massifs spill down into the azure gulf, with Sinai's mountains rising beyond. The cave where Anthony spent his last 25 years contains medieval graffiti and modern *tilbas*, scraps of paper bearing supplications inscribed with "Remember, Lord, your servant", which pilgrims stick into cracks in the rock. **Birdlife** – hoopoes, desert larks, ravens, blue rock thrushes and pied wagtails – is surprisingly abundant, and you might glimpse shy **gazelles**.

The Monastery of St Paul

The **Monastery of St Paul** has always been overshadowed by St Anthony's. Its titular founder (not to be confused with the apostle Paul) was only 16 and an orphan when he fled Alexandria to escape Emperor Decius' persecutions, making him the earliest known hermit. Shortly before his death in 348, Paul was visited by Anthony and begged him to bring the robe of Pope Athanasius, for Paul to be buried in. Anthony departed to fetch this, but on the way back had a vision of Paul's soul being carried up to heaven by angels, and arrived to find him dead. While Anthony was wondering what to do, two lions appeared and dug a grave for the body, so Anthony shrouded it in the robe and took Paul's tunic of palm leaves as a gift for the pope, who subsequently wore it at Christmas, Epiphany and Easter.

The monastery (called Deir Amba Bula or Deir Mari Bolus) was a form of posthumous homage by Paul's followers: its turreted walls are built around the cave where he lived for decades. To a large extent, its fortunes have followed those of its more prestigious neighbour. In 1484 all its monks were slain by the Bedouin, who occupied St Paul's for eighty years. Rebuilt by Patriarch Gabriel VII, it was again destroyed near the end of the sixteenth century.

The monastery is much smaller than St Anthony's and a little more primitive looking. It boasts four churches, but the **Church of St Paul** is its spiritual centre, a cave-church housing the remains of the saint. The church walls are painted with murals generally thought inferior to those of St Anthony's, though they have been well preserved. A monk will show you round the chapels and identify their icons: notice the angel of the furnace with Shadrach, Meshach and Abednego, and the ostrich eggs hung from the ceiling – a symbol of the Resurrection. The southern sanctuary of the larger **Church of St Michael** contains a gilded icon of the head of John the Baptist on a dish. When Bedouin raided the monastery, its monks retreated into the five-storey **keep**, supplied with spring water by a hidden canal. Nowadays this is not enough to sustain the monks and their guests, so water is brought in from outside.

There is a small shop selling supplies and a reasonably priced cafeteria just outside the monastery grounds.

Ain Sukhna and El Gouna

Without private transport or a desire to visit the Red Sea monasteries (see p.589), it's hardly worth stopping between Suez and Hurghada. Heading south past the numerous oil and natural gas refineries, you'll see parched highlands rising inland. The **Jebel Ataqa** is the northernmost range in the Eastern Desert and an old Bedouin smuggling route.

From Suez, a seventy-kilometre series of beaches and coves marks the area around **AIN SUKHNA**. The name derives from the **hot springs** (35°C) originating in the Jebel Ataqa, but it's the sea that attracts visitors, largely affluent Egyptians, but few foreigners. Light patches offshore indicate **coral reefs**, while barbed-wire fences delineate areas sown with landmines (mainly beneath the cliffs). There are paying **beaches** (£E20–50) in front of the *Ain Sukhna* and *Mena Oasis* hotels; other stretches are free.

If you haven't got a car, Ain Sukhna is best reached by **bus from Suez**, 10km south of which is the welcoming *Palmera* (Ⓣ062/341-0816, Ⓦwww.palmerabeachresort.com; ❼), with three enormous swimming pools, and several restaurants and bars. Other swish places to stay include the *Mena Oasis* (Ⓣ062/329-0850, Ⓕ329-0855; half-board ❼), 67km south of Suez, with a disco and over a kilometre of beach. The only budget accommodation in the area is the *Sahara Inn* motel (no phone; ❷–❸), about 10km south of **Za'farana** along the desolate, windblown highway, with austere rooms with or without air conditioning.

The next stop for buses south of Ain Sukhna is the ugly oil town of **Ras Gharib**, which only really appeals to mountaineers keen to tackle **Jebel Gharib** (1757m).

El Gouna

Approximately 22km north of Hurghada lies the vast tourist resort of **El Gouna** (Ⓦwww.elgouna.com), popular with the Egyptian jet set and Western package tourists. Built on a series of islands linked by purpose-built bridges and canals, El Gouna covers 37 square kilometres of land, and packs a lot in. There's an eighteen-hole **golf** course, a **casino**, two shopping centres, (the main one having an open-air **cinema**), cafés, restaurants, bars, nightclubs, **banks**, travel agencies, a **museum**, **aquarium** and a **post office,** plus a brewery, a winery, a cheese factory, and an international airport. A free half-hourly shuttle bus to the resort from Hurghada is run by El Gouna Transport. Most hotels have **dive centres** attached (a list of dive sites in the vicinity appears on p.581), and watersports, horseriding, go-karting, tennis, squash and microlight flights are also on offer. The state-of-the-art private **hospital** (emergencies Ⓣ065/354-0011, Ⓦwww.elgounahospital.com.eg) has a decompression chamber (Ⓣ012 218-7550).

A **private airstrip** is served by weekly flights from Cairo run by the charter company SunAir (Ⓣ02/335-7440).

Accommodation, eating and drinking

There are more than a dozen three- to five-star **hotels** in El Gouna, plus numerous private villas. Among the profusion of **eating, drinking and dancing** venues are poolside snackbars, karaoke joints, discos, Bedouin tents, formal restaurants and *sheesha* cafés. Holidaymakers on full-board packages can use the "dine around" system to patronize other hotels; details are listed on Ⓦwww.elgouna.com.

Mövenpick Resort Ⓣ065/354-4501, Ⓦwww.moevenpick-elgouna.com. Luxurious a/c rooms with bath and balcony or patio overlooking the sea, lagoon or gardens. There are four pools, a dive centre (Ⓦwww.divetribe.com), kiteboarding, a 3km stretch of beach, and a spa, massage and aromatherapy centre. Wheelchair friendly. ❼–❽

Sheraton Miramar Ⓣ065/354-5606, Ⓦwww.starwoodhotels.com. Built on nine islands, its 339 a/c rooms (each accessed via a small bridge) have terraces, sea views and satellite TV. There are two main pools, three more for children, and a dive centre. Wheelchair friendly. ❼

Steigenberger Golf Resort Ⓣ065/358-0140, Ⓦwww.steigenberger.com. Swish German-owned hotel, designed by US architect Michael Graves, with an 18-hole championship golf course and spa. It's won awards for both its outstanding architecture and environmental policies. ❼–❽

Three Corners Rihana Inn Ⓣ065/358-0025, Ⓦwww.threecorners.com. A/c studios featuring terraces with pool or mountain views, kitchenettes and satellite TV, as well as access to the beach and better facilities of its four-star sister hotel *Three Corners Rihana Resort*. Home to the Colona Dive Centre (Ⓣ065/358-0113, Ⓦwww.colona.com) and Easy Divers (Ⓣ012 230-5202, Ⓦwww.easydivers-redsea.com). 7

Hurghada (Ghardaka)

In two decades, **HURGHADA** has been transformed from a humble fishing village into a booming town of well over 150,000 people. This phenomenal growth is almost entirely due to **tourism**, which accounts for 95 percent of the local economy. However, it's worth taking Hurghada's claims to be a seaside resort with a handful of salt: its public beaches are distant or uninviting, while the best marine life is far offshore. If you're not into diving or clubbing, you'll soon find that Hurghada lacks charm – though you have to admire its commercial gusto.

While package tourists laze in their resorts, independent travellers often feel hard done by. Paying for boat trips and private beaches is unavoidable if you're to enjoy Hurghada's assets, and although conditions for diving, windsurfing and deep-sea fishing are great, the **cost** is high, with real bargains limited to accommodation. Nor will you save much by self-catering; everything in the shops is more expensive than in Cairo or the Nile Valley. As tour groups come year round, there's no "off" season; **peak times** are the European Christmas and Easter holidays and the Russian vacation period of August and September, Hurghada being extremely popular with Russians, hundreds of thousands of whom visit each year. While their custom is welcomed by the resorts, cultural differences – notably over alcohol and sex – often cause tension with the locals. Budget hotels are most in demand over winter, when backpackers use Hurghada as a transit point between the Nile Valley and the Sinai peninsula.

The town itself is a hotchpotch of utilitarian structures, garish hotels, gaudy shops and sporadic patches of waste ground. Coming in from the north, look out for the windmill fields, built to harness wind power and generate electricity.

Within Hurghada, most of the coastline from Ed-Dahar in the north to the so-called New Hurghada in the south is shielded from view by the line of resorts, so

Approaches to Hurghada

Hurghada is more accessible by public transport than its location might suggest.

- **From Alexandria** Superjet has one bus daily to Hurghada (9hr).
- **From Cairo** There are frequent buses daily to Hurghada from the Turgoman terminal (6-7hr). El Gouna Transport Company (Ⓣ02/574-1533) also runs fourteen comfortable a/c buses throughout the day and night (6hr) from their office near the Ramses Hilton, just north of the Egyptian Antiquities Museum. You can also catch these buses half an hour later at Nasser City Station (Autostrad Rd). There are also numerous daily EgyptAir flights (1hr).
- **From Suez** The 410-kilometre journey from Suez can be covered in around five hours by service taxi, or at a less perilous speed by around a dozen daily buses (6–7hr).
- **From Sinai** The catamaran trip from Sharm el-Sheikh is quick and convenient; see p.534 for details.
- **From the Nile Valley** Many travellers come to Hurghada by bus from Aswan (3 daily; 7hr) and Luxor (around 7 daily; 5hr) via Qena and Safaga. There are also a couple of buses daily from Assyut. Service taxis cross the desert between Beni Suef and Za'farana, or Qift and El-Quseir but foreigners are not permitted to use these routes. EgyptAir may run flights from Luxor during peak travel periods.

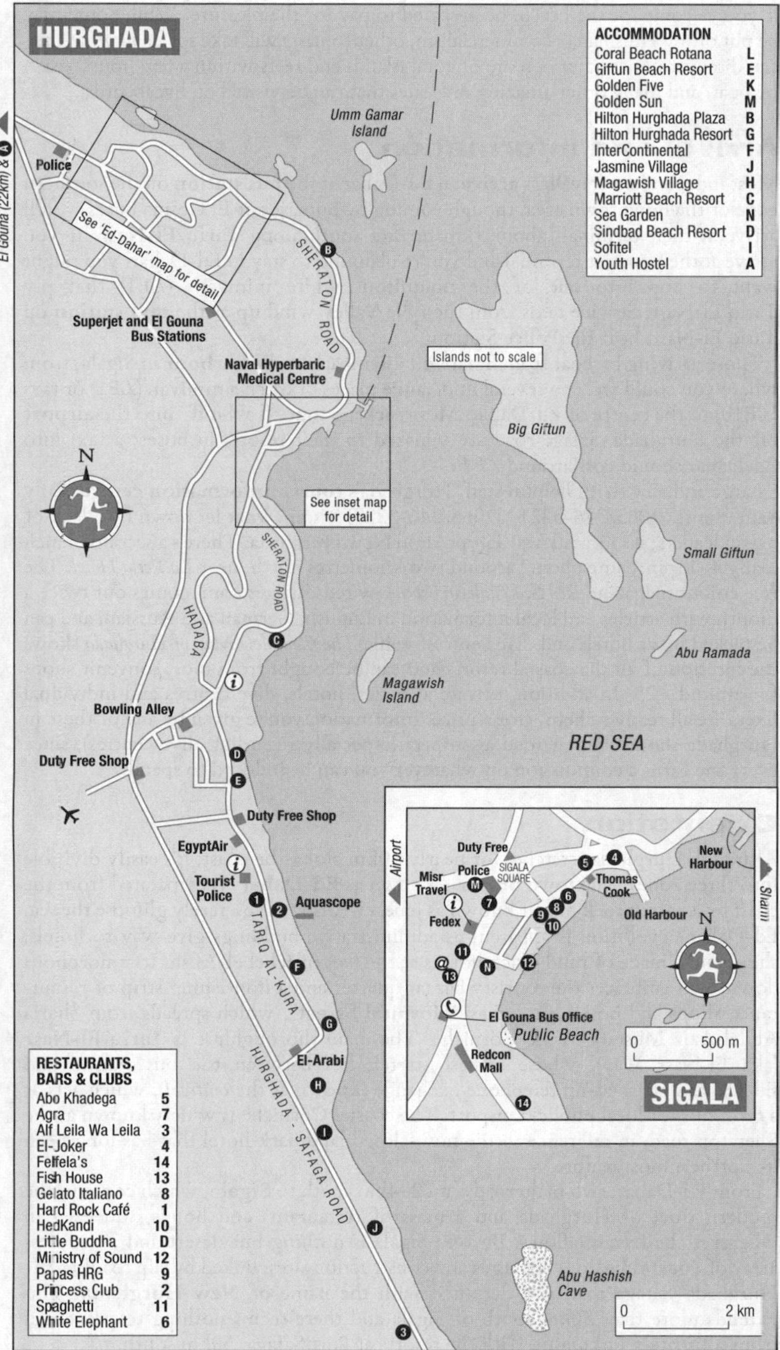

HURGHADA
Sharm el-Sheikh
El Gouna (22km) & A
K, L & Port Safaga (45km)
ACCOMMODATION
Coral Beach Rotana L
Giftun Beach Resort E
Golden Five K
Golden Sun M
Hilton Hurghada Plaza B
Hilton Hurghada Resort G
InterContinental F
Jasmine Village J
Magawish Village H
Marriott Beach Resort C
Sea Garden N
Sindbad Beach Resort D
Sofitel I
Youth Hostel A
Umm Gamar Island
Police
See 'Ed-Dahar' map for detail
Sheraton Road
Superjet and El Gouna Bus Stations
Naval Hyperbaric Medical Centre
Islands not to scale
Big Giftun
N
See inset map for detail
Small Giftun
Hadaba
Abu Ramada
Magawish Island
Bowling Alley
RED SEA
Duty Free Shop
Duty Free Shop
EgyptAir
Tourist Police
Aquascope
Tariq al-Kura
El-Arabi
Hurghada - Safaga Road
RESTAURANTS, BARS & CLUBS
Abo Khadega 5
Agra 7
Alf Leila Wa Leila 3
El-Joker 4
Felfela's 14
Fish House 13
Gelato Italiano 8
Hard Rock Café 1
HedKandi 10
Little Buddha D
Ministry of Sound 12
Papas HRG 9
Princess Club 2
Spaghetti 11
White Elephant 6
Airport
Duty Free
Police
Sigala Square
Misr Travel
Thomas Cook
New Harbour
Sharm
Old Harbour
Fedex
El Gouna Bus Office
Public Beach
Redcon Mall
0 500 m
SIGALA
Abu Hashish Cave
0 2 km

7 THE RED SEA COAST

if you've come for the beach, be prepared to pay for the pleasure. While some may be put off by Hurghada's commercialism, other tourists will take solace in what they can discover underwater: a score of coral islands and reefs within a few hours' reach by boat, and many other amazing dive sites that can be visited on liveaboards.

Arrival and information

Most independent travellers **arrive** in Ed-Dahar at the **bus station** on the southern edge of the downtown area, though coming by Superjet or El Gouna buses, you'll arrive at their terminals about 1km further south along **Tariq El-Nasr**. If you arrive at the Superjet terminal and you're planning to stay in Ed-Dahar, you might want to hop into one of the ubiquitous white minivans (£E1) that ply Tariq El-Nasr. Service taxis from the Nile Valley wind up at the **taxi station** on Tariq El-Nasr, near the Police Station.

Those arriving by boat from Sinai will disembark at the **harbour** in Sigala, from where you could walk to several mid-range places or catch a minivan (£E1) or taxi (£E10) to the centre of Ed-Dahar. Most package tourists who fly into the **airport** off the Hurghada–Safaga road are whisked to their resorts in buses; a taxi into Ed-Dahar should cost around £E40.

Large and airy, with helpful staff, Hurghada's **tourist information centre** (daily 8am–8pm; Ⓣ065/346-3221, Ⓕ065/346-3220) is somewhat let down by a lack of useful leaflets; it's located near EgyptAir in New Hurghada. There's a second branch (daily 4–11pm; same phone) around two kilometres north, near *La Perla Hotel*. The free colour magazine *Red Sea Bulletin* (Ⓦwww.redseapages.com) comes out twice a month with articles and local information in English, German and Russian, and can be picked up at hotels and dive centres, while *The Complete Map of Hurghada* shows the location of all the coastal resorts and can be bought from most souvenir shops for around £25. In addition, private agencies, hotels, dive centres and individual fixers are all ready to help – for a price. Information you're given by any of these in Hurghada should be regarded as suspect (especially regarding dive centres), since everyone earns a commission on whatever you can be induced to spend.

Orientation

Although Hurghada stretches for nearly 40km along the coast, it's easily divisible into three zones. The town proper – known as **Ed-Dahar** – is separated from the coast by a barren rock massif known as Jebel el-Afish, so you rarely glimpse the sea. Ed-Dahar's evolution is apparent as administrative buildings give way to hotels, shops and a maze of mud-brick homes at the feet of Jebel el-Afish. Its amorphous downtown embraces the touristy bazaar quarter and a flourishing strip of restaurants, shops and hotels known as **"Hospital Street"**, which spreads from Sharia Abdel Aziz Mustafa to the Corniche. The main thoroughfare is **Tariq El-Nasr** (aka El-Nasr Way), whose busiest stretch lies between the bus station and Ed-Dahar's boarded-up telephone exchange (known as the *centraal*), which acts as a terminus for local public transport. The coastal Corniche is widely known as the Sheraton road, in reference to the now-closed landmark hotel that has long been its northernmost feature.

From Ed-Dahar, two main roads run 2–4km south to **Sigala**, which contains the modern **port** of Hurghada and a mass of restaurants and hotels, squeezed in wherever the terrain allows. Beyond Sigala is nothing but desert and an endless array of **coastal holiday villages** and construction sites, linked by slip roads to the Hurghada–Safaga road and dignified with the name of **New Hurghada**. This extends more than 30km south of Sigala and there seems nothing to prevent it from ultimately linking up with the resorts at Port Safaga, 50km south.

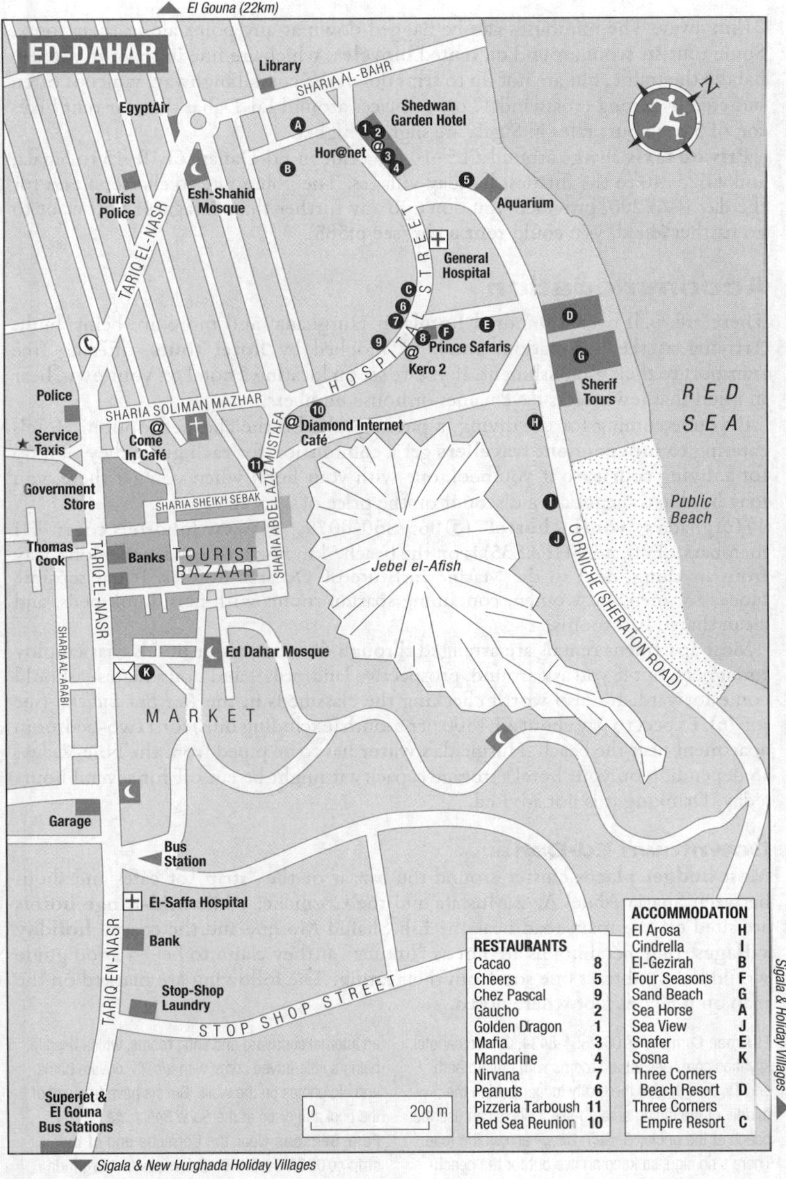

Transport

While **walking** is fine for getting around Ed-Dahar, transport is needed to reach Sigala or anywhere further south. **Private minibuses** run up and down the coast along the Corniche 24 hours a day, as well as Tariq El-Nasr to the airport and beyond. You'll pay £E0.50 for a short hop or £E1 for rides between Ed-Dahar, Sigala and New Hurghada, and £E3 for a trip as far south as the *Jasmine Village*,

21km away. The minibuses can be flagged down at any point along their route. Some tourists scoot around on rented **bicycles**, which are fine in town if you can handle the traffic, but are not up to trips down the coastal highway, which is often buffeted by strong crosswinds. Lots of places around Ed-Dahar's bazaar rent bikes for £E5 per hour; rates in Sigala are slightly higher.

Private taxis charge around £E5–10 for a ride in Ed-Dahar, £E10–15 to Sigala, and £E25–40 to the furthest holiday villages. The going rate to charter a taxi for the day is £E200, provided you don't go any further than Safaga. If you want to go further afield, you could **rent a car** (see p.585).

Accommodation

There are well over a hundred **hotels** in Hurghada, and more are being built. Arriving at the bus station, you'll be mobbed by **hotel touts**, offering free transport to their establishment. If you're set on locating a hotel on your own, bear in mind that few streets have names or house numbers.

If you're coming for the diving, a **package deal** is the cheapest option. Hotels catering to **independent travellers** get a commission for each guest they sign up for a diving course, so if you book one with your hotel when you get there, you may be able to negotiate a discount on the price of a room.

Hurghada's **youth hostel** (ⓣ065/350-0079, ⓦwww.hihostels.com; HI members £E30, non-HI £E35) is on the beach 5km north of town and a long way from anything, next to the Marine Institute of Oceanic Studies. It has separate blocks for men and women, containing spartan rooms with fans, bunk beds, and clean shared bathrooms.

Most apartment rentals are arranged through dive centres or hotels that employ foreigners, but if you ask around, prospective landlords – and housemates – should come forward. It's also worth checking the classifieds in the *Red Sea Bulletin* (see p.576). Expect to pay about £E1800 per month (excluding bills) for a two-bedroom apartment near the beach. Hurghada's **water** has to be piped from the Nile Valley, so depending on your hotel's storage capacity it might be cut off for several hours a day. Drinking it is not advised.

Downtown Ed-Dahar

Most **budget places** cluster around the bazaar or the "strip" of cafés and shops between Sharia Abdel Aziz Mustafa and the Corniche, while **mid-range hotels** are sited off the main road near the Esh-Shahid Mosque and the coastal **holiday villages**. In general hotels are not as "luxury" as they claim to be – a good guide would be to subtract one star from their rating. The following are marked on the map on p.577 except where noted.

El Arosa Corniche ⓣ065/354-8434, ⓔelarosahotel@yahoo.com. Decent a/c rooms with private bath and TV, though give the grotty indoor pool in the middle of the dining area a miss. Guests can use the beach at the pricier *Geisum Village* across the road. There's no sign, so keep an eye out for the peach-coloured exterior. ❹

Cindrella Corniche ⓣ065/355-6571. The somewhat gaudy decor in the clean a/c rooms – all with private baths – may not be to everyone's taste, but *Cindrella* is good value, friendly and offers wi-fi. It has an on-site pizza restaurant and bar. ❸

El-Gezirah Off Sharia al-Bahr ⓣ065/354-7785, ⓕ354-3708. An orange, yellow and turquoise confection, with an internal courtyard and snug rooms, which despite being a little frayed come with a/c, TV, private baths and old photos on the walls. Guests have free use of the pool and disco at the *Sand Beach*. ❹

Four Seasons Near the Corniche end of the strip ⓣ065/354-5456, ⓔforseasonshurghada@hotmail.com. The rooms – with a/c, TV and private bath are scruffy but acceptable for the price at this slightly shambolic place where, fittingly, a stopped clock stands motionless in the lobby. Not to be confused with the smart international chain of the same name. ❷–❸

Hilton Hurghada Plaza South end of the Corniche (see map, p.575) ⓣ065/354-9745, www.hiltonworldresorts.com. Massive but isolated five-star resort perched on an arid hill between Ed-Dahar and Sigala. Still, it does have understated en suites with sea views, tubs and wi-fi, plus the full range of facilities. 8

Sand Beach Corniche 065/354-7992, www.sandbeach-hurghada.net. The rooms don't quite match the over-the-top marble lobby, but they are blandly comfortable. There are three pools, a beach, diving centre and disco, but service can be abrupt. Popular with Russians. 6

Sea Horse Off Sharia al-Bahr 065/354-8704, seahorse.hotel@gmail.com. This welcoming place has a relaxed atmosphere, airy en suites, a central garden and a pool. Residents can use its beach, and the one at the *New Sea Horse*, by *Hilton Hurghada Plaza*. 5–6

Sea View Corniche 065/354-5959, www.seaviewhotel.com.eg. A bit away from the action, *Sea View* has clean a/c rooms with white and green decor, prints of Ancient Egypt and small balconies overlooking the sea across the busy Corniche. Residents have free use of the *Sea Horse*'s beach. 3–4

Snafer Near the Corniche end of the strip 065/354-0260, ashrafhurghada@hotmail.com. A pleasant hotel with courteous staff and well-kept a/c rooms with private bath and TV – they vary, so ask to see a few. The upper floors have good sea views, but there's no elevator. It's probably Ed-Dahar's best-value hotel in this price bracket. 3

Sosna Off Tariq El-Nasr 065/354-6647. Budget place with carpeted rooms with fan and bedside lamps; private bathrooms are optional. With a relaxed atmosphere, it's used mainly by Egyptians. 2

Three Corners Beach Resort Corniche 065/354-7816, www.threecorners.com. Slightly smarter than the *Empire Hotel*, with its own beach and manicured gardens. The comfortable a/c en suites have satellite TV; the more expensive also have sea views. It's less opulent than some of the other hotels on this part of the beach, but the rooms are a shade cheaper. 5–6

Three Corners Empire Hotel Hospital St 065/354-7186, www.threecorners.com. Dominating the skyline, this large, somewhat dated, hotel has spacious and very clean a/c en-suite rooms with satellite TV and balconies overlooking the pool. Guests can use the beach at the *Three Corners Beach Resort*. 4–5

Sigala

Despite a decent range of places to eat and drink, it's hard to see why anyone would want to stay in Sigala, since there are better mid-range options in Ed-Dahar and ritzier holiday villages in New Hurghada. However, if everywhere else is full, you could try the following.

Golden Sun Just off Sheraton Rd 065/344-4403, goldenkhalid@hotmail.com. With a small garden out front, fake papyrus prints on the walls, an internet café and clean, functional a/c rooms, *Golden Sun* does the best with what it has. 2

Sea Garden Hotel Off Sheraton Rd 065/344-7493, www.seagarden.com.eg. The clean but plain rooms could do with a touch-up, but all have a/c, private facilities and wi-fi. There's a nice garden and pool, and it's close to the attractions of Hurghada Marina. BB 6

New Hurghada

The fully-contained **holiday villages** of New Hurghada take independent travellers if trade is slack. Unless stated otherwise, all the resorts below (see map, p.575) have air conditioning, at least one pool, a diving centre, beach and disco. Where the clientele is mainly from certain countries, you may feel at a disadvantage if you don't speak the right language. The distances stated below are measured from Ed-Dahar's bus station.

Coral Beach Rotana 28km 065/346-1610, www.rotana.com. Large en suites in blues and yellows have minibar and satellite TV; some also have French windows. Facilities include two pools, tennis, squash and horseriding, and there's a large beach with reefs offshore. Mainly caters to Italians. An upgrade was planned at the time of research. 7

Giftun Beach Resort 14km 065/346-3040, www.giftunbeachresort.com. A mix of Spanish-style chalets with pretty gardens and standard hotel rooms with bright decor, fronting a good beach and windsurfing lagoon. All-inclusive of meals and activities except for watersports. 7

Golden Five 25km ⓣ065/344-7744, ⓦwww.golden5.com.eg. A vast Vegas-style combination of theme park and hotel complex, with daily shows, a replica Egyptian village, aqua park, enormous pools, a cable-car lift and dozens of bars and restaurants. Smart service and family-friendly. ⑧

Hilton Hurghada Resort 17km ⓣ065/346-5036, ⓦwww.hiltonworldwideresorts.com. With a full range of facilities and the same five-star rating as its sister *Plaza* hotel (see p.578), but the rooms have been brightened up recently and the health and fitness centre revamped. ⑧

InterContinental 17km ⓣ065/346-5100, ⓦwww.ichotelsgroup.com. Opulent complex of rooms with bath, satellite TV, sea views and tea/coffee makers; some also have Arabic-style latticework features. Amenities include a very large marina, health club and tennis courts. ⑦

Jasmine Village 21km ⓣ065/346-0475, ⓦwww.jasminevillage.com. Straightforward rooms with satellite TV and fridge. Great little beach with reef and windsurfing lagoons. Other amenities include a playground, zoo, aviary, mini-golf and tennis and squash courts. Disabled access. Half-board ⑦

Magawish Village 19km ⓣ065/346-2621, ⓦwww.magawish.com. A former Club Med, offering simple mid-range rooms with kitchenettes, plus a big beach and decent sports facilities, especially for wind- and kitesurfing, and a children's playground. Half-board ⑦

Marriott Beach Resort 11km ⓣ065/344-6950, ⓦwww.marriott.com. Five-star complex with a large pool and a small sandy beach, a marina, health club and residents-only disco. The suites (around $250) are particularly good if you have the money to upgrade. Standard rooms ⑧

Sindbad Beach Resort 13km ⓣ065/344-3261, ⓦwww.sindbad-group.com. Family-oriented four-star complex, popular with Russians and Eastern Europeans, with lots of nightlife, a huge water chute on the beach and an entertainment complex offering dolphin shows. Patchy service. Half-board ⑧

Sofitel 20km ⓣ065/346-4646, ⓦwww.sofitel.com. Classy pseudo-Moorish complex, with marble floors, lattice windows and a vast curvaceous pool. The management puts on events like themed dinners for which guests are encouraged to dress up. Good online deals. Half-board ⑦–⑧

Diving and snorkelling

Diving really put Hurghada on the map. Its topography favours island corals over reefs, with sharks, giant moray eels and manta rays in its deeper, rougher waters. There are about ten islands within day-trip range and over a score of sites that can be visited on extended dive safaris, or liveaboards.

Hurghada welcomes hordes of tourists each week, and has more than a thousand tour boats. To help combat the environmental impact of this, the **Underwater National Parks of the Red Sea and Protected Islands** (aka Marine Park) enforces a daily "environmental tax" (€2–3) for all divers and snorkellers, the proceeds of which are being ploughed back into Red Sea environmental projects. This is in addition to the standard per-person charge of €3 per day to dive the Giftun Islands and the nearby reefs and €5 per day for sites further south, such as Brothers and Zabargad. The problem is also being tackled by **HEPCA** (Hurghada Environmental Protection and Conservation Association; ⓦwww.hepca.com), which is trying to raise ecological awareness – though few of the local dive centres show much interest. Tourists can help by favouring dive centres which belong to HEPCA and which display a certificate from the **Egyptian Underwater Sports Federation**.

A four- or five-day PADI Open Water course costs €300–350 including the dive certificate. Beginners can expect to pay around €80 for two supervised dives. Scuba **equipment** is included in the price of courses, but otherwise costs around €23 extra per day; renting snorkelling gear for a day costs about €5. The average rate for a day's **boat diving** is €40–60; most trips include two dives and lunch. Never hand over cash to someone on the street who promises to arrange a trip; book through a dive centre (see below).

For longer trips, the Colona Dive Centre (see p.581) can arrange **liveaboards** and diving packages (mostly lasting for a week) taking you further south to sites near Safaga, Mersa Alam, Wadi Gimal and Wadi Lahami, or even as far as the Zabargad Islands, about 100km southeast of Berenice. Expect to pay at least €80 per person per day.

There are **decompression chambers** in El Gouna's hospital (see p.573) and the Mubarak Naval Hyperbaric & Emergency Medical Centre, in Ed-Dahar about 500 metres northwest of the police station (☎065/354-9150 or 354-4195).

Dive centres

Your life may depend on **choosing the right diving centre**; always check that the instructor is qualified, with valid ID and insurance, not merely photocopies. Many are freelancers who frequently change jobs, so even the best centres sometimes get bad instructors. As a rule of thumb, it is safer to dive with the large outfits attached to holiday villages than with backstreet operators taking clients sent by budget hotels (whose recommendations can't be trusted). Of the hundred or so dive centres in Hurghada, most are run by Europeans and tend to have higher standards than the locally managed outfits. The ones listed below are affiliated to HEPCA and are thus subject to monitoring.

The thirty or so dive centres which are members of the **Diving Emergency Centre Organization** (DECO; ☎012 218-7550, Ⓦwww.deco-international.com) encourage clients to pay €6 for three weeks' cover, which includes free use of the decompression chambers in Hurghada, El Gouna or Mersa Alam, doctor's fees, as well as equipment and medicines used in treatment, though not hospitalization or any transport for the injured person.

Aquanaut Blue Heaven *Regina Resort*, Sigala ☎065/344-0892, Ⓦwww.aquanaut.net.

Aquarius Diving Club *Marriott Beach Resort* ☎065/344-6950, Ⓦwww.aquariusredsea.com.

Colona *Magawish Village* ☎065/346-4631, Ⓦwww.colona.com.

Divers International *Sofitel* ☎065/354-9745 ext 5507, Ⓦwww.diversintl.com.

Easy Divers *Three Corners Beach Resort* ☎012 230-5202, Ⓦwww.easydivers-redsea.com.

El-Samaka *El-Samaka Diving Centre* ☎065/354-3681, Ⓦwww.elsamaka.com.

Emperor Divers *Tourist Harbour*, Sigala ☎012 737-2125, Ⓦwww.emperordivers.com.

James & Mac *Giftun Beach Resort* ☎012 311-8923, Ⓦwww.james-mac.com.

Jasmin Diving Center *Grand Seas Resort* ☎065/346-0334, Ⓦwww.jasmin-diving.com.

Subex Downtown off the Corniche ☎065/354-3261, Ⓦwww.subex.org.

Dive sites

Most sites within day-trip range are to the east and northeast of Hurghada. Inexperienced divers should be wary of the northerly reefs, where the currents are strongest. While many liveaboards go as far north as Ras Mohammed, sites to the south are regarded as more prestigious. All of the following are within day-trip range unless stated otherwise.

Abu Hashish Cave An underwater cave in the reef, once used as a dope smugglers' cache.

Abu Ramada Three coral blocks covered in psychedelic-hued soft corals, off Giftun Island.

Abu Ramada Gota (aka "Aquarium") Amazing standing *ergs* and 1500-year-old stony corals, with a profusion of bannerfish, sweetlips and spotted groupers.

Brothers Several *ergs* emerging from the deeps of the Red Sea, 80km northeast of El-Quseir. A popular liveaboard destination, open only to boats with permits.

Careless Reef North of Giftun Island, and only accessible in mild weather conditions, this reef is the home of an extended community of moray eels.

Dolphin House A horseshoe-shaped reef 15km south of Mersa Alam, widely used by dolphins as a nursery for their young. HEPCA has recently installed buoys to prevent boats from entering. An excellent site for snorkelling.

El-Fanadir Beautiful reef slope and large table corals, to the north of Sigala.

El-Fanous Coral gardens just off Big Giftun Island, good for snorkelling as well as diving.

Giftun Island Most of the reefs on the Big and Small Giftun have been ruined by years of dive boats dropping their anchors onto the coral, and are now mostly visited by craft packed with snorkellers (around €25 per person including equipment and lunch, but excluding entrance fee). Two notable spots are the Small Giftun Drift (fine reef wall and lovely fan corals), and the Stone Beach on the northeast side of Big Giftun.

Shadwan Island Halfway to Sharm el-Sheikh, so out of day-trip range. Sheer walls and deep trenches here attract reef and oceanic sharks. Its lighthouse was of keen interest to de Monfreid, when he navigated his boat through these waters in the early 1920s, with six hundred kilos of hashish secreted in its hold.

Thistlegorm This wreck (see p.526) is cheaper and slightly easier to reach from Sharm el-Sheikh.

Um Gamar Island Sheer walls and caves, brilliant for drift diving. You can swim through a cave filled with thousands of silvery glassfish.

Snorkelling

The small reefs offshore from the *Shedwan* hotel complex in Ed-Dahar and the *Jasmine Village* in Hurghada have been subject to noticeable damage, though they do offer snorkellers a glimpse of fish and corals further out to sea. Most dive centres offer snorkelling trips and can recommend good locations at Giftun Island or elsewhere. An especially good deal is offered by Prince Safaris on Dr Sayed Koryem Street (Ⓣ065/354-9882 or Ⓣ012 248-4015, Ⓦwww.prince-diving.com), near the *Three Corners Empire Hotel*; it's run by friendly Bedouin brothers, who can arrange snorkelling to Giftun Island for around €20 (with lunch).

Beaches, pools and watersports

Diving apart, Hurghada presents itself as an all-round beach resort. While the **public beach** in Sigala (daily 8am–sunset; £E5) has been transformed from a wasteland where no foreign tourist would be seen dead to a tidy shore with sunshades and a small refreshment kiosk, to sunbathe without unwanted attention you'll have to go for the **private beaches**. In Ed-Dahar, the *Shedwan Golden Beach* (next to the *Shedwan Garden Hotel*), *Three Corners Empire Beach Resort* and *Sand Beach* open their beaches to outsiders for £E20–60 (you can also use the pools at the *Shedwan* and *Sand Beach*). Most holiday villages allow outsiders to use their beaches and pools for a fee (£E3).

Powerful gusts make Hurghada a great place for **windsurfing** and **kiteboarding**. Several holiday villages have lagoons and centres where you can rent boards (for around €15/hr) or kites (around €35/hr), plus wetsuits, and some places offer instruction. Happy Surf (Ⓣ012 240-9888, Ⓦwww.happy-surf.de) organizes windsurfing and has branches at *Sofitel* and *Hilton Hurghada Plaza*. For kiteboarding, try Pro Center at *Jasmine Village* (Ⓣ010 667-2811, Ⓦwww.tommy-friedl.de); and Colona Watersports at *Magawish Village* (Ⓣ010 344-1810, Ⓦwww.colonawatersports.com).

If you book one or two days ahead, Prince Safaris (see snorkelling above) can arrange **deep-sea fishing** day-trips for around €100 per boat including equipment. An international fishing competition, sponsored by the Egyptian Fishing Federation, is held off Hurghada's shores every February.

The Aquarium, Sindbad Submarine and Sindbad Quest

If you want a glimpse of the Red Sea's wonders without getting wet, visit the **Red Sea Aquarium** (daily 9am–2pm & 6–9pm; £E5, camera £E2) on the Corniche.

Alternatively, there are the much-hyped **Sindbad Submarines** (€40), two craft which can take you to depths of 22m in comfort. Disappointingly, however, half the time is spent getting to and from the sub's mooring offshore from the *Sindbad Beach Resort* in New Hurghada, and after submerging a diver swims alongside trailing bait to attract wrasses, groupers and parrotfish past the portholes. Book through any of the major hotels, or at the resort (Ⓣ065/344-4688, Ⓔsubmarine@sindbad-club.com).

Another window on the underwater world can be had from the *Sindbad Quest*, a space-age glass-bottomed speedboat (€30 for a two-hour trip; ⓣ065/344-4688, ⓔquest@sindbad-club.com). A more traditional glass-bottomed boat experience can be arranged through most of the hotels for around £E50 per hour.

Eating

Hurghada is good for **eating out**, with a wide choice of cuisines suited to all budgets. The holiday villages all have restaurants, mostly upmarket and with **live music** (provided by cover bands or Egyptian floor shows) in the evening. For an inexpensive meal, check out the many (often nameless) fish restaurants and pizza parlours in Ed-Dahar and Sigala. **Opening hours** are generally mid-morning until 11pm or midnight (sometimes later in high season), though the choice of food dwindles after 10pm. Almost everywhere adds around ten percent in **service taxes** to the bill – some resorts bump things up by as much as twenty percent.

For cheap eats, there are two good *fuul* and falafel stands on the street running south of, and parallel to, Sharia Sheikh Sebak; there are *kushari* diners near the bus station. In Sigala, there's a pair of falafel stands on Sigala Square near the police station, and a place with refrigerated display cabinets outside that does tasty kebab, *kofta* and pizzas.

Some of the smartest restaurants (and bars, clubs and clothing boutiques) are to be found at the new Hurghada Marina in Sigala, which has good Thai, Indian, Italian and Lebanese restaurants, with several others being set up at the time of research.

Ed-Dahar

Chez Pascal Hospital St. Good Belgian-inspired nouvelle cuisine like prawn cocktail, lobster thermidor, seafood platters and *crêpes suzette* though service can be slow and prices (mains £E45–85) are a little higher than the norm.

Gaucho *Shedwan Garden Hotel*. Argentine-style steakhouse (though it's mainly Australian beef) with sizzling entrecote, T-bone and fillet cuts. It has a vaguely Spanish colonial feel, with cane furniture, leather placemats and Latin music. Mains £E65–110.

Golden Dragon *Shedwan Garden Hotel* ⓣ065/355-5051. Kitsch, faux oriental decor – snarling dragons, red lanterns and pagoda-style roofs – but a genuine Chinese chef and great food: try the salt and pepper squid. Mains £E50–65.

Mafia *Shedwan Garden Hotel* ⓣ065/354-7007. With checked tablecloths, bunches of plastic grapes hanging from the ceiling and marble fittings, *Mafia* serves decent Italian pastas and wood-fired pizzas (mains £E32-38).

Mandarine *Shedwan Garden Hotel* ⓣ065/354-7007. Excellent Lebanese restaurant with mixed grills, shawarmas and kebabs from £E45. The house speciality is grilled pigeon with tomato and onion.

Pizzeria Tarboush Sharia Abdel Aziz Mustafa. Flashing palm-tree lights stand outside this economical café and takeaway, where a small margarita pizza sets you back just £E9. No alcohol.

Red Sea Reunion Hospital St ⓣ065/354-9630. Seafood, Indian and Italian dishes (mains from £E35) are on offer at this low-key joint, which has a canopied roof terrace with views of the Esh-Shahid minarets in the distance.

Sigala

Abo Khadega East of Sigala Square. A small workers' café where you can get a tasty meal of soup, rice, salad, beans and grilled meat from £E10.

Agra South of Sigala Square. Good Indian joint serving a variety of dishes, including lamb biryani and tandoori chicken for £E30–50.

El-Joker Near the police station in Sigala Square. Excellent seafood restaurant with generous portions at very good prices (£E25–40) – try the calamari soup. Daily 11pm–1am.

Felfela's Sheraton Rd, south of Redcon Mall ⓣ065/344-2410. This spacious branch of the Cairo chain serves decent Egyptian food at reasonable prices, and has a great view of the harbour. Good for vegetarians. Daily 8.30am–midnight.

Fish House Next to *McDonald's*. A smart seafood restaurant with a/c and large picture windows overlooking Sheraton Rd, and a sushi bar. The simpler dishes are usually the best bets. Mains from £E25, sushi from around £E50. Very good value.

Gelato Italiano Hurghada Marina. Home-made Italian ice cream (£E9 per scoop), waffles and smoothies, as well as proper illy espressos, lattes and cappuccinos.

Spaghetti Near *McDonald's*. Steak and seafood restaurant with large outdoor seating area. Good value, and popular with families.

White Elephant Hurghada Marina. Tasty and nicely-presented Thai food including red and yellow curries, pad thai, *tom yam gung* and the house speciality, blue shell crab. Mains £E35–85.

Drinking

A lot of drinking goes on in discos, restaurants and hotels, though there aren't that many independent bars; some of the best are to be found at Hurghada Marina (see above). Most restaurants don't sell alcohol during Ramadan and before 1pm on Fridays, but the holiday villages are exempt from these restrictions. There are **duty-free shops** in the AKA mall near the EgyptAir office in New Hurghada, in Sigala Square opposite the police station, and next to the *Ambassador Hotel* on the road to the airport. The following **bars** are open until at least midnight.

Ed-Dahar

Cacao Near the Corniche end of the strip. Busy bar with regular drinks promotions, live music and plenty of wooden seats to perch on, plus pizzas and snacks if you need something to soak up the alcohol.

Cheers Near the Aquarium. Open 24hr for serious drinking, with a wide range of cocktails for around £E25 and very cold beer. There's a wide-ranging menu with good breakfasts.

Nirvana Hospital St. Dark pub-like bar with a few tall stools out front, a dart board, live sport on TV and rock tunes. Popular with Russians. Open until 2am.

Peanuts Hospital St. Cheesy Dutch-run spot, with funky lighting, pub grub and pitchers of sangria for £E75. Karaoke in five languages on Wed, ladies night on Thurs, disco on Sat and free sangria with meals on Sun. Open until 2am.

New Hurghada

Hard Rock Café Across from the *El-Smaka* hotel Ⓦwww.hardrock.com/hurghada. Popular branch of the international chain, decorated in the standard rock memorabilia. A spacious outdoor area, pool tables, live music and DJs after midnight. Noon–3am.

Little Buddha *Sindbad Beach Resort* Ⓦwww.littlebuddha-hurghada.com. Offshoot of the Parisian bar of the same name, with slick decor, subdued lighting, Southeast Asian fusion food and great cocktails. Turns into a DJ bar later on. 4pm–4am.

Sigala

Papas HRG Hurghada Marina Ⓦwww.papasbar.com. This buzzing Dutch-run bar, now in a new location, is a Hurghada institution and very popular with foreigners. It has an attached deli and a wide range of events. The *Shade* bar next door is another cool spot.

Nightlife

Hurghada has some of the liveliest nightlife in mainland Egypt, but the music is mostly mainstream. Posh places balk at shorts or trainers; smart-casual **dress** is universally acceptable. A £E20 minimum charge is standard almost everywhere, rising to more than £E50 in some venues. A Stella, Sakkara Gold or Meister will set you back £E10–25, imported beer or a cocktail £E25–40. Few discos get going before 11pm, and while most are advertised as staying open till 4–5am, they do close early if things are quiet.

Papas HRG (see above) in Hurghada Marina is one of the most popular hangouts in Hurghada, with live music and a sociable crowd. The nearby *HedKandi Beach Bar* (Ⓦwww.hedkandibeachbar.com), which has played host to the likes of Brandon Block, draws hordes of clubbers, particularly to its full moon parties. Just to the south is the *Ministry of Sound Beach Club* (Ⓦwww.ministryofsoundegypt.com), a spin-off of the iconic 90s London club playing hip hop, r 'n' b, funky and deep house, and club classics. Other favourites are in holiday villages; try the *Dome* at the *InterContinental* or the discos at the *Sand Beach*, *Princess Club Sindbad Beach Resort*, *Giftun Beach Resort* or the *Sofitel*.

▲ Clubbers at the Ministry of Sound

Occasionally you can see **bellydancing** at some clubs, with one of the best shows at *Alf Leila Wa Leila* ("1001 Nights"), on the southern outskirts of Hurghada. Tickets, including transport, can be bought at most hotels ($35 including dinner, $25 with soft drinks; 9pm–midnight). Some resort discos also put on "Russian Shows" featuring tawdry dance troupes between songs.

Listings

Banks Of the two close together on Tariq El-Nasr in Ed-Dahar, the Banque Misr (daily 9am–9pm) has an ATM and gives cash advances on Visa and MasterCard, while the National Bank of Egypt (Sat–Thurs 8.30am–2pm & 6–9pm) takes travellers' cheques. ATMs are numerous in Ed-Dahar and Sigala, including at most of the larger hotels. In New Hurghada there are ATMs at the HSBC on Sheraton Rd, near Redcon Mall, at the *InterContinental* and at Banque Misr just north of the tourist office.

Car rental Avis, opposite *Aqua Village* (☎065/344-4146), has a good range of 4WDs. There's also Hertz at the airport (☎065/344-4146).

Hospitals The general hospital in Ed-Dahar (☎065/334-6740) and the private El-Saffa on El-Nasr St (☎065/354-6965) have improved, but it's better to try El-Salam Hospital (☎065/354-8787, ⓦwww.elsalamhospital.com) on the Corniche between the *Hilton* and the port, or the hospital in El Gouna (see p.573). Hotels and holiday villages have physicians on call.

Internet cafés In Ed-Dahar, try Come In Café on Sharia Soliman Mazhar, Diamond Internet Café on Hospital Street or Hor@net in the *Shedwan Garden Hotel* mall. Sigala has dozens of internet cafés, particularly around *McDonald's*.

Laundry Stop-Shop off Tariq El-Nasr, 300m south of the bus station in Ed-Dahar. Many hotels have in-house laundries, charging £E5–20 per item.

Pharmacies There are several on Sharia Abdel Aziz Mustafa and Tariq el-Nasr in Ed-Dahar, and outside the hospitals.

Post office On Tariq el-Nasr, 200m north of the bus station (daily except Fri 8.30am–2.30pm).

Travel agent Thomas Cook is in Sigala at 8 Sheraton Rd (daily 9.30am–5pm & 5.30–9pm; ☎065/344-3338) and in Ed-Dahar at 2 Tariq el-Nasr (same hours; ☎065/354-1807).

Tourist police Next to the tourist office in New Hurghada (24hr; ☎065/344-7773). To contact the police in Ed-Dahar, call ☎065/354-3365.

Tours Most hotels and scores of travel agencies offer excursions to Luxor, Karnak, Sinai, Cairo and the Red Sea Monasteries as day-trips or overnight packages, and can book tickets for the catamaran to Sharm el-Sheikh. Two recommended companies are Misr Travel at *Magawish Village* in New Hurghada (Ⓣ065/344-2131, Ⓦwww.misrtravel.net) and Prince Safaris in Ed-Dahar (Ⓣ065/354-9882, Ⓦwww.prince-diving.com).

Work Distinctly feasible if you have diving qualifications (Divemaster upwards) or foreign languages (especially Japanese or Russian). Ask other foreigners working here which firms are dodgy, and don't hand over your passport lightly. Whatever you do, do not invest any money in Hurghada – the biggest sharks aren't found in the Red Sea.

Moving on

The numerous daily EgyptAir **flights** are the quickest way of reaching **Cairo**. You can book flights at the airline's offices in New Hurghada (Ⓣ065/346-3034) or Ed-Dahar (Ⓣ065/354-7891); both are open daily 8am–8pm. The **airport** (Ⓣ065/344-3974) is 15km south of Ed-Dahar, off the Hurghada–Safaga road.

Buses

For travel by **bus** to Cairo or Luxor, it's a good idea to buy your tickets in advance from the main bus station (Ⓣ065/354-7582). East Delta runs eleven a/c buses daily to Cairo's Turgoman garage (6–8hr). The **El Gouna Transport Company** (Ⓣ065/354-1561) runs fourteen daily buses from Hurghada, via El Gouna, to Cairo. The High Jet Company has eight daily buses to Cairo.

Suez is served by a dozen buses daily (6-7hr); tickets are sold on the bus. Around seven daily buses go to Luxor (5hr), and are routed via Safaga and Qena, with a couple of services continuing to Aswan (7hr). Other buses travel to Safaga hourly (1hr), which is also accessible by buses bound for Mersa Alam (8hr) via El-Quseir (4hr) at 8pm, 1am and 3.30am. Other buses go daily to Assyut (8am) and Sohag (7am).

Besides the above, a/c **Superjet** buses depart four times a day for Cairo (noon, 2.30pm, 5pm & 12.30am) from the Superjet station (Ⓣ065/355-6188), 1km south of Ed-Dahar's main bus station; the 2.30pm bus carries on to Alexandria (9hr). There's also a 7am bus to Luxor (5-6hr). Buy tickets in advance to be sure of a seat.

Bus timetables in Egypt are notoriously subject to change, so it's advisable to ask around to find out the latest information.

Taxis

Mornings are the best time to catch seven-seater **service taxis** to Suez (5hr), Cairo (6–7hr), Port Safaga (45min), El-Quseir (1hr 30min) or Mersa Alam (3–4hr). A fair price for seven people to hire a **taxi** to Luxor is £E200 per person; don't believe anyone who says there's a "convoy charge" for foreigners. Groups can also consider taking one all the way to Sharm el-Sheikh (at least £E1000) – which is one way to avoid a tedious interlude at Suez (see p.508).

By sea

The **catamaran** to **Sharm el-Sheikh** is run by International Fast Ferries (Ⓣ065/344-7571) and takes an hour and a half (Mon at 4am, Tues, Thurs & Sat at 9am; adults £E250 one way, children aged 3–11 £E150, under 3s free). Times are subject to change, so check before you set out. Space for cars (£E245) must be booked in advance. Tickets can be bought from a wide variety of outlets: Sherif Tours (Ⓣ065/354-5147), next to the *Sand Beach Hotel* on the Corniche; any travel agent (including Thomas Cook); EgyptAir; most of the hotels; or the El Gouna office at their bus station in Ed-Dahar.

Excursions to the Red Sea Mountains

Inland of Hurghada, the barren plains erupt into the **Red Sea Mountains**, which follow the coast southwards towards Ethiopia. This geologically primitive range of granite, porphyry and breccia contains Egypt's highest mountains outside Sinai. They are home to a few thousand Bedouin, who are perfectly at ease in the wilderness – unlike isolated groups of miners and soldiers, who feel almost as exiled as the slaves who quarried here in ancient times. As far as Europeans are concerned, the Red Sea Mountains were first climbed in the 1920s and 1930s, and have hardly been scaled since; as Sinai becomes increasingly commercialized, this may become the next wilderness to attract tourists.

Twenty kilometres north of Hurghada, a track quits the highway and climbs inland towards Jebel Abu Dukhaan, the 1161-metre-high "Mountain of Smoke". Anciently known as **Mons Porphyrites**, this was the Roman Empire's main source of fine red porphyry, used for columns and ornamentation. Blocks were dragged 150km to the Nile, or by a shorter route to the coast, from where they were shipped to far-flung sites such as Baalbek in Lebanon, or Constantinople. Round about the extensive quarries lies a ruined town of rough-hewn buildings with two large cisterns and an unfinished Ionic temple.

Under the emperors Trajan and Hadrian, the pale, black-flecked granite quarried at **Mons Claudianus**, 50km from Mons Porphyrites, was used to construct the Pantheon and Trajan's Forum in Rome. Around the quarries, beneath Jebel Fatira and Jebel Abu Hamr, you'll find numerous abandoned columns.

Between the two quarries rise the highest mountains in the Eastern Desert: **Jebel Gattaar** and **Jebel Shaayib el-Banat**. Jebel Gattaar (1963m) is esteemed by the Bedouin for its permanent springs and comparatively abundant vegetation. Further south, Jebel Shaayib el-Banat (at 2187m the highest in mainland Egypt) rises to a summit that the geographer and mountaineer George Murray likened to a "monstrous webbed hand of seven smoothed fingers".

The Red Sea Mountains are best visited through travel operators on **day excursions** from Hurghada. Many companies offer half-day camel or jeep safaris at sundown, including a barbecue and Bedouin entertainments for around €35; try Prince Safaris in Ed-Dahar (see p.582). The experienced Red Sea Desert Adventures (see p.593) in Mersa Alam offers similar excursions, and can organize longer trips lasting several days that take in Mons Porphyrites and Mons Claudianus (around €100 per day). From Mersa Alam they also organize stargazing trips to a desert amphitheatre where images from a telescope are projected on to a large screen (€30).

The coast south of Hurghada

Down the coast from Hurghada, the stream of holiday resorts becomes less dense until three belated spurts of development on the outskirts of **Port Safaga** (58km), **El-Quseir** (a further 85km), and **Mersa Alam** (a further 132km). Little more than an overgrown, grubby port, Safaga has few charms, though it is within boat range of some stunning offshore reefs, while El-Quseir retains a sleepy quality unlike anywhere else on the Red Sea. The region around Mersa Alam is home to a few isolated diving camps and not much else, but this is set to change as a new tourist development, **Port Ghalib**, is presently under construction.

Further south, communications become tenuous and bureaucratic obstacles loom as you head towards the Sudanese border. From **Bir Shalateen**, you need military permission to proceed further south, or into the mountains, and the allure of the far south depends primarily on its reefs, which can be reached by dive boats operating out of Hurghada, Safaga, El-Quseir and Mersa Alam.

The highway initially runs several kilometres inland before regaining the coast. About 40km after Hurghada and 18km before Safaga, a signpost indicates the turn-off for **SHARM EL-NAGA**, a wide bay where the attractive *Sharm El-Naga Resort and Diving Centre* (Ⓣ010 111-2942, Ⓦwww.sharmelnaga.com; ❻) has forty comfortable en-suite chalets, a vast swimming pool, beach bar and restaurant (rates are all-inclusive). The main attraction here is the **beach diving** and **snorkelling** (the dive centre can be contacted on Ⓣ010 123-4540) and day-trippers from overcrowded Hurghada often come here to use the beach (£E25 fee for non-guests).

The luxury development of **Soma Bay**, 2km further south (Ⓦwww.somabay.com), boasts a Gary Player-designed eighteen-hole golf course and Les Thermes Marins des Cascades, a spa and thalassotherapy centre, among other delights. There are several top-notch hotels offering similar facilities, of which the *Sheraton Soma Bay* (Ⓣ065/354-5845, Ⓦwww.sheraton-somabay.com; ❾) is the most appealing, with over three hundred rooms, several restaurants and bars, a nightclub and elaborate mosaic pool. Further south, just before Safaga, is **Makadi Bay**, a similar-style complex with a *Le Meridien* and several four- and five-star *Iberotel* hotels; the *Iberotel Makadi Beach* has the best range of facilities and a choice of half-or full board (Ⓣ065/359-0000, Ⓦwww.iberotel.com; ❼).

Port Safaga

PORT SAFAGA (Bur Safaga in Arabic) amounts to very little. Coming in from the north, you pass a slip road curving off to six holiday villages on a headland, which cater to groups on diving holidays. The town, whose economy is driven by the nearby phosphate mines, begins 3km later and consists of a single windswept avenue running straight on past concrete boxes with bold signs proclaiming their function, until the bus station and a final mosque, 4km south. Silos and cranes identify the port, which runs alongside (but remains out of bounds) for most of this distance. Safaga's only attraction is the **reefs** to the north, and there's not much reason to hang around otherwise.

The **bus station** is near to the port, while most of Safaga's facilities are along the main drag, including the **police** station and **EgyptAir**, 200m south of the City Council, followed by a **hospital** 500m on. There's a **petrol station** beyond the next turn-off, across the main road from the Bank of Alexandria; further south on the other side are Banque Misr and the National Bank of Egypt, and a **telephone exchange**. Tourists staying at the holiday villages can change money at the **bank** inside *Shams Safaga* or at the Banque du Caire in the shopping arcade near the *Holiday Inn*. There's no tourist office.

Accommodation

In Safaga itself, accommodation includes several pricey **hotels** near the beach and a few mid-range options on the Corniche. If you're diving, you'll probably be staying at one of the cluster of holiday resorts with dive centres, all of which are around 3–5km north of town unless otherwise stated; minibuses (£E1–2) run out to the *Shams Safaga*, the furthest of the resort complexes.

Amira Safaga On the Corniche between the port and the town Ⓣ065/325-3821, Ⓦwww.amirasafaga.com. Smart hotel with a decent range of facilities, including its own beach, bar and disco, but isolated from the other resorts. Half-board ❻

Holiday Inn Resort (also known as Safaga Palace) Ⓣ065/326-0100, Ⓦwww.ichotelsgroup.com. Safaga's most stylish tourist village, with an outsized pool, an English-style pub and fine sea views; rooms have a/c, fridge and satellite TV. ❻

Lotus Bay Resort & Gardens Cairo Ⓣ02/748-2639, Ⓦwww.lotusbay.com. This spacious array of villas in a nice garden has all mod cons, plus tennis, squash, a big pool, a kids' club, and a dive and windsurfing centre. Italian/Swiss clientele. Half-board ❻

Menaville Village ⓣ065/326-0064, ⓦwww.menaville.com. The climbing plants that cover the whitewashed buildings give a Mediterranean feel to this resort, which also boasts a large pool, gardens and reasonable rates. It's also home to the Thermal Karlovy Vary Centre, which offers treatment for psoriasis and rheumatism, capitalizing on Safaga's supposedly propitious natural circumstances – including high UV levels in the sunshine and some radioactivity in the sands. ❼

Nemo ⓣ065/325-6777, ⓦwww.nemodive.com. This European-owned hotel, located on the Corniche (coming from Hurghada, take the first left before entering town), has eager management, bright rooms, its own reef and a vague Disney theme. There's also a colourful children's playground and regular film screenings in the bar. Weekly all-inclusive packages start from €230. ❺–❻

Shams Safaga ⓣ065/325-1781, ⓦwww.shams-dive.com. Popular with British tour groups, this lavish resort has more than 300 bungalows and hotel rooms, a private reef, good sports facilities and a children's playground. A Club Mistral windsurfing and kiteboarding centre is based here (ⓦwww.club-mistral.com). Half-or full board; rates include local alcoholic drinks. ❼

Diving and snorkelling

Boats and instructors at the main **dive centres** tend to be committed to groups, though they will take on independent travellers if they have space: expect to pay around €330 for a four-day PADI Open-Water course, or €50 for two boat dives. As in Hurghada, an **environmental fee** of €3 a day is levied on all diving and snorkelling trips.

The main diving grounds lie 6–8km offshore from the holiday villages between Safaga Island and the Ras Abu Soma headland to the north. **Tubiya Island** is ringed with corals only just off its beach, while dive boats drop their clients directly over the sunken **North and South Fairway Reefs** or the twin pairs of sites known as **Tubiya Kebir**, **Tubiya Soraya**, **Gamul Soraya** and **Gamul Kebir**. Other sites include the **Seven Pillars** off Ras Abu Soma, and the **Panorama Reef** and **Shark Point**, 10km east of Safaga Island. Most of them are notable for their coral pillars and strong currents.

Dive centres in the vicinity include the Alpha Red Sea at the *Amira Safaga Hotel* and *Menaville Village* (ⓣ065/325-3229, ⓦwww.alpharedsea.com); Barakuda at *Lotus Bay* (ⓣ065/325-3911, ⓦwww.barakuda-diving.com); Ducks, *Holiday Inn Resort* (ⓣ065/326-0100, ⓦwww.ducks-dive-center.de German-language site only); Orca at *Sun Beach* (ⓣ065/326-0111, ⓦwww.orca-diveclubs.com) and Shams Safaga at the *Shams Safaga* (ⓣ065/325-1781, ⓦwww.shams-dive.com).

Note that among the big fish prevalent in these waters are aggressive **hammer head sharks**.

Eating

Aside from the **restaurants** at the holiday resorts, there are several **cafés** offering sandwiches or *shawarmas* on the main drag. For grilled meat, pizza, pasta and salads, however, you're better off at the *Aly Baba* restaurant (daily noon–10pm), 2km north of the town centre, or the *El-Joker* restaurant, 3km north of town opposite the *Lotus Bay*.

Moving on from Safaga

There are around nine **buses** daily to Hurghada and seven to Cairo. Sticking to the Red Sea Coast, three buses a day (9pm, 2am & 4.30am) run down to El-Quseir and Mersa Alam. Six buses a day ply the desert road to Qena and Luxor, a couple of which go all the way to Aswan. **Service taxis** leave from the depot 500m south of the port entrance and run in between buses to Hurghada and Qena for similar rates, though it can take a long time to muster enough passengers for El-Quseir.

El-Quseir

EL-QUSEIR, 85km from Safaga, is also a phosphates extraction centre, though with fewer inhabitants and more appeal. In pharaonic times, boats sailed from here to the "Land of Punt" (thought to be Yemen or Somalia), as depicted in reliefs within Hatshepsut's temple at Deir el-Bahri. The Romans knew it as Leukos Limen ("White Harbour"), while under Arab rule El-Quseir was the largest Red Sea port until the tenth century, remaining a major transit point for pilgrims until the 1840s, when Flaubert caught its last flickers of exoticism.

Today, El-Quseir is a sleepy place, mostly unaffected by tourism, despite the holiday villages on its outskirts. The main **orientation** point is a traffic roundabout where service taxis drop and wait for passengers, near a co-op garage and the *Sea Princess Hotel*. The road off to the right leads to a small **harbour** where you can watch men building boats, or stroll past shuttered and balconied houses to a thirteenth-century **mosque** and a nineteenth-century **quarantine hospital**.

Smack in the town centre, just past the main traffic roundabout, sits El-Quseir's most impressive landmark, the sixteenth-century crumbling **walled fortress** (daily 9am–5pm; £E10), now housing a museum. Designed to protect trade routes used by the Ottomans, the fortress declined after trade was diverted around the Cape of Good Hope. Napoleon's army raised the French flag here in 1799, only to attract the attention of British warships sailing off the coast. The French survived a brief assault, but abandoned the fort two years later. Its most recent occupant was the Egyptian army, stationed here until 1975. The cistern, watchtower (climb up for excellent views), and rooms built into the walls of the fortress each contain small exhibits on the history and traditions of the Red Sea coast.

Aside from the fortress, El-Quseir's main diversion is strolling along the beach-side **promenade**. Life moves at a pretty slow pace, except on Fridays, when Ma'aza and Ababda Bedouin flock in for the weekly **market**. The best **dive sites** nearby are the Brothers, east of El-Quseir, and the Elphinstone and Abu Dabbab reefs, down towards Mersa Alam, although the Quei and Wizr reefs are closer. All the **dive centres** are attached to the resort hotels, and may not allow outside divers to join their trips; it's best to book a dive package deal from the start.

Arrival and information

The **bus station** and the **service taxi stand** are side-by-side in the heart of town, a ten-minute walk or a short minibus hop (50pt) from the main roundabout. There are five daily buses to **Cairo** (6am, 7.30am, 9am, 7pm & 8.30pm; 10–11hr); all services stop at Safaga (2hr) and Hurghada (3hr), and the 6am also stops at Suez (9–10hr). Heading south, there are four daily buses to **Mersa Alam** via the coastal route (5am, 9am, 7pm & 8pm; 2hr). **Service taxis** depart when full for Cairo, Hurghada, Safaga and Mersa Alam. To reach **Luxor**, you could charter a taxi via Safaga (expect to pay £E300 plus for seven people) or get a bus to Safaga and an onward bus from there.

El-Quseir's **bank** (no ATM) is on Sharia el-Gumhorriya, 150m north of the roundabout, while the road that turns right at this point leads to an old-fashioned **telephone exchange** (24hr). For **internet access**, Hot Line is about 100m east of the *Sea Princess Hotel* on Sharia Port Said, just south of the roundabout.

Accommodation

Accommodation is limited to two hotels in the centre and a clutch of holiday villages outside town.

El Quseir Hotel Sharia Port Said, town centre ⊕065/333-2301. A refurbished 1920s home with charming rooms: although rates may seem a bit high for rooms that aren't en suite, this atmospheric hotel is a welcome break for mid-range travellers tired of boxy concrete bungalows, and boasts ocean views from its balcony. It's not signed, so look for the

Eco-tourism or greenwashing?

The Red Sea Coast's booming tourism industry has prospered at serious cost to the **environment**. Rampant development, over-fishing, pollution, the degradation of coral reefs and increased pressure on water supplies are just a few of the problems. As the Hurghada Protection and Conservation Association (Ⓦwww.hepca.com), a local NGO, warns: "Environmental deterioration is no longer a threat but a reality. Each day in the Red Sea we are witness to the depletion of the very resource base that attracts so many visitors here in the first place."

In recent years numerous "ecolodges" have sprung up in the region. While some – such as those run by Red Sea Diving Safari (see p.593 & 594) – have genuine green credentials, many others are simply indulging in greenwashing. Similarly not all the dive centres and travel agencies are as conservation-minded as their promotional literature might suggest. The key thing for eco-minded travellers to do is to ask lots of questions – such as: How is waste disposed of? What is recycled? How is power usage minimized? How does the local community benefit? What conservation efforts are being made? – before making their decisions.

"Diving world – Red Sea Egypt" emblem above the door. BB ❸

Flamenco Beach Resort 7.5km north of town Ⓣ065/335-0200, Ⓦwww.flamencohotels.com. A kitsch pinkish three-star complex with reasonable diving packages including half-board accommodation. ❻

Mövenpick Resort El Quseir 7km north of town Ⓣ065/333-2100, Ⓦwww.movenpick-hotels.com. A spacious five-star with every facility imaginable, including a dive centre and spa. The European-managed, Nubian-style resort is one of the few in this part of Egypt that has managed to blend with the local environment and native culture, while running development projects. Good online deals. BB ❽

Radisson Blu 3km north of town Ⓣ065/335-0260, Ⓦwww.radissonblu.com. At the luxury end, it's hard to beat the beautifully-designed *Radisson Blu*. Built Bedouin-style with domed roofs, it features three pools, a dive centre, private beach and lagoon, and an Ayurvedic spa. BB ❺

Rocky Valley Diver's Camp 10km north of town Ⓣ065/326-0055, Ⓦwww.rockyvalleydiverscamp.com. A handful of bungalows and Bedouin-style tents, with a restaurant and snorkelling and diving gear rental. It's booked up for twenty weeks a year by tour groups, so independent travellers should call in advance. BB ❺

Sea Princess Sharia Port Said, town centre Ⓣ065/333-1880. This central hotel is a scruffy little place decked out with film posters and vintage banknotes. The friendly staff and clean, shared bathrooms just about make the claustrophobic rooms tolerable. ❷

Eating and drinking

Among the handful of **places to eat** around El-Quseir, the best is the *Old Restaurant*, a popular Bedouin-themed place some 50m north of the *El-Quseir Hotel*, with offerings ranging from inexpensive grilled chicken to a seafood platter (mains £E20-60). The *Citadel Restaurant*, on the main road near the fortress, is more a local favourite serving authentic Egyptian fare. **Alcohol** and nightlife are confined to the holiday villages, which sometimes feature bellydancing; non-residents may attend at the management's discretion.

El-Quseir to Mersa Alam

The coastal road south of El-Quseir (sections of which are being moved slightly further inland to protect the coast and wildlife) runs through some of the most amazing landscape and desert in Egypt. It's sprinkled with holiday resorts all along the 132km stretch to Mersa Alam. Although this southern Red Sea Coast is growing in popularity with holiday-makers and divers, its tourist infrastructure is far from developed. Telephone use is limited and some resorts have to rely on expensive satellite communications, though mobile phone coverage is reasonable in the area.

A few of the **resorts** along the coast, such as *Helio* and *Utopia*, won't take independent travellers, but others will, such as the huge *Akassia Swiss Resort*, 26km south of El-Quseir (Ⓣ065/339-0040, Ⓦwww.akassia.com; half board ⑧), with 470 a/c en suites, an enormous domed lobby, and five swimming pools; there's a water park with several slides next door. Alternatively, there's the three-star *Mangrove Bay Resort*, 30km south of El-Quseir (Cairo Ⓣ02/748-6748, Ⓦwww.mangrovebayresort.com; half board ⑦–⑧). Rooms come with a/c, fridge and terrace, and the hotel has its own beautiful white sandy beach.

Further south, 50km north of Mersa Alam, is **Mersa Alam International Airport** (Ⓦwww.marsa-alam-airport.com), served by several daily flights from Europe, and five-six weekly from Cairo. There's no public transport from the airport, and most arrivals are ferried to their resorts in shuttle buses.

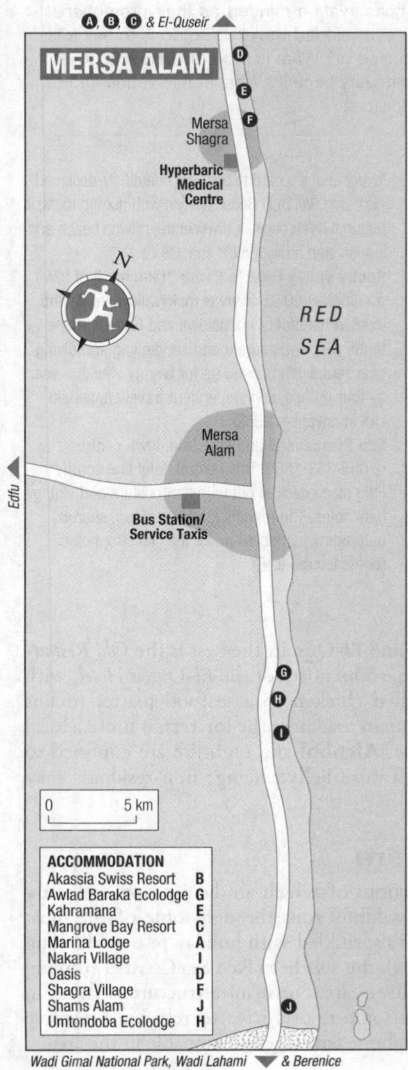

Adjacent to the airport is the Kuwaiti-funded **Port Ghalib** development (Ⓦwww.portghalib.com), currently under construction, and pretty quiet at the time of writing. Essentially a new town (similar to El Gouna, see p.573), when completed it will occupy 18km of coast, and comprise shops, a golf course, accommodation units, hotels, a promenade and a three-hundred-berth yacht marina. A few resorts are already open, such as the *Marina Lodge (*also known as *Coral Beach Diving Hotel;* Ⓣ065/370-0222, Ⓦwww.millenniumhotels.com; ⑦), proffering four-star luxury in bright, modern rooms and a dive centre (Ⓦwww.emperordivers.com).

Twenty-five kilometres north of Mersa Alam is the German-run *Oasis* (Ⓦwww.oasis-marsaalam.de; ⑤) with a collection of bungalows, each with different decor and assembled to mimic a small village; try to get room 23, which has red decor and a bath tub with sea views. It also features a restaurant, bar, pool and dive centre (Ⓦwww.sinaidivers.com). A little to the south is the five-star *Kahramana* (Ⓣ02/748-0883, Ⓦwww.kahramanaresort.com/k_marsa/home.htm ⑦), whose Mexican-inspired architecture and 70s decor is set against beautiful and empty sandy beaches.

A ten-minute walk south of the *Kahramana*, at **Mersa Shagra**, is the northernmost of three ecolodges run by Red Sea Diving Safari. *Shagra Village* (Ⓣ02/338-0022, Ⓦwww.redsea-divingsafari.com; full board ❺–❻) is a friendly beachside dive centre that aims to minimize the impact of diving and tourism; it has environmentally friendly tents on the beach, huts and chalets – the latter two options have a/c and fridge, and the chalets are en suite. Rates include all meals and unlimited soft drinks; underwater weddings are a speciality, with the bride and groom in full scuba gear for the ceremony. It's also home to Red Sea Desert Adventures (Ⓣ012 399-3860, Ⓦwww.redseadesertadventures.com), whose jeep and camel safaris run from October to March (see p.587), as well as Egypt's most southerly decompression chamber, the Hyperbaric Medical Centre (Ⓣ012 165-3806); divers are encouraged to take out cover in case they have to use it (around €6 for three weeks).

In December 2008 two Danish tourists and one Egyptian went missing, presumed drowned, on a private diving trip just off the coast of Mersa Shagra – a pertinent reminder of the importance of following the full diving safety procedures.

Mersa Alam

The town of **MERSA ALAM** itself is undistinguished, consisting of a large army base, some government buildings and apartment blocks constructed for the expected influx of hotel staff to the area, grafted onto a fishing port where liveaboards now moor. Opposite is a coffee shop patronized by local divers. The **bus stand** is on the edge of town, 800m west of the traffic circle, with daily buses to Hurghada (5hr; 5am, 7am, noon, 2.30pm & 5pm, though departure times fluctuate so ask locally) via El-Quseir (2hr) and irregular buses and **service taxis** to Bir Shalateen (4hr). There is also regular transport to Edfu and Aswan in the Nile Valley. The only bank, with an ATM, is 25km away at the *Kahramana Hotel*.

In 2001 HEPCA (see p.580) and government agencies set up a new crescent-shaped national park, the "Dolphin House Reef", close to Mersa Alam to protect the area's spinner dolphins. Tourist numbers to the reef have been capped at two hundred per day (previously there were up to 2,500 per day). The Environment Ministry is also planning to set up similar reserve nearby for sharks. There is also a need for tourists to act responsibly, as a highly publicised case in June 2009 showed: a Frenchwoman on a boat trip near Mersa Alam mistook a shark for a large fish, jumped into the water to have a closer look, and was attacked and killed by it.

South of Mersa Alam

For keen divers that have made it this far, there are several camps and two hotels to the south of town offering **accommodation**. All arrange transfers from either Mersa Alam or Hurghada airports. This eerily empty and barren region of just mountains, ocean and reefs is far removed from the commercialized northern Red Sea coast but it does give the opportunity to explore the most remote dive sites in the south Red Sea, such as **Samaduy**, **Abu Dabab**, **Elphinstone** and the **Fury Shoal**.

Fourteen kilometres south of Mersa Alam, the Bedouin-style *Awlad Baraka Ecolodge* (Ⓣ021/248 8062, Ⓦwww.aquariusredsea.com; full board ❻), has comfortable huts with shared facilities and en-suite bungalows, a restaurant and café, and offers PADI Open Water courses. A similar setup can be found at the nearby *Umtondoba Ecolodge* (Ⓣ012 792-3336, Ⓦwww.ecolodge-redsea.com; ❻), where the diving is run by Deep South Diving (Ⓦwww.deep-south-diving.com), which organizes day-trips and open-water diving courses. There's another Red Sea Diving Safari ecolodge at *Nakari Village*, 18km south of Mersa Alam (Ⓣ02/337-1833, Ⓦwww.redsea-divingsafari.com; full board ❻), with accommodation in tents or domed Bedouin stone huts.

Rock art

The **rock art** of the Eastern Desert is one of Egypt's best-kept secrets. Spread over 24,000 square kilometres of desert east of Luxor and Edfu, the sites vary from a single boulder to walls of cliff face dotted with pictures of people and animals, flotillas of boats and herds of giraffes, ostriches and elephants. They are difficult to reach, however, and it's easy to get lost – at least one group has died in the area – so it's vital to go with a guide. There are three main places of interest: two are partially accessible by 2WD, using the roads between El-Quseir and Qift or Mersa Alam and Edfu, but all of the wadis between them require 4WD.

Created before the unification of Egypt (c.3100 BC), the rock art sheds light on the origins of Egyptian civilization. The oldest human figures are gods or chieftains in ostrich-feather headdresses, brandishing maces; they are intriguingly similar to the "Conquering Hero" motif in pre- and Early Dynastic art at Hierakonopolis in the Nile Valley. They often appear standing in boats, and are frequently surrounded by ostriches, elephants or cattle. Both Hans Winkler, who did seminal research in the 1930s, and David Rohl, who made recent studies, believe the oldest boats represent "Eastern Invaders" from Mesopotamia, who reached Egypt by the Red Sea and conquered the indigenous people of the Nile Valley, kick-starting Egyptian civilization.

Permits are required for visiting these sites: both Red Sea Desert Adventures (see p.593) and Ancient World Tours (UK ⓣ020 7917 9494, ⓦwww.ancient.co.uk) can obtain them and organize excursions.

Fifty kilometres south of Mersa Alam is *Shams Alam Hotel* (ⓣ012 244-4932, ⓦwww.shams-dive.com; full board ➐), with 160 fully equipped rooms surrounding a pool and a dive school offering trips to **Wadi Gimal National Park**, a unique protected area covering 6000 square kilometres of land and 4000 square kilometres of sea; its entrance is just 100m beyond the hotel. Inside the park's borders, three ranger stations, built to look like ancient Roman domiciles, are used as base camps by scientists surveying the land and studying plant and animals species. Spring and autumn are particularly good times to observe bird migrations, including osprey, falcons, white-eyed gulls and the occasional flamingo. The park headquarters, next to the Wadi Gimal Diving Centre, is not yet equipped for travellers, but there are plans to build an on-site information centre. To **camp** in the park, foreigners need permission from the Coast Guard in Mersa Alam; Red Sea Desert Adventures (see p.593) may be able to help with these, or you could contact Mohamed Abbas (ⓔmatahoon2004@yahoo.com), a researcher at the park.

Around 80km south of the park, and 5km south of the village of **Hamata**, is the *Zabargad Dive Resort* (ⓣ012 215-2775, ⓦwww.zabargad.net; ➏), which has attractive, fully equipped Nubian-style domed bungalows with pool, restaurant and bar and is popular with German divers. Four kilometers further south is the third of the Red Sea Diving Safari ecolodges, *Wadi Lahami Village* (Cairo ⓣ02/338-0021, ⓦwww.redsea-divingsafari.com; ➏–➐), which caters for experienced divers only and has full-board accommodation in standard and "royal" tents, and chalets. Just beyond the turnoff for the *Wadi Lahami Village* is the southernmost resort on the Red Sea Coast, the five-star *Lahami Bay* (Cairo ⓣ02/753-7100, ⓦwww.lahamibay.com; ➑), which is filled with Mediterranean and Far Eastern touches, stylish en suites decorated with local artwork, several restaurants, cafés and bars, and tennis courts, sauna, fitness centre and windsurfing facilities. Its dive area is a further 50km south at the port of **Ras Banata**, whose island reefs are home to one of the few undisturbed breeding grounds for **sea turtles** on the Red Sea Coast.

The far south: Berenice to the Sudanese border

As the coast road heads southwards to the Sudanese border, the seemingly endless coastline is almost completely empty except for the occasional mangrove, grazing camel or cluster of tanks left by the military. One hundred and forty-five kilometres south of Mersa Alam is the town of **BERENICE**, named after Ptolemy II's wife, on whose suggestion a trading port was established here in 275 BC. Abandoned during the fifth century AD, the site was excavated in 1818 by Belzoni, who found a Temple of Semiramis. Nowadays, Berenice amounts to a few characterless buildings clustered together in a windswept bay. Its hinterland, however, has several would-be attractions. For climbers, there is the challenge of Egypt's "most aggressive peaks", **Jebel Farayid** and the **Berenice Bodkin** – one of the largest rock spires in the whole of North Africa and the Middle East. Here, too, are the Ancient **Emerald Mines of Wadi Sakait**. Nearby is a small Ptolemaic rock temple, dedicated to Isis and Serapis. Red Sea Desert Adventures (see p.593) can organize safaris from Mersa Alam, taking in both Berenice and Wadi Sakait.

For geopolitical reasons, this area has long been off-limits. During the early 1980s, following the Iranian Revolution, the US military staged war games here. More recently, the **far south** has been a bone of contention between Egypt and Sudan, whose common border was arbitrarily set by the British in 1899. After independence, both countries agreed this was unfair on the Bishari nomads whose tribal grounds straddled the border, so a slice of Egyptian territory was placed under Sudanese administration – this worked fine until Sudan granted a Canadian oil company offshore exploration rights, and Egypt responded by sending in troops to reassert its sovereignty. Since 1992, the region from **Bir Shalateen** down to **Halaib** has been under military rule, and Egypt has launched a crash programme of "development" to cement its hold on this previously neglected, potentially oil-rich region.

In 1999, some restrictions were lifted and tourists can now travel at least as far as Bir Shalateen, which has a daily camel market; with some advance warning, Red Sea Desert Adventures (see p.593) will run a very informative day-trip to the village, and can also help you obtain a camping permit. The area is still a very sensitive military zone and anyone not obtaining permission is likely to be treated with extreme suspicion.

Off the coast 100km southeast of Berenice is **Zabargad Island**, whose deep reefs teeming with fish and corals are a favourite destination for liveaboards.

Contexts

Contexts

History

The present borders of Egypt are almost identical to those in pharaonic times, territories such as Sinai and Nubia being essentially marginal to the heartland of the Nile Valley and its Delta, where Egyptian civilization emerged some five thousand years ago. The historical continuity is staggering: the pharaonic era alone lasted thirty centuries before being appropriated by Greek and Roman emperors.

Egypt's significance in the ancient world was paramount, and the country has never been far from the front line of world history. Although neither Christianity nor Islam was born in Egypt, both are stamped with its influence. In modern times, when the Arab world sought to rid itself of European masters, Egypt was at the forefront of the anti-colonial struggle, while its peace treaty with Israel altered the geopolitics of the Middle East.

Prehistoric and Predynastic Egypt

Stone tools from the gravel beds of Upper Egypt and the Gilf Kebir in the Western Desert attest to the presence of **hunter-gathering hominids** over 250,000 years ago, when the Sahara was a lush savanna that supported zebras, elephants and other game. Between around 70,000 and 24,000 BC, there were fluctuating wet and dry periods, when lakes rose or shrank and grasslands expanded or receded, and tribes are assumed to have moved backwards and forwards between the Nile and the oases. While most still lived by hunting and fishing, herding cattle emerged even before cereal cultivation, sheep and goat herding filtered through from the Near East (c.7000 BC).

During the **Neolithic** era, Middle Egypt and the Delta had **settled communities** that cultivated wheat and flax, herded flocks and wove linen. Although some reverted to nomadism after the rains of the Neolithic era checked the process of desertification, others remained to develop into agricultural societies. Between 6600 and 4700 BC, human occupation of the Western Desert reached its peak, giving rise to the **rock art** in the Cave of the Swimmers and other sites at the Gilf Kebir and Jebel Uwaynat.

The impetus for development came from southern Egypt. At **Nabta Playa**, 100km west of Abu Simbel, archeologists have identified the world's **oldest calendar** of standing stones and sculpted monoliths – dating from around 6000 BC – that attests to a Neolithic culture with a knowledge of astronomy and the resources and organization to create such a site. And then there are the mysterious **boats** drawn in the Eastern Desert perhaps a thousand years later, which some believe represent "Eastern Invaders" who conquered the indigenous people of the Nile Valley.

Evidence of later agricultural societies is less impressive. The **Naqada I** period, from about 4000 BC onwards, was characterized by larger settlements and a distinctive style of pottery. Clay and ivory figurines show Naqada menfolk sporting beards and penis shields, like their Libyan neighbours. More extraordinary are the narrow-necked vases carved from basalt, which can't be reproduced by twenty-first-century technology. **Naqada II** graves (containing copper tools, glazed beads, and lapis lazuli from Asia) evolved from simple pits into painted tombs lined with mats and wood and, later still, brick.

The development of extensive **irrigation** systems (c.3300 BC) boosted productivity and promoted links between communities in Upper and Lower Egypt, giving rise to two loose **confederations**. As power coalesced around Naqada in the south and Behdet in the Delta, each confederation became identified with a chief deity and a symbol of statehood: Seth and the White Crown with **Upper Egypt**, Horus and the Red Crown with the **Delta.**

Later, each acquired a new capital (Hierakonpolis and Buto, respectively) and strove for domination; the eventual triumph of the southern kingdom resulting in the **unification of the Two Lands** (c.3100 or 2090 BC) under the quasi-mythical ruler **Menes** (aka Narmer). Some identify him as pharaoh Aha, whose tomb is the earliest found at Saqqara, but if the Greek name "Menes" is derived from the Egyptian *mena* ("Establisher"), it may not refer to any actual individual.

The Archaic Period and the Old Kingdom

The **Early Dynastic** or **Archaic Period** was the formative epoch of Egyptian civilization. Its beginnings are a mix of history and myth, relating to the foundation – supposedly by Menes – of the city of **Memphis**, located at the junction between Upper and Lower Egypt: the first imperial city on earth. From Memphis, the third and fifth kings of the **I Dynasty** (c.3100–2890 or 2920–2770 BC) attempted to bring Sinai under Egyptian control. Writing, painting and architecture became increasingly sophisticated, while royal tombs at Saqqara and Abydos developed into complex mastabas. At this time, royal burials were accompanied by the deceased's servants – a practice that later dynasties abandoned.

Also indicative of future trends was the dissolution of the unified kingdom as centralized authority waned. Although briefly restored by Raneb, regional disputes persisted throughout the **II Dynasty** (c.2890–2686 or 2770–2645 BC), inspiring the mythological **contendings of Seth and Horus**. Rivalry between the regions and their respective deities appears to have been resolved under Khasekhemwy, the last king of the dynasty – paving the way for an era of assurance.

Alternative chronologies

Egyptology is riddled with uncertainties, not least in its chronology of dynasties and kingdoms (not an Egyptian concept, but a modern invention enabling scholars to get a handle on three thousand years of history). In *A Test of Time*, **David Rohl** argues that only one of the "Four Pillars" of synchronicity between Ancient Egyptian and Biblical history is impeccable, and that evidence calls for the Third Intermediate Period to be shortened by 300 years, with knock-on effects on earlier times. Rohl's **New Chronology** puts the Exodus in the XIII rather than the XIX Dynasty, and makes Akhenaten a contemporary of David and Saul. In the 1990s, disputes over the age of the Sphinx provided support for the theory advanced by **Anthony West** in *Serpent in the Sky*, that the Egyptian temples embody the legacy of a far older, greater civilization. In this book we've stuck to **orthodox chronologies**, about which even mainstream Egyptologists differ and acknowledge margins of error. These are up to a hundred years in the period around 3000 BC, seventy-five years around 2000 BC, and between ten and fifteen years around 1000 BC. From 500 BC onwards, dates are fairly precise until the Ptolemaic era, when the chronology gets hazy, only firming up again in Roman times.

During the **III Dynasty** (c.2686–2613 or 2649–2575 BC), technological advances and developments in culture raised Egypt to an unprecedented level of civilization. The dynasty's foremost ruler was **Zoser** (or Djoser), whose architect, **Imhotep**, built the first **Step Pyramid** at Saqqara in the 27th century BC. Its conception and construction was a landmark, and later generations deified Imhotep as the ultimate sage. The III Dynasty also sent expeditions into Sinai, to seek gold and copper and subjugate the local Bedouin.

Scholars differ over whether the III Dynasty belongs to the Archaic Period or the succeeding **Old Kingdom**, when pyramid-building and expansionism were likewise pursued during the **IV Dynasty** (c.2613–2494 or 2575–2465 BC), whose first king, **Snofru** (aka Sneferu), raised two pyramids at Dahshur and raided Nubia and Libya. His successors, **Cheops** (Khufu), **Chephren** (Khafre) and **Mycerinus** (Menkaure), erected the **Pyramids of Giza**, expanded trade relations with the Near East, and developed mining in Nubia. Though Snofru's line expired with the death of **Shepseskaf**, his widow Queen **Khentkawes** is believed to have married a high priest to produce an heir.

During the **VI Dynasty** (c.2345–2181 or 2323–2150 BC), nobles were buried in their own **nomes** (provinces) rather than at Saqqara, and these nomarchs became increasingly powerful, until the situation reached the point of no return under **Pepi II** (aka Neferkare), whose death heralded the **end of the Old Kingdom**.

The Middle Kingdom

There followed a century of internal strife, known to Egyptologists as the **First Intermediate Period**. The Greek historian Manetho records seventy rulers during the brief VII Dynasty; no one knows the number during the VIII Dynasty. When famine struck, weak principalities allied themselves with **Herakleopolis**, the capital of the Twentieth Nome, whose ruler, **Achthoes**, gained control of Middle Egypt and founded the **IX Dynasty** in 2160 or 2154 BC. While this controlled the north, Upper Egypt was contested by the rulers of Edfu and Luxor (known to history as **Thebes**), until the Theban ruler Inyotef Sehertowy triumphed, founding the **XI Dynasty**.

The struggle between north and south was finally resolved by **Nebhepetre Mentuhotep II**, who reunited the Two Lands in 2055 or 2050 BC, establishing the **Middle Kingdom**. During his fifty-year reign, mines and trade routes reopened; incursions into Libya, Nubia and Sinai resumed; and arts and crafts flourished again. His successors sent expeditions to the Land of Punt, one of them commanded by **Amenemhat** (or Ammenemes), who returned the capital to Memphis, annexed northern Nubia, furthered trade with Palestine and Syria, and founded the **XII Dynasty** (c.1991–1786 or 1985–1795 BC).

Under **Senusret I** (aka Sesostris I), the administrative capital was transferred to the **Fayoum**, where massive waterworks were undertaken. Amenemhat II curbed the power of the nomarchs, while Senusret III may have abolished the office completely. These kings also built **the last pyramids**, at Lahun, El-Lisht and Hawara, where the final pyramid was erected by Amenemhat III.

According to Rohl's New Chronology, it was **Amenemhat III** who took **Joseph** as his vizier and let the **Israelites** settle in the Delta. Graves at Avaris suggest a large Semitic population stricken by calamities, akin to the Biblical account of the events leading up to the Exodus, which Rohl assigns to the reign of the XIII Dynasty pharaoh **Dudimose**. These attributions are utterly at variance with orthodox chronology, which places the Exodus during the New Kingdom, over two hundred years later.

Yet there's no doubt that the late XII Dynasty was a **troubled time**, with floods bringing poor harvests and famine in their wake. The faces of the statues of pharaohs of this era are uniquely stern and careworn. Whether or not Egypt was also smitten by plagues and disrupted by an exodus from the Delta, it was obviously in poor shape to resist an invasion.

The Hyksos invasion

Under the XIII Dynasty Egypt slid towards an era of disorder termed the **Second Intermediate Period**. For the first time, Lower Egypt fell into the hands of "rulers of foreign lands" or *heka kaswt* – later rendered by the historian Manetho as **Hyksos**. Manetho relates that "invaders of obscure race" appeared in the reign of Dudimose, but many archeologists believe that they gradually filtered into the Delta and only took over later. They had weapons and technology which gave them an edge over the Egyptians: chariots, bronze armour, helmets and swords, and recurved bows that outranged the Egyptian ones. Although Egyptian chronicles describe their rule as anarchic, the *Rhind Mathematical Papyrus* suggests that the Hyksos fostered aspects of native culture, and their introduction of the *shaduf* (counterweighted draw-well) irrigation device proved of lasting benefit to Egyptian agriculture.

Ruling Lower Egypt from the Delta city of **Avaris**, the Hyksos tolerated a separate XIV or Xois Dynasty in the western Delta until about 1650 BC, and pursued peaceful trade with Thebes until the **Theban XVII Dynasty** ruler Sekenenre Tao II resumed war with Lower Egypt. His son **Khamose** was within striking distance of Avaris when he died, whereupon his brother, **Ahmosis I**, finally expelled the Hyksos from Egypt (in 1567 or 1550 BC), ushering in a new era.

The New Kingdom

The **XVIII Dynasty** (c.1567–1320 or 1550–1295 BC) founded by Ahmosis I inaugurated the **New Kingdom**, a period of stability, wealth and expansion, whose rulers include some of the most famous names in Egyptian history. Their formidable war machine subdued **Nubia** (yielding gold, ivory, ebony, gems and slaves) and established colonies or local satrapies in Syria and Palestine. An influx of immigrants into Egypt introduced new customs, ideas and technology.

The effects are evident at **Thebes**, capital of the New Kingdom, where a spate of temples and tombs symbolize the pre-eminence of the god **Amun** and the power of the pharaohs. While **Tuthmosis I** (c.1525–1512 or 1504–1492 BC) built the first tomb in the Valley of the Kings, his daughter **Hatshepsut** raised the great mortuary temple of Deir el-Bahri, ruling as pharaoh (c.1503–1482 or 1473–1458 BC) despite her stepson's claim on the throne. Having belatedly assumed power, **Tuthmosis III** embarked on conquests beyond the Fourth Cataract in Nubia and across the Euphrates to the borders of the Hittite Empire. Many biblical scholars believe that Tuthmosis III was the pharaoh of the Exodus (though other XVIII rulers have also been fingered). His successor **Amenophis II** (c.1459–1425 or 1427–1400 BC) penetrated deeper into Nubia, and **Tuthmosis IV** (c.1425–1417 or 1400–1390 BC) strengthened the empire by marrying a princess of Mitanni, a state bordering the Hittites.

The zenith of Egyptian power coincided with the reign of **Amenophis III** (c.1417–1379 or 1390–1352 BC), who devoted himself to the construction of great edifices such as Luxor Temple. During the same period, a hitherto minor aspect of the sun-god was increasingly venerated in royal circles: the **cult of Aten**, which the pharaoh's son would subsequently enshrine above all others. By changing his name from Amenophis IV to **Akhenaten** and founding a new capital at Tell el-Amarna, he underlined his commitment to a new monotheistic religion that challenged the age-old priesthood and bureaucracy (see p.231).

This **Amarna Revolution** barely outlasted Akhenaten's reign (c.1379–1362 or 1352–1336 BC) and that of his successor, **Smenkhkare**, for the boy king **Tutankhamun** (1361–1352 or 1336–1327 BC) was easily persuaded to abjure Aten's cult and return the capital to Thebes, heralding a **Theban counter-revolution** that continued under **Ay** and **Horemheb**. Though Horemheb (c.1348–1320 or 1323—1295 BC) effectively restored the *status quo ante*, his lack of royal blood and, more importantly, an heir, brought the XVIII Dynasty to a close.

The Ramessid dynasties

The **XIX Dynasty** (c.1320–1200 or 1295–1186 BC) began with the brief reign of Horemheb's vizier, **Ramses I** (c.1320–1318 or 1295–1294 BC), whose family was to produce several warrior-kings who would recapture territories lost under Akhenaten. **Seti I** (c.1318–1304 or 1294–1279 BC) reasserted pharaonic authority in Nubia, Palestine and the Near East, and began a magnificent temple at Abydos. His son **Ramses II** (c.1304–1237 or 1279–1213 BC) completed the temple and the reconquest of Asia Minor, commemorating his dubious victory at Qadesh with numerous reliefs, but later concluding a treaty with the Hittites. At home, Ramses usurped temples and statues built by others, and raised his own monumental edifices – notably the Ramesseum at Thebes and the sun temples at Abu Simbel.

His son **Merneptah** (c.1236–1226 or 1213–1203 BC) faced invasions by the "Sea Peoples" from the north and Libyans from the west, but eventually defeated them in the Delta. He is also popularly believed to be the pharaoh of the **Exodus**, though most scholars reckon that this occurred under the XVIII Dynasty. The XIX Dynasty expired with **Seti II** (c.1210 or 1194 BC), to be followed by some years without a ruling dynasty.

The **XX Dynasty** (c.1200–1085 or 1186–1069 BC), begun by Sethnakhte, was the last of the New Kingdom. His successor **Ramses III** (c.1198–1166 or 1184–1153 BC) repulsed three great invasions by the Libyans and Sea Peoples, and built the vast temple-cum-pleasure palace of **Medinet Habu**. Under the eight kings who followed (all called Ramses), Egypt lost the remains of its Asiatic empire, and thieves plundered the royal necropolis. **Ramses XI** (c.1114–1085 or 1099–1069 BC) withdrew to his palace in the Delta, delegating control of Upper Egypt to **Herihor**, high priest of Amun, and Lower Egypt to Vizier **Smendes**.

The Late Period

Their successors consolidated this division, ruling their respective halves of Egypt from **Thebes** and **Tanis**, with the Theban priest-kings acknowledging the Tanite pharaohs' superiority; scholars designate both ruling houses as the **XXI Dynasty** (c.1069–945 BC). Towards the end of this era, **Shoshenk I** founded the **XXII Dynasty** (c.945–715 BC) of **Libyan** extraction, which ruled Egypt from **Bubastis** in the Delta until a rival line seized power in Upper

Egypt, precipitating civil war between the Bubastite monarchs and the Theban **XXIII Dynasty** (818–720 BC), which was further complicated by a brief **XXIV Dynasty** (727–715 BC) of **Ethiopian** kings.

The lifespan of these four dynasties – termed the **Third Intermediate Period** (TIP) – is one of the murkiest eras of Egyptian history, yet crucial to Rohl's New Chronology hypothesis, as the accepted dates for the New Kingdom hinge on the length of the TIP. Rohl contends that the XXI and XXII dynasties overlapped for generations, and that the duration of the TIP should therefore be reduced accordingly – with knock-on effects down the line.

In 747 BC, Egypt's prolonged instability was brought to an end by the intervention of neighbouring Nubia. The Nubian king **Piankhi** advanced as far north as Memphis, while his brother **Shabaka** went on to conquer the Delta and reunite the Two Lands. The **XXV Dynasty of Nubian kings** (c.747–656 BC) was marked by a revival of artistic and cultural life. The dynasty's later, **Ethiopian**, rulers had to contend with the **Assyrians**, who were thrown back from the gates of **Thebes** in 671 BC and eventually sacked the city in 664 BC.

After the Assyrians withdrew from Egypt to defend their homeland from the Babylonians, the vacuum was filled by **Psammetichus I**, the first ruler of the **XXVI Dynasty** (664–525 BC). Known as the Saïte Dynasty after its capital at **Saïs** in the Delta, this was the last great age of pharaonic civilization – termed the **Late Period** - harking back to the glories of the Old Kingdom in art and architecture, but also adopting new technologies and allowing colonies of Greek merchants at Naucratis and Jewish mercenaries at Elephantine.

Necho II (610–595 BC) defeated Josiah, King of Judah, at Megiddo, and is credited with starting to build a canal to link the Nile with the Red Sea. Though **Psammetichus II** (595–589 BC) enjoyed several victories, his successor was overthrown following defeat in Libya, the throne passing to **Amasis** "the Drunkard", who relied on Greek allies to stave off the Persian Empire.

The **Persian invasion** of 525 BC began a new era of rule by foreigners that essentially lasted until Nasser overthrew Egypt's monarchy in 1952. The Persian emperors **Cambyses** and **Darius I** completed Necho's canal, founded a new city near Memphis, called **Babylon-in-Egypt** (today's Old Cairo), and built and restored temples to enhance their legitimacy, yet **rebellions** attested to Egyptian hatred of this foreign **XXVII Dynasty**. After this was ousted the native **XXX Dynasty** faced repeated Persian assaults, which **Nectanebo I** repulsed with Greek help, but resulted in a crushing defeat for **Nectanebo II** in 343 BC. Egypt remained under Persian control until 332 BC, when their entire empire succumbed to **Alexander the Great**.

The Ptolemies, Roman rule and Christianity

During his brief stay in Egypt, Alexander offered sacrifices to the gods of Memphis and visited Amun's temple at Siwa; reorganized the country's administration, installing himself as pharaoh; and founded the coastal city of **Alexandria**; he then went off to conquer what remained of the known world. Upon his death in 323 BC, Alexander's Macedonian generals divided the empire, Ptolemy becoming ruler of Egypt and establishing the **Ptolemaic Dynasty** in 332.

Under Ptolemy I, **Greek** became the official language, and Hellenistic ideas had a profound effect on Egyptian art, religion and technology. Although Greek deities were also introduced, the Ptolemies cultivated the Egyptian gods and ruled much like Egyptian pharaohs, erecting great cult temples such as Edfu and Kom Ombo. They also opened new ports, established the great Library of Alexandria and had Hebrew scriptures translated into Greek by rabbis.

All this did nothing to check growing **Roman intervention** in Egyptian affairs. In 54 BC **Julius Caesar** took Alexandria by force, only to be seduced by **Cleopatra VII**, the last of the Ptolemies, who bore a son by him – Caesarion - and after Caesar's death formed a similar alliance with **Mark Antony**. However, their joint fleets suffered disaster against **Octavian** at the Battle of Actium, and both committed suicide rather than face captivity. Octavian had Caesarion murdered and reduced Egypt to the status of a province of the Roman Empire (30 BC).

Like the Ptolemies, the **Roman emperors** adopted many of the Egyptian cults, building such monuments as Trajan's kiosk at Philae and temples at Dendara and Esna. Their main interest in the new colony was as a grain supplier to Rome. In terms of culture, language and administration, **Hellenistic influence** barely diminished and Alexandria continued to thrive as an important centre of Greek and Hebrew learning.

Although the **Holy Family's flight to Egypt** from Palestine cannot be proven, Egypt's Jewish colonies would have been a natural place of refuge, and many sites remain associated with the episode. According to Coptic tradition, **Christianity** was brought to Egypt by **St Mark**, who arrived in the time of Nero. Mark converted many to the new underground faith, founding the Patriarchate of Alexandria in 61 AD.

Politically, the most significant ruler was **Trajan** (98–117), who reopened Necho's Red Sea Canal. Trade flourished, but the *fellaheen* were growing increasingly discontented with heavy taxation and forced recruitment into the Roman army.

The Copts

First-century Egypt was fertile ground for the spread of **Christianity**. The old gods had lost credibility over the millennia of political manipulations and disasters, while the population – Egyptians and Jews alike – was becoming increasingly anti-Roman and nationalistic in its outlook. The core of Christianity, too, had a resonance in ancient traditions, with its emphasis on resurrection, divine judgement and the cult of the great mother.

As Egypt's Christians – who became known as **Copts** – grew more assertive, there was conflict with the Roman authorities. **Persecutions** began in 202, reaching their height under Emperor **Diocletian** (284–305), when thousands of Coptic Christians were massacred. Copts date their calendar from the massacres in 284.

The legalization of Christianity and its adoption as the imperial religion by **Constantine** in 313 did little to help the Copts. The Roman rulers, in their new capital at **Byzantium**, embraced an orthodox faith that differed fundamentally from that of their Egyptian co-religionists. Attempts at reconciliation at the **Council of Nicaea** (325) failed, and the split had become irrevocable by the time it was formalized at the **Council of Chalcedon** (451), following which the Copts established their own completely separate Patriarchate at Alexandria.

The same period also saw the emergence of **monasticism**, which took root in the Egyptian deserts. The monasteries of St Catherine in the Sinai, those of Wadi Natrun and Sohag, and St Anthony's and St Paul's in the Red Sea Mountains, all originated in these years.

The Caliphal era

Egypt remained under **Byzantine rule** until the **advance of Islam** in the seventh century. The Muslim armies, led by the Prophet Mohammed's successor, Abu Bakr, defeated the Byzantine army in 636. General Amr Ibn al-As then advanced on the fortress town of Babylon-in-Egypt, which soon surrendered, followed by the capital, Alexandria, in 642.

Amr built his own capital, **Fustat**, north of Babylon-in-Egypt, in what is today Old Cairo. However, Egypt was merely a province in the vast Islamic **Caliphate** that was governed from Damascus and Baghdad; as in Roman times, Egypt was regarded as a bread basket for the empire. Inside Egypt, **Arabization and Islamicization** were hastened by the discriminatory poll-tax (*jiziya*) levied on Copts and Jews by Caliph Omar. Much depended on the character of the caliphs and clannish power struggles, whose impact was felt throughout the empire. In 750, the ruling **Umayyad** dynasty was defeated by the armies of Abu al-Abbas (a descendant of Abu Bakr), and an **Abbassid** caliphate came to power in Baghdad, administering Egypt, along with its other territories, for the next two centuries.

The Tulunids and Ikhshidids

In 868, **Ahmed Ibn Tulun**, sent to administer Egypt on behalf of Caliph al-Mu'tazz, declared the territory independent and founded a dynasty that ruled Egypt for 37 years. Like previous rulers, he built a new capital city, **Al-Qitai**, whose vast mosque still remains. But the **Tulunid dynasty** proved ephemeral; all his heirs were assassinated, and by 905 Abbassid rule was reimposed.

Egypt remained under the direct control of Baghdad until 935, when Mohammed Ibn Tughj was granted the title Ikhshid (ruler or king) by the caliph. Like the Tulunids, the **Ikhshidid dynasty** functioned virtually independently, until a combination of famine, drought and instability opened the way for an invasion of the **Shia Fatimids** from Tunisia in 969, whose armies swept on to conquer Syria. Now it was Egypt's turn to host the imperial capital.

The Fatimid caliphs

The early **Fatimid caliphs** ruled half the Muslim world, with Egypt forming the central portion of an empire that included North Africa, Sicily, Syria and western Arabia. **Gohar**, commander of the caliphal forces, built the city of **Al-Qahira** (the Triumphant) as a new capital in 969, its walls containing opulent palaces and the great mosque-university of Al-Azhar. From there, **Caliph al-Muizz** ruled an empire with a vast multiracial army including Europeans, Berbers, Sudanese and Turks.

Whereas Al-Muizz and his successor were efficient, tolerant rulers under whom Egypt flourished, the third caliph – **Al-Hakim** (996–1021) – was a capricious despot, whose destruction of the Church of the Holy Sepulchre in Jerusalem later provided a pretext for the First Crusade. By the long reign of his grandson, **Al-Mostansir** (1035–94), decay had set in. Though able governors restored order and prosperity for a further century, the Fatimid Empire felt increasingly vulnerable after the loss of Syria to the Seljuk Turks, and confronted by new forces in Europe.

The **Crusades** (after 1097) obliged the Fatimids to fight for their possession of the Holy Land, and defend Egypt itself after 1167. Outraged by the feebleness of the Fatimids and fraternization between Muslims and Crusaders in Palestine, the Seljuk Sultan, Nur al-Din, sent an expedition to repel the Europeans. His nephew,

Salah al-Din al-Ayyubi – known to Europe as Saladin – took possession of Alexandria and routed the Crusaders.

The Ayyubid sultans

On the death of the last Fatimid caliph in 1171, **Salah al-Din** became ruler of Egypt. To this day he remains an Arab hero, renowned for his modesty, generosity and wisdom. Having no pretensions to religious leadership, he took the secular title of Al-Sultan ("The Power") rather than that of caliph. Of his 24-year reign, he spent only eight years in Cairo, the rest being spent at war against the Crusaders. By 1183, Syria had been won back and in 1187 Jerusalem was recaptured.

In Cairo, he built a fortress – today's Citadel – and expanded the Fatimid walls to enclose the city. To propagate Sunni orthodoxy, he introduced the Seljuk institution of the **madrassa** or teaching mosque, thus turning Cairo into a great centre of learning.

Following his death in 1193, the Sultanate's eastern territories fragmented, but Egypt remained united under the **Ayyubids**. His nephew, **Al-Kamil** (1218–38), repulsed the Fifth Crusade, and the last of the dynasty, **Ayyub** (1240–49), built up a formidable army of Qipchak slaves from the Black Sea region.

When Ayyub died without leaving an heir, his widow **Shagar al-Durr** took power, ruling openly as sultana until the Abbassid caliphs insisted that she take a husband, quoting the Prophet's words: "Woe to the nations ruled by women." Having wed she had him murdered by a henchman, **Beybars the Crossbowman**, who clawed his way to power after she was killed in 1250.

The Mamlukes

Beybars was a commander (amir) among the **Mamlukes**, the foreign slave-troops on whom the later Ayyubids depended. Originally drawn from Central Asia and later from all over the Near East and the Balkans, they became a self-perpetuating caste whose amirs ruled Egypt for the next three centuries, each sultan intriguing his way through the ranks to assume the throne by *coup d'état* or assassination. Frequent changes of ruler were preferred, since contenders had to spread around bribes.

The Turkic **Bahri** ("River") **Mamlukes** (so-called after their garrison by the Nile) gave rise to the first Mamluke dynasty, founded by **Qalaoun**, who poisoned Beybars' heirs in 1279. He sponsored many buildings in Cairo, established relations with potentates around the Indian Ocean and concluded treaties with European sovereigns. **Mohammed al-Nasir** (1294–1340) was another great builder and power-broker, who concluded treaties with the Mongols after defeating them in Syria – but his heirs struggled to hold the throne amidst perpetual intrigues by Mamluke factions.

In 1382 the sultanate was seized by **Barquq**, of the Circassian **Burgi** ("Tower") **Mamlukes** garrisoned below the Citadel. To finance his campaigns against the **Mongols** in Syria, he imposed taxes that beggared the economy. Hardships were exacerbated by famine and plague during his son's reign, and it was only under Sultan **Barsbey** (1422–37) that Egypt regained some of its power, establishing friendly relations with the Ottoman Turks and expanding trade in the Indian Ocean.

Though Egypt enjoyed peace and prosperity during the long reign of **Qaitbey** (1468–95), his lavish building programme was unsustainable by his successors. Egypt's spice-trade monopoly was dealt a crippling blow by the discovery of the

Cape route to the Indies, depriving the 46th (and penultimate) sultan, **Qansuh al-Ghuri** (1501–16), of revenue, just as the **Ottoman Turks** attacked Mamluke domains in Syria. Following Al-Ghuri's death in battle at Aleppo, his successor **Tumanbey** was crushed by the Ottoman onslaught and executed in Cairo in 1517.

Ottoman and French occupation

Even after the Turkish conquest, the Mamlukes remained powerful figures in the administration of what was now a province of the **Ottoman Empire**. Government was provided by a series of **pashas**, officials trained in Istanbul. The Mamluke army continued to grow with the import of Caucasian slaves; by the end of the sixteenth century its senior **Beys** were infamous for their intrigues, arbitrary taxes and profligate ways. Egypt's **decline** was accelerated by a plague epidemic in 1719, which left the country depopulated, its capital crumbling away amidst mounds of rubbish, as the French traveller Volney described it in 1784.

At the end of the century, Egypt became a pawn in the struggle between France and Britain. **Napoleon** saw it as a means to disrupt British commerce and rule in India. In 1798, his fleet landed at Alexandria, where he issued a proclamation that began with the Islamic *bismillah* ("In the name of God"), promising to liberate Egypt from the "riffraff of slaves", and that he respected Islam more than the Mamlukes did.

Although Napoleon routed the Mamlukes and occupied Cairo, he left his fleet exposed at Abu Qir Bay, where it was destroyed by the British under Nelson. With his grand vision in tatters, Napoleon returned secretly to France, leaving the army behind. After General Menou proclaimed Egypt a **French protectorate** the British invaded Alexandria, combining with Ottoman forces to take Cairo, forcing the French to surrender. Under the Capitulation Agreement, the archeological treasures gathered by Napoleon's savants were surrendered to Britain – which is why the **Rosetta Stone** ended up in the British Museum rather than the Louvre.

While Europeans marvelled at the wonders of Ancient Egypt, Egyptians were left awed by the defeat of the "invincible" Mamlukes and such wonders of Western technology as printing presses and hot-air balloons (which the French introduced to Cairo). While Ottoman rule had been restored, things would not be the same.

Mohammed Ali and his heirs

Among the Turkish officers left in charge was **Mohammed Ali** of the Albanian Corps, whose dynasty was to change Egypt more radically than any ruler since Salah al-Din, and is thus regarded as the founder of modern Egypt. Having been confirmed as **Pasha** in 1805, he proceeded to decapitate the Mamluke leadership (see p.126), confiscated private land and set about modernizing Egypt with European expertise, building railways, factories and canals. His son Ibrahim led a murderous campaign to subjugate northern **Sudan**, of which the only positive result was the introduction of a special kind of **cotton** – henceforth Egypt's major cash crop.

When Mohammed Ali died insane in 1849, his successor **Abbas** (1848–54) closed the country's factories and secular schools and opened Egypt to free trade, thus retarding industrialization. **Said Pasha** (1854–63) granted a concession to a French engineer, Ferdinand de Lesseps, to build the **Suez Canal** (see p.504) – a project completed in 1869, by which time **Khedive Ismail** (1863–79) was in power. He transformed Cairo, spending lavishly on modernization, but exorbitant interest rates had to be paid on European loans. To stave off bankruptcy, he sold his Suez Canal shares to the British government in 1875.

Ismail was deposed by his son **Tewfiq** (1879–92), whose own fiscal power was limited by the French and British, to the disgust of patriotic Egyptians. A group of army officers forced him to appoint their leader, **Ahmed Orabi**, as Minister of War. France and Britain responded by sending in the gunboats, shelling Alexandria and landing an army which routed Orabi's forces at Tell el-Kebir and restored Tewfiq as a puppet ruler under British control.

British occupation and Egyptian nationalism

Britain's stated intention was to set Egyptian affairs in order and then withdraw, but its interests dictated a more permanent involvement. From 1883 to 1907, Egypt was controlled by the British Consul-General, Sir Evelyn Baring, later **Lord Cromer**, who coined the term **Veiled Protectorate** to describe the relationship between the two countries. Egyptian resentment at this usurpation of authority found expression under **Abbas II**, who came to power in 1892, and in a nationalist movement led by the lawyer **Mustafa Kamel**. Egypt was effectively a colony, with Britain supplying all the country's manufactured goods, and encouraging Egyptian dependence on cotton exports.

When Turkey entered **World War I** on the side of Germany in 1916, Egypt was still nominally a province of the Ottoman Empire, so to safeguard its strategic interests Britain declared Egypt a protectorate and tightened its grip. By 1917, **Fouad**, the sixth son of Ismail, was *khedive* of Egypt, with Reginald Wingate its High Commissioner. The **nationalist movement** flourished under wartime conditions; in 1918 its leader, **Sa'ad Zaghloul**, presented Wingate with a demand for autonomy, which was rejected. The request to send a delegation (*wafd*) to London led to Zaghloul's arrest and deportation to Malta (rescinded after nationwide riots). In 1922 Britain abolished the protectorate and recognized Egypt as an independent state but kept control of the judiciary, communications, defence and the Canal, while Fouad assumed the title of king.

The next twenty years saw a struggle for power between the king, the British and the nationalist **Wafd Party**. Fouad's son, **King Farouk**, succeeded him in 1935 and signed a twenty-year **Anglo-Egyptian treaty**, which ended British occupation but empowered their forces to remain in the Canal Zone. In 1937, Egypt joined the League of Nations, but the outbreak of World War II halted its move to complete independence.

World War II and postwar manoeuvrings

World War II saw Rommel's **Afrika Korps** coming within 111km of Alexandria, though they were repulsed by the **Eighth Army** under General Montgomery at the **Battle of El-Alamein** in October 1942. Thereafter the tide of war turned in the Western Desert campaign and the Allies continued to advance across North Africa, through Libya and Tunisia.

During the war, the Wafd leadership kept dissent muted on the tacit understanding that full independence would be granted after the war, when they demanded the evacuation of British troops and unification with Sudan (contrary to Britain's plans for its self-government). Popular resentment was expressed in riots and strikes, supported by the **Muslim Brotherhood** (see "Islam", p.616), which led to clashes with British troops in the Canal Zone.

Following the declaration of the state of **Israel** in May 1948, Egypt joined Iraq, Syria and Jordan in a military invasion. The defeat of the Arab forces was followed by a UN-brokered treaty that left the **Gaza Strip** under Egyptian administration. Many of the Egyptian officers who fought in this war were disgusted by the incompetence and corruption of their superiors: these veterans formed the core of a revolutionary conspiracy known as the **Free Officers**.

The 1952 Revolution

Following Egypt's first **elections** in ten years, the Wafd won a majority and formed a government with Nahas Pasha as prime minister. In 1952, Nahas was dismissed by King Farouk after abrogating the Anglo-Egyptian treaty, and the Egyptian army was sent out onto the streets to quell protests. On July 23, the Free Officers staged a bloodless **coup**, forcing **Farouk's abdication** three days later. Their nominal leader, General Naguib, became head of the armed forces and prime minister, but real power lay in the hands of the nine officers of the **Revolutionary Command Council** (RCC), foremost among who was Colonel **Gamal Abdel Nasser**.

The constitution was revoked, political parties dissolved, the monarchy abolished and Egypt declared a **republic** (July 26, 1953). Meanwhile, a struggle for power raged behind the scenes, as Naguib attempted to step beyond his figurehead status and moderate the RCC's radicalism. After being implicated in an attempt on Nasser's life in 1954, Naguib was placed under house arrest; Nasser became acting head of state and in June 1956 was confirmed as president.

The Nasser era

President Nasser dominated Egypt and the Arab world until his death in 1970, his ideology of **Arab nationalism** and socialism making him supremely popular with the masses from Iraq to Morocco. Under his leadership, Egypt was at the forefront of **anti-colonialism**, supporting liberation struggles in Algeria and sub-Saharan Africa, and co-founding the Non-Aligned Movement.

In 1954 he reached agreement for the withdrawal of British troops from the Canal Zone, though the Canal's management and profits were to remain in foreign hands. Meanwhile he was seeking credits from the World Bank to finance construction of the Aswan High Dam, and weapons to rearm Egyptian forces. When the Soviet Union offered to supply arms, the United States vetoed loans for the dam, leaving Nasser with no alternative but to **nationalize the Canal** to secure revenue, in July 1956.

This was regarded by Britain and France as a threat to their vital interests. Both concluded a secret agreement with Israel, whose **invasion of Sinai** in October 1956 was to provide the pretext for their own intervention to "safeguard" the Canal. Following bombardments and British paratroop landings in Port Said, the United States stepped in, threatening to destabilize Britain's economy unless its forces withdrew. The canal reopened under full Egyptian control and Nasser emerged from the **Suez Crisis** as a champion of Arab nationalism.

On a wave of **pan-Arab** sentiment, Egypt and Syria united to form the **United Arab Republic** in 1958, an unworkable arrangement that foundered within three years. Egypt moved closer to the Soviet Union, accepting technical and military assistance on a massive scale, to build the Aswan High Dam and counter an increasingly well-armed Israel by staging *Fedayeen* raids from Gaza.

When Israel threatened to invade Syria in 1967, Nasser sent Egyptian forces into Sinai and blockaded the Tiran Straits, cutting shipping to the Israeli port of Eilat. Israel responded with a pre-emptive strike, destroying Egypt's air force on the ground and seizing Sinai, Gaza, the West Bank and the Golan Heights. The **Six Day War** was a shattering defeat for the Arabs and Nasser in particular, who proffered his resignation, only resuming the presidency after mass demonstrations of support on the streets. The conflict had no formal resolution, subsiding into a **War of Attrition** which dragged on for the next two years, with Israeli forces shelling the Canal cities from Sinai while Egypt rearmed and struggled to host millions of refugees.

Amid the drama of Suez and wars with Israel, it's easy to overlook the **social achievements** of the Nasser era. One of the RCC's first acts was to break up the old feudal estates, transferring **land** to the *fellaheen*. As a result of the **Aswan High Dam,** the amount under cultivation increased by fifteen percent (surpassing population growth for the first time) and the dam's turbines powered a huge **industrial base**, created virtually from scratch. There was similar progress in **education and health care**; average life expectancy rose from 43 to 52 years. The downside was a Soviet-style system where all political parties were merged into the **Arab Socialist Union** (ASU), and censorship, torture and internment were widespread. Nevertheless, **Nasser's death** – from a heart attack – in 1970 came as a profound shock to the whole Arab world. His funeral procession in Cairo was the largest Egypt has ever seen.

Egypt under Sadat

Nasser's deputy, **Anwar Sadat**, was confirmed as president by the ASU hierarchy to reform a country demoralized by defeat, stagnation and austerity. His "**corrective revolution**" reversed decades of centralized economic control, while the mass-expulsion of Soviet advisers masked secret planning with Syria and Jordan to launch a new campaign against Israel. On October 6, 1973, Egyptian forces crossed the Canal, storming the "invincible" Bar-Lev Line to enter Israeli-held Sinai. This **October War** (aka 10th Ramadan/Yom Kippur War) ultimately turned against the Arabs, but enhanced their bargaining position and dealt a blow to Israeli self-confidence; Egypt also regained a strip of territory to the east of the Canal, enabling Sadat to claim victory.

After the war, an amnesty was granted to political prisoners, censorship was lifted and some political parties, including the Muslim Brotherhood, were allowed. Equally important was Sadat's *infitah* or "**open door**" policy, to encourage private and foreign investment and reduce the role of the state in the economy. Helped by Gulf Arab investments – a reward for the October War – and stimulated by the reconstruction of the Canal cities, the economy boomed. However, while the number of millionaires rose from 500 to 17,000 and an affluent middle class developed, the condition of the urban poor and *fellaheen* worsened. Some five million families subsisted on less than $30 a month, and one and a half million Egyptians migrated to work in the Gulf States.

In 1977, when the International Monetary Fund insisted on the removal of subsidies on basic foodstuffs, there were nationwide **food riots**. Needing an injection of Western capital and convinced that Israel's acquisition of nuclear weapons made an Arab victory impossible, Sadat became the first Arab leader to visit Jerusalem, signing the **Camp David Agreement** (1978), whereby Egypt recognized Israel's right to exist and Israel agreed to withdraw from Sinai. Outraged, the Arab League severed links with Egypt and moved its headquarters from Cairo to Tunis.

At home, Sadat had encouraged the rise of Islamic groups to counter leftist influences, but as the Muslim Brotherhood grew stronger and protested against the Camp David accord he ordered wholesale arrests – resulting in **Sadat's assassination** by Islamic militants in October 1981.

Mubarak's Egypt

Sadat's successor, **Hosni Mubarak**, is the third president to have emerged from the armed forces, and has ruled Egypt since 1981 through an authoritarian system essentially unchanged since Nasser's time. Under the **emergency laws** passed after Sadat's murder – still in force today – demonstrations are illegal unless licensed by the police (who violently suppress unauthorized ones); **torture** by the security forces goes unpunished; human rights activists are arrested, and **elections** are rigged.

Although Mubarak had to open the presidential election to other candidates when he ran for a fifth term in 2005, his opponent **Ayman Nour** was jailed on charges of forging signatures as MP of a new liberal party, Al-Ghad ("Tomorrow"), while meetings of the reformist alliance **Kifaya** ("Enough") were broken up by government thugs. Manipulation of elections for the National Assembly was less successful, with the banned Muslim Brotherhood winning a quarter of the seats under the guise of independent candidates – an unprecedented protest vote that the regime had to swallow.

Despite being a taboo subject in the media, it's widely believed that the ailing octogenarian president wants his younger son, **Gamal Mubarak**, to succeed him. A small Westernized minority may consider Gamal a modernizer like King Mohammed VI of Morocco, but most Egyptians view him as a playboy set to inherit the family fortune. Few doubt that a **succession** crisis looms in the not so distant future.

Meanwhile, Egypt's problems are mounting. Only three percent of its land is usable for agriculture, while the **population** rises by a million every nine months (at the time of writing, it stands at 83 million). Egypt must import half the food it needs, and without $2 billion a year in **US aid** the economy would collapse. Society is increasingly polarized between the masses for whom living standards are no higher than in Nasser's time – or have fallen – and wealthy elites who benefit most from the pervasive **corruption** in government and the private sector. In 2009, anger at **inflation** led to violent strikes and factory occupations in the textile towns of the Delta.

Another woe for Egyptians since 2006 has been **bird flu**, which has killed 22 people (mostly women, who rear poultry at home and employ an ancient method of feeding, whereby they chew grain and blow it into the birds' mouths). When the World Health Organization declared a **swine flu** pandemic two years later, the government ordered the killing of all pigs in Egypt – a culling that provoked riots among the *zebaleen* (rubbish-collectors) who live on the outskirts of Egyptian cities.

Regime change in Egypt?

Mubarak's **regime** has long been a thinly-disguised military dictatorship allied to an oligarchy. Ex-military and police officers hold top jobs in civilian life; the army is a profit-making entity (owning farms, factories and construction businesses using conscript labour); and senior officials and wealthy entrepreneurs (often from the "Menoufi Mafia" promoted from the Delta governorate where Sadat and Mubarak were born) collude in a web of mutual corruption. Most Egyptians refer to the ruling elite as the "band of thieves" – but see little hope of getting rid of them.

The regime's resilience was demonstrated in the 1990s, when **Islamic militants** and the security forces fought a low-level war in Middle Egypt, during which over 1200 people were killed, 10,000 wounded and scores of thousands detained under the emergency laws. The Luxor massacre of 1997 proved to be the swansong of the Gamaat Islamiya – whose imprisoned leaders denounced the massacre and announced a ceasefire – while the other militant group, Jihad Islami, was forced to decamp to Afghanistan after its network in Egypt was eradicated and it was expelled from its base in Sudan. When a new group, Al-Tawhid w'al Jihad, began bombing Sinai resorts in 2004, the terrorists were tracked down and wiped out within two years.

The regime's Achilles heel is Mubarak's mortality. In poor health, he cannot rule for much longer, nor expect his son Gamal to inherit the presidency without opposition. **Mayehkomsh** (literally, "He will not rule") is a coalition of diverse groups and prominent individuals, pledged to contest the 2011 presidential election; the respected former head of the International Atomic Energy Agency, **Mohammed El Baradei**, may be a candidate whom all factions can support. Even within the ruling National Democratic Party there are many who would prefer **General Omar Suleiman**, Egypt's spy supremo, to Gamal Mubarak – though the general's weak heart is said to disqualify him from running for the presidency. Or perhaps another candidate will emerge from the armed forces with the backing of the oligarchy, to perpetuate the kleptocracy…

The resurgence of Islamic **terrorism** since 2004 has seen bombings at Sinai tourist resorts and attacks in Cairo. While security forces crushed the terrorist bases in the hinterland of El-Arish, the **Gaza border** became an increasing concern as smugglers' tunnels conveyed terrorists into Egypt. When Israel invaded Gaza in 2008 to stop Hamas rocket attacks, Egypt kept the Rafah border crossing shut and deployed troops to prevent refugees from fleeing. In 2009 Egypt began building a subterranean barrier to prevent further tunnels being dug, reinforcing the blockade of Gaza.

While Egyptian public opinion remains solidly pro-Palestinian, senior officials make little secret of their wish to see **Hamas** humbled. General Omar Suleiman, Egypt's spymaster, regards it as an extension of the Muslim Brotherhood, and an Iranian proxy like Lebanon's Hezbollah – whom he has accused of establishing sabotage cells in the Canal cities. **Iran** is seen as bent on acquiring nuclear weapons and hegemony over the Middle East. The Egyptian government's decision to build a nuclear power station on the Mediterranean coast suggests it is contemplating its own nuclear weapons option, though this aim has yet to be openly stated.

With little effective political opposition except the Muslim Brotherhood, a soaring population and a creeping **environmental crisis** in the Delta – where land is being lost to rising sea-levels and soil-salinization – it's hard to be optimistic about Egypt's future.

Islam

Islam was born on the Arabian Peninsula, beyond the periphery of Greco-Roman civilization. Its founder, **Mohammed**, was a merchant from the city of Mecca, in what is now Saudi Arabia. At the age of forty (c.609 AD), he began to have visions of an angel commanding him to recite divine revelations. As "God's Messenger", he proclaimed the oneness of **Allah** (God), the evil of idolatry in a city worshipping several deities (of whom Allah was one) and the need for submission (*islam*) to Allah's will. Forced to flee Mecca with his followers in 622 (the *hijra* that marks the beginning of the Muslim calendar), he spent eight years uniting the Bedouin tribes of Medina to finally conquer Mecca, dying two years later.

Mohammed's recitations – he was illiterate – were later transcribed into the Islam's holy book, the **Koran** (or "recitation"), which asserted that Allah was the same God worshipped by Jews and Christians, but that the message of Abraham (Ibrahim), Moses (Musa) and Jesus (Issa) had been distorted and was only truly expressed by Mohammed, the "Seal of the Prophets".

The Pillars of Faith

Muslims (believers) face five essential requirements, the so-called "**Pillars of Faith**": prayer five times daily, the pilgrimage (*hajj*) to Mecca, the Ramadan fast, giving alms (*zakat*), and – most fundamental of all – the belief that "there is no God but Allah and Mohammed is His Prophet". Ritual prayers are the most visible of these obligations, punctuating the Islamic day (which begins at sunset) at dawn, noon, mid-afternoon, sunset and after dark. Prayers can be performed anywhere, but preferably in a mosque.

In the past, a muezzin (prayer crier) would climb his minaret each time and summon the faithful. Nowadays, the call is most likely pre-recorded; even so, this most distinctive of Islamic sounds has a beauty all of its own. The message is simplicity itself: "God is most great (*Allahu Akbar*). I testify that there is no God but Allah. I testify that Mohammed is His Prophet. Come to prayer, come to security. God is great." Another phrase is added in the morning: "Prayer is better than sleep."

Prayers are preceded by ritual ablutions. Facing Mecca (the direction indicated in a mosque by the *mihrab* or niche), worshippers recite the *Fatihah*, the first chapter of the Koran, and then repeat the same words twice in the prostrate position, with interjections of *Allahu Akbar. A* highly ritualized procedure whose obeisance symbolizes Muslims' submission to God, the sight of thousands of people going through the same motions simultaneously in a mosque is a powerful one. On Islam's holy day, Friday, all believers are expected to attend prayers led by local imams, who also deliver a *khutba*, or sermon.

Ramadan is the name of the ninth month in the lunar Islamic calendar, the month in which the Koran was first revealed to Mohammed. For the whole of the month, believers must obey a rigorous fast (the custom was originally modelled on Jewish and Christian practice), forsaking all forms of consumption between sunrise and sundown; this includes food, drink, and any form of sexual contact. Only certain categories of people are exempted: travellers, children, pregnant women and warriors engaged in *jihad* (see below). Given the climates in which many Muslims live, the fast is a formidable undertaking, but in practice it becomes a time of intense celebration.

The pilgrimage, or **Hajj**, to Mecca is an annual event, with millions flocking to Mohammed's birthplace from all over the world. Here they go through several days of rituals, the central one being a sevenfold circumambulation of the sacred Ka'ba shrine. Islam requires that all believers go on a *Hajj* as often as is practically possible, but for the poor it may well be a once-in-a-lifetime occasion, and is sometimes replaced by a series of visits to lesser, local shrines – in Egypt, for instance, to the mosques of Saiyida Zeinab or El-Hussein in Cairo.

Development in Egypt

Mohammed's successors – the four Rightly Guided Caliphs – spread Islam far beyond Arabia in a great **jihad** ("holy struggle"); within a century of the Prophet's death they had forged an Islamic Empire extending from the Atlantic Ocean to Central Asia. Egypt fell readily in 640, its Byzantine rulers hated by a native population who acquiesced to, or welcomed, the Muslim conquest after its leader, Amr, promised to respect Egypt's Christians and Jews as "people of the book".

In accordance with Koranic precepts codified by Caliph Omar, they had to pay a poll-tax (*jizia*) and submit to restrictions affirming their inferior status, in return for which their lives and property were protected. Even these weren't guaranteed under Caliph al-Hakim, who destroyed many churches and synagogues during his reign. Despite such powerful incentives to convert to Islam, it was not until the eleventh century that Cairo attained a **Muslim majority**, and not until the thirteenth century for Egypt as a whole.

The original Arab dynasties of Egypt subscribed to **Sunni Islam** – the more "orthodox" branch of the religion, dominant then, as now, in most parts of the Arab world. However, the Fatimid dynasty, which took control of Egypt in 969, signalled a shift to **Shiite Islam**, which was to continue (among the rulers, at least) until late in the twelfth century. Under the Ayyubid dynasty that followed, Egypt reverted, permanently as it turned out, to Sunni adherence, with orthodoxy propagated through the new institution of the **madrassa** – a theological college attached to a mosque.

The Grand Sheikh of Cairo's **Mosque of Al-Azhar** is the ultimate theological authority for most Sunnis outside the Gulf Arab states, issuing *fatwas* (opinions) on a wide range of questions submitted by believers, from family matters to financial affairs – in person, by post or email.

Sheikhs and Sufis

Alongside this formal religious establishment, Egypt also developed **a popular religious culture**, manifested in the veneration of sheikhs and the formation of Sufi brotherhoods – both of which remain important today. **Sheikhs** are basically local holy men: people who developed reputations for sanctity and learning.

Although the Koran prohibits monasticism and isolation from the community, Islam soon developed religious orders dedicated to asceticism and a mystical experience of God. Collectively known as the **Sufis**, these groups generally coalesced around a charismatic teacher, from whom they derived their name. The largest of these brotherhoods (*tariqas*) in Egypt are the **Rifai**, the **Ahmediya** and the **Shadhiliyya** – who can be seen at moulids ("saint's day" festivals) parading with their distinctive banners.

Towards crisis

While Europe was in the Dark Ages, the Islamic world, straddling the Near East, India and the Mediterranean, developed and disseminated **knowledge** from Classical civilizations and Asia, in fields from chemistry to cartography. The medical treatises of Ibn Sina (known in Europe as Avicenna) and the piped water and sewage systems of Fustat are just two Egyptian examples. Yet despite this contribution to the European Renaissance and the lucrative trade in spices and other luxuries, relations between Islam and Christendom were more antagonistic than amicable. The Crusades, and Saracen and Ottoman attacks on Europe, had an enduring impact on both sides.

As Europe moved towards the Age of Enlightenment, the Islamic world grew more introverted and hostile to innovation, and by the end of the eighteenth century Europe was poised to take advantage. Napoleon's expedition to Egypt in 1798 marked the beginning of a century in which virtually every Islamic country came under the control of a **European power**. While Islam couldn't be held solely responsible, its centrality and the reality of European technological superiority posed a question that provoked a **crisis in religious self-confidence**: Why had Islam's former power now passed to infidel foreigners?

The Islamist response

Responses to this question veered between two extremes. There were those who felt that Islam should try to incorporate some of the West's secularism and materialism; on the other side, there were movements holding that Islam should turn its back on the West, purify itself of all corrupt additions and thus rediscover its former power.

The earliest exponent of the latter view was the **Muslim Brotherhood** (Il-Ikhwan il-Muslimeen), founded in Ismailiya by **Hassan el-Banna** in 1928. The Brotherhood preached a moral renewal of Islam, established a network of schools and training centres, and later set up clandestine paramilitary groups. Aimed as much against corrupt feudal institutions as against Western imperialism, the Brotherhood spread throughout Egypt and spawned offshoots across the Middle East. Its terrorist activities prompted a violent state response, being banned by King Farouk, whose bodyguards assassinated el-Banna in 1949.

His mantle was assumed by Sayyid Qutb, whose conversion to radical Islam followed two years in the USA, where he was appalled by American women, the "animal-like" mixing of the sexes and jazz music. Jailed for ten years after an abortive attempt by two Brothers to assassinate Nasser, Qutb wrote a manifesto, *Milestones* (smuggled out of prison), asserting that Muslim states had reverted to Jahiliyya (the pagan era before Islam) by failing to apply Sharia law. On the day of Qutb's execution in 1966, a 15-year-old follower vowed to continue his work by forging an Islamist vanguard: Ayman al-Zawahiri, the future founder of Jihad Islami and Al-Qaida's deputy leader.

In Egypt, the Brotherhood remained underground until the Sadat era, when the government regarded it as a useful counterweight to the Left. Its tacit cooperation with the state led to the emergence of more radical groups; the most effective was **Al-Jihad**, which assassinated Sadat and attempted to launch a revolution in Assyut in 1981. Under Mubarak, the mainstream Islamist opposition was allowed to establish clinics and schools for the poor, **Gamaat Islamiya** ("Islamic Societies") captured the professional unions, and thousands of Egyptians put their savings into Islamic investment houses. When these went bankrupt amid accusations of fraud the Islamic movement's credibility was badly dented, but its prompt distribution of aid after the 1991 Cairo earthquake redeemed its reputation amongst the urban poor.

The following year **Islamic militants** launched an insurgency in Middle Egypt, killing tourists, policemen and Copts. Gamaat Islamiya (not to be confused with the aforementioned Islamic Societies, despite their overlapping membership and ideology) and the smaller Jihad Islami ("Islamic Jihad") claimed divine sanction for attacks on the "Pharaonic regime", "infidel" tourists, and Christians who refused to pay *jizia* (extortion money).

While the insurgency was crushed following the 1998 Luxor massacre and the ceasefire declared by imprisoned leaders of Gamaat Islamiya, the authorities have since deferred to the Islamist agenda by jailing three hundred Egyptians for converting to Christianity, and turning a blind eye to sectarian rapes and other violence directed against the Copts, from Alexandria (in 2006) to Middle Egypt (2010).

Meanwhile the exiled leaders of the Jihad Islami, **Ayman al-Zawahiri** and Mohammed Atef, joined Osama Bin Laden in Afghanistan, merging with Al-Qaida to form the "World Islamic Front Against Jews and Crusaders". Their assault on the World Trade Center on 9/11 was a devastating reprise of an earlier attack in 1993. In Egypt, a new terrorist group – Al-Tawhid w'al Jihad – wreaked havoc on Sinai's resorts in 2004–05. That its members were Sinai Bedouin – a people who had previously showed no radical inclinations – especially alarmed the authorities.

Since the 2005 elections the Muslim Brotherhood has had 88 out of 454 seats in the National Assembly. While some credit them with being a responsible opposition, nudging Egypt towards democracy, others reckon that their true agenda is summed up by the phrase "One man, one vote, once" – meaning that, having taken power by democratic means, the Brotherhood would abolish democracy. Their English-language website (Ⓦwww.ikhwanweb.com) is couched in more moderate terms than their Arabic one.

While many Egyptians doubt that Islam offers a solution for *everything* – and the lifestyle aspirations of Egyptian youth are far from fundamentalist – the Islamists' view of world events is broadly shared at every level of society. The Brotherhood has a large following in universities and legal associations, with activists willing to risk arrest and torture. Besides using intimidation, the authorities have tried to marginalize them by attempting to introduce a unified nationwide **azan** (call to prayer) in place of the cacophony of individual muezzins (which critics fear could provide a pretext to silence preachers linked to the Brotherhood). The training of **female imams** at Al-Azhar University is another aspect of the government's strategy to "modernize" Islam (Morocco is likewise training women to be imams).

Egypt's most popular cleric is Sheikh Yusuf al-Qaradawi, who opines on the Al Jazeera show 'Sharia and Life' and IslamOnline (Ⓦwww.islamonline.net). In the West he has been condemned for stating that homosexuals deserve the same punishment as fornicators, and that suicide bombings against Israeli soldiers and civilians in the Occupied Territories are a legitimate form of resistance. Yet he has also been denounced by Saudi clerics for saying that "The enmity that is between us and the Jews is for the sake of land only, not for the sake of religion", and for favouring Sufism and music – all of which are anathema to hardline Wahhabis.

Chronology

The chronology below is designed for general reference of monuments and dynasties or rulers. For simplicity, only the **major figures of each dynasty** or era are listed, and likewise with monuments and artefacts.

The following abbreviations are used: EAM (Egyptian Antiquities Museum in Cairo), IAM (Islamic Arts Museum in Cairo) and BM (British Museum in London).

c.250,000 BC ▸ **Hunter-gathering hominids** roam the savannas. Stone tools from this time have been discovered in gravel beds of Upper Egypt and Nubia.

c.25,000 BC ▸ **Late Paleolithic era**. Onset of desertification, until rains of Neolithic era. Ostrich eggs and flints have been found beneath dunes of Great Sand Sea.

c.6000 BC ▸ **Middle Neolithic era**. Intensive occupation of the Western Desert by hunter-gatherers. Rock art at the Gilf Kebir; solar calendar at Nabta Playa.

Predynastic Egypt

c.5000 BC ▸ Pastoralism becomes widespread in the Eastern and Western deserts, while **Badarian culture** takes root in the Nile Valley. Pottery, jewellery and ivory excavated at village of El-Badari in Upper Egypt.

c.4000 BC ▸ **Naqada I culture** Burnished pottery and granite maceheads have been found near Qus in Upper Egypt.

Early Dynastic or Archaic Period (c.3100–2686 or 2920–2575 BC)

c.2920–2770 BC ▸ **I Dynasty** Aha; Djer; Den.

c.2920 or 3100 BC ▸ **Unification of the Two Lands** (Upper and Lower Egypt) by **Menes**. Foundation of Memphis; Palette of Narmer (EAM); Stele of Peribsen (BM); Scorpion Macehead (Ashmolean Museum, Oxford).

2686–2613 or 2469–2575 BC ▸ **III Dynasty** Zoser; Sekhemkhet; Huni. Step Pyramid and Unfinished Pyramid built at Saqqara; Collapsed Pyramid at Maidum.

Old Kingdom (c.2686–2181 or 2575–2134 BC)

2613–2494 or 2575–2465 BC ▸ **IV Dynasty** Snofru; Cheops; Chephren; Mycerinus. Bent Pyramid at Dahshur; Great Pyramids of Giza.

2494–2345 or 2465–2323 BC ▸ **V Dynasty** Userkaf; Sahure; Neferefre; Nyuserre; Unas. Sun Temples and Pyramids at Abu Sir; several further pyramids at Saqqara.

2345–2181 or 2323–2150 BC ▸ **VI Dynasty** Teti; Pepi I; Pepi II. More pyramids at Saqqara.

First Intermediate Period (c.2181–2050 or 2134–2040 BC)

2181–2160 or 2150–2134 BC **VII and VIII dynasties** Period of anarchy and fragmentation of power.

2160–2130 or 2154–2040 BC ▸ **IX and X dynasties** Achthoes. Capital at Herakleopolis, near Beni Suef.

2133–1991 BC ▸ **XI Dynasty** Inyotef Sehertowy; Nebhepetre Mentuhotep II reunites Two Lands in 2050 BC. Ruined mortuary temple at Deir el-Bahri; Mentuhotep's statue (EAM).

Middle Kingdom (c.2055–1650 or 2050–1786 BC)

1991–1786 or 1985–1795 BC ▸ **XII Dynasty** Amenemhat I; Senusert I and II; Amenemhat III. Pyramids at Lahun, Lisht and Hawara; rock tombs at Beni Hassan and Aswan; site of Medinet Madi.

1795–1650 BC ▸ **XIII Dynasty.**

Second Intermediate Period (c.1786–1567 or 1650–1550 BC)

1786–1603 or 1650–1550 BC **XIV Dynasty.**

1674–1567 ▸ **XV and XVI (Hyksos) dynasties** Khyam; Apophis I and II. Capital at Avaris in the Delta (with Minoan frescoes); Rhind Mathematical Papyrus (BM).

1684–1567 BC ▸ **XVII Dynasty** Expulsion of the Hyksos by Ahmosis. Tombs at Qarat Hilwah, in Bahariya Oasis.

New Kingdom (c.1567–1085 or 1550–1070 BC)

1567–1320 or 1550–1295 BC ▸ **XVIII Dynasty** Two Lands reunited; period of imperial expansion. Ahmosis; Amenophis I; Tuthmosis I and II; Hatshepsut; Tuthmosis III; Amenophis II and III; Akhenaten; Smenkhkare; Tutankhamun; Ay; Horemheb. Temple of Deir el-Bahri; site of Tell el-Amarna; royal tombs in the valleys of the Kings and Queens at Thebes; Luxor and Karnak temples; Tutankhamun's gold (EAM).

1320–1200 or 1295–1186 BC ▸ **XIX Dynasty** Ramses I; Seti I; Ramses II; Merneptah; Seti II. Serapeum at Saqqara; temples at Abydos and Abu Simbel; Ramesseum and royal tombs at Thebes.

1200–1085 or 1186–1069 BC ▸ **XX Dynasty** Sethnakhte; Ramses III (and eight other minor and hopeless Ramses). Temple of Medinet Habu and further royal tombs at Thebes; some are plundered by workmen.

Third Intermediate Period (c.1069–747 BC)

1069–945 BC ▸ **XXI Dynasty** Authority divided between Tanis and Thebes. Smendes; Herihor; Psusennes I and II. Capital at Tanis; Treasure of Tanis (EAM); Book of the Dead (BM).

945–715 BC ▸ **XXII Dynasty** Shoshenk; Osorkon. Ruins at Tanis; Shoshenk's relief at Karnak.

818–715 BC **XXIII and XXIV dynasties.**

Late Period (747–332 BC)

747–656 BC ▸ **XXV (Nubian) Dynasty** Piankhi; Shabaka; Taharqa; Tanutamun. Reliefs at Luxor; Kiosk of Taharqa at Karnak; statue of Amenirdis (EAM).

664–525 BC ▸ **XXVI (Saïte) Dynasty** Psammetichus I; Necho II; Psammetichus II; Apries; Amasis. Ruins of Naucratis; stelae at Ismailiya.

525–404 BC ▸ **XXVII (Persian) Dynasty** Persian invasion. Cambyses; Darius I; Xerxes; Artaxerxes I. Temple of Hibis at Kharga Oasis; completion of Nile–Red Sea canal; foundation of Babylon-in-Egypt (Cairo).

404–380 BC ▸ **XXVIII and XXIX dynasties** Amyrtaeus; Amasis "The Drunkard". Temple of El-Ghweeta, Kharga Oasis; tomb of Amunhotep Huy, Bahariya Oasis.

380–343 BC ▸ **XXX Dynasty** Nectanebo I and II. Additions to Philae and Karnak; ruined temple of Amun at Siwa Oasis.

Ptolemaic Era (332–30 BC)

332–30 BC ▸ **Alexander the Great** conquers Egypt and founds Alexandria. His successors, the **Ptolemies**, make the city a beacon for the Mediterranean world, where Hellenistic and Judaistic culture mingles. Their line expires with Cleopatra VII (51–30 BC), vanquished by the power of Rome. In Nubia, the kingdom of Meröe reaches its apogee. Construction (or modification) of temples of Edfu, Esna, Kom Ombo, Dendara and Philae; catacombs in Alexandria; Sanctuary of Amun at Siwa Oasis; ruins of Karanis and Qasr Qaroun in the Fayoum; Valley of the Mummies at Bahariya Oasis; temple of Dakka, Lake Nasser.

Roman and Byzantine Period (30 BC–640 AD)

30 BC ▸ Octavian (Augustus) annexes Egypt to the **Roman Empire**. Tomb of Kitnes and Temple of Dush in Kharga Oasis.

45 AD St Mark brings **Christianity** to Egypt. Muzawaka Tombs in Dakhla Oasis.

249–305 ▸ **Persecution of Coptic Christians** under Decius and Diocletian. "Pompey's Pillar" at Alexandria.

313 ▸ Edict of Milan **legalizes Christianity**. Foundation of monasteries of Wadi Natrun, St Anthony, St Paul and St Catherine.

395 ▸ Partition of Roman Empire into East and West; Egypt falls under Eastern, **Byzantine**, sphere. Necropolis of El-Bagawat at Kharga Oasis.

451 Council of Chalcedon leads to **expulsion of Copts from Orthodox Church**. Numerous objects in Coptic Museum (Cairo).

Arab Dynasties (640–1517)

640–642 ▸ **Arab conquest** of Egypt; introduction of **Islam**. Mosque of Amr and ruins of Fustat in Cairo.

661–750 ▸ Egypt forms part of **Umayyad Caliphate**, ruled from the dynasty's capital at Damascus. Ceramics and pottery (IAM).

750–935 ▸ **Abbassids** depose Umayyads and form new dynasty, ruling from Baghdad. In 870 Egypt's governor, **Ibn Tulun**, declares independence, founding a dynasty which rules until 905. Mosque of Ibn Tulun in Cairo.

935–969 ▶ **Ikhshidid dynasty** takes power in Egypt.

969–1171 ▶ **Shiite Fatimid dynasty** conquers Egypt and seizes the Islamic Caliphate, which it rules from Cairo. Mosques of Al-Azhar, Al-Hakim and Al-Aqmar, Mausoleum of Imam Al-Shafi'i, and various fortified gates, in Cairo.

1171–1250 ▶ **Salah al-Din** founds **Ayyubid dynasty** and liberates land conquered by the Crusaders. Egypt returns to **Sunni Islam**. Intrigues of **Shagar al-Durr** open the way to **Mamluke** takeover. Madrassa-Mausoleum of Al-Silah Ayyub and the Aqueduct in Cairo; ruins of Shali in Siwa Oasis. Mausoleum of Shagar al-Durr in Cairo.

Mamluke Dynasties (1250–1517)

1250–1382 ▶ **Bahri Mamlukes** Qalaoun; Khalil; Mohammed al-Nasir. In Cairo: Qalaoun's Maristan-Mausoleum-Madrassa, Mosques of Al-Nasir, House of Uthman Katkhuda, and Qasr Bashtak.

1382–1517 ▶ **Burgi Mamlukes** Barquq; Farag; Barsbey; Qaitbey; Qansuh al-Ghuri. In Cairo: Barquq's Mausoleum, Madrassa and Khanqah of Barsbey, Mosque of Qaitbey, and the Ghuriya. Also, Fort Qaitbey in Alexandria.

Ottoman Period (1517–1798)

1517 ▶ **Selim the Grim conquers Egypt**. For the next three centuries the country is ruled as an Ottoman province from Istanbul. In Cairo: Mosques of Suleyman al-Silahdar and Suleyman Pasha; Sabil-Kuttab of Abd al-Rahman Katkhuda. Terbana Mosque in Alexandria.

1798–1802 ▶ French occupation of Egypt. Capitulation Agreement of 1802 leaves British in effective control of the country. Treasures shipped off to Louvre/British Museum. European graffiti left on numerous temples.

Pashas, khedives and kings (1805–1952)

1805 ▶ **Mohammed Ali** seizes power and begins a programme of ruthless **modernization**. Mohammed Ali Mosque in Cairo; Ras el-Tin Palace and Mahmudiya Canal in Alexandria. Belzoni, Mariette and others pioneer digs at pharaonic sites in the Nile Valley and Delta.

1848–54 ▶ Reign of **Abbas I**.

1854–63 ▶ Reign of **Said Pasha**. Suez Canal begun.

1863–79 ▶ Reign of **Khedive Ismail**. Completion of **Suez Canal**; Central Cairo boulevards constructed.

1879–92 ▶ Reign of **Khedive Tewfiq**. British crush the **Orabi Revolt** (1882–83). Tewfiq reinstated as a puppet ruler under British control. Howard Carter discovers **Tutankhamun's tomb** at Thebes (1922) at the tail end of a period of intensive excavations throughout Egypt.

1935–52 ▶ Reign of **King Farouk**; during World War II Egypt stays under British control.

1952–53 Farouk overthrown by Free Officers. Egypt declared a **republic**. Construction of Midan Tahrir in Cairo.

Modern Egypt (1952–)

1956 ▶ **Nasser** becomes President; **Suez Crisis**. Major industrialization programme, and construction of schools, hospitals and public housing.

1967 ▶ **Six Day War** with Israel; massive damage to Canal cities.

1970 ▶ **Nasser dies** and is succeeded as president by **Sadat**. **Aswan High Dam** completed.

1973 ▶ **October War** with Israel.

1977–78 ▶ Food riots. Sadat's trip to Jerusalem leads to **Camp David** agreement. Mohandiseen district of Cairo built, along with hundreds of new hotels, shops, etc. First line of Cairo metro completed.

1981 ▶ **Assassination of Sadat**. Presidency assumed by **Mubarak**.

1990 ▶ **Gulf War**.

1991 ▶ **Cairo earthquake** Many buildings damaged, but the second metro line is pushed to completion.

1994 ▶ **Underwater finds at Alexandria** Divers and archeologists begin exploration of the ruins of the ancient Lighthouse of Pharos and the royal quarters in the harbour at Alexandria.

1995 ▶ Tomb of Ramses II's sons found in the Valley of the Kings.

1996 ▶ **Valley of the Mummies** Egypt's largest cache of mummies is discovered in Bahariya Oasis.

1997 ▶ Fifty-eight foreigners killed by Islamic militants at Hatshepsut's Temple, near Luxor. **Toshka Project** inaugurated.

2000 ▶ The interior of the **Red Pyramid** at Dahshur is reopened after many years.

2001 ▶ Discovery of the underwater city of **Herakleion** at Abu Qir on the Mediterranean coast.

2002 ▶ Inauguration of the **Bibliotheca Alexandrina**, and the completion of the main branch of the **Sheikh Zayid Canal** at Toshka.

2004 ▶ Opening of the Alexandria National Museum. Bombing of Taba Hilton in Sinai.

2005 ▶ **Mubarak** wins a fifth term as president. Bombings at Sharm el-Sheikh in Sinai.

2006 ▶ Discovery of **tomb KV63** at the Valley of the Kings. Bombings at Dahab in Sinai.

2008 ▶ Tombs of V Dynasty officials found at Saqqara.

2009 ▶ Strikes in Delta textile towns. Discovery of VI Dynasty pyramid and mummy of Queen Seshestet at Saqqara, and New Kingdom fortresses near Qantara.

2010 ▶ Sectarian clashes in Middle Egypt. Temple of Bastet unearthed in Alexandria.

Music

Egypt's traditions in music, as with other cultural spheres, date back to pharaonic times, though the primary influences are Arab and Islamic. Cairo is the centre of the Arab recording industry – a dominance partly acquired thanks to the decline of its rivals in Lebanon, Libya and Kuwait, but one which is now being challenged by studios and labels in Saudi Arabia and the Emirates. Still, Egypt's vast and youthful population makes it the most important market for Arab music; what follows is the briefest of introductions to the various major genres.

Ancient Egyptian music

Nobody is sure what **Ancient Egyptian music** sounded like, but enough is known about the instruments for musicologists to have tried to recreate the hymns and songs that accompanied rituals and court life in ancient times. Flutes and clarinet-type instruments go back to the Old Kingdom (if not Predynastic times), as do harps, trumpets, cymbals and castanets. By the Middle Kingdom, harps were accompanied by the *sistrum* (a kind of rattle associated with the goddess Hathor), tambourines, clappers and a type of guitar. The lute and lyre were probably introduced by the Hyksos, while other instruments came into Egypt as a result of the various foreign invasions after the fall of the New Kingdom.

Religious music

Although the call to prayer and the recitation of the Koran are not regarded in Egypt as music, they are certainly listened to for pleasure. The *tajwid*, or musically elaborate style of Koranic recitation, reached its apogee in Egypt; virtuosity is maintained by rigorously testing reciters before they are awarded the title of *moqri*. Among the masters of this genre are **Sheikh Mohammed Mahmoud al-Tablawi**, **Sheikh Abdelbasset Abdessamad** and **Mohammed Rifaat**.

Performers may be **munshids** – professionals who move from one festival to another – or simply the **muezzin** or **imam** of the local mosque. In everyday life, all muezzins have their individual styles of phrasing, and the government's proposal to replace diverse voices with a single nationwide **azan** has been fiercely resisted. Recitals at **moulids** are often more participation than performance, with lines of Sufi devotees chanting and swaying to the accompaniment of a drum. These recitals, known as **zikrs**, can last for days. **Sufi music** gained a wider following in Egypt in the late 1990s thanks to **Yassin al-Tuhami**, who revitalized a once-forgotten moulid in the Muqattam Hills that now draws *fellaheen*, Cairene and foreign Sufi enthusiasts alike.

Coptic liturgical music is quite different in spirit and only to be heard at church services. Some maintain that it is descended from Ancient Egyptian temple chants, as the Coptic language has many similarities with Ancient Egyptian and cymbals are played during the liturgy (distinguishing Coptic from Orthodox ritual music, which is purely choral). Much Coptic music on the Web actually hails from churches in the US rather than Egypt (see links on ⓦwww.copticchurch.org and www.coptic.org), but CDs of local Coptic choirs are sold at churches and monasteries in Egypt.

Another form – which many would deny is religious at all – is **zar** music, performed at rituals that are often likened to exorcisms, though their aim is not to expel a spirit from its host but to harmonize relations between them. *Zars* are usually private events reserved for women but occasionally occur at public moulids.

Classical Arabic music

The antecedents of **classical Arabic music** can be traced back to the **Bedouin** war bards of the Arabian Peninsula, whose metre matched that of a camel's stride, but also to the refined **court music** of the great caliphal cities of Baghdad and Damascus, and Ottoman Constantinople, which nurtured instrumental and compositional skills for generations.

During the twentieth century the form was characterized by oriental scales, orchestras and male choirs, bravura rhetoric and soloists filled with yearning. **Sayyid Darwish** was its father, blending Western instruments and harmony with Arab musical forms and Egyptian folklore, but its greatest exponent was **Um Kalthoum**, whose fifty-year career spanned the advent of gramophones, radio and long-distance broadcasting, making her the most popular singer in the Arab world. In Egypt she was a national institution, accorded a weekly concert on radio and, later, TV; her funeral in 1975 drew the largest crowd since that of President Nasser (who timed his speeches around her broadcasts).

Almost as revered was **Mohammed Abdel Wahab**, a nightclub singer who composed the music for Egypt's national anthem, "Biladi, Biladi". His career was linked to the birth of the Egyptian film industry in the 1930s, which also saw the rise of Lebanese-born **Farid al-Atrache** and his sister **Asmahan** (killed in a car crash in 1944). Another superstar was the actor/singer **Abdel Halim Hafez**, the "Nightingale of the Nile", whose film recordings are still loved though he died in 1977. Wahab survived all of the above, but lay low for nearly twenty years before releasing his last song shortly before his death in 1991. His protégée, **Warda al-Jaza'iriya**, is a true Mediterranean – French, Algerian, Lebanese and Egyptian by birth, heritage and residency – who has been at the forefront of Arab music for decades but rejects comparisons with Um Kalthoum.

Regional/ethnic music

The different types of folk or popular music you'll come across vary greatly with the region and environment: Cairo, the Nile Valley, the Delta and the desert all have their own characteristic sounds, rhythms and instruments.

Saiyidi

The music of Upper Egypt – known, like its people, as **Saiyidi** – has a characteristic rhythm, which horses are trained to dance to. It is based upon two instruments: the *nahrasan*, a two-sided drum hung over the chest and beaten with sticks; and the *mismar saiyidi*, a kind of wooden trumpet. **Omar Gharzawi** is known for his rebuttals of the stereotyped image of stupid, hot-headed Saiyidis; **Sayed Rekaby El-Genena** revels in poetic rapping competitions (a tradition in his home village); while **Rabia el-Bakaria**'s music and lyrics are likened by admirers to Egyptian reggae. On a more official standing is *Raïs* ("Boss") **Met'al Gnawi**, who has represented Egypt at music festivals abroad, with a band promoted as **Les**

Musiciens du Nil. At home he is best known for his hit "Ya Farula!" ("My Strawberry"), full of fruity sexual allusions.

Fellahi

The northern counterpart to Saiyidi music, found in the Delta, is known as **fellahi** (peasant) music. It is generally softer, with a fondness for the *matsoum* (4/4) rhythm, and use of instruments like the *rababa*, a two-stringed viol, and the *mismar*, a kind of oboe.

Sawaheeli

Found along the Mediterranean coast and in the Canal Zone, **Sawaheeli** music is characterized by the use of a harp-like stringed instrument, the *simsimiya*. Another form, specific to Alexandria, also features the accordion, the result of the city's Greek and Turkish influences. The most famous Sawaheeli singers are **Aid el-Gannirni** from Suez and **Abdou el-Iskanrani** from Alex, while Port Said is home to Zakaria Ibrahim's band **El Tanbura**.

Bedouin

There are two kinds of Bedouin music in Egypt: one found in the Western Desert, the other in the Eastern Desert and Sinai. Both have songs recounting old tales to a strong rhythmic accompaniment featuring handclapping and frame drums called *duf* or *darabukka*, depending on their size. This polyrhythmic sound has been a major influence on *shababi* music (see p.626), but **Awad al-Malki** aside, Bedouin artists have yet to achieve widespread popularity in Egypt or the international success of Nubian musicians.

Nubian

Nubian music found a global audience in the 1990s, when **Ali Hassan Kuban** hit the world-music charts with *From Nubia to Cairo* and *Walk Like a Nubian*. Born in 1933, he sang on boats as a child, played at weddings and founded a succession of bands that introduced brass sections, electric guitars and soul vocals to Nubian music, releasing his last album shortly before his death in 2001. Kuban, the female vocalist **Tété Alhinho** and other Nubian musicians cut several CDs under the name **Salamat** for the Piranha label (Ⓦwww.piranha.de).

Drummer **Mahmoud Fadl** began his career as a limbo dancer at weddings and has produced four albums of his own plus *Um Kalthoum 7000*, a Nubian homage to the Arab diva featuring the singer **Salma Abu Greisha**, who also appears on Fadl's *The Drummers of the Nile Go South*, with drummers **Gaafar Hargal** and **Hamdi Matoul**. Until his death in 2006, another international star was **Hamza el-Din**, whose compositions for the *oud* (lute) and *tar* (single-skinned frame drum) were influenced by his Sufi beliefs and conservatory training. His haunting *Escalay* ("The Waterwheel") was a lament to his birthplace, drowned by Lake Nasser; he also wrote pieces for ballet companies and the Kronos Quartet.

Pop music

In Cairo and other cities, rural traditions have mixed with more elite styles and adapted to reflect urban preoccupations. By the mid-1980s two main types of music had developed: **shaabi** and **shababi**. Nowadays, some would say that the distinction between them is moot, and artists such as Hakim can rightfully claim to have a foot in each camp, while pop idol Amr Diab has spearheaded attempts to stake a claim on the world market. For news and clips of stars, visit **websites** Ⓦwww.mazika.com, www.albawaba.com and www.sotwesoora.com, or Internet **radio stations** like Al Madina FM (Ⓦwww.almadinafm.com).

Shaabi

Shaabi ("people") music was born in the working-class quarters of Cairo, and blends the traditional form of the *mawal* (plaintive vocal improvisations) with a driving beat; the lyrics are often raunchy, satirical, or provocative. You will rarely hear this music via the media, but it is popular at weddings and parties throughout working-class Cairo, at nightclubs along Pyramids Road – and played on battered cassettes in taxis, buses and cafés.

The original *shaabi* singer was **Ahmed Adaweyah**, who, from 1971 on, introduced the idea of street language, to which later imitators added elements of rap and disco, in the manner of Algerian *raï* music. The genre is still frowned upon in official cultural circles. **Sha'ban Abdel Rahim** was a laundry ironer until a television appearance catapulted him to stardom. His earthy persona infuriated Egypt's cultural arbiters, but eventually he was embraced by the government and recorded "The Word of Truth", a paean to Mubarak crediting him with making running water and mobile phones available to the masses. Rival *shaabi* superstar **Hakim** has tried to reach an international crossover audience with a remix of his hits by Transglobal Underground, following the example of Amr Diab (see below).

Shababi

Shababi or "youthful" music – also known as **al-jeel** ("the generation") music – followed hot on the heels of *shaabi* in the 1980s. It took disco elements like drum tracks and synthesized backing and mixed them with Nubian and Bedouin rhythms – the latter introduced by Libyan musicians who had fled to Cairo after Gaddafi's "cultural revolution", notably **Hamid el-Shaeri**, whose 1988 back-room recording of "Lolaiki" sung by **Ali Hamaida** launched the genre. Some fans and critics now call *shababi* "Mediterranean" music, acknowledging the crosscurrents of influences within the Arab world and its European diaspora – while others simply see it as classic Arabic pop.

Whatever the name, it's big business – though piracy means that most artists receive relatively little from sales of tapes and CDs, earning their money from appearances at weddings and concerts instead. That said, Egypt's foremost pop idol, **Amr Diab**, broke into the international market with the song "Nour el Ain", and had another international hit with "Akhtar Wahed". **Mohammed Mounir** is almost as popular in the Arab world for his plaintive songs of city life and pan-Arab yearning.

Shababi has a galaxy of female stars that compete on satellite channels across the Arab world. Many are foreigners – the Moroccan **Samira Saeed** and the Lebanese **Elissa**, **Nancy Ajram** and **Haifa Wahbe** – who are based in Cairo or at least sing in the Egyptian dialect, but the most controversial singer is homegrown. Born in the Islamist stronghold of Assyut, **Ruby** has set Egyptian eyes agog with the sexuality of her videos and the assertiveness of her lyrics, which got her expelled from the musicians' union in 2007. By contrast, **Shireen Abdel Wahab** is seen as respectable and performs at official functions and benefit concerts. Other popular artists include the musician and actor **Mustafa Amar** and the lutist and singer **Ehab Tawfik**.

Discography

Although CDs are catching on fast in Egypt, cassettes remain the medium of choice, being robust, cheap and very easy to copy. For details of music shops in Cairo, see p.203; recordings of traditional music are issued by the Centre for Culture and Art (www.egyptmusic.org). In Europe or North America you can find a more limited range of vintage albums – mostly Um Kalthoum and the like – with a few more contemporary releases on labels such as Mondo Melodia, Piranha or Axiom.

Ancient Egyptian music

Michael Atherton *Ankh: The Sound of Ancient Egypt* (Celestial Harmonies). Haunting suites developed from songs or poems.

Religious music

Mohammed Rifaat and Sheikh Abdelbasset Abdessamad *Le Saint Coran* (Club du Disque Arabe). Two masters of Koranic recitation featured on a series of CDs issued in France.

Al-Hamidiyah Brotherhood *Saint Egypt: La Châdhiliya – Sufi Chants from Cairo* (Institut du Monde Arabe). An offshoot of the Shadhiliyya Sufi order.

Um Sameh, Um Hassan and Nour el-Sabah *Mazaher*. Three *zar* priestesses on CD and video, available in Cairo from the Egyptian Center for Culture and Art.

Classical Arabic music

Um Kalthoum *Al-Awia fil Gharam*; *Al-Atlaal*; *Enta Omri* (Sono Cairo). Three of her greatest live recordings, available in CD or DVD format.

Mohammed Abdel Wahab *Treasures* (EMI Arabia). A double CD featuring works from his later period including "The Last Blessing", an amazing 40-minute recital.

Abdel Halim Hafez *Abdel Halim Hafez – Twentieth Anniversary Memorial Edition* (EMI Arabia). This double CD includes some of his 1930s film-score songs and experimental arrangements from the 1960s.

Farid al-Atrache *Les Années '30* (Club Du Disque Arabe). Remastered songs from the 1930s when Farid was at his hottest.

Warda *Warda* (EMI Hemisphere). A CD compilation of her more recent work.

Saiyidi music

Les Musiciens du Nil *Charcoal Gypsies* (Real World). Met'al Gnawi's ensemble fuses African and Middle Eastern percussion with traditional Saiyidi sounds, to irresistible effect.

Sayed Rekaby El-Genena *Jaafra*. Poetic rapping, *oud* and *duf* music from his home village, available on CD from the Egyptian Center for Culture and Art.

Nubian music

Ali Hassan Kuban *From Nubia to Cairo, Walk Like a Nubian and Real Nubian* (Piranha). An infectious mix of wedding songs, brass bands and African percussion.

Hamza el-Din *Escalay* (Nonesuch). Classical *oud* music inspired by Nubian sounds and Sufism.

Mahmoud Fadl *The Drummers of the Nile Go South; The Drummers of the Nile in Town* (Piranha). The Nubian master-percussionist whips up a storm with Saiyidi musicians and the Hasaballah brass band.

Salamat *Mambo El Soudani – Nubian Al Jeel Music from Cairo and Ezzayakoum* (Piranha). Stonking percussion and frenzied sax and trumpet riffs.

Sawaheeli

El Tanbura *The Simsimiyya of Port Said* (Institut du Monde Arabe); Friends of Bamboute (Proper). Their debut album features Sufi and traditional songs; their twentieth-anniversary release, also dance music and trancelike chanting.

Shaabi

Ahmed Adaweyah *Al-Tareek*; *Adaweat*. Two soulful albums featuring the father of *shaabi* at his best, both widely available in Egypt.

Hakim *Lela* (EMI Arabia). Sizzling *shaabi* with guest appearances by Stevie Wonder and the late James Brown.

Shababi

Amr Diab *Akhtar Wahed*; *Kemmel Kalamak* (Rotana). The first is an excellent introduction to Diab's singing, while the second marks his debut as a composer.

Mohammed Mounir *Ahmar Shafayef* (Mondo Melodia). Plaintive songs of life and the city, with a political edge.

Ruby *Fein Habibi* (MSM Egypt). This 2004 album set a new benchmark for the daring of its lyrics and video clips; her 2007 *Meshit Wara Ehsasy* is tamer.

Books

Most of the books listed below are in print; those that are out of print (o/p) should be easy to track down in secondhand bookstores. Books that are only published in Egypt are generally most easily available in Cairo.

Books aside, there are a few **periodicals** which are worth seeking out if you're seriously into Egyptology. The *Journal of Egyptian Archeology*, published annually by the Egyptian Exploration Society (EES, ⓦwww.ees.ac.uk) is the world's leading Egyptology forum: all the new theories and discoveries get printed here first. The EES also publishes the magazine *Egyptian Archeology*, illustrated and with a popular slant. Or you can subscribe to *Ancient Egypt* magazine, featuring easy-to-read articles by academics, plus details of lectures, conferences and events held by Egyptology societies in Britain; go to ⓦwww.ancientegyptmagazine.com.

Travel

General

Amelia Edwards *A Thousand Miles up the Nile*. Verbose, patronizing classic from the 1870s. All books on Egypt have their Amelia quotes – the *Rough Guide to Egypt* included.

Gustave Flaubert *Flaubert in Egypt*. A romp through the brothels, baths and "native quarters" of Egypt, by the future author of *Madame Bovary*.

Amitav Ghosh *In An Antique Land*. Wry tales of modern-day life in a Delta village, interspersed with snippets of less absorbing historical research.

E.W. Lane *Manners and Customs of the Modern Egyptians*. Facsimile edition of this encyclopedic study of life in Mohammed Ali's Cairo, first published in 1836. Highly browsable.

Christopher Pick *Egypt: A Traveller's Anthology*. By a mixed bag of observers from the eighteenth and nineteenth centuries, including Disraeli, Mark Twain, Vita Sackville-West, Flaubert, E.M. Forster and Freya Stark.

Paul William Roberts *River in the Desert*. Chiefly interesting for its eyewitness account of a *zar* (exorcism) and a chapter on the Kushmaan Bedouin of the Eastern Desert.

Anthony Sattin *The Pharaoh's Shadow*. Fascinating discourse on the "survival" of Ancient Egyptian religious beliefs and practices in modern-day Egypt.

Cairo

Mamluk Art: The Splendour and Magic of the Sultans. A guide to Mamluke architecture in Cairo, Alexandria and Rosetta, with concise essays illustrated with colour photos, plans and walking routes.

Maria Golia *Cairo: City of Sand*. Focuses on the domestic life, housing and nitty-gritty of contemporary Cairo, including its satellite cities, ring road and other prestige projects.

Khaled Al Khamissi *Taxi*. Fifty-eight conversations with Cairo cabbies, making up a brilliant portrait of daily life in the nation's capital, the joys, the frustrations and the resilience of its inhabitants as they negotiate the daily grind. After reading this, you'll never look the same way at a taxi driver again.

Max Rodenbeck *Cairo: The City Victorious*. This superb history of Cairo includes the best anecdotes from earlier histories and follows events up until 1999.

Catherine Williams *Islamic Monuments of Cairo: A Practical Guide*. A detailed handbook to the monuments and history of seventh- to nineteenth-century Cairo, illustrated with black and white and colour photos.

Alexandria

Andrew Chugg *The Lost Tomb of Alexander the Great*; *Alexander's Lovers*. Chugg's theory, expounded in *The Lost Tomb*, that Alexander's body is buried in Venice under the guise of St Mark caused a stir in 2004. The follow-up focuses on Alexander's wives and lovers.

Jean-Yves Empereur *Alexandria Revealed*; *Alexandria Rediscovered*. As director of the Centre d'Etudes Alexandrines, responsible for excavating the Pharos, the Catacombs and lesser-known sites, Empereur has unearthed a mass of evidence about the ancient city. In *Alexandria Rediscovered* he writes about the problems of working in a city whose buried past is all too fragile. Both books are very readable and profusely illustrated.

E.M. Forster *Alexandria: A History and a Guide*. This 2004 Abinger Edition is replete with erudite notations to Forster's 1922 guidebook, and includes his collection of essays on Alexandrian life, *Pharos and Pharillon*.

Michael Haag *Alexandria: City of Memory*. An evocative and beautifully written account of the city as experienced by Forster, Cavafy and Durrell, illustrated with many rare photographs from the 1920s, 1930s and 1940s.

The desert

Wael Abed *The Other Egypt: Travels in No Man's Land* (Zarzora Expedition). A *tour d'horizon* of the natural wonders of the Western Desert, illustrated with eighty colour photos, plus rare black-and-white photos from the 1920s and 1930s.

Ahmed Fakhry *The Oases of Egypt*. Volume I, covering Siwa, is fascinating and has been republished in paperback; Volume II, on Bahariya and Farafra, is heavier going and remains out of print, but can be found in Cairo bookshops.

Saul Kelly *The Hunt for Zerzura: The Lost Oasis and the Desert War*. A detailed account of the real drama that inspired *The English Patient*.

Cassandra Vivian *The Western Desert of Egypt: An Explorer's Handbook*. This exhaustive, recently updated guidebook covers all the oases and off-the-beaten-track sites, with maps and GPS waypoints. Fits the dashboard of a 4WD, but too heavy for a rucksack. Sold in Cairo and Bahariya Oasis.

Ancient history

General

Mark Collier & Bill Manley *How to Read Egyptian Hieroglyphics: A Step-By-Step Guide To Teach Yourself.* A bestseller, thanks to its clarity and the exciting sense of knowledge that it confers.

George Hart *British Museum Pocket Dictionary of Egyptian Gods and Goddesses; Routledge Dictionary of Egyptian Gods and Goddesses.* Both are highly useful guides to the deities and myths of Ancient Egypt, illustrated with line drawings. The former is easier to carry when visiting temples in Egypt.

Colin J. Humphreys *The Miracles of Exodus: A Scientist's Discovery of the Extraordinary Natural Causes of the Biblical Stories.* With a title like that, who could resist a look? Some of the explanations therein seem quite plausible, others less so.

Dieter Kurth *The Temple of Edfu: A Guide by an Ancient Egyptian Priest.* A complete translation of the hieroglyphic inscriptions on the enclosure wall of Edfu Temple, describing the rituals and daily life within its walls.

Dimitri Meeks & Christine Favard-Meeks *Daily Life of the Egyptian Gods.* Scholarly study of the rituals and beliefs surrounding the gods; a TV spin-off focused on the more salacious bits.

David Rohl *A Test of Time: The Bible – From Myth to History; Legend: The Genesis of Civilisation.* The former is a stimulating argument for revising the chronology of Ancient Egyptian and Biblical history; the latter advances an unusual theory of Egypt's pre-dynastic era. Both are closely argued and worth reading even if you're sceptical (as most Egyptologists are).

Ian Shaw *The Oxford History of Ancient Egypt.* An excellent survey taking in theories and discoveries up until 2003, with many fine illustrations and site plans.

Ian Shaw and Paul Nicholson *British Museum Dictionary of Ancient Egypt.* Richly illustrated, paperback-sized dictionary, especially good for site plans and assessments of fairly recent discoveries.

Joyce Tyldesley *Hatshepsut: The Female Pharaoh; Nefertiti: Egypt's Sun Queen; Ramses: Egypt's Greatest Pharaoh.* Readable and illuminating biographies of some of the most famous rulers of the New Kingdom.

Jean Vercoutter *The Search for Ancient Egypt.* Pocket-size account of Egypt's "discovery" by foreigners, packed with drawings, photos and engravings.

Kent Weeks *The Lost Tomb; The Treasures of Luxor and the Valley of the Kings; Atlas of the Valley of the Kings.* The first describes Weeks' discovery and excavation of the mass tomb of the sons of Ramses II; the second is an illustrated guide to treasures from Luxor and its necropolis; and the third is the first volume of an ongoing *magnum opus*, showcased on the Theban Mapping Project's website, ⓦwww.kv5.com.

John Anthony West *Serpent in the Sky: High Wisdom of Ancient Egypt;*

The Traveler's Key to Ancient Egypt: A Guide to the Sacred Places of Ancient Egypt. New Age interpretations of Ancient Egyptian culture. *Serpent* is quite heavy going and marred by rants, but *Traveler's Key* is a lively on-site guide that points out inconsistencies in orthodox Egyptology and presents alternative theories.

Pyramidology

Guillemette Andreu *Egypt in the Age of the Pyramids*. Nicely illustrated study of the pyramids' evolution in the context of Ancient Egyptian life and culture, by a French Egyptologist.

Robert Bauval *The Orion Mystery*. Postulates that the Giza Pyramids corresponded to the three stars in Orion's Belt as it was in 10,500 BC.

I.E.S. Edwards *The Pyramids of Egypt*. Lavishly illustrated, closely argued survey of all the major pyramids, overdue for an update since it was last revised in 1991.

Graham Hancock *Fingerprints of the Gods*; *The Message of the Sphinx*; *The Mars Mystery*; *Heaven's Mirror*. Asserts that the pyramids, Angkor Wat temple and the statues of Easter Island were all created by a lost civilization propagated by extraterrestrials.

Peter Hodges *How the Pyramids were Built*. As a professional stonemason, Hodges has practical experience, rather than academic qualifications, on his side. An easy read and quite persuasive.

The Amarna Period/Tutankhamun

Cyril Aldred *Akhenaten, King of Egypt*. A conventional account of the Amarna period by a British Egyptologist.

Michael Haag *The Rough Guide to Tutankhamun*. A pocket-sized guide, covering not just the life of its subject but also the history of the Valley of the Kings and the lives of Howard Carter and Lord Carnarvon. Illustrated throughout with both archive and modern photographs.

Dominic Montserrat *Akhenaten: History, Fantasy and Ancient Egypt*. An interesting study of how Akhenaten's image has evolved and resonated in popular culture since he was "discovered" in the nineteenth century.

Ahmed Osman *Moses and Akhenaten*; *Stranger in the Valley of the Kings*. These two books argue that Akhenaten was actually Moses, and his grandfather Yuya the Biblical Joseph, in a substantial rewrite of the Exodus story.

Julia Samson *Nefertiti and Cleopatra*. Fascinating account of Egypt's most famous queens, by an expert on Amarna civilization. Samson concludes that Smenkhkare, Akhenaten's mysterious successor, was actually Nefertiti; her coverage of Cleopatra is rather less controversial.

Ptolemaic, Roman and Coptic Egypt

Christian Cannuyer *Coptic Egypt – The Christians of the Nile*. A pocket-sized, easy to read study of Coptic history and culture, fully illustrated throughout.

Dominic Montserrat *Sex and Society in Graeco-Roman Egypt*. In-depth study of sexual mores and practices in a famously licentious era.

Győző Vörös *Taposiris Magna: Port of Isis*. A richly illustrated look at the ancient port city whose lighthouse is commonly thought to be a scaled-down copy of the Pharos at Alexandria, though Vörös argues it was actually a prototype.

Medieval and modern history

Said K. Aburish *Nasser: The Last Arab*. A new look at an old hero, who embodied the aspirations and contradictions of Arab nationalism. As the author of books on Saddam Hussein, Arafat and the House of Saud, Aburish mourns the lack of a new Nasser to inspire the Arabs today.

Raymond William Baker *Islam Without Fear: Egypt and the New Islamists*; *Sadat and After*. The first is a social profile of Egypt's contemporary Islamists, the second consists of critiques of Egyptian society from across the political spectrum.

Stephen Bungay *Alamein*. Concise, highly readable and enlightening on the interplay between strategy, tactics, logistics and intelligence during the Western Desert campaign.

Derek Hopwood *Egypt: Politics and Society 1945–90*; *Sexual Encounters in the Middle East: The British, the French and the Arabs*. The first is an accessible and useful survey of the modern era, now in its third edition; the second focuses on the Orientalist fascination for "the other".

Amin Maalouf *The Crusades through Arab Eyes*. A Lebanese Copt, Maalouf has used the writings of contemporary Arab chroniclers to retrace two centuries of Middle Eastern history, and concludes that present-day relations between the Arab world and the West are still marked by the battle that ended seven centuries ago.

Sociology and feminism

Galal Amin *Whatever Happened to the Egyptians?*; *Whatever Else Happened to the Egyptians?* Two insightful, wryly readable accounts of social changes from the 1950s to the present. Subjects covered range from car ownership and Westernization in the first book, to TV, fashions and weddings in the second.

Nayra Atiya (ed.) *Khul-Khaal: Five Egyptian Women Tell Their Stories*. Gripping biographical accounts by women from diverse backgrounds, revealing much about Egyptian life a generation ago that still holds true today. Widely sold in Egypt.

R. Critchfield *Shahhat: An Egyptian*. A wonderful book, based on several years' resident research with the Nile Valley *fellaheen*, across the river from Luxor. Moving, amusing and shocking, by turn. Widely sold in Egypt.

Nawal el-Saadawi *The Hidden Face of Eve*. Egypt's best-known woman writer, this is her major polemic, covering a wide range of topics – female circumcision, prostitution, divorce and sexual relationships. Her website (@www.nawalsaadawi.net) embraces literature, sociology and politics (see also opposite).

Islam

A.J. Arberry (trans.) *The Koran* (Oxford University Press). This translation is the best English-language version of Islam's holy book, whose revelations and prose style form the basis of the Muslim faith and Arab literature.

Karen Armstrong *Muhammed: A Prophet for Our Times*; *Islam: A Short History*. Two widely acclaimed books by a religious scholar and former nun, sympathetic to Islam and its Prophet.

Titus Burckhardt *Art of Islam: Language and Meaning* (o/p). Superbly illustrated, intellectually penetrating overview of Islamic art and architecture.

Robert Spencer *The Truth about Muhammed: Founder of the World's Most Intolerant Religion*. A forensic indictment of the Prophet's life and legacy, to be read as an antidote to Armstrong's biography (or vice versa), but not taken to Egypt.

Wildlife

Bertel Bruun *Common Birds of Egypt*. A slim illustrated guide you can slip into your pocket.

Guy Buckles *Dive Guide: The Red Sea*. An illustrated guide to over 125 diving and snorkelling sites from Sinai to Eritrea, with notes on access, visibility and diving conditions, as well as the species that you'll see.

David Cottridge & Richard Porter *A Photographic Guide to Birds of Egypt and the Middle East*. This ornithology guide is better illustrated than Brunn's, but heavier to carry around.

Egyptian fiction and poetry

Alaa Al-Aswany *The Yacoubian Building; Chicago*. Al-Aswany's first novel was a controversial bestseller in the Arab world, portraying the tenants of a Cairo apartment block as a microcosm of Egyptian society. His second, *Chicago*, set among Egyptian émigrés abroad, is equally perceptive about Egyptians, but its American characters verge on caricature.

Salwa Bakr *The Golden Chariot*; *The Wiles of Men and Other Stories*. A novel set in a women's prison near Cairo; the inmates' tales highlight different facets of women's oppression in contemporary Egypt. Touching and disturbing.

C.P. Cavafy *The Collected Poems of C.P. Cavafy: A New Translation*. Elegiac evocations of the Alexandrian myth by the city's most famous poet, in a new translation by Aliki Barnstone.

Gamal al-Ghitani *The Zafarani Files*; *Zayni Barakat*; *Pyramid Texts*. *The Zafarani Files* is a dark satire about paranoia and credulity, while *Zayni Barakat* is a convoluted drama set in the last years of Mamluke rule. His latest novel, *Pyramid Texts*, is a series of Sufistic parables about the human condition, inspired by the Sphinx and the Giza Pyramids.

Yusuf Idris *The Cheapest Nights*; *Rings of Burnished Brass* (o/p). Two superb collections by Egypt's finest writer of short stories, who died in 1991. Uncompromisingly direct, yet ironic.

Naguib Mahfouz *Palace Walk*; *Palace of Desires*; *Sugar Street*; *Miramar*. The late Nobel laureate's novels have a nineteenth-century feel, reminiscent of Balzac or Victor Hugo. His "Cairo Trilogy", comprising the first three books listed here, is a tri-generational saga set during the British occupation, while *Miramar* looks back on the 1952 Revolution from the twilight of the Nasser era. Favoured themes include the discrepancy between ideology and human problems, and hypocrisy and injustice.

Nawal el-Saadawi *Woman at Point Zero*; *The Fall of the Imam*; *God Dies by the Nile*; and others. Saadawi's novels are informed by her work as a doctor and psychiatrist in Cairo, and by her feminist and socialist beliefs, on subjects that are virtually taboo in Egypt. *Point Zero*, her best, is a powerful and moving story of a woman condemned to death for killing a pimp. You will find very few of her books on sale in Egypt, though *The Fall of the Imam* is the only one officially banned (see also opposite).

Ahdaf Soueif *Aisha*; *In the Eye of the Sun*; *The Map of Love; I Think of You*. Born in Cairo, Souief was educated in Egypt and England. Her semi-autobiographical novels are acclaimed for their sensibility: *In the Eye of the Sun* explores love and destiny in the Middle East during the 1960s and 1970s; *The Map of Love* (shortlisted for the Booker Prize) and *I Think of You* focus on sexual politics.

Bahaa Taher *Aunt Safiyya and the Monastery*. Beautifully crafted novella set in a village in Upper Egypt, where a blood feud is challenged by a Muslim farmer and a Coptic monk.

Foreign fiction

Michael Asher *The Eye of Ra*; *Firebird*. Two gung-ho thrillers with a supernatural edge, involving outlaw desert tribes and the lost oasis of Zerzura.

Noel Barber *A Woman of Cairo*. Ill-starred love and destiny amongst the Brits and Westernized Egyptians of King Farouk's Cairo; from that perspective, a good insight into those times.

Agatha Christie *Death Comes at the End*; *Death on the Nile*. The latter is a classic piece of skullduggery solved by Poirot aboard a Nile cruiser. *Death Comes at the End* is a lamer effort, set around Luxor.

Len Deighton *City of Gold*. Hard-boiled thriller set in 1941, when vital information was being leaked to Rommel. Its period detail is excellent.

Paul Doherty *The Mask of Ra*. A pharaonic whodunit set at the time of Hatshepsut's accession.

Lawrence Durrell *The Alexandria Quartet*. Endless sexual and metaphysical ramblings, occasionally relieved by a dollop of Alex atmosphere or a profound psychological insight.

Ken Follet *The Key to Rebecca*. Fast-paced thriller based on the true story of a German spy who operated in Cairo during 1942, with a walk-on role for Sadat.

Robert Irwin *The Arabian Nightmare*. Paranoid fantasy set in the Cairo of Sultan Qaitbey, where a Christian spy contracts the affliction of the title. As his madness deepens, reality and illusion spiral inwards like an opium-drugged walk through a *medina* of the mind.

Michael Ondaatje *The English Patient*. The novel takes liberties with the truth when portraying Almássy and his co-explorers (see p.433) but its brilliance is undeniable, and its equal focus on Kip and Dorothy make it more multi-layered than the film.

Michael Pearce *The Mamur Zapt and the Donkey-vous*; *The Mamur Zapt and the Girl in the Nile*; *The Mamur Zapt and the Men Behind*; *The Mamur Zapt and the Return of the Carpet*; *The Mamur Zapt and the Spoils of Egypt*. A series of yarns set in *khedival* Egypt, featuring the chief of Cairo's secret police.

Dan Richardson *Gog – an End Time Mystery*. Set in a flood-ravaged Egypt after terrorists destroyed the Aswan High Dam, this near-future thriller abounds with savage plot twists and memorable Egyptian characters.

Wilbur Smith *River God*; *The Seventh Scroll*; *Warlock*. A blockbuster trilogy that crams the Hyksos invasion and liberation of Ancient Egypt into two volumes, interspersed by the search for the lost tomb of pharaoh Mamose in modern times.

Language

Language

Language

Although Arabic is the common and official language of 23 countries, the spoken dialect of each can vary considerably. **Egyptian Arabic**, however, is the most widely understood in the Arab world, because of Egypt's vast film, television and music industry.

Egyptians are well used to tourists who speak only their own language, but an attempt to tackle at least a few words in Arabic is invariably greeted with great delight and encouragement. Most educated and urban Egyptians will have been taught some English and are only too happy to practise it on you, but a little Arabic is a big help in the more remote areas.

Transliteration from Arabic script into English presents some problems, since some letters have no equivalents. The phonetic guide below should help with **pronunciation**:

ai as in *eye*
aa as in *bad* but lengthened
aw as in *rose*
' a glottal stop as in *bottle*
' as when asked to say *ah* by the doctor
ey/ay as in *day*
ee as in *feet*
gh like the French r (back of the throat)
kh as in Scottish *loch*

Note that every letter should be pronounced, and that double consonants should always be pronounced separately. In the following vocabulary, **bold** type is used to indicate **stress**.

Vocabulary

Whatever else you do, at least make an effort to learn the Arabic numerals and polite greetings. The phrases and terms in this section represent only the most common bits of vocabulary you might need; for a comprehensive list, try the *Rough Guide Egyptian Arabic Phrasebook*. For Cairo language schools, see p.205.

Basics

Yes	**ai**wa or na'am
No	la
Thank you	**shok**ran
You're welcome	**af**wan
Please (to m/f)	min **fad**lak (m)/**fad**lik (f)
Come in, please (to m/f)	it**fad**dal (m)/ itfad**dali** (f)
Excuse me	low sa**maht** (m)/ samahti (f)
Sorry	aasif (m)/asfa (f)
God willing	in**shal**lah

Greetings and farewells

Welcome/hello	**ah**lan w-**sah**lan
(response)	**ah**lan bik (m)/biki (f)/ bikum (pl)
Hello (formal)	assal**aam**u al**ei**kum
(response)	wa-al**ei**kum assal**aam**
Greetings	mar**haba**/sa'eeda
Nice to meet you	fursa sa'eeda
Good morning (morning of goodness)	sa**bah** il-kh**ee**r
(response: morning of light)	sa**bah** in-n**u**r
Good evening (evening of goodness)	mas**a'** il-kh**ee**r
(response–evening of light)	mas**a'** in-n**u**r
How are you (m/f) ?	iz**zay**ak (m)/iz**zay**ik (f)
[I'm] Fine, good (m/f)	kway**yis** (m)/kwayy**isa** (f)
Thanks be to God	il-ham**du** lil**lah**
Good night	tis**bah** (m)/tisbahi (f) 'ala kh**ee**r
And to you (m/f)	**wen**ta (m)/**wen**ti (f) bikheer
Goodbye	m**a'a** sal**aa**ma

Directions

Where is…	**fey**n…
Hotel (name) ?	**fu**nduk (name) ?
(name) restaurant?	mat**'a**m (name) ?
the bus station?	ma**hat**tat il-autobees?
the train station?	ma**hat**tat il-atr?
the service taxi depot?	el-m**o**gaf?
the airport?	il-mat**aa**r?
the hospital?	il-mus**tash**fa?
the toilet?	il-twalet?
Left/right/straight ahead	shim**aal**/yim**ee**n/ 'ala **tool**
Near/far	areeb/ba'eed
Here/there	**hin**a/**hin**ak
When does the bus leave?	il-autob**ee**s yisafir imta?
When does the train leave?	il-atr yisafir imta?
…arrive?	…yoosal?
What time (is it)?	is**sa'a** kam?
First/last/next	il-awwil/il-akhir/ et-tani
Nothing	walla**haaga**
Not yet	lissa

Shopping

Do you (m/f) have…?	fi **'an**dak (m)/ **'an**dik (f)…?
…cigarette(s)	…sig**aa**ra/sagayir
…matches	…kibr**ee**t
…newspaper	…gurn**a**l
I (m/f) want something	…**ay**yiz (m)/**ay**yiza (f) haaga…
else	t**a**ni
…better than this	…ahsan min da
…cheaper	…arkhas min da
…like this	…zay da
(but)	(wa-laakin)
bigger/smaller	**ak**bar/asghar
How much (is it)?	bi-kam (da)?
It's too expensive	da ghaali **a**wi
big	keb**ee**r
small	sughayyar
That's fine	maashi
There is/is there?	fi?
This/that	di/da
I (m/f) want my change	**ay**yiz/**ay**yiza fakka

Accommodation

Do you (m/f) have a room?	fi **'an**dak (m)/ **'an**dik (f) ouda?
I (m/f) would like to see the room	**ay**yiz/**ay**yiza ashu**f** il-**ow**ad

Can I see the rooms?	mumkin ash**u**f il-**ow**ad?
Is there…?	fi…?
…hot water?	…mayya **sukh**na?
…a shower?	…doush?
…a balcony?	…balcona?
…air conditioning?	…takyeef **ha**wa?
…a telephone?	…telif**oo**n?
How much is the bill?	kam il-hi**sab**?

Useful phrases

What is your (m/f) name?	**is**mak (m)/**is**mik (f) ey?
My name is…	**is**mi…
Do you (m/f) speak…	tit**kal**lim (m) /titkal**limi**…(f)
Arabic?	**'ar**abi?
English?	ingl**ee**zi?
French?	fran**sa**wi?
I speak English	ana bat**kal**lim ingl**ee**zi
I don't speak Arabic	ana ma-bat**kal**lim **'a**rabi
I understand (a little)	ana **fa**hem (sh**wai**ya)
What's that in English?	ya**'a**ni ey bil- ingl**ee**zi?
I (m/f) don't understand	**a**na mish **fa**hem (m)/**fah**ma (f)
I (m/f) don't know	ana mish **'aa**rif (m)/**'aar**fa (f)
I (m/f) am tired/ unwell	ana ta'a**baan** (m)/ ta'a**baa**na (f)
I (m/f) am hungry	ana gaw**'aan** (m)/ gaw**'aana** (f)
I (m/f) am thirsty	ana 'atshaan (m)/'atshaana (f)
I (m/f) (don't) want…	(mish) **ay**yiz (m)/ **ay**yiza (f)…
I (m/f) am (not) married	ana (mish) mit**gaw**wiz (m)/ mitgaw**wiza** (f)
It's not your business	mish **shugh**lak
Don't touch me!	ibni le wadi!
Behave yourself	hatirim nassak
Let's go	**ya**lla
Slowly	baraahah
Enough! Finished!	khalas!
Never mind	maalesh
It doesn't matter	mish muhim
There's no problem	ma **fee**sh mush**kil**a
May I/is it possible?	**mum**kin?
It's not possible	mish **mum**kin

Calendar

day	youm
night	leyla
week	usboo'a
month	shahr
year	sana
today	inna**har**da
tomorrow	**buk**ra
yesterday	imbaarih
later	ba**'deen**
Saturday	youm is-sabt
Sunday	youm il-ahad
Monday	youm il-it**nay**n
Tuesday	youm it-tal**aat**a
Wednesday	youm il-arb**'a**
Thursday	youm il-kha**mees**
Friday	youm il-**gum**'a

Money

Where's the bank?	**fey**n il-bank?
I (m/f) want to change…	**ay**yiz/ayyiza aghayyar…
…money	…fl**oo**s
…British pounds	…gi**nay** sterlini
…US dollars	…dolar am**ri**kani
…Euros	…euro
…travellers' cheques	…shikaat siyahiyya
Egyptian pound	gi**ney**
half pound (50 piastres)	nuss gi**ney**
quarter pound (25 piastres)	roba' gi**ney**
piastre	**ir**sh

Numbers and fractions

Though Arabic numerals may seem confusing at first, they are not hard to learn and with a little practice you should soon be able to read bus numbers without any problems. The one and the nine are easy enough; the confusing ones are the five, which looks like a Western zero, the six, which looks like a Western seven, and the four, which looks like a three written backwards. In practice, once you've got the hang of it, the trickiest are the two and the three, which are sufficiently similar to be easily confused. Note that unlike the rest of the Arabic language, the numerals are written from left to right.

0	٠	**sifr**	21	٢١	**wahid wa 'ashreen**
1	١	**wahid**	30	٣٠	**talaateen**
2	٢	**itnayn**	40	٤٠	**arb'aeen**
3	٣	**talaata**	50	٥٠	**khamseen**
4	٤	**arb'a**	60	٦٠	**sitteen**
5	٥	**khamsa**	70	٧٠	**sab'aeen**
6	٦	**sitta**	80	٨٠	**tamaneen**
7	٧	**sab'a**	90	٩٠	**tis'een**
8	٨	**tamaanya**	100	١٠٠	**miyya**
9	٩	**tes'a**	121	١٢١	**miyya wa-wahid wa 'ashreen**
10	١٠	**'ashara**			
11	١١	**hidarsha**	200	٢٠٠	**mitayn**
12	١٢	**itnarsha**	300	٣٠٠	**talaata miyya**
13	١٣	**talatarsha**	400	٤٠٠	**arb'at miyya**
14	١٤	**arb'atarsha**	1000	١٠٠٠	**alf**
15	١٥	**khamastarsha**	2000	٢٠٠٠	**alfayn**
16	١٦	**sittarsha**	3000	٣٠٠٠	**talaat alaaf**
17	١٧	**sab'atarsha**	4000	٤٠٠٠	**arb'at alaaf**
18	١٨	**tamantarsha**	1/2		**nuss**
19	١٩	**tis'atarsha**	1/4		**roba'**
20	٢٠	**'ashreen**	1/8		**tumna**

Egyptian food and drink terms

Some basics

We'd like the menu please	Ayyzeen el-menu min **fad**lak	**…fresh**	…taaza
With little sugar	Sukkar aleel	**…meat**	…lahm
Without sugar	Bid**oo**n sukkar	**…cooked enough**	…mistiwi **kway**yis
We'd like to have…	Ihna ayy**zeen**…	**This is very tasty**	Da lazeez awi
I can't/don't eat…	**A**na makulsh…	**Give me/us…**	Iddini/iddina…
What is this?	'Ey da?	**The bill, please**	El-hi**saab**, min **fad**lak (m)/min **fa**dlik (f)
I didn't order this	Ma'alabtish da	**Plate**	taba'
We don't want this	Ihna mish ayy**zeen** da	**Napkin**	futa
This is not…	Da mish…	**Bottle**	Izaaza

Glass	kub**baaya**
Fork	showka
Knife	sik**kee**na
Spoon	mala'a
Table	tara**bey**za
Menu	lista/menoo

The bill (check)	el-hi**saab**
Very sweet	ziyaada
Little sugar	'ariha
No sugar	saada
Medium	mazb**oo**t

Menu reader

'Aish	Bread
Zibda	Butter
Beyd	Eggs
Samak	Fish
Gibna	Cheese
Gibna rumi	Yellow cheese
Gibna beyda	White cheese
Murabba	Jam
'Asal	Honey
Lahma	Meat
Firakh	Chicken
Zeit	Oil
Zeitun	Olives
Filfil	Pepper
Melh	Salt
Sukkar	Sugar
Khudaar	Vegetables
Salata	Salad
Fawaakih	Fruit
Zabaadi	Yoghurt

Drinks

Shai	Tea
Shai bi-na'ana	Tea with mint
Shai bi-laban	Tea with milk
Shai kushari	Tea made with loose-leaf
Shai lipton	Tea made with a tea bag
Laban	Milk
Ahwa	Coffee (usually Turkish)
Ahwa fransawi	Instant or filter coffee
Mayya	Water
Mayya ma'adaniyya	Mineral water
Beera	Beer
Nibeet	Wine
Zibiba	Ouzo
'Aseer	Juice
'Aseer asab	Sugar-cane juice
'Aseer burtu'an	Orange juice
'Aseer limoon	Lemon juice
'Aseer manga	Mango juice
Karkaday	Hibiscus
Tamar hindi	Tamarind (cordial)
'Er' sous	Liquorice-water
Helba	Fenugreek infusion
Irfa	Cinnamon infusion
Yansoon	Aniseed infusion
Sahleb	Milky drink made with ground orchid root

Soups, salads and vegetables

Shurba	Soup
Shurbit firakh	Chicken soup
Shurbit 'ads	Lentil soup
Shurbit khudaar	Vegetable soup
Melokheya	Jew's mallow, a leafy vegetable stewed with meat or chicken broth and garlic to make a slimy, spinach-like soup
Salata	Salad
Salatit khiyaar	Cucumber salad
Salatit tamatim	Tomato salad
Salatit khadra	Mixed green salad
Tarboola	Salad of bulghur wheat, parsley and tomato
Basal	Onion
Fasuliyya	Beans
Gazar	Carrots
Baamya	Okra (gumbo, ladies' fingers)
Bisilla	Peas

Bataatis	Potatoes
Ruz	Rice
Torshi	Pickled vegetables
Bidingaan	Eggplant (aubergine)

Main dishes

Kofta	Mincemeat flavoured with spices and onions, grilled on a skewer
Shish kebab	Chunks of meat, usually lamb, grilled on a skewer with onions and tomatoes
Shish tawook	Kebab of marinated, spiced chicken
Firakh	Chicken grilled or stewed and served with vegetables
Fatta	Mutton or chicken stew, cooked with bread
Hamam mashwi	Grilled pigeon
Lahm dani	Lamb
Kibda	Liver, stewed with green peppers and chili
Kalewi	Kidney
Mokh	(Sheep) brains
Dik rumi	Turkey
Samak mashwi	Grilled fish served with salad, bread and dips
Balti	A Mediterranean fish similar to mackerel
Bouri	Mullet
Soubeit	Sole
Gambari	Prawns
Calamari	Squid

Appetizers and fast food

Fuul	Boiled fava beans served with oil and lemon, sometimes also with onions, meat, eggs or tomato sauce
Taamiya	Felafel; balls of deep-fried mashed chickpeas and spices
Shawarma	Slivers of pressed, spit-roasted lamb, served in pitta bread
Tahina	Sesame seed paste mixed with spices, garlic and lemon, eaten with pitta bread
Hummus	Chickpea paste mixed with tahini, garlic and lemon, sometimes served with pine nuts and/or meat (but also just the Arabic for chickpeas/garbanzo beans; indeed, more commonly used with that meaning in Egypt)
Babaghanoug	Paste of aubergines mashed with tahina
Kushari	Mixture of noodles, lentils and rice, topped with fried onions and a spicy tomato sauce
Shakshouka	Chopped meat and tomato sauce, cooked with an egg on top
Makarona	Macaroni "cake" baked in a white sauce or mincemeat gravy
Mahshi	Literally "stuffed", variety of vegetables (peppers, tomatoes, aubergines, courgettes) filled with mincemeat and/or rice, herbs and pine nuts
Wara einab	Vine leaves filled as above and flavoured with lemon juice
Fiteer	A sort of pancake/pizza made of layers of flaky filo pastry with sweet or savoury fillings

Desserts, sweets, fruits and nuts

Mahalabiyya	Sweet rice or cornflour pudding, topped with pistachios
Balila	Milk dish with nuts, raisins and wheat
Baklava	Flaky filo pastry, honey and nuts
Basbousa	Pastry of semolina, honey and nuts
Um (or Om) Ali	Corn cake soaked in milk, sugar, raisins, coconut and cinnamon, usually served hot
Gelati or ays krim	Ice cream
'Ishta	Cream
Tuffah	Apples
Mishmish	Apricots
Mawz	Bananas
Balah	Dates
Teen	Figs
Teen shawqi	Prickly pear (cactus fruit)
Shammam	Melon
Battikh	Watermelon
Farawla	Strawberries
Fuul sudaani	Peanuts
Lib batteekh	Watermelon seeds
Lawz	Almonds

Glossary

Common alternative spellings are given in brackets.

Ablaq Striped. An effect achieved by painting, or laying courses of different coloured masonry; usually white with red or buff. A Bahri Mamluke innovation, possibly derived from the Roman technique of *opus mixtum* – an alternation of stone and brickwork.

Ain (Ayn, Ein) Spring.

Amir (Emir) Commander, prince.

Ba The Ancient Egyptian equivalent of the soul or personality, often represented by a human-headed bird; also used to describe the physical manifestation of certain gods.

Bab Gate or door, as in the medieval city walls.

Bahr River, sea, canal.

Baksheesh Alms or tips.

Baladi National, local, rural or countrified; from *balad*, meaning country or land.

Baraka Blessing.

Beit (Beyt) House. Segregated public and private quarters, the *malqaf*, *maq'ad* and *mashrabiya* are typical features of old Cairene mansions.

Bey (Bay) Lord or noble; an Ottoman title, now a respectful form of address to anyone in authority.

Bir (Beer) Well.

Birka (Birqa, Birket) Lake.

Burg (Borg) Tower.

Calèche Horse-drawn carriage.

Caliph Successor to the Prophet Mohammed and spiritual and political leader of the Muslim empire. A struggle over this office caused the Sunni–Shia schism of 656 AD.

Canopic jar Sealed receptacle used in funerary rituals to preserve the viscera of the deceased after embalming. The stomach, intestines, liver and lungs each had a patron deity, sculpted on the jar's lid.

Cloisonné A multi-step enamelling process used to produce jewellery, vases and other decorative objects.

Corniche Seafront or riverfront promenade.

Dahabiya Nile houseboat.

Darb Path or way; can apply to alleyways, thoroughfares, or desert caravan routes.

Deir Monastery or convent.

Djed pillar Ancient Egyptian symbol of stability, in the shape of a pillar with three or four horizontal flanges, possibly derived from a pole around which grain was tied.

Feddan A traditional measure of land equivalent to 4200 square metres.

Fellaheen (sing. fellah) Peasant farmers who work their own land or as sharecroppers or hired labourers for wealthier farmers.

Felucca Nile sailing boat.

Finial Ornamental crown of a dome or minaret, often topped by an Islamic crescent.

Galabiyya Loose flowing robe worn by men.

Gezira Island.

Ghard (Ghird) Extended belt of sand dunes.

Hajj (Hadj) Pilgrimage to Mecca.

Hagg/Hagga One who has made the pilgrimage to Mecca.

Haikal Sanctuary of a Coptic church.

Hammam Turkish bathhouse.

Haramlik Literally the "forbidden" area, ie women's or private apartments in a house or palace.

Heb-Sed An Ancient Egyptian festival symbolizing the renewal of the king's physical and magical powers, celebrated in the thirtieth year of his reign and every three years thereafter.

Islamist(s) Groups aiming to replace secular with Sharia law and realign Egypt's foreign policy – some by peaceful means, others violently.

Ithyphallic Decorous term for a god with an erection; Min, Amun and Osiris were often depicted thus by the Ancient Egyptians.

Jebel (Gebel, Gabal, etc) Hill or mountain.

Jedid/Jedida (Gadid/Gadia) "New" in Arabic; the ending depends on whether the subject of the adjective is masculine or feminine. In Upper Egypt, the first syllable is pronounced as a soft *je*; in Lower Egypt, as a hard *ga* sound.

Ka Ancient Egyptians believed that an individual's life-force served as the "double" of his or her physical being and required sustenance after their death, through offerings to the deceased's *ka* statue, sometimes secluded in a *serdab*.

Khan Place where goods were made, stored and sold, which also provided accommodation for travellers and merchants, like a *wikala*.

Khedive Viceroy.

Kom Mound of rubble and earth covering an ancient settlement.

Kufic The earliest style of Arabic script; Foliate *kufic* was a more elaborate form, superseded by *naskhi* script.

Kuttab Koranic school, usually for boys or orphans.

Leyla kebira "Big night": the climactic night of a popular religious festival.

Liwan An arcade or vaulted space off a courtyard in mosques and madrassas; originally, the term meant a sitting room opening onto a covered court.

Madrassa Literally a "place of study" but generally used to designate theological schools. Each madrassa propagates a particular school of Islamic jurisprudence.

Malqaf Wind scoop for directing cool breezes into houses; in Egypt, they always face north, towards the prevailing wind.

Mamissi Birth House. A pseudo-Coptic term coined to describe a structure attached to temples from the Late Period to Roman times, where rituals celebrating the birth of Horus and the reigning king were performed.

Mashrabiya An alcove in lattice windows where jars of water can be cooled by the wind; by extension, the projecting balcony and screened window itself, which enabled women to watch street-life or the *salamlik* without being observed.

Masr (Misr, Musr) Popular name for Egypt, and Cairo, dating back to antiquity.

Mastaba Mud-brick benches outside buildings; Egyptologists use the word to describe the flat-roofed, multi-roomed tombs of the Old Kingdom, found at Saqqara and other sites.

Merlons Indentations and raised portions along a parapet. Fatimid merlons were angular; Mamluke ones crested, trilobed (like a fleur-de-lis) or in fancier leaf patterns.

Midan An open space or square; in Tulunid Cairo most were originally polo grounds.

Mihrab Niche indicating the direction of Mecca, to which all Muslims pray.

Minaret Tower from which the call to prayer is given; derived from *minara*, the Arabic word for "beacon" or "lighthouse".

Minbar Pulpit from which an address to the Friday congregation is given. Often superbly inlaid or carved in variegated marble or wood.

Mosque A simple enclosure facing Mecca; in its original form, the mosque acquired minarets, *riwaq*s, *madrassa*s and mausolea as it was developed by successive dynasties.

Moulid Popular festival marking an event in the Koran or the birthday of a Muslim saint. The term also applies to the name-days of Coptic saints.

Muezzin A prayer-crier (who nowadays is more likely to broadcast by loudspeaker than to climb up and shout from the minaret).

Muqarnas Stalactites, pendants or honeycomb ornamentation of portals, domes or squinches.

Naos The core and sanctuary of a Coptic or Byzantine church, where the liturgy is performed.

Naskhi Form of Arabic script with joined-up letters, introduced by the Ayyubids.

Nomarch A Greek title, used to describe a provincial governor in Ancient Egypt.

Nome A Greek term, used to describe a province of Ancient Egypt.

Nomen The name that a pharaoh was given at birth, which equates more or less with a family name, eg Tuthmosis in the XVIII Dynasty or Ramses in the XIX Dynasty.

Ostracon (pl. ostraca) A Greek term used by archeologists to describe potsherds or flakes of limestone bearing texts and drawings, often consisting of personal jottings, letters or scribal exercises.

Pasha (Pacha) Ruler – a lord or prince. Nowadays, a respectful term of address for anyone in authority, pronounced "basha".

Prenomen The "throne name" assumed by a pharaoh at his coronation. When inscribed in a cartouche it is usually preceded by the symbols for Upper and Lower Egypt, and followed by the suffix Re.

Pronaos Vestibule of a Greek or Roman temple, enclosed by side walls and a row of columns in front.

Pylon A broad, majestic gateway that formed the entrance to temples from the XVIII Dynasty onwards, or a series of gateways within large complexes such as Karnak.

Qadim/Qadima (masc./fem.) "Old", as in Masr al-Qadima, or Old Cairo.

Qalaa Fortress, citadel.

Qasr Palace, fortress, mansion. Also used to describe semi-fortified villages in the oases, such as Qasr al-Farafra.

Qibla The direction towards Mecca in which Muslims pray, indicated in mosques by the wall where the *mihrab* is located.

Qubba Dome, and by extension any domed tomb or shrine.

Ras Cape, headland, peak.

Repoussé A technique in which malleable metal is ornamented by hammering from the reverse side to form a raised design on the front, which is often combined with the opposite technique of chasing (hammering from the front) to form a finished piece.

Riwaq Arcaded aisle around a mosque's *sahn*, originally used as residential quarters for theological students; ordinary folk may also take naps here.

Sabil Public fountain or water cistern. During the nineteenth century it was often combined with a Koranic school to make a *sabil-kuttab*.

Sahn Central courtyard of a mosque, frequently surrounded by *riwaqs* or *liwans*.

Salamlik The "greeting" area of a house; ie the public and men's apartments.

Sanctuary The *liwan* incorporating the *qibla* wall in a mosque, or the shrine of a deity in an Ancient Egyptian temple.

Senussi An Islamist movement, strong in the Libyan Desert between 1830 and 1930, which resisted British and Italian colonialism in Egypt and Libya.

Serdab The Arabic word for a cellar beneath a mosque. Also used by Egyptologists to describe the room in mastaba tombs where statues of the deceased's *ka* were placed, often with eye-holes or a slit in the wall enabling the *ka* to leave the chamber, and offerings to be made to the statue from the tomb's chapel.

Shabti (ushabti) Ancient funerary figurines, whose purpose was to spare their owner from having to perform menial tasks in the after-life.

Sharia Street (literally "way"). With the Arabic feminine ending added (the resulting word is sometimes transliterated Shariah), it refers to laws based on Koranic precepts.

Sharm Bay.

Squinch An arch spanning the right angle formed by two walls, so as to support a dome.

Sufis Islamic mystics who seek to attain union with Allah through trance-inducing *zikrs* and dances. Whirling Dervishes belong to one of the Sufi sects.

Supreme Council for Antiquities (SCA) The state organization responsible for Egypt's ancient monuments, formerly called the Egyptian Antiquities Organization.

Tariqa A Sufi order or dervish brotherhood.

Tell Another word for *kom*.

Thuluth Script whose vertical strokes are three times larger than its horizontal ones; *Thuluth* literally means "third".

Tuf-tuf A form of transport in some tourist areas, consisting of an engine pulling open-sided carriages, but running along roads; similar to a Noddy train.

Uraeus (pl. uraei) The rearing cobra symbol of the Delta goddess Wadjet, worn as part of the royal crown and often identified with the destructive "Eye of Re".

Wadi Valley or watercourse (usually dry).

Wahah Oasis.

Wikala Bonded warehouse with rooms for merchants upstairs. Here they bought trading licences from the *muhtasib* and haggled over sales in the courtyard. *Okel* is another term for a *wikala*.

Yardang Freestanding, wind-eroded rock formation, typical of the White Desert.

Zikr Marathon session of chanting and swaying, intended to induce communion with Allah.

Small print and Index

A Rough Guide to Rough Guides

Published in 1982, the first Rough Guide – to Greece – was a student scheme that became a publishing phenomenon. Mark Ellingham, a recent graduate in English from Bristol University, had been travelling in Greece the previous summer and couldn't find the right guidebook. With a small group of friends he wrote his own guide, combining a highly contemporary, journalistic style with a thoroughly practical approach to travellers' needs.

The immediate success of the book spawned a series that rapidly covered dozens of destinations. And, in addition to impecunious backpackers, Rough Guides soon acquired a much broader and older readership that relished the guides' wit and inquisitiveness as much as their enthusiastic, critical approach and value-for-money ethos.

These days, Rough Guides include recommendations from shoestring to luxury and cover more than 200 destinations around the globe, including almost every country in the Americas and Europe, more than half of Africa and most of Asia and Australasia. Our ever-growing team of authors and photographers is spread all over the world, particularly in Europe, the US and Australia.

In the early 1990s, Rough Guides branched out of travel, with the publication of Rough Guides to World Music, Classical Music and the Internet. All three have become benchmark titles in their fields, spearheading the publication of a wide range of books under the Rough Guide name.

Including the travel series, Rough Guides now number more than 350 titles, covering: phrasebooks, waterproof maps, music guides from Opera to Heavy Metal, reference works as diverse as Conspiracy Theories and Shakespeare, and popular culture books from iPods to Poker. Rough Guides also produce a series of more than 120 World Music CDs in partnership with World Music Network.

Visit www.roughguides.com to see our latest publications.

Rough Guide credits

Text editor: Róisín Cameron
Layout: Sachin Gupta
Cartography: Rajesh Chhibber
Picture editor: Harriet Mills
Production: Rebecca Short
Proofreader: Stewart Wild
Cover design: Dan May, Chloë Roberts
Photographer: Eddie Gerald
Editorial: **London** Andy Turner, Keith Drew, Edward Aves, Alice Park, Lucy White, Jo Kirby, James Smart, Natasha Foges, James Rice, Lara Kavanagh, Emma Traynor, Emma Gibbs, Kathryn Lane, Monica Woods, Mani Ramaswamy, Harry Wilson, Lucy Cowie, Alison Roberts, Joe Staines, Matthew Milton, Tracy Hopkins, Ruth Tidball; **Delhi** Madhavi Singh, Lubna Shaheen, Jalpreen Kaur Chhatwal
Design & Pictures: **London** Scott Stickland, Dan May, Diana Jarvis, Mark Thomas, Nicole Newman, Sarah Cummins, Emily Taylor; **Delhi** Umesh Aggarwal, Ajay Verma, Jessica Subramanian, Ankur Guha, Pradeep Thapliyal, Sachin Tanwar, Anita Singh, Nikhil Agarwal
Production: Liz Cherry
Cartography: **London** Ed Wright, Katie Lloyd-Jones; **Delhi** Ashutosh Bharti, Rajesh Mishra, Animesh Pathak, Jasbir Sandhu, Karobi Gogoi, Alakananda Roy, Swati Handoo, Deshpal Dabas
Online: **London** Faye Hellon, Jeanette Angell, Fergus Day, Justine Bright, Clare Bryson, Aine Fearon, Adrian Low, Ezgi Celebi; **Delhi** Amit Verma, Rahul Kumar, Narender Kumar, Ravi Yadav, Debojit Borah, Rakesh Kumar, Ganesh Sharma, Shisir Basumatari
Marketing & Publicity: **London** Liz Statham, Jess Carter, Vivienne Watton, Anna Paynton, Rachel Sprackett, Laura Vipond; **New York** Katy Ball, Judi Powers; **Delhi** Ragini Govind
Digital Travel Publisher: Peter Buckley
Reference Director: Andrew Lockett
Operations Assistant: Becky Doyle
Operations Manager: Helen Atkinson
Publishing Director (Travel): Clare Currie
Commercial Manager: Gino Magnotta
Managing Director: John Duhigg

Publishing information

This eighth edition published August 2010 by
Rough Guides Ltd,
80 Strand, London WC2R 0RL
11 Community Centre, Panchsheel Park,
New Delhi 110017, India
Distributed by the Penguin Group
Penguin Books Ltd,
80 Strand, London WC2R 0RL
Penguin Group (USA)
375 Hudson Street, NY 10014, USA
Penguin Group (Australia)
250 Camberwell Road, Camberwell,
Victoria 3124, Australia
Penguin Group (Canada)
195 Harry Walker Parkway N, Newmarket, ON,
L3Y 7B3 Canada
Penguin Group (NZ)
67 Apollo Drive, Mairangi Bay, Auckland 1310,
New Zealand
Cover concept by Peter Dyer.

Typeset in Bembo and Helvetica to an original design by Henry Iles.

Printed in Singapore

664pp includes index

A catalogue record for this book is available from the British Library

ISBN: 978-1-84836-501-8

1 3 5 7 9 8 6 4 2

Help us update

We've gone to a lot of effort to ensure that the eighth edition of **The Rough Guide to Egypt** is accurate and up-to-date. However, things change – places get "discovered", opening hours are notoriously fickle, restaurants and rooms raise prices or lower standards. If you feel we've got it wrong or left something out, we'd like to know, and if you can remember the address, the price, the hours, the phone number, so much the better.

Please send your comments with the subject line "**Rough Guide Egypt Update**" to ⓔ mail@roughguides.com. We'll credit all contributions and send a copy of the next edition (or any other Rough Guide if you prefer) for the very best emails.

Have your questions answered and tell others about your trip at ⓦ www.roughguides.com

Acknowledgements

Thanks from **Dan Richardson** to Hagg Ibrahim, Hamada and Karin El-Khalifa, Aladin Al-Sahaby, Ayman Simaan, Ziggy, Amr and Hassan in Luxor; Mahmoud Yussef and Mohsen in Kharga Oasis; Talat Mulah and Yehiya Abdallah in Bahariya; Mahdi Hweiti and Hugo Gaarden in Siwa; and Zahraa Adel Awad in Alexandria. In London, thanks are due to Róisín Cameron for her incisive pruning of the text and forbearance of missed deadlines, and to Harriet Mills for the snazzy pictures.

Daniel Jacobs would like to thank Hisham Youssef (*Berlin Hotel*, Cairo), Salah Mohammed (Samo Tours), Hamdi Ghazali (Samo Tours), Hamdi Shora (Adventure in Egypt), Humphrey Davies, Caroline Evanoff, and big thanks also to Shafik and Dan for their input.

Shafik Meghji: A special *shukran* must go to: Róisín Cameron for her help and advice; Alex at Prince Travels in Ed-Dahar; Yousri at the Hurghada Tourist Office; Salaama on the road to Suez; Mohammad at the Port Said Tourist Office; Alad at Sun 'N Fun in Na'ama Bay; Friday at Sinai Divers in Na'ama Bay; the staff at Christina Beach Palace in Dahab; Tom Steiner of Fantasea in Dahab for his diving expertise; Hilary Gilbert and family in St Catherine's for their insight into Bedouin life; Angela at Nature Travel in Nuweiba; Dina Naeem in Cairo; Jean and Nizar Meghji for all their encouragement; Nina Meghji for her invaluable cartography skills; and Sioned Jones for her quick-fire translations, film-making skills and, above all, love and support.

Readers' letters

Thanks to all the readers who have taken the time to write in with comments and suggestions (and apologies if we've inadvertently omitted or misspelt anyone's name):

Zahraa Adel Awad; Mariam Banahi; Derek Belcher; Louise Bochardt; Lindsay Cabble; Jill Cameron; Alicia Choo; Jeff Clausen; Julie Colburn; Jennie Cole; Vivien Conrad; D.J. Coode; Gordon Davies; Jan Deckers; K. Delvaux; Ron Dupuis; Sonia Fankhauser; Alan Hakim; Christopher Horn; Mags Humphrey; Laura Hussey; Peggy Jay; Gwen Jennes; Ben Johnson; Esther Klink; David Lebon; Joyce Mills; Anna Moore; Silvia Muff; Saki Onda; Guilio Perroni; Lene Petersen; Ian Renner; Jim Saddler; Barrie Singleton; Sylvia Smith; Ben Spencer; Michael Smyth; Richard Thomson; H.J. van Vliet; Lisa Walker; Antony Waterman; Erik Weijers; John Woodhouse.

Photo credits

All photos © Rough Guides except the following:

Introduction

Khan el-Khalili bazaar, Cairo © Ian Cumming/Axiom Photographic
Bread sellers, Cairo © Photononstop/Tips Images
Street names, Cairo © Gary Cook/Alamy
Flamingos © M. & C. Denis-Huot/Bios/Tips Images
Sufi followers attend Tanta Moulid © Shawn Baldwin/Corbis

Things not to miss

01 Abu Simbel, The Great Temple of Ramses II © Richard Passmore/Getty Images
02 Tomb of Peshedu, Deir el-Medina, Valley of the Kings © Sylvain Grandadam/Superstock
03 Man selling roasted peanuts, Alexandria © Bill Lyons/Alamy
04 Belly dancer © Roger Ressmeyer/Corbis
06 Camel riding near Sharm el-Sheikh © Alan Copson/awl-images.com
07 Karkaday © Marka/Alamy
08 Mezze dishes, Egypt © Jean Dominique Dallet/Alamy
09 Khan el-Khalili bazaar district, Cairo © Ashok Sinha/Getty Images
10 Felucca on the Nile © panicpanda/istockphoto.com
11 Red Sea reef with butterflyfish and diver © Martin Strmko/istockphoto.com
12 Street vendor selling orange juice, Cairo © Design Pics/Superstock
13 Catacombs of Kom es-Shoqafa © Stuart Franklin/Magnum Photos
14 White Desert © Mike Nelson/epa/Corbis
16 Hot air balloons over the Ramesseum, Theban Necropolis © Tony Roddam/Alamy
17 Dahabiya Assouan interior © Dylan Chandler/courtesy www.nourelnil.com
19 Elephantine Island and the Nile, Aswan © Robert Harding
21 Tutankhamun's funerary mask, Egyptian Antiquities Museum © Jamie Marshall/DK Images
22 Dahshur, Snofru's Bent Pyramid © Peter Wilson/DK Images
23 *Dunraven* wreck, Ras Mohammed © Reinhard Dirscherl/Tips Images
24 Sofianopoulo Coffee Store, Alexandria © James Morris Phot242/Axiom Photographic
25 St Catherine's Monastery chapel, Sinai © Dmitriy Kazachenko/istockphoto.com
26 The Sphinx, Giza © Alistair Duncan/DK Images

Egyptian temple architecture colour section

Colossi of Ramses II, Abu Simbel © Alistair Duncan/DK Images
Pylons at Edfu © Robert Partridge: The Ancient Egypt Picture Library
Hypostyle Hall at Karnak © Robert Partridge: The Ancient Egypt Picture Library
Dendara astronomical ceiling © Robert Partridge: The Ancient Egypt Picture Library
Deir el-Bahri © Pat Glover/istockphoto.com

Egypt's underwater world colour section

Snorkelling in the Red Sea © Westend61/Superstock
Gorgonian sea fan, St Johns Reef, Red Sea © WaterFrame/Wolfgang Poelzer/Photolibrary
Golden butterflyfish over coral reef with soft corals, Red Sea © Georgie Holland/Superstock
Steephead parrotfish, Red Sea © Richard Carey/istockphoto.com
Clownfish © Jodi Jacobson/istockphoto.com
Green turtle © Ron Masessa/istockphoto.com
Crown jellyfish © Reinhard Dirscherl/Superstock
Diver and coral reef, Red Sea © Brandelet Didier/Bios/Tips Images
Spinner dolphins, Red Sea © Jean Cassou/Tips Images
Old motorcycle on the *Thristlegorm* wreck © Miguel Angelo Silva/istockphoto.com

Black and whites

p.91 Men sitting on a park bench in Midan Tahrir, Cairo © Jon Spaull/DK Images
p.214 Detail of Ramses II, Temple of Nefertari, Abu Simbel © Alistair Duncan/DK Images
p.241 Assyut grain merchant's shop © Seth Lazar/Alamy
p.301 Colossi of Memnon and hot air balloons © Max Alexander/DK Images
p.376 Jeep safari, Great Sand Sea © F1 Online/Tips Images
p.393 Maidum pyramid © Geoff Brightling/DK Images
p.408 Eroded limestone in the White Desert © Michael Hoefner/istockphoto.com
p.424 Souk in El-Kharga © René Mattes/Photolibrary
p.434 Rock art in the Mestekawi-Foggini Cave (Cave of the Beasts) © András Zboray/www.fjexpeditions.com
p.470 Engraving of the Pharos of Alexandria by Fischer von Erlach © Historical Picture Archive/Philip de Bay/Corbis
p.502 Women sitting by the Suez Canal © epa/Corbis
p.559 St Catherine's Monastery, Sinai © Valeriy Kalyuzhnyy/istockphoto.com
p.568 Giant moray with scuba diver, Hurghada © Reinhard Dirscherl/Photolibrary
p.585 DJ Suzee at Ministry of Sound, Hurghada © www.MinistryofSoundEgypt.com

Index

Map entries are in colour.

D

E

F

G

INDEX

Q

R

S

T

U

V

W

Y

Z

Map symbols

maps are listed in the full index using coloured text

Chapter division boundary	Lighthouse
International boundary	Battlefield
Main road	Shipwreck
Minor road	Restaurant
Tunnel	Hotel
Footpath/track	Statue
River	Transport stop
Ferry route	Garage/fuel station
Railway	Telephone
Metro line & station	Post office
Fortified Wall	Information point
Point of interest	Internet access
Airport	Hospital
Cliff face/escarpment	Parking
Crescent dune	Temple
Oasis/palm grove	Tomb
Spring	Monastery/convent
Waterfall	Synagogue
Fountain	Building
Swimming pool	Stadium
Viewpoint	Church
Mountain range	Mosque
Mountain peak	Christian cemetery
Reef	Muslim cemetery
Crater	Park/national park
Pyramid	Beach/dunes
Cave	Delta
Mountain pass	Saltpan
Checkpoint	